About Pearson

Pearson is the world's learning company, with presence across 70 countries worldwide. Our unique insights and world-class expertise comes from a long history of working closely with renowned teachers, authors and thought leaders, as a result of which, we have emerged as the preferred choice for millions of teachers and learners across the world.

We believe learning opens up opportunities, creates fulfilling careers and hence better lives. We hence collaborate with the best of minds to deliver you class-leading products, spread across the Higher Education and Test Preparation spectrum.

Superior learning experience and improved outcomes are at the heart of everything we do. This product is the result of one such effort.

Your feedback plays a critical role in the evolution of our products and you can contact us – reachus@pearson.com. *We look forward to it.*

Reviews of the First Edition

Professor Singh seems to have given us a singularly learned, well-written, and detailed introduction to the study of ancient India... It is possible to have disagreement with Professor Singh on various issues, but that, in fact, lends charm to what she writes because what would a book like this be worth unless it can generate debates in the class-room?

—**Dilip K. Chakrabarti**, University of Cambridge

[The book's] unusual format consists of not only a narrative text, but boxed information from original sources and research works, and on key concepts, which the students will find instructive.... The website for further references and reading makes a supplement to the narrative. The list of further readings is impressive. Due attention is paid to regional histories, especially South India and sources in regional languages...

—**R. Champakalakshmi**, *The Hindu*

...a well illustrated, marvellously produced textbook covering the vast history from the Stone Age to the 12th century... Singularly impressive for its make-up and appearance, this textbook is the first of its kind in the country...

Each chapter of the book contains a critical reappraisal of sources and the development of historical knowledge... helping students understand the rigorous methodology that underlies the process.... '[U]nsettled' issues have been dealt with through the debates without losing their complexity and thus creating awareness of various scholars' valuable contributions towards the construction of historical knowledge...

Singh's book... educates its readers as to how history can stake claims on various areas of knowledge in the domain of interdisciplinary studies like gender studies, environmental history, human geography, landscape archaeology and human ecology.

—**Rajan Gurukkal**, *The Book Review*

Professor Singh has succeeded in her venture of producing a balanced and stimulating textbook on the early Indian past. She has followed recent trends in historiography, incorporating into her book new theoretical perspectives, scientific technologies, and the enormously growing archaeological data. Often neglected South Indian history is also adequately represented.

—**N. Karashima**, University of Tokyo

With its in-depth assessment of the literary and archaeological sources and theoretical discourses, [this book] provides a unique and long overdue introduction to the study of Indian history to the 12th century, which gives full coverage also to peninsular India.

—**Hermann Kulke**, University of Kiel

This is the first work on ancient India where the text has been constructed at different levels. Ten chapters pan across the whole canvas, from prehistory and protohistory to ancient and early medieval history. The panorama is interspersed with inset capsules where some themes are picked out to illustrate larger elements in the chapters...

Singh's deep affection for all kinds of ancient Indians has ensured that she does not lose sight of ordinary people, or for that matter, their eating habits, or even their pets.

Early India is not merely humanised through such capsules and sources, it is also illuminated by the roughly 450 illustrations that accompany the text.

—**Nayanjot Lahiri**, *India Today*

This up-to-date, lavishly illustrated, and thoughtfully designed volume is clearly the new standard against which future texts will be measured. Singh's overview of early Indian history deftly integrate[s] archaeological data in a way few, if any, other reviews have achieved or ventured....

[Singh] stresses the complexity and diversity of experience while also crafting a composite image, a mosaic, of a unified Indian past. That she is able to do justice to regional specificity, occupational diversity, and cultural complexity is a testament to [her] powerful historical vision....

The most enduring value of Upinder Singh's new synthesis is the way in which it aims to create not simply consumers but producers of historical thought.

—**Kathleen D. Morrison**, *Seminar*

Singh... writes with a refreshing openness, and her constant aim is to communicate clearly, without simplifying the complex subject matter before her. This is the major contribution of the book...

In an era when most historians are torn between different and contending theories, Singh remains rooted to facts and analysis without ever committing the error of claiming that she has said the last word on the subject.

—**Rudrangshu Mukherjee**, *The Telegraph*

...a fascinating and up-to-date account of South Asia's past, from the dim beginnings of the hunter-forager way of life to the early medieval period. It is based on an objective assessment of both literary and archaeological sources... the book will be useful to students of history and archaeology at all levels and to all educated laymen who desire to know about South Asia's past.

—**K. Paddayya**, Deccan College, Pune

The language is refreshingly gender-sensitive and direct. The visuals are chosen with care and several of them are spectacular. Access to primary sources (both visual and textual) enriches the book enormously. It is more than apparent that the author has carefully deliberated over each sentence in order to create a text that is comprehensive.

—**Kumkum Roy**, *IIC Quarterly*

SECOND EDITION

A HISTORY OF ANCIENT AND EARLY MEDIEVAL INDIA

From the Stone Age to the 12th Century

Upinder Singh

This book is dedicated to the students I have taught at St. Stephen's College, the University of Delhi, and Ashoka University

Senior Editor—Acquisitions: Anindita Malhotra
Senior Editor—Production: C. Purushothaman

ISBN 978-93-570-5148-4

First Impression, 2024
Third Impression, 2025
Fourth Impression, 2026

Published by Pearson India Education Services Pvt. Ltd, CIN: U72200TN2005PTC057128.

Head Office: 1st Floor, Berger Tower, Plot No. C-001A/2, Sector 16B, Noida - 201 301, Uttar Pradesh, India.
Registered Office : 6th Floor, Tower A, Unit A and B International Tech Park, Capita Land Chennai, 200 Feet Radial Road, Zamin Pallavaram, Old Pallavaram Chennai – 600117, Tamil Nadu, India
Website: in.pearson.com; Email: companysecretary.india@pearson.com

Compositor: DigiWorld Creative, Pune, Maharashtra
Book designed by Idesign
Printed in India by ***Rajkamal Electric Press, Kundli, Haryana-131 028.***

**Please note that there are a few updates to the first impression of this edition, which have been incorporated in subsequent printings. If you have the first impression, kindly refer to the Errata sheet via the eLibrary QR code on the back cover of the book.*

Brief Contents

Contents

Photographs

Maps

Figures

About the Author

Upinder Singh

Upinder Singh is Professor in the Department of History at Ashoka University. Previously, she taught at St. Stephen's College and the Department of History, University of Delhi. She studied history in St. Stephen's College and went on to receive her M.A. and M.Phil. from the University of Delhi, specializing in ancient Indian history. She obtained her Ph.D. from McGill University, Montreal. She has been a recipient of several international fellowships. In 2009, she was awarded the Infosys Prize for Social Sciences—History.

Professor Singh's wide range of research interests and expertise range over various aspects of ancient Indian history and archaeology, the history of ideas, and India's interactions with the wider world. Her research papers have been published in various national and international journals. She is the author of several books—*Kings, Brāhmanas, and Temples in Orissa: An Epigraphic Study (AD 300–1147)* (1994); *Ancient Delhi* (1999), *The Discovery of Ancient India: Early Archaeologists and the Beginnings of Archaeology* (2004), *The Idea of Ancient India: Essays on Religion, Politics, and Archaeology* (2016; new edn, 2024), *Political Violence in Ancient India* (2017), and *Ancient India: Culture of Contradictions* (2021). She has edited *Delhi: Ancient History* (2006), *Rethinking Early Medieval India* (2011); and has co-edited *Ancient India: New Research* (2009), *Asian Encounters: Exploring Connected Histories* (2014), *Buddhism in Asia: Revival and Reinvention* (2019), and *The World of India's First Archaeologist: Letters from Alexander Cunningham to J.D.M. Beglar* (2021).

Preface to the Second Edition

The first edition of *A History of Ancient and Early Medieval India: From the Stone Age to the 12th Century* was published in 2008. Since then, new discoveries, research, and perspectives have further enriched our understanding of the early Indian past. My own perspectives and interests too have evolved. Hence the need for this new edition.

I continue to feel strongly about the central tenets of the first edition. These include the need to integrate archaeology and history, to include subordinated groups in social history, to recognize the importance of religion and philosophy, and to be sensitive towards the intellectual and aesthetic domains. Readers of history books should be exposed to the exciting world of primary sources and to the challenges of interpretation they present. Discussions of historical debates should encourage readers to approach them with an open mind, a spirit of questioning, and an ability to critically evaluate evidence and arguments. Historical inquiry is an on-going process, and in history, there can never be a last word.

Over the years, my perspective on ancient Indian history has expanded as a result of my own research and what I have learnt from the research and writings of other historians. This is reflected in my collection of essays, *The Idea of Ancient India: Essays on Religion, Politics, and Archaeology* (second edition, 2023). My book, *Political Violence in Ancient India* (2017) reflects my increased interest in the history of ideas, recognizing continuities and overlaps as well as ruptures and differences across time. My belief that visual sources are powerful, evocative historical sources—relegated in most history books to a separate section on art and architecture—has grown stronger. My understanding of the subcontinent as a complex, variegated mosaic of regions has expanded into an awareness of the need to view these regions as part of many intricate networks of interaction that connected various parts of Asia, Europe, and Africa. This is reflected in my co-edited volume, *Asian Encounters: Exploring Connected Histories* (2014). A global history approach offers a comparative lens that helps understand cultural connectivities and affinities as well as specificities and differences. —The incorporation of all these ideas makes the second edition of this book significantly different from the first.

Readers will find many other new elements scattered through the book, in the form of new details and new emphasis. For instance, the early chapters refer to the latest scientific methods used in archaeology, and to how genome research is contributing to our knowledge of prehistory and protohistory by throwing light on human ancestry and migration. The forest is recognized as an important part of the ecology, subsistence base, and trade networks of ancient societies, but I have emphasized that forest people were also an important part of ancient Indian political history over the centuries. In the sphere of intellectual history, this edition contains a more detailed treatment of the history of science and mathematics. The last chapter discusses Islam and the advent of the Turks, which are important parts of the history of early medieval India. There is an attempt to include more material on relatively neglected areas within the subcontinent such as Kashmir and the North-east. There is also more on the regions of South Asia beyond the modern boundaries of India, namely Pakistan, Bangladesh, Nepal, Bhutan, and Sri Lanka. Across all the chapters, readers will find a highlighting of new writing, research, and ideas that have pushed forward the frontiers of early Indian history.

History has always been connected with politics and identity. Historians cannot help looking at the past through the eyes of their present. But this is different from judging the past and manipulating the evidence to suit political agendas. All hypotheses are not equally valid; it is important for readers to understand the difference between historical interpretations that are grounded on sound analysis and argument, and those that are not. This requires that historians clearly explain the methods and debates of the discipline to non-specialists and students. This is one of the major aims of this book.

From the start, I visualized this book as simultaneously addressing two audiences—students and general readers; in fact, anyone who is curious about India's ancient past. As I say in my book, *Ancient India: Culture of Contradictions*, the past can be beautiful, uplifting, and inspiring; it can also be ugly, unsettling, and disturbing. Understanding history requires abandoning simplistic stereotypes and preconceived notions; it requires a sensitivity to the nuances and complexities of the subject. I hope that this new edition of *A History of Ancient and Early Medieval India* will convey these nuances and complexities to readers. I think that the joy and wonder arising from learning about the lives and experiences of people who lived long ago is an exciting adventure that can add meaning to our lives. I hope this new edition fulfills these aims.

My understanding of history has been defined in a major way by my journey as a teacher. This journey began in 1981, when I joined St. Stephen's College as a lecturer. In 2004, I moved to the History Department of the University of Delhi, and in 2018, I joined Ashoka University, Sonepat. I have learnt a great deal through teaching my students in these three institutions. This new edition of this book is dedicated to them.

Upinder Singh

Upinder Singh
December 2023

Acknowledgements to the Second Edition

My indebtedness to many friends, colleagues, scholars, and others is recorded in the Acknowledgements to the first edition of this book, as well as in its references. In addition, I would like to thank the following for helping me in various ways in preparing this second edition:

Vijay Tankha was, as always, an editorial advisor and fellow traveller along historical tracks. Nayanjot Lahiri was a sounding board for ideas and a source of helpful suggestions. Osmund Bopearachchi sent me reading material and generously offered several photographs. Farhat Hasan suggested many useful readings on early medieval India. Other scholars who helped me in various ways include Joel P. Brereton, P. P. Divakaran, George L. Hart, Ravi Korisettar, Stephanie W. Jamison, Timothy Lubin, Patrick Olivelle, Shanti Pappu. K. Rajan, David Shulman, and Y. Subbarayalu.

Ashoka University, where I presently teach, has provided me an ideal working environment, one which nurtures a lively spirit of inquiry and interdisciplinarity, both inside and outside the classroom. I have learnt much from the Ashoka community, including my colleagues in the History Department as well as from those in other Departments. Among the latter, I would especially like to thank Rajendra Bhatia, L. S. Shashidhara, and Mali Skotheim. The Library staff of Ashoka University has been a rock of support. I owe them special thanks.

I would like to thank the following for the many new images that adorn this book: Naman Ahuja, Robert Arlt, Hans Bakker, Tanmay Haldar, Rima Kalita, Ravi Korisettar, Srikumar Menon, Kathleen Morrison, Shanti Pappu, Alka Patel, K. Rajan, Ingo Strauch, Pankaj Tandon, Rakesh Tewari, and Supriya Varma. Thanks are also due to the Kerala Council of Historical Research, the American Institute of Indian Studies, and the Metropolitan Museum of Art, New York.

Readers of this book will recognize that it looks very different from the first edition. I am grateful to Rohit Kathuria for designing the basics of the new layout.

The most heartening thing for me was that the entire Pearson team understood what this book was supposed to be—a text-book, but much more than that; a book that aimed at giving state-of-the art information to readers, as well as arousing curiosity and interest in the subcontinent's early past. I must acknowledge the enthusiastic support extended by the Pearson senior management—Vinay Swamy (Country Head—India), Sojan Jose (Director—Product) and Vishal Dhawan (Director—Sales). Anindita Malhotra (Senior Editor) who steered the project forward with efficiency, energy, and a meticulous attention to detail. Rahul Kumar worked tirelessly to perfect the layout and cover design. Daljeet Kaur worked hard on the permissions. It has truly been a pleasure working with members of the Pearson team on the second edition of this book and I would like to thank them all.

Upinder Singh

Upinder Singh

Preface to the First Edition

From 1981, I spent over twenty years teaching the undergraduate course on ancient and early medieval India at St. Stephen's College, Delhi. It was a daunting course, demanding coverage of many different areas and issues over enormous spans of time. I was fortunate to have students with sharp and inquisitive minds, whose questions constantly forced me to re-think my perspectives and conclusions, and who made me realize that teaching is ultimately about the quality of communication between student and teacher. Undergraduate teaching, with its enormous pressures of teaching and marking work, left very little time for research. Nevertheless, I did manage to keep my research going, and explored issues related to social and economic history, religious institutions, inscriptions, archaeology, and the modern histories of ancient sites and monuments.

A History of Ancient and Early Medieval India: From the Stone Age to the 12th Century emerged from the intersection of my experiences as a teacher and researcher. Primarily a textbook and reference work for both undergraduate and postgraduate students, this book will, I hope, also appeal to the general reader. Its aim is to provide an introduction to ancient and early medieval India through a comprehensive overview of historical issues and details within a firm chronological framework; explanations of basic concepts and terminology; an exposure to the flavour of textual, material, and visual historical sources; and a highlighting of new discoveries and research. Perhaps most importantly, this book focuses on the process through which historical knowledge is formed, and the intellectual inquiry and debate that form part of this process.

This book is not a mere summary of existing knowledge. Rather than offer students a smoothened narrative, which they will then be expected to absorb passively, it is necessary to expose them to the complex details and textures of history. Where there are unresolved issues, they have been presented as such, rather than conveying a false sense of certainty. Where there are debates, the different perspectives have been presented, along with my own assessment of which arguments are convincing and which ones are not.

Historians and teachers invest far too much time and energy in telling students what to think, rather than how to think for themselves. Students need to learn to evaluate evidence and hypotheses, to relentlessly question and critique what they read or are told, and formulate and express their independent views. It is essential to acknowledge the valuable contributions made by various scholars towards the construction of historical knowledge and to understand the rigorous methodology that underlies this process. However I hope that this book encourages readers to think courageously and creatively beyond the current boundaries of academic discourse and debate.

Since this is a macro-history of the Indian subcontinent, and in a single volume at that, it outlines broad trajectories, always aware of the fact that these are only a few of multiple trajectories. Thus, for instance, while the account of the beginnings of food production may suggest that this was the inexorable direction in which things were moving, emphasis is still placed on the fact that hunting and gathering remained a preferred subsistence activity for many communities across the centuries. Similarly, the discussion of the early historical period may seem to suggest that everything was making way for the emergence of city life, but it must not be forgotten that most people of the subcontinent continued to live in villages.

The privileging of certain processes over others is partly the result of the training and tendency of a historian to focus on what appear to be significant changes, and also due to the inherent nature and inadequacies of sources and available data. The fact is that whether we look at the archaeological or literary sources, we know much more about agricultural groups than hunter-gatherers, and much more about city-dwellers than village folk. Nevertheless, it is important to constantly remind ourselves about the partial and inadequate nature of our historical narratives.

Prehistory to *c.* 1200 CE is an enormous span of time, and it is not possible to be exhaustive on each and every issue. The structure of this book involves breaking this vast period into broad chronological units. For earlier periods, all radiocarbon dates mentioned in this book are calibrated dates. Following current usage, BCE (Before Common Era) is used instead of BC, and CE (Common Era) instead of AD. Against the background of the controversy over the dates of the Buddha's life, *c.* 480 BCE has been taken as the date of the parinibbana.

Within the broad chronological units, profiles have been constructed of the various geographical regions, incorporating the range of available literary and archaeological evidence, bringing out the complex strands of historical processes within and across different regions. The coverage of regions is necessarily dependent on available information, and the gaps and inadequacies in this information should inspire young scholars to take on the challenge of addressing them.

Each chapter looks at various aspects of a particular period on the basis of a critical survey of the available sources. The narrative is punctuated by boxes focusing on key concepts, primary sources, further discussion of specific issues or details, recent discoveries, and new directions in research. From the beginning of the historical period, the chapters start with a synopsis of political history and a discussion of political processes. This is not because these are necessarily the most important aspects of history, but because it is useful for students to have a basic understanding of political context and chronology. Political narrative has been accompanied, to every possible extent, with a discussion of political structures and processes.

Political, social, economic, religious, and cultural history are discussed sequentially in order to bring out their inter-connectedness within a chrono logical and contextual frame. The discussion of social history looks at issues such as class, caste, gender, and subordinate and marginalized groups. Philosophical ideas are treated as an important part of the intellectual life of different periods. Religious doctrines and practices are discussed as important areas requiring detailed investigation, and not merely as part of an ideology reflecting existing power structures. I hope that the many excerpts from original sources and photographs create sensitivity towards the aesthetic dimensions of Indian cultural traditions reflected in literature, art, and architecture.

As far as possible, references have been cited to enable the interested reader to go to the original source. Translations have often been slightly modified to make them more accessible. Punctuation has been altered to suit the style of the book, especially since diacritical marks have been dispensed with. Since historical literature generally uses such diacritics and students should understand them, the conventionally used systems of transliteration for Sanskrit and Tamil have been provided towards the end of the book.

It is a matter of great satisfaction for me that this book contains over 400 illustrations—line drawings, photographs, and maps—many of a quality and range that are not to be found in any book on ancient and early medieval India. The visual element is as important for understanding prehistoric stone tools as for appreciating art and architecture. The illustrations are much more than an adjunct or supplement to the text. In many cases they convey much more than words possibly can, illuminating the past and making it vivid, meaningful, and exciting.

In spite of my best effort, I am aware that this book has certain limitations. For instance, largely because the book was already very long, the last chapter does not discuss the Delhi Sultanate or the history of Islam in the subcontinent, which are very important parts of the early medieval period. For similar reasons, the rich and varied cultural developments of this period could not be surveyed exhaustively. I have instead given a brief overview, with a focus on South India, hoping that the photographs will to some extent make up for the lack of detailed discussion.

This book provides students and scholars with a foundation, encouraging them to pursue further reading, depending on their needs and interests. The historical narrative given in the book relies not only on my own research but also on a vast array of writing and research produced by others. My debt to this scholarship is acknowledged in the in-text references and the readings suggested at the end of the book. Readers are encouraged to follow these references for more detailed treatment of various issues.

The Web supplement carries forward the features of this book, especially in terms of excerpts from original sources and illustrations. This resource allows a reader access to constant additions and updates to the material. This open-endedness is essential, given the fact that new data and changes in perspective are an integral part of the discipline of history.

I hope that this book communicates how exciting and challenging an exploration of the history of ancient and early medieval India can be. My students, initially at St. Stephen's College, and subsequently in the History Department of the University of Delhi, have been an important part of my own exploration of this history. That is why this book is dedicated to them.

Upinder Singh
Delhi, 2008

Acknowledgements to the First Edition

It gives me great pleasure to acknowledge and thank the many people who have helped me in different ways in seeing this book through.

Several ideas emerged in the course of conversations with my friend and colleague, Nayanjot Lahiri. K. P. Shankaran was a relentless source of ideas, which, to his apparent surprise, I always took very seriously. Rajni Palriwala gave prompt help and advice on sociological concepts and issues. Other members of the Delhi academic community who helped me at various points of time with ideas or material include T. K. V. Subramanian, B. D. Chattopadhyaya, Amar Farooqui, Mahesh Rangarajan, Brij Tankha, D. E. U. Baker, Vijaya Ramaswamy, Parul Pandya Dhar, and Vikas Kumar Verma. Valuable long-distance help was given by Dilip K. Chakrabarti in the University of Cambridge and Leslie Orr in Concordia University, Montreal. Rukun Advani offered sound advice on several critical occasions. The library staff of St. Stephen's College, were always extremely helpful in locating material.

The grant of the Daniel Ingalls fellowship (2005) by the Harvard–Yenching Institute allowed me to exploit the formidable resources of the Harvard libraries and also enabled me to do a great deal of writing. The Institute is a very lively and warm place, and this is due to Tu Weiming, Peter Kelly, Elaine Witham, Susan Alpert, Ruohong Li, and other members of the faculty and staff. I thank them all. I am confident that the Yenching Institute will continue to play an important role in providing a meeting ground for much-needed interaction between South Asian and East Asian scholars.

While I was at Harvard, S. R. Sarma and Parimal Patil provided timely suggestions on readings on science, philosophy, and religion. Neelam and Balbir Sihag gave me a home away from home, and the latter gave me access to his interesting ideas and writings on Kautilya. Sugata Bose, Ayesha Jalal, Neeti Nair, and Seema Alavi gave me friendship, which made those months at Harvard a lot of fun, apart from academically productive.

Special thanks are due to the readers who read this book and gave valuable suggestions and constructive criticism, which helped improve the text immensely—P. S. Dwivedi, Uma Chakravarti, Nayanjot Lahiri, Rupendra Kumar Chattopadhyay, Aloka Parasher-Sen, Naina Dayal, Shonaleeka Kaul, Meera Vishvanathan, and Mudit Trivedi. It is a source of great personal satisfaction to me that one of them—P. S. Dwivedi—is my former teacher, who kindled an interest in ancient Indian history in me when I was an undergraduate student at St. Stephen's College. And four of them—Naina, Shonaleeka, Meera, and Mudit—are my former students and now young scholars in their own right. I feel privileged to have had such relationships with my teachers and students.

I owe thanks to several institutions for the photographs in this book. Foremost among these is the Archaeological Survey of India, which provided many photographs from its Photographic Section. Souvan Chatterji, Rajbir Singh, and Teja Singh gave ready and invaluable help, and cheerfully tolerated the enormous, messy piles of photo catalogues which Jai Prasad and I left on their tables for days on end. I would also like to thank the Archaeological Survey for permission to photograph certain artefacts in its Central Antiquities Collection in the Purana Qila, and Sarjun Prasad and his assistants for being so helpful during our shoots there.

Among the officers of the Survey who helped me source or obtain photographic material, I must especially thank R. S. Fonia, D. V. Sharma, K. P. Poonacha, R. S. Bisht, B. R. Mani, and Alok Tripathi. I hope that the photographs provided by the Underwater Archaeology Wing of the Archaeological Survey will inspire an interest in marine archaeology among young students. I would also like to thank Jithendra Das and his colleagues in the Hyderabad Circle of the Archaeological Survey for helping source photographs of Nagarjunakonda.

Thanks are also due to the National Museum, New Delhi, the Indian Museum, Kolkata, and the Government Museums at Chennai, Mathura, Lucknow, Patna, and Chandigarh for permission to use several photographs. At the National Museum, J. E. Dawson, Rita Devi Sharma, D. P. Sharma, Amarendra Nath Tripathi, and Byanktesh K. Singh were very helpful. I would especially like to acknowledge the permission given by the museum to use its beautiful coin photographs that are scattered throughout this book.

I would like to thank the American Institute of Indian Studies for providing some of the photographs reproduced in this book. I would also like to thank Kansai University, Osaka for photographs of Shravasti excavations.

Very special thanks are due to my old friend and photographer, Aditya Arya. In the past too, Aditya has somehow or other got entangled in my book ventures, but this time, his contribution, again at the cost of his time and work, was major. Watching him painstakingly photograph artefacts at the Purana Qila, and looking at the extraordinary results, made me acutely aware of the immense power of the photograph to communicate historical information. Apart from the photographs of ancient pottery and other artefacts in the Central Antiquities Collection, a large proportion of the exquisite colour photographs of ancient sculptures that appear in this book (e.g., those of Sanchi, Ajanta, and Ellora) have been shot by Aditya. The fact that he felt so passionately about making high quality photographs of both ordinary and extraordinary artefacts available to students, transformed this book into much more than what I imagined it could be.

I would like to thank Benoy Behl for allowing me to use his photographs of Ajanta, Alchi, and Tabo. I am especially grateful for the Alchi and Tabo photographs because I think it is high time students were made aware of the extraordinary natural beauty of Ladakh, Lahul, and Spiti, and the historical importance of the continuing Buddhist tradition in these areas.

Goutam Dey of Berachampa contributed photographs of the Chandraketugarh terracottas. I hope that his photographs will stir concern for this important yet neglected site. Photographs of Bhita, Kaushambi, and Hire Benkal were contributed by Mudit Trivedi, those of Angkor Vat by K. P. Shankaran, and the view of Tabo monastery by Raghav Tankha. M. R. Mughal of Boston University generously stepped in to give me photographs of Mohenjodaro. Thanks to them all.

Thanks are due to Tarak Sharma for the illustrations in this book; to Uma Bhattacharya for the beautiful maps and discussions over delicious cookies; Satwinder Singh Channey and Rohit Kathuria for the design and final layout of the book; and Pooja Sharma for efficiency combined with cheer while doing the preliminary layout work. Rimli Borooah did an excellent job of tidying up the text.

At Pearson, I must, first of all, thank Kamini Mahadevan who visited St. Stephen's College many years ago and instigated a train of thought that led to the writing of this book. Jai Prasad believed in this book and worked long and hard on it for many years, stoically bearing the brunt of my barrage of relentless e-mails and phone calls. Praveen Dev provided crucial last-minute editorial help. Debjani M. Dutta was consistently supportive. The production of this book involved inputs from many members of the Pearson team, and I thank them all. I am convinced that this kind of book could not have been produced, at this price and quality, by any other publishing house in India.

I would also like to acknowledge the role of my husband Vijay Tankha for living through my obsessive involvement with this project and for offering, as always, invaluable advice on style and content.

Upinder Singh
Professor, Department of History
University of Delhi

A Reader's Guide to *A History of Ancient and Early Medieval India, 2e*

A first of its kind in India, this book has been developed and designed as a textbook for students of ancient Indian history as well as a book meant for anyone interested in India's early past. It provides an exhaustive coverage of a vast span of India's ancient past in a lucid and engaging narrative style. Pedagogic elements built into the book make the study of history a thought-provoking and enjoyable experience.

In order to help you make the best use of this book, this section provides a window into its various components.

Each chapter constitutes a chronological unit within a larger framework, providing a comprehensive overview of historical issues and details, constructing profiles of various geographical regions of the subcontinent. The **Chapter Outline** provides an overview of the organization of the chapter. The **Chapter Opener** image encourages readers to ask questions about the period. Each chapter begins with a story which represents an important strand in its rich thematic coverage.

564 | A History of Ancient and Early Medieval India

A little over 1,500 years ago, a guild of silk weavers of Lata (in Gujarat) set out on a long journey along with their families. It is not clear what compelled them to move from their homes, but they ultimately reached and settled down in a town called Dashapura in Central India. During the reign of emperor Kumaragupta I, at a time when Bandhuvarman governed the town, the guild financed the building of a temple dedicated to the sun god, Surya. It was a magnificent temple with broad and lofty spires, and its consecration ceremonies were performed in the winter of 437–38 CE. As the years passed, a part of the temple was damaged, possibly by lightning. The guild decided to intervene and finance repairs and renovation. The work began in the spring of 473–74 CE. All these details are given in an inscription discovered at Mandasor, which corresponds to the Dashapura of the inscription. The text of the inscription was composed by Vatsabhatti, a devotee of Surya. He was also the very person whom the guild had entrusted with building and repairing the temple.

The Mandasor inscription is one of many epigraphs of the period *c.* 300–600 CE, which is often referred to as the Gupta period. Dynastic labels have fallen into disfavour among historians. Even if they are used, in this case, it must be remembered that although the political history of North India during these centuries was dominated by the Guptas, the Vakatakas carved out a large kingdom in the western Deccan and were a dominant political force at the time. It is also necessary to take into account political developments in other parts of the subcontinent.

Indian historians who lived and wrote during the period of Nationalist resistance to colonial rule portrayed the Gupta period as a 'golden age'. The glorification of the Gupta period can be viewed as a reaction of Nationalist historians to Imperialist historiography. The features that were highlighted included the political unification of a large part of the subcontinent under what was presumed to be a centralized government, the production of exceptionally fine works of Sanskrit literature, significant developments in the spheres of stone sculpture and architecture, and a presumption that all this was based on eco-

Boxes

Five kinds of boxes appear throughout the book. Each plays a distinct role in helping you explore and understand different dimensions of India's exciting past.

Several important concepts and terms used by historians (sometimes drawn from different disciplines) are explained with their specific and complex meanings in KEY CONCEPTS. This helps in understanding the conceptual vocabulary used by historians, and draws attention to the inherent interdisciplinary nature of history.

KEY CONCEPTS | **Lineage, clan, tribe**

Historians use several sociological terms and concepts while describing ancient cultures. Kinship refers to socially and culturally recognized relationships among people, commonly assumed to be based on natural or biological ties. These ties may be based on birth/descent (con- mance of rituals, and even in matters of inheritance. For example, in a patrilineal society, a son or daughter may inherit property from their mother's kin, and the mother's brother may have a significant role to play in the lifecycle rituals of his sister's children.

PRIMARY SOURCES | **Black and Red Ware**

As its name indicates, Black and Red Ware (BRW) refers to a pottery that is both red and black. The two colours may appear on the same surface of the pot, or one surface may be black, the other red. BRW should not be confused with black-on-red ware (e.g., the typical Harappan Black-and-red pottery occurs in many parts of the subcontinent in several different cultural contexts. For example, it occurs at neolithic sites (Chirand, Piklihal, etc.), pre-Harappan Lothal, many Harappan sites in Gujarat (e.g., Lothal, Surkotada, Rojdi, Rangpur, and

An exposure to the original sources of history and how they can be interpreted is essential to evaluate historical arguments. It also makes history exciting. The PRIMARY SOURCES boxes provide you with descriptions and illustrations of archaeological source material, interesting information about textual sources and their authors, translated excerpts from ancient texts and inscriptions, and discussions of visual sources.

FURTHER DISCUSSION | **The making of long carnelian beads**

The city of Khambhat (Cambay) in Gujarat is one of the largest centres of stone bead- making in the world today. Mark Kenoyer, Massimo Vidale, and Kuldeep K. Bhan conducted an ethno-archaeological study, examining the techniques used by modern bead makers morphic rock which was heated to make an extremely hard and durable tool. This material has been given the name of 'Ernestite', after the archaeologist Ernest J. H. Mackay, who was the first to discover the drills and understand their significance. It could have taken a

A more detailed examination of specific issues is essential for a nuanced understanding. FURTHER DISCUSSION boxes reveal the multi-layered nature of our past and encourage readers to think more deeply about a variety of historical themes and issues.

RECENT DISCOVERIES | **Attirampakkam**

The site of Attirampakkam has been long recognized as an important palaeolithic site. Recent excavations by a team led by Shanti Pappu and Kumar Akhilesh were marked by a comprehensive, multidisciplinary approach and revealed valuable new evidence. These excavations, accom- west Asia. The new dates for the lower palaeolithic from the recent excavations at Attirampakkam have changed the situation radically.

The lower palaeolithic age in South Asia has been generally placed in

Historical knowledge is constantly growing. New discoveries can often radically change our understanding. RECENT DISCOVERIES boxes direct attention to some of these exciting discoveries, the people who made them, and their impact on our understanding of India's ancient past.

Many times, it is not new discoveries but new questions, methodologies, and debates that lead to important breakthroughs. NEW DIRECTIONS IN RESEARCH boxes bridge the gap between readers and researchers by presenting samples of interesting new research, and explaining their methodology and results in a clear and accessible way. This exposes you to new trends in history writing, and provides a sense of the constantly changing understandings of the past.

NEW DIRECTIONS IN RESEARCH | **Betel-bag bearers in royal courts**

The cultivation and use of betelnut is known from the early centuries CE. The Sanskrit word *tambula* can refer to the betel leaf vine (*Piper betle* L.), as well as to a roll consisting of a leaf of this vine, smeared with slaked lime, enclosing sliced areca nut, and other

Betel leaves seem to have been part of the lives of aristocrats and affluent people at least from the Gupta period onwards. During the 9th/10th centuries, the gift and exchange of betel increased in many roles, including rituals of welcome and social and political alliances.

Maps, Photographs, and Figures

Moving ahead from the dull, text-heavy narrative of other books on ancient India, *A History of Ancient and Early Medieval India* has over 550 illustrations—maps, photographs, and drawings—that bring history alive. These make you understand history with greater clarity and enable you to truly appreciate the richness of our subcontinental past and culture.

Maps are essential to understand history. Note the use of different colours for topographical and elevation details, latitude and longitude coordinates to define the mapped area, a scale to give an idea of distances, and modern place markers to convey a sense of relative location.

Over 450 photographs of various artefacts, such as stone tools, terracottas, pottery, coins, archaeological sites, religious monuments, and sculptures, enliven the text.

Further Readings at the end of each chapter encourage you to read more extensively on various topics to deepen your understanding of the subcontinental past.

FURTHER READINGS

Bakker, Hans. 1997. *The Vakatakas: A Study in Hindu Iconology*. Groningen: Egbert Forsten.
Banerjea, J. N. [1956] 1975. *The Development of Hindu Iconography*. 2nd rev. edn. New Delhi: Munshiram Manoharlal.
———. 1966. *Pauranic and Tantric Religion: Early Phase*. Calcutta: University of Calcutta.
Chakrabarti, Kunal and Kanad Sinha. (Eds.). 2018. *State, Power and Legitimacy: The Gupta Kingdom*. Delhi: Primus Books.
Chatterjee, Asim Kumar. 2000. *A Comprehensive History of Jainism. Vol. 1: From the Earliest Beginnings to AD 1000*. New Delhi: Munshiram Manoharlal. Chapters 7, 8.
Chattopadhyaya, B. D. [1994] 1997. *The Making of Early Medieval India*. Delhi: Oxford University Press.

See chapter 3, p. 116 For a discussion of plant and Animal domestication and food Production

It is easier to identify and describe stone tools than to know whether, or to what extent, a community was producing its food through plant or animal domestication. Sometimes, there

In order to help you understand a certain idea in detail, or to follow up a topic dealt with across different chapters, **Cross References** are provided in the margins. These are indicated by a cross reference icon with relevant page numbers.

Diacritic marks, used extensively in academic writing, have been avoided to facilitate easy reading. However, the conventionally used systems of transliteration for Sanskrit and Tamil have been provided at the end of the book to help you navigate through academic writings.

A Note on Diacritics

अ	आ	इ	ई	उ	ऊ	ऋ	ए	ऐ	ओ	औ	•	ः
a	ā	i	ī	u	ū	ṛ	e	ai	o	au	ṁ	ḥ

क	ख	ग	घ	ङ	च	छ	ज	झ	ञ
ka	kha	ga	gha	ṅa	ca	cha	ja	jha	ña
ट	ठ	ड	ढ	ण	त	थ	द	ध	न
ṭa	ṭha	ḍa	ḍha	ṇa	ta	tha	da	dha	na

Glossary

Acheulian tools: an assemblage of stone tools marked by advanced and increasingly symmetrical handaxes and cleavers; primarily associated with the lower palaeolithic, they continue into later parts of the stone age as well
***agrahara*:** land or village gifted by a king
***ahimsa*:** non-injury, non-violence
Ajivikas: An ancient religious sect, associated with Makkhali Gosala
***akam*:** Sangam love poems
Alvars: the Vaishnava saint-poets of early medieval South India
***bhikkhuni*:** a Buddhist nun
biface: handaxe
Black and Red Ware (BRW): Pottery whose surface is partly black and partly red, found in various different chronological and cultural contexts
blade: a flake tool, the length of which is more than twice its width
***bodhisattva*:** a future Buddha
boustrephedon style: a style of writing in which consecutive lines start in opposite directions

The **Glossary** explains certain specific terms used in the book. Words listed in the Glossary are given in bold on their first occurrence in the book.

The **References** at the end of the book provide the key to in-text references in the various chapters.

References

Abraham, Meera. 1988. *Two Medieval Merchant Guilds of South India*. New Delhi: Manohar.
Acri, Andrea ed. 2016. *Esoteric Buddhism in Mediaeval Maritime Asia: Networks of Masters, Texts, Icons*. Singapore: ISEAS.
Acri, Andea, Roger Blench, and Alexandra Landmann eds. 2017. *Spirits*
______. 2010. *Bodhgaya*. New Delhi: Oxford University Press.
______. 2015. *Nalanda: Situating the Great Monastery*. Mumbai: Marg Foundation.
Asher, Frederick M. and Walter Spink. 1989. *Maurya Figural Scultpure Reconsidered*. Ars Orientalis 19: 1–25.

We hope that this book will prove to be an important contribution towards transforming the way ancient Indian history is understood, taught, and learnt. It is our endeavour to constantly improve this book, and we would be glad to receive suggestions from all our readers. Please write to us with your feedback to https://in.pearson.com/support/product-support.html

INTRODUCTION

Ideas of the Early Indian Past

The main physiographic zones of the subcontinent

Ways of dividing the Indian past

Changing interpretations of early Indian history

New histories, unwritten histories

The Puranas describe a universe shaped like an egg, vertically divided into the celestial worlds, earth, and netherworlds. The earth is a flat disc, consisting of seven land masses (*varshas*) arranged in concentric circles, alternating with seas of salt water, molasses, wine, butter, curd, milk, and fresh water. Situated in the centre of the earth is Jambudvipa, in whose southernmost part lies Bharatavarsha, the golden Meru mountain rising from its midst. One of several explanations of the name Bharatavarsha connects it with the Bharata people, descendants of the legendary king Bharata, son of Dushyanta and Shakuntala. Cosmography blends with geography in the Puranas. Bharatavarsha is said to consist of nine divisions (*khandas*), separated from one another by seas. The places of pilgrimage described in the Puranas extend across many parts of the subcontinent. The mention of its mountains, rivers, and places—some of which can be identified—suggests that the composers of such texts were familiar with various areas of the Indian subcontinent, and perceived them as parts of a larger cultural whole.

For people of other lands, the major subcontinental landmark was the river Sindhu (Indus). Persian inscriptions include Hidu among the provinces of the empire of king Darius, Greek texts talk about India, and ancient Chinese sources refer to the land of Shendu. These terms initially referred to the Indus valley, but their connotations swiftly expanded. For Megasthenes, the Greek emissary who visited the court of Chandragupta Maurya in the 4th century BCE, 'India' meant the entire subcontinent. Many centuries later, the Arab geographers used the term al-Hind, for North India or the entire subcontinent; some of them extended it up to Southeast Asia. Medieval Persian texts used the word Hindustan for the subcontinent, 'stan' being a Persian suffix for territorial terms.

Ancient Indian texts have the idea of the subcontinent as a geographical and cultural unit but also recognize its distinct parts. In the *Vishnu Purana*, the land of Bharatavarsha is said to lie south of the snow-clad mountains and north of the ocean. Bharatavarsha is understood not merely as a geographical area but as the only land where the cycle of the four *yugas*, *karma*, and *dharma* operate (see B. D. Chattopadhyay, 2019: 1–30). Within this land, the Puranas list and describe different geographical regions and people (S. M. Ali, 1966: 109–77). The *Raghuvamsha*, a long poem composed by the 4th/5th century Sanskrit poet and playwright Kalidasa, recounts the *digvijaya* (victory over the quarters) of the legendary king Raghu as a circumambulation of the subcontinent, describing the various political units, physical landscapes, and produce of the regions he traversed with his army. There were other ways of visualizing and describing geographical space. Ancient Tamil poems talk of the land of the Tamils known as Tamilakam and divide it into five ecological zones known as *tinai*. The 12th century *Rajatarangini* of Kalhana talks about the beauty and distinctiveness of Kashmir, while aware of its connections with other regions.

In the early medieval period, the word 'Hindu' acquired religious connotations. But at the same time, Hind or Hindustan continued to have a broader geographical meaning. For instance, the *Nuh Sipihr* of the Sufi intellectual Amir Khusraw describes Hind as the best of countries, and Abul Fazl's *Ain-i-Akbari* extolls the people of this land.

Although the idea of South Asia forming a geographic and cultural unit within which there was regional diversity is a very old one, its nation-states—India, Pakistan, Nepal, Bhutan, Bangladesh, and Sri Lanka—emerged in recent times, in the 20th century. When exploring ancient history, it is necessary to ignore modern political boundaries and to treat the Indian subcontinent and its many regions and sub-regions as a complex, ever-changing mosaic. The history of the subcontinent is really about the historical trajectories and interactions of many regions and sub-regions which at certain points of time attained some measure of political unity. Further, the subcontinent was never an isolated unit in ancient times. Across the centuries, there were various kinds of interaction—political, economic, social, religious, and cultural—with other parts of Asia, Europe, and Africa.

The Main Physiographic Zones of the Subcontinent

The Indian subcontinent has fairly well-defined geographical frontiers within which there is enormous ecological diversity. This ecology has changed greatly over time. The earth is about 4.5 billion years old. *Homo sapiens* appeared on the planet only about 200,000 years ago. The drama of life on earth unfolded against the drama of geology and natural history, long before humans arrived on the scene. There were massive tectonic movements (changes in the earth's crust), volcanic eruptions, continental collisions and separations, water replacing land and vice versa. For instance, the alluvial Ganga plain was once a sea; the Deccan plateau was the product of a series of volcanic eruptions that emitted molten floods of hot lava; the now highly

FURTHER DISCUSSION | South Asian landscapes—then and now

Pranay Lal points out that if you travel from Bengaluru to Jammu, you will cover 2700 km in distance, but over 3 billion years of the earth's history by just looking out of the window. The Nandi Hills, not far from Bengaluru, belong to a rock formation known as the Dharwad Craton, formed about 3.5 billion years ago, and are among the oldest rocks in India. The rugged granite terrain near Ramanagara near Bengaluru, where Sholay—the blockbuster Hindi film of the 1970s—was shot, was formed about 2.5 billion years ago.

The history of the earth includes massive tectonic movements—movements in the earth's crust. India, Sri Lanka, Australia, Madagascar, and East Antarctica were once a single huge landmass that geologists call Gondwanaland. Thiruvalluvar rock at Kanyakumari, the southernmost tip of India, is the point at which they broke away as a result of three huge volcanic eruptions that happened between 180 million and 80 million years ago. The discovery in 2000 of the Indian purple frog (*Nasikabatrachus sahyadrensis*) in the Nilgiris is interesting because its closest relative is a frog found in the Seychelles, a group of islands in the western Indian Ocean, about 1,600 km away from the coast of Kenya. These distant cousins tell the story of these and other islands forming land bridges between India and Madagascar millions of years ago, and then getting separated.

The story of the subcontinent's mountains and rivers is a story of change. The Himalayas are very young fold mountains, formed due to three massive tectonic upheavals that pushed the Eurasian plate against the Indian plate. The first uplift occurred between 41 and 32 million years ago; the second between 13 and 9 million years ago; and the third between 4 million years ago and 300,000 years ago.

Events in one area of the world could have an impact in very distant places. About 75,000 years ago, a massive volcanic eruption occurred at what is today lake Toba in Sumatra. Tephra ash deposits from this eruption have been found embedded in river valleys in peninsular India. This eruption led to a series of environmental changes, the precise nature of which are still being debated.

Source Pranay Lal, 2016

The rocky terrain at Ramananagara

eroded Aravallis are the oldest fold mountains in the subcontinent, the Himalayas are the youngest.

Today, the climatic patterns of the Indian subcontinent are similar to those prevailing in other areas on the same latitude, but are significantly modified by the Himalayas and the Western Ghats. The Himalayas block the icy northern winds from sweeping across the Indo-Gangetic plains in winter as well as the rain-laden monsoon winds from the south-west in summer. The barrier of the Western Ghats similarly leads to rainfall in the western coastal strip. Most of the subcontinent gets its rains from the south-west monsoon, except for the north-west and Sri Lanka, which rely on winter rains.

In the north, the subcontinent is bordered by the Himalayas. The process of their uplift and folding is still going on, making them geologically unstable. The Himalayas can be divided into the western, central, and eastern zones, each with its own specific characteristics. To their north is the Karakoram range and to the west are the Hindu Kush mountains which run through modern Pakistan and Afghanistan. The north-western part of the subcontinent includes the arid mountainous North-West Frontier Province and the Baluchistan province of Pakistan. Leaving aside the fertile river valleys, this area is not especially suited for agriculture, but the many routes running along its valleys and passes connect the subcontinent with areas lying to its west.

Even more arid conditions prevail in the Thar desert of Rajasthan, where low hills and sand dunes rise over the underlying low, rocky plateau. Between the desert and the north-western mountains lies the Sindh province of southern Pakistan, the Indus providing precious water in an area of very low rainfall. The northern course of this river lies in Tibet and Ladakh, and along with its tributaries, it flows through the fertile plains of Indian and Pakistani Punjab. To the east of the Indus is the shrivelled course of a once mighty river, the Ghaggar-Hakra.

The fertile northern alluvial plain of the Ganga and its tributaries is another major geographical zone of the subcontinent. The western part of this plain is known as the doab ('the land between two rivers', the Ganga and Yamuna). The middle part of the plains corresponds roughly to the modern state of Bihar and the eastern part of Uttar Pradesh. The eastern part includes the delta of the Ganga and Brahmaputra, comprising of modern West Bengal, Assam, and Bangladesh. To the north, the Ganga plain veers into the Nepal terai, and to the north of the terai lie rugged mountain ranges. The Vindhyan ranges separate the northern plains from peninsular India, while the Aravalli hills divide the Thar desert from Central India. The Malwa plateau, with its two major rivers, the Narmada and Tapi, lies between the Aravallis and the Central Indian mountains.

Peninsular India is an old and relatively stable geological formation, its landscape marked by plateaux, plains, and the fertile valleys of rivers such as the Mahanadi, Krishna, Godavari, Pennar, and Kaveri. The Deccan plateau, formed by the lava flows from very ancient volcanoes, constitutes the dominant part of the peninsula. It is bordered by the Eastern and Western Ghats, beyond which are the narrow Coromandel and Malabar–Konkan coastal plains. The Nilgiri, Annamalai, and Cardamom hills lie in the extreme south of the peninsula. The island of Sri Lanka, geologically an extension of peninsular India, is separated from it by the shallow Palk Strait. The central highlands in the south-central part of the island are surrounded by plains which are traversed by many rivers.

The various geographical zones of the subcontinent should not be viewed as isolated units. From very early times, human interaction took place through routes cutting across mountains, rivers, and regions, dictated by geographical features and human needs. The Hindu Kush could be crossed at points such as the Khyber, Gomal, and Bolan passes, and a network of overland routes connected the subcontinent to China, Central Asia, West Asia, and Europe.

Our view of history tends to be land-oriented. We often forget that about 71% of the earth's surface is covered by water and that the seas and oceans carry about 96.5% of that water. Across the centuries, the over 7,500 km subcontinental coastline was

FURTHER DISCUSSION | **The mighty Brahmaputra**

The Brahmaputra is one of the mightiest Indian rivers. It comes into its own during the monsoons, when its waters swell enormously and result in massive floods. There are no storage dams and no major hydro-electric projects on this river. It can be pacific as well as volatile. It is unpredictable.

The river rises in the Himalayan glaciers, flows some 1,100 km through Tibet, Arunachal Pradesh, and Assam, and then into Bangladesh. It meets the Ganga (known as the Padma in this lower stretch) and Meghna, creating a massive delta which debouches into the Bay of Bengal. The Ganga and Brahmaputra carry massive amounts of sediments during the monsoon floods—estimated at an average of about 13 million tons per day. Together, these two rivers discharge the greatest volume of water among the world's rivers—carrying about 170,000 cubic metres of water per second into the Bay of Bengal.

The Brahmaputra drains over 700,000 sq km of land, and its course has been marked by numerous changes over the centuries, especially due to tectonic movements. Its deeply braided course is marked by shallow marshy lakes known locally as *beels* and many sandy islands known as *chars*.

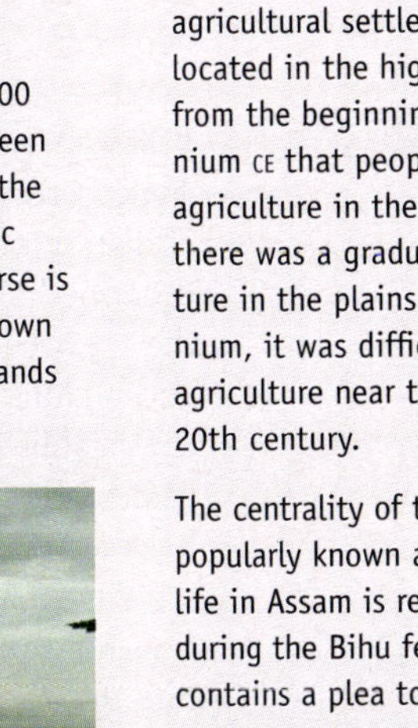

From early times, the history of Assam has been intertwined with the Brahmaputra. The river, hills, and floodplain are parts of a complex and delicate ecosystem. The one-horned rhinoceros is today found only on the floodplain of the Brahmaputra. The earliest neolithic agricultural settlements in Assam were located in the highlands and it is only from the beginning of the first millennium CE that people experimented with agriculture in the floodplain. Although there was a gradual extension of agriculture in the plains during the first millennium, it was difficult to practice settled agriculture near the river until the early 20th century.

The centrality of the Brahmaputra—popularly known as Luit—to everyday life in Assam is recognized in songs sung during the Bihu festival. One of these contains a plea to the powerful river:

> The Barhamthuri on the banks of the Brahmaputra, the place where we gathered firewood, do not wash it away.
> O God Brahmaputra, you will lose those who offer you areca nut.

Source Saikia, 2019

home to numerous fishing, trading, and sailing communities. This long coastline linked the subcontinent to the larger Indian Ocean world and to other parts of Asia, Europe, and Africa.

The natural landscape has always been an important part of human life, and has affected and influenced people's thought and action in many ways. The topography, climate, soil, and natural resources of any land influence modes of subsistence, settlement patterns, population density, and trade. This issue can be discussed in specific as well as global contexts. In recent times, scholars have used the term Anthropocene to refer to an epoch when human activities began to leave an indelible mark on global ecological processes. Assessments of when this epoch began vary widely, although most scholars place it in the 18th century, with the beginning of the Industrial Revolution in Europe. There is also a critique of the idea of the Anthropocene—that it is essentially based on European experience and presents a homogenized picture of realities that were much more diverse and complex. Although the human impact on the environment in the past three centuries has been qualitatively different from that in earlier times, it is necessary to acknowledge the enormous environmental impact of human activities in much earlier times, for instance, due to the invention of fire or the beginnings of agriculture, and the human contribution to the extinction of several animal species (see Cederlöf and Rangarajan, 2018: xiii–xxiv).

The global crisis created by the impact of carbon emissions on climate has forcefully brought home the fact that the history and future of humankind are inextricably tied up with the environment and climate, land and water, plant and animal species. It is hence essential to understand human history in relation to ecology.

Ways of Dividing the Indian Past

The English word 'history' comes from the Greek *historia* (inquiry or investigation). History is essentially a discipline that inquires into the experiences of people who lived in the past. Historians often classify the past by dividing it into different periods. Labels are necessary for the sake of convenience, but their basis should be meaningful and consistent, and their limitations should be recognized.

For a long time, historians divided Indian history into the Hindu, Muslim, and British periods. This classification can be questioned on several grounds. What about polities ruled by non-Muslim elites after the advent of Turkish rule? Is the religious affiliation of a ruling elite the best basis for labelling a period? Why is the third period described as the British and not the Christian period? From when can we start using the term Hindu meaningfully as a basis of religious identity? What about the periods and regions where Buddhism or Jainism flourished? While the historical significance of the establishment of the Delhi Sultanate and the spread of Islam in the subcontinent is undeniable, did this event create a fundamental rupture in the fabric of the everyday lives of ordinary people?

Due to such questions that can be posed, most historians have discarded the Hindu–Muslim–British periodization of the Indian past in favour of a more neutral classification into the ancient/early, early medieval, medieval, and modern periods. The dividing lines may vary, but the ancient or early period can be considered as stretching roughly from the earliest times to the 6th century CE; the early medieval from the 6th to the 12th/13th centuries; the medieval from the 13th to the 18th centuries; and the modern from the 18th century to the present. The 18th century is sometimes referred to as the early modern period. Periodization is convenient but it is important to remember that these are not hard lines. Dividing the past into neat categories can also be limiting. Some of the most exciting themes in Indian history require taking a long-term view and breaking through the lines of periodization.

The ancient or earliest parts of the human past can be further divided into prehistory and history. The enormously long period before the invention of writing and the study of that period are known as prehistory. The part of the past that comes *after* the invention of writing, and the study of that part of the past (i.e., of literate societies) constitute what is considered history.

A language consists of spoken symbols of communication. A script, or writing, is a system of visual communication using signs or symbols associated with specific meanings or sounds, written down on some surface. Human beings used languages long before they invented **scripts**. The cuneiform script of Mesopotamia (in ancient Iraq) was invented in *c.* 3400 BCE and Egyptian hieroglyphics in *c.* 3100 BCE. The ancient Mesopotamians pressed letters onto moist clay tablets, while the ancient Egyptians wrote on papyrus sheets made of reeds. In the Indian subcontinent, the earliest substantial evidence of writing is associated with the Harappan civilization and dates from *c.* 2600 BCE, but recent discoveries push back the origins of the script to the second half of the 4th millennium BCE. The Harappan script is mostly found on seals and sealings. But apart from the specimens of writing that have actually survived, it can be assumed that people must have written on perishable material as well. Writing marked a new stage in human expression and communication. It opened new possibilities for storing and transmitting ideas and knowledge across distance and time. Rulers used writing to advertise and exercise power, merchants to record business transactions, priests to preserve religious texts, and poets to give permanence to their creative expression. We can speculate about the precise impulses that led to the invention of writing, but all over the world (with

Map 1 The physical geography of the Indian subcontinent

a few exceptions) it coincided with the emergence of cities and states. For these reasons, historians consider the beginning of writing an important watershed in the story of ancient cultures.

However, the impact of writing was gradual, complex, and by no means uniform. In a situation where relatively few people knew how to read or write, writing gave power and privilege to those who knew it and denied it to those who did not. Further, the invention of writing did not mean the end of oral transmission. The spoken word has always held a special significance in many cultural traditions, and this significance continued even after manuscripts of texts came to be made. Oral versions of many written texts continued to circulate and often had a far greater outreach and impact. And some written texts existed simultaneously in oral, written, and performative forms.

Apart from its impact, the beginning of writing is also an important watershed in the study of the past because written evidence becomes available to the historian. Nevertheless, it must be remembered that such evidence covers only a very small portion of the human past. The past before writing (prehistory) and the history of non-literate people who did not leave behind written sources are also extremely important and have to be recovered. And even when written sources are available, archaeological sources continue to be important for historians.

In the Indian subcontinent, the story of writing is a bit complicated. Although the Harappans were a literate people, their script has not yet been deciphered. So, historians cannot use the written material they left behind to reconstruct history. Another mystery is: what happened to writing after the decline of the Harappan civilization in *c.* 1900 BCE? While it is possible that people continued to write, although on perishable material, there are hardly any surviving specimens of writing between *c.* 1900 BCE till we come to the 4th century BCE. The oldest script in the subcontinent is the Harappan script, but the oldest *deciphered* script is **Brahmi**, known from at least the 4th century BCE, and the two scripts seem to be quite different.

For these reasons, it is not easy to draw the dividing line between history and prehistory in India and the term **protohistory** is useful. This word carries different meanings. In the European context, it is sometimes used to refer to people who did not themselves have writing, but who are mentioned in the written records of a contemporary literate group. In the Indian subcontinent, the Harappan civilization—a literate culture with an undeciphered script—is included in protohistory. This term can also include the period *c.* 1500–500 BCE, for which there is an orally transmitted literature (the Vedas), but no evidence of writing. Archaeologists often use the word protohistory for the long period between the beginning of food production and the advent of iron technology. This would include **neolithic** and **chalcolithic** cultures in different parts of the subcontinent.

The subcontinent is a huge geographical area, and the transition to literacy did not take place everywhere at the same time. For instance, areas outside the literate Harappan zone were inhabited by non-literate people. Going by the earliest surviving samples of deciphered writing, the beginning of the historical period in North India would have to be placed in the 4th century BCE. On the basis of **Tamil-Brahmi** inscriptions and **Sangam literature**, the transition to the historical period in South India is generally placed during the 3rd or 2nd centuries BCE. But the evidence of earlier Brahmi inscriptions from Anuradhapura in Sri Lanka and more recently, from Kodumanal and Keezhadi in Tamil Nadu, suggest that the date needs to be pushed back to at least the 4th century BCE. If the Harappan script is deciphered some day, the dates for the beginning of the historical period in northern India will have to be pushed back to the 3rd millennium BCE, or even earlier.

Changing Interpretations of Early Indian History

The past is gone and cannot be revisited directly. It can only reveal itself through historical sources and skillful interpretations and reconstructions of the past by historians. Writing history does not mean collecting and assembling a set of self-evident facts. It involves a rigorous analysis of the primary sources, reasoned argument, and interpretation. Like all other disciplines, over time, the academic discipline of history has been marked by a great deal of diversity and change in focus, perspectives, and methods.

All societies have a sense of the passage of time and of the past. In ancient India, texts such as the epics and Puranas reflect the existence of a cyclical concept of time—of the idea of four *yugas* (ages) of *krita*, *treta*, *dvapara*, and *kali*, which together form a *mahayuga*. But a sense of linear time also existed, for instance, in the use of eras and sequential accounts of dynasties and kings. A historical consciousness is reflected, for instance, in the king lists in the Puranas, the idea of *itihasa*, the epic narratives, accounts of saints and teachers in Jaina texts, royal biographies, and the genealogies and accounts of political events preserved in royal inscriptions. (See Chapter 1 for further discussion of this issue.) As is the case with other ancient cultures, the historical consciousness reflected in the traditional histories of ancient India is significantly different from the ways in which history is researched and taught in modern universities.

The **historiography** (the scholarly activity of constructing and writing history) of ancient and early medieval India reveals many significant changes over time; these can be understood against the background of the political and intellectual contexts in which they emerged and flourished. The various 'schools' of history writing are often presented and understood in terms of one school making way for the other in a neat, forward progression. The reality is, however, much more complex. There was considerable variety within the various schools; some of them co-existed (and still do so) in dialogue or conflict with each other; and there are many examples of writings that do not easily fit into the dominant historiographical trends of their time.

Harappan writing on seal; Egyptian hieroglyphics; Mesopotamian cuneiform (from top)

The 18th and 19th centuries were dominated by the writings of European scholars, usually referred to as the Orientalists or Indologists, although they often described themselves as 'antiquarians'. Many of them were employees of the East India Company and later, the British Government of India. The founding of the Asiatic Society of Bengal in 1784 provided an institutional focus for scholars working in a number of related fields such as textual study, **epigraphy**, **numismatics**, and history. A major contribution of the Indologists lay in their efforts to collect, edit, and translate ancient Indian texts. In this, they depended heavily on information provided by Indians, whose contribution was rarely acknowledged. Indology soon spread beyond the confines of the British empire and became a subject of study in European universities. There was also a gradual increase in the number of Indian scholars who devoted themselves to the study of India's early past.

Apart from the study of ancient texts, the 19th century also witnessed important developments in the field of epigraphy, numismatics, **archaeology**, and the study of art and architecture. The decipherment of the Ashokan Brahmi and **Kharoshthi** scripts were major breakthroughs. The analysis of coins contributed to the construction of a framework of political history. Officers of the Geological Survey discovered prehistoric stone tools and laid the basis of Indian prehistory. The Archaeological Survey of India was established in 1871, and over the succeeding decades, this institution made an important contribution towards unearthing and analyzing the material remains of India's past. The Burma Circle of the Archaeological Survey of India and the Archaeological Survey of Ceylon (established in 1890) laid the foundations of archaeological research in Myanmar and Sri Lanka.

The contributions and breakthroughs of the 18th and 19th centuries were rooted in a colonial context, and this is evident in certain features of Indological writing. The Brahmanical perspective of ancient Sanskrit texts was often uncritically taken as reflecting the Indian past. Social and religious institutions and traditions were critiqued from a Western viewpoint. Indian society was presented as static and its political systems as unwaveringly despotic over the centuries. Race, religion, and ethnicity were often confused with each other and there was a tendency to exaggerate the impact of foreign influence on ancient India. This is the time when the classification of the Indian past into the Hindu, Muslim, and British periods took root.

Indian scholars of the late 19th and first half of the 20th centuries made major contributions towards constructing a connected narrative of ancient India. Writing against the background of an emergent, and later increasingly strong, national movement, these historians are generally referred to as Nationalist historians. They were responsible for meticulously weaving together data from texts, inscriptions, coins, and other material remains to amplify the contours of the ancient Indian past. Especially important contributions were made in the field of political history. South India was brought into the narrative and progress was made in the study of regional polities.

The nationalist tinge in the writings of these scholars can be seen in their insistence on the indigenous roots of all major cultural developments. It is also reflected in their search for golden ages, which led to their exalting the age of the Vedas and the Gupta empire. Non-monarchical polities were discovered described as republics, and were celebrated to counter the idea that India had never known anything but despotic rule. The periodization of the Indian past into the Hindu, Muslim, and British periods was, however, retained. It coalesced with a communal tendency to valorize the 'Hindu period' and

R. C. Majumdar (1888–1980), a leading historian of the Nationalist school

to project the advent of the Turks and Islam as a calamity which led to a fundamental fracture in the fabric of Indian society.

From the 1950s, inspired by Marxism, left-oriented historians came to play an influential role in the construction of the history of ancient and early medieval India. In the long run, their major achievements include shifting the focus from dynastic history to social and economic structures and processes, giving importance to modes of production, class stratification, and agrarian relations. The Nationalist historians' search for golden ages was replaced by a more critical approach, acknowledging the existence of tensions and conflicts in the ancient past. There was a concerted attempt to democratize history by moving the spotlight away from political and social elites to recover the histories of ordinary people, especially those who had suffered centuries of subordination and marginalization.

While making these valuable interventions and contributions, up to around the 1980s, left-oriented historians often tended to work with unilinear historical models derived from Western historical and anthropological writings. Texts were sometimes read uncritically, with insufficient attention paid to their problematic chronology and peculiarities of genre. Archaeological data was included, but the basic framework of the historical narrative remained text-centric. Religion and culture were often sidelined or mechanically presented as reflections of socio-economic structures and change.

In recent years, against the background of the ascendency of right wing politics, there is an increasing circulation of right wing interpretations of the early Indian past in the academic and popular domains. These usually attempt to push back the dates of ancient texts, emphasize indigenous origins and elements, and go back to the old idea of ancient India being a 'Hindu period' marked by glorious achievements which came to an end with the advent of the Turks. These perspectives, which are frequently connected with communal agendas, tend to ignore the complexities of the ancient Indian past. In their search for pure origins, they forget the fact that mixture, migration, and cultural confluence have important parts of human history from early times and that the Indian subcontinent is no exception to this.

The influence of political ideologies on the interpretation of the past is not only seen in India. For instance, a history of ethnic conflict in Sri Lanka has played an important role in promoting competing Aryan/Sinhala and Dravidian/Tamil versions of the island's past (see Gunawardana, 1995, 2000). In recent years, Sri Lankan historians have questioned the over-reliance on the Pali chronicles for the construction of the island's early history; they have urged a more nuanced understanding of the past based on a more critical reading of the texts, and the incorporation of epigraphic and archaeological evidence. In Pakistan and Bangladesh too, nationalism and religion have had an impact on the writing of history, and the dilemmas on how to treat the pre-Islamic past are especially reflected in school text-books. The use of history to serve political agendas of the present can, in fact, be seen all over the world.

While history has always been connected with the ideologies and concerns of the present, it is extremely important to interrogate all constructions of the past and to distinguish those based on a rigorous analysis of the sources and convincing argument from those that not.

As mentioned earlier, not all history writing can be subsumed under the labels of historiographical schools. Changes in the historiography of ancient India over the past few decades can also be understood by focusing on some of their specific themes and features.

The continuing growth in the volume of archaeological data and the use of scientific techniques in archaeology have been transforming our understanding of the early Indian past. Genome analysis is bringing to light new evidence on the migrations and mingling of people across the world. Palaeo-environmental studies are reconstructing the changing profiles of the environment and climate and their impact on human life. The study of ancient flora and fauna is contributing to a more precise understanding of subsistence practices, nutrition, health, and disease. Animal histories are adding a new, important dimension to our understanding of the human past.

D. D. Kosambi (1907–66), a pioneer of Marxist historiography

Studies of ancient texts and inscriptions have become more nuanced than before and view them as discourses that must be understood in the light of their time, genre, authorial perspective, and audience. It is recognized that visual sources have an importance beyond art history. The history of ideas and emotions are new areas that are opening up. Most historians are conscious of the urgent need to break through the boundaries and cocoons created by conventional periodization and the need to write histories that cut across the centuries.

Historians continue to be acutely conscious of the impact of power structures and social inequality on history writing and they recognize that history has to become more inclusive for it to be meaningful to more people. Most ancient textual sources were produced by and for members of elite groups and therefore reflect their ideas and interests. But there are ways of getting around these limitations. These include reading texts against the grain, being attentive to their silences and nuances, and drawing on the evidence of archaeology. Efforts continue to be made to recover the past of subordinated and marginalized groups that have often been hidden from history—such as the labouring poor, lower castes, tribal communities, and groups that were once labeled 'untouchables.' The inequalities embedded in institutions such as slavery, ***varna***, ***jati***, and the patriarchal family need to be viewed from long-term perspectives, to understand how they intersected and changed over time.

During the last few decades, a small group of historians (mostly women) working on gender relations has made a strong impact on ancient Indian social history. They have asked new questions, broken the artificial divide between the private and political domains, revealed the power hierarchies within the family and household, and demonstrated the close relationship between gender, class, caste, and political power. Women and gender are now recognized as important parts of social history. In more recent times, the awareness that gender cannot be limited to the binaries of male and female is likely to push the understanding of gender and sexuality forward in interesting ways.

A significant feature of the historiography of the early medieval period is the detailed study of the changing profiles of regions and sub-regions. Based on careful empirical examination of epigraphic and textual sources, these studies have identified changes in political, economic, and social structures, with a special focus on agrarian relations and the legitimation of political power. These have been accompanied by studies of the emergence and development of regional languages, literature, and cultural traditions. Such studies have revealed the varied historical textures and trajectories in different parts of the Indian subcontinent in early medieval times.

Histories of early India should ideally represent the diverse regions and communities of the subcontinent. However, while the heartlands of great empires and kingdoms are well represented, many regions, for instance the Northeast, are not. Greater effort needs to be made to redress this balance. Histories of the subcontinent need to pay greater attention to the areas that today form the nation states of Sri Lanka, Pakistan, Nepal, Bhutan, and Bangladesh. More attention also needs to be paid to the relationships between the regions of the subcontinent with other parts of the world. Apart from trade networks, there are many exciting and relatively unexplored aspects of cultural transactions across the regions of the ancient world, which would help situate the history of ancient South Asia within a global context.

New Histories, Unwritten Histories

There can never be a last word in history. The achievements made by historians over the years are many, but there are still many challenges in expanding and deepening our understanding of the complexities and diversities of historical processes in the various regions of the subcontinent, and in incorporating the textures of the lives of ordinary people, especially marginalized and subordinated groups, into our understanding of the ancient past. A critical understanding of historiography is essential in order to have a sense of where the history of ancient and early medieval India stands today. However, the major advances of the future are likely to be the result of asking new questions, looking for new answers to old questions, highlighting new themes, and thinking boldly and creatively beyond the boundaries of existing historical frameworks. The infinite possibilities and open-endedness of history make it an exciting discipline.

Some people seem to think that ancient history is distant, difficult to relate to, even irrelevant to our present times and concerns. However, there is great value in understanding ourselves and our times within a larger historical context. The most important thing that history can do is to teach us to think historically. It can make us realize the diversity and complexity of human experiences across cultures, across time. If we look carefully, we will find that the tangled roots of several social practices, institutions, and ideas of the present lie in the remote past. But history is marked not only by continuities, but also by major ruptures and changes. So it would be a mistake to expect to find in the ancient past a mirror of the present. In fact, more interesting than the aspects that are familiar to us are those that are startlingly different. The story of the past contains much that is surprising and exciting. This is enough justification for reading and writing history.

FURTHER READINGS

Bhattacharya, Sabyasachi. 2011. *Talking Back: The Idea of Civilization in the Indian Nationalist Discourse*. New Delhi: Oxford University Press.

Chakravarti, Uma. 2006. *Everyday Lives, Everyday Histories: Beyond the Kings and Brahmanas of 'Ancient' India*. New Delhi: Tulika.

Chattopadhyaya, B. D. 2019. *The Concept of Bharatavarsha and Other Essays*. Ranikhet: Permanent Black. Chaps. 1–3.

Rangarajan, Mahesh and K. Sivaramakrishnan. (Eds.). 2012. *India's Environmental History*. Vol. 1: *From Ancient Times to the Colonial Period*. Ranikhet: Permanent Black.

Roy, Kumkum. 2018. *The Power of Gender and the Gender of Power: Explorations in Early Indian History*. New Delhi: Oxford University Press.

Terracotta plaque depicting a rapturous scene of a dance and musician, *c.* 1st century BCE; the two holes on top suggest that it was meant to be strung or hung.

CHAPTER 1

Understanding Sources

Reading ancient texts from a historical point of view

Archaeology and the early Indian past

Epigraphy: the study of inscriptions

Numismatics: the study of coins

Visual sources

Conclusions

On 21st October 1880, U. V. Swaminatha Aiyar, a learned Tamil scholar and teacher at the Government College in Kumbhakonam, paid a courtesy call on Ramaswami Mutaliyar, who had recently come to town as a *munsif* (civil judge). Aiyar introduced himself as a pupil of the great Tamil scholar Minakshisundaram Pillai. Mutaliyar was unimpressed and started questioning him about the texts that he had studied. Aiyar reeled off a long list of titles. The judge interrupted him impatiently and asked, "What's the use of studying all of this?" Aiyar reeled off some more titles, ending with Kamban's *Ramayana*. "It's fine that you have studied all of these recent books. But have you studied any of the old works? Have you studied the *Chivaka-chintamani*? Have you studied the *Manimekalai*? Have you studied *Shilappadikaram*?" Aiyar was astonished and confused. He had spent many years acquiring mastery over texts of various genres and he thought he knew everything. But he had never heard of these. Aiyar's interest was aroused. He devoted the rest of his life to looking for palm leaf manuscripts of ancient Tamil texts, editing and publishing them. He published 93 books, including collections of the old Tamil 'Sangam' poetry, the epics known as the *Shilapaddikaram* and *Manimekalai*, and his own essays. We know about Aiyar's fateful encounter with Ramaswami Mutaliyar from his unfinished autobiography, *En Charittiram* (My life story). This is just one of many exciting stories of discovery or rather, re-discovery, that we read about in history.

The past, like the present, is complex and can be looked at from many different perspectives. There can never be a single, final, perfect history. There can never be a complete or exact picture of what happened in the past; the task of the historian is to bring us as close as possible to such a picture. This involves carefully studying the available sources of information, searching for fresh evidence, and rigorous analysis and interpretation. Debate and disagreement are an important part of the growth of all forms of knowledge, and history is no exception.

All historical interpretations are ultimately based on evidence derived from the sources of history, which are conventionally divided into two categories—textual and archaeological. From a historian's point of view, **textual sources** include all compositions—long or short, written or oral; **archaeological sources** include all tangible, material remains. But these distinctions are not absolute. Most remains of the past, including literary **manuscripts**, are actually material in nature. And certain kinds of archaeological sources which have writing on them—inscriptions, coins, and inscribed images—can be considered material objects and texts. Visual sources, which include architecture, sculpture and painting, can be seen as a distinctive type of material source.

The ways in which historians have used different kinds of sources to construct the history of ancient and early medieval India will become clear as you read this book. This chapter gives a broad overview of the major sources, highlighting their general features, and the important issues that have to be kept in mind while using them as windows into the past.

Reading Ancient Texts from a Historical Point of View

Throughout history, in all cultures, in all parts of the world, subordinated and marginalized social groups have been deprived of opportunities to participate in the production and dissemination of knowledge. Hence, ancient texts largely reflect the perspectives and ideas of political, social, or religious elites. Almost all of them were written by upper-class men for other upper-class men.

PRIMARY SOURCES | **Ancient palm leaf manuscripts**

Paper was invented in China in about the 2nd century BCE. Block printing too was invented in that land in about the 8th century and printing from moveable type in the 11th century. These technologies gradually spread to other parts of Asia and eventually to Europe. In India, traditional writing materials and methods continued to be used for many centuries. Ancient Indian manuscripts were often made with palm leaves. Here is a description of how such manuscripts (known as *talapatra* in Sanskrit, *olai* in Tamil) were usually made:

The leaf used was either from the talipot palm (*Corypha umbraculifera; tali* in both Sanskrit and Tamil) or palmyra palm (*Borassus flabelliformis*, Sanskrit *tala*, Tamil *panai*). The talipot leaf is larger, thinner, and more flexible and durable than that of the palmyra. Talipot leaves may measure about 90 × 8–9 cm, and the palmyra ones about 50 × 3–4 cm. The selected leaves were cut to the right shape and size. They were then pierced in one, two, or three places (on the left, middle, and right top). A string was woven through these holes, and then wound around the leaves. One end of the string was knotted or was tied to a small object (e.g., a shell, wooden peg, or button) to prevent it from slipping out of the holes. The cover of the palm leaf manuscript was made of wood, dry palm petioles, or in rare cases, ivory.

The writer engraved letters on the leaf with a stylus (a pointed, pen-like object). The leaf was then smeared with soot or powdered charcoal mixed with vegetable juice, so that the black mixture filled the grooves and the writing was easy to read. The letters ran parallel to the length of the leaves. In some cases where the leaf was very long or when the text was in verse, the words were written in two or three columns. If there was a commentary, it was usually written above, below, or sometimes around the text. Page numbers were often given in the right margin.

Palm leaf manuscripts had to be stored very carefully as they were vulnerable to many natural hazards such as heat, insects, water, fungus, dust, and fire as well as the danger of destruction by human hands. Scribes kept the manuscript tradition alive by repeatedly making copies of old manuscripts. This vibrant tradition started declining around the 19th century with the coming of the printing press.

There are special techniques for treating and preserving old palm leaf manuscripts. First, the manuscript is fumigated or treated with insecticides (e.g., thymol, chloromate solution, formaldehyde, phosphene gas, or ethylene oxide). The leaves are then cleaned using solvents such as water, detergents, or ethyl alcohol. Next, any split, broken, or damaged portions are repaired. This can be done using special, thin paper and a water soluble mixture including small quantities of polyvinyl acetate and methyl cellulose. Once the repairs are complete, the leaves are oiled to make them flexible and polished gently with a soft, dry cloth. They can then be restrung and the covers attached. The repaired manuscript has to be stored carefully so that it is protected from any fresh damage.

The discovery, preservation, and care of ancient manuscripts are crucial parts of the preservation of historical heritage. There are thousands of old manuscripts in various parts of the subcontinent whose contents have not yet been studied or published. It is impossible to estimate just how many have been destroyed and how many are waiting to be discovered.

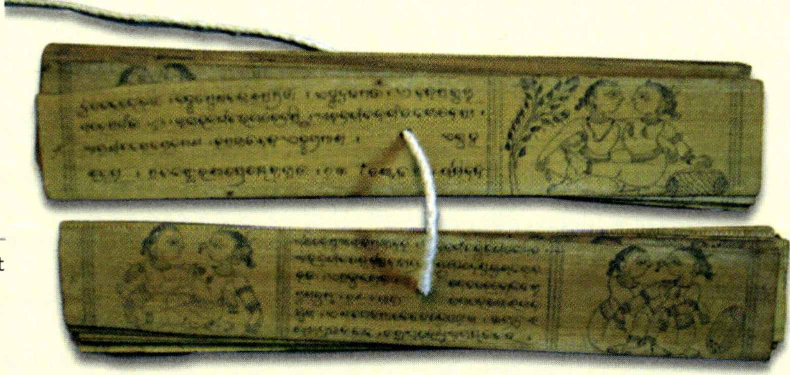

A palm leaf manuscript in the proto-Bangla script, *c.* 12th century

A text is any composition consisting of words. The general term 'text' is here being distinguished from the more specific term 'literature.' Literature is very hard to define, but can be understood as a type of text that uses language in creative, expressive, and imaginative ways, for instance, a work of drama or poetry.

All texts are connected to the historical contexts in which they are produced and in which they circulate. However, an ancient text does not give a simple or direct reflection of the society of its time. It offers a complex representation of that society and a refracted image of the past. Information has to be prised out with great care, skill, and ingenuity to make historical inferences. Many early religious texts were not primarily meant to be read but to be recited, heard, and performed. They were passed on orally from one generation to the next, even after they were available in the form of written manuscripts.

A text can be read in many different ways from a historical point of view, but certain important issues have to be kept in mind. Foremost among these are its age and authorship. Ancient texts are much older than their surviving manuscripts. Some of them grew and changed over time and this process of growth and change—the period of composition—in some cases lasted for hundreds of years before they were compiled or given a more or less final shape. A text can be used as a source of historical information for the period during which it was composed, but if the composition stretched over many centuries, it becomes essential to try to identify its different chronological layers and the various additions or interpolations made over time. This is not easy and requires a very skillful analysis of language, style, and content, on the basis of which older and newer portions can be identified. Scholars have prepared critical editions of some of the texts. A critical edition is prepared on the basis of a careful comparative study of different manuscripts of a text and considers the parts that are common to all as the original core. The critical apparatus attached to a critical condition directs attention to variations across manuscripts and different commentarial interpretations. When analyzing a text from a historical point of view, it is necessary to be aware of the period over which it was composed and when it was compiled.

Many early texts were the work of not one, but many authors. Even if the authors remain anonymous, it is important to identify their background and the perspectives and biases they reflect, such as those of class, religion, and gender. Other questions that can be asked about texts include: Where were they composed? Where and in what forms did they circulate? Who transmitted them and how did they go about doing so? Who was their target audience? What was the place of these texts within prevailing social and political power structures and cultural traditions?

Analyzing a text from a historical point of view does not mean mechanically plucking out self-evident 'facts'. The information a text provides has to be understood within the framework of its particular genre or type. In the case of poetry or drama, the analysis requires sensitivity to the literary conventions and aesthetic sensibilities of the time and the writer's style and imagination. Some texts are normative or prescriptive. They do not directly describe what was actually going on, but present an ideal situation from the point of view of their authors. The intersection between what they say and what was happening on the ground has to be skillfully reconstructed. Ancient texts often contain myths, and although myths can tell us indirectly about history, myth and history are not the same thing. It is possible to tease out hidden meanings from texts by reading them creatively against the grain and by comparing what they say with other sources.

The classification of textual sources: language, genre, and content

Ancient and early medieval texts can be divided into categories on the basis of language, genre, content, age, and the tradition to which they belonged. Linguists and philologists (scholars who study old languages) have divided the languages of the world into different families. Languages belonging to the same family have certain structural similarities and share a significant number of similar, related words (or cognates). For instance, Hindi, Punjabi, Marathi, Bengali, Assamese, Gujarati, Sindhi, Odia, Nepali, and Kashmiri belong to the **Indo-European** family. So do Persian, Greek, Latin, German, French, Dutch, Italian, Spanish, Armenian, and many other languages of Europe and Asia. Languages of the **Dravidian** family—Tamil, Malayalam, Telugu, Kannada, and Tulu—are today largely spoken in South India. Exceptions include Brahui, which is spoken in the Baluchistan area of Pakistan, Gondi in Central India, and Malto in the Rajmahal hills of Eastern India. Santali, Khasi, Mundari, and some other languages of eastern India belong to the Austro-Asiatic family. Certain languages of the Northeast, such as Manipuri, Bodo, Garo, and Lushai belong to the Tibeto-Burmese family. Andamanese, one of the languages spoken in the Andaman Islands, is not apparently related to any of the known language families.

The oldest surviving texts in the Indian subcontinent—the **Vedas**—are in Sanskrit. Sanskrit belongs to the Indo-Iranian branch of the Indo-European family of languages, as do ancient **Pali** and **Prakrit** (also known as Middle Indo-Aryan or Middle Indic). There were various dialects of Prakrit—e.g., Maharashtri, Shauraseni, and Magadhi. **Apabhramsha** is a term used for the further development of Prakrit up to the end of the 1st millennium CE; it contains a blend of later Prakrit with elements of regional languages. Among the Dravidian languages, Tamil has the oldest literature, followed by Kannada. Many of the other Indian regional languages and dialects we are familiar with today took shape between *c.* 1000 and 1500. The worlds of the various languages and

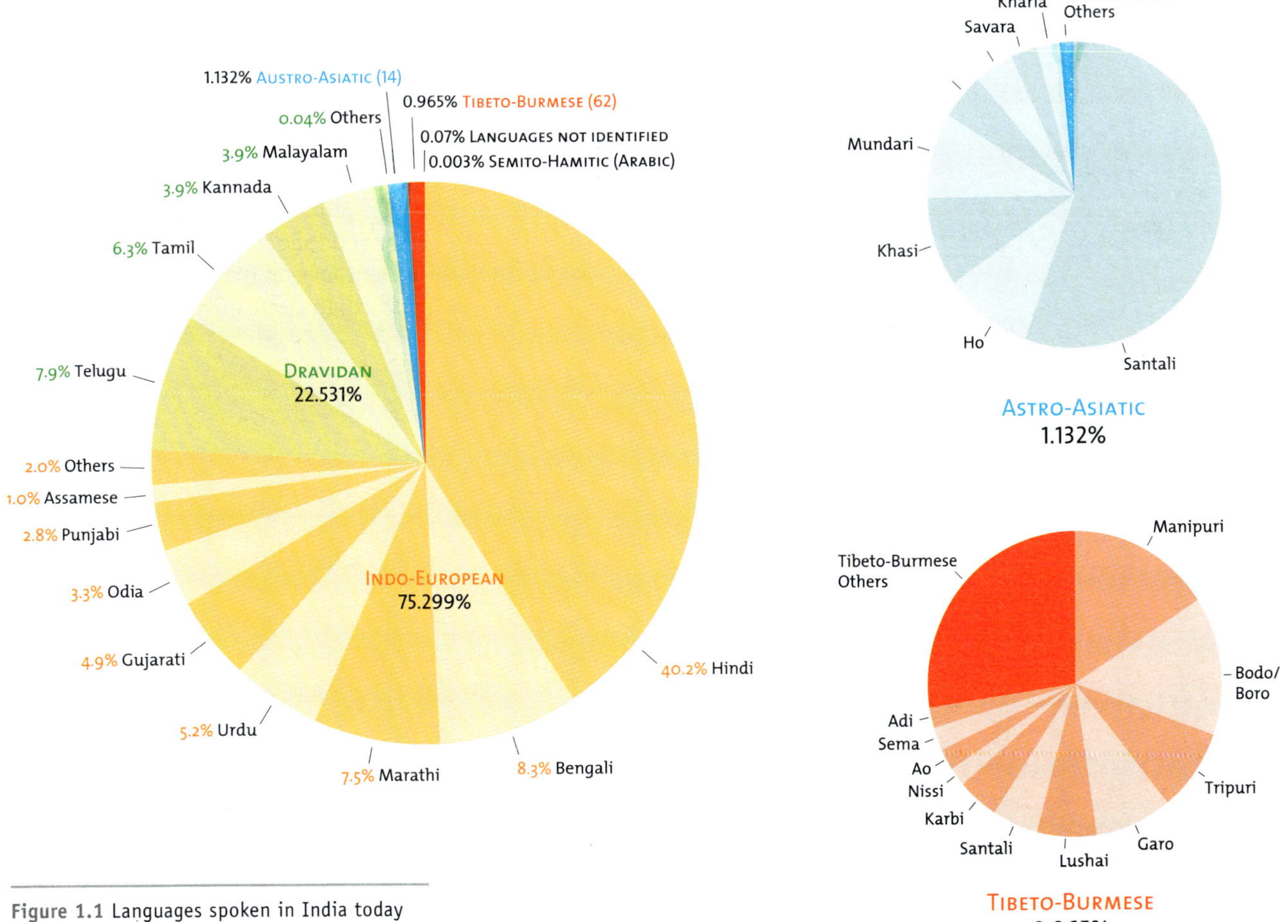

Figure 1.1 Languages spoken in India today

people who used them for speech or writing were not closed or separate, but overlapping and interacting (see Mohan, 2021).

Languages have histories and change with the times. The pre-classical Sanskrit of the *Rig Veda* is different from the classical Sanskrit of Kalidasa's poetry. The term 'classical Sanskrit' refers to the language whose rules were codified by the 5th/4th century BCE grammarian Panini in his *Ashtadhyayi*. Another important Sanskrit grammatical work is Patanjali's *Mahabhashya* (2nd century BCE). The oldest surviving Prakrit grammar is Vararuchi's *Prakritaprakasha*, whose date is debated. The ancient Tamil of the Sangam poems is different from modern Tamil. The *Tolkappiyam* is the oldest surviving Tamil grammar; parts of it go back to the early centuries CE. Such grammatical texts tell us about the structure of ancient languages and they also contain incidental historical references.

Ancient Indian texts are sometimes divided into religious and non-religious (or 'secular') texts. Although this is a handy distinction, there are a few things worth keeping in mind. The English word 'religion' attaches great importance to belief, and suggests fixed, rigid, mutually exclusive boundaries and distinct religious identities. No ancient Indian word has such a meaning. The Sanskrit ***dharma*** or the Pali ***dhamma***, for instance, had a broader reference to a path that people should follow or an exemplary way of life. They included many different kinds of things—codes of conduct, social practices, forms and foci of worship, ritual activity, traditions, and philosophical ideas. Ancient societies did not make the kind of distinction between the religious and the secular domains with which we are familiar in modern times. Therefore, we should not be surprised to find an interweaving of what appear to be religious and non-religious themes and content in many ancient texts.

Some of the major textual sources for the history of ancient and early medieval India are discussed in the following sections. (For additional details, see the various volumes of Gonda. [Gen. Ed.], [1973–87] 2022.) As the variety and volume of texts is enormous, these should only be considered a sample. The idea is to give a brief introduction to their range, with a special focus on texts frequently used and cited by historians. While some of these reflect a historical consciousness, that is, an attempt to preserve the memory of certain aspects of the past, most of them were not written with such an intention. But, as we shall see in the course of this book, texts of any kind can be used as sources of history. Texts are not only sources of history, they are also an important part of history, and some texts had a life and influence long after the period of their composition. Historians usually study ancient texts in their original languages. However, general readers who do not know these languages can get a flavor of these texts through good translations.

The Vedas

In the Hindu tradition, the Vedas have the status of ***shruti*** (literally, 'that which has been heard'). They are thought to embody an eternal, self-existent truth realized by the *rishis* (seers) in a state of meditation or revealed to them by the gods. The category of ***smriti*** (literally, 'remembered') texts includes the Vedanga, Puranas, epics, Dharmashastra, and Nitishastra.

The word Veda comes from the root *vid* (literally, 'to know') and means 'knowledge'. There are four Vedas—*Rig, Sama, Yajur*, and *Atharva*. The *Rig Veda* contains the world's oldest surviving poetry, some of it of extraordinary beauty and philosophical depth. Each Veda has four parts, the last three of which sometimes blend into each other—the **Samhita**, Brahmana, Aranyaka, and Upanishad.

The *Rig Veda* Samhita is a collection of 1,028 hymns (*suktas*) arranged in 10 books (Mandalas). The *Sama Veda* consists of 1,810 verses, mostly borrowed from the *Rig Veda*, arranged according to the needs of musical notation. The original melodies are, however, lost. The *Yajur Veda* deals with the details of the performance of sacrificial rituals (***yajnas***). The *Atharva Veda* is the latest Veda and contains hymns (some from the *Rig Veda*), but also spells and charms which reflect popular beliefs and practices. The **Brahmanas** (this term should not be confused with the Brahmana *varna* or caste) are prose explanations of the Samhita portions and give details and explanations of sacrificial rituals and their outcome. The **Aranyakas** ('forest books') interpret sacrificial rituals in a symbolic and philosophical way. There are 108 **Upanishads**, among which 13 are considered the principal ones. The Upanishads contain a great variety of philosophical ideas about sacrifice, the body, and the universe, but are most closely associated with the concepts of ***atman*** and ***brahman***. Within the Vedic corpus as a whole, Books 2–7 (known as the family books) of the *Rig Veda* Samhita are considered the oldest; the later portions of this Samhita, along with all the other Vedic texts, comprise later Vedic texts.

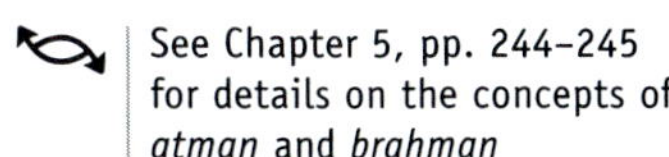
See Chapter 5, pp. 244–245 for details on the concepts of *atman* and *brahman*

There are several recensions (*shakhas*) of the Vedas, associated with different schools (*charanas*) of Vedic study and interpretation. (The terms *shakha* and *charana* are often used interchangeably.) The Shakala *shakha* is the only surviving recension of the *Rig Veda*. The texts of the *Yajur Veda* are divided into those of the Shukla (White) school and Krishna (Black) school. The recensions of the Shukla (also known as Vajasaneya) *Yajur Veda* are the Madhyandina and Kanva. The Black school is represented by the Kathaka, Kapishthala, Maitrayani, and Taittiriya recensions. The main difference between the texts of the two schools is that the Samhitas of the White school contain only the *mantras* (prayers and sacrificial formulae), while in the texts of the Black school the *mantras* are accompanied by a commentary describing and discussing various aspects of the sacrificial rituals. The Kauthuma, Ranayaniya, and Jaiminiya (or Talavakara) are recensions of the *Sama Veda*, and the Shaunaka and Paippalada of the *Atharva Veda*. References in inscriptions mention other recensions of the Vedas that once existed but are now lost.

Vedic texts are religious and ritualistic texts, and references to possible historical events are few. For example, Book 7 of the *Rig Veda Samhita* refers to a battle of 10 kings, in which Sudas defeated a number of adversaries who had confederated against him. Historians have tried to reconstruct various aspects of the **culture** represented in the Vedas, but it is not easy to interpret this vast and complex corpus.

A major problem in using the Vedas as a source of history is that of dating the *Rig Veda*. The dates that have been suggested for the composition of this text range from *c*. 6000 BCE to 1000 BCE. The very early dates are not acceptable because the cultural context of the *Rig Veda*, for instance, the use of metals, was not known at the time. Many historians take *c*. 1500–1000 BCE as the period of composition of early Vedic literature and *c*. 1000–500 BCE as that of later Vedic texts.

Vedic texts form an important part of the Brahmanical tradition—texts composed, preserved and transmitted by a section of Brahmana men. It reflects their religious beliefs, practices, and points of view. As a source of history, these texts are used for the history of parts of north-western and northern India during the 2nd and 1st millennia BCE. But apart from the question of dates, as we shall see later on, there are several problems in co-relating the evidence from the Vedas with archaeology.

A number of supplementary texts known as Vedanga (literally, 'limbs of a Veda') aimed at helping the proper recitation, use, and understanding of the Vedas. These include works on phonetics (*shiksha*), metre (*chhanda*), grammar (*vyakarana*), etymology (*nirukta*), ritual (*kalpa*), and astronomy (*jyotisha*). The broad period of composition of Vedanga texts is *c*. 500–200 BCE. Yaska's *Nirukta*, a work on the etymology of words in the *Rig Veda*, belongs to around the 5th century BCE.

The two Sanskrit epics: the *Mahabharata* and the *Ramayana*

The two Sanskrit epics, the *Mahabharata* and the *Ramayana*, fall within the category of *smriti* as well as *itihasa* (traditional history), although the *Ramayana* is sometimes classified as *kavya* (literature). (For overviews, see Fitzgerald, 2004; Goldman and

Sutherland Goldman, 2004.) Similarities in language and style suggest that they emerged from a common cultural milieu. The *Mahabharata* refers to Valmiki and the *Ramayana,* and outlines the Rama story in a section called the *Ramopakhyana*. The *Ramayana* in turn mentions the Kurus, Hastinapura, and Janamejaya, although it does not mention the Mahabharata war. The two epics were clearly aware of each other, at least in their later stages of development. The composition of the *Mahabharata* can be placed between *c.* 400 BCE and *c.* 400 CE, and the *Ramayana* between the 5th/4th century BCE and the 3rd century CE. Hiltebeitel (2001: 18–20) suggests a shorter period of composition for the *Mahabharata*, from the mid-2nd century BCE to the year zero. J. L. Brockington (1984) identifies five distinct chronological and cultural stages in the development of the *Ramayana*. The fact that the different stages in the composition and development of the epics could well have spanned many centuries, possibly even a thousand years, should make it obvious why most historians no longer use the term 'epic age'.

The epics are magnificent texts with powerful stories that have captured the imagination of millions of people over the centuries. To use them as historical sources, it is necessary to identify their internal chronological layers, which is not an easy task. According to tradition, Rama lived in the *treta yuga* (age) and the Mahabharata war happened later, in the *dvapara yuga*. However, some historians argue that the events and characters associated with the *Mahabharata* reflect a slightly earlier period than those of the *Ramayana*. This is because the setting of the *Mahabharata* is the Indo-Gangetic divide and the upper Ganga valley, while in the *Ramayana*, the centre of political gravity had clearly shifted eastwards, to the middle Ganga valley. The strong women characters of the *Mahabharata* suggest an earlier stage of social development, when women were less subordinated to men compared to later times. The practice of ***niyoga*** (levirate; i.e., when a husband deputes his conjugal rights over his wife to another man in order to produce an heir) in the *Mahabharata* also suggests a social stage that is prior to that of the *Ramayana*, which reflects much stricter controls over women.

The *Mahabharata* consists of 18 Parvas (books) and has two main recensions—a northern and southern. The core story concerns a conflict between two sets of cousins—the Kauravas and the Pandavas—and a great war that was fought between them at Kurukshetra. But the text also contains a huge amount of material that has little or no connection with the main story. According to tradition, it was composed by Vyasa (he is also an important character in the epic), but in its present form, it is clearly not the work of a single individual. The *Mahabharata* is truly an encyclopaedic work, and it boasts of this fact. A heroic story formed the core to which many other stories, and didactic portions containing teachings, were added over centuries. The additions include the stirring discourse of Krishna to Arjuna on the eve of the war, known as the *Bhagavad Gita*.

Whether a bitter war between the Pandavas and the Kauravas ever happened is difficult to prove or disprove. It is possible, even likely, that there was a small-scale conflict between two sets of cousins that was gradually transformed into a gigantic epic war by bards and poets. Some historians and archaeologists have argued that this conflict may have occurred in about 1000 BCE.

The *Ramayana* exists in the form of two main recensions—northern and southern; the northern recension can be further divided into the north-eastern, north-western, and western. The language of the northern recension is more elaborate and polished than that of the southern one. The epic consists of seven Kandas (books), of which the first (Bala Kanda) and last (Uttara Kanda) are later interpolations. The basic story of the *Ramayana* is about Rama, prince of Kosala; his banishment to the forest due to the intrigues of his wicked stepmother; the abduction of his wife Sita by Ravana, the demon king of Lanka; Sita's rescue; and Rama's return to the capital, Ayodhya, to become king. The compact vocabulary and style indicate that the core of the text was the work of a single individual, traditionally identified as Valmiki. Valmiki appears in the Bala Kanda, where he is inspired to compose the epic, and in the Uttara Kanda, where he gives

PRIMARY SOURCES | Archaeology and the *Mahabharata*

Archaeological explorations and excavations at places mentioned in the *Mahabharata*—e.g., Hastinapura, Kurukshetra, Panipat, Tilpat, Baghpat, Mathura, and Bairat—have given evidence of a pottery called **Painted Grey Ware** (**PGW**) which goes back to *c.* 1000 BCE. This shows that these sites were inhabited around this time, and the nature of the remains suggests that the people who lived here shared a pastoral-cum-agricultural lifestyle.

There is another sort of evidence from Hastinapura: The *Matsya* and *Vayu Puranas* state that during the reign of king Nichakshu (fifth king after Parikshit, grandson of Arjuna, who became king after the war), due to a flood in the Ganga, the capital was shifted from Hastinapura to Kaushambi. Excavations at Hastinapura gave evidence of a flood in the Ganga, after which the site was deserted for several centuries. However, it is not necessary that this was the same flood mentioned in the Puranas.

There is a strong local tradition that the Purana Qila in New Delhi marks the place where Indraprastha, the capital of the Pandavas, once stood. Shams Siraj Afif's *Tarikh-i-Firuz Shahi* (14th century) states that Indraprastha was the headquarters of a *pargana* (district). A 14th century stone inscription found in Naraina village in west Delhi also mentions Indraprastha. The 16th century *Ain-i-Akbari* of Abul Fazl states that Humayun's fort was built at the place where Indraprastha, capital of the Pandavas, was located long ago. In fact, till the end of the 19th century, there was a village called Indarpat inside the fort walls.

Excavations carried out at the Purana Qila between 1954 and 1971 revealed several archaeological levels ranging from the 4th century BCE to the 19th century CE. The discovery of a few stray pieces of PGW indicated the possibility that an older settlement was located somewhere nearby. However, there is no way of knowing for sure whether this settlement had any connection with the Mahabharata legend. The recent excavations conducted during 2013–14 and 2017–18 yielded more material remains of the different phases, including what appears to be a pre-Maurya level.

Archaeology cannot really prove or disprove the historicity of epic events or characters. The crux of the matter is that there is a qualitative difference between the nature of literary and archaeological evidence. The epic imaginatively weaves together an event-centred narrative about people and places. Archaeology, on the other hand, tells us about general patterns of material culture, and cannot easily be used to corroborate textual details about individuals or events.

Purana Qila excavations in progress, 1954

refuge to Sita. As direct references to Rama being an incarnation of the god Vishnu are concentrated in the first and last books of the *Ramayana*, some scholars argue that it was originally a heroic epic that became imbued with religious significance at a later point of time. Others argue that the *Ramayana* was pervaded by the idea of Rama's divinity from the very outset.

Excavations at the site of Ayodhya (in Ayodhya district, UP) indicated the existence of a settlement here from the **Northern Black Polished Ware (NBPW)** phase, which is usually dated from *c.* 700 to 2nd/1st century BCE. The 2002–03 excavations, conducted by the ASI at the direction of the Allahabad High Court, focused on the remains that lay beneath the Babri Masjid, which was destroyed by a mob in 1992. These excavations revealed material remains from the NBPW phase onwards. According to the excavation report (Manji, Mani, et al., 2003: 268), this phase at Ayodhya can be dated *c.* 1000–300 BCE on the basis of radiocarbon dates.

The dynamism of the epics is evident from the existence of many vibrant epic traditions which have moulded the characters and events in various ways. In Jaina tellings of the *Mahabharata*, the central figure is the 22nd *tirthankara* Arishtanemi, who is said to have resolved to become an ascetic when he saw animals being killed for his wedding feast. The war that takes place is between king Jarasandha (with the Kauravas on his side) and the Yadavas (with the Pandavas on their side). The 16th century *Razmnama* is a Persian telling of the *Mahabharata* which was part of a translation project sponsored by the Mughal emperor Akbar. The tellings of Rama's story include the Buddhist *Dasharatha Jataka* in Pali, the Jaina *Paumachariu* of Vimalasuri in Prakrit, Kamban's Tamil *Iramavataram*, and Tulsidas' 16th-century *Ramcharitmas* in Awadhi. Rama's story was narrated in Tibet, Myanmar, Laos, Cambodia, and Indonesia. Apart from written and oral versions, the stories of the *Ramayana* and *Mahabharata* have also been the subject of art and performance sculpture, painting, stories, plays, novels, dance dramas, television serials, and films (for the *Ramayana*, see Richman, 1992; Dhar. [Ed.], 2021).

The epics can be read in many different ways from the historical point of view. While most scholars have focused on debating the historicity of their events, some have tried to understand their many different cultural layers against the background of changing historical processes. Another approach is to read such texts as a response to a specific kind of historical context. For instance, James L. Fitzgerald (in Mittal and Thursby, 2005: 54) has argued that the *Mahabharata* was a Brahmanical response to certain specific historical developments: the increasing popularity of religious traditions such as Buddhism and Jainism, and the rise of dynasties such as the Nandas and Mauryas, who extended support to them, were perceived by a section of the Brahmanas as threatening the Brahmanical order. The *Mahabharata* was their response to this perceived crisis. Regardless of their historicity, across the centuries, the *Mahabharata* and *Ramayana* have inspired many powerful narratives and have played important roles as purveyors of a variety of social, political, and cultural values.

The Puranas

The word 'Purana' means 'old'. According to tradition, the Puranas were composed by Vyasa, but it is clear that in the form in which they have come down to us, they were not the work of one person nor of one age. There are 18 Mahapuranas (great Puranas), and many more Upapuranas (secondary Puranas). The standard list of the 18 Mahapuranas includes the *Vishnu*, *Narada*, *Bhagavata*, *Garuda*, *Padma*, *Varaha*, *Matsya*, *Kurma*, *Linga*, *Shiva*, *Skanda*, *Agni*, *Brahmanda*, *Brahmavaivarta*, *Markandeya*, *Bhavishya*, *Vamana*, and *Brahma*. The origins of Puranic composition may back to much earlier times, but it stretched forward into the 4th–5th centuries CE, and in some cases, even later.

The Puranas are supposed to have five characteristics (*pancha-lakshanas*), i.e., they are supposed to discuss five topics—the creation of the world (*sarga*); re-creation (*pratisarga*); the periods of the various Manus (*manvantaras*); the genealogies of gods and *rishis* (*vamsha*); and an account of royal dynasties (*vamshanucharita*), including the Suryavamshi and Chandravamshi kings, whose origin is traced to the sun and the moon. Actually, not all Puranas deal with all these five topics, and most of them deal with much more.

The conception of time in the Puranas is mind-boggling. There are four ages or *yugas*—*krita, treta, dvapara,* and *kali*, all consisting of thousands of years. These four *yugas* make up a *mahayuga*, and 1,000 *mahayugas* constitute a *kalpa*. Every *kalpa* is divided into 14 *manvantaras*, each presided over by a Manu. One *yuga* follows the other, and the periodic destruction of the world is followed by its re-creation. This cycle of time is connected with the cyclical decline and revival of *dharma*. Within the cylical framework of the *yugas*, there are linear narratives of political history.

The earliest parts of the Puranic genealogies are either entirely or partly mythical. The later genealogies of kings of the *kali* age, after the Kurukshetra war, have historical material. The account is given in the future tense in the form of a prophecy, because Vyasa is supposed to have lived at the end of the *dvapara yuga* and the beginning of the *kali yuga, before* the events he is supposed to be describing. The *Bhavishya Purana* is mentioned in some Puranas as the original authority for the genealogies, but the present versions of this text have incomplete material on the subject and seems quite late.

Although their details do not always match, the Puranas—especially the *Vayu, Brahmanda, Brahma, Harivamsha, Matsya,* and *Vishnu*—do provide useful information on ancient political history. They refer to historical dynasties such as the Haryankas, Shaishunagas, Nandas, Mauryas, Shungas, Kanvas, and Andhras (Satavahanas). They also mention certain kings with names ending in the suffix 'naga', who ruled in Northern and Central India in the early centuries CE, about whom very little else is known. The dynastic lists end with the Guptas (4th–6th centuries), indicating that most of the Puranas were compiled at about this time. However, some are later—e.g., the *Skanda Purana* belongs to the 6th/7th century and the *Bhagavata Purana* to the 10th century.

The Puranas have accounts of mountains, rivers, and places, which are useful for the study of historical geography. They also reflect the emergence of a religiosity based on devotion, especially towards the gods Vishnu and Shiva and the goddess Shakti. This devotion was expressed through the worship of deities in image form in temples, pilgrimage (*tirtha*), and vows (*vrata*). The Puranas had a very important function in the Brahmanical tradition as vehicles of Brahmanical social and religious values. At the same time, they also reflect the interaction of Brahmanical and non-Brahmanical cultural traditions and the emergence and development of Hindu religious practices.

Dharmashastra

The Sanskrit word *dharma* (from the root *dhri*, meaning 'to maintain, support, or sustain') is very rich in meaning and difficult to translate. It has an interesting history, which will be discussed in Chapters 5, 6, and 7.

In its classical form, *dharma* refers to the proper, ideal conduct of a person living in society, a course of action which leads to the fulfilment of the goals of human life. These goals, known as *purusharthas*, are *dharma* (righteous conduct), *artha* (material well-being), and *kama* (sensual pleasure). At some point, ***moksha*** (deliverance from the cycle of rebirth) was added to the list. In this scheme of things, material gain and sensual pleasure are considered appropriate goals, if pursued in moderation in accordance with *dharma*. The concept of *dharma* is closely tied up with the idea of *samsara*—the cycle of birth, death, and rebirth. The fruits of *dharma* include the acquisition of spiritual merit (*punya*), and its impact is supposed to be felt not only in this life but in future lives as well. The obligations of *dharma* are considered as applicable to and binding on everybody. Therefore, *dharma* also means duty.

A special corpus of Sanskrit texts dealing specifically with *dharma* are collectively known as **Dharmashastra**. These texts can be subdivided into three groups. The first two are the **Dharmasutras** and the Smritis. The third includes brief and elaborate commentaries (*tikas* and *bhashyas*, respectively), collections with comments and conclusions (*nibandhas*), and compendia of views from different texts (*sangrahas*), all composed between the 9th and the 19th centuries. The Dharmasutras are earlier than the Smritis, but it is not easy to assign absolute dates to individual works. Kane ([1941b] 1974: xixii) dates the beginning of the composition of the Dharmasutras to about the 6th century BCE, Olivelle ([2000] 2003: 10; 2010) to the 3rd century BCE.

The Dharmasutras are part of the Vedanga as well as Dharmashastra corpus. Vedanga texts include the Kalpasutras ('aphorisms on ritual'), which are divided into Shrautasutras, Grihyasutras, and Dharmasutras. *Sutra* (literally, 'thread') refers to a style in which ideas are expressed in very short, condensed statements. The Shrautasutras deal with Vedic sacrifices that required the use of at least three fires. The Grihyasutras deal with the simpler domestic sacrifices involving the use of only one fire. The rituals they discuss include daily sacrifices to be performed by a householder, mainly involving oblations of ghee or offerings of flowers and fruits. They also describe the ***samskaras*** (literally, 'preparation', 'arrangement')—rituals marking important life stages of the upper three *varnas*, such as *upanayana* (initiation), *vivaha* (marriage), and *antyeshti* (funerary rites). The Dharmasutras deal with *dharma*.

Dharmashastra recognizes three sources of *dharma*—*shruti* (i.e., the Vedas), *smriti* (i.e., the Smriti texts), and *sadachara* or *shishtachara* (good custom or the practices of the learned, cultured people). The Samhitas of the Vedas do not contain direct discussion of rules of conduct, so the second and third sources of *dharma* are very important. A person's *dharma* depends on gender, age, marital status, *varna*, and ***ashrama***. The four *varnas* are—Brahmana, Kshatriya, Vaishya, and Shudra. The first three of these were eventually included in the category of ***dvija*** (literally, 'twice-born') as they alone have the right to the sacred-thread ceremony, which is considered similar to a second birth. The *ashrama* system went through several stages of development and in its classical form, divided the life of a *dvija* male into four stages—***brahmacharya*** (celibate studenthood), ***grihastha*** (the householder stage), ***vanaprastha*** (partial renunciation), and ***sannyasa*** (complete renunciation). The fourth *ashrama* was not considered obligatory. The *ashramas* represent an ideal scheme and it should not be imagined that people in ancient India necessarily followed it in real life. Further, it was not supposed to apply, even as an ideal, to women or Shudras.

There was also the concept of *samanya dharma* or *sadharana dharma*, which was applicable to all people. This included virtues such as nonviolence, truthfulness, non-stealing, and control of the senses, but Dharmashastra did not consider this *dharma* as important as the *dharma* of the *varnas* and *ashramas*. There was also a recognition that different lands, people, and ages had different *dharmas*.

Apart from norms of social behaviour, Dharmashastra deals with a number of other issues including personal, civil, and criminal law. However, the 'laws' of these 'law books' are not like the provisions of the Indian civil or penal codes. We do not know to what extent their recommendations were actually used or applied in early times. These texts are normative and prescriptive—they talk about the way things *should* be, from the point of view of Brahmana 'dharma experts' who composed them and were also the implied subject for many of the rules.

Although Dharmashastra texts do not directly describe the society of their time, inferences about social practices can be made on their basis. Contradictions within or across texts may indicate the range of opinions among experts, differences in customary practices in different areas, or changes in social norms over time. The Brahmanical tradition had some amount of in-built elasticity in order to come to terms with social reality and change.

PRIMARY SOURCES | Theory and practice in the Dharmashastra

Dharmashastra texts reveal the tension between theory and practice within the Brahmanical tradition. They divide society into four *varnas*, but also refer to the more numerous *jatis* (castes), which they explain as the result of the mixture of varnas (***varna-samkara***). Although they assert that everybody must follow the *dharma* of their *varna*, they concede that in times of emergency or acute distress, people can follow the duties of other *varnas*. They refer to the *dharma* of different regions (*desha-dharma*), castes (*jati-dharma*), and families (*kula-dharma*).

Consider the following examples based on the *Manava Dharmashastra*, often referred to as the *Manu Smriti*, a text which was composed in the 2nd–3rd centuries CE:

A. The *Manu Smriti* forbids marriage between a man and the daughter of his maternal uncle or paternal aunt. Medatithi, the 10th century commentator on the text, states that such cross-cousin marriages are against *dharma*. But Madhava, the 14th century commentator on the *Parashara Smriti*, gives detailed arguments to show that there was nothing wrong with such marriages, citing Vedic passages and custom.

B. The *Manu Smriti* condemns marriage between a *dvija* man and a Shudra woman. But when it talks of the division of property, it specifies the shares to be given to the sons born of a Brahmana, Kshatriya, or Vaishya father by a Shudra woman.

C. The text states that a widow should not remarry. But it fixes the length of time a woman should wait for a husband who is missing, and lays down the inheritance rights of sons with one mother and two fathers (i.e., a son whose mother has married a second time).

D. In one place, the *Manu Smriti* forbids the eating of meat. However, elsewhere, it includes meat among the items to be offered to a Brahmana invited to a *shraddha* (ceremonies in honour of and for the benefit of ancestors).

Example A shows that the author or authors of the *Manu Smriti* and the commentator Medatithi clearly disapproved of cross-cousin marriage. But Madhava apparently lived in a part of South India where such marriages were socially accepted, and so he defended them. Examples B and C indicate that the authors of the *Manu Smriti* disapproved of marriage between a *dvija* male and Shudra female, and did not approve of women, including widows, remarrying. But as such things did happen they had to regulate prevailing practice by laying down some rules. Example D similarly shows that the authors of the *Manu Smriti* did not approve of meat eating among Brahmanas, but had to acknowledge the prevalence of non-vegetarianism.

The authors of the Dharmashastra texts had to confront and try to regulate a wide variety of social practices. This, to a large extent, accounts for the variations in their opinions and prescriptions.

Buddhist texts

Early Buddhist texts are generally divided into canonical and non-canonical texts. Canonical texts are the books which lay down the basic tenets and principles of a religion, religious school, or sect. The various Buddhist schools classify their canonical literature in different ways, some into 9 or 12 Angas, others into 3 Pitakas.

There are Pali, Chinese, and Tibetan versions of the ***Tipitaka*** (The Three Baskets/Collections). The Pali *Tipitaka* of the Theravada school is the oldest of them all. Pali was a literary language which developed out of a mixture of dialects, particularly those spoken in the Magadha area of Eastern India. The *Tipitaka* consists of three books—the *Sutta*, *Vinaya*, and *Abhidhamma*. In the Buddhist context, *sutta* (from the Sanskrit *sutra*) refers to texts that are supposed to contain what the Buddha himself said. The *Sutta Pitaka* contains the Buddha's discourses on various doctrinal issues in dialogue form. The *Vinaya Pitaka* has rules for monks and nuns of the **sangha** (monastic order). It includes the *Patimokkha*—a list of transgressions against monastic discipline and atonements for these. The *Abhidhamma Pitaka* is a later work, and contains a thorough study and systemization of the teachings of the *Sutta Pitaka* through lists, summaries, and questions and answers.

The three Pitakas are divided into books known as the Nikayas (analogous but not identical to the Agamas of the Buddhist Sanskrit tradition). For instance, the *Sutta Pitaka* consists of five Nikayas—the *Digha*, *Majjhima*, *Samyutta*, *Anguttara*, and *Khuddaka Nikayas*. The ***Jatakas***—stories of the previous births of the Buddha—are one of the 15 books of the *Khuddaka Nikaya*. The *Khuddaka Nikaya* also contains the *Dhammapada* (a collection of verses dealing mainly with ethical sayings), and the *Theragatha* and *Therigatha* (songs of Buddhist monks and nuns). The *Therigatha*, which describes women's experience of renunciation, is especially important because it is one of the very few surviving ancient Indian texts composed by or attributed to women.

According to Buddhist tradition, the *Sutta* and *Vinaya Pitakas* were recited at the first council of monks at Rajagriha immediately after the Buddha's death, and 100 years later at the second council at Vaishali. But their composition must have extended over several centuries. The composition of the basic core of the Pali *Tipitaka* can be placed between the 5th and 3rd centuries BCE. The canon is supposed to have been written down in the 1st century BCE in Sri Lanka under the patronage of a king named Vattagamani, by which time it must have undergone further modifications. Although the *Tipitaka* is generally used by historians as a source for the history of early historic North India, it is important to note that its compilation and status as a canon has to do with events in Sri Lanka several centuries later. It was produced by the Mahavihara monks in order to legitimize and define themselves at a time when their Abhayagiri rivals were enjoying political support (see Collins, 1990).

Non-canonical Buddhist texts in Pali include the *Milindapanha* (1st century BCE–1st century CE) which consists of a dialogue on various philosophical issues between king Milinda—no doubt the Indo-Greek Menander—and the monk Nagasena. The *Nettigandha* or *Nettipakarana* (The Book of Guidance) belongs to the same period and gives a connected account of the teaching of the Buddha. Commentaries on the *Tipitaka* include a 5th century work by Buddhaghosha. The first connected life story of the Buddha occurs in the *Nidanakatha* (1st century). The Pali or Sri Lankan chronicles—the *Dipavamsa* (4th–5th centuries) and the *Mahavamsa* (5th century)—contain a historical-cum-mythical account of the Buddha's life, the Buddhist councils, the Maurya emperor Ashoka, the kings of Sri Lanka, and the arrival of Buddhism on that island.

See Chapter 8, pp. 520–521 for details of the various Buddhist schools

Apart from texts in Pali, there are several Buddhist works in Sanskrit, and in a mixture of Prakrit and Sanskrit that is often referred to as Buddhist Sanskrit or Buddhist hybrid Sanskrit. The trend towards the use of Sanskrit intensified in the **Mahayana** schools, but some non-Mahayana texts were also composed in Sanskrit or mixed

PRIMARY SOURCES | **Songs of Buddhist nuns**

Ubbiri's song

Ubbiri was a woman of Shravasti, who attained ***nibbana*** (enlightenment) as an *upasika*, i.e., lay-woman. The turning point in her life was an encounter with the Buddha, which took place while she was lamenting the death of her daughter Jiva. The following song is in the form of a dialogue between the Buddha and Ubbiri.

[Buddha:]

Mother, you cry out 'O Jiva' in the woods.
Come to yourself, Ubbiri.
Eighty-four thousand daughters
all with the name 'Jiva'
have burned in the funeral fire.
For which one do you grieve?

[Ubbiri:]

I had an arrow hidden in my heart
and he took it out—
that grief for my daughter.
The arrow is out,
the heart healed of hunger.
I take refuge in the Buddha-sage,
the *Dharma*, the *Sangha*.

Mitta's song

Mitta was a Sakya woman of Kapilavastu. The first verse of her song speaks of the observances she followed as a lay-woman, the second of her life after she became a nun.

To be reborn among the gods
I fasted and fasted
every two weeks,
day eight, fourteen, fifteen
and a special day.

Now with a shaved head
and Buddhist robes
I eat one meal a day.
I don't long to be a god.
There is no fear in my heart.

Source Murcott, 1991: 81, 21

Prakrit-Sanskrit. The *Mahavastu* contains a **hagiography** (sacred biography) of the Buddha and describes the emergence of the monastic order in Buddhist hybrid Sanskrit. The *Lalitavistara* (1st/2nd century), a hagiography of the Buddha associated with the Sarvastivada school but strongly tinged with Mahayana elements, is in Sanskrit and Buddhist hybrid Sanskrit.

Sanskrit Buddhist texts include Ashvaghosha's *Buddhacharita* (1st/2nd century) and the Avadana texts. The latter contain stories of noteworthy deeds with a moral; they include the *Avadanashataka* (2nd century) and the *Divyavadana* (4th century) which have stories connected with the Buddha and the Maurya emperor Ashoka. The 1st century *Ashtasahasrika-prajnaparamita* and *Saddharma-pundarika* offer accounts of the various future Buddhas known as **bodhisattvas** (the word is also spelt *bodhisatva*) and Mahayana doctrines. Later works of Mahayana thinkers such as Nagarjuna, Vasubandhu, Asanga, Aryadeva, Buddhapalita, and Dignaga are in Sanskrit.

Buddhist texts are important sources for the history of Buddhism, its doctrines, monastic order, and royal patrons such as Ashoka, revealing many other facets of the polity, society, and economy of their times as well. They offer a non-Brahmanical window into ancient India; however, the Brahmanical perspective is replaced by a Buddhist one.

Jaina texts

The sacred books of the Jainas are collectively known as the Siddhanta or Agama. The language of the earliest texts is an eastern dialect of Prakrit known as **Ardha-Magadhi**. The Jaina monastic order came to be divided into the **Shvetambara** and **Digambara** schools, perhaps in about the 3rd century CE. The Shvetambara canon includes the 12 Angas, 12 Uvamgas (Upangas), 10 Painnas (Prakirnas), 6 Cheya Suttas (Cheda Sutras), 4 Mula Suttas (Mula Sutras), and a number of individual texts such as the *Nandi Sutta* (*Nandi Sutra*) and *Anugodara* (*Anuyogadvara*). There is some overlap in the content of the canonical texts of the two schools. For instance, the Digambaras accept and give prime importance to the Angas, and some of the texts they club together as the Angabahyas have corresponding Shvetambara texts.

According to Shvetambara tradition, the Angas were compiled at a council held at Pataliputra. The compilation of the entire canon is supposed to have taken place in the 5th or 6th century at a council held in Valabhi in Gujarat, presided over by Devarddhi Kshamashramana. Some of the material in the canon may go back to the 5th or 4th century BCE, but changes and additions continued to be made till the 5th–6th centuries CE. In order to use such texts as historical sources, a clearer identification of their internal chronology is required.

See Chapter 8, pp. 523–525 for details on the Shvetambara and Digambara schools

The non-canonical Jaina works are partly in Prakrit dialects, especially Maharashtri, and partly in Sanskrit, which started being used in the early centuries CE. Commentaries on the canonical works include the Nijjuttis (Niryuktis), Bhashyas, and Churnis in Maharashtri Prakrit; the early medieval Tikas, Vrittis, and Avachurnis are in Sanskrit. The genealogical lists in the Jaina Pattavalis and the Theravalis contain very precise chronological details about the Jaina saints, but they sometimes contradict each other.

The Jaina Puranas (the Shvetambaras call them Charitas) are hagiographies of the Jaina saints known as *tirthankaras* (literally 'ford makers'), but they contain other material as well. The *Adi Purana* (9th century) narrates the life of the first *tirthankara* Rishabha, also known as Adinatha. The 8th century *Harivamsha Purana* gives a Jaina version of the stories of the Kauravas, Pandavas, Krishna, Balarama, and others. The *Trishashti-lakshana Mahapurana* by Jinasena and Gunabhadra (9th century) has life stories of various Jaina saints, kings, and heroes. It also has sections on topics such as life-cycle rituals, the interpretation of dreams, town planning, the duties of a warrior, and how a king should rule. The *Parishishtaparvan* (12th century) by Hemachandra gives a history of the earliest Jaina teachers and also mentions certain details of political history. A number of Prabandhas (12th century onwards) from Gujarat offer semi-historical accounts of saints and historical characters. Jaina texts also include hymn texts and lyrical poetry. The vast Jaina didactic story (*katha*) literature in Sanskrit, Prakrit, and Apabhramsha can offer historians clues on the everyday life of their time. The Jaina texts in the Kannada language are discussed further on in this chapter.

Jaina texts offer information regarding the history and doctrines of Jainism, the doctrines of rival schools, the life stories of the saints, and the life of monks and nuns in the *sangha*. The texts can also be used for information on other aspects of the cultural history of their times. Jaina texts have not, however, been studied or used as extensively by historians as Buddhist sources. Much more work needs to be done on ancient Jaina manuscripts and texts.

Sangam literature and later Tamil works

Tamil has a long and rich history (see Shulman, 2016). Its earliest literature consists of a group of texts in old Tamil, often collectively referred to as Sangam literature. A tradition recorded in post-7th century works speaks of three Sangams or literary gatherings in ancient times. The first is supposed to have been held in Madurai for 4,440 years, the second at Kapatapuram for 3,700 years, and the third in Madurai for 1,850 years. Although the details of this legend obviously cannot be considered historical, the similarity of language and style within the texts of the Sangam corpus suggests the possibility that they were products of some sort of literary gathering. The case for the historicity of at least the third Sangam is that some of the kings and poets associated with it are historical figures. On the other hand, there is a possibility that the legend of the Sangams may have been based on a very different event—the establishment of the Jaina *sangha* in Madurai in about the 5th century. In view of the controversy surrounding the tradition of the three Sangams, some scholars prefer to use the term 'early classical Tamil literature' rather than 'Sangam literature'.

The Sangam corpus includes six of the eight anthologies of poems included in the *Ettutokai* (The Eight Collections), and nine of the ten *pattus* (songs) of the *Pattuppattu* (The Ten Songs). The style and certain historical references in the poems suggest that they were composed between the 3rd century BCE and the 3rd century CE. They were compiled into anthologies in about the mid-8th century. A few centuries later, these anthologies were collected into the super-anthologies (i.e., anthologies of anthologies) called the *Ettutokai* and the *Pattuppattu*. The earliest parts of the first two books of the *Tolkappiyam* can also be included in Sangam literature. The *Tolkappiyam* is essentially a work on grammar, but it also includes a discussion of phonology, semantics, syntax, and literary conventions.

There are two kinds of Sangam poems—***akam*** and ***puram***. *Akam* poems have love as their theme, while *puram* poems are mostly about war. A. K. Ramanujan (1999) describes *puram* poetry as 'public poetry' which dealt with all kinds of themes other than love, such as good and evil, community and kingdom. The poems were modelled on the bardic songs of older times and were orally transmitted for an indefinite period before they were written down. The anthologies include a total of 2,381 poems ascribed to 473 poets, 30 of whom were women. The poets came from cities and villages and had varied social and professional backgrounds. They included teachers, merchants, carpenters, astrologers, goldsmiths, blacksmiths, soldiers, ministers, and kings. Due to their varied themes and authorship, Sangam poems offer a useful window into the time when they were composed.

A number of Tamil didactic works were written in the post-5th century period. The most famous of these is Tiruvalluvar's *Tirukkural*, a work on ethics, polity, and love (5th–6th centuries). The author Tiruvalluvar may have belonged to a community of weavers or drummers. The *Tirukkural* contains didactic poems which offer advice on

PRIMARY SOURCES | The stories of the two Tamil epics

Although the *Mahabharata* and *Ramayana* were known in early historical South India, the origins of Tamil epic narratives seem to lie in late Sangam compositions such as the *Kalittokai* and *Paripatal* rather than in northern influence.

The *Silappadikaram* (The Song of the Anklet) by Ilankovatikal ('prince ascetic') consists of 30 cantos arranged in three books. The outline of the story is as follows: Kovalan (the son of a wealthy merchant) and Kannaki are a young, happily married couple living in Puhar. Kovalan falls in love with a beautiful courtesan named Madhavi and abandons his wife. He eventually returns home after quarrelling with Madhavi. Kannaki welcomes him back and offers him her golden anklet to raise some money. They travel to Madurai, capital of the Pandya king, accompanied by a Jaina nun named Kavundi. Kovalan goes off to sell his wife's anklet. He is accused of stealing the queen's anklet, which looks just like Kannaki's, and is executed. Kannaki is devastated. She proves her husband's innocence by bursting open her other anklet—it contains a ruby, whereas the queen's was filled with pearls. The king, who had executed a man unjustly, dies of remorse; his wife dies of grief. Kannaki tears off her left breast and hurls it onto the city in fury. Madurai is engulfed in flames. Kannaki joins her husband in heaven; on earth she comes to be worshipped as the ideal wife.

Zvelebil points out that the epic's complex treatment of guilt and evil is one of its strengths. So are its multi-layered characters with human flaws and frailties, which evolve as the story progresses. The anklet has an important symbolism—Kannaki wears her anklets in the beginning of the story, when she is happy; she removes them after she is abandoned by Kovalan. The anklet is the cause of Kovalan's tragic end and the symbol of truth which ultimately proves his innocence. When Kannaki is united with her husband in heaven, she again wears both her anklets. Although the epic no doubt catered to an elite, educated audience, it tells us a great deal about the lives of ordinary people of the time.

The *Manimekalai* (The Jewel Belt) of Sattanar consists of 30 cantos and a preamble. The outline of the story is as follows: Prince Udayakumara is in love with Manimekalai, who is not interested in him because she wants to renounce the world and become a Buddhist nun. In order to escape the attentions of the prince, Manimekalai assumes the form of a woman named Kaya-Chandikai. She distributes food to the needy people of Madurai, using a magic alms-bowl. The husband of the real Kaya-Chandikai sees Manimekalai with the prince and kills him in a fit of jealousy. Manimekalai is put in prison, where she survives many ordeals to which she is subjected. Realizing that she is a saintly person, the queen begs forgiveness and sets her free. Manimekalai eventually reaches Kanchi, where a famine is raging and feeds the poor with her magic alms-bowl. She ultimately fulfils her heart's desire by joining the Buddhist *sangha*.

The *Manimekalai* is often considered somewhat inferior to the *Silappadikaram* in terms of its formal literary features. While the *Silappadikaram* has a Jaina flavour, the *Manimekalai* has a strong, strident Buddhist tone. Its characters are either good or bad, with few shades of grey, and the narrative is marked by many more miracles and supernatural interventions.

Source Zvelebil, 1974: 131–35, 140–42

many matters, including virtue, love, friendship, kingship, honour, and nonviolence. Of the several Tamil epics, two of the best known are the *Silappadikaram* and *Manimekalai*, composed in about the 5th/6th century CE.

Early medieval Tamil texts include the inspired and intense devotional poetry of the Vaishnava saints (**Alvars**) and Shaiva saints (**Nayanars** or **Nayanmars**) and their hagiographies. Vaishnava poetry took off with the compositions of Peyalvar, Puttalvar, and Poikaialvar. In the 10th century, Nathamuni collected the Alvar hymns into the canon known as the ***Nalayira Divya Prabandham***. The *Alvarvaipavam* is a sacred biography of the Vaishnava saints. Shaiva devotional literature began with the compositions of Tirumular and Karaikal Ammaiyar. The hymns of the Nayanmar saints were compiled in the 10th century by Nambi Andar Nambi and this compilation formed the core of the Shaiva canon, the ***Tirumurai***. Nambi also wrote a work called the ***Tiruttondar Tiruvantati*** about the saints. In the 12th century, the accounts of the Shaiva saints were collected in a text called the ***Periyapuranam***. All these texts provide valuable insights into the religious and social history of early medieval South India.

New genres of Tamil poetry emerged in early medieval times, many in praise of kings and gods. The Kalampakams were poetic compositions in which the last line, word, foot, or syllable of the preceding poem formed the beginning of the succeeding one. Kovai were poems in which the verses are arranged in a thematic sequence. Compositions in this genre included: the *Pantikkovai*, a 6th/7th century work written in honour of the Pandya king Netumaran; Manikkavachakar's *Tirukkovaiyar* (9th century) in praise of the god Shiva; and Poyyamolip Pulavar's *Tanchaivanan Kovai* (13th century) about Tanchaivanan, a minister and general of a Pandya king. Ula literature comprised songs in praise of gods, sung when the image of the deity was taken out in procession. Tutu poetry consisted of poems in which a message is delivered to a god, lover, or someone else. The moral aphorisms and sayings of Avvaiyar (9th/10th century), the second of three poetesses by this name, are still popular among Tamil-speaking people today.

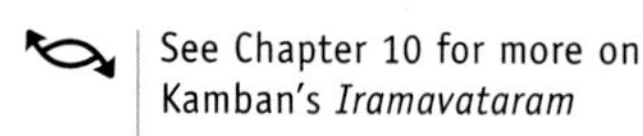
See Chapter 10 for more on Kamban's *Iramavataram*

Of the many Tamil renderings of the story of Rama, the most famous is Kamban's *Iramavataram*. Tamil versions of the Mahabharata story were also written, of which some fragments survive. Several Tamil lexicons and grammatical works belong to the early medieval period.

Early Kannada and Telugu texts

The earliest Kannada inscriptions date from the 5th/6th century onwards, but the oldest surviving piece of literature in this language is the *Kavirajamarga* (The Royal Road of the Poets), a 9th century work on poetics. A well-developed tradition of prose and poetry must have existed for some time, as this work mentions many earlier writers and their works which have not survived.

The Karnataka area was a stronghold of Jainism and a significant part of early medieval Kannada literature had Jaina themes. The best known poets of the 10th century were Pampa, Ponna, and Ranna, all of whom wrote Jaina Puranas. Pampa, author of the *Adi Purana* (an account of the life of the first *tirthankara* Rishabha or Adinatha), also wrote the *Vikramarjunavijaya*, based on the Mahabharata story. Ponna wrote both in Sanskrit and in Kannada, and was given the title of *Ubhaya-kavi-chakravarti* (imperial poet in both languages). Chavunda Raya, a general and minister under the Ganga kings, wrote a Kannada version of Jinasena and Gunabhadra's Sanskrit *Trishashtilakshana Mahapurana*, an account of the 24 Jaina saints, in continuous prose. In the 12th century, Nagachandra or Abhinava Pampa wrote the *Ramachandracharitra Purana*, one of many Jaina versions of Rama's story. The interesting Kannada works of the 12th century include Neminatha's *Lilavati*, in mixed verse and prose, which tells the love story of a Kadamba prince and a beautiful princess.

Place names in inscriptions from the 2nd century CE suggest the antiquity of Telugu, while epigraphs of the 5th–6th centuries CE reflect the shaping of the classical form of the language. Early medieval inscriptions used verse and are marked by a literary flavour and style. Although there may have been older works, the earliest surviving work of Telugu literature is Nannaya's 11th century rendering of the first two-and-a-half books of the *Mahabharata* in mixed verse and prose. This work was written at the request of the eastern Chalukya king Rajarajanarendra. Nannaya laid the foundations of Telugu poetic style, and Telugu tradition gave him the epithet *Vaganushasanundu* (Maker of Speech). His style is marked by the use of a variety of Sanskrit and regional metres, and a combination of lengthy Sanskrit compounds with Telugu words.

Tikkana, a minister associated with the court of Manumasiddhi, a ruler based in the Nellore area, added 15 Parvas to Nannaya's *Mahabharata* and set new trends in narrative style. He also composed a work called the *Uttararamayanamu*. Another writer who seems to have lived in about this period was Nanne Choda—author of the *Kumara-sambhavamu*—who describes himself as a ruler of a small principality called Orayuru. Telugu literature reached a level of maturity in the 14th century during the Kakatiya period and its highest point of achievement during the reign of the Vijayanagara king Krishnadevaraya (1509–29 CE).

Other ancient texts, biographies, and histories

As mentioned earlier, literature is something hard to define, but uses language in creative, expressive, and imaginative ways. Instead of looking at literature in isolation, it is useful to see it as part of literary culture. This involves looking at the connections between language, literature, culture, society, and polity. It also means trying to understand what texts meant to the people for whom they were composed (see Pollock. [Ed.]., 2003). While using literature for historical reconstruction, it is necessary to understand its aesthetic and stylistic conventions.

Early Indian literature includes a number of masterpieces of poetry and drama which can be read and appreciated for their sheer beauty and fine literary qualities. Such texts are used by historians as sources of information about the times in which they were composed. The earliest Sanskrit poets and playwrights include Ashvaghosha and Bhasa. Ashvaghosha was the author of the *Buddhacharita* (which he describes as a *mahakavya*), *Sariputraprakarana*, and *Saundarananda*. Bhasa wrote several dramas, including the *Pancharatra, Dutavakya, Balacharita*, and *Svapna-Vasavadatta*. One of the most celebrated names among Sanskrit writers of the 1st millennium is that of Kalidasa (4th–5th centuries), author of the dramas *Abhijnanashakuntala, Malavikagnimitra, Vikramorvashiya*, and poetic works such as the *Raghuvamsha, Kumarasambhava*, and *Meghaduta*. The many early medieval poets and writers include Bharavi, Rajashekhara, and the poetess Vijayanka.

Ancient dramas on historical themes are of special interest to historians, although it is necessary to remember that they were literary works and not historical accounts. Vishakhadatta's *Mudrarakshasa* (5th/6th century) revolves around the manoeuvres of Chanakya to win over Rakshasa, a minister of the Nandas, to Chandragupta's side. Narrative literature such as the *Panchatantra* (3rd/4th century) and the *Kathasaritsagara* (Ocean of Streams of Stories, 11th century) are based on popular folk tales that ordinary people may have known, listened to, and enjoyed.

There is a vast body of ancient and early medieval technical literature on varied subjects such as grammar, mathematics, statecraft, astronomy, medicine, architecture, poetics, dramaturgy, and philosophy. Reference has already been made to grammatical texts such as Panini's *Ashtadhyayi* and Patanjali's *Mahabhashya*. Kautilya's *Arthashastra* is a major work on statecraft. Aryabhata's *Aryabhatiya* and Varahamihira's *Brihatsamhita* are important astronomical texts. Other technical treatises include the *Natyashastra* (on drama and the performing arts), *Kamasutra* (on sensual pleasure), the *Charaka Samhita* and *Sushruta Samhita* (on medicine), and the Shilpashastras (on architecture and sculpture). Apart from indicating the level of expertise and knowledge in their respective fields, such treatises also provide other kinds of useful historical information.

See Chapter 8, pp. 503–505 for a discussion of these schools

Philosophical texts and commentaries reflect the vibrant intellectual debates of their times. Apart from Buddhist and Jaina texts, which have already been mentioned, there are many philosophical works belonging to the **Samkhya**, **Yoga**, **Nyaya**, **Vaisheshika**, **Purva Mimamsa**, and **Uttara Mimamsa** schools. These also mention the philosophical ideas of schools whose texts have not survived, such as the materialist **Charvaka** or **Lokayata** school.

The courts of early medieval kings attracted writers and poets, some of whom wrote biographical compositions in praise of their royal patrons. The famous Sanskrit biographies include Banabhatta's *Harshacharita* (7th century) about king Harshavardhana. Vakpati wrote the Prakrit *Gaudavaho* (8th century) about Yashovarman of Kanauj. Bilhana's *Vikramankadevacharita* (12th century) is woven around the Chalukya king Vikramaditya VI.

Royal biographies in Tamil include the anonymous *Nandikkalambakkam* (9th century), a long poem about the events of the reign of the Pallava king Nandivarman III. An 11th century work, the *Kalinkattupparani* by Cheyankontar, is based on the war between the Chola king Kulottunga and Anantavarman Chodaganga, the ruler of Kalinga. The poet describes and praises the heroism of the Chola king and his army commander, presenting the war as a divine conflict between the principles of good and evil.

Sandhyakara Nandi's *Ramacharita* is a Sanskrit work with double meaning, simultaneously narrating the story of the *Ramayana* and of Ramapala, an 11th/12th century king of Bengal. The 12th century *Kumarapalacharita* by Hemachandra is a long poem in Sanskrit and Prakrit, which tells the story of the Chaulukya kings of Gujarat and

PRIMARY SOURCES | Banabhatta and his royal biography

Banabhatta's *Harshacharita* is the oldest surviving biography in India. Apart from painting a glowing picture of his patron Harsha of the Pushyabhuti dynasty, the writer also speaks about himself. The early part of Bana's pedigree is mythical and narrates the origins of the Vatsyayana branch of the Bhargava Brahmanas, to which he belonged. The later part is historical.

Bana was born in Pritikuta, a Brahmana village in the Kanyakubja area, famed for the learning and stature of its residents. His mother Rajadevi died when he was a small child, and he was brought up by his father who died when he was 14. Bana was taught by an illustrious teacher named Bharchu. In his youth, he set out on a series of travels, accompanied by his half-brothers and a colourful entourage including poets, philosophers, artists, actors, monks, ascetics, a gambler, singer, goldsmith, and dancing girl. It is no wonder that he acquired a bit of a reputation.

The story goes that one day Bana received a letter summoning him to present himself in Harsha's court. The meeting started off badly. The king had apparently believed the gossip about Bana's wayward ways and treated him with scant regard. Bana was quick to defend himself, arguing that although he may have been a bit wild in his youth, he came from a respectable Brahmana family and was currently living a blameless married life. Within a few days, he became a court favourite and many lavish presents and honours were showered on him. Bana went on to write the *Harshacharita*, a eulogistic biography of his patron, as well as a prose romance called the *Kadambari*.

Bana describes the *Harshacharita* as an *akhyayika*, a genre of texts related to the *itihasa* tradition. The episodes in the biography are selected and narrated from a literary and aesthetic perspective. Its descriptions are vivid and literary, and sometimes show a touch of humour. The work displays Bana's skills as a master of Sanskrit prose. Typical of the genre of royal biographies are long, elegant passages eulogizing the king. Consider, for example, the following sentence:

> He (i.e., Harsha) was embraced by the goddess of Royal Prosperity, who took him in her arms, and, seizing him by all the royal marks on all his limbs, forced him, however, reluctant, to mount the throne—and this though he had taken a vow of austerity and did not swerve from his vow, hard like grasping the edge of a sword; clinging closely to duty through fear of stumbling in the uneven path of kings, and attended with all her heart by Truth who had been abandoned by all other kings, but had obtained his promise of protection, and waited on reverentially by the reflected images of a fair handmaid standing near, which fell on his toe-nails, as if they were the ten directions of space impersonate.

According to some scholars, the *Harshacharita* is incomplete because it ends after Harsha's rescue of his sister Rajyashri from the flames of the pyre on which she sought to end her life, and his accession to the thrones of Thanesar and Kanauj. However, V. S. Pathak argues that the work is complete as it has all the five well-defined thematic stages of a beginning, effort, the hope of achieving the end, certainty of success, and a conclusion. Rajyashri was Harsha's sister, but her name also means royal glory, and Harsha's rescuing her symbolically represents his successful acquisition of royal glory. Although Bana paints Harsha as an ideal, exemplary ruler, traces of a less perfect picture can be found in the nuances of the narrative. For instance, there are hints of a fratricidal struggle for the throne behind the portrayal of the deep brotherly love between Harsha and Rajyavardhana.

Source Cowell and Thomas, 1993: 57; Pathak, 1966: 30–32

simultaneously illustrates the rules of Sanskrit and Prakrit grammar. The *Prithvirajaraso* by Chand Bardai is an epic poem in Braj-bhasha, woven around the Rajput king Prithviraja Chauhan. The establishment of the Delhi Sultanate in the 11th century gave rise to a series of Persian chronicles narrating the history of various dynasties. The aim of ancient and early medieval biographers and chroniclers was as much to display their literary skills as to produce a work that would flatter their royal patrons. Their motives, perspectives, and audience have to be kept in mind when using their works as sources of history.

Kalhana's *Rajatarangini* (River of Kings) is a 12th century Sanskrit text which offers a connected account of the kings of Kashmir from the early ones of legend to the historical rulers of the 12th century. Kalhana belonged to a well-connected Brahmana family of Kashmir. His father Canpaka was at one time closely associated with the royal court, but by the time Kalhana was born, the family had fallen out of favour. The *Rajatarangini* consists of almost 8,000 verses arranged in eight cantos, each called a *taranga* (wave). Kalhana refers to earlier historians and chronicles. Apart from the *Nilamatapurana*, he mentions eleven works of earlier scholars, none of which have survived. Kalhana is often described as India's first historian, but he considered himself a great poet (*mahakavi*) who could make the past come vividly alive.

Summaries of ancient textual sources tend to miss out on unusual texts that do not fall within any of the main categories. These include a Sanskrit work on agriculture called the *Krishi-Parashara*, composed in Bengal some time between the 6th and 11th centuries CE. The early medieval texts of this region also include the *Dakar Bachan* and *Khanar Bachan* in old Bengali. These contain aphorisms and wise sayings mostly concerning agriculture, but also other things such as medicine, family life, and astrology.

The nature of ancient Indian historical traditions

As we have seen, the textual sources for ancient and early medieval India include a large variety and volume of texts. Do any of them reflect a historical tradition, i.e., an interest in preserving the memory of the past? Romila Thapar (2000) has made a useful distinction between 'embedded' and 'externalized' forms of history. Embedded history is where the historical consciousness has to be prised out, as in myth, epic, and genealogy. Externalized history reflects a more evident and self-conscious historical consciousness, reflected for instance in chronicles and biographies. Thapar points out that the embedded forms of historical consciousness tended to be connected with lineage-based societies and the externalized ones to state societies.

Apart from lists of teachers, later Vedic texts contain certain types of compositions that reflect a historical consciousness. These include the *dana-stutis*, *gathas, narashamsis*, and *akhyanas*. The *dana-stutis* are hymns praising the generosity and exploits of kings. The *gathas* are songs in praise of kings, sung on the occasion of certain sacrifices. *Narashamsis* were used in rituals and are preserved in texts such as the Brahmanas and Grihyasutras. *Akhyanas* are narrative hymns in dialogue form, and referring to mythical and possibly historical events. It is interesting to note that all these types of compositions were directly connected with the performance of sacrifices (*yajnas*).

The king-lists in the Puranas and epics represent more substantial evidence of an ancient Indian historical tradition. As mentioned earlier, the *Mahabharata* is considered traditional history or *itihasa*, and is supposed to record things that actually happened; whether they did happen in the way in which they are described is another issue (see Kanad Sinha, 2021). Bards known as *sutas* and *magadhas* played an important role in maintaining these historical traditions. The poets and bards of the ancient Tamil land who eulogized their royal patrons can also be seen as creators and transmitters of a historical tradition. The Buddhist *Dipavamsa* and *Mahavamsa*, which offer a mythico-historical account of how Buddhism travelled to Sri Lanka, represent a historical tradition as well. Mention may also be made of sacred biographies in the Buddhist, Jaina, and Hindu traditions.

Notwithstanding their eulogistic nature, royal biographies too reflect a historical tradition. Mention can also be made of royal inscriptions, many of which have a ***prashasti*** (panegyric) containing the king's genealogy and references to his exploits, usually with a view to shower praise on him. The *Arthashastra* and the Chinese pilgrim Xuanzang mention royal archives preserving official records in every Indian city, while Al-Biruni's 11th century *Tahqiq-i-Hind* refers to the archives of the Shahi kings of Kabul. Unfortunately, no such ancient archives survive.

Mention was made above to Kalhana's *Rajatarangini*, a literary work which offers a history of Kashmir. Kalhana describes the landscape of Kashmir with pride and feeling, wove lively character sketches, and gave dramatic descriptions of political events. His narration includes his comments, references to *karma* and fate, and to the morals and lessons offered by past events. Other works called *Rajatarangini* were composed in Kashmir between the 14th and 16th centuries.

In our time, history is an academic discipline based on research, linked to modern institutions such as universities and research institutes. The historical traditions of ancient India were connected with religious, ritualistic, and court contexts. Modern historians distinguish between myth and history, ancient texts do not. Ancient texts often combine narrative and didactic elements, in contrast to modern historical writings which self-consciously aim (or should aim) at a certain level of objectivity and distance. Accounts of the past in ancient sources are very different from what we read in university history books; they reflect a historical consciousness that has to be understood within the context of their own time and genre.

Accounts of India from outside the subcontinent

As mentioned earlier, the subcontinent was never an isolated geographical area. Since early times, traders, travellers, pilgrims, settlers, soldiers, goods, and ideas moved to and fro across its frontiers, covering vast distances over land and water. It is, therefore, not surprising that there are many references to India in texts written by authors who belonged to areas outside the subcontinent. Such texts reveal how people from other lands viewed India and its people, what they noticed and found worthy of description. Distinctions can be made between statements based on hearsay and those grounded in personal experience, between perceptive observations and cases where the writer simply got things wrong. An example of a very unreliable account is the *Indica* of Ktesias (4th century BCE), which is full of bizarre stories about India and Indians, apparently collected by the author while living in Persia as a royal physician.

The earliest references to India in Greek texts date from the 5th century BCE and their frequency increases thereafter. One of the most famous works is the *Indica* of Megasthenes, a Greek envoy who came to the court of Chandragupta Maurya. The book is lost, but later Greek works preserve paraphrases of some of its sections. The many Greek and Latin texts of the 2nd century BCE to the 2nd century CE which refer to India include the works of Arrian, Strabo, and Pliny the Elder, and the anonymous *Periplus Maris Erythraei* (Periplus of the Erythraean Sea). These texts are especially important for the history of Indian Ocean trade.

Many Chinese monks made long and arduous journeys to India, crossing mountains, plateaux, deserts and sometimes oceans, in order to collect authentic manuscripts of Buddhist texts, meet Indian monks, and visit places of Buddhist learning and pilgrimage. The best known among those who wrote accounts of their Indian travels are Faxian (*c.* 337–422 CE) and Xuanzang (*c.* 600–664 CE). Faxian's travels and were confined to northern India. Xuanzang spent over 10 years travelling the length and breadth of the country. Yijing (*c.* 635–713 CE), another Chinese monk, took the sea route both ways and spent ten years in the great monastery of Nalanda. The accounts written by these monks throw light on the history of Buddhism and various other aspects of their time. It is important to keep the authors' perspectives and motives in mind while using these texts as historical sources.

The rapid political expansion of the Arabs, the unity given to them by Islam, the spread of urban centres, and the patronage of the Caliphs had important and far-reaching impact on the circulation of ideas and technology across Asia and Europe. Al-Mamun, the 9th century Abbasid Caliph, established an academy called the Beyt-al-Hikma (House of Wisdom) in Baghdad. Scholars of this academy busied themselves with an ambitious project of translating Greek, Persian, and Sanskrit texts on philosophy and science into Arabic. The flexibility of Arabic lent itself to the creation of a very precise scientific and technical vocabulary. Moreover, since this was a spoken language, the knowledge of ancient texts became theoretically available to anybody in the swiftly expanding Arab-speaking world. Within the span of a few centuries, the learning and accomplishments of different cultures spread far beyond their original geographical frontiers. There was also a dissemination of elements of folk tales. For instance, the Arabic *Kalila-wa-Dimma* was based on stories in the *Panchatantra*.

Abu Rihan or Al-Biruni, a native of Khwarizm or Khiva (in modern Turkmenistan), was one of the greatest intellectuals of early medieval times. Only 40 of the 180 books he wrote have survived. Al-Biruni travelled to India to satisfy his curiosity about the land and its people, and

PRIMARY SOURCES | **Al-Biruni on the writing of the Hindus**

The tongue communicates the thought of the speaker to the hearer. Its action has therefore, as it were, a momentary life only, and it would have been impossible to deliver by oral tradition the accounts of the events of the past to later generations, more particularly if they are separated from them by long periods of time. This has become possible only by a new discovery of the human mind, by the art of writing, which spreads news over space as the winds spread, and over time as the spirits of the deceased spread. Praise therefore, be unto Him who has arranged creation and created everything for the best!

The Hindus are not in the habit of writing on hides, like the Greeks in ancient times. Socrates, on being asked why he did not compose books, gave this reply: 'I do not transfer knowledge from the living hearts of men to the dead hides of sheep.' Muslims, too, used in the early times of Islam to write on hides, e.g., the treaty between the Prophet and the Jews of Khaibar and his letter to Kisra. The copies of the Koran were written on the hides of gazelles, as are still nowadays the copies of the Torah.... The *kirtas* (or *charta*) is made in Egypt, being cut out of the papyrus stalk.... It was in China that paper was first manufactured. Chinese prisoners introduced the fabrication of paper into Samarkand and thereupon it was made in various places, so as to meet the existing want.

The Hindus have in the south of their country a slender tree like the date and coco-nut palms, bearing edible fruits and leaves of the length of one yard, and as broad as three fingers one put beside the other. They call these leaves *tari* and write on them. They bind a book of these leaves together by a cord on which they are arranged, the cord going through all the leaves by a whole in the middle of each.

In Central and Northern India people use the bark of the *tuz* tree, one kind of which is used as a cover for bows....

As for the writing or alphabet of the Hindus, we have already mentioned that it once had been lost and forgotten; that nobody cared for it, and that in consequence people became illiterate, sunken into gross ignorance, and entirely estranged from science. But then Vyasa, the son of Parashara, rediscovered their alphabet of fifty letters by an inspiration of God. A letter is called an *akshara*.

Some people say that originally the number of their letters was less, and that it increased only by degrees. This is possible, or I should even say necessary....

The great number of the letters of the Hindu alphabet is explained, firstly, by the fact that they express every letter by a separate sign if it is followed by vowel or a diphthong or a *hamza* (*visarga*), or a small extension of the sound beyond the measure of the vowel; and, secondly, by the fact that they have consonants which are not found together in any other language, though they may be found scattered through different languages—sounds of such a nature that our tongues, not being familiar with them, can scarcely pronounce them, and that our ears are frequently not able to distinguish between many a cognate pair of them.

The Hindus write from the left to the right like the Greeks. They do not write on the basis of a line, above which the heads of the letters rise whilst their tails go down below, as in Arabic writing. On the contrary, their ground-line is above, a straight line above every single character, and from this line the letter hangs down and is written under it. Any sign above the line is nothing but a grammatical mark to denote the pronunciation of the character above which it stands....

After describing these characteristics of 'Hindu' writing, Al-Biruni goes on to acknowledge the existence of many different scripts in the land of Hind—Siddhamatrika, the most widely known and used in Kashmir, Varanasi, and the country around Kanauj; Nagara in Malwa; Ardhanagari in Bhatiya and some parts of Sindh; Malwari in Sindh; Karnata in Karnatadesha; Andhri in Andhradesha; Dirwari in Dravidadesha; Lari in Latadesha (in Gujarat); Gauri (i.e., Gaudi) in Purvadesha, i.e., the eastern country; and the Bhaikshuki, used in Udunpur in Purvadesha, described as the writing of the Buddha.

Source Sachau, 1964: 170–73

to study their ancient texts in their original language. His *Tahqiq-i-Hind* covers a large number of topics including Indian scripts, sciences, geography, astronomy, astrology, philosophy, literature, beliefs, customs, religions, festivals, rituals, social organization, and laws. Apart from the historical value of his descriptions of 11th century India, Al-Biruni helped modern historians identify the initial year of the Gupta era. The *Tahqiq-i-Hind* states that the Gupta era began 241 years after the beginning of the Shaka era. Since the Shaka era began in 78 CE, this places the beginning of the Gupta era in 319–20 CE.

Several Arabic geographical and travel accounts were written in the early medieval period. Some of these, such as the account of the traveller Sulaiman, refer to India. This is not surprising considering that both Arabs and Indians were actively involved in Indian Ocean trade. Such works throw light on various aspects of Indian political history.

Persian was the language of royal courts and high culture in Central and West Asia in early medieval times, and a number of Persian texts refer to India. The *Chachnama* describes how a Brahmana named Chach usurped the throne of Sindh in the mid-7th century and narrates the subsequent Arab conquest of that region by Muhammad bin Qasim. The *Shahnama* of Firdausi, a classic of Persian poetry, and the *Gulistan* by the famous poet Saadi, refer incidentally to aspects of Indian trade.

In early medieval India, the Sanskrit and Persianate worlds intersected with each other and with emerging regional literary cultures. Many texts reveal the importance of bilingualism and multilingualism at that time across the world. Translation was as important then as it is now, and the massive translation projects of the Arabs are one of many examples. Several ancient texts travelled across geographical spaces and time and were part of global circulations of knowledge.

Archaeology and the Early Indian Past

We turn now from texts to archaeology. Archaeology—the study of the human past though material remains—is closely connected with history (for an overview, see Renfrew and Bahn, [1991] 2020). Material remains range from vestiges of grand palaces and temples to the small, discarded products of everyday human activity such as pieces of broken pottery. They include different things such as structures, artefacts, bones, seeds, pollen, seals, coins, sculptures, and inscriptions. Methods and ideas have changed greatly between the beginnings of Indian archaeology in the late 19th century and now.

Historians, anthropologists, and archaeologists understand 'culture' as something that includes all patterns of people's learnt behaviour, the ways of thinking and doing things that they learn from the social group of which they are a part. Archaeologists also use the word culture in a more specific, technical sort of way connected with certain other important terms—**artefact, industry**, and **assemblage**. An artefact is any portable object made or altered by human hands (e.g., pottery, tools). Similar artefacts made of the same material found at a site comprise an industry (e.g., a **microlith** industry, **blade** and **burin** industry). All the industries found at a site form its assemblage. If similar assemblages are found at several sites, these sites are said to belong to the same archaeological culture.

Material evidence is a key to understanding human behaviour and experience. It is not enough to describe a stone tool or pot; the challenge is to get the stone tool or pot to tell their stories about the people who made and used them. As the products of craft traditions and part of the lifestyles of people, artefacts are rooted in specific cultural contexts. So, the narrow technical meaning of 'culture' in archaeology can be stretched to correspond to the wider meaning mentioned earlier. The rhythms and patterns of material culture are generally much slower than those of historical events, and archaeological cultures do not coincide with the rise and fall of dynasties or kingdoms.

Field archaeology deals with the exploration and excavation of sites. **Sites** are places where material remains of past human activity can be identified. In the plains, in areas where mud and brick were used for making houses, archaeological sites occupied by people for a very long time are often visible as mounds. Mounds get formed over the centuries due to the rebuilding of structures and the accumulation of rubbish, wind-blown sand, and other sediments.

Sites are often discovered by sheer accident. They can also be discovered by using clues in texts, through regional or village surveys, or with the help of aerial photography. Sites buried underground can be detected by simple methods like inserting metal probes or rods into the ground. There are also the more sophisticated remote-sensing techniques such as LANDSAT imagery. Scanners of LANDSAT satellites create digital images of the earth's surface and can help identify features such as ancient river courses, canals, embankments, and buried settlements.

Archaeological evidence does not provide a complete picture of the material culture of ancient people. Artefacts found in the archaeological record generally consist of things that have been thrown away, lost, forgotten, hidden, or left behind (intentionally or unintentionally) by people when they moved elsewhere. Furthermore, not all material traits survive. Archaeological reconstruction depends on the amount and kind of material that is preserved, and this in turn depends on the objects themselves and on environmental factors, particularly soil and climate. Inorganic materials like stone, clay, and metal are most likely to survive in the archaeological record. Stone age people must have used tools of wood and bone as well, but it is the stone tools that have survived in large numbers. Tropical regions, with heavy rains, acidic soils, warm climates, and dense vegetation are not favourable for preservation. These things have to be kept in mind when assessing archaeological evidence. Sites can get destroyed by the forces of nature (e.g., floods, tectonic movements, volcanic eruptions), but they are more often destroyed by people when they clear land for farming or build houses, factories, roads, and dams.

Sites can be explored by carefully examining what lies on the surface or they can be excavated, i.e., dug. Sites are not excavated just to see what they contain, but rather to uncover their stratigraphic sequence. The basic principle of stratigraphy is that if there are several layers, strata, or levels at a site, the lower ones are older. Of course, if a site gets disturbed, this principle does not apply. It is very important to know the **stratigraphic context** of artefacts, i.e., the precise level at which they were found, and what other kinds of things were found along with them.

Excavations can be horizontal (where a large surface area is exposed) or vertical (where the digging involves a small surface area), and are accompanied by careful recording, mapping, photographing, labelling, and preserving of artefacts. Recording is very important because excavation is destructive—some features of the upper layers have to be destroyed as archaeologists move from one layer to the next. Equally important is the publication of results, otherwise no one except the excavators will know what was discovered at the site.

These days, an important trend within field archaeology is to try to understand sites within their larger landscape and context. Archaeologists are also increasingly moving towards non-destructive methods of investigation, such as remote-sensing and regional surveys. Regional surveys are conducted by walking over carefully selected sections of an area, observing the distribution and nature of surface features and finds. These are recorded and the surface finds are collected. A great deal of valuable archaeological information can be gathered in this way.

The Hastinapura mound

FURTHER DISCUSSION | Letters from Alexander Cunningham to J. D. M. Beglar

The beginnings of archaeology in India go back to the 19th century. Alexander Cunningham was India's first professional archaeologist and when the Archaeological Survey of India was established in 1871, he was appointed its first Director General. Cunningham's achievements and limitations have to be assessed in the context of the time, when India was a British colony.

In 2005, Victoria Memorial Hall in Kolkata acquired a set of hand-written letters written by Cunningham to his Archaeological Assistant and friend, J. D. M. Beglar, between 1871 and 1886. The 193 letters tell the story of the history of Indian archaeology in the 1870s and 1880s in the words of Cunningham himself.

The letters describe the nitty gritty of the archaeological expeditions. Cunningham often travelled on horseback or elephant. There were other modes of transport such as bullock trains, carriage dak, carts, tongas, carriages, and phaetons. The journeys sometimes involved difficult river crossings. Writing from Shekohabad in February 1877, Cunningham reported:

> All my Books in Nos. 3 & 4 Boxes are destroyed. The Camel sat down in the middle of the Ahsin River with them & nearly killed my cook also.

The expeditions required buying equipment such as ropes and pegs; arranging for tents; and collecting provisions and food such as bread, meat, butter, and tea for the time spent in camp. The weather is a regular refrain in the letters, and the heat is mentioned most often:

> The heat came on suddenly at the end of February. I managed to carry on until I got to Uchera ... I went to Allahabad by Rail, and was devoured by musquitoes [*sic*] while waiting for money.

The letters describe many exciting discoveries as they were made. For instance, in the autumn of 1875, Cunningham announced to Beglar:

> I have got a proof that Pâtaliputra was on the Son! Therefore, the Son was the Erannoboas of the Greeks, as I have always told you.

In December 1875, he wrote from Rajgir:

> I spent 3 days at Râjgir where I discovered several new caves two of which are close to our so called Sattapanni cave ... my men reached your cave from the upper side first! Just above it there are two real caves upwards of 70 feet long each but they have never been inhabited except by bears.

He announced a fine sculptural find in Mathura in March 1882:

> I found only one sculpture of any value. This is however, a really valuable ones group of Herakles killing the Nemean Lion! I have the sculpture with me now. It is more than 3 feet high. I found it forming the side of a trough for bullocks to drink out of and covered with a bit of wall of bricks & mud. Before I recognized the subject I noticed the artistic merit of the sculpture. I intend to have it photographed at Simla by Craddock.

Cunningham's letters refer frequently to money and accounts, occasionally to family matters. What stands out in the letters is how the archaeological work was carried out in the midst of frequent illness. The letters reveal that during the most productive years of his life, Cunningham was afflicted by debilitating physical ailments, especially as he grew older. This did not, however, reduce his passion for his work.

Source Upinder Singh. [Ed.]., 2021

Alexander Cunningham (1814–93)

J. D. M. Beglar

FURTHER DISCUSSION | H. D. Sankalia: Born for archaeology

Hasmukh Dhirajlal Sankalia (1908–89) was one of the greatest archaeologists in independent India. He was born in a middle-class Gujarati family in Bombay (Mumbai). A frail and sickly child, young Hasmukh's imagination was fired by stories from the *Mahabharata*, *Ramayana*, and Puranas, and of the lives of Napoleon, Shivaji, and Rana Pratap. A Gujarati translation of Lokmanya Bal Gangadhar Tilak's *The Arctic Home in the Vedas* especially inspired him to study ancient Indian history.

At St. Xavier's College, where he studied Sanskrit and English, Sankalia was mentored by the learned Jesuit priest, Father Heras. In Bombay University, he wrote his MA thesis on Nalanda. His father wanted him to follow the family profession and become a lawyer, but the young man had other ideas. During the 1920s, he was attracted towards the political and social ideals of Mahatma Gandhi. Eventually, on Father Heras' advice, he made his way to University College, London. He wrote his PhD thesis on the archaeology of Gujarat under the supervision of F. J. Richards, a retired British civil servant with a keen understanding of Indian prehistory and historical geography. He learnt the latest excavation techniques while participating in the Mortimer Wheeler's excavations at Maiden Castle in Dorset.

H. D. Sankalia (1908–89), a pioneer of Indian archaeology

Back home in India, Sankalia started looking for a job. After being rejected twice for a position in the Archaeological Survey of India, in 1939, he took up the position of Professor of Proto-Indian and Ancient Indian History in the recently established Deccan College Postgraduate and Research Institute in Pune. His distinguished colleagues included the scholar of linguistics and Sanskrit, S. M. Katre, and the anthropologist Iravati Karve. Sankalia was an institution builder. Under his leadership, Deccan College came to be recognized as the premier institution of archaeological research in India. Sankalia retired from Deccan College in 1973 after 36 years, continuing there as Emeritus Professor.

Sankalia's work had enormous range and impact. He opened up the fields of Indian prehistory and protohistory. K. N. Dikshit, the then Director General of the ASI, invited him to lead the first Gujarat Prehistoric Expedition in 1941–42. Many sites were identified and the mesolithic phase of Indian prehistory was discovered. The first skeletal remains of stone age humans in India were found at Langhnaj. The Gujarat work was followed by a study of palaeolithic sites in the Godavari valley. Over the decades, Sankalia criss-crossed the length and breadth of India. He conducted excavations at Jorwe, Nashik, Nevasa, Chirki, and Inamgaon (in Maharashtra); Langhnaj, Akhaj, Valasna, and Dwarka (in Gujarat); Navdatoli, Maheshwar, and Tripuri (in MP); Tekkalakota and Sanganakallu (in Karnataka); and Ahar (in Rajasthan). He excavated a few early historic sites—Kolhapur, Dwarka, and Tripuri. He is known for the prompt publication of the results of his excavations. He also wrote important general books such as *Indian Archaeology* (1962), *Prehistory and Proto-history of India and Pakistan* (1962–63), *Stone Age Tools, Their Techniques and Probable Functions* (1964), and *An Introduction to Archaeology* (1966). He was open to new ideas and approaches such as ethnoarchaeology and New Archaeology.

Although his reputation rests on his being a field archaeologist, Sankalia was interested in texts, inscriptions, and ethnography. He was not afraid to court controversy. For instance, in *Ramayana in Historical Perspective* (1982), he questioned traditional views about the epic's age and evolution, and suggested that Lanka may have originally been located in eastern Madhya Pradesh.

As a teacher, Sankalia became the guru of an entire generation of distinguished Indian archaeologists. The excavations at Inamgaon (1968–83) were carried out under the supervision of Sankalia and his former students, M. K. Dhavalikar and Z. D. Ansari. The report of these excavations (1986) gives a detailed picture of the lives of chalcolithic farmers of Western India; it represents a high watermark in rigorous investigation, the use of scientific methods, and meticulous reporting. Sankalia strongly believed that the results of archaeological research should be disseminated to the public. He tried to explain archaeology to ordinary people through lectures and articles written in English, Gujarati, Hindi, and Marathi. The title of his autobiography, *Born for Archaeology*, admirably sums up his life and his work.

Table 1.1 The cultural sequence at Hastinapura

Period	Date	Cultural traits
V	Late 11th–15th centuries	Pottery—very different from earlier periods; coarse to medium-grained red ware; glazed wares with floral designs. Structures made of broken bricks from remains of earlier periods; four structural sub-periods identified. Many types of iron objects including nails, arrowheads, spearheads, hoes, knife blades, etc. A stone image of Parvati and Rishabhadeva. Terracottas of poor workmanship. Bangles of glass, ivory, shell, bone, etc. A coin of Balban (1266–87) from the middle level.
Site deserted		——
IV	Early 2nd century BCE–late 3rd century CE	Pottery—red ware, some with stamped designs; black-on-red painted pottery found in the upper levels. Houses mostly made of burnt bricks (14½ × 9 × 2½ inches); squarish bricks (11 × 11 × 4 inches) used for floors. Several house plans were reconstructed and seven structural sub-phases identified. Copper objects. Iron objects including nails, an axe/adze, sickle, and pan. A fine and varied range of moulded terracotta figurines (including many of the humped bull), wheels, carts, and votive tanks and a fine headless figure of the *bodhisattva* Maitreya. Well-made rings and beads. Inscribed potsherds and a seal. Coins of the rulers of Mathura, the Yaudheyas, and imitation coins of the Kushana king Vasudeva.
Site deserted		Evidence of a massive fire
III	Early 6th century–early 3rd century BCE	Pottery—Northern Black Polished Ware (NBPW), coarse grey ware, unslipped red ware. Houses of mud-bricks and kiln-burnt bricks (17.5 × 10 × 2.7 inches). Brick-lined drains. Terracotta ring wells. Copper objects. Iron arrowhead, chisel and sickle. Punch-marked and uninscribed cast coins. Human and animal figurines (many of elephants) made of terracotta. Beads of etched carnelian and crystalline quartz. Rings made of copper, chalcedony, gold, and horn.
Site deserted		Evidence of a flood in the Ganga
II	*c.* 1100–800 BCE	Pottery—Painted Grey Ware (PGW), black-slipped ware, and ordinary red and red-slipped ware. House walls of mud, mud-brick, reed, and mud plaster; one fragmentary burnt brick. Copper artefacts. Iron slag in the uppermost levels. Chert and jasper weights. Glass bangles. Terracotta objects including animal figurines. Bone needles. Charred grains of rice. Bones of horse, pig, cattle, etc.
Site deserted		——
I	Pre-1200 BCE	Pottery—fragments of **Ochre Coloured Pottery** (**OCP**). No structures found, maybe because a very limited area was excavated. Habitation seems to have been sporadic
Natural soil		——

Note The mound of Hastinapura in Meerut district, Uttar Pradesh, was excavated by a team led by B. B. Lal in 1950–52 (see Lal, 1954–55). Its cultural sequence extended over an enormously long stretch of time, with four breaks in occupation. The earliest settlement belonged to the period before *c.* 1200 BCE and the latest level to the early 15th century CE. This table gives a brief synopsis of some of the main features of the various levels known as Periods I–V. Read the table from bottom to top, starting from the lowest and earliest level, Period I. Note the range of evidence and the remarkable snapshot it gives of the life of people who lived at this site over the centuries. The cultural sequence at Hastinapura is a very important reference point for other sites in the upper Ganga valley.

While archaeologists generally work on land, marine or underwater archaeology is a rapidly growing area. In most other countries, marine archaeology deals mainly with shipwrecks. But in India, there are instances of entire settlements that have been submerged by the sea. Marine archaeology involves many specialists such as oceanographers, geologists, geophysicists, and diver-photographers. It also requires the use of special equipment and scientific instruments. For instance, an echo-sounding system registers a rise when a boat passes over an underwater object. A side scan electronic system gives a view of the sea floor. Underwater metal detectors held by divers give a signal if they sense any kind of metal object between 3 and 4 m away. Exciting underwater discoveries have been made off the coast of Dwarka and Bet Dwarka in Gujarat. At Dwarka, there are remains of a submerged port-city, including fortification walls and stone anchors, perhaps going back to *c.* 1500 BCE.

Bangaran Island, Lakshadweep: ancient ship anchor; marine archaeologist at work

Scientific techniques in archaeology

Archaeologists increasingly rely on various scientific techniques in order to obtain precise information about the lives of past communities. These are especially useful in dating archaeological material. Many dating methods are based directly or indirectly on the principle of radioactive decay. **Carbon-14** or radiocarbon dating is the best known of these, but others include **thermoluminescence**, potassium-argon, electron spin resonance, uranium series, and fission-track dating.

The word **archaeometry** refers to a range of scientific techniques and analyses involving the use of measurement to analyze ancient objects or materials. The chemical analysis of pottery and metal artefacts can give clues about how they were produced. A comparison of the chemical composition of metal artefacts and ores can help identify the source of ores. Chemical analysis of soil can be used to determine the degree of human presence and activity at a site. For instance, the decomposition of animal excreta increases the nitrogen content of the soil. At the **chalcolithic** site of Inamgaon in Maharashtra, the soil in the courtyards had higher nitrogen content than that inside the house. This shows that people tied their animals in their courtyards.

Palaeontology is the study of the remains of dead organisms over enormous spans of time. Within this discipline, molecular biology and DNA studies have been used to understand **hominin** evolution, to answer questions about what ancient people looked like, and to plot patterns of migration. In recent years, the rapid advances in genome analysis have especially contributed towards understanding patterns of migration and changes in population in different parts of the world (see Reich, 2018).

Human teeth and bones provide a great deal of information. The dental structure of humans is connected to subsistence patterns and methods of food preparation. Trace element analysis of human bones and scanning electron microscopic (SEM) analysis of tooth enamel can help identify the kind of food people ate and whether they suffered from nutritional deficiencies. Diseases such as arthritis and tuberculosis leave their mark on bones. **Palaeo-pathology** is the study of diseases ancient people suffered from by analyzing their bones. Human bones are also examined to make inferences about population size, density, mortality, fertility, and life expectancy. Since food and nutrition are related to social standing, assessing the nutritional inputs in the bones of men and women at a site can indicate whether there were marked status differences between groups of people or between men and women. Of course, all the scientific techniques mentioned here require specialized laboratories, equipment, and skilled specialists.

The distribution of faunal remains (animal bones) at a site can indicate which areas were used for butchering, cooking, eating, bone tool making, and refuse dumping. **Faunal analysis** gives information about the animals people hunted and domesticated, the age of animals at death, and the diseases that afflicted them. The bones of wild and domesticated species can usually be differentiated. The joints of animals used for agriculture or draught purposes get fused and can be identified. Faunal remains can lead

FURTHER DISCUSSION | **Radiocarbon dating**

Discovered by an American chemist named Willard Libby in 1949, radiocarbon dating is today a very widely used dating method in archaeology and Carbon-14 (C-14) is a radioactive isotope of carbon. It is formed due to the influence of cosmic radiation on nitrogen in the atmosphere. Plants absorb C-14 in the atmosphere through their intake of carbon dioxide during the process of photosynthesis. C-14 passes into animals as they feed off plants or herbivorous animals. The intake of C-14 stops when the plant or animal dies, after which the C-14 in the physical structure of the dead plant or animal tissue begins to disintegrate at the rate of one half every 5,730 years (this is known as the 'half-life' of C-14). By measuring the amount of C-14 remaining in the dead plant or animal tissue, scientists can figure out when it died, i.e., how old it is. The radiocarbon method can be used to date various organic materials such as wood, charcoal, bone, and shell.

Like all other scientific dating methods, the C-14 method provides approximate, not exact dates, and a standard error margin (known as the standard deviation) is recognized. Radiocarbon dates are accompanied by a plus/minus factor. Take the following date: 2500 ± 100 BP. This means a date range between 2600 and 2400 BP. 'BP' stands for 'Before Present', and the year 1950, which was about the time the radiocarbon method of dating was introduced, is taken as the base line, i.e., year one. Archaeologists sometimes resort to multiple dates from the same sample in order to arrive at mean dates with a smaller standard deviation. Sometimes radiocarbon dates can be way off the mark. This could be because the sample has got contaminated, or due to some procedural error.

Scientists have known for some time that the amount of radiocarbon produced in the atmosphere has not been constant over time. They have also noticed a discrepancy between the more accurate dates produced by tree-ring dating and those arrived at by the radiocarbon method. Therefore, it is clear that some calibrations, i.e., corrections, have to be made while converting radiocarbon dates to calendar dates, i.e., BCE and CE dates. In view of the fact that there is still some debate regarding calibration procedures, some archaeologists prefer to publish uncalibrated dates. However, certain calibration tables have been more or less accepted by many scholars. Calibrated radiocarbon dates are usually preceded by the abbreviation 'Cal.'

Radiocarbon dates have made a dramatic difference to our understanding of the chronology of ancient cultures. But why is it that radiocarbon dates for cultures given in different books are not always the same? This could be because some dates are calibrated, while others are uncalibrated. Another reason is that there is an element of interpretation and judgement involved even in the use of radiocarbon dates. When there is a string of radiocarbon dates for a site, which one is to be highlighted? Since radiocarbon dates give us a date bracket, which end of the bracket should be emphasized? Sometimes, instead of giving a whole string of radiocarbon dates with the standard deviation, archaeologists calculate the mean date and give that as a single radiocarbon date. There are thus, choices to be made in the use of radiocarbon dates. How an archaeologist interprets and presents them depends on his/her larger understanding of the relative chronology of cultures.

to inferences about aspects of environment such as climate and vegetation and the season during which a site was occupied. Sometimes, bones reveal contacts between communities. For instance, the identification of marine fish bones and shells at Inamgaon, at least 200 km from the sea, shows that its inhabitants had contacts with coastal communities.

Environments are not just backdrops to human activity; they are an important *part* of human experience. The relationship between people and their environmental landscape is an interactive, reciprocal one. Human interactions with the environment do not only have to do with subsistence or economic activities. They also depend on communities' social and political organization and their ideas about the world and their place in it. Archaeological landscapes include natural and human-made features that are associated with various activities as well as symbolic meaning. An understanding of the interactions between humans and their natural environment is, therefore, an important aspect of **prehistory**, **protohistory**, and history. Environmental archaeology, which aims at understanding how societies adapted to their environment and how they used environmental resources, involves the collaboration of scientists and archaeologists. **Palaeo-botanical** studies include the analysis of pollen and other minute plant remains, seeds, charcoal, sediments, and geological strata.

In recent years, the use of remote sensing and Geographical Information Systems (GIS) tools has been increasingly used to identify changes in the physical landscape and subsurface archaeological remains, such as palaeo-channels of rivers, structures, moats,

Table 1.2 Some dating methods used in archaeology

Dating method	Used on	Time range/Lower time limit (ya=years ago)
Carbon-14	Organic material, e.g., charcoal, wood, seeds, plant remains, bones	From 50,000 to 80,000 ya
Thermoluminescence	Inorganic material that has been heated rapidly to 500°C or above, e.g., pottery, terracotta, burnt flint	Even objects older than 50,000–80,000 ya
Potassium-Argon	Volcanic rocks older than about 100,000 years	Hundreds of millions of ya
Electron spin resonance	Bone, shell	Hundreds of thousands ya
Uranium series	Rocks rich in calcium carbonate	50,000–500,000 ya
Fission track	Certain kinds of rocks and minerals, obsidian, glass, mica, etc.	About 300,000 ya to millions of ya
Palaeomagnetic dating	Magnetized sediments, volcanic lava, clay baked to 650–700°C	Can only be used to date very old deposits from hundreds of thousands ya to millions of ya
Amino acid analysis	Bone	Up to 100,000 ya
Dendrochronology (tree-ring dating)	Timber in areas outside the tropics	Up to about 8,000 ya
Optically stimulated or infrared stimulated luminescence	Any sediment which is believed to have been undisturbed after its burial under other sediments	Still undefined as refinements in the process continue; extends up to at least 17,000 ya; more accurate than C-14 calibrations for CE dates

and roads (Rajani, 2021). Electro-optical sensors and cameras mounted on LANDSAT, IRS, and SPOT satellites yield images of value to archaeologists. Non-invasive techniques are of especial value in areas that are heavily built up and where regular excavations cannot be carried out. Geospatial techniques have enabled the identification of the relationship between human activities and the landscape in very specific ways. They also have important implications for identifying areas of archaeological potential and for drawing up conservation plans.

Since the volume of archaeological data related to the early Indian past is steadily increasing, it is necessary to consult the most archaeological publications to keep pace with new discoveries.

Interpreting archaeological evidence

Interpretation is as crucial in archaeology as in using textual sources. It is involved at all levels, from the seemingly simple stage of classifying artefacts to the framing of historical hypotheses. Just as it is possible to identify trends in history writing, similarly, there have been several changes in approach and method within the disciple of archaeology. For example, in the 1960s, the traditional cultural history perspectives were challenged by the emergence of what came to be known as **New Archaeology** and a school known as 'processualism'. Closely allied with anthropology, this school tried to understand cultures and cultural processes holistically, especially in relation to ecology, human adaptation, and the interaction of different kinds of variables. It advocated a problem-oriented approach, and emphasized the importance of explanation, generalization, and theory building. **Post-processual archaeology**, which emerged subsequently, is not a single school. It is an umbrella term which refers to several approaches that challenged many of the assumptions, methods, and goals of processualism. This included questioning the possibility of objective knowledge about the past as well as questioning the older explanatory models and generalizations. Rather than seeing material culture as a simple reflection of past societies, post-processual approaches recognized that material culture was an active, dynamic part of human experience, representing the thought processes, actions, and choices made by people. This includes recognizing the importance of the cognitive and symbolic aspects of material culture. In recent years, archaeologists have tended to combine the insights of different approaches.

Archaeology usually provides an anonymous history, one that sheds light on cultural processes rather than events. It is the only source for prehistory, the longest part of the human past, during which many major discoveries and developments took place. It is also the only source for those parts of the past covered by non-deciphered written records, and it continues to provide valuable information even after the beginning of the historical period. Unfortunately, once textual sources become available, historians tend to use archaeology as a secondary, corroborative source. One of the current challenges for early Indian history is to adequately incorporate archaeological evidence into the larger historical narratives.

Archaeology often tells us about aspects of everyday life that are not revealed or emphasized in texts. It provides information on the history of human settlements and can give very specific details about modes of subsistence—the food people procured in order to live, and how they obtained it. In recent years, the study of food has expanded into a study of foodways, which includes various aspects of the procurement, production, and consumption of food, including the larger social, political, and cultural contexts. Archaeology offers details about the crops people grew, the agricultural implements they used, and the animals they hunted and tamed. It is an excellent source of information on various aspects of the history of technology—raw materials, their sources, the techniques used to make artefacts of various kinds. Archaeology also helps reconstruct routes and networks of exchange, trade, and interaction between communities.

There are many problems involved in translating archaeological cultures into history. An archaeological culture need not necessarily correspond to a linguistic group, political unit, or a social group such as a **lineage**, **clan**, or **tribe**. One of the most important issues is how to explain changes in material culture, especially in pottery traditions.

Ethno-archaeology

Ethnography is the study of living cultures and communities. **Ethno-archaeology** studies the behaviour and practices of living communities in order to interpret the archaeological evidence related to communities of the past.

The Indian subcontinent is an area where many traditional features and methods survive—for instance in agriculture, animal husbandry, house building, the clothes people wear and the food they eat. Modern craftspersons are an important guide for understanding the ways in which ancient craftspersons may have made things. Technology involves much more than the techniques used for making artefacts. It is necessary to explore the social organization of craftspersons, the customs and beliefs that material objects were part of, how goods were marketed, the relationship between craftspersons and traders, and between craftspersons and customers. Ethno-archaeology helps answer these sorts of questions as well. For instance, a tradition of carnelian bead manufacturing exists these days in Khambhat, in Gujarat. Studying modern bead making in this area gives valuable clues about the way in which the Harappan beads may have been made and the possible social organization of the bead makers.

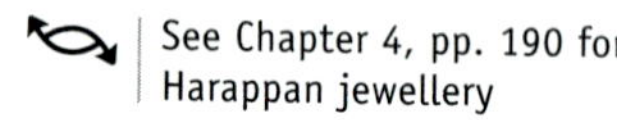

See Chapter 4, pp. 190 for Harappan jewellery

Ethno-archaeology can contribute towards filling the silences and gaps in history. For instance, it has helped archaeologists make inferences about women's role in

Harappan carnelian beads

PRIMARY SOURCES | The social and cultural aspects of technology

Gundiyali and Lodai are two pottery manufacturing villages in Kutch, Gujarat. Archana Choksi's case study explores the social and cultural aspects of technology and raises several important points that archaeologists and historians need to keep in mind when interpreting ancient pottery traditions:

1. Pots of different shapes, sizes, and forms are found in both villages. The form of vessels is connected to their specific function. For example, the mouth of a vessel used for storing dry material like grain and flour is wide so that it is easy to put a hand into it. Vessels used to carry water into fields have small mouths to minimize spillage. Cooking vessels have wide mouths to allow stirring and enlarged, thick rims so that they can be handled when hot. Vessels used for eating are open and shallow, with rim bases that give them stability. The connection between the form and function of pots can help archaeologists interpret the function of the pots they find at sites.
2. The potters of Gundiyali and Lodai produce rather different vessels. This is because Gundiyali is dominated by farmers, labourers, and the service class, while Lodai is dominated by farmers and herders. These groups have different life-styles and needs and they use different kinds of pots. It is clear that potters make the sorts of pots their clients want, and consumer demand for pottery is shaped by occupation, family and community identity, food habits, and ritual practices. Inferences about patterns of social and economic organization can be made on the basis of the range of pots found at a site.
3. The potters of Gundiyali and Lodai are reluctant to experiment or change the forms and designs of the vessels they make. Pots change when there are significant socio-economic changes. For instance, the shapes of some of the traditional vessels have been modified to suit urban kitchens, although the decoration remains the same. This is relevant to understanding general patterns of continuity and change in ancient ceramic traditions.

Source Choksi, 1995

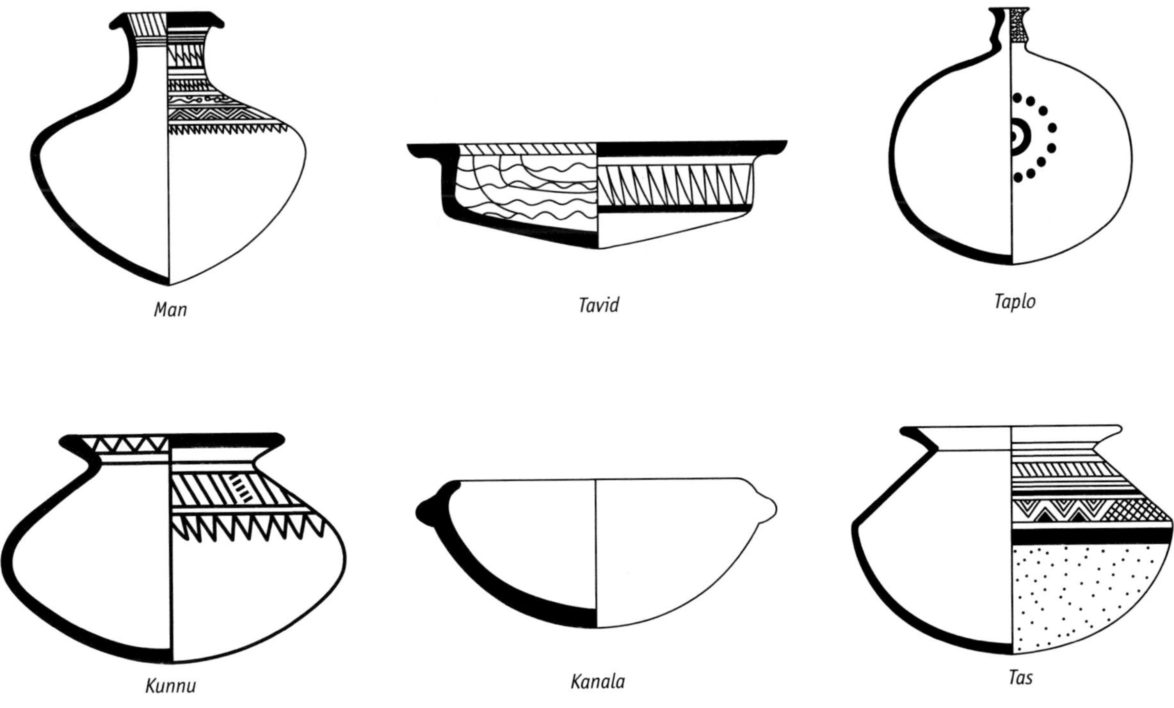

Figure 1.2 Pots from Gundiyali and Lodai

subsistence and craft-related activities in early times. Studies of modern communities of hunter-gatherers and shifting cultivators can help understand the life-ways of people who followed similar subsistence strategies in the past. Such studies have pointed out that tribal communities were never completely isolated, and they have also highlighted the important link between the ways in which people obtain their food and their identity as a community. Of course, ethno-archaeological evidence must be used cautiously, and it should be seen as suggesting *possible* and not necessarily conclusive ways of interpreting the archaeological data, always keeping in mind the differences between the present and past contexts.

The salvage operations at Nagarjunakonda, 1954–60

Protecting sites

The processes of rural and urban expansion pose constant threats to archaeological sites and their protection is crucial to the protection of the cultural heritage. **Salvage archaeology** aims at identifying endangered sites and saving them from destruction.

Many decades ago, the site of Nagarjunakonda in the Guntur district of Andhra Pradesh was submerged in water when the Nagarjunasagar dam was built across the Krishna. Before this happened, between 1954 and 1960, officers of the Archaeological Survey of India thoroughly explored, excavated, and documented the valley. The next step was a massive salvage operation. Nine of the most important structures were transplanted and re-built on top of the Nagarjunakonda hill and on the banks of the reservoir. Replicas of 14 other structures were made.

Apart from such spectacular sites and huge salvage projects, there are thousands of smaller sites all over the subcontinent that need to be noticed, documented, and cared for. Protecting the archaeological heritage is an important responsibility of the Government and the Archaeological Departments. But it is also essential for ordinary people to realize the importance of protecting and cherishing these fragile links to the past.

Epigraphy: The Study of Inscriptions

Ancient and early medieval scripts

Inscriptions and coins come under the general umbrella of archaeology and archaeological sources, but they are subjects of specialized study in their own right. The study of inscriptions is known as epigraphy. An inscription is any writing that is engraved on something—stone, wood, metal, ivory plaques, bronze statues, bricks, clay, shells, pottery, etc. Epigraphy includes deciphering the text of inscriptions and analyzing the information they contain. It also includes palaeography, the study of ancient writing. (For overviews of Indian epigraphy, see Sircar, 1965 and the more up-to-date Salomon, 1998).

As mentioned earlier, the oldest inscriptions in the Indian subcontinent are in the yet undeciphered Harappan script. The oldest deciphered inscriptions belong to the late 4th century BCE, and are in Brahmi and Kharoshthi (sometimes spelt Kharoshti). These include those of the Maurya emperor Ashoka, which are in a number of different languages and scripts, but mostly in the Prakrit language and Brahmi script. As there are no obvious links between the Harappan script and Brahmi or Kharoshthi, what happened to writing in between remains a mystery. There is no direct mention of writing in Vedic texts, but references to poetic metres, grammatical and phonetic terms, very large numbers, and complex arithmetical calculations in later Vedic texts are taken by some historians to indicate the possibility that writing may have been known at the time.

The first definite textual references to writing and written documents occur in the Buddhist Pali texts, especially the Jatakas and the *Vinaya Pitaka*. Panini's *Ashtadhyayi* refers to the word *lipi* (script). The Brahmi of Ashoka's inscriptions seems a fairly developed script, and it must have had a prior history of at least a few centuries. More recently, important direct evidence that Brahmi existed in pre-Maurya times has come from Anuradhapura in Sri Lanka, where archaeologists unearthed potsherds with short inscriptions (probably names of people) that can be dated to at least the early 4th century BCE. Short Tamil-Brahmi inscriptions have also been found on potsherds at Porunthal, Kodumanal, and Keezhadi in Tamil Nadu. Most of these represent post-firing graffiti. (These will be discussed in Chapter 6).

J. F. Fleet (1847–1917), one of the leading epigraphists in colonial India

There are three main types of scripts. In a logographic script, written symbols stand for a word, in a syllabic script for a syllable, and in an alphabetic script for a single phonetic sound. In the strict sense of the term, in an alphabet, the vowels should have a separate and fully independent status equal to that of consonants. Both the Brahmi and Kharoshthi scripts stand midway between alphabetic and syllabic scripts, and can be described as semi-syllabic or semi-alphabetic.

Kharoshthi's core area lay in the north-west—in and around the Indus, Swat, and Kabul river valleys, the land known as Gandhara in ancient times. Ashoka's Shahbazgarhi and Mansehra inscriptions are in this script. Kharoshthi was later used in North India under the Indo-Greek, Indo-Parthian, and Kushana kings, and was also used in certain records outside the Gandhara area, including in parts of Central Asia. Written from right to left, Kharoshthi seems to have been derived from the north Semitic **Aramaic** script.

D. C. Sircar (1907–85), a distinguished epigraphist and scholar

The origins of Brahmi, a script written from left to right, are not as clear. Some scholars have suggested an indigenous origin, others an Aramaic origin. A problem in accepting the latter theory is that the direction of writing and the forms of the letters in Brahmi and Kharoshthi are different, so it is unlikely that they were derived from the same script. Kharoshthi declined and died out in about the 3rd century CE. Brahmi, on the other hand, became the parent of all the indigenous scripts of South Asia, and also of those used in parts of Central and Southeast Asia.

The different stages of the Brahmi script are often labelled on the basis of dynasties, e.g., Ashokan Brahmi, Kushana Brahmi, and Gupta Brahmi. The epigraphist D. C. Sircar identified three stages of development in the history of this script in northern India: early Brahmi (3rd–1st centuries BCE); middle Brahmi (1st century BCE–3rd century CE); and late Brahmi (4th–6th centuries CE). In the late 6th century, Gupta Brahmi evolved into a script known as **Siddhamatrika** or Kutila, which had sharp angles at the lower right-hand corner of each letter. Regional differences became sharper after this point of time.

The modern North Indian scripts gradually emerged out of Siddhamatrika. Nagari or Devanagari was standardized by about 1000 CE and an eastern script (known as proto-Bengali or Gaudi) took shape between the 10th and 14th centuries. From here, it was a short step to the emergence of the Bengali, Assamese, Odia, and Maithili scripts in the 14th–15th centuries. This is also the time when the Sharada script emerged in Kashmir and adjoining areas.

The earliest inscriptions in the Tamil language (with some Prakrit elements) are engraved in rock shelters and caves, mostly in Tamil Nadu, especially in the area near Madurai. They are in a script known as Tamil-Brahmi, an adaptation of Brahmi for writing the Tamil language. Iravatham Mahadevan (2003) has identified two phases in the evolution of the Tamil-Brahmi script—early Tamil-Brahmi (*c.* 2nd century BCE–1st century CE) and late Tamil-Brahmi (2nd–4th centuries CE).

Three southern scripts emerged in the early medieval period—**Grantha**, Tamil, and **Vatteluttu**. The first of these was used for writing Sanskrit, the second and third for writing Tamil (Mahadevan, 2003: 210–14). The Grantha script is derived from the southern Brahmi script of the Prakrit inscriptions of the early Pallavas. Vatteluttu emerged from Tamil-Brahmi in about the 5th century, and its history continues for many centuries, especially in the Chera kingdom. The Tamil script first appeared in the Pallava territory in the 7th century CE and became widespread in the far south in the Chola period. Although the ancestry of the Tamil script can be traced to Brahmi, it was not directly derived from Tamil-Brahmi. It was formed by simplifying the Grantha script

PRIMARY SOURCES | Deciphered and undeciphered scripts

The story of the decipherment of ancient scripts is an exciting one. Ashokan Brahmi was deciphered as a result of the slow, painstaking efforts of a number of administrator-scholars working in India as employees of the East India Company. They included Charles Wilkins, Captain A. Troyer, W. H. Mill, J. Stevenson, and James Prinsep. These scholars first tried to read early medieval Brahmi inscriptions and then worked at deciphering the older Brahmi letters. The final step in the decipherment of the 3rd century BCE Maurya Brahmi was made by Prinsep in 1837.

Even though Prinsep managed to read these inscriptions, he had no idea about the identity of the king Piyadasi mentioned therein. The answer came soon enough, when George Turnour, an officer of the Ceylon Civil Service, identified the king as Ashoka on the basis of references in the Pali chronicle, the *Dipavamsa*.

Prinsep also played a role in the decipherment of Kharoshthi, along with other scholars such as Christian Lassen, Charles Masson, Alexander Cunningham, and E. Norris. The decipherment of Kharoshthi was easier because of the availability of bi-script coins in Greek and Kharoshthi issued by the Indo-Greek kings.

Apart from the Harappan script, there are some other scripts that are still undeciphered or difficult to read. These include highly stylized, calligraphic variations of Brahmi known as ornate Brahmi, found on short inscriptions in various parts of the country. Another script referred to by scholars as *shankhalipi* (because its characters look like *shankhas*, i.e., conch shells) is found in various parts of India except the far south between the 4th and 8th centuries CE. Both ornate Brahmi and *shankhalipi* seem to have been used mainly for names and signatures. There is a still undeciphered script similar to Brahmi found on terracotta seals at sites such as Chandraketugarh and Tamluk in Eastern India. An undeciphered script similar in some ways to Kharoshthi has been found in Afghanistan.

Source Salomon, 1998

Kharoshthi Script

Vowels

ā ī ū e o ạm

Consonants

ka	kha	ga	gha	
cha	chha	ja	jha	ña
ṭa	ṭha	ḍa	ḍha	ṇa
ta	tha	da	dha	na
pa	pha	ba	bha	ma
ya	ra	la	va	
śa	ṣa	sa	ha	

Brahmi Script

Vowels

a	i	u	e	o	aṁ
ā	ī	ū	ai		

Consonants

ka	kha	ga	gha	ṅa
cha	chha	ja	jha	ña
ṭa	ṭha	ḍa	ḍha	ṇa
ta	tha	da	dha	na
pa	pha	ba	bha	ma
ya	ra	la	va	
śa	ṣa	sa	ha	

The development of some Brahmi letters

	Maurya (3rd c. BCE)	Shunga (2nd–1st c. BCE)	Shaka/Kushana (1st–3rd c. CE)	Gupta (4th–6th c. CE)	Siddhamatrika (7th–9th c. CE)
ka					
ja					
ta					
pa					
ya					
sa					

Development of the letter *ṇa* in Brahmi and its derivative scripts

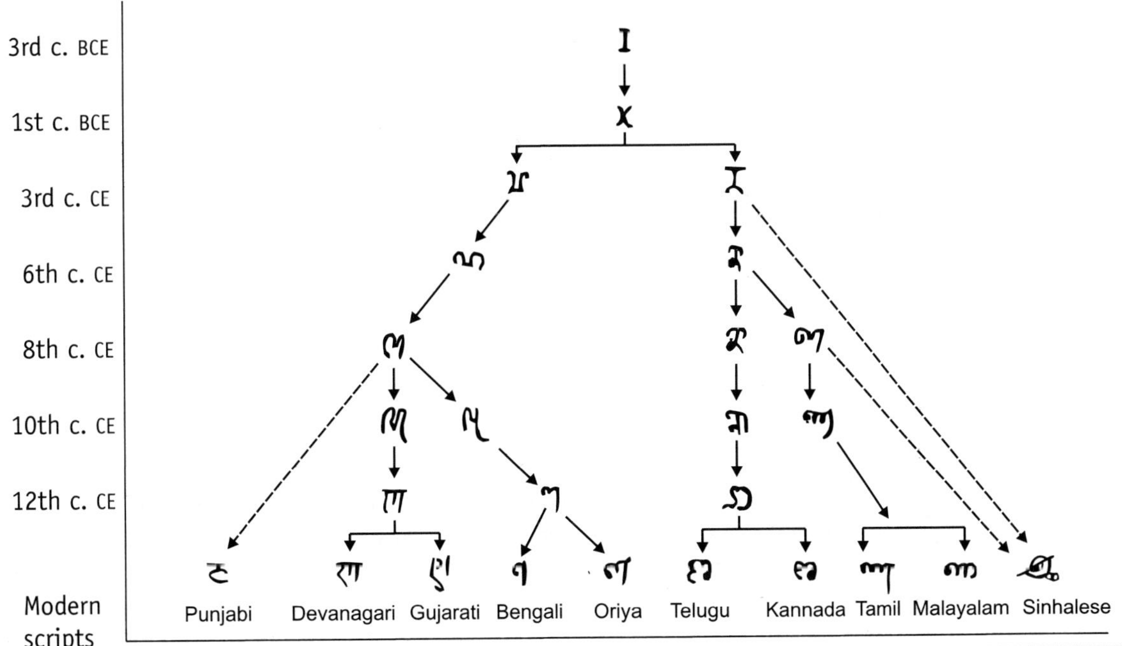

Figure 1.3 Kharoshthi and Brahmi scripts (after Salomon, 1998: 32, 33)

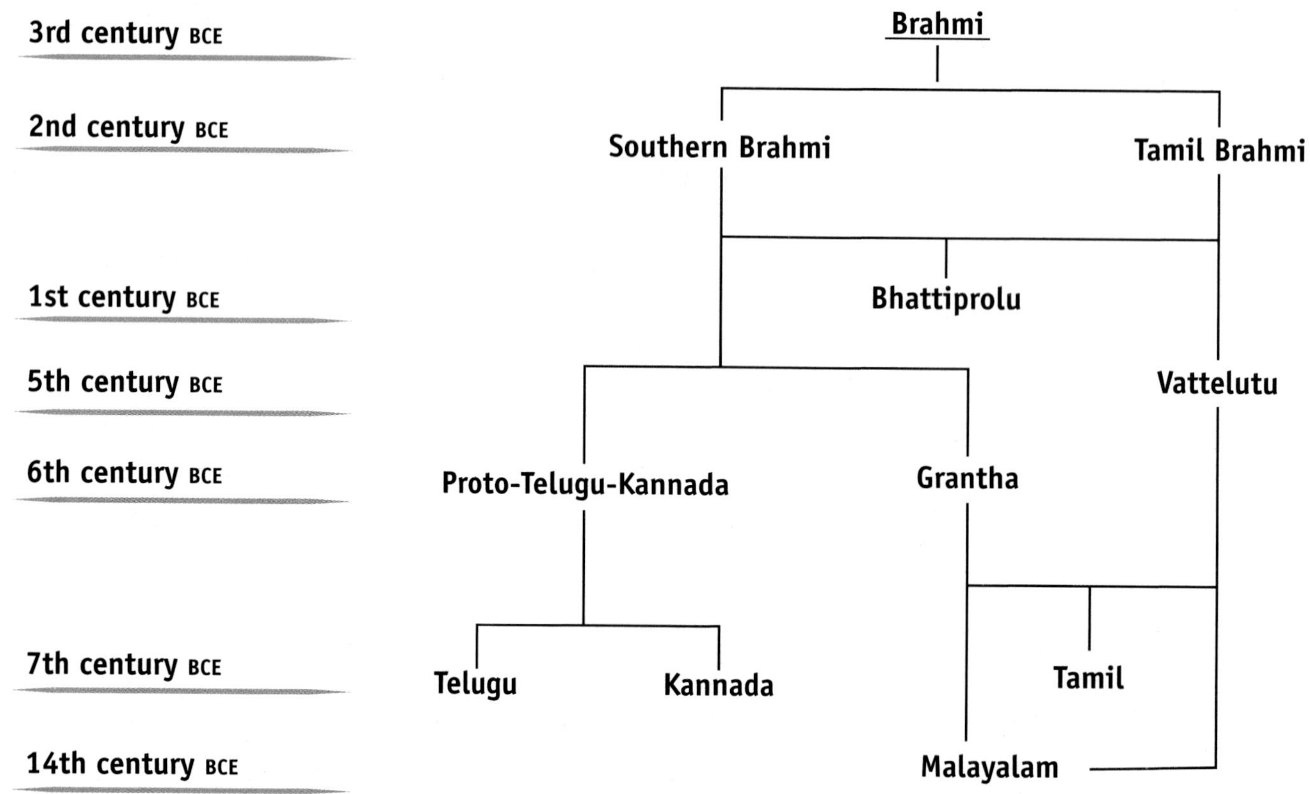

Figure 1.4 Evolution and chronology of South Indian scripts (after Mahadevan, 2003: 215)

and adding Vatteluttu letters to suit the needs of the Tamil Language. Something similar to the modern Telugu and Kannada scripts took shape in the 7th/8th century, while the Malayalam script developed out of Grantha by the 14th century.

Ancient Indian inscriptions include a few bi-script documents, in which the text is given in the same language written in two different scripts. Most of the instances come from the north-west and consist of short bi-script Brahmi–Kharoshthi inscriptions. The longer records include an 8th century Pattadakal pillar inscription of the Chalukya king Kirttivarman II. The language is Sanskrit; the text is written both in the North Indian Siddhamatrika script and in the local southern proto-Telugu–Kannada script.

Languages of ancient and early medieval inscriptions

The earliest Brahmi inscriptions, including those of Ashoka, are in dialects of Prakrit (also known as **Middle Indic**). Between the 1st and 4th centuries CE, many inscriptions were written in a mixture of Sanskrit and Prakrit. The first pure Sanskrit inscriptions appeared in the 1st century BCE. The first *long* Sanskrit inscription is the Junagadh rock inscription of the western **Kshatrapa** king Rudradaman. By about the end of the 3rd century CE, Sanskrit had gradually replaced Prakrit as the language of royal inscriptions in northern India.

In the Deccan and South India, Sanskrit inscriptions appeared along with Prakrit ones in the late 3rd/early 4th century CE, for instance at Nagarjunakonda in Andhra Pradesh. The Sanskrit element gradually increased. In the transitional phase of the 4th and 5th centuries, there were bilingual Sanskrit–Prakrit inscriptions, as well as those in a mixture of the two languages. Thereafter, Prakrit fell into disuse.

Between the 4th and 6th centuries, Sanskrit emerged as the premier language of royal inscriptions all over India. Thereafter, it attained the status of a language associated with high culture, religious authority, and political power not only in the subcontinent but also in certain parts of Southeast Asia. However, in the post-Gupta period, there was also an important trend towards the evolution of regional languages and scripts.

Even Sanskrit inscriptions show the influence of local dialects in spellings and words of non-Sanskritic origin.

In South India, inscriptions in the old Tamil language (and the Tamil-Brahmi script) appeared in the 2nd century BCE and the early centuries CE. Tamil became an important language of South Indian inscriptions under the Pallava dynasty. There are examples of bilingual Tamil–Sanskrit Pallava inscriptions from the 7th century onwards. In these, the invocation, genealogical portion, and concluding verses are often in Sanskrit and the details of the grants in Tamil. Kings of the Chola and Pandya dynasties also issued Tamil and bilingual Sanskrit–Tamil inscriptions. Hundreds of donative Tamil inscriptions were inscribed on temple walls in various parts of South India in early medieval times.

The earliest Kannada inscriptions belong to the late 6th/early 7th century CE. From this period onwards, there were many private donative records in Kannada, and this language was also used in some royal grants. There are some bilingual Sanskrit–Kannada inscriptions and a 12th century inscription found at Kurgod (in Bellary district, Karnataka) is in three languages—Sanskrit, Prakrit, and Kannada. The late 6th century epigraphs of the early Telugu Chola kings mark the beginnings of Telugu as a language of inscriptions. Thereafter, there are many private donative records in this language. Malayalam inscriptions appeared in about the 15th century. There are also a few late inscriptions in Tulu, a Dravidian language which is similar in some ways to Kannada and is spoken in parts of Karnataka.

As for inscriptions in the modern North Indian languages, Marathi and Odia inscriptions can be identified from the 11th century. Inscriptions in dialects similar to what is referred to today as Hindi appear in Madhya Pradesh from the 13th century onwards, and Gujarati can be identified in epigraphs from the 15th century.

Arabic inscriptions appeared in the subcontinent with the establishment of Arab control over Sindh and the expansion of Arab trade activities, especially on the western coast. The 9th century Kollam copper plates is mostly in Tamil inscribed in the Vatteluttu script, with a few words in the Grantha script. The sixth plate, however, contains signatures of witnesses in three languages and scripts—Arabic written in the Kufic script; Pahlavi; and Judaeo-Persian written in the Hebrew script.

Dating the inscriptions

Inscriptions are usually dated in regnal years or eras. The dates of eras are given in words, numerals, or both. The ancient Indian calendar system often had a combination of lunar as well as solar units. Inscriptions sometimes specify the month, lunar fortnight (*paksha*), lunar day (*tithi*), weekday (the civil day or solar day), and may give additional astronomical details. The specification of the year and day began in the 2nd century BCE. Some later inscriptions give the date in the form of chronograms (known as *bhuta-sankhya*). Instead of numbers, words standing for these numbers are used—e.g., *bhumi* (the earth) = 1; *kara* (hand) = 2; *loka* (the worlds) = 3; *veda* = 4, etc. These words are given in the reverse sequence of the numbers in the date, and are to be read backwards. For example, 'kara-veda-bhumi' means the year 142. If an inscription is not dated, it can be assigned a rough date on palaeographic grounds.

Many different eras were used in ancient and early medieval India. To cite a few examples—the Vikrama era of 58 BCE, the Shaka era of 78 CE, the Kalachuri-Chedi era of 248 CE, and the Gupta era of 319–20 CE. The Kollam era of 824 CE was used in inscriptions of Kerala and adjoining parts of Tamil Nadu, while the Chalukya-Vikrama era of 1076 was used in some inscriptions of Karnataka and adjoining areas. The eras marked important events, usually the accession of a king. Subordinate kings used the era of their overlord, and some eras continued to be used long after their founding dynasty had disappeared. While the initial year of most ancient and early medieval eras is known, uncertainty still surrounds a few. For instance, the suggested dates for the beginning of the Harsha era include 612, 619, and 648 CE. Similarly, the dates for the era of the Ganga kings of Odisha range from the 4th to the 9th century CE.

FURTHER DISCUSSION | **How to convert ancient era dates into modern ones**

How do you convert a date in an ancient era into BCE/CE dates of the Common Era, which is based on the Christian calendar? All that is required is a bit of simple arithmetic. For a date in an era that began in a BCE year, subtract the initial BCE year of that era from it. If the era began in a CE year, add the initial CE date.

For example, year 179 of the Vikrama era (which began in 58 BCE) = 179 - 58 = 121 CE; year 179 of the Shaka era (which began in 78 CE) = 179 + 78 = 257 CE.

There can be a bit of variation in the conversion of ancient dates, depending on whether the months mentioned are solar or lunar months. The month is also relevant because the traditional Indian year did not begin in the same month as the Western year, which begins in January. Another point that can create some confusion is whether the year mentioned in the inscription is to be understood as expired or current; this is sometimes, but not always, indicated in the text. To give an example, when we celebrate a child's first birthday, going according to expired years, she has completed one year, but going by current years, she has begun his second year of life. In spite of these kinds of issues, if an inscription is dated in a known era, it is possible to pin it down within a very narrow margin.

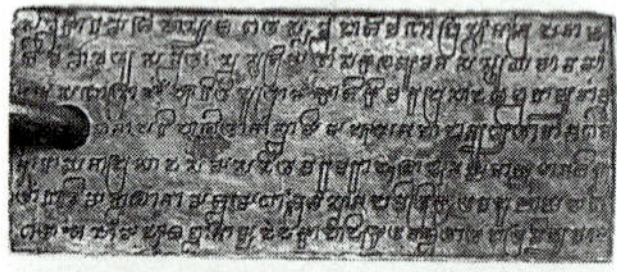

A Pala period image with a donative inscription on the base; copper plate inscriptions

The classification of inscriptions

Inscriptions can be classified in several different ways, for instance according to the surface they are engraved on, language, age, and geographical region. They can also be classified into official and private records, depending on whose behalf they were inscribed. Ashoka's edicts and royal land grants are examples of official records. Inscriptions recording grants made by private individuals or guilds to temples, or to Buddhist or Jaina establishments are examples of private records.

Inscriptions can also be classified according to their content and purpose into types such as donative, dedicative, and commemorative inscriptions. For instance, the Lumbini pillar inscription of Ashoka is a royal commemorative inscription, recording a specific event—the visit of the king to the Buddha's birthplace. In many parts of India, there is evidence of an ancient practice of erecting memorials to the dead. Thousands of memorial stones are found all over the country, not always connected with burials. Some only have sculpted scenes (realistic or symbolic), others also have inscriptions. The most common memorial stones were erected in memory of dead heroes or women who committed *sati*. But there are other kinds as well. Stones were set up in honour of Jaina men and women who performed voluntary ritual death. On the Konkan coast, many stones were erected in memory of sailors who lost their lives in sea battles. Some memorial stones were worshipped.

Donative inscriptions in favour of religious establishments were inscribed on shrine walls, railings, and gateways. The excavation and donation of caves to ascetics was recorded in inscriptions in the caves. Donative inscriptions include records of the installation of religious images, often inscribed on the images themselves. Others record investments of money made by people, out of the interest of which lamps, flowers, incense, etc. were to be provided for the worship of the deity.

Royal land grants are an important category of donative records. There are thousands of such inscriptions, some on stone, but mostly inscribed on one or more copper plates. Most of them record grants made by kings to Brahmanas and religious establishments. The earliest stone inscriptions recording land grants with tax exemptions are 1st century CE Satavahana and Kshatrapa epigraphs at Nashik. The oldest known copper plate grant is the late 3rd century Patagandigudam grant of the Ikshvaku king Ehavala Chantamula. Copper plate grants increased in number and frequency in the early medieval period.

Royal inscriptions include *prashastis* (panegyric). Most royal inscriptions (and some private ones too) usually begin with a *prashasti*, but some inscriptions are entirely devoted to eulogizing their subject. Well-known examples are the Hathigumpha inscription of Kharavela, a 1st century BCE king of Kalinga in Odisha, and the Allahabad *prashasti* of the 4th century Gupta emperor Samudragupta.

PRIMARY SOURCES | Memorializing death in stone

Memorial stones and their inscriptions reflect the values and ideals that ancient communities associated with life and death. In the Andhra region, such stones are known as *chhaya stambhas*. At Nagarjunakonda, there are memorial stones in memory of kings, queens, soldiers, chieftains, generals, holy people, and an artisan. At the base of a 12 ft high limestone pillar is an inscription recording the names of 29 royal women—sisters, mothers, and queens of the Ikshvaku family, collectively mourning king Chantamula I. Above the inscription are five panels of relief carving, one on top of the other, depicting the dead king in different poses. In the first (lowest) scene, he appears as a plump figure distributing gifts during the performance of a religious ceremony. In the next one, he is riding an elephant. In the panel above this, he is surrounded by women, three seated on the floor (perhaps musicians), the fourth dancing. In the next scene, he is sitting on a throne, flanked by women, two of whom may represent his queens. The topmost panel depicts a building, possibly a palace or heaven.

The Nagarjunakonda memorial pillar in honour of an artisan is naturally much simpler. It just gives the name of the artisan Mulabhuta and states that he came from a place called Pavayata. Above the inscription is a narrow-necked vase, which may have been the emblem of the guild to which Mulabhuta belonged.

The largest concentration of memorial stones is in Karnataka. Almost 3,000 hero stones dated between the 5th and 13th centuries have been found here. Inscriptions on some of these give only a name, others offer details of the circumstances in which the person died. Hero stones usually commemorated male heroes, but two inscriptions from Siddhenahalli and Kembalu refer to the heroic death of a woman and of a queen who launched a cattle raid. An inscription from Shikaripur refers to a woman laying down her life to defend others.

Hero stone from Khanapur, Karnataka

There are also some interesting memorials for pets. An inscription from Gollarahatti is in memory of a hunting dog named Punisha who died after killing a wild boar, while another one from Atkur commemorates the death of a dog named Kali who died fighting a wild boar during a hunt. A 12th century inscription at Tambur mourns the death of the pet parrot of a king of the Kadamba dynasty of Goa. The parrot was eaten by a cat in the palace and the inscription tells us that the king was so overwhelmed with grief at this event that he killed himself.

The tradition of memorial pillars lives on in certain parts of the country today, e.g., in Karnataka and among tribal communities of Gujarat and Madhya Pradesh. The Maria and Muria Gond tribes of the Bastar region of Madhya Pradesh still erect memorials of stone and wood. Some are plain, others are beautifully carved or painted. These memorials are linked with beliefs and rituals related to death and afterlife, and are a very important part of the culture and identity of the people.

Source Settar and Sontheimer, n.d.; Postel and Cooper, 1999

Certain inscriptions record the building of waterworks, wells, and charitable feeding houses by private individuals. Certain royal initiatives related to water are recorded on a granite rock at Junagadh (Girnar) in Gujarat. Apart from a set of Ashokan edicts, this rock bears two other important inscriptions. A *c.* 150 CE inscription of the Shaka Kshatrapa ruler Rudradaman records the beginning of the construction of a water reservoir known as Sudarshana lake in the 4th century BCE during the time of the Maurya emperor Chandragupta, its completion during the reign of Ashoka, and its repair in the 2nd century CE. A 5th century inscription on the *same* rock, of the time of the Gupta king Skandagupta, describes how the lake burst its banks due to excessive rains and was repaired after two years' work. What we have here is an amazing history of the building and repair of an ancient water reservoir over a period of about 1,000 years!

There are other miscellaneous types of inscriptions—labels, graffiti left by pilgrims and travellers, religious formulae, and writing on seals. Certain inscriptions from Madhya Pradesh give a condensed summary of the basics of Sanskrit grammar. 'Footprint inscriptions' are found in many parts of the country, accompanying a pair of engraved footprints of a holy man, king or other noteworthy person.

Inscriptions as a source of history

Compared with manuscripts of texts, inscriptions have the advantage of durability. They are usually contemporaneous to the events they speak of and their information can be connected to a time and place. Changes and additions made to them can usually be detected without great difficulty. The text of inscriptions may be brief, but a large number of short inscriptions can often provide important historical information. Compared to textual sources, which tend to give a theoretical perspective, inscriptions often reflect what people were actually doing. And although epigraphs of different categories usually follow a standard format, some of them do have the ability to surprise. Inscriptions are inscribed texts and their contents have to be analyzed as carefully as those of other texts, keeping in mind their purpose and audience.

Inscriptions are a valuable source of information on political history. The geographical spread of a king's inscriptions is often taken as indicating the area under his political control. But the discovery of inscriptions depends on chance and not all the inscriptions inscribed during a king's reign need necessarily be found. Furthermore, moveable inscriptions are not always found ***in situ***, i.e., in their original place.

The earliest royal inscriptions do not contain much genealogical material, but later ones generally do. Their *prashastis* give details about the history of dynasties and the reigns of kings. Of course, there are problems. Royal inscriptions naturally tend to exaggerate the achievements of the ruling king. Sometimes, confusion is created when a genealogy mentions kings with the same name, or when different inscriptions contradict each other on particular details. Sometimes genealogies skip names. This kind of skipping occurs, for instance, in the case of Skandagupta and Ramagupta, who are ignored in Gupta genealogies because they did not come in the direct line of succession of later rulers.

There are cases where inscriptions of different dynasties make conflicting claims. For instance, a Gurjara-Pratihara inscription states that king Vatsaraja conquered all of Karnataka. However, the contemporary Rashtrakuta king claims in his inscriptions to have defeated Vatsaraja and to have ruled over the Karnataka area. Wherever possible, details of political events given in inscriptions have to be cross-checked.

Apart from factual details, royal inscriptions are a rich source of information on political ideology, revealing the many ways in which rulers in different parts of the subcontinent sought to convert their power into legitimate authority.

Inscriptions, especially those of the early medieval period, have been used as a major source of information on political structures and administrative and revenue systems. They can also shed light on the history of settlement patterns, agrarian relations, forms of labour, and class and caste structures. Analyzing epigraphic evidence involves unravelling the technical vocabulary of inscriptions—for instance, the designations of officials, fiscal terms, and land measures—the meanings of which are not always clear.

There are very few ancient records of secular land transactions and records of land disputes, but these take us straight to the heart of social and economic issues. For instance, an inscription of the time of the Chola king Rajaraja III (1231 CE) states that farmers of a certain village found the burden of arbitrary levies in money and paddy and the demand of compulsory labour made on various pretexts by several agencies so unbearable that they could no longer carry on cultivation. A meeting of the Brahmana assembly and the leading men of the locality was held in the village temple. Decisions were taken, fixing the dues that farmers were to give to the Brahmanas and royal tax collectors, and the labour services that they were expected to perform.

Inscriptions provide dateable information on the history of religious sects, institutions, and practices. Donative records help identify the sources of patronage enjoyed by ancient religious establishments. They also give glimpses into sects and cults that were once important but did not leave any texts of their own—e.g., the Ajivika sect and the ***yaksha*** and ***naga*** cults.[1] Inscriptions can help identify and date sculptures and struc-

[1] The term 'cult' is used here to refer to beliefs and practices associated with the worship of a particular deity.

PRIMARY SOURCES | An ancient theatre, an ancient love story

The Sitabenga and Jogimara caves on Ramgarh hill (in Chhattisgarh) are located in the midst of a dense jungle in the Surguja district of Chhattisgarh. Both caves have inscriptions in a Prakrit/ Middle indic dialect, engraved in Brahmi letters of the 3rd or 2nd century BCE.

In front of the entrance of the Sitabenga cave is a row of rock-cut benches arranged in terraces in the shape of a crescent, with aisles. The two-line inscription in the cave cannot be read clearly or fully. It seems to talk of venerable poets who kindled the heart of others with their poetry, and people tying garlands of jasmine flowers around their necks at the swing festival of the full moon, when there was much fun, frolic, and music. The inscriptions and the layout of the cave and the area around it suggest that this may have been an ancient theatre, a place where poets recited their poems and where plays were performed long ago.

The Jogimara cave lies to the south of Sitabenga. Here, there is a five-line inscription which can be translated as follows:

> Sutanuka by name, a *devadasi*. The excellent among young men, Devadinna by name, the *rupadaksha*, loved her (*kamayitha*).

In later times, the word *devadasi* referred to a temple woman, but its meaning in this early context is unclear. *Rupadaksha* can be interpreted in different ways—it could mean someone skilled in sculpture, or a scribe, or an officer connected with coinage. But there are paintings on the roof of the cave, so maybe the word means painter or artist.

The inscription raises many questions: Who was Sutanuka? Her name literally means 'one who has a slender or beautiful body.' Perhaps she lived up to her name. Did she inscribe this epigraph? A woman knowing how to write would have been unusual for that time. Who was Devadinna? Was he an artist who sat desolately in this cave and inscribed his love for his beloved? Is it possible that someone else was the inscriber someone who knew one or both of the lovers, or had heard of their love? What sort of love was Devadinna and Sutanuka's? The inscription is in the past tense, and it has a melancholy tone. Did one of the lovers fall out of love, or were they separated by circumstance, family pressure, or death?

'Love' is a complex word that means different things in different times and places. We will never know the full story of Sutanuka and Devadinna's love. But the Jogimara cave inscription reminds us that although the lives of ancient people were very different from ours, they too experienced a variety of deep emotions. The history of emotions is an exciting new field of history.

Source Upinder Singh, 2021b: 40–41

tures, and thus, throw light on the history of iconography, art, and architecture. They are also a rich source of information on historical geography. In fact, the location of several ancient Buddhist monastic sites such as Kapilavastu (identified with Piprahwa in Basti district, UP) has been fixed on the basis of inscribed monastic seals.

Inscriptions reflect the history of languages and literature and a few refer to the performing arts. For instance, the 7th century Kudumiyamalai inscription gives the musical notes used in seven classical ragas. Inscriptions from Tamil Nadu refer to the performance of various kinds of dances. The pillars of the eastern and western gateways of the Nataraja temple at Chidambaram have label inscriptions describing the dance poses of 108 sculpted figures carved on them, quoting verses from the *Natyashastra* of Bharata.

The epigraphic process included the conceptualization, execution, and reception of inscriptions. Inscriptions are material remains and have to be understood in relation to the larger archaeological contexts in which they are found. They are also texts, connected with other texts, religious and cultural ideas, and with structures of power, authority, and social status. If they are associated with sculptures, they have to be understood in relation to them. Whether fragmentary or complete, whether consisting of one word or hundreds of lines, an inscription has to be read and analyzed carefully. Its contents can then be compared with those of other inscriptions and with information from other kinds of sources. In all cases, inscriptions have to be understood within their larger context.

Numismatics: The Study of Coins

In its most general sense, money is a medium of exchange and measure of value that is widely accepted within a community as a means of making payments for goods or services or for settling debts. Currency and coinage are more specific terms. Currency is a medium of exchange backed by an issuing authority, one that can be used to immediately discharge any kind of financial obligation. Coinage is metal currency. It has a definite size, shape, and weight standard, and bears the stamp of an issuing authority. The main message-bearing side of a coin is known as the obverse and the other side the reverse. In the world context, the earliest coins appear in Lydia in West Asia in *c.* 700 BCE and were made of electrum, a natural alloy of gold and silver.

Numismatics or the study of coins includes the analysis of the material out of which coins were made; the identification of the sources of the metals; the classification and study of the form of coins on the basis of their fabric (size, shape, thickness, design, workmanship), **metrology** (weight), design, metallic composition, techniques of manufacture, and message content. Ancient coins are usually discovered by accident. A very small proportion finds its way into the hands of coin collectors or governments; the majority end up getting lost, melted down, or destroyed. Coins occur as stray individual finds or as part of coin hoards. Hoards are especially valuable for monetary history and consist of coins withdrawn from human custody (due to being buried underground for safety, or fire, floods, loss, etc.) and subsequently found.

Metrology—the measurement and arrangement of coins by weight—is an important aspect of numismatics. In the course of circulation, coins are subjected to wear and tear and their weight gradually decreases. This fact enables numismatists to arrange them in a chronological sequence and to distinguish between coins of a hoard that have been in circulation for greater and less periods of time. Various techniques are used for ascertaining the metal content of coins. One method is to carefully inspect their colour and lustre. There are other informal physical procedures such as testing for resonance by dropping the coin on a hard surface to produce a sound or testing its ductility by biting it. A water displacement test can be conducted to measure a coin's specific gravity. There are also several chemical testing procedures for ascertaining metal composition. These are more accurate but generally damage the coin. Non-destructive scientific techniques such as X-ray fluorescence (XRF) spectrometry, which are now being used to analyze the elemental composition of coins, provide quick and accurate results.

Mint towns can be identified by noting sites where large numbers of coin moulds have been found. An analysis of coin dies can help identify the number and sequence of issues and estimates of the volume of coins produced by these dies can be made by extrapolation.

A brief history of Indian coinage

Stone age people had neither currency nor coinage and conducted exchange via barter. Chalcolithic cultures too conducted trade without the use of coins. The Harappans, for instance, had a very extensive trade network without using coinage. The *Rig Veda* mentions words such as *nishka* and *nishka-griva* (gold ornaments), and *hiranya-pinda* (gold globules), but these cannot be understood as coins. Later Vedic texts use terms such as *nishka*, *suvarna*, *shatamana*, and *pada*. These may have been metal pieces of definite weight, not necessarily full-fledged coins.

The earliest definite textual and archaeological evidence of coinage in the Indian subcontinent dates from the 6th–5th centuries BCE in a context of the emergence of states, urbanization, and expanding trade. Buddhist texts and the *Ashtadhyayi* refer to words

Ratti **seeds**

such as *kahapana/karshapana*, *nikkha/nishka*, *shatamana*, *pada*, *vimshatika*, *trinshatika*, and *suvanna/suvarna*. The basic unit of Indian coin weight systems was a red-and-black seed of the *gunja* berry (*Abrus precatorius*) known as the *raktika*, *ratti*, or *rati*. In South India, the standard weight of coins was theoretically calculated on the basis of the relationship between two kinds of beans—the *manjadi* (*Odenathera pavonina*) and the *kalanju* (*Caesalpinia bonduc*). The advent of coinage did not mean the disappearance of barter or the use of other media of value and exchange—these co-existed for a very long time. (For overviews of Indian coinage, see Sircar, 1965; Gupta, [1969] 1996; Cribb, 2005.)

The oldest coins found in the subcontinent are punch-marked coins, made mostly of silver, some of copper.[2] They are usually rectangular, sometimes square or round. The blanks for making these coins were generally cut from a metal sheet or made from flattened metal globules. The symbol or symbols were then hammered on separately, using dies or punches. These coins are often irregular in shape, their corners sometimes snipped off to adjust their weight. Most of the silver punch-marked coins weighed 32 *ratti*s or about 56 grains (grain is a weight measure used for metals; 1 grain). Punch-marked coins are found all over the subcontinent, and continued to circulate in many places till the early centuries CE, with a longer period of circulation in peninsular India.

The punch-marked coins of Northern India can be divided into four main series on the basis of their weight, the number and nature of punch marks, and their area of circulation—the Taxila-Gandhara type of the north-west with a heavy weight standard and a single punch type; the Kosala type of the middle Ganga valley, with a heavy weight standard and multiple punch marks; the Avanti type of Western India, with a light weight standard and single punch mark; and the Magadhan type with a light weight standard and multiple punches (Mitchiner, 1973). Changes in coinage patterns mirrored political changes. With the expansion of the Magadhan empire, the Magadhan type of punch-marked coins came to gradually replace those of other states.

Although these coins do not have any legends (i.e., anything written on them), it is likely that most of them were issued by states. In later times, there is evidence of city issues and guild issues, and it is possible that this practice also prevailed in the period of the punch-marked coins. Symbols on these coins include geometric designs, plants, animals, the sun, wheel, mountain, tree (including tree-in-railing), branches, and human figures. Some symbols may have had a religious or political importance, but their precise significance is not always certain. The coins often have primary and secondary punch marks. The latter are 'counterstamps' or 'countermarks' which were added on later, without heating the coins.

Uninscribed cast coins made of copper or alloys of copper appeared soon after the punch-marked coins. They have been found in most parts of the subcontinent except the far south. Some types have a fairly wide distribution, while others (such as those found at Ayodhya and Kaushambi, which seem to have been issued in the late 3rd or early 2nd century BCE) have a more restricted range of circulation. Cast coins were made by melting metal and pouring it into clay or metal moulds. Clay moulds have in fact been found at many sites and a bronze mould was found at Eran in Central India. The discovery of punch-marked and uninscribed cast coins in the same archaeological level at some early historical sites indicates that they overlapped in time.

Other early Indian coin types include uninscribed die-struck coins, mostly in copper, rarely in silver. The symbols, some similar to those on the punch-marked coins, were struck onto coin blanks with metal dies that were carefully carved with the required designs. The minting of such coins may have begun in about the 4th century BCE and they have been found in large numbers at sites such as Taxila and Ujjain.

The next stage in the history of Indian coinage is marked by the die-struck Indo-Greek coins of the 2nd/1st century BCE. These are very well-executed, usually round (a few are square or rectangular) and mostly in silver (a few are in copper, billon

Silver punch-marked coin of Magadha; uninscribed cast copper coin of Kaushambi; silver coin of Indo-Greek king Demetrius (obverse and reverse, from top)

[2] For excellent images and descriptions of ancient Indian coins of different periods, see numismatist Pankaj Tandon's website, https://coinindia.com

[a silver–copper alloy], nickel, and lead). They bear the name and portrait of the issuing ruler on the obverse. Coins of Menander and Strato I show them slowly aging from teenagers to old men, indicating their long reigns. Coins issued jointly by kings reflect the practice of conjoint rule. The reverse of these coins usually had religious symbols. The Indo-Greeks issued bilingual and bi-script coins, the name of the issuer appearing on the obverse in Greek and on the reverse in the Prakrit language and usually in the Kharoshthi script (rarely in Brahmi). The coins of these kings also have certain symbols referred to as monograms by numismatists, the precise significance of which is not certain. Coins of the Shakas, Indo-Parthians, and Kshatrapas follow the basic features of Indo-Greek coinage, and include bilingual and bi-script issues.

The Kushanas (1st–4th centuries CE) were the first dynasty of the subcontinent to mint large quantities of gold coins; their silver coins are rare. They also issued many copper coins of low denominational value, which indicates the increasing spread of the money economy. Kushana coins have the figure, name, and title of the king on the obverse. On the reverse are deities belonging to Greek, Iranian, Indian, and other pantheons. The legends are either entirely in Greek, or in some cases in the Prakrit language and Kharoshthi script on the reverse. From the time of Kanishka, the Bactrian language (written in the Greek script) began to be used on Kushana coins.

A number of coin types ranging from the 3rd century BCE to the 4th century CE, referred to by numismatists as indigenous, tribal, ***janapada***, or local coins form an important source of information on the history of the dynasties of northern and Central India. These coins are mostly cast or die-struck in copper or bronze, but there are some silver coins and a few rare examples of ones made of lead and potin (an alloy of copper, lead, tin, and dross). They include those issued by chieftains, kings, and non-monarchical states such as the Arjunayanas, Uddehikas, Malavas, and Yaudheyas. There are also coins bearing the name of cities such as Tripuri, Ujjayini, Kaushambi, Vidisha, Airikina, Mahishmati, Madhyamika, Varanasi, and Taxila, presumably issued by the administration of these cities. Some coins with the word *negama* seem to represent coins issued by merchant guilds. Certain Taxila coins with the legend *pancha-nekame* may have been issued jointly by five guilds.

In the Deccan, the pre-Satavahana coinage was followed by the copper and silver coins of the Satavahana kings. Rulers of this dynasty also issued coins of small denominational value made of lead and potin. Most Satavahana coins were die-struck, but there are some cast coins, and a combination of techniques was also used. The legends were generally in the Prakrit language and Brahmi script. However, the portrait coins (mostly in silver, but also in lead) use a Dravidian language (which can be identified as Tamil) and Brahmi script. Punch-marked coins continued to circulate alongside the Satavahana issues.

There was a greater demand for silver currency in the western Deccan, perhaps due to commercial reasons. The Shaka Kshatarapa ruler Nahapana introduced a silver currency in the Nashik area. Like the Satavahanas, the Kshatrapas also issued bilingual coins. Roman gold coins flowed into peninsular India in large quantities in the early centuries CE and may have been used as a medium of exchange for large-scale transactions or as currency reserves and capital deposits. Locally made imitations of Roman gold coins have also been found. So, in the early centuries CE in the western Deccan, there was a co-existence of Satavahana, Kshatrapa, punch-marked, and Roman coins. Currencies of the western Deccan also flowed into the eastern Deccan.

Some of the punch-marked coins found in various parts of South India have been identified as dynastic issues on the basis of their symbols. For example, coins found in a hoard at Bodinaikkanur near Madurai had a double carp fish—the symbol of the Pandya kings. In recent years, there has been increasing evidence of dynastic issues (some with portraits) with legends of the Cholas, Cheras, and Pandyas. This evidence has largely come from private collections and as surface and stray finds. Coins with the legend *Valuti* have been assigned to the Pandyas. Silver coins with the portrait of a Chera king and the legend *Makkotai* have been found in the Krishna riverbed near Karur. There are also coins with the legends *Kuttuvan Kotai* and *Kollippurai* along with the Chera symbols of the bow and arrow and the double fish and tiger.

Gold coins (obverse and reverse) of Kushana king Vima Kadphise and Gupta king Kumaragupta I (from top)

The imperial Gupta kings issued well-executed die-struck gold coins with metrical legends in Sanskrit. Known as *dinaras*, these coins have been mostly found in North India. The obverse depicts the reigning king in various poses, usually martial ones, but there are interesting instances of coins of Samudragupta and Kumaragupta I showing them playing the *vina* (a stringed instrument). The reverse of the Gupta coins have religious symbols indicating the kings' religious affiliations. There was a decline in the metallic purity of gold coins in the later part of Skandagupta's reign. The Guptas also issued silver coins, but their copper coins are rare.

In the post-Satavahana period in the eastern Deccan, the Ikshvakus of the lower Krishna valley (3rd–4th centuries) issued lead coins similar in fabric to those of the Satavahana. Some copper issues have been attributed to the Shalankayana dynasty (early 4th–mid-5th centuries) and the Vishnukundins (mid-5th–mid-7th centuries). Coins of the Traikutakas (3rd–4th centuries) circulated in the western Deccan and silver issues of the early Kalachuris (6th century) in the Maharashtra area.

The numismatic history of the early medieval period has been the subject of continuing debate. Historians who describe this period as marked by a feudal order talk of a decline in coinage along with a decline in trade and urban centres, followed by a revival in the 11th century. This hypothesis can be questioned. There was certainly a decline in the aesthetic quality of coins, in the number of coin types, and in their message content. Many are devoid of names or titles, and are therefore, difficult to associate with a particular king. However, as demonstrated by John S. Deyell (1990), there does not seem to have been a decline in the *volume* of coins in circulation.

A number of base metal alloy coin series were issued by dynasties in early medieval times. In the Ganga valley, billon coins circulated in the Gurjara-Pratihara kingdom, while other coin types circulated in Rajputana and Gujarat. Copper coins were minted by the Arab governors of Sindh between the mid-8th to mid-9th centuries. In Kashmir, copper coins were supplemented by bills of exchange (***hundikas***) denominated in terms of coins or grain, and the use of cowries. During the 6th–7th centuries, kings of Bengal such as Shashanka issued gold coins. A few gold coins have been identified as Pala issues. It has been suggested that the references to currency units in their inscriptions do not represent actual coins but theoretical units of value made up by a fixed number of objects such as **cowries**. A number of silver coins known as Harikela coins were circulating in Bengal between the 7th and 13th centuries and these had corresponding local eastern series, issued in the name of various localities.

In the western Deccan, some early medieval coin types have been tentatively identified with the Chalukyas of Badami. Although gold and silver coins found in the Andhra region have been attributed to the early eastern Chalukyas, there seems to be a subsequent gap of about three centuries till the end of the 10th century, when there was a revival of gold and copper coinage under the later kings of this dynasty. The attribution of certain gold and silver coins to the Chalukyas of Kalyana and to the Kalachuri Rajputs remains uncertain. Coins issued by the Kadambas of Goa have been identified, and a few gold coins have been attributed to the Shilaharas of the western Deccan.

In the far south, coins with lion and bull motifs, some inscribed with titles, have been associated with the Pallavas. The tiger crest is the emblem on Chola coins. The seals of several Chola copper plate inscriptions show the tiger, fish (the Pandya emblem), and bow (the Chera emblem), indicating that the Cholas had achieved political suzerainty over these two dynasties. The appearance of these three emblems on many gold, silver, and copper coins suggests that these were Chola issues. Gold coins found at Kavilayadavalli in the Nellore district of Andhra Pradesh have the motifs of the tiger, bow, and some indistinct marks. The obverse has the Tamil legend *sung* which seems to be a short form of *sungandavirttarulina* (abolisher of tolls), one of the titles of the Chola king Kulottunga I. The legends on the reverse—either *Kanchi* or *Ne* (maybe short for Nellur)—may indicate the names of mint towns. The last phase of Chola rule is only represented by copper coins. Coins—mostly copper ones—of the early medieval Pandyas have been found largely in Sri Lanka. A few bear names like Vira Pandya or

Silver Gurjara-Pratihara coin; copper Pallava coin (obverse and reverse, from top)

Sundara Pandya; the problem is one of figuring out which of the several kings of these names they refer to.

The Ghaznavid and Ghurid invasions introduced new coin types made of gold, silver, and billon in the north-west. Some of these retained some of Indian motifs, languages, and scripts. For instance, a coin type of Mahmud of Ghazni from Lahore has the *shahada* (the Islamic profession of faith) in Arabic on one side and Sanskrit written in the Nagari script on the reverse. Some coins of Muhammad Ghuri have bull and horseman motifs (seen on Rajput coins); others depict the Hindu goddess Lakshmi (see images on p. 683).

Coins as a source of history

At first glance, coins may appear to carry little historical information, but they provide clues to several important historical processes.

The wide distribution of Kushana coins indicates the flourishing trade of the period. The ship on certain Satavahana coins reflects the importance of maritime trade in the Deccan during this period. Roman coins found in various parts of India provide information on Indo-Roman trade. The few coin series issued by guilds indicate the importance of these institutions. Coins are often taken to indicate levels of economic prosperity (or the lack of it) or the financial condition of ancient states. Historians frequently interpret the debasement of coins as an indication of a financial crisis in the state or more general economic decline, for instance, in the time of the later Guptas. However, in a situation where the supply of precious metals is restricted or reduced, alloying or debasement can be a response to an increase in the demand for coins created by an increase in the volume of economic transactions (Deyell, 1990). As already indicated, the numismatic record of early medieval India is closely tied up with broader debates about the nature of political, social, and economic structures of the time.

Dates appear rarely on early Indian coins. Exceptions are some western Kshatrapa coins which give dates in the Shaka era and some Gupta silver coins which give the regnal years of kings. Whether dated or undated, coins discovered in archaeological excavations often help date the layers. An example is the site of Sonkh near Mathura, where the excavated levels were divided into eight periods on the basis of coin finds.

As important royal message-bearing media, coins form a vital source of political history. The area of circulation of dynastic issues is often used to estimate the extent and frontiers of empires. However, caution has to be exercised, because coins made of precious metals had an intrinsic value and often circulated beyond the borders of the state issuing them. They also sometimes continued to circulate for some time after a dynasty faded from power. Several different currency systems could prevail in an area, and it is necessary to visualize multiple overlapping and intersecting spheres of coin circulation.

Numismatic evidence is an especially important source for the political history of India between *c.* 200 BCE and 300 CE. Most of the Indo-Greek kings are known almost entirely from their coins. Coins also offer information on the Indo-Parthians, Shakas, Kshatrapas, Kushanas, and Satavahanas. The coins of over 25 kings with names ending in the suffix 'mitra' have been found in the area from east Punjab to the borders of Bihar. Coins found in various parts of North and Central India (Vidisha, Eran, Pawaya, Mathura, etc.) mention kings whose names end in the suffix 'naga', about whom little is known from other sources. Coins also offer information on ancient political systems. The term ***gana*** on coins of the Yaudheyas and Malavas points to their non-monarchical polity. City coins are suggestive of the importance and possible autonomy of certain city administrations.

Sometimes, numismatic evidence offers more than just the names of kings and provides biographical details. For instance, the only specific detail we know about the life of the Gupta king Chandragupta I is that he married a Lichchhavi princess, and this detail comes from coins commemorating the marriage. Coins have helped prove that a Gupta king named Ramagupta ruled between Samudragupta and Chandragupta II.

PRIMARY SOURCES | Counter-struck coins of the Kshatrapas and Satavahanas

In 1906, a spectacular discovery was made in Jogalthembi, a small village on the outskirts of Nashik in Maharashtra. It was a hoard of 13,250 silver coins of Nahapana, a king belonging to the Kshaharata house of the Kshatrapa rulers, who established his base in the Gujarat area in the first century CE. As many as 9,270 of these coins had marks of counter-striking by Gautamiputra Satakarni, a king of the Satavahana dynasty, which was a major political force in the Deccan in the early centuries CE.

Counter-striking is the phenomenon of coins issued by one authority being re-struck by another authority. Numismatists refer to the original strike of counter-struck coins as the 'undertype' and the new one as the 'overtype'. When properly done, re-striking can completely erase the original undertype. However, in many cases, if the re-striking is not forceful enough, some of the motifs of the undertype can be seen along with the overtype. The authority that originally struck the coin must in all cases have been earlier than or contemporary to the one responsible for the overtype.

Shailendra Bhandare describes how counter-striking can provide important historical information about the relative chronology and political history of the Kshatrapa and Satavahana rulers. The design of Nahapana's silver coins were based on the Indo-Greek silver drachms. The obverse bore his portrait along with a legend in a corrupt form of the Greek script. On the reverse was his dynastic emblem—a thunderbolt and arrow—along with inscriptions in the Brahmi and Kharoshthi scripts. All the coin legends were in the Prakrit language and proclaimed Nahapana as the Kshatrapa of the Kshaharata house. Gautamiputra Satakarni counter-struck Nahapana's coins with his own symbols. These included an arched hill surrounded by a Prakrit legend giving his name on the obverse. On the reverse was his dynastic emblem—four circles joined by a cross, with a small crescent on top of one of the circles. (Numismatists call this the 'Ujjain' symbol.)

Another interesting example of counter-striking comes from certain coins issued by Nahapana with counter-strikes by an otherwise unknown Satavahana king named Shiva Satakarni. There are also coins issued by Shiva Satakarni, counter-struck by Nahapana. The fact that these two rulers were counter-striking each other's coins indicates that they must have been contemporaries.

Counter-striking is generally interpreted as a graphic indication of political rivalry and contest, showing which king had the upper hand over the other at a particular point of time. The rivalry between the Kshaharata and Satavahana rulers is well known from other sources, including inscriptions. However, Bhandare points out that counter-striking was a way of efficiently and swiftly providing an acceptable exchange medium when the political authority in an area had changed, announcing the change to money users.

Continuity was an important factor in ensuring that people had faith in the authenticity and value of money, and a sudden change in coin types could create a situation of 'circulatory shock'—uncertainty and mistrust among coin users. Therefore, when a new political authority took over, it often tried to ensure that its coins did not look too different from those of its predecessors. This is why when Nahapana took over the Nashik area, his coins retained the elephant and a modified form of the tree-in-railing motifs of the earlier Satavahana coins that were in circulation here. Similarly, his Junnar coins retained the lion emblem of earlier coins. At the same time, while trying to maintain continuity, Nahapana made his point on the reverse of the new coins issued from Nashik and Junnar, where the Satavahana "Ujjain symbol" was replaced by his own thunderbolt and arrow emblem.

Source Bhandare, 2006

Silver coin (obverse and reverse) of Nahapana, re-struck by Gautamiputra Satakarni

Cowrie shells

The performance of the *ashvamedha* sacrifice by Samudragupta and Kumaragupta I is represented on coins. The archer and battleaxe coin types of Samudragupta predictably advertise his physical prowess, while the lyrist type, which shows him playing the *vina*, represents a completely different aspect of his personality.

The depiction of deities on coins provides information about the personal religious preferences of kings, royal religious policy, and the history of religion. For instance, representations of Balarama and Krishna appear on 2nd century BCE coins of the Indo-Greek king Agathocles at Aï-Khanoum (in Afghanistan), indicating the popularity and importance of the worship of these gods in this region. The depiction of a great variety of figures from Indian, Iranian, and Graeco-Roman religious traditions on the coins of the Kushana kings is generally interpreted as a reflection of their eclectic religious views. But it can equally be read as evidence of the many religious cults prevailing in their empire and the wide range of religious symbols through which the Kushanas chose to legitimize their political power.

In premodern times, different types of monetary systems co-existed and interacted with each other (Deyell, 2019). It is necessary to go beyond the study of coins and coin types to understand the different ways in which societies engaged in exchange and trade. In many parts of Asia, across many centuries, cowrie shells functioned as money, sometimes along with coins (see Yang, 2011). The evidence for this comes from textual references and archaeological excavations. The type of cowries most preferred in India were those found in the Maldive islands. The market value of cowries fluctuated, depending on demand and supply. Apart from coins and cowries, bills of exchange were often used for complex, 'cashless' economic transactions.

Visual Sources

As will become apparent as you read this book, visual sources form a rich and evocative window into many aspects of the history of ancient and early medieval India. The discipline of Indian art history has changed over the years (see Dhar, 2011) and now historians recognize visual sources as an important source of history.

A great deal of what we call ancient Indian art was not art for art's sake but was religious in theme and context. Distinctions are sometimes made between art and craft but the dividing lines are fluid. The creators of the paintings at Bhimbetka, the bronze Harappan 'dancing girl,' the relief sculptures at Sanchi and Ellora, and the terracottas of Chandraketugarh were all artists, working in different times, with different media, for different clientele. Most ancient Indian artists remain anonymous, leaving their work rather than their names to speak for them. Artistic skills were passed on from one generation to the other and practitioners were sometimes organized in guilds (see Misra, 1975). Artists and artisans were often peripatetic, moving around from one place to another, commissioned by different patrons to execute works that cut across religious boundaries.

The history of architecture, sculpture, and painting in ancient and early medieval India is a history of continuity, change, and diversity (for a good overview, see Huntington, 1985). Art reveals culturally rooted attitudes towards beauty. As pointed out by Vidya Dehejia (2009: 24), the acceptance and celebration of the sensuous bodily form in premodern Indian art is unparalleled. The sensuous refers to that which is aesthetically pleasing to the senses. (The sensual is that which is related to amorous or sexual pleasures, while the erotic has stronger and direct connections with sexual desire.) Bodies in ancient art—whether of ordinary men and women, gods and goddesses, demi-gods, even saints—are usually beautiful and very often sensuous, that is, aesthetically pleasing to the eye. Physical beauty was seen as a concomitant of political as well as spiritual power. Of course, the idealized bodily forms in ancient Indian art should not be seen as direct reflections of what ordinary people looked like!

As we shall see in this book, material evidence, including architectural and sculptural remains, sometimes gives us information about ideas and practices that are not present in texts. As is the case with other sources, analyzing visual sources involves skillful interpretation. Just as text can be read in many different ways, a piece of sculpture or painting too can be read in many different ways. A great deal depends on the questions that are asked. Apart from reflecting aesthetic ideas, art is an important source for the history of religion. There are connections between the aesthetic sensibilities reflected in ancient Indian texts and art. Religious iconography (the conventions of representation used for making religious images) can be seen in conjunction with how texts describe deities and saints. But the work of artists cannot be seen as simple translation of what is contained in texts. Apart from conceptualization and execution of art works, their reception, that is, how people in ancient times may have viewed them, is also a relevant issue.

The patronage of religious sculptures and structures was considered a means of accumulating merit and asserting social and political status. In fact, much more is known about patrons who financed works of art compared to the artists who created them. Sometimes art conveys a powerful message that can be interpreted in multiple ways. Artists, like poets, sometimes used double entendre that is, double meaning. Art sponsored by rulers sometimes shows political allegory (see Asher, [1983] 2018). Donative inscriptions on sculptures tell us about religious patronage and reveal a great deal about social and political processes. Artistic styles sometimes reveal cultural contacts and confluence. Portable religious icons often travelled long distances and were potent transmitters of religious ideas that got transformed in the process of travel and settling down in new cultural niches. Whether it is a small artefact, a sculpture, or a huge monument, the art of ancient and early medieval India can be appreciated as an important source of history or for its own sake.[3]

Bharhut Chanda *yakshi*

CONCLUSIONS

As we move back centuries or millennia, the quantum and type of data available for more recent history is simply not there; the life stories of specific individuals and events are difficult to locate and are replaced by broad brush strokes of historical processes. The primary sources include texts, archaeological remains, inscriptions, coins, and visual sources, all of which need to be carefully contextualized and analyzed, keeping in mind their nature, potential, and limitations. Wherever several sources are available, their evidence has to be co-related. The co-relation of evidence from texts and archaeology is especially important for a more comprehensive and inclusive history of ancient and early medieval India. However—as will become evident in later chapters—given the inherent differences in the nature of textual and archaeological data, it is not always easy to integrate them into a smooth and seamless narrative. The written word, material artefact, and visual image do not capture the entire range of human experience. They offer partial, refracted images of the past. Many important aspects of everyday life such as the oral, personal, and emotional, are very dimly visible. The discipline of history requires a skillful examination of sources, the use of reason, rigorous analysis, and a conscious attempt at objectivity. It also requires asking new questions. All histories are partial and provisional and subject to revision, but all histories are not equally reliable or acceptable. They have to be supported by evidence from the sources and must stand up to scrutiny when subjected to rigorous analysis. Many aspects of the lives and experiences of our remote ancestors will remain elusive. The challenge for the historian is to use historical analysis to uncover as much as possible about those lives and experiences.

[3] Works of ancient Indian art can be appreciated *in situ*, in illustrations in art books or online sources, or by visiting museums. Visuals of collections of some of the world's great museums, and their publications, can be accessed on their websites. These include the British Museum in London and the Metropolitan Museum in New York. For collections in Indian museums, a useful sources is the repository available at http://museumsofindia.gov.in. The Huntington Archive of Buddhist and Asian art is another useful source.

FURTHER READINGS

Chakrabarti, Dilip K. 1988. *A History of Indian Archaeology from the Beginning to 1947*. New Delhi: Munshiram Manoharlal.

Chattopadhyaya, B. D. 1977. *Coins and Currency Systems in South India c. 225–1300*. New Delhi: Munshiram Manoharlal.

Cribb, Joe. 2005. *The Indian Coinage Tradition: Origins, Continuity and Change*. Nashik: Indian Institute of Research in Numismatic Studies.

Deyell, John and Rila Mukherjee. (Eds.). 2019. *From Mountain Fastness to Coastal Kingdoms: Hard Money and 'Cashless' Economies in the Medieval Bay of Bengal World*. New Delhi: Manohar.

Gonda, Jan. (Gen. Ed.). (1973–87) 2022. *A History of Indian Literature*. 10 Vols. New Delhi: Manohar.

Gupta, P. L. (1969) 1996. *Coins*. 4th Edn. New Delhi: National Book Trust.

Lahiri, Nayanjot. 2017. *Monuments Matter: India's Archaeological Heritage Since Independence*. Mumbai: Marg. Vol. 68, No. 4.

Mahadevan, Iravatham. 2003. *Early Tamil Epigraphy: From the Earliest Times to the Sixth Century AD*. Chennai: Cre-A and the Department of Sanskrit and Indian Studies, Harvard University.

Mohan, Peggy. 2021. *Wanderers, Kings, Merchants: The Story of India Through its Languages*. Gurgaon: Penguin.

Mittal, Sushil and Gene Thursby. (Eds.). 2005. *The Hindu World*. Indian rep. New York and London: Routledge. Chaps. 2–5.

Mugali, R. S. 1975. *History of Kannada Literature*. New Delhi: Sahitya Akademi.

Pollock, Sheldon. (2006) 2007. *The Language of the Gods in the World of Men: Sanskrit, Culture and Power in Premodern India*. Delhi: Permanent Black.

Rao, Velcheru Narayana and David Shulman. (Eds. and Trans.). 2002. *Classical Telugu Poetry: An Anthology*. Delhi: Oxford University Press. Introduction, pp. 75–122.

Ray, H. P. and C. Sinopoli. (Eds.). 2004. *Archaeology as History in Early South Asia*. New Delhi: Indian Council of Historical Research and Aryan Books.

Renfrew, Colin and Paul Bahn. (1991) 2020. *Archaeology: Theories, Methods, and Practice*. 8th Edn. London: Thames and Hudson.

Salomon, Richard. 1998. *Indian Epigraphy: A Guide to the Study of Inscriptions in Sanskrit, Prakrit, and the other Indo-Aryan Languages*. New Delhi: Munshiram Manoharlal.

Shulman, David. 2016. *Tamil: A Biography*. Cambridge, MA: The Belknap Press of Harvard University Press.

Singh, Upinder. 2004. *The Discovery of Ancient India: Early Archaeologists and the Beginnings of Archaeology*. Delhi: Permanent Black.

Sircar, D. C. 1965. *Indian Epigraphy*. Delhi: Motilal Banarsidass.

———. 1968. *Studies in Indian Coins*. Delhi: Motilal Banarsidass.

Thapar, Romila. 2000. 'Society and Historical Consciousness: The *Itihasa-purana* Tradition.' In Romila Thapar, *Cultural Pasts: Essays in Early Indian History*. New Delhi: Oxford University Press, pp. 123–54.

Winternitz, M. 1985–1993. *History of Indian Literature*. 3 Vols. Rep. Edn. Delhi: Motilal Banarsidass.

Zvelebil, K. V. 1975. *Tamil Literature*. Leiden/Koln: E. J. Brill.

Twelfth century sandstone sculpture of a dancer, perhaps an *apsara*, from Madhya Pradesh; to be repatriated by the Metropolitan Museum of Art to India.

CHAPTER 2

Hunter-Gatherers of the Palaeolithic and Mesolithic

The geological ages and hominin evolution

Hominin remains in the Indian subcontinent

Palaeo-environments

Classifying the Indian stone age

The palaeolithic

The mesolithic

Conclusions

In the summer of 1863, Robert Bruce Foote, an officer of the Geological Survey of India, was busy with his routine survey duties at Pallavaram (in Chennai). A stone embedded in a gravel pit caught his eye and he picked it up. It was a seemingly unremarkable piece of brownish quartzite, with one end chipped off, but Foote recognized the unmistakable signs of human workmanship in its form. He had discovered a handaxe, the first palaeolithic tool identified in India. The Pallavaram handaxe was the oldest but not the first prehistoric tool discovered in India. In 1856, Le Mesurier, a railway engineer, had found a small chert arrowhead near Nyagurhee village in Central India. Prehistoric tools were subsequently reported from many areas, including the eastern Vindhyas, the Jabalpur area, Sindh, the Andaman islands, and Bengal. The geologists who played a major role in these discoveries shared their evidence and ideas with European geologists such as Charles Lyell and archaeologists such as John D. Evans. In 1868, Foote travelled to England to inform the scholarly community about his work, and in 1873, some of the prehistoric tools he had discovered in India were displayed at the International Exhibition held at Vienna. Foote went on to discover and document hundreds of prehistoric and protohistoric sites in South and Western India. Through his meticulous research and writing, he laid the foundation of Indian prehistory and South Indian geology. His writings and catalogues of his stone tool collection remain an important resource for scholars even today. It is fitting that an archaeological museum in Ballari, Karnataka, an area where Foote carried out intensive investigations, is named after him.

Since the 19th century, hundreds of prehistoric sites have been identified in the Indian subcontinent and new methodologies and perspectives have enhanced our understanding of the stone age—the longest part of the human past. The sources of information include structural remains, burials, plant remains, bones of humans and animals, and rock art. However, the most prolific and important sources are the tools, mostly of stone, made and used by prehistoric humans. The skills represented by these tools must have been developed through experimentation over centuries and carefully transmitted from one generation to the next. It took time, skill, strength, labour, and patience to make stone tools. Some of them are so aesthetically fashioned that they look like works of art.

Stone tools are found in different contexts. They may occur overground as surface finds, embedded in river deposits, at habitation sites, or at **factory sites** (places where tools were made). It is important to know whether the artefacts were found in a primary context (in the place where they were made or used), semi-primary (slightly removed from their original place), or secondary context (far removed from their original position).

There are various ways in which prehistorians try to ascertain how stone tools may have been made and what they were used for. They can experiment and try to make similar tools, or they can study communities who make and use stone tools today. Another method of understanding the functions of stone tools is **microwear analysis**. In the course of its frequent use, as a tool comes into repeated, regular contact with certain kinds of materials, its surface and edges develop wear marks and a polish or gloss. Different kinds of activities—cutting plants, chopping meat, cutting hides, etc.—leave different kinds of wear marks and polish. By carefully examining these under a powerful microscope, it is possible to make inferences about what the tool was used for. The question of *who* made the tools is more difficult to answer. However, considering the active involvement of men and women in subsistence activities, it is very likely that both sexes participated in making stone tools.

Stone tools were a very important part of the lives of stone age humans and are, therefore, an important key to understanding their world. But prehistory is not only about describing and classifying stone tools. It is about using these and other remains to try to understand the life-ways of prehistoric people.

The Geological Ages and Hominin Evolution

Humans like to think that they have always been the centre of the universe, but science has proved that this is not so. Our planet and its innumerable species are part of an amazingly long, complex, and continuing drama of evolution, in which human beings made a very late entry. The earth is about 4.5 billion years old and humans appeared on it only some 200,000 years ago. The many advances in the physical sciences in the 20th and 21st centuries have greatly amplified our understanding of the earth's history, while genetic science has unveiled the complex mechanisms that underlay the biological evolution of species. In recent years, advances in DNA analysis have provided important scientific evidence regarding the process of human evolution and migration.

The foundations of geological and biological evolutionary theories were laid in the 19th century. Charles Robert Darwin's path-breaking book, *The Origin of Species* (1859) explained how new species arose due to adaptation and how the process of natural selection led to the survival of the fittest. Darwin had been deeply influenced by Charles Lyell's *Principles of Geology* (1830–33), which explained the past changes in the earth's surface as results of still-continuing processes such as wind action, erosion, earthquakes, and volcanic eruptions. Thomas Henry Huxley's *Evidence as to Man's Place in Nature* (1863) extended Darwin's idea of evolution to human beings. The authoritative writings of such scholars ultimately revolutionized prevailing ideas about how and when human beings appeared on the earth.

Evolutionary theory had enormous and unsettling implications, and it is not surprising that many 19th-century Europeans found it difficult to accept. Religion and science have often been at loggerheads. The theory of evolution ran counter to the biblical theory of creation, which held that nature and humans were created in all their perfection by a divine agency according to a divine plan. It was not easy to accept the idea that reptiles and insects had appeared on the earth long before human beings, or to recognize certain similarities between humans and chimpanzees, or to think of the world as millions of years old. Just as disconcerting was the fact that evolutionary theory suggested that change in nature was continuing, unpredictable, and unstoppable.

The breakthroughs in the natural sciences had an immediate and major impact on prehistoric archaeology. Stone tools had been found and reported in earlier decades, but what was absent was a theoretical perspective within which such finds could be understood. For instance, in 1836, a French customs officer named Jacques Boucher de Perthes had discovered flint tools in the Somme valley. He argued that such tools, in some instances found along with bones of extinct animals, were remains of humans who had lived long before the biblical flood. De Perthes' work was greeted by general scepticism until his finds were authenticated many years later by the geologists Hugh Falconer and Joseph Prestwich, and the archaeologist John D. Evans.

What was initially difficult to accept eventually became recognized as established scientific fact. Geologists divide the history of the earth into four eras or ages related to the evolution of life forms: **Primary** (**Palaeozoic**), **Secondary** (**Mesozoic**), **Tertiary**, and **Quaternary**. The Tertiary and Quaternary together form the **Cenozoic** or the age of the mammals, which began about 100 million years ago (mya). The Cenozoic is divided into seven epochs, of which the last two—the **Pleistocene** and **Holocene**—are especially important for the story of hominin evolution. The Pleistocene began about 2.6 mya (it was earlier thought to have begun about 1.6 mya), and the Holocene (or Recent period, in which we live) about 12,000 years ago.

In biology, evolution refers to the gradual changes in the heritable features of a **species** population over successive generations due to changes in gene frequencies and the process of natural selection, which favours traits that help the species adapt to the environment. Over time, this process can give rise to a new species. The terms species (or specie) and **genus** are central to discussions of evolution. A species includes organisms that are genetically distinct, similar in physical structure and behaviour and which normally interbreed with each other, or which could do so if they had access to each other. A genus is an assemblage of related species. Take the following example: *Canis familiaris* (the domesticated dog), *Canis lupus* (wolf), and *Canis aureus* (jackal) all belong to the same genus—*Canis*—which is mentioned first. The second word is the name of the species they represent. There are many differences in skin colour, facial features, hair colour, body build, height, etc. among modern human beings living in different parts of the world, but we all belong to the same species of anatomically modern humans—*Homo sapiens sapiens* (the second *sapiens* refers to our sub-species). ***Homo sapiens*** is a Latin term, meaning 'thinking man'.

In current usage, hominid is a term with wide connotations, used for a group consisting of all modern and extinct Great Apes and humans (that is, modern humans, chimpanzees, gorillas, and orangutans plus all their immediate ancestors). Hominin is a narrower group consisting of modern humans, extinct human species, and all our immediate ancestors.

Palaeo-anthropologists have used fossil evidence to piece together the fascinating story of the biological and cultural evolution of early humans (see Roberts, 2011). This is not an easy task. It is sometimes difficult to identify a species on the basis of incomplete skeletal material and it is not always clear whether these remains are representative of the entire population of an area. Different stages in the process of human evolution can be identified on the basis of crucial biological markers, such as increase in **cranial capacity** (brain size), changes in pelvic structure and the beginnings of bipedalism (walking erect on two legs), and the modification of dental structure due to changing food habits. Some important aspects of the cultural evolution of early humans include the making of stone tools, the emergence of some kind of social organization, the beginnings of language, and the capacity for symbolic thought.

In recent years, the rapid advances in genome analysis have contributed towards understanding patterns of hominin migration and population changes in different parts of the world (see Reich, 2018). The genome consists of two sets of 23 chromosomes contained in the nucleus of each human cell, one inherited from the mother, one from the father. It is the full genetic code inherited from both parents. Earlier genetic studies focused on mitochondrial DNA, which is located outside the cell nucleus in the mitochondria, and is passed down from mother to daughter. Genome-wide studies (studies of the full genome) which track genetic mutations and variations over time have the potential of revealing unknown facets of human ancestry and migrations. The Human Genome Project (1990–2003) was a massive collaborative scientific project aimed at determining the complete DNA sequence of the human genome (see https://www.genome.gov). In 2001, scientists associated with this project succeeded in sequencing about 90% of the human genome. In 2022, scientists of the Telomere-to-Telomere (T2T) consortium announced an important breakthrough—the sequencing of the full human genome.

The earliest known hominins were members of the *Australopithecus* genus, who lived roughly between 4.4 and 1.8 mya; their remains have so far only been identified in Africa. The earliest of these, *Ardipithecus* (or *Australopithecus ramidus*), seems to have evolved from some common ancestor of the hominid and pongid ape lines in sub-Saharan Africa about 4.4 mya. While the Australopithecines may have used naturally available material as tools, there is no conclusive evidence that they were tool makers. Fossil evidence of the earliest representatives of the genus *Homo*—***Homo habilis*** (hand-using man)—was

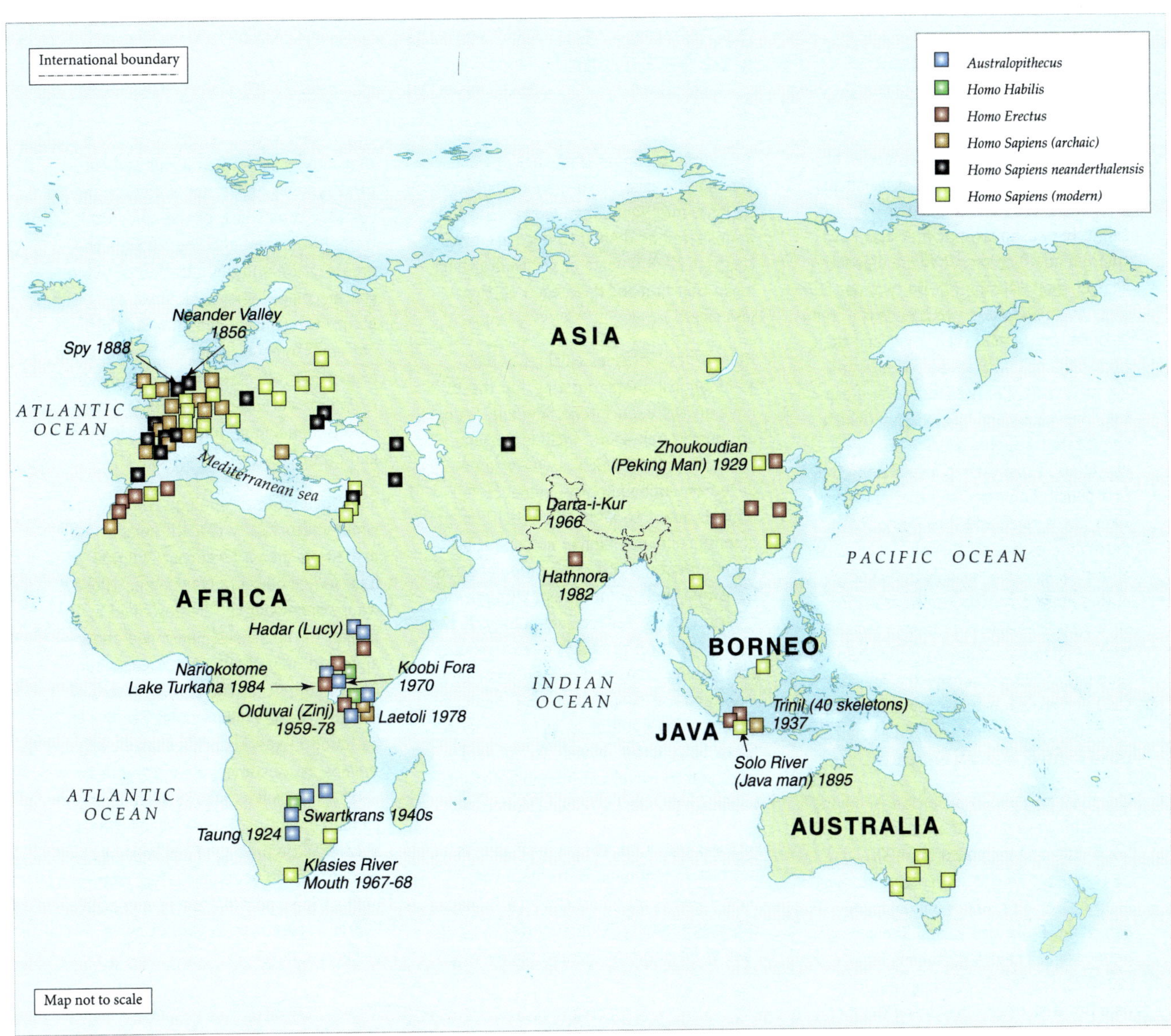

Map 2.1 Some hominin sites

found at sites such as Koobi Fora in Kenya and the Olduvai gorge in Tanzania, and is dated about 2 mya. The earliest stone tools have been found at Hadar in Ethiopia and have been dated about 2.5 mya.

Homo erectus (named for his/her fully erect posture) appeared in East Africa around 1.7 mya. From here, this species seems to have spread to various parts of Africa, Asia, and Europe. Remains of *Homo erectus* in Java have been dated between 1 to 2 mya and were associated with bones of many animal species but no stone tools. *Homo erectus* remains discovered in the Zhoukoudian caves, 50 km south-west of Beijing, are dated between 800,000 and 400,000 years ago. This site also yielded over 20,000 stone tools and bones of 96 mammalian species. *Homo erectus* remains have also been found at Dmanisi in Georgia.

In 2013, remains of a new species, *Homo naledi*, were discovered in South Africa and were subsequently dated to about 285,000 years ago. Although this species had a small cranial size, it was associated with evidence of ritual burials. The evidence suggests that around 315,000 years ago, three human species existed in Africa—*Homo sapiens*, *Homo heidelbergensis* (also known as *Homo rhodesiensis*), and *Homo naledi* (for details, see Galway-Witham et al., 2019: 5–6, 34, 6).

KEY CONCEPTS | **What does it mean to be human?**

Homo sapiens are one of 180 species of primates (the highest order of mammals). They share some characteristics with certain other mammals, but they also have their unique features. They are bipedal, that is, they walk upright on two, not four legs. As an adaptation to bipedalism, their legs are longer than their arms, and their back-bone has an S-shape. Their hands are prehensile, i.e., well suited to grasping. The fingers and large thumb (which can rotate through a 45 degree angle) can be used together to grip a stone tool or a pencil. Compared to other animals, their jaw is small and they do not have protruding canine teeth. Females of most animal species are sexually active only during limited periods known as *estrus;* such a cycle is absent in human females. Human infants are born with undeveloped brains (only 25 per cent of the full adult size) and remain helpless and dependent on maternal care for a very long time compared to other mammalian species.

The story of hominin evolution is, among other things, a story of an increase in brain size, and increased brain size can be connected to greater memory storage, learning abilities, and more complex behaviour. Brain size varies. The average brain size of modern humans is large (1350 cc, i.e., cubic centimetres), compared to that of chimpanzees (393.8 cc), *Australopithecines* (507.9 cc), and *Homo erectus* (973.7 cc). However, the issue is not just one of absolute brain size or weight, but brain size and weight in proportion to the total body size. The brain of an elephant is more than three times as heavy as that of a human; this doesn't make the elephant smarter than us. Similarly, the brain size of men tends on average to be larger than that of women. This doesn't mean that men are necessarily more intelligent than women. Human brains size has tended to decrease over the past 20,000 years or so. That doesn't mean that humans have been getting less smart!

Human-ness includes cultural as well as biological characteristics and these have always been interdependent. 'Modern human behaviour' includes several traits, not all of which are easy to deduce from archaeological evidence. All animals adapt to and interact with their environment, but human communities have a greater ability to manipulate and transform their environment through the creation of specialized technology. It has been argued on the basis of experiments that chimpanzees and orangutans can make and use simple tools. But humans have a unique ability to make specialized tools, both varied as well as standardized, and to travel considerable distances to obtain the desired raw materials.

Animals communicate through sounds but human language is far more complex. There is no doubt that the human thinking capacity is far superior to that of members of the ape family, and that human social behaviour and cultural systems are far more diverse and complex than those of the apes. Other traits of human behaviour include the organization and delimitation of living space (camp floors, structures, etc.), the ability to adapt to changing and different environments, symbolic thought and expression reflected in art, ceremonial or ritualistic activity (e.g., burials), community behaviour, and ideas of individual and group identity.

Some palaeo-anthropologists argue that while anatomically modern humans appeared on the earth almost 200,000 years ago, *fully* modern humans—i.e., those whose *behaviour* can be described as human in the senses mentioned above—appeared only about 40,000 years ago. Others argue that the earliest traces of some of these 'human' traits can in fact be found in species other than *Homo sapiens*, for instance, among the Neanderthals as well as among some of the archaic hominins. Before Neanderthals became extinct all over the world by around 39,000 years ago, they interbred with *Homo sapiens* and produced hybrid populations in various parts of Europe and Asia.

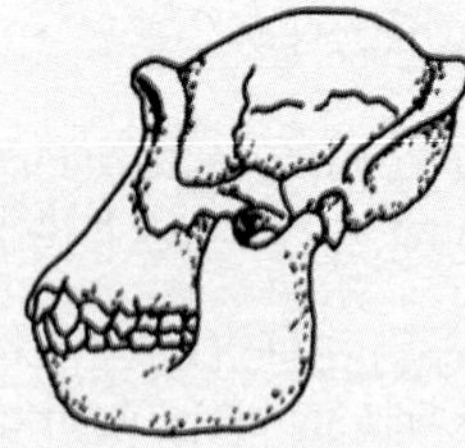
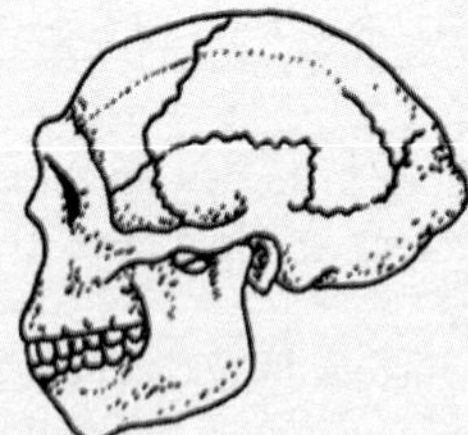
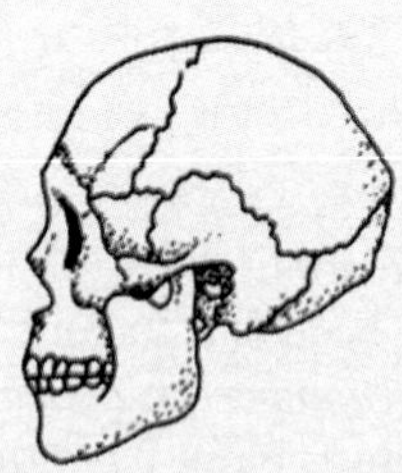

Figure 2.1 Skull structure of gorilla, *Homo erectus, Homo sapiens sapiens*

Homo sapiens, who are today the only surviving member of the hominins, appeared in Africa about 200,000 years ago. Early fossil remains have been found in the Omo basin and Herto in Ethiopia, Singa in Sudan, Laetoli in Tanzania, and Klasies River Mouth and Border Cave in South Africa. The sustained expansion of *Homo sapiens* out of Africa, which eventually led to the spread of this species all over the world, seems to have started about 100,000 years ago. The recent discovery of a new species, *Homo floresiensis* from Floris island in Indonesia, dated to about 60,000 years ago, has raised questions about the nature and timing of the hominin expansion out of Africa.

From about 130,000 years ago, there is evidence of Neanderthals in various parts of Western and Central Asia and in Europe. There is also evidence that Neanderthals and *Homo sapiens* inter-bred and produced hybrid populations in various parts of Eurasia. This has led to a debate on whether Neanderthals were a distinct species of the genus *Homo* (*Homo neanderthalensis*) or a subgroup of *Homo sapiens* (*Homo sapiens neanderthalensis*). In 2008, a finger bone discovered in the Denisova Cave in southern Siberia gave evidence of a new hominin species, which was given the name Denisovian.

Ultimately, *Homo sapiens* replaced all other Homo species.

Evolution was not a neat unilinear process, with one species making way for another. The rapidly increasing evidence from ancient DNA has made it evident that representing evolution through simple tree diagrams does not work, and that the story of hominin evolution includes the simultaneous existence of different species and continuing migrations and mixtures of populations on a scale not hitherto imagined.

There are continuing debates among palaeoanthropologists and archaeologists about how hominin evolution and dispersal should be understood. While African origins are central to the story, there are several unresolved questions about hominin evolution and migration. The number, reasons, timing, and routes of major hominin migrations from Africa are the subject of continuing debate. There are currently two 'Out of Africa' models. Both accept the idea that archaic humans started migrating out of Africa into Asia and Europe about 1.8 to 2 mya. According to the recent African origin (RAO) model, subsequently, modern humans arose in one or several parts of Africa about 250,000 years ago and started expanding to other parts of the world some time between about 60,000 and 90,000 years ago. According to the multiregional evolution (MRE) model, modern humans evolved in different parts of the world without any recent dispersal from Africa or elsewhere (Stoneking, 2016). New evidence and research are likely to rapidly add to our understanding of the story of human ancestry. South Asia is clearly an area of rich potential in this respect.

Hominin Remains in the Indian Subcontinent

In sharp contrast to the widespread occurrence of animal fossils and stone tools all over the subcontinent, the evidence of hominin fossils is at present very meagre (Kennedy, 2000; Chakrabarti, 2006: 10–16; Chauhan, 2016). This is no doubt due to inadequate investigations.

From the 19th century onwards, several remains of fossil apes were discovered in the Siwalik hills. These hills, which form the outermost range of the Himalayas known as the sub-Himalayan zone, stretch across Pakistan, India, Nepal, and Bhutan. Given rather dramatic names such as Ramapithecus, Sivapithecus, and Brahmapithecus, the fossils came to be collectively known as the 'God-Apes of the Siwaliks'. Remains of Ramapithecus were subsequently found in other parts of Asia, Africa, and Europe as well, and were dated between 10–14 mya. Ramapithecus, who lived in the Miocene–Pliocene transition, was once thought to represent the oldest direct ancestor of modern humans. However, this idea and the relationship between the various fossil types were questioned on the basis of new dating methods and a reassessment of the fossil evidence (see Gaur, 2016).

Authenticated early human remains in South Asia are relatively recent. In 1966, Louis Dupree discovered a fragment of a right temporal bone at the cave site of Darra-i-Kur in north-eastern Afghanistan. The deposit in which it was found gave a radiocarbon date of 30,000 ± 1900–1200 BP, i.e., 28,950 ± 1960–1235 BCE. The fragment was considered consistent with Neanderthals as well as anatomically modern humans. The associated stone tools seem to belong to a **middle palaeolithic** context.

In 1982, Arun Sonakia of the Geological Survey of India made an important discovery near Hathnora village on the northern bank of the Narmada, about 40 km north-east of Hoshangabad. Here, embedded in thick, closely packed sandy, pebbly gravel, he found a fossilized fragment of a cranium (skull cap) along with some fossils of vertebrates (*proboscideans* and *bovids*) and a few late **Acheulian tools**. The skull fragment

See p. 83 for an explanation of Acheulian tools

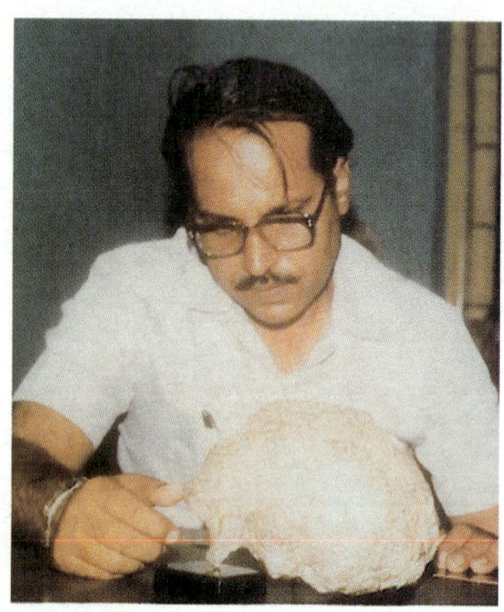

Arun Sonakia holding the Hathnora skull cap

seems to have belonged to a woman, between 27 to 32 years old. Sonakia suggested that she represented an advanced variety of *Homo erectus*—'advanced' because of her larger cranial capacity range of 1155 to 1421 cc—and named her *Homo erectus narmadensis*. However, according to other scholars, the cranium belongs to an archaic (early) variety of *Homo sapiens*. It is also possible that this 'Narmada Woman' belonged to an intermediate species.

Between 1983 and 1992, the Anthropological Survey of India launched an intensive search for human fossils and tools in the central Narmada valley. This led to the discovery of hundreds of palaeolithic tools and some animal fossils. In 1997, important discoveries were made in the same boulder conglomerate deposit at Hathnora where the cranial fragment had been found some years earlier. These included a hominid clavicle (collar bone) along with animal fossils and several late or middle palaeolithic tools. Subsequently, fragments of a femur and humerus were discovered at a site called Netankheri. According to A. R. Sankhyan (2016), the fossils found in the central Narmada valley may represent at least two different hominin species; the approximate dates suggested for them and their associated palaeolithic context ranges from 300,000 to 75,000 years ago.

In 2001, P. Rajendran, a teacher in the Department of History of Kerala University, found a complete fossilized human baby skull in Odai in the Villupuram district of Tamil Nadu. Rajendran was excavating a trench which had microliths in the upper levels and **upper palaeolithic** tools in the lower ones. At a depth of 6 m, just under the upper palaeolithic deposit, there was a ferricrete deposit (a mineral conglomerate consisting of sand and gravel, cemented into a hard mass by iron oxide). The skull was found close to this trench, embedded in a similar ferricrete deposit which was later dated 166,000 BP, placing it in the middle or upper Pleistocene.

Map 2.2 Hominin discoveries in the subcontinent

The antiquity of certain other reported hominin finds is uncertain. This is the case with the two human mandibles of an adult male and female *Homo sapiens* found by H. D. Sankalia and S. N. Rajaguru on the bank of the Mula-Mutha river in Pune district, Maharashtra. The age of the mandible of an adult male found by V. S. Wakankar in a cave at Bhimbetka in Madhya Pradesh is similarly uncertain. Several cave sites in Sri Lanka—Fa-Hien Lena, Batadomba Lena, Beli Lena, and Alu Lena—have yielded remains of anatomically modern humans in contexts falling in the date range of 37,000–10,500 BP.

The growing body of data throws light on the movements of modern human populations, plants, and animals in South Asia (see Petraglia and Allchin. [Eds.]., 2007), but there is much more that needs to be understood. More concerted efforts are likely to add to the data and may transform the larger story of human evolution, which has so far concentrated more on Africa and Europe than on South Asia.

Palaeo-environments

The environments in which prehistoric people lived were very different from ours. Some of the major changes that gave the subcontinent its present form took place millions of years ago, in some instances long before hominins appeared on the planet. As mentioned in the Introduction, hundreds of millions of years ago, the peninsula was part of a huge land mass that geologists call Gondwanaland, which included Australia, Africa, Madagascar, South America, the Arabian peninsula, Sri Lanka, and Antarctica. At some point of time, this land mass broke up and the Indian landmass started drifting northwards at the rate of 20 cm a year, eventually joining up with the Asian landmass, between 50 and 35 mya. All this was the result of the movement of massive tectonic plates embedded within the earth. The collision and intermittent pressure of the Indian and Asian plates led to uplifts that resulted in the creation of the Tibetan plateau and the Himalayas. Rivers brought down immense volumes of eroded sediments from the mountains, and this resulted in the creation of the fertile northern alluvial plain. The process of **plate tectonics** (the word 'tectonic' means movements in the earth's crust) is not over. The Indian plate continues to press into Asia at the rate of 5 cm a year. The Himalayas and the Tibetan plateau are still rising at an average of 5–10 mm per year. Occasional movements in the tectonic plates lead to intermittent earthquakes and changes in the course of rivers in the northern parts of the subcontinent.

All over the world, the Pleistocene era, which began about 2.6 mya, was marked by dramatic climatic changes. The earlier idea of a sequence of four ice ages and four interglacial periods for the higher latitudes has been questioned. There seem to have been more than four ice ages and interglacials, corresponding to alternating periods of cold and warmer climate. During the cold phases, when ice sheets covered one-third of the earth's landmass, sea levels fell dramatically. When the climate became warmer, the ice melted and sea levels rose. It is believed that the tropical and semi-tropical regions went through alternating dry and wet phases (interpluvial and pluvial phases), but the rhythm of Pleistocene climatic changes in these parts of the world is not fully understood.

The Pleistocene environments of the subcontinent were influenced by larger global patterns of climate, but sometimes also by distant seismic events. For instance, about 75,000 years ago, a gigantic volcanic super-eruption occurred in Sumatra at a place today represented by lake Toba. Tephra ash deposits arising from this eruption have been found embedded in river valleys in peninsular India. There is continuing debate over the impact of the Toba eruption. Some scholars argue that it had major impact on global climate, ecology, and hominin evolution and migration. Others argue that it had little impact on hominin populations in South Asia, or that its impact was uneven across regions.

About 12,000 years ago, the Pleistocene era made way for the Holocene era (which continues into our own time) and the basic climatic patterns that prevail in the world today were established. This does not mean that there have been no significant climatic changes in the last 12,000 years. It is just that these changes have not been as enormous as those that occurred within the Pleistocene. The beginning of the Holocene was marked by wetter climatic conditions than those of the late Pleistocene.

The study of the specific features of palaeo-environments is a very important part of prehistory. Detailed palaeo-environmental studies are so far available for very few parts of the subcontinent. One of the earliest such studies was conducted in 1935 by H. de Terra and T. T. Paterson on the Soan (Sohan) river in the Potwar plateau, between the Pir Panjal and Salt ranges in Pakistan. Their team found a large number of tools, mostly of the middle and upper palaeolithic, some of the **lower palaeolithic** as well. De Terra and Paterson identified five tool-bearing terraces (a terrace is an old bed of a river) of the Soan and tried to correlate these terraces with the theory of a four-fold glacial cycle in Kashmir, and further, with a four-fold European glacial cycle. This framework was extended, through comparisons, to the Narmada and the area around Chennai. Although most of the correlations, sequences, and conclusions of the de Terra–Paterson study are no longer accepted, it marked an important stage in the history of prehistoric research in India. In 1930, L. A. Cammiade and M. C. Burkitt carried out a similar study, correlating the stratigraphy of prehistoric stone tools and their environment in the Eastern Ghats of Andhra Pradesh. The Soanian contexts are now considered to probably belong to the late Pleistocene.

Studies of the Son valley (in northern MP) and Belan valley (in southern UP) have thrown light on the connections between the changes in river systems, climate, and stone age sites in the valleys of these southern tributaries of the Ganga (Clark and Williams, 1986). During the late Pleistocene, the climate in this area was much cooler and drier than it is today. At the same time, hippopotamus and crocodile bones show that some permanent water was available in rivers and streams. In the early Holocene, the climate seems to have become warmer and wetter, probably leading to an expansion of forests and shrinking of grasslands.

The Thar desert today has very little naturally occurring surface water, except for short periods in the rainy season, and people have to rely on rain water stored in tanks, wells, tube wells, and canals. A study of the western Rajasthan section of the Thar desert (Misra and Rajguru, 1985), especially around Didwana in Nagaur district, indicates that the present environment of the Thar is very different from what it was like in the Pleistocene era. Except for a phase in the upper Pleistocene (25,000–13,000 BP), during most of that era, surface water in some quantity was always available; as a result, the flora and fauna was much more abundant than it is today. The sediments of the salt lakes indicate a significant increase in rainfall in the mid-Holocene (6,000–4,000 BP). It is not a coincidence that the most widespread prehistoric occupation in this area belongs to that period.

Classifying the Indian Stone Age

The three-age system—the idea that there was an age of stone tools, followed by one dominated by those of bronze and then of iron—was first put forward in the late 18th and early 19th centuries by the Danish scholars P. F. Suhm and Christian Thomsen. The accuracy of this theory was proved by excavations by another Danish scholar, Jacob Worsaae. The next important step was to identify changes within the stone age. In 1863, John Lubbock divided the stone age into two parts, the **palaeolithic** and **neolithic**. A few years later, Edouard Lartet suggested the division of the palaeolithic into the lower, middle, and upper palaeolithic, largely on the basis of changes in fauna associated with the different tool types. Archaeologists gradually identified distinct tool-making traditions within the palaeolithic and also recognized the significance of changes in subsistence patterns within the stone age. The use of the term **mesolithic** is relatively recent.

The Indian stone age is divided into the palaeolithic, mesolithic, and neolithic on the basis of geological age, the type and technology of stone tools, and subsistence base. The palaeolithic is further divided into the lower, middle, and upper palaeolithic.

Table 2.2 Important features of the stone age

Terminology	Geological age	Typical Indian stone tool types	Main subsistence base
Lower palaeolithic	Lower Pleistocene	**Pebble** and **core tools** like handaxes, **cleavers,** and **chopping tools**	Hunting and gathering
Middle palaeolithic	Middle Pleistocene	Flake tools, including those made by prepared core techniques such as the **Levallois technique**	Hunting and gathering
Upper palaeolithic	Upper Pleistocene	Blade tools made on flakes—e.g., parallel-sided blades and burins	Hunting and gathering
Mesolithic	Holocene	**Microliths**	Hunting, gathering, fishing, with instances of animal domestication in a few places
Neolithic	Holocene	**Celts** (ground and polished handaxes)	Food production based on animal and plant domestication

A general time range for the lower palaeolithic is from about 2 mya to 100,000 years ago, the middle palaeolithic from about 100,000 to 40,000 years ago, and the upper palaeolithic from about 40,000 to 10,000 years ago. However, there is a great deal of variation in the dates for different sites. According to the standard classification, palaeolithic cultures belong to the Pleistocene geological era, while the mesolithic and neolithic cultures belong to the Holocene era.

While Table 2.2 explains the basic features of the different phases of the stone age, it also tends to over-simplify matters. It must be remembered that this classification is an analytical tool used by scholars to identify patterns across a very long and complex span of the human past. The reality was much more complex. Further, there is continuing debate on how to explain the behavioural changes of prehistoric people. Why did people decide to change their mode of subsistence? What was the impact of environmental change of their way of life? Were changes in stone tool forms and technologies the result of influx of new populations, local innovation, or both?

Except for the dividing line of the Holocene, stone age cultures did not evolve uniformly in a neat unilinear fashion all over the subcontinent. There are regional variations in some of their features and their dates also vary considerably. The 'typical Indian tool types' column in Table 2.2 indicates the tools that are considered characteristic of that particular phase. However, it does not mean that there is complete uniformity in tools found at different sites, or that tools typical of one phase were absent in another. For example, celts are associated with the neolithic, but are known to occur as late as the historic period in certain parts of Eastern India. Similarly, with regard to subsistence base, it should be noted that hunting and gathering did not come to an end with the beginning of **animal and plant domestication**. Many agricultural communities continued to hunt and forage for food. In fact, these subsistence activities (also known as foraging) continue to be prevalent in certain niches of the subcontinent even today.

It is easier to identify and describe stone tools than to know whether, or to what extent, a community was producing its food through plant or animal domestication. Sometimes, there is insufficient data to reach a conclusion. Finally, there is the issue of overlap. Although there are some 'pure' neolithic sites in India, early agricultural sites frequently show an intermixture of neoliths with copper and copper-alloyed objects.

See Chapter 3, pp. 116–121 for a discussion of plant and animal domestication and food production

The Palaeolithic

Lower palaeolithic sites

Palaeolithic tools have been found in almost all parts of the subcontinent (Chakrabarti, 1999: 54–75; Allchin and Allchin, 1997: 47–85; Chauhan, 2016). Although hardly any sites have so far been discovered in the alluvial stretches of the Indus or Ganga valleys (with some notable exceptions such as Kalpi in UP), they have been identified on rocky areas within or on the margins of these valleys, e.g., in the Rohri hills in Sindh and the northern fringes of the Vindhyas. Sites are prolific in other parts of the subcontinent, especially in peninsular India, leaving aside the coastal plains. Comparatively few palaeolithic habitation sites have been identified, but it can be assumed that people lived close to sources of food, water, and stone in different kinds of habitats—for instance, along the banks of rivers or streams and in caves and rock shelters.

Excavated sites are comparatively few and most of the evidence comes from surface finds of stone tools. Because of insufficient data from most sites, it is necessary to focus on the published results of stone tools found in clearly defined stratigraphic contexts. Some sites were inhabited over many stages of the stone age.

Even in the absence of detailed studies, some broad inferences about Pleistocene climate can be made on the basis of the deposits in which palaeolithic tools are found. For instance, tools often get embedded in river terraces. Although a number of other factors are also involved, the erosion and deposition activity of rivers can be related to rainfall. Cemented gravel (a deposit in which small pebbles are packed tightly together in soil) is generally taken to represent a wet climatic phase. A boulder conglomerate (a deposit where larger boulders are packed together) is interpreted as representing a drier phase, while clay or silt deposits represent still drier conditions.

The typical lower palaeolithic tools are fairly large core tools made of quartzite or other hard rocks. They include chopping tools, handaxes, and cleavers. Apart from directly breaking off pieces of stone from large boulders, which would have required considerable strength, it is possible that people lit fires against rocks and threw water over them so that large fragments broke off more easily. Within the palaeolithic, there is a gradual increase in the range and variety of stone tools and a shift in preference from coarse-grained to fine-grained stone.

In recent years, important evidence of dates for lower palaeolithic contexts has come from the Potwar plateau and the Siwaliks. At Dina and Jalalpur in the Jhelum basin, members of a British archaeological team discovered 15 artefacts including three handaxes in a boulder conglomerate deposit dated *c.* 700,000–500,000 years ago by the **palaeo-magnetic method**. There are much earlier dates reported from Riwat near Rawalpindi in Punjab province of Pakistan. Here, in 1983, members of the British Archaeological Mission to Pakistan's Potwar Project, working with the Department of Archaeology and the Geological Survey of Pakistan, discovered stone artefacts embedded in a stone conglomerate deposit dated to about 2.01 mya by the palaeo-magnetic method. At the sites of Gurha Sahan and PS-57, stone tools were found embedded in the Pinjor bed of the Siwaliks, dated between 2.4 and 2 mya. Stone tools reported in the Jammu and Himachal sections of the Siwalik hills seem to belong to about the same age. For instance, at Uttarbaini in the Jammu area, early palaeolithic tools were found in a deposit dated 2.8 ± 0.5 mya. This date has, however, been questioned.

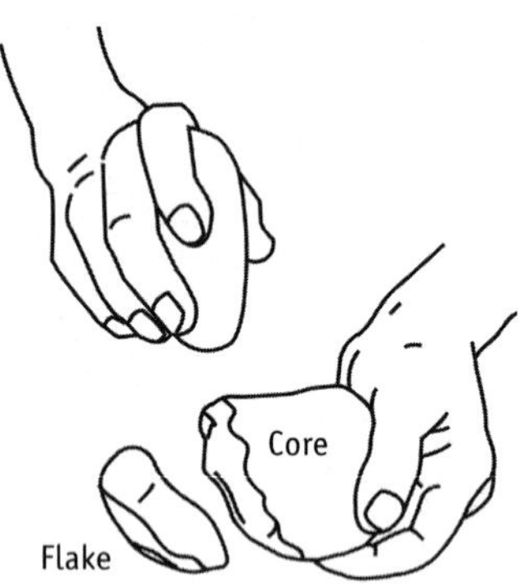

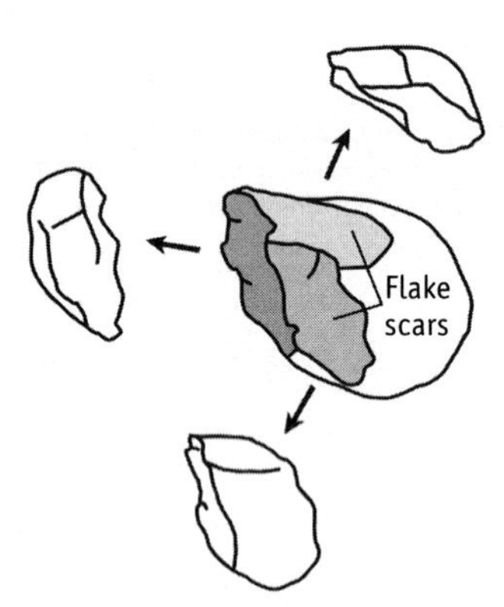

Figure 2.2 The percussion technique of making flakes

Some absolute dates are now available for lower palaeolithic contexts in other areas as well. The tephra layer at Bori in Maharashtra (below which a stone tool was found) has been dated to 1.4 mya by the potassium-argon method. Didwana in Rajasthan has been dated 390,000 BP (by the uranium/thorium series dating method). In the Hiran valley in Gujarat, the lower palaeolithic context is dated 190,000–69,000 BP (via the uranium/thorium series dating method). Recently, late Acheulian assemblages from the site of Patpara and Bamburi in the middle Son valley (MP) have been dated to between 140,000 to 120,000 years ago through the single grain optically stimulated luminescence method. Nevasa (in Maharashtra) has given a date of 350,000 BP (via uranium/thorium series dating). In Karnataka, the site of Yedurwadi has been dated 350,000 BP.

Factory sites are generally located close to the sources of raw materials and are marked by a profusion of stone tools in various stages of preparation. In many instances, they were visited and used during several phases of the stone age, sometimes even later. In Sindh, there are a number of such sites in the limestone hills capped by flint nodules. In lower Sindh, stone tools belonging to the lower, middle, and upper palaeolithic were

PRIMARY SOURCES | Typical lower palaeolithic tools

Stone tools are an important key to understanding the lives of prehistoric humans. It is, therefore, very important to understand the meaning of terms used by prehistorians for different stone tool types, especially since some of them can be rather misleading.

If you take a piece of stone and break it into two or more pieces, the largest piece is called a core and the smaller piece or pieces are called flakes. A stone tool made out of the largest piece (core) is called a core tool, while tools made out of the smaller pieces (flakes) are called flake tools. Removing slivers or pieces from a rock is called flaking. The depressions or marks formed on the surface of a stone when flakes are removed are known as flake scars.

A handaxe is generally a core tool. It is also known as a biface, because it is usually worked on both sides. Generally made on a core, it is roughly triangular in shape, broad at one end and pointed at the other. Not all handaxes were hand-held tools; some of them could have been hafted onto handles.

Pebble tools are tools of different types made on pebbles, in which only the working edge is flaked, the rest of the tool remaining untouched.

A chopping tool is a tool made on a core or a pebble and is flaked alternately on both sides to produce a wavy cutting edge.

A chopper is a large, unifacial tool, i.e., worked on one side only.

A cleaver is a flattish tool made on a broad rectangular or triangular flake, on one end of which is a broad and straight cutting edge.

The term Acheulian is often used to refer to an assemblage of stone tools marked by advanced and increasingly symmetrical handaxes and cleavers. These are associated with the lower palaeolithic, but continue well afterwards as well.

Source Sankalia, (1964) 1982: 45–58

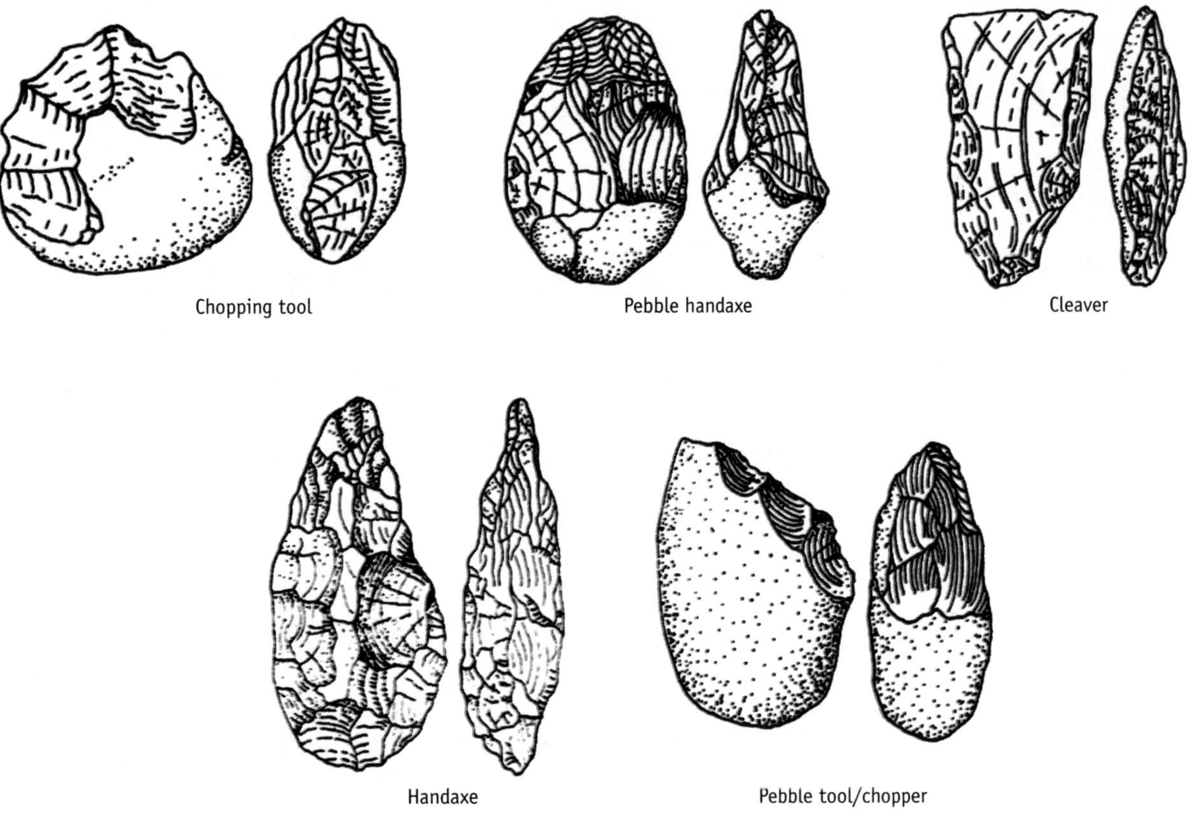

Figure 2.3 Lower palaeolithic tools

Map 2.3 Major palaeolithic sites

found at sites such as Jerruk and Milestone 101. In upper Sindh, there are factory sites in the Sukkur and Rohri hills.

Many people tend to think of stone age sites as distant, isolated places. As a matter of fact, stone age tools are often found in places that are today bustling with activity. A good example are the many sites found in and around the modern city of Delhi. Four lower palaeolithic stone tools were found in 1956 on the Delhi Ridge, near the main gate of the University of Delhi, and more were subsequently discovered on the northern Ridge. In 1983, a late Acheulian handaxe was found on the campus of Jawaharlal Nehru University. A systematic study of stone age sites in south Delhi and adjoining areas (Chakrabarti and Lahiri, 1986) identified 43 sites ranging from the lower palaeolithic to the microlithic. Excavations at Anangpur in the Badarpur hills to the south of the city revealed thousands of early and late Acheulian tools along with traces of several **palaeo-channels** of the Yamuna river. The evidence indicates that this was a large lower palaeolithic habitation and factory site.

In Rajasthan, lower, middle, and upper palaeolithic tools have been found around Ajmer and stray finds of lower palaeolithic tools occur in the Luni valley. There is a detailed profile of the Didwana area of the Nagaur district in western Rajasthan, with a sequence extending from the early to the middle palaeolithic. The Mogara hill near

Jodhpur seems to have been a factory site where lower, middle, and upper palaeolithic as well as mesolithic tools were made.

In Gujarat, lower palaeolithic tools have been found in the valleys of the Sabarmati, its Orsang and Karjan tributaries, and in the Bhadar valley in Saurashtra. Lower palaeolithic and later artefacts have been found all along the Konkan coast up to Goa. In Maharashtra, palaeolithic tools have been found in many places along the coast and in the Wardha–Wainganga valleys. Stratigraphic profiles of sections of the Mula-Mutha, Godavari, Pravara, and Tapi rivers are available. Lower and middle palaeolithic tools have been found in stratigraphic contexts in the Dattawadi area of the Mutha river in Pune. Lower palaeolithic tools have been found in a stratigraphic context in the Gangawadi area on the Godavari at Nashik. Lower palaeolithic tools were found in a cemented gravel bed at Bori on the left bank of the Kukadi river in Pune district, Maharashtra.

Prehistoric remains occur in various parts of Central India in Damoh, Raisen, and the Narmada, upper Son, and Mahanadi valleys. The Narmada valley is an especially rich and well-researched area. Excavations at Adamgarh hill, not far from Hoshangabad, revealed a sequence of lower and middle palaeolithic tools. However, the most spectacular finds come from hundreds of rock shelters at Bhimbetka (in Raisen district, MP), 30 km north of Hoshangabad, which have given evidence of an enormously long sequence of occupation stretching from the lower palaeolithic to the historic period.

The Bhimbetka hillside is composed of sandstone and quartzite. There are three perennial freshwater springs in the area, and several creeks filled with water. A study of the present-day flora and fauna indicates the presence of at least 30 plant types which yield edible fruits, tubers, and roots. There are fish in the streams, and the hillside is home to many animals such as deer, boar, *nilgai*, leopard, wolf, hare, and fox. Of course, in prehistoric times, conditions wouldn't have been exactly like this. Nevertheless, it is clear that this site must have been attractive for stone age people from the points of view of shelter, food, and raw material for tools. Most of the stone tools at Bhimbetka were made of a yellowish quartzite available in plenty in the area, but a grey quartzite was also obtained from further away. Five floors paved with flat stone slabs belonging to the lower palaeolithic were identified. No bones have been found so far, perhaps because of the acidic soil.

In the Belan valley in Uttar Pradesh, detailed studies revealed a sequence of stone age industries from the lower palaeolithic to neolithic to protohistoric. In Bihar in Eastern India, a lower palaeolithic living and working floor was excavated at Paisra in the Kharagpur forests near Munger (Pant and Jayaswal, 1991). The whole area was rich in finished and unfinished artefacts, broken pieces of stone, and anvils. Eight post-holes were found, marking places where wooden posts had been dug into the ground to support thatched huts.

The river valleys and foothills of the Chota Nagpur plateau in Jharkhand and the adjoining areas of West Bengal have yielded lower palaeolithic tools. In Odisha, tools of all three phases of the palaeolithic have been found in many places. A large number of lower and middle palaeolithic tools were found in explorations at Dari-dungri in Sambalpur district, and lower palaeolithic tools have also been found along the valleys of the Budhabalan and Brahmani rivers.

In her detailed discussion of the Indian lower palaeolithic, Sheila Mishra (2006–07) points out that lower palaeolithic in peninsular India is almost entirely Acheulian. The Acheulian sites in peninsular India can be divided into early and late Acheulian. The early Acheulian sites include Chirki-Nevasa, Morgaon, Bori, Lalitpur, Aganwadi, Singi Talav, Hunsgi, Yediapur, and Isampur. These have two types of stone tools—large hand-held ones (handaxes, hammerstones and choppers) and small finger-held ones. The small, sharp flake tools hardly show any secondary retouching.

The Bhimbetka rock shelters; quartzite handaxe from the Narmada valley (from top)

At one time, it was believed that the lower palaeolithic industry of the south (which was given the name 'Madrasian') was different from that of other parts of the country because of a supposed absence of pebble tools. The research of the past few decades has proved that this is incorrect, and that pebble tools such as choppers and chopping tools are found along with handaxes at several sites.

Jwalapuram in Kurnool district (AP) has yielded an archaeological sequence from the lower palaeolithic to the iron age (see Korisettar and Janardhana, 2014). The site is also notable for paintings in hundreds of rock shelters; the earliest paintings have been ascribed to the Pleistocene. The evidence of tephra ash from the Toba volcanic eruption at a level containing middle palaeolithic tools is important in discussions of migrations of hominins out of Africa and environmental changes during the Pleistocene.

A stratigraphic sequence of lower and upper palaeolithic tools was identified in the Malaprabha–Ghataprabha valleys in Karnataka. Lower palaeolithic tools have also been found in the Hunsgi–Baichbal and Krishna valleys. Lower palaeolithic tools occur at many places at Hunsgi (in the Gulbarga district of Karnataka), on the banks of the Hunsgi, a tributary of the Krishna river (Paddayya, 1982). Here, sites with very few types of artefacts may represent places where certain specific activities, such as making tools or

FURTHER DISCUSSION | Isampur: a centre of stone tool manufacture

Isampur (Gulbarga district, Karnataka) is a village located in the north-western part of the Hunsgi valley, drained by a small seasonal stream known as the Kamta Halla. The palaeolithic site lies about 2 km north-west of the village, close to the bank of the stream, covering an area of about 7,200 sq m. It was discovered in 1983, when the silt deposits overlying the limestone floor of the valley were exposed due to quarrying activity carried out as part of a major irrigation project.

This site offered some obvious advantages to prehistoric humans. Water and a variety of wild animal and plant food were available. Another advantage was that siliceous limestone blocks and slabs occur plentifully in the area at the intersection of flat and steep surfaces. There is evidence of Acheulian as well as middle palaeolithic occupation at the site.

The Acheulian material mostly consisted of cores in different shapes, large flakes, and debitage (waste material). The main tool types were chopping tools, knives, handaxes, cleavers, and scrapers. While unfinished tools occurred in large numbers, there were relatively few finished ones. Hammer stones of different sizes, made of hard rocks such as quartzite, basalt, and chert were found in very large numbers on the surface and in the excavated levels. There is evidence of quarrying and of different stages in tool manufacture. The middle palaeolithic assemblage consisted of flake tools, mostly made out of locally available chert nodules. These included finished tools, cores, hammer stones, flakes, and debitage. There were also tools made of quartzite and limestone. Scrapers of various types were the most numerous. Tools were made both by simple flaking and through the use of a prepared core technique.

The site consisted of four sub-localities, each measuring 300–400 sq m, within which there were many limestone slabs and blocks suitable for making tools. These rocky patches must have been centres of tool-making activity. Given the large extent of the site and the huge number of tools found here, it seems that Isampur was one of several hubs of stone tool manufacture in the Hunsgi–Baichal valleys, from where hominins must have ranged out to the valley floor and the uplands for foraging. Some of the tools found here are weathered and have use-marks, showing that the site was also a habitation site where people lived and carried out subsistence activities such as food processing.

Source Paddayya et al., 1999–2000

Figure 2.4 Isampur tools

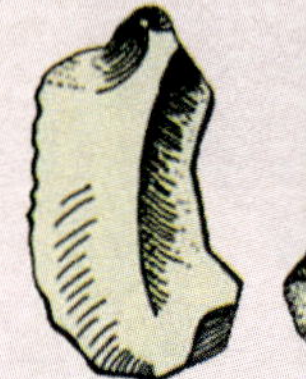

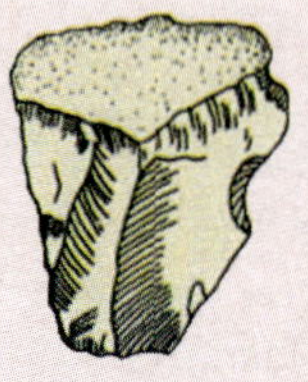
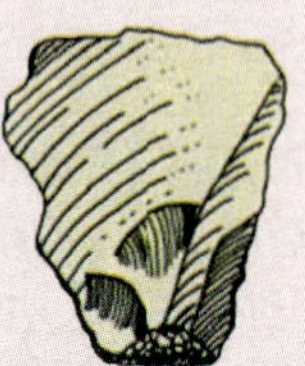
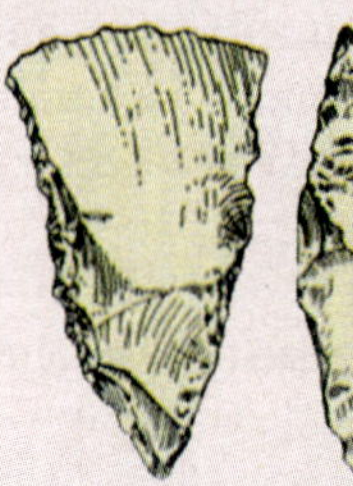

killing game, were carried out. Sites where tools occur in larger number and variety may have been temporary camp sites. Still larger sites, where stone tools have been found in great profusion and variety, may have been places where groups of people lived for longer periods of time. The Hunsgi tools were mostly made of various kinds of stone, including limestone, sandstone, quartzite, dolerite, and chert, some of which were not locally available. In one of the excavated areas, huge granite blocks were arranged around a 63 sq m area, perhaps used as a support for temporary shelters made of branches, grass, and leaves. Today, the area around Hunsgi supports about 40 types of wild edible plants as well as plenty of small game.

Isampur in the Hunsgi valley of Karnataka is the largest palaeolithic site found so far in India (see Paddayya 2014). Geoarchaeological investigations and excavations at this site between 1997 to 2001 revealed evidence from the lower palaeolithic onwards. The site yielded thousands of stone tools made of limestone, chert, and quartzite. Apart from handaxes and cleavers, a large number of scrapers (usually associated with the middle palaeolithic) were found at Acheulian levels. Surface explorations in the area revealed many other small sites within a 5–6 km radius of Isampur, where traces of hominin activity were found. Three samples of enamel from bovid teeth excavated from Isampur were dated to 1.2 mya through the Electronic Spin Resonance (ESR) method. This is one of the earliest dates for the lower palaeolithic in the Indian subcontinent.

In recent years, although there has been a gradual accumulation of valuable archaeological data pertaining to the northeastern part of India—a vast area which includes the modern states of Assam, Manipur, Mizoram, Nagaland, Tripura, Arunachal Pradesh, and Sikkim—there is still a great deal that remains to be discovered (see Sarma and Hazarika, 2014). The prehistoric sequence in this region emerges with clarity only in the neolithic. However, stone artefacts dated to late Pleistocene and early Holocene contexts have been found. These display affinities with the Hoabinhian culture sites of south China and various parts of Southeast Asia, which are placed between the palaeolithic and neolithic. The typical Hoabinhian tools include pebble tools, utilized flakes, and a few edge-ground tools and bone tools; pottery and fully ground axes appear at a later stage (Hazarika,

Lower palaeolithic tools from Attirampakkam

2017: 83–84). Excavations at Ranyak Khen (RYK) cave near Mimi in Nagaland have given evidence of edge-grinding tools fashioned from river pebbles of serpentine and limestone, some hammer stones, disc-shaped scrapers, bone tools, cord-impressed pottery, and a human burial. There is no evidence of animal or plant domestication. The site has yielded an AMS date of c. 5,560+/40 BP and has been assigned to an early pre-neolithic context. While the Northeast has been considered by some scholars as an inhospitable region during the Pleistocene, Manjil Hazarika has argued that it could possibly have been a corridor for early hominin dispersals and migrations to various parts of Southeast Asia (Hazarika, 2017: 261–62). Whatever may be the case, there is no doubt that the northeastern states of India present great potential for future investigations.

The prehistoric sequence in Bangladesh is not yet adequately documented or understood (see Jahan, 2016). Most of the evidence consists of surface finds from the Chittagong Hill Tracts and the Lalmai-Mainamati area, and there are also some sites in the Sylhet hills in the north-east. In the Lalmai-Mainamati hills in Comilla district and Chaklapunji Tea State in Habiganj district, petrified or fossil wood is the most readily available rock and was the main material used by prehistoric people to make tools. This fossil wood industry has affinities with that of the Haora and Khowai river valleys of Tripura and the Irrawaddy valley of Myanmar.

Many prehistoric sites have been identified in western Nepal. The earliest evidence is an Acheulean handaxe discovered by Gudrun Corvinus in the Babai river valley (Darnal, 2016). Handaxes were also found at Jhaijri in Gadari and Satpati near the confluence of the Narayani and Satpati rivers. Soanian-type tools occur as surface finds in the Siwaliks.

In Andhra Pradesh, lower palaeolithic tools have been found in inland areas as well as the coastal Visakhapatnam area, where they have been connected to a sea level over 7 m above the present one. Nagarjunakonda, one of the sites that have been studied extensively, has given palaeo-climatic evidence of three alternating wet and dry cycles. Choppers and scrapers made of quartz have been found in the Palghat district of Kerala.

In Tamil Nadu, there is a stratigraphic sequence from the early palaeolithic to the mesolithic from near Chennai. Gudiyam cave, not far from Chennai, has yielded a sequence of lower, middle, and upper palaeolithic tools. The fewness of the tools and the absence of other remains suggest that the site was occupied for short periods of time.

Attirampakkam, in the Kortallaiyar river basin, is one of the richest palaeolithic sites in Tamil Nadu (Pappu et al., 2003). The site was discovered in 1863, and explored for stone tools for many years thereafter. The excavations conducted here since 1999 have produced dramatic results, which have important implications for understanding the palaeolithic in South Asia and the 'Out of Africa' dispersals of hominins.

Middle palaeolithic sites

Within the palaeolithic, there were gradual changes in stone tools. Handaxes, chopping tools, and cleavers did not altogether disappear, but the balance shifted towards smaller, lighter flake tools, some of them made by prepared core techniques, including the Levallois technique.

Middle palaeolithic tools have been found in many parts of the subcontinent, often in river gravels and deposits, which give clues about prevailing climatic conditions. There are some dates for middle palaeolithic contexts. Didwana (Rajasthan) has given two thermoluminescence dates of 150,000 BP and 144,000 BP. The Hiran valley (Gujarat) has yielded a uranium–thorium series date of 56,800 BP.

In the north-west, lots of stone tools, mostly of the middle palaeolithic, have been found in the Potwar plateau between the Indus and Jhelum rivers. The over 3 m thick deposit in the Sanghao cave in the North-West Frontier Province of Pakistan revealed a sequence of middle and palaeolithic occupation. Thousands of stone tools were found, along with bones (of animals, some perhaps of humans) and hearths. All the tools are made of quartz, which is easily available around the site. Many of the tools of Period I were made from flakes stuck from prepared cores, and there were lots of burins.

Borer from Nellor district (AP)

RECENT DISCOVERIES | Attirampakkam

The site of Attirampakkam has been long recognized as an important palaeolithic site. Recent excavations by a team led by Shanti Pappu and Kumar Akhilesh were marked by a comprehensive, multidisciplinary approach and revealed valuable new evidence. These excavations, accompanied by detailed palaeo-environmental studies, revealed a long stratigraphic sequence and resulted in the discovery of thousands of stone tools.

A sequence of eight stratified deposits comprising fluvial sediments was exposed at Attirampakkam, reaching a maximum thickness of about 9 m. The site was obviously attractive for stone age humans over thousands of years as archaeologists found evidence of Acheulian assemblages as well as of a transition from a later Acheulian to late middle palaeolithic toolkit. Four fossil animal teeth, 17 animal footprints, and 5 hoofmarks are among the exciting discoveries.

The Acheulian is a phase of the lower palaeolithic marked by an assemblage of large cutting tools, mainly consisting of bifaces. The evidence from Africa suggests that the Acheulian phase began about 1.6 mya. Evidence of the Acheulian phase in other parts of the world is considerably later than that from Africa and Southwest Asia. The new dates for the lower palaeolithic from the recent excavations at Attirampakkam have changed the situation radically.

The lower palaeolithic age in South Asia has been generally placed in the middle Pleistocene. Palaeomagnetic and direct Al/Be burial dating of stone artefacts date the earliest Acheulian levels at Attirampakkam at not less than 1.07 mya, with a pooled average of 1.51+/- 0.07 mya. These dates are not only the earliest in India, but are contemporary with some of the lower palaeolithic Acheulian sites in Africa and Southwest Asia.

Attirampakkam has also given evidence of gradual changes from the Acheulian assemblage towards a disuse of bifaces, an increasing number of small tools, various kinds of Levallois flake and point making techniques, and the evolution of blade making techniques. The changes in artefact trends point to significant behavioural changes. Luminescence dates indicate that the end of the Acheulian culture and beginning of the middle palaeolithic phase took place 385+/-64 thousand years ago (ka) and that the middle palaeolithic continued here till 172+/- 41 ka.

Due to the absence of human fossils, it is not possible to connect the changes in the Attirampakkam assemblages to a particular hominin species. But the dates from the site indicate that India was populated by hominins using an Acheulian tool making technology and a tool kit including handaxes and cleavers much earlier than imagined. It also suggests that the transition to the middle palaeolithic in South India took place much earlier than imagined. At Attirampakkam, this transition occurred at a time comparable to the timing of the transition to the middle palaeolithic in Africa and Europe.

The evidence and dates from Attirampakkam point to the need for a fresh look at the dating of other Acheulian sites in South Asia and raise important questions about the timing of hominin dispersals out of Africa.

Source Pappu et al., 2011; Akhilesh et al., 2018

PRIMARY SOURCES | **The Levallois technique**

The Levallois technique is an advanced method of making flake tools. It is named after a place called Levallois Perret near Paris, where this technique was first noticed on prehistoric stone tools. Instead of breaking off a flake and working on it to produce the desired shape, first the core was carefully prepared. Its sides were trimmed, and flakes were then systematically removed from its surface, from the centre outwards in all directions. Then, a striking platform was created by flattening the top of the prepared core, and perpendicular blows were struck at that point, either directly or through an intermediary tool.

The flake detached in this way was thin, roughly triangular or oval in shape, with a clean undersurface, and shallow, centrally directed flake scars on the upper side. It would need very little further working, because its edges were already sharp. Because the core of a Levallois flake looks like the shell of a tortoise, it is sometimes referred to as a tortoise core.

There are other prepared core techniques as well. For instance, in the discoid core technique, flakes are scalloped from the circumference of a large core or flake with at least one flat side. The remaining core has a bevelled rim and is flat in the centre. The Levallois technique can be used to produce only one flake at a time, while the discoid core technique can produce several flakes. Flakes produced by the latter method tend to be small.

Source Sankalia, (1964) 1982: 29–30

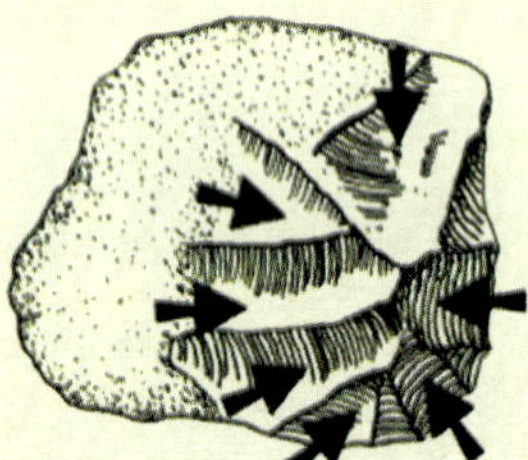

Preparation of Levallois core

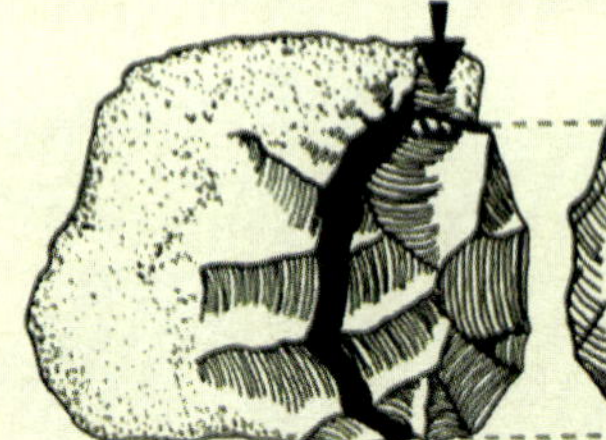

Levalloisian core with the flake (replaced) to show where the blow was struck

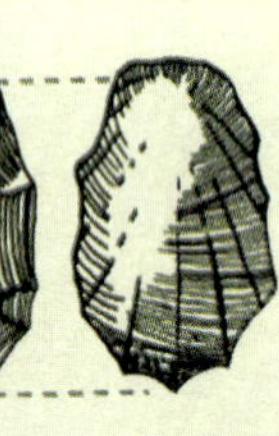

Levallois flake showing the prepared platform and 90° angle

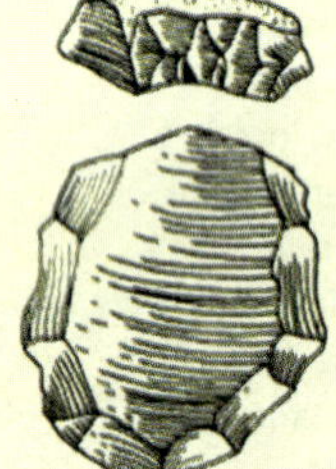

'Tortoise' or Levallois core after removal of the flake

Figure 2.5 Preparation of a Levallois flake

In the Thar region, middle palaeolithic artefacts occur in reddish brown soil, which indicates more abundant vegetation, more surface water, and a cooler, wetter, and more humid climate compared to lower palaeolithic contexts. Small factory sites and camp sites have been found in various parts of the Thar, especially near rivers and lakes. A large number of stone age sites belonging to the middle palaeolithic phase onwards are located around Budha Pushkar lake, an area which offers advantages of the easy availability of water and stone. Middle and upper palaeolithic tools are also found around Ajmer. There is evidence of middle palaeolithic working floors at Hokra and Baridhani, close to the now dried-up lakes. In the Jaisalmer area, upper palaeolithic material is not as abundant as are artefacts of the middle palaeolithic. Middle palaeolithic sites have also been located along the now virtually extinct Luni river system. The term Luni industry is used for middle palaeolithic assemblages west of the Aravallis, and can be contrasted with the industry of the regions lying east of the Aravallis. Although certain forms are common to both areas, sites to the west of the Aravallis display more variety in stone tool types and larger numbers of reworked flakes. Middle and upper palaeolithic tools have also been found along the eastern margin of the Gujarat plain.

The Belan valley has so far yielded 87 middle palaeolithic sites (Varma et al., 2014). These include Mahua Kaccha, Panchoh, Daiya, Belarahi and Karaundahia, Itaha, and Nagini-ki-pahari. Although some core and pebble tools occur, most of the artefacts are made on flakes. A total of 86 middle palaeolithic sites have so far been identified in the valleys of the Son and its tributaries; these include several factory sites. The sites include Kukaraon, Kotar, Hatwa, Kuradih, Khairahia, and Dhoman-ki-Pahari. Chert is the most frequently used raw material; quartzite, flint, and jasper are among the other types of stone used.

The middle palaeolithic industry of Central and peninsular India is sometimes referred to as the Nevasan industry after the site of Nevasa, where the pioneering

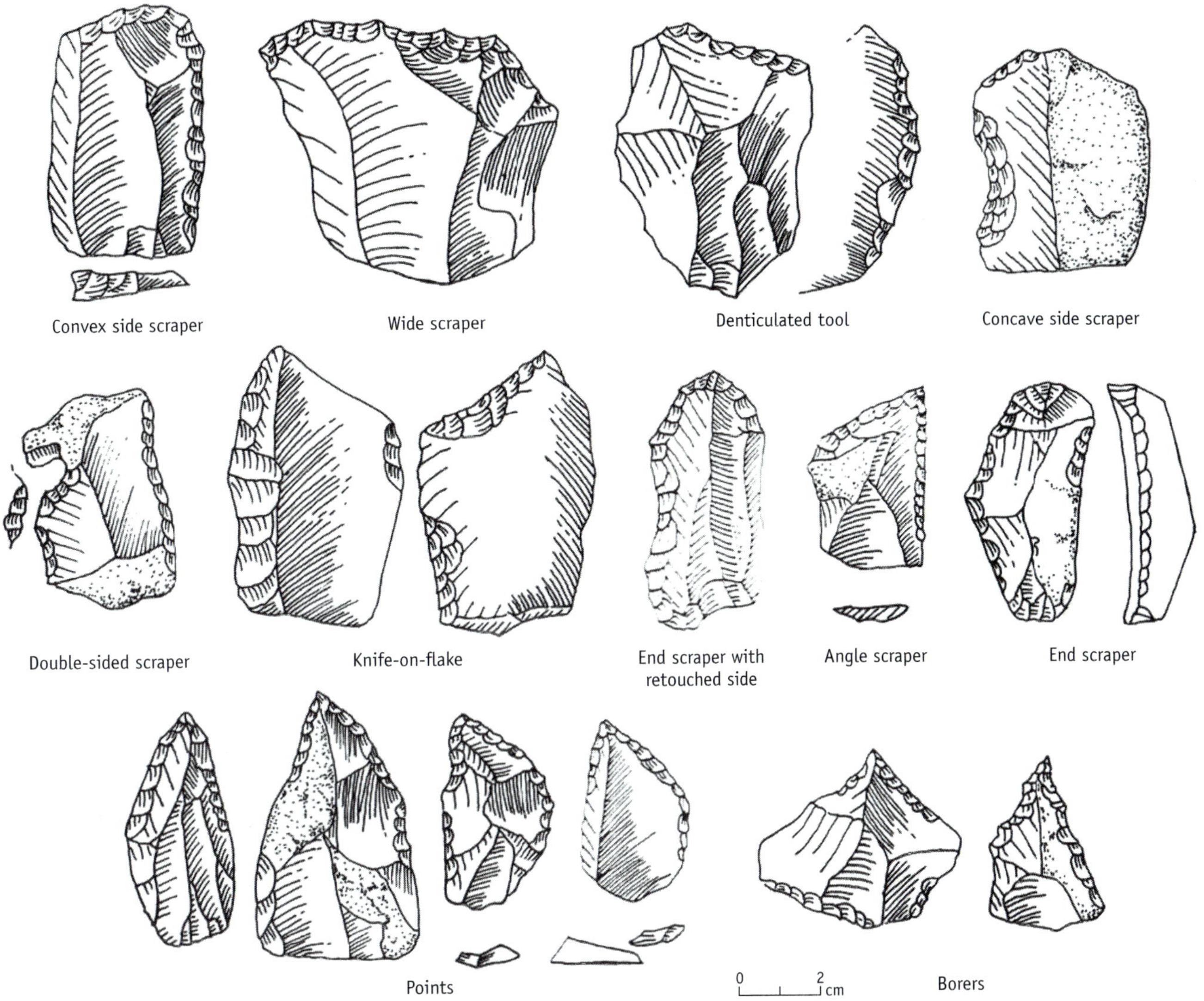

Convex side scraper
Wide scraper
Denticulated tool
Concave side scraper
Double-sided scraper
Knife-on-flake
End scraper with retouched side
Angle scraper
End scraper
Points
0 2 cm
Borers

Figure 2.6 Middle palaeolithic tools

archaeologist H. D. Sankalia first discovered middle palaeolithic artefacts in a stratified context. The tools, which include a wide variety of scrapers, are made of smooth, fine-grained stone such as agate, jasper, and chalcedony. Patne in the Tapi valley revealed a stratigraphic sequence of middle and upper palaeolithic and mesolithic tools. There is evidence of a middle palaeolithic living and factory site at Chirki near Nevasa.

The earliest trace of human occupation in the Ganga plain is found embedded in a 20 m thick cliff section at Kalpi (in Jalaun district, UP), on the southern bank of the Yamuna. A number of vertebrate fossils—elephant tusk, shoulder blade of elephant, molars of *Equus* and bovids—were found here. Middle palaeolithic stone tools (including pebble tools, points, and side scrapers) and bone tools (such as end scrapers, points, and burins) were found along with them. The tool-bearing level at Kalpi has been dated to about 45,000 years ago. There are several middle and upper palaeolithic sites further east, especially in the western part of West Bengal.

In South India, the middle palaeolithic culture is marked by a flake tool industry. On the Visakhapatnam coast, quartzite, chert, and quartz were frequently used to make stone tools. There is evidence of tools made by the Levallois technique at many places. In addition to smaller handaxes, cleavers, and choppers, the middle palaeolithic tool kit included new tool types such as scrapers of different shapes. A C-14 date for the middle palaeolithic at Nandipalli (Kadapa district) indicates that it is older than 23,000 years ago. The important site of Attirampakkam (TN) has been discussed earlier.

Middle palaeolithic scraper from Attirampakkam

Upper palaeolithic sites

The important technical advance of the upper palaeolithic was the making of parallel-sided blades. There was also an increase in the number of burins. The trend was towards smaller tools, and this must have been due to adaptations to environmental changes. It is known, for instance, that the climate of Northern and Western India seems to have become increasingly arid during the upper palaeolithic. Older tool types continued to be made for activities that required heavier tools.

There are some dates for upper palaeolithic contexts. Site 55 at Riwat gives an early date for the upper palaeolithic—*c.* 45,000 years ago. C-14 dates from the Sanghao cave range from 41,825 ± 4,120 BCE to 20,660 ± 360 BCE. In Central India, the Son valley has given radiocarbon dates within the range of 12,000–10,000 BP. Two dates from the Kurnool caves (in AP) are 19,224 BP and 16,686 BP (based on the electron spin resonance method).

In the north-west, the Sanghao cave has given evidence of middle and upper palaeolithic tools, hearths, animal bones, and what appear to be burials. Upper palaeolithic tools have also been found in the Rohri hills in upper Sindh and Milestone 101 in lower Sindh. In North India, the Kashmir upper palaeolithic has been dated to about 18,000 BP and coincides with the onset of a milder climate.

In the Thar, the number of upper palaeolithic sites is fewer than those of the preceding phase, due to increasing aridity. However, there was continuing human occupation around the Budha Pushkar lake. In Central India, upper palaeolithic habitation sites have been found in caves and rock shelters of the Vindhyas.

The upper palaeolithic context in the Belan valley has been dated between 25,000 and 19,000 years ago, and that of the Son valley to about 10,000 years ago. Chopani Mando in the Belan valley seems to be a habitation site with a cultural sequence from the upper palaeolithic to neolithic. The upper palaeolithic assemblage consisted of tools made from chert, a stone available in the nearby Vindhyas. The animal bones discovered in the Belan valley included those of wild cattle, sheep, and goats. Since sheep and goats do not seem to be indigenous to this area, they may have been brought here from the north-west. If this was indeed the case, it could represent an early stage of animal domestication.

In Siddhi district of Madhya Pradesh, in the valley of the Son river, an archaeological team led by G. R. Sharma and J. D. Clark excavated the upper palaeolithic site of Baghor I. A subsequent microwear study of the site Baghor III (not far from Baghor I) (Sinha, 1989) threw light on the subsistence activities of this phase. The study identified the different kinds of activities that the stone tools found at the site were used for. Some of these activities, such as boring, scraping, and whittling, were probably related to craft work. Others, such as cutting, slicing, piercing, and chopping, could have been associated with food processing, hunting, or craft work. Microwear analysis identified the proportion of tools used on vegetal materials, those used for processing non-vegetal material, and those used to work on wood or bamboo to make hunting and gathering gear. Some tools showed a kind of wear and polish that indicated they had been hafted onto handles.

There are many upper palaeolithic sites in the Chota Nagpur region and the Damin area of the Rajmahal hills. These include Paisra in Munger district. Upper palaeolithic tools have been found in the various districts of West Bengal. There is not enough evidence of the palaeolithic phase in Assam and other parts of the north-east. But in the Lalmai hills of Bangladesh and in the Haora and Khowai river valleys in western Tripura, a number of tools, including typical upper palaeolithic types such as blades, burins, points, etc. made out of fossil wood have been found. Similar tools have been found in the upper Irawaddy valley in Myanmar.

Upper palaeolithic chert blades from the Narmada valley; Burin from Mukat Manipur [West Bengal] (from top)

A distinctive feature of the cave sites of Kurnool and Muchchatla Chintamanu Gavi in Andhra Pradesh are tools made of animal bones found in an upper palaeolithic context. In one of the caves, as many as 90 per cent of the excavated tools were made

PRIMARY SOURCES | Upper palaeolithic tools

A blade is a flake tool, the length of which is more than twice its width. A blade with more or less even, parallel sides is known as a parallel-sided blade. A burin is a small tool made on a blade. It has a sharp but thickset working border, similar to that of a modern screwdriver. Burins may have been used as engraving tools or for making grooves in wood or bone for hafting stone tools.

Source Sankalia, (1964) 1982: 66–68

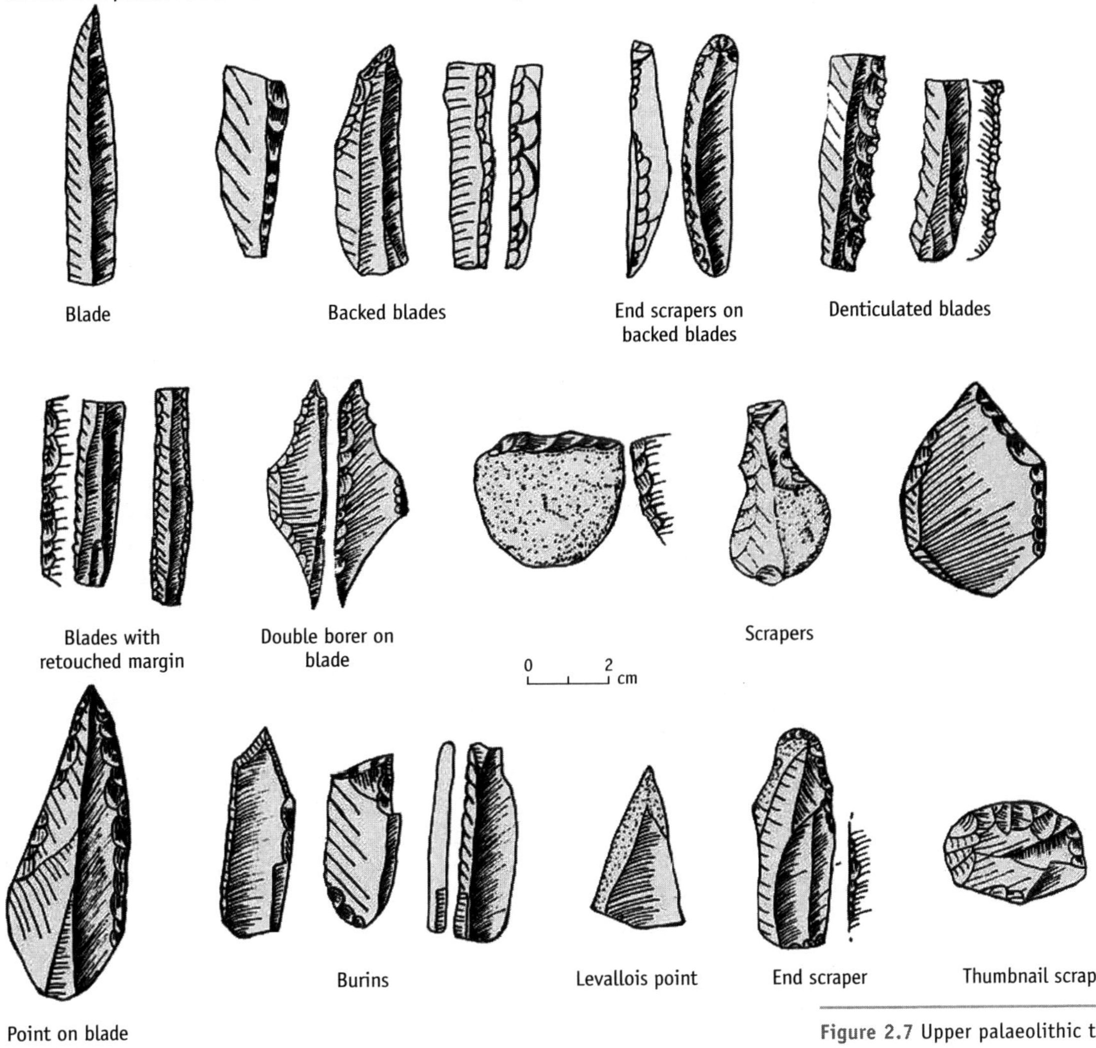

Figure 2.7 Upper palaeolithic tools

of this material. The faunal remains reported from the site included those of the bat, *nilgai*, four-horned antelope, gazelle, *chital*, *sambar* deer, barking deer, mouse deer, wild boar, tiger, leopard, jungle cat, rusty-spotted cat, spotted hyena, civet, fresh-water fish, mongoose, sloth bear, porcupine, bandicoot rat, gerbil (a rodent), mouse, bush rat, black-naped hare, grey *langur*, baboon, ass, rhinoceros, shrew, and giant pangolin. Apart from giving valuable information about the animals with whom upper palaeolithic people shared their landscape, this list also suggests that thick forests and more humid conditions prevailed in this area. Upper palaeolithic artefacts were also found in a cave at Renigunta in Chittoor district of southern Andhra Pradesh. Stone tools of this phase occur at many places along the east coast of peninsular India, and their antiquity ranges between 25,000 and 10,000 years ago.

Palaeolithic art and cults

Prehistoric art marks the beginning of the history of art. It is also an important window into the world of prehistoric people. Apart from paintings on rocks, rock art includes **petroglyphs**, a word used when some substance of a rock surface is removed through engraving, bruising, hammering, chiselling, or scooping. Prehistoric art can occur in permanent places (e.g., cave paintings) or can be portable (e.g., figurines). Such remains were clearly an integral and important part of community life and some of them seem to have had some sort of cultic or religious significance.

In Europe, Australia, and southern Africa, there is clear and considerable evidence of upper palaeolithic rock paintings and engravings. Animals are the predominant motifs, and some of the representations may have been part of hunting rituals. Female figurines known as 'Venus figurines' may represent fertility beliefs and rituals. In India, however, there is very little evidence of palaeolithic art. This is partly because most of the evidence must have perished over time, and partly because much still remains to be discovered. We may, in fact, have to redefine what we consider as 'art' in order to recognize the remains of artistic activity of prehistoric people. In recent years, the volume of evidence of prehistoric art in India has increased substantially and in some cases, seems to go back to the lower palaeolithic.

There are problems in dating and interpreting prehistoric art, and in ascertaining if an object was simply utilitarian or whether it had some other sort of function and significance. For instance, a very damaged upper palaeolithic carved bone object found at Lohanda Nala in the Belan valley (UP) has been identified as a mother goddess figurine by some and as a harpoon by others. Animal teeth found in a cave at Kurnool have grooves which suggest that they may have been attached to a string and worn as ornaments. A circular disc made of chalcedony at Bhimbetka and a soft sandstone disc at Maihar (south-west of Allahabad) were found in Acheulian contexts; neither seem to be tools. A piece of ostrich eggshell engraved with two panels of criss-cross designs was discovered at Patne. Four perforated beads and one incomplete bead made of ostrich eggshell came from Patne and one from the Bhimbetka rock shelters, all from upper palaeolithic contexts.

Dramatic evidence of artistic-cum-cultic activity comes from Cave III F-24 at Bhimbetka, known as the 'auditorium cave'. This seems to belong to the lower palaeolithic. A roomy tunnel, about 25 m long, leads into a hall which has three other entrances. In the middle of the cave is a large rock. The part of the rock facing the tunnel is flat and vertical. On it are seven cupules (cup-like depressions), up to 16.8 mm deep. A few metres away from this rock, at the bottom of a pit, is another huge rock. This has one single large cup mark, along with a meandering line carved on its surface. One interpretation is that the rock with multiple cupules was used as a rock gong and that the marks were made when it was hit repeatedly. It is likely that they were deliberately made as part of some important prehistoric community ritual. The cupules in the Bhimbetka cave may be the oldest surviving rock art in the world. Interestingly, prehistoric cupules have been found in other parts of the world as well; they are unlikely to represent the oldest rock art ever made; it is just that they had better chances of surviving than paintings (Bednarik, 2001).

The site of Baghor I in Madhya Pradesh has given fascinating evidence of an upper palaeolithic shrine dated *c.* 9000–8000 BCE. Here, there was a roughly circular platform made of sandstone rubble, about 85 cm in diameter. In the centre was a piece of natural stone with a striking pattern of concentric triangular laminations in colours ranging from a light yellowish red to a dark reddish brown. Archaeologists found nine other fragments of this stone, mostly on or near the platform. When the ten pieces were joined together, they formed a triangle, about 15 cm high, 6.5 cm wide, and 6.5 cm thick. This triangular stone was evidently originally placed on the platform. It is interesting to note that the Kol and Baiga tribal people who live in this part of the Kaimur hills today make circular

FURTHER DISCUSSION | **Ostrich eggshell beads**

The ostrich (*Struthio camelus* sp.), the largest living bird in the world, is today found in its natural habitat only in Africa, where it teeters on the verge of extinction. However, ostriches once roamed over many parts of Asia, including India, till the end of the Pleistocene or early Holocene. Ostriches may have been hunted for food, and their eggs must also have been eaten. The eggs are big—their size ranges from about 127 × 103 mm to 160 × 129 mm, with an average thickness of 1.97 mm. They weigh between 775 g to 1618 g. The shell is smooth, yellowish white, speckled with black. It is so hard, that you have to use a hammer and saw to break it. The shells could have been used as bowls or containers.

Fragments of ostrich eggshell have been found in upper palaeolithic contexts in India. The first discovery was made in the 1860s in the Ken river in Banda district of Uttar Pradesh. Since then, pieces of ostrich eggshell have been found at Patne in Maharashtra and about 50 discoveries have been made in various parts of Rajasthan, Madhya Pradesh, and Maharashtra. A few of the eggshell pieces have been dated. Patne gives a date of 25,000 years BP; Chandresal (in Rajasthan) gives two dates—38,900 ± 750 BP and 36,500 ± 600 BP; Ramnagar (in Madhya Pradesh) gives a date of over 31,000 years BP. Some eggshell pieces have patterns on them. When examined carefully under the microscope, most of these seem to be the result of natural weathering. However, the fragment found at Patne is clearly engraved with criss-cross patterns made long ago by human hands.

Beads and discs for ornaments were also made out of ostrich eggshell. Some of them had a hole through which they could be strung. About 41 Indian sites have given evidence of such beads in Pleistocene contexts ranging from 39,000 to 25,000 BP. For instance, ostrich eggshell beads occur in upper palaeolithic contexts at Patne and Bhimbetka. The Patne beads have a diameter of about 10 mm and the Bhimbetka ones of 6 mm. The Bhimbetka beads were discovered in an upper palaeolithic burial in a rock shelter, on the neck of the skull of a buried man. He must have been wearing a necklace with different kinds of beads; the others had decayed, but the two ostrich eggshell beads survived.

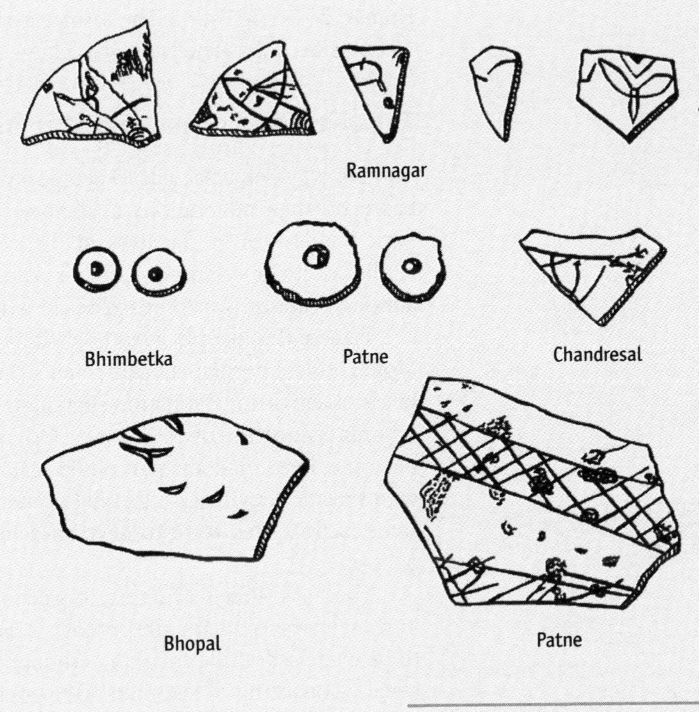

Figure 2.8 Decorated ostrich eggshell objects

Making such beads must have required considerable skill and care, and some scholars have tried to replicate them experimentally. G. Kumar worked with heavily weathered ostrich eggshell and used mesolithic tools, drilling through both sides, to produce two perforated beads. It took him 10–12 minutes. R. G. Bednarik used fresh ostrich eggshell. He found that it was best to work with tools made of coarse-grained quartizites and quartz, and managed to drill through the shell of a complete egg in 70–90 seconds. Through experimentation, he also reconstructed the process whereby beads of this material must have been made.

Although the number of surviving beads is small, these must represent a very small proportion of those made and used by prehistoric people. Small beads could not have achieved a decorative result singly or in small numbers. The role and function of such beads must have been non-utilitarian, symbolic, or ideological. They must have been produced with such care and perfection because they were imbued with important cultural meaning. The beads also display an appreciation of an essentially abstract form.

Beads made of ostrich eggshell have also been found in upper palaeolithic contexts in Siberia, inner Mongolia, China, and Africa. Clearly, ornaments made out of this material were the fashion in many parts of the prehistoric world. Bushmen of southern Africa are known to have used ostrich eggshell for making beads and as water vessels till recently.

Source Bednarik, 1997

rubble platforms and worship similar triangular stones as a symbol of the female principle or as an icon of a goddess.

More recently, the sites of Daraki-Chattan and Chaturbhujnath Nala (Mandasaur district, MP) have given dramatic evidence belonging to the palaeolithic (see Giriraj Kumar, 2014: 307–08). The former is a small but deep cave, with over 500 cupules on its two side walls. The latter has a large number of rock paintings.

The life-ways of palaeolithic hunter-gatherers

The life-ways of palaeolithic people living in different parts of the subcontinent were based on their adaptations to their specific environments. However, there were some basic similarities in the lives of these hunting-gathering communities. Ethnographic studies of modern hunter-gatherers can supplement the information from archaeology, although caution has to be exercised while drawing parallels and conclusions.

Palaeolithic people lived in shelters made of rock, branches, grass, leaves, or reeds. More and less permanent settlements can be identified and some sites represent specific kinds of activities. Habitation sites such as Bhimbetka and Hunsgi give evidence of continuous occupation over centuries. Other sites indicate temporary camp sites, where people came, lived for some part of the year, and then moved on. Still others were connected with specific activities—e.g., kill or butchery sites and factory sites. As mentioned earlier, some factory sites seem to have attracted many different communities over thousands of years.

The basic social structure of palaeolithic hunter-gatherers may have corresponded in some ways to what anthropologists call a 'band society', although caution always has to be exercised while invoking ethnographic parallels. **Bands** are small communities, usually consisting of less than 100 people. They tend to be mobile or nomadic to some extent, moving from one place to another, depending on the seasonal availability of the animals they hunt and the plant food they gather. Members of a band are usually related to each other through kinship, and their division of labour is based on age and sex. The exchange of goods is based on rules of reciprocity, not on commercial exchange. Within a band, no single person or persons 'owns' the natural resources they all depend on. There are no institutions of formal government, no formal or permanent leaders, not even the powerful chiefs seen in more complex tribal societies. The behaviour of members of the group is not regulated by force but through customs, norms, and social etiquette.

One of the stereotypes about the life of hunter-gatherers is that theirs was a constant, relentless struggle for survival with little or no leisure time. The material desires and wants of palaeolithic humans must have been relatively limited and their technology did not permit them to hoard food beyond a point. These two factors meant that their subsistence-related activities ceased when they had obtained enough food. This must have given them some time for other kinds of activities. Ethnographic evidence in fact shows that not all modern hunter-gatherers live a hand-to-mouth existence and many of them have plenty of leisure time to sleep, chat, play games, and relax.

Another commonly held view is that hunting-gathering is an inefficient mode of subsistence. This can be questioned on the basis of the long history of this mode of subsistence and its continuation (of course on a much reduced scale) even into our own time. Further, ethnographic studies have shown that many hunting-gathering groups do not fully exploit the natural resource potential of their area and that they consciously practise sensible restraint in their exploitation of the environment in order to conserve its resources.

Modern hunter-gatherers tend to obtain a significant amount of their food through gathering rather than hunting. This suggests that the 'hunting' part of the term 'hunter-gatherer' has perhaps been over-emphasized by scholars and the 'gatherer' part neglected. This conclusion has important implications for understanding subsistence patterns as well as gender roles and relations in palaeolithic societies. In most modern hunting-gathering communities, men hunt and women gather food, and a similar

FURTHER DISCUSSION | **Food resources—now and then**

Due to the lack of organic plant and animal remains, archaeologists often draw on ethnographic evidence of present communities living in areas that once supported prehistoric populations. Some important case studies have tried to understand palaeolithic sites within their broader environmental and settlement contexts.

K. Paddayya's study of the settlement and subsistence patterns of the lower palaeolithic culture of the Hunsgi valley identified about 40 species of wild edible plants growing in the valley today, including fruits, berries, pods, leafy vegetables, mushrooms, and seeds. The valley does not support any large wildlife today, except perhaps the gazelle and blackbuck. But fossilized bones of wild cattle (*Bos* sp.) and a horn fragment of a deer were found at the middle palaeolithic site of Hagargundigi on the Bhima river, about 80 km to the north-east. Kodekal, a neolithic site situated 8 km from the Hunsgi valley, yielded remains of three species of deer (*barasingha*, gazelle, and spotted deer). It is reasonable to assume that thousands of years ago, such animals were present in the Hunsgi valley as well. The valley still supports a variety of small mammals, birds, reptiles, and aquatic animals. These include the hare, porcupine, birds such as the sandgrouse, partridge, and quail, reptiles such as the monitor lizard, many varieties of fish, and several types of insects. Some of these resources are routinely exploited for food by local communities living in the area today.

The present flora and fauna of the Hunsgi valley gives an idea of the range of wild plant and animal food available to prehistoric people who lived in this area thousands of years ago. Of course, in those times the area must have had a much thicker vegetation of savannah woodland and must have supported a much richer range of flora and fauna. Paddayya suggests that in view of the fact that the plant resources of the area shrink in the dry summer months, prehistoric people must have had to rely more on hunting animals for food during that period.

M. L. K. Murty's study focused on present-day hunting-gathering tribes of Andhra such as the Yerukulas, Yanandis, Chenchus, and Boyas, as well as incipient agricultural groups such as the Gonds and Konda Reddis. These communities still depend on wild forest food, small game, reptiles, riverine and sea fauna, insects, and honey. Murty listed about 80 edible wild plants used by these people, including fruits, berries, seeds, tubers, pods, pulps, and vegetables. He pointed to a broad congruence of the location of prehistoric hunter-gatherer sites and those inhabited by present-day tribal communities relying significantly on hunting and gathering. This indicates that the ecological niches that were exploited by prehistoric communities who lived by foraging and hunting still manage to support communities who rely on similar subsistence strategies.

Source Paddayya, 1985; Murty, 1985

division of labour probably existed in palaeolithic times. But if plant food had a greater dietary importance, it can be inferred that women must have contributed in a major way to the subsistence base of palaeolithic communities.

The artistic, social, and cultic implications of some of the specimens of palaeolithic art have already been mentioned. Modern hunter-gatherers regard themselves as part of a larger world of nature because of their daily and direct encounter with it. Animals, plants, and aspects of the landscape may be treated as kin or foe; they may be worshipped or may form the focus of rituals. Since modern hunter-gatherers maintain some degree of contact with more complex societies, it would be a mistake to assume that prehistoric people had identical beliefs. However, it is possible that there were some very broad similarities arising out of a similar type of subsistence base.

The Mesolithic

Mesolithic sites

The Pleistocene geological era made way for the Holocene about 12,000 years ago. Many environmental changes took place during this transition and there are detailed profiles of climatic patterns for some parts of the subcontinent. For instance, an analysis of soil samples from Birbhanpur in West Bengal shows a trend of increasing aridity. On the other hand, the study of the salt lake sediments and pollen grains at Didwana in western Rajasthan suggests higher rainfall at this point of time. In eastern Madhya Pradesh, the climate of the early and middle Holocene seems to have been wet and warm, with heavy

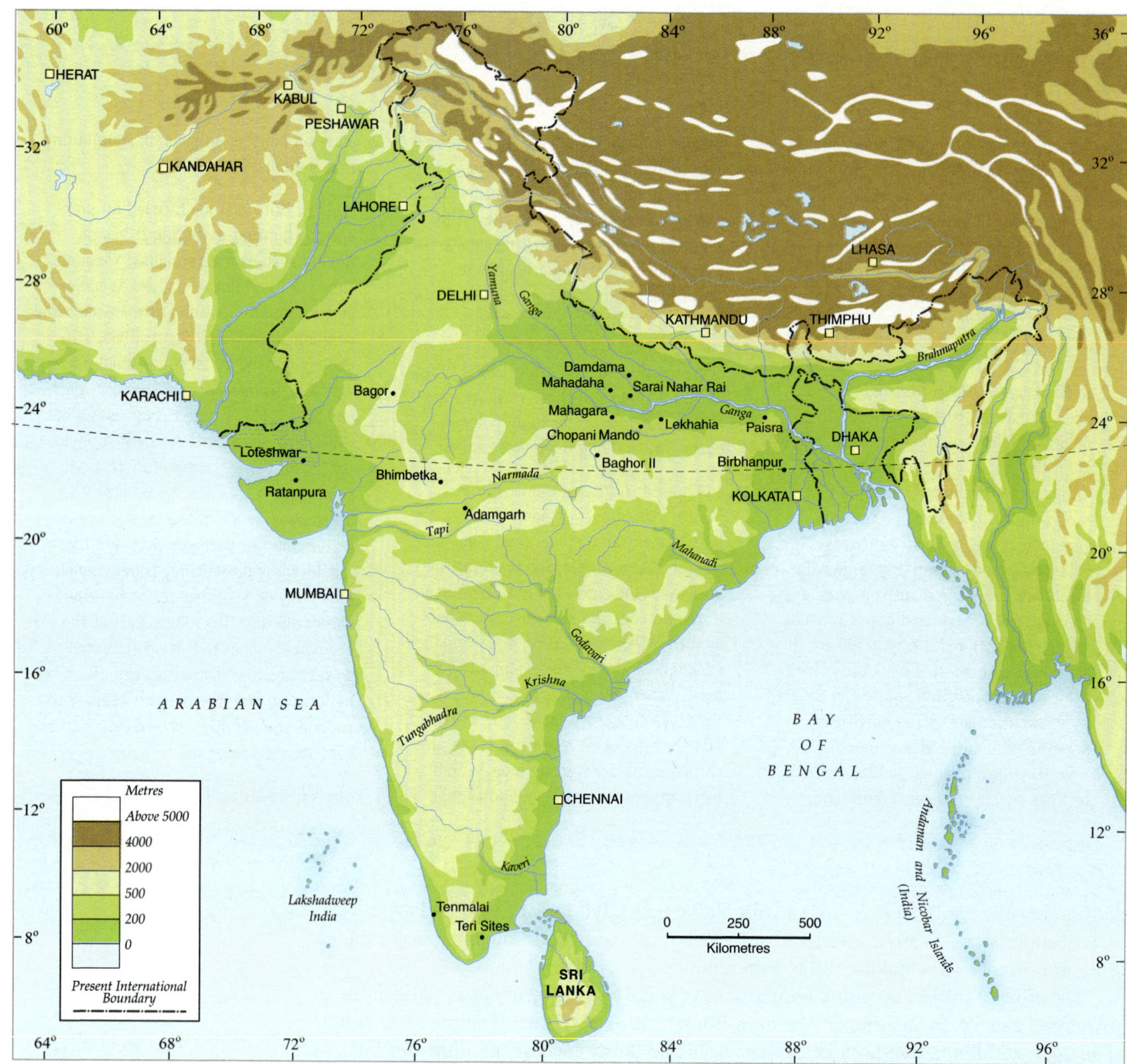

Map 2.4 Some early mesolithic sites

rainfall in the summer monsoon months and moderate levels of rainfall in winter. A drier spell seems to have set in about 4,000–3,000 years ago.

The term mesolithic is used in Indian prehistory for post-Pleistocene (i.e., Holocene) hunting-gathering stone age cultures marked by the use of very small stone tools referred to by archaeologists as microliths. At sites such as Patne, where there is a long and continuous stratigraphic sequence of prehistoric occupation, the gradual decrease in the size of stone tools can be seen very clearly. The term **epi-palaeolithic** is sometimes used for the transitional stage of tools that are smaller than those typical of the upper palaeolithic, but bigger than microliths. Changes in tool kits may have been related to changes in environmental factors, but such detailed connections have not been fully worked out.

It is not easy to define or identify the mesolithic phase with any precision. The sites are located in very diverse ecological contexts and some of them are clearly pre-Holocene. Sites such as Patne (in Maharashtra) and Fa-Hien Lena, Batadomba Lena, and Beli Lena (in Sri Lanka) have given evidence of microliths in late Pleistocene contexts. Further, microliths are known to have been made and used well into the historical period. Mehtakheri (MP) has given evidence of a micro-blade technology from about

PRIMARY SOURCES | Microliths

Microliths range in length from under 1 cm to 5 cm. The tools are mostly made on short parallel-sided blades made of cryp-to-crystalline silica stone such as quartzite, chert, chalcedony, jasper, and agate. Microliths include miniature versions of some of the upper palaeolithic tool types such as burins, points, and scrapers. But there is also the introduction of tools in regular geometric shapes such as lunates (crescents), triangles, rhomboids, trapezes, and trapezoids. Microliths are usually classified into 'geometric' and 'non-geometric' types.

What was the use of such tiny tools? This question can be answered by supplementing the archaeological data with ethnographic evidence from communities in different parts of the world who still make and use such stone tools in their daily lives.

Some microliths may have been used as tools in themselves, but many must have been hafted, singly or in large numbers, onto wooden or bone handles to make composite tools. In some instances, the original hafts have survived. Microliths could have been used to make spear-heads, arrowheads, knives, daggers, sickles, and adzes. It is possible that poison was applied to microlithic tips and barbs to add to the lethal effect of the weapons. Microliths were also embedded in a wooden matrix to make sickles for harvesting plants.

Microwear analysis of microliths from the northern Vindhyas and Ganga plains indicates artefacts were used for various activities related to hunting. Ethnoarchaeological research among tribal communities who still make and use microliths has added to the understanding of this technology.

Did the beginning of microlith technology originate from local innovations in response to changing environmental conditions? Was it introduced by new incoming populations? Were a combination of factors involved? These questions are the subject of debate.

Source Sankalia, (1964) 1982: 69–77; Misra, 1974

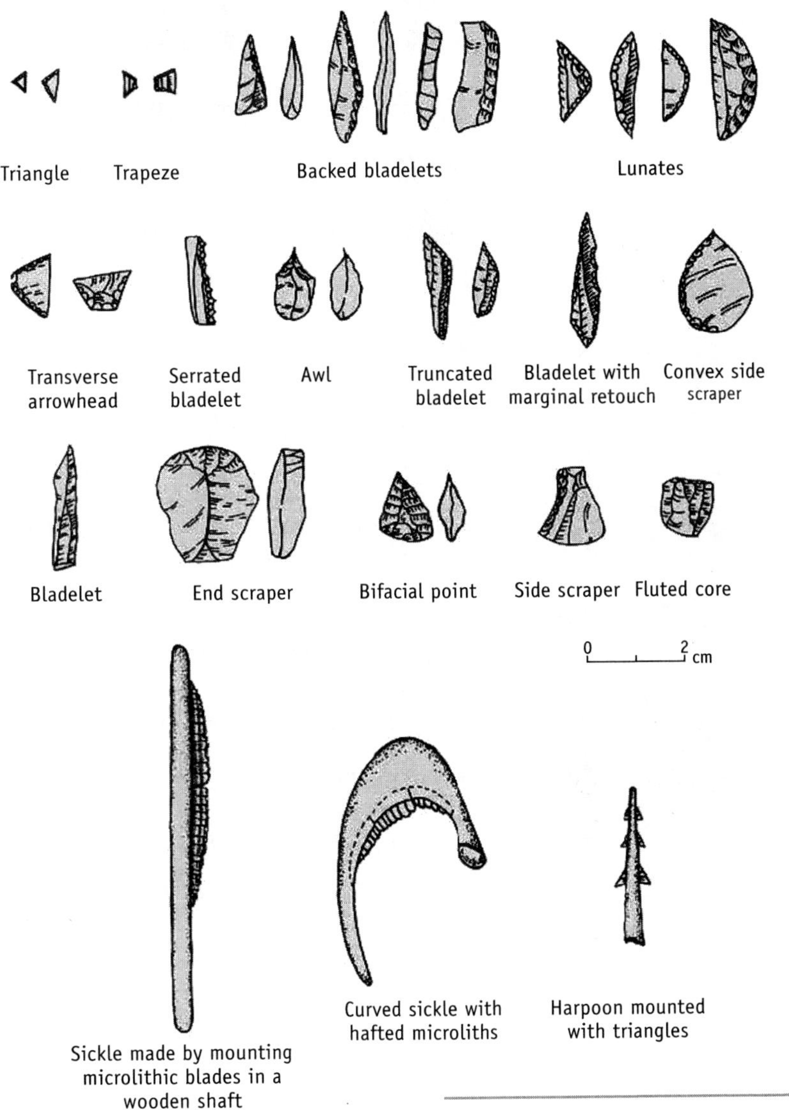

Figure 2.9 Microliths

48,000 to 3,000 years ago (Sheila Mishra et al., 2013). The mesolithic economy was based on a diverse subsistence base involving hunting and gathering, but some sites have given evidence of the domestication of animals. Mesolithic sites reflect different levels of sedentariness. Some seem to have been permanent or semi-permanent settlements, or at least settlements that were repeatedly inhabited over long periods of time. Pottery is absent at most mesolithic sites, but hand-made pottery occurs at Langhnaj in Gujarat and at sites such as Morahana Pahar, Baghai Khor, Chopani Mando, and Lekhahia in

Microliths from various sites

Mirzapur district (UP). The analysis of skeletal remains found at mesolithic sites has given information about people's physical stature, nutrition, physical activity, health, and disease (see, for instance, Lukacs, 2016). The burials also give insights into funerary beliefs and practices. Rock art, found at many mesolithic sites, enlivens our understanding of mesolithic communities. All this adds up to a much greater volume of information than is available for the Indian palaeolithic.

One of the features of the Indian mesolithic phase is the spread of settlements to new ecological niches (for site details, see Allchin and Allchin, 1997: 88–110; Chakrabarti, 2006: 98–110; V. D. Misra and Pal. [Eds.]., 2002; Pal, 2014; V. N. Misra, 2019). This is generally seen as a result of an increase in population due to more favourable environmental conditions (increased rainfall) as well as technological innovations. There is a calibrated range of dates from various mesolithic sites, e.g., Bhimbetka (6556–6177 BCE; 4895–4580 BCE), Baghor (7416–6622 BCE; 4246–3991 BCE), Bagor (5418–4936 BCE; 4575–4344 BCE), Sarai Nahar Rai (9958–9059 BCE), and Paisra (6377–6067 BCE). Barkhera has given a date of 5520+/-130 BCE, Adamgarh 5505+/-125 BCE, and Damdama has given two dates —6690+/-65 BCE and 6915+/-65 BCE.

A large number of mesolithic sites have been identified in the northern Vindhyas and Ganga valley. The transition from a hunting-gathering stage to the beginnings of settled agriculture can be traced at Chopani Mando in the Belan valley (Sharma et al., 1980). Excavations revealed a 1.55 m thick occupational deposit, divided into three periods. The first was epi-palaeolithic, while the second and third were clearly mesolithic. Period II was divided into two phases—IIA and IIB. Period IIA had non-geometric microliths such as blades, points, scrapers, and borers, mostly made of chert. In Period IIB, there were a large number of geometric microliths. The microliths continued into Period III, which was also marked by handmade pottery with cord-impressed patterns, anvils and hammer stones, querns and mullers (used for grinding and food processing), and ring stones. There were bones of wild cattle and sheep/goats. Pieces of burnt clay with reed impressions showed that the mesolithic people of Chopani Mando lived in wattle-and-daub huts. Excavations revealed the outlines of two round huts belonging to Period IIA and five round huts of Period IIB. In Period III, there were remains of 13 round and oval huts, clustered very close to each other. The round huts had an average diameter of 3.3 m, and the oval ones 4.7 x 3.3 m. Outside the huts were three hearths and traces of what seemed to be the bases of storage bins made of bamboo and clay. Wild rice is reported from late mesolithic levels at this site.

FURTHER DISCUSSION | **Animal bones at mesolithic sites**

Bones of wild and domesticated animals have been found at some mesolithic sites. However, there is considerable difference of opinion among experts when it comes to the identification of the animal species.

Bagor (Rajasthan): The mesolithic context here dates to the 5th and 4th millennia BCE. There are differences in opinion about the identification of the animal bones. P. K. Thomas identified domesticated cattle (15.7 per cent of the identifiable bones in the assemblage) and sheep/goats (64.4 per cent; it is not always possible to distinguish between sheep and goat bone fragments). The site also yielded bones of wild boar and pig (3.7 per cent), buffalo (0.8 per cent), blackbuck and gazelle (4.4 per cent), spotted deer (4.8 per cent), *sambar* (4.3 per cent), hare (0.6 per cent), Indian grey mongoose (0.8 per cent) and Indian fox (0.5 per cent). Other species include porcupine, rat, tortoise, fish, and frog. D. R. Shah does not mention the occurrence of such domesticated species, but lists river turtle and monitor lizard.

Tilwara (Barmer district, Rajasthan): According to V. N. Misra, the late mesolithic level (its dates are uncertain) gave evidence of wild goat, a canid (jackal or dog), pig, spotted deer, hog deer, mongoose, and domesticated humped cattle. Thomas only reported cattle and goat/sheep from this site.

Langhnaj (north Gujarat): The mesolithic context in which the animal bones were found was dated 2550–2185 BCE. Only wild animals were represented. These include a canid (probably wolf), mongoose, rhinoceros, wild boar, *chital*, hog deer, swamp deer, *nilgai*, and blackbuck. The presence of wild buffalo or wild cattle has also been suggested. V. N. Misra suggested that the climate of the area during mesolithic times must have been arid. However, the presence of the rhinoceros and the possible presence of the water buffalo go against this theory. The rhinoceros is known to prefer large stretches of marshland and grassland. The animal bones at Langhnaj suggest that the area was covered by a combination of savannah and forest with interspersed wetlands.

Kanewal (north Gujarat): This site has given evidence of bones of rhinoceros, buffalo, spotted deer, swamp deer, *nilgai*, and wild boar. Bones of domesticated cattle, sheep, and goats have also been identified. The occurrence of camel bones is interesting and shows contact with people using these animals.

Loteshwar and Ratanpur (north Gujarat): Bones of domesticated sheep, goats, and cattle have been reported from these sites.

Adamgarh (MP): Bones of domesticated cattle, sheep, goat, pig, and dog have been reported here, along with those of wild animals such as spotted deer, *barasingha*, *sambar*, porcupine, hare, lizard, and a species of the genus *Equus*. There are two very different radiocarbon dates for these finds, one falling in the 6th millennium BCE, the other in the 1st millennium BCE. Due to the uncertain dates and stratigraphy of the finds, the evidence of early animal domestication at Adamgarh has been questioned.

Bhimbetka (MP): This site has given bones of domesticated cattle along with those of wild animals such as *barasingha*, hog deer, and rhinoceros. It is interesting to note that mesolithic paintings at this site have representations of Indian humped cattle (zebu) as well as its wild progenitor, *Bos namadicus*.

Sarai Nahar Rai, Mahadaha, and Damdama (UP): The faunal evidence from these sites is controversial. K. R. Alur identified wild cattle and sheep/goat. According to U. C. Chattopadhyaya, there is no evidence of sheep or goats, wild or domesticated, at these three sites. Thomas and Joglekar identified over 30 species including cattle, *gaur*, goat, gazelle, *chital*, *sambar*, barking deer, mouse deer, rhinoceros, wild boar, pygmy hog, hippopotamus, elephant, wolf, jackal, sloth bear, porcupine, rat, and bandicoot. No domesticated animals are represented.

Chopani Mando (UP): Bones of wild cattle and goat/sheep are reported from this site.

Source Chattopadhyaya, 2002

The three excavated sites of Sarai Nahar Rai, Mahadaha, and Damdama lie very close to each other. Sarai Nahar Rai (in Pratapgarh district, UP) is located on the banks of a dried oxbow lake which marks an old course of the Ganga. Geometric microliths were found here, along with shells and animal bones (of bison, rhinoceros, stag, fish, and tortoise). Within the habitation area, there were 11 human burials in oblong pits—those of 9 men, 4 women, and a child. The age of the men was estimated to be in the range of 16–35 years, and that of the women 15–35 years. One of the buried skeletons had an arrow embedded in its ribs. A multiple burial contained the remains of four persons. Microlithic tools, animal bones, and shells were placed in graves as grave goods. An analysis of the skeletal material revealed that the dental health of the people was on the whole good, but that some of them suffered from osteo-arthritis. The mesolithic level at Sarai Nahar Rai has been dated *c.* 8400 ± 150 BCE by the radiocarbon method.

Mahadaha is also on the banks of an oxbow lake. Excavations revealed a 60 cm thick occupational deposit and distinct areas associated with habitation and

FURTHER DISCUSSION | **Graves, subsistence, and settlement patterns**

Umesh C. Chattopadhyaya has explored the connections between the emergence of formal burials among hunter-gatherers and the subsistence patterns and settlements of the mesolithic Ganga valley. His study is based on the faunal remains and burials at Sarai Nahar Rai, Mahadaha, and Damdama.

An initial study of Sarai Nahar Rai suggested that the site was occupied seasonally and that in summer, groups living in the Vindhyan stretches migrated into the Ganga valley due to water and food scarcity. Excavations at Mahadaha and Damdama led to a questioning of this hypothesis, largely on the basis of the thickness of the occupational deposits and the occurrence of many heavy non-transportable grinding stones. Chattopadhyaya has carried forward this questioning.

This area had diverse food resources. The plant remains at Damdama suggest the availability of various types of wild edible plants. The animal bones found at these sites included those of wild animals exploited for food. The subsistence base of the mesolithic people had a special emphasis on the hunting of swamp deer (*Cervus duvauceli*) and hog deer (*Axis procinus*) and must have been supplemented by an intensive use of aquatic resources such as tortoise and fish.

Mahadaha and Damdama yielded teeth of hog deer and swamp deer. As the breeding season of these animals is known, April and July can be identified as the months of birth of the two species respectively. On the basis of the analysis of some of the teeth remains, the age of the animal at the time it was killed and the month in which this happened can be ascertained. This gives us an idea about the months/seasons in which the sites were occupied by humans. Chattopadhyaya's analysis of such teeth remains shows that Mahadaha and Damdama were occupied during summer as well as winter. The presence of a commensal species (one that depends on humans for its food) such as bandicoot rat (*Bandicota bengalensis*) at these sites is also significant, as this species cannot establish itself at a habitation site unless food is available to it all year round.

The evidence of burials at the three sites confirms the above conclusions. All three display similar burial practices—the bodies were buried in shallow rectangular graves, usually in an extended position. Male burials outnumber female burials; there are a few instances of child burials at Mahadaha and Damdama. Differences in grave goods suggest some level of social ranking. At Mahadaha, the cemetery-cum-habitation area revealed 35 pit-hearths containing burnt clay, ash, and charred animal bones, which seem to have been associated with funerary rituals. What is most significant for Chattopadhyaya's argument is the orientation of the burials. With a few exceptions at Damdama, the graves were broadly aligned west–east or east–west. Archaeological and anthropological evidence suggests that it is likely that they were aligned towards the point of sunrise or sunset at the time of burial. The precise points of the east–west orientation would have varied to some extent in summer and winter. Many of the burials at these sites fall broadly within the calculated range of the annual solar path across the horizon, suggesting that burials took place both in summer and in winter. This too indicates that the sites were occupied all year round.

Anthropologists have identified a close relationship between the designation of formal areas for the disposal of the dead and the existence of corporate group rights over critical resources. These rights are based on lineal descent from deceased ancestors. The mesolithic burials of Mahadaha are suggestive of this sort of situation. But what were the reliable but restricted resources over which these people may have tried to stake their claim through descent? Chattopadhyaya suggests that they consisted of aquatic resources such as tortoise and fish, which have rich nutritional value and are very productive and reliable food resources. The growing population in the Ganga valley during the mesolithic phase may have led to competition and conflict over these resources. This may have been the impetus for people to come together and function as corporate groups and to stake their claim to territory through burial practices and burial symbolism.

Source Chattopadhyaya, 1996

butchering. The microliths were made of chert, quartz, chalcedony, crystal, and agate, all of which must have been brought over fairly long distances across the river from the Vindhyas. Twenty-eight burials of 30 individuals, including two instances of a man and woman buried together, were found within the habitation area. The burials were elliptical and their base sloping. The grave goods included microliths, shells, burnt pieces of animal bones, bone arrowheads and rings, and ochre pieces. The bones found in the butchering area included those of wild cattle, hippopotamus, deer, pigs, and turtles. Thousands of animal bones were found in the lake area. The mesolithic people of Mahadaha were tall (men were up to 1.90 m and women 1.62–1.76 m). Their dental health was good, but many of them suffered from osteo-arthritis. Of the 17 males, 7 females, and 3 children identified in the skeletal record, 5 represented persons less than 18 years old, 6 belonged to the 18–40 age group, and only 1 (a female) represented a person between 40–50 years old. These figures provide an idea of average life expectancy.

NEW DIRECTIONS IN RESEARCH | **The journey to get chalcedony**

The general picture of the mesolithic phase is one of small, mobile bands of people exploiting the resources available in their environment with their microlithic tools. Recent studies have indicated that the reality was far more complex. Gurcharan S. Khanna's study of chalcedony at Bagor in eastern Rajasthan has highlighted how a focus on this one raw material reveals patterns of movement, exchange, and resource procurement. Here are some of the findings:

1. The microliths of Bagor are mostly made of chert and quartz, but some are of chalcedony. Tools made of quartz form about 79 per cent of the total stone tool assemblage, those made of chert about 20 per cent, and chalcedony tools about 1 per cent. However, if only the finished tools are considered, the percentages are different—chert tools represent the greater proportion and quartz tools are much less. The proportion of chalcedony finished tools is variable but not insignificant; this stone was preferred for making smaller blade tools.
2. Chalcedony is a member of a group of crypto-crystalline minerals, which includes chert, jasper, opal, flint, agate, and carnelian. Compared to other rocks, chalcedony has higher water content and a fibrous grain structure. These qualities make it easy to control flaking and to make standardized tools, especially small ones. This is why mesolithic people may have preferred chalcedony over other stones for making such tools.
3. While chert and quartz are available within walking distance, the chalcedony found in this area is of poor quality. Good quality chalcedony is available in the Deccan Traps, 90 km to the south-east of Bagor. That is probably the area from where the mesolithic people obtained it.
4. There could have been another reason for moving south-eastwards seasonally. Bagor is located on the eastern side of the Aravalli hills, which is an intermediate zone as far as rainfall is concerned. The mesolithic people of Bagor may have moved south-eastwards in the dry post-monsoon season in order to find grazing land for their animals (there is evidence of animal domestication at this site).
5. The people of Bagor could have obtained chalcedony from the Deccan Traps either through direct procurement or through exchange with intermediate groups.
6. In the later part of the mesolithic phase, there is evidence of copper. It is possible that the introduction of copper at this site had to do with the interaction of its people with the farmers and metallurgists of Ahar, a settlement which lay at considerable distance to its south.

Source Khanna, 1993

Damdama is situated at the confluence of a small stream belonging to the Sai river system. Within the 1.5 m thick occupational deposit, excavators discovered microliths, bone objects, querns and mullers, anvils, and hammer stones. There were hearths, patches of burnt floor plaster, charred wild grain, and animal bones. There were 4 multiple burials (of a male and female) among the 41 human burials. In one of the graves, an ivory pendant was found among the grave goods. Dates for Damdama fall within the early 7th millennium BCE. Recently, domesticated rice has been reported from mesolithic levels at this site.

Rock shelters excavated at Lekhahia (in Mirzapur district of southern UP) have yielded blade tools and microliths. There is a clear tendency of tools to become progressively smaller in the upper levels of the deposit. Burials were found, and so was pottery. Baghai Khor is another rock shelter site in the same area. This has a pre-ceramic and a ceramic microlithic phase. Two **extended burials** were identified, the first belonging to the pre-ceramic phase and the second to the ceramic phase.

A 105 sq m section of a mesolithic floor was excavated at Paisra. Apart from microliths, there was evidence of large and small fireplaces positioned very close to each other. The thinness of the deposit suggests a short period of mesolithic occupation.

Birbhanpur is close to the Damodar river in Burdwan district in West Bengal. Mesolithic stone tools made of quartz, some of chert and chalcedony, were found here. This seems to have been both a habitation and a factory site. A study has shown that the climate during the mesolithic phase at Birbhanpur was drier than in the immediately preceding phase, which was more wet and humid.

Bagor (in Bhilwara district of eastern Rajasthan) is one of the best documented mesolithic sites. It is located on a sand dune, about 25 km west of Bhilwara in Rajasthan, close to the Kothari river. The three occupational levels represented continuous human occupation over more than 5,000 years. Period I (*c.* 5000–2800 BCE, according to radiocarbon dates) was labelled mesolithic, Period II (*c.* 2800–600 BCE) chalcolithic, and Period III (*c.* 600 BCE–200 BCE) gave evidence of iron. The 2000–01 excavations, which brought to light further information about the mesolithic period, revised the dates and suggested on the basis of calibrated radiometric dates that it be subdivided into two phases—a-ceramic (beginning in 5700–4500 BCE) and ceramic (*c.* 4500–3500 BCE). Microliths were found in the greatest numbers in Period I but continued into the later phases as well. The microliths of Period I were mostly made of locally available chert and quartz. Most of them were made on blades and they included a large number of geometric microliths such as triangles and trapezes. House floors paved with stone slabs were found, and in some places, there was evidence of roughly circular arrangements of stone that may have marked the outlines of shelters. Certain stone-paved areas with a large number of animal bones were probably butchering areas. Only one burial was unearthed and there was no definite evidence of grave goods. Other discoveries included ring stones (perhaps used as hammer stones to make microliths), pieces of red ochre, querns, and rubbing stones (for grinding food). Bones of wild animals included those of wild cattle, two kinds of deer, pigs, jackals, rats, monitor lizards, turtles, and fish; bones of domesticated sheep/goats and cattle were also reported. There is a possibility that small bits of pottery found at the site may belong to the mesolithic phase.

Arunima Kashyap (2006) undertook a wear analaysis of stone tools at Bagor using reflected light Scanning Electron Microscope (SEM) along with Energy Dispersive Analysis (EDS), and starch grain analysis of tools and soil samples to document continuities and change in subsistence practices from the a-ceramic mesolithic phase (*c.* 5700–4500 BCE) to the ceramic phase (*c.* 4500–3500 BCE). Use wear analysis indicated the increasing use of tools on various kinds of plants. This suggests that while hunting and meat and fish processing continued during the ceramic phase, there was a significant increase in plant processing activities, suggesting intensified plant use and incipient agriculture. Kashyap argues that in view of this, along with traces of copper residue found on the edges of three microliths, the use of the label 'mesolithic' for Period I at Bagor seems to be a misnomer.

Microliths have been found in the valleys of the Tapi, Narmada, Mahi, and Sabarmati. One of the important sites is Langhnaj. The occupational deposit here was divided into three periods. Period I was mesolithic and yielded microliths, human burials, bones of wild animals, and some potsherds. Mehtakheri in the Narmada valley has given evidence of microliths dated to as early as 48,000 years ago, the earliest date so far for microliths in the subcontinent.

Adamgarh hill near Hoshangabad has already been mentioned among the palaeolithic sites of Central India. Its upper layers represented a mesolithic level, which in turn made way for a neolithic–chalcolithic one. Shells found between 15–21 cm from the top of the mesolithic deposit were dated by the radiocarbon method to *c.* 5500 BCE, so the mesolithic level belongs at least to the 6th millennium BCE. Thousands of microliths were found here, mostly made of chert, chalcedony, jasper, and agate, raw materials which are available in the riverbed of the Narmada about 2 km away. Geometric microliths (triangles and trapezes) were very common. Mace heads or ring stones and hammer stones were also found. The wild animal bones comprised those of the hare, lizard, various kinds of deer, and porcupine. Bones of domesticated cattle, sheep, goat, dog, and pig have also been reported, but this evidence has been questioned. This site has given evidence of pottery at mesolithic levels.

Painting of boar, Bhimbetka (after Neumayer, 1983)

Baghor II in the Son valley has already been mentioned in the discussion of the palaeolithic sites of Central India. This site also has a mesolithic phase. The tools are of chert and chalcedony, and geometric microliths occur. Fragments of grinding stones, one hammer stone, and pieces of red ochre were found. There were very few finished stone tools, and as much as 96.7 per cent of the total mesolithic lithic material that was

RECENT DISCOVERIES | **Prehistoric hunter-gatherers in the Sri Lankan rain forests**

Caves and rock shelters excavated in Sri Lanka, belonging to the late Pleistocene and early/middle Holocene eras, have provided important evidence for understanding the life of prehistoric hunter-gatherers in South Asia. Fa-Hien Lena is a large cave in Yatagampitiya village in the Kalutara District of the Western Provinces in the tropical evergreen forest in the southwestern part of Sri Lanka. Another important site in the Wet Zone is Batadomba Lena which has yielded a stone tool assemblage starting from *c.* 38,000–36,000 cal. BP. Both Batadomba-lena and Fa-Hien Cave have yielded early fossil remains of *Homo sapiens*, stone tools, and abundant faunal remains, representing the life-ways of prehistoric hunter-gatherers living thousands of years ago in the Sri Lankan tropical rainforests.

Fa-Hien Lena was first excavated during 1986–88 and later, between 2009 and 2012. The earlier excavations at the site revealed the fossil remains of a 5.5–6.6 year old child, along with the remains of at least two infants and a young woman, which were dated (on the basis of associated charcoal) to 30,000 +/- 60 BP. Later excavations confirmed the early dates and divided the occupation at the site into four phases. This site has given some of the earliest evidence of dated microliths (mostly made of quartz) and bone tool technology in South Asia.

Microliths are often thought to have appeared at the end of the Pleistocene or the beginning of the Holocene, but there is increasing evidence of earlier beginnings. In European prehistory, these small stone tools have been linked to the hunting of medium and large sized game in grasslands or woodlands, or as adaptations to environmental challenges created due to climatic change. The recent multi-disciplinary study of the Fa-Hien cave shows that the microlith assemblage remained fairly stable over a long period of time (*c.* 48,000 to 45,000 cal. BP to 4,000 cal. BP) and that it was connected with the procurement of small to medium size semi-arborial and arboreal prey and rain forest plants. Remains of rainforest mammals, reptiles, molluscs, and plants have been documented at the site. A total of 14,485 bone and teeth fragments were analyzed, and over half were identified. Small mammals dominated the faunal assemblage throughout, and included carnivores such as the civet cat. Monkeys and tree squirrels accounted for over 70% of the total faunal remains in all periods of occupation. Evidence of cut marks and charring on bones indicate that these animals were hunted and killed for food. Animal bones were also used to make tools.

The fact that the Fa-Hien cave stone tool assemblage did not change significantly over the long period of occupation of the site, from the late Pleistocene into the Holocene indicates that it represents a stable and successful adaptation to the tropical environment. The evidence also shows that microliths were part of a flexible and diverse tool kit, and were made and used in diverse ecological settings.

Source Wedage, et al., 2019, 2019a

Dancers, Lakhajoar (after Neumayer, 1983)

excavated consisted of waste material of stone tool working. This suggests that the tools were made here and taken away to other places. The location of five or six large shelters can be identified by a series of post-holes. Three hoof prints of a *sambar* deer were preserved in the excavated deposit.

Bhimbetka has also already been mentioned in the section on palaeolithic sites. The site shows a gradual reduction in the size of tools. Mesolithic tools include blades and geometric microliths like triangles, trapezes, and crescents. Quartz was used a great deal in the palaeolithic stage, but in the mesolithic phase there was a shift to chalcedony. Bhimbetka is famous for its mesolithic paintings, which will be discussed further on.

In peninsular India, microlithic sites found in the vicinity of Mumbai seem to represent coastal mesolithic communities who exploited marine resources for food. Microliths have been found in other parts of Maharashtra as well. Further south, the microliths are mostly made out of milky quartz. They have been found at Jalahalli and Kibbanhalli near Bengaluru in Karnataka, in Goa, and at Nagarjunakonda (in southern AP), and Renigunta (in Chittoor district, AP). Jwalapuram Locality 9, a rock shelter site in Andhra Pradesh, has yielded over 53,000 microliths in upper palaeolithic levels that go back to about 35,000 BP.

Microliths occur at many places along the east coast of India and seem to mark camps of mesolithic fishing communities. South of Chennai, tiny stone tools, mostly of quartz and chert, have been found on old sand dunes known as *teris*. On the Visakhapatnam coast, stone tablets and ring stones have been found at sites such as Chandrampalem, Paradesipalem, and Rushikonda. Similar stones are used today by local fishermen in the area as net sinkers. Apart from the coastal areas, rock shelters, flat hilltops, river valleys, and lakesides were also inhabited during the mesolithic phase.

The island of Sri Lanka is rich in prehistoric remains (see Deraniyagala, [1988] 2004; Perera, 2010; Kulatilake, 2016). During periods of lower sea levels, Sri Lanka was connected for long periods of time to the mainland. The evidence suggests the arrival of *Homo sapiens* during the late Pleistocene, around 40,000 years ago. Upper palaeolithic tools have been found at Bundala on the southeastern coastal region. The more prolific and dramatic evidence, however, occurs in a microlithic context, especially in caves and rock shelters in the rain forest area at Fa-Hien Lena, Batadomba Lena and Belilena Kitugala, which have been assigned dates between 40,000 to 8,000 years ago. Human skeletal remains found at Fa-Hien Lena (in western Sri Lanka) in association with non-geometric microliths have been dated to about 37,000 years ago. The human remains at Batadomba Lena and Belilena Kitugala are associated with geometric microliths. The skeletal remains from these sites are the oldest remains of anatomically modern humans found so far in South Asia. Burials with grave goods are indicative of modern human behaviour. At Fa-Hien Lena, there is a burial sequence stretching from the late Pleistocene to the middle/late Holocene. The open air site of Bellanbandi Palassa in the dry southeastern plains has revealed the remains of at least 16 individuals.

The evidence from mesolithic sites from different parts of the subcontinent suggests movement and interaction among communities. Factory sites located at sources of raw materials must have been meeting grounds for different groups. The fact that mesolithic tools found north and south of the Ganga are made of the same kinds of stone indicates that either the raw materials or the tools themselves were moved across the river. The mesolithic people of Sarai Nahar Rai, Damdama, and Mahadaha would have had to travel over 75 km to reach the stone resources of the Vindhyas. Clearly, the communities living in the northern alluvial plain and the hill people of the northern fringes of the Vindhyas must have been interacting with each other. In later times, mesolithic communities must have interacted with early agriculturists who lived in their neighbourhood.

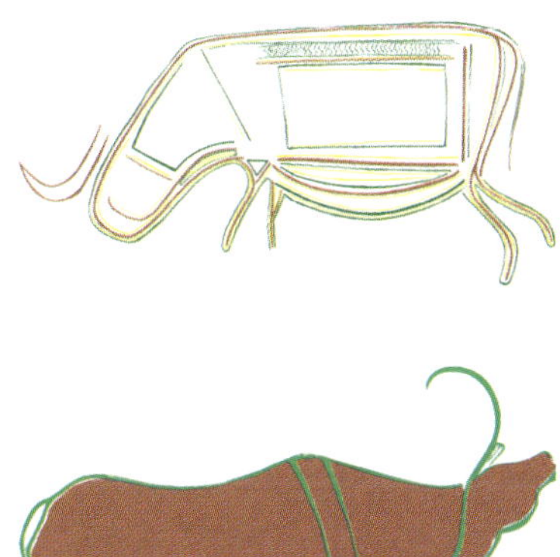

Polychrome boar, Bhimbetka; bull, Jaora (after Neumayer, 1983)

There are many instances of temporary mesolithic camp sites in various parts of the subcontinent, but sites such as Sarai Nahar Rai, Damdama, Mahadaha, and Chopani Mando were inhabited continuously. This can be inferred from the nature of the archaeological evidence and also certain more specialized studies of the faunal material. The evidence from several sites of formal, ceremonial burials, with the bodies usually laid out in a west–east direction (occasionally the other way around) with grave goods suggests rituals associated with death. The presence of grave goods is often taken as an indication of some sort of belief in afterlife. This may well be so, but there is ethnographic evidence of societies in which certain belongings of the deceased are considered to bring bad luck to the living, and these are therefore, buried along with the body. Instances of jewellery found on the body suggest a custom of adorning the body before burial, and may indicate high-rank individuals within the community.

The magnificence of mesolithic art

There are very few examples of portable mesolithic art. A chert core engraved with an interesting geometric design was found at Chandravati in Rajasthan. It is assumed to be mesolithic because lots of microliths have been found at the site. A few engraved bone objects have been discovered at sites such as Bhimbetka. A human tooth with faint geometric marks on it was found in a jaw fragment along with some other teeth.

The most spectacular remains of the mesolithic are rock paintings and engravings (the latter are known as petroglyphs). The first rock paintings in India (and in fact anywhere in the world) were discovered by A. C. L. Carlleyle, an assistant surveyor with the Archaeological Survey of India in 1867–68 at Sohagighat in the Kaimur hills in the present Mirzapur district (UP). Today, hundreds of rock art sites are known in various parts of the subcontinent (for overviews, see Chakravarty. [Ed.], 1984; Neumayer, 1983, 1993; Giriraj Kumar, 2014; Ajit Kumar. [Ed.], 2015). These are an important source of information on the lives of prehistoric communities and show some similarities but also several variations.

Bovine animal, Kathotia; elephant, Lakhajoar (after Neumayer, 1983)

Lakhajoar: Hunting scene; feeding a pig and preparing food, Kathotia (after Neumayer, 1983)

In 1957, the archaeologist V. S. Wakankar noticed the Bhimbetka rocks out of a train window while travelling from Bhopal to Itarsi and got off at the nearest railway station to explore. This is how one of the most magnificent rock art sites in the world was discovered. Bhimbetka is one of seven hills marked by a very picturesque natural environment. There are 642 rock shelters here, nearly 400 of which have paintings, engravings, and bruisings. Their style, theme, and worn state indicate that they belong to very old times. Mesolithic paintings have also been found at other sites in Madhya Pradesh such as Kharwar, Jaora, Kathotia, and Lakhajoar.

In Europe, most prehistoric paintings tend to be located in dark, relatively inaccessible parts of the caves, but those in Indian rock shelters are usually in well-lit areas and are easily seen. The best paintings were not, however, made in shelters that were living spaces. Some of the big paintings on high surfaces would have required scaffolding and

Lakhajoar: fishing scene; family scene (after Neumayer, 1983)

the cooperation of many people. Such paintings, and those made in layers, suggest some kind of ritualistic significance.

The Bhimbetka paintings have been studied by V. S. Wakankar (2005), Yashodhar Mathpal (1974), and Erwin Neumayer (1983, 1993), and the results of their research illuminate many aspects of the lives of the painters. Mathpal identified three main phases of the rock paintings, with further sub-phases within these. The first five sub-phases are mesolithic, the sixth is transitional, and the last three belong to the historic period. Sixteen colours or shades can be identified, with white and light red used most often. The colours were made from minerals which were ground and then mixed with water or some other substance like animal fat, marrow, or egg white. The red was made out of iron oxide (*geru*), white from limestone, and green may have been made from green chalcedony. Some paintings are monochrome (in one colour), while others are polychrome (in

more than one colour). The handles of brushes must have been made from twigs, and the brush itself out of squirrel tail, animal fur, or *semal* (silk cotton).

As at most mesolithic rock art sites, animals dominate the scenes at Bhimbetka. Twenty-nine species of animals are depicted, including the *chital* (this occurs most often), leopard, tiger, panther, elephant, rhinoceros, antelope, deer, and squirrel. Different kinds of birds, fish, lizards, frogs, crabs, scorpions, and small centipedes also make an appearance. Although the Bhimbetka hillsides are still home to many animals, the elephants, rhinoceroses, lions, wild buffalo, *gaur*, and blackbuck depicted in the mesolithic paintings have disappeared. Bhimbetka was declared a World Heritage Site by UNESCO in 2003.

In mesolithic art at Bhimbetka and elsewhere, animals are represented on their own or as part of hunting scenes. Hunters hunt singly or in groups, sometimes wearing masks and head-dresses crowned with antlers and horns. They are adorned with ornaments such as necklaces, bangles, wrist bands, elbow bands, and knee bands with tassels. Some are unarmed; others carry sticks, spears, bows and arrows, or slings. The hunters are sometimes accompanied by dogs. There are scenes showing traps and snares, others of animals running after hunters.

While some of the animal figures are rather abstract, many of them are very realistic. Animals are sometimes shown in outline; in other instances, their bodies are decorated with designs. A few paintings are in the 'x-ray style', showing the inner organs, including foetuses in the womb of female animals. Apart from hunting scenes, animals appear in more peaceful, sympathetic scenes such as those depicting pregnant animals, a panther or tiger with cubs, stag, and *chital* running after a fawn, grazing buffaloes, rabbits hopping, and monkeys leaping about. There is a lot of movement in the scenes. There are also fantastic animals—the famous Bhimbetka 'boar' has the body of a boar, but a snout like a rhinoceros, the underlip of an elephant, and the horns of a buffalo.

Mesolithic paintings at Bhimbetka and other sites also depict men and women, young and old. Male figures often look like matchsticks, women are sometimes given fuller forms. Some men wear loincloths, probably made of leaves, animal skin, or pieces of tree bark. Men wear their hair loose, women braided. Some figures are broad and decorated with geometric designs, and from their attitude seem to represent men of authority. Masked dancers (referred to by prehistorians as 'dancing sorcerers') may represent ritual specialists. Hand, fist, and finger prints are also found, similar to those that people make on their houses these days on auspicious occasions.

The Bhimbetka paintings reflect a division of labour on the basis of gender. Men hunt and women are shown gathering and preparing food, for instance grinding food on querns. It is difficult to identify what sort of vegetable food was being processed. Basket-like containers must have been used to store food, but no pottery is depicted. Dry gourds and leather bags may have been used to hold water. There are scenes of people collecting fruit and honey. Some scenes depict sexual activity, others show people dancing. The dancers convey a sense of rhythmic movement; occasionally they lose their balance and fall.

Prehistoric rock art sites have been found in many other parts of India as well, including in Ladakh and Kumaon. The importance of the rock art sites in the Vindhyan stretches in Mirzapur district of Uttar Pradesh have been long known, but recent research has revealed new sites (Pratap, 2016).

In Eastern India, rock art sites have been found in Jharkhand and Bihar. Over 55 rock shelters with rock art have been identified in western Odisha, especially in the Sundargarh and Sambalpur districts. Microliths found in some of the rock shelters have confirmed mesolithic occupation in the area. The richest area for rock paintings are the 12 rock shelters of the Lekhamoda group in the reserve forests of Chhengapahad and Garjanpahad. Excavations in one of these rock shelters revealed a cultural sequence from the mesolithic to the chalcolithic. An interesting feature of the rock art of Odisha is the occurrence of paintings and engravings in the same shelter. Also, the art is mostly non-figurative, with an emphasis on abstract patterns and decorative designs, both geometric and non-geometric. Animals occur infrequently and humans are even more rare.

Hunter with basket/net filled with animals, Jaora; pair of hunters, Bhimbetka (from top)

Kerala has many rock art sites with paintings and carvings. One of the oldest is the cave known as Ezhuthu Guha, situated in the midst of a dense sandalwood forest in

Idukki district. Geometric figures predominate and animal and human depictions are infrequent. One problem is that although some of the paintings have been assigned to the late mesolithic phase, no mesolithic tools have been found so far in any of the Kerala rock shelters. Rock art sites are abundant in Andhra Pradesh, Karnataka, and Tamil Nadu as well (Chandramouli, 2002). Many of the rock art sites in the Deccan are dominated by depictions of cattle and seem to belong to a stage of agro-pastoralism.

It is not easy to date rock art. Relative or approximate dating is based on an analysis of theme, content, style, technique, contexts, a careful study of superimpositions, and comparative analysis. There are some scientific ways of dating as well (Bednarik, 2002). Carbon-14 dating can be used to date organic pigments or mineral accretions on the surface on which the art has been made. Deposits or patina on rock art can be dated using thermoluminescence, OSL, and uranium/thorium techniques, giving indirect evidence of the age of the art itself. Examining the art through field microscopy can also give clues about its age. The results of such methods, which have not so far been used much in India are, however, open to interpretation and questioning, as are those based on the more traditional methods. Apart from the problems of dating, other challenges in Indian rock art studies include connecting them with their specific archaeological context, larger landscape, and settlement patterns in the area (see Blinkhorn et al., 2012).

Why did prehistoric people make such paintings and engravings? Probably for many different reasons—to express their creative urges, to decorate their homes, or to tell a story in pictures. Some scenes may be an expression of community identity or solidarity, some may commemorate memorable events. Others may have been associated with rituals connected with hunting or fertility. It is difficult to know whether the paintings were made by men or women, or both. Apart from the scenes of animals and people, there are a few more enigmatic paintings and engravings. Ethnographic evidence is sometimes used by scholars to try to reconstruct various aspects of rock art, but has to be used with great caution.

A very interesting, rather abstract painting has been found in a rock shelter at Jaora (MP). Perhaps it reflects a view of the world consisting of air, earth, and fire. But it is possible that it means something completely different. The mesolithic artist who painted it would have known for sure, but since he/she is not around to tell us, we have to use our imagination to try to unravel its possible meanings. Rock art is an evocative window into the prehistoric mind and prehistoric life, but many aspects of these will always remain mysterious and elusive to the modern investigator.

Abstract painting, Jaora (after Neumayer, 1983)

CONCLUSIONS

Prehistory represents the longest part of the human past, and is associated with the emergence of anatomically modern humans and important developments in stone tool technology and subsistence strategies. Palaeo-environmental studies form the essential background for the reconstruction of the life-ways of prehistoric people. The data on of the lower, middle, and upper palaeolithic phases in the subcontinent is gradually increasing, but still largely consists of stone tools. Mesolithic communities fanned out into new ecological niches and the evidence of rock art provides valuable information about their lives and aesthetic sensibilities. Palaeolithic and mesolithic people obtained their food through hunting and gathering. However, animal bones found at some mesolithic sites indicate that the beginnings of animal domestication can be traced to this phase. The major transition from hunting-gathering to food production based on the domestication of plants and animals is associated with the next cultural stage—the neolithic.

FURTHER READINGS

Allchin, Raymond and Bridget Allchin. 1997. *Origins of a Civilization: The Prehistory and Early Archaeology of South Asia*. New Delhi: Viking. Chapters 3–5.

Bhattacharya, D. K. 1972. *Prehistoric Archaeology*. Delhi: Hindustan Publishing Corporation, pp. 24–46.

Chakrabarti, Dilip K. 2006. *The Oxford Companion to Indian Archaeology: The Archaeological Foundations of Ancient India, Stone Age to AD 13th Century*. Delhi: Oxford University Press. Chapters 2, 3–5.

Chakrabarti, Dilip K. and Makkhan Lal. (Eds.). 2014. *History of Ancient India*. Vol. 1. New Delhi: Vivekanand International Foundation and Aryan Books International.

Hazarika, Manjil. 2017. *Prehistory and Archaeology of Northeast India: Multidisciplinary Investigations in an Archaeological Terra Incognita*. New Delhi: 2017.

Jamir, Tiatoshi and Manjil Hazarika. (Eds.). 2014. *50 Years after Daojali-Hading: Emerging Perspectives in the Archaeology of Northeast India. Essays in Honour of Tarun Chandra Sharma*. New Delhi: Research India Press.

Kennedy, Kenneth A. R. 2000. *God-Apes and Fossil Men: Palaeoanthropology of South Asia*. Ann Arbor: University of Michigan Press.

Kumar, Ajit. (Ed.). 2015. *Rock Art: Recent Researches and New Perspectives (Festschrift to Padma Shri Dr. Yashodhar Mathpal)*. 2 Vols. Delhi: New Bharatiya Book Corporation.

Misra, V. D. and J. N. Pal. (Eds.). 2002. *Mesolithic India*. Allahabad: Allahabad University.

Misra, V. N. 2019. *The Mesolithic Age in South Asia: Tradition and Transition*. New Delhi: Aryan Books International.

Neumayer, Erwin. 1983. *Prehistoric Indian Rock Paintings*. Delhi: Oxford University Press.

Pappu, Shanti, Yanni Gunnell, Kumar Akhilesh, Régis Braucher, Maurice Taieb, François Demory, and Nicolas Thouveny. 2011. 'Early Pleistcene Presence of Acheulian Hominins in South India.' *Science* 331: 1596–99.

Petraglia, Michael D. and Bridget Allchin. (Eds.). 2007. *The Evolution and History of Human Populations in South Asia: Interdisciplinary Studies in Archaeology, Biological Anthropology, Linguistics and Genetics*. Dordrecht: Springer.

Robbins Schug, Gwen and Subhash R. Walimbe. (Eds.). 2016. *A Companion to South Asia in the Past*. Wiley Blackwell. Chaps. 2–8.

Roberts, Alice. 2011. *Evolution: The Human Story*. London: Dorling Kindersley.

Reich, David. 2018. *Who We Are and How We Got Here: Ancient DNA and the new science of the human past*. Oxford: Oxford University Press.

Settar, S. and Ravi Korisettar. (Eds.). n.d. *Prehistory: Archaeology of South Asia*. Archaeology and Interactive Disciplines. Vol. 3. New Delhi: Indian Council of Historical Research and Manohar.

Mesolithic animal paintings showing the X-ray style at Kathotia and Lakhajoar.

CHAPTER 3

The Transition to Food Production: Neolithic, Neolithic–Chalcolithic, and Chalcolithic Villages

c. 7000–2000 BCE

Lahuradeva is a seemingly ordinary village in Sant Kabir Nagar district of Uttar Pradesh, girded on three sides by a large lake, with houses, a modern temple, and *dharamshala* (rest house). But sherds of ancient pottery found on the surface of farmers' fields are clues to its remarkable history. There are also remains of an ancient mound, which rises to a height of about 4 m above the plain, but has been mostly levelled due to agricultural activity. The archaeological potential of Lahuradeva was recognized in the 1980s, and it was excavated by the Uttar Pradesh State Archaeology Department between 2001 and 2006. Core deposits of the lake and palaeobotanical remains were analyzed by the Birbal Sahni Institute of Palaeobotany in Lucknow and the Geology Department of Lucknow University in order to reconstruct the climate and flora of the site. The results of the investigations have changed our understanding of the origins of agriculture in the subcontinent. The site of Mehrgarh in Baluchistan was long recognized as an early centre of plant domestication, where wheat and barley were being grown in the 7th millennium BCE. The remains at Lahuradeva revealed that the middle Ganga valley was an early centre of agriculture based on another crop—rice.

The world's first agricultural villages appeared in *c.* 8000–6000 BCE. West Asia was an early centre of wheat and barley farming, and the earliest domesticated animals in this area included sheep and goats. Early neolithic villages have been identified at Jericho and 'Ain Ghazal in the Jordan valley, Tepe Guran and Ali Kosh in Iran, Çatal Höyük in Turkey, and Abu Hureyra and Çayönü in Syria. In *c.* 7000 BCE, at sites such as Cishan in north China, farmers were growing millet and domesticating pigs, dogs, and chickens. In south China, at sites such as Baliligang, Hemudu, and Tianluoshan, villagers were growing rice and domesticating water buffalos, dogs, and pigs. The excavations at Mehrgarh, which gave evidence of barley and wheat cultivation, and cattle, sheep, and goat domestication, indicated that Baluchistan in South Asia was another zone of early agriculture in the 7th millennium BCE. The evidence from Lahuradeva and other sites in the middle Ganga valley suggests that this was an early centre of rice cultivation.

Over the next few millennia, the domestication of plants and animals was being practised in various other parts of the world as well. The people of Mexico were growing corn, beans, squash, gourds, avocados, and chilli pepper, and were domesticating turkeys, dogs, and honeybees. At about the same time, communities living in the Peruvian highlands were cultivating beans, gourds, tomatoes, and potatoes, and may have domesticated the llama and alpaca. In Southeast Asia, excavations at the Spirit Cave in Thailand revealed several plant species including almond, pepper, cucumber, betel nut, beans, and peas. Although it is not certain whether all of them were cultivated, the wide range of plant remains suggests more than a simple food-gathering community. In sub-Saharan Africa, the cultivation of finger millet, sorghum, rice, teff, and yams, and the domestication of sheep, goats, and cattle came to be established in various ecological niches. The primary domestication of plants and animals took place in areas where the concerned species were native, but these swiftly spread to secondary areas of domestication in different parts of the world (see Bellwood, 2005).

The Neolithic Age and the Beginnings of Food Production

The domestication of animals and plants was the outcome of a long series of collective experiments involving many generations of men, women, and children, stretching out over hundreds, perhaps thousands, of years. We will never know the names of the people who

Map 3.1 Centres of agriculture

took part in these experiments and made the critical choices and changes in their strategies of obtaining food. But the processes they set in motion marked one of the greatest achievements of humankind. Archaeological evidence records a fairly late stage in the story of animal and plant domestication, when it was already well underway. Although many details of these processes still elude us, it is possible to reconstruct various aspects of the transition from hunting-gathering to domestication in different parts of the world.

The domestication of plants and animals marked a special kind of human interference in nature and a new stage in the relationship between people, plants, and animals. It involved removing plants and animals from their natural habitat, a process of selective breeding and rearing under artificial conditions under human control for purposes of human gain. There are differences between plant collection and plant domestication, and between animal keeping and animal domestication. When grain is harvested and *all* of it is consumed, this is a stage of food collection. If, after harvesting, some grain is consumed for food and the rest put aside and later intentionally planted, this is the stage of plant domestication. When certain species of animals are captured and kept, this is a stage of animal keeping. When wild animals are removed from their natural habitat and maintained and bred under artificial conditions by people for their profit, this is the stage of animal breeding or domestication.

It is possible to identify gradual shifts in the balance of subsistence strategies from hunting and gathering towards animal rearing and agriculture. For instance, the background to the beginnings of plant domestication was the transition from simple foraging (food collection) to complex foraging, the latter representing a stage of intensive exploitation of wild plants. The next stage was that of incipient (early) agriculture, which, over time, led to the stage of developed agriculture. In the long run, such shifts were associated with technological changes, greater food availability, a rise in population, an increase in the number and size of human settlements, and more complex social and political organization.

Hundreds, probably thousands, of years must have elapsed between the initial domestication of plants and animals in an area and the increased reliance of people on these resources for their food. A distinction can be made between societies in which a small amount of food is obtained through animal and/or plant domestication and those which obtain a significant or substantial amount of food through these activities. It is the latter that can be described as food producing societies. A working definition of a **food-producing society** is one which meets at least half its food needs for at least part of the year through the domestication of animals and/or plants, in a context wherein animals and plants are not tied to their natural habitat. Of course, since precise statistics are unavailable for ancient societies, the extent to which a group depended on domestication for its food can only be gauged subjectively.

In the classification of the stone age, the neolithic age is associated with innovations in stone tool technology, specifically the making of ground, pecked, and polished stone tools and the advent of food production. Changes in stone tools were related to shifts in subsistence strategies. Other features of the neolithic phase include the invention of pottery, a greater degree of sedentary living, the emergence of small and relatively self-sufficient village communities, and a division of labour based on sex. V. Gordon Childe coined the phrase **neolithic revolution** to highlight the enormous significance of these changes. This was a gradual revolution, which took place several times in different regions, with varied features and results.

Why Domestication?

After thousands and thousands of years of hunting and gathering, why did some groups of people start domesticating animals and plants? One of the earliest attempts to answer this question was made by V. Gordon Childe (1952), who suggested that environmental changes at the end of the Pleistocene were the impetus towards food production. Childe argued that about 10,000 years ago, the climate in parts of West Asia became drier due to a northward shift of the summer rains. This desiccation (i.e., drying up) led to a concentration of people, plants, and animals close to water resources such as rivers and oases. This enforced closeness eventually led to new relationships of dependence between humans, plants, and animals, resulting in domestication.

Childe's theory was questioned by Robert J. Braidwood (1960), who rejected the focus on environmental change as the crucial factor leading to agriculture. He pointed out that environmental changes had occurred *within* the Pleistocene as well and had not led to agriculture. Braidwood argued that domestication took place in certain **nuclear zones**, which supported a variety of wild plants and animals that had the potential for domestication. In such areas, domestication was the natural outcome of human experimentation and people getting to know their environment better. This theory does not really explain the pressures or incentives that may have led to domestication. There is ethnographic evidence of many hunting-gathering communities who know their environment very well and are even aware of agriculture, but do not see the point of practising it themselves. There have to be good reasons for a community to radically change its way of life.

Braidwood's theory was rejected by Lewis R. Binford (1968) on the grounds that it could not be archaeologically tested, and that there are some specific, concrete factors that can explain the beginnings of agriculture. Binford asserted that ethnographic evidence indicates that in areas where environment and population have remained constant, a stable balance between the human population and food resources is achieved and people do not have to look for new sources or strategies of getting food. Such groups in fact tend to live at food consumption levels far below the resource potential of their environment. Two factors can upset the balance between people and food: stress produced by environmental change or by demographic (population) growth. Binford identified two kinds of demographic stress—internal demographic stress, which occurs when the number of people within a community increase; and external demographic stress, caused by immigration into an area by people from another area.

In the context of the origins of agriculture, Binford emphasized external demographic stress. He argued that at the end of the Pleistocene era, as a result of a rise in sea levels, people living along the coasts migrated to less populated inland areas. This upset the people–food equilibrium in inland areas and gave an impetus to the search for new strategies to increase food supplies. The problem is that evidence of a migration of people from the world's sea coasts to inland areas at the end of the Pleistocene is lacking. Internal demographic stress may have been a factor in upsetting the people–food balance in some areas, but a question that can be raised is: can we really talk about 'over-population' and 'food crisis' in times when human communities were small and resources abundant?

Kent Flannery (1969) shifted the focus from the search for an event that might have led to the beginnings of food production to the *process* of food production itself and the adaptive advantages of plant and animal domestication over foraging and hunting. He distinguished two types of food procurement systems—negative and positive feedback food procurement systems. **Negative feedback food procurement systems** involve a balanced exploitation and use of various food resources within an area and discourage any change. **Positive feedback systems** are those in which the productivity of resources actually *increases* as a result of human interference and exploitation.

Flannery gave the example of the maize plant: When people transplanted maize from areas within its natural habitat to other areas, over time the plants responded to the process of domestication by a series of changes such as an increase in the size of the cob and in the number of grains. Genetic changes resulting from the process of cross-fertilization increased the productivity of this resource, and once people recognized this increased productivity, they turned more and more towards the domestication of maize. This hypothesis explains why people found agriculture more advantageous than food gathering, but it does not explain why the initial experiments in domestication were made in the first place.

Recent studies have suggested that the key may in fact lie in environmental change, although not the sort suggested many years ago by Childe. The extinction of big game, which took place in Europe, was not really a factor in zones of early agriculture such as West Asia. Here, gazelles, wild cattle, onagers (wild ass), deer, and wild goats remained the main sources of meat during much of the Pleistocene as well as in the early Holocene. On the other hand, what does seem to be relevant is the fact that in many parts of the world, the Holocene was marked by the onset of a milder, warmer, wetter climate. Such changes may have led to an expansion of the natural habitat area of wild cereals that had the potential for domestication. Perhaps it was not an environmental crisis but environmental amelioration that was responsible for the beginnings of domestication.

Given the limitations of the evidence and the fact that we are looking at very slow, gradual processes that must have varied in pace and detail, we may never be able to fully comprehend the details of the initial stages in the processes of animal and plant domestication or identify the impulses that lay behind them. It should also be remembered that in the case of complex cultural processes, the archaeological evidence often provides little 'hard data' on social and political factors that may have had an important role to play. More important than isolating a single factor responsible for the origins of domestication is to try to track down the process as it unfolded in different regions. Given the variety in ecology and resources in the various centres of early plant and animal domestication, it is very possible that different factors may have operated in different parts of the world.

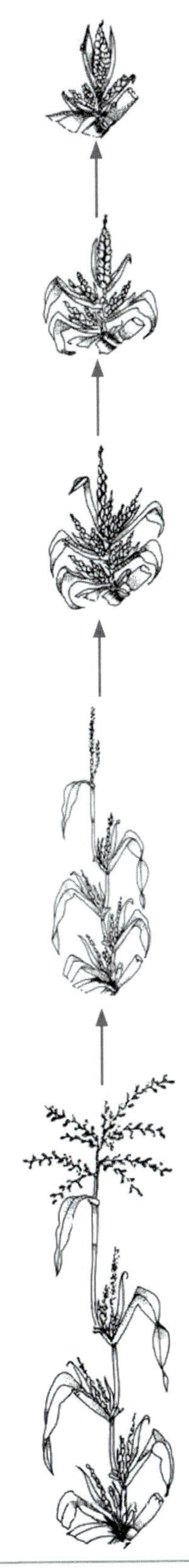

Figure 3.1 The evolution of maize from the wild grass *teosinte*; the number of grains in the cob gradually increased and the husks eventually became enclosures for corn ears

The Identification of Domestication and Food Production in the Archaeological Record

When wild animals or plants are domesticated over long periods of time, certain morphological changes (i.e., changes in their form) tend to take place. In the case of animals, early domesticates tend to be smaller than their wild counterparts (later, when conditions of feeding and breeding reach an optimal level, their size tends to increase).

The face becomes shorter in relation to the cranium. There are changes in dental structure—teeth become smaller, some teeth (such as the premolars and third molars) may disappear. Horns tend to reduce in size. Domesticated cattle have weak muscle ridges and poorly defined joint facets, while in the case of draught animals there is a strengthening of certain muscles. Domestication also leads to a shortening of the animal's hair and changes in its coloration.

Morphological changes of the sort listed above appear only when domestication has been underway for a long time and will not be apparent in the early stages. For example, it has been estimated that it took *thousands* of years of domestication for such changes to become apparent in the case of the horse, while they were faster in the case of cattle, goats, and sheep. Nevertheless, once such changes manifest themselves, it is usually possible for scientists to study the animal bones and teeth found at an archaeological site and to identify not only the animal they represent, but also whether this animal was wild or domesticated. The task of identifying the bones of a domesticated variety of an animal is made easier if bones of wild or transitional forms are also present at the site.

Apart from the direct scientific analysis of animal bones, there are other ways of inferring animal domestication. Animals found outside their natural habitat—for instance, mountain goats found in the plains—suggest domestication. Age and sex ratios reflected in the faunal assemblage can also provide important clues. In the wild, the male–female proportion among animals is 1:1. However, when they are bred, males and castrates are killed quite young and females are killed in old age. These patterns can be identified in the faunal record.

Just as in the case of animals, wild and domesticated plant grains and seeds can also be differentiated. Under conditions of domestication, over a long period of time, plants undergo certain morphological changes. For example, the grains of wild wheat and barley are larger than those of domesticated varieties. Wild varieties of wheat and barley have brittle ears and fragile spikes and their ears break apart immediately on reaching maturity. This is the natural way in which plants maximize their seed dispersal. In the case of domesticated wheat and barley, on the other hand, the ears break up only at the stage of threshing. Not all plants have an equally good chance of surviving or being recognized in the archaeological record. Root crops such as potatoes and yams lack hard parts and are, therefore, less likely to survive. Further, since they reproduce asexually, they do not necessarily undergo significant genetic changes during the process of domestication, and they may have so many different varieties that it is difficult to distinguish between wild and domesticated ones.

Direct evidence of plant domestication can be obtained by a careful analysis of grains or seeds found at a site, especially those that get carbonized due to contact with fire. Even an analysis of impressions of grain or husk on lumps of clay or pottery can help identify domestication.

Indirect evidence of animal or plant domestication can be inferred from art remains such as representations of people capturing or tending animals, harvesting grain, or processing food. However, none of these are conclusive. Animal capture could indicate hunting, tending animals could reflect a stage of animal keeping, and harvesting grain and food processing are perfectly compatible with a stage of food collection. Certain kinds of artefacts and tools such as grinding stones and sickles are sometimes taken as indicative of plant domestication, but their evidence is not conclusive. Grinding stones can be used to grind collected wild grain and sickles can be used to reap wild plants. Evidence from the natural sciences—the analysis of pollen grains, molluscs, remains of insects, etc.—can indicate changes in land use and indirectly, the presence or absence of agriculture.

However, ascertaining the food-producing status of a community is more difficult and subjective. While some sites give clear evidence of the importance of animal and/or plant domestication in their subsistence base, in many more cases, there is insufficient evidence to make an assessment. In fact, in the Indian subcontinent, sites are often labelled 'neolithic' simply on the basis of the presence of ground and polished stone tools.

PRIMARY SOURCES | The analysis of ancient plant remains

The study of ancient plant remains is known as **palaeobotany** or **archaeobotany**. Botanical remains from ancient sites often include macro-botanical remains such as seeds or grains. These can get preserved through desiccation, waterlogging, or charring. It is possible to collect seeds or grains manually in the course of an excavation. However, this can damage them and smaller pieces may be missed. A more efficient method is the use of the flotation technique. There are different kinds of flotation apparatuses, but the basic principle in all of them is the same. This involves slowly and steadily pouring dried carbonized plant material along with its soil matrix into a liquid medium such as water. The inorganic material will sink to the bottom and the carbonized seeds will float on the surface and can be retrieved. These are then collected and analyzed under microscopes to determine what types of plants they represent and whether these were wild or domesticated.

Plant remains can also take the form of micro-botanical remains. Tiny particles of silica called phytoliths are found in certain specific parts of a plant (e.g., the root, stem, or flower). Their recovery from a site can help differentiate between wild and domesticated species. Analysis of plant parenchyma (soft tissue of roundish, thin-walled cells in a plant stem or in the pulp of fruits) can be used for a similar purpose.

Palynology—the analysis of pollen and spores—is another important technique. Pollen are the tiny reproductive bodies of flowering plants. Their strong outer exine (shell) can survive in certain kinds of sediments for thousands of years. Scientists can study pollen grains under microscopes and identify the plants they belong to. Changes in pollen profiles in different archaeological layers may suggest climatic change, forest clearance, or agriculture.

These days, several new techniques are available. For instance, it is possible to directly date tiny pieces of squash seeds and maize cobs through the use of accelerator mass spectrometric (AMS) dating. DNA studies can identify the chromosome structure in different plant genotypes. This can help establish links between domesticated and wild species of plants and identify the area where wild progenitors of domesticated species were originally located.

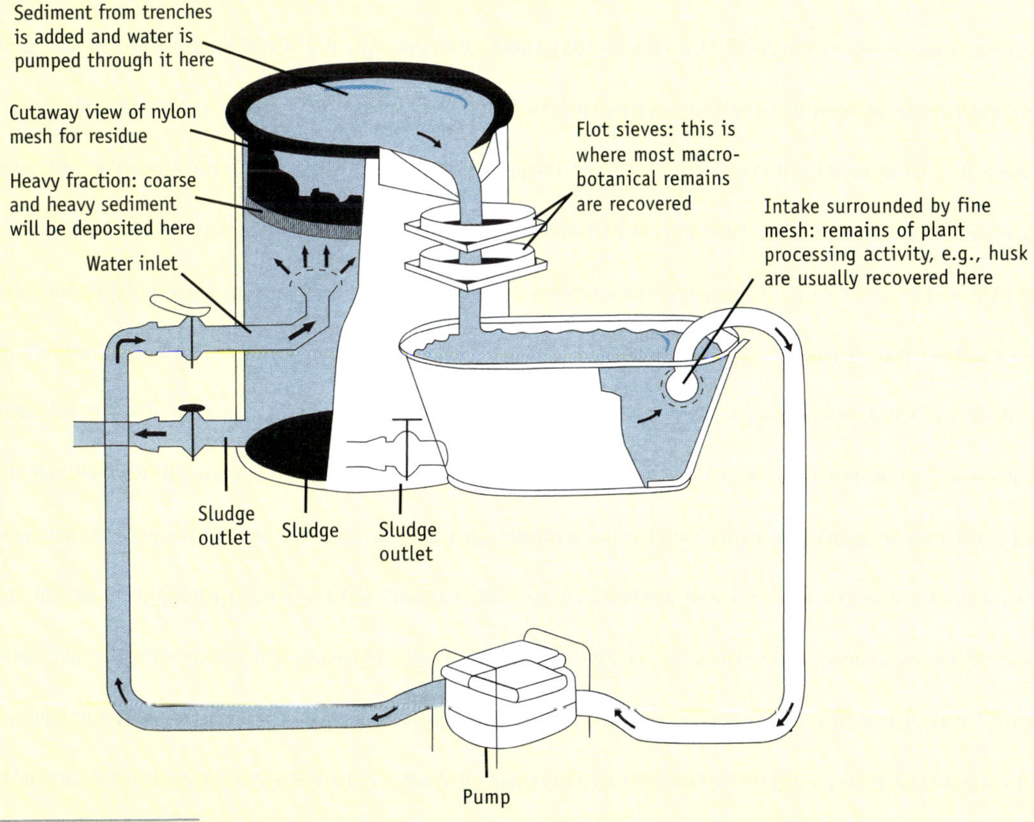

Figure 3.2 A flotation apparatus

The Transition to Food Production in the Indian Subcontinent

In classifications of the stone age, the neolithic age is generally associated with food production, pottery, and sedentary living. The reality is much more complex. In the Indian subcontinent, the roots of some of the features associated with the neolithic can be traced to the mesolithic phase. In the last chapter, there were references to the evidence of pottery and animal domestication at certain mesolithic sites. On the other hand, as we shall see, there are some neolithic sites without pottery. The issue of sedentism (i.e., sedentary living) is also complex. As we have already seen, some mesolithic hunter-gatherer communities led a fairly sedentary life. And there were some communities practising animal and/or plant domestication who did not live for very long in the same place. Further, instead of thinking of sedentary and nomadic life as two alternatives, it is necessary to recognize different *degrees* of sedentism in the lifestyle of various communities.

The beginnings of animal and plant domestication did not mean the end of the hunting-gathering way of life. Communities that practised animal rearing and agriculture usually continued to hunt and forage for food. Moreover, there were numerous communities who retained their hunting-gathering way of life and never switched over to domestication at all. This chapter, however, focuses on those that did make the transition. Given the great ecological diversity in different parts of the subcontinent—especially in climate, soil, and the availability of plant and animal species that could be potentially domesticated—it is not surprising that the details of the various adaptations made by early pastoralists and agriculturists varied quite a bit.

One reason why the title of this chapter highlights the beginnings of food production rather than the neolithic is because food production is the most important aspect of the neolithic phase. Secondly, the history of early food-producing settlements in the subcontinent consists of different regional profiles and trajectories. In certain regions (e.g., the northern fringes of the Vindhyas), the food-producing neolithic culture emerged out of an earlier mesolithic phase. In other areas (such as the north-west), there is no mesolithic phase and the earliest settlements seem to belong to neolithic agriculturists and pastoralists. Another important point to note is that while there are some 'pure neolithic' sites, there are many more neolithic–chalcolithic cultures which have elements of the neolithic along with the use of metal (mainly copper).

Since we are dealing with a vast expanse of time, and in order to convey the idea of the complex and variegated cultural mosaic, in this book, the discussion of food-producing agricultural–pastoral communities of the subcontinent has been divided into three overlapping phases: Phase I—*c.* 7000–3000 BCE; Phase II—*c.* 3000–2000 BCE; and Phase III—*c.* 2000–1000 BCE onwards. The first two phases are discussed in this chapter, while the third will be discussed in Chapter 5. In the case of sites which have a long cultural sequence, only the earliest phases that fall within the first two chronological phases are discussed here; the later phases will be discussed in Chapter 5. The various geographical zones of early food-producing communities are discussed in terms of their chronology, general features, and specific traits, against the background of the cultural sequence of that particular area (for site details, see Chakrabarti, 2006; Allchin and Allchin, 1997; Chakrabarti and Lal. [Eds.], 2014, Vol. 2).

The earliest village settlements, *c.* 7000–3000 BCE

THE NORTH-WEST

Several sites in Baluchistan illustrate the change from a semi-nomadic pastoral life towards settled agriculture. The oldest and best documented evidence comes from Mehrgarh (Jarrige et al., n.d.). This site is located in the Bolan valley in the northern part of the Kachi plain, near the point where the river emerges from the hills through the Bolan pass. The Bolan valley was an important link between the Indus plains and the mountainous valleys of north Baluchistan, and people and animals must have moved along this route from very early times. Excavations at Mehrgarh revealed the remains of ancient settlements scattered over an area of about 200 ha on a low mound and the surrounding plain. Seven occupational levels were identified, giving striking evidence of continuous occupation and of cultural continuity and change over many millennia. The first six levels, i.e., Periods, are relevant for us here.

Periods I and II at Mehrgarh are considered neolithic, even though there is a small amount of copper present. The remains of Period I (sub-divided into Periods IA and IB) were located in an 11 m thick deposit at the northern end of the site, on the high bank of the Bolan river. The chronology of this phase is somewhat uncertain due to inconsistent radiocarbon dates. The majority of the dates fall between 6000 and 5500 BP (*c.* 5000 BCE, calibrated). The problem is that although Period I seems to have lasted for a very long time, most of the radiocarbon dates for the middle levels of Period IA also fall within the range of 5800 and 5530 BP. Furthermore, the excavators point out that there are also some much earlier radiocarbon dates—9385 ± 120 BP for Period IA; 7115 ± 120 BP for Period IIB; and 6500 ± 80 BP for Period III. This series of earlier dates has the advantage of providing a coherent chronological framework for the Mehrgarh neolithic sequence from the 8th to 6th millennia BCE.

The people of Period I (this includes both Periods IA and IB) lived in houses made of handmade mud-bricks with small, rectangular rooms. One of the rooms at the lowest levels of Period I, measuring 2 × 1.8 m, had reed impressions on the floor and a grinding stone. The bricks used for house walls were of a standardized size, with distinctive rounded ends and finger impressions on their upper surface. Some of the structures divided into small units may have been granaries.

The stone tools of Period I included thousands of microliths, most of them based on blades. A few ground neolithic handaxes (celts) were also found. Some of the blades were set into wooden handles with a thick layer of bitumen and may have been used as sickles to harvest grain. Grinding stones indicate food processing. There were a few stone vessels and objects such as perforated discs and spatulae incised with a criss-cross design. Bone tools, including needles and awls, were also found, as was a handmade clay female figurine. Mehrgarh I was basically a-ceramic, i.e., it had no pottery; the first few pieces of pottery appeared in Period IB.

The people of Period I buried their dead in the open spaces between their houses. The bodies were placed in oval pits in a flexed (bent) position. The bones were often covered with red ochre, suggesting some sort of fertility beliefs. In at least two burials, young goats had been placed near the feet of the body. Grave goods included bitumen-lined baskets and food offerings, and ornaments such as necklaces made of stone or shell beads, bone pendants, and anklets. A copper bead was found in one of the burials. The occurrence of turquoise and lapis lazuli beads is especially interesting. The lapis lazuli could have come from Afghanistan. Turquoise could have come from eastern Iran or Central Asia. The nearest source of marine shells is the Makran coast, about 500 km away. The presence of such items in the graves indicates that the people of Mehrgarh were engaged in some amount of long-distance exchange.

In Period IB, a graveyard consisting of 150 burials covering over 220 sq m was unearthed. The burials were more elaborate than before. A small niche was cut into one side of a pit, and the body and grave goods were placed inside. The niche was then sealed with a wall made of mud-brick, after which the pit was filled up. A few copper beads were found in the burials. There are some instances of double burials and also of **secondary burials**, where the bones of one or more people were collected and buried after exposing the body to the elements. The significance of these changes in burial practices is unclear.

Period II at Mehrgarh, dated *c.* 6000–4500 BCE, is divided into three sub-phases—A, B, and C. The size of the settlement increased during this period and there were several mud-brick structures divided into small cell-like compartments. Some of these may have been houses, but others may have been used for storage. For instance, double rows of small rooms with a passage in between, with barley seeds on the floors, may have been used to store grain. The stone and bone tool types of Period I continued. There were two sickles made of microliths hafted onto a bitumen matrix. P. Vaughan's microwear study of stone tools found in an area of Period IIA indicates that most of them were connected with the working of animal products—activities such as butchery, cooking, hide processing, and the making of bone artefacts. Small amounts of handmade pottery occurred in the early part of Period II and wheel-made pottery appeared in Period IIC. In Period IIB, a copper ring and bead and a small ingot of copper were found. Other finds of Period II included an ivory tusk, pieces of red ochre, grinding stones, and a small unbaked clay figurine of a male torso. There were two flexed burials, the bodies covered with red ochre, unaccompanied by any grave goods.

Mehrgarh III belongs to the second half of the 5th millennium BCE and is chalcolithic. There is evidence of a significant increase in craft activities, including large-scale production of wheel-made pottery with painted decorations, marked by innovations and refinement in pottery-making techniques. A pottery-manufacturing area was found, where the bases of three ovens were exposed on top of an accumulation of 6 m of pottery debris. The frequent occurrence of ornaments such as necklaces and bracelets made out of tiny steatite beads indicates that bead making was another important craft. There were also beads of semi-precious stones such as lapis lazuli, turquoise, and agate, as well as of terracotta and shell. Stone micro-drills may have been used to make engravings on shell. There were a few terracotta humped bulls. Terracotta crucibles with traces of copper suggest the beginning of metallurgy.

Period III had storage complexes divided into compartments, similar to those of earlier phases. A large cemetery containing the burials of about 99 people shows changes in burial practices. The niches walled in by cigar-shaped bricks, known in Period II, were absent. The heads of some of the skeletons were placed on bricks. There was one collective burial with two wheel-made painted pots as grave goods (pots are not found in any other burial). In another burial, a copper or bronze object that looks like a fragment of a segmented seal was found near the skull. Ornaments, mostly made of steatite micro-beads, occurred frequently among the grave goods. There were also pendants of lapis lazuli, carnelian, turquoise, chrysoprase, agate, terracotta, and seashell.

The most remarkable aspect of Periods I–III is that they provide the earliest and most comprehensive evidence of subsistence activities in the region, revealing the transition from hunting and food gathering to a heavy reliance on animal domestication and agriculture. Thousands of plant specimens were collected in the course of the Mehrgarh excavations. These included charred grains and seeds as well as impressions of grain on mud-brick. Barley seems to have been the most important crop. In Period I, the predominant type of barley was six-row naked barley (*Hordeum vulgare nudum*). There were also other varieties—hulled six-row barley (*Hordeum vulgare vulgare*) and wild and domesticated hulled two-row barley (*Hordeum vulgare spontaneum* and *Hordeum vulgare distichum*). The fact that wild, transitional, and domesticated varieties of barley were found at the site proves that north Baluchistan fell within the natural habitat zone of wild barley and that Mehrgarh was part of a large nuclear area of barley domestication.

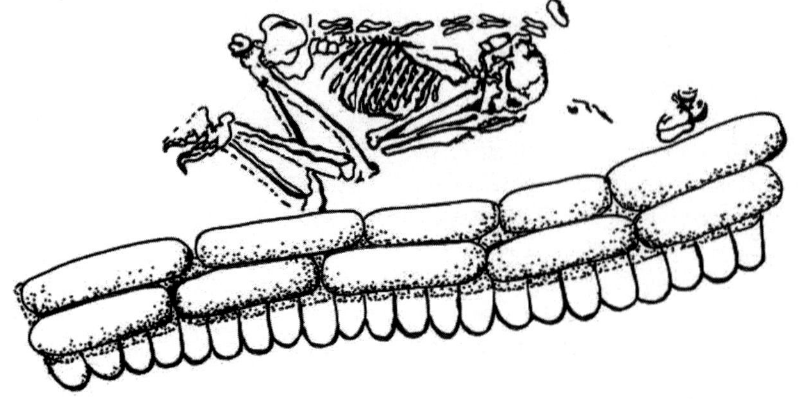

Figure 3.3 Burial with stone blades, cores, and a celt as grave goods, Mehrgarh, Period I

Wheat was another important crop. Grains of domesticated hulled einkorn wheat

(*Triticum monococcum*), emmer wheat (*Triticum diococcum*), and naked wheat (*Triticum durum*) were found in Period I. In later periods, a large proportion of the wheat grains belonged to the *Triticum sphaerococcum* variety. Whether Mehrgarh fell within the natural habitat zone of wild wheat is a matter of debate, as no clear evidence of wild wheat has so far been found in the area. But there is no doubt that the people of Mehrgarh were domesticating this cereal.

Seeds of *ber* (*Zizyphus jujube*) and dates (*Phoenix dactylifera*) were also found in Periods I and II. In Period II, in addition to barley and wheat, there were numerous seeds of cotton (*Gossypium* sp.) found in a hearth. Period III showed continuity with the earlier period, but also a diversification of agriculture. Two new varieties of wheat (*Triticum aestivum compactum, Triticum aestivum sphaerococcum*) and one of barley (*Hordeum hexastichum*) and a new cereal—oats (*Avena* sp.)—were identified. Wheat had become more important than barley.

Not much is known about the methods of cultivation practised by the neolithic and early chalcolithic people of Mehrgarh. Farmers must have relied on winter rains and may have channelized water into their fields by building mud or stone embankments similar to the *gabarbands* made in the region today. Stone sickles made by hafting tiny microliths onto wooden handles with bitumen must have been used for harvesting grain.

Neolithic Mehrgarh gives clear evidence of the transition from hunting to animal domestication. The lower levels of Period I were dominated by the bones of wild animals—deer (mostly gazelle, but also some blackbuck, *sambar,* and *chital*), *nilgai*, goat, onager (wild ass), water buffalo, cattle, pig, and perhaps elephant. There is also evidence of domesticated goats, and the decreasing size of sheep and cattle suggests that their domestication too was underway. By the end of Period I, the frequency of bones of gazelles and other wild animals had drastically decreased, while those of domesticated cattle, goats, and sheep had greatly increased. Cattle were now the most important domesticated animal. In Period III, cattle still dominated, but there was an increase in the proportion of sheep and goat bones. Interestingly, Period III also showed an increase in the number of bones of wild animals, suggesting resurgence in hunting activity.

J. R. Lukacs' study (1985) of the human dental remains shows a low rate of dental caries (cavities) in the early levels. This may have been due to the high fluoride levels in the drinking water available in the area. Other features of the teeth suggest that people had a coarse diet. There is evidence of tooth probing (people poking their teeth either to sooth pain or prise out food). Dental health declined in Period III, and this may have been due to changes in food habits, for instance, the consumption of more refined foods.

The evidence from Period IV onwards shows a further expansion of the settlement, diversification of agriculture and crafts, and more and better decorated pottery. In Period IV, there were larger structures, with rooms separated from each other by wide walls and doors with wooden lintels. One door, only 1.10 m high (people must have had to bend down to go through) led into a room crammed with many objects such as stone flakes, blades, grinding stones, pestles, and many bones. Other items found in this room included a storage jar, a crushed basin with ridges and snake designs painted on the inner side, fine goblets, and beautifully painted vessels. The pottery of Period IV included polychrome wares. A new style of terracotta female figurine with a tubular body, pinched nose, and joined legs made its appearance. There are continuities in pottery designs between Periods IV and V. In Period VI, there were some changes—the appearance of a red ware decorated with *pipal* leaves, and a well-fired grey ware. This is also the time when similar styles of pottery began appearing in various parts of Baluchistan, suggesting an increase in interaction. A large pottery kiln was found in Period VI. A distinctive feature of this period are terracotta female figurines with elaborate hairstyles, heavy breasts, and joined legs, which may have had a cultic significance. Several large mounds in the Kachi plain may represent unexplored sites contemporary to the later periods of Mehrgarh.

The Bolan pass leads from Mehrgarh into the Quetta valley, where there are a number of sites. Today, farmers of this valley compensate for meagre rainfall by using water drawn from wells and streams to irrigate their fields. Kile (also spelt Kili) Gul Mohammad and Damb Sadaat are two of the important excavated sites in this area. Kile Gul Mohammad is about 3.2 km from Quetta city, on the banks of the Hannah river. The mound is a small one—about 90 × 55 m. Walter A. Fairservis (1950) conducted a small excavation over a 3.5 sq m area up to a depth of 11.14 m, reaching natural soil. The excavation revealed four periods of occupation—KGM I, KGM II, KGM III, and KGM IV. Radiocarbon dates from the upper levels of neolithic KGM I fall between *c.* 5000 and 4500 BCE, but the beginning of the settlement could go back to *c.* 5500 BCE, or even earlier. There was no evidence of pottery at this stage. Bones of domesticated cattle, sheep, goat, and ass/horse were found. There were no cereals, but two sickle blades were discovered.

The people of Kile Gul Mohammad may initially have been nomadic pastoralists, but by the end of Period I, they were living in houses made of mud or wattle-and-daub (interlaced rods and twigs plastered with mud). The artefacts included microliths and blades of chert, jasper, and chalcedony. There were a few ground tools and bone points. Handmade and basket-marked pottery made its appearance in KGM II. In KGM III, there was wheel-made pottery, including a fine black-on-red ware with geometric designs painted on it. Remains of mud-brick houses, some resting on stone foundations, have been found. The first copper objects made their appearance in Period III.

The uppermost level of Kile Gul Mohammad (KGM IV) was contemporary with the first period of occupation at Damb Sadaat (DS I), and there was a broad similarity in their cultural remains. KGM IV and DS I showed a distinctive type of pottery known as Kechi Beg Ware after the site where it was first found. This was a well-fired, thin, buff-coloured pottery. The shapes included deep and wide vases, bowls, and jars. The pots were painted with geometric designs in black, sometimes also in red.

Calibrated dates for Period II of Damb Sadaat indicate *c.* 3000 BCE as its midpoint. In this phase, there were multi-roomed mud-brick structures, many with limestone blocks used in the foundations. Hearths for cooking, similar to modern *tandoors*, were found in houses. The pottery included a type known as Quetta ware—a buff-coloured ware decorated with black painted designs, with shapes such as jars with flaring or straight rims, small-mouthed bowls with a sharp angle between the shoulder and base, and jars with pedestals. There was also a grey pottery known as Faiz Mohammad Grey Ware. This was represented by shallow plates and deep, open bowls, painted with geometric and naturalistic designs. Terracotta objects included cattle figurines, some painted with black stripes, and female figurines similar to those found in Mehrgarh VI. There were also small terracotta models of houses, rattles, and seals. A copper/bronze blade of a dagger or knife, a bone spatula, and an alabaster vessel are other artefacts associated with Period II at Damb Sadaat.

Anjira and Siah Damb in the Kalat plateau were excavated by Beatrice de Cardi, the former in 1948 and 1957, and the latter in 1957. Five periods of occupation were identified; the earliest occupation was apparently contemporaneous with Period II at Kile Gul Mohammad. In the Kalat plateau, Period I represented a semi-nomadic settlement, with no traces of structures. The pottery included a fine wheel-made buff ware, sometimes with a burnished red **slip** (coating). Chert blades were also found. In Period II, there were mud structures made on stone boulder foundations. The pottery included a red-slipped ware and a burnished grey ware. In Period III, the foundations of houses were made of blocks of stone cut into rough squares. The earlier pottery made way for Togau ware, a red pottery with black painted designs. The main shapes were open bowls, and designs of stylized ibexes, birds, and goats were painted on the interior, just under the rim. There was also another kind of pottery (known as Zari ware) with paintings in white with black outlines. In Period IV, the stone used for making houses was properly dressed into square blocks and there was pottery similar to that found at Nal. Period V of the Kalat sites has been co-related with Damb Sadaat III.

Mundigak is located on a now dry tributary of the Arghandab river in south-east Afghanistan. Excavations at this site were carried out by J. M. Casal in the 1950s and

1960s. The dates for Period I (which is divided into several sub-phases) fall within *c.* 4000–3500 BCE. The early settlers seem to have been semi-nomadic, as no structures were found in the lowest levels of Period I. In phase 4 of Period I, there were small oblong cells with walls made of pressed earth. In phase 5, there were larger houses consisting of square or oblong rooms made of sun-dried bricks. Cooking hearths were initially situated outside the houses and later perhaps in the courtyards. There were wells in between the houses. Pottery was found throughout Period I and was mostly wheel-made. There were bone awls, alabaster vases, stone blades, and beads made of stone, lapis lazuli, and frit (a calcined mixture of sand and fluxes). The few copper objects included a needle and a small bent blade. A terracotta figurine of a humped bull was found in phase 3 of Period I. Period II at Mundigak gave evidence of plant remains—club wheat (*Triticum compactum*) and *ber*, and there were bones of domesticated cattle, sheep, and goats.

Explorations in the Zhob–Loralai area of Baluchistan have identified many early village sites in the plains of the Gomal, Zhob, Anambar, and Thal rivers. Sur Jangal, Dabar Kot, and Rana Ghundai are three important sites in the Anambar valley. The people living at these sites must have been practising some form of irrigation, otherwise it is difficult to understand how they sustained themselves. The early phase of occupation at Sur Jangal seems to be contemporaneous to Kile Gul Mohammad IV. People lived in small mud houses. The large quantities of cattle bones indicate the importance of cattle rearing. Some of the pottery found at Sur Jangal was decorated with painted designs of humped and humpless cattle. Terracotta items included small house models. There were also goggle-eyed female figurines, similar to those found at other contemporary and slightly later sites in the Zhob valley (such as Periano Ghundai and also at Mehgarh VI and Damb Sadaat III). These figurines have been given the label 'Zhob mother goddess', and are assumed by some scholars to have had some sort of cultic significance.

Rana Ghundai in the Loralai valley was excavated by Brigadier Ross in the 1930s and re-investigated by Fairservis in 1950. Five occupational levels were identified. The calibrated dates for Period I gave a range of *c.* 4500–4300 BCE, while those for the early levels of Period III gave a range of *c.* 3500–3100 BCE. Period I consisted of a 4 m thick deposit and seems to represent a settlement of a semi-nomadic community. Traces of living surfaces and hearths were found, but there were no well-defined structural remains. Almost all the pottery was handmade and plain. There were bones of domesticated cattle, sheep, and goat. Four teeth, either of a horse or ass, were found. Brigadier Ross, a veterinary officer, was certain that they were horse teeth, but this has been contested by others. Microlithic blades, bone points, and needles with eyes were other artefacts found in Period I. In Period II, the typical pottery was wheel made, with a buff to red surface. Decorations included friezes of stylized humped bulls, and in one instance, blackbuck, all painted in black. The main pottery forms were bowls or cups with a wide shoulder, often with a ring base or hollow pedestal. In Period III, there were some changes in the style of painted pottery.

In the valley of the Gomal river (a tributary of the Indus), there are several early sites in Dera Ismail Khan district. Of these, Gumla and Rahman Dheri have been excavated. Gumla was excavated by a team from Peshawar University in 1971. Six cultural phases (i.e., periods) were identified, the first two of which are of interest to us here. Period I revealed a small settlement, just a little over 0.40 ha in size. There were microliths, bones of domesticated cattle, hearths, and large community ovens. Period I was a-ceramic; pottery made its appearance in Period II. Pots with a rough surface were followed by finer pottery painted with geometric designs, cattle, and fish. Terracotta female figurines were also found. There were microliths and a few objects of copper and bronze. Terracotta objects included bangles, cart models, gamesmen, and cattle and female figurines. There are similarities between some of the pottery designs and the female figurines of Gumla and certain sites in Turkmenistan in Central Asia.

There are several sites to the north of Gumla and Rahman Dheri. One of them is Sheri Khan Tarakai, in the Bannu basin, where calibrated radiocarbon dates gave a range of *c.* 4500–3000 BCE for the earliest levels. Many of the houses here were made of

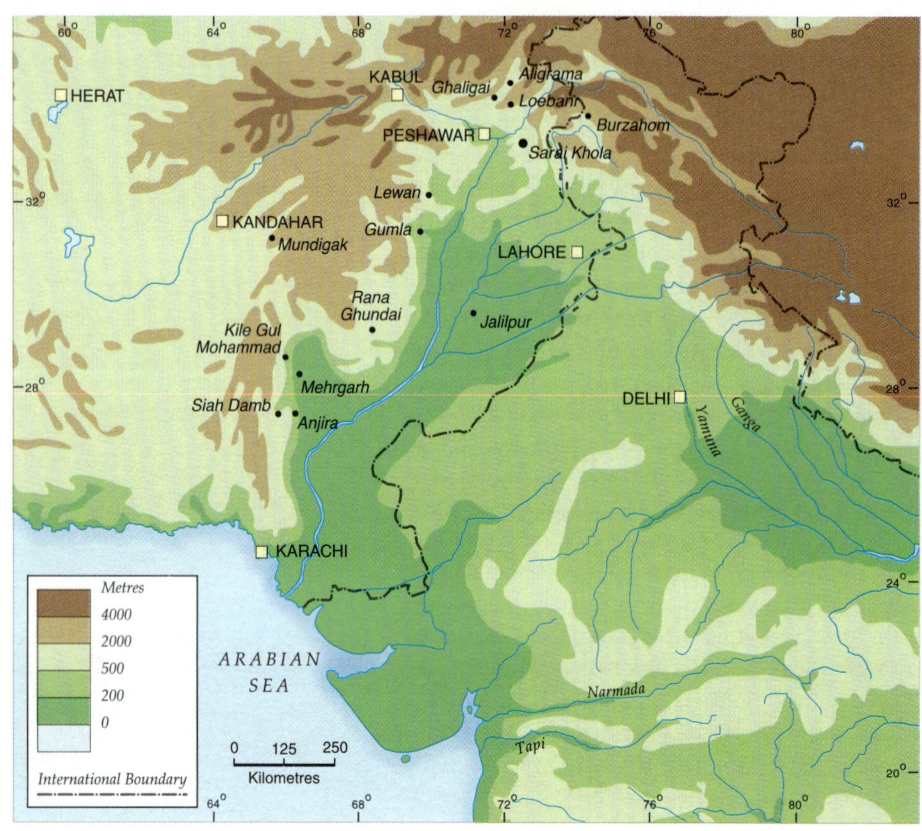

Map 3.2 Early village settlements in the north-west

mud-bricks built over stone foundations. Artefacts included ground celts, microliths, saddle querns and mullers, ring stones, and bone tools. Terracotta spindle-whorls and female and bull figurines (some painted) were found. There was evidence of the cultivation of barley. Bones of sheep, goats, cattle, and buffalo were found, as were freshwater molluscs and chank shells from the coast. There were two main types of pottery. One was a coarse handmade pottery with a black slip on the outside and a burnished pinkish buff to cream-slipped interior, with designs (including representations of goats) painted on in black or brown. The body of the other type of pottery had a rusticated surface (i.e., roughened with a thick slurry of clay); sometimes the neck-and-shoulder portion were left smooth and unroughened and were decorated with painting.

In the northern part of the Punjab province of Pakistan, the site of Sarai Khola, lying on the edge of the Potwar plateau, revealed a neolithic occupation going back to about the 4th millennium BCE. The site was excavated in 1968–71 by the Pakistan Archaeological Department. Here, in Period I, there was a handmade plain red or brown burnished pottery with mat impressions on the base. There were ground and polished stone celts, blades, microliths, and lots of bone points. Terracotta wheels and toy carts were also found.

The 5 ha site of Nal, located in the Khozdar area which links north and south Baluchistan, was first excavated in 1925. Some of the structures discovered here were made of boulders from a nearby riverbed, while others were made of stone quarried from the nearby hills. Several burials were found, most of them **fractional burials** in pots, but there were also some complete skeletons laid out in clearly defined and sometimes undefined graves. There was one instance of a child buried in a grave consisting of a small mud-brick chamber with grave goods including a bead necklace and crystal pendant.

The typical Nal pottery was polychrome and includes a variety of shapes, many with disc bases—ovoid, narrow-mouthed pots; carinated pots with a narrow mouth; almost straight-walled jars; open bowls; carinated bowls with an inward-turning upper body; and canisters with a flat bottom and a round, straight-edged mouth. Geometric and naturalistic designs (including fish and ibex) were painted onto the pots in blue, red, and/or yellow. The many artefacts found at Nal included stone balls, discs, ring stones and grinding stones; silver foil; beads made of agate, crystal, carnelian, lapis lazuli, and paste; and cattle figurines. Several copper objects and an adze made of copper alloyed with nickel and lead were also found. Nal pottery is considered contemporaneous with that of Periods I and II at Damb Sadaat and Period IV of Anjira and Siah Damb.

Nal pot

Nal-related sites are associated with two types of water management systems. One was the building of stone embankments across hill slopes to block soil washed down by rains; crops were grown on such terraces after the rains were over. The second was a system wherein water that accumulated in low-lying basins was channelized into fields through a system of small dams and canals.

Kulli in the Kolwa tract is a 12 ha site, only the upper levels of which have been excavated. Here, there were multi-roomed stone structures. The artefacts included stone querns and rubbing stones, beads made of semi-precious stones such as lapis lazuli, agate, and carnelian, bone bangles, and a small quantity of copper, gold, and glass. The Kulli pottery is profusely ornamented; a typical motif is cattle with an elongated body and large round eyes, usually set in a landscape. Analogous remains have been found at the sites of Mehi, Niai Buthi, Adam Buthi, Nindowari, and Edith Shahr. Adam Buthi, dated 3500–3000 BCE, is the earliest of these sites.

Bala Kot is a 2.8 ha site on the Makran coast of south Baluchistan, at the mouth of the Windar river. Period I represented a neolithic occupation dated from the late 5th to early 3rd millennium BCE. The houses were made of mud-bricks. Some of the wheel-made pottery was similar to that found at Nal. Microliths, terracotta figurines of humped bulls; beads of stone, lapis lazuli, shell, and paste; terracotta, shell, and bone artefacts; and a small number of copper objects were found. There is evidence of the cultivation of barley and the domestication of cattle, sheep, and goats. The bones of buffalo, deer, pig, and hare were found. Apart from Bala Kot, there are other early village sites in the Makran area, such as Miri Qalat and Shahi Tump.

Figure 3.4 Nal pottery (after Hargreaves, 1929)

In the Cholistan desert of Bahawalpur, a number of early village settlements are located on the alluvial plain of the Ghaggar-Hakra river. This river flowed to the east of the Indus, and although it is now dried up, it must once have been a mighty stream. The typical handmade and wheel-made pottery found in the earliest settlements in this area included large and small vessels with a coating of mud mixed with pieces of pottery applied to the outer surface; thick and thin pottery with multiple incised lines; and carinated or globular vases with a black slip on the exterior. These pots are known as Hakra wares, and the sites where they are found are known as Hakra wares sites.

M. R. Mughal's (1997) research in this area revealed that the Hakra settlements go back to the middle of the 4th millennium BCE, if not earlier. As many as 99 Hakra wares sites have so far been identified. They range from small settlements below 5 ha to fairly large ones of 20–30 ha. About 52 per cent of the sites seem to be camp sites, while 45 per cent appear to represent more permanent settlements. Some seem to have been centres of craft specialization. Artefacts found at Hakra wares sites include microliths, grinding stones, terracotta cattle figurines, bangles made of shell and terracotta, and pieces of copper. Bits of copper were found at Valwali, a site where 32 terracotta figurines, including those of the humped bull, were found.

Hakra wares have also been found outside the Ghaggar-Hakra valley, for instance at Jalilpur in the Punjab plains of Pakistan, near the left bank of the Ravi. Period I at this site gave evidence of Hakra wares in association with artefacts such as beads of stone, gold, coral and semi-precious stones, chert blades, and bone points. Terracotta net sinkers (used to weigh one end of the fishing net to keep it under water) indicate that fishing was an important part of the subsistence base of the people. Bone remains of sheep, goat, cattle, and gazelle were also found.

Harappa, on the banks of the Ravi, has given evidence of an early period designated the Ravi aspect of the Hakra phase, dated c. 3500/3300–2800 BCE (Meadow and Kenoyer, 2001). Remains of a small village with huts made of wooden posts and walls of plastered reeds were identified. Some mud-brick fragments of what may have been a kiln were found, but there was no evidence of mud-brick structures. Other artefacts included pottery, stone and bone tools, broken necklaces, terracotta spindle whorls, steatite beads, and bangles made of shell and terracotta. The most important evidence were potsherds with pre-firing marks and post-firing graffiti representing the formative stage of the Harappan script.

Period IA at Kunal in Hissar district of Haryana has also yielded Hakra wares. In the early level, the settlement was small (about 1 ha). Pottery designs included *pipal* leaves and a bull with very curved horns. Artefacts included bone tools, micro-blades made of chalcedony, copper fishhooks and arrowheads. People built their houses on an artificially raised area. House floors were made by digging a pit and paving it with rammed

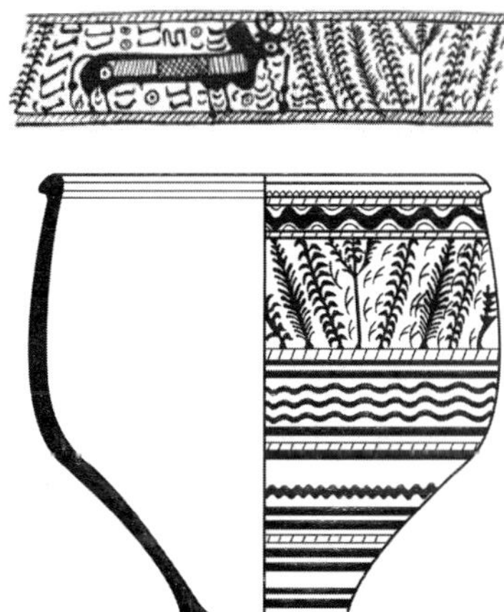

Figure 3.5 Kulli pottery from Nindowari (after Casal, 1966)

earth. The floors were below ground level and walls were plastered with mud. Post-holes around the circumference show the places where wooden posts supported a wattle-and-daub superstructure.

Bhirrana is a recently excavated site in the Fatehabad district of Haryana (Rao et al., 2004–05). Period IA belongs to the Hakra wares culture. People lived in shallow mud-plastered pit dwellings varying from 34 to 58 cm in depth and 230 to 340 cm in diameter. Apart from dwelling pits, pits used for sacrifices or industrial activity and refuse pits were also identified. In addition to the typical Hakra wares, there were other types of pottery such as mud applique ware, incised ware, tan slipped/chocolate slipped ware, black burnished ware, brown on buff ware, bi-chrome wares, black-and-red ware, and red wares. The artefacts included beads of carnelian, agate, jasper, and lapis lazuli; plain and painted terracotta bangles; sling balls of sandstone and terracotta; an unbaked triangular cake; a sandstone quern and pestle; a crucible; a clay hopscotch; and a chert blade and bone point.

THE VINDHYAN FRINGES, MIDDLE GANGA PLAINS, AND OTHER AREAS

The reason why so much detail has been given about early agricultural villages in the north-west in the above section is because there is much more data about this zone compared to other areas. However, another early centre of agricultural–pastoral communities lay in the Vindhyan fringes in southern Uttar Pradesh, where over 40 neolithic sites have been identified in the course of explorations in the Belan, Adwa, Son, Rihand, Ganga, Lapari, and Paisuni rivers. Neolithic levels have been identified at several excavated sites such as Koldihwa, Mahagara, Pachoh, and Indari. The key issues are those of dates and whether the rice remains that have been found at several sites belong to wild or domesticated varieties.

The neolithic culture in this area emerged out of a well-established mesolithic phase. Some of the mesolithic features such as microlith blades and the range of heavier stone tools continued, but there are also important new features such as the domestication of cattle and the cultivation of rice. Reference was made in the previous chapter to the discovery of wild rice at mesolithic levels at Chopani Mando in the Belan valley. Recently, domesticated rice has been reported from mesolithic levels at Damdama as well. The fact that wild rice is found in the area even today shows that it fell within the natural habitat zone of this cereal, and this explains the early dates for the domestication of rice.

Koldihwa and Mahagara (both in Allahabad district, UP) are two important excavated sites, located on the northern fringes of the Vindhyas on the banks of the Belan river. Koldihwa showed cultural continuity from the neolithic to the iron age. Remains of rice and impressions of rice husk embedded in pieces of burnt clay were found here at neolithic levels. The examination of rice imprints on pottery suggests that the people were familiar both with wild rice and cultivated rice (*Oryza sativa*). Other discoveries included stone blades,

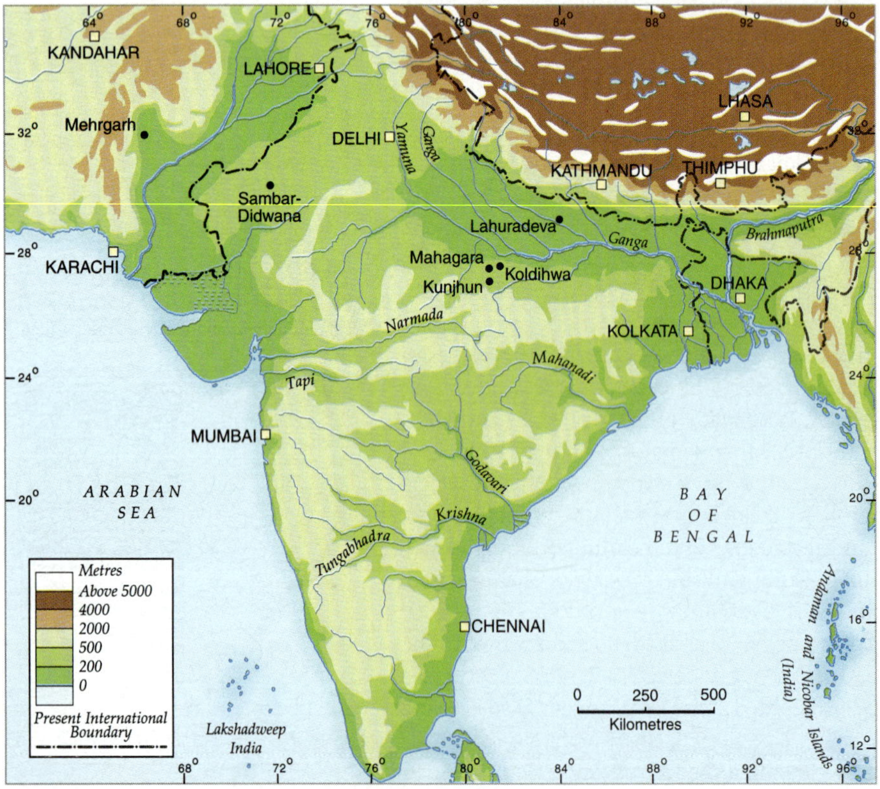

Map 3.3 Early centres of agriculture in the subcontinent

polished stone celts, microliths (mostly made on chert), querns and mullers (used for grinding), and bone tools. The pottery was handmade and consisted of three varieties—net-marked or cord-marked pottery; a plain red pottery; and a black-and-red ware. Deep bowls and storage jars were the dominant shapes. Some of the red ware showed soot marks, suggesting that these pots may have been used for cooking. There is currently a debate about the dates of the neolithic phase at Koldihwa. Three of the calibrated C-14 dates from the site are early and fall between the 8th and 6th millennium BCE (7505–7033, 6190–5764, 5432–5051), but the other dates are much later.

Mahagara on the right bank of the Belan river (not far from the mesolithic site of Chopani Mando) is another important neolithic site. Floors and post-holes associated with 20 huts were identified here. Reed or bamboo impressions on clumps of mud suggest that hut walls were made of wattle and daub. There were neolithic stone blades, microliths, celts, querns, mullers, and sling balls on floors. Pottery, bone arrowheads, terracotta beads, and animal bones were also found at the site. An interesting discovery was a cattle pen (about 12.5 × 7.5 m) located in the middle of the settlement. This was irregular in plan, with a fence marked by 20 post-holes and spaces left for at least three openings. Inside the fenced area were clusters of hoof marks left by cattle of different ages. The number of such marks suggests that about 40–60 animals may have been penned here. Rows of hoof marks of sheep or goats were also found outside the pen, near the huts, suggesting the frequent movement of animals between the huts and the enclosure. Animal bones included those of cattle, sheep, goat, horse, deer, and wild boar, out of which the first three seem to have been domesticated. The botanical remains included rice husk embedded in pottery. The bone and plant remains suggest that people hunted wild animals, collected wild plant food, and domesticated plants and animals.

The site of Kunjhun is in the Son valley in Sidhi district of Madhya Pradesh, not far from Koldihwa. The neolithic settlement here, which goes back to the 4th millennium BCE, yielded wild and domesticated rice. Kunjhun seems to have been a factory site specializing in the making of stone artefacts. Archaeologists identified several areas where stone was heated to improve its colour and workability and then made into blades. Taken together, the evidence from Koldihwa and other sites in its vicinity suggests that the northern fringes of the Vindhyas constituted an early, independent centre of rice domestication.

Early agricultural settlements also spread into the central Ganga plain. This is indicated by the excavations at Lahuradeva in Sant Kabir Nagar district in eastern Uttar Pradesh. The earliest period of occupation at this site belongs to the neolithic and was sub-divided into Periods IA and IB. Period IA was represented by a 45–50 cm deposit. Small burnt clay pieces showed that people lived in wattle-and-daub huts. They made and used hand-made red and black and red pottery. Some of the pottery had cord impressions, some had incised and applied designs and a fine red slip. The shapes included water vessels and pedestalled and knobbed bowls. The most notable finds of Period I were the remains of domesticated rice that can be dated to a 7th millennium BCE context. In Period IB, the size of the settlement increased substantially. The subsistence base expanded to include wheat and barley, and apart from wild animals, there was evidence of domesticated animals such as cattle and goat. People lived in wattle and daub huts. New pottery shapes included the beaker, spouted vessel, perforated vessel, dish, and bowl-on-stand. In some cases, the black and red pottery had a slip, burnishing, or painted designs. Artefacts included beads of steatite, agate, carnelian, chalcedony, and terracotta. A few copper artefacts (v-shaped arrowhead, fishing hook, etc.) were found. A piece of bangle made of marine shell was also found. Period II (*c.* 2000–1300 BCE) showed a further increase in the size and population of the settlement. There was evidence of over 40 earthen silos for storing grain; a cluster of such bins associated with some structural remains was identified as a granary. A new thin type of black slipped ware with painted white or creamy patterns made its appearance. Beads made of steatite, semi-precious stone, and terracotta increased, as did bone arrowheads. New artefact

RECENT DISCOVERIES | **Plant and animal remains from neolithic Lahuradeva**

Excavations at the 220 × 140 m mound at Lahuradeva revealed the following five-fold cultural sequence extending from the neolithic phase to the early centuries CE:

Periods IA and IB: Early farming phase
Period II: Developed farming phase
Period III: Advanced farming/early iron phase
Period IV: NBPW phase
Period V: Early centuries BCE/CE (labelled as Shunga-Kushana)

Here, we will focus on Periods IA, IB and II.

Period IA: the archaeological excavations and the micro-charcoal, pollen, and phytoliths in the lake core sediments indicated that the earliest human activity at the site goes back to about 10,500 BP. This took place during a short wet spell (*c.* 10600–10300 BP), followed by drier climate (*c.* 10300–9200 BP).

The plant remains for the period between 8300 to 5000 BP (*c.* 6500–3000 BCE) included those of wild and domesticated rice. Wild rice (*Oryza rufipogon*) remains were found from the beginning of the occupation, but domesticated rice (*Oryza sativa*) made its appearance in the 7th millennium BCE. AMS dating of a piece of husk of domesticated rice gave a date of 8360 BP (*c.* 6500 BCE). Cultivated rice phytoliths and diatoms appeared in about 8300 BP and 9720 BP respectively; these are considered to be related to paddy fields. Also found were remains of foxtail millet, job's tear (which is native to various parts of southeast asia), goosefoot/*bathua*, mugawort, and catchfly. The plant remains indicate that the early neolithic people of Lahuradeva were obtaining their food through gathering wild plants with a limited amount of rice cultivation. Eleven types of wood remains were also identified.

The faunal remains included bones of wild animals such as *gaur*, *nilgai*, *sambar*, and spotted deer, many with cut marks and evidence of charring, indicating that they were killed for food. Bones of small animals such as hare, squirrel, and mongoose were also identified. Aquatic animals included the Indian mud turtle, various kinds of freshwater fish, water bird, crab, and mussel. There were no bones of domesticated animals.

Period IB (*c.* 5000–4000 BP) was marked by increasing aridity in climate. The occurrence of domesticated and wild rice increased substantially. The appearance of new crops—including wheat, barley, lentil, and field pea—indicated the practice of double cropping. Various wood taxa were identified. Wild animal bones included those of *gaur*, spotted deer, chowsingha, wild pig, small game, fish, and reptiles. Charred bones of a panther, rat, and bandicoot rat were also found, along with a fragment of elephant ivory and a bone piece that may have belonged to an elephant or rhinoceros. The bones of domesticated cattle, goats, and cats were also found. Cattle and goats were killed for food.

Period II was marked by a wetter climate. The analysis of charcoal remains revealed 30 taxa that were known in earlier periods, with the addition of *bhang*, *heena/jhiri*, *karonda*, *arni*, *tendu*, *pipal*, and *bakar*. The faunal remains were dominated by domesticated animals, namely cattle, sheep, goat, buffalo, and a few bones of pig. Bones of wild animals included *sambar*, various kinds of deer, wild pig, wild wolf, and porcupine. Cut marks and charring indicated that the meat of these was consumed. Bird and turtle bones were also found. A significant find belonging to the upper level of Period IB or lower level of Period II were a large number of bones of cattle (*Boz indicus*) found in one place, many with cut marks and charring. These seem to have been butchered somewhere else and then brought to the spot, as the bones consisted only of high value meat parts. It was estimated that the culled animals could have supplied about 1,800 kg of meat, which suggests that they were the remains of a feast, perhaps connected with some important community ritual.

Source Tewari et al., 2022

Lahuradeva remains: (clockwise from top left) Period IA: domesticated rice (*Oryza sativa*); Period IA–IB: rice husk inclusions in a potsherd; Period IA–IC: corded ware; Period IB: steatite beads; Period II: painted black slipped ware; mat impressed pottery, painted pottery; tile (centre)

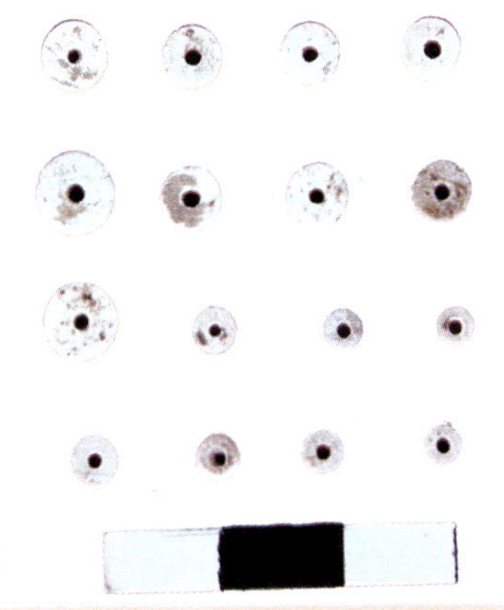

types included a few stone celts, hammer, and ball. Copper artefacts included fish hook and antimony rod.

Jhusi is located at the confluence of the Ganga and Yamuna rivers in Allahabad (UP). The site was excavated from 1995 onwards, and revealed a 16.5 m thick occupational deposit, with levels ranging from the neolithic to the early medieval period. The material belonging to the neolithic period included various types of hand-made pottery (cord impressed, burnished black, burnished red, and black and red wares), querns and mullers, microliths, bone points, steatite micro-beads, and beads made of semi-precious stone. The analysis of palaeobotanical remains indicated that rice (*Oryza sativa*) was the dominant cereal, accompanied by bread wheat, dwarf wheat, and barley. Also identified were lentils, green gram, grass pea, field pea, horse gram, sesame, linseed/flax, *anwala*, grape vine, common vetch, and Job's Tear. Radiocarbon analysis of charcoal from the levels where the cultivated rice was found revealed dates as early as the 7th millennium BCE (see Pokharia et al., 2009).

Pollen studies of the salt lakes of Didwana, Lunkaransar, and Sambhar in Rajasthan indicate a marked increase in cereal-type pollen in this area in *c.* 7000 BCE. This, along with the discovery of tiny charcoal pieces, may indirectly suggest the clearance of forests and the beginning of agriculture. However, no food-producing sites of such an early date have so far been identified in the area.

Neolithic, neolithic–chalcolithic, and chalcolithic communities, *c.* 3000–2000 BCE

During *c.* 3000–2000 BCE, village settlements spread to new areas. It can be noted that these settlements were roughly contemporaneous with the urban Harappan civilization, which is the subject of the next chapter. The volume of information for this period is more substantial than for the preceding millennia, and certain distinctive characteristics of the various geographical zones can now be identified.

THE NORTH AND NORTH-WEST

In the Kashmir valley, there are several neolithic sites near Srinagar and between Baramulla and Anantnag. These include Burzahom, Gufkral, Hariparigom, Jayadeviudar, Olchibag, Pampur, Panzgom, Sombur, Thajiwor, Begagund, Waztal, Gurhoma Sangri, and Damodara. During the Pleistocene era, the Kashmir valley was a gigantic lake and the neolithic sites are located on the remnants of the ancient lake beds known as *karewas*.

Burzahom, one of the important excavated sites in this region, is located on a terrace of *karewa* clay above the flood plain of the Jhelum river, 16 km north-east of Srinagar. The site offers a beautiful view of green fields and the Dal lake, which is only about 2 km away. Burzahom is a Kashmiri word meaning 'place of birch', and the discovery of burnt birch in the excavations indicates that birch trees grew in the area in neolithic times as well. The site must have been surrounded by forests, with water close by, and the neolithic people must have cut down some of the trees in order to establish their settlement.

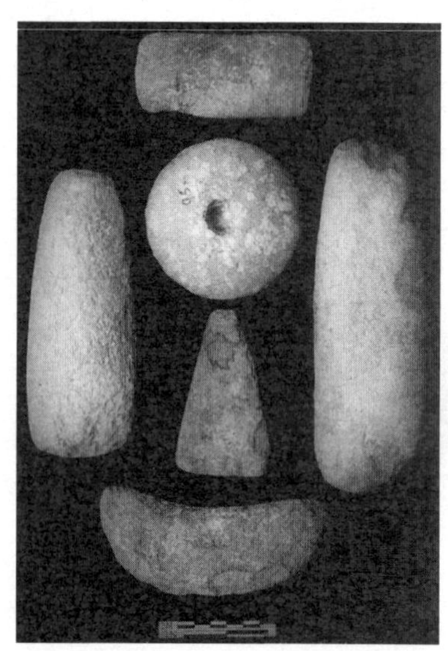
Neolithic stone tools, Burzahom

The site was discovered in 1935 by de Terra and Paterson, who thought it belonged to the Harappan civilization. Its real significance was understood much later, when excavations were carried out by the Archaeological Survey of India in 1960–71 under T. N. Khazanchi. There are four periods of occupation at Burzahom. The first two are neolithic, the third megalithic, and the fourth early historical. Period I was dated by the radiocarbon method to before *c.* 2920 BCE.

A distinguishing feature of Period I at Burzahom is the presence of mud-plastered pit dwellings. Most of the pits were round or oval, narrower at the top and widening out towards the base. The largest is 3.96 m deep, with a diameter of 2.74 m at the top and 4.57 m at the bottom. Post-holes around the circumference of the pits at ground level show where wooden poles would have supported a roof made of pinewood thatched

FURTHER DISCUSSION | **Did people actually live in the Burzahom pits?**

Pits have been found at neolithic levels at Burzahom and Gufkral in Kashmir and at Loebanr III and Kalako-deray in the Swat valley. They have generally been interpreted as winter homes of neolithic people. The steps, ash, charcoal, and potsherds in them have been cited as proof of the fact that people lived here. Pit dwellings are seen as a strategy adopted by neolithic people to cope with the harsh Kashmir winter. It is presumed that people moved to the ground level in summer.

This interpretation has been questioned by R. A. E. Coningham and T. L. Sutherland on the basis of a fresh analysis of pits found at British iron age sites. They point out that the British iron age pits too were once considered dwellings, but some scholars have rejected this idea. Experiments carried out by P. J. Reynolds showed that as soon as a fire was lit inside such a pit, the atmosphere became intolerably thick with smoke. It is also argued that the lighting of fires inside the pits does not necessarily indicate domestic activities such as cooking or an attempt to warm the living space. The firing of pits could have been in order to prolong their life, to clear mould or damp, or to speed up the drying of the mud plaster. Moreover, if the pits were dwelling units where fires were regularly lit, their sides should have been black with soot, but this was not the case. An alternative explanation of the British iron age pits is that they may have been underground grain storage units.

Coningham and Sutherland suggest that the function of the Kashmir-Swat pits too should be reconsidered. They argue that sites such as Burzahom may not have been occupied all year round, with people living in pits in the winters and moving to ground level in summer. They may have been occupied only during spring and summer, and abandoned during the winter. After the harvest, surplus grain could have been stored and sealed in the underground pits. When winter set in, people may have migrated to the less severely cold areas of the plains or the lower valleys, leaving the sealed grain to be used for sowing next spring.

While the majority opinion among scholars currently interprets the Kashmir-Swat pits as dwellings, the hypothesis cited here shows how the evidence can be interpreted in a different way.

Source Coningham and Sutherland, 1997

with birch. Some of the deeper pits had a few steps, but these did not extend to the bottom, perhaps because this would have narrowed the space too much. Ladders may also have been used to climb in and out of the deeper pits. Charcoal, ash, potsherds, and hearths made of stone or clay were found inside the pits. There were some square and rectangular pit chambers too, about 1 m deep. One of them measured 6.4 × 7 m. Some of the pit chambers had stone or clay hearths. It is interesting to note that the square/rectangular pit chambers were found in the centre of the settlement, while the round/oval ones were at the periphery. Close to the living pits were smaller storage pits with a 60–91 cm diameter, containing stone and bone tools and animal bones. Stone hearths near the mouths of some of the dwelling pits suggest that people also lived in the open at ground level, probably during the warm summers.

Other finds of Period I at Burzahom included ill-fired, handmade, coarse pottery in grey, red, brown, and buff colours. The shapes included simple rimless bowls and bottle-shapes with flared rims. Mat impressions on the base of many of the pots showed that they were made on mats. The stone tools included oval and oblong stone axes (some pecked and ground), chisels, adzes, grinding stones, ring stones, and mace heads. Also found were 'harvesters'—distinctive rectangular stone choppers or knives with two or more holes on the blunt side. Burzahom had a well-developed bone tool industry; artefacts such as points, harpoons, needles (with and without eyes), awls (probably for stitching animal skins), spear heads, daggers, and scrapers were found here. Tools were also made from antlers. No burials were found in Period I, suggesting that people may have adopted some other method of disposal of the dead.

In Period II, the people of Burzahom moved out of the pits and built houses on ground level. Some pits were filled up with *karewa* soil, their surface plastered with mud and covered with a thin layer of red ochre. These formed the floors of huts made of mud, mud-brick, and timber. Several burials were found in Period II, mostly within the habitation area. The dead were usually buried under house floors or in the compounds, in oval pits plastered with lime. Both **inhumation** and secondary burials were practised. In the case of secondary burials, the bones were sometimes covered with red ochre. In the

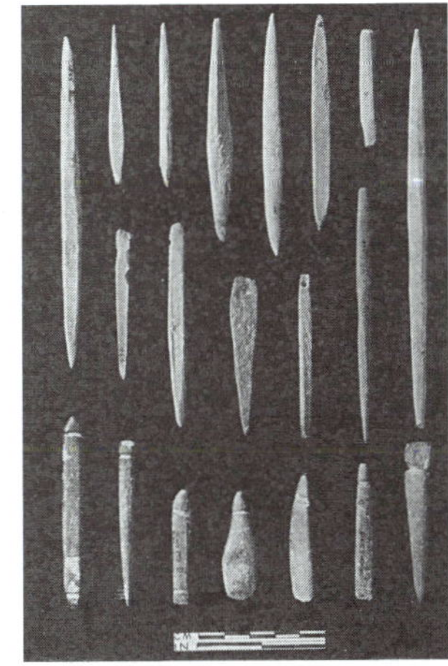

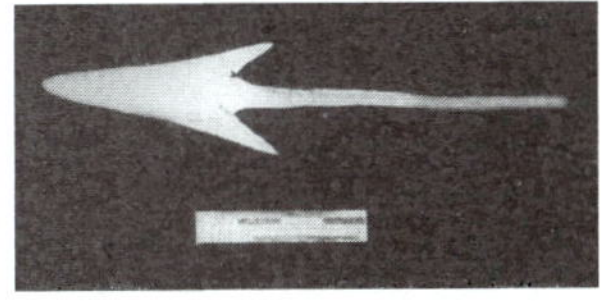

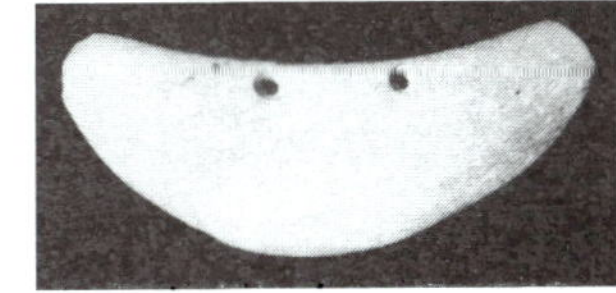

Burzahom: bone tools including needle with eye; bone arrowhead; perforated harvester (from top)

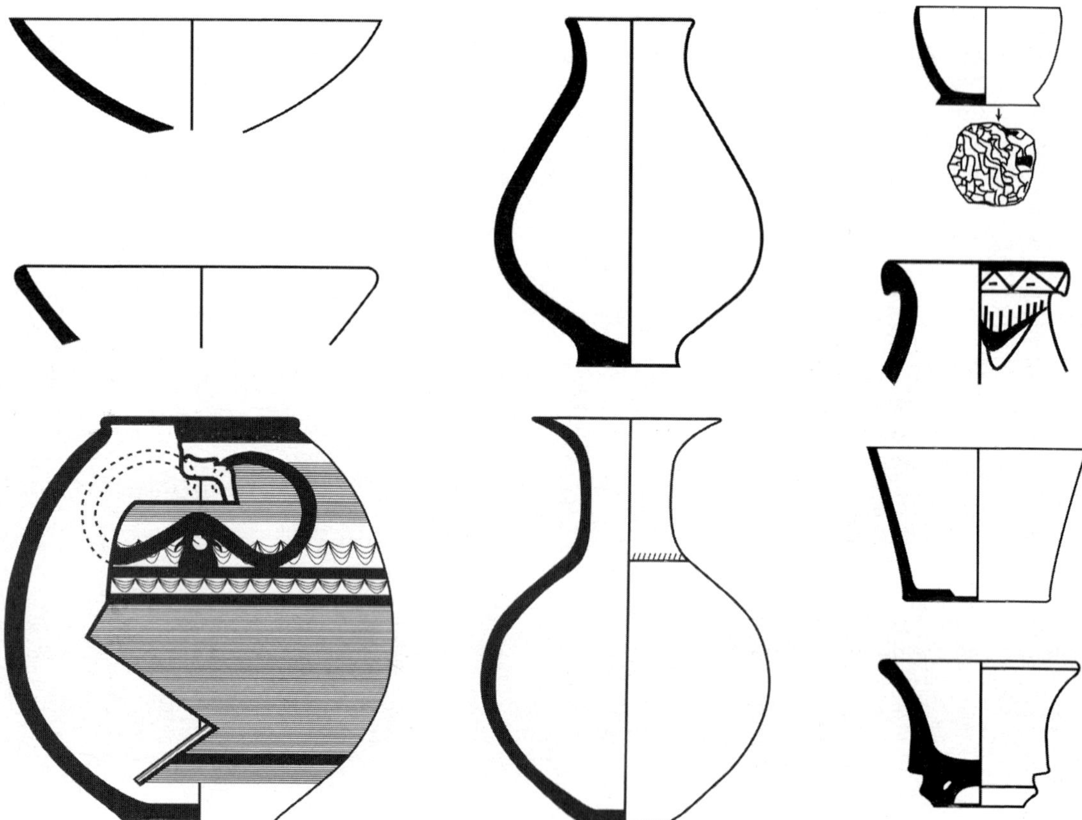

Figure 3.6 Burzahom pottery

primary burials, the body was placed in a flexed position. Apart from the occasional beads around the neck of some of the bodies, there were usually no grave goods. Holes in one of the skulls gave evidence of trepanning (boring holes in skulls). Period II at Burzahom continued till at least *c.* 1700 BCE.

An interesting feature of Period II of neolithic Burzahom is that humans were sometimes buried along with wild animals such as deer, wolf, ibex, *nilgai*, snow leopard, and pig, and domesticated animals such as cattle, buffalo, dog, sheep, and goat. The animals may have been killed and buried along with the deceased humans or their meat may have been placed in the grave as part of the grave goods. The interment of dogs with humans suggests that pets were sometimes buried along with their masters. There were also separate pit burials for animals within the habitation area. In one case, five dogs were buried along with antlers.

Artefacts from Period II included pottery, mostly handmade. There were a few new shapes and a black burnished pottery, which seems to have been a deluxe ware. The shapes included dish with hollow stand, globular pots, jars, stems with triangular perforations, and a funnel-shaped vase. A distinctive type in the black burnished ware is a high-necked jar with a flaring rim, globular body, and base, with oblique notches incised on the lower part of the neck. Stone and bone tools continued, similar to those of Period I, but they were more numerous and had a better finish. The stone tools included harvesters. A single copper arrowhead was found towards the end of Period II. Microwear analysis of Burzahom neolithic tools by R. K. Pant (1979) has shown that the tools were often re-ground and re-shaped. Some of the handaxes had clearly been used for cutting, chopping, and dressing wood, while others were probably used for chopping meat. The study also showed that the ring stones functioned as mace heads.

Two engraved stone slabs were found in Burzahom Period II. The engraving on one of these is indistinct. Its pattern has been tentatively identified as a hut with a thatched conical roof, to the right of which is the hind portion of some sort of animal, whose tail can be seen clearly. The other engraving is clearer (see p. 153, Fig. 3.7). It covers an area of 48 × 27 cm of a stone slab and depicts a hunting scene. A stag with large antlers is being pierced from behind by a (female?) hunter with a long spear, while another hunter shoots an arrow at it from the front.

Hunting and fishing were important parts of the lives of the neolithic people of Burzahom. This is clear from the animal bones, the engraved hunting scene, and the high percentage of weapons such as spearheads, arrowheads, and harpoons. Initially, there was no direct evidence of agriculture from the site, and scholars interpreted harvesters, stone querns, flake knives, mace heads, and seeds of wild plants as indirect evidence of some level of cultivation. However, a later analysis of botanical remains from different strata of Periods I and II provided direct evidence of cultivated wheat, barley, and lentils (*Lens culinaris*).

The distinctive features of the Kashmir neolithic include a wide range of stone and bone tools, pit dwellings, perforated 'harvesters', and animal burials. Some of these features also occur at sites in Central Asia and China. A wheel-made red pot containing 950 beautiful agate and carnelian beads was found in the early levels of Period II. Another globular pot had the painting of what seems to be a horned deity, a motif which occurs at **early Harappan** levels at Kot Diji. This suggests some contact between the neolithic communities of Burzahom and the Indus area.

The cultural sequence at Gufkral (41 km south-east of Srinagar, near Tral) extends from the neolithic to the historical period. Period I of the sequence is neolithic and is divided into three sub-phases: Period IA, IB, and IC. There is a calibrated date of 2468–2139 BCE from Period IB, so Period IA could go back to *c.* 3000 BCE or even earlier. As at Burzahom, here too, in Period I, there were pit dwellings, circular or oval, wide at the base and narrower above, varying in diameter from 3.80 to 1.50 m at the top. The larger dwelling pits mostly belonged to the earlier phase and were only 20 to 30 cm deep. The dwelling pits were surrounded by storage pits and hearths. Post-holes around the pits and hearths indicated the places where wooden posts were erected to support a superstructure of grass and reed. The bases of houses may have been plastered with mud to prevent the entry of water and snow. In the earlier dwelling pits of Period IA, floors were plastered with red ochre paste. Some pits were subsequently enlarged, and there were also two-chambered dwelling pits. In the early part of Period IA, hearths were rectangular in shape, while in the later phase, circular and rectangular hearths of clay were found. Interestingly, no hearth or fireplace was found *inside* the dwelling pits.

Period IA at Gufkral was a-ceramic. The finds included polished stone tools and a large quern with ochre paste sticking to the depression in the middle. There were tools made of bone and horn, including small arrowheads and a bone needle with an eye. In most cases, the tips of bone tools were charred to strengthen the working edge. Other artefacts include steatite beads and a broken terracotta marble. Bones of wild animals—sheep, goat, cattle, red deer, Himalayan ibex (a wild goat), wolf, and bear—were found. There were also some bones of domesticated sheep and goats. The people of Gufkral were clearly heavily dependent on hunting, but were beginning to domesticate certain animals. Plant remains included barley, wheat, and lentils.

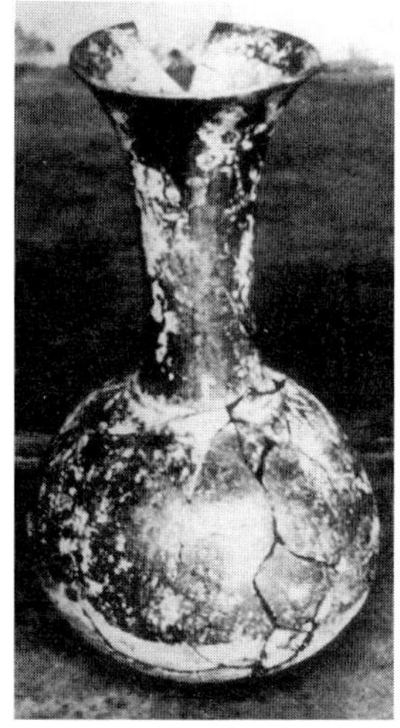

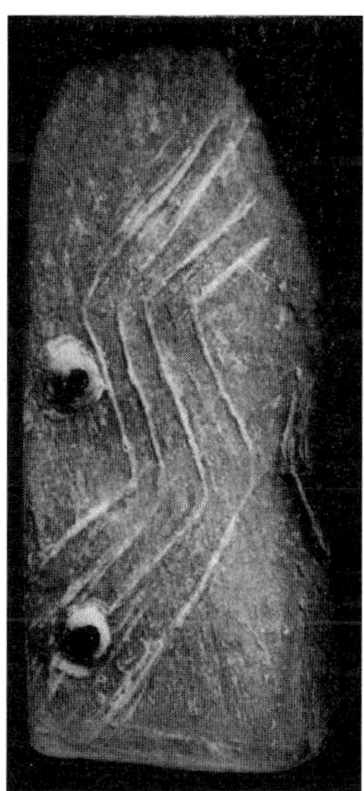

Burnished globular jar with long neck, Burzahom; Decorated stone harvester, Gufkral (from top)

The first pottery at Gufkral appeared in Period IB. It was handmade and mostly grey (there were a few red pots), with mat impressions on the base. Big jars, bowls, and basins were the common shapes. The pit dwellings disappeared in this period. A 5–7 cm thick compact clay floor mixed with lime was found extending over the excavated area. There was also a mud and rubble wall and another compact 70 cm wide wall-like structure. Polished stone tools, as well as bone tools, continued.

Bones of red deer, ibex, bear, sheep, goats, cattle, and fowl occurred in Period IB. Many bones had sharp cut marks on them. The proportion of wolf bones decreased and those of dogs increased. The animal bones indicate that although hunting remained important, there was a significant increase in the domestication of sheep, goats, and cattle. The grains of Period IA continued into IB, with the addition of the common pea (*Pisum arvense*). The presence of large quantities of charcoal and charred wood pieces indicated the occurrence of an extensive fire. A radiocarbon date from Period IB gave a range of 2468–2139 BCE.

The upper levels of Period IC at Gufkral were dated *c.* 1620–1300 BCE, so the beginning of this period can be placed in *c.* 2000 BCE. In this phase, there were many refuse pits and dumps. Wheel-made pots appeared and included grey, burnished grey, red, and black wares. There were new shapes like long-necked jars and dish-on-stand with triangular perforated designs on the stem. There were stone querns, pounders, and double-holed harvesters. Only one neolithic celt was found. Stone and terracotta spindle whorls with large holes suggest the weaving of woollen cloth. There were terracotta bangles and potsherds with graffiti marks. One copper hairpin with a flattened spiral head was discovered. The largest number of bone tools were found in this period. Animal bones included those of domesticated sheep, goat, cattle, pig, and dog. There were also bones of fish, hare, rodents, hedgehog, and beaver. All the grains of Period IB continued in this period. Hunting continued to decline in importance and the scale of animal breeding correspondingly increased.

There are some similarities between the neolithic sites of Kashmir and those in the Swat valley in north Pakistan. The archaeological sequence in the Ghaligai cave in the Swat valley may go back to *c.* 3000 BCE. Here, at the lowest levels, there was coarse handmade pottery. Some pots had a slip and others a burnished interior. Pebble tools and bone points were also found. Although there are some similarities with the pottery types found at Burzahom Period I, polished stone tools are absent in the Ghaligai cave.

A number of grave sites have been explored in the Swat valley. These include Loebanr, Aligrama, Birkot Ghundai, Kherari, Lal-batai, Timargarha, Balambat, Kalako-deray, and Zarif Karuna. Various kinds of burials have been identified—flexed burials, cremation, urn burials, fractional burials, and multiple burials. Loebanr III and Aligrama have given evidence of wheat and barley. Rice, lentils, and field or common pea were found at Loebanr III, and a grape seed (*Vitis vinifera*) was also identified. Remains of pit-dwellings, some which must have had thatched roofs on wooden superstructures, were found at Loebanr III and Kalako-deray. Jade beads found at the former site suggest exchange with Central Asia.

Surface finds of neolithic axes, chisels, and ring stones occur at sites such as Ror, Baroli, and Dehra Gopipur in the Kangra district of Himachal Pradesh. These tools were found along with choppers and flake tools, but the dates of the neolithic context in this area are uncertain.

RAJASTHAN

In the areas of Rajasthan, Malwa, and the northern Deccan, the beginnings of settled life are associated with a chalcolithic rather than a neolithic phase. Reference was made in the previous chapter to Bagor in eastern Rajasthan, where there is evidence of animal domestication and intensive exploitation of plants and possibly incipient agriculture in what is labelled a 'mesolithic' phase (Kashyap, 2006). The mesolithic phase at this site is followed by a chalcolithic phase. Substantial evidence of early sedentary chalcolithic sites comes from areas rich in copper ores. Copper ores occur in many parts of India—Rajasthan, Gujarat, Bihar, Uttar Pradesh, and Andhra Pradesh—but the richest mines are in Rajasthan, Gujarat, and Bihar. There is evidence of the use of copper in certain parts of the subcontinent from about 3000 BCE onwards. The chalcolithic communities of Rajasthan engaged in a variety of subsistence practices.

Many of the protohistoric cultures discussed in this and the subsequent sections are named after sites where they were first discovered. Archaeological cultures are also sometimes named after a pottery type. This does not mean that this is the *only* pottery type that occurs, simply that it is a *diagnostic* type. Cultures can also be named after the region in which they are concentrated. This does not necessarily mean that their sites are not found outside that particular area. For instance, Malwa culture sites are also found outside Malwa in Maharashtra. Similarly, some Ahar culture sites are found in Malwa, outside their nuclear zone in south-east Rajasthan. These are all archaeological cultures, which means that they shared a range of associated material remains. What else they shared, apart from material culture, is a matter of interpretation.

The Ganeshwar–Jodhpura culture was located in the north-eastern part of Rajasthan. Over 80 sites of this culture have so far been identified. The largest concentration is in Sikar district, but sites also occur in neighbouring Jaipur and Jhunjhunu districts. The site concentration can be connected with the copper ore resources of the Baleshwar and Khetri areas, where traces of ancient copper working have been found. The Ahar culture was located in the south-eastern part of Rajasthan. The profiles of these sites show that they were part of an important process of metallurgical growth in Rajasthan, the roots of which go back to the 4th millennium BCE.

Jodhpura, on the banks of the Sahibi river, is the first site where evidence of the Ganeshwar–Jodhpura culture was identified. The typical pottery here is wheel-made, orange to red in colour, with incised designs. Shapes include dish-on-stand with a thick slip. The calibrated dates from Jodhpura begin in *c*. 2800/2700 BCE, though some archaeologists take them back to 3000–2800 BCE.

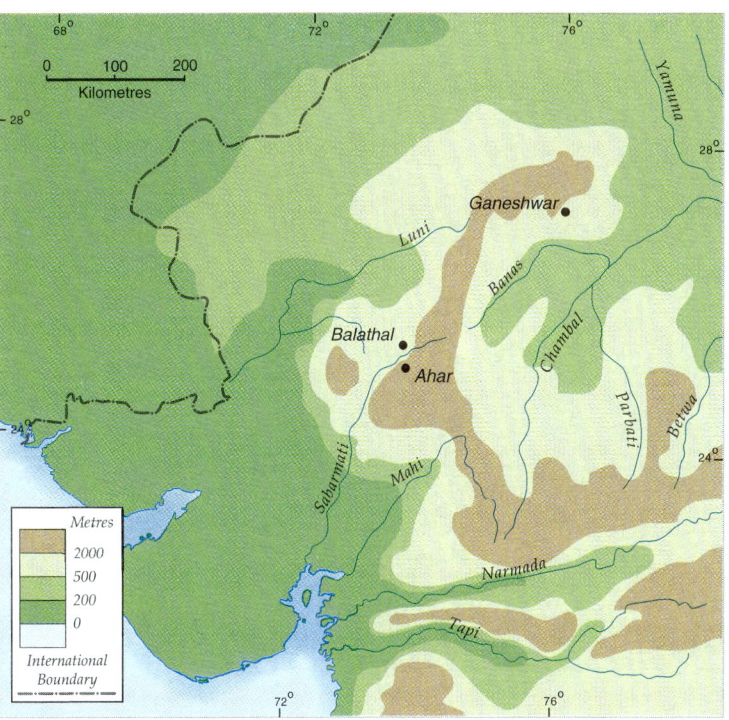

Map 3.4 Three major chalcolithic sites of Rajasthan

Pottery similar to that found at Jodhpura was discovered at Ganeshwar, near Nim-ka-Thana. There are three cultural phases at Ganeshwar. The dates for Period I are from *c*. 3800 BCE onwards; Period II can be dated between *c*. 2800–2000 BCE. Period I reflects a hunting-gathering community using microliths made of chert and quartz. Charred bones, almost all belonging to wild animals, were found. The lower levels of Period I showed a predominance of bones of small animals, while the higher levels were dominated by those of larger animals. Period II was divided into two phases—I and II. The first phase was marked by the beginning of metallurgy. A few copper objects were found—five arrowheads, three fishhooks, one spearhead, and one awl. People lived in circular huts with floors paved with pebbles and rock fragments. There were lots of microliths and animal bones. Both hand-made and wheel-made pottery was found. There was a profusion of Ganeshwar–Jodhpura ware, a poorly fired pottery made of micaceous clay, with a bright red slip. There were also a few pots made of well-fired, well-levigated clay. The second phase had a wide range of pots and was marked by an expansion in copper metallurgy. Hundreds of copper objects of different types—arrowheads, spearheads, celts, chisels, rings, bangles, balls, etc.—dominated the assemblage, with a corresponding decline in the number of microliths and animal bones. Period III at Ganeshwar belongs to the iron age.

The reports on Ganeshwar do not mention any direct evidence of copper smelting (furnaces, crucibles, etc.). But the over 1000 copper objects found at this small 1.2–1.6 ha site suggest that it had emerged as a copper-working centre and that its people were supplying these items to communities elsewhere. There are similarities between the wheel-made pottery of Ganeshwar Period II and early Harappan pottery. The early Harappans may have been obtaining their copper from here. This site may also have been one of the major suppliers of copper to the **mature Harappan** culture. Harappan pottery was found on the surface at two Ganeshwar culture sites. At Ganeshwar itself, there is a reserved slip ware which is only found in the Harappan context at Banawali and a few other places. Double spiral-headed pins from Ganeshwar have been found at some Harappan sites. All this suggests cultural contact between the Ganeshwar and Harappan cultures.

In south-east Rajasthan, over 100 sites of the Ahar or Banas culture have been identified in the Banas and Berach river systems, roughly between Udaipur and Jaipur. Some sites also occur in the Malwa plateau of Madhya Pradesh. Ahar, Gilund, and Balathal are

Map 3.5 Ahar culture sites, Rajasthan

three excavated sites. Ahar was excavated in 1953–54 and 1961–62, Gilund in 1959–60, and Balathal in 1994–98. The typical Ahar pottery is a black-and-red ware with linear and dotted designs painted on in white. Ahar culture sites tend to be located along river banks and generally range in size from a few ha to over 10 ha. However, Ahar itself is at least 11 ha and Gilund is about 10.5 ha. Many of the sites were located within 8–17 km of each other.

Ahar is located on the outskirts of Udaipur. Period I is divided into three phases—Ia (Early), Ib (Mature), and Ic (Late). The calibrated dates for these three phases are *c*. 3300–2600 BCE, 2600–2000 BCE, and 2000–1500 BCE. Fifteen building phases were identified in Period I. Ordinary houses were made of mud and rested on stone foundations. Walls were strengthened by bamboo screens or quartz nodules, and roofs were probably sloping. Floors were made of black clay mixed with yellow silt, sometimes paved with gravel from the riverbed. No complete house plan was exposed, but there were vestiges of a house, about 10.31 m long, partitioned off by a mud wall. Multiple-mouthed ovens were also found. Artefacts included microliths. There were plenty of copper objects—rings, bangles, antimony rods, a knife blade, and four socketless axes. Copper sheet and slag indicated that copper was smelted locally. Saddle querns and beads of semi-precious stones (including one made of lapis lazuli) and terracotta beads or spindle whorls were discovered. Rice grains and bones of cow, buffalo, goat, sheep, deer, pig, fish, turtle, and fowl were identified.

An iron ring and nail occurred in Period Ib at Ahar, and iron objects (arrowhead, chisel, peg, and socket) are quite common in Period Ic. Whether the levels at which these artefacts were found were intact or disturbed is a subject of debate. There is every possibility that this constitutes one of the earliest occurrences of iron in the subcontinent.

The discoveries at Gilund were broadly similar to those at Ahar. The structural remains included a mud-brick complex, measuring about 30.48 × 24.38 m, and part of a wall made of burnt bricks resting on a foundation of stone rubble. Storage pits were also found. The artefacts included microliths, fragments of copper, and beads of semi-precious stones. There were terracotta gamesmen and figurines of animals, including humped bulls with long horns.

Balathal in Udaipur district is an important Ahar culture site. The first phase of occupation (Period I) is relevant here. The size of the site was about 2 ha. In the early phase of Period I, there were remains of small, circular wattle-and-daub huts with mud-plastered floors and two plastered storage pits. In the later phase, a striking discovery was the remains of a massive mud fortification wall in the centre of the mound. The wall was reinforced in places with stone and there was clear evidence of bastions. The width of the walls ranged from 4.80 m to over 5.0 m, and the fortifications enclosed an area of over 500 sq m. A street (ranging from 2 to 4.8 m in width) running north-west to south-east, along with a small lane, were also exposed. In the second phase of Period I, the houses were larger rectangular units made of mud, mud-bricks, and stone, resting on stone foundations. Three multi-roomed structural complexes were discovered, within which kitchens and storage areas were identified. Two potters' kilns were also found.

The Balathal pottery was of many different types. It included thin red, tan, black-and-red, and buff-coloured pots. There was also a reserve slip ware, in which the pots were first treated with a thin red wash and then with a thick dark red slip, on which designs were made with a comb-like instrument while the slip was still wet. The thick, coarse wares included a red-slipped ware, plain red ware, burnished grey ware, and plain grey ware. There were very few stone microliths or blades. Lots of copper artefacts were found—choppers, knives, razors, chisels, and barbed and tanged arrowheads. There were also bone tools such as points and scrapers; stone querns, grinders, and hammer stones; and terracotta balls and stylized figurines of bulls and sheep. Ornaments included necklaces made of terracotta, steatite, faience, and semi-precious stones like carnelian, agate, and jasper. There were also bangles of copper, shell, and terracotta.

The large quantity of animal bones found at Balathal included those of *gaur*, *nilgai*, *chausingha*, blackbuck, fowl, peafowl, turtle, fish, and molluscan shells. Wild animals accounted for only 5 per cent of the bones. Much more numerous were bones of domesticated cattle, buffalo, sheep, goat, and pig. Cattle bones constituted almost 73 per cent of the faunal remains. The plant remains included wheat, barley, at least two varieties of millet, black gram, green gram (*moong*), pea, linseed, and fruit such as jujube (*ber*). Cereals and lentils seem to have been grown in large quantities and stored in storage bins, of which several have been found. Grain was ground into flour on stone querns, and the bread was probably cooked on handmade flat pans (*tawas*) on u-shaped *chulhas*, similar to those used in the village even today. Calibrated dates suggest that the time span for the chalcolithic settlement at Balathal was from *c*. 3700 BCE to 2000 BCE. This would make it contemporary with the early Harappan phase at Kot Diji and as early as the Jodhpura–Ganeshwar culture of north-east Rajasthan.

The site of Ojiyana is located on a hillside in Bhilwara district. Ahar culture levels at this site (3rd/2nd millennium BCE) yielded carbonized remains of a wide variety of plants including hulled barley, naked barley, bread wheat, dwarf wheat, rice (*Oryza sativa L.*), *jowar* millet, *ragi* millet, foxtail millet, lentil, field pea, chickpea, grass pea, green gram, black gram, moth bean, horse gram, linseed, sesame, safflower, and several varieties of grasses and weeds (Pokharia, 2008). The site has also given evidence of house complexes made of stone, and some wattle and daub structures in the late stage. There is reported evidence of a stone fortification wall and a stone wall plastered with mud, which may have been associated with storing grain.

Sites of the Ahar culture show the use of a great variety of raw materials including steatite, shell, agate, jasper, carnelian, lapis lazuli, copper, and bronze. Although the shell objects were locally made, the shell itself must have come from the Gujarat coast. The discovery of etched carnelian beads and Rangpur-type lustrous red ware in Ahar Period IC suggests a connection with Harappan sites in Gujarat.

THE MALWA REGION

Stone celts discovered in various parts of Central India may belong to a neolithic context, but the evidence has not been adequately studied. There is, however, a good deal of evidence on the sequence of chalcolithic farming cultures in the Malwa region, beginning with the Kayatha culture, followed by the Ahar culture, and then the Malwa culture. Calibrated radiocarbon dates place the Kayatha culture between *c*. 2400 and 2000 BCE. This culture gets its name from the site of Kayatha in Ujjain district, on the banks of the Chhoti Kali Sindh, a tributary of the Kali Sindh, which is in turn a tributary of the Chambal river.

Three types of pottery have been found at Kayatha culture sites. The typical Kayatha pottery is a fine, sturdy, wheel-made ware. It has a thick brown slip, usually from lip to shoulder, and sometimes up to the base. Linear designs are painted on in violet or deep red only on the upper part of the vessel, especially on the rim. The shapes include bowls and basins, vases with a globular profile and concave neck, and large storage jars. Other kinds of pottery associated with Kayatha ware include a buff ware with a thin, fine fabric and linear and geometric designs painted on in red. The shapes are rather limited and include *lotas*, high and short concave-necked jars, and basins. Thirdly, there is a red 'combed ware' with a fine fabric, usually without any slip or wash. It is decorated with multiple wavy and zigzag lines made with some kind of comb-like instrument. The shapes consist only of bowls and basins.

As the Kayatha excavations were restricted in scope, no complete house plans were uncovered. But houses were apparently made of mud and reed with mud-plastered floors. Bones of domesticated cattle and horses were found, and the people seem to have eaten tortoises. No grain remains were identified. There was a rich repertoire of stone and copper artefacts. The stone tools included plenty of microliths (blades, points, lunates, etc.) made out of locally available chalcedony. A mace head or ring stone may have been used as an agricultural implement for turning soil. The people were well versed in copper technology. There were two copper axes cast in moulds, a fragmentary chisel, and 28 copper bangles found in two pots. Two beautiful necklaces made of agate and carnelian beads (and one faceted crystal) were discovered in two pots—one consisting of 175, the other of 160 beads. Another pot contained 40,000 steatite micro-beads, strung in threads. The copper axes, bangles, and necklaces were all found in a small area of what must have been a house. It seems that the people who lived here had to leave suddenly, abandoning their valuable possessions on the floor.

Kayatha ware is similar in some respects to early Harappan pottery, and there is also a similarity in the steatite micro-beads of these two cultures. The axes found at Kayatha have indentation marks that are similar to those found on Ganeshwar specimens, and it is quite possible that they came from Ganeshwar. All this suggests connections, whose precise nature is difficult to determine. There was an abrupt break in occupation at Kayatha in about 1800 BCE, and the site remained deserted for about a century. When reoccupied, it represented an Ahar/Banas culture phase.

THE WESTERN DECCAN

The earliest farming culture in the western Deccan is the Savalda culture, named after the site of this name in the Tapi valley. This culture can be dated *c*. 2450–1700 BCE, and its sites are found between the Tapi and Godavari rivers in north Maharashtra. The typical Savalda ware is a wheel-made chocolate-coloured pottery, of medium to coarse fabric, with a thick, crackled slip. The variety of shapes includes the high-necked jar, dish, dish-on-stand, bowl, basin, ring stand, vase, beaker, and knobbed lid. A remarkable aspect of Savalda pottery is that the designs painted over the thick, crackled slip include tools, weapons, and geometric motifs.

Kaothe is a site belonging to the Savalda culture. It is a 20 ha site, and the shallow 50 cm thick deposit suggests a short-duration, nomadic occupation. The houses seem to have been round or oval, with a sloping roof. Many bone tools and beads made of shell, opal, carnelian, and terracotta were found. Bones of wild deer and domesticated cattle, buffalo, sheep/goat, and dog were identified. Plant remains included a variety of millet and two kinds of pulses—gram and *moong*. The pottery consisted of a sturdy ware with geometric and naturalistic designs.

Daimabad on the banks of the Pravara river (a tributary of the Godavari) in Ahmednagar district of Maharashtra also has a Savalda culture phase. The evidence here did not indicate a semi-nomadic community. There were mud houses, some large and multi-roomed, with hearths, storage pits, and jars. Sometimes there were courtyards in front, and a lane has been traced in one place. The excavations yielded microliths, bone and stone artefacts, and a few beads of shell, carnelian, steatite, and terracotta. A phallus-shaped object made of agate was found inside a house. Plant remains included wheat, barley, pea, lentil, black gram, and green gram.

THE MIDDLE GANGA PLAIN AND EASTERN INDIA

In a previous section, reference was made to early evidence of food-producing settlements in the northern Vindhyan fringes at Koldihwa, Mahagara, and Kunjhun, and in the middle Ganga valley at Lahuradeva. Sites of a subsequent period have been found in the Sarayupara plain in the north-eastern part of Uttar Pradesh. This is part of the middle Ganga plain, bound on the south and west by the Ghaghara and on the east by the Gandak, extending up to the foothills of the Himalayas. An important site in this area is Sohagaura in the Bansgaon sub-division of Gorakhpur district, at the confluence of the Rapti and Ami rivers. The village lies on a mound about 60 ha in area. Excavations in the 1960s and 1970s brought out a six-fold cultural sequence at Sohagaura, ranging from the neolithic (Period I) to the medieval (Period VI). The remains of Period I included small pieces of ill-fired, handmade pottery with a coarse or medium fabric, most of the sherds either rusticated or cord impressed.

There are several neolithic and neolithic-chalcolithic sites in the alluvial plains of north Bihar. Chirand, Senuar, Chechar-Kutubpur, Maner, and Taradih have been excavated. All these sites mark 3rd/2nd millennium BCE villages located on the banks of streams and show the presence of full-fledged agricultural villages in the Gangetic plains of Bihar. Chirand (in Saran district) is a huge mound, about 1 km long, situated at the confluence of the Sarayu and Ganga rivers. A 3.5 m thick occupational deposit was excavated here. The beginning of the occupation may go back to before the mid-3rd millennium BCE. Stone celts and hammer stones were made out of quartzite, basalt, and granite. Various other kinds of tools, pestles, querns, and balls were found. Microlithic blades and points were made from materials like chalcedony, chert, agate, and jasper. There were a large number and variety of bone and antler implements such as celts, scrapers, chisels, hammers, needles, points, borers, awls, diggers, and pins. Bone ornaments included pendants, earrings, bangles, discs, and combs, and there were also bangles made of tortoise bone and ivory.

The pottery of neolithic Chirand included red, grey, and black wares. There was also a black-and-red ware. Most of the pottery was handmade, though there were some examples of the turntable method. Some pots had painted (usually red ochre) and scratched designs on their surface, generally linear or geometric. The exterior of many grey pots was burnished. The shapes included various kinds of vases and bowls.

There were different varieties of beads of agate, carnelian, jasper, marble, steatite, and faience—long tubular, long barrel, short barrel, cylindrical, triangular, and disc-shaped. Some of them were unfinished, indicating they were locally made. No copper objects were found. Terracotta figurines included representations of humped bulls, birds, and snakes. There were also terracotta beads, bangles, wheels, balls, and what seem to be two fragments of a brooch. A small perforated stem had traces of soot inside—perhaps it was a smoking pipe. A few terracotta discs with holes in the centre may have been spindle whorls.

The neolithic people of Chirand lived in circular wattle-and-daub huts with rammed floors. In the early stage, floors were below ground level, but later they were at ground level. Hearths were found in the houses. A semi-circular hut had several oblong ovens, perhaps for community cooking. Mud boundary walls of houses were traced. Burnt chunks of clay with reed or bamboo impressions suggest that the houses were destroyed by a fire. Plant remains included rice, wheat, barley, and lentils such as *moong* and *masoor*. Lots of bones of animals, birds, and fish were identified, indicating the prevalence of hunting and fishing. Clusters of fish scales and remains of river shells and snails give additional information on the food habits of the people. Animal remains included bones of wild elephants, rhinoceros, and deer, and those of domesticated cattle. Chirand had a later, chalcolithic occupation level as well.

Chechar-Kutubpur is a site located on the banks of the Ganga, across the river from Patna, near Biddupur. The neolithic deposit here was divided into three phases (A, B, and C) on the basis of changes in pottery. People lived in circular wattle-and-daub huts with mud floors. There were hearths in the centre of the floors. Lots of bone and antler tools and micro-beads of steatite and chalcedony were found here.

The ancient mound of Senuar (B. P. Singh, 2003) is on the banks of the Kudra river at the foot of the Kaimur range, in Rohtas district of Bihar, not far from Sasaram. There are four periods of occupation at the site: Period I is neolithic, Period II chalcolithic, Period III represented the Northern Black Polished Ware (NBPW) culture, and Period IV belongs to the early centuries CE. The lower levels of Period IB were dated by radiocarbon to *c.* 1770–1400 BCE; therefore, the beginning of Period IA probably goes back to

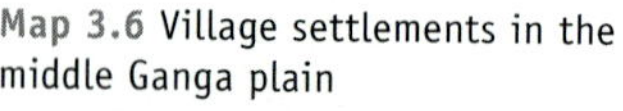

Map 3.6 Village settlements in the middle Ganga plain

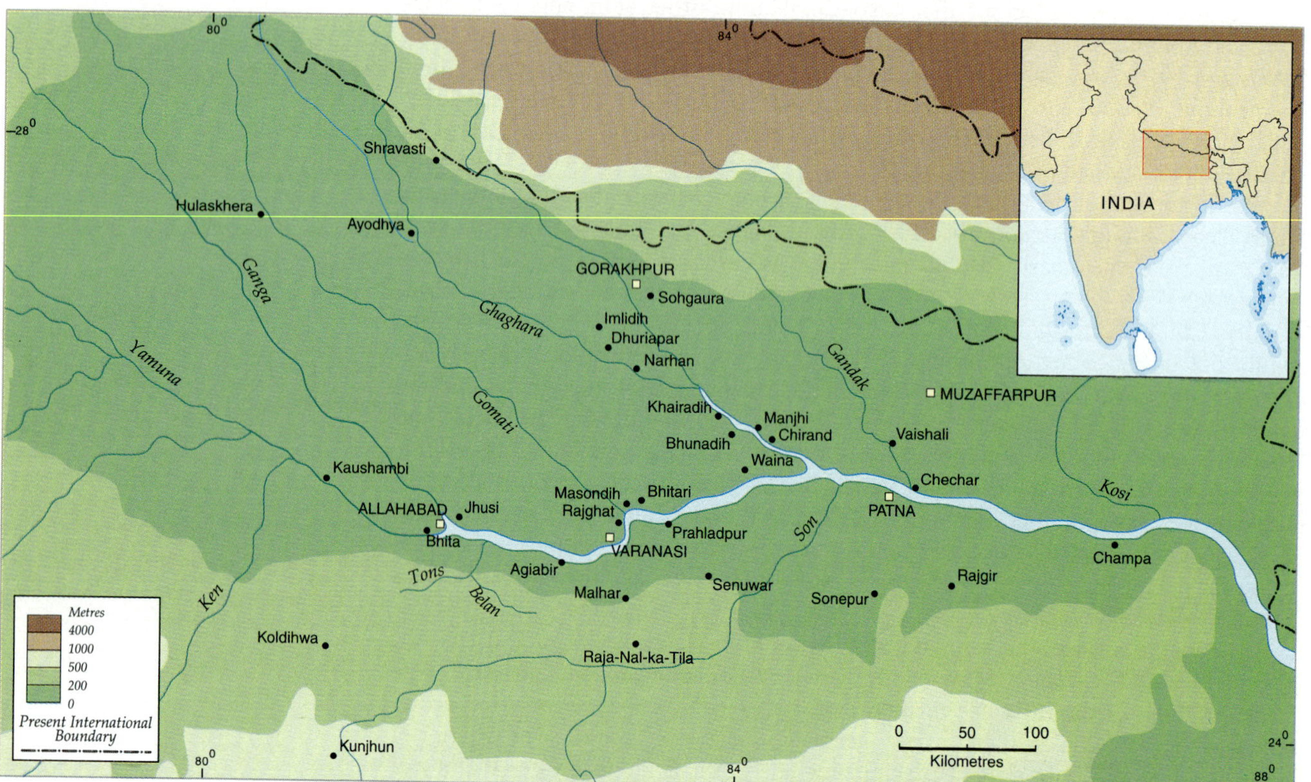

the latter half of the 3rd millennium BCE. Here we are concerned with Period I, which is divided into Periods IA and IB.

Period IA at Senuar was a 1.5 m thick neolithic deposit with remains of wattle-and-daub houses. There were three main kinds of pottery—a red ware, burnished red ware, and burnished grey ware. Some of the pottery was rusticated, some had designs made by cord impressions. The shapes included the wide-mouthed shallow bowl, channelled bowl, vase, and spouted vessels. Most of the pottery was wheel-made, but there was also some handmade pottery. Lots of microliths (small bladelets, also flakes and blades) made of chert, chalcedony, agate, quartz, and quartzite were found. There were a few triangular polished celts, stone pestles, saddle querns, hammer stones, and sling balls of various sizes. Bone tools included points, with use marks at the tip. Beads of semi-precious stones were also discovered.

The animal bones from Senuar have been carefully studied. The domesticated animals included cattle, buffalo, sheep, goat, pig, cat, and dog. Wild animals included *nilgai*, antelope, and *chital*. The charring and cut marks on many of the bones showed that the animals were killed for food. That the people ate shell food from the river is clear from the remains of molluscs and large numbers of shells. Considering that the site is on the banks of a river, it is odd that no fish bones were reported. Carbonized grains show that people grew two crops a year. Rice (*Oryza sativa*) was the main crop, but people also grew barley, dwarf wheat (*Triticum sphaerococcum*), sorghum millet, ragi millet, lentil, grass pea (*Lathyrus sativus*), and field pea (*Pisum arvense*).

Period IB at Senuar was neolithic–chalcolithic and consisted of a 2.02 m thick deposit. House floors were made of well-rammed earth mixed with *kankar* and potsherds, and there were marks of post-holes in some places. Nineteen copper objects were found, including a fishhook, wire, some rings, a broken needle, and several broken and indeterminate objects. There was also a fragmentary lead rod. Chemical analysis of the copper wire showed that it was made of almost pure copper and that the metal was probably obtained from the neighbouring Rakha mines. The artefacts of Period IB were more or less similar to those of Period IA, but there was a marked improvement in the pottery, especially in surface treatment. Although most of the pots were wheel-made, there were some handmade pieces as well. The vessels had a fine slip and a high grade of burnishing. Post-firing red ochre coloured paintings—earlier only found on the burnished grey ware—were now also found on the burnished red ware. Painted decoration was much more frequent, and pots were often also decorated with thumb or finger impressions, rope, or notched patterns on appliqué bands of clay.

There were more stone tools in Period IB than in the earlier phase, including many polished stone celts, mostly made of black basalt. Microliths were also found in large numbers. The material of the tools was the same as in Period IA, but there were a few new shapes. Shell ornaments included triangular pendants. There were lots of finished and unfinished beads of semi-precious stones such as agate, carnelian, and jasper. Twenty-five faience beads were also found. Terracotta artefacts included beads, pottery discs, a bull figurine, and maybe a whistle. Some of the pottery discs may have been wheels for toys or gaming counters used by children. Those with holes may represent spindle whorls. Apart from the grains that continued from Period I, in Period IB, there were some more plant remains—those of bread wheat (*Triticum aestivum*), chickpea or gram (*Cicer arictinum*), and *moong* (*Vigna radiata*). There are some cultural similarities between neolithic Chirand and Senuar.

The site of Maner is located on the banks of an old course of the Ganga, not far from Patna. The neolithic deposit here was 3.45 m thick and yielded handmade red ware and burnished red and grey wares. The shapes included the long-necked vase, bowl with short stem, lipped bowl, and spouted bowl. Other artefacts included stone microliths, bone points, and terracotta spindle whorls.

Taradih is situated close to the Mahabodhi temple at Bodh Gaya. There are two phases of the neolithic occupation here—Period IA had hand-made burnished and unburnished red wares and cord-impressed wares. Period IB was marked by a handmade burnished

Celts from Nayapur and Kuchai; shouldered celt from Kuchai

grey ware, sometimes with post-firing ochre-coloured painting. The other artefacts included neolithic celts, microliths, and bone tools. There were remains of wattle-and-daub houses with hearths. Bones of cattle, goat, buffalo, pig, sheep, deer, bird, fish, and snail were identified. Plant remains included grains of rice, wheat, and barley.

Neolithic tools—ring stones, shouldered celts, and triangular and rectangular axes—have been found in various parts of West Bengal, but the dates of the finds remain uncertain. Kuchai is an excavated site in Odisha which yielded faceted hoes, chisels, pounders, mace heads, and grinding stones. There was also a reddish brown pottery tempered with coarse grit, some with a slip and incised decoration. Neolithic material such as faceted and shouldered celts, bar chisels, rounded butt axes, wedges, and hammer stones occur as surface finds in Mayurbhanj district, but there is a lack of clarity about their dates and cultural contexts.

The archaeological profiles of the north-eastern states of Assam, Meghalaya, Nagaland, Arunachal Pradesh, Tripura, Mizoram, Manipur, and Sikkim are gradually emerging. Large numbers of polished stone tools have been found in various parts of the Khasi, Garo, Naga, and Cachar hills, but their cultural context and dates are uncertain. We have to keep in mind the fact that polished celts are found even at historical levels at certain sites. Sarutaru, Daojali Hading, and Marakdola—all in Assam—have been excavated. These sites will be discussed in Chapter 5, as the neolithic levels here seem to be fairly late.

SOUTH INDIA

The dates of the southern neolithic sites mostly fall within the broad time bracket of *c.* 2900–1000 BCE, but they can be further divided on the basis of chronology and geographical region. The earliest dates so far range between *c.* 2900 and 2400 BCE and come from Utnur, Pallavoy, Kodekal, and Watgal. These and other early sites are discussed in this section, while the later ones will be discussed in Chapter 5. The widespread palaeolithic and mesolithic occupation in peninsular India was discussed in the previous chapter. At present, there is insufficient information on the dates of the mesolithic phase in the far south, and the connections between the mesolithic and neolithic phases have not been properly worked out.

The meagre evidence of neolithic sites along the south-east coast of India is surprising, considering that this area has yielded evidence of palaeolithic and mesolithic artefacts. Apart from a neolithic site at Puducherry on the Tamil Nadu coast, there seems to be an absence of sites in the deltas of the Pennar, Krishna, and Godavari rivers. This may be due to sites being swallowed up by the riverine silts or due to inadequate exploration. However, there are many sites in the middle and lower Krishna valley.

FURTHER DISCUSSION | The mystery of the ash mounds

The first reports of the ash mounds appeared in the 1830s and 1840s. They were described as 'cinder mounds' or 'cinder camps', and many thought they were of volcanic or limestone origin. T. J. Newbold carried out the first excavation of an ash mound site during this period. In the course of his excavation at Kupgal, he found remains of pottery, animal bones, and a rubbing stone. This convinced him that the mounds were not natural geological formations but were created by people. In the late 19th century, the geologist-prehistorian Robert Bruce Foote became the first to connect the ash mounds with the neolithic culture. On the basis of his excavation at the site of Budikanama (also known as Kudatini) and a chemical analysis of the ash mound material, he argued that the ash mounds were heaps of excessively burnt cow dung, created by neolithic cattle herders.

Few were convinced by Foote's argument. Robert Sewell argued that not all the ash mounds represented cattle camps and that some of them might belong to the medieval period. G. Yazdani suggested that the mounds may have been created by metal workers in gold or iron. There were many others who bought the argument that ancient iron-smelters were responsible for the creation of the ash mounds.

In the 1950s, Raymond Allchin and F. E. Zeuner made important contributions towards the understanding of the ash mounds. Zeuner submitted the ash of Kudatini to a chemical and microscopic study. This established beyond all doubt that the mounds were made out of dung, most likely cattle dung. Allchin undertook an archaeological survey of the Raichur doab and excavated the habitation site of Piklihal and the ash mound site of Utnur. The Utnur excavation connected the ash mound at this site with a rectangular enclosure surrounded by post-holes, which Allchin interpreted as a cattle pen. Zeuner and Allchin's investigations indicated that Foote had been right after all. It also became evident that the accumulations of cattle dung had been burnt not once but many times; this repeated burning seems to have been deliberate, not accidental.

A number of questions remained: Did the ash mounds represent *in situ* burning of dung that had accumulated naturally over time, or was the dung collected, deliberately heaped up, and then burnt? Why was it burnt at regular intervals? Was it in order to periodically clean up the cattle pens or did this activity have some sort of symbolic significance? Allchin suggests that the ash fires may represent annual seasonal rituals of purification.

Another problematic issue was the relationship between the ash mounds and the settlements. Allchin suggested that there were two kinds of ash mounds—those in or near permanent settlements (such as Kupgal and Gadiganur) and others not associated with any settlements (including some of the largest ones, e.g., Kudatini and Utnur). On the other hand, on the basis of his excavations at Budihal, K. Paddayya suggested that the ash mound and habitation areas were not two separate, different types of sites, but were, in fact, partly contemporaneous and related to each other. He also argued that the ash mounds were not an *in situ* accumulation of dung, but that dung and garbage cleared from penning and house areas was piled up here and then burnt. According to this view, the ash mound sites are part of a sedentary neolithic village culture.

Ash mounds do not occur at all southern neolithic sites. In the Pennar basin in Cuddapah district of Andhra Pradesh, there are neolithic sites but no ash mounds. The mounds are similarly absent from sites in the upper Tungabhadra valley and southern Karnataka. It has been suggested by P. C. Venkatasubbaiah that the absence of ash mounds in the Cuddapah district may be because of differences in subsistence systems. In this area, people practised animal breeding, but they also relied on millet and pulse farming. Due to the importance of agricultural activity, cow dung was used as manure and was therefore, not burnt for ceremonial or other purposes. An alternative explanation is that even if agriculture was practised (and there is increasing evidence that it was) at many southern neolithic sites, manuring was not necessary. In such a situation, dung and dung ash could have been used for plastering houses, but they were not the valuable resources they represent for villagers today. The reasons for the presence or absence of ash mounds at southern neolithic sites would, in this case, have more to do with differences in cultural traditions rather than in subsistence practices.

The relative dates of the ash mound and non-ash mound sites are not yet fully clear. The duration of the ash mound phase and their relationship with sedentary villages are the subject of debate (see Fuller et al., 2007). More investigations are required, and it is likely that not all the ash mound sites represent the same sort of settlement pattern.

Source Korisettar et al., 2003

In the southern part of the Deccan plateau, where granite hills rise from the black cotton soil, the earliest neolithic villages were generally located on hillsides and plateaux, sometimes along minor streams, and occasionally along the banks of major rivers. A distinctive feature of many sites in this region is that they are marked by ash mounds. Research into the southern neolithic has in fact been dominated by a discussion of the ash mounds. The two key areas are the Raichur doab, between the Krishna and the Tungabhadra, and the Shorapur doab, between the Bhima and the Krishna. Ash mounds have been excavated at Utnur, Kupgal, Kodekal, and Pallavoy.

The ash mound sites are large accumulations of ash and vitrified material, created by the repeated burning of heaps of cow dung. They mark neolithic cattle pens which were surrounded by heavy enclosures made of tree trunks. Even today, cattle breeders in parts of Central and South India pen their animals in similar enclosures. Some of the neolithic pens were attached to permanent settlements, while others may have been temporary camps. The periodic burning of heaps of dung may have been connected with seasonal festivals marking the beginning or end of annual migrations to the forest grazing grounds. Modern pastoralists in peninsular India still burn bonfires on such occasions, and cattle are driven through fire, as it is believed that this will protect them from diseases.

Excavations at Utnur (in Mahbubnagar district, Telangana) have shown that the wooden enclosure of the cattle pen here was rebuilt many times, and the dung within it was likewise burnt repeatedly. Cattle hoof-prints were found in the ash. The size of the enclosure indicated that it could have held about 540–800 cattle. Utnur gave evidence of a small amount of ground stone axes, stone blades, and a handmade coarse pottery. The latter included a burnished grey or buff ware (usually plain, sometimes with post-firing designs painted on in red ochre), and also a ware with a red, black, or brown dressing applied to it before burnishing and firing (sometimes with pre-firing black or purple painted designs). Calibrated dates from Utnur range between 2800 and 2200 BCE. The earliest ash mounds here may be dated to *c.* 2500 BCE.

Piklihal revealed evidence of occupation at several areas across granite outcrops. The cultural sequence extends from the neolithic into the iron age and further into the early centuries CE.

Excavations at Watgal and Budihal incorporated new archaeological approaches and techniques, and were marked by an especially careful collection and analysis of faunal and botanical remains. Watgal (Devaraja et al., 1995) is located in Raichur district of north Karnataka. The earliest calibrated radiocarbon date from this site gives a range starting from 2900–2600 BCE, and occupation continued into the 1st millennium BCE. Period I had a microlithic industry consisting mainly of blades and lunates made of chert and quartzite. There were also large flakes of basalt and dolerite.

The calibrated date range for Period IIA at Watgal is *c.* 2700–2300 BCE. This period was marked by increasing diversity in stone tools. There were underground storage pits. Two carbonized seeds of betel nut (*Areca catechu*) were found. This is the earliest evidence of the use of betel nuts in South Asia. Period IIA was dominated by microliths made of chert. Most of the pottery was handmade, while some may have been made on a slow wheel. It was ill-fired and consisted of coarse red and grey wares, as well as a burnished grey ware with post-firing painting in red ochre. There were other artefacts such as beads made of marine shell. The burials included one urn burial and two extended burials marked by stones, without grave goods.

The calibrated range for Watgal Period IIB is *c.* 2300–2000 BCE. Here, as in the earlier sub-phase, there were numerous storage pits. The burials included both urn burials and extended burials marked by stones. But there was a new feature—pots appeared as grave goods. The range and number of artefacts were also greater. They included microliths and milling stones, beads of marine shell, stone, and terracotta, and a shell pendant. A small iron fragment may have been an intrusion from later levels. Animal and human terracotta figurines (one clearly representing the torso of a female) were found. There was a continuity of earlier pottery types, with a slight increase in the amount of wheel-made pottery. Periods III and IV at Watgal are post-2000 BCE and show evidence of copper/bronze and iron.

Budihal (in Gulbarga district, Karnataka) has been excavated by K. Paddayya and others (Paddayya, 1993). One of the aims of the excavations was to understand the ash mounds in relation to their ecology and the material evidence around them. The site is located on a sandstone plateau covered with thin brown soil. A complex of four localities (I–IV) within a 400 × 300 m area was identified. Each locality consisted of an ash mound as well as habitational deposit. In the extreme west of the site, an extensive area (about 4.5 ha) was found littered with a huge number of chert tools and waste chert material, and nothing else. Huge sandstone boulders found nearby showed marks of small and big grinding

Map 3.7 Some important neolithic sites in South India

grooves, places where people must have worked at grinding and polishing stone tools. This was clearly a chert blade-working area. It is possible that chert tools made at this site were sent to other neolithic settlements in the Shorapur doab and perhaps even further.

Excavations in Locality I (the main part of the site) at Budihal clearly showed that the ash deposits were located in the centre. Within the ash mound area, two distinct parts were identified—a cattle-penning area on the east and a cow dung disposal area on the west. There were several episodes of cattle penning, dung accumulation, and burning. A dozen structures were identified in the 1.34 ha habitational area around the ash deposit. One was a platform-like surface for chert working (chert was available 5–6 km north of the site) and another was a place for storing pottery. The rest were round dwelling units with low walls made of blocks of stone packed in mud. A total of 10 child burials (some in pits, others in pots) were found in the habitational area. The artefacts found from the ash mound and residential area included red and grey pottery, ground stone tools, chert blades, bone tools including axe heads, and beads of shell, bone, and semi-precious stones.

NEW DIRECTIONS IN RESEARCH | **Community feasting at neolithic Budihal**

In one of the trenches excavated to the south of the ash mound, within the habitational area of Locality I at Budihal, the archaeological team discovered patches of floor made of *kankar*-like material. Chemical analysis showed these to be made of fine ash, clay, small pieces of potsherds, bone, and charcoal, mixed with water and then rammed together in order to produce a hard surface. This floor seems originally to have covered an area of 200–250 sq m.

Strewn over this were huge numbers of animal bones—mostly those of cattle, but also of sheep, goat, buffalo, and wild animals. The large number of bones and stone tools of various kinds, including chopping tools and chert blades, indicated that this was a butchering area. Sandstone blocks found on the floor may have been used for chopping meat. Splinters of bone and bone artefacts show that some bone tools were made on the spot and were probably used for marrow extraction and hide working.

Three small pits (20–25 cm wide and 15–20 cm deep) were found in the northern part of the butchering area. These contained ashy soil, pieces of charcoal, and burnt bones. This was probably where people roasted meat.

The large size of the butchering floor, its location between the ash mound and the settlement area, the fact that it was plastered to create a hard and permanent working area, the occurrence of such a large number of bones and tools, and the cooking area nearby—all this suggests that the area was used not by a single person but by the entire community or at least a substantial large part of it. Perhaps it was used on special or ceremonial occasions, when animals were killed for a feast and their meat shared among those present.

Source Paddayya et al., 1995

Seeds of three types of wild plants were identified through the flotation of soil samples—*ber*, Indian cherry, and *amla* (*Emblic myrabolans*). A few grains of domesticated horse gram were also found. Faunal remains of about 15 domesticated and wild animal species were identified. Bones of domesticated cattle were the most numerous. This shows that the neolithic people of Budihal specialized mainly in cattle rearing and to a lesser extent on sheep, goat, buffalo, and fowl. The bones of wild fauna included *nilgai*, blackbuck, antelope, monitor lizard, tortoises, birds, fish, crabs, and molluscs. An even more interesting discovery was that of a butchering area within the settlement area, on the southern side of the ash mound. Calibrated dates for the ash mound at Budihal give a range of *c*. 2450–2100 BCE and for the village settlement *c*. 2450–1600 BCE.

The Budihal excavations demonstrated the presence of a habitation site directly associated with ash mounds, and Paddayya made some general observations on this basis. He emphasized that neolithic ash mounds and habitation sites were closely related to each other, and that the ash mound sites are best described as neolithic pastoral settlements with ash deposits. Ash mound sites tend to occur in hilly tracts, close to perennial sources of water, with good pasture land but soils too poor for agriculture. Garbage accumulated from the penning of cattle and other animals was dumped along with household refuse at spots close to the settlement and was periodically burnt. The reasons for the cow dung accumulation and burning were in part practical—to keep the settlement clean, to protect people and animals from health hazards posed by vermin-infected dung heaps, and to scare away wild animals. The burning could also have been part of rituals aimed at promoting the fertility of cattle. Some of the ash mounds are so large that the sites could have served as regional or local centres where people came from afar to attend periodic cattle fairs.

While the evidence from Budihal is important because it shows the complementary relationship between ash mounds and what seems to be a long-duration habitation site, it is not yet established beyond all doubt that a similar situation prevailed in other places. It is possible to visualize variations among sites—some may have been single, independent sites, others seem to consist of pairs or clusters (e.g., Kupgal, Budihal, Palavoy). Some may represent short-term camps of pastoralists, others more long-term habitation.

There are different views on the subsistence base of the southern neolithic sites. One view is that the neolithic people were fully sedentary farmers who made clearances in forests to carry out agriculture. Another view is that while these people may have practised some amount of agriculture, they were basically nomadic pastoralists. A third view is that they were sedentary pastoralists who did not practise any agriculture whatsoever. Raymond and Bridget Allchin (1997: 104) argue that ash mound sites such as those at Utnur and Kudatini represent seasonal cattle camps. They also suggest that the evidence reflects a transition from cattle pastoralism (represented at the early ash mound sites) towards agriculture (in the later sites). However, the early date from Watgal, which does not have any ash mounds, shows that the ash mound sites were not necessarily the earliest.

The faunal remains, ash mounds, terracotta figurines of humped cattle, and rock bruisings of cattle on rocks around some of the settlements testify to the importance of cattle rearing in the southern neolithic. Cattle (*Bos indicus*) dominate the faunal assemblage, both in the ash mound and non-ash mound sites. Sheep and goat bones also occur, but in much smaller quantities. Horse (*Equus*) remains have been reported, but it is not clear whether a wild or domesticated species is represented. Bones of water buffalo and pig (probably both wild and domesticated) occur occasionally. Other faunal remains include the bones of wild and domesticated fowl.

Till recently, there was not much evidence of agriculture at South Indian neolithic sites. There were the occasional discoveries of charred grain and the indirect evidence of grinding stones, but cattle rearing seemed to dominate the picture. In fact, some scholars argued that the terrain, soil, and dry climate of the area made it unsuitable for agriculture. Recent research has changed this picture and has highlighted the range of plant remains found at southern neolithic sites (see Korisettar et al., 2003). Millets seem to have been the staple crop, but grains of pulses and seeds of *ber* have also been found. Fragments of areca nut, probably wild, were found at Watgal. Chickpea (*Cicer arietinum*) has been identified at Piklihal.

So far, there is not much evidence of craft or trade activities at these sites. Although copper and bronze objects occur at several sites, there is no indication of the local smelting or working of copper. Did these objects come via exchange or trade from elsewhere? A pair of gold earrings was found at neolithic Tekkalakota and the Kolar fields of Karnataka are the likely source of the gold found in Harappan contexts. This would imply trade between the urban Harappans and the neolithic communities of South India. Marine shell and marine shell artefacts found at Watgal indicate exchange with coastal areas, probably the western coast.

We can note the beginning of the chalcolithic phase at sites such as Singanapalli and Ramapuram in the Kurnool district of Andhra Pradesh. The calibrated range of a date from Ramapuram is *c.* 2455–2041 BCE. This site gave evidence of house floors plastered with lime, wheel-made painted pottery (mostly black-on-red), microliths, and beads of semi-precious stones.

The Life of Early Farmers

As mentioned at the beginning of this chapter, hunting-gathering and food production do not represent two ends of a unilinear evolutionary scheme. The advent of food production based on animal and plant domestication did not lead to a complete eclipse of the hunting-gathering way of life. Many communities living in the Holocene continued to practise these activities, and continue to do so in some parts of the world, even in the 21st century. Further, archaeological data clearly indicates the practice of hunting and/or gathering at most early farming sites. Since hunting-gathering communities often lived in forested areas rich in various kinds of valued produce (for instance wood, spices, gums, honey, wax, and wild animal products), they often engaged in exchange with agrarian communities. It is, therefore, best to see hunting and gathering (also known as foraging) as a set of strategic practices rather than a label applied to certain cultures or communities (see Morrison, 2007).

The neolithic stage is generally associated with relatively self-sufficient village communities with equilibrium between food production and population. However, the issue is not only one of the *quantity* of available food. Food is an essential prerequisite for human survival, but it is much more. The obtaining and consumption of food is generally a social activity; food items may be part of systems of hospitality, gift giving, trade, and social taboos. Food preferences and ways of preparation are important parts of social life, both within the family and in the larger social group. The site of Budihal gives a graphic image of community food preparation and feasting at a neolithic site.

Although certain inferences can be made about the social and political organization of early food-producing communities, it is necessary to recognize the fact that they were not identical to each other. Some sites reflect small communities with a relatively simple social organization, while larger sites represent more complex societies. The details of the subsistence patterns of the communities would have varied, depending on the resource potential of the environmental niche they lived in and on their methods of adapting to it. Differences in material equipment such as tools, pottery, and houses suggest differences in craft traditions and lifestyles. Burial practices and objects of possible cultic significance reflect divergent belief systems and customs.

There is a view that compared to the struggle for existence and lack of leisure time that marked the lives of prehistoric hunter-gatherers, the life of farmers was much easier. As indicated in the previous chapter, the first part of such a view can be questioned. Similarly, it would be an oversimplification to think of the life of early farmers as one marked by comfort and ease. Farmers were in fact a vulnerable lot (see Scott, 2017). As is the case today, lack of rain could mean a bad harvest, pests or disease could wipe out an entire crop, and mould and rodents could destroy precious reserves of stored grain.

In spite of the differences in the ways of life of early farmers and the need to abandon stereotypical notions, it is possible to identify certain general features of the impact of the transition from hunting-gathering to food production. It was earlier pointed out that elements of sedentary living can be seen among certain hunting-gathering groups, while some farmers and pastoralists retain a migratory lifestyle. Further, there are different views on whether sedentary living preceded or followed the beginnings of agriculture. However, there is no doubt that in the long run, the transition to agriculture did lead to increasing levels of sedentariness among most communities.

See Chapter 5, p. 272 for details of Deccan chalcolithic skeletal remains

Studies of nutrition and disease based on an analysis of human bones suggest that hunter-gatherers had a high-protein diet, one that was more varied, balanced, and healthy compared to that of early farmers, whose diet tended to be high in carbohydrates, with an emphasis on cereals or root crops. Sedentary people were also more vulnerable to infectious diseases and epidemics than nomadic groups. This may help explain the high incidence of disease reflected in the bones of certain early farming communities.

Living for long periods of time in one place would have led to a more enduring relationship between people and their environmental niche. A sedentary life and the diet associated with agriculture would have meant less stress on women during pregnancy and more stable conditions for mother and child after childbirth. Further, high-carbohydrate diets are connected with decreased birth intervals. All these factors would have combined to produce higher birth rates. Sedentary living would have been easier on children and old people, and may have resulted in reduced death rates and increased life expectancy. Due to such reasons, the advent of food production would, in the long run, have led to an increase in population and changes in the age profiles within communities.

Food production required new tool kits and equipment. It also involved a new kind of scheduling of subsistence activities and shifts in the contributions of men and women, children, and aged folk. There would also have been a change in the food ethic—hunter-gatherers generally collect as much food as they can immediately consume on a short-term basis. Farmers would have had to produce and store quantities of food for future use. The focus would no longer have been on the acquisition of food to satisfy immediate needs on a daily basis, but rather on strategies that required much more long-term planning (for a detailed discussion, see Bellwood, 2005).

Figure 3.7 Hunting scene engraved on stone, Burzahom

It has been argued that women may have been in the forefront of experiments related to plant domestication. This argument is largely based on ethnographic studies that connect women with horticulture activities. If, in hunting-gathering societies, men generally hunted and women did the food gathering, then it is indeed likely that the early experiments in agriculture were made by women. Further, since pottery was connected to food storage and cooking, tasks that are generally associated with women, they may have had a significant role to play in technical advances related to pottery making. Studies of modern potters have pointed out that making pots is an elaborate, lengthy process that involves more than the hands of the potter who gives the pot its final shape. Women and children may have been involved in these other activities, including collecting and processing clay, collecting fire wood, piling it in the kiln, and decorating the pots. While ethnographic evidence is never conclusive, in these instances, it is fairly persuasive, and there is good ground to assume the involvement of women in the important cultural advances made in the transition to food production.

Although the neolithic stage is generally associated with subsistence-level activities, there is evidence of specialized crafts and long-distance exchange at sites such as Mehrgarh. Kunjhun and Ganeshwar indicate fairly well-developed craft traditions and site specialization. Many sites give evidence of separate areas within the settlement being earmarked for different activities (cattle rearing, craft production, butchering, etc.). This reflects conscious, collective decisions made by members of the community for organizing space and activities. Evidence cited in earlier sections clearly indicates that some neolithic communities were interacting with proto-urban and urban cultures.

When larger groups of people started living together in settled villages, they would have had to devise new ways and norms of interaction and co-operation, ones that were different from those associated with bands of hunter-gatherers. The communities of early farmers and pastoralists must have been internally differentiated on the basis of age and sex. At some sites, differences in the size of houses and in the quantity and quality of grave goods suggest the existence of social ranks. Among larger groups, the regulation of economic activities and social relations would have required some sort of effective political control and organization.

Changes in Cultic and Belief Systems

Changes in subsistence practices would have involved shifts in symbolic and belief systems. One problem is: How are we to define religious or cultic activities, and how can their traces be identified in the archaeological record? In the previous chapter, we noted that some of the palaeolithic and mesolithic art remains may have been

FURTHER DISCUSSION | **Female figurines—ordinary women or goddesses?**

At one time, scholars tended to use the 'Mother Goddess' label for all female figurines found at sites. This was largely because of the belief that the worship of fertility goddesses was an important part of agricultural societies all over the world, and also due to a tendency to look at ancient remains through the lens of later-day Hinduism, in which goddess worship had an important place. However, scholars are now increasingly aware of the stylistic and technical differences among assemblages of female figurines. Further, all goddesses need not have been part of a single goddess cult, and not all ancient goddesses were necessarily associated with maternity.

In the light of such problems, the term 'Mother Goddess' should be replaced by the longer but more neutral phrase—'female figurines with likely cultic significance.' This does not mean that none of these figurines might have had a religious or cultic significance. It is indeed possible that some were either images that were worshipped or votive offerings that were part of some domestic cult or ritual. However, not all female figurines necessarily had such a function. Whether we are looking at human or animal figurines, in all cases, their possible significance or function has to be assessed, and cannot be assumed. Apart from their form, the context in which they were found is crucial.

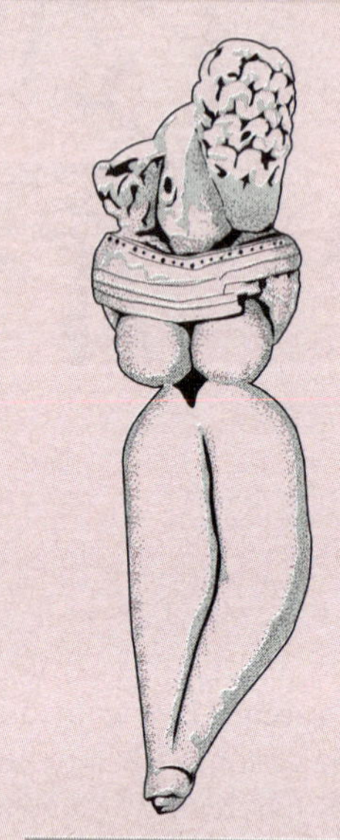

Female figurine, Mehrgarh

connected with magico-religious beliefs and hunting rituals. The cultivation of crops and the domestication of animals must have led to increased concerns with fertility and magico-religious ways of controlling it. Terracotta female figurines found from neolithic levels onwards at certain sites (e.g., in the north-western zone) have often been given the label of 'Mother Goddesses'. It is very likely that farming communities connected women with fertility because of the fact that women give birth. It is also possible that they worshipped images of goddesses associated with fertility. However, the interpretation of female figurines is very subjective. Were these figurines goddesses, or were they toys, decorative items, or clay portraits of ordinary women? Similarly, were the humped bull figurines found at sites such as Rana Ghundai, Mehrgarh, Mundigak, Bala Kot, Gilund, Balathal, and Chirand cult objects? Unless their form or context suggest religious or cultic significance, it is necessary to be cautious while making inferences about the role and function of terracotta figurines. Many rock art sites show activities during the neolithic, with changes in theme and style (these will be discussed in Chapter 5).

Purposeful, standardized burials do not appear for the first time in the neolithic or neolithic–chalcolithic phase, but they do increase in number. Such burials imply significance attached to the bodily remains of the deceased. In cases where burials occur within the habitation area, it is difficult to be certain whether the dead were respected or feared, or both. Patterns in the orientation and form of burials show the existence of funerary customs followed by at least some members of the community. Multiple burials may indicate simultaneous death or the strength of kinship ties. The practice of covering bodies with red ochre prior to burial at Mehrgarh suggests a fertility ritual. The joint burials of humans and animals at Burzahom reflect a close relationship between people and the animals concerned. Simple versus more elaborate graves can be seen as reflections of differences in funerary customs associated with people of different ranks. Food items among the grave goods suggest a belief in afterlife. Secondary burials suggest multi-stage funerary practices and rituals. The social implications of changes in burial practices at certain sites need to be investigated further.

CONCLUSIONS

There is considerable variation in the chronology of the early food-producing societies and in the details of their adaptation to their environment. In *c.* 7000–3000 BCE, food-producing villages emerged in Baluchistan, the northern fringes of the Vindhyas, and the middle Ganga valley. The number and geographical spread of such settlements increased in *c.* 3000–2000 BCE. The beginnings of animal and plant domestication did not lead to the extinction of hunting and gathering. One of the striking features of this period was the co-existence and interaction among neolithic, neolithic–chalcolithic, rural chalcolithic, urban chalcolithic, and hunter-gatherer communities. In the long run, the importance of the advent of food production lay not only in its immediate consequences, but also in the potential it created for future changes. In certain areas, the process of food production and its associated cultural developments eventually led to the emergence of proto-urban settlements, and then full-fledged cities.

FURTHER READINGS

Chakrabarti, Dilip K. 2006. *The Oxford Companion to Indian Archaeology: The Archaeological Foundations of Ancient India, Stone Age to AD 13th Century*. New Delhi: Oxford University Press. Chapters 6, 7.

Chakrabarti, Dilip K. and Makkhan Lal. (Eds.). 2014. *History of Ancient India*. Vol. 2. New Delhi: Vivekanand International Foundation and Aryan Books International. Chaps. I.1, I.2.

Jarrige, Catherine, Jean–François Jarrige, Richard H. Meadow, and Gonzague Quivron. (Eds.). n.d. *Mehrgarh: Field Reports from Neo-lithic Times to the Indus Civilization*. Karachi: Department of Culture and Tourism, Government of Sindh, Pakistan, in collaboration with the French Ministry of Foreign Affairs. Korisettar, Ravi, P. C. Venkatasubbaiah, and Dorian Q. Fuller. 2003. 'Brahmagiri and Beyond: The Archaeology of the Southern Neolithic.' In S. Settar and Ravi Korisettar. (Eds.)., *Indian Archaeology in Retrospect,* Vol. 1: *Prehistory: Archaeology of South Asia*. New Delhi: Indian Council for Historical Research and Manohar, pp. 151–237.

Robbins Schug, Gwen and Subhash R. Walimbe, Subhash R. (Eds.). 2016. *A Companion to South Asia in the Past*. Wiley Blackwell.

Sharma, G. R., V. D. Misra, D. Mandal, B. B. Misra and J. N. Pal. 1980. *From Hunting and Food Gathering to Domestication of Plants and Animals: Beginnings of Agriculture (Epi-Palaeolithic to Neo-lithic: Excavations at Chopani-Mando, Mahadaha and Mahagara)*. Allahabad: Abinash Prakashan.

Tewari, Rakesh and R. K. Srivastava (with contributions by A. Saxena, B, Seth, H. J. Tobschall, I. B. Singh, K. K. Singh, K. S. Saraswat, N. S. Tyagi, P. P. Joglekar, Randall Law, S. C. Yadava, S. Krumm, S. R. Dubey, and V. von Seckendorff). 2022. 'Excavations at Lahuradewa: 2001–02, 2002–03, 2004–05, 2005–06.' Part 1 and 2. *Pragdhara 27–28* (Joint Issue). *Journal of the U.P. State Archaeology Department*.

Valuable details and case studies of the sites mentioned in this chapter (and others too) can be found by browsing through the various volumes of *Indian Archaeology–A Review (https://asi.nic.in/wp-content/uploads/2015/12/IAR_Review_2010_11.pdf)*, *Man and Environment*, *Puratattva*, and *Pragdhara*.

In the hunting scene engraved on stone at Burzahom, one of the hunters appears to be a woman; also note the two suns.

CHAPTER 4

The Harappan Civilization

c. 2600–1900 BCE

In 1826, Charles Masson, an adventurer who had deserted the East India Company army, stood on the mounds of Harappa, a village in Sahiwal district of Punjab. He was convinced that this must have been the very place where, in the 4th century BCE, the Macedonian invader Alexander had defeated king Porus in battle. A few years later, a traveller named Alexander Burnes visited Harappa. He thought it was an important site, but was clueless about its precise significance. Many decades later, in the 1850s, Harappa was visited by Alexander Cunningham, a military engineer with the East India Company who was keenly interested in archaeology. He conducted a small excavation and discovered the remains of some structures, but was not impressed.

When Cunningham re-visited Harappa in 1872, he came as Director General of the newly established Archaeological Survey of India (ASI). He was dismayed to find the mounds badly disturbed by railway contractors who had been busy extracting free bricks. Cunningham found stone tools and ancient pottery, and also obtained a seal with a bull and some strange writing. He was intrigued, but concluded that since the bull did not have a hump, the seal must be a foreign one. He missed a very important clue.

John Marshall, Director General, ASI, 1902–28

The officers of the Archaeological Survey of India who explored Harappa and Mohenjodaro in the early 20th century were unenthusiastic about the sites. Pandit Hirananda Sastri reported that he did not think there was any point in excavating Harappa, and D. R. Bhandarkar's assessment was that Mohenjodaro could not be more than 250 years old! The sites were, however, eventually excavated. In 1920, Daya Ram Sahni started excavations at Harappa and in 1921, R. D. Banerji started excavating Mohenjodaro. But it took a few more years for the true significance of the discoveries at these sites to be understood. The formal announcement of the discovery of the Indus or Harappan civilization was made in 1924 by John Marshall, Director General of the Archaeological Survey, almost a century after Charles Masson had wandered over the mounds of Harappa and sensed that there was something significant about the place (see Lahiri, 2005 for the details of this fascinating story). The implications of Marshall's dramatic announcement were enormous. An important and exciting fragment of India's past had been uncovered, and the beginnings of civilization in the subcontinent were pushed back some 2,500 years, to a time roughly contemporaneous with the civilizations of Mesopotamia and Egypt.

Civilization and Urbanization: Definitions and Implications

There is considerable overlap in scholarly discussions on the themes of civilization, urbanization, and state formation. The word 'civilization' originated in 18th century France and its use spread across Europe along with imperialist expansion, which brought European societies in close contact with those of Africa and Asia. The theories of superior and inferior cultures and races, and the idea of a dichotomy between 'civilized' and 'primitive' people were rooted in this historical context. Historians and archaeologists have long abandoned such value-laden uses of the term civilization. They generally use it for cultures that are marked by cities, a state, and writing. Civilizations share certain broad features such as urban centres, a certain amount of social, economic, and political complexity, and ceremonial or monumental architecture. However, they also have their unique character and trajectories. A comparative approach is useful in order to identify what is similar but also what is very different among early civilizations (see Scarre et al., [1997] 2021).

The word 'urbanization' means the emergence of cities. In a few instances, archaeologists have described neolithic settlements as urban on the basis of a settlement's size and architecture, even in the absence of writing. This is the case with 8th millennium BCE Jericho in the Jordan valley and the 7th millennium BCE settlement at Çatal Höyük in Turkey. The Mayan civilization of Mesoamerica and Mycenaean civilization of Greece did not have true cities, while the Inca civilization of Peru did not have a system of true writing. However, apart from a few such exceptions, cities and writing tend to go together. Urbanization and civilization are more or less synonymous and are associated with the state.

One of the earliest attempts to define a city was made by V. Gordon Childe (1950). Childe described the city as the result and symbol of a revolution that marked a new economic stage in the evolution of society. Like the earlier 'neolithic revolution', the 'urban revolution' was neither sudden nor violent; it was the culmination of centuries of gradual social and economic changes. Childe identified 10 abstract criteria, all supposedly deducible from archaeological data, which distinguished the first cities from the older and contemporary villages.

Rakhaldas Banerji, who excavated Mohenjodaro in 1921

Childe's observations were the starting point of an important debate on the diagnostic features of urban societies. Some scholars did not agree with his use of the word 'revolution' to describe urbanization, as it suggests sudden, deliberate change. Further, his 10 criteria seem to be a loose assemblage of overlapping features, and are not arranged in any sequence of relative importance. For instance, were sophisticated artistic styles as important as an agricultural surplus or a state structure? Further, all 10 features (e.g., exact and predictive sciences) are not directly deducible from the archaeological data. Another objection is that some features, such as monumental architecture, specialized crafts, and long-distance trade are occasionally found in non-urban contexts as well. However, if we consider the 10 characteristics collectively instead of individually, it has to be conceded that Childe did succeed in identifying the most significant features and implications of city life.

Over the years, there have been three different sorts of trends in defining the city. One is to narrow down the diagnostic features, focusing, for instance, on writing, monumental structures, and a large population. A second trend is to identify more specific criteria such as settlement size, architectural features (e.g., fortifications and the use of stone and brick), and a uniform system of weights and measures. A third trend is towards a more abstract definition, highlighting features such as cultural complexity, homogeneity, and far-reaching political control.

The various hypotheses that have been put forward to explain the rise of the world's first cities are reflective of how different scholars view and understand the dynamics of historical processes. Childe emphasized the importance of technological and subsistence factors such as increasing food surpluses, copper-bronze technology, and the use of wheeled transport, sailboats, and ploughs. Scholars such as Robert McC. Adams emphasized social factors, while Gideon Sjoberg asserted that political factors played the pivotal role in the emergence of cities.

An important aspect of McC. Adams' contribution to our understanding of city life is his highlighting the relationship between cities and their hinterlands (see McC. Adams, 1966, 1968). City and village are not two opposite poles, but interdependent and interacting parts of a larger cultural and ecological system. While cities were no doubt ultimately sustained by agricultural surpluses produced in villages, the generation, appropriation, and deployment of agricultural surpluses were neither automatic nor purely economic phenomena and were governed by social and political factors. McC. Adams also highlighted the multiple roles played by cities: They were nodes for the appropriation and redistribution of agricultural surpluses. They provided a

KEY CONCEPTS | **The 10 characteristics of cities, according to Childe**

1. The world's first cities were larger and more densely populated than villages.
2. While the city population may have included some farmers and herdsmen, it also comprised full-time craftspersons, merchants, transporters, officials, and priests. These groups were supported by the surplus food produced by farmers.
3. Farmers had to hand over their surplus produce as tax or tribute to a ruling elite.
4. Monumental public buildings were hall marks of cities and reflected the concentration of social surplus (i.e., surplus produce and wealth generated in a society) in the hands of the elite.
5. There was a trade-off between the ruling class and the rest of society. Rulers lived off the surplus produced by farmers and in return provided them with peace, security, planning, and organization.
6. The invention of systems of recording—writing and numeral notation—helped meet the needs of administration.
7. The invention of writing led to the development of exact but practically useful sciences such as arithmetic, geometry, and astronomy, and the creation of a calendar.
8. Conceptualized and sophisticated styles of artistic expression made their appearance.
9. Cities implied a significant amount of long-distance trade.
10. They also implied a state organization based on residence in a territory rather than on kinship. The state provided security and materials to specialist craftspersons, enabling them to live a settled rather than an itinerant life.

There have been enormous increases in data and theoretical advances since Childe put forward his hypothesis. Historians and archaeologists are much more aware of the complexities and variations in city life, and the difficulties in making a list of diagnostic features that fits all early cities. There is also an awareness that the textures of urban experience for the many people who lived in ancient cities are not easy to reconstruct on the basis of archaeological and/or limited textual evidence.

Source Childe, 1950

Daya Ram Sahni, who excavated Harappa in the 1920s

permanent base for new social and political institutions that regulated the relationships between specialized producers occupying different econiches. They were centres for the safe storage of surpluses, concentration of wealth, and for expenditure on public building programmes by elite groups. They were centres of learning, artistic creativity, philosophical debate, and the development of religious ideas.

Gideon Sjoberg (1964) emphasized the close connection between the history of cities and the rise and fall of empires. He argued that political control was crucial in maintaining the social organization of empires and provide the stability necessary for the development of trade and commerce. He also elaborated on the many facets of the city's functions and features. The concentration of population in a relatively small space in a city allowed a greater level of protection and security than possible in a village. It also facilitated communication and the exchange of goods and services among specialists. Elite groups tended to be concentrated in the city and usually lived near its centre. The city was hence a place where political decisions were taken and military strategies planned. Apart from being centres of intellectual and commercial activity, since elite groups were usually also patrons of the arts, cities also became centres of cultural and artistic activity.

In recent years, there have been vigorous discussions among scholars about various aspects of urbanization (the emergence and growth of cities) and urbanism (the form of the city) (see Marcus and Sabloff. [Ed.], 2008; Monica L. Smith, [2003] 2010). The issues include whether premodern and modern cities have similar features, whether it is possible to draw a clear dividing line between the rural and urban, whether or not a definition of the city is necessary or possible, and the nature of the relationship between cities and states. The role of political leadership and community initiative, neighbourhoods and households, economic interactions and exploitation, social cooperation and conflict, have also been highlighted. Various factors such as population growth, long-distance trade, irrigation, war, and conflict have been suggested as having played an important role in the emergence of cities. Actually, as is the case with all complex cultural phenomena, a variety of factors—social, political, economic, technological, and ideological—must have been involved, in *conjunction* with each other, and the details of their interplay would have varied from city to city. Since archaeology forms the primary source for reconstructing the emergence of the world's first cities, there is more direct information on the material and technological aspects rather than other factors, which can be understood only in very general terms.

The emergence of cities has to be viewed as part of a longer history of human settlements, both rural and urban. The story of urbanization is one of increasing cultural complexity, a widening food resource base, greater technological sophistication, expanding craft production, social stratification, and the emergence of a level of political organization that can be described as a state.

Recent Discoveries and Changing Perspectives

Over the almost hundred years since the significance of the momentous discoveries at Mohenjodaro and Harappa, information about the Harappan civilization has increased enormously. New sites have been discovered and excavated, already known sites have been re-excavated, and there are several new interpretations based on the earlier and newer discoveries. The amount of data and information has been steadily growing and continues to grow. Yet, many aspects of the civilization remain mysterious and subjects of vigorous debate.

Madho Sarup Vats, who excavated Harappa in the 1920s and 1930s

In the initial years after its discovery, the Mesopotamian links were crucial for dating the Harappan civilization, and archaeologists tended to compare the two (Shaffer, 1982a). This led to many questionable theories about Harappan origins and the nature of the Harappan economy and polity. In recent decades, scholars have become very conscious of the earlier bias and acknowledge the need to view the Harappan civilization independently rather than through a Mesopotamian lens.

Another feature of the early decades of Harappan studies was an emphasis on urban settlements, especially Mohenjodaro and Harappa. Apart from being the first sites of the culture to be excavated, these two cities seemed to stand out by virtue of their size and architectural features. However, several other sites are now known to be as large or even larger than them, e.g., Lurewala and Ganweriwala in Cholistan, Rakhigarhi in Haryana, and Dholavira in Gujarat. Scholars have increasingly directed attention to the smaller, less imposing sites, including towns and villages. These include Allahdino (near Karachi), a village settlement that measures only about 5 ha, but which reveals all the main features of the Harappan civilization. Another relatively recently excavated site is Balu in Kaithal district of Haryana, a small fortified rural settlement that has yielded a rich variety of plant remains. Profiles of different kinds of Harappan settlements are now available, and the understanding of the networks that connected cities, towns, and villages has increased substantially.

Although Harappan sites share certain common features, there are also significant regional and inter-site differences. These are visible, for instance, in the layout of settlements and in the crops that people grew. There are also differences in the types, range, and frequency of artefacts. For instance, at Allahdino, the typical black-on-red Harappan pottery formed only 1 per cent of the total pottery finds. The mud-brick platforms in the southern part of the citadel complex at Kalibangan, which have been interpreted as 'fire altars', do not occur at most other sites. There are also differences in the frequency of various funerary practices across sites. For instance, post-cremation burials were much more numerous at Harappa than at Mohenjodaro. All this suggests a variety of subsistence strategies, food habits, craft traditions, religious beliefs, cultic practices, and social customs.

Over the years, the nature and function of certain structures have also been reconsidered. For instance, there is good reason to question whether the 'great granaries' at Mohenjodaro and Harappa were granaries at all (Fentress, 1984). Less acceptable is Leshnik's suggestion (1968) that the dockyard at Lothal was not a dockyard but an irrigation reservoir. The re-interpretation of structures has important implications for the

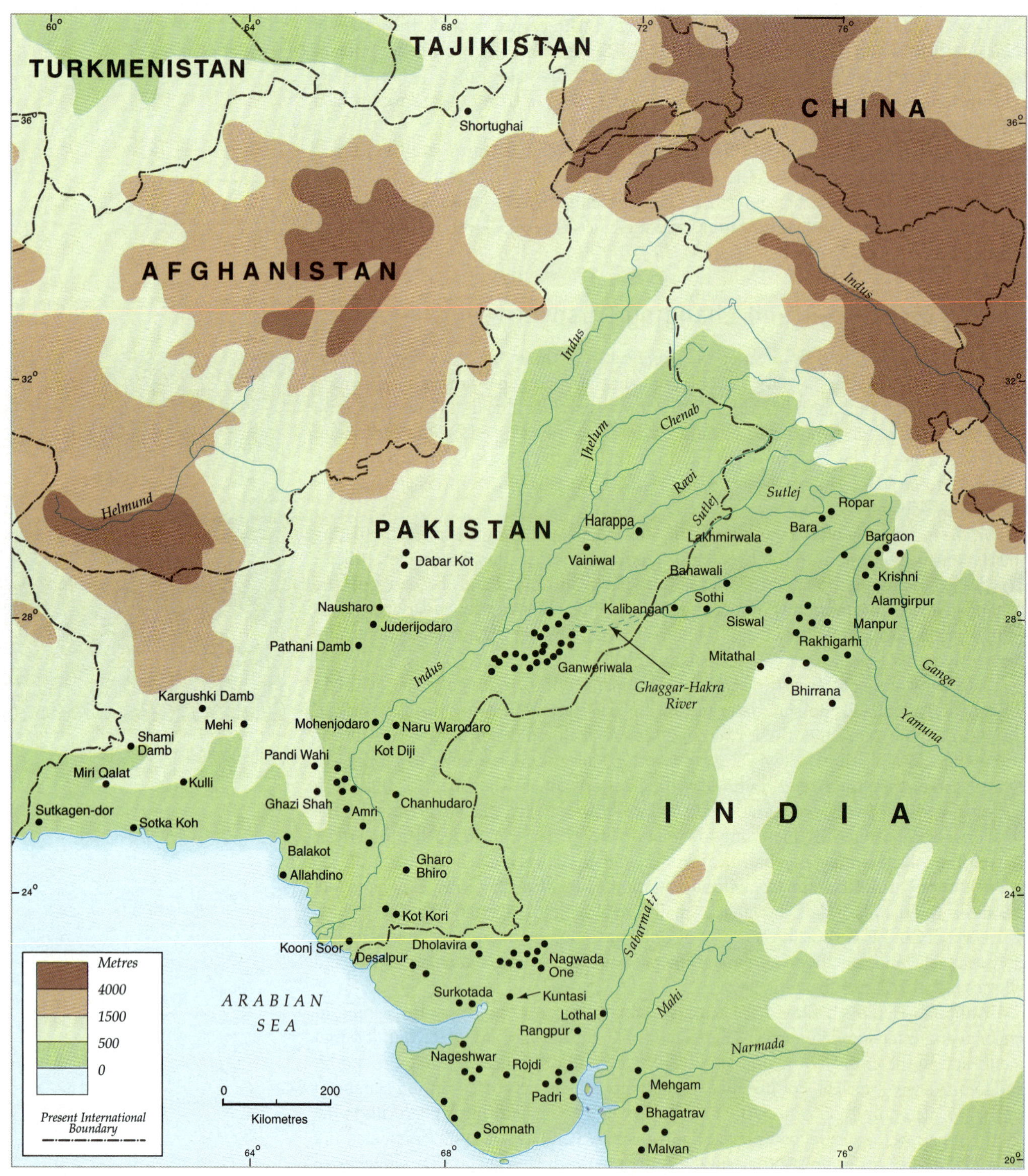

Map 4.1 Distribution of major Harappan sites

understanding of the Harappan social and political systems. For instance, the so-called 'granaries' used to be cited to support the theory of a strong, centralized state.

Recent excavations at Harappan sites reflect the changes in approaches, goals, and techniques within the discipline of archaeology. For instance, compared to earlier excavations, the more recent ones have been marked by much more careful analysis of the cultural sequence and details of various parts of the residential areas. Several studies have contributed to a better understanding of the cultural processes that preceded and followed Harappan urbanism. As more sites have been discovered, explored, excavated, and studied, there is a clearer understanding of the settlement patterns in different parts of the Harappan culture zone. Although there is no unanimity so far on how to read the Harappan script, various studies have sought to document the changes in written material and motifs over time. There has also been a greater use of scientific techniques, including the analysis of plant and bone remains, which provide very specific information about the diet and health of the Harappans. In the future, genome analysis is likely to provide significant information about the Harappan people.

The debates about various aspects of the Harappan civilization reflect both the potential of archaeology as a window into the ancient past and the important role of interpretation in this discipline. There are many different theories about almost every aspect of the Harappan civilization. Not all are equally acceptable; each has to be carefully examined. Conclusions can be reached on certain issues, while in other cases, it is necessary to acknowledge the current limits of our knowledge.

Harappan, Indus, or Sindhu-Sarasvati Civilization?

The first sites of this civilization were discovered in the valley of the Indus and its tributaries. Hence it was given the name 'Indus valley civilization' or 'Indus civilization'. Today, the count of Harappan sites has risen to well over a thousand. The area covered by the Harappan culture zone is huge, ranging between 680,000 to 800,000 sq. km. Sites have been found in Afghanistan; in the Punjab, Sindh, Baluchistan, and North-West Frontier Province of Pakistan; in Jammu, Punjab, Haryana, Rajasthan, Gujarat, and western Uttar Pradesh in India. The northernmost site is Manda in Jammu district of Jammu and Kashmir, the southernmost is Malvan in Surat district in southern Gujarat. The western-most site is Sutkagen-dor on the Makran coast of Pakistan, and the easternmost is Alamgirpur in the Saharanpur district of Uttar Pradesh. There is an isolated site at Shortughai in Afghanistan.

The vast geographical extent of the civilization should make the objection to the terms 'Indus' or 'Indus valley' civilization obvious. The terms 'Indus–Sarasvati' or 'Sindhu–Sarasvati' civilization are also used by many scholars. This is because a large number of sites are located on the banks of the Ghaggar-Hakra river, which is identified by some scholars with the ancient Sarasvati mentioned in the *Rig Veda*. However, the sort of objection to the terms 'Indus' or 'Indus valley' civilization can also be applied to the terms 'Indus–Saraswati' or 'Sindhu–Saraswati' civilization. Since the civilization was not limited to the valleys of the Indus or Ghaggar-Hakra, the best option is to use the term 'Harappan' civilization. This is based on the archaeological convention of naming a culture after the site where it is first identified. The use of the term Harappan civilization does not imply that all other sites are identical to Harappa or that the culture developed first in this place. In fact, Possehl asserts that it is necessary to break the Harappan monolith into sub-regions, which he calls 'Domains' (Possehl, 2003: 6–7). The Harappan civilization simultaneously displays elements of cultural uniformity and regional specificity.

We sometimes hear news about the discovery of new sites of the Harappan civilization. This is done on the basis of a checklist of archaeological features. Pottery is an important marker. The typical Harappan pottery is red, with designs painted on in black, and has a certain range of forms and motifs. Other material traits associated with the civilization include terracotta cakes (pieces of terracotta, usually triangular, sometime round, whose precise function is unclear), a standardized brick size in the 1:2:4 ratio, and certain types of stone and copper artefacts. When the basic set of Harappan material traits are found associated with each other at a site, it is described as a Harappan site.

The Harappan culture was actually a long and complex process consisting of at least three phases—the early Harappan, mature Harappan, and late Harappan. The early Harappan phase was the formative, proto-urban phase of the culture. The mature Harappan phase was the urban phase, the full-fledged stage of civilization. The late Harappan phase was the post-urban phase, when the cities declined. Some archaeologists use other terminology. For instance, Jim Shaffer (1992) uses the term 'Indus valley tradition' for the long series of human adaptations starting from the neolithic–chalcolithic stage to the decline of the Harappan civilization. Within this larger sequence, he uses the term 'regionalization era' for the early Harappan phase, 'integration era' for the mature Harappan phase, and 'localization era' for the late Harappan phase. The early Harappan–mature Harappan transition and the mature Harappan–late Harappan transition are also treated as separate, distinct phases. In this book, the simple and straightforward terminology of early Harappan, mature Harappan, and late Harappan will be used. When the unqualified term Harappan culture/civilization is mentioned, the reference is to the *urban* phase.

Before the advent of radiocarbon dating, the civilization was dated by cross-referencing with the Mesopotamian civilization, with which the Harappans were in contact and whose dates were known. Accordingly, John Marshall suggested that the Harappan civilization flourished between *c.* 3250 and 2750 BCE. When the Mesopotamian chronology was revised, the dates of the Harappan civilization were revised to *c.* 2350–2000/1900 BCE. In more recent times, archeologists have discussed and debated the dates of the royal graves of Ur, where Harappan beads have been found. The dates suggested for these graves have usually ranged from 2600 BCE to 2500 BCE. Julian Reade (2008) has pointed out that the dates in early Mesopotamian archaeology are not as fixed or secure as often imagined, and has suggested a revision of the dates of the royal graves of Ur to *c.* 2400–2300 BCE. There are differences in the dates of individual graves within this span.

The advent of radiocarbon dating in the 1950s offered the prospect of a more scientific basis for dating the civilization, and the number of sites for which radiocarbon dates are available have gradually increased. The 1986–1996 Harappa excavations gave over 70 new radiocarbon dates, but none from the earliest levels, which were submerged in water. Calibrated C-14 dates give a time frame of about 2600–1900 BCE for the urban phase in the core regions of the Indus valley, the Ghaggar-Hakra valley, and Gujarat. This is quite close to the dates arrived at through cross-dating with Mesopotamia. The dates of individual sites vary.

Collating the calibrated radiocarbon dates from various sites gives the following broad chronology for the three phases of the Harappan culture: early Harappan, *c.* 3300–2600 BCE; mature Harappan, *c.* 2600–1900 BCE; and late Harappan, *c.* 1900–1300 BCE. Readers will find some variations on these dates in different publications. For instance, Chakrabarti (2014, Vol. 2: 95) gives the following dates—early Harappan: 3500 BCE onwards; mature Harappan: 2700 BCE onwards; and late Harappan: 2000 BCE onwards. His dating of the mature phase rests on radiocarbon dates and what he describes as 'hard evidence,' namely the presence of Harappan artefacts in the royal graves of Ur, which he assumes to be datable to *c.* 2600 BCE. However, as mentioned above, the dating of the Ur graves is not as secure as is often presumed. In any case, the dates of the phases of the Harappan culture should be understood as approximate dates, subject to revision as more radiometric dates become available.

Origin: The Significance of the Early Harappan Phase

Issues of origins are always complex and often contentious. In his report on Mohenjodaro, John Marshall asserted that the Indus civilization must have had a long antecedent history on the soil of India (see Chakrabarti, 1984 for a summary of the various theories). However, there were others who put forward **diffusionist** explanations. According to E. J. H. Mackay, a migration of people from Sumer (southern Mesopotamia) may have led to the Harappan civilization; other proponents of the migration theory included D. H. Gordon and S. N. Kramer. Mortimer Wheeler argued for a migration of ideas, not people—the idea of civilization was in the air of West Asia in the 3rd millennium BCE and the founders of the Harappan civilization had a model of civilization before them.

The fact that city life emerged in Mesopotamia a few centuries before it appeared in the Egyptian and Harappan contexts does not mean that the latter were derived from the Mesopotamian civilization in a direct or indirect way. There are in fact several striking differences between the Harappan and Mesopotamian civilizations. The Mesopotamians had a completely different script, a much greater use of bronze, different settlement layouts, and a large-scale canal system of the kind that is absent in the Harappan civilization.

If the Harappan civilization cannot be explained as an offshoot or offspring of the Mesopotamian civilization, what is the alternative? The story of its origins can, in fact, be traced to the emergence of settled farming communities in Baluchistan in the 7th millennium BCE. Its more immediate prelude was the cultural phase that used to be known as pre-Harappan, and is now usually referred to as the early Harappan phase.

Amalananda Ghosh (1965) was the first archaeologist to identify similarities between a pre-Harappan culture and the mature Harappan culture. Ghosh focused on the pre-Harappan Sothi culture of Rajasthan. He asserted that there were similarities between Sothi pottery and the pottery of (*a*) Zhob, Quetta, and other Baluchi sites; (*b*) pre-Harappan Kalibangan, Kot Diji, and the lowest levels of Harappa and Mohenjodaro; and (*c*) mature Harappan levels at Kalibangan, and perhaps also at Kot Diji. In view of these similarities, he argued that the Sothi culture should be described as proto-Harappan. A limitation of this hypothesis was that it was based exclusively on a comparison of pottery, and did not consider other material traits. And in emphasizing ceramic similarities, Ghosh had ignored the many differences between the Sothi and Harappan cultures. The result was an over-emphasis on the Sothi element in the account of the emergence of the Harappan civilization.

The first comprehensive analysis of the evidence from pre-Harappan sites in the greater Indus valley and north Baluchistan was made by M. R. Mughal (1977). Mughal compared the whole range of evidence (pottery, stone tools, metal artefacts, architecture, etc.) from pre-Harappan and mature Harappan levels, and explored the relationship between the two stages. The pre-Harappan phase showed large fortified settlements; a fairly high level of expertise in specialized crafts such as stone working, metal crafting, and bead making; the use of wheeled transport, and the existence of trade networks. The range of raw materials used by the pre-Harappans was more or less the same as that used in the mature Harappan phase (except for jade, which is absent in the early Harappan context). The two things lacking were large cities and increased levels of craft specialization. Mughal argued that the 'pre-Harappan' phase actually represented the early, formative phase of the Harappan culture and that the term 'pre-Harappan' should, therefore, be replaced by 'early Harappan'.

Painted designs on early Harappan pottery, Nal (from top right); Kulli (left)

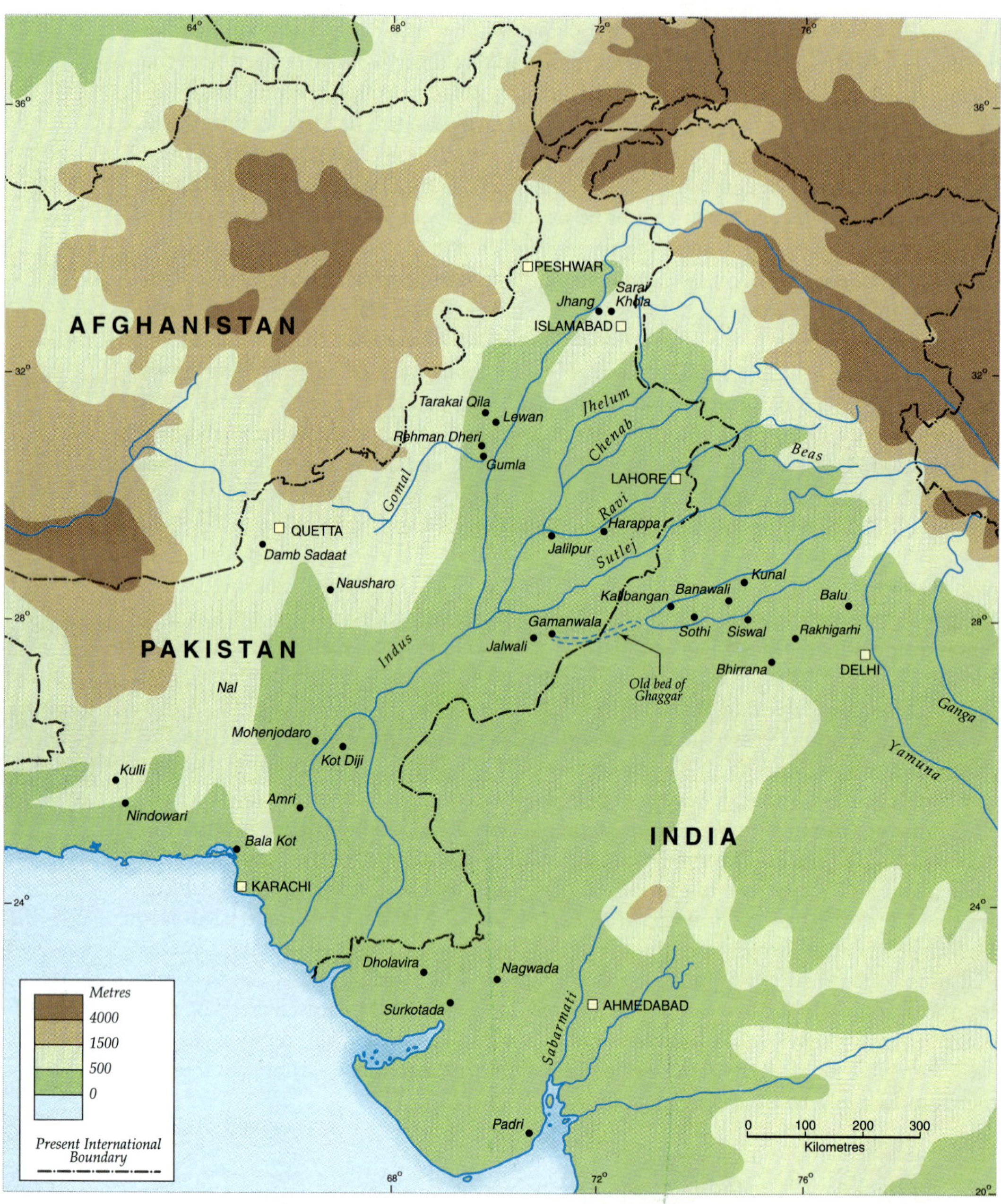

Map 4.2 Some early Harappan sites

Early Harappan levels have been identified at a large number of sites, a few of which are discussed below. At some sites, the early Harappan phase represents the first cultural stage, at others it is part of a longer cultural sequence. The dates vary from site to site, but the general range is *c.* 3300–2600 BCE. The early Harappan phase is extremely important, not merely as a stepping-stone to urbanization, but in its own right as well.

At Balakot (on the coastal plain of Sonmiani Bay on the Makran coast), Period II is early Harappan. The pottery was wheel-made and painted, some of it similar to the polychrome ware of Nal. There were microliths, humped bull figurines, a few copper objects, miscellaneous artefacts made of terracotta, shell, and bone, and beads of lapis lazuli, stone, shell, and paste. Remains of barley, vetch, legumes, and *ber* were found and bones of cattle, sheep, goat, buffalo, hare, deer, and pig were identified.

Mention was made in Chapter 3 of the site of Nal in the Khozdar area of Baluchistan. Nal- and Amri-related sites represent the early Harappan phase in the southern part of the Indus valley and Baluchistan.

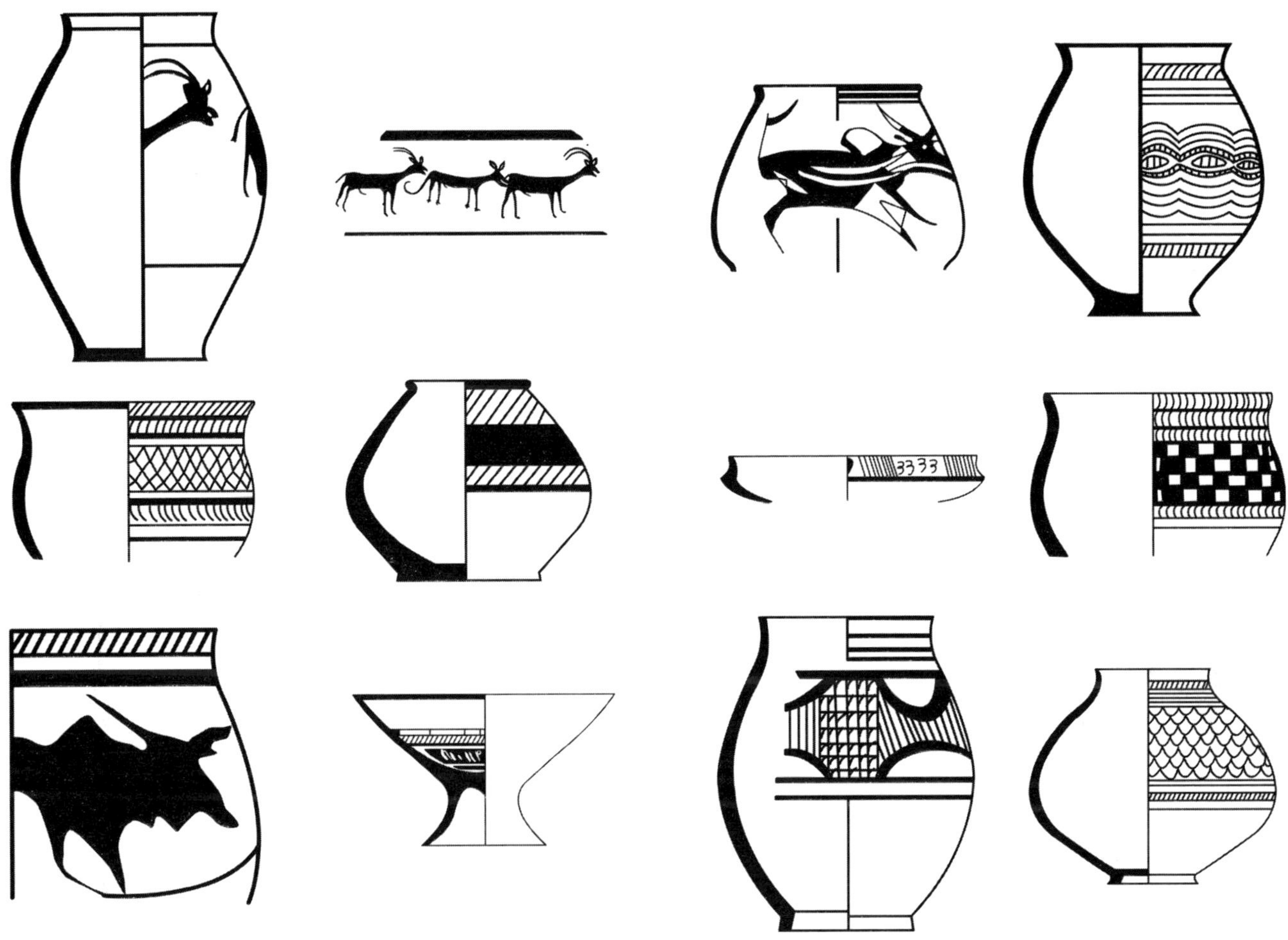

Figure 4.1 Amri pottery

Amri in Sindh lies about 2 km from the right bank of the Indus. The settlement goes back to *c.* 3500 BCE. Period I at Amri is early Harappan and is further sub-divided into four phases—1A, 1B, 1C, and 1D. Period II represents a transitional phase and Period III is mature Harappan. Within Period I, there was a gradual increase in the refinement and variety of pottery. Mud-brick structures, sometimes supplemented with stone, made their appearance. Artefacts included chert blades, stone balls, bone tools, and a few fragments of copper and bronze. In Period IC, there were multiple cellular compartments, perhaps used for storing grain or as platforms for buildings. The pottery was dominated by wheel-made wares and showed a great variety of forms and painted designs, mostly geometric. The painting was monochrome or polychrome, using brown, black, and ochre.

Kot Diji lies about 160 km north-east of Amri, on the left bank of one of the old flood channels of the Indus. Here, there is an early and mature Harappan level with a burnt deposit in between. Early Harappan Period I was dated from *c.* 3300 BCE. Fortified with a massive wall made of limestone rubble and mud-brick, the settlement consisted of a citadel complex and a lower residential area. House walls of stone and mud-brick were found in the upper levels. Artefacts included objects of stone, shell, and bone; terracotta figurines (including a bull figurine), bangles, and beads; and a fragment of a bronze bangle. There is a great variety of pottery in Period I, mostly wheel-made and decorated with brownish bands of paint. The distinctive pottery is a short-necked ovoid pot, painted with designs such as the 'horned deity', *pipal* leaves and 'fish scales'. Artefacts similar to those at Kot Diji Period I have been found at other sites as well, and such levels are known as 'Kot Dijian'.

At Mehrgarh, the excavators noted the occurrence of Kot Diji style vessels, fragments of triangular terracotta cakes, very long flint blades, and fragments of perforated jars,

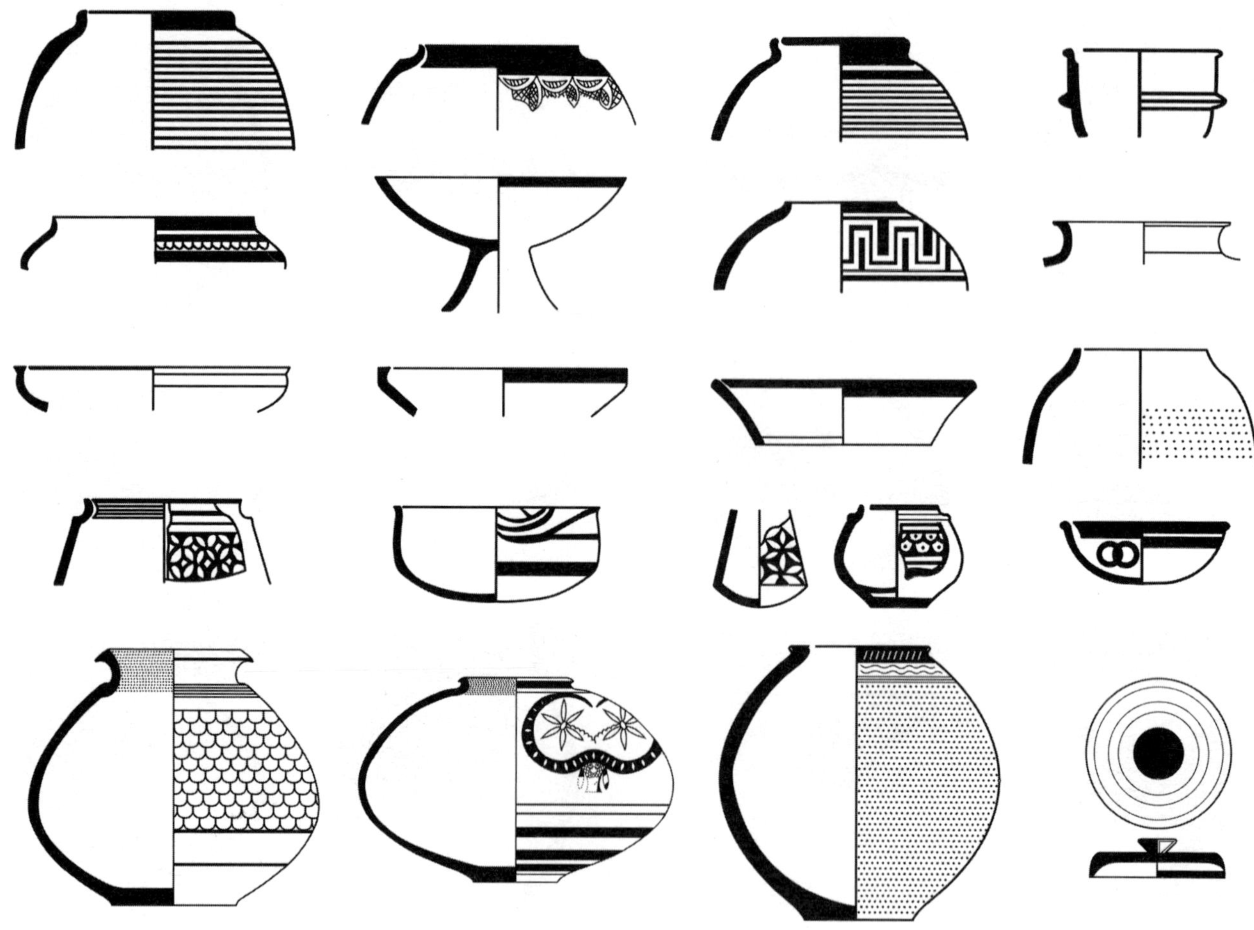

Figure 4.2 Kot Dijian pottery from various sites

which suggest links with the Indus valley by the end of Period VII. However, these links are not so strong as to constitute true Harappan influence. At nearby Nausharo, there is a clear transition from the early Harappan to a transitional and then mature Harappan phase. The pottery of Period IC (the later part of the early Harappan levels) at Nausharo was similar to that of Mehrgarh Period VIIC. Jarrige (Jarrige et al., n.d.: 87) suggests that these two phases were contemporaneous and can be dated *c.* 2600–2550 BCE.

There are a number of early Harappan sites in the Dera Jat area in the western Indus plains. At Gumla in the Gomal valley, new pottery styles, including some similar to the Kot Dijian, appeared in Period II. Period III was dominated by Kot Dijian pottery forms and designs including the 'horned deity'. Period IV at Gumla belonged to the mature Harappan phase.

Period I at Rehman Dheri in the Gomal valley is early Harappan and its earliest levels are dated *c.* 3380–3040 BCE. The settlement was over 20 ha in size. Aerial photographs showed a planned, rectangular settlement with a regular grid of streets and houses, surrounded by a massive wall that belonged to a later phase, contemporary with the mature Harappan. However, it is clear that there was a wall made of mud and mud-brick around the settlement in the early Harappan phase as well. The pottery designs show Kot Dijian elements and some of the pots have graffiti. Artefacts included stone blades, copper and bronze tools, and terracotta figurines. Beads of lapis lazuli and turquoise were found, indicating exchange with Afghanistan and Central Asia. Plant remains comprised grains of wheat and barley. Bones of cattle, sheep, and goat were identified.

Similar discoveries were made at several sites in the Bannu basin. The early Harappan settlement at Lewan may go back to the early 3rd millennium BCE. Apart from a small habitation area, excavations revealed an area measuring about 450 × 325 m, littered with various kinds of stone tools in different stages of production—microliths (mostly of chert) as well as heavy stone artefacts, including various types of querns, stone balls, long triangular stone axes, ring stones, and pointed hammer stones. Lewan was clearly a factory site where various kinds of stone tools were made. Beads and bead making material were also found in a part of this industrial area. Tarakai Qila gave evidence of wheat, barley, lentils (*Lens culinaris*), and field pea (*Pisum arvense*), and there were stone blades with the sheen typical of sickles used for harvesting grain. Bones of cattle, water buffalo, sheep, and goat were found.

Early Harappan pottery: Zangian; Shahi Tump

Period II at Sarai Khola in the northern part of Punjab province of Pakistan is early Harappan. There was a transition within this period from pit dwellings to mud-brick houses. The dominant pottery type was Kot Dijian. Stone artefacts included microliths, celts, and chisels. There were other objects such as terracotta figurines, terracotta and shell bangles, beads made of steatite paste, and one of lapis lazuli. Some copper artefacts, including bangles, pins, rings, and rods, also made their appearance.

In the previous chapter, mention was made of more recent excavations at Harappa in Punjab province of Pakistan, which indicate that the first occupation of the site (Period I) belongs to the Ravi aspect of the Hakra phase. The settlement of the early Harappan phase at Harappa (Period II) was over 25 ha in area (Meadow and Kenoyer, 2001). It was divided into two mounds, each with massive mud-brick platforms and fortifications. The layout of the houses and streets suggest elements of planning. Remains of mud-brick walls, hearths, and a small circular kiln were found. Craftspeople used a variety of raw materials to produce a diverse range of items. Pottery included types similar to those found at Kot Diji. Other artefacts included chert blades, a few stone celts, terracotta female figurines and bangles, and beads made of lapis lazuli, carnelian, and steatite. There is evidence of writing (on pottery and seals), inscribed seals, and standardized weights. Certain types of artefacts found in the early Harappan phase—including some pottery types, figurines, triangular terracotta cakes, toys, and bangles—continued into the mature Harappan phase.

As mentioned in Chapter 3, the first village settlements in the Cholistan tract of the Hakra plain belong to the Hakra wares phase. The next cultural phase in this area is Kot Dijian, i.e., early Harappan. In fact, the greatest concentration of Kot Dijian sites lies in the Cholistan region. In this phase, there was a dramatic change from a nomadic life to permanent settlement. M. R. Mughal's study (1997) shows a drop in the number of camp sites from 52.5 per cent (Hakra wares phase) to 7.5 per cent. Many of the settlements had kilns, indicating a sharp increase in specialized craft activities. About 60 per cent of the sites are under 5 ha, and 25 per cent are between 5 and 10 ha. There are a few larger sites, namely Jalwali (22.5 ha) and Gamanwala (27.3 ha).

Period I at Kalibangan on the banks of the Ghaggar river is early Harappan (see B. B. Lal et al., 2003). Calibrated radiocarbon dates give a range of *c.* 2920–2550 BCE. The settlement of Period I was about 4 ha in size and was surrounded by massive mud-brick fortifications. Houses were made of mud and mud-brick, and were built around courtyards. There was a standardization of brick size (3:2:1). Hearths, lime-plastered storage pits, and saddle querns were found in houses. Artefacts included stone blades, terracotta cakes, shell bangles, disc beads made of steatite, carnelian, faience, gold, and silver, and over a hundred copper objects. The pottery of Period I showed great variety. Some of the pots were similar to Kot Dijian pottery. The distinctive pottery was red or pink in colour with designs painted on in black, sometimes also in white. The designs included a moustache-like scroll, plants, fish, and cattle. Some of the graffiti on pottery is similar to the script of the mature Harappan phase. One of the most exciting finds in Period I was made to the south of the site—a ploughed field surface, showing the north–south and east–west furrow marks left by a plough several thousand years ago.

There are a number of early Harappan sites in the Indo-Gangetic divide. At Kunal, Banawali, and Rakhigarhi in Hissar district of Haryana, the early Harappan phase was

Figure 4.3 Painted motifs on pre-Harappan pottery from Kalibangan

succeeded by a mature Harappan phase. At Kunal, Period IA belonged to the Hakra wares phase. Period IB showed a continuation of the traits of the earlier phase, but also a large quantity of pottery of the type found at Kalibangan I. There was also the first occurrence of sturdy red beakers and jars of the Harappan type. Period IC was transitional between the early and mature Harappan. The below ground-level houses of the earlier phases made way for ground-level houses made of standardized mud-bricks (in the 1:2:3 and 1:2:4 size ratios). Six steatite seals and one shell seal bearing geometric patterns were found. Thousands of beads made of semi-precious stone were found at early Harappan levels at Kunal. One of the houses revealed a silver pot containing a hoard of jewellery, including two silver tiaras, a silver armlet and bangles, six round gold pendants, and beads made of semi-precious stones such as lapis lazuli and agate.

At Banawali, the early Harappan phase was marked by mud-brick houses with hearths and plastered storage pits in the courtyards. The pottery was similar to that found at Kalibangan I. Artefacts included stone blades, copper objects, beads of gold and semi-precious stones, and a cubical chert blade. Nearby, along the Ghaggar-Hakra, early Harappan levels were identified at Siswal and Balu in Haryana and Rohira and Mahorana in Punjab.

Rakhigarhi gives evidence of a planned settlement and mud-brick structures in early Harappan Period I (see Amarendra Nath, 2004). The range of pottery types was similar to that of Kalibangan I. Artefacts included uninscribed seals, pottery with graffiti, terracotta wheels, carts, rattles, and bull figurines, chert blades, weights, a bone point, and a muller. A lot of animal bones were found during the excavations, indicating the importance of animal husbandry. A stacked set of hopscotches was found in an open area behind the structural complex. This suggests the possibility that a game similar to *pithu*, which is popular among children in India and Pakistan, goes back to early Harappan times!

Bhirrana in Fatehabad district of Haryana (Rao et al., 2004–05) has given valuable information on the processes leading to the Harappan civilization. Period IA belongs to the Hakra wares culture, Period IB is early Harappan, Period II early mature Harappan, and Period IIB mature Harappan. The remains of Period IB included vestiges of structures made of mud-bricks in the ratio of 1:2:3, including a house complex consisting of six rooms, a central courtyard, and *chullahs*. There were many different kinds of pottery, including the types known from Kalibangan, as well as the bi-chrome wares, a few sherds of light incised wares, and tan/chocolate wares known from Period IA. Some of the pottery had graffiti. Other artefacts included copper arrowheads, rings, and bangles; beads of carnelian, jasper, steatite, shell, and terracotta; terracotta marbles, pendant, bull figurine, female figurines, rattle, cake, wheel, toy carts with solid wheels (a few have radiating lines which may possibly represent spokes), and gamesmen (small pieces that may have been used as counters in some sort of ancient board game); plain and segmented terracotta bangles; faience bangles; bone objects; and sandstone sling balls, marbles, and pounders. A shale button seal and a steatite seal with a boss, both with concentric circle designs, were found.

Excavations at sites such as Padri and Kuntasi in Saurashtra have shown the existence of a well-developed early Harappan horizon in Gujarat. The site of Dholavira in the Rann of Kutch has early Harappan levels. The settlement was fortified with an imposing wall made of stone rubble set in mud mortar. Buildings were made of standardized (1:2:4) mud-bricks. Pottery included perforated jars and dish-on-stand, and there was evidence of copper artefacts, stone blades, shell objects, terracotta cakes, and stone beads.

The Relationship Between the Early and Mature Harappan Phases

Apart from the fact that some features of the mature Harappan culture were already in place in the early Harappan phase, what is also visible is a gradual transition from a variety of regional traditions towards a level of cultural uniformity cutting across regions, a process that the Allchins call 'cultural convergence' (Allchin and Allchin, 1997: 163). Some inferences can also be made about the social and political processes that were underway. Specialized crafts imply specialized craftspersons, trade implies traders, and planned settlements imply planners, executors, and labourers. Seals have been found at Kunal and Nausharo and may have been connected with traders or elite groups. The discovery of hoards of jewellery at Kunal, including a silver piece that has been interpreted as a crown, suggests a fairly high level of concentration of wealth and may also have political implications. The discovery of symbols similar to Harappan writing at early Harappan levels at Padri in Gujarat, Kalibangan in Rajasthan, Banawali in Haryana, Dholavira in Kutch, and Harappa in west Punjab shows that the roots of the Harappan script go back to this phase.

Another notable feature is the appearance of the 'horned deity' at a number of places. He is painted on a jar found at Kot Diji and on several jars found at early Harappan Rehman Dheri, in contexts dated *c.* 2800–2600 BCE. At Kalibangan Period I, his figure was incised on one side of a terracotta cake, on the other side of which was a figure with a tied animal. All this suggests that the process of 'cultural convergence' was also operating in the religious and symbolic spheres.

But how did this convergence come about? What led to the transition from the proto-urban early Harappan phase to full-fledged city life? Was it the result of increased inter-regional contact, or long-distance trade? Trade with Mesopotamia has been suggested as a factor, but the importance of this trade has been exaggerated even in the context of the mature Harappan phase. According to Chakrabarti (1995b: 49–52), the catalyst for the transition may have been an increasing level of craft specialization, instigated especially by the development of copper metallurgy in Rajasthan. He suggests that another crucial factor for the spread of settlements in the active floodplain of the Indus may have been agricultural growth based on an organized irrigation system, but direct evidence of this is lacking. The answer may lie in the emergence of a new, decisive political leadership, significant changes in social organization, or perhaps a new ideology. Unfortunately, such changes are difficult to deduce from the archaeological data.

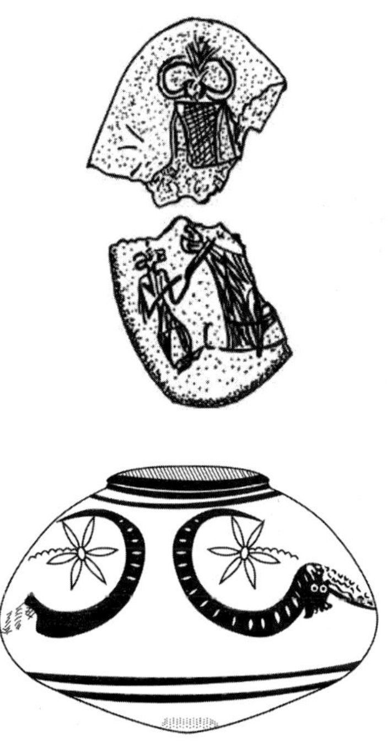

Figure 4.4 Horned deity on terracotta cake and pot, Kalibangan, Period I

There are several other gaps in our understanding of the relationship between the early and mature Harappan phases. The information about the earliest levels at sites such as Mohenjodaro and Harappa is inadequate. There are several mature Harappan sites where there is no early Harappan level, e.g., Lothal, Desalpur, Chanhudaro, Mitathal, Alamgirpur, and Ropar. There are several early Harappan sites in the Potwar plateau which do not have mature Harappan levels. In Cholistan, only a few of the many early Harappan sites—Chak 76, Gamanwali, and Sandhanawala Ther—continued to be occupied in the mature Harappan phase. Further, there are no early Harappan sites in the active Indus plain. And at sites where there are both early Harappan and mature Harappan levels, the transition from one to the other is not always smooth. At Kot Diji and Gumla, a burnt deposit between the two suggests a major fire. Evidence of burning was also found at Amri and Nausharo. At Kalibangan, the break in occupation may have been due to an earthquake.

The General Features of Mature Harappan Settlements

The fact that the Harappan civilization was urban does not mean that all or even most of its settlements had an urban character. A majority were villages. The cities depended on villages for food and perhaps also labour, and various kinds of goods produced in cities found their way into the villages. As a result of the brisk urban–rural interaction, the typical range of Harappan artefacts reached even small village sites.

It is not easy to estimate the exact size of ancient settlements, as they are often spread over many mounds and buried under layers of alluvium. Nevertheless, it is clear that the Harappan sites varied a great deal in size and function, from large cities to small pastoral camps. The largest settlements include Mohenjodaro (over 200 ha), Harappa (over 150 ha), Ganweriwala (over 81.5 ha), Rakhigarhi (over 100 ha), and Dholavira (about 100 ha). Lurewala in Cholistan, with an estimated population of about 35,000, seems to have been as large as Mohenjodaro. Other large sites (about 50 ha) are Nagoor, Tharo Waro Daro, and Lakhueenjo-Daro in Sindh, and Nondowri in Baluchistan. Some very large Harappan sites have been reported in Punjab—Dhalewan (about 150 ha) in Mansa district and Gurni Kalan I (144 ha), Hasanpur II (about 100 ha), Lakhmirwala (225 ha), and Baglian Da Theh (about 100 ha) in Bhatinda district, but details are lacking. The second rung of Harappan settlements are moderate-sized sites ranging between 10 and 50 ha, such as Judeirjodaro and Kalibangan. Then, there are the even smaller sites of 5–10 ha, such as Amri, Lothal, Chanhudaro, and Rojdi. The many settlements in the 1–5 ha range include Allahdino, Kot Diji, Rupar, Balakot, Surkotada, Nageshwar, Nausharo, and Ghazi Shah. There are also settlements even smaller than these.

View of Mohenjodaro (Sindh, Pakistan)

The streets and houses of Harappan cities were once thought to be laid on a grid-pattern oriented north–south and east–west. Actually, even Mohenjodaro does not show a perfect grid system. Roads in the Harappan cities were not always absolutely straight and did not always cross one another at right angles. But the settlements were clearly planned. There is no strict correlation between the level of planning and the size of a settlement. For example, the relatively small site of Lothal shows a much higher level of planning than Kalibangan, which is twice its size. The details of the plans differ. Mohenjodaro, Harappa, and Kalibangan have a similar layout, consisting of a raised citadel complex and a lower city. At Lothal and Surkotada, the citadel complex is not separate;

Mohenjodaro: well flanked by house walls

it is located within the main settlement. In its most fully developed phase, Dholavira consisted of not two but three parts—the citadel, middle town, and lower town.

A major difference between the buildings in large cities and those in smaller towns and villages was in the type and combination of raw materials used. In villages, houses were made mostly of mud-brick, with the additional use of mud and reeds; stone was occasionally used for foundations or drains. Buildings in towns and cities were made of sun-dried and burnt bricks. In the rocky areas of Kutch and Saurashtra, however, there was extensive use of stone. The massive fortification walls with a veneer of dressed stone at Dholavira and the remains of stone pillars in the citadel are very distinctive and are not found at any other Harappan site.

The fact that some house walls at Mohenjodaro survive upto a height of 5 m is a tribute to the strength of the bricks and the brick-laying skill of the Harappans. There were various styles of laying bricks, including what is known as the 'English bond style'. In this, bricks were laid together in a sequence of long side (stretcher) and short side (header), with an alternate arrangement in consecutive rows. This gave the wall maximum load-bearing strength. A striking feature of Harappan structures is the uniformity in the average size of the bricks—7 × 14 × 28 cm for houses and 10 × 20 × 40 cm for city walls. Both these brick sizes have an identical ratio of thickness, width, and length (1:2:4). This ratio first makes its appearance at a few sites in the early Harappan phase, but in the mature Harappan phase, it is found in all the settlements.

People lived in houses of different sizes, mostly consisting of rooms arranged around a central courtyard. Doorways and windows generally faced the side lanes and rarely opened onto the main streets. The view from the lane into the courtyard was blocked off by a wall. There are remains of staircases that may have led to the roof or a second storey. The fact that some of the houses at Mohenjodaro were two stories high or more is also suggested by the thickness of their walls. Floors were usually made of hard-packed earth, often re-plastered or covered with sand. The ceilings were probably over 3 m high. Roofs may have been made of wooden beams covered with reeds and packed clay.

The doors and windows of houses were made of wood and mats. Clay models of houses show that doors were sometimes carved or painted with simple designs. Windows had shutters (perhaps made of wood or reeds and matting), with latticework grills above and below to allow in light and air. A few pieces of carved alabaster and marble latticework have been found at Harappa and Mohenjodaro; such slabs may have been set into the brickwork. Small houses attached to large ones may have been the quarters of service groups working for wealthy city dwellers. In the larger houses, passages led into inner rooms, and there is evidence of frequent renovation activity.

Bathrooms and toilets are facilities people use every day but which most books on ancient history rarely discuss. In the case of the Harappan civilization, there is quite a bit of information on this aspect (Kenoyer, 1998: 59–60). Many houses or groups of houses had separate bathing areas and toilets. Bathing platforms with drains were often located in rooms next to a well. The floor of the bathing area was usually made of tightly fitted bricks,

Mohenjodaro: main street

frequently set on edge, to make a carefully sloped watertight surface. A small drain led from here, cut through the house wall, and went out into the street, connecting ultimately with a larger sewage drain.

Although some people may have used the area outside the city walls to relieve themselves, toilets have been identified at many sites. They ranged from the simple hole in the ground above a cesspit to more elaborate arrangements. Excavations at Harappa uncovered toilets in almost every house. The commodes were made of big pots sunk into the floor, many of them associated with a small *lota*-type jar, no doubt for washing up. Most of the pots had a small hole in the base, through which water could seep into the ground. The waste from the toilets was in some cases discharged though a sloping channel into a jar or drain in the street outside. Some people must have had the job of cleaning the toilets and drains on a regular basis.

Well laid-out streets and side lanes associated with an efficient and well-planned drainage system are other notable features of Harappan settlements. Even the smaller towns and villages had impressive drainage systems. The sewage chutes and pipes were separate from drains for collecting rain water. Drains and water chutes from the second storey were often built inside the wall, with an exit opening just above the street drain. At Harappa and Mohenjodaro, terracotta drain pipes directed waste water into open street drains made of baked bricks. These connected into large drains along the main streets, which emptied their contents into the fields outside the city wall. The main drains were covered by corbelled arches made of brick or stone slabs. There were rectangular soak-pits for collecting solid waste at regular intervals. These must have been cleaned out regularly, otherwise the drainage system would have become choked and a health hazard.

The Harappans made elaborate arrangements for water for drinking and bathing. The emphasis on providing water for bathing, evident at several sites, suggests that they were very particular about personal hygiene. It is possible that frequent bathing also had a religious or ritualistic aspect. The sources of water were rivers, wells, and reservoirs or cisterns. Mohenjodaro is noted for its large number of wells. Harappa had much fewer wells but a depression in the centre of the city may represent a tank or reservoir that served the city's inhabitants. There are a few wells at Dholavira, which is noted more for its impressive water reservoirs lined with stone.

Profiles of Some Harappan Cities, Towns, and Villages

A very small proportion of identified Harappan sites have been excavated. And where excavations have taken place, only sections of the settlements have been exposed (for site details, see, for instance, Kenoyer, 1998; Possehl, 2003; Lal, 1997; Chakrabarti and Lal. [Eds.], 2014, Vol. 2).

Mohenjodaro in Sindh lies about 5 km away from the Indus; in protohistoric times, the river may have flowed much closer. The site consists of two mounds, a higher but smaller western mound and a lower but larger eastern mound. There is an extensive area to the east that has not yet been explored. The size of the site has been estimated as about 200 ha. On the basis of the density of houses in the excavated area, Fairservis (1967) suggested that the lower city may have housed about 41,250 people.

The western mound at Mohenjodaro (known as the citadel) rises up to 12 m above the plain. The structures here were built on an artificial mud and mud-brick platform, about 400 × 200 m. The mound was circled by a 6 m thick mud-brick retaining wall or platform with projections on the south-west and west, and a tower has been identified on the south-east. It has been suggested that the elevated area at Mohenjodaro does not represent a defensive fortification but was part of a civic design to create an elevated symbolic landscape. However, the defensive nature of the walls here and at other cities cannot be ruled out.

The buildings on the citadel mound of Mohenjodaro are among the things we associate most closely with the Harappan civilization. In the north are the Great Bath, the so-called 'granary', and 'college of priests'. The Great Bath, an example of the Harappans' engineering skill, measures about 14.5 × 7 m, with a maximum depth of 2.4 m. A wide staircase leads down into the tank from the north and south. The floor and walls of the tank were made water-tight by finely fitted bricks laid edge to edge with gypsum mortar. A thick layer of bitumen was laid along the sides of the tank and probably also below the floor, making this one of the earliest examples of waterproofing in the world. The floor slopes towards the south-west corner, where a small outlet leads to a large corbelled brick drain, which would have taken the water out to the edge of the mound. Remains of brick colonnades were discovered on the eastern, northern, and southern sides of the bath and a similar colonnade must have existed on the western side as well. Two large doors lead into the complex from the south and there were also entrances from the north and east. There are a series of rooms along the eastern edge of the building. One of them has a well that may have supplied water to the tank. Immediately to the north of the Great Bath is a large building consisting of eight small rooms with common bathing platforms.

Across the street from the Great Bath are the remains of a large, imposing building (69 × 23.4 m) consisting of several rooms, a 10 m square courtyard, and three verandahs. Two staircases led either to the roof or an upper storey. Because of its size and proximity to the Great Bath, it was tentatively identified as the house of the chief priest or several priests, and was labelled the 'college of priests'.

On the western edge of the citadel mound, at the south-west corner of the Great Bath, raised on a tapered brick platform, is a structure that was originally identified as

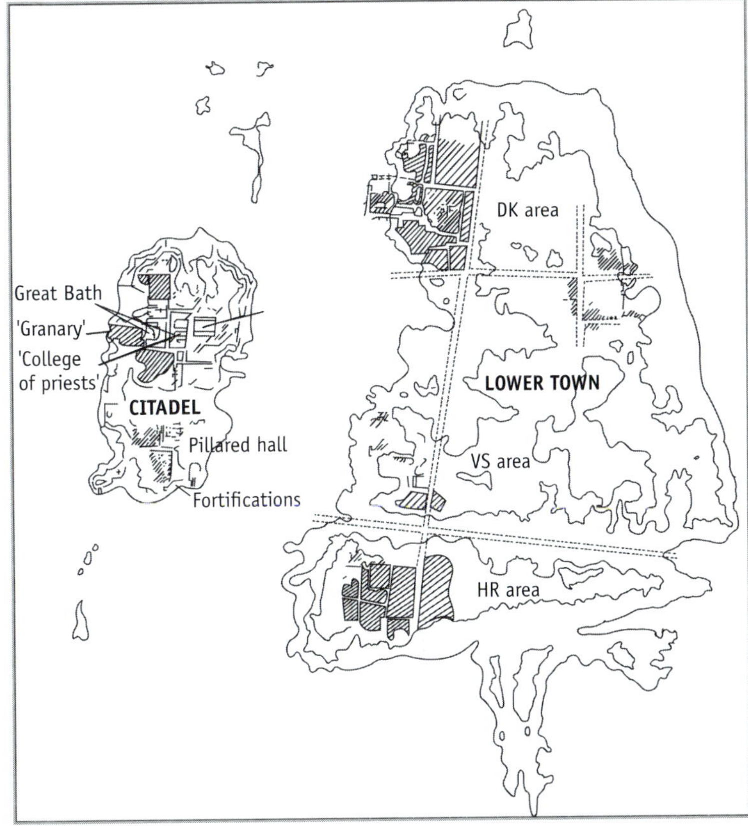

Figure 4.5 Citadel and lower town, Mohenjodaro

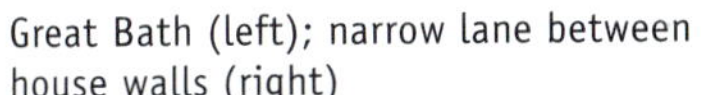

Great Bath (left); narrow lane between house walls (right)

a *hammam* or hot-air bath, and later as the 'great granary'. The 50 × 27 m solid brick foundation was divided into 27 square and rectangular blocks by narrow passageways, 2 running east–west and 8 running north–south. The entire superstructure may have been made of wood. A 4.5 m wide brick staircase led from the south-western edge of the building to the level of the plain. There was a small bathing platform at the top of the stairs and a brick-lined well at their foot. To the north was a burnt brick platform, identified by Wheeler as a loading dock. As it was excavated without recording the artefacts found in the passageways or the rooms, it is difficult to be sure about its function. But the absence of reports of charred grain or storage containers has led some scholars to question its identification as a granary.

In the southern part of the citadel mound, there is a large building (27 × 27 m) that has been labelled an 'assembly hall'. It is roughly square in shape and is divided into five aisles by rows of rectangular brick piers.

The lower town to the east, covering over 80 ha, may also have been surrounded by a fortification wall. It was divided into major blocks by four north–south and east–west streets and numerous smaller streets and alleys. The main streets were about 9 m in width, the rest in the range of 1.5–3 m. The houses varied in size, suggesting differences in wealth and status. In the HR area (the sections of Mohenjodaro are named after the excavators: HR stands for H. Hargreaves, DK for K. N. Dikshit), there were remains of a large building where many seals and fragments of a stone sculpture of a seated man with a shawl over his left shoulder (similar to the so-called 'priest-king' found in the DK area) were found. This building was tentatively interpreted as a temple or the house of an important leader. In the western part of the HR area, there was a double row of 16 houses, each consisting of a single room with a bathroom in front and 1 or 2 smaller rooms in the back. These were tentatively identified as shops or workers' quarters. A number of shops and workshops associated with copper working, bead making, dyeing, pottery making, and shell working were identified in the lower town.

Figure 4.6 Citadel and adjacent area, Harappa

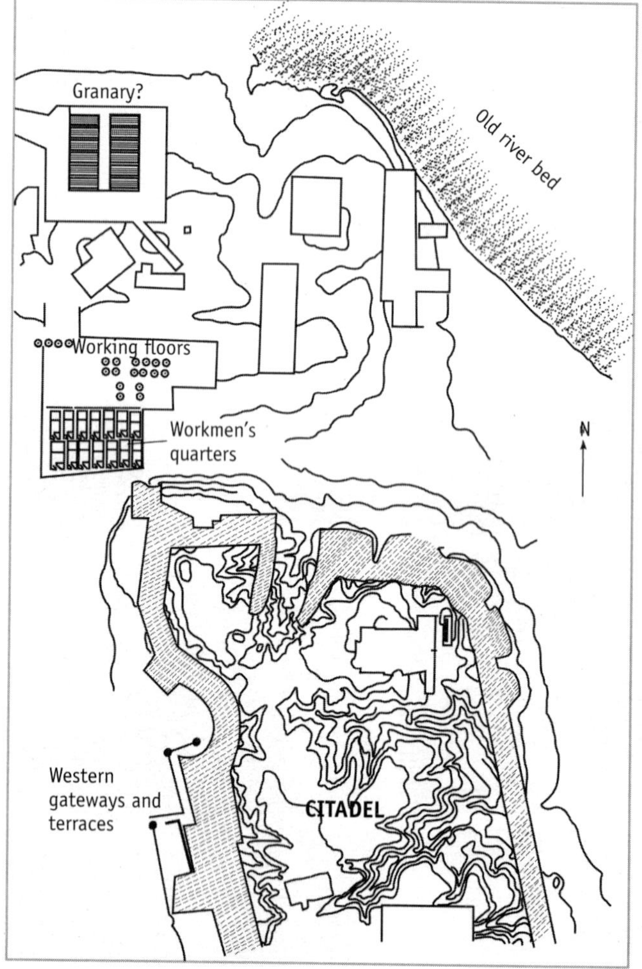

There may have been over 700 wells in the city of Mohenjodaro (Jansen, 1989). This gives a very high average frequency of about one in every third house. The wells were 10–15 m deep and were lined with special wedge-shaped bricks. Deep grooves at the top edges show the spots where the ropes attached to buckets rubbed against them. Most houses or house blocks at Mohenjodaro had at least one private well. Many neighbourhoods had public wells along the main street. We can imagine people meeting here, exchanging news and gossip as they waited to fill their pots with water. The rising water table and soil salinity have endangered the survival of the structures of the excavated structures at this important site.

Chanhudaro is a 4.7 ha site, about 130 km south of Mohenjodaro. Today, the river flows 20 km to its west; in protohistoric times it may have been closer. This is a single mound site with no fortifications. There are mud-brick platforms with remains of various structures. The traces of at least three streets have been identified. The main one was 5.68 m wide, and had two covered drains made of burnt bricks on both sides. Chanhudaro was clearly an important centre of craft activity. Some of the houses yielded raw material such as carnelian, agate, amethyst, and crystal as well as finished and unfinished beads and drills. More striking was the discovery of a bead factory, with lots of finished and unfinished beads, mostly made of steatite. Seal making, shell working, and the making of stone weights seem to have been other important crafts practised here.

The mounds of Harappa cover an extensive area of about 150 ha. The Ravi river flows some 10 km away from the site. The higher citadel mound lies to the west, with a lower but larger lower town to its south-east. South of the citadel mound is a cemetery of the mature Harappan phase. The citadel at Harappa was shaped roughly like a parallelogram, about 415 m north–south and 195 m east–west. It was surrounded by a mud-brick wall with massive towers and gateways, and the structures inside were raised on one or more high platforms. Because of the damaged nature of the mound, clear profiles of the main citadel structures, such as those available for Mohenjodaro, are lacking.

To the north of the citadel complex, a number of structures were located on a mound (Mound F) surrounded by a mud-brick wall. This seems to represent a northern suburb connected with craft activity. One walled complex had at least 15 units (about 17 × 7 m), each consisting of a courtyard in front and a room at the back, arranged in 2 rows with a lane in between. This has been interpreted as workmen's quarters. To the north of this complex were at least 18 circular brick platforms, with an average diameter of a little over 3 m, made of bricks set on edge. These may have been threshing platforms for grain. A wooden mortar for pounding grain may have been fitted into their centre, as husked barley and straw were found here. The 'granary' was located to the north of these platforms. It consisted of 12 units arranged in 2 rows of 6 rooms, divided by a central passage. Each unit measured 15.2 × 6.1 m, with three sleeper walls with air space in between. There was probably a wooden superstructure supported in places by large columns. As in the case of the Mohenjodaro 'granary', no grains were reported from this building. Its interpretation as a granary was mainly based on comparisons with structures found in Rome.

Kalibangan: main street; house walls

In the lower walled town of Harappa (Mound E), a large open area inside the southern gateway may have been used as a market or as a place where goods coming into the city were inspected. Various workshops where shell, agate, and copper artefacts were made have been identified. Outside the southern gateway, a small mound revealed houses, drains, bathing platforms, and perhaps a well. This may have been a halting or resting spot for travellers or traders.

Kalibangan (literally, 'black bangles') gets its name from the thick clusters of black bangles lying all over the surface of its mounds. The site lies on the banks of the dry bed of the Ghaggar river, in the Hanumangarh district of Rajasthan. It is fairly small, with a perimeter ranging from 1 to 3 km. There is a smaller western mound (known as KLB-1) and a larger eastern one (known as KLB-2), with an open space in between. KLB-1 has evidence of early and mature Harappan occupation, while KLB-2 represents only a mature Harappan occupation. There is also a smaller, third mound, which only has a large number of fire altars. Both the citadel complex and lower town were fortified.

The mature Harappan settlement on the western mound at Kalibangan was divided into two parts by an inner wall with stairs on either side (see B. B. Lal et al., 2020). The southern sector had no houses, but is noted for a series of mud-brick platforms with a row of seven clay-plastered pits. Nearby were a well and bath pavements. The pits have been interpreted as fire altars, i.e., sacrificial pits in which offerings were made into the fire, and the area seems to have been associated with community rituals. The buildings in the northern part of the citadel mound seem to have been houses where people associated with the rituals performed in the southern sector may have lived. There is a burial ground about 200 m west–south-west of the citadel. Apart from regular extended burials, there were also some circular pits with grave goods (pottery, bronze mirrors, etc.), but no human remains.

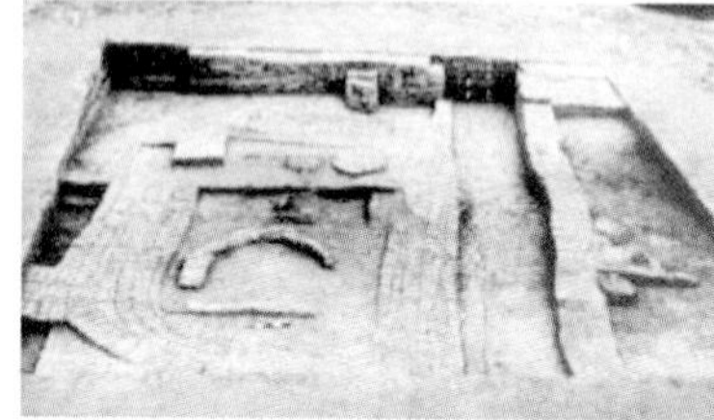

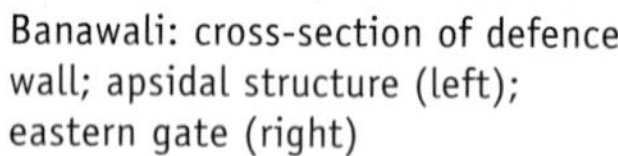

Banawali: cross-section of defence wall; apsidal structure (left); eastern gate (right)

The lower town was a rough parallelogram in plan, enclosed by a mud-brick wall. Several streets were traced here. Oblong fire altars were found in houses, with a central stele (rectangular piece) around which terracotta cakes, ash, and charcoal were found. While corbelled drains made of bricks have been found on the citadel mound, street drains of the Mohenjodaro type were absent in the lower town at Kalibangan. The sewage from houses was discharged into troughs or large jars embedded in the ground outside. The large number of bangles of terracotta, shell, alabaster, steatite, and faience at the site indicate that bangle making was an important craft. Other interesting artefacts include an ivory comb, a copper buffalo or bull, what appears to be a stone phallic emblem with a base, and a terracotta fragment incised with a horned figure.

Banawali in Hissar district (Haryana) is a fortified site measuring about 300 × 500 m, close to the dry bed of the Rangoi river. The site shows evidence of the early, mature, and late Harappan phases. Period II represents the mature Harappan culture. A wall divided the fortified area into two sections—a higher citadel area and a lower town. The citadel was semi-elliptical in plan and had its own mud-brick fortifications, surrounded by a moat. A few streets and structures were identified inside. A ramp led from the citadel into the lower town. The mud-brick houses had raised platforms (*chabutaras*) outside. Baked bricks were used only for wells, bathing pavements, and drains. Excavations revealed a multi-roomed house, where archaeologists identified a kitchen and a toilet with a jar that seemed to have functioned as a washbasin. Since many seals and weights were found in this house, it may have belonged to a wealthy merchant. There was another big house with a large number of beads of gold, lapis lazuli, and carnelian, tiny weights, and a 'touchstone' showing steaks of gold. This must have been a jeweller's house. Interestingly, seals were only found in the lower town, not in the citadel complex. Lots of stone weights in small denominations were found at the site, as was a terracotta model of a plough. Several houses at Banawali gave evidence of fire altars. In one place, these altars were associated with an apsidal structure which may have had some sort of ritualistic function.

Five mounds have been identified at Rakhigarhi (Hissar district, Haryana) (see Amarendra Nath, 2004). The citadel mound, surrounded by a mud-brick fortification wall, had platforms, a brick well, fire altars, some streets, and drains of various sizes. A lapidary workshop was identified, with remains of about 3,000 unfinished beads and roughly cut pieces of stone, mostly carnelian, chalcedony, agate, and jasper; bead polishers for smoothening the beads; and a hearth for heating the stones. In another part of the site, bones, antlers, ivory pieces, and finished and unfinished bone points, combs, needles, and engravers gave clear evidence of bone and ivory working. A cemetery revealed eight burials consisting mostly of brick-lined pits; in one case there was a wooden coffin. The results of the DNA analysis of one of the human bones found at the site is part of the ongoing investigations at the site and will be discussed below.

Lothal: well and drains

At Bhirrana in Haryana, Period IIA has been described as early mature Harappan and Period IIB as mature Harappan. The mature Harappan settlement was surrounded by a massive fortification wall made of mud-brick. Three multi-roomed house complexes were exposed. One of them, in the central part of the mound, consisted of four rooms. Two house complexes, separated from each other by a lane, were exposed in the eastern part of the mound. One of these consisted of 10 rooms with a verandah and a courtyard; terracotta cakes mixed with ash and clay were found on the floors. Yet another house complex in the north-western part of the mound consisted of six rooms, a kitchen, a central courtyard, three additional courtyards, and an open verandah. The floors were paved with mud-brick, and the brick walls were plastered with mud. A circular *tandoor* and *chullah* were found in one of the courtyards, and another *chullah* was discovered in the kitchen. Charred bones and the skull of a bovine animal were found next to one of the *chullahs*. A 4.80 m wide street ran north–south along the fortification wall. Three lanes were also identified. The artefacts included a fragment of a thick, sturdy red ware with an incised female figure, whose pose is reminiscent of that of the bronze Mohenjodaro 'dancing girl'.

Farmana in Rohtak district revealed two phases of occupation—Period I (Hakra phase) and Period II (mature Harappan) (see Shinde et al., 2011). The latter phase was subdivided into Period IIA (*c.* 2600–2400 BCE); IIB (*c.* 2400–2200 BCE); and IIC (*c.* 2200–2000 BCE). Period II revealed a planned settlement with remains of structures arranged along a main street and smaller streets. The structural complexes included multi-roomed units made of mud brick (occasionally burnt brick), often arranged around an open courtyard. A variety of pottery types and remains of a pear-shaped potter's kiln were found. Artefacts included objects made of stone, terracotta, copper, and bone. The remains of 70 burials were found, including extended burials, secondary burials, and symbolic burials (with pottery and ornaments, but no skeletal remains). The botanical remains included various types of barley, wheat, and pulses, as well as garlic, ginger, turmeric, and clove.

Lothal is located between the Sabarmati river and its tributary, the Bhogavo, in Saurashtra in Gujarat. The sea is now about 16–19 km away, but at one time, boats from the Gulf of Cambay could have sailed right up to the place. It was a modest-sized settlement (280 × 225 m), roughly rectangular in plan, surrounded by a wall which was initially made of mud and later of mud and burnt bricks, with the entrance on the south. There was a burial ground in the north-west, outside the enclosing walls. The citadel (called the 'Acropolis' by the excavator S. R. Rao) was roughly trapezoidal in plan and consisted of an area elevated on a mud-brick platform in the southern part of the site. Remains of residential buildings, streets, lanes, bathing pavements, and drains were traced here. To the south of the residential area was a complex identified as a warehouse, where goods may have been packed and stored. Sixty-five terracotta sealings with impressions of reed, woven fibre, matting, and twisted cords on one side and impressions of Harappan seals on the other were found here.

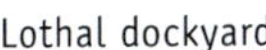

Lothal dockyard

Some of the houses in the main residential area were quite large, with four to six rooms, bathrooms, a large courtyard, and verandah. A few had fire altars—small pits with terracotta cakes or round lumps of clay and ash. The streets were paved with mud-brick, with a layer of gravel on top. Houses belonging to artisans such as coppersmiths, bead makers, etc. were identified on the basis of the occurrence of kilns, raw materials, and finished and unfinished artefacts. One of the streets was identified as a 'bazaar street', the rooms lining it interpreted as shops.

The most distinctive feature of Lothal is the dockyard, which lies on the eastern edge of the site. This is a roughly trapezoidal basin, enclosed by walls of burnt bricks. The eastern and western walls measured 212 m and 215 m respectively in length, while those

Dholavira: tank (left); northern gate (right)

on the north and south measured 37 m and 35 m. The dockyard had provisions for maintaining a regular level of water by means of a sluice gate and a spill channel. A mud-brick platform along the western embankment may have been the wharf where goods were loaded and unloaded. An alternative interpretation of this structure as a water reservoir is not convincing.

Dholavira is located on Kadir island in the Rann of Kutch in Gujarat (see Bisht, 2015). In protohistoric times, water levels in the Rann may have been higher than they are today, allowing boats to sail from the coast right up to the site. The architecture of Dholavira shows a large-scale use of sandstone, combined in places with mud-brick—a feature of the Harappan sites of Gujarat. The layout of this settlement is unlike that of any other Harappan site. It is surrounded by an outer fortification wall made of mud-brick with a veneer of stone blocks on the outer face, with imposing bastions and two major gateways in the middle of the northern and southern walls. Within the outer walls, at least three different sections were identified. There was a small 'castle' area, a 'bailey' area to its west, and a larger 'middle town' to the north, all with their own enclosing walls. A lower town lay to the east. An interesting feature is a large open area (called the 'stadium') between the castle–bailey and the middle town, which may have been used for special ceremonial occasions. There was also substantial evidence of habitation outside the fortification wall, which may represent a suburb of the city. The site seems to be looking out towards the sea and it must have been an important stopping point on busy maritime trade routes. The fortified sites of Desalpur, Kuntasi, Bagasra, Shikarpur, and Juni Kuran indicate that there were many Harappan settlements in the Kutch area.

Figure 4.7 Plan of Dholavira

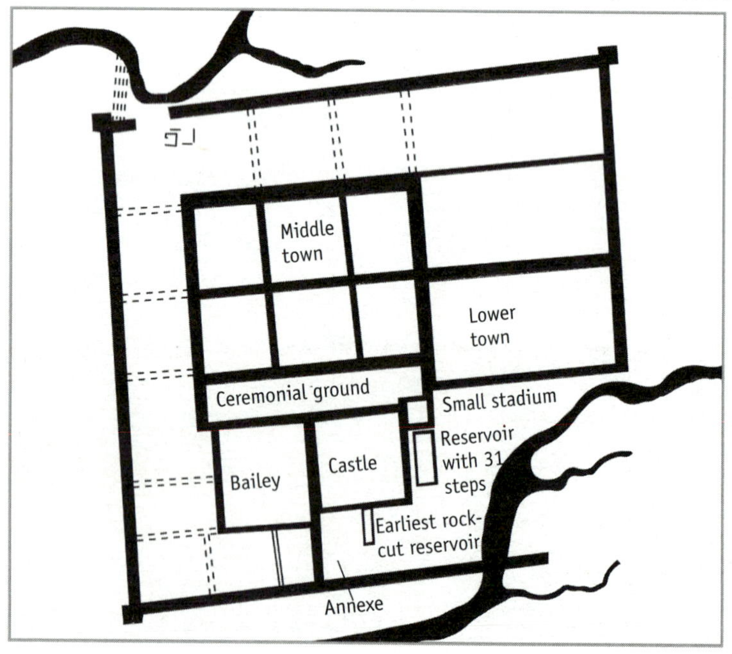

The fortified acropolis of Dholavira covered an area of 300 × 300 m, with gateways in the centre of its four walls. Remains of limestone pillar bases and pillar fragments with a highly polished surface were found in the eastern gateway. This discovery has taken the history of monumental stone sculpture/architecture in the subcontinent back from the 4th century BCE (the Maurya period) to the 3rd millennium BCE. In one of the side rooms of the northern gateway of Dholavira lay what seems to be a fallen signboard. An inscription had been made with white gypsum paste inlaid into a wooden board. The wooden board had fallen flat on its

Dholavira citadel: eastern gate with pillar fragments (left); well; massive drain (right)

face, and although the wood had decayed, the gypsum was found intact. The symbols, each measuring about 37 × 25–27 cm, perhaps announced the name of the city or the title of its ruler. The acropolis had a large well, an elaborate drainage system, and large buildings which may have had administrative or ritualistic functions.

The middle town of Dholavira was surrounded by a 360 × 250 m wall with four gateways. The lower town gave evidence of houses and areas where various types of craft activities such as bead making, shell working, and pottery making were carried out. Outside the city walls, there was evidence of additional habitation and burials. The cemetery area revealed rectangular pit burials lined with blocks of stone, but there were no skeletal remains. These may have been memorials to the dead.

The city had an impressive and unique water harvesting and management system. It can be noted that this area receives less than 160 cm of rain every year and is very prone to droughts. The site is flanked by two streams—the Manhar and Mandsar. Dams were built across these to channelize their water into reservoirs. Several large, deep water cisterns and reservoirs (at least 16) located in the citadel and lower town preserved precious stores of rain water.

Kanmer in the Rapar taluka of Kachcch district has five periods of occupation: Period I is early Harappan; Period II mature Harappan; Period III late mature Harappan; Period IV historic; and Period V medieval (see Kharakwal et al., 2012). The mature Harappan phase has been subdivided into Periods IIA and IIB. The phase saw the building of a massive fortification wall around the settlement and several phases of structural activities. There was a furnace which may have been used for making faience beads. Two perforated terracotta sealings with a 'unicorn' (a mythical one-horned bovine animal) impression are among the various artefacts found. The analysis of palaeobotanical remains identified various types of barley, wheat, millet, rice, field pea, green gram, and cotton. There were bones of domesticated animals such as cattle, buffalo, sheep, goats, and pigs; the wild animals included deer, nilgai, and antelopes. The remains of various birds, fish, reptiles, and molluscs were also identified.

Allahdino is a small (1.4 ha) unfortified village site of the Harappan civilization, about 40 km east of Karachi. Houses made of mud-brick, often resting on stone foundations, were laid out in a west–south-west to east–north-east orientation. A large multi-roomed building on a large mud-brick platform in the north-eastern part of the excavated area seems to have had some special significance. Another building was associated with three wells. The wells at Allahdino had very small diameters, and their mouths ranged from 60 cm to 90 cm. This may have been to enable the ground water to rise higher due to hydraulic pressure. It has been suggested that well water may have been used to irrigate the nearby fields.

The artefacts found at Allahdino included a large number of copper items, seals, terracotta toy carts, and triangular terracotta cakes. The most spectacular discovery was a small terracotta jar containing a profusion of gold, silver, bronze, agate, and carnelian ornaments. These included a massive belt or necklace consisting of 36 long carnelian beads and bronze spacer beads and a multi-strand necklace of silver beads. The discovery of ornaments of precious metals and stone at a village site shows that at least some of the inhabitants of this Harappan village were very rich.

The Diversity of the Harappan Subsistence Base

The Harappan civilization covered an enormous area within which there was great ecological variety—alluvial plains, mountains, plateaux, and sea-coasts. The resource potential of this area was rich enough to generate the food surpluses that are an important aspect of urbanization and urbanism. The diversity of the subsistence base may also have been an important sustaining factor—if one food resource failed, people could turn to others. Agriculture was the mainstay, supplemented by animal husbandry and hunting. Riverine and marine food resources were tapped, where available. The sources of information on the subsistence patterns of the Harappans consist of plant remains, animal bones, artefacts, motifs on seals and pottery, and analogies with modern practices.

Subsistence is closely related to environment, and the nature of the Harappan environment is the subject of continuing debate. Archaeologists such as Mortimer Wheeler and Stuart Piggott suggested a wetter climate in Harappan times on the basis of the following arguments: (*a*) the large number of burnt bricks found at Harappan sites would have required large quantities of fuel, which would only have been possible with a heavy forest cover, supported by heavier rainfall; (*b*) the *gabarbands* (embankments) constructed in the Baluchistan area suggest heavier rain; (*c*) the depiction of animals such as the tiger, elephant, and rhinoceros on seals indicates a forest and grassland vegetation that could only have been supported by heavier rainfall; (*d*) the elaborate drainage system of the cities was geared towards carrying off rain water. The first and last points can be refuted most easily. It is not easy to estimate just how much wood (and forest) would have been required to make the burnt bricks, and the Harappan drains were largely part of a system of sewage disposal.

Many scholars hold that climatic conditions in the greater Indus valley have remained more or less constant since Harappan times. However, some studies suggest otherwise. Plant palynologist Gurdip Singh (1971) analyzed pollen from the three salt lakes of Sambhar, Didwana, and Lunkaransar, and the freshwater Pushkar lake, and constructed a profile of rainfall in this part of Rajasthan from *c.* 8000 BCE to 1500 BCE. He concluded that there was an increase in rainfall in *c.* 3000 BCE and a decrease in 1800 BCE. However, a study of the Lunkaransar lake (Enzel et al., 1999) suggests that it had dried up by 3500 BCE and that the climate had become drier long before the emergence of the Harappan civilization. The issue of the nature of climatic conditions in Harappan times, thus, remains unresolved.

Given the area covered by the civilization, naturally there were regional variations in the plants grown by farmers (see Ranjit Pratap Singh, 2014). Wheat has been found at Mohenjodaro and Harappa; barley at Mohenjodaro, Harappa, and Kalibangan; and sesamum at Harappa. Harappa has also given evidence of watermelon seeds, peas, and dates. Rice occurs at Harappa, Kalibangan, Lothal, and Rangpur. Millets have been identified at Harappa, Surkotada, and Shortughai. Grapes were known, so was henna (*mehendi*). Cotton may also have been grown. Detailed evidence of the plant economy of the early and mature Harappan phase is available from Balu (in Haryana) (Saraswat and Pokharia, 2001–02). The crop remains identified here included various types of barley, wheat, rice, horse gram, green gram, chickpea, field pea, grass pea, sesamum, melon, watermelon, date, grapes, and the earliest evidence of garlic. Rohira (Sangrur district, Punjab) has given evidence of various kinds of plant remains at early Harappan (IA) and mature Harappan (1B) levels. Those found at mature Harappan levels include various types of barley and wheat, lentil, something resembling *kulthi* or

Terracotta plough found at Banawali

horsegram, and fenugreek. Apart from the wide range of cereals, pulses, vegetables, and fruits grown by the Harappans, another striking point is the similarity of the past and present plant economies in the various regions.

Modern cropping practices provide some clues to protohistoric patterns. Today, in Sindh, rainfall levels are low, but the Indus brings down flood waters and silt. The fertile land requires no deep ploughing, irrigation or manuring. Sesamum and cotton were probably sown in June/July and reaped in September/October, as *kharif* (summer) crops. Crops such as wheat and barley would have been sown in November and reaped in March/April as *rabi* (winter) crops. In Gujarat, rice is a *kharif* crop, and it must have been so in Harappan times as well.

Reference has already been made to the discovery of a ploughed field at early Harappan levels at Kalibangan. The continuing use of the plough into the mature Harappan phase can be inferred. Terracotta models of ploughs at Bahawalpur and Banawali give further evidence of the use of this implement. The fact that no actual ploughs have survived is no doubt because they were made of wood.

Farmers must have built *bunds* (embankments) of mud or stone to divert river water, as they do today in areas like Baluchistan. Irrigation canals have been found at Shortughai. Fairservis suggested that a well and associated drains at Allahdino may represent an irrigation system, but the evidence is far from conclusive. Similarly, Leshnik's hypothesis that the dockyard at Lothal is actually an irrigation reservoir is not convincing. Even if the Harappans did dig canals in the alluvial plains, it would be very difficult to identify them. However, H. P. Francfort (1992) identified remains of a small-scale canal network in the Haryana area, and some of the ancient canals traced in the Ghaggar-Hakra plain may belong to the Harappan phase.

The bones of many types of wild and domesticated animals found at Harappan sites (see Joglekar and Goyal, 2014) indicate that apart from agriculture, the Harappans practised hunting and animal husbandry, and/or that they were interacting with hunters and pastoralists. Bones of wild animals found at Harappan sites include many varieties of deer, pig, boar, sheep, goat, and possibly ass. Bones of tortoise and fish have also been found. Rhinoceros bones occur only at Amri, although this animal is depicted on numerous seals and in terracotta figurines (see Divyabhanusinh et al., 2018; Bose, 2020). Elephant bones occur in very small quantities at Harappan sites, although this animal appears on seals. (On the elephant in Indian history, see Trautmann, 2015.) Tigers are represented often in figurines, leopards more rarely. Rabbits, peacocks, pigeons, ducks, monkeys, and wild fowl are represented in figurines and paintings on pottery. The Harappans exploited riverine and marine resources where these were available. At coastal sites, fish, turtles, and molluscs must have provided an important protein-rich element in people's diet. The discovery of marine catfish bones at Harappa suggests that coastal communities may have traded in dried fish in inland cities.

Harappan sites have also yielded many remains of domesticated animals such as humped and humpless cattle, buffalo, sheep, and goat. Cattle and buffaloes were the most important domesticated animals. They would have been used for meat, milk, and also as draught animals. Goats and sheep could have been used for meat, wool, milk, and as pack animals (they are still used to carry loads of salt and grain in some of the Himalayan stretches). Dogs and cats were domesticated, probably as pets. The issues of the domestication of the pig, camel, and horse are the subject of debate and hinge on the identification of the bone remains and the cultural level with which they should be associated. Pig bones have been found at several Harappan sites but whether they belong to wild or domesticated pigs is debated. Camel bones have been reported from Harappa, Mohenjodaro, Surkotada, Kalibangan, Kanewal, and Nagwada, but it is not clear whether they can be associated with the Harappan phase. It is also not certain whether the camel bones belong to the dromedary (one-humped camel) or the two-humped Bactrian camel. It is possible that the Harappans were aware of camels due to their contacts with the west but that they did not use them to any significant extent.

NEW DIRECTIONS IN RESEARCH | **The rhinoceros and the Harappans**

Shibani Bose points out that across the centuries, big mammals or megafauna, have inspired both fear and as well as fantasy. Her work focuses on three animals – the rhinoceros (*Rhinoceros unicornis*), elephant (*Elephus maximus*), and tiger (*Panthera tigris*). Bose uses these animals to try to understand the ecology of ancient India and analyzes the perceptions and attitudes towards these animals across the centuries. She emphasizes out that megafauna species played important roles in the ecological niches they inhabited. Bose's analysis is based on a study of the faunal remains from sites in North and Central India, a large variety of textual sources, and visual representations of animals in art. Here, we will look at a small part of her discussion of the rhinoceros, an animal which (like the tiger) has received much less attention than the elephant, cheetah, and lion.

The rhinoceros inhabits the alluvial grasslands and floodplains of rivers with marshy, swampy terrain. The earliest fossilized fragments of the bones of various species belonging to the rhinoceros genus go back to the late Pleistocene and have been found in Central and peninsular India. Rhinoceros bones are also found in mesolithic and neolithic contexts. The animal also appears in early rock art in Mirzapur in Uttar Pradesh, Rajasthan, and Gujarat.

Rhinoceros bones occur at many Harappan sites, such as Nausharo (Baluchistan), Harappa (Punjab), Madina (Haryana), Kalibangan and Karanpura (Rajasthan), and sites in Gujarat such as Lothal, Surkotada, Shikarpur, Khanpur, Kuntasi, and possibly Oriya Timbo. Rhinoceros shoulder blades seem to have been used as anvils for making stone tools and Bose argues that the meat of this animal may also have been consumed.

The rhinoceros is also frequently represented in Harappan terracottas. What stands out in these is the naturalistic depiction, suggesting that the Harappans were able to closely observe the animal's anatomical features. For instance, the rhinoceros figurines found at Mohenjodaro depict the wrinkled skin realistically by hatching or pitting, or by adding strips of clay to show the folds in the hide. On seals too, the animal is depicted with naturalistic details, such as tiny eyes, thick hide, and rough, wrinkled skin, shown in some cases with hatched lines or by holes made by a fine drill. These make it clear that it is rhinoceros *unicornis* that is represented. The animal is shown standing in front of a manger-like object which could represent a trough, which suggests a religious or ritualistic significance. The frequency and nature of the rhinoceros' appearance shows that it had an important place in the Harappan people's belief systems.

In later times, the rhinoceros is mentioned in Vedic texts, the Pali *Tipitaka*, Dharmashastra, *Ramayana*, and *Mahabharata*. *Khadga* is the word usually used for it. This unusual animal also figures in ancient Greek accounts of India. However, when its history is traced in post-Harappan times, the presence of the rhinoceros in the cultural space seems to have waned, especially when compared with animals such as the elephant and the horse. Bose argues that this was not the result of reduced numbers but reflects changes in social and cultural perceptions, perhaps due to new forms of settlement and production. With the increasing importance of agriculture and the clearance of forests, animals such as the elephant and horse assumed greater importance as they fulfilled important needs as draught animals and in armies. The rhinoceros had less practical utility and was also encountered less often by humans.

Due to the fact that the rhinoceros and tiger have a low reproduction rate and due to human activities such as poaching and destruction of their natural habitats, the survival of these animals is precarious. Conservation attempts continue to be made but preserving the lives and habitats of these animals is uphill task.

Source Bose, 2020

The issue of the horse is the most debated. It is not easy to ascertain whether bones reported from some sites belong to the half-ass (*Equus hemionus khur*) or domesticated horse (*Equus caballus*). Horse remains have been reported at Harappa, Lothal, Surkotada, Kuntasi, and Kalibangan, and at superficial levels at Mohenjodaro. Sàndor Bökönyi (1997) examined the equid bone samples from Surkotada and concluded that at least six of them probably belonged to the true horse. His conclusions were challenged by Meadow and Patel (1997). Brigadier Ross (1946) reported horse teeth at pre-Harappan levels at Rana Ghundai, but this identification was questioned by Zeuner (1963). While horse bones are not completely absent at Harappan sites, they are not prolific

FURTHER DISCUSSION | **Animal bones at Shikarpur**

Shikarpur is a Harappan site in Kutch district in Gujarat, excavated by the Gujarat State Department of Archaeology in 1987–90. The excavation was a small one. It revealed an over 3 m thick deposit, of which the lower layers (layers 10–19) represented an early Harappan phase and the upper layers (layers 1–9) the mature Harappan phase. The animal remains found at the site were sent to the Archaeozoology Laboratory at Deccan College, Pune. The results of the detailed investigations by P. K. Thomas, P. P. Joglekar, Arati Deshpande-Mukherjee, and S. J. Pawankar give important information about the subsistence patterns of the Harappans in Gujarat:

A total of 15,483 pieces of bone were unearthed in the excavations. It was possible to identify 53.46 per cent of them, i.e., 8,267 fragments. There were cut marks and signs of charring on some of the bones, indicating slaughtering and cooking. The faunal assemblage consisted of 47 species—23 mammals, 3 birds, 2 reptiles, 5 fish, 13 molluscs, and 1 *crustacea*. The wild animals included wild buffalo, *nilgai*, *chowsingha*, blackbuck, gazelle, various kinds of deer, wild pig, wild ass, jackal, hare, and rhinoceros. The domesticated animals included cattle, buffalo, sheep/goat, horse, pig, and dog.

The bones of domesticated animals comprised over 85 per cent of the total faunal assemblage in both the early and mature Harappan phases. Cattle bones were most numerous. In the early Harappan phase, 77.48 per cent of the bones were of cattle, while in the mature Harappan phase, their percentage was 77.84 per cent. Sheep/goat bones (it is difficult to distinguish the two) amounted to 11.26 per cent of the early Harappan phase, and were reduced to 4.63 per cent in the mature Harappan phase. Buffalo bones were 4.28 per cent and 4.61 per cent in the early and mature Harappan phases, respectively. Dog bones were only found in the mature Harappan phase, and that too in very small quantities (0.116 per cent). Very few horse bones were found (0.13 per cent), and these occurred only in the mature Harappan phase.

The evidence shows that the consumption of meat of domesticated animals was an important part of the diet of the people of Shikarpur. The contribution of wild and aquatic animals varied considerably in different layers.

The analysis of bones and teeth showed that domesticated animals were killed at different ages. Most of the cattle and buffaloes lived up to the age of maturity—about 3 years—and were killed at various ages up to the age of about 8 years. The fact that some were older than 8 years suggests that they were also valued for secondary products and used for draught purposes. Sheep/goats were killed at relatively younger ages—between 6 months to their respective ages of maturity, suggesting they were primarily reared for meat.

Towards the end of the mature Harappan phase at Shikarpur, there seems to have been an increase in the exploitation of wild animals. It is not clear whether this was the result of a decline in agricultural production, failure of rains, population pressure, or a combination of several such factors.

Source Thomas et al., 1995

either. Some scholars have identified representations of horses in terracotta figures and seals, but these are not conclusive. Horses are known to have been first domesticated in the Pontic-Caspian steppes, initially for meat, later for riding. The horse and the wheel had tremendous and far-reaching impact. Horses formed the basis for new kinds of mobility—to help humans herd animals, pull wheeled carts and chariots, and much later, as the mount of cavalry warriors. Between *c.* 3500–3000 BCE, horses spread beyond the Pontic-Caspian steppes, as is evident from the increase in horse bones in southeastern and central Europe, the Caucasus, and northern Kazakhstan (see Anthony, 2007). It is not surprising that some domesticated horses found their way into some Harappan sites. However, the horse did not play an important role in the Harappan civilization.

Harappan Crafts and Techniques

Diverse, well-developed craft traditions are one of the hallmarks of the Harappan civilization. Early writings tended to contrast the plainness of Harappan artefacts with the opulence of their Egyptian and Mesopotamian counterparts. Nowadays, the technological sophistication and beauty of some of the Harappan artefacts are recognized. There is a great variety of standardized, mass-produced craft items at Harappan sites (see Bhan and Vidale, 2014). The artefacts are far greater in quantity and range, and show greater technical finesse than those found in earlier cultural phases. While some sites specialized in the production of a single or a few items, others such as Harappa manufactured a wide range of goods. Craft activity was often localized in a certain part of the settlement.

Ceramics include all items involving the heating of clay such as bricks, terracotta, and faience. Harappan pottery reflects efficient mass production. Pottery kilns were

Figure 4.8 Harappan pottery

found at Mohenjodaro, Harappa, Nausharo, and Chanhudaro. The pots were fired in funnel-shaped up-draft closed kilns, although open-firing kilns may also have been used. There is a great variety of pottery, including black-on-red, grey, buff, and black-and-red wares. Most pots were wheel-turned. Both fine and coarse fabrics occur and their thickness varies. The typical Harappan pottery is a fine, sturdy, wheel-made ware with a bright red slip. Some pots are decorated with painted black designs. Polychrome painting is rare. The red colour for the slip was made from red ochre (iron oxide, known as *geru*), while black was made by combining dark reddish-brown iron oxide with black manganese. Distinctive shapes include the dish-on-stand, vase with s-profile, small vessel with knobbed decoration, large slender-footed bowl, cylindrical perforated jar, and goblet with pointed foot. The decorative patterns range from simple horizontal lines to geometric patterns and pictorial motifs. Some of the designs such as fish scales, *pipal* leaves, and intersecting circles have their roots in the early Harappan phase. Human figures are rare and crude. At the earliest levels of Mohenjodaro, a burnished grey ware with a dark purplish slip and vitreous glaze may represent one of the earliest examples of glazing in the world. Although there is a certain level of uniformity in pottery styles and techniques across the Harappan culture zone, this coexists with regional pottery traditions. For instance, at the Gujarat sites, the typical Harappan pottery occurs along with micaceous read ware, black and red ware, and pottery that has been labelled Sorath Harappan and Prabhas Ware.

Inferences can be made about the functions of some of the Harappan pots. The large jars may have been used to store grain or water. The more elaborately painted pots may

Miniature perforated pot; beaker; pot with pointed base (with seal impression); ring stand (from left)

0 2 cm

have had a ceremonial use or may have belonged to rich people. Small vessels may have been used as glasses to drink water or other beverages. The function of the perforated jars is not clear. One suggestion is that they may have been wrapped in cloth and used for brewing fermented alcoholic beverages. Another possibility is that they may have had a ceremonial or ritualistic use. Shallow bowls probably held cooked food; flattish dishes were used as plates. Cooking pots of various sizes have been found. Most of them have a red- or black-slipped rim and a rounded bottom; the lower part of the pot is often strengthened by a thick slurry or clay mixed with ground pottery or chaff. The rims of the cooking pots are strong and project outwards to help pick them up or move them around. Some of the forms and features of the pots used by the Harappans can be seen in traditional kitchens even today. Apart from ceramic vessels, the Harappans also made and used metal ones.

Harappan sites have yielded a profusion of terracottas. There are figurines of animals such as bulls, buffaloes, monkeys, and dogs. There are toy carts with solid wheels (a few with lines suggesting spokes). Human figurines include male figurines and more numerous female figurines of various types. The Harappan craftspersons also made terracotta bangles.

Pottery designs; terracottas: human and animal figurines; mask; circular and triangular cakes (from top)

0 2 cm

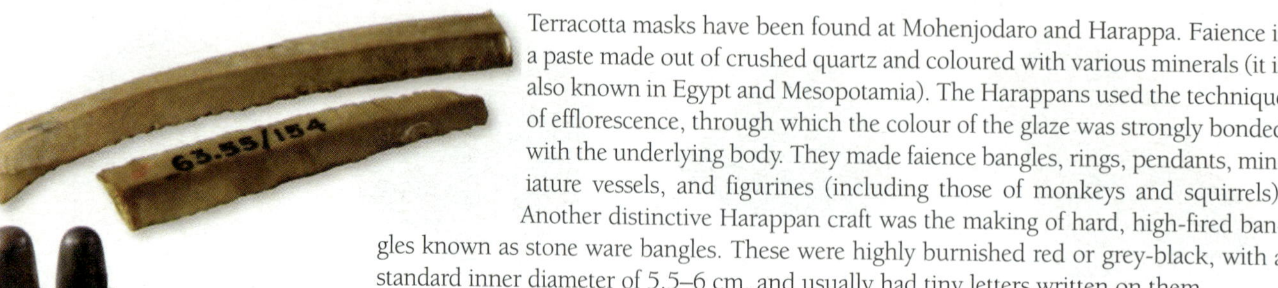

Terracotta masks have been found at Mohenjodaro and Harappa. Faience is a paste made out of crushed quartz and coloured with various minerals (it is also known in Egypt and Mesopotamia). The Harappans used the technique of efflorescence, through which the colour of the glaze was strongly bonded with the underlying body. They made faience bangles, rings, pendants, miniature vessels, and figurines (including those of monkeys and squirrels). Another distinctive Harappan craft was the making of hard, high-fired bangles known as stone ware bangles. These were highly burnished red or grey-black, with a standard inner diameter of 5.5–6 cm, and usually had tiny letters written on them.

Stone work was another important craft. Reference was made earlier to the stone masonry and fine polished pillars at Dholavira. More visible at all Harappan sites were the mass-produced chert blades made by the crested guided ridge technique. Some of these may have been used as knives for domestic use, others as sickles. Harappan stone quarries have been identified in the Rohri hills of Sindh. Some of the stone blades may have been obtained from contemporary hunter-gatherer communities. The fact that stone flakes and cores occur in many houses at Mohenjodaro suggests that at least some of the tools were made by people in their homes. Datrana in north Gujarat has revealed abundant evidence of stone blade and bead manufacture.

The Harappan civilization is marked by a well-developed metal crafting traditions (Ravindra N. Singh, 2014). Apart from making artefacts out of pure copper, Harappan craftspersons alloyed copper with arsenic, tin, or nickel. Copper and copper alloy artefacts included vessels, spears, knives, short swords, arrowheads, axes, fishhooks, needles, mirrors, rings, and bangles. The axes were flat, without a shaft hole, and were probably hafted in a split and bound handle. The number of pure copper artefacts was far greater than alloyed bronze ones. Usually, tools like knives, axes, and chisels, which needed hardened edges, were alloyed. Alloys increased over time—for instance, at Mohenjodaro, bronze tools increased from 6 per cent to 23 per cent from the lower to the higher levels. The large number of pure copper may suggest cultural preference rather than technological backwardness, and the variations in the composition of copper alloys suggests a tradition of metal recycling (Lahiri, 1995).

Sixteen copper furnaces were found at Harappa, and copper workshops were found at Lothal. A large amount of copper oxide was discovered in a brick-lined pit at Mohenjodaro. That metal objects were considered precious is clear from the fact that they were buried in hoards for safekeeping by their owners. One hoard found at Harappa consisted of a large cooking pot with a bronze cover. Inside were several types of copper tools and weapons, including various types of axes, daggers, spearheads, arrowheads, chisels, and a bowl. Some of the objects were unused, others used and worn.

Beautifully worked gold and silver jewellery including necklaces, bracelets, brooches, pendants, and earrings have been found at Harappan sites. A hoard of jewellery made of gold, silver, and semi-precious stones was found at the small village site of Allahdino. The Harappans used silver to emboss conch shells and to make vessels. The technique of mixing gold and silver seems to have been known. Lead was used to make plumb bobs and in copper casting. It may be noted that two metal objects found at Lothal contain 39.1 per cent and 66.1 per cent iron. Iron pieces have been reported from a few other chalcolithic sites in the subcontinent as well, so it is not surprising that the Harappans may have had some familiarity with iron smelting.

Chert blades; stone gamesmen; copper arrowhead and celt; stone sealing; seal (from top)

Seal making was another important Harappan craft. Most of the seals are square or rectangular. The average size of the square seals is about 2.54 cm, but there are larger ones, a little over 6.35 cm. Some have a perforated boss at the back for handling and suspension. A few cylindrical and round seals have also been found. Most of the seals are made of steatite, but there are a few silver, faience, and calcite ones as well. Two fine silver seals with the unicorn motif were discovered at Mohenjodaro, and some copper and soapstone ones were found at Lothal. To make the stone seals, the stone was sawed and shaped with knives, and then carved, using fine chisels and drills. The seal was coated with an alkali and heated, giving it a white lustrous surface. The carving is in

FURTHER DISCUSSION | **Sculpture in stone and metal**

Apart from utilitarian items made of stone and metal, a few pieces of stone and metal sculpture have been found at Harappan sites. Most of them are small, but they display fine artistic skills and sensibilities. They include the stone bust (17.78 cm high) of a male figure found at Mohenjodaro, which has been labelled the 'priest-king'. Two fine stone torsos of a male figure (about 10 cm high) were found at Harappa, a seated stone ibex or ram (49 × 27 × 21 cm) at Mohenjodaro, and a stone lizard at Dholavira. The only large piece of sculpture is that of a broken, seated male figure from Dholavira.

Two bronze female figurines were found at Mohenjodaro. One of them has become famous as the 'dancing girl'. This figurine was found in a small house in the south-western quarter of the city (in the HR area) during the 1926–27 excavations. The figure is 10.8 cm high and was made by the lost-wax method.

This method involves first making a wax model and then covering it with a clay coating, leaving some holes as passageways. When the clay-covered moulds are heated in ovens, the wax melts out.

The 'dancing girl'

Molten bronze is then poured in, and takes the place of the wax. When the mould has cooled, the outer clay envelope is chipped off and the craftsperson can then put the finishing touches to the solid bronze statue. This technique is still used in certain parts of India.

But to get back to the 'dancing girl': She represents a very thin woman standing with her right hand on the back of her hip and left hand resting on her left thigh, just above the knee. She may have once held some object in this hand. She is naked. She wears a necklace and has 24–25 of bangles on her left arm and just 4 on her right arm. Her arms are unnaturally long. Her head is tilted back, and she has a defiant, nonchalant air about her. Her hair is swept back in a low, loose bun at the nape of her neck. John Marshall named her the 'dancing girl' because he thought she had the air of a semi-impudent 'nautch girl', hand on hip, beating time to the music with her feet. The name has stuck. But the 'dancing girl' may not have been dancing at all, and even if she was, she may not represent a professional dancer.

intaglio—i.e., it is a sunken engraving, with the impression appearing in relief. Motifs include the elephant, tiger, antelope, crocodile, hare, humped bull, buffalo, rhinoceros, and the one-horned mythical animal referred to as a unicorn. There is often a small feeding trough or stand in front of the animal. There are also composite animals, human figures, and plants. Most of the seals have a short inscription. Some rectangular seals have writing, but no motif.

Bead making was a craft known in earlier cultures, but in the Harappan civilization new materials, styles, and techniques came into vogue. A new type of cylindrical stone drill was devised and used to perforate beads of semi-precious stones. Such drills have been found at sites such as Mohenjodaro, Harappa, Chanhudaro, and Dholavira. The Harappan craftspeople made beads out of steatite, agate, carnelian, lapis lazuli, shell, terracotta, gold, silver, and copper. The Harappan long barrel cylinder beads made out of carnelian were so beautiful and valued that they found their way into royal burials at Ur in Mesopotamia. Tiny micro-beads were made of steatite paste and hardened by heating. Beads were also made of faience.

Bead making factories with tools, furnaces, and beads in various stages of preparation have been found at Chanhudaro and Lothal. At Bagasra in Gujarat, there is evidence of the production of artefacts of shell, faience, and beads of semi-precious stones (agate, carnelian, amazonite, lapis lazuli, and steatite). Clay-lined silos, varying from 0.30 to 1 m in diameter and 0.15 to 0.30 m in depth, were used to store semi-precious stones. Sites such as Dholavira, Shikarpur, and Kanmer also seem to have been involved in bead-making. The Harappan bead-makers used efficient drilling techniques and had

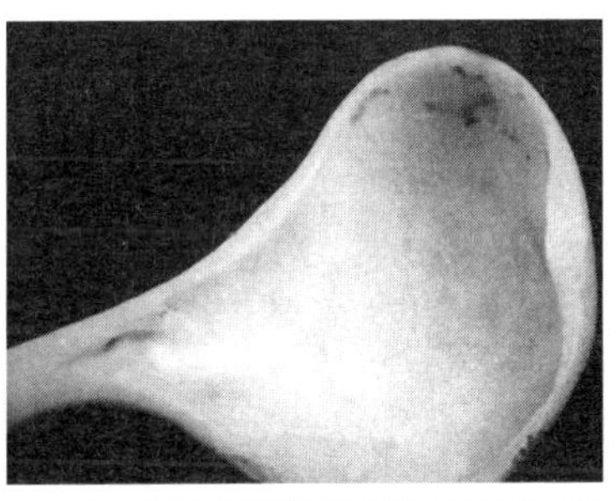

Shell ladle, Lothal

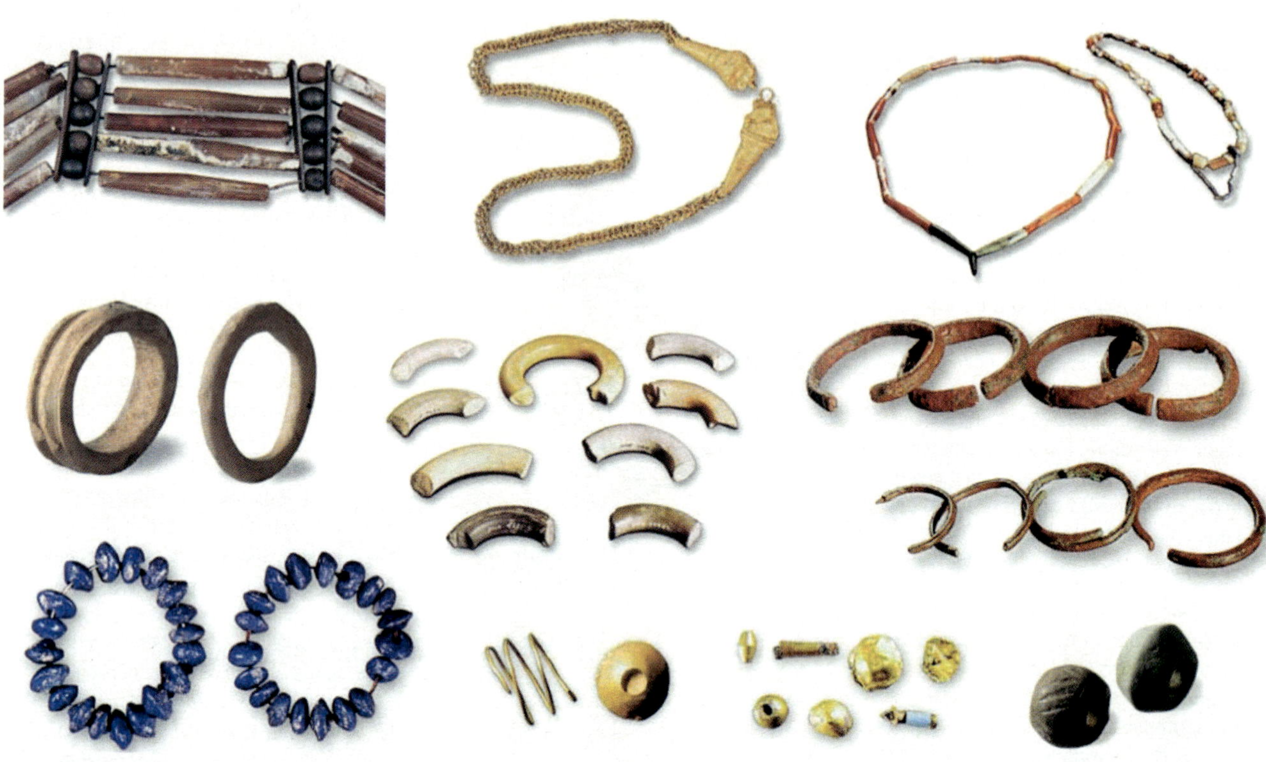

Jewellery: necklaces of carnelian beads, gold (1st row); bangles of terracotta, copper, stoneware (2nd row); lapis lazuli beads, gold spiral pin, gold and terracotta beads (3rd row)

perfected the technique to change the colour of agate beads. The bead-making tradition in Gujarat today gives us clues on how the Harappan craftspeople may have made their beads.

Beads, bracelets, and decorative inlay work of shell show the existence of craftspersons skilled in shell working. Bangles were often made from conch shell. Chanhudaro and Balakot were important centres of shell work. Further evidence of site specialization comes from Gujarat. An intensive surface survey and excavations at Nageshwar (in Jamnagar district) have shown that this site was exclusively devoted to shell-working and specialized in making bangles. Evidence of shell working also comes from Kuntasi, Dholavira, Rangpur, Lothal, Nagwada, and Bagasra. This craft was clearly very important in the Gujarat region of the Harappan culture zone. Bone working was another specialized craft. Beads, awls, and pins were made out of bone. There are a few examples of ivory carving in the form of combs, carved cylinders, small sticks, pins, gamesmen, and a carved plaque.

It can be inferred that the Harappans made cotton and woollen textiles. The terracotta figurines wearing clothes (shawls, skirts, etc.) reflect the kinds of clothes people wore. Mesopotamian texts mention cotton as one of the imports from Meluhha (an area which included the Indus valley). Traces of cotton cloth were found at Mohenjodaro, preserved over the centuries due to their being in contact with a corroding silver jar. Several examples of cotton thread and cloth were identified on copper tools. At Harappa, cotton threads were found wrapped around the handle of a small copper mirror in a burial and also around the handle of a curved copper razor. Harappa also gave evidence of woven textile impressions on the inside of faience vessels. The uniform thickness and uniformity of the weave suggest the use of spinning wheels. Various kinds of spindle whorls for spinning thread have been found at Harappan sites. Weaving may have been a cottage industry practised in villages, and also to some extent in the cities. Impressions on clay floors and fired clay lumps suggest traditions of making baskets and mats out of reeds and grasses.

More recently, microscopic analysis of thread fragments found in copper/copper alloy ornaments from Harappa and steatite beads from Chanhudaro have given evidence of silk fibres in contexts dated to *c.* 2450–2000 BCE (Good et al., 2009). A scanning electron

FURTHER DISCUSSION | **The making of long carnelian beads**

The city of Khambhat (Cambay) in Gujarat is one of the largest centres of stone bead-making in the world today. Mark Kenoyer, Massimo Vidale, and Kuldeep K. Bhan conducted an ethno-archaeological study, examining the techniques used by modern bead makers of this place. They supplemented this with experimentation and an analysis of the remains of bead manufacture at the site of Chanhudaro in south Pakistan. The results throw light on how the Harappan craftspersons may have made their beautiful long barrel cylinder beads. The process must have been something like this:

Long nodules of carnelian (a reddish orange variety of agate) were brought from Gujarat to Chanhudaro. The best were chosen and separated. These were dried in the sun for many months and then heated in shallow ovens to make the stone easier to work. The heating also deepened the red colour. The bead roughouts were made using a copper-tipped stake and an antler or horn hammer, using indirect percussion or pressure flaking techniques. Larger nodules were cut lengthwise and chipped to make bead roughouts. These roughouts were then partially ground on grooved sandstone or on quartzite grinding stones.

Then came the drilling of holes through the beads. This was done using a special cylindrical drill made out of a rare metamorphic rock which was heated to make an extremely hard and durable tool. This material has been given the name of 'Ernestite', after the archaeologist Ernest J. H. Mackay, who was the first to discover the drills and understand their significance. It could have taken a craftsperson a whole day of work—heating, chipping, and grinding—to make a drill. The Harappan bead makers used many different sizes of drills (at least six sizes) to make a single bead. The drilling was probably done with a hand-held bow drill. The friction would have produced intense heat, so the work may have been done under water, or at least by dripping water continuously on the drill hole.

The study conducted by Kenoyer and his team showed that even with these superior drills, it would have taken over 24 hours or three 8-hour days of steady drilling to perforate a single 6 cm long bead. The beads on the belts found at Mohenjodaro and Allahdino vary from 6 to 13 cm in length. It would have taken 3–8 days to make one of the longer beads, probably more, considering that the bead makers of Khambhat take long breaks after a couple of hours of work, as it is a very strenuous and tiring process. Once the beads were perforated, there was a laborious polishing process.

Taking the process from start to finish, it would have taken over 480 work days to make a belt of 36 beads of the kind found at Allahdino. Even if more than one worker was put on the job, it would still have taken up to a year. These beads must have been highly valued and worn only by the rich. For people who could not afford the expensive long carnelian beads, Harappan craftspeople made imitations in terracotta and painted them red.

Kenoyer, Vidal, and Bhan also analyzed the archaeological patterns of manufacturing waste and finished artefacts, the structural evidence, and settlement layout in order to make inferences about the way in which bead manufacture was organized and controlled. Why did the Harappans transport carnelian nodules from Gujarat to Chanhudaro, instead of getting at least some of the preliminary work, such as discarding poor quality nodules, done near the source of the raw materials? The evidence suggests that all stages of carnelian bead manufacture at Chanhudaro were centralized and controlled by a powerful and wealthy group of merchants. This also explains the uniformly good quality of the raw materials used and the high level of standardization. This is in contrast to evidence from the Moneer area at Mohenjodaro, which is suggestive of short-term production by several entrepreneurs.

Source Kenoyer et al., 1995

micrographic survey of the silk fibres from Harappa indicated that they belonged to the *A. assamensi* silk moth, which is found in North-eastern India and *A. mylitta*, which is found on the west coast. It is not clear which species of silk moth the Chanhudaro fibres belonged to—they may have belonged to *A. assamensis* or a species of *Philosamia* (Eri silk). This is the earliest evidence for silk outside China and indicates that silk-making based on wild silk worms was practised in South Asia at a very early date.

The Harappan crafts display an impressive level of standardization. Standardization extended to units of weights and measure. Cubical weights made of chert, chalcedony, black stone, etc. have been found at all excavated sites, and their accuracy all over the Harappan culture zone is remarkable. The system is binary in the smaller weights (1:2:8:16:32:64) and decimal in the higher weights (with a ratio of 160, 200, 320, and 640). The largest weight found at Mohenjodaro weighs 10.865 g. A shell scale was found at Mohenjodaro and an ivory scale at Lothal; a shell object found in Saurashtra was probably used to measure angles.

Stone weights, Dholavira

Kenoyer (1998: 149–50) has suggested that state control may have been responsible for the high level of standardization in crafts that were considered to have a value in maintaining the socio-economic or ritual order and which used non-local raw materials and highly complex technologies (e.g., the making of seals, stoneware bangles, and stone weights). Leaving aside pottery and bricks, crafts using local materials and simple technologies tend to show greater variation. But what is the explanation of the high level of standardization in crafts such as pottery-making and brick making? Does it imply centralized control by merchants or rulers? Some element of central direction is suggested, but its nature and degree are far from certain. If not direct, it may have taken the indirect form of facilitating or controlling the flow of at least some of the raw materials and finished goods. On the other hand, the level of standardization could also indicate the fanning out of hereditary craft specialists over large areas, or a well-developed network of internal trade. It is possible that craftsmen and traders may have been organized in corporate groups similar to guilds, but there is no proof of this.

Apart from engineering skill evident in architecture, some inferences can be made about Harappan mathematical knowledge. As pointed out by P. P. Divakaran (2018: 74, 77), the exceptional degree of regularity of form that marks this civilization reveals a strong sense of geometry. Apart from the regularity of the proportions of brick size, the use of trapezoidal bricks in wells of different dimensions reflect the first known attempt in the subcontinent to reduce the properties of a circle to an associated regular polygon. The details of Harappan science are not yet well worked out. It is likely that some elements of the scientific and mathematical knowledge of the Harappans lived on and influenced later Indian thought, but the details are difficult to ascertain.

Networks of Trade

The discovery of the Harappan civilization generated a great deal of interest in Harappan–Mesopotamian trade links. This is because before the advent of radiocarbon dating, these links gave vital clues for dating the Harappan culture, and also due to the prevailing interest in cross-cultural comparisons. Over the years, however, many scholars have come to the conclusion that Harappan–Mesopotamian trade may not have been as substantial as earlier held. Other areas such as the Persian Gulf have been identified as important zones of interaction as far as the long-distance trade of the Harappans is concerned. However, it is clear that trade networks within the Harappan culture zone and those linking the culture with other areas in the subcontinent were extremely significant; they are crucial for understanding the structure of the Harappan civilization as well as its striking level of cultural homogeneity. The importance of such trade is clear from the very wide range of raw materials and finished goods that found their way to different parts of the vast Harappan culture zone. This was an age before the advent of coinage, and the vibrant trade of the Harappans was based on barter or some other media of exchange.

One of the important aspects of trade is the identification of the sources of major raw materials. The best way of doing this is to scientifically analyze the artefacts and to compare the results with raw materials from various possible sources. Unfortunately, there are not enough studies of this kind so far. Another method is to plot the location of the known resources of various raw materials, especially those closest to the Harappan culture zone. Proof that these were being used in protohistoric times would, of course, give clinching evidence. Unfortunately, this is not usually available, and the earliest evidence of the exploitation of these resources is often contained in 18th/19th century textual references. In spite of its limitations, this kind of exercise is useful in helping identify probable sources of raw materials used by the Harappans. Randall William Law's geological provenance study (2011) of the rock and mineral assemblage of Harappa (discussed below) has confirmed some of the earlier hypotheses based on this sort of methodology and has given a new perspective on others.

The discovery of factory sites in the limestone hills of Sukkur and Rohri indicates that chert blades were mass produced here and sent to various Harappan settlements in Sindh. The Khetri deposits of Rajasthan must have been an important source of copper. The Ganeshwar–Jodhpura complex of Rajasthan was probably a major source of copper artefacts for the Harappans, especially given the fact that Harappan sites such as Rakhigarhi and Kalibangan are located close by. Lead and zinc probably also came from Rajasthan. Tin is available in the Tosam area of modern Haryana, but other possible sources are Afghanistan and Central Asia. Gold may have come from the Kolar fields of Karnataka, where it may have been obtained via trade from the neolithic people who lived there. These neolithic herders may also have been exporters of cattle. (Fine disc beads, probably of steatite paste, found at Piklihal may have been obtained from the Harappans.) Gold could also have been panned from the sands of the upper Indus. Semi-precious stone used for bead manufacture came from Gujarat. Lapis lazuli was probably obtained from the Badakhshan mines in Afghanistan, although it is also reported as occurring in the Chagai hills in Baluchistan. Traders must also have been engaged in a brisk trade in grains and other food products, transporting these between villages and cities.

Two-wheeled carts were an important mode of transport for people and goods. Bronze and terracotta models of carts with solid wheels have been found at various sites. No carts survive, but their tracks have been found at several sites, indicating spans roughly similar to those used today. Traders must also have transported their merchandise across long distances in caravans of pack animals such as oxen, sheep, goats, and donkeys. Towards the end of the mature Harappan phase, there is possible evidence of the use of the camel. The use of the horse seems to have been very minimal. Boats are depicted on seals and moulded tablets, and clay models have been found at Harappa and Lothal. River boats had cabins, ladders leading to the roof, and a high seated platform on the stern for navigation. Seafaring boats had a sharp keel, pointed prow, high flat stern, and mast and ropes for sails.

Several routes of trade and communication connected the various parts of the Harappan culture zone—Baluchistan, Sindh, Rajasthan, Cholistan, Punjab, Gujarat, and the upper doab. These routes can be reconstructed by studying the geographical landscape, settlement patterns, and the distribution of raw materials and finished products. Lahiri (1992: 112–43) points out that major trade routes connected the following areas: Sindh and south Baluchistan; coastal Sindh, upper Sindh, and the central Indus plains; the Indus plains and Rajasthan; the regions lying to the north of the Indus and Harappa; Sindh and east Punjab; east Punjab and Rajasthan; and Sindh and Gujarat. Some of the routes were already well defined in the early Harappan phase—e.g., the Baluchistan–Sindh route via the Kirthar mountains, and the route from east Punjab and Rajasthan via the Cholistan tract. The route connecting north Afghanistan, the Gomal plain, and Multan with a feeder route going to the Taxila valley also continued to be important. Certain routes that were being used in the earlier period became more important in the mature Harappan phase—e.g., the routes within Sindh, between Sindh and the central Indus plains, and between Sindh and Baluchistan via Kutch and Kathiawar. It is likely that the Indus saw a certain amount of riverine traffic. There was also a coastal route linking the Gujarat sites such as Lothal and Dholavira to sites such as Sutkagen-dor on the Makran coast. The location of some of the important sites can in fact be explained in relation to the trade routes of the time. For instance, Mohenjodaro lay at the intersection of the water-route of the Indus and the east–west land route that linked the Quetta valley and the Bolan river to Kot Diji and the western Nara.

Terracotta cart, Harappa

The main sources of information on long-distance trade include a number of Harappan or Harappan-related (i.e., similar to Harappan types) artefacts found at sites outside the subcontinent, and foreign objects found at Harappan sites. These are supplemented by textual sources in the case of Indus–Mesopotamian trade (see Chakrabarti, 1990; Ratnagar, 1981).

A number of Harappan and Harappan-related objects have been found in south Turkmenistan at sites such as Altyn Depe, Namazga, and Khapuz. These include ivory

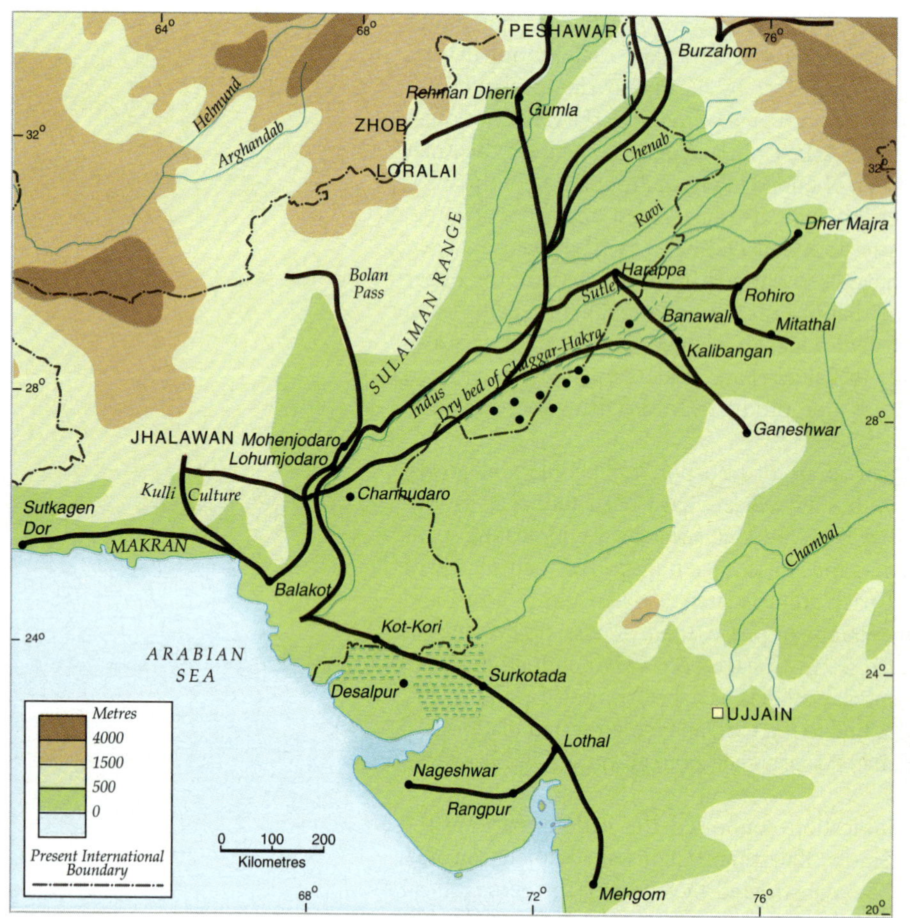

Map 4.3 Harappan routes of internal trade (after Lahiri, 1992)

dice, two types of metal objects (a spearhead and ladle), an ithyphallic terracotta, perforated ware, a segmented bead, and a silver seal. The most definite evidence comes from Altyn Depe, in the form of a rectangular Harappan seal bearing the Harappan script. The sites in Iran which have yielded Harappan and Harappan-related artefacts are Hissar, Shah Tepe, Kalleh Nisar, Susa, Tepe Yahya, Jalalabad, Marlik, and Jiroft. The main evidence consists of seals and carnelian beads (both the etched and long barrel cylinder types). The most important evidence of trade with Afghanistan comes from an isolated Harappan trading outpost at Shortughai.

Many years ago, a round seal with a short-horned bull motif and Harappan writing was found at Failaka in the Persian Gulf. In recent years, there has been a substantial increase in the evidence of Harappan trade contacts with the Persian Gulf area. Harappan and Harappan-related artefacts (including a piece of ivory, a *linga*-shaped object, a circular mirror, and seals with Harappan motifs and/or writing) have been found at Ras-al-Qala on the island of Bahrain. Excavations near Hamad in Bahrain yielded a typical Harappan seal and carnelian beads in burials. A seal with the bull motif and Harappan script was found at the site of Hajjar. From Failaka, apart from the 'Persian Gulf seal' mentioned above, there was a flat, round seal with the Harappan script. Jar fragments with Harappan writing have been found at many sites in the Persian Gulf. These were probably containers used to transport perishable goods from the Harappan culture zone to this region.

The Harappans were also trading with the Oman peninsula. An etched carnelian bead of the Harappan type was found at Umm-an-Nar. There are similarities between certain other types of objects found at this site (a square steatite seal, fragments of pottery, carnelian beads, a cubical stone weight, etc.) and Harappan artefacts. Maysar, an excavated copper-smelting site, has yielded evidence (e.g., pottery decorations and motifs on a seal) that suggests Harappan influence. Ras al-Junayaz yielded a Harappan seal, Harappan inscribed potsherd, and an ivory comb. The major imports from Oman may have included chlorite vessels, shell, and perhaps mother-of-pearl. Copper has been mentioned as another Omani export to the Harappans, but this is unlikely, as the metal was available closer, in Rajasthan. As for Harappan exports to Oman, the items that survive in the archaeological record include beads, chert weights, and ivory objects.

There is textual as well as archaeological evidence for Harappan trade with Mesopotamia. Mesopotamian records of the time of king Sargon (2334–2279 BCE) refer to ships from the lands of Dilmun, Magan, and Meluhha tied along the quay of the capital city, Akkad. Dilmun can be identified with Bahrain, and Magan with the Makran coast and Oman. Meluhha may have been a generic term for areas lying to the east of Mesopotamia, including the Indus valley, or it may refer specifically to the Indus valley. The archaeological evidence for Harappan–Mesopotamian trade consists mainly of a few

Map 4.4 Long-distance trade routes

Harappan or Harappan-related seals and carnelian beads at Mesopotamian sites such as Kish, Lagash, Nippur, and Ur. Carnelian beads (both the etched type and the long barrel-cylinder type) were also found in the royal graves at Ur. Certain motifs such as the bull on Mesopotamian seals have been cited as reflecting Harappan influence. Cylinder seals (which are common in West Asia) with Harappan-type motifs suggest interaction between merchants of these two areas. The absence of Mesopotamian seals and sealings in the Harappan context suggests that Mesopotamian traders were not directly involved in the Harappan–Mesopotamian trade interactions.

Carnelian beads were clearly an important Harappan export to West Asia. Textiles and conch shell objects were other possible exports. Ivory and ivory objects may have been exported by the Harappans to Afghanistan, Turkmenistan, and perhaps the Persian Gulf. Mesopotamian texts mention the following items as imports from Meluhha: lapis lazuli, carnelian, gold, silver, copper, ebony, ivory, tortoiseshell, a chicken-like bird, dog, cat, and monkey. Mesopotamia's general exports included fish, grain, raw wool, woollen garments, and silver. It is possible that wool and silver found their way to Meluhha, but there is no archaeological proof of this.

There are two very different assessments of Harappan–Mesopotamian trade. Ratnagar (1981) highlights the importance of this trade, especially the trade in lapis lazuli, and even argues that its decline was a reason for the decline of the Harappan civilization. Notwithstanding the long list of items mentioned in texts, the fact remains that there are very few Harappan artefacts found in Mesopotamia and even fewer Mesopotamian artefacts found at Harappan sites. A few Mesopotamian-type stone weights have been reported from Mohenjodaro and Harappa. Three motifs found on some Harappan seals

NEW DIRECTIONS IN RESEARCH | **Sources of rocks and minerals**

Randall William Law's study focuses on identifying the sources of the stone and metal artefacts excavated at the site of Harappa during different phases in its settlement history, beginning with Period I (the early Harappan Ravi phase) to Period V (the late Harappan Cemetery H phase).

In order to answer these questions, Law took into account the entire assemblage of stone and metal artefacts excavated by the Harappa Archaeological Project. From this assemblage, he compared almost 3000 objects made of different rock or mineral types with geological samples collected from various possible sources located across the Greater Indus region. He argues that since rock and mineral artefacts functioned both as prestige and utilitarian items, they were essential parts of the political economy of Harappan society, as essential for the development and sustenance of urbanized societies as were grain or livestock. His study is, therefore, more than a catalogue of rocks, metals, and sites. It asks questions about who the inhabitants of Harappa were interacting with while acquiring rocks and minerals, the ways in which inter-regional patterns of interaction changed over time, and whether there were variations in rock and mineral acquisition and use between groups of people living in different parts of sites.

The study examined artefacts made of material including steatite, chert, agate—jasper, lapis lazuli, limestone, alabaster, crystaline quartz, copper, lead, gold, and silver. The stages in the study were as follows: References in geological works were examined to locate potential sources of metals and mineral artefacts found at Harappa. This was followed by geological fieldwork. Potential sources (in India, Pakistan, and Oman) were visited and samples obtained. Information was gathered from traditional jewellery makers and sellers. The methods used to identify the archaeological and geological materials include visual inspection, basic mineralogical testing, X-ray diffraction analysis (XRD), electron microprobe analysis (EMPA), spectrometric analysis, and instrumental neutron activation analysis (INAA). The data was then analyzed using a statistical method known as canonical discriminant analysis (CDA). The "provenance postulate" that forms the basis of Law's study is that it is possible to determine the source of a stone or metal object provided that the qualitative or quantitative chemical or mineralogical differences *between* the natural sources is greater than the qualitative or quantitative differences *within* each source.

Through this study, Law was able to determine the provenance of over 2,100 stone and metal artefacts found at Harappa (and almost 120 found at other sites). Some of the findings corroborate hypotheses put forward by earlier scholars, others suggest that a few need to be revised. External trade was a feature of all the phases of the site, but most of the areas involved in this trade were located in the neighbouring highland areas. There was a steady intensification of inter-regional exchange networks during the period leading to the mature Harappan phase. This included a significant change, namely the acquiring of chert and grinding stone through long distance trade networks. Most of the sources of metal and mineral artefacts were located north of the Indus basin, indicating that these were more important than hitherto assumed. Pb isotope assays of metal artefacts indicated that the people of Harappa were obtaining lead ores from deposits in Jammu and Kashmir, Baluchistan, and another unidentified source. The sources of the copper artefacts that were analyzed seem to lie west of the Indus region or in Oman. Lapis lazuli clearly came from the Sar-i-Sang area mines in the Badakhshan region of Afghanistan. Although Law did not visit the Chagai hills of Baluchistan, on the basis of his close reading of reports, he considers it unlikely that lapis lazuli actually occurs in that region.

The study confirms the hypothesis that except for lapis lazuli and turquoise, the raw materials used to make artefacts at Harappan sites were available within the Harappan culture zone or not far from it. Clear evidence for long-distance trade with distant areas such as Mesopotamia, Iran, or Arabia was lacking. The conclusion is that trade with these areas does not seem to have been an important factor in Harappan urbanism.

Source Law, 2011

are seen by some scholars as reflecting Mesopotamian influence—the whorl design, a man grappling with two animals (lions or tigers), and the gatepost motif. The evidence as a whole is not very substantial. Chakrabarti (1990) and Shaffer (1982b) argue that Harappan trade with Mesopotamia was not direct, extensive or intensive. This trade does not seem to have been particularly important for the development or sustenance of the Harappan civilization. More recently, Reade (2008) has argued for the need to reassess Harappan–Mesopotamian trade relations in the light of growing evidence of interactions along the Arabian Sea coast. He also argues that Mesopotamian chronologies should be lowered by two centuries, which would suggest that the Harappan cities existed well before the trade with Mesopotamia began.

Among the Harappan imports via long-distance trade, lapis lazuli was probably an import from Afghanistan (or it could have been obtained closer from the Chagai hills of Baluchistan). Jade must have come from Turkmenistan. Tin may have been obtained from

FURTHER DISCUSSION | Shortughai—a Harappan trading post in Afghanistan

Shortughai is located near the confluence of the Oxus and its tributary, the Kokcha, in north-east Afghanistan. It is a small site, only about 2 ha. The cultural deposit is 2.5–3 m thick, within which four periods of occupation have been identified. Period I (50 cm thick) was dated by radiocarbon to the end of the 3rd millennium BCE.

The discoveries of Period I included the following: pottery with Harappan designs, terracotta cakes, fragments of toy carts, copper and bronze objects, pieces of gold and lead, a discoidal gold bead; lapis lazuli, agate, carnelian, steatite, small barrel-shaped agate beads; long tubular and etched carnelian beads; flint micro-blades and drill heads; shell bangles; and mud-bricks of the typical Harappan size. Harappan graffiti occurred on the rims of jars and on beakers. There was a square Harappan seal with the motif of a rhinoceros and the Harappan script. The discovery of so many typical Harappan artefacts and manufacturing techniques proves that this was not a site which had mere *contact* with the Harappan civilization, but a site *belonging* to the Harappan civilization.

Shortughai also has some unique features. A ploughed field covered with flax seeds was found in an area unsuitable for irrigation, showing the practice of dry farming. Small irrigation canals drawing on the water of the Kokcha, located about 25 km away, were found in other parts of the site.

What were the Harappans doing at Shortughai? This site seems to have been connected with the lapis lazuli mines nearby. However, lapis lazuli objects are not particularly numerous at Harappan sites. A second possibility is that Shortughai owed its importance to its proximity to the tin mines of Afghanistan and Ferghana. A third possibility is that it had a role to play in camel trade.

Source Chakrabarti, 1990: 1–2, 86–89

Ferghana and eastern Kazakistan in Central Asia. Carved chlorite and green schist vessels were a popular item of trade in West Asia and the Persian Gulf, and a few fragments have been found at Mohenjodaro. These may have been imported from southern Iran or from Baluchistan. Very few West Asian artefacts have been found in Harappan contexts. A seal of the Persian Gulf type was found at Lothal as a surface find. A lapis lazuli bead from Mohenjodaro and a pendant with lapis lazuli inlay found at Cemetery-H levels at Harappa were possibly imports from West Asia. A cylinder seal (as mentioned earlier, cylinder seals were common in West Asia) with Indian motifs was found at Kalibangan.

Harappan objects in Mesopotamia can be dated from the Early Dynastic IIIA period (which began in *c.* 2600/2500/2400 BCE) to the Isin–Larsa period (*c.* 2000/1900 BCE) in the Mesopotamian sequence, which corresponds to the entire span of the mature Harappan phase. The finds from other parts of West Asia also belong roughly to this period. However, the discovery of a Harappan seal at the site of Nippur in a 14th century BCE context suggests that Harappan contact with Mesopotamia may have continued, although in a diminished form, into the late Harappan phase. The continuation of some amount of trade with the Persian Gulf region is suggested by two Harappan seals found at Failaka in a 14th century BCE context, and a late Harappan seal found at Bet Dwarka. The latter has Harappan writing and a three-headed animal motif similar to that found on certain Persian Gulf seals.

The importance of overland routes from the Harappan civilization through Afghanistan is evident from the location of Harappan sites near each of the passes and routes that lead through Baluchistan into Afghanistan. Pathani Damb is near the Mula pass, Nausharo near the Bolan pass, Dabarkot in the Gomal valley, and Gumla and Hathala in the Derajat, along the route via the Gomal pass. The Gomal route seems to have been the most important.

Two main overland routes connected the Harappan civilization with West Asia. The northern one passed through northern Afghanistan, north Iran, Turkmenistan, and Mesopotamia, crossing sites such as Shortughai, Tepe Hissar, Shah Tepe, and Kish. A southern route passed through Tepe Yahya, Jalalabad, Kalleh Nisar, Susa, and Ur. The maritime route to Mesopotamia may also have been used. It is likely that sites such as Sutkagen-dor, Balakot, and Dabarkot (the latter two may at that time have been located at the coast instead of some distance away) were important points along this route. Lothal (10 km away from the Gulf of Cambay) and Kuntasi (on the Phulki river, 4 km from the coast), Dholavira (in the Rann of Kutch), and the sites along the coast of Kutch no doubt played an important role in maritime trade.

The argument that the quantum of Harappan long-distance trade was not great is persuasive. Unlike the resource-poor area of Mesopotamia, the Harappan culture zone was rich in a variety of natural resources. Food requirements and most of the raw materials required by Harappan craftspersons could have been met by resources available within the Harappan culture zone. The diverse, well-developed craft traditions meant that most of the finished goods required by the Harappans were likewise available from within this area. A few raw materials and products were obtained from other parts of the subcontinent and from areas such as Afghanistan and Central Asia. Very few essential items had to be imported from distant places. Harappan trade must have involved highly organized merchant groups as well as nomadic peddlers in the mountainous stretches. The extent of state control over this activity is a matter of debate.

The Nature and Uses of Writing

Among the biggest mysteries about the Harappan civilization are the language (or languages) the Harappans spoke and their writing system. It is likely that people living in various parts of the Harappan culture zone spoke different languages and dialects. The writing on the seals was probably in the language of the ruling elite. Some scholars have suggested that this language belonged to the Indo-Aryan family. However, Iravatham Mahadevan (1977) and Asko Parpola (1994) have presented substantial evidence to argue that the Harappan language belonged to the Dravidian family of languages. An argument made by Steve Farmer, Richard Sproat, and Michael Witzel (2004) that the Harappans had non-linguistic symbols but no real system of writing has been effectively refuted by Asko Parpola (2008).

Over 6,000 inscribed objects have been found at Harappan sites (for details, see Mahadevan, 1977; Parpola, 1994). Most of the writing appears on seals and sealings (seal impressions), some on copper tablets, copper/bronze implements, pottery, and other miscellaneous objects. About 50 per cent of the inscribed objects have been found at Mohenjodaro, and the two sites of Mohenjodaro and Harappa together account for about 87 per cent of all inscribed material. Most of the inscriptions are very short, with an average of five signs. The longest one has 26 signs. The script seems to have emerged in a fully evolved state and does not show any significant changes over time. This conclusion may, however, be the result of the inadequacies of earlier excavations, which did not record the stratigraphic context of all objects, making it difficult to sort out earlier and later samples of writing.

Writing on the Dholavira 'signboard'

There are 400–450 basic signs and the script is **logo-syllabic**—i.e., each symbol stood for a word or syllable. It was generally written and meant to be read from right to left (this is reversed on the seals). This is evident from that fact that in inscriptions, the letters are cramped on the left side, where space had clearly run out, and from overlapping letters scratched onto pottery. There are a few instances, however, of writing from left to right. Longer inscriptions that consisted of more than one line were sometimes written in the **boustrophedon style**—with consecutive lines starting in opposite directions.

What was the connection between the motifs on the seals and the writing? What was the extent of literacy among the Harappans? What was writing used for? In order to understand the uses of writing in the Harappan civilization, it is necessary to try to interpret the functions of the inscribed objects. Writing appears very frequently on the seals. Some of these were impressed onto small moist clay tablets known as sealings, probably by merchants to authenticate their bales of merchandise. The evidence of textile impressions on some sealings supports this interpretation. However, more seals than sealings have been found, and the seals are generally worn at the edges and not inside. Some seals have a hole in them, suggesting that a string was passed through them. This suggests that some of the so-called seals may have had other functions. They may have been tokens used in the buying and selling of goods. They may also have been worn as amulets or used as identification markers (like modern identity cards) by well-to-do people like landowners, merchants, priests, artisans, and rulers. Those no longer in use must have been intentionally broken so that they could not be misused by anybody. Tablets with narrative scenes may have had a religious or ritualistic function. The so-called 'seals' were, thus, used for multiple purposes.

Writing also appears on miniature tablets made of steatite, terracotta, and faience. Since these objects were not used to make impressions, unlike the seals, the writing on them was not reversed. Many of the objects were discovered at Harappa and other large cities. Rectangular copper tablets with writing and animal motifs were found at Mohenjodaro, while a few tablets with raised writing were found at Harappa. The limited number of places where they occur suggests a restricted use. Interestingly, there are many duplicates of both the miniature and copper tablets.

The evidence of writing on pottery suggests a wider use in craft production and economic transactions. Harappan potters sometimes inscribed letters onto pots before firing. At other times, inscriptions were made on pots after they were fired (this is termed 'graffiti'). Even if the potters who made the marks on their pots were themselves illiterate, they must have been able to recognize the symbols. Pointed goblets sometimes have seal impressions, which may have indicated the name or status of the person for whom the pot was made.

Items like copper and bronze tools, stoneware bangles, bone pins, and gold jewellery were sometimes inscribed. A copper vessel found at Mohenjodaro contained a large number of gold objects. These included four ornaments with tiny inscriptions, all apparently written by the same hand, probably giving the name of the owner. Some of the writing inscribed or painted on personal possessions such as bangles, tools, beads, and bone rods may have had some sort of magico-religious or ritualistic significance.

The Dholavira 'signboard' may or may not indicate a high level of urban literacy, but it does indicate a civic use of writing. Compared with the Mesopotamian and Egyptian civilizations, the written material in the Harappan civilization appears significantly less in terms of length and volume. However, it is likely that a very small proportion of Harappan written material survives, and that people wrote on perishable material as well. Two terracotta representations (one is broken) of what look like wooden writing tablets from Mohenjodaro are interesting. The intact one measures 18 × 8 cm, and on one side has a small rectangular projection with a hole, presumably for hanging. The evidence of a common script all over the vast Harappan culture zone shows a high level of cultural integration. The virtual disappearance of the script by *c.* 1700 BCE suggests both a close connection of writing with city life and the lack of sufficient downward percolation of writing.

Religious and Funerary Practices

The basic elements of what can be loosely described as 'Harappan religion' were outlined by John Marshall in 1931. Although some aspects of Marshall's interpretation can be criticized—especially his tendency to read elements of later Hinduism into the evidence—he did succeed in identifying several important features of Harappan religion. Hypotheses about this issue are bound to be subjective, especially in view of the fact that the script is undeciphered.

The worship of female goddesses associated with fertility has long been held as one of the major features of Harappan religion. This conclusion is based on the following factors: (*a*) the concerns that agricultural societies are invariably known to have with fertility; (*b*) cross-cultural parallels with other ancient civilizations; (*c*) the importance of goddess worship in later Hinduism; and (*d*) the discovery of a large number of terracotta female figurines that were labelled 'Mother Goddesses'. Certain representations on seals are also relevant. For instance, a seal showing a nude woman, head downwards, with her legs apart and a plant issuing from her vagina is often interpreted as a prototype of Shakambhari, the Earth Mother.

Harappan seals; the script—the 'jar' sign (ƱF) and the 'marker' sign (*II*) are the most frequently occurring symbols (from top)

Female figurine with fan-shaped headdress

As discussed in Chapter 3, describing all female figurines as representations of a single great 'Mother Goddess' associated with fertility and maternity clearly over-simplifies the situation. The attributes of the figurines and the contexts in which they were found have to be considered carefully before assigning them a religious or cultic significance. As pointed out in an earlier chapter, not all female figurines necessarily represented goddesses (let alone a single goddess), and not all goddesses necessarily had maternal associations. Some of the Harappan female figurines may have had a cultic significance and may have been part of household rituals. Others may have been toys or decorative items.

A study of the Harappan terracottas by Alexandra Ardeleanu-Jansen (2002) underlines the great variety in the form of female figurines. The type which is frequently interpreted as having a religious significance is a slim female figure with a distinctive fan-shaped headdress, wearing a short skirt. She is heavily ornamented with necklaces, armlets, bangles, anklets, and earrings. Some of the figurines have cup-like attachments and flowers on either side of the head. In certain cases, the cup-like attachments have traces of black residue, suggesting that they were used to burn oil or some sort of essence. Such figurines may have been religious images worshipped in households, votive offerings made to a deity, or part of the paraphernalia of domestic rituals. It is interesting to note that such figures do not appear on Harappan seals and tablets or in stone or metal sculpture.

There is also a matronly, pot-bellied type of female figurine who may represent either a pregnant woman or a prosperous woman. She is naked and sometimes wears some jewellery and a turban or headdress. Both the 'matronly type' and the 'slim type' of female figurines may hold a baby in their arms. The 'matronly type' can stand without support, while the youthful, 'slim type' needs support. It is interesting to note that female figurines—including those with possible religious significance—are found in large numbers at sites such as Mohenjodaro, Harappa, and Banawali, but not at sites such as Kalibangan, Lothal, Surkotada or Mitathal.

Most of the terracotta figurines (including the female ones) were found broken and discarded in secondary locations. None were found in a context that could be interpreted as a temple. This was one of the reasons why Marshall suggested that they were votive offerings rather than cult images. The fact that so many of them were broken suggests that they may have been part of a ritual cycle and were made for short-term use for certain specific occasions. The relationship between the female figurines and the male and animal figurines with which they are associated needs to be explored.

Marshall suggested that the Harappans also worshipped a male god represented on a steatite seal discovered at Mohenjodaro, usually referred to as the Pashupati seal. This shows a male figure with a buffalo horn headdress seated on a dais with his legs bent double under him, heels together, toes pointed down. His outstretched arms are adorned with bangles, his hands rest lightly on his knees. He is flanked by four animals—an elephant, rhinoceros, water buffalo, and tiger. Beneath the dais are two antelopes or ibexes. Marshall thought the male figure was three-headed and ithyphallic. He saw a striking resemblance between this deity and the Shiva of later Hindu mythology, who is also known as Mahayogi (the great *yogi*) and Pashupati (lord of the animals).

Another aspect of the fertility-related beliefs of the Harappans was the worship of male and female creative energy in the form of stone icons of the type later known as *lingas* and *yonis*. The *linga*-type objects vary in size and shape. The smallest ones (1.5–30 cm in height) are mostly made of limestone and alabaster; some are made of other materials such as terracotta, shell, or faience. The large ones (mostly in the 60 to 90 cm height range) are made of stone. The ring stones vary in diameter from 1.5 to 1.30 cm. The larger ones are made of stone, while the smaller ones are made of stone, shell, faience, or paste. George Dales argued that the contexts in which these stones were found do not suggest cultic significance. Some of the ring stones had lines on them and may have had architectural use, either to guide masons in pillar building or to measure angles; or they may have been used to make astronomical calculations. Marshall had suggested that some of the *linga*-shaped objects may have been grinders or unfinished

Female figurine, Banawali

FURTHER DISCUSSION | **Man, god, or goddess?**

The 'Pashupati seal'

Marshall concluded that this seal showed that the Harappans worshipped a god who seems to have been a proto-Shiva. This conclusion has not gone unchallenged. The questions that have been asked include the following:

1. Is the figure really sitting in a yogic posture of ritual discipline?
2. Is he really three-headed?
3. Is he ithyphallic?
4. Is the figure a male?
5. Shiva as Pashupati in later Hindu mythology protects domesticated cattle, while the figure on the seal is associated with wild animals. In view of this difference, can the two really be connected?

The figure has been variously identified as a chieftain, a divine bull-man, Indra, or the demon Mahisha of the Puranas.

M. K. Dhavalikar and Shubhangana Atre (see Atre, 1985–86) have suggested that it represents a goddess—a 'lady of the beasts'. Notwithstanding all these alternative interpretations, the basics of Marshall's interpretation are still persuasive. The figure can be accepted as that of a male seated in a yogic posture, although it is not certain that he was three-headed. The similarities between the deity—for he seems to be no ordinary man—and certain attributes of the later-day Shiva remain striking. Of course, we do not know what name the Harappans gave him.

We can recall here the 'horned deity' that appears on a Kot Diji pot, Kalibangan terracotta cake, and the Padri jar. This indicates that the worship of a horned deity goes back to the early Harappan phase.

weights. However, a terracotta piece which closely resembles a *linga* with a *yoni-pitha* (*yoni* base) has been found at Kalibangan. The evidence suggests that at least some of these artefacts were icons with religious significance.

The Harappan seals, sealings, amulets, and copper tablets depict a number of trees, plants, and animals, some of which may have had cultic significance. The *pipal* (*Ficus religiosa*) tree appears often and may have been venerated. Sometimes, there is a figure peering out from between its branches, possibly a tree-spirit. A seal found at Mohenjodaro shows a row of seven figures with long braids standing in front of a *pipal* tree which has a horned figure standing in it. It is not clear whether the figures are male or female, but because they are seven in number, scholars have speculated that there may be a connection with the later traditions of the seven *rishi*s or the seven mothers.

Some of the animals depicted on seals and sealings—for instance, the humped and humpless bull, snake, elephant, rhinoceros, antelope, *gharial*, and tiger—may have had cultic significance. The bull, a symbol of male virility in many ancient cultures, seems to have been especially important. We can note the steatite bull statuettes discovered at certain sites, including a very sophisticated terracotta bull found at Mohenjodaro. It is possible that some of the terracotta animals on wheels may have been cult images rather than toys. Two Harappan sealings appear to represent animals being carried in processions; one of them resembles a bull or cow. The composite animals (tiger–human, bull–elephant, ram–bull–elephant, etc.) and the 'unicorn' depicted on some seals and sealings may also have had some sort of religious or mythological significance. That this not a two-horned bovine depicted in profile but a mythical one-horned animal is proved by small terracottas which have one horn. Especially interesting are certain representations on seals that consist of a combination of body parts of a human with those of assorted animals such as snake, tiger, goat, elephant, and 'unicorn.' These composite motifs must have had some religious or magical significance. Some of the terracotta, shell, faience, and metal tablets found at Harappan sites may have been amulets. Their motifs, such as the *svastika*, may have been associated with a protective function or auspiciousness. Terracotta masks and puppets found at Mohenjodaro and Harappa include those in the

FURTHER DISCUSSION | **The 'fire altars'**

The citadel complex at Kalibangan consists of a northern and southern unit, separated from each other by a wall. In the southern sector, archaeologists found five or more mud-brick platforms, separated from each other and from the back of the fortification wall by streets. Steps or ramps led up to the platforms. On one of these platforms, there was a row of seven clay-lined pits, each about 75 × 55 cm. These have been identified as 'fire altars', i.e., pits in which offerings were made into the fire as part of sacrificial rituals. Ash, charcoal, the remains of a rectangular clay piece, and terracotta cakes were found in them. To the west of this row of pits, within easy reach of whoever sat in front of them, was the lower half of a jar containing ash and charcoal, embedded into the ground. Nearby was a well and the remains of bath pavements with attached drains, all made of burnt bricks. A 'fire altar' and a well were discovered on another platform in the southern sector of the citadel complex. There was also a 1.25 × 1 m brick-lined rectangular pit, containing cattle bones and antlers. This suggests the practice of animal sacrifice. The southern sector of the Kalibangan citadel complex seems to have been a place where sacrificial rituals of a congregational character were performed. The northern part of the citadel complex contained houses. B. B. Lal suggests this may have been where the priests who performed the rituals lived.

'Fire altars' have also been reported at Banawali, Lothal, Amri, Nageshwar, and Vagad in Gujarat and at Rakhigarhi in Haryana. But it is only at Kalibangan and Banawali that they may have signified some community event; in the other cases, they seem to have been associated with domestic rituals. Again, as in the case with female figurines, the fact that the 'fire altars' have been found at a few sites but are absent at most, indicates variations in religious practice within the vast area of the Harappan culture.

Source B. B. Lal, 1984

Harappan seals with depictions of tiger, elephant

form of real and mythical animals, and these may have been used in religious, political, or politico-religious rituals.

The Great Bath was probably the scene of an elite ritual activity involving ceremonial bathing. A triangular terracotta cake found at Kalibangan has a carving of a horned deity on one side and an animal being dragged by a rope by a human on the other. The latter has been tentatively interpreted as suggesting the practice of animal sacrifice. A Kalibangan cylinder seal shows a woman flanked by two men who hold her with one hand and raise swords over her head with the other; this may represent a scene of human sacrifice. The most striking evidence suggesting ritualistic practices comes from the 'fire altars' found on the citadel mound at Kalibangan.

Harappan cemeteries have been located at sites such as Harappa, Kalibangan, Lothal, Rakhigarhi, and Surkotada. The most common method of burial was to place the body of the deceased in an extended position, with the head towards the north, in a simple pit or brick chamber. Grave goods including food, pottery, tools, and ornaments were placed along with the body, but they were never too many or lavish. Clearly, the Harappans preferred to use wealth in life rather than bury it with their dead. At Harappa, there was a coffin with a shroud made of reeds. Symbolic burials with grave goods but no skeletons were found at Kalibangan. Fractional burials (where the body was exposed to the elements and the bones then gathered and buried) were found at Mohenjodaro and Harappa. These two sites also gave evidence of urn burials suggestive of cremation. Multiple burials of men and women were discovered at Lothal and Rakhigarhi.

The religious and funerary beliefs and practices of the Harappans show great variety. While there are dangers in viewing these through the lens of later-day Hinduism, it is interesting to note that the Harappan civilization does display a few features reminiscent of later traditions, except, however, the important element of temple worship. Not a single structure found at any Harappan site can conclusively be identified as a temple.

The Harappan People

What did the Harappan people look like? What sorts of clothes and ornaments did they wear? How did they relax and have fun? Terracotta, stone, and bronze sculptures (some of which have been described in earlier sections) help answer such questions. The form of human terracotta figurines was connected to their function, stylistic conventions, and audience, and they may not be realistic representations of what all or even most Harappans looked like. Nevertheless, they do help insert three-dimensional people into our picture of the Harappan civilization.

The human terracottas can be divided into female and male figurines, those whose sex is not clear, a few that are androgynous, that is with both female and male attributes (e.g., a figurine from Harappa which has breasts and a beard), and a few males in feminine dress. Going by the figurines, Harappan women wore a short skirt made of cotton or wool. They wore their hair variously in braids, rolled into a bun at the back or side of the head, arranged in separate locks or ringlets, and wrapped around the head like a turban, or left loose. What looks like a fan-shaped headdress could actually represent hair stretched over a frame made of bamboo or some other material. At Harappa, it is supplemented by flowers or flower-shaped ornaments. Such hairstyles or headdresses could indicate women of distinction or deities. Female figurines wear ornaments such as necklaces, chokers, hair ornaments, bangles, and belts. We can recall the beautiful jewellery found at many Harappan sites.

Male figurines are usually bare headed, though some are turbaned. Most of them are nude, so it is difficult to say what sort of clothes men wore. Certain stone sculptures suggest the use of a *dhoti*-like lower garment and an upper garment consisting of a shawl or cloak worn over one shoulder and under the other. There are various hairstyles—braids, buns, and hair hanging loose. Most of the male figurines have beards, in styles ranging from the 'goatee' to the more common combed and spread-out style as in the case of the 'priest-king'. There is some degree of overlap in male and female hairstyles and ornaments, but also some differences. For instance, men and women both wear bangles and necklaces, but men rarely wear multi-strand necklaces made of graduated beads.

Children of all cultures and all times play with toys, and Harappan children were no exception. Terracotta toys of various kinds have been found at Harappan sites. They include balls, rattles, whistles, gamesmen, carts with moveable parts, and animals on wheels. There are spinning tops made of terracotta and shell. Some have a shallow depression, while others have a copper tip to make them spin around a long time. Clay marbles have been found in courtyards of houses. Miniature terracotta cooking vessels, beds, and other toy furniture have been found, with which children must have played house. There are figurines of children playing with toys. One of them holds what seems to be a clay disc. Many clay discs have in fact been found at Harappan sites, and it is possible that these are remnants of a *pithu*-like game played with a ball and piled-up pieces of clay or stone. Lots of terracotta figurines of dogs have been found at Harappan sites, some with collars, suggesting that people kept dogs as pets. Some of the terracotta figurines of people and animals have a comic appearance, reflecting a sense of humour.

The social implications of the worship of female deities are complex. Although such worship reflects the ability to visualize divinity in feminine form, it does not necessarily translate into power or a high social position for ordinary women. While some of the female figurines found at Harappan sites may represent goddesses, many seem to represent ordinary, mortal women. Terracotta figurines of women at work are few. Figurines depicting women grinding or kneading something (food/clay?) have been found at Nausharo, Harappa, and Mohenjodaro, suggesting the association of women with food-processing activities. In ancient societies, childbirth was a process fraught with danger. Some of the fat female terracotta figurines may represent pregnant women. Excavations at Harappa yielded a burial with a woman and baby, perhaps a case of death in childbirth. Some female figurines found at Harappan sites carry a suckling infant on the left hip; others show women carrying infants close to their breast. An unusual terracotta figurine found at Nausharo (Period ID) shows a male with feminine headdress holding an infant. Tiny terracotta figurines of small children have been found at most sites. Were all of them toys or could they be votive objects? Can a statistical analysis of the child figurines help us identify whether there was a cultural bias in favour of male or female children? This is a very interesting question, but answers can only be speculative.

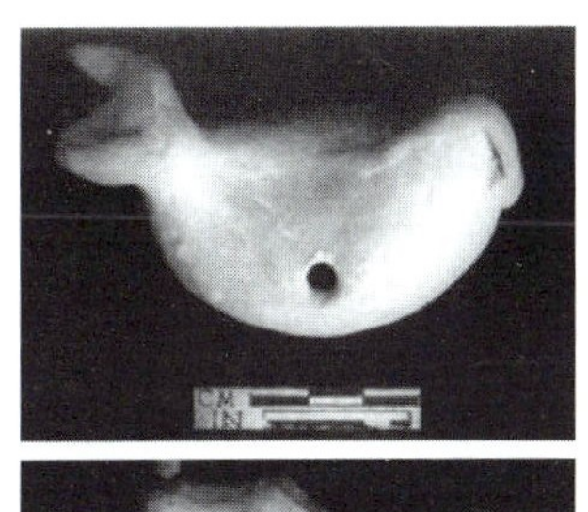

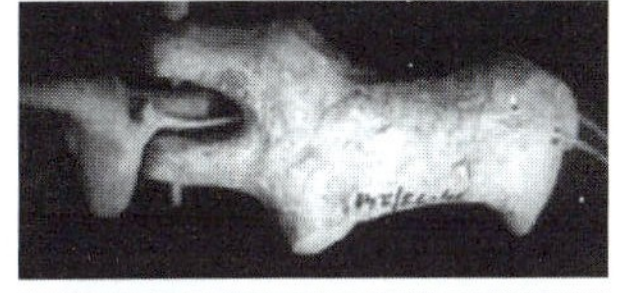

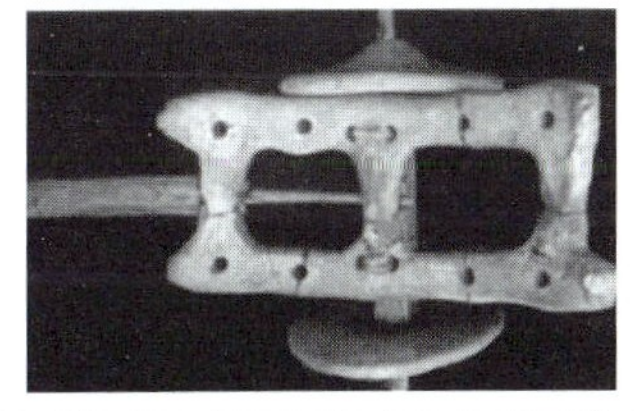

Terracottas (from top): figurine; games and dice; perforated bird-shaped rattle; bull with moveable head; cart

NEW DIRECTIONS IN RESEARCH | **How healthy were the Harappans?**

The early excavations at Harappa focused on architecture and artefacts. The more recent excavations carried out during the 1980s and 1990s reflect the advances in the field of archaeology and included a careful collection and scientific analysis of bone remains. The results give us important information about the health and nutrition of the Harappans.

Cemetery R-37 is located in the southern part of the site. Excavations were carried out under the supervision of J. M. Kenoyer. A team of four physical anthropologists—K. A. R. Kennedy, John R. Lucacs, Nancy Lovell, and Brian Hemphill—had the special job of carefully excavating the skeletons and removing them to the laboratory for analysis. Ninety skeletons were recovered from the cemetery. Most of them represented females. The number of skeletons in different age ranges were as follows:

Children (< 16 yrs)	:	15
Young adults (17–34 yrs)	:	35
Middle-aged adults (35–55 yrs)	:	27
Older adults (> 55 yrs)	:	13

The general health of this sample of the Harappan population was quite good. The skeletons showed a low incidence of traumatic injury, chronic infectious diseases, and neoplastic diseases (tumours). There were no traces of nutritional inadequacy such as rickets, scurvy, or anaemia. There were, however, three cases of arrested growth lines, suggesting that growth during childhood was halted temporarily. This could have been due to malnutrition or some serious illness. The most common ailment suffered by the people buried in this cemetery was arthritis. Signs of this appeared in the spine and in the joints of knees, hands, and feet. There were also several instances of severe arthritis in the neck, which may have been the result of unusual stress on the neck vertebrae, perhaps due to carrying heavy loads on the head over a long period of time.

The teeth of the people were analyzed and the dental pathology profile was what would be expected in a community of agriculturists. The most common dental problem was gross enamel hypoplasia (pitted or missing enamel) and the least common was hypercementosis (excessive deposit of cementum, a calcified hard tissue covering the root surface). Dental caries (cavities) were present in 43.6 per cent of the individuals examined. The dental caries rate was worked out as 6.8 per cent, which is a high rate typical of agricultural groups. Tooth loss, calculus (hardened plaque or tartar), and alveolar resorption (wasting away of the bony socket) occurred with moderate frequency. There were differences between males and females in the incidence of tooth loss and enamel hypoplasia. But the frequency of dental abscesses, calculus, and alveolar resorption were more or less the same for men as for women.

The study showed that the Harappans buried in Cemetery R-37 were relatively healthy agriculturists. A statistical analysis of the crania of the skeletons shows biological similarity among the people buried in the cemetery, a similarity between them and the skeletons found in the late Harappan Cemetery-H, and with the modern populations inhabiting this area today. This shows a broad biological continuity between the inhabitants of the area from mature Harappan to late Harappan into more recent times.

Source Dales and Kenoyer, 1991: 191–99, 210–12

Early studies of Harappan skeletons focused on classifying the Harappans into racial types. More recent studies have abandoned the old, rather arbitrary racial classifications. They have asked different questions and given an interesting set of conclusions. Kenneth A. R. Kennedy's study (1997) of skeletons found at Harappan sites shows biological heterogeneity between the different regions, and similarity with the people who live in these areas today. This means that the Harappans of Punjab resembled the present-day Punjabis in appearance, while the Harappans of Sindh resembled the modern inhabitants of Sindh. Kennedy also identified the incidence of malaria among the Harappans.

Recently, DNA analysis of data from a female skeleton (labelled 16113) from the Rakhigarhi cemetery has revealed interesting results (see Shinde et al., 2019). The results of the study fit with a mixture of people related to the ancient Iranian and Southeast Asian hunter-gatherers. These results were correlated with ancient DNA samples from 11 sites located in Iran and Turkmenistan, which had connections with the Harappan civilization, and were found to be similar. The study suggests that the Harappans had little or no immediate genetic contribution from steppe pastoralists or from Anatolian and Iranian farmers or herders. The Iranian component in the genetic profile goes back to a much *earlier* time, to a lineage that was ancestral to the hunter-gatherers, herders, and farmers of ancient Iran. The genetic profile of the Harappans is also seen to have had a primary impact on the ancestry of later South Asians. This is the first genomic-wide study of a Harappan skeleton and marks an important beginning. In the coming years,

NEW DIRECTIONS IN RESEARCH | What exactly did the Harappans eat?

This question has already been partly answered in the earlier discussion of the Harappan subsistence base and the plant and animal remains found at Harappan sites. However, recent scientific analysis of lipid residues in Harappan pottery has given further valuable information.

A study conducted by Kalyan Sekhar Chakraborty, Greg F. Slater, Heather M.-L. Miller, Prabodh Shirvalkar, and Yadubirsingh Rawat analyzed the absorbed lipid residues from 59 potsherds from Kotada Bhadli (in Nakhatrana Taluka of Kachchh district, Gujarat), a mature Harappan agro-pastoral site. AMS dates suggest that it was occupied between 2300 and 1950 BCE. The walled settlement, excavated between 2010 and 2013, was about 3.11 ha and included a central residential complex with ten rooms. The preliminary report on the faunal remains indicates that the main domesticated animals whose meat was consumed by people who lived here were cattle, possibly water buffalo, goats and sheep. Remains of *Sus* (pig) were also found, but it is not certain whether it was of the wild or domesticated variety. A preliminary study of 20 tooth samples of the animals suggests that most of the cattle and water buffalo died at an older age, suggesting that they were reared for secondary products. Most of the goat/sheep were killed young, indicating that they were killed for meat. The culling patterns from Harappan sites in Gujarat further indicate that many male cattle (bulls and bullocks) and perhaps some water buffalo were kept alive till a late age for traction and labour.

The analysis of the lipid residues in the pottery fragments revealed dairy fat. It is possible to identify fats originating from animals that mainly consumed C-3 type vegetation and those of animals that predominantly consumed C-4 type of vegetation. (C-3 type of vegetation and C-4 type of plants differ in their mode for the dark reaction of photosynthesis.) Analysis of the tooth enamel of animals makes it possible to identify which of the two types of plant food they mainly consumed. The study indicated that dairy products were an integral part of the diet of the Harappans who lived in Kotada Bhadli, and that these dairy products were derived from cattle and possibly water buffalo. This is the first direct proof of the importance of dairy product processing in South Asia.

Another study of lipid residues in Harappan pottery was conducted by Akshyeta Suryanarayan, Oliver Edward Craig, Miriam Cubas, and Ravindra Nath Singh. A total of 172 pottery pieces from one city (Rakhigarhi), one town (Farmana), and five rural settlements (Alamgirpur, Masudpur I, Masudpur VI, Lohari Ragho, and Khanak) in North India were analyzed. The analysis showed that the following had been cooked in the pots—dairy products; ruminant animal meat (most ruminant animals have a 4-chambered stomach and two-toed feet); and either non-ruminant adipose fats, plants, or mixtures of these products. The study revealed a similarity in vessel use in rural and urban sites and between the mature Harappan and late Harappan phase. The animal bones from the study region showed cattle to be the dominant domesticated species, and among these, there were a larger number of castrated bulls and females. This suggests a herding strategy connected with dairying.

These two studies indicate the potential of scientific methods to throw light on the food habits of Harappans.

Source Chakraborty et al., 2020; Suryanarayan et al., 2021

genome analysis of more human remains found at Harappan sites will no doubt shed valuable light on the genetic profiles of the Harappans.

There is the larger question of the analysis and assessment of the structure of Harappan society. The absence of deciphered written evidence is a major handicap, and inferences have to be made very carefully on the basis of archaeological data. The people who lived within the Harappan culture zone comprised villagers and city folk. Harappan society included occupational groups such as farmers, herders, hunter-gatherers, craftspeople, fisherfolk, merchants, sailors, rulers, administrative officials, ritual specialists, architects, carpenters, brick masons, well diggers, boat makers, sailors, sculptors, shopkeepers, sweepers, garbage collectors, and so on. Some farmers may have lived in the cities and tilled their fields nearby. Terracotta net sinkers and arrow points found at Mohenjodaro and Harappa suggest that the city population included hunters and fisher-folk. The level of social differentiation may not have been as great as in Mesopotamia and Egypt, but differences in house sizes and the hoards of jewellery do indicate a concentration of wealth and differences in social and economic status. The affluent social groups would have comprised rulers, land owners, and merchants. Class and rank differences based on occupation, wealth, and status must have existed. Claims that the caste system existed in Harappan society are highly speculative.

The Ruling Elite

Political organization includes a range of issues related to the exercise of power and leadership in a society. The debate on the nature of the Harappan political system has focused largely on whether or not a state existed, and if so, what sort of state it was. A great deal depends on our definition of a state and the interpretation of the archaeological evidence. Cultural uniformity does not necessarily mean political unification; therefore, there is the additional question of whether the evidence suggests the existence of one state or many.

Many scholars have observed that the elements of warfare, conflict, and force in the Harappan civilization seem weak compared to contemporary Mesopotamia and Egypt. Weapons are not a dominant feature of the artefacts found at Harappan sites. There are few depictions of conflict between people in the narrative reliefs on terracotta and faience tablets. However, fortifications, especially the imposing ones at sites such as Dholavira, cannot be overlooked. It seems that the element of force in the Harappan culture has been underestimated (Ratnagar, 2016: 61–60).

That the Harappan civilization lasted for some 700 years and its artefacts, traditions, and symbols seem to have continued more or less unchanged through this long period, suggests a strong element of political stability. There must have been groups of rulers in the various cities. Just who they were and how they were related to each other remains a mystery. These groups would have been responsible for the maintenance of the city facilities—walls, roads, drains, public buildings, etc. Some of the seals may bear names, titles, and symbols of these elites and could throw important light on the Harappan rulers, if the writing could be read.

One of the earliest hypotheses regarding the Harappan political structure was put forward by Stuart Piggott and was supported to some extent by Mortimer Wheeler (for details of the various theories, see Jacobson, 1986). Piggott suggested that the Harappan state was a highly centralized empire ruled by autocratic priest-kings from the twin capitals of Mohenjodaro and Harappa. This view was based on a number of features, including the level of uniformity in material traits, the use of a common script, and standardized weights and measures. Mohenjodaro and Harappa seemed to clearly stand out in the midst of the other settlements. Urban planning and monumental public works implied the mobilization of a specialized labour force. The 'granaries' at Mohenjodaro and Harappa fitted in with a view of the Harappan rulers as exercising a high level of control over everything, even maintaining buffer stocks of grain to tide over times of food scarcity. The apparent lack of internecine warfare between the settlements suggested that they were united under a single rule.

This view of the Harappan state soon came in for criticism. Walter A. Fairservis (1967) argued that the Harappans did not have an empire, not even a state. He pointed to the absence of evidence of priest-kings, slaves, standing armies, or court officials. According to him, Mohenjodaro was a ceremonial centre, not an administrative one. He argued that the sort of control reflected in the Harappan civilization could have been exercised by an elaborate village administration. Later, Fairservis modified his views to some extent and agreed that there may have been some element of centralized control and a class structure. But he still maintained that force did not play a significant role and that interdependence, religion, and tradition were responsible for regulating social behaviour.

Another view of the Harappan political system came from S. C. Malik (1968), who argued that the lack of imposing monuments and supreme gods goes against the idea of a strong, centralized state. The Harappan polity, according to Malik, is an example of what Elman Service described as the chiefdom stage, transitional between a **kinship society** and civil state society.

The two trends in more recent writings are, paradoxically, a return to the idea of a Harappan empire and a complete rejection of such an idea. Ratnagar (1991) analyzed the archaeological evidence and used cross-cultural parallels with other early state societies to conclude that we do seem to be looking at a Harappan empire. The strongest critique

KEY CONCEPTS | Defining a state

The word 'state' is used very often in historical and anthropological analysis; therefore, it is important to know the various meanings attached to it. Here are some of the frequently cited and used definitions:

Elman R. Service (1975: 14) identified four stages of social organization marked by increasing complexity. The band is a small (usually less than a hundred people), mobile hunter-gatherer group, lacking formal leadership, whose members are linked to each other by kinship. The tribe is a larger and more complex group with a subsistence based on sedentary agriculture and/or mobile animal domestication, among whom kinship ties were still important. The **chiefdom stage** is characterized by 'centralized direction, hereditary hierarchical status arrangements with an aristocratic ethos, but no formal, legal apparatus of forceful repression.' Service adds that leadership in a chiefdom is exercised by an authority that possesses neither formal legal power nor a bureaucracy. There are social ranks, but no classes. A state is characterized by the existence of civil law and formal government that are 'institutionalized, enacted, official', and which 'employ, threaten, or imply the actual use of force'. For Service, the essential ingredients of a state are the power of force and authority.

Ronald Cohen (1978: 69–70) identified the state as a specific type of political system characterized by a centralized bureaucracy and dominant control of the mechanisms of force by a central authority. He further emphasized that an important difference between a chieftaincy and state was the latter's ability to counter forces of political fission (breakaway groups or splintering).

The central element in Morton H. Fried's (1978) conception of the state is social stratification based on differential access of the members of a society to basic productive necessities. Fried makes a distinction between **pristine states** and **secondary states**. A pristine state is one which emerges from indigenous stimuli, usually with no pre-existing models. A secondary state is one which has the model of an already existing state at hand and whose origins are related to pressures from this already existing state.

Henri J. M. Claessen and Peter Skalnik (1978) define an early state in the following way: a centralized socio-political organization for the regulation of social relations in a complex, stratified society, which is divided into at least two basic strata or emergent social classes—the rulers and the ruled—and in which the relations of political dominance and tributary obligations between the rulers and the ruled are legitimized by a common ideology founded on reciprocity (mutual relations of give and take). They also suggest that early states can be divided into three types on the basis of increasing levels of complexity—the inchoate early state, the typical early state, and the transitional early state.

Since state formation is a gradual process, it is often difficult to say precisely when something that can be called a 'state' appeared. Service's chiefdom stage represents a transitional period between a pre-state kinship society and a state society.

Part of the problem in defining a state is that the many different kinds of state systems that have existed in history make it difficult to formulate a universal definition. For instance, although Fried directs attention to the element of social stratification in state societies, his emphasis on centralization simply does not fit all states. Apart from the problem of definition, in the case of early states, there is also the problem of identifying levels of social and political complexity on the basis of archaeological evidence.

Recent studies of the state have questioned various aspects of the older unilinear evolutionary models and terminology. For instance, Norman Yoffee (2005) has challenged various 'myths' related to the evolution and nature of the earliest states. These myths include the ideas that all these states were basically similar; that they were ruled by powerful totalitarian elites who exercised a monopoly of control over goods, services, and information; that they were marked by territorial integration of large areas; and that their social structure can be understood by invoking modern ethnographic parallels.

James C. Scott (2017) emphasizes the difficulties in identifying 'stateness' and suggests that we look for markers of territoriality and a specialized state apparatus—walls, tax collection, and officials. Other pointers include a specialized class of scribes, soldiers (possibly full-time ones) with armour, and efforts to standardize weights and measures. He also points out that only cereal grains could form a basis of regular taxation; in this sense, they can be seen as premier political crops. The concern for the acquisition and control of population was central to statecraft, and this involved coercion, frequent warfare, and various types of bondage, including slavery. Scott also emphasizes the fragility of early states. They were vulnerable to the spread of infectious diseases due to large concentrations of populations and armies on the move. Crop failure and the disastrous results of over-utilization of the environment led to deforestation and soil salinization. Even after the appearance of states, more people lived outside than inside them. The outsiders included nomads, who were difficult to govern or control, and were often considered barbarians. Flight from the demands of the state was quite common.

In the older evolutionary models, the state was seen as the apex of a unilinear model of political development; sedentary living and agriculture were considered its essential ingredients. However, the evidence of large, complex, non-state polities, and the existence and persistence in Eurasia of nomadic states (even empires, e.g. those of the Xiongnu and Mongols) that subsisted on mobility, multi-resource pastoralism, and a leadership structure involving power sharing underlines the need to question these assumptions. Scholars have increasingly recognized the diversity of states, questioned their inevitability, and underlined their fragility.

How states emerged is a complex issue. At a general level, factors such as ecological setting, a diverse subsistence and resource base, technological capacity, interaction networks, conflict, warfare, political leadership, collective action, religion, and ideology have been seen as relevant, but the specifics of the situation varied from case to case.

Source Claessen and Skalník. (Eds.)., 1978; Feinman and Marcus. (Eds.)., 1998; Yoffee, 2005; Scott, 2017; Grinin et al., (Eds.)., 2004

FURTHER DISCUSSION | **A priest-king?**

Ancient India does not display a strong tradition of royal portraiture. In ancient Mesopotamia and Egypt, rulers are portrayed extensively in stone reliefs and sculptures; their palaces, tombs, and temples further proclaim their power. The Harappan case is strikingly different. The stone bust of a male figure found at Mohenjodaro has been given the label 'priest king'. The figure is that of a man with a close-cropped beard, half-closed eyes, and a fillet with an encrusted diadem around his head. An armlet with a similar but smaller ornament is tied around his right arm. A robe decorated with a trefoil design passes over his left shoulder and under his right arm. However, whether he represents a priest or king or both is far from certain. The same is the case with a large damaged seated figure found at Dholavira. While large houses have been found at Harappan sites, none of them matches our idea of a palace, although it is possible that certain buildings on the citadels of cities such as Mohenjodaro were the functional equivalent of palaces.

of such a view has come from Jim Shaffer (1982b). Shaffer questions the level of homogeneity in the Harappan civilization and suggests that it could have been the result of a well-developed network of internal trade rather than a strong, centralized government. He underlines the absence of huge royal tombs, palaces, and temples, and the absence of marked social differentiation of the kind visible in ancient Egypt and Mesopotamia. At Harappan sites, artefacts of various types are distributed throughout the occupational levels rather than clustered in elite residences or structures. All the typical Harappan artefacts (including ornaments of precious metals and semi-precious stones, seals and sealings, and the script) occur in small village settlements. This suggests an equality of access to wealth or the symbols of wealth among village and city dwellers, which goes against the idea of a centralized empire.

The fact that some form of state structure did exist in the Harappan civilization cannot be denied. The absence of marked social or economic differences and tombs or palaces of the Egyptian or Mesopotamian kind does not mean that a state did not exist, rather that it was a different sort of state. The communications system, standardization in artefacts, site specialization, mobilization of labour for public works, the establishment of the trading outpost of Shortughai—all these things indicate a level of economic complexity and the existence of a state. So does the level of cultural homogeneity and the use of a common system of writing across areas in which many different languages and dialects must have been spoken. The levels of social differentiation indicate some degree of class stratification. Some of the buildings on the citadel complex seem to have had an administrative function. Centralized control is apparent in the Harappan civilization. The questions are: How much and by whom?

Jacobson (1986) suggests that the Harappan state was an early state with the following characteristics: a sovereign or sovereigns closely linked to a mythical character and seen as benevolent; a military component lacking the dominance characteristic of more mature states; and weakly developed economic stratification. According to Possehl (2003: 57), Harappan society was highly disciplined and had a strong corporate element; the Harappans may have been ruled by councils rather than kings. Kenoyer (1998: 100) suggests that the Harappan state must have comprised many competing classes of urban elites, such as merchants, ritual specialists, and those who controlled resources such as land and livestock, with different levels and spheres of control.

A 'Unicorn' seal

Kenoyer also suggests that the animals on the square stamp seals represent totemic symbols standing for a specific clan, perhaps along with some additional information. At least 10 clans or communities are represented by these animals—the unicorn, humped bull, elephant, water buffalo, rhinoceros, humpless bull with short horns, goat, antelope, crocodile, and hare. The unicorn motif (there are variations in its representation) is found at almost all sites where the seals have been found, including in Mesopotamia. At Mohenjodaro, over 60 per cent of the seals have this motif, while it occurs on about 46 per cent of the seals at Harappa. The large number of unicorn seals at major cities led Ratnagar to suggest that the unicorn was the symbol of the Harappan ruling elite. Kenoyer, on the other hand, argues that the 'unicorn clan' probably represented the aristocracy or merchants who had an important executive role in the government. It is in fact the *less* frequent motifs such as the bull, elephant, rhinoceros, and tiger that may have been symbols of the most powerful rulers at the apex of the Harappan power structure.

While Mohenjodaro stands out in some ways (for instance, no other site has a structure comparable to the Great Bath), there are other large Harappan cities such as Rakhigarhi, Lurewala, Ganweriwala, and Dholavira. Were they provincial centres knit together through a well-worked-out system of political control? Were they the capitals of separate states? Were they city-states? In the past, scholars tended to simply presume highly centralized political structures, whereas now there is a greater acceptance of the possibility of decentralization. It is not, however, certain whether there was a large Harappan empire or a number of separate, perhaps inter-related states. Another possibility that cannot be ruled out is that there may have been several states with different kinds of political organization.

The Decline of Urban Life

At some point of time, things started going wrong in the Harappan cities. Decline had set in at Mohenjodaro by 2200 BCE and the settlement had come to an end by 2000 BCE. In some places, the civilization continued till 1800 BCE. Apart from the dates, the pace of decline also varied. Mohenjodaro and Dholavira give a picture of gradual decline, while at Kalibangan and Banawali, city life ended all of a sudden (see Lahiri. [Eds.]., 2000 for the various theories regarding Harappan decline).

One of the most popular explanations of the decline of the Harappan civilization is one for which there is least evidence. The idea that the civilization was destroyed by Aryan invaders was first put forward by Ramaprasad Chanda (1926)—he later changed his mind—and was elaborated on by Mortimer Wheeler (1947). Wheeler argued that references in the *Rig Veda* to various kinds of forts, attacks on walled cities, and the epithet *puramdara* (fort destroyer) given to the god Indra must have a historical basis and reflect an Aryan invasion of the Harappan cities. He identified a place called Hariyupiya in the *Rig Veda* with Harappa. Wheeler also pointed to certain skeletal remains found at Mohenjodaro as proof of the Aryan massacre. He subsequently modified his hypothesis, to the extent that he acknowledged that other factors such as floods, decline in trade, and over-utilization of natural resources may have had a role to play. But he insisted that the ultimate blow was given by an Aryan invasion. The Cemetery-H culture, he suggested, represented the culture of the Aryan invaders.

Many scholars such as P. V. Kane (1955), George Dales (1964), and B. B. Lal (1997) have effectively refuted the Aryan invasion theory. The evidence from the *Rig Veda*, a religious text of uncertain date, is far from conclusive. Moreover, if there had been an invasion, it should have left some traces in the archaeological record. There is, in fact, no evidence of any kind of military assault or conflict at any Harappan site. The 37 groups of skeletal remains at Mohenjodaro do not belong to the same cultural phase and, therefore, cannot be connected to a single event. Not one of these skeletons was found on the citadel mound, where we would have expected a major battle to have taken place. The fact that there is a sterile layer between the mature Harappan and Cemetery-H levels goes against Wheeler's hypothesis that the latter represents the settlement of the Aryan invaders. Moreover, K. A. R. Kennedy's analysis (1997) of the skeletal remains does not show any discontinuity in the skeletal record in the north-west at this point of time, making it clear that there was no major influx of new settlers with a different physiognomy. The Harappan civilization was not destroyed by an Indo-Aryan invasion.

Natural disasters, not necessarily sudden or single, did have a role to play. Several layers of silt at Mohenjodaro give evidence of the city being affected by repeated episodes of Indus floods. M. R. Sahni (1956), and later Robert L. Raikes (1964) and George F. Dales (1966), argued that the floods at Mohenjodaro were the result of tectonic movements. Dales suggested that these may have occurred at a place called Sehwan, about 90 miles downstream from Mohenjodaro, where there is evidence of rock faulting. The theory is that tectonic movements led to the creation of a gigantic natural dam that prevented the Indus from flowing towards the sea, turning the area around Mohenjodaro into a huge lake. The theory of several such episodes of flooding induced by tectonic movements is not, however, convincing. Neither is H. T. Lambrick's hypothesis (1967), based on what he himself describes as purely circumstantial evidence, that the Indus changed its course, moving some 30 miles eastwards, starving Mohenjodaro and its inhabitants of water.

While Mohenjodaro may have got worn out due to repeated episodes of naturally occurring floods, Harappan sites in the Ghaggar-Hakra valley were affected by gradual desiccation. The Sutlej or the Yamuna once flowed into the Ghaggar. Tectonic movements led to river capture—either the Yamuna joined up with the Ganga system or (what is more likely) the Sutlej was captured by the Indus, drastically reducing the water flowing into the Ghaggar. M. R. Mughal's (1997) study of settlements in this region shows a drastic reduction in the number of sites as the river dried up.

A sudden rise in the Arabian Sea coastline of west Pakistan could have caused floods and a rise in soil salinity. Such an uplift along the coast and in the lower Indus valley could also have seriously disrupted the coastal communications and trade of the Harappans.

Reference has already been made to the debate on the nature of the climate, especially rainfall, in protohistoric times. On the basis of his study of pollen from Rajasthan lakes, Gurdip Singh suggests a connection between the onset of a drier climate and the decline of the Harappan civilization. However, a study of the sediments of the Lunkaransar lake indicates that the onset of drier conditions in this area may have happened well before the emergence of the Harappan civilization. Whether climatic change played a role in the decline of the Harappan civilization, therefore, remains unclear.

The issue of environmental change can be connected to the ways in which the Harappans were treating their environment. Perhaps they were over-exploiting it through over-cultivation, over-grazing, and excessive cutting of trees for fuel and farming. This would have resulted in decreasing soil fertility, floods, and increasing soil salinity. Making estimates of population, land, food, and fodder requirements on the basis of modern data, Fairservis suggests that the civilization declined because the growing population of people and cattle could not be supported from resources within the Harappan culture zone.

Shereen Ratnagar (1981) has argued that the decline in the lapis lazuli trade with Mesopotamia was a factor in the decline of the Harappan civilization. Whether this trade was particularly important for the Harappans is, however, debatable; consequently, this could not have been a factor responsible for the decline.

There must have been different factors at work in different sites and parts of the Harappan culture zone. Archaeological evidence does not give direct access to the possible social and political dimensions of the decline of the Harappan civilization. What it does indicate very clearly is that the Harappan culture underwent a gradual process of de-urbanization. The mature Harappan phase was followed by a post-urban phase, known as the late Harappan phase.

The Significance of the Late Harappan Phase

The late Harappan phase had a wide geographical spread but there was a distinct decline in the level of cultural homogeneity that marked the mature Harappan phase. The late Harappan phase is best understood in the following geographical contexts: Sindh; west Punjab and the Ghaggar-Hakra valley; eastern Punjab and Haryana; the Ganga–Yamuna doab; and Kutch and Saurashtra. In Sindh, the late Harappan phase is represented by the Jhukar culture at sites such as Jhukar, Chanhudaro, and Amri. The transition from the mature to the late Harappan phase in this region does not show any sudden discontinuity. There were gradual changes in the seals, a decrease in the frequency of cubical weights, and writing came to be confined only to pottery. The evidence of pottery suggests reciprocal contacts between the Jhukar culture of Sindh and the late Harappan culture at Lothal and Rangpur.

In the Punjab province of Pakistan and the Ghaggar-Hakra valley, the late people of Rojdi in Saurashtra were expanding and rebuilding their settlement. The data suggests an eastward and southward shift of settlements and people.

In 2000, an anonymous tip-off led to the discovery of a huge hoard of jewellery (weighing about 10 kg) in Mandi (Muzaffarnagar district, UP), including beads of gold, banded agate, onyx and copper (see. D. V. Sharma et al., 1999–2000). In 2004–05, burials with rich grave goods were discovered during excavations at Sanauli (Baghpat district, UP). The style of the artefacts and surface finds of pottery from the site suggest affinities with the Harappan or late Harappan culture. Sanauli seems to have been contemporary to the late Harappan phase, but has some unique features (these will be discussed in Chapter 5). The picture of opulence presented by these sites is very different from the image of economic decline generally associated with 2nd millennium BCE sites.

The evidence from mature and late Harappan sites shows a complex interplay of elements of continuity and change. Compared to mature Harappan pottery, the slip of late Harappan pottery is less bright. The pots tend to be thicker and sturdier. Some of the classic Harappan shapes—e.g., the beaker, goblet, perforated jar, s-shaped jar, and pyriform (pear-shaped) jar—disappear. Other shapes—e.g., jars of different shapes and the dish-on-stand—continue. Various elements of Harappan urbanism such as the cities, script, seals, specialized crafts, and long-distance trade declined in the late Harappan phase, but did not completely disappear. Some of the late Harappan sites such as Kudwala (38.1 ha) in Cholistan, Bet Dwarka in Gujarat, and Daimabad (20 ha) in the upper Godavari valley can be described as urban, but they are few and far between. Graffiti on pottery occurs in Saurashtra and northern Gujarat as well as in the eastern regions. Four potsherds with Harappan letters were found at late Harappan levels at Daimabad. Some circular seals occur at Daimabad and Jhukar; rectangular seals minus motifs were found at Dholavira. A rectangular conch shell seal with the motif of a three-headed animal, similar to that found on seals of the Persian Gulf, was found at Bet Dwarka. This suggests that contact with the Persian Gulf continued in the late Harappan phase, at least in the Gujarat region. The late Harappan phase at Bhagwanpura shows flourishing specialized craft activity; there are 2 clay tablets and 19 sherds with graffiti, which could represent a script. In Punjab and Haryana, there are faience ornaments, beads of semi-precious stones, terracotta cart frames, kilns, and fire altars.

A notable development in the late Harappan phase was the diversification of agriculture. At Pirak in Baluchistan, there was the beginning of double cropping—wheat and barley were being grown as winter crops and rice (with irrigation), millet, and sorghum as summer crops. In the Kachi plain, there were fairly large settlements, growing a variety of crops, supplemented with irrigation. In Gujarat and Maharashtra, various kinds of millets were being grown as summer crops. Rice and millets were found at late Harappan levels at Harappa. Excavations at Hulas gave evidence of diverse plant remains. Grains included rice, barley, dwarf wheat, bread wheat, club wheat, oats, jowar, and finger millet. Pulses included lentil, field pea, grass pea (*khesari*), *kulthi*, green gram (*moong*), and chickpea. Almond and walnut shells were found, and a single carbonized seed of cotton was identified. A diverse agricultural base in the late Harappan phase is also revealed at sites such as Mahorana (Sangrur district, Punjab), Daulatpur (Kurukshetra district, Haryana), Kanmer (in Kachchh district, Gujarat), and Oriyo Timbo (Bhavnagar district, Gujarat).

The general picture presented by the late Harappan phase is one of a disintegration of urban networks and an expansion of rural ones. There is an overlap between the late Harappan and **Painted Grey Ware (PGW)** culture at sites such as Bhagwanpura and Dadheri in Haryana, and Katpalon and Nagar in Punjab. Also significant is the overlap between late Harappan and **Ochre Coloured Pottery (OCP)** levels in western Uttar Pradesh at sites such as Bargaon and Ambakheri. The evidence from this area, Gujarat, and north Maharashtra suggests an eastward and southward migration of the Harappans due to a combination of pressures such as those discussed in the earlier section.

CONCLUSIONS

The Harappan civilization was the first urban culture in South Asia, and is known from a large number of urban and rural settlements. The urban phase of the Harappan culture emerged from the proto-urban early Harappan phase. Archaeological evidence reveals a great deal about this civilization—its varied subsistence base, sophisticated craft traditions, and extensive subcontinental and long-distance trade networks—but given the non-decipherment of the script, conclusions about many other aspects such as religion, society, and polity remain speculative. There was cultural homogeneity as well as diversity within the vast Harappan culture zone. Some of the neolithic, neolithic–chalcolithic, and chalcolithic sites mentioned in Chapter 3 were roughly contemporaneous with the Harappan civilization and interacted with it. The Harappan civilization did not come to a sudden end. The urban phase was followed by the late Harappan phase, which was marked by the decline of urban features and the diversification of agriculture.

FURTHER READINGS

Chakrabarti, Dilip K. 1990. *The External Trade of the Indus Civilization*. New Delhi: Munshiram Manoharlal.

———. 2006. *The Oxford Companion to Indian Archaeology: The Archaeological Foundations of Ancient India, Stone Age to AD 13th Century*. Delhi: Oxford University Press. Chapters 8–11. Dilip K. Chakrabarti. (Eds.). 2004. *Indus Civilization Sites in India: New Discoveries. Marg* 55(3). Mumbai: Marg Publications.

Chakrabarti, Dilip K and Makkhan Lal. (Eds.). 2014. *History of Ancient India*. Vol. 2. New Delhi: Vivekanand International Foundation and Aryan Books International. Parts II, VII.

Dales, George F., J. M. Kenoyer, and the staff of the Harappa Project. 1991. 'Summaries of Five Seasons of Research at Harappa (District Sahiwal, Punjab, Pakistan), 1986–1990.' In R. H. Meadow. (Eds.). *Harappa Excavations. 1986–1990: A Multidisciplinary Approach*. Monographs in World Archaeology. Vol. 3. Madison: Prehistory Press.

Kenoyer, Jonathan Mark. 1998. *Ancient Cities of the Indus Valley Civilization*. Karachi: Oxford University Press and American Institute of Pakistan Studies.

Lahiri, Nayanjot. 1992. *The Archaeology of Indian Trade Routes (up to c. 200 B.C.)*. Delhi: Oxford University Press.

———. 2005. *Finding Forgotten Cities: How the Indus Civilization was Discovered*. New Delhi: Permanent Black.

———. (Eds.). 2000. *The Decline and Fall of the Indus Civilization*. Delhi: Permanent Black.

Lal, B. B. 1997. *The Earliest Civilization of South Asia (Rise, Maturity and Decline)*. New Delhi: Aryan Books International.

——— and S. P. Gupta. (Eds.). 1984. *Frontiers of the Indus Civilization*. New Delhi: Books and Books.

Law, Randall. 2011. *Inter-regional Interaction and Urbanism in the Ancient Indus Valley. A Geologic Provenance Study of Harappan Rock and Mineral Assemblage*. Kyoto: Research Institute for Humanity and Nature.

Mahadevan, Iravatham. 1977. *The Indus Script: Texts, Concordance and Tables*. New Delhi: Archaeological Survey of India.

Marcus, Joyce, and Jeremy A. Sabloff. (Eds.). 2008. *The Ancient City: New Perspectives on Urbanism in the Old and New World*. New Mexico: School for Advanced Research Resident Scholar Series.

Parpola, Asko. 1994. *Deciphering the Indus Script*. Cambridge, Cambridge University Press.

_______. 2008. 'Is the Indus Script Indeed not a Writing System?' In *Airāvati: Felicitation Volume in Honour of Iravatham Mahadevan*. Chennai: Varalaaru.com. pp. 111–31.

Mughal, M. R. 1997. *Ancient Cholistan: Archaeology and Architecture*. Lahore: Ferozsons.

Possehl, Gregory L. 2003. *The Indus Civilization: A Contemporary Perspective*. New Delhi: Vistaar Publications.

———. (Ed.). 1979. *Ancient Cities of the Indus*. New Delhi: Vikas Publishing House.

———. (Ed.). 1982. *Harappan Civilization: A Contemporary Perspective*. New Delhi: Oxford University Press and IBH.

———. (Ed.). 1993. *Harappan Civilization: A Recent Perspective*. New Delhi: American Institute of Indian Studies, Oxford University Press, and IBH.

Ratnagar, Shereen. 1991. *Enquiries into the Political Organization of Harappan Society*. Pune: Ravish.

———. 2001. *Understanding Harappa: Civilization in the Greater Indus Valley*. New Delhi: Tulika.

———. 2016. *Harappan Archaeology: Early State Perspectives*. New Delhi: Primus.

Scott, James C. 2017. *Against the Grain: A Deep History of the Earliest States*. New Haven and London: Yale University Press.

Settar, S. and Ravi Korisettar. (Eds.). 2002. *Indian Archaeology in Retrospect*, Vol. II: *Protohistory: Archaeology of the Harappan Civilization*. New Delhi: Indian Council of Historical Research and Manohar.

WEBSITES

www.harappa.com
http://asi.nic.in (the website of the Archaeological Survey of India)

Harappan perforated pot, animal figurine, toy cart; the function of perforated pots is debated.

CHAPTER 5

Cultural Transitions: Images from Texts and Archaeology

c. 2000–600 BCE

Janaka, king of Videha, was performing a great sacrifice, and Brahmanas had come from far and wide to attend. The king announced a prize of 1,000 cows with 10,000 gold pieces fastened to their horns for the wisest among all the assembled Brahmanas. At this, sage Yajnavalkya asked his pupil Shamashravas to herd the cows home. The other Brahmanas grew furious at his audacity and an intense philosophical contest ensued. One by one, eight interlocutors posed a series of questions to Yajnavalkya on matters related to the sacrifice, the senses, the worlds to which great men departed, the nature of the *atman*, the making of the universe, and the resting places of the gods and spirits. One of the interlocutors was a woman named Gargi. As her questions built up to a crescendo, Yajnavalkya thundered at her to stop or else her head might fall off. Gargi retreated, but spiritedly subjected the sage to a second round of queries. Vidagdha, the last questioner, had to pay the price of defeat with his head. All had been silenced by Yajnavalkya's brilliant responses.

This episode is narrated in the *Brihadaranyaka Upanishad*, a text belonging to the Vedic corpus. Is there a historical basis to this incident? Did a great sage named Yajnavalkya ever exist? Did a woman named Gargi participate in a philosophical quest dominated by men? Was the price of defeat in such contests really death? How many people were actually interested in such esoteric issues? It is difficult to answer such questions with certainty, but the episode does conjure a dramatic scene of philosophical inquiry in which the stakes were very high—of reputation and life itself.

The poets who composed the Vedic hymns of praise and supplication to the gods and the priests who explained how the rituals were to be performed were not historians. Vedic texts are religious and ritualistic texts, not works of history. However, combined with the available archaeological evidence, they can be used as *sources* of information on various aspects of the life of people who lived in the greater Indus valley, the Indo-Gangetic divide, and the upper Ganga valley in the 2nd and 1st millennia BCE.

When discussing this period, most accounts of ancient Indian history make a decisive shift from a narrative based on archaeology to one based on Vedic texts. In general, archaeological evidence is cited only when it supports what the texts suggest. This approach has resulted in an undue focus on the northern and north-western regions of the subcontinent and a neglect of other areas. It has also led to the sidelining of substantial archaeological evidence from neolithic–chalcolithic, chalcolithic, and early iron age cultures that tells us about the lives of ordinary people living in the various regions of the subcontinent during *c.* 2000–500 BCE.

The challenge is to incorporate both textual and archaeological evidence, wherever they are available. However, evidence from these two sources does not always match. When dealing with material culture, priority should be given to archaeological evidence. Vedic texts, on the other hand, are a rich source of information on the development of philosophical concepts and religious ideas and practices in the regions where they were composed. Another challenge is to explore and expand the historical potential of the archaeological evidence from regions for which no texts are available, and where archaeology remains the only window into the past.

In order to understand the complex historical jigsaw puzzle of the subcontinent in *c.* 2000–500 BCE, it is necessary to carefully juxtapose the archaeology-based and text-and-archaeology-based profiles of the various regions, recognizing that in some cases, the pieces do not fit together perfectly.

Perspectives from Texts

Using the Vedas as a historical source

Extracting history from a textual corpus as ancient, vast, and complex as the Vedas is no easy task. Unfortunately, critical editions identifying the original core of the texts are not available. The 19th century translations cannot be relied upon, and recent authoritative translations, whether in the European or Indian languages, are few (see, for instance, Jamison and Brereton trans., 2014). A great deal depends on the interpretation of words and phrases, whose meanings may vary from one text and context to another.

The Vedic corpus was not a popular literature and, therefore, does not represent popular ideas or practices. It was composed, preserved, and transmitted by and for a section of the Brahmanas. (Here, the reference is to Brahmanas as a social group. The Brahmanas are also a category of Vedic texts.) The texts were transmitted orally for many centuries and it is not certain when they were first written down. The earliest surviving manuscripts belong to the 14th century CE. The texts are, however, much older than that.

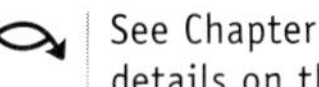

See Chapter 1, pp. 22–23 for details on the Vedic corpus

The dates of composition of the *Rig Veda* are the subject of debate. Astronomical references in the text have been used to date it, but have given different results. For instance, Ludwig concluded that the text was composed in the 11th century BCE, while Jacobi arrived at a 3rd millennium BCE date. More recently, Subhash Kak (2001) has argued that the astronomical references in the *Rig Veda* suggest a *c.* 4000–2000 BCE time bracket. A 1380 BCE inscription found at Bogaz Koi in north-eastern Syria records a treaty between a Hittite and Mitanni king. It mentions the gods Indara (Indra), Mitras (Mitra), Nasatia (Nasitya, i.e., the Ashvins), and Uruvanass (Varuna)—deities who are mentioned in the *Rig Veda*. While a majority of the Mitanni people spoke the local Hurrian language, the inscription indicates that their rulers had Indo-Aryan-sounding names and invoked Indo-Aryan gods. Belonging to about the same period is a Hittite text inscribed on a clay tablet, about horse training and chariotry, written by a Mitannian named Kikkuli. This uses several technical terms which resemble Indo-Aryan ones. While these inscriptions are relevant for the history of the Indo-Aryan languages and gods, they do not give direct or definite information about the date of the *Rig Veda*. There are close similarities between the language and culture reflected in the *Rig Veda* and an ancient Iranian text called the *Avesta*. This could be an important clue to dating the *Rig Veda*, but unfortunately, the dates of the *Avesta* are not certain. Its oldest parts may go back to *c.* 1500 BCE. Very early dates for the *Rig Veda* that fall within the 7th or 6th millennium BCE are clearly not acceptable. One reason is that we know from archaeology that the north-western part of the subcontinent was at that time still in the stone age, and the *Rig Veda* clearly belongs to the chalcolithic age. Most historians use a rough chronology of *c.* 1200–1000 BCE or *c.* 1500–1000 BCE for the composition of the earliest sections of the *Rig Veda*.

Books 2–7, the oldest books of the *Rig Veda Samhita*, are also known as the family books because their composition is attributed to the families of certain seer-poets—Gritsamada, Vishvamitra, Vamadeva, Atri, Bharadvaja, and Vasishtha. Books 1, 8, 9, and 10 seem to be of a later period. The hymns of this Samhita are arranged in a precise pattern. In the family books, they are arranged according to deity, number of stanzas, and metre.

The pattern of arrangement makes it possible to detect interpolations. Hymns that disrupt the pattern must have been added to the collection later. This does not necessarily mean that they were later in terms of their period of *composition*. The 'later', i.e., less old books of the *Rig Veda Samhita* may actually contain some very old hymns, and the 'earlier' books may contain some not-so-old hymns. Sometimes, certain hymns are assigned a later date because their content or ideas seem different. However, such differences could be due to their originating in a different milieu or reflecting different ideas current at the time.

The deliberate, careful arrangement of the hymns of the *Rig Veda Samhita* was the work of its compilers. The language, and possibly also the content, of the hymns may have been modified in the process of compilation, which may have taken place in *c*. 1000 BCE. The Vedas may have been arranged and compiled because of the desire of priests to create an authoritative text for the sacrifices they performed. We know from other sources that there were various recensions of the *Rig Veda*, which may have differed from each other in content, arrangement, and traditions of interpretation. Of these recensions, only the Shakala has survived into our own time.

Vedic texts can be used as sources of history for the areas in which they were composed. The family books of the *Rig Veda Samhita* were composed in the land of *Sapta-Sindhu* or the seven rivers. The rivers in question were the Indus, its five tributaries, and the Sarasvati (which can probably be identified with the modern Ghaggar-Hakra). The core geographical area of later Vedic texts was Kuru–Panchala, which comprised the Indo-Gangetic divide and the upper Ganga valley.

Many different kinds of histories of the Indo-Aryans have been derived from the Vedas. Nationalist historians extracted historical details from the texts but tended to idealize the Vedic age (Altekar, [1938] 1991; Majumdar et al., [1951] 1971). A subsequent trend was more dispassionate in approach and concentrated on using the texts to reconstruct social, economic, and political history using unilinear historical and anthropological models (R. S. Sharma, 1983; Thapar, 1990). There are other studies (e.g., Witzel, 1997a, 1997b) based on a detailed textual analysis. Nevertheless, when we talk of the 'Vedic age' or 'Vedic culture', we must be conscious of the problem of dating the *Rig Veda*, the religious and elite nature of the texts, their specific geographical contexts, and the availability of substantial archaeological data for these and other regions.

Who were the Indo-Aryans?

The use of Vedic texts as a source of history is linked to a number of questions about the people to whom these texts belonged. Who were the Indo-Aryans? Where did they come from? What was the relationship between the Vedic and Harappan cultures? These issues have not always been treated as purely academic ones. They have political implications, and have been used to serve diverse political agendas, from colonial times till the present.

During the 19th and early 20th centuries, when large sections of Africa and Asia were colonized by European nations, many scholars thought about history in terms of the movement and interaction of different races. Some scholars used the term 'race' loosely in the sense of an ethnic or cultural group. However, another trend was to classify people of the world into different races such as Caucasian, Mongoloid, Negroid, etc. on the basis of physical and other characteristics. These classifications appeared to be objective and scientific on the surface, but most of them were racist. They provided a pseudo-scientific justification for the European subjugation of Asian and African people, whom they presented as inferior races. Linguistic theory became entwined with race theory to produce flawed racial interpretations of the early Indian past in the colonial period (see Trautmann, 2005). The theory of a superior white, blond-haired, and blue-eyed Aryan race, which became a part of Nazi propaganda in 20th century Germany, is a myth and is not based on historical facts. (On the myth of a superior Aryan race and how it was a misappropriation of a linguistic concept, see Mallory, 1989: 266–72.) This is the case with all theories that claim that a particular group of people are inherently superior to others. Today, most anthropologists have abandoned racial classifications. There is no doubt that people living in different parts of the world look different. But the old, prejudiced category of race, which presented people in different parts of the world as separate, unrelated, and unchanging entities, frozen in time, has been replaced by more meaningful and objective ways of classifying and understanding human cultures. In fact, genetic studies show that there are no 'pure' races or communities in the world. From the time of the human origins in Africa and the subsequent dispersals of populations across different parts of the world, the story of is one migration and inter-mixture.

The composers of the *Rig Veda* described themselves as *Arya*, which can be understood as a cultural or ethnic term. The word literally means kinsman or companion. The terms 'Indo-European' and 'Indo-Aryan', as used by linguists and historians, have nothing to do with racial classifications. They are linguistic terms, referring to families of languages and their speakers. The Indo-Aryans were the speakers of a sub-group of the Indo-Iranian branch of the Indo-European family of languages. The Vedas reflect a close connection with Iran. But we do not know when, where, or why the Indo-Iranians and Indo-Aryans parted ways.

The original homeland of the Indo-Europeans and Indo-Aryans is the subject of continuing debate among philologists (scholars who study old languages), linguists, historians, archaeologists, and others. The dominant view is that the Indo-Aryans came to the subcontinent as immigrants. Another view, advocated mainly by some Indian scholars, is that they were indigenous to the subcontinent. Over the years, many original homelands have been proposed for the Indo-Aryans (see Bryant, 2002). These include Tibet, Afghanistan, Iran, the Aral Sea, the Caspian Sea, the Black Sea, Lithuania, the Arctic, the Caucasus, the Urals, the Volga mountains, southern Russia, the central Asian steppes, West Asia, Turkey, Scandinavia, Finland, Sweden, the Baltic region, and India. All these claims are not supported by equally convincing evidence.

One of the most widely accepted views locates the original homeland of the Indo-Europeans in the Pontic-Caspian steppes of Eastern Europe (see Mallory, 1989). This is largely based on using philological evidence to make inferences about where a lost parent language, referred to by scholars as proto-Indo-European (PIE), was originally spoken. In recent years, a substantial increase in archaeological data has reinforced this argument. Horses, horse-drawn wagons, and chariots are important parts of this story. David W. Anthony (2007) has argued that linguistic and archaeological evidence indicate that proto-Indo-European was probably spoken in the Pontic-Caspian steppes north of the Black and Caspian Seas (in the modern countries of Ukraine and Russia) between *c.* 4500 and 2500 BCE. The westward and eastward spread of this language can be associated with the spread of elements of the Yamnaya culture or horizon (*c.* 3300–2500 BCE; because of its regional diversity, many archaeologists prefer not to call it a 'culture'). The Yamnaya horizon reflects a new kind of life marked by increased mobility due to the use of wheel-drawn wagons and horseback riding. This led to the emergence of more productive kind of nomadic pastoralism on the steppes. Whether features of this culture spread due to migration and/or emulation is the subject of debate.

The discoveries at the site of Sintashta (*c.* 2100–1800 BCE), located in the northern steppes to the east of the Ural mountains, revealed a large, fortified settlement with evidence of metal working. The most dramatic remains were burials which, apart from human remains, included the remains of horses, chariots with spoked wheels (these are the first chariots to be found in the world), and many copper and bronze weapons. Some similarities have been suggested with the funerary rituals of the *Rig Veda* and there is a hypothesis that the Sintashta sites may represent the material remains of Indo-Iranian speakers. Many pieces of the puzzle remain, but a coherent linguistically and archaeologically attested picture of migrations across Europe and Asia seems to be gradually emerging.

In recent years, DNA analysis has been marshalled in the debate on the Indo-Aryan homeland and this too suggests migrations across Eurasia, and eventually into India. There are very few studies of ancient DNA from the Indian subcontinent. A study by Narasimhan and others (2019) was based on a genome-wide study of ancient DNA from 523 individuals who lived in Central Asia and northern South Asia. This study documented a series of movements during the bronze age of people from the Eurasian steppes to the northern part of the Indian subcontinent, which seems to explain the spread of Indo-European languages. More studies of ancient DNA from South Asian sites, based on a larger and diverse population base, are likely to shed more light on genetic profiles and patterns of migration. However, it must be kept in mind that putting together archaeological, linguistic, and genetic evidence is not always easy as the three types of evidence are qualitatively different.

It must be emphasized that there is no evidence of an Aryan invasion of northwestern India, nor of a massive wave of immigration. The evidence suggests a series of migrations of relatively small groups of people. Studies indicate that language spread does not necessarily have to be the result of large-scale events. Superior military technology, and the use of the horse and chariot may have given the immigrants the crucial initial advantage, enabling them to establish their homes and political dominance in the land of the seven rivers, gradually leading to a process of language replacement. Sanskrit has a series of dental consonants, sounds produced by touching the tip of the tongue to the upper teeth (*t, th, d, dh, n*). But it also has a parallel set of retroflex consonants, produced by curling the tongue upwards to touch the palate (*ṭ, ṭh, ḍ, ḍh, ṇ, ṣ*). As pointed out by Madhav Deshpande (1979), the retroflex consonant is found in all the Dravidian languages, and must have come into Sanskrit from a Dravidian source. There are differences of opinion among scholars about when this might have happened. However, retroflexion is only found in India, and is absent in all other Indo-European languages. (On retroflexion in Indian languages, see Mohan, 2021: 19–25.)

Some scholars argue that the theory of Indo-Aryan migrations into India is unacceptable and that the Aryans were indigenous to India (Danino, 2016). There are various versions of the 'Indigenous Aryanist' theory (see Bryant, 2001: 141–156). Some argue that the Harappan civilization represents the Vedic culture. There are, however, many problems in this hypothesis. One is the gap in dates. There is also the issue of the script. Scholars such as Iravatham Mahadevan and Asko Parpola, who have worked on the Harappan script, argue that it encodes a Dravidian language, which also goes against the theory of the equation of the Harappan and Vedic cultures. The absence of the retroflex consonant in other Indo-European languages, and its wide prevalence in the Indian subcontinent also goes against the 'out of India' theory. There are many differences between the urban Harappan civilization and the rural Vedic culture. The world of the *Rig Veda* is dominated by spoked-wheel chariots drawn by horses. Even if it is accepted that some horse remains have been found at a few Harappan sites, the remains are very few; there is also very little evidence of vehicles with spoked wheels.

Many pieces of the puzzle remain to be found and understood, but the evidence suggests that the advent of the Indo-Aryans into India was part of a long and complex story of migrations and mixtures of populations. The *Rig Veda* contains many loanwords and elements from the Dravidian and Munda language families. This indicates the co-existence and interaction of people speaking these different languages. DNA analysis too tells a story of population mixtures. It indicates that the people of India today represent a mixture of two highly differentiated populations—the Ancestral North Indians (ANI) and the Ancestral South Asians (ASI). The ANI are genetically related to Europeans, Central and West Asians, and the people of the Caucasus. The ASI are descendants of a population that is not related to any present-day populations outside India (Reich, 2018: 135). So, everyone who lives in India today (including the tribal groups) represent genetic mixtures that took place thousands of years ago.

While the issue of the Aryans has often dominated historical discourse, it should be remembered that the history of India cannot be equated with the history of the Aryans.

The culture reflected in the family books of the *Rig Veda Samhita*

Historians divide the Vedic corpus into two parts—early and later Vedic texts, although recent studies suggest a more complex internal chronology. Early Vedic texts refer to the family books of the *Rig Veda Samhita*. Later Vedic texts include Books 1, 8, 9, and 10 of the *Rig Veda Samhita*, the Samhitas of the *Sama*, *Yajur*, and *Atharva Vedas*, and the

Brahmanas, Aranyakas, and Upanishads attached to all the four Vedas. (Among these later texts, the Mantra portions are the earliest, followed by the Brahmanas, Aranyakas, and Upanishads.) The cultural stages reflected in the two broad strata of early and later Vedic texts have come to be known as the early and the later Vedic cultures.

TRIBES AND WARS

The *Rig Veda* is pervaded with the aura of warring tribes. About 30 tribes and clans are mentioned. Five tribes—the Yadu, Turvasha, Puru, Anu, and Druhyu—are collectively known as the 'five peoples' (*pancha-jana*, *pancha-kristya*, or *pancha-manusha*). The Purus and Bharatas are the two dominant tribes. Initially, they seem to have been allies, but at some point, they fell apart. The *Rig Veda* mentions a chief of the Purus named Trasadasyu. It also mentions a famous Bharata king named Divodasa and describes his victory over the Dasa ruler Shambara, who had many mountain fortresses.

Many Rig Vedic hymns beseech the gods for victory in battle. It is difficult to distinguish between mythical and historical events, between demons and real enemies. There are several references to conflicts with the Dasas and Dasyus. One view is that these were the aboriginal people encountered by the Indo-Aryan tribes. However, they may actually represent earlier (pre-Vedic) waves of Indo-Aryan immigrants. Prayers to Indra to defeat not only the Dasa but also the Arya enemies indicate that there were conflicts among the Aryas too.

There are about 300 clearly non-Indo-European words in the *Rig Veda*. These 'loan words' show that the Rig Vedic people were interacting with people speaking Dravidian and Munda languages. There are many tribes with non-Indo-Aryan names in the *Rig Veda*, such as the Chumuri, Dhuni, Pipru, and Shambara. The text also refers to Arya chieftains with non-Indo-Aryan names, e.g., Balbutha and Bribu. All this is indicative of processes of cultural interaction.

The 'battle of ten kings' (*dasharajna*), recounted in Book 7 of the *Rig Veda Samhita* may refer to an actual historical incident. In this battle, the Bharata chief Sudas, grandson of Divodasa, fought against a confederacy of 10 tribes. The mention of the Purus, their former allies, as a part of this confederacy indicates that political alliances were fluid and shifting. Vishvamitra, the Bharata *purohita*, seems to have been replaced by Vasishtha before the battle, reflecting another sort of behind-the-scenes re-alignment. The great battle took place on the banks of the river Parushni (Ravi). The Bharatas won by breaking a natural dam on the river. Marching on to the Yamuna, they defeated a local ruler named Bheda. Sudas eventually settled down along the Sarasvati and celebrated his victory and position of political paramountcy by performing the *ashvamedha* sacrifice.

The word *rajan* (or *raja*) occurs many times in the family books of the *Rig Veda*. Since a full-fledged monarchical state had not yet emerged, this word is best translated as 'chieftain' or 'noble', rather than as 'king'. It is not always clear from the hymns whether the *rajan* was the chief of a tribe, clan, clan segment or several clans. But his main task was to protect his people and to lead them to victory in war. The reference to the chieftain as *gopa* or *gopati* (lord of the cattle) indicates that protecting and increasing the cattle herd was his other major role. The royal priest accompanied the *rajan* to battle, recited prayers, and supervised the performance of rituals. The importance of royal priests such as Vasishtha and Vishvamitra is reflected in many Vedic hymns. *Bali* refers to an offering made to a god; it also means tribute periodically offered by the clansmen to the *rajan*. Tribute was no doubt also extracted from tribes defeated in battle. A regular taxation system had not yet emerged.

The *Rig Veda* mentions assemblies such as the ***sabha*** and *samiti*. The distinctions between their functions are not entirely clear. The *sabha* seems to have been a smaller, more elite gathering, whereas the *samiti* appears to have been a larger assembly presided

PRIMARY SOURCES | The hymn to arms (*Rig Veda Samhita* 6.75)

The following benediction was recited by the *purohita* (royal priest) either before the chieftain set out on a military expedition or in order to bless the warriors accompanying the consecrated horse in the *ashvamedha* sacrifice. Note how the various weapons are described and praised, one by one:

His mien is like that of a thundercloud, when he drives armoured into the
lap of battles.
With an unpierceable body, conquer! Let the greatness of your *armour*
carry you through.

With the *bow* may we win cattle, with the bow the contest, with the bow
may we win the sharp battles.
The bow banishes the (battle-)lust of our rival. With the bow may we
win all the quarters.

Just like (a woman) about to speak, she keeps going up to his ear, while
embracing her dear partner.
Like a maiden (with her anklets?), she jangles when stretched out on the
bow: this *bowstring* here that makes (the arrow) cross over into the
melee (as if to a [festive] gathering).

The two faring forth to the melees, like a maiden to (festive) gatherings—
let them carry (the arrow) as a mother does a child in her lap.
Let them pierce our rivals when the two find each other: these *bow-ends*
here when they spring apart (against) the enemies.

Father of many (daughters [=arrows]), he (also) has many a son; he
makes a clattering when he descends into the melees.
The *quiver*, tied onto the back, wins clashes and battles—all of them—
when it is thrust into action.

Standing on the chariot, he leads the prizewinners [=horses] forward
wherever he desires: the good charioteer.
Admire the greatness of the *reins*. The cords guide, following the
(charioteer's) mind (though it is) behind them.

They make their sharp cries—the bullish-hooved *horses* along with the
chariots, as they seek the prize,
trampling down the enemies with their forefeet, they destroy our rivals,
without (even) divesting (them of their armor).

The *chariot-stand*, "Oblation(-deposit)" its name, where his weapon, his
armour is deposited—
there may we reverently approach the powerful chariot always when we
seek its benevolence.

The *forefathers*: assembling for the sweet (soma), conferring vigour, they
who are props in distress, skillful, deep,
with glittering weapons, arrow-strong, not shirking, entirely heroic,
broad, overwhelming the troops.

O Brahmanas, forefathers, deserving of soma, let Heaven and Earth,
blameless ones, (be) kindly to us;
let Pushan protect us from difficult passage, you who are strong through
truth. Guard (us): let none who curse hold sway over us.

She wears the fine-feathered (eagle); a wild deer is her tooth. Lashed
together with cows, she flies when propelled forth.
Where men clash and separate, there will our *arrows* provide shelter
for us.

You (arrow, though) of straight course, avoid us. Let our body become
a rock.
Let Soma speak on our behalf; let Aditi provide us shelter.

It smashes hard on their back, keeps beating at their haunches—
o *horsewhip*, impel the cautious horses into battles.

Like a snake with its coils, it encircles the arm, parrying the blow of the
bowstring—
the *handguard*, knowing all the trajectories (of the bowstring): as a male
let it protect the male all around.

She who is smeared with poison, with the head of a deer, but whose
mouth is metal:
here is lofty reverence to her who has (received) the semen of Thunder,
to the goddess *Arrow*.

Once released, fly away, you arrow, sharpened by a sacred formulation.
Go to the enemies; fall on them. Do not leave a single one of them
standing.

Where the darts fly together, like lads with unruly hair,
there let Brahmanaspati, let Aditi provide us shelter—always provide
shelter.

Your vulnerable places I cover with armour; let Soma the king clothe you
with immortality.
Let Varuṇa make (a space) wider than wide for you; let the gods cheer
you on as you win.

Whoever wishes to smite us—one of our own or a foreigner, or even
one outside the pale—
him let all the gods injure. The sacred formulation is my inner armour.

Source Jamison and Brereton. (Trans.). 2014: 876–78

KEY CONCEPTS | **Lineage, clan, tribe**

Historians use several sociological terms and concepts while describing ancient cultures. Kinship refers to socially and culturally recognized relationships among people, commonly assumed to be based on natural or biological ties. These ties may be based on birth/descent (consanguinal relations), marriage (affinal relations), adoption, or fosterage. There are also other culturally specified kinds of kinship—e.g., in North India, there is the custom of the *rakhi* brother–sister relationship and the '*muh-bola-bhai*' (a man declared to be a brother). Kinship is so important in Indian society that its language has spread far and wide. Younger people routinely address their elders as 'uncle' and 'aunty' and people who are not even remotely related may address each other as 'brother', 'sister', 'mother', or 'father'.

Kinship systems can be unilineal or multi-lineal. **Unilineal kinship systems** which recognize descent relationships through the father are known as **patrilineal** or agnatic. Unilineal kinship systems which recognize descent through the mother are known as **matrilineal. Multi-lineal** or cognatic systems are those in which descent through both the mother and father is recognized. In both patrilineal and matrilineal systems, relationships through the other parent also receive recognition for different purposes at different times—for instance, at times of marriage, during the performance of rituals, and even in matters of inheritance. For example, in a patrilineal society, a son or daughter may inherit property from their mother's kin, and the mother's brother may have a significant role to play in the lifecycle rituals of his sister's children.

A lineage is a group of unilineal kin. In view of the problem of drawing the dividing line between family and lineage, the latter term can be used to refer to relations beyond the three or four generation family. Several unilineal descent groups who trace their descent from a common ancestor, actual or mythical, form a **clan.** Members of a clan sometimes claim a common place of origin and may have clan property or a clan god. A number of related clans constitute a tribe.

Discussions of early Indian history often use the framework of transition from tribe to territorial state. As mentioned in Chapter 4, it is difficult to give a universal definition of the word 'state.' The same can be said for 'tribe.' Earlier, the term was routinely used by anthropologists to refer to people they considered primitive, who lived in economically less-developed areas, and lacked a script. These days, sociologists and anthropologists are careful to avoid value-laden terms such as 'primitive' and are aware of the pitfalls in defining a tribe. Some have stopped using the category of tribe. André Beteille ([1960] 1977) suggests that a tribe can be defined as a society with a political, linguistic, and somewhat vaguely defined cultural boundary, based on kinship, and lacking in social stratification. Within this very general definition, tribes differ from one another in many ways.

In the context of early Indian history, historians often use the term 'tribal' to refer to pre-chiefdom and pre-state societies. The relationship between tribe and state has often been seen in terms of an evolution from a less complex to a more complex political system, but it can also be seen in terms of coexistence and conflict. As pointed out by Sumit Guha (2021), tribalism in the sense of decentralized political systems which do not have a single, powerful head at the apex, is a recurring phenomenon in history, not an extinct type of political formation. Tribes are political organization created in reaction to threats from other tribes or from centralized states such as kingdoms.

In this book, the term 'tribe' is used for the sake of convenience to refer to non-monarchical political formations which have comparatively less rigid structures of social and political hierarchy and control. However, it is important to recognize the complexities of the meanings of such terms and the difficulties in identifying their diagnostic features in ancient societies.

over by the *rajan*. Such assemblies may have played an important role in the redistribution of resources. Hymns express the desire for harmony among members ('Assemble, speak together; let your minds be all of one accord.'). The *vidatha* has been understood as a tribal assembly with diverse functions. However, it actually seems to refer to a local congregation of people meeting to perform socio-religious rituals and ceremonies for the well-being of the settlement.

The family books contain several terms for socio-political units, many of which were based on kinship. These include *jana*, *vish*, *gana*, *grama*, *griha*, and ***kula***. Their precise meaning, however, is not always clear. The *jana* of the *Rig Veda* can be translated as tribe, *vish* is often translated as people in general or as clan, and *gana* as lineage. *Grama*, which later came to mean village, seems to have originally referred to a mobile group of people who may or may not have been related to each other through kinship.

PASTORALISM, AGRICULTURE, AND OTHER OCCUPATIONS

Animals such as horses, goats, and sheep are mentioned in the family books, but cattle were clearly prized the most. R. S. Sharma (1983: 24) has drawn attention to the many derivations of the word *gau* (cow) in the *Rig Veda*. Words for war with the infix *gau*—such as *gavishti*, *gaveshana*, *goshu*, and *gavya*—suggest that many battles were in effect cattle raids. Further indications of the importance of cattle come from other words containing the *gau* infix. The tribal chief was known as *janasya gopa*. Measures of time included *godhuli* (dusk) and *samgava* (morning), measures of area/distance included *gavyuti* and *gocharman*. The buffalo was known as *gauri* or *gavala*. The daughter was *duhitri* (she who milks cows). *Gojit* (winner of cows) was a word for a hero. A wealthy person was known as *gomat* (owner of cattle). One of the epithets of the god Indra was *gopati* (lord of cattle).

Some scholars have used the number of references to pastoral versus agricultural activities in the family books as an index of their relative importance, and have concluded that while cattle rearing was of overwhelming importance, agriculture was either a subsidiary activity or one that was practised by non-Indo-Aryans. However, the frequency of usage in religious or ritualistic texts and contexts may not be an accurate indicator of the relative importance of these activities in everyday life. Apart from word frequencies, it is necessary to examine the nature and content of the references.

R. N. Nandi (1989–90) has drawn attention to the many references to agricultural activity in the *Rig Veda* and argues that it was by no means marginal. The verbs *vap* (to sow) and *krish* (to cultivate) occur, along with references to various agricultural implements. *Phala*, *langala*, and *sira* are words for the plough, which must have been made of wood. Other implements included the hoe (*khanitra*), sickle (*datra*, *srini*), and axe (*parashu*, *kulisha*). The word *kshetra* has a range of meanings, including a cultivated field. Hymns refer to the levelling of fields for cultivation, the desire for fertile fields (*urvara*), and furrows (*sita*) drenched by rain, producing rich harvests. The only terms for cereals are *yava* (barley or a generic term for cereal) and *dhanya* (a generic term for cereals). There are references to seed processing, food prepared from cereals, and large jars that were probably used to store grain. Some hymns refer to conflicts among people for the protection of sons, grandsons, cattle, water courses, and fertile fields. Prayers to Indra beseech him to grant or enrich the fields. This god is described as the protector of crops, winner of fertile fields (*urvarajit*), and one who showers such fields on those who perform sacrifices to him. The later parts of the family books invoke Kshetrapati, who seems to have been a guardian deity of agricultural fields. Wars were fought for cattle, but also for land.

Hymns refer to warriors, priests, cattle-rearers, farmers, hunters, barbers, and vintners. The crafts mentioned include chariot-making, cart-making, carpentry, metal working, tanning, the making of bows and bowstrings, sewing, weaving, and making mats out of grass or reeds. Some of these occupations and crafts may have been the jobs of full-time specialists.

There are hardly any references to metallurgical activities in the *Rig Veda*, and very few of these occur in the family books (Chakrabarti, 1992). The word *ayas* occurs in several contexts. There are references to Indra's thunderbolt of *ayas*; the chariot of Mitra and Varuna having columns of *ayas*; and the home of Indra and Soma made of *ayas*. A hymn to Agni compares his splendour to the edge of *ayas*. Another hymn to Agni beseeches him to be like a fort of *ayas* to his worshippers. A prayer to Indra asks him to sharpen his worshipper's thought as if it were a blade of *ayas*. The family books also refer to the Dasyus' cities of *ayas*, forts of *ayas*, a horse's jaws of *ayas*, and a vessel of *ayas*. The few metal objects mentioned in the *Rig Veda* are *kshura* (razor), *khadi* (maybe a bangle), and *asi/svadhiti* (axe). But it is not clear precisely which metal these objects were made of. A hymn (4.2.17) refers to the doers of good deeds having freed their birth from impurity in the same way as *ayas* is purified. The medieval commentator Sayana explains this reference as follows: 'As the smiths heat metal using bellows.' There are a few references in the *Rig Veda* to the words *dham* and *karmara*, but these occur in the late books 9 and 10, and it is far from certain whether they refer to iron-welding or iron smiths.

Some scholars have interpreted the references to *ayas*, metal objects, and metallurgical activity in the *Rig Veda* as indicative of iron artefacts and iron working. However, there is no definite evidence that this was so. There is in fact no clear or conclusive reference to iron in the family books. *Ayas* could have meant copper, copper-bronze, or may have been a generic term for metals.

Anthropological studies have brought out the importance of gift exchanges in simple societies, and some of their observations are useful for understanding the culture reflected in the *Rig Veda*. In his classic work on the gift, Marcel Mauss, [1954] 1980) pointed out that such exchanges may appear on the surface to be voluntary and spontaneous, but are actually strictly obligatory and governed by conventions that have to be observed. It is not the individual but groups (families, clans, tribes) who make the exchanges and are bound by their obligations. Such exchanges—known as **prestations**—do not only involve material goods of economic value. They also involve the exchange of other things such as courtesies, entertainments, military assistance, ritual, women, children, dances, feasts, and hospitality. The rules of the game in gift exchange are different from the logic that operates in ordinary sorts of economic exchanges. The offering, receiving, and reciprocating of gifts are acts that establish and cement social relationships and social hierarchies. In the *Rig Veda*, we have noted that gifts (*bali*) were received by the *rajan* from members of the clan. Priests received ***dana*** (ritual gifts) and ***dakshina*** (sacrificial fees) at the conclusion of sacrificial rituals.

Gift-giving and receiving do not rule out other kinds of exchange, but trade in the Rig Vedic context was probably minimal. Cattle were considered an important unit of value. The word *nishka* seems to have meant 'a piece of gold' or 'gold necklace'. These may have been used for exchange, but they are not the same thing as coinage. Exchange was conducted through barter and/or by using other units of value. There are prayers to the gods to 'give broad paths to travel' and ensure a safe journey. Mention is made of chariots and carts drawn by oxen, mules, or horses. The *panis* (literally, 'those who possess wealth') in some instances refer to merchants and in others to stingy people who did not perform sacrifices and hid their wealth. There are references to boats (*nau*) and the ocean (*samudra*). *Rig Veda* 1.116.3 refers to the Ashvins rescuing Bhujya in the ocean with the help of a ship with a hundred oars. Book 10 refers to the eastern and western oceans. But both Books 1 and 10 are later books, and historians differ on the extent to which composers of the early sections of the *Rig Veda* were familiar with sea travel, let alone sea trade.

War booty was a major source of wealth (*pana*, *dhana*, *rayi*, etc.). The references to wealthy people and those worthy of attending the assemblies suggest differences in wealth and rank. The *rajan* and the assemblies must have had a say in the redistribution of war booty, and the *rajan* and his immediate kinsmen must have got a larger share. Apart from cattle, other items solicited in prayers and sacrifices include houses, horses, gold, fertile fields, friends, plentiful food, wealth, jewels, chariots, fame, and children. The notion of individual private property ownership as we understand it—associated with the right to buy, sell, gift, bequeath, and mortgage—did not exist. The clan as a whole enjoyed rights over major resources such as land and herds.

The household was the basic unit of labour, and there is no mention of wage labour. The *Rig Veda* is, however, familiar with slavery. Slavery is an extreme form of social subordination that was known in many ancient societies and continued into later times as well. Generally speaking, a slave—whether male or female—was considered socially and legally the property of the master. The *Rig Veda* refers to enslavement in the course of war or as a result of debt. The fact that in later times, *dasa* and *dasi* are terms used for male and female slaves, suggests that initially, ethnic differences may have been an important basis of enslavement. Slaves, male and female, generally worked in the household, but were not used to any significant extent in production-related activities. As pointed out by Gerda Lerner (1986), in all cultures, throughout history, there was an important difference in the experience of enslavement for men and women. For women slaves (as well as some male ones), enslavement generally involved sexual exploitation in addition to exploitation of their labour.

Although the family books reflect differences in rank and some inequalities in wealth, these do not add up to distinct socio-economic classes in the sense of significant differences in access to and control over basic productive resources. However, the absence of a class hierarchy does not mean that Rig Vedic society was egalitarian. The family books reflect inequalities between masters and slaves, and between men and women. The *rajan* stood at the top of the ladder of political and social power and status, the *dasi* stood at the very bottom.

The *Rig Veda* mentions food and drink, clothes, and leisure-time pursuits of people. There are references to the consumption of milk and milk products, *ghrita* (*ghee*, clarified butter), grains, vegetables, and fruits. Vedic texts refer to meat eating, and the meat of animals such as sheep, goat, and oxen seems to have been consumed on special occasions (Majumdar et al., [1951] 1971: 393). The reference to cows as *aghnya* (not to be killed) suggests a disapproval of their indiscriminate killing. The drink known as *soma* consisted of the juice of the *soma* plant, mixed with milk, sour milk, or *yava* (cereal). *Sura* seems to have been an intoxicating drink made out of fermented grain. There are references to clothes of cotton, wool, and animal skin, and the wearing of ornaments. There is mention of singing and dancing, and to musical instruments such as the *vina* (lute), *vana* (flute), and drums. The *Rig Veda* suggests that chariot racing and dicing were popular pastimes.

VARNA IN THE *RIG VEDA*

The word *varna* occurs in many places in the family books and usually means light or colour. However, in some passages, it is associated with the Aryas and Dasas. The fact that similar epithets are applied to Dasas and Dasyus, and that both these terms are used to describe certain enemies, indicate an overlap in their connotations. The *Rig Veda* describes them as *a-vrata* (people who do not obey the ordinances of the gods) and *a-kratu* (those who do not perform sacrifices). Another adjective used for them is *mridhra-vacha*. This can be interpreted in different ways—as referring to their speech being indistinct, unclear, soft, unintelligible, uncouth, hostile, scornful, or abusive. The fact that this epithet is used in one place for the Purus, an Indo-Aryan tribe, makes it unlikely that it meant 'unintelligible'. In three places in the *Rig Veda*, the term *krishna-tvach* or *asikni-tvach* is applied to the Dasyus. This can be interpreted literally as 'dark skinned', or as a figurative use of darkness. In one passage, the Dasas are described as *anasa*. Whether this means noseless (i.e., flat-nosed), faceless (in some metaphorical sense) or mouthless (i.e., whose speech is incomprehensible) is uncertain.

The old view highlighted the supposed physical differences, and described the Dasas and Dasyus as the dark-skinned, flat-nosed aboriginal people of India who were displaced and pushed southwards by the fair-skinned Aryans. The references cited above should make it clear that the epithets used for the Dasas and Dasyus can be interpreted in different ways. Whether or not there were stark differences in physical appearance can be debated. What *is* certain is that there were a range of cultural differences, including those of religious practice, and possibly in mode of speech, language, or dialect. Many scholars think that the Dasas and Dasyus were not non-Aryan tribes but earlier waves of Indo-Aryan immigrants who arrived in the subcontinent before the Vedic Aryans. A connection has been suggested between an Iranian tribe called the Dahae and the Dasas of the *Rig Veda*, and between the Dahyu tribe and the Dasyus. Although the *Rig Veda* talks of conflicts between the Aryas and the Dasas and Dasyus, there were also conflicts and military engagements among the Indo-Aryan tribes as well—the conflict between the Bharatas versus the Purus and their allies in the 'battle of ten kings' is a case in point.

The words 'Brahmana' and 'Kshatriya' occur frequently in the family books, but the term *varna* is not associated with them. There is mention of Brahmanas drinking *soma* and reciting hymns, and although they seem to have been a group who enjoyed respect, there are no indications that membership of this group was based on birth. The words 'Vaishya' and 'Shudra' are absent. The earliest reference to the division of society into four strata occurs in the *Purusha-sukta*, a hymn in Book 10 of the *Rig Veda Samhita*. As this is a later book, the four-fold *varna* order is seen as a feature of later Vedic texts.

The absence of a strict social hierarchy and the existence of an element of social mobility is suggested in *Rig Veda* 3.44–45. In this hymn, the poet asks Indra: 'O, Indra, fond of *soma*, would you make me the protector of people, or would you make me a king, would you make me a sage who has drunk *soma*, would you impart to me endless wealth?' This suggests that a man could aspire to different sorts of vocations and goals in life.

WOMEN, MEN, AND THE HOUSEHOLD

Nineteenth-century socio-religious reformers and nationalist historians of the early 20th century often presented the Vedic age as a golden age for women. They pointed out that the Vedic people worshipped goddesses; the *Rig Veda* contains hymns composed by women; there are references to women sages; women participated in rituals along with their husbands; they took part in chariot races and attended the *sabha* and various social gatherings. Such a presentation of the 'high' position of women in Vedic society can be seen as a response to the oppression and humiliation of colonial rule. The idea was to show that in ancient times, Indians were better than the Westerners, at least in the way they treated women. This could also be used as an argument to improve the prevailing condition of women in Indian society (see Uma Chakravarti, 2006).

Feminist historians shifted the focus from discussing women in isolation to an analysis of gender relations. Unlike sex, which is biological, gender refers to culturally defined roles associated with men and women. In recent times, there is a realization that studies of gender need to move beyond binaries of male and female to take into account transgender identity and experience. Earlier, historians tended to focus on the public, political domain, relegating the family, household, and gender relations to the private, domestic domain. However, the distinction between the private and political domains is an artificial one. Ideologies and hierarchies of power and authority exist within the family and household, in the form of norms of appropriate conduct based on gender, age, and kinship relations. Further, there is a close connection between relations within the household, marriage and kinship systems, the control of women's sexuality and reproduction, class and caste relations, and larger political structures. These are all like the interlocking building blocks of a vast and complex social pyramid. For these reasons, gender relations form an important part of social history.

The experiences of women belonging to different groups in society varied and it is, therefore, necessary to break down the category of 'women' into more specific subcategories based on rank, class, occupation, and age. Women have to be understood in relation to men, and their relationships are embedded in wider social, economic, and political contexts. For all periods, the vague issue of the 'status of women' therefore, has to be replaced by more meaningful questions, such as: What were the relations between men and women in the domestic sphere? How was a person's descent recognized? What were the norms of property and inheritance? What was the role of women in production-related activities? Did they have control over these activities or the fruits of their labour? How was the sexuality and reproductive potential of women controlled and regulated? What was the role of women in the religious and ritual spheres? Did they have access to education and knowledge systems? Did they have direct or indirect access to political power? Further, structures of subordination and control were not total or all-encompassing, and an analysis of gender relations has to move beyond seeing women as passive victims of oppressive social structures. In spite of their subordination, women occupied a variety of social spaces, performed different roles, and were participants and active agents in history.

KEY CONCEPTS | The family and the household

The word 'family' means different things to different people. If you ask a person about the members of her family, she might mention herself, her siblings, and her parents. Another person might include grandparents and great-grandparents, dead or alive. Yet another person might include aunts and uncles, cousins, nephews, nieces, etc.

As pointed out by A. M. Shah ([1964] 1998: 15), the word 'family' can refer to:

1. the household, i.e., all people living in one house or under one head, including parents, children, and household employees
2. parents and their children, whether living together or separately
3. all those who are held to be close relatives by birth or marriage
4. all those who are either descended or claim to be descended from a common ancestor
5. a property-holding unit
6. a ceremonial unit, for instance, including all those who have the right to perform the *shraddha* rites in honour of deceased ancestors.

Definitions of the family that are based on the issue of property holding or the performance of the *shraddha* do not help in understanding social groups that are property-less or who do not perform the *shraddha* rituals in the prescribed way.

Because the word 'family' can mean so many different things, sociologists often qualify it with an adjective that makes it more specific. So, for instance, the terms '**elementary family**' and 'nuclear family' refer to a married couple and their children, who may or may not live together. An extended family means two or more elementary families (or parts of them) joined together. This can take the form of a patrilineal joint family—sons and their families living with their father—in societies based on patrilineal descent, and a matrilineal joint family in societies based on the principle of matrilineal descent. It is not easy to draw the dividing line between the joint or extended family and the lineage.

The **household** is more specific and easier to identify. Members of a household share a common residence. They perform different economic activities, some within, others outside the home. The household is the site of people's most intimate and profound experiences in life. It is a place where many different kinds of human emotions and experiences are played out every day—those involving love and hatred, conflict and cooperation, oppression and compassion, violence and concern.

Households come to be related to other households, families, and lineages through ties of kinship and marriage. The institution of marriage grants social approval to a union of two people assumed to be sexual partners and grants legitimacy to their offspring. Marriage and the household do not necessarily go hand in hand. For instance, among certain matrilineal groups in Kerala and the Lakshadweep islands, the husband does not live with his wife, but visits from time to time.

Families can be divided into different types on the basis of descent, residence, membership, and the number of partners. Mention was made earlier of patrilineal and matrilineal social systems. Some societies recognize cognatic descent—i.e., descent in both the mother's and the father's line. Patriliny and matriliny are not equivalent to patriarchy and matriarchy. Patriarchy means societies in which males (usually the eldest male) exercise dominant power and authority within the family. Matriarchy refers to a system in which such power and authority is vested in women. While there are several instances of matrilineal societies, no known society of the past or the present can be described as matriarchal.

Patriarchy is not uniform. In patriarchal, patrilineal caste society, strict control over women's sexuality and reproductive potential is essential for the transmission of property and for the maintenance and perpetuation of the endogamous caste system. There are other varieties of patriarchy which offer different degrees of autonomy to women. For instance, tribal patriarchal societies may give more freedom to women than others. Patriliny dominates in South Asia. But there are a few pockets where matriliny is practised, for instance in India among the Khasi, Garo, and Lalung communities in North-east, the Nairs of Kerala, and the people of Lakshadweep. In these societies, although descent through the mother's line is recognized, the management of property is usually in the hands of men.

Social norms that valorize sons and curtail the freedom of women are typical of patrilineal societies. For instance, if we compare India with Sri Lanka, Indonesia, Thailand, or the Philippines, where many communities follow cognatic or bilateral kinship systems, the picture is different (Leela Dube, 1994). These are, broadly speaking, patriarchal societies but as a result of the fact that descent and property are transmitted both through women and men, the extreme forms of discrimination against women (reflected, for instance, in dowry killing, female infanticide, and neglect of the girl child) do not exist. Further, in North American and European societies, although children often still take the surname of the father, property rights and ideas of closeness and distance with the mother's or father's side do not vary significantly.

Families in which the wife moves to live in her husband's father's house (or his grandfather's or uncle's house, if the father is not alive) are known as patrilocal or virilocal. Families in which the husband moves in with his wife's mother's family are known as matrilocal or uxorilocal (e.g., the Nairs of Kerala and Khasis of Meghalaya). Another type of arrangement is called duolocal—where the husband and wife continue to live with their respective families even after their marriage (e.g., in the Lakshadweep islands and central Kerala).

Family types can also be distinguished from each other on the basis of the number of mates. Monogamy is a system in which a person has only one spouse at a time. In **polygamy**, one person can have more than one spouse at the same time. There are two types of polygamy—polygyny is a system in which a man can have several wives, while polyandry is a system in which a woman can have several husbands. There is a form of polyandry where the marriage ritual may be between a woman and one man, but the woman may either be considered the wife of all the brothers, or the latter may have access to her sexual and domestic services.

Sociological studies reveal a great deal of diversity among families and households in different parts of the subcontinent today. Similar diversity must have prevailed in ancient times as well.

In the older writings, a great part of the discussion about women of the Vedic age focused on elite women, ignoring the less privileged members of this sex. Although the *Rig Veda* mentions goddesses, none of them are as important as the major gods. The social implications of the worship of female deities are complex. While such worship does at least mark the ability of a community to visualize the divine in feminine form, it does not automatically mean that real women enjoyed power or privilege. The proportion of hymns attributed to women in the *Rig Veda* is miniscule (just 12–15 out of over 1,000), as is the number of women sages. This suggests that women had limited access to sacred learning. There are no women priests in the *Rig Veda*. While women participated as wives in sacrifices performed on behalf of their husbands, they did not perform sacrifices in their own right; nor do they appear as givers or receivers of *dana* or *dakshina*. The Vedic household was clearly patriarchal and patrilineal, and women enjoyed relatively little control over material resources. Their sexuality and reproductive resources were controlled through the ingraining of norms of what was considered appropriate behaviour.

Early Vedic texts have several words for household units—*durona*, *kshiti*, *dam/dama*, *pastya*, *gaya*, and *griha*—which may have corresponded to different kinds of households. Considering that this was a patriarchal and patrilineal society, it is not surprising that Rig Vedic prayers are for sons, not daughters, and that the absence of sons is deplored. The *Rig Veda* attaches importance to the institution of marriage and refers to various types of marriage—**monogamy**, **polygyny**, and **polyandry**. The rituals indicate post-puberty marriages, and there are references to women choosing their husbands. A woman could remarry if her husband died or disappeared. There are also references to unmarried women, such as the Rig Vedic seer Ghosha.

Male dominance and the subordination of women is a feature of all known historical societies. The issue is one of the *degree* of dominance and subordination, and the structures in which these were embedded. Compared to later Vedic texts, the family books of the *Rig Veda Samhita* reflect a situation in which social status was not as rigidly defined or polarized as it came to be in later times. However, it was not a society of equals—rank and gender were the two main bases of inequality.

RELIGION: SACRIFICES TO THE GODS

The *Rig Veda* reflects the beliefs and practices of a religious elite and its patrons, and there are several striking similarities with ideas reflected in the Iranian *Avesta*. The *Rig Veda* indicates a diversity of religious practice. For instance, there is mention of people who did not worship Indra, and the Dasas and Dasyus are described as not honouring the Vedic gods and not performing sacrifices.

The Vedic hymns divide the universe into the sky (*dyu*), earth (*prithvi*), and the middle realm (*antariksha*). The word *deva* (literally, 'shining', 'luminous') is frequently used for the gods. The gods are sometimes also called *asuras* in the *Rigveda*. Initially, this word referred to a powerful being; in later times it came to be used exclusively in a negative sense for demons. The *Rig Veda* asserts that there are 33 gods associated with the sky, earth, and the intermediate region, but the actual number of deities mentioned in the text is more. Some gods are mentioned more often than others, but there is no fixed order of importance nor a fixed pantheon. Whichever deity is invoked in a particular hymn is spoken of as a supreme god. Max Müller described this phenomenon as **Henotheism** or **Kathenotheism**. Apart from the gods, the *Rig Veda* mentions *gandharvas* (celestial beings), *apsaras* (celestial nymphs, wives of the *gandharvas*), and malevolent beings such as *rakshasas* (demons), *yatudhanas* (sorcerers), and *pishachas* (spirits of the dead). Different ideas of how the world was created are mentioned in passing—e.g., as a result of a great cosmic battle, the separation of heaven and earth, or the actions of the gods.

The performance of *yajnas* (sacrificial rituals) was central to Rig Vedic religion. The sacrifice marked a movement from the everyday, mundane sphere of activity and experience to the sacred sphere. It involved reciprocity and exchange. The gods were seen

PRIMARY SOURCES | Hymn to Indra (*Rig Veda* 2.12)

This hymn praises Indra, describing various aspects of his personality and referring to various myths connected with him. Note the reference in the fifth verse to people who doubt his existence:

Who, even when just born, was the foremost thinker, the god who by his
own will tended to the gods,
before whose explosiveness the world-halves trembled in fear because of
the greatness of his manliness—he, o peoples, is Indra.

Who made firm the wavering earth, who settled the quaking mountains,
who gave the midspace wider measure, who propped up the heaven—he, o peoples, is Indra.

Who, having smashed the serpent, let flow the seven rivers, who drove
away the cattle by uncovering Vala,
who produced the fire between two stones, gathering the winnings in
contests—he, o peoples, is Indra.

By whom all these exploits have been done: who has put the Dasa tribe
below and hidden away,
who, has taken the riches of the stranger, as a winning gambling
champion does the wager—he, o peoples, is Indra.

The terrifying one about whom they always ask, "Where is he?"—and
they say of him, "He does not exist!"—
he diminishes the riches of the stranger like the stakes. Put trust in him!
—he, o peoples, is Indra.

Who is the invigorator of the enfeebled, who of the starving, who of the
formulator of hymns, of the weak one needing help,
who with fair lips is the helper of the one who has yoked the pressing
stones, of him with soma pressed—he, o peoples, is Indra.

Under whose direction are the horses, under whose the cows, under
whose the nomadic bands, and under whose all the chariots,
who has given birth to the sun and who to the dawn, who is the guide
of the waters—he, o peoples, is Indra.

Whom the two war-cries, clashing together, call upon in rivalry—the
enemies on both sides, here and over there—
even the two who have mounted the same chariot [=the chariot-warrior
and charioteer] call on him separately —he, o peoples, is Indra.

Without whom peoples do not win, whom they call upon for help
as they fight,
who has become a match for everyone, who is the mover of the
immovable - he, o peoples, is Indra.

Who has struck with his arrow those constantly creating for themselves
great guilt, the unthinking ones,
who does not concede arrogance to the arrogant man, who is the
smasher of the Dasyu—he, o peoples, is Indra.

Who in the fortieth autumn discovered Shambara dwelling in the
mountains,
who smashed the serpent displaying its strength, the son of Danu,
(thereby) lying (dead)—he, o peoples, is Indra.

The mighty seven-reined bull who let loose the seven rivers to flow,
who, with his mace in his arms, kicked away the son of Rohini as he
was ascending to heaven—he, o peoples, is Indra.

Even heaven and earth bow to him; even the mountains fear his
explosiveness.
The soma-drinker who is renowned as the one bearing the mace in
his arms, as the one bearing the mace in his hands—he, o peoples, is Indra.

Who helps through his help the one pressing soma, the one cooking (an
offering), the one praising, the one labouring,
whose is the strengthening formulation, is the soma, is this gift—he, o
peoples, is Indra.

You who rip free the prize of victory for the one pressing, the one
cooking, even before a stubborn (foe)—you are certainly real!
We (will be) dear to you throughout all the days, Indra. Having good
heroes, we would announce the ritual distribution.

Source Jamison and Brereton, 2014: 416–17

as powerful, mostly benevolent beings, who could be made to intervene in the world of men via the performance of sacrifices. Sacrifices took place in the house of the ***yajamana*** (the person for whom the sacrifice was performed and who bore its expenses) or on a specially prepared plot of land nearby. They consisted mostly of oblations of milk, ghee, and grain poured into the fire, accompanied by the recitation of appropriate sacrificial formulae. Some *yajnas* involved the sacrifice of animals. The gods were supposed to partake of the offerings as they were consumed by the fire. A part of the offerings was eaten by the officiating priests. The goals of Rig Vedic sacrifices included wealth, good health, sons, and a long life for the *yajamana*.

Some sacrifices were simple, domestic affairs, performed by the householder. Others required the participation of ritual specialists. Seven types of sacrificial priests are mentioned

FURTHER DISCUSSION | The *soma* plant and its juice

In the *Rig Veda*, *soma* is a plant, the juice extracted from a plant, and the name of a god. *Soma* can be identified with the *haoma* of the *Avesta*. The *Rig Veda* describes *soma* as a divine drink that confers immortality and many hymns describe its exhilarating effect. It is the drink of the gods and Indra is particularly fond of it. For humans, *soma* seems to have had the ability to alter physiological functions, alter states of mind, and sharpen creativity. It is described as endowing men with strength in battle, keeping them awake and alert at night, and inspiring poets to compose their hymns. The descriptions suggest that the juice of this plant had hallucinogenic, intoxicating, or sympathomimetic (stimulating the sympathetic nervous system or producing similar results) properties. At some point of time, the *soma* plant seems to have become difficult to obtain and substitutes had to be used.

The pressing, straining, and drinking of *soma* juice was an important part of Vedic rituals. The juice seems to have been extracted by laying the plant on a skin and pressing it with stones. It was filtered through sheep's wool and then offered to the gods. The juice was sometimes mixed with water and milk.

Over 100 different identifications have been suggested for the *soma* plant. It has been identified with plants such as *Cannabis sativa L.* (hemp, *bhanga*), *Panax ginseng C.A.M.* (ginseng), *Peganum harmala L.* (Syrian rue), *Papaver somniferum L.* (opium poppy), and *Amanita muscarita* (fly agaric, a mushroom with hallucinogenic properties). The plants of the *Ephedra* genus are strong candidates. Varieties of these leafless plants grow in many parts of Asia and Europe, but they are not common in India. They have been used in folk medicine for a long time, and are identified as the original *haoma* by members of the Parsi community even today. The *Ephedras* contain ephedrine or pseudo-ephedrine, both of which have sympathomimetic effects. Studies have shown that their effects on human physiology can include the following: a rise in blood pressure, increase in heart muscle contraction, decrease in pulse rate, stimulation of metabolism, increased perspiration, hyperglycaemia followed by hypoglycaemia, stimulation of insomnia, tremor, nausea, and dilation of eye pupils. However, it is possible that the *soma* juice consisted of the extract of not one, but more than one, type of plant.

Source Nyberg, 1997

in the *Rig Veda*—the Hotri, Adhvaryu, Agnidh, Maitravaruna, Potri, Neshtri, and Brahmana—each with his particular tasks clearly laid down. Priests were given a fee (*dakshina*) in return for the important duties they performed. The *Rig Veda* does not mention temples or the worship of deities in image form.

The *Rig Veda* reflects a naturalistic **polytheism**—a belief in many gods who personified natural phenomena. The connection is clear in some cases from the very name of the deity, as in the case of Agni (Fire), Surya (the Sun), and Ushas (Dawn). However, the mythology of some deities stretched far beyond their association with a particular natural phenomenon. For instance, although Indra seems to have been originally associated with the thunderstorm, he rapidly outgrew this connection to develop a much more complex personality. The gods were conceived of as anthropomorphic, i.e., as having a physical form similar to that of humans. The level of detail varies, but mention is often made of their head, face, mouth, hair, hands, feet, clothes, and weapons. There is an overlap in some of their physical features, epithets, and exploits.

Indra is the most frequently invoked god in the *Rig Veda*. This powerful god, who quaffs *soma* and kills his enemies with his thunderbolt, represents the strong masculine warrior ethos that pervades the *Rig Veda* (Whitaker, 2011). The hymns vividly describe his appearance and personality. He is vigorous and strong, a great warrior, who leads the Aryas to victory in battle. He is bounteous (*maghavan*). There is reference to his mother and father (Tvashtri is often mentioned as his father). Indrani is his consort and the Maruts his companions. There are many references to Indra defeating hostile forces and demons such as Vala, Arbuda, and Vishvarupa. The most important myth connected with him is his victory over the serpent demon Vritra. He kills Vritra with his thunderbolt and frees the waters that had been obstructed by the demon. The *Rig Veda* often mentions Indra as Vritra-han, slayer of Vritra. Many scholars interpret the conflict between Indra and Vritra as a creation myth, in which Vritra symbolizes chaos.

Agni is another important god and is often invoked along with Indra. He represents many aspects of fire—the fire of the cremation pyre, the fire that engulfs forests, the fire that burns enemies, the heat generated by *tapas* (austerity), and the heat of sexual desire. Most important of all, as the sacrificial fire, he is the intermediary between gods and humans. In this role, he functions as a divine priest. Soma—the personification of the *soma* plant—is closely associated with Indra and Agni and is credited with many similar exploits. He is described as a wise god, one who inspires poets to compose hymns, a great god who rules over the earth and all humans. In later hymns, Soma is identified with the moon.

Varuna and Mitra are frequently invoked together in the *Rig Veda* and are members of an eight-member group of gods known as the Adityas. Varuna is associated with ***kshatra*** (secular power), sovereignty, and kingship. He restricts and punishes evil-doers with the fetters or bonds that he has at his command. Although the hymns mention his eye and golden mantle, they do not give vivid descriptions of his physical appearance. He is associated with *maya*, an ability to construct forms. He is an all-seeing god who knows what everybody is up to.

Other deities of the *Rig Veda* include the sun god Surya, son of Dyaus. Surya drives away the darkness by riding in his chariot across the sky, and is sometimes visualized as a white horse or an eagle. Vayu is the wind god. The Ashvins are twin gods associated with war and fertility. Vishnu is mentioned infrequently in the Rig Vedic hymns. He is a benevolent god, and is in places associated with Indra. The *Rig Veda* mentions his three gigantic strides which encompassed the entire universe.

Very few Rig Vedic hymns are addressed to Rudra, a deity associated with great destructive potential. These refer to several attributes similar to those associated with Shiva of the later-day Puranas. Rudra is a god who inspires fear. The Maruts are Rudra's sons who drive across the sky in horse-drawn chariots, creating rain and storms.

Ushas, goddess of the dawn, is mentioned 300 times in the *Rig Veda*, and 20 hymns are addressed to her. Representing the victory of light over darkness, she is generous and is invoked by those desiring wealth. Aditi, mother of the Adityas, is another important goddess. Her name means freedom, and she is invoked to bestow freedom from sickness, harm, and evil. Some hymns speak of her as a mother and connect her with the earth and the cow. Raka is a benevolent, bountiful goddess. Sinivali bestows children. Prithvi (Earth) is a minor goddess, most often invoked together with Dyaus. Vach (speech), Ida (literally, 'the milk and butter offered in the sacrifice'), and Sarasvati (representing the river of this name) are some of the other goddesses mentioned in the *Rig Veda*. However, except for Ushas, goddesses have a relatively insignificant presence in the text.

The hymns of the *Rig Veda* contain fleeting allusions to myths involving gods, humans, and semi-divine beings. Many of these myths are elaborated on in later texts. For instance, *Rig Veda* 10.95 is a dialogue hymn consisting of a conversation between king Pururavas and the water nymph, Urvashi. Pururavas implores Urvashi to come back to live with him: 'My wife, turn your heart and mind to me.' Urvashi refuses: '… What use to me are these words of yours? I have left you, like the first of the dawns. Go home again, Pururavas. I am hard to catch and hold, like the wind.' The details of the Urvashi–Pururavas myth are given in later texts. Such dialogue hymns may have been part of ritual performances.

The Rig Vedic concept of *rita* corresponds to the ancient Iranian concept of *asha*. This is the principle that governs the closely-related orders of nature, the gods, humans, and sacrifice (*yajna*). It refers to the order of the universe, the order of the sacrifice, and the moral order that human beings should adhere to. Some hymns refer to Varuna and Mitra as the guardians or furtherers of *rita*. In the later Book 10, there is a dialogue hymn in which Yami appeals to her brother Yama (in later mythology, the first son of the sun, the first mortal man, and king of the dead) to commit incest with her in order to procreate. Yama rejects her overtures, stating that to do so would be contrary to *rita* and to the ordinances of Mitra and Varuna. The word *dharma* occurs in the *Rig Veda*, but is less important than *rita*. Derived from the root *dhri* (to support or maintain), it is associated with foundation of the world and all beings. This foundation is created by and for the sacrificial rituals and is associated with certain gods and with royal authority.

As far as funerary practices are concerned, the *Rig Veda* refers to both cremation and burial. The ideas of a vital force (*asu*) or spirit (*manas*) that survive death occur in the text. There are references to a heavenly paradise as well as a terrible hell. These issues are discussed in greater detail in later Vedic texts.

The historical milieu of later Vedic texts

ASPECTS OF EVERYDAY LIFE

Compared to the *Rig Veda Samhita*, later Vedic texts reveal greater complexity in political organization, social life, and economic activities. Agriculture increased in importance. Cereals such as barley (*yava*), wheat (*godhuma*), and rice (*vrihi*) are mentioned, and there are several references to agricultural operations such as sowing, ploughing, reaping, and threshing. The *Atharva Veda* has charms to ward off pests and to avert drought, reflecting the anxieties that farmers must have had. Land was occupied by extended families, and the clan seems to have exercised general rights over land. The institution of private property in land had not yet emerged. The household was the basic unit of labour. Slaves were not used for productive purposes to any significant degree, and there are no words for hired labour.

Hymns in praise of gifts (*dana-stutis*) in the later books of the *Rig Veda* refer to generous presents of cows, horses, chariots, gold, clothes, and female slaves made by kings to priests. This indicates the items valued in society, the concentration of wealth in the hands of rulers, and the relationship and exchanges between kings and priests. The earliest references to the gift of land occur in later Vedic texts, but the attitude towards this practice was still ambivalent. The *Aitareya Brahmana* suggests that the king should gift 1,000 pieces of gold, a field, and cattle to the Brahmana who anoints him. Yet the same text says that when king Vishvakarman Bhauvana wanted to make a gift of land as *dakshina* to his Brahmana priest Kashyapa, the earth goddess herself appeared before him and said that no mortal should give her away. A similar story occurs in the *Shatapatha Brahmana* in the context of the performance of the *sarvamedha* sacrifice.

The earliest clear textual references to iron in the Indian subcontinent are found in later Vedic texts (Chakrabarti, 1992). The terms *krishna-ayas*, *shyama*, and *shyama-ayas* (the black or dark metal) in the *Yajur Veda* and *Atharva Veda* clearly refer to this metal. There are indications of the use of iron in agriculture. The *Taittiriya Samhita* (5.2.5) of the Black *Yajur Veda* mentions ploughs driven by 6 or even 12 oxen. These must have been heavy and may have been made of iron. The *Atharva Veda* (10.6.2–3) mentions an amulet born of a ploughshare, smitten away with a knife by a skilful smith. The reference to the smith and the fact that iron is definitely known in the *Atharva Veda* suggest that the ploughshare in question was made of iron. In the context of implements used in the *ashvamedha* sacrifice, the *Shatapatha Brahmana* (13–2.2.16–19) connects iron with the peasantry. Elsewhere, the same text (13–3.4.5) connects this metal with the subjects or people (*praja*).

Early Buddhist texts belonging to *c*. 600–200 BCE contain several references to iron. The *Suttanipata* refers to many objects (a goad, stake, ball, and hammer) made of *ayas*. Especially important is a simile that mentions a ploughshare that has got hot during the day, and which 'splashes, hisses, and smokes in volumes' when thrown into water. This seems to be a reference to the process of quenching iron objects. The term *ayovikara kushi* in Panini's *Ashtadhyayi* has been translated as 'iron ploughshare'. All these references suggest that between *c*. 1000 BCE and 500 BCE, the use of iron in agriculture became prevalent in the Indo-Gangetic divide and the upper and middle Ganga valley.

Later Vedic texts mention various kinds of artisans, such as carpenters, chariot makers, bow-and-arrow makers, metal workers, leather workers, tanners, and potters. The *Vajasaneyi Samhita* and *Taittiriya Brahmana* mention occupations including the following: doorkeeper, charioteer, attendant, drummer, mat maker, smith, ploughman, astrologer, herdsman, maker of bowstrings, carpenter, wood-gatherer, basket maker, jeweller, vintner, elephant keeper, and goldsmith. Vocations mentioned in other later Vedic texts include those of the physician, washerman, hunter, fowler, ferryman, servant, barber, cook, boatman, and messenger. Wagons drawn by oxen were probably the most frequent mode of transport. Chariots (*rathas*) were used for war and sport, and there is mention of riding on horses and elephants. Boats are mentioned, but it is not clear whether they were for riverine or sea travel. There is still no clear reference to coinage. The general milieu as can be gathered from the texts is a rural one, although towards the end of the period, there are traces of the beginnings of urbanism—the *Taittiriya Aranyaka* uses the word *nagara* in the sense of a town.

Although only philosophical and religious texts of the time have survived, these allude to other branches of learning. The *Chandogya Upanishad* (7.1.2) gives a list of subjects of study including the Veda, *itihasa*, *purana*, grammar, astronomy, military science, and knowledge of portents (*daiva*). Later Vedic texts only indicate how sacred knowledge was imparted. Great importance was attached to the relationship between teacher and pupil and to oral instruction. The *Shatapatha Brahmana* refers to the *upanayana* ceremony, which initiated the young boy into *brahmacharya*—the stage of celibate studenthood. Education—of whatever kind—seems to have been largely restricted to elite males.

The leisure pastimes mentioned in later Vedic texts are similar to those referred to in the family books of the *Rig Veda*. Chariot racing and dicing were popular, as were music and dancing. Lute players, flute players, conch blowers, and drummers are mentioned. So are musical instruments such as the cymbals, drums, flutes, lutes, and a harp or lyre with 100 strings. The *Yajur Veda* mentions a *vansha-nartin* which could mean an acrobat.

As for the food people ate, *apupa* was a cake mixed with ghee, or made out of rice or barley. *Odana* was made by mixing grain variously with milk, water, curds, or ghee. *Karambha* was a porridge made of grain, barley or sesame. Rice was sometimes fried, or else cooked with milk and beans. *Yavagu* was a gruel made out of barley. Milk products such as curds, sour milk, and butter were consumed. Meat was eaten on special occasions, such as when honouring guests. There are references to an intoxicating beverage called *sura*.

Apart from cotton, clothes made of woollen thread (*urna-sutra*) are also mentioned often, and were probably made of sheep's wool or goat's hair. There is mention of turbans and leather sandals. Ornaments such as *nishka* were worn around the neck, and jewels or conch shells were worn as amulets to ward off evil.

THE EMERGENCE OF MONARCHY

Warfare is a striking aspect of the milieu of both early and later Vedic texts. Book 1 of the *Rig Veda Samhita* refers to a battle of 20 kings, involving 60,099 warriors (the numbers need not be taken literally). But the nature of political units was changing. The 6th century BCE political map of North India showed the existence of different kinds of political systems—monarchical states (*rajyas*), oligarchic states (*ganas* or *sanghas*), and tribal principalities. The roots of these developments lie in the period *c.* 1000–600 BCE. While some communities retained their tribal character, others were making the transition towards statehood. Larger political units were formed through the coalescing of tribes. The Purus and Bharatas came together to form the mighty Kurus, the Turvashas and Krivis formed the Panchalas, and the Kurus and Panchalas seem to have been allies or confederates.

Later Vedic texts reflect a transition from a tribal polity based on lineage to a territorial state. Some historians argue that this transition was not yet complete. Witzel (1995) argues that the Kurus represent the first state in India. He suggests that it was the Kurus under their king Parikshit (and their Brahmana priests) who initiated the collection and codification of the Vedic corpus into a canon. This included the re-arrangement of old and new poetic and ritual material, and was necessary to fulfil the needs of the newly developed *shrauta*, ritual presided over by various ritual specialists.

NEW DIRECTIONS IN RESEARCH | The invention of the war elephant

The elephant had an extremely important place in ancient Indian political and economic life, and it also features in religious thought and imagery. Asiatic elephants were once found from Mesopotamia to China to South India, Eastern India, Bangladesh, and Sri Lanka. In West Asia, the extinction of the elephant took place in about the first half of the 1st millennium BCE, probably due to the great demand for ivory. Thomas R. Trautmann has discussed the relationship between elephants and kings in South and Southeast Asia.

Why were elephants important? They were the mounts of kings, they were used to carry heavy materials, they led temple processions, and they provided ivory. But their most important function was in war. Elephants were not usually bred in captivity. The main reason is their high maintenance costs. They eat a lot (over 150 kg a day) and reach a working age at 15 years. So, it was more economical to capture adult elephants in the forests. Trade in elephants never really caught on. There were two main ways of acquiring them—capturing wild elephants and taking them as part of plunder or tribute. Elephants were captured and tamed, but they were not domesticated in the way in which cattle, horses, sheep, or goats were. Captured and trained elephants were neither fully domesticated nor wild.

Elephants were the backbone of ancient Indian armies. Trautmann argues that the war elephant was invented in India in *c*. 1000 BCE. What he means by the invention of the war elephant is the mastery of techniques of capturing wild male elephants and training them for use in war. He suggests that this happened in the late Vedic period and soon spread all over North India. This invention was connected with the establishment of kingship, the long tradition of domesticating large animals, and the use of elephants in contexts other than war.

Elephants were known to the Harappans. Harappan seals have many representations of this animal. There are also some terracottas and a few elephant bones, and ivory beads recovered from Harappan sites. However, there are no representations of humans riding elephants. The Harappans may have captured and displayed elephants, but there is no evidence that they trained and rode on them. The great gods and warriors of the *Rig Veda* ride in horse-drawn chariots. Armies included horse-riding warriors and those fighting on foot. The Rigvedic people knew the elephant but did not ride on them or use them in war.

The situation changed radically in later Vedic texts with the eastward movement of the Indo-Aryan people into lands where elephants were found in plenty in the forests. During the period 1000–500 BCE, the war elephant became increasingly important. The inclusion of the elephant in the army lead to the idea of the four-fold army (*chaturanga-bala*) consisting of foot soldiers, chariots, cavalry, and elephant corps. Elephants appear as gifts made by kings to poets and priests.

One of Trautmann's important observations is that once elephants were incorporated into armies, a certain logic unfolded: Indian kings needed elephants and needed the forests in which elephants lived. The forest was, therefore, considered an important part of the kingdom. The continued acquisition of elephants for use in armies depended on the continued availability of wild elephants in forests. So, it was in the interests of kings to preserve the forest habitat of elephants.

In later centuries, Indian armies were repeatedly defeated by cavalry-based armies. Did their reliance on elephants prove to be their undoing in the long run?

Source Trautmann, 2015

FURTHER DISCUSSION | The ceremony of the jewel offering

The *ratnahavimshi* (ceremony of the jewel offering) was a part of the *rajasuya* sacrifice. It involved the *rajan* going on successive days to the homes of certain people—the *ratnins* (literally, 'jewels')—and offering oblations to certain gods.

There is some variation in the names and order of the list of *ratnins* in different texts. They included the following:

1. the Brahmana or *purohita* (he usually heads the list)
2. the *rajanya* (nobles)
3. *mahishi* (chief queen)
4. *parvrikti* (the discarded queen; it is necessary to visit her to ward off evil)
5. *senani* (commander of the army)
6. *suta* (charioteer or bard)
7. *gramani* (village headman)
8. *kshattri* (royal chamberlain)
9. *sangrahitri* (charioteer, master of treasury, or collector of tribute?)
10. *bhagadugha* (literally, 'milker of shares', distributor of food or perhaps collector of the king's share of the produce)
11. *akshavapa* (literally, 'thrower of dice', a functionary connected with dicing or perhaps with the maintenance of accounts)
12. *govikartana* (chief huntsman)
13. *takshan* (carpenter)
14. *rathakara* (chariot maker)
15. *palagala* (courier)
16. *sthapati* (probably a judge or a local chief)

The *ratnahavimshi* ceremony indicates the status of the *ratnins* and the king's dependence on them. Some *ratnins* were related to the king through kinship, whereas others were functionaries with whom he had no kinship relations. This illustrates the transitional nature of the later Vedic polity—it was in between a polity based on kinship and one marked by an elaborate military and bureaucratic machinery.

Curiously, the Brahmana texts state that some of the *ratnins* were inferior both to the Brahmanas and to the Kshatriyas. So, immediately after the ceremony, the *rajan* was supposed to perform two rites to atone for the sin of associating these unworthy persons with the sacrifice.

Source R. S. Sharma, (1959) 1996: 143–58

As explained in Chapter 4, the transition to a state polity is always the culmination of a number of complex political, social, and economic processes. The emergence of a monarchical state would have involved multiple processes of conflict, accommodation, and alliances. Monarchy involves the concentration of political power in the hands of a king. The supremacy of the *rajan* was achieved by sidelining rival claimants to power, establishing coercive mechanisms, and control over productive resources. Apart from the monarchies, there were polities that maintained their tribal moorings and where political power was in the hands of assemblies, not kings.

The *rajan* of later Vedic texts is, like his Rig Vedic counterpart, a leader in battle. But he is also a protector of settlements and of people, especially Brahmanas. He is a custodian of the social order and sustainer of the *rashtra* (this term does not necessarily refer to a well-defined territory). Hereditary kingship was emerging. The *Shatapatha* and *Aitareya Brahmanas* refer to a kingdom of 10 generations (*dasha-purusham rajyam*). There are a few references (e.g., *Atharva Veda* 1.9; 3.4) to the election of the king, but these probably amounted to a ratification of hereditary succession. There is an interesting reference to the Srinjayas expelling their king Dushtaritu Paumsayana from the kingdom, in spite of his 10 generations of royal descent. This was probably an exception to the rule. Later Vedic rituals exalted the supremacy of the king, both over his kinsmen and over his people. Terms such as *samrajya* and *samrat* reflect the idea of empire, although empires had not yet appeared on the scene.

The emergence of monarchy was accompanied by speculations on the origins of the institution and attempts to provide a legitimizing ideology. Some of these speculations refer to the divine realm, others to the human sphere. The *Aitareya Brahmana* (1.1.14) states that on being defeated in battle by the demons, the gods realized that the reason for their defeat was that they had no king. So they elected a king, who led them to victory against the demons. Elsewhere in the same text (8.4.12), it is said that the gods, led by Prajapati, decided to install Indra as their king on the grounds that he was the most vigorous, strong, valiant, and perfect among them all, and the one who best carried out tasks that needed to be done.

Later Vedic texts emphasize the close connection between kings and gods. The *Shatapatha Brahmana* asserts that a king gains identity with Prajapati through the performance of the *vajapeya* and *rajasuya* sacrifices. As the visible representative of Prajapati, although one, he rules over many. Such statements should be understood as attempts to exalt the status of the king, not as a theory of the divinity of kings, nor as indicative of their worship.

The emergence of the *rajan* as wielder of supreme political power involved his distancing himself from those closest to him—his kinsmen. This distancing was emphasized in ritualized contests such as the chariot race in the *vajapeya* sacrifice, and the cattle raid and game of dicing in the *rajasuya* sacrifice. In earlier times, such contests may have decided who was worthy of becoming king, but now they were ritual enactments in which the outcome—the victory of the *rajan*—was already decided and known.

Another aspect of the *rajan*'s increasing power was his acquiring greater control over productive resources. *Bali*, which was initially a voluntary offering, probably consisting of agricultural produce and cattle, gradually became obligatory. The *Shatapatha Brahmana* (1.3.2.15) states that the Vaishya offers *bali* because he is under the *vasha* (control) of the Kshatriya, and has to give up what he has stored when he is told to do so. The *rajan* is referred to as *vishamatta*—eater of the *vish* (people), indicating that he lived off what the people produced. The *rajan*'s appropriation of *bali* from the people does not, however, quite amount to a clearly defined and organized system of taxation.

References to the *sabha* and *samiti* continue in later Vedic texts. But with the increase in royal power, the power of the assemblies must have correspondingly declined.

Later Vedic texts indicate a close relationship between the king and his *purohita* (his Brahmana priest and counsellor). *Purohita* literally means 'one who is put in front' (by the king). The relationship between king and *purohita* is likened to that between earth and heaven. The importance of the *purohita* is graphically illustrated in the *rajasuya* ceremony, where he introduces the king to the assembled people and announces: 'This man is your king. Soma is the king of us Brahmanas' (*Shatapatha Brahmana* 5.3.12, 4.2.3). The system of administration seems to have been fairly rudimentary.

Kumkum Roy (1994b) underlines the close connection between the emergence of the monarchical system, the *varna* hierarchy, the organization of kinship relations, and the structure of households. The grand *shrauta* sacrifices performed by the king legitimized the king's control over the productive and reproductive resources of his realm, while the domestic sacrifices performed by the *grihapati* (head of the household) legitimized his control over the productive and reproductive resources of his household. Brahmanical texts implicitly recognize the connections between the political and domestic spheres in their description of the *rajan* as a custodian of the social order.

THE *VARNA* HIERARCHY

Although kinship ties were still very important, later Vedic texts indicate the beginnings of a class structure in which social groups had different degrees of access to productive resources. *Varna* was partly an ideology that reflected the increasing social differentiation of the times. It was even more an ideology that justified this differentiation from the point of view of the elite groups. In dividing society into four hereditary strata, this ideology defined social boundaries, roles, status, and ritual purity. Members of the four *varnas* were supposed to have different innate characteristics, which made them naturally suited to certain occupations and social rank. The *varna* hierarchy was to remain an important part of the social discourse of the Brahmanical tradition for many centuries, and the duties and functions of the four *varnas* are elaborated on in the Dharmashastra texts of later times.

The *Purusha-sukta* (Purusha hymn) in Book 10 of the *Rig Veda Samhita* refers to four social groups—Brahmana, Rajanya (instead of Kshatriya), Vaishya, and Shudra, though the word *varna* is not mentioned. It describes the four groups, and a whole lot of other things as well, as originating from different parts of the body of a primeval giant named Purusha, in the course of a sacrifice supposed to have been held long, long ago, in which Purusha was the sacrificial offering. The body symbolism in the Purusha hymn indicates that the four *varnas* were visualized as inter-related parts of an organic whole. At the same time, it clearly indicates a *hierarchy* of ranks, with the Brahmana at the top and the Shudra at the bottom. The fact that the *varnas* are described as being created at the same time as the earth, sky, sun, and moon indicates that they were supposed to be considered a part of the natural, eternal, and unchangeable order of the world. In fact, as pointed out by Brian K. Smith (1994), the *varna* scheme was extended beyond society to the classification of other aspects of the world, the gods, and nature.

Initially, there seems to have been some ambiguity about the relative positions of the higher *varnas*. In the *Panchavimsha Brahmana* (13, 4, 17), where Indra is associated with the creation of the *varnas*, the Rajanya are placed first, followed by the Brahmana and Vaishya. The *Shatapatha Brahmana* (13.8.3.11) also places the Kshatriya first in the list. Elsewhere, in the same text (*Shatapatha Brahmana* 1.1.4.12) the order is as follows: Brahmana, Vaishya, Rajanya, and Shudra. However, the order of the four *varnas* in the Brahmanical tradition became fixed from the time of the Dharmasutras onwards.

The relationship between the Brahmana and Kshatriya *varnas* was close but complex. Later Vedic texts emphasize the importance of the *purohita* for the king, and the close relationship between the Rajanya and at least a section of the Brahmana community. On the other hand, the texts also emphasize differences between the three *varnas*. The *Aitareya Brahmana* (8.36.4) states that the *rajasuya* sacrifice endowed each of the four *varnas* with certain qualities—the Brahmana with *tejas* or lustre, the Kshatriya with *virya* or valour, the Vaishya with *prajati* or procreative powers, and the Shudra with *pratishtha* or stability. The conflict between the gods Mitra and Varuna has been seen as symbolic of a conflict between the first two *varnas*. Mitra represented the principle of *brahma* (sacred power) and Varuna the principle of *kshatra* (secular power). There are several statements about the relationship between ***brahma*** and *kshatra*, describing them variously as antagonistic, complementary, or dependent on each other. Upanishadic philosophy has also been viewed as a reflection of the Kshatriya challenge to Brahmanical supremacy in the field of ultimate knowledge. However, it should be remembered that the Upanishads were recognized as part of the Vedic corpus.

The Brahmanas had an exalted status in the *varna* hierarchy, associated as they were with the performance of sacrifices and with knowledge, specifically the study and teaching of the Vedas. The *Shatapatha Brahmana* (11.5.7.1) associates the Brahmana with four special attributes: purity of parentage, good conduct, glory, and teaching or protecting people. He is also associated with receiving four privileges from the people—honour, gifts, freedom from being harassed, and freedom from being beaten. The Kshatriyas or Rajanya were connected with strength, fame, ruling, and warfare. The Vaishyas were associated with material prosperity, animals, food, and production-related activities such as cattle rearing and agriculture. In the *soma* sacrifice, prayers were offered for the protection of the *brahma*, *kshatra*, and *vish*. The goals varied, depending on the *varna* to which the *yajamana* belonged. For the Brahmana, the goal was priestly lustre (*brahma-varchas*), for the Rajanya it was prowess (*indriya*), and for the Vaishya, it was animals and food (*pashu* and *anna*).

The position of the Shudra at the bottom of the *varna* ladder was fixed from the very beginning. He was associated with serving the higher *varnas* and performing menial tasks. He could not perform Vedic sacrifices. A *dikshita* (one who had undergone initiation for a Vedic sacrifice) was not supposed to speak to a Shudra. According to *Aitareya Brahmana* 35.3, the Shudra is at the beck and call of others, can be made to rise at will, and can be beaten at will (*yatha-kama-vadhya*).

There were groups in society who were considered even lower than the Shudras. Slaves (*dasas* and *dasis*) are mentioned among gift items in the *dana-stutis*. However, on occasion, children born of slave women could aspire to high status. For instance, in Book 1 of the *Rig Veda*, there is a reference to Kakshivan, son of the sage Dirghatamas

PRIMARY SOURCES | The *Purusha-sukta* (*Rig Veda* 10.90)

The Man has a thousand heads, a
thousand eyes, and a thousand feet.
Having covered the earth on all
sides, he extended ten fingers'
breadth beyond.

The Man alone is this whole
(world): what has come into being
and what is to be.
Moreover, he is master of
immortality when he climbs
beyond (this world) through food.

So much is his greatness, but the
Man is more than this:
a quarter of him is all living
beings; three quarters are the
immortal in heaven.

With his three quarters the Man
went upward, but a quarter of him
came to be here again.
From there he strode out in
different directions toward what
eats and what does not eat.

From him the Viraj was born; from
the Viraj the Man.
Upon his birth, he reached beyond
the earth from behind and also
from in front.

When, with the Man as the
offering, the gods extended the
sacrifice, spring was its melted
butter, summer its firewood,
autumn its offering.

On the ritual grass they
consecrated that sacrifice, the Man,
born at the beginning.
With him the gods sacrificed, (also)
the Sadhyas and those who were seers.

From that sacrifice, when it was
offered in full, the clotted-butter
mixture was collected.
It [=the sacrifice] was made into
the animals: those of the air (and
both) those that belong to the
wilderness and those that belong
to the village.

From this sacrifice, when it was
offered in full, the verses and
chants were born.
Metres were born from it. The sacrificial
formula—from it that was born.

From it horses were born and
whatever animals have teeth in
both jaws.
Cows were born from it. From it
were born goats and sheep.

When they apportioned the Man, into
how many parts did they arrange him?
What was his mouth? What his two
arms? What are said to be his two
thighs, his two feet?

The Brahmana was his mouth. The
ruler [Rajanya, i.e., Kshatriya] was
made his two arms.
As to his thighs—that is what the
freeman [Vaishya] was. From his
two feet the servant [Shudra] was born.

The moon was born from his mind.
From his eye the sun was born.
From his mouth Indra and Agni,
from his breath Vayu was born.

From his navel was the midspace.
From his head the heaven developed.
From his two feet the earth, and the
directions from his ear. Thus they
arranged the worlds.

Its enclosing sticks were seven; the
kindling sticks were made three
times seven,
when the gods, extending the
sacrifice, bound the Man as the
(sacrificial) animal.

With the sacrifice the gods
performed the sacrifice for
themselves: these were the first
foundations.
These, its greatness, accompanied
(it) to heaven's vault, where the
ancient Sadhyas and the gods are.

Source Jamison and Brereton, 2014: 1539–40

by a woman slave of the queen of Anga. Kavasha Ailusha, author of a Vedic hymn in Book 10, is also described as the son of a woman slave. These were probably exceptional instances.

Although there are no clear indications of the practice of untouchability in later Vedic texts, groups such as the Chandalas were clearly looked on with contempt by the elites. The *Chhandogya Upanishad* and *Taittiriya* and *Shatapatha Brahmanas* mention the Chandala in a list of victims to be offered in the presumably symbolic *purushamedha* (human sacrifice), and describe him as dedicated to the deity Vayu (wind). The dedication to Vayu has been interpreted as indicating that the Chandala lived in the open air or near a cemetery, but this is far from certain. The *Chhandogya Upanishad* (5.10.7) states that those who perform praiseworthy deeds in this world swiftly acquire rebirth in a good condition—as a Brahmana, Kshatriya, or Vaishya, while those who perform low actions acquire birth in a correspondingly low condition—as a dog, boar or Chandala.

The *Shatapatha Brahmana* (1.4.1.10) gives the story of a king named Videgha Mathava who originally lived on the banks of the Sarasvati and crossed the Sadanira (Gandak) river with his priest Gotama Raghugana, preceded by Agni Vaishvanara. Historians have often interpreted this story as reflecting the eastward movement of the Indo-Aryans and the first agricultural 'colonization' of the eastern lands through burning down the forests. On the other hand, giving an early Videhan king a respectable north-western origin may have been a way of legitimizing his power, and the reference to Agni may allude to the extension of Brahmanical sacrificial ritual to these areas.

Later Vedic texts reflect processes of social interaction, conflict, and assimilation. According to the *Aitareya Brahmana* (33.6), when Vishvamitra's 50 sons did not accept Shunahashepa (Devarata) as his son, the sage cursed them to become the Andhras, Pundras, Shabaras, Pulindas, and Mutibas. This story reflects the attempt of the Brahmanical tradition to extend some amount of recognition to 'outsiders'. Some non-Indo-Aryan groups were assimilated into the *varna* hierarchy, usually at the lower rungs. In fact, the Shudras may have been a non-Indo-Aryan tribe living in the north-west, who later lent their name to the fourth *varna* (R. S. Sharma, [1958] 1980: 34–35). However, not all tribal groups were assimilated. Some were simply acknowledged. Later Vedic texts mention forest people such as the Kiratas and Nishadas. They also show the emergence of the concept of *mlechchha*, a category that included various tribal groups and foreign people considered to be 'outsiders' in the Brahmanical tradition (see Parasher, 1991).

While later Vedic texts suggest that society in the upper Ganga valley was becoming increasingly stratified, there was still a certain amount of fluidity in occupations. This is suggested in *Rig Veda* 9.112.3, where the poet says: 'I am a reciter of hymns, my father is a physician, and my mother grinds (corn) with stones. We desire to obtain wealth in various actions.'

GENDER AND THE HOUSEHOLD

The household was an important institution, not only for its members, but also for the larger social and political units of which it was a part. A series of household rituals legitimized the householder's control over the productive and reproductive resources of the household (Roy, 1994b). In later Vedic texts, the variety of household forms of earlier times made way for an idealized *griha* unit headed by the *grihapati*. Only a married man, accompanied by his legitimate wife, could become the *yajamana* in a sacrifice. Marriage (*vivaha*) was important for the continuation of the patrilineage. Relations between husband and wife (*pati* and *patni*) and father and son were hierarchically organized. Women came to be increasingly identified in terms of their relations with men. Words such as *stri*, *yosha*, and *jaya* were closely associated with wifehood and motherhood, actual or potential. The *grihapati* had control over the productive resources of the household unit and the reproductive potential of his wife. This control was maintained by a domestic ideology that clearly laid down the structures of dominance and subordination within the family. The productive resources of the household were transferred from father to son, and rituals such as the *agnyadheya* emphasized the importance of ties with the patrilineal ancestors (*pitris*).

Gender relations were embodied in ideas and rituals related to marriage (for details, see Kane, [1941b] 1974; Roy, 1994b; Leslie, [1991] 2015). Later Vedic texts refer to marriage by capture, and to a woman choosing her spouse. Polygyny was more prevalent than polyandry. Kings could have many wives and concubines. The *Aitareya Brahmana* (3.5.3.47) states that even though a man may have several wives, one husband is enough for one woman. A woman was considered married not only to a man but into his family. There are references in a later Rig Vedic hymn and in the *Atharva Veda* to the practice of a widow marrying her younger brother-in-law.

The later Vedic ideas and ceremonies of marriage are reflected in a complex hymn in the tenth Mandala, often referred to as the *Surya-sukta* (Surya hymn) (*Rig Veda* 10.85). This hymn suggests that the bride was simultaneously considered a precious asset and a stranger with destructive potential. The marriage ceremonies seem to have been largely confined to the bride, groom, and their immediate families. In the marriage hymn in the *Atharva Veda* (14.1–2), the priest is assigned a more prominent role in neutralizing the dangerous potential of the bride and in ensuring her incorporation into her new home.

Women are praised and exalted in some places in later Vedic texts. For instance, the *Shatapatha Brahmana* (5.2.1.10) states that the wife is half her husband and completes him. The *Brihadaranyaka Upanishad* (6.4.17) mentions a ritual for obtaining a learned daughter. On the other hand, women were generally excluded from the study of the Vedas. Although their presence as wives was required in the *shrauta* sacrifices, they could not perform such sacrifices independently in their own right. Later texts even introduce the possibility of an effigy of gold or grass in place of the wife. Most of the *samskaras* (except, of course, marriage) did not apply to them.

Later Vedic texts reflect the idea that the menstrual blood of women is dangerous and polluting (Smith, 1991). A menstruating wife is not supposed to participate in sacrifices. The sacrifice has to be postponed or it has to be performed without her. The *Taittiriya Samhita* reflects other taboos as well—it was inappropriate to talk to, sit near, or eat food cooked by a menstruating woman. According to this text, when Indra killed Vishvarupa, son of the god Tvashtri, he transferred one-third of the stain of killing a Brahmana to women. This 'stain' is said to have taken the form of women's menstrual periods (*Taittiriya Samhita* 2.5.1).

Women were expected to conform to a docile role. *Shatapatha Brahmana* (10.5.2.9) states: 'A good woman is one who pleases her husband, delivers male children, and never talks back to her husband.' The desire for sons is borne out in many hymns. The *Aitareya Brahmana* (7.15) describes a daughter as a source of misery, and states that only a son can be the saviour of the family. A gestation rite called the *pumsavana* was prescribed to ensure the birth of a male child. The *Atharva Veda* contains charms for changing a female foetus into a male one. The *Maitrayani Samhita* (4.7.4) says: 'Men go to the assembly, not women.' Women appear as gifts and commodities of exchange, for instance in the references to *rajas* gifting their daughters to win over sages. The only form of ritual gift giving or exchange that women could be part of was giving the first alms to the *brahmachari*, who was supposed to begin his stint by begging from his mother or his teacher's wife. The increasing social differentiation and emergence of a state was accompanied by an increasing subordination of women.

References to women's work in later Vedic texts include tending cattle, milking cows, and fetching water. There are also the *vayitri* and *siri* (female weaver), *peshaskari* (female embroiderer), *bidalakari* (female splitter of bamboo), *rajayitri* (female dyer), and *upalaprakshini* (woman corn grinder). The *Shatapatha Brahmana* mentions women carding wool. Apala is described in the *Rig Veda* as having taken care of her father's fields. Vishpala was a woman warrior who lost a leg in battle, and there are references to other women warriors such as Mudgalini and Vadhrimati. A few women—Gargi and Maitreyi—participated in philosophical debate with Upanishadic sages.

RELIGION, RITUAL, AND PHILOSOPHY

Later Vedic texts contain a variety of ideas on creation. The *Purusha-sukta* describes creation as the result of a primordial sacrifice, while other hymns describe creation as emanating from the sun or from Hiranyagarbha (the golden embryo). A hymn to the god Vishvakarman (10.81) imagines the creator god as an artisan—as a sculptor, smith, woodcutter, or carpenter—and as the first sacrificer and the sacrificial offering. A hymn in Book 10 of the *Rig Veda Samhita*, often referred to as the Nasadiya, has one of the most abstract and profound explorations of the mysteries of creation.

In later Vedic texts, the concept of *rita* receded into the background. The frequency of the word *dharma* decreased and its connotations shrank. It came to be especially connected with kingship and with the royal consecration ritual known as the *rajasuya* (Olivelle, 2004).

PRIMARY SOURCES | **Creation (*Rig Veda* 10.129)**

The nonexistent did not exist, nor did
the existent exist at that time.
There existed neither the airy space
nor heaven beyond.
What moved back and forth? From
where and in whose protection? Did
water exist, a deep depth?

Death did not exist nor deathlessness
then. There existed no sign of night
nor of day.
That One breathed without wind by
its independent will.
There existed
nothing else beyond that.

Darkness existed, hidden by darkness,
in the beginning. All this was a
signless ocean.

What existed as a thing coming into
being, concealed by emptiness—that
One was born by the power of heat.

Then, in the beginning, from thought
there evolved desire, which existed
as the primal semen.
Searching in their hearts through in-
spired thought, poets found the
connection of the existent in the
nonexistent.

Their cord was stretched across: Did
something exist below it? Did
something exist above?
There existed placers of semen and
there existed greatnesses. There was
independent will below, offering
above.

Who really knows? Who shall here
proclaim it?—from where was it born,
from where this creation?
The gods are on this side of the
creation of this (world). So then who
does know from where it came to be?

This creation—from where it came to
be, if it was produced or if not—
he who is the overseer of this (world)
in the furthest heaven, he surely
knows. Or if he does not know...?

Source Jamison and Brereton, 2014:
1608–09

In the family books of the *Rig Veda*, certain gods were brought together by invoking them in the same sacrificial rituals. In the later parts of the text, some hymns emphasized the connections among them. There are 40 hymns in the *Rig Veda* addressed to Vishvadevas—all the gods. Some hymns speak of the various gods as manifestations of the same divine being. Thus, *Rig Veda* 1.164 points out the differences in the names Agni, Indra, and Vayu, and goes on to assert that there is one being, whom the poets speak of as many (*ekam sad vipra bahudha vadanti*).

The sacrificial ritual of the Brahmana texts

The Brahmana texts reflect a situation where sacrifices had become longer, more elaborate, and expensive. The sacrifice is presented as the act that created the world, and the correct performance of sacrifice was seen as necessary to regulate life and the world. While some sacrifices involved the participation of just one priest, others involved many more, and the ritual specialists were extremely important. The god Prajapati, who is associated with creation and the sacrifice, is the most important deity in the Brahmanas. Later Vedic texts frequently refer to the conflict between *devas* and *asuras*; the latter, by this time were considered demons.

The ritual of *agnyadheya* (establishment of the fires) was essential for a householder to perform the *shrauta* sacrifices. After performing this ritual, he became *ahitagni* (one who has established fires). The *agnihotra* was a simple domestic sacrifice, to be performed daily by the head of a *dvija* household, morning and evening. It involved the pouring of oblations of milk, and sometimes vegetal substances, into the fire, to the god Agni. There were also the periodic new-moon and full-moon sacrifices, and those performed at the beginning of the three seasons. There were even grander, longer, more elaborate ones which involved the participation of many different ritual specialists along with their assistants, which must have been performed by wealthy people and kings. The *yajamana* underwent a *diksha* (consecration) before the sacrifice, and had to follow a number of rules until its completion. The *dakshina* was an important part

FURTHER DISCUSSION | **The sacrificial arena**

The elaborate *shrauta* (Vedic) sacrifices involved the use of three fires—the *garhapatya* (householder's fire), *ahavaniya* (offeratorial fire), and *dakshinagni* (southern fire). These fires were supposed to be placed in pits of different shapes. The pit for the *garhapatya* was supposed to be round, that of the *ahavaniya* square, and that of the *dakshinagni* crescent shaped.

The position of the fires—and everything else—was fixed. The *garhapatya* was located in the west, the *dakshinagni* in the south, and the ahavaniya to the east. The *garhapatya* was lit first of all, and the other two fires were then lit from its coals. The *vedi* was a rectangular area with concave sides, situated between the *garhapatya* and *ahavaniya* fires. It was covered with sacred grass, and the equipment required for the sacrifice was placed here.

The positions of the priests such as the Hotri (the priest of the *Rig Veda*, responsible for recitation), the Adhvaryu (the priest of the *Yajur Veda*, responsible for the various ritual actions), the Udgatri (priest of the *Sama Veda*, responsible for the singing), and the Brahmana were specified. The *yajamana* and his wife also had their assigned places.

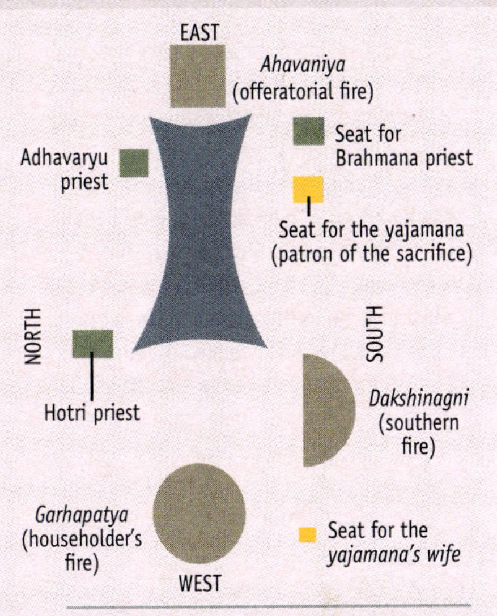

Figure 5.1 Diagram of sacrificial arena

of the sacrifice, and as the sacrifices became longer and more complicated, it became larger and larger.

A number of complex sacrificial rituals were associated with kingship. The *vajapeya* sacrifice was connected with the attainment of power and prosperity, and also contained a number of fertility rites. It included a ritual chariot race in which the *rajan* raced against his kinsmen and defeated them. The *ashvamedha* was a sacrifice associated with claims to political paramountcy and incorporated several fertility rites as well. The *rajasuya* was the royal consecration ceremony. Apart from a number of agrarian fertility rites, it included a ritual cattle raid, in which the *rajan* raided the cattle of his kinsmen, and also a game of dice, which the king won. At a larger, symbolic level, in the *rajasuya*, the king was presented as standing in the centre of the cyclical processes of the regeneration of the universe (Heesterman, 1957).

The Upanishads

The word 'Upanishad' (literally, 'to sit near someone') is usually understood as referring to pupils sitting near or around their teacher. Alternatively, it could mean connection or equivalence; the Upanishads were constantly suggesting connections and equivalences between things. The knowledge that was to be imparted and absorbed was no ordinary knowledge. It was all-encompassing, the key to liberation from the cycle of birth, death, and rebirth, something that could only be taught to select, deserving pupils. It was difficult to explain and even more difficult to comprehend. It was revealed through dialogue, discussion, debate, and contest among seekers, using a variety of devices—stories, images, analogies, and paradoxes.

The oldest Upanishads are in prose, the later ones in verse. The *Brihadaranyaka* and *Chhandogya* are among the earliest. The Upanishads and Aranyakas deal with similar things, and the distinction between the two categories of texts is not always clear. For instance, the *Brihadaranyaka Upanishad* is considered both an Aranyaka and Upanishad. While the early Upanishads belong to the period *c.* 1000–500 BCE, many others are of a later period.

PRIMARY SOURCES | **The *atman*, according to Uddalaka Aruni**

The *Chhandogya Upanishad* tells the following story: One day, Uddalaka Aruni told his son Shvetaketu to go forth and take up the celibate life of a student, as their family was Brahmana only in name and none had so far devoted themselves to study. So Shvetaketu went off to become a student when he was 12 years old. He learnt all the Vedas and came back swollen headed when he was 24, thinking that he knew everything. His father Uddalaka Aruni saw this. He instructed Shvetaketu on a number of issues about which the son knew nothing, and soon made him realize just how little he knew. In the following conversation between father and son in the *Chhandogya Upanishad* (6.13.3), Uddalaka uses graphic analogy to explain the nature of the *atman* to Shvetaketu. The first speaker is Uddalaka, and the father and son speak alternately:

'Bring a banyan fruit.'
'Here it is, sir.'
'Cut it up.'
'I've cut it up, sir.'
'What do you see there?'
'These quite tiny seeds, sir.'
'Now, take one of them and cut it up.'
'I've cut one up, sir.'
'What do you see there?'
'Nothing, sir.'

Then he told him:

'This is the finest essence here, son, that you can't even see—look, on account of that finest essence, this huge banyan tree stands here. Believe, my son: the finest essence here—that constitutes the self of this whole world; that is the truth; that is the self (*atman*). And that's how you are, Shvetaketu.'

Source Olivelle, 1998: 255

Considering the fact that the Upanishads were the work of many different people living in various parts of North India over many centuries, it is not surprising that they do not contain a single, cohesive, uniform system of ideas. They deal with many issues, but are especially concerned with the two fundamental concepts of *atman* and *brahman* (not to be confused with the god Brahma). A major concern of Upanishadic thought is to explore and explain their meaning and mutual relationship.

The word *brahman* comes from the root *brih*, which means to be strong or firm. It means something that grants prosperity, a vital force that strengthens and animates. In the Upanishads, there are many efforts to describe *brahman*. The *Kena Upanishad* (2.1) asserts that the gods themselves were unable to understand *brahman*, and even those who think they have understood it do not. The *Taittiriya Upanishad* (3.1.1) states that *brahman* is that from which all beings are born, that by which they are sustained, and that into which they enter on death. *Brahman* is the eternal, imperishable reality in the universe. In the *Brihadaranyaka Upanishad* (3.8.11), the sage Yajnavalkya tells Gargi that the imperishable *brahman* sees but can't be seen, thinks but can't be thought of, perceives but can't be perceived. Besides *brahman*, there is no one that sees, hears, thinks, or perceives. The *Mundaka Upanishad* (1.1.7) explains that just as a spider spins and gathers its web, just as plants grow upon this earth, and just as head and body hair grow from a living person, even so does everything in this world arise from the imperishable *brahman*. Later Upanishads speak of *brahman* as of a god.

If *brahman* is the ultimate reality pervading the universe, the *atman* is the ultimate reality within the self of an individual, i.e., the imperishable essential self. There are many explanations of the *atman* in the Upanishads. The *Brihadaranyaka Upanishad* (3.7.23) describes it as the immortal inner controller, who sees but can't be seen, hears but can't be heard, thinks but can't be thought of, perceives but can't be perceived. Besides the *atman*, there is none who sees, hears, thinks, or perceives. In the *Chhandogya Upanishad* (3.14.2–3), the *atman* is described as lying deep within the heart, smaller than a grain of rice, barley, or mustard seed, smaller even than a millet grain or millet kernel. Paradoxically, it is also described as larger than the earth, the intermediate region, and the sky, larger than even all the worlds put together.

The word *maya* occurs in the *Shvetashvatara Upanishad*. Scholars disagree on whether the idea or something similar is present in earlier Upanishads as well. *Maya*, often translated as 'illusion', can be interpreted in other, different ways. It can mean ignorance (*avidya*), the inability to realize oneness with *brahman*, or the creative power of *ishvara* (god) from the human point of view.

The idea of a cycle of birth and death is present in the Brahmanas and Upanishads. The *Shatapatha Brahmana* states that those who do not perform the sacrificial rites correctly will be born again and suffer death again. It also talks of a world where material pleasures are enjoyed by those who perform the sacrifices, and of a hell where evil-doers are punished. The same text refers to the dead as having to face two fires—good people pass through the flames, while evil-doers perish. A person is born again after death and is punished or rewarded for his/her deeds. Some of the Upanishads explain the doctrine of transmigration. Death and rebirth are connected with ignorance and desire, and deliverance can be attained through knowledge. The Upanishads refer to three worlds—the worlds of humans, ancestors (*pitris*), and gods. Those who will be reborn go after death to the world of the fathers, while those who are destined for immortality go to the world of the gods. According to Johannes Bronkhorst (2007), the doctrines of rebirth and karmic retribution were features of the culture of Greater Magadha (Magadha and surrounding areas) that were eventually incorporated into the Brahmanical tradition.

The goal of Upanishadic thought is the realization of *brahman*. Liberation (*moksha, mukti*) from the cycle of *samsara* could only be achieved through such knowledge. This knowledge (*jnana*) could not be obtained through mere intellectual exertion. This was knowledge of an inner, intuitive, experiential kind, that could only come upon the seeker as a sort of revelation that would transform him instantaneously. Later Upanishads such as the *Shvetashvatara* point towards yogic meditation as a means of realizing *brahman*. Performing of sacrifices and following an ethical code of conduct were of no use towards this end. In the *Chhandogya Upanishad* (3.8.11), Yajnavalkya tells Gargi that even if a man were to make offerings, perform sacrifices, and indulge in austerities for thousands of years, it wouldn't amount to anything. The same text (2.23.1) states that people who performed sacrifices, recited the Veda, and gave gifts (*dana*), those who devoted themselves to the performance of austerities (*tapa*), and those who led a celibate life of studenthood in their teacher's house studying the Veda—all these people gain worlds earned by merit. A person steadfast in the knowledge of *brahman*, on the other hand, attains immortality.

In later times, there were many different interpretations of Upanishadic thought, which came to be known as Vedanta (literally, 'end of the Veda'; also known as Uttara Mimamsa). Upanishadic thought reflects different ideas about *atman*, *brahman*, and the world, and statements such as *tat tvam asi* (you are that), *aham Brahm-asmi* (I am *brahman*), and *brahma-atma-aikyam* (unity of *brahman* and *atman*) can be interpreted in different ways. The *Bhagavad Gita* combined certain aspects of Upanishadic philosophy with an emphasis on *varna-dharma*. One of the most influential interpretations of the Upanishads was that of the late 8th/early 9th century thinker Shankara. According to Shankara's monistic Advaita Vedanta (non-dualist Vedanta), the Upanishads tell us that there is only one single, unified reality—*brahman*—and everything else is not fully real. However, there is also a pantheistic strand in Upanishadic thought which identifies the universe with *brahman*. There is also a theistic strand of thought, which visualizes *brahman* as a god who controls the world. Given the diversity and complexity of Upanishadic ideas, it is not surprising that later thinkers interpreted them in very different ways.

The Upanishads are often seen as anti-sacrifice and anti-Brahmana. The *Brihadaranyaka Upanishad* states that the performance of sacrifice leads to the world of the fathers (*pitriyana*), but knowledge leads to the world of the gods. Upanishadic knowledge is in several places associated with kings or Kshatriyas. There are references to Brahmanas being instructed in the knowledge of *brahman* by kings such as Ajatashatru, Ashvapati, and Pravahana. In the *Chhandogya Upanishad* (1.8–9), Pravahana tells Uddalaka Aruni that this knowledge has never till the present been in the possession of a Brahmana. In the *Brihadaranyaka Upanishad* (3–4), Yajnavalkya's ideas are contradicted by Brahmanas, but are received with enthusiasm by king Janaka.

However, the fact that the Upanishads were included in the Vedic corpus as part of *shruti* should caution us against stretching this argument too far. For one thing, there are connections between the ideas of the Upanishads and early Vedic texts. Furthermore, the Upanishads do not reject sacrifice; rather, they employ the vocabulary of sacrifice to new ends. Ritual is re-described symbolically and allegorically. The link between humans and the cosmos is not the ritual itself but knowledge of the forces symbolically represented in the ritual. Knowledge of this symbolic meaning becomes more important than the performance of the ritual. An example of this is the re-description of the *ashvamedha yajna* in the *Brihadaranyaka Upanishad*. In this re-description, the various parts of the horse's body are identified with different parts of the cosmos—his head is dawn, his eye is the sun, his breath is the wind, and his mouth is fire. The horse and the horse sacrifice take on new, symbolic meaning. Nevertheless, although ritual was not rejected, the emphasis was on the attainment of a new kind of knowledge.

POPULAR BELIEFS AND PRACTICES

The Brahmanas were manuals for sacrificial priests, and the Upanishads reflect an esoteric quest for a special kind of self-knowledge. Although some of the ideas in these texts may have had a wider circulation, the Brahmanas, Upanishads, and Aranyakas cannot be described as texts reflecting popular beliefs and practices. The *Atharva Veda*, on the other hand, contains a number of charms and spells—for wealth, children, prosperity, health, etc.—reflecting the concerns of ordinary people. It also has hymns dealing with marriage and death. Although considered the latest Veda from the point of view of language and form, some of the ideas and practices reflected in this text are clearly very old.

PRIMARY SOURCES | *Atharva Veda* spells

To win the love of a woman (*Atharva Veda* 6.9):

As the creeper holds the tree in a tight embrace, so embrace me: be my lover and do not depart from me!

As the eagle which seizes its prey beats its wings at the sun, so I beat at your heart: be my lover and do not depart from me!

As the sun during the same day encircles the sky and the earth, so I encircle your heart: be my lover and do not depart from me!

Against fever (*Atharva Veda* 5.22):

May Agni drive the fever away from here—and so also may Soma, and the stone of the press, and Varuna of pure will, and the altar and the strewing and the flaming logs of wood! May enmities disappear!

You who make yellow all those whom you burn as in the fire, whom you consume—well, fever, may you be without strength: flee away there, flee away below!

That wrinkled fever, daughter of wrinkles, red like a powder, throw it down, drive it away, O herb possessed of all powers!

You are not comfortable in a strange land. Although you are powerful, have pity on us! Fever has found its proper occupation, it will go back among the Bahlika (people of the north-west).

So cold, then burning, you make us shake with coughing, terrible are your characteristics, O fever; spare us from them!

Do not take as allies the lingering sickness, nor the cough, nor shortness of breath; never come back again from where you have gone, O fever, I implore you!

O fever, with your brother the lingering sickness, with your sister the fit of coughing, with your cousin the itch, go away and stay with other people!

The fever which returns on the third day and that which dies down on the third day, the persistent fever and the autumn fever, the cold, the burning, the summer fever, and that of the rainy season, make them all disappear!

To the people of Gandhara and of Mujavant, to those of Anga and of Magadha, we send the fever, like a messenger, like a treasure!

Source Renou, 1971: 23–24

SCIENCE AND MATHEMATICS IN VEDIC TEXTS

Discussions of ancient Indian science tend to be marked by two extreme approaches that either minimize the achievements or make exaggerated claims. An objective assessment has to avoid these extreme positions. The idea that the major discoveries and achievements of modern science were already known to ancient Indians is unacceptable. A concern that often drives the analysis is whether the knowledge was indigenous or the result of external influence. Here too, objective analysis is required, keeping in mind the circulation of people and knowledge in the ancient world, and the fact that learning from other cultures can go hand in hand with originality and creativity.

Vedic texts refer to the sun and moon, seasons, constellations, year, and months (Plofker, 2009: 28–35). The performance of sacrifices at certain fixed times such as at the new moon, full moon, solstices, and equinoxes required observing the celestial bodies and time. References in the texts indicate an attempt to regulate a luni-solar calendar. What is not clear is how precise the astronomical observations and the calendar schemes based on them were.

Vedic texts show a fascination for numbers and contain the concepts of finite and infinite quantities. The word *sankhya* is used for counting and for numbers. The texts reflect an elaborate number word system based on the decimal system, that is, a word system that uses ten as the basic unit to express higher numbers. (The idea of using a base to express greater numbers is there in Old Babylonian texts dated to *c.* 1800 BCE, but the unit used there is 60.) There are about 3000 number names in the *Rig Veda* (for details, see Divakaran, 2018:113–25). The highest power of 10 is 10,000; the highest number is 99,000. Numbers were believed to have more than a mundane application—they had an important role in relation to religion, ritual, and cosmology.

Later, the Vedanga texts (supplementary texts to the Vedas) contain more details of astronomical and mathematical ideas. Jyotisha-vedanga contains the earliest mathematical expressions of astronomy and calendrics. *Shulba/shulva* means cord or rope (used for measurement), and these texts contain a ritual geometry, explaining the form and dimensions of sacrificial fire altars made of bricks. This includes a discussion of various area-preserving transformations of plane figures—for instance, changing rectangles or squares into circles and *vice versa* while maintaining the same area. This required an understanding and application of various geometric principles. The Shulbasutras reflect an understanding and application of the idea that the sum of the squares on the width and length of a rectangle are equal to the square on its diagonal; this was also applied to right angle triangles. The principle of the 'theorem of the diagonal' was stated in words in the *Baudhayana Shulbasutra*. Greek Euclidian geometry expressed the principle in the form of a theorem; this later came to be known as the Pythagoraean theorem (Divakaran, 2018: 46–55).

Archaeological Profiles of Different Regions of the Subcontinent, *c.* 2000–500 BCE

We now move from texts to archaeology. The following sections of this chapter give a summary of the cultural sequences in different parts of the subcontinent as reflected in archaeological evidence (for site details, see Allchin and Allchin, 1997; Dilip K. Chakrabarti, 2006; Chakrabarti and Lal. [Eds.], 2014, Vol. 2). The discussion takes off from where Chapters 3 and 4 ended, and is organized into two parts—the first deals with neolithic–chalcolithic and chalcolithic cultures, and the second with early iron age cultures. The reason why more space has been given to certain regions and sites is not necessarily because they were more important, but because they have been more intensively studied. Full published reports are available for comparatively few sites, and there are some regions for which properly worked-out archaeological sequences and secure dates are unavailable. We can assume the continued existence throughout these centuries of hunter-gatherer communities, who must have interacted with agricultural–pastoral groups.

Neolithic–chalcolithic and chalcolithic cultures

THE NORTH-WEST AND NORTH

As mentioned in Chapter 4, in the north-west, the mature Harappan culture was followed by the late Harappan phase, represented by the Jhukar culture in Sindh and the Cemetery-H culture in Punjab. In both cases, there are elements of continuity and change; the most clear change is the virtual disappearance of urban features.

The Jhukar culture is known from excavations at Jhukar, Chanhudaro, and Amri. The distinctive pottery is a buff ware with a red or cream slip, with paintings in black, showing some continuity with mature Harappan pottery traditions. The cubical stone weights and female figurines of the Harappan type became rare. The typical rectangular Harappan seals were replaced by circular stamp seals, and writing was confined to potsherds.

The Cemetery-H culture is represented, among other sites, at Harappa. Here, at the lower Cemetery-H levels, the graves consisted mostly of extended burials. The pottery showed some continuity with earlier levels, but there were also new forms and designs. In the upper levels, there were urn burials with disarticulated bones. M. R. Mughal's study of the Bahawalpur area indicates changes in the number, frequency, and nature of settlements in the Cemetery-H phase. Although there were some fairly large settlements (e.g., Kudwala, 31.1 ha, and four sites—Lurewala, Lundewali II, Gamuwala Ther, and Shahiwala—between 15 and 20 ha), most of the sites were small, under 5 ha. Several of the mature Harappan settlements were abandoned, and late Harappan settlements were established in new locations. The number of sites dropped from 174 (mature Harappan) to 50 (late Harappan). There was a decline in the number of industrial sites, and an increase in multi-functional sites combining habitation with craft production. There was also a notable increase in short-duration camp sites. The decline in settlements and population in this area was the result of the drying up of the Hakra river.

In the area between Peshawar and Chitral, on both sides of the Hindu Kush mountains, there are a number of cemeteries belonging to the Gandhara Grave culture. The C-14 dates for this culture range between *c.* 1710 and 200 BCE. The sites include Loebanr, Aligrama, Birkot Ghundai, Kherari, Timargarha, Lalbatai, Kalako-deray, Balambat, and Zarif Karuna. The graves generally consist of an oblong pit, sometimes with stone-lined walls, usually closed in with a stone slab. This pit was often dug into the base of a larger upper pit, which was filled with soil and charcoal, and often surrounded by a circle of stones. There were three types of burials—flexed burials, post-cremation burials including those in urns, and fractional burial. Both single and multiple burials occur. The site of Katelai yielded two burials of horses along with their masters. The grave goods included lots of plain, buff-red, or grey pottery in a range of shapes such as tall goblets, pedestal cups, beakers with flared mouths, and bottles with long and slender necks. Some graves yielded flat, female figurines with appliqué breasts, occasionally with incised eyes and necklaces. There were copper/bronze objects such as pins with decorated tops, and a bronze model of a horse was found at Katelai. Iron objects were rare.

Figure 5.2 Gandhara Grave culture burial, Loebanr

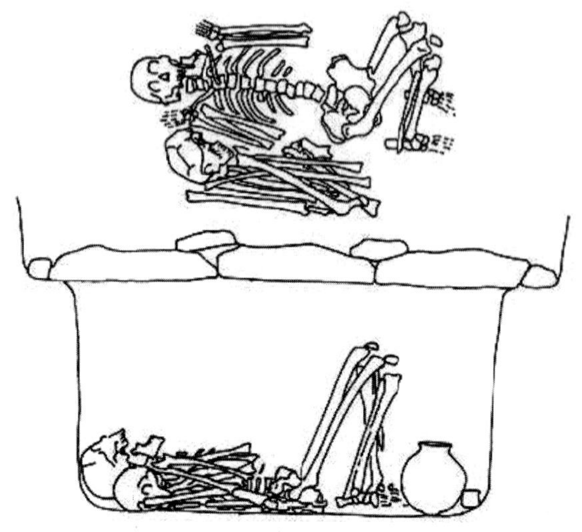

The Ghaligai cave sequence is an important reference point in this area. In this cave, Phases V, VI, and VII correspond to the early, middle, and late phase of the Gandhara Grave culture. Phase V was associated with a number of graves located on the hill-sides. There were **cist** graves made of vertical and horizontal stone slabs (see the later section on megaliths for an explanation of the different types of megaliths). Post-cremation burials outnumbered inhumations. Remains of rectangular stone houses were identified, and many different types of wheel-made pots and copper and bone artefacts were found. In Phase VI, there were more inhumations than post-cremation burials. Copper artefacts continued, and there was a fine wheel-made pottery in many different shapes, including chalices and cup-on-pedestal. Phase VII represented a

FURTHER DISCUSSION | **Mythological motifs on Cemetery-H pottery**

The Cemetery-H urns bear naturalistic designs (leaves, trees, stars), but also an interesting series of what seem to be mythological motifs. The latter include peacocks with a human form drawn in the middle, and bulls/cows with plant-like attachments to their horns. In one scene, there are two long-horned animals facing each other, held by a man with long wavy hair; a dog seems to be skipping menacingly behind one of the animals.

These scenes have been interpreted in various ways. Some scholars have tried to connect them with the ideas of death and afterlife in the Vedas. However, all these interpretations remain speculative.

Figure 5.3 Designs on Cemetery-H pots

late phase of the Gandhara Grave culture and yielded wheel-made red pottery and human terracotta figurines. Iron made its appearance. There is a similarity between some of the pottery types of Periods V–VII and those found in parts of Central Asia.

In Kashmir, at sites such as Burzahom and Gufkral, the neolithic phase was followed by a megalithic phase. Megaliths are monuments made of large, roughly dressed slabs of stone. At Burzahom, there are massive **menhirs** (single, tall stones) and a large megalithic stone circle. Grey or black burnished ware made way for a coarse red ware. Bone and stone tools typical of the earlier period continued, but in fewer numbers. There were a few metal objects.

At Gufkral, the megalithic phase (Period II) is marked by fallen menhirs, and was represented by a 50–60 cm thick habitational deposit. There was a nearly 10 cm thick floor, running throughout, with a few breaks marked by pits. Many of the latter were refuse pits, going down to natural soil levels, and contained lots of broken pottery and animal bones. The pottery of Period II showed continuity with neolithic Period I and included a burnished grey ware, gritty red ware, and thick dull-red ware, but the proportion of thick dull-red ware and wheel-made pottery had increased. There were lots of large finished and unfinished ring stones. Other artefacts included a copper point, a wooden bead, pestles, spindle whorls, a fine awl, and a miniature pot. The number of bone tools decreased, but there were innovations such as handles for tools, mostly made from the tibia of sheep/goat and bone marrow sockets. All the grains of the preceding neolithic period continued. Rice and millet made their appearance towards the end of Period II. Faunal remains included the bones of cattle, sheep, goat, dog, pig, and fowl. The bones of sheep and goats outnumbered those of cattle. Hunting seems to have declined, because the only wild animal bones found were those of ibex. Iron has been reported at megalithic Gufkral.

Kiari in Ladakh yielded handmade pottery, similar to that found in Period II at Burzahom. Structural remains consisted of hearths. There were stone artefacts such as saddle querns, pestles, and burnishers. Bones of domesticated cattle, sheep, and goats were found. There is a calibrated date of 1000+ BCE from Kiari (Chakrabarti, 2006: 207).

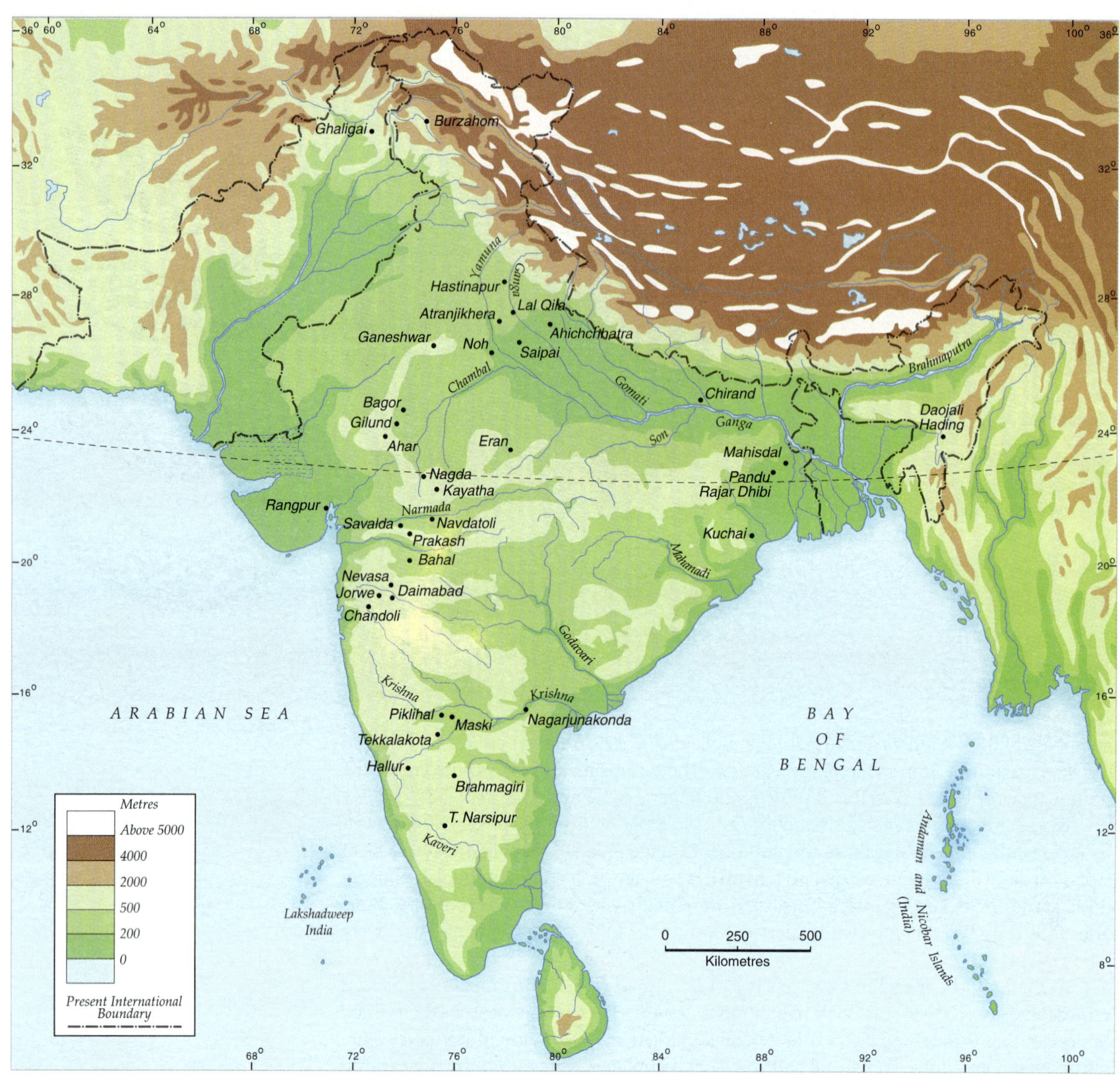

Map 5.1 Major neolithic-chalcolithic sites in the Indian subcontinent

In the Almora area of the Uttarakhand Himalayas, there are various kinds of megalithic burials—dolmens, cairns, menhirs, and cists (see the later section on the megaliths for explanations of these terms). The cist burials of this area are associated with red, grey, and black pots, including pedestalled bowls and spouted pots, and also with horse burials.

THE INDO-GANGETIC DIVIDE, THE UPPER GANGA VALLEY, AND THE DOAB

The late Harappan phase

Over 500 late Harappan sites have been identified in the area between the Yamuna and Sutlej. Most of the settlements are small, under 5 ha. Evidence of mud floors with post holes and hearths, mud-brick structures, storage pits, kilns, and a fire altar were found from Sanghol in Ludhiana district of Punjab. The late Harappan settlement at Dadheri consisted of mud houses built on a mud platform. Artefacts found here included copper and terracotta objects and beads of carnelian and lapis lazuli. At Banawali

RECENT DISCOVERIES | **The Sanauli cemetery**

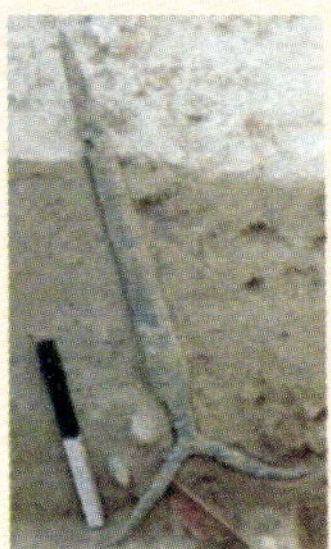

Excavations at Sanauli (Baghpat district, UP) in 2004–05 have revealed what appears to be a vast late Harappan cemetery (D. V. Sharma et al., 2005–06). The Yamuna river flows about 6 km west of the site today, but it may have been closer in protohistoric times. The discoveries at Sanauli, tentatively dated *c.* 2200–1800 BCE, are similar in some respects to those found at other mature or late Harappan sites, but they also have certain unique features.

During the 2004–05 excavations, 116 graves were excavated from different depths. All of them were laid in a northwest–southeast orientation; 52 were extended burials, 35 were secondary burials, and 29, which did not contain any human remains, seem to be symbolic burials. A double burial (Burial 27) at middle levels contained the skeletons of two males, aged 30–35 years. The grave goods included four flask-shaped vessels and a small rimless bowl near the head. A dish-on-stand with a splayed outer rim was placed in the middle of the grave, below the hip portion of the skeletons. A beautifully decorated long steatite bead and another bead of white-banded agate were also found. Only one skull was found among the skeletal material. There was also a triple burial (Burial 69) along with two urn burials. This was a secondary burial. Only one skull was found, placed upside down. The absence of skulls may have been due to the peculiar circumstances of death of the individuals concerned. This grave contained 21 pieces of pottery of different types, including three dish-on-stand and two pitchers with lids in the shape of bull heads.

One of the symbolic burials (Burial 28) in the upper levels contained two mushroom-shaped dish-on-stands. It also had a violin-shaped copper container with 28 tiny, paper-thin, stylized copper objects arranged in six rows. A burnt brick wall with a finished inner surface ran parallel to the burial in the east. Another symbolic burial (Burial 106) contained patterns of steatite inlays, the outer lines of which resembled a human effigy. A completely burnt clay trough found at middle levels of the site may have been used for cremating the dead.

The grave goods in this cemetery comprised copper objects, gold ornaments including heart-shaped bracelets, beads of semi-precious stones, steatite, faience, and glass. One burial contained a copper antennae sword, along with a sheath. There is evidence suggestive of animal sacrifice in some middle and upper level burials.

The dish-on-stand was clearly an important part of the grave goods. Its form evolved over time and the mushroom shape found in the upper levels has not been found elsewhere. In most burials, it occurred either below the hip or near/below the head of the buried person; in a few instances, it was close to the feet. It was also used as an offering stand, in one case, holding the head of a goat.

A preliminary study of about 40 skeletons by S. R. Walimbe identified the skeletons of 10 males and 7 females. The sex of 17 skeletons could not be determined. The bones of five child burials were analyzed; one of them was 1–2 years old, two were 3–5 years, and two were about 10 years. There were also remains of six sub adults.

The 2018 excavations at Sanauli revealed further dramatic evidence (Manjul and Manjul, 2018). Eight burials were unearthed. Three were coffin burials containing human skeletal remains, three were secondary burials (including one burial with two individuals buried together), and two were symbolic burials which did not contain any human remains

but those of a bird and dog. The human burials were contained in legged wooden coffins (the wood had decayed) and were accompanied with grave goods—pottery, beads (made of agate, faience, paste, and gold), weapons (dagger, antennae swords, helmet, shield), the wooden shaft of a whip decorated with copper, and a chalice-shaped copper pot with a tortoise base. The most spectacular finds were the remains of three chariots—these were open vehicles with two solid wheels decorated with copper triangles. One of them had a pole and yoke *in situ*. These are the oldest finds of wheeled vehicles in India.

Were these chariots pulled by horses or carts pulled by bulls (Parpola, 2020)? Are there some connections with the Bactria Margiana Archaeological Complex (BMAC) culture of South Central Asia (which has also given evidence of bull-drawn carts) which in turn, was connected with the Sintashta culture? Do they provide archaeological evidence for an early wave of Indo-Aryans, who arrived and interfaced with the late Harappan culture? The picture is not yet clear. The full implications of the Sanauli finds still remain to be understood.

Source D. V. Sharma et al., 2005–06; Manjul and Manjul, 2018; Parpola, 2020

in Haryana, there is evidence of mud houses and a rich range of artefacts including faience ornaments, beads of semi-precious stones, and objects made of copper, clay, and terracotta.

Sanghol yielded evidence of a wide range of plant remains in a late Harappan context that was dated *c.* 1900–1400 BCE. An analysis of the palaeo-botanical remains (Saraswat, 1996–97) identified hulled barley, naked barley, dwarf wheat, bread wheat, jowar millet, Italian millet, *khesari*, field pea, lentil, chickpea (gram), horse gram, Egyptian clover (*barseem*), linseed, and sesame (*til*). The remains of hyacinth bean (*sem*), fruits (grape, lemon, *karaunda*, *anwala*), and opium poppy seeds were also found. The plant remains identified at Mohrana comprised hulled and naked six-row barley, dwarf wheat, club wheat, lentil, and grape pips.

The chalcolithic cultural sequence in the doab includes the late Harappan phase, the Ochre Coloured Pottery (OCP) culture, the **copper hoards**, and the **Black and Red Ware (BRW)** phase. Some of these phases spilt out into adjoining areas as well. There are almost 70 late Harappan sites in the doab region, mostly along the higher banks of the tributaries of the Yamuna—the Hindon, Krishni, Kathanala, and Maskara. Most of the settlements are small (the largest measures 200 × 200 m), and the average distance between settlements is 8–12 km. The thickness of the deposits is 1–2 m. Three sites have been excavated—Alamgirpur in Meerut district and Hulas and Bargaon in Saharanpur district. The late Harappan occupation at Hulas may go back to before 2000 BCE and it seems to have continued till about 1000 BCE.

There is very little structural evidence from late Harappan sites in the doab. Houses were generally made of wattle and daub. At Hulas, however, rectangular mud-brick structures with rammed floors, post-holes, and hearths were identified in the earliest phase. In the middle phase, clusters of two or three circular wattle-and-daub structures—perhaps storage bins—were found inside some of the rectangular mud houses. In the final stage, five round furnaces were found in some of the structures. A few burnt bricks were found at this site and at Alamgirpur.

The late Harappan pottery of this area is made of well-levigated clay and included both handmade and wheel-made types, with both coarse and fine fabrics. It has a thin cream wash or a bright red slip, over which geometric and naturalistic designs were painted in black. A small proportion of the pots also have incised designs. The other artefacts found at these sites included chert blades, stone querns and pestles, and bone points. There were a few copper objects—a broken blade from Alamgirpur, and a fragmentary chisel and some rings from Bargaon. Ornaments included bangles of terracotta, carnelian, and steatite, and beads of terracotta, steatite, agate, carnelian, and faience. Circular and triangular terracotta cakes and terracotta animals, carts, and wheels were also found.

It can be inferred that people living at these sites continued to grow crops such as wheat and barley, which were known in the area in the mature Harappan phase. Rice husk was found embedded in the cores of potsherds at Hulas and Un. The list of plant remains from late Harappan Hulas is impressive—rice, barley, dwarf wheat, bread wheat, club wheat, oats, sorghum (*jowar*), finger millet (*ragi*), lentil, field pea, grass pea, *kulthi*, green gram (*moong*), chickpea (gram), a broken cowpea, cotton, castor, almond, walnut, fruits, and wild grasses. This was clearly an agricultural community with a diverse and well-established agricultural base.

The Ochre Coloured Pottery culture

The Ochre Coloured Pottery (OCP) was discovered in 1950–51 in western Uttar Pradesh at the sites of Bisauli (Badaun district) and Rajpur Parsu (Bijnaur district). It is an ill-fired, wheel-made ware with a fine to medium fabric, and a thick red slip, sometimes decorated with black bands. Some potsherds have incised designs and post-firing graffiti. The pottery was given its name because when it was rubbed, it left an ochre colour on the fingers. This could be because of water-logging, wind action, poor firing, or a combination of such factors.

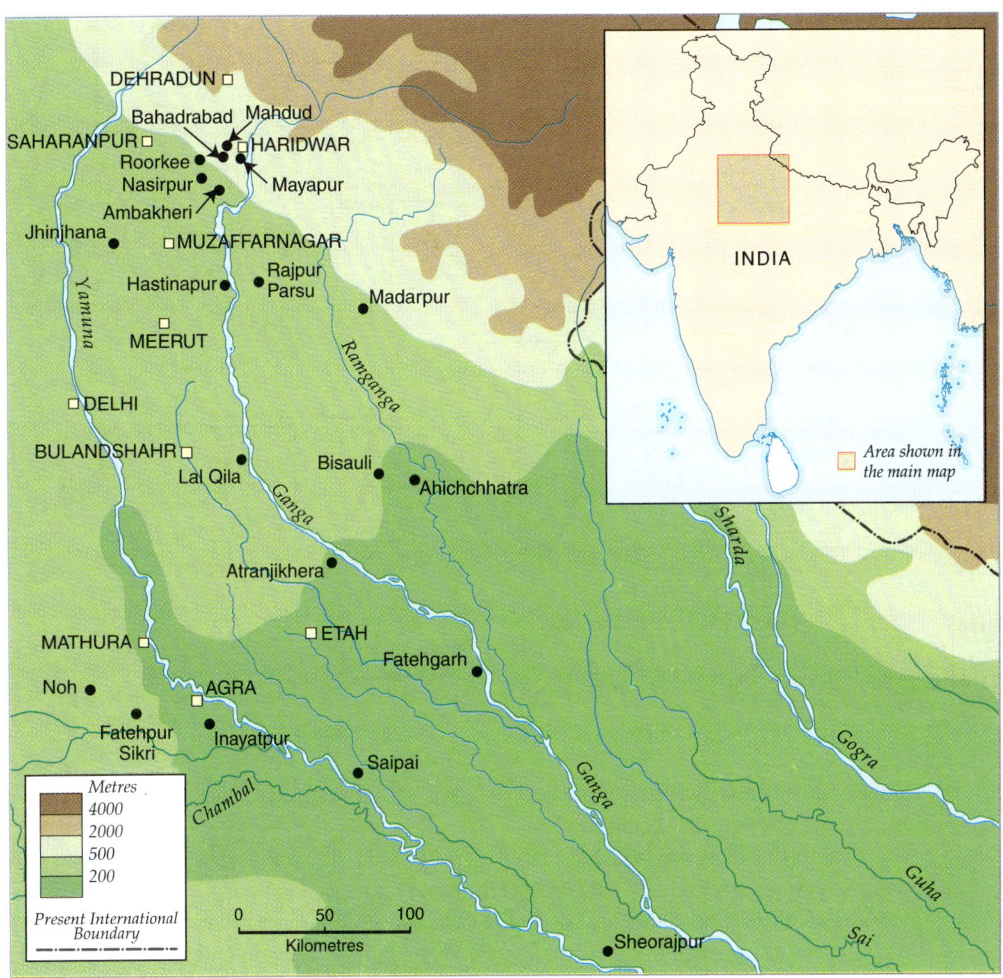

Map 5.2 Ochre Coloured Pottery sites

Subsequently, OCP was found to be widely distributed in the doab, with a concentration in the Saharanpur, Muzaffarnagar, Meerut, and Bulandshahr districts of western Uttar Pradesh. Over 80 sites have been identified in Saharanpur district alone. This pottery has been found outside this area as well, and its distribution extends north–south from Bahadarabad near Haridwar in Uttarakhand to Noh and Jodhpura in Rajasthan, and east–west from Katpalon near Jalandhar in Punjab to Ahichchhatra near Bareilly. The OCP phase in Rajasthan seems to be earlier than that in the doab.

OCP occurs in two sorts of stratigraphic contexts. At Hastinapura, Ahichchhatra, and Jhinjhana, the OCP level was followed by a break in occupation and a Painted Grey Ware (PGW) level. At Atranjikhera and Noh, the OCP level was followed by a Black and Red Ware (BRW) level, and then a PGW level. Certain sites such as Bargaon and Ambakheri show an overlap between the late Harappan and OCP phase. Some scholars maintain that OCP is just a degenerate form of late Harappan pottery. According to others, it was an independent ceramic tradition that was influenced in some areas by the Harappan pottery tradition. At least two broad categories of OCP can be identified—a western zone (represented at sites such as Jodhpura, Siswal, Mitathal, Bara, Ambakheri, and Bargaon) that shows links with the Harappan tradition, and an eastern zone (represented at sites such as Lal Qila, Atranjikhera, and Saipai) that does not display any such links.

Major excavated sites include Lal Qila (Bulandshahr district), Bahadrabad and Ambakheri (both in Saharanpur district), Atranjikhera (Etah district), Ahichchhatra (Bareilly district), and Saipai (Etawah district). The OCP deposits are generally shallow, ranging from 0.5 to 1.5 m in thickness. The settlements are usually small (upto 200–300 sq m), although there are a few larger settlements such as Lal Qila (632 sq m). The

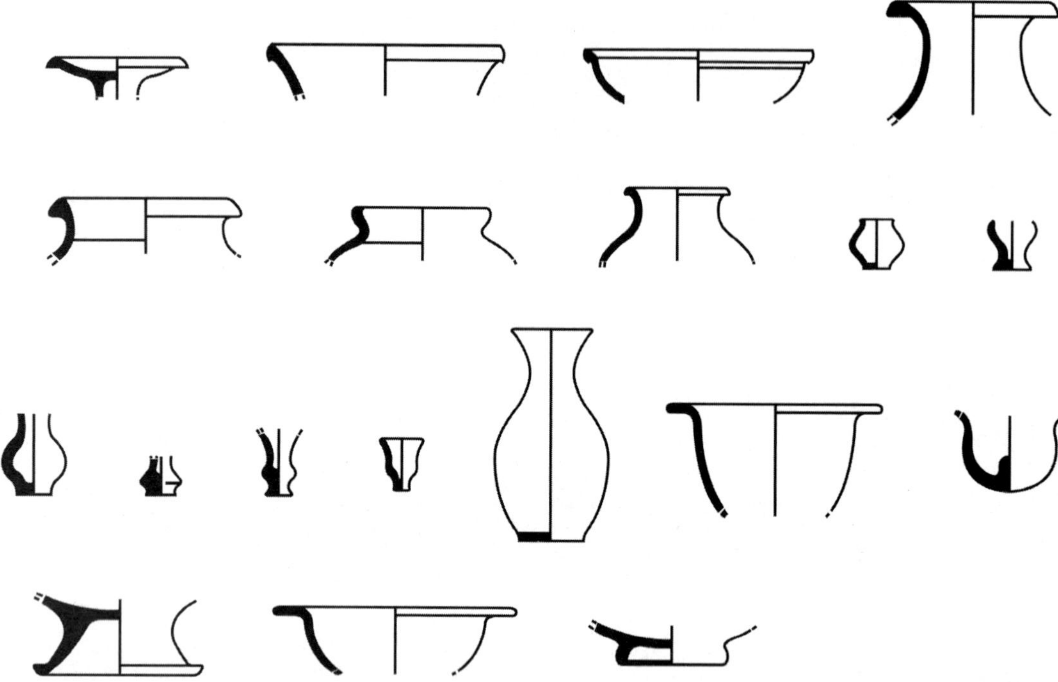

Figure 5.4 Ochre Coloured Pottery from Ambakheri

average distance between two sites is 4–6 km in Saharanpur district, and 5–8 km in other parts of the upper Ganga valley.

Due to the disturbed nature of the deposits and the small area covered by excavations, very few structural remains were found at most OCP sites. There were some remains of wattle-and-daub houses at Lal Qila, Atranjikhera, Daulatpur, and Jodhpura. Very few mud- or burnt bricks were found. At Atranjikhera, people lived in mud houses with frames made of posts of *babul*, *sissoo*, *sal*, and *chir* pine trees. An unlined well was also found. At Jodhpura, a mud-brick structure with the bricks joined together with mud mortar was discovered. Lal Qila must have been an important settlement, going by its size, structures, and range of artefacts. There were remains of oblong wattle-and-daub structures with mud floors and post-holes, and a few sun-dried bricks with mud mortar. An unlined pit may have functioned as a well.

Apart from pottery, very few artefacts have been found at OCP sites. Stone objects included querns and beads. Bone tools were found at Lal Qila. A few copper artefacts also occur at various sites. A piece of copper and fragments of a terracotta crucible containing copper granules were discovered at Atranjikhera. A hooked spearhead and harpoon made of copper were found at Saipai. Lal Qila yielded five copper objects—two pendants, one bead, an arrowhead, and a broken celt. The terracotta objects found at this site included anthropomorphic and animal figurines, wheels, bangles, balls, tablets, gamesmen, crucibles, discs, beads, grinders, and querns. Terracotta figurines of humped bulls were found at Ambakheri. The Lal Qila pottery included a vase painted with a semi-naturalistic humped bull with long, curved horns.

The people who lived at OCP sites obtained their food from agriculture, animal husbandry, and hunting. Plant remains at Lal Qila included wheat, barley, and rice. Atranjikhera yielded rice, barley, gram, and *khesari*. This suggests that people grew two crops a year—rice in summer and barley and legumes in winter. At Saipai, sandstone pounders, querns, and pestles were found, and there were bones of domesticated *Bos indicus*. Lal Qila yielded complete animal skeletons on floors, and there were circular fire pits with charred bones of domesticated cattle, buffalo, goat, sheep, pig, horse, dog, and wild deer. Many of the bones had cut marks, indicating that the animals were killed for their meat.

Most of the OCP sites in the doab seem to belong to the first half of the 2nd millennium BCE, but the dates from Atranjikhera are a few centuries earlier. The dates from Jodhpura in Rajasthan go back to the early 3rd millennium BCE. The OCP culture can be seen as a contemporary of the mature Harappan and late Harappan cultures, with certain sites showing contact between them.

The copper hoards

In 1822, a copper harpoon was discovered at Bithur in Kanpur district. Since then, over 1300 copper objects of a similar range have been found in various parts of India, mostly in hoards. Archaeologists refer to them as copper hoards.

Copper hoards have been found at about 100 sites across an area stretching from the upper Ganga valley to Bengal and Odisha. There have also been several discoveries in Haryana, Rajasthan, and Madhya Pradesh, and a few in Gujarat, Karnataka, Kerala, and Tamil Nadu. However, the largest concentration of sites is in the doab region of

Map 5.3 Copper hoard sites

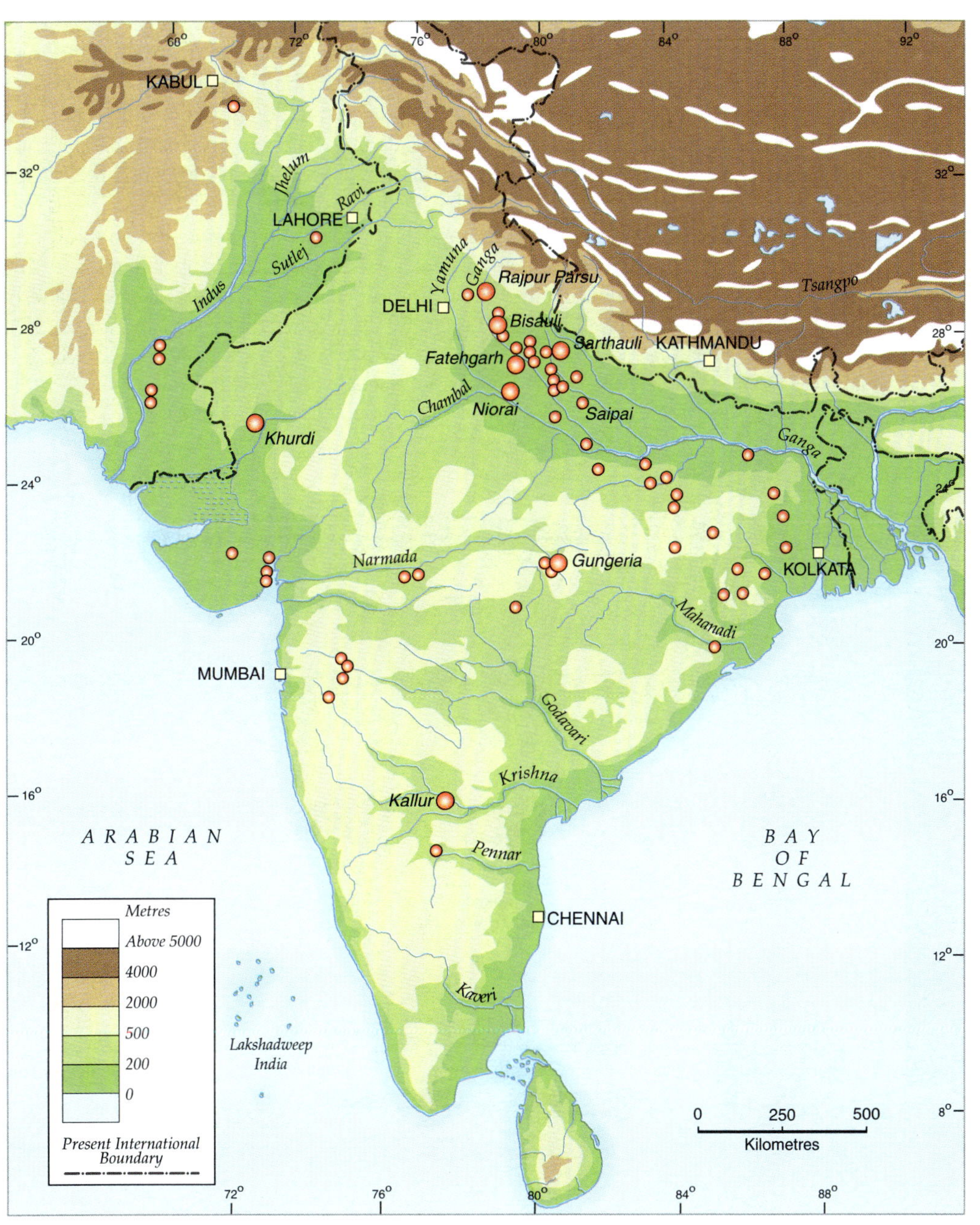

Uttar Pradesh. The number of objects found together varies from 1 to 47, except in the case of Gungeria in Madhya Pradesh, where 424 objects weighing over 200 kg were found in a single hoard, along with 102 silver objects. Since most of the copper hoard discoveries were accidental and the objects were not found in a stratified context, it is very difficult to date them. The hoards found in Bihar and West Bengal may in fact belong to the historical period. In view of this, the site of Saipai (in Etawah district), where the copper objects were found in the course of an excavation in an OCP level, is especially important.

The copper hoards include many different kinds of objects such as flat celts, shouldered celts, bar celts, harpoons, antennae swords, and anthropomorphic figures. Most of them seem to be part of hunting equipment. Typological differences can, to some extent, be associated with geographical areas. For instance, in the eastern zone of Bihar, West Bengal, and Odisha, there is a predominance of flat celts, shouldered celts, bar celts, and double axes. In the Uttar Pradesh and Haryana areas, these types occur along with anthropomorphs, antennae swords, hooked swords, and harpoons. Sites in Rajasthan have yielded mainly flat celts and bar celts.

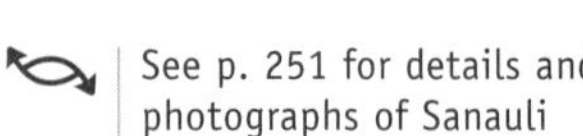
See p. 251 for details and photographs of Sanauli

A comparison of the Harappan copper artefacts and the copper hoard objects shows striking differences in typology and alloying techniques. About 46 per cent of the copper hoard objects had up to 7 per cent arsenic alloying. On the other hand, only 8 per cent of analyzed Harappan artefacts show arsenic alloying. The site of Sanauli has recently yielded two antennae swords of the copper hoard types in a late Harappan context. One of these was found *in situ* in a grave, and has a copper sheath.

The evidence of the copper hoards suggests that between the mid-3rd and 2nd millennium BCE, the upper Ganga valley had emerged as a distinct copper-manufacturing area, with interactions extending into the regions of Haryana, Gujarat, Madhya Pradesh, the Deccan, Kerala, and Tamil Nadu. What is not clear is whether it was an independent

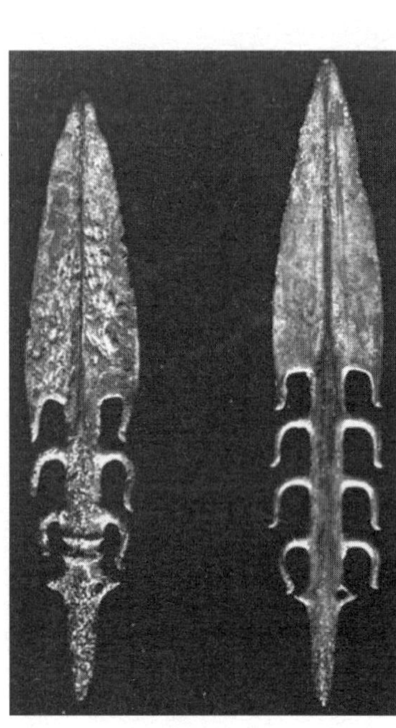

Copper harpoons from Sisupalgarh and Hastinapura

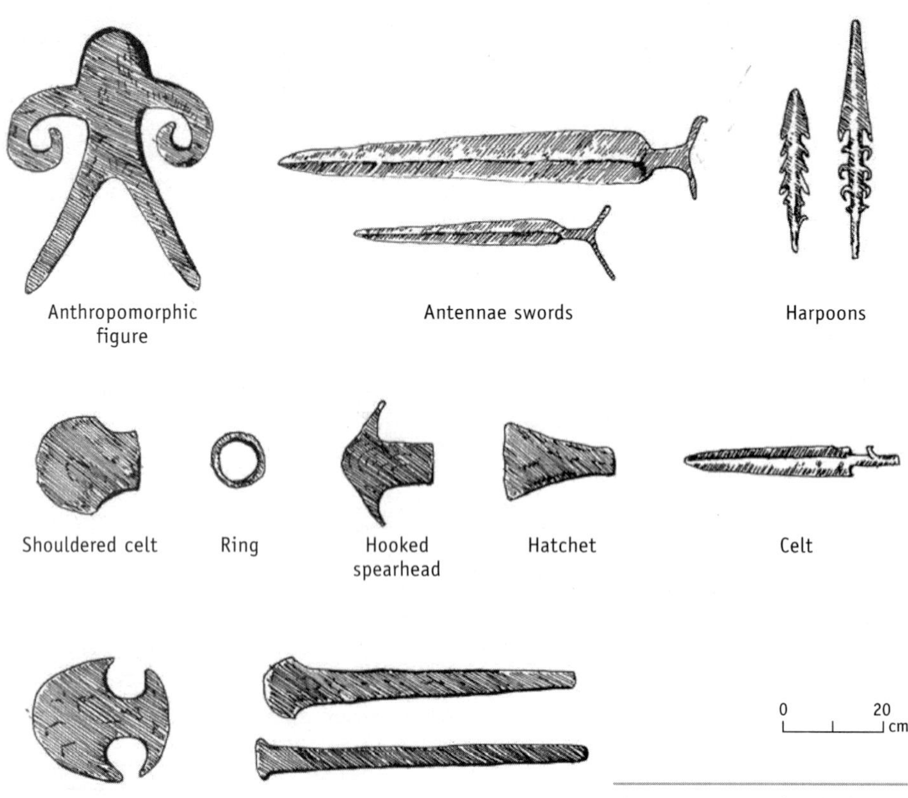

Figure 5.5 Copper hoard objects

FURTHER DISCUSSION | **The enigma of copper anthropomorphs**

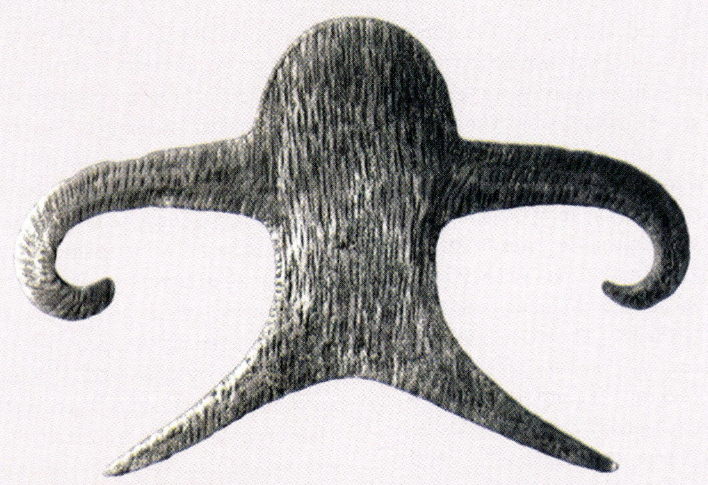

The most enigmatic artefact among the copper hoard objects is the anthropomorph. This is a large object, between 25 and 45 cm in length, 30 and 43 cm in breadth, and weighing up to 5 kg. The length is in almost all cases greater than its breadth (the Bisauli piece is an exception to this rule). The object usually has in-curved arms, sharpened on the outer edge, and plain outstretched legs. The arms are thinner than the head, which was thickened by beating the top.

In 2001, a hoard of 31 copper anthropomorphs was found at Madarpur in the Moradabad district of Uttar Pradesh (D. V. Sharma et al., 2001–02). They were discovered by workers digging the soil for the preparation of mud-bricks. The artefacts were *in situ*, stacked one on top of the other. Such a large number of anthropomorphic figures have not been found elsewhere. What is also intriguing is that the shapes are not identical, and there are some that do not occur anywhere else. The artefacts were found in a deposit which also yielded OCP. Madarpur seems to have been a place which specialized in the production of copper anthropomorphs.

What was the anthropomorph used for? One suggestion is that it was a weapon. D. P. Agrawal suggests that when thrown, it has a sort of whirling boomerang effect, and that it may have been a missile used to kill birds. However, why such elaborate artefacts should have been made for this purpose is not clear. The different shapes of the objects also go against this theory. Another possibility is that they had a religious or ritualistic function. It may be noted that tiny anthropomorphic figures, similar to the copper hoard types, are worshipped in parts of northern India as the god Shani.

centre of copper working or whether it represents an extension of the older and better documented centre of copper metallurgy in north-eastern Rajasthan.

The Black and Red Ware phase in the doab

Black and Red Ware (BRW) was long known to occur at several archaeological sites in association with various other pottery types, in many different cultural contexts. However, the existence of a distinct and independent Black and Red Ware phase in the doab was first recognized during excavations at Atranjikhera in the 1960s. Here, a BRW level was found sandwiched between OCP and PGW levels. A similar stratigraphic sequence was later identified at Noh and Jodhpura in Rajasthan. Some archaeologists maintain that there are links between the BRW of the doab and Rajasthan, while others disagree.

BRW levels at Atranjikhera did not yield any stone or metal artefacts. There were only fragments of stone, waste flakes, chips, and cores of quartz, chalcedony, agate, and carnelian. Three beads (of carnelian, shell, and copper) and a fragment of a comb made of bone were also found. BRW levels at Noh yielded a shapeless piece of iron, terracotta bead, and bone spike.

As for evidence of subsistence patterns, rice, barley, gram, and *khesari* were found from OCP levels at Atranjikhera, and it is likely that the cultivation of these crops continued into the BRW phase. Grains of rice and *moong* were found at BRW levels at this site.

BRW pot, megalithic level, Maski (Karnataka)

PRIMARY SOURCES | **Black and Red Ware**

As its name indicates, Black and Red Ware (BRW) refers to a pottery that is both red and black. The two colours may appear on the same surface of the pot, or one surface may be black, the other red. BRW should not be confused with black-on-red ware (e.g., the typical Harappan pottery), in which both the inner and outer surfaces of the pot are red, and designs are painted in black.

Many of the BRW pots are black inside and red outside. This could be a result of the inverted firing technique: In this, the pots are positioned upside down in the kiln with some vegetal material placed inside them. When the pot is fired, its outer part is exposed to oxidizing conditions and turns red, while its inner part is subjected to reducing conditions and turns black. Another possibility is that the pots went through two rounds of firing (double firing)—i.e., they were first fired red and then re-fired, so that one of the surfaces became black, or vice versa.

Black-and-red pottery occurs in many parts of the subcontinent in several different cultural contexts. For example, it occurs at neolithic sites (Chirand, Piklihal, etc.), pre-Harappan Lothal, many Harappan sites in Gujarat (e.g., Lothal, Surkotada, Rojdi, Rangpur, and Desalpur), chalcolithic sites in the middle and lower Ganga valley (Chirand, Pandu Rajar Dhibi, etc.), sites of the Ahar/Banas culture (Ahar, Gilund), Malwa culture (Navdatoli, Inamgaon), Kayatha culture (Kayatha), and Jorwe culture (Chandoli), iron age PGW sites (Atranjikhera, Hastinapur, etc.), South Indian megalithic sites (Brahmagiri, Nagarjunakonda, etc.), and at early historical levels all over the subcontinent. At certain sites in the doab (e.g., Atranjikhera) and Rajasthan (e.g., Noh), there is a distinct BRW level between the OCP and PGW levels.

Not all of this black-and-red pottery is identical. There is in fact a great deal of variation in technique, fabric, and shape among the black-and-red pottery that occurs in different geographical and chronological contexts. In view of all this, it is clear that all black-and-red pottery cannot be treated as representing a single ceramic culture, a single community of artisans, or a single community of consumers. The existence of different varieties of black-and-red pottery at various sites does not necessarily show the existence of cultural uniformity or cultural contact. When we talk about black-and-red pottery in Indian archaeology, its specific geographical and cultural context must always be indicated.

The case of Black and Red Ware shows that we must always be very careful in making historical inferences on the basis of superficial similarities in pottery.

Source H. N. Singh, 1979

WESTERN INDIA

In Chapter 3, there was a discussion of the early phase of the Ganeshwar–Jodhpura culture of north-eastern Rajasthan, with special reference to the sites of Jodhpura and Ganeshwar. The early phase of the Ahar/Banas culture of south-east Rajasthan, represented at sites such as Ahar, Gilund, and Balathal was also discussed. Rajasthan continued to be a major region for copper metallurgy during the succeeding centuries as well.

At Ganeshwar, Period III is dated from *c.* 2000 BCE onwards. There was a wide range of pottery in this phase. Hundreds of copper artefacts, e.g., arrowheads, rings, bangles, spearheads, chisels, balls, and celts were found. This shows that Ganeshwar was a major centre for the manufacture of copper artefacts. Compared to Period II, there was a decline in the number of microliths and animal bones, suggesting a decline in hunting.

Period I at Ahar is divided into three periods—Ia (dated from 2500 BCE), Ib (dated from 2100 BCE), and Ic (dated from 1900 BCE). Period Ia was discussed in Chapter 3. Here we will look at Periods Ib and Ic. As far as pottery is concerned, there is continuity in BRW throughout Periods Ia, Ib, and Ic, but there are some changes in the types and proportions of the associated wares. For instance, in Period Ia, there were mostly convex-sided BRW bowls, buff and imitation buff-slipped wares, red wares, and some grey ware. In Period Ib, the BRW continues, and there is a lot of grey ware and red ware, but no buff and buff-slipped ware. Period Ic was marked by deeply carinated BRW bowls and lustrous red ware.

The artefacts discovered in Period Ib at Ahar included microlithic fluted cores and a blunt-backed blade of quartz; beads of agate, calcite, carnelian, faience, jasper, schist, shell, steatite, bone, and terracotta; terracotta objects such as ear studs, skin rubbers, head scratchers (?), votive tanks, crucibles, dice, bangles, finials, pipes, pendants, and human and animal (bull, horse, and maybe elephant) figurines. Copper objects included rings, bangles, kohl sticks, celts, and a knife blade. In Period Ic, there were microlithic scrapers and borers; beads of carnelian, crystal, glass, jasper, lapis, schist, shell, and terracotta; terracotta skin rubbers, ear studs, a 'votive tank', crucible, bull and elephant figurines, stoppers, pendants, bangles, balls, and pipes. The copper items comprised rings and kohl sticks.

Evidence from Ahar indicates that the people who lived here cultivated rice, and possibly millet. The evidence of structures and pottery suggest that in Period Ib, the site was more thickly populated than in the preceding and succeeding periods. It is also likely that there was interaction between the chalcolithic agricultural people of Ahar and the 'mesolithic' hunter-gatherers who lived at sites such as Bagor.

Investigations at the late Ahar culture settlement at Purani Marmi (Chittoorgarh district, Rajasthan) near Balathal yielded important information on the subsistence base of the people who lived here. A total of 545 animal bones from 4 habitational layers were analyzed and identified as those of cattle, sheep, goat, buffalo, blackbuck, spotted deer, and domestic fowl. Two types of freshwater molluscs were also found. The relative quantities of the bones indicate that the people were mainly pastoralists engaged in cattle and buffalo rearing. They supplemented this with some amount of sheep and goat herding and a limited amount of hunting.

Mention should also be made of a number of megalithic sites in the Aravalli stretches of Rajasthan, for instance, Khera, Satmas, and Daosa. Very few details or dates are available for them. The most common type of megalith found in this region is the cairn.

In Gujarat, the mature Harappan phase was followed by a late Harappan phase. As mentioned in Chapter 4, Kutch and Saurashtra show a marked increase in the number of settlements.

The late Harappan settlements in Gujarat can be divided into two phases—the pre-lustrous red ware sites (Lothal B, Rojdi, Babar Kot, Padri) and the lustrous red ware sites. Lothal (in Period B, also known as Phase V) revealed remains of houses made of mud and reed. Short blades of jasper and chalcedony replaced the long chert blades of the mature Harappan phase. Jasper and carnelian beads made way for biconal terracotta beads, and cubical weights of chert and agate were gradually replaced by larger, truncated ones made of schist and sandstone. There was a decrease in the use of copper. Rectangular steatite seals with the Harappan script continued, but without animal motifs. Rojdi IA, Rangpur IIB and IIC also represent the late Harappan phase.

The settlement at Rojdi was about 7 ha in size. The main settlement area was surrounded by a stone rubble wall on three sides (the Bhadar river lay on the east), with a double-bastioned gateway in the western wall. There were other structures of stone masonry as well. Various types of metal artefacts were found, e.g., an axe, bar celt, bangles, rings, a fishhook, pieces of wire, and a pin. The plant remains included millets, barley, mustard, *khesari*, lentil, linseed, pea, vetches/beans, various kinds of gram, jujube, and a number of weeds, medicinal plants, and grasses (which may have been used for animal fodder). The late Harappan site of Babar Kot measured about 2.7 ha and had a stone fortification wall. The plant remains included millets and gram.

Prabhas Patan II (Somnath Patan in Junagadh district) on the banks of the river Hiran is divided into two sub-phases—the earlier one has late Harappan pottery but no lustrous red ware, and the later one has late Harappan pottery associated with lustrous red ware. A structural complex made of stone blocks set in mud mortar and divided into smaller compartments was interpreted as a warehouse. Artefacts included a steatite seal amulet, segmented beads made of faience, and cubical chert blades. There were copper objects and beads of chalcedony, carnelian, and agate, and a gold ear ornament.

Dwarka: marine archaeologists diving near Samudra Narayan temple; diver measuring submerged structure; circular stone structure in the inter-tidal zone

At Dwarka (Jamnagar district, Gujarat), marine archaeologists found the remains of a submerged settlement and identified its inner and outer walls, bastions, and a large stone jetty. Stone anchors and lustrous red ware were found at the site. The island of Bet Dwarka also revealed a submerged site. The settlement seems originally to have been 4 × 0.5 km, and there are remains of fortifications. A Harappan seal carved with a three-headed animal, lustrous red ware, BRW, and a jar inscribed with Harappan writing were found. Other discoveries included a coppersmith's stone mould and some shell bangles. There is a thermoluminescence date of 1570 BCE from Bet Dwarka, which is considered to be a late Harappan site.

There are many late Harappan sites in the Rupen valley in north Gujarat, with and without lustrous red ware. The settlements tend to be located on old sand dunes, close to sources of water. Most of them are small and have a thin occupational deposit. The late Harappan sites in this area seem to mostly represent seasonal camp sites of pastoralists.

There is more information from the site of Kanewal in Kheda district at the mouth of the Gulf of Cambay. Here, there were circular wattle-and-daub huts with rammed floors. The artefacts included oblong terracotta cakes; beads of carnelian, faience, shell, and terracotta; terracotta spindle whorls and net sinkers; copper objects; and various types of pottery including lustrous red ware. Some of the pottery found at sites in this area has graffiti in the Harappan script, indicating some level of literacy among the people who lived here.

THE MIDDLE GANGA VALLEY

There are a large number of protohistoric sites in this region, especially in the trans-Sarayu area. Narhan in Gorakhpur district (UP) is on the northern bank of the Sarayu (Ghaghara), about 30 km east of Imlidih (Purushottam Singh, 1994). Excavations at this site revealed a cultural sequence stretching from the second half of the 2nd millennium BCE to the 7th century, CE. Period I at Narhan (labelled the Narhan culture) was dated *c.* 1300–700 BCE. Remains of wattle-and-daub houses with post-holes and hearths were found. The pottery was marked by a white-painted BRW, along with some white-painted black-slipped ware, red-slipped ware, and plain red ware. Other artefacts included bone points; pottery discs; terracotta beads, dabbers, and balls; and one polished stone axe. The copper objects included a ring and fishhook. Chemical analysis of these objects, as well as of those found in later periods indicates that they were made of a low-tin bronze. The metal workers were familiar with techniques such as alloying, cold working, annealing, and casting. The source of the copper ores seems to have been the Rakha mines of Bihar.

An exceptionally wide range of plant remains were found at Narhan. Period I remains included cultivated rice (*Oryza sativa*), hulled and six-row barley (*Hordeum vulgare*), three kinds of wheat (*Triticum compactum, T. aestivum,* and *T. compactum*), pea, green gram, gram or chickpea, and *khesari*. Oilseeds—mustard and flax (*alsi*)—were found, as were seeds of jackfruit (*katahal*). Fragments of *mahua*, *sal*, tamarind, teak, *siris*, *babul*, mulberry, *ganiyari*, *Nux vomica*, holy basil (*tulsi*), mango, *katahal*, and bamboo were identified. Animal bone remains included those of humped cattle and sheep/goat, wild deer or antelope, horse, and fish. An interesting find was the impression of a fish-hook and thread on a mud clod. Iron rust showed that the hook was made of iron, and the analysis of a tiny surviving fibre revealed that the thread was made of ramie (*Boehmeria nivea*), a strong, water-resistant fibre. Two iron pieces (a 13 cm long bar and another fragmentary piece), were found in the upper deposits of Period I. Iron objects increased in the subsequent period. The Narhan sequence is repeated at many places in the middle Ganga plains, including in the area south of the Sarayu.

At Khairadih, Period I was marked by BRW and associated pottery. Calibrated dates gave a range of 1395–848 BCE. At Rajghat near the Ganga, the early occupation was marked mainly by a black-slipped ware. The many BRW sites in the area to the south of

Mirzapur include Raja Karna Ka Tila on the Karamnasa river. Period I at this site yielded BRW, microlith chips, a clay sling ball, shells, terracotta beads and discs, and bone points and arrowheads. Rice, barley, *ragi*, foxtail millet, lentil, field-pea, *khesari*, and *moong* were identified. Period II began in about 1300 BCE and gave evidence of iron.

Imlidih Khurd is a site on the banks of the Kuwana river. Period I represents the pre-Narhan culture and goes back to *c.* 1300 BCE. It yielded a crude, handmade cord-or-mat-impressed red ware, including spherical bowls, pedestalled bowls, vases with flaring rims, and *handi*-like and spouted vessels. There were remains of wattle-and-daub houses, a storage pit (1.95 m in diameter), a circular bin-like structure (about 85 cm in diameter), and ovens. Artefacts included beads of agate, faience, and terracotta, a few steatite micro-beads, bone points, and pottery discs. The faunal remains included bones of domesticated cattle, sheep/goat, and pig. Cattle bones were the most numerous, and had cut marks. Bones of freshwater turtle, fish, and freshwater molluscs were also found. The plant remains were extremely varied and included rice, barley, bread wheat, dwarf wheat, *jowar*, pearl millet (*bajra*), lentil, *moong*, field pea, grass pea, mustard, and sesame. The seeds of fruits—wild jujube, *anwala*, and grape—were also found. The evidence indicates that agriculture based on two crops a year was already established in the trans-Sarayu plain in the first half of the 2nd millennium BCE.

Period II at Imlidih Khurd belongs to the Narhan culture and is dated *c.* 1300–800 BCE. It was marked by intense structural activity in the form of at least two successive mud floors with several post-holes and ovens. The typical pottery was a white-painted BRW, similar to that found at Narhan. Other artefacts included bone points, pottery discs, terracotta beads, a copper arrowhead, two copper beads, and some curious terracotta pieces that may have been legs or pedestals of some indeterminate object, possibly for ritualistic use. The plant remains comprised rice, barley, wheat, kondon-millet, lentil, chickpea, *moong*, and *anwala*, along with various weeds and wild plant species. The faunal remains included the bones of domesticated cattle, goat/sheep, horse, and dog. The bones of wild animals comprised those of boar, hog deer, *chital*, and *barasingha*. Except for the molluscs, the aquatic fauna of Period I continued into Period II.

Excavations at the 40 ha site of Agiabir in Mirzapur district revealed a long cultural sequence extending from the Narhan phase to the early medieval period. In Period I (the Narhan culture phase), the main pottery types were BRW, black-slipped ware, and red ware. The pottery showed some differences with the typical range of Narhan ware. People lived in wattle-and-daub huts, and two silos used for storing grain were found. There were lots of beads, especially those made of agate. A bead-making workshop was identified. Faience objects, microliths, terracotta beads, bone points, terracotta discs, one copper fishhook, and a clay lamp or incense burner were found. Fireplaces associated with charred animal bones gave evidence of peoples' food habits. Period II at Agiabir has been described as pre-NBP with iron. Iron and copper objects were the noteworthy finds of this phase.

There are a number of sites marked by megaliths in and near the northern fringes of the Vindhyas in Allahabad, Banda, Varanasi, and Mirzapur districts of south-eastern Uttar Pradesh. These include Kakoria, Jang Mahal, and Kotia. The main types of megaliths that occur are cairns and stone circles. Some of the graves gave evidence of fractional burial. Others were associated with animal burials. At Kotia, the graves yielded few human skeletal remains, but three contained the remains of domesticated sheep, pig, and cattle. Cut marks suggest that the animals were killed at the time of burial. Many of the megaliths in this area are devoid of skeletal remains of any kind, and may represent memorials for the dead.

The habitation site of Kakoria lies on both sides of the Chandraprabha river, immediately to the north-west of the megalithic cemetery at the base of a hillock. The pottery from the habitation and burial sites included BRW, black-slipped ware, and red ware. Most of it was wheel made, and the main forms included dishes, bowls, perforated vessels, lids, pedestalled cups, and elliptical and globular jars. Lots of microliths made of agate, chalcedony, and chert were found. Beads of terracotta and semi-precious stones, sling balls, grinding stones, and a few copper objects also occurred.

Most of the megaliths of southern Uttar Pradesh belong to a pre-iron age. Kotia in the Belan valley is an exception. Here there were many iron tools, including a spearhead, two sickles, an arrowhead, and an adze, all indicating advanced metallurgical techniques. The Kotia pottery included BRW, red ware, black-slipped ware, and a dull, coarse black or grey ware, all with a thick fabric. There were many bone fragments of domesticated animals such as ox, sheep, and pig, some with cut marks.

A date ranging from the 2nd millennium BCE (or earlier) to the 7th century CE has been suggested for pre-iron Kakoria. The megaliths of Jang Mahal have been estimated as belonging to the beginning of the 1st millennium BCE. Kotia is placed later, between *c.* 800 BCE and 300 BCE.

EASTERN INDIA

The early phase of occupation at sites such as Chirand and Senuar in eastern India was discussed in Chapter 3. These sites continued to be occupied into the 2nd millennium BCE (for details, see R. N. Chattopadhyaya, 2014). At Chirand, chalcolithic Period II is in many respects a continuation of neolithic Period I. There were microliths, polished celts, beads of terracotta, steatite, and semi-precious stones. The pottery was dominated by BRW along with grey/buff, black- and red-slipped wares. Copper made its appearance in Period II, and the upper levels yielded evidence of many iron objects. The earliest calibrated dates for Period II give a range of 1936–1683 BCE.

At Senuar, Period II is neolithic–chalcolithic. The 2.02 m thick deposit showed a basic continuity with the preceding period. The new elements were some copper objects—a fishhook, piece of wire, needle, and an indeterminate object. A fragmentary rod of lead was also found. The plant remains showed the introduction of bread wheat, kondon millet (*Pasupalum scrobiculatum*), chickpea, green pea, and horse gram (*Dolichos bilorus*). There was an increase in the number of faunal remains compared to the earlier period.

Barudih in the Singhbhum district, in the Chota Nagpur plateau of Jharkhand, yielded interesting evidence of microliths, neolithic celts, iron slag, and wheel-made pottery in the same 'neolithic' level. The iron objects included a sickle. The earliest radiocarbon dates give a range of 1401–837 BCE for this site.

There seem to be close connections between the cultural patterns in Bihar and West Bengal. Over 65 BRW sites have been found in West Bengal. On the basis of size, the settlements can be divided into three categories—0.5–2 acres, 4–5 acres, and 8–9 acres. The BRW phase began in this region in about the middle of the 2nd millennium BCE. The problem is that 'Black and Red Ware settlements' are found upto about 400 BCE, stretching across a period of over a thousand years. Clearly, they belong to different periods, and there is a need to identify their chronological moorings.

There is overall similarity in the range of artefacts found at the Bengal BRW sites—in the pottery, stone tools, beads of semi-precious stones, and fairly limited copper objects. Rice must have been the most important crop. The abundance of deer bones and antlers suggest the presence of large tracts of forests and grassy land. The agriculturists of the plains must have been interacting with communities, including hunter-gatherers, living in the Chota Nagpur plateau, an area rich in stone and metal (especially copper and tin). Many BRW sites show some familiarity with iron, but the iron industry in this area really emerged in a major way only towards the end of the BRW phase.

Pandu Rajar Dhibi in the Ajay valley is an important site in West Bengal. Period I, with calibrated dates from *c.* 1500 BCE onwards, revealed microliths, ground stone tools, bone tools, and pottery. No metal was found, but this may be due to the limited area covered by the excavations. In chalcolithic Period II, there were a few copper artefacts, beads of semi-precious stones, terracotta figurines, iron spearheads and points, slag, and ovens. The pottery included a BRW with designs painted on in white, along with other associated wares such as a red-slipped black-painted pottery, black-slipped pottery, and a buff/grey plain ware. The faunal remains included the bones of domesticated cattle, buffalo, goat, and deer, along with those of hog deer, *sambar*, fish, turtles, and fowl.

At Bharatpur in the Damodar valley, Period I yielded microliths, small neolithic celts, bone tools, steatite beads, copper objects, and pottery dominated by BRW. The earliest calibrated date range for this period is 1735–1417 BCE. Period I at Mahisdal in the Kopai valley gave evidence of house floors rammed with terracotta nodules, lots of microliths and bone tools, beads of steatite and semi-precious stones, terracotta bangles, a terracotta phallus, and one flat copper celt. The pottery consisted of BRW and associated wares. A storage pit with lots of charred rice grains was found. The earliest calibrated range of dates for Period I at Mahisdal is 1619–1415 BCE.

The neolithic sites in Odisha include Kuchai in Mayurbhanj district. Domesticated rice was found at the neolithic site of Baidipur. Sankarganj in Dhenkanal district gave a calibrated date of *c.* 800 BCE for a level yielding neolithic celts and copper artefacts. Recently, a neolithic celt manufacturing site was discovered at Sulabhdihi in the Sundargarh district of Odisha (Behera, 1991–92).

At the excavated site of Golbai Sasan on the Mandakini river, neolithic Period I showed traces of floors and post-holes. There was red and grey handmade pottery with cord or tortoiseshell impressions, and a few pieces of worked bone. Period IIA was chalcolithic. The outlines of circular huts (3.9–7.9 m in diameter), with hearths and post holes along the circumference, were identified. Both handmade and wheel-made pottery was found, including BRW, dull red ware and burnished black, chocolate brown, and red wares. Copper artefacts included a chisel, bangle, fishhook, and ring. The polished stone tools included axes, adzes, and shouldered celts. Bone artefacts included weapons and ornaments (such as earstuds and pendants). Spindle whorls, sling balls, and a crude human figurine were among the other artefacts. The features of Period IIA continued into Period IIB, with the addition of an iron tool shaped like a stone celt. The plant remains of Periods IIA and IIB included rice, *moong*, and *kulthi*. Faunal remains comprised bones of cattle, goat, deer, and elephant. The occupation of Golbai Sasan seems to fall within the 2nd millennium BCE, if not earlier.

THE NORTH-EAST

The north-eastern states of India, comprising Assam, Arunachal Pradesh, Meghalaya, Tripura, Manipur, Nagaland, Mizoram, and Sikkim are rich in archaeological finds and potential, but require much more intensive archaeological investigation. The evidence mainly consists of stone artefacts and data regarding subsistence is meagre. There are several neolithic sites, especially in the hilly areas, but unlike in other parts of the subcontinent, there is no clear archaeological documentation of the transition to the neolithic. Much of the evidence consists of surface finds, but there are a few excavated sites (for details, see Hazarika 2017: 94–117). The few dates available are fairly late.

At Sarutaru, 25 km south-east of Guwahati, excavations yielded slate and sandstone shouldered celts and round-butted axes. The pottery included handmade brown, buff, and grey wares, some with parallel lines or criss-cross patterns on the exterior made by cord or basket impressions. However, the 'neolithic' phase at Sarutaru may be as recent as the early centuries CE. Excavations at nearby Marakdola revealed a 1 m thick deposit which yielded wheel-made pottery of fine kaolin clay, some with cord impressions. Similar pottery was found at Ambari near Guwahati, in contexts dated between the 7th and 12th centuries CE.

In the north Cachar hills, at Daojali Hading, the 1.5 m thick deposit yielded stone and fossil wood axes, adzes, chisels, hoes, grinding slabs, querns, and mullers. Locally available shale, sandstone, quartzite, and fossilized wood were used. Three types of pottery were found—grey and red cord impressed pottery; dull-red stamped pottery, and plain red pottery. The querns and mullers are indirect evidence of food processing.

NEW DIRECTIONS IN RESEARCH | **Early agriculture in Nagaland**

The early history of agriculture in the north-eastern part of the subcontinent is not well understood. A recent study based on plant remains and radiocarbon dates from six excavated sites in Nagaland offers the first direct archaeobotanical evidence from the area.

Anil K. Pokharia, Tiatoshi Jamir, David Tetso, and Zokho Venuh studied plant remains from several sites in Nagaland. These sites were excavated between 2008 and 2010 by the Department of Art and Culture, Government of Nagaland, and the Anthropological Society of Nagaland.

The sites are New Phor, Chungliyimti, Khusomi, Khezhakeno, Movolomi, Phor, and Ranyak Khen. Apart from various remains including stone tools and pottery, iron artefacts were found at some of them (Chungliyimti, Khusomi, Khezhakeno, and Phor).

Forty-six soil samples from various levels from these sites were collected and analyzed. The remains of wild/domesticated rice (*Oryza sp.*) and various kinds of millet were most numerous, but there were also remains of wheat, horse gram, grass pea, cotton, silk cotton, Job's tears, *anwala*, *tumburu*, weeds, and wild taxa.

The food staples were wild/domesticated rice and millets, combined with collected or cultivated legumes. The presence of *anwala* and *tumburu* suggests that the people who lived here centuries ago were aware of their medicinal properties. *Tumburu* is also used as a spice.

Charcoal and ash were collected from these sites and sent for radiocarbon dating. The calibrated radiocarbon dates indicate that the dates of the botanical remains ranged from the late 1st millennium BCE to the 2nd millennium CE.

It is interesting to note that the six excavated sites which have yielded evidence of early occupation have megaliths and the people who live in the area today associate these megaliths with many legends about their ancestors.

Source Pokharia et al., 2013

Neolithic tools and handmade grey ware have been found at several places in Nagaland, but few sites have been excavated. Purakha yielded a sequence including pre-neolithic and neolithic levels. A charcoal sample from Stratum 3 yielded a C-14 date of 2,580 ±200 BP.

The site of Napachik in Manipur, located on a hillock near the Manipur river, has given a thermoluminescence date of 1650 ± 350 BCE for handmade cord-impressed ware. The excavation revealed stone choppers, scrapers, flakes, an edged knife, grinding stone, and polished celts. Some of the flake tools were very small and looked like non-geometric microliths. Most of the pottery was reddish-brown, but there were also grey and whitish sherds. Decorations with cord marks make their appearance. Some pots had tripod legs, a feature that shows affinities with pottery found at certain sites in south China, Thailand, and Malaysia.

Neolithic tools have been found at various sites in Meghalaya. An excavation conducted at Selbalgiri, on a terrace of the Rongram river, yielded a microlithic level, followed by a 60 cm deposit containing stone celts and pottery. The handmade pottery included grey, grey-brown, and dull brown ware with a coarse and gritty fabric. An excavation at Pynthorlangthen in the Jowai area revealed a 1 m thick neolithic deposit containing adzes, axes, chisels, points, blades, and scrapers. Most of the celts were chipped, while some were partially ground. Sherds of a coarse, handmade red ware with cord impressions were found. This seems to have been a factory site.

In Arunachal Pradesh, the site of Parsi-Parlo yielded a 50–100 cm thick neolithic deposit with two phases. In the first phase, stone tools included scrapers and large cutting tools made of sandstone and quartzite, with traces of pecking and grinding. In Phase II, the scrapers and large cutting tools disappear; there are pecked and ground tools, axes, and faceted tools. A poorly levigated, gritty pottery makes its appearance. Neolithic tools have also been found at Daporijo.

Not all the sites in the North-east that have yielded polished and ground stone tools and handmade pottery are necessarily early; some are positively late. In Meghalaya, the site of Myrkhan gave a date range of 1885 to 1765 BCE, and Lawnongthroh a calibrated C-14 date of 1220 BCE. On the other hand, the 'neolithic' level at the Kanai Gaon Reserve in Dibrugarh district has given a date of 1440 ±80 BP, i.e., the 6th century CE. Chungliyimti in Nagaland, which yielded a variety of artefactual remains, including finished and unfinished celts made of sandstone and phyllite, buff-coloured wheel-made pottery, beads of semi-precious stone, as well as archaeo-botanical remains, gave a very late date range of 980 to 1647 CE (Hazarika, 2017: 114–15). This indicates that polished stone celts continued to be made and used for a long period of time in these areas, well after the introduction of copper and iron. More excavations and a better idea of the chronology of the sites are required for a clearer picture of the neolithic and neolithic–chalcolithic horizons in the north-eastern part of the subcontinent. There are similarities between some of the pottery and stone tool types of this region and those found in East and South-east Asia.

THE CULTURAL SEQUENCE IN CENTRAL INDIA

There is some evidence of late Harappan pottery in the north-western part of the Malwa plateau at sites such as Sihoniya, Khudai, and Bassaiya. Late Harappan pottery has also been reported at Manoti in Mandasore district. However, at present, little detail is available. There is, however, quite a bit of data on the well-established cultural sequence of the Kayatha, Ahar, and Malwa cultures (Dhavalikar, 1979a). The first of these was discussed in Chapter 3. Here, we will discuss the Ahar and Malwa phases.

The Ahar culture

As mentioned in Chapter 3, the Ahar culture that flourished in south-eastern Rajasthan also spread to the Malwa region of Central India. Ahar culture levels have been identified at Kayatha and at several sites in the Chambal valley. The typical Ahar pottery is a coarse, wheel-made Black and Red Ware, with designs painted on in white (usually on the outer surface, but sometimes also on the inner one). There are bowls and dishes of various kinds; the bowls usually have thin incised grooves on the neck. Another associated pottery type is the red-slipped ware, which includes variants such as tan-, orange-, chocolate-, and brown-slipped pottery, all highly burnished. Coarse handmade red and grey wares are also found.

The other artefacts include necklaces made of short, cylindrical beads. Unlike the meagre remains of stone artefacts at Ahar culture sites in Rajasthan, there was a prominent blade tool industry at Ahar levels at Kayatha. One of the unique features of the Ahar culture in Central India are the terracottas. The animal terracottas mostly consist of naturalistic or stylized bull figurines, made of very fine clay with few impurities, baked at a uniformly high temperature. Many of the figurines have prominent humps and long, pointed horns. There is no decoration on their surface, only nail marks. An interesting find was a pair of short horns on a pedestal. It is possible that such figurines may have had a cultic significance.

People lived in small mud houses with walls made of reed screens, thickly plastered with mud. Sometimes house floors were made of gravel and cobble, rammed in hard, compact clay. At Kayatha, there is evidence of a large-scale fire towards the end of the Ahar phase.

The Malwa culture

The Ahar culture phase was followed by the Malwa culture. Navdatoli (west Nimar district), on the southern banks of the Narmada, is the largest settlement of this culture. Calibrated dates for the beginning of the settlement are in the range of 2000–1750 BCE. Other important sites are Maheshwar (Nimar district), Nagda (Ujjain district), and Eran (Sagar district). The cultural sequence at the recently excavated site of Chichali (Khargaon district, MP) consists of Ahar, Malwa, Jorwe, and early historical levels.

The typical Malwa pottery has a somewhat coarse core and a thick buff or orange slip. Designs were painted on in black or dark brown, usually just on the upper part of the pots. The pottery includes *lotas*, concave-sided bowls, channel-spouted bowls, and pedestalled goblets. Malwa ware is exceptionally rich in form and designs. Over 600 different kinds of motifs occur on the pots, mostly geometric, but some naturalistic. Plants,

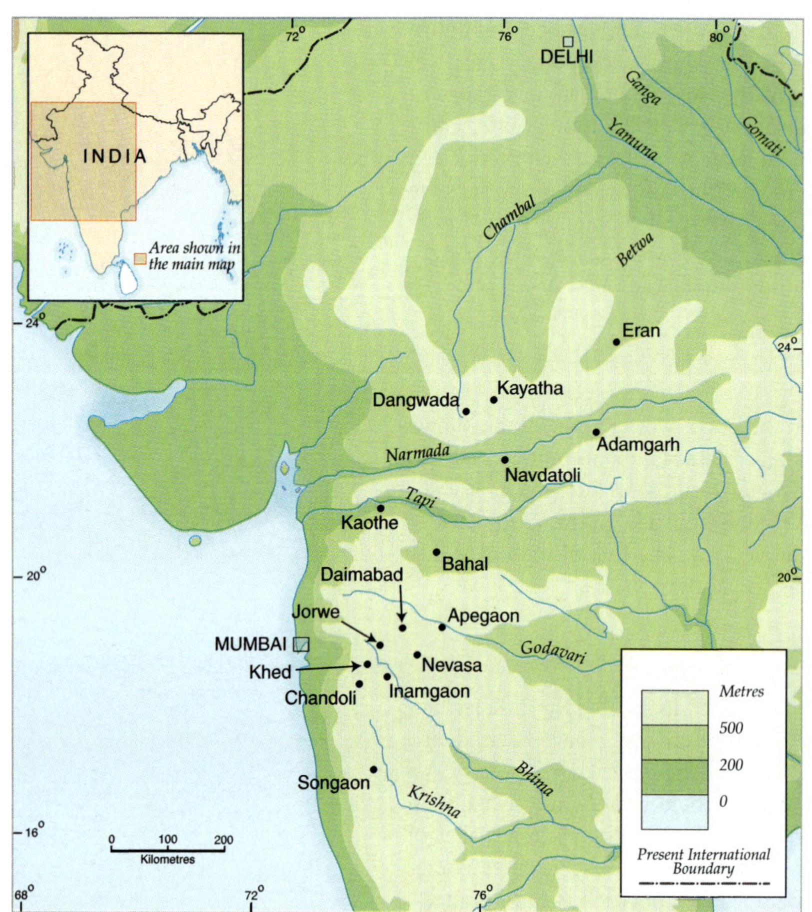

Map 5.4 Major chalcolithic sites in Malwa and the Deccan

animals, and even humans are painted on the pots. There are representations of the black-buck, bull, deer, peacock, pig, tiger, panther, fox, tortoise, crocodile, and insects.

Navdatoli does not show any signs of planning; the houses were built haphazardly, with lanes in between. People lived in circular or oblong wattle-and-daub houses with floors plastered with lime. Houses had wooden posts all around to support a roof that was probably conical. The walls were low; sometimes there was no wall, the sloping sides of the roof coming down to ground level. Mud was often plastered over screens of split bamboo. The diameter of the circular houses ranged from 1 to 4.5 m. The rectangular houses were 5–6 m long. *Chulhas* and storage jars were found in houses. At Nagda, on the banks of the Chambal, there was evidence of the use of mud-brick. At Eran, there was a massive mud fortification wall and a moat.

More artefacts of stone than copper are found at Malwa culture sites, probably because of the scarcity of copper. There are lots of stone blades. Over 23,000 microliths were found in the Navdatoli excavations (Sankalia et al., 1958), most of them made of chalcedony, but a few also made of carnelian, agate, jasper, and quartz. The fact that all the tool types were evenly distributed in all layers and areas of the site suggests that every household in Navdatoli made its own tools. Some tools were hafted, others hand-held. Stone artefacts included saddle querns, rubbers, hammer stones, and mace heads or weights. Copper artefacts included flat axes, wire rings, beads, bangles, fishhooks, chisels, nail parers, thick pins, and a broken mid-ribbed sword. The axes had round indentation marks, similar to those found at Ganeshwar. An analysis of some of the copper objects revealed tin and lead alloying. Navdatoli also yielded beads of steatite, terracotta, faience, agate, amazonite, carnelian, chalcedony, glass, jasper, lapis lazuli, and shell. There were terracotta animal figurines and spindle whorls. Plant remains included wheat, barley, linseed, black gram, *moong*, lentil, *anwala*, *ber*, and *khesari*. Rice was found in the later levels. The faunal remains comprised bones of wild deer and domesticated cattle, sheep, goat, and pig.

Excavations at Malwa culture sites yielded some remains of religious or ritualistic activity. At Navdatoli, a 2.3 × 1.92 × 1.35 m pit was dug into the middle of the floor of a house of the earliest occupational phase. The sides and base of the pit were plastered with mud. Wood was found inside, and there were charred wooden posts at its four corners. This pit can be identified as a fire altar where sacrifices were performed. Another interesting discovery at Navdatoli was a huge storage jar decorated with a female figure (a goddess? a worshipper?) on the right, a lizard or alligator on the left, and what looks like a shrine in between. The shrine seems to have been associated with the lizard. There were four such shrines on the four sides, and the shoulder of the jar was ornamented with appliqué patterns. On the other side of the jar was a shrine with a tortoise to its left (the figure on the right cannot be made out). It can be noted that a shell amulet in the shape of a tortoise was found at Malwa culture levels at Prakash (in Maharashtra). A standing human figure with dishevelled hair on a fragmentary channel-spouted bowl found at Navdatoli is identified by some scholars as a proto-Rudra.

Mention may also be made of the bull figurines found at some Malwa culture sites. The evidence from Dangwada suggests the worship of bulls, trees, snakes, and female deities, and there are fire altars where sacrifices were probably performed. Malwa culture sites have given evidence of burials within houses. At Azadpur near Indore, there was a child burial under a house floor. The body was laid in a north–west orientation, with the feet cut off after death, suggestive of some ritual. A serrated blade and a small terracotta tablet were placed below the head, and a stone to its right.

THE CHALCOLITHIC FARMERS OF THE DECCAN

The late Harappan and Malwa cultures

Discoveries at Daimabad suggest that the late Harappan culture extended into the Deccan. Elsewhere in this region, the general chalcolithic cultural sequence consists of the Savalda culture, followed by the Malwa and Jorwe cultures (Dhavalikar, 1979b). The Savalda culture was discussed in Chapter 3. Here, we will look at the late Harappan phase, and more so at the Malwa and Jorwe cultures, with special reference to the sites of Daimabad and Inamgaon. The detailed excavation reports for both these sites provide an exceptionally detailed range of information about the lives of the early chalcolithic farmers of the Deccan.

As mentioned earlier, the Malwa culture spread from Central India to the Deccan. The main concentration of sites in the Deccan was in the Tapi valley, with fewer settlements in the Pravara–Godavari and Bhima valleys. The Malwa ware of the Deccan is a little different from that of Central India. The fabric is fine, not gritty and unevenly baked, and the pots were uniformly fired at high temperatures. The typical forms are deep bowls and spouted vessels with flaring mouths (the latter are not found in Central India). A coarse handmade red or grey ware, similar to that of the southern neolithic, was also used. Important Malwa culture sites include Daimabad, Inamgaon, and Prakash.

Daimabad (Ahmednagar district, Maharashtra) is a deserted village on the banks of the Pravara, a tributary of the Godavari. It was excavated during 1976–79 by an Archaeological Survey of India team under the direction of S. A. Sali. This important site has a long, well-documented chalcolithic sequence. Period I (before 2300/2200 BCE) belongs to the Savalda culture, Period II (2300/2200–1800 BCE) is late Harappan, Period III (1800–1600 BCE) has been labelled the 'Daimabad culture', Period IV (1600–1400 BCE) represents the Malwa culture, and Period V (1400–1000 BCE) the Jorwe culture (Sali, 1986).

In Daimabad Period II (late Harappan), the size of the settlement increased to about 20 ha. The houses were arranged on either side of a 30–50 cm thick wall made of black clay. The largest house measured 6.3 x 6 m. There was a grave lined with mud-bricks containing a skeleton laid out in an extended position. The body seems to have been originally covered with reeds of fibrous plants. The main pottery type was a fine red ware with linear and geometric designs painted on in black; the shapes included the dish-on-stand, bowl-on-stand, dishes, and vases. There was also a burnished grey ware, a thick, coarse hand-made ware, and a few specimens of ribbed bichrome and deep red wares. Two button-shaped seals with Harappan writing and four inscribed potsherds were among the singular discoveries. Other artefacts included stone tools such as microlithic blades, stone and terracotta beads, shell bangles, gold beads, and a terracotta measuring scale. The presence of copper slag indicated that copper was smelted locally. The plant remains included millets, gram, and *moong*—all of which were present in Period I—with horse gram making its appearance for the first time.

Bone knife, Daimabad

There was a break in occupation for about half a century between the end of Period II at Daimabad and the beginning of Period III, which has been called the 'Daimabad culture'. The typical pottery of Period III was a black-on-buff/cream ware. Other artefacts included microlithic blades, bone tools, beads, and a single piece of worked elephant

Pottery from different phases, Daimabad

tusk. Part of a copper-smelting furnace was found, as were three different types of burials—a pit burial, post-cremation urn burial, and symbolic burial. Hyacinth bean was the new addition to the plant remains.

Period IV at Daimabad belonged to the Malwa culture. Many structural remains of this period were identified. People lived in fairly spacious, usually rectangular mud houses, with mud-plastered floors, wooden posts embedded in the thick mud walls, and steps leading up to the doorway from outside. A house with two furnaces, one with a copper razor, was identified as a coppersmith's workshop. On the basis of the occurrence of fire altars, certain structures were tentatively identified as religious structures. An elaborate structural complex including a mud platform with fire altars of different shapes, and an apsidal temple associated with sacrificial activity were identified. There were 16 burials, either pit or urn burials. Twigs of a fibrous plant were laid out at the bottom of the pits. The artefacts of Period IV included microlithic blades, copper objects, faience beads, and terracotta and bone objects. The plant remains included barley, three kinds of wheat, *ragi*, lentils, pulses, and *ber*. *Sugandha bela* (*Pavonia odorata*) may have been used to make a perfume.

Inamgaon (in Pune district) is located on a terrace of the Ghod, a tributary of the Bhima. It is one of the largest, most intensively and extensively excavated chalcolithic sites in Maharashtra. The excavations, undertaken by a team from Deccan College, Pune, under the direction of M. K. Dhavalikar, H. D. Sankalia, and Z. D. Ansari, lasted for 12 seasons between 1968 and 1983, and provided a lot of information about the lives of the farmers who lived in this place hundreds of years ago. According to the report, Period I (*c.* 1600–1400 BCE) belonged to the Malwa culture, Period II (*c.* 1400–1000 BCE) to the

FURTHER DISCUSSION | **The Daimabad bronzes**

In 1974, a farmer named Chhabu Laxman Bhil discovered a hoard of metal objects while digging at the base of a shrub in Daimabad village. The headman of nearby Ladgaon village reported the discovery to the police. The objects were subsequently acquired by the Archaeological Survey of India from the district authorities.

The hoard consisted of the following four objects:

1. A man (16 cm high) standing on and driving a simple two-wheeled chariot (45 cm long and 16 cm wide) attached by a long pole to two yoked oxen standing on two cast copper strips. There is a small figure of a dog standing on the central pole of the guard of the chariot. The man holds the upper horizontal bar of the guard with his left hand and a long stick curved at both ends in his right. His chest and belly are somewhat elongated. His upper chin and lower lip are protruding. He has a short nose, wide open eyes, and curved eyebrows. His curly hair is parted in the middle and rolled into a bun at the nape of his neck. His knees are slightly bent and his penis is surmounted by four hoods of a cobra;
2. a water buffalo (31 cm high and 25 cm long) on a four-legged platform attached to four solid wheels;
3. an elephant (25 cm long) on a similar platform (27 cm long), but with the axles and wheels missing; and
4. a rhinoceros (25 cm long and 19 cm high) standing on the axles of four solid wheels.

The objects were solid cast and heavy, weighing 60 kg altogether. They reveal considerable casting skill and aesthetic finesse. Chemical analysis showed that they were made of bronze with varying, but low, tin content.

Although the hoard was not found in the course of the initial excavation, later excavations near the find-spot correlated its find-spot to the late Harappan phase.

These artefacts do not seem to have been utilitarian objects. They may have had a religious or ritualistic significance, and the fact that they are on wheels suggests that they were part of a procession. S. A. Sali was tempted to identify the human figure as the god Shiva, lord of the beasts, but this is very conjectural. Metal figures of this kind have not been found elsewhere in India, and the Daimabad hoard remains an enigma.

Source Sali, 1986: 477–79

early Jorwe culture, and Period III (*c.* 1000–700 BCE) to the late Jorwe culture. Here, we will focus on Period I (Dhavalikar et al., 1988).

The floors of as many as 134 houses were exposed in the course of the Inamgaon excavations. Out of the 32 houses of Period I, 28 were rectangular, 1 circular, and 3 were pit dwellings. The rectangular houses had rounded corners with very low mud walls, over which must have been a wattle-and-daub construction and a thatched, conical roof. These are the kinds of houses that villagers of this area live in even today. The houses were spacious, 8 × 5 m on the average, and were often divided into two by a wattle-and-daub screen. Oval-shaped hearths for cooking were found inside. Sometimes, there was an additional hearth in the courtyard; this may have been used for roasting meat. There were two kinds of storage structures—overground bins made of wickerwork and silos dug into the ground, inside or outside the houses.

The early chalcolithic farmers of the Deccan obtained their food by farming, hunting, and fishing. The fact that barley was the main crop is not surprising, considering this area does not get the amount of rainfall required for wheat cultivation. The faunal remains at Inamgaon included the bones of domesticated animals such as humped cattle, buffalo, goat, sheep, dog, and pig. The bones of wild animals included those of *sambar*, *chital*, blackbuck, hare, and mongoose, as well as birds, reptiles, fish, and molluscs.

Tools of stone and copper have been found at various Malwa culture sites. Siliceous stone such as chalcedony and agate were mostly used, and the tools were usually made on blades or flakes. Polished stone axes occur rarely. Microwear analysis has identified tools used for different purposes—plant working, meat cutting, antler or bone working, and hide scraping. Copper artefacts included knives, chisels, fishhooks, axes, and ornaments such as bangles and beads. At Inamgaon, there were lots of beads and pendants, mostly of terracotta, jasper, ivory, and carnelian; also of shell, steatite, faience, paste, amazonite, serpentine, cipper, gold, and calcite. Among the semi-precious stones, jasper and carnelian, which were locally available, were used more than those obtained from distant sources. The fact that shell beads were found at Inamgaon is interesting, as this is an inland site, with the sea about 200 km away.

In Period I at Inamgaon, the only burials discovered were child burials. In all three periods, children were buried in pits in two urns placed mouth to mouth horizontally. Human and animal terracotta figurines were found at all levels. The features and contexts of some of the female figurines suggest a possible cultic significance. The large number of bull figurines suggests that this animal may have been venerated.

The Jorwe culture of the Deccan

The Jorwe culture was first discovered at the site of Jorwe, and was later found to have extended over a large area, covering practically the whole of modern Maharashtra, except the coastal Konkan district. The Pravara–Godavari valleys seem to have been the nuclear zone of this culture. The peripheral zone extended up to the Tapi river in the north and the Krishna in the south. The main excavated sites are Daimabad, Inamgaon, Theur, Songaon, Chandoli, Bahal, Prakash, Jorwe, and Nevasa. Prakash is the largest Jorwe site in the Tapi valley, Daimabad in the Godavari valley, and Inamgaon in the Bhima valley. All three settlements were 20 ha or more in size. These large sites represented permanent agricultural villages. Jorwe, Bahal, and Nevasa are medium-sized settlements. The average Jorwe culture settlements were, however, much smaller—usually 1–2 ha. This category includes Walki and Gotkhil, which seem to have been sites of predominantly seasonal agricultural-cum-pastoral occupation, while Garmals appears to have been a temporary camp site located close to a source of chalcedony. These facts point to the existence of a settlement hierarchy. Radiocarbon dates from Nevasa, Chandoli, and Songaon suggest a time frame of *c.* 1300–1000 BCE. At Inamgaon, on the other hand, the dates for the early Jorwe culture are *c.* 1400–1000 BCE, while the late Jorwe phase is dated *c.* 1000–700 BCE.

Jorwe pottery is fine, well baked, and rich in form and design. The pots have a red or bright-orange matt surface on which designs—usually geometric—were painted in black. The shapes include a concave-sided bowl with sharp carination, spouted jar with flaring mouth, and high necked jar with globular profile. There is also a coarse, hand-made red and grey pottery. Oval lamps of red and grey ware are also found. A pottery kiln has been identified at Inamgaon.

At Daimabad, Period V represents the Jorwe culture. The settlement grew to about 30 ha in this period. There were traces of a mud fortification wall with bastions. The excavators identified the houses of a butcher, lime maker, potter, bead maker, and merchant. There was an elliptical structure with approach paths plastered with cow dung; clusters of pots seem to have contained offerings including copper objects, shaped stones, and tool hafts made of cattle bones. The artefacts included microliths, copper objects, beads, and terracotta figurines. There was also a terracotta cylinder seal depicting a horse-drawn cart or chariot. The crop list of this phase is more or less the same as that of the preceding period, with the addition of three new types of millets (kodon millet, foxtail millet, and *jowar*). Out of the 48 burials, 44 were urn burials, three were extended pit burials, and one was an extended burial in an urn. One of the curious things about the Daimabad burials belonging to all phases is that except for one burial belonging to the late Harappan phase, all of them were of infants and young people. An analysis of teeth remains

Inamgaon (from top): Period I (Malwa phase) pot; Period II (early Jorwe) terracotta lamp

Pottery from different periods, Prakash

of the skeletons showed the presence of dental caries, gross enamel hypoplasia, tartar accumulation, and calculus deposits. There was one instance of infantile scurvy.

At Inamgaon, Periods II (early Jorwe) and III (late Jorwe) revealed rectangular houses, similar to those of Period I (Malwa culture). The fact that the houses were laid out almost in rows, with an open space (perhaps a lane or road) in between, suggests an element of planning. The houses had fire pits, usually with a flat stone at the bottom daubed with mud, serving as a stand for the cooking vessel. The nitrogen in the soil in the courtyards shows that animals were tied here.

On the basis of the discoveries in various houses, it was possible to reconstruct who lived where. The houses of artisans such as potters, goldsmiths, lime makers, bead makers, and ivory carvers were on the western periphery of the settlement, while the farmers and other well-to-do people lived in the middle. A large, five-roomed Period II structure in the centre of the settlement was identified as the house of the ruling chief. This had a granary next to it. In Period III, the chief seems to have lived in the eastern part of the settlement, on the river front. One of the structures was identified as a granary or a temple for fire worship. Other public works that must have involved community effort included a stone embankment wall, geared towards protecting the settlement from floods and for storing water. Irrigation channels were also identified. Inferences about the social and political organization of the people were made on the basis of the details of material evidence. The settlement layout and the burials suggest a ranked society.

FURTHER DISCUSSION | **Food, nutrition, and health among the people of Inamgaon**

Scientists conducted trace element analysis on 165 human bone samples found in the Inamgaon burials. The aim was to investigate the relationship between subsistence, age, status, and changes in diet over time. They reached the following conclusions:

1. The people of the early Jorwe phase consumed a diet containing relatively more agriculturally produced plant food, animal food, and dairy food.
2. The late Jorwe phase people had a diet rich in animal food, fish, and locally gathered plants.
3. Burials were generally under house floors, sometimes in the courtyard. The bones found in the rectangular houses in the central part of the mound reflected a more nutritious diet than those found in the round huts. The diet-related elements suggest some sort of status difference within the community.
4. There does not seem to have been any difference in the diet of males and females in any phase.
5. The rise in weaning age in the late Jorwe period may be associated with a gradual shift from an agricultural to a semi-nomadic lifestyle.
6. The microscopic analysis of the skeletons showed evidence of infantile scurvy, other types of degenerative joint diseases, and fractures.
7. The dental health of the people was good—the incidence of dental caries and gross enamel hypoplasia was low, but people seem to have lost their teeth somewhat early in life.

Source V. D. Gogte and Anupama Kshirsagar in Dhavalikar et al., 1988, Vol. 1, Part 2: 991–98

Period III (late Jorwe) pottery, Inamgaon

The subsistence base at Inamgaon included farming, hunting, and fishing. Grains/seeds of barley, wheat, lentil, *kulthi*, grass pea, *ber*, and a very few grains of rice were found. Barley was the main crop, followed by wheat. The domesticated animals included cattle, buffalo, goat, sheep, pig, and horse (the horse is rare, occurring towards the end of Period II). Cattle were the most important domesticated animal throughout. People hunted animals such as deer. The horse, ass, and four-horned antelope were the new animals added to the list of faunal remains known from Period I. The evidence of fish-hooks indicates fishing.

Period II (early Jorwe) was the most prosperous period at Inamgaon and reflected an intensification of farming and animal domestication. Irrigation was probably used to grow winter crops such as wheat, peas, and lentils. The population of the settlement also seems to have increased. In Period III (late Jorwe), on the other hand, there was a gradual but drastic change in productivity. The cultivation of winter crops such as wheat and pea declined, and the reliance on hardier crops such as barley, lentil, and horse gram increased. There was also a greater dependence on hunting and collecting wild plants.

A rich assemblage of artefacts has been found at Jorwe culture sites. Blade flakes were made of siliceous stones such as chalcedony and agate. Polished stone axes and chisels of dolerite occurred rarely. Ornaments included beads of chalcedony, agate, carnelian, and jasper. Gold occurred occasionally in the form of beads at Daimabad and spiral ear ornaments at Inamgaon. At Inamgaon, pottery kilns and many lime kilns were identified. Copper was scarce, and was used sparingly for axes, chisels, knives, and fishhooks, and also for bangles and beads. A furnace for extracting copper from ore was found at this site.

Inferences can be made about networks of exchange on the basis of the evidence from Jorwe levels at Inamgaon. Gold and ivory were probably obtained from Karnataka, conch shell from the Saurashtra coast, and amazonite from Rajpipla in Gujarat. Apart from tapping the locally available copper and nearby chalcopyrites, this metal may also have been obtained from Rajasthan and from the Amreli district in Gujarat. Haematite, marine fish, and marine shell must have come from the Konkan coast, and hyacinth bean from the upper Ghod valley. Both these regions were occupied by hunter-gatherers, to whom the chalcolithic farmers may have offered beads and pottery in exchange. Within the Jorwe culture zone, Inamgaon and Daimabad may have been major suppliers of pottery to other settlements.

The occurrence of Jorwe pottery at Navdatoli in Central India and T. Narsipur in Karnataka suggests that the Jorwe people had contact with neolithic farmers of north

FURTHER DISCUSSION | **Goddesses with and without heads**

Female figurines of clay—both baked and unbaked—have been found at Inamgaon and Nevasa. Some of them are headless. It is likely that these figurines represented goddesses connected with fertility.

At Inamgaon, an interesting discovery was made under a house floor belonging to Period II (the early Jorwe phase). There was a female figurine in a clay receptacle. Over this was a headless female figurine and a bull. All the figurines were unbaked, showing that they were meant for temporary use. The headless figurine had a hole in its abdomen, and the bull had a hole in its back. When a stick was inserted through both the holes, the headless female figurine was found to sit perfectly on the bull's back!

The fact that the figurines were buried under a house floor suggests they were part of an important household ritual. It is possible that the headless figurine represented a goddess connected with fertility, childbirth, or the welfare of children.

Source Dhavalikar et al., 1988, Vol. 1, Part 1: 571–79

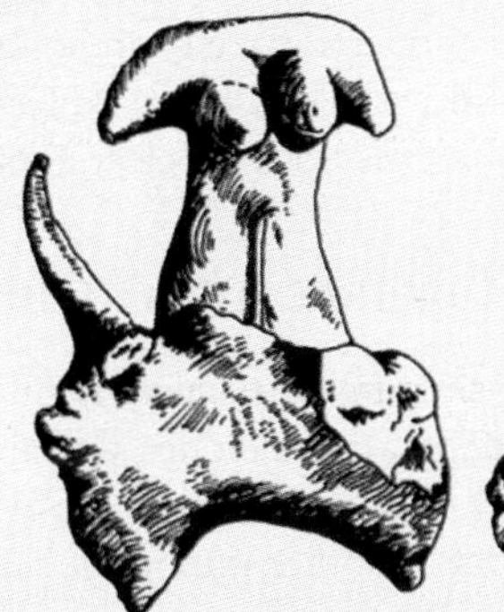

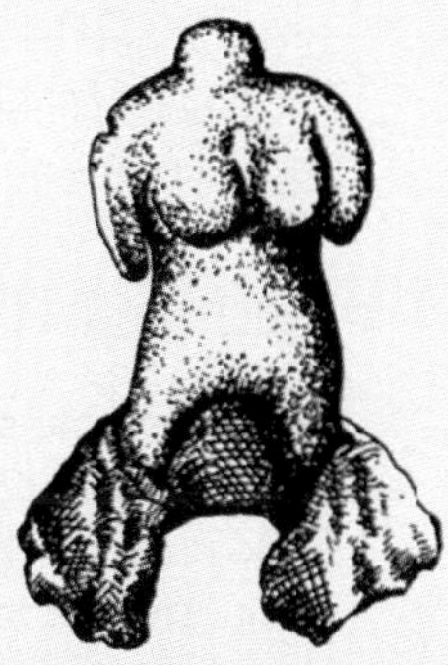

Figure 5.6 Inamgaon figurines

Karnataka and chalcolithic communities of Central India. There were also connections with the late Harappans and lustrous red ware users of Gujarat. The precise nature of these contacts is, however, not clear.

At Jorwe culture sites, adults were usually buried in an extended position, children in urns placed horizontally mouth to mouth. Burial pits were dug into house floors, occasionally in the courtyard. An unusual feature was that in the case of adults, the feet were deliberately cut off, perhaps to keep the spirit of the deceased within the house. At Inamgaon, there was a curious urn burial in the courtyard of the large five-room house. The burial belonged to the transitional phase between Periods II and III, and is dated *c*. 1000 BCE. The urn was made of unbaked clay and had four stumpy legs. The jar was 80 cm high and 50 cm wide, and had a painting of a boat with long oars. One of its sides was modelled to resemble a woman's abdomen. Inside was the skeleton of a male, about 40 years old, seated in foetal position with the knees flexed up to his knees, his chin pressed down to his chest. Unlike the skeletons found in other burials, his feet were intact, not cut off. Close to this burial, but belonging to an earlier phase, was a burial consisting of a four-legged jar along with a similar jar cut into half and placed by its side. It contained no skeletal remains, only a painted globular jar with a lid. This might have been the symbolic burial of a person whose body could not be found, perhaps someone who had died in battle. Going by their location and nature, these two burials seem to have been those of important people; perhaps they represent two generations of ruling chiefs.

Excavations at Walki (Pune district, Maharashtra) on the Bhima river brought to light another Jorwe culture site. A total of 106 structural features were identified here. The houses, most of them circular, were arranged in clusters of five or six huts. The high nitrogen content in some floors points to animal dung, indicating that animals used to be tethered here. Some of the floors may have been used as threshing floors. In each hut cluster, there was a circular silo with lime-plastered sides and base, probably used to store grain. The fact that these huts did not have walls suggests they were not occupied in the

Period III (late Jorwe) terracotta figurine, Inamgaon

rainy season. There were some other large, squarish or rectangular huts with low mud walls in the central part of the habitation. These seem to have been occupied all year. X-ray diffraction analysis of the pottery suggests that Inamgaon, which is located 27 km away, provided earthen pots to Walki. Two unique agricultural implements were found here—a bone ploughshare and a seed drill made of antler. Walki seems to have been a pastoral-cum-agricultural satellite farmstead of Inamgaon (Shinde, 1994: 171).

By *c.* 1000 BCE, practically all Jorwe settlements in the northern Deccan were suddenly deserted, although the one at Inamgaon continued till *c.* 700 BCE. One theory is that the settlements were abandoned because of increasing aridity, which may have led to food scarcity. On the other hand, the evidence of burnt structures points to some other sort of disaster. At Inamgaon, the small huts and coarse pottery at late Jorwe levels contrast sharply with the spacious homes and fine pottery of the early Jorwe phase. They suggest increasing poverty, a time of trouble. Recent studies of the late Jorwe phase, especially at sites such as Sheriwadi, Pimpalsuti, and Talegaon in the Bhima basin have brought out the connections (e.g., in pottery) between the late Jorwe culture and the succeeding megalithic and early historic phases in the Deccan, but the relationship between these various phases is not very clear at present.

NEOLITHIC-CHALCOLITHIC SITES OF SOUTH INDIA

Early neolithic sites in Karnataka, Tamil Nadu, Andhra Pradesh, and Telangana were discussed in Chapter 3. Reference was also made there to the beginning of the chalcolithic phase in the Kurnool district of Andhra Pradesh. Garapadu and Nagarjunakonda in Guntur district are other important sites which have given evidence of neolithic and microlithic tools. We take the story on from there.

The early occupation of sites such as Utnur, Watgal, and Budihal comprised the first stage of the neolithic in South India. The second stage is represented at some of the older sites, as well as in a number of new sites that came to be occupied in

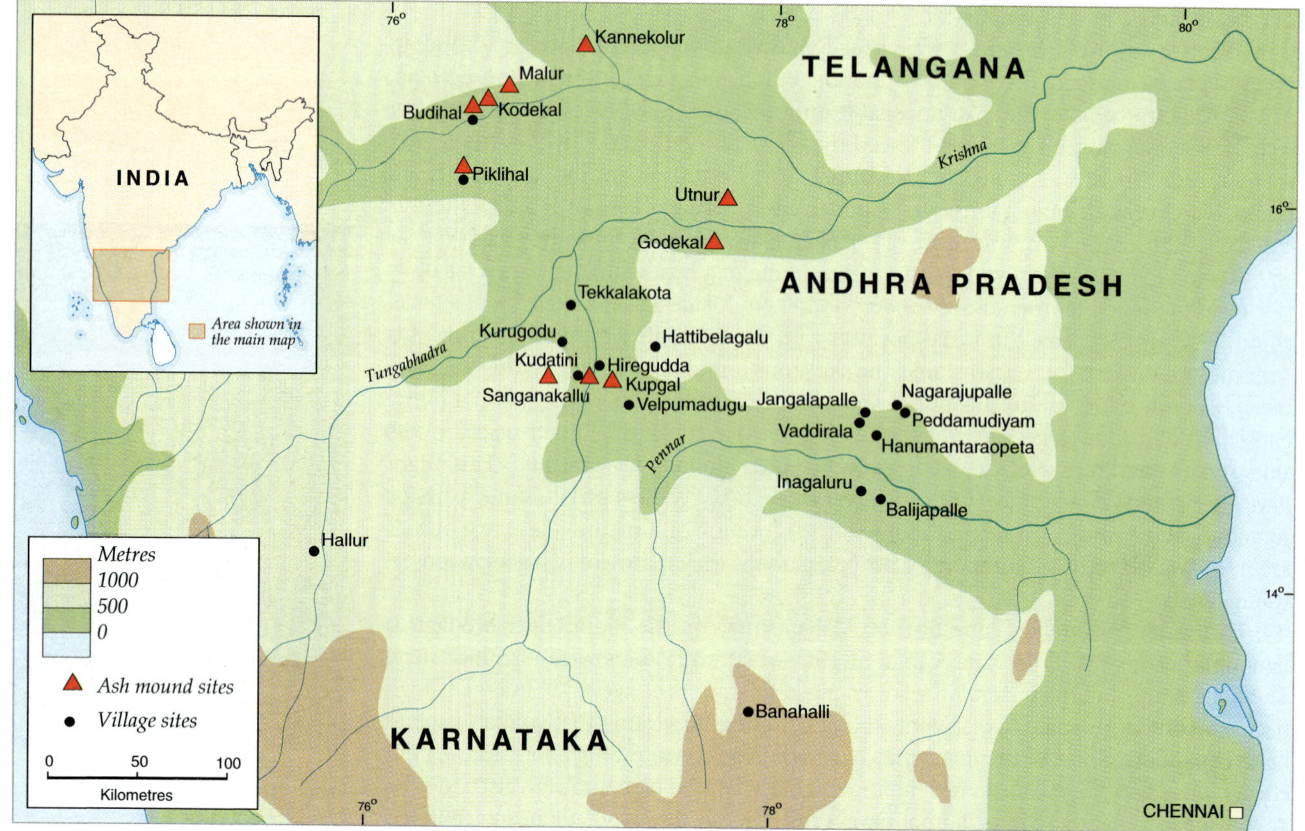

Map 5.5 Some neolithic-chalcolithic settlements in South India

NEW DIRECTIONS IN RESEARCH | **Images and soundscapes in neolithic rock art**

Pictures made on granite rocks can be seen in many places in Karnataka and Andhra at sites such as Kupgal, Piklihal, and Maski. They are difficult to date, but a rough chronology can be worked out on the basis of style, content, and weathering. Some of the images may belong to the mesolithic, some to the neolithic–chalcolithic stage, and others are much later. Many of the pictures were made by crayoning (rubbing dry colours on to the stone surface) rather than painting. There are also many rock bruisings, made by hammering or pecking the motifs onto the rock surface. Cattle are the dominating theme.

At Kupgal (Bellary district, Karnataka), there is an outcrop of granite hills, locally known as Hiregudda (literally, 'big hill'). It is part of the site of Sanganakalli. These hills have hundreds of rock pictures, mostly bruisings, ranging from neolithic to modern times. Humped cattle with long horns are the most common theme. They are usually depicted singly, occasionally in pairs; they sometimes have anthropomorphic figures riding on them or surrounding them, with bows and arrows in hand. Individual anthropomorphic figures are the next frequently occurring theme. Many of them are ithyphallic. There are also several scenes depicting heterosexual intercourse. Some scenes show people standing in a chain-like formation; they are usually interpreted as dancers. Other less frequently occurring motifs include the elephant, tiger, deer, buffalo, birds, footprints, and abstract designs. In general, the scenes tend to be small and simple; large, complex scenes are absent.

N. Boivin's study of the Kupgal rock art points out that some of the locations where the images were made must have been difficult to access for artists as well as viewers. Boivin suggests that certain images seem to celebrate male prowess and sexuality, as well as links between men and cattle. Perhaps they were made by young men associated with cattle herding, maybe even cattle raiding. Kupgal was evidently a major stone quarrying and tool production centre. Another possibility is that the pictures were made by men who came here to quarry stone. The making and viewing of these pictures may have been part of ritualized activity, involving 'rock music' as well. This is suggested by the fact that some of the dolerite boulders at the site seem to have been used for percussion purposes—they have grooves which emit a deep sound like a bell or gong when hit with a granite stone, producing sound that resounded across the hills. This suggests that apart from the visual aspect, the aural/acoustic aspect is also important in understanding the meanings and functions of rock art. Soundscapes are as important as landscapes.

The point emphasized by Boivin is that it is necessary to look beyond the images in isolation and to take into account the wider physical and social landscape. It can be noted that neolithic ash mounds once stood at the base of the Kupgal hill. It is also important to note the fact that this rock art site continues to hold a special meaning for groups living in the area today. Rock bruisings are still made; cattle continue to be the main subject, although the style has changed.

Source Boivin, 2004

this period. Watgal is one of the older sites which continued to be occupied in the 2nd millennium BCE. Period III at this site is dated post-2000 BCE. This level revealed three burials and many large storage pits. Artefacts included BRW sherds, agate beads, carved steatite earrings, human and animal figurines, six copper/bronze artefacts, and three iron objects that may have belonged originally to a later period. Horse gram and *ragi* were the new grains in this period. Period IV was post-1500 BCE. Artefacts included terracotta figurines (fewer than in Period III) and beads of lapis lazuli, dolerite, copper/bronze, and marine shell. There were megalithic chamber graves. One of these contained an iron knife, a small piece of gold-wrapped silver wire, and various kinds of pottery spread out over four large stones. The infant burials were both of the urn and extended types.

The second stage of the southern neolithic–chalcolithic is also represented at the earlier levels of sites such as Sanganakallu, Brahmagiri, Piklihal, Maski, Tekkalakota, and Hallur (all roughly falling within the time bracket of *c.* 2100–1700 BCE). Settlements were established on top of granite hills, on levelled terraces on hillsides or on plateaux between the hills. People lived in round wattle-and-daub huts. Stone tools

Neolithic celt, Brahmagiri

such as celts and blades were made and used, but there is also evidence of many copper and bronze artefacts. The Karnataka region is well-known for its gold mines, so it is not surprising that gold objects have been found at Tekkalakota. The pottery range of this stage is similar to that found at the earlier neolithic sites in the area, with some new features such as perforated and spouted vessels and the roughening of the outer surface of pots. Extended burials were located within the habitation area and usually contained grave goods such as stone tools and pottery. Children were buried in urns.

The third phase followed the second at these sites. Stone tools continued, but there was an increase in the number of copper and bronze tools such as chisels and flat axes. The new elements in pottery were a grey and buff ware with a harder surface, and there was also a wheel-made unburnished ware with purple paint. There are few radiocarbon dates for this phase, but it may be roughly dated *c.* 1500–1050 BCE. The upper levels of most of the sites merge into a megalithic phase.

At Sanganakallu (Bellary district, Karnataka), the earlier neolithic phase was a-ceramic and devoid of copper; this was followed by a phase with copper tools and wheel-made pottery. In both phases, there were ground and polished stone tools, microliths and bone points, and chisels. The pottery of the neolithic–chalcolithic phase included black-on-red ware (some painted with designs in red ochre) and pale grey, burnished grey, and brown wares. There was also a coarse brown and black pottery. Terracotta figurines mostly comprised bulls and birds. Bones of cattle, sheep, goat, and dog were identified. The neolithic phase at Sanganakallu seems to have begun in about 2000 BCE.

At Brahmagiri (in the Chitradurg area), neolithic Period IA was marked by remains of wattle-and-daub huts with wooden or bamboo posts, supported by stone. The artefacts included ground and polished stone tools, microlithic blades, and grey pottery (mostly handmade). Copper–bronze objects made their appearance in Period IB. Extended burials of adults and urn burials of children were found at the site.

Pottery from different periods, Maski

Period I (2nd millennium BCE) neolithic pot-sherd

Period II (1st millennium BCE) megalithic Black and Red Ware

Period III (1st–3rd century CE) coarse grey ware; russet-coated painted ware

Period IV (medieval period) burnished brown ware; grey ware with incised designs

At Piklihal, the lower levels yielded floors of circular huts, neolithic tools, and microlithic blades. The pottery was handmade and consisted mostly of grey and burnished grey wares. There were also some specimens of black, buff, red/brown wares, some with paintings in red ochre and purple. Terracotta figurines of humans, animals, and birds were discovered. Bones of domesticated cattle, goat, and sheep were found. The upper neolithic levels gave evidence of rectangular wattle-and-daub huts, one of them with a hearth inside and a saddle quern outside. The artefacts included fragments of a copper bowl and pottery made on a slow wheel. New pottery types included painted black-on-red ware and a green ware with mottled surface. Beads of carnelian, shell, and magnesite were found.

At Maski, Period I is neolithic–chalcolithic. This yielded ground and polished stone tools, microlithic blades, and a fragment of a copper rod. There were beads of carnelian, agate, amethyst, chalcedony, shell, coral, glass, and paste. The pottery included a dull-red ware and a pinkish buff ware. There were also a few potsherds of painted black-on-red ware and a dull grey ware with incised designs. Animal bones included those of short-horned humpless cattle, buffalo, sheep, and goat. Rock bruisings and paintings have been found in the area.

At Tekkalakota (Bellary district), the early neolithic phase was marked by a handmade grey pottery, both plain and burnished, in some cases with designs painted on in black, purple, or violet. The second phase had black-and-red and dull brown pottery. Apart from the typical neolithic stone tools, both phases yielded microliths, bone tools, beads of steatite and semi-precious stones, and copper and gold artefacts. The structural remains suggested that people lived in round huts with conical roofs, sometimes supported by stones at the base. Extended and fractional burials in urns were found. Animal bones comprised those of cattle, sheep, and tortoise. Charred grains of *kulthi* and hyacinth bean were identified. Calibrated dates for the site are *c.* 2100–1800 BCE.

Hallur is located on the banks of the river Tungabhadra in the Dharwar region, in the Haveri district of Karnataka. Period I is neolithic and is divided into an earlier and later phase. The floors of the round wattle-and-daub huts were made of stone chips and river sand. The first phase mainly had handmade plain and burnished grey wares, as well as some reddish-brown ware with purple paintings. In the second phase, a painted Black and Red Ware made its appearance. The stone tools comprised ground and polished tools and microliths. Other artefacts included copper fishhooks and double axes, as well as beads of steatite, quartz, bone, and shell. A double urn burial was discovered. Animal bones comprised those of cattle, sheep, and goat, with the addition of horse bones in the second phase. Calibrated dates for Hallur Period I range between *c.* 2000 and 1400 BCE.

The subsistence base of the southern neolithic–chalcolithic communities included agriculture, animal domestication, and hunting. Horse gram and *ragi* were found at Tekkalakota and Hallur. Paiyampalli yielded horse gram and green gram. These are the staple food crops of the area even today. The neolithic–chalcolithic farmers probably made terraces on the hillsides for cultivation. The numerous cattle bones, many with cut marks, found at all sites reflect the importance of cattle rearing. There are numerous figurines of humped cattle, and these animals also occur in rock paintings at sites such as Maski. Mesolithic and neolithic paintings of humped bulls in a distinctive style have been reported in the rock shelters at Budagavi (Anantapur district, AP).

A re-investigation of the plant and animal remains of seven neolithic sites in Karnataka and Andhra Pradesh (Korisettar et al., 2001) has provided detailed information regarding patterns of subsistence across the southern neolithic sites. Evidence from seven sites was examined—Hallur, Sanganakallu, Tekkalakota, Hiregudda, Kurugodu, Hattibelagallu, and Velpumadugu. Cattle were the most important domesticated animals; goats and sheep were less important. Chickens may also have been domesticated. There were some water buffalo bones, but it is not clear whether they belonged to domesticates. Wild animals that were hunted included the antelope, deer, and pig. There was occasional use of freshwater resources such as fish and molluscs, even at sites that were a bit far from rivers. Measurement of cattle bones indicated that the cattle herded by southern neolithic

NEW DIRECTIONS IN RESEARCH | **Sanganakallu**

Sanganakallu is a cluster of sites scattered across the tops, slopes, and valleys of the Sanganakallu-Kupgal hills, north of Sanganakallu village, 7 km northeast of Ballari/Bellary. There are five hills—Sannarachammagudda, Sadasivagudda, Choudammagudda, Suddalamattigudda, and Hiregudda. The largest amount of material remains are found on Hiregudda. The neolithic and megalithic remains on these hills have been known and studied from the late 19th century onwards.

The Bellary District Archaeological Project, directed by Ravi Korisettar and Nicole Boivin, focused on a holistic study of the site through a meticulous documentation of its various interrelated features. Surface surveys were accompanied by excavations at several places, and the materials collected were analyzed in laboratories. A total station digital mapping of the cultural features of the entire 1000 acre occupational area was accomplished. It is, therefore, possible to visualize the larger landscape of the site between *c*. 2000 to 1000 BCE and how it changed from the neolithic to the megalithic phase.

Hiregudda: view of site; dolerite axe making debitage (from top)

The granite hills have stone resources that were utilized from prehistoric communities. Numerous active springs supplied water to them. The plains around the hills had shallow water bodies and swampy terrain. Soil rich in clay suitable for making pottery was also available.

The habitation areas on the hills ranged from 0.5 and >1.0 ha. The site has seven ash mounds, some buried under later deposits, some totally destroyed. AMS dates and the stratigraphic sequence help date the neolithic period at Sanganakallu between 1950 and 1350 BCE. The ashmound phase of the neolithic came to an end in about 1750 BCE. Stone circles and menhirs are among the megalithic monuments found on the hills. Rocks that functioned as gongs have been identified through multiple cupule marks on their surface, indicating their use for music and/or ritual.

There were two major stone tool manufacturing areas, one associated with microliths, the other with stone axes or ground stone tools. Hiregudda seems to have been the largest ground stone axe factory site in the region. Analysis of the pottery indicates that it was made by the coiling method. The shapes of some of the cooking pots, with a narrow mouth and rounded body, suggest that boiling was an important part of cooking. This would have been the way in which millet—the staple food—was cooked.

Hiregudda: bull engraving; axe grinding marks (from top)

Archaeobotanical studies of plant remains from the Sannarachamma hill and Hiregudda revealed millets, pulses, and some wheat and barley at neolithic levels. Large quantities of hyacinth bean, a pulse of West African origin, were found. Large numbers of goat and sheep bones indicate the consumption of the meat of these animals. Cattle meat may have been consumed on special, ceremonial occasions. The symbolic importance of cattle in the southern neolithic is also evident from their frequent occurrence in rock art.

About 1 km northeast of Hiregudda is a rock shelter called Birappa which has rock paintings and a dense deposit of microliths. The pictographs here are in various shades of red. These include hand prints, geometric shapes, and various animals including deer, antelope, and possibly a boar. The rock art at Hiregudda ranges from the mesolithic to recent times. The motifs in the earliest scenes include bulls, especially long-horned humped bulls. Later motifs include sexual scenes and dancing scenes. Hiregudda also has petroglyphs consisting of interlinked bulls and conjoined heads of cattle.

There is evidence of beads of steatite, carnelian, shell, and crystal quartz at neolithic levels, suggesting bead making. Over 50 spindle whorls were found, indicating spinning activity.

The excavations at Sanganakallu and the analysis of the remains have added substantially to our understanding of the South Indian neolithic and megalithic.

Source Korisettar and Boivin, 2014

people were of medium to medium–heavy build. The cropping pattern consisted of an emphasis on *kharif* (summer) crops such as small millets, pulses (*moong* bean), and horse gram. Additional crops such as wheat, barley, pigeon pea, pearl millet, and hyacinth bean were selectively grown. Wheat and barley must have been winter crops. Fruits and tubers must have been gathered during the dry season. The evidence of plants cultivated in different seasons of the year matches the evidence of the thickness of the occupational deposit at these sites, indicating that they were occupied all year round.

At several sites, the neolithic–megalithic transition seems to have begun between 1400 and 1250 BCE (see Fuller et al., 2007). However, as discussed below, Brahmagiri has given very early dates for the megalithic phase. There is much more that needs to be understood about the relationship between the South Indian neolithic and megalithic.

From copper to iron: early iron age cultures of the subcontinent

All over the world, the iron age comes after the copper-bronze age. The transition from copper to iron raises a number of questions: Was iron smelting an accidental by-product of copper smelting? Were the smelting and working of iron well within the range of the technical expertise of coppersmiths, or did they involve a gigantic technological leap? After using metals such as copper and bronze for so many centuries, why did some communities start making and using iron tools?

There are certain important technological aspects to these issues. Copper melts at 1083°C, while iron melts at the much higher temperature of 1534°C. Therefore, the smelting of iron requires furnaces that can maintain very high temperatures. Iron ore is associated with many more impurities than copper ores and requires the maintenance of a number of conditions for successful smelting. A temperature of 1250°C has to be maintained in the furnace for the separation of unwanted gangue materials from smelted material. A good blast of air has to be supplied to the furnace, along with constant supplies of fuel. Another important prerequisite is the efficient use of fluxes. A flux is a smelting aid, a substance added to molten ore, which combines with impurities to form slag that can be extracted. The technology of **carburization**—heating the iron in association with carbon to make steel—was another important step that had to be mastered before iron came into widespread use.

The evidence of iron lumps, pieces, or artefacts from chalcolithic levels at sites such as Lothal, Mohenjodaro, Mundigak, Pirak, Allahdino, Said Qalas Tepe, Deh Morasi, and Ghundai, and Ahar indicates that certain chalcolithic communities were familiar with iron and were able to smelt it from the ores. Iron may have initially been extracted accidentally in the copper-smelting furnace when sufficiently high temperatures were attained, if there was iron oxide in the copper ore, or if a haematite flux was used to smelt these ores. But this represented an initial, experimental stage. The large-scale use of iron and the achievement of technical finesse in iron working was something that happened gradually and at a later stage.

Copper ores are not as widely available as iron ores, and it is possible that a shrinking of trade networks may have given an impetus towards the increasing replacement of copper with iron. This was especially so once the requisite technological knowledge of iron smelting and working had been achieved, and people realized the superiority of iron over copper and bronze in terms of hardness and durability.

The beginning of iron technology is not the same thing as the beginning of the iron age. A distinction has to be made between the presence of a few iron objects at a site and a significant use of iron. But how is 'significant use' to be assessed? This has to be done on the basis of the total volume of iron artefacts in themselves and in relation to those of other metals and materials, and by their nature and purpose. It is necessary to try to identify when people started using iron for everyday activities, especially for production purposes. In the case of the agricultural societies, it is necessary to try to identify when iron implements started being used in agricultural operations for making tools such as ploughs, hoes, and sickles. This marks the beginning of the iron age.

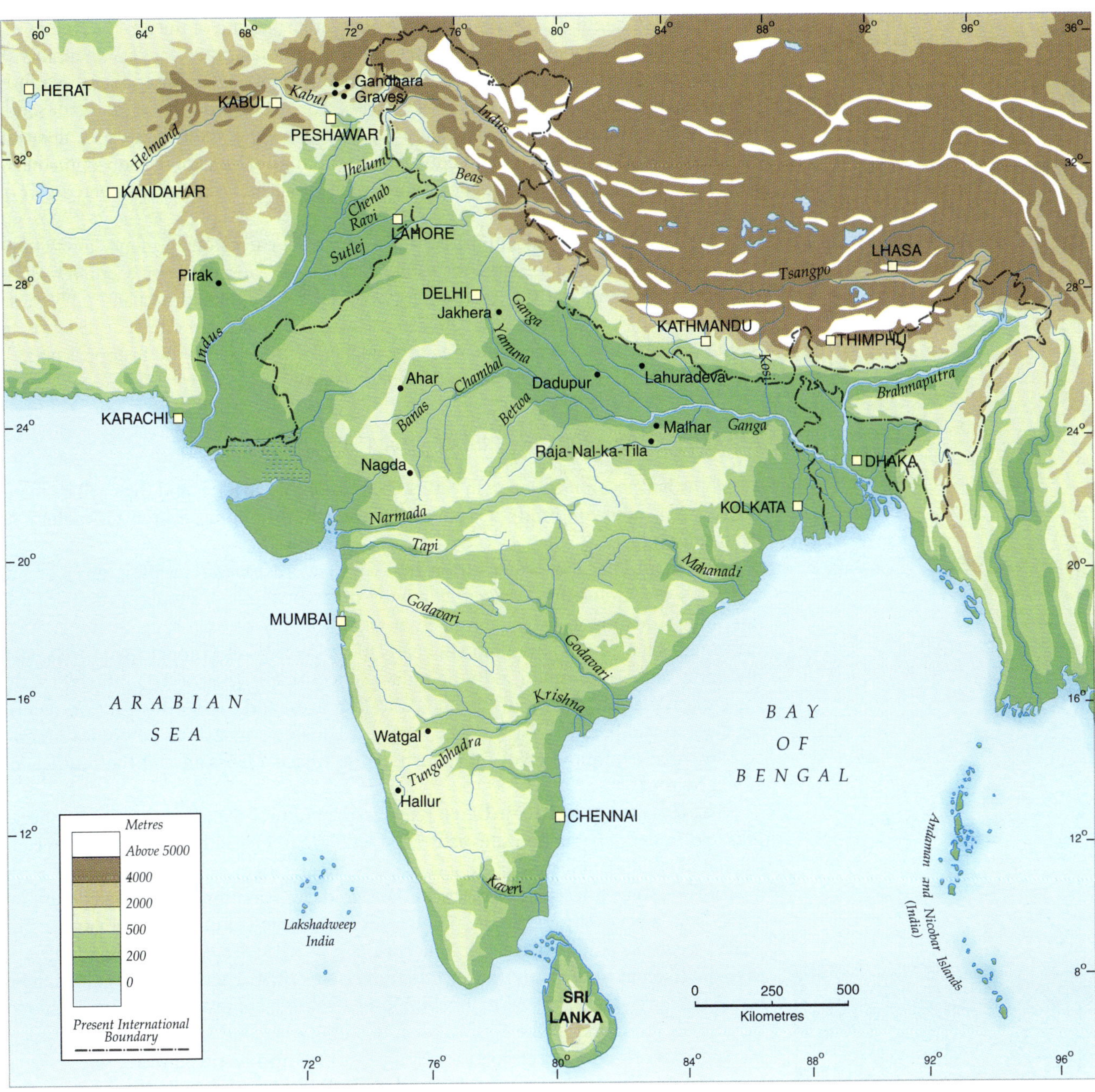

Map 5.6 Early finds of iron in the subcontinent

As pointed out by Chakrabarti (1992: 33), iron ores suitable for pre-industrial smelting are found in all parts of the subcontinent, leaving aside the alluvial river valleys. Evidence from later Vedic texts (cited in earlier sections in this chapter) suggests familiarity with iron and the use of iron in agriculture in the Indo-Gangetic divide and upper Ganga valley in *c.* 1000–500 BCE. The evidence from archaeology gives more detailed and specific evidence for the beginning of iron technology and the beginning of the iron age in various parts of the subcontinent, in some cases from dates that are earlier than what the texts suggest. Although lists of artefact types are available from several sites, more information on iron-smelting and iron-working sites is required.

Several early iron-using zones can be identified in the subcontinent: Baluchistan and the north-west; the Indo-Gangetic divide and the upper Ganga valley; Rajasthan; eastern India; Malwa and Central India; Vidarbha and the Deccan; and South India. All these zones are located in or near iron ore resources and all of them have given evidence of pre-industrial smelting. It should be noted that the growing amount of archaeological evidence and scientific dates are reshaping our understanding of the advent and development of iron technology in different regions of the Indian subcontinent. Chakrabarti's analysis indicates that there is no evidence that iron technology diffused into the Indian subcontinent from West Asia or anywhere else. The use of iron in Central and South India seems to have started earlier than in the north-west or the Ganga valley, and this metal seems to have entered the productive system in most parts of the subcontinent by *c.* 800 BCE. However, recent evidence from certain Uttar Pradesh sites has altered part of this picture.

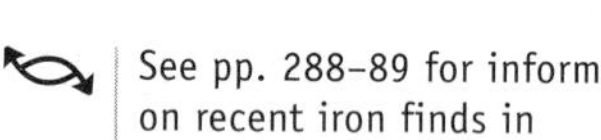

See pp. 288–89 for information on recent iron finds in Uttar Pradesh

The following section summarizes the evidence of early iron age zones in the subcontinent (for details of the sites, see Chakrabarti, 1992; Tewari, 2014). Certain regions do not find mention, either because they have not been explored properly or because they are areas where iron made its appearance at a somewhat later date. For instance, in Assam, Odisha, and Gujarat, there is no evidence of iron before the historical period. The picture in the Punjab plains and Sindh is unclear.

A CLARIFICATION ABOUT THE INDIAN MEGALITHS

Megaliths have been mentioned in earlier sections of this chapter, and they will be mentioned even more frequently in connection with the beginning of iron technology in peninsular India.

The word 'megalith' comes from two Greek words, *megas* meaning great or big and *lithos* meaning stone. Megaliths include different kinds of monuments that have one thing in common—they are made of large, roughly dressed slabs of stone. Such monuments have been found in many parts of the world—in Europe, Asia, Africa, and in Central and South America. In the Indian subcontinent, they occur in the far south, the Deccan plateau, the Vindhyan and Aravalli ranges, and the north-west (for details, see Basa et al. [Eds.], 2015). The practice of making megaliths continues among certain tribal communities of India such as the Khasis of Assam and the Mundas of Chota Nagpur.

The term **megalithic culture** refers to the cultural remains found in the megaliths and from the habitation sites associated with them. Megaliths once used to be considered the dominant feature of a homogeneous, independent, and distinct culture. Such a view is no longer accepted. In view of the significant variations in associated cultural remains, it is necessary to use the plural term 'megalithic cultures' rather than the singular 'megalithic culture'. Megaliths reflect certain burial styles that emerged at different times in different places and continued for quite some time. The origins of some of these burial practices can be traced to a neolithic–chalcolithic context. For instance, pit and urn burials are found in the South Indian neolithic–chalcolithic sites, and two burials marked by stones have been found at Watgal. It may also be noted that a sarcophagus burial occurred in the upper level of the chalcolithic Jorwe phase at Inamgaon. The megalithic chamber tombs, however, appear to be a new development.

Topikal, Kochi; sarcophagus in dolmenoid cist, Sanur

The three basic types of megaliths are the chamber tombs, unchambered tombs, and megaliths not connected with burials (Sundara, 1975: 331–40). The chamber tombs usually consist of a chamber (the size and shape of which may vary) composed of two or four vertical slabs of stone (known as **orthostats**), topped by a horizontal capstone. If the chamber is underground, it is known as a **cist**. If it is partly underground, it is known as a **dolmenoid cist**. If it is fully above the ground, it is known as a **dolmen**. Chamber tombs can have a hole known as a 'port hole' in one of the vertical slabs. They may also have a passage leading up to them. The chamber is sometimes divided into sections by vertical slabs called **transepts**. The chamber tombs include the *topikals* (literally, 'hat stones') and *kudaikals* (literally, 'umbrella stones'), which are found in Kerala and Karnataka. In the *topikals*, the burial urn is placed in an underground pit and is covered by a low, convex, circular capstone. In the *kudaikals*, the urn is placed in a chamber consisting of four orthostats capped by a large hemispherical capstone.

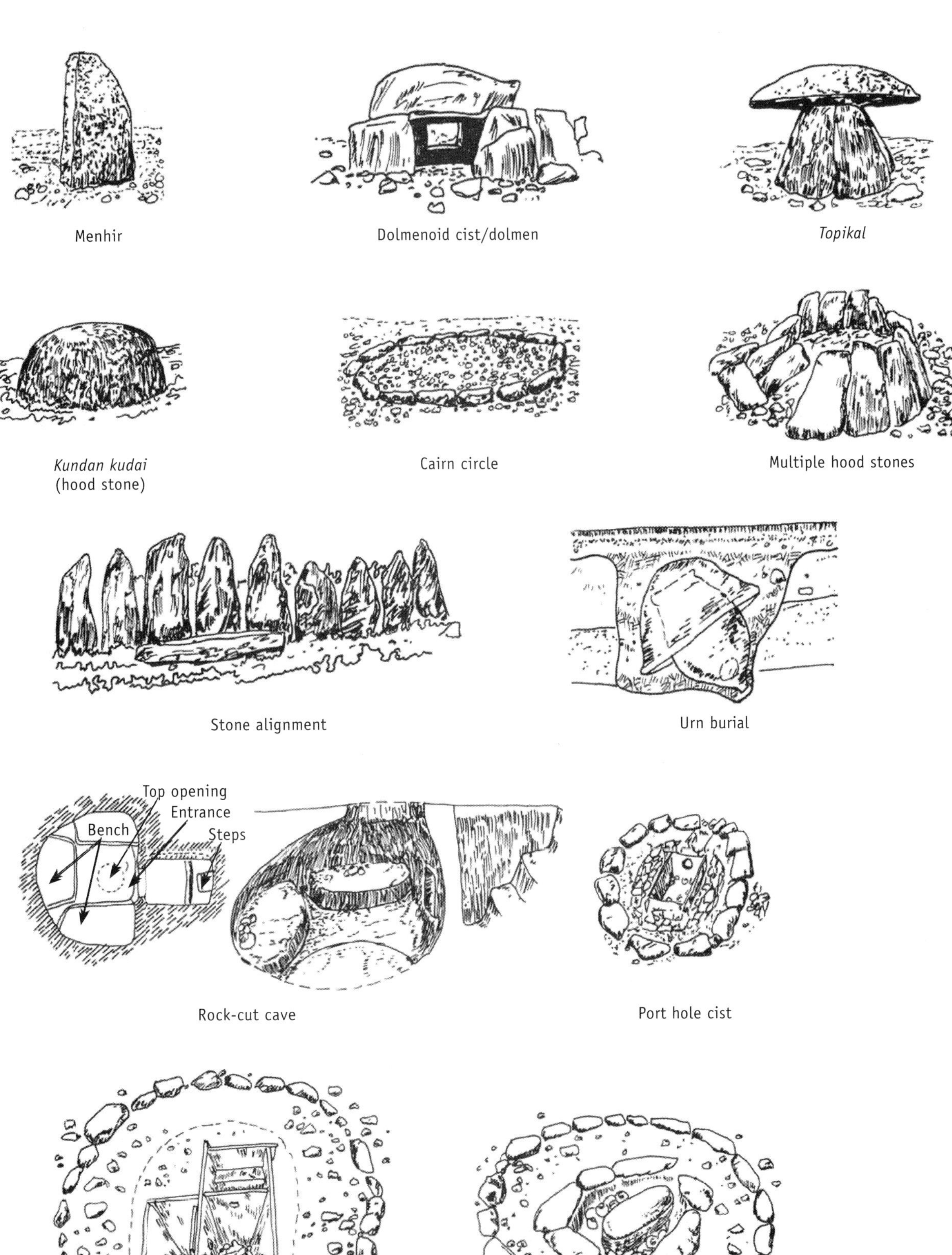

Figure 5.7 Different types of megalithic monuments (after Ghosh, 1989)

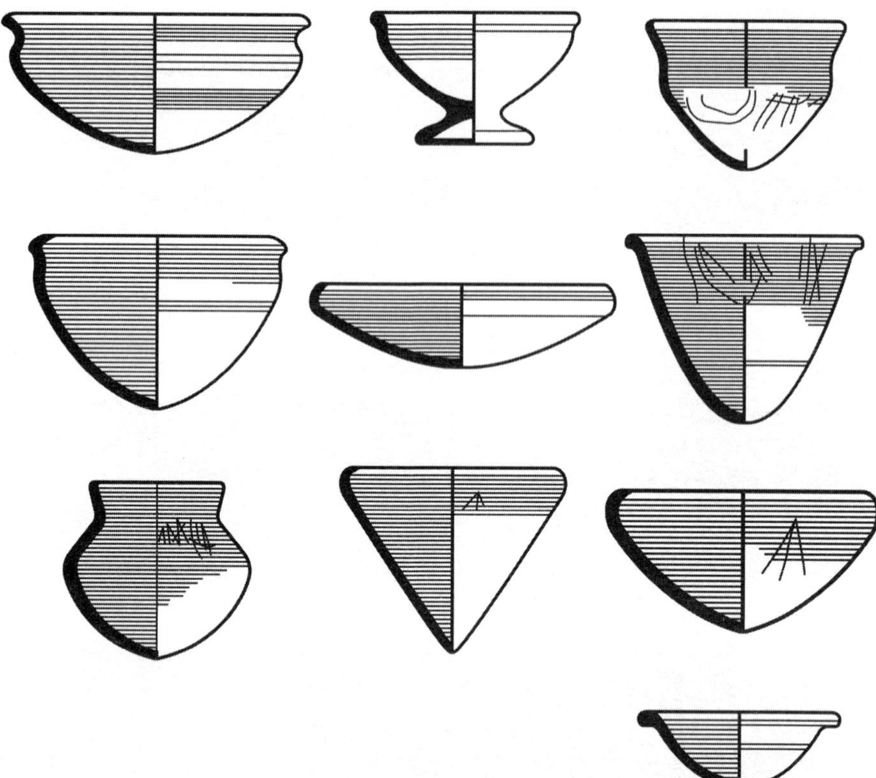

Figure 5.8 Black and Red Ware from megalithic sites in the Deccan and South India

The unchambered burials are of three types—pit burials, urn burials, and **sarcophagus burials**. In pit burials, the funerary remains are buried in a pit. If a pit burial is marked by a circle of large stones, it is known as a **pit circle**. If it has a heap of large stones piled on top, it is known as a **cairn**. If both a stone circle and piled-up stones are present, the burial is known as a **cairn stone circle**. A pit burial marked by a single large standing stone slab is called a **menhir**. A sarcophagus burial consists of a terracotta trough (often with legs and lid) containing the funerary remains. Urn burials consist of funerary remains placed in a large pot or urn, the mouth of which is sometimes covered by a stone slab. Urn and sarcophagus burials are often included among megalithic burials, even if they are not marked by stones, as are burials in rock-cut caves. Not all megaliths are connected with burials. Some of them consist of alignments of large stones arranged in a geometric pattern. Although such monuments seem to be related to the megalithic tradition, their precise function and significance is not always clear.

It is easier to describe the shape and size of the megaliths than to understand the beliefs they reflect. These structures must have been an important part of the lives and belief systems of the people who constructed them. Unlike the burials of the neolithic–chalcolithic phase, which tend to be within the habitation, megalithic burials are located in a separate area. The separation of the abodes of the living and the dead is significant, and is indicative of a shift in social organization. The megaliths reflect many different kinds of funerary practices—extended, fractional, post-excarnate, and post-cremation burials. There are instances of graves containing the remains of more than one person. Some group burials may represent family vaults. But cases where there are no signs of repeated opening are suggestive either of simultaneous death or ritual suicide. The presence of grave goods—weapons, pottery, ornaments—suggests a belief in afterlife. Some of the megaliths are clearly funerary sites, while others may have been memorials for the dead.

Reference was made in earlier sections to the megaliths in the Vindhyas, which belong to a pre-iron chalcolithic context. The megaliths of peninsular India, on the other hand, are generally associated with iron. Not all megalithic sites are contemporaneous. Some are as early as *c.*1300 BCE (as discussed below, Brahmagiri has given much earlier date), while others are as late as the early centuries CE. The important thing to remember is that in view of their extensive distribution and the wide range in their dates and contexts, the megaliths cannot be treated as representing a single, homogeneous, or contemporaneous culture. The diversity of funerary monuments within and across sites suggests significant differences in cultural practice.

THE NORTH-WEST

Iron objects of various types—vessels, javelin heads, sword blades, arrowheads, spearheads, a horseshoe, and fishhook—have been found in cairn burial sites in Baluchistan such as Damba Koh, Jiwanri, Gatti, Nasirabad, Zangian, Mughal Ghundai, and Bishezard. It is, however, difficult to date these burials. Some scholars date them between *c.* 1100 and 500 BCE, but they may actually be much later.

At Pirak in the Kachi plain of Baluchistan, there was a limited amount of iron in Level VI; iron artefacts increased in Levels IV and III. Arrowheads were the only iron artefact type. A blacksmith's furnace shows that iron objects were made at the site. There was basic cultural continuity in pottery types and stone blades between the chalcolithic and early iron-bearing levels. However, a new type of pottery—a grey or black ware—made its appearance. The excavated area of Level IV revealed a set of rooms within an enclosing wall. The niches and doors had wooden lintels. There were ovens and fireplaces, and a few storage jars were found half-buried in the ground. In Level III, the houses were rebuilt, and the larger number of fireplaces, ovens, and artefacts may indicate an increase in craft activity. Some terracotta seals with compartmented designs and beads decorated with zigzag and circular patterns were also found. There were a large number of bone points, mostly made of antler, frequently decorated with an incised circlet on each side. The earliest evidence of iron at Pirak can be dated between *c.* 1000 and 800 BCE.

In an earlier section in this chapter, reference was made to the Gandhara Grave culture in the North-West Frontier Province of Pakistan and the cultural sequence in the Ghalighai cave. Iron objects appear in Period VII of the Gandhara Grave culture and can be dated to the beginning of the 1st millennium BCE. There was a basic cultural continuity between the earlier chalcolithic phase and the iron bearing levels. The iron objects included spearheads, arrowheads, pins/nails, spoons, rings, forks, and an axe. One of the graves at Timargarha yielded what appears to be the cheek bar of a horse's harness.

At Saraikhola, iron makes its appearance in the second phase of graves of Period III. The artefacts comprised two rings, a rod, and the iron clasp of a necklace. These may perhaps belong to the first half of the 1st millennium BCE.

Iron objects have been found at megalithic levels at Gufkral in Kashmir (discussed earlier), and on the basis of C-14 dates for the site, may be as early as about 1850 BCE. However, the real development of the iron industry at this site took place in the early historical Period III.

Burzahom menhir

The Kumaon–Garhwal region is rich in metals and minerals. Heaps of slag and many iron objects were found at the site of Uleni in the upper Ramganga basin in the Almora district of Kumaon. Uleni was clearly an iron smelting and working site and has given a calibrated date range of 1022–826 BCE.

MEGALITHS IN THE NORTH-EAST

Megalithic monuments are prolific in various parts of the North-east. However, they are difficult to date as the megalithic tradition in this region continues into contemporary times. There are several ethno-archaeological studies of living megalithism in this part of the country.

FURTHER DISCUSSION | **Living megalithism, landscapes, and memory**

The megalithic monuments of the north-eastern states of India are difficult to date, but what makes them especially interesting is the fact that they are part of living cultural traditions. This makes it possible to study modern perceptions and memories of these monuments, adding new dimensions to our understanding of modern megalithism and also presenting the possibilities of ethno-archaeology. Rammathot Khongreiwo's analysis of the pre-Christian belief systems and socio-religious practices of the Nagas does precisely this. He situates the megaliths of Nagaland within their larger landscape, understanding landscape as consisting of the interface of the physical landscape with human cultural activity. This interface may take the form of marking the terrain materially; it also includes perceptions, beliefs, and practices associated with natural or monumental features.

The traditional view among the Nagas is one where nature is considered living, powerful, and animated with spirits. Mountains, rivers, caves, and trees are seen as the abode of supernatural beings, including guardian spirits. There is also an old tradition that uses stones as witnesses to oaths and as important landmarks, and megaliths are seen as possessing supernatural powers. The Tangkul Nagas are known to take oaths on the *rihailung*—talismanic stones placed on raised stone altars called *rihai*. The *rihailung* were associated with rituals, traditional systems of justice, and with prophesying the future of the village. Some of the megaliths are associated with the ancestors; some are seen as the abode of deities; others are deified and worshipped.

Certain megaliths are thought to be men or women transformed into stone and the legends associated with them are still remembered. For instance, there is the legend of Sopfunuo of Rusoma, an Angami Naga village about 5 km north of Kohima. According to this legend, Sopfunuo was a beautiful girl of this village who married a man of another village and loved him dearly. Some jealous women poisoned the husband's mind against her and instigated him to abandon her. She left her house for her ancestral home with her son, carrying a burning pine torch. On the way, she was attacked and killed by an evil spirit. The child was pierced by a rib bone of her corpse and died. The mother and child are believed to have been metamorphosed into stones of human shape. The people of Rusoma heard of the incident and found the stones; they tried to move the mother stone away, but a fierce storm prevented them. The two stones had to be pulled together, and were brought back to Rusoma. This is the local tradition connected with the megaliths located at the site.

Among the Nagas, beliefs and practices associated with nature and megalithic monuments are important parts of collective memory and cultural identity even today.

Source Khongreiwo, 2014

Sopfunuo stones

THE INDO-GANGETIC DIVIDE AND THE UPPER GANGA VALLEY: THE PAINTED GREY WARE CULTURE

Painted Grey Ware (PGW) sites in the Ghaggar-Hakra area (including Bhagwanpura) and in the Bikaner region have not given evidence of iron artefacts. Elsewhere, at sites such as Jakhera and Kaushambi (and also Noh in Rajasthan), iron has been found at pre-PGW BRW levels. But in the Ganga–Yamuna doab, the earliest iron objects are generally associated with PGW.

PGW was first identified at Ahichchhatra (in Bareilly district) in the 1940s, but its full significance was understood only after excavations at Hastinapur were carried out by B. B. Lal in 1954–55. PGW has a very extensive distribution, stretching from the Himalayan foothills to the Malwa plateau in Central India, and from the Bahawalpur region

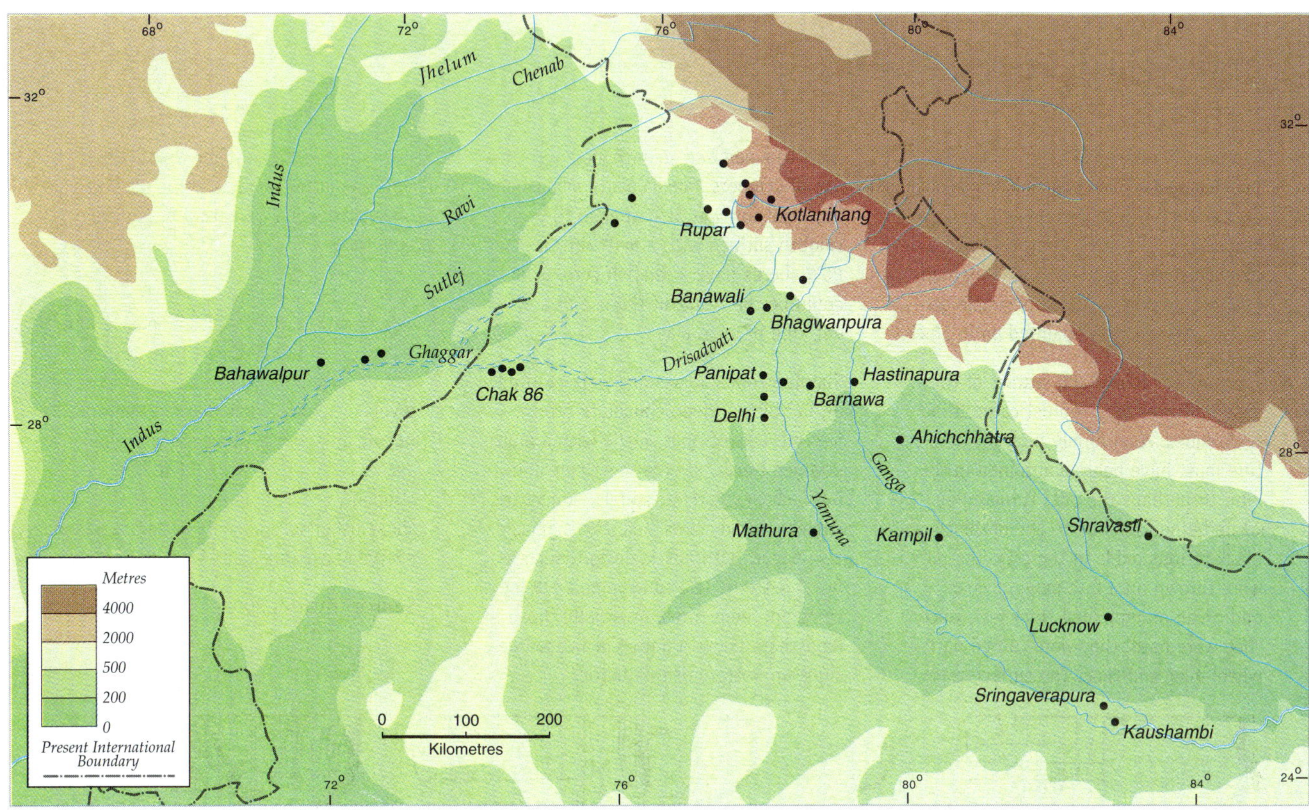

Map 5.7 Some Painted Grey Ware sites

of Pakistan to Kaushambi near Allahabad in Uttar Pradesh. Apart from the plains, it has been found at sites such as Kashipur, Thapli, and Purola in the hilly regions of Kumaon and Garhwal. Sporadic sherds have been found at other places as well—at Vaishali in Bihar, Lakhiyopir in Sind, and Ujjain in Madhya Pradesh. The main concentration of sites are, however, in the Indo-Gangetic divide, Sutlej basin, and upper Ganga plains. The dates of the PGW culture range from *c.* 1200 to *c.* 500/400 BCE, and the sites in the north-west are probably earlier than those in the Ganga valley. Given its wide geographical distribution and chronological range, it is not surprising that there are regional variations both in the pottery as well as in associated remains. In the archaeological sequence of the Ganga valley, the PGW phase is followed by the Northern Black Polished Ware (NBPW) phase, the beginning of which goes back to *c.* 700 BCE at Sringaverapura. The evidence from various PGW sites suggests a proto-urban phase.

Important evidence of the PGW material culture is available from excavated sites such as Hastinapur, Alamgirpur, Ahichchhatra, Allahpur, Mathura, Kampil, Noh, Jodhpura, Bhagwanpura, Jakhera, Kaushambi, and Shravasti. PGW occurs in four kinds of stratigraphic contexts. At some sites (e.g., Rupar and Sanghol in Punjab, Daulatpur in Haryana, and Alamgirpur and Hulas in western UP), it is preceded by a late Harappan level, with an intervening break in occupation. At other sites (e.g., Dadheri, Katpalon, and Nagar in the Punjab and Bhagwanpura in Haryana), there is an overlap between the PGW and late Harappan phase. At some sites (e.g., Hastinapura and Ahichchhatra in UP), it is preceded by the OCP culture, with a break in between. And at other sites (e.g., Atranjikhera in UP and Noh and Jodhpura in Rajasthan), the PGW phase is preceded by a BRW phase, with a break in between. At the upper end, PGW overlaps with the NBP culture.

Structural remains at PGW levels consist mainly of wattle-and-daub and mud huts. Unbaked bricks and one baked brick were found at Hastinapura. Large baked bricks, possibly used for ritualistic purposes, were found at Jakhera. At Bhagwanpura, there were remains of a large, 13-room house made of baked bricks, but it is not clear whether this was built in the PGW or preceding late Harappan phase. There were artefacts made of stone, bone, and terracotta. Chert and jasper weights were found at Hastinapur.

Painted Grey Ware sherds from Hastinapura and Ahichchhatra

PRIMARY SOURCES | **Painted Grey Ware**

Painted Grey Ware (PGW) is a very fine, smooth, and even-coloured pottery, with a thin fabric. Its shades range from a soft silvery grey to a strong battleship grey. It was made out of well-worked, very high quality clay. Designs, mostly simple geometric patterns, were painted on in black.

The uniform colour and texture of the pots indicates very sophisticated firing techniques. A uniformly high temperature must have been maintained in the kiln. Or perhaps the pots turned grey while being fired due to the presence of black ferrous oxide in the clay. The pots were thrown on a fast-moving wheel and given an egg-shell thickness. Once they were hard, they were turned on the wheel a second time. The surface was then trimmed and smoothened with the use of scrapers. Some sort of smoothening emulsion was also applied to give a smooth surface with a matt finish. Some PGW sherds have a reddish core, which could be the result of the use of a different kind of local clay.

Simple geometric designs were painted on in black or deep chocolate brown. Several rows of lines, made with a multi-pronged brush, are the most common. Dots, dashes, circles, spirals, concentric circles, checks, *swastikas*, and sigmas also occur. Naturalistic designs such as floral patterns and sun symbols are less common. Some sites, especially those in Rajasthan, show stamped or incised designs on pottery of this fabric.

PGW shows comparatively few shapes. Open-mouthed bowls and dishes occur often, *lotas* and miniature pots infrequently.

PGW seems to have been a deluxe table ware, used by well-to-do people. It forms a very small percentage (3–10 per cent) of the total pottery assemblage at the levels at which it has been found, and occurs along with other pottery types such as plain grey ware, BRW, and black slipped ware. People must have used these other sorts of pottery for cooking, everyday use, and food storage.

Source Tripathi, 2002

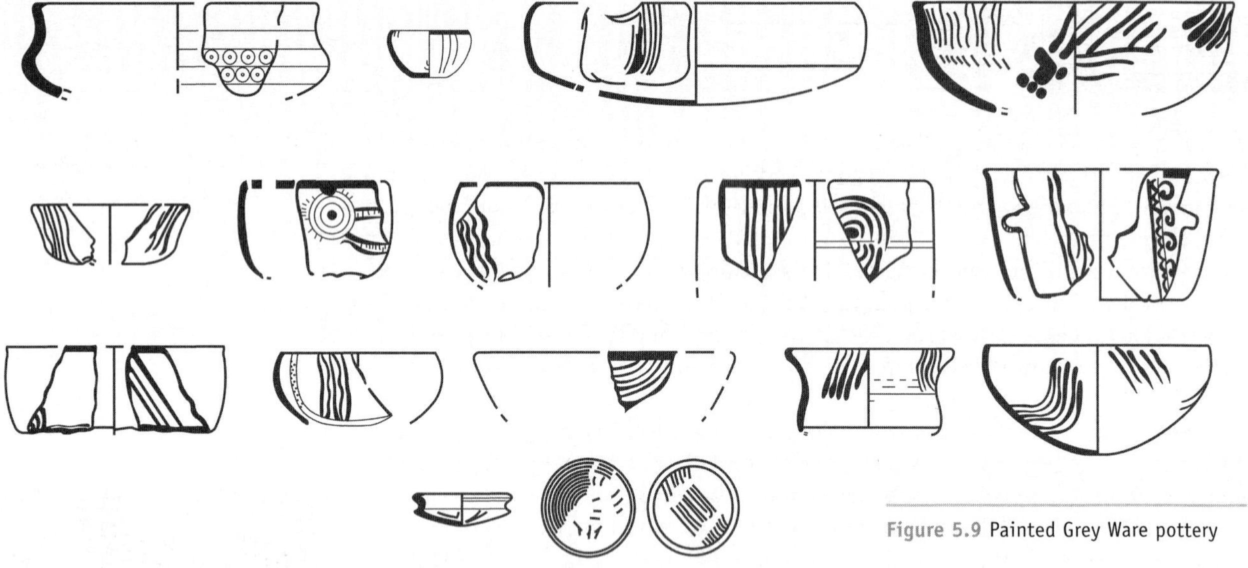

Figure 5.9 Painted Grey Ware pottery

At Jakhera, iron makes its appearance in Period II in association with BRW, black slipped ware, and red wares in a context that can be dated before 1200 BCE. Period III at Jakhera represents a fairly evolved, proto-urban or semi-urban stage of the PGW culture. An interesting piece of evidence from this site is a water channel and a bund associated with a 60 m long water channel, suggesting water management strategies. Remains of houses (many with multiple hearths), roads and lanes paved with potsherds, and an uneven mud-brick platform associated with a fire altar have also been found. A fire pit with a terracotta hooded snake, a crude handmade figurine, and a bowl were among the interesting discoveries. Square and roundish storage bins suggest surplus food production. The rich range of artefacts from Jakhera included gold and copper ornaments, 106 beads of semi-precious stones, copper artefacts of various kinds, geometric stone pieces, and ivory objects. A large number of iron objects, including agricultural implements such as hoes and sickles, were also found.

Abhaipur (Pilibhit district) revealed a four-fold cultural sequence marked by OCP, BRW, PGW, and NBPW. A set of calibrated C-14 dates for Period III range from 1344 BCE to 980 BCE. There is a 30–50 cm deposit below the level from which the sample was taken and this indicates that the iron-bearing PGW level is even older than this (Tewari, 2014: 579).

The PGW sites indicate a subsistence base that included the cultivation of rice, wheat, and barley. People were growing two crops a year. There is no actual evidence of irrigation facilities, but a few deep circular pits outside the habitation area at Atranjikhera are indicative of *kachcha* wells. People living in the area today use such wells to irrigate their fields. Animal husbandry was also practised. PGW sites have yielded bones of cattle, sheep, and pigs, many of them charred and bearing cut marks. Fish bones and fishhooks indicate fishing. Horse bones have been found at Hastinapura.

Most of the artefacts found at PGW levels seem to be connected with war or hunting—arrowheads, spearheads, blades, daggers, and lances. But there are also clamps, sockets, rods, rings, pins, chisels, axes, adzes, borers, and scrapers, some of which would have been useful in carpentry. The mature PGW phase (Period IIB) at Jakhera has also given important evidence of iron implements used in agriculture—a sickle, ploughshare, and hoe. The wide range of iron objects at PGW levels at Atranjikhera and the agricultural implements found at Jakhera show that the iron industry was well-developed in this area during this period.

The chemical analysis of iron artefacts from PGW levels at Atranjikhera has indicated that they were made of wrought iron and were then carburized, probably by keeping them on a bed of charcoal for a long time at a high temperature. The composition of the objects and pieces of iron slag at the site matched that of the iron-rich rocks found in the stretch of hills between Agra and Gwalior, indicating that these were the source of the iron ore.

There are some detailed studies of settlement patterns associated with the PGW phase. Makkhan Lal's study (1984) of the Kanpur district (UP) identified 46 PGW sites. Of these, 26 were below 1 ha, 14 between 1 and 1.99 ha, 2 between 2 and 2.9 ha, 3 between 3 and 3.99 ha, and 1 between 4 and 4.99 ha. The sites away from the rivers were smaller than those along riverbanks. The average spacing between two settlements was 10–14 km. Erdosy's study (1988) traces the history of settlements in Allahabad district (UP) between *c.* 1000 BCE and 300 CE. Period I (100–600 BCE) concerns us here. There was a two-tier hierarchy of settlements. Fifteen sites were 0.42–2.80 ha in size, the average size being 1.72 ha. One site—Kaushambi—was 10 ha and clearly stood out among all the others. Its location in an area of poor soil and rugged terrain may have been in order to access the mineral resources of the Vindhyas. Assuming an average density of 160 people per ha, Erdosy estimates that between 60 and 450 people lived in these villages. A two-tier site hierarchy is also visible in northern Haryana—of the 42 PGW sites here, one site was 9.6 ha and none of the rest were more than 4.3 ha. This evidence can be compared with Mughal's analysis of PGW settlements in the Bahawalpur area, where there are 14 sites ranging between 0.5 and 13.7 ha. Except for Satwali (13.7 ha), most of them were under 5 ha.

Painted Grey Ware sherds from various sites

THE EVIDENCE FROM RAJASTHAN

Noh near Bharatpur shares a similar cultural sequence with sites in the neighbouring upper Ganga valley. Here, Period I yielded OCP and Period II was marked by BRW. Some shapeless pieces of iron were found in Period II. Period III was marked by PGW and yielded iron artefacts such as a spearhead, arrowhead with a socketed tang, and an axe with a broad cutting edge.

In eastern Rajasthan, PGW levels at Jodhpura revealed a crucible-shaped furnace used for the direct reduction of ore, where the bloom was heated in an open furnace and forged on an adjacent platform.

The most important evidence comes from Ahar in south-east Rajasthan. Here, there were three chalcolithic phases, and iron occurred in Phases Ib and Ic of the chalcolithic occupation. In Phase Ib, there was an arrowhead, a ring, and slag. In Phase Ic, there were four arrowheads, two chisels, one nail, one peg, and a socket. Calibrated dates for the iron-bearing chalcolithic levels at Ahar fall within the first quarter of the 2nd millennium BCE. However, according to some scholars, the finds come from disturbed layers.

THE MIDDLE AND LOWER GANGA VALLEY

The evidence suggests the beginning of iron technology in the middle Ganga valley in the early and mid-2nd millennium BCE (see Tewari, 2004 for details). Calibrated radiocarbon dates from BRW levels at Period I at Dadupur (Lucknow district) suggest that iron was introduced at this site in the first half of the first millennium BCE. On the basis of calibrated radiocarbon dates, the iron-bearing Period II at Malhar (Chandauli district) was dated to the 18th/17th century BCE. Iron artefacts included a nail, clamp, arrowhead, spearhead, awl, knife, bangle, ploughshare, and sickle. Malhar also yielded the remains of two clay furnaces filled with iron slag, as well as sherds of red, grey, and black slipped ware, an axe, and tuyeres (terracotta pipes used to force air into a furnace). Similar furnaces have been found at other sites in the neighbourhood, and haematite is available in the Geruwatwa hill. All this suggests that the area around Malhar was a centre of iron smelting and the making of iron artefacts. Iron was found at Raja Nal ka Tila (Period II) in the upper Belan valley and the calibrated radiocarbon date range is 1431–1135 BCE. Both these sites have given evidence of iron smelting and iron working. Iron at Jhusi (Period IB) (Allahabad district) is dated to *c.* 1100 BCE.

Elsewhere in the middle Ganga valley, for instance at Ganweria, iron often appears in association with black-slipped ware. At Koldihwa, iron-bearing levels follow the chalcolithic levels, without any break. The iron objects included axes and arrowheads, and crucibles and slag were also found. At Panchoh, iron nodules were found with ill-fired handmade corded and plain red wares, microliths, and small neolithic celts.

At Narhan, on the banks of the Sarayu, the beginning of iron can be placed in *c.* 1000–900 BCE. Iron objects made their first appearance in Period I (marked by BRW) and increased significantly in Period II (marked by black-slipped ware and red wares). Period II showed an increase in the number and variety of arrowheads and bone points. There were beads of glass, agate, and terracotta; terracotta balls and dabbers; bone and terracotta dice; terracotta gamesmen; glass bangles; bone pendants; two crude terracotta female figurines; and two animal figurines representing a bull or *nilgai*. Crucibles made of a vitreous substance as well as of terracotta may have been connected with metallurgy or medicine. Copper objects included antimony rods, a nail parer, bangles, and a fishhook. The iron objects comprised arrowheads, spearheads, chisels, and nails. The discovery of carbonized grains of rice, barley, pea, and green gram indicate a basic continuity in agricultural practices with Period I, the only new element being safflower seeds. Remains of *sisoo* and *jamun* were found. Period I at Narhan is dated *c.* 1300–800 BCE and Period II *c.* 800–600 BCE.

Period I at Aktha (Varanasi district, UP) has yielded iron in association with BRW, black slipped ware, and red wares. The level has been dated between 1800 and 1450 BCE.

In eastern India, the earliest iron artefacts appear in a BRW context at sites such as Chirand, Sonpur, Taradih, Bahiri, Mahisdal, and Bharatpur. Many sites show cultural continuity from the chalcolithic BRW phase to the early iron BRW phase. On the other hand, at Mahisdal (on the banks of the Kopai river), early iron artefacts occurred along with microliths, and at Barudih, iron was associated with neoliths.

Mention was made earlier of iron artefacts found at chalcolithic levels at Pandu Rajar Dhibi in the Ajay valley in West Bengal. Iron artefacts have been found in Period I at Tulsipur and Dihar in association with BRW. The sites of Bahiri and Mangalkot are also in the Ajay valley. Period I at Bahiri has given calibrated C-14 dates ranging from 1189–1180 BCE to 795 BCE; there is evidence of rammed floors of wattle-and-daub houses, bone tools, BRW and associated wares, some microliths, and an extensive deposit of iron ore and slag. A piece of copper wire found at Bahiri was analyzed and found to contain about 10 per cent tin alloying. Period I at Mangalkot yielded iron slag, ingots, and iron artefacts such as points and arrowheads in Period I, which is dated *c.* 1200–700 BCE. Here, there were remains of wattle-and-daub houses with mud floors plastered with cow dung and sometimes rammed with potsherds and granular gravels. The artefacts included stylized human terracotta figurines, miscellaneous terracotta objects (beads, bangles, sling balls, net sinkers), beads of semi-precious stones, some microliths, lots of different kinds of bone tools, and copper spiral bangles and fishhooks. Iron artefacts included a point, spearhead, and knife; iron slag and bloom have also been found.

CENTRAL INDIA

Iron is found at BRW levels at sites such as Nagda on the banks of the Chambal and Eran on the banks of the Bina river. There is broad cultural continuity between the chalcolithic and early iron age levels.

At Nagda, Period I belongs to the Malwa culture. The site was reoccupied after a short break of occupation. Period II was marked by BRW, although the earlier pottery types continued, as did the microliths. Iron objects occurred throughout and included a double-edged dagger, an axe socket, axe with broad cutting edge, spoon, ring, nail, arrowhead, spearhead, knife, and sickle. There was a red or cream pottery with designs (mostly geometric) painted on in black. Similarly at Eran, Period I belonged to the Malwa culture, while Period IIA had BRW and iron. At Ujjain, the iron artefacts found at BRW levels included a spearhead, arrowhead, knife, crowbar, and spade. The dating of the early iron bearing levels at these sites is the subject of debate.

There are a number of iron-bearing megalithic sites in Madhya Pradesh. The important ones include Dhanora, Sonabhir, Karhibhandari, Chirachori, Majagahan, Kabrahata, Sorara, Sankanpalli, Timmelwada, Handaguda, and Nelakanker.

THE DECCAN

The earliest iron artefacts in the Deccan occur at BRW levels, and many of them are associated with megaliths. The relationship between these levels and the preceding chalcolithic Jorwe culture is not clear. Many of the Jorwe sites seem to have been deserted for four to five centuries, and were reoccupied in about the 6th/5th century BCE. At other places, there seems to be some cultural continuity between the Jorwe phase and the succeeding iron age phase.

Prakash has a cultural sequence similar to that of Nagda: Malwa culture levels, followed by a short break in occupation, then a BRW deposit yielding iron artefacts, followed by an early historical NBPW level. The iron artefacts found at BRW levels at Prakash comprised the following types—tanged arrowhead, celt-like axe head, knife blade, sickle, chisel-edged tanged object, clamp, lance or spearhead, ferrule (a metal joint or protective cap), and nails. Similar evidence was found at Bahal.

Several megalithic burials and associated habitational deposits in Maharashtra have yielded iron objects. Important sites include Takalghat-Khapa, Naikund, Mahurjhari, Bhagimohari, Borgaon, Ranjala, Pimpalsuti, and Junapani. Cup marks or circular incisions have been found on the outer stones of the stone circles at several sites in Vidarbha. Takalghat-Khapa yielded remains of a habitation site associated with the megalithic burial ground and a date range from 8th/7th century BCE to 4th century BCE. The calibrated range of dates from Naikund are 800–420 BCE and 785–410 BCE. These sites seem to have been flourishing agricultural settlements. Barley, rice, and lentil grains were found on house floors at Naikund. There were a wide range of copper and iron artefacts. The iron artefacts included ladles, nails, dagger blades, arrowheads, knives, chisels, spikes, axes, double-edged adzes, blades, bars/rods, fishhooks, horse bits, bangles, nail-parer-cum-earpicks (?), tridents, a spearhead, sword, and cauldron. Iron hoes were found at Naikund, and there was also evidence of the local smelting of iron. The remains of a workshop included a furnace made of small curved bricks with a cylindrical terracotta pipe. Iron ore was found in a *nala* about a kilometre away from the smelting site. Mahurjhari was an important bead-manufacturing site and the exceptional richness of grave-goods in the burials may be related to this fact. Bead manufacture at this site continued from the megalithic to the early historic phase (Mohanty, 1999).

The remains of horses, replete with iron bits and bedecked with copper ornaments, were found at almost all the stone circles at Mahurjhari and Naikund. One of the Mahurjhari burials revealed the complete skeleton of a horse, cut marks suggesting that it had been sacrificed and then buried with the human. There were two other dramatic burials—one grave contained the remains of an adult male, his mouth gaping, an arrow embedded near his collarbone. The second contained the top part of the body of an adult male, a dagger with an iron blade and copper hilt rested on his chest. Such burials speak eloquently of a warrior tradition.

SOUTH INDIA

In South India, the earliest iron objects appear in the overlap between the neolithic and megalithic phases. The transition from the neolithic-chalcolithic to the megalithic phase in South India may have taken place by *c.* 1400 BCE. At a few sites (e.g., Velpumadugu in Andhra Pradesh), the ash mounds continue into the early megalithic phase. The change in ritual behaviour from ash mounds to stone megaliths marks a significant ritual and symbolic shift.

Among the important megalithic sites in Karnataka are Brahmagiri, Maski, Hanamsagar, Terdal-Halingali, T. Narsipur, and Hallur. Hallur has a radiocarbon date of *c.* 1000 BCE. Kumarnahalli has an earlier thermoluminescence date of 1300–1200 BCE. Kathleen Morrison's reconsideration of the evidence from Brahmagiri (2005: 258) included dates for two pieces of charred pieces of wood excavated by Wheeler in 1947–48 in Megalith 6. The wood samples were dated by AMS and conventional radiocarbon dating and gave an unexpectedly early date range between 2140 and 1940 BCE, which falls within the time frame of the South Indian neolithic.

Megaliths at Hire Benakal; Rajan Kolluru (from top)

Excavations at Sannarachamma hill near Sanganakallu (in Karnataka) have given evidence of the transition from an ash mound site to one marked by megaliths. There is a thick ash mound layer followed by later neolithic deposits. The ash mound phase can be dated from *c.* 1950–1900 BCE and continued till *c.* 1700 BCE. The village settlement continued for several centuries thereafter. This made way for a megalithic phase which had pottery, but no iron. The neolithic–megalithic transition at this site is placed between 1400–1250 BCE (Korisettar et al., 2003). The site of Hiregudda too has an ash mound and neolithic phase followed by a megalithic phase. The large number of stone axes found here suggests that the transition to the megalithic phase may have been connected with an increase in specialized craft production (Fuller et al., 2007).

The discovery, explorations, and excavations at a large number of iron age sites in Tamil Nadu have greatly enhanced our understanding of the iron age. The megalithic sites in the state include Adichanallur, Amritamangalam, Kunnattur, Sanur, Vasudevanallur, Tenkasi, Korkai, Kayal, Kalugumalai, Perumalmalai, Pudukkotai, Tirukkampuliyar, and Odugattur. Recent evidence from excavations at Kodumanal, Mayiladumparai, Thandikudi, and Porunthal is of special importance. Megaliths, BRW, and iron have often been considered a package and a site has been labelled as 'megalithic' even when these stone monuments have not been found there, simply on the basis of BRW and iron. It should be noted that not all megaliths have iron and these monuments continued to be made well into the early historic phase. The broad date range is *c.* 1500 BCE to 500/300 BCE. There is considerable variety in the megalithic types in Tamil Nadu (Rajan, 2014). A new type of cist burial was found at Kodumanal. Six burials at the site had a transepted cist made towards the eastern side of the stone circle, with two simple subsidiary cists placed on both sides of it towards the front. Porunthal and Thandikudi revealed three double cist graves. BRW urns have been found at Adichanallur and Perur. Especially intriguing are large anthropomorphic megaliths found at Moddur (Chengam taluk) and Udyayarnattam (Villupuram taluk). The picture from the Tamil Nadu megaliths is one of some widespread shared features along with diversity.

Important sites in Kerala include Pulimattu, Tengakkal, Cenkotta, Muthukar, Peria Kanal, Machad, Pazhayannur, and Mangadu. On the basis of the typology of the artefacts, Machad and Pazhayannur have been dated between the 2nd century BCE and the 2nd century CE. The megaliths at Mangadu in Kollam district of Kerala have a range of *c.* 1000–100 BCE.

Grave goods in cist, Porunthal (left); Kodumanal megalith (right)

Sites in Andhra include Kadambapur, Nagarjunakonda, Yelleswaram, Gallapalli, Tadapatri, Mirapuram, and Amaravati. Megaliths associated with BRW have also been found in Sri Lanka. Some of the megalithic types are associated with specific regions—for instance, the *kodaikal*s and *topikal*s with Kerala and Karnataka, and the menhirs with Kerala, Andhra Pradesh, and Karnataka.

Megalithic sites were initially understood as settlements of nomadic pastoralists. However, the evidence from several sites indicates that early iron age communities in the far south lived on a combination of agriculture, hunting, fishing, and animal husbandry. There is also evidence of well-developed craft traditions. These features, along with the megalithic monuments themselves, suggest sedentary living.

People grew cereals, millets, and pulses. Charred grains of horse gram, green gram, and possibly *ragi* were found at Paiyampalli. Rice husk occurred at Coorg and Khapa (in Karnataka), and Hallur yielded charred grains of *ragi*. Rice grains were found in one of the tombs at Kunnatur (in Tamil Nadu). Naturally, there were some regional variations in the crops grown. Pestles and grinding stones have been found at some megalithic sites. For instance, a granite grinding stone was found in a cist at Machad (in Kerala). K. Rajan's recent (2003) study of the megaliths of the Pudukottai region of Tamil Nadu suggests that the location of megalithic sites close to irrigation tanks (mostly rain fed, some fed by streams) was more than a coincidence.

Some clues to subsistence practices also come from paintings and figurines. Hunting scenes are depicted at Marayur and Attala (in Kerala). At Hire Benkal (in Karnataka), there are scenes of hunting, showing peahens, peacocks, stags, and antelopes, as well as scenes of people dancing in groups. The frequent occurrence of animal bones—of both wild and domesticated species—indicates domestication and hunting. The cow, sheep, dog, and horse were among the domesticated animals. Cattle were the most important domesticated animal, and in this respect, there was continuity in subsistence practices from the earlier neolithic–chalcolithic phase. Fishhooks have been found in some megalithic graves in Tamil Nadu.

The megalithic sites of South India give evidence of well-developed traditions of specialized crafts. Different kinds of pottery have been found, including BRW. Some pots with lids with decorated finials in the shape of birds or animals appear to be ceremonial wares. There is evidence of bead making. Grave goods included etched carnelian beads and beads of other material as well. There are copper and bronze artefacts such as utensils, bowls, and bangles; a few silver and gold ornaments also occur.

Brahmagiri (from top): chamber tomb with port hole; close-up of chamber

FURTHER DISCUSSION | **The enigma of the megalithic anthropomorphs**

Over two decades ago, a huge anthropomorphic figure was discovered at Mottur in Chengam taluka of Tamil Nadu. The figure was part of an arrangement of stones in three concentric circles. The two outer circles were made of stone slabs. The anthropomorph stood in the innermost circle, facing south. It had been embedded in the ground by digging out the bedrock to a depth of 75 cm, and was given additional support by stone packing on both sides at ground level.

The anthropomorph was 3.25 m wide and 3.25 m tall. It had curved arms, 0.92 m long, and the neck and head were represented by a semi-circular projection above the shoulder. Instead of legs, there was a pedestal, making it look like a sitting figure. An identical figure had been discovered a few years earlier at Udayarnattam at Villupuram taluk. This figure—3 m tall and 1 m around the waist—formed part of a stone circle marking a cist burial. A small triangular projection above the shoulder looked like a neck.

Local tradition has an interesting explanation for such figures. It tells us that long ago, the Valiyars (pygmies) learnt that a 'rain fire' was about to break out. They decided to flee southwards to save themselves. They requested their god to come with them, but he refused. So, as they left, they cut off his head and took it along with them. Hence, the figure stands headless.

Anthropomorphic figures have been found at 15 megalithic sites stretching from the central Godavari valley to the Tamil Nadu hills. These include Kaperlaguru on the Godavari, Amabala Vayal in Kerala, Midimalla near Chittoor, and Kumati in Bellary district. At Eguvakantala Cheruvu in Chittoor district, three anthropomorphic figures were found associated with each other; the one on the east had a round port hole. Anthropomorphs with heads but no arms have also been reported from northern Andhra Pradesh, particularly at sites on the south bank of the Godavari such as Tottigutta and Dongatogu.

What exactly these giant anthropomorphs symbolized is difficult to say. They usually occur in association with chamber tombs and dolmens. They may have been connected with ancestor worship.

Source Rajan, 1998a

Iron objects generally outnumber objects made of other metals at megalithic sites. The large volume and variety of iron artefacts—utensils, weapons (arrowheads, spearheads, swords, knives, etc.), carpentry tools (axes, chisels, adzes), and agricultural implements (sickles, hoes, coulters—the vertical blade fixed in front of a ploughshare)—indicate the metal's widespread use in everyday life. Other more elaborate objects found in burials may have had ritualistic functions.

Different sorts of metallurgical techniques were used in the manufacture of metal artefacts. Some of the copper and bronze objects were evidently cast in moulds, others were hammered into shape. Some communities knew how to alloy metals. An analysis of iron artefacts at Pazhayannur and Machad (Mehta and George, 1978) indicates that the metal was relatively pure with very small traces of other elements. Most of the metal objects at these two sites seem to have been made by forging thin strips, which were then joined by beating them together. One of the objects, a hook, was moulded. There is evidence of local smelting of iron at Paiyampalli (Karnataka).

Some megalithic sites must have been centres of craft production linked to networks of exchange. This is suggested by the location of several large megalithic settlements on the trade routes of the early historical period. Inter-regional trade is also suggested by the distribution of non-local items of precious metals and semi-precious stones.

Megalithic cist, Brahmagiri

Excavations at Kudatini in the Bellary district have revealed an exceptionally well-preserved late neolithic/early iron age sarcophagus burial (Mushrif et al., 2002–03). This was a secondary burial. The sarcophagus and the pots around it contained the remains of a single individual—a child who probably died at the age of 6 or 7. Excavations at

RECENT DISCOVERIES | From the neolithic to the iron age at Kadebakale

Kadebakale is a vast site in Koppal District, Karnataka, stretching across a dramatic landscape of rocky hillside and terraces, to the north of the Tungabhadra river. A series of pedestrian surveys, excavations, and remote sensing studies conducted here over many years revealed a great deal of information about the settlement history of the area from the neolithic phase to the 16th century, a period of over 2,500 years. During two survey projects—Kathleen Morrison and Carla Sinopoli's Vijayanagara Metropolitan Survey and the prehistoric survey conducted by A. M. Bauer—as many as a hundred prehistoric sites were identified. These include settlements, ash mounds, megaliths, and occasionally occupied hill terraces and rock shelters. Here, we are interested in the transition from the neolithic to the early iron age (for the sake of convenience, we will refer to the iron-bearing levels as belonging to the iron age). Although the focus on habitation did not remain the same and the data for both stages is not as yet equal in volume, it is sufficient to frame conclusions about pattern of continuity and change across these two phases.

Structural remains of the neolithic phase at Kadebakale were meagre and may reflect permanent or semi-permanent settlement. So far, no ashmounds have been found here. There are 21 radiocarbon dates for one of the settlements (Block B) with a range of 1613–1134 BCE. Above this were iron age deposits which gave a date range of 937–357 BCE. The early iron age occupation at the site was marked by larger settlements, well-developed specialized craft production (iron working and pottery making), and megalithic complexes. The megaliths include stone circles and reveal several rounds of repair, firing, and ritualistic offerings. A central megalith (in Block A) seems to have been especially important. Social differentiation appears to have increased in the iron age phase. The pottery of the iron age phase shows greater diversity of types and forms than that of the neolithic. Black and Red Ware makes its appearance towards

Kadebakale; excavation in progress (from top)

the end of the neolithic. Copper artefacts are absent in the neolithic levels and are very few in iron-bearing ones.

In this region, the main neolithic crops were millets and pulses, some of which were locally domesticated; some were of African origin. These were supplemented with some non-local crops such as rice, wheat, and barley. At Kadebakale, this pattern continues in the iron age levels. Analysis of botanical remains indicates a greater reliance on pulses rather than cereals, with hyacinth bean being dominant. A major change in the iron age was the construction of small containment reservoirs, indicating initiatives for irrigation, perhaps to grow winter crops that needed more water.

The neolithic people of Kadebakale relied on both hunting and breeding animals. As at other neolithic sites in the region, the faunal remains include bones of domesticated and wild animals. The domesticated animals were cattle (*zebu* and water buffalo), sheep/goats, dogs, fish, and the Indian hare. Although age structure data was inadequate to determine animal age at killing, which would throw light on their use, there are many cattle toe bones which display traction-related pathologies. There is a greater volume of data on animal use at iron age levels. Hunting continued to be important. Almost half of the faunal assemblage consisted of bones of wild animals; locally available birds, fish, snakes, lizards, and turtles dominated. The sex and age structure data (animals being killed at a young age) indicate that goats/sheep were raised to maximize milk output. The pattern for cattle was different—apart from dairy produce, they were also used for traction. The fact that cattle were allowed to live for longer periods may also be due to the greater religious/symbolic importance attached to them.

The study of Kadebakale indicates the difficulty in identifying diagnostic features of the South Indian neolithic and early iron age. It also points to differences in the profiles of sites within the same region. Ash mounds, which are found at many South Indian neolithic sites, are not found here. Megaliths seem to have been constructed by late neolithic communities and continued to be built for a long time. Chipped stone tools continued to be made and used beyond the neolithic phase, and are found along with metal artefacts in the early iron age. Hunting wild animals was important across the phases.

A preliminary study of charred food lumps found in an iron age pit (labelled as Feature 40) at Kadebakale moves beyond listing plant remains to try to understand how people made food from plants. Food lumps sometimes (but not always) represent the remains of cooked food, leftovers, or cooking mistakes. The study of food lumps found in the iron age pit indicates that people at this site were using both millets and pulses to make food items employing different culinary techniques, including making food from dry doughs and wet batters. The archaeology of foodways—which includes the processing, preparation, consumption, and discard of food, as well as the social and cultural aspects of food—is an exciting area that is opening up through the use of a variety of scientific and interpretative techniques.

Source Morrison et al., 2017; Bates et al., 2022

Iron-age structures and artefacts (from top left); cave painting (right)

megalithic Kodumanal in Erode district, Tamil Nadu, revealed several new features. A cist contained a deer buried in an urn along with etched carnelian beads, a sword, and axes. It seems that in cist burials, the function of the passage was to provide enough space to perform rituals against the port hole. Graffiti marks in archaic Tamil–Brahmi on the grave goods were another major discovery at Kodumanal (Rajan, 1998b).

Some megalithic graves reveal continued use of the same burial area over many centuries. However, it seems that the graves were not used more than once or twice in a generation. They probably represent a small elite group within a ranked society. Compared to the earlier neolithic–chalcolithic burials, fewer megalithic graves contain burials of children and young adults, and there is a very high percentage of burials of adult males.

Rock paintings found at megalithic sites show fighting scenes, cattle raids, and hunting scenes. At the megalithic habitation site of Mallapadi in Tiruppattur Taluk in Tamil Nadu, rock shelters contained paintings made with white kaolin. One scene showed two horse riders fighting each other with poles. Another showed a human figure with raised arms, holding a stick or weapon. At Paiyampalli, the paintings include a fighting scene, dancing figure, horse raiders, flora, birds, and sun motifs. Such paintings give interesting insight into the lives and experiences of megalithic communities.

The construction of megaliths must have involved community endeavour. These monuments must also have been sites of rituals that formed an important part of the social and cultural lives of people. Ethnographic studies of modern megalithic communities suggest that the building of such monuments may have been connected with feasting, gift exchange, and the forging of alliances.

Recently, there have been some indications of a possible connection between the Harappan civilization and megalithic sites. Sulur is a late megalithic–early historic site near Coimbatore in Tamil Nadu. Iravatham Mahadevan (2007) pointed out that a *c.* 1st century BCE inscription inscribed on a dish found here is similar to an inscription found on a Harappa miniature tablet and that 3–4 of the Sulur signs occur in the same order on other Harappa miniature tablets. According to Mahadevan, such evidence suggests that the Harappan writing tradition was continued in megalithic graffiti and that the languages of the two cultures may have been related to each other.

The impact of iron technology

There is often a time lag between the beginnings of a technology, its maturation, and its significant impact. Iron is found at a few sites in early 2nd millennium BCE contexts. The metal became more widely prevalent in *c.* 1000–800 BCE. During *c.* 800–500 BCE, the use of iron was known in virtually all regions of the subcontinent, and by this time, most regions (including the Ganga valley) seem to have entered the iron age. However, in certain areas, this transition took place much later.

There has been a decades-long debate over the impact of iron technology on the history of ancient India (see Sahu, 2006 for the different perspectives). This debate has to do partly with the larger question of the role of technology in history, and partly with assessing the literary and archaeological evidence of iron in different areas at different points of time. The debate has especially focused on the Ganga valley in the 1st millennium BCE. Some of the older hypotheses, thought provoking as they were in their time, are not supported by evidence and need to be discarded. For instance, many decades ago, D. D. Kosambi suggested that the eastern movement of the Indo-Aryans was in order to reach the iron ores of south Bihar, and that a near-monopoly over these ores was responsible for the political dominance attained by the state of Magadha (in south Bihar) in early historical times. These hypotheses are untenable, given the very wide distribution of iron ores in the subcontinent. As mentioned earlier, chemical analysis of early iron artefacts at Atranjikhera points to the hills between Agra and Gwalior, not Bihar, as the probable source of ores.

R. S. Sharma highlighted the role of iron axes in clearing the forests of the Ganga valley and iron ploughs in agricultural expansion in this area. He argued that the use of these implements was responsible for generating an agricultural surplus, which paved the way for the second phase of urbanization. Religions such as Buddhism were a response to the new socio-economic milieu generated by iron technology. Many aspects of this hypothesis were questioned. A. Ghosh and Niharranjan Ray argued that the forests of the Ganga valley could have been cleared through burning. It was pointed out that Sharma's argument was not supported by archaeological data, that the impact of iron technology was gradual, that it manifested itself properly in the mid-NBPW phase when urbanization was well underway, and that socio-political factors had an important role to play in the historical transformations of the Ganga valley in the 1st millennium BCE. Makkhan Lal questioned the idea of large-scale forest clearance through the use of the iron axe and the generation of an agricultural surplus through the use of the iron plough. He argued that there was no significant increase in the use of iron from PGW to NBPW levels, that iron technology was not an essential prerequisite for an agricultural surplus or urbanization, that the Bihar iron ores were not tapped during this period, and that the Ganga plains in fact remained heavily forested till as late as the 16th and 17th centuries CE.

Technology is certainly an extremely important factor in history, but it has to be considered along with other variables. Archaeological data indicates that the beginning of iron technology in parts of the Ganga valley can be traced to the 2nd millennium BCE. The earliest iron artefacts occur in BRW or PGW contexts. The use of iron and its impact increased gradually over the centuries and is reflected in the increase in the number and range of iron objects in the NBPW phase. While the expansion of agriculture must certainly have involved some amount of land clearance, large tracts of land continued to be forested. Massive deforestation in the Ganga valley and in the subcontinent in general is actually a feature of the colonial period, when the extension of the railways, increase in population, and the commercialization of agriculture led to a dramatic, unprecedented reduction in forest cover (Williams, 2003: 346–69).

Detailed studies of archaeological data from the various regions and sub-regions highlight the complexity of the relationship between technological change and history. For instance, in the far south, the early advent of iron was not followed swiftly by socio-economic transformations. Rajan Gurukkal ([1981] 2006) points out that iron ploughshares tended to be restricted to the wetland areas. He also argues that notwithstanding the knowledge of iron technology, the larger socio-political context of war and plunder hindered the process of agrarian growth in Tamilakam. Iron technology was important, but its impact was gradual and was not uniform in all areas.

The Problem of Correlating Textual and Archaeological Evidence

A great deal of the contentious debate about the co-relation of texts and archaeology during the period *c.* 2000–500 BCE revolves around the Aryan issue and the relationship between the Vedic and Harappan cultures. The possible co-relations between Sangam literature and the later stage of the megalithic culture of South India, which will be discussed in a later chapter, are considerably less polemical.

Many attempts have been made to identify the Indo-Aryans in archaeology. As discussed in Chapter 4, some scholars argue that the Harappan and Vedic cultures can be equated, but this is a problematic hypothesis. Others have identified the Cemetery-H culture with the Indo-Aryans. Others have identified foreign elements in the post-urban phase at Chanhudaro (although M. R. Mughal emphasizes cultural continuity rather than discontinuity at that site). Some have sought to identify the Aryans with changes in funerary practices, fire worship, and the use of the horse at Gandhara Grave culture sites. The copper hoards have been variously connected with the early Indo-Aryans, Harappan refugees, and the pre-Aryan inhabitants of the doab. A connection between PGW and the later Vedic Aryans has been suggested on the basis of a chronological and geographical overlap and some similarity in their cultural elements. The PGW culture has also been linked to the *Mahabharata* events. The chalcolithic cultures of Rajasthan, Central India, and the Deccan have been variously identified with pre-Aryans, Aryans, or non-Vedic immigrants. Out of all these co-relations, many scholars accept the later Vedic culture–PGW correlation.

However, the central problem that has not been properly worked out is: On what basis are connections between material culture—especially pottery—and historically known groups of people to be drawn? It is clear that ceramic cultures cannot be mechanically identified with specific linguistic groups, ethnic groups, lineages, or political units. The spread of similar craft products may have to do with the spread of craft traditions or trade rather than the migration of people. Historians and archaeologists need greater methodological clarity and consistency in how to interpret continuity and change in ceramic traditions and how to correlate cultures known from texts with archaeological cultures.

Issues of origins are contentious. While the debate about the original home of the Indo-Aryans is likely to continue, it is necessary to look beyond it. As we have seen, there is a considerable amount of archaeological evidence that throws light on cultural patterns and cultural change in different regions of the Indian subcontinent during the period *c.* 2000 BCE–600 BCE.

CONCLUSIONS

Texts and archaeology reveal the varied cultural mosaic of the subcontinent between *c.* 2000 and 500 BCE. During these centuries, many parts of the subcontinent made the transition from the chalcolithic to the iron age. Historians have used the Vedic texts to reveal broad patterns of historical change in the north-west and the upper Ganga valley. Archaeology outlines the features of the everyday life of people living in these and other parts of the subcontinent. The evidence indicates a large number of settlements, many relying on a well-established and stable agricultural base with a two-crops-a-year cycle, supplemented by animal domestication and hunting. In some areas, there was a two-tiered hierarchy of settlements, with a small number of fairly large settlements, sometimes fortified, supporting substantial populations. Traditions of specialized crafts and metallurgical techniques for iron crafting become visible in most areas. There is also evidence of inter-regional and long-distance trade in raw materials and finished goods. All this suggests increasing levels of socio-economic complexity. Towards the end of this period, North India stood on the threshold of urbanization.

FURTHER READINGS

Anthony, David W. 2007. *The Horse, the Wheel, and Language: How bronze age riders from the Eurasian steppes shaped the modern world*. Princeton and Oxford: Princeton University Press.

Basa, Kishor K., Rabindra K. Mohanty, and Simatri B. Ota. (Eds.). 2015. *Megalithic Traditions in India: Archaeology and Ethnography*. 2 Vols. Bhopal: Indira Gandhi Rashtriya Manav Sangrahalaya and New Delhi: Aryan Books International.

Bryant, Edwin. 2002. *The Quest for the Origins of Vedic Culture: The Indo-Aryan Migration Debate*. Delhi: Oxford University Press.

Chakrabarti, Dilip K. 1992. *The Early Use of Iron in India*. Delhi: Oxford University Press.

———. 2006. *The Oxford Companion to Indian Archaeology: The Archaeological Foundations of Ancient India, Stone Age to AD 13th Century*. Delhi: Oxford University Press. Chapter 14.

Chakrabarti, Dilip K. and Makkhan Lal. (Eds.). 2014. *History of Ancient India*. Vol. 2. New Delhi: Vivekanand International Foundation and Aryan Books International.

Chakravarti, Uma. 2006, *Everyday Lives, Everyday Histories: Beyond the Kings and Brahmanas of 'Ancient' India*. New Delhi: Tulika.

Dhavalikar, M. K., H. D. Sankalia, and Z. D. Ansari. 1988. *Excavations at Inamgaon*. Vol. 1, Parts I and II. Pune: Deccan College.

Erdosy, George. (Ed.). 1997. *The Indo-Aryans of Ancient South Asia: Language, Material Culture and Ethnicity*. New Delhi: Munshiram Manoharlal.

Fuller, Dorian Q., Nicole Boivin, and Ravi Korisettar. 2007. 'Dating the Neolithic of South India: New Radiometric Evidence for Key Economic, Social, and Ritual Transformations.' *Antiquity* 313: 755–78; DOI: https://doi.org/10.1017/S0003598X00095715.

Guha, Sumit. 2021. *Tribe and State in Asia through Twenty-Five Centuries*. Asia Shorts series, No. 10. Ann Arbor: Association for Asian Studies.

Hazarika, Manjil. 2017. *Prehistory and Archaeology of Northeast India: Multidisciplinary Investigations in an Archaeological Terra Incognita*. New Delhi: 2017.

Hooja, Rima. 1988. *The Ahar Culture and Beyond: Settlements and Frontiers of 'Mesolithic' and Early Agricultural Sites in South-Eastern Rajasthan c. 3rd–2nd Millennia* BC. BAR International Series 412. Oxford.

Jamison, S. W. and Michael Witzel. 1992. *Vedic Hinduism* (available on Michael Witzel's homepage: http://www.people.fas.harvard.edu).

Korisettar, Ravi, P. P. Joglekar, Dorian Q. Fuller, and P. C. Venkatasubbaiah. 2001. 'Archaeological Re-investigation and Archaeozoology of Seven Southern Neolithic Sites in Karnataka and Andhra Pradesh.' *Man and Environment* 26(2): 46–66.

Lal, Makkhan. 1984. *Settlement History and Rise of Civilization in Ganga-Yamuna Doab (from 1500 BC to 300 AD)*. Delhi: Orient Book Distributors.

Lukacs, J. R. and S. R. Walimbe. 1986. *Excavations at Inamgaon, Vol. 2. The Physical Anthropology of Human Skeletal Remains*. Pune: Deccan College.

Moorti, U. S. 1994. *Megalithic Culture of South India*. Varanasi: Ganga Kaveri Publishing House.

Nandi, R. N. 1989–90. 'Archaeology and the *Rigveda*.' *Indian Historical Review* 16(1–2): 35–79.

Parasher, Aloka. 1991. *Mlecchas in Early India: A Study in Attitudes towards Outsiders upto AD 600*. Delhi: Munshiram Manoharlal.

Roy, Kumkum. 1994. *The Emergence of Monarchy in North India: Eighth–fourth Centuries BC as Relected in the Brahmanical Tradition*. Delhi: Oxford University Press.

———. (Ed.). 1999. *Women in Early Indian Societies*. New Delhi: Manohar.

Sahu, Bhairabi Prasad. (Ed.). 2006. *Iron and Social Change in Early India*. Oxford in India Readings: Debates in Indian History and Society. Delhi: Oxford University Press.

Sastry, V. V. Krishna. 1983. *The Proto and Early Historical Cultures of Andhra Pradesh*. Hyderabad: The Government of Andhra Pradesh.

Sharma, R. S. 1980. *Sudras in Ancient India: A Social History of the Lower Order Down to circa AD 600*. 2nd Rev. Edn. Delhi: Motilal Banarsidass. Chapters 2, 3.

———. 1983. *Material Culture and Social Formations in Ancient India*. Delhi: Macmillan India.

———. (1959) 1996. *Aspects of Political Ideas and Institutions in Ancient India*. Delhi: Motilal Banarsidass.

Singh, H. N. 1979. 'Black and Red Ware: A Cultural Study.' In D. P. Agrawal and Dilip K. Chakrabarti. (Eds.). *Essays in Indian Protohistory*. Delhi: B. R. Publishing Corporation. pp. 267–83.

Singh, Purushottam. 1994. *Excavations at Narhan (1984–89)*. Varanasi: Banaras Hindu University; Delhi: B. R. Publishing Corporation.

Sundara, A. 1975. *The Early Chamber Tombs of South India*. Delhi: University Publishers.

Smith, Brian K. 1994. *Classifying the Universe: The Ancient Indian Varna System and the Origins of Caste*. New York and Oxford: Oxford University Press.

Sundara, A. 1975. *The Early Chamber Tombs of South India*. Delhi: University Publishers.

Trautmann, Thomas R. 2015. *Elephants and Kings: An Environmental History*. Ranikhet: Permanent Black in association with Ashoka University.

_______. (Ed.). 2005. *The Aryan Debate*. Oxford in India Readings: Debates in Indian History and Society. Delhi: Oxford University Press.

Witzel, Michael. 1997. 'Rgvedic History: Poets, Chieftains and Polities.' In George Erdosy. (Ed.). *The Indo-Aryans of South Asia*. pp. 307–52.

Bronze rhinoceros figure standing on axles of wheels; one of four animal figures found in a horde at Daimabad (Maharashtra); note that the wheels are solid and do not have spokes.

CHAPTER 6

Cities, Kings, and Renunciants: North India

c. 600–200 BCE

- The sources: textual and archaeological
- The 16 great states
- The *ganas* or *sanghas*
- The forest tribes
- Political conflicts and the growth of the Magadhan empire
- The Persian and Macedonian invasions
- Land and agrarian expansion
- Archaeological and textual profiles of early historic cities
- Urban occupations, crafts, guilds, and money
- The new social elites: *gahapati* and *setthi*
- Trade and traders
- Class, kinship, *varna*, and *jati*
- Gender, family, and household
- The renunciatory tradition
- The Ajivikas
- Early Buddhism
- Early Jainism
- Conclusions

The Buddha arrived in a grove outside Kusinara accompanied by his disciple Ananda, weary after a long journey. The two talked of many things, and the conversation turned to the Buddha's imminent demise. The Buddha instructed Ananda that his remains should be treated in the same manner as those of a king of kings. The disciple implored him not to die in Kusinara. This small, nondescript town with mud huts in the middle of a jungle was unworthy of being the scene of the Buddha's final passing away. There were other great cities such as Champa, Rajagaha, Savatthi, Saketa, Kosambi, and Varanasi, Ananda argued, more worthy of this honour.

The Buddha brushed aside these objections. He told Ananda that long ago, Kusinara was a great city named Kusavati, capital of a mighty king named Maha-Sudassana. It measured 12 *yojana*s east to west and 7 *yojana*s north to south. Crowds of people thronged its streets and there was prosperity everywhere. Day and night, the city resounded with the sounds of elephants, horses, chariots, drums, tabors, lutes, songs, cymbals, gongs, and with the cry, 'Eat, drink, and be merry!' Kusavati was no less than Alakananda, the royal city of the gods. It was indeed worthy of being the place where the Buddha would breathe his last.

This conversation between the Buddha and Ananda takes place in the *Mahaparinibbana Sutta* of the *Digha Nikaya*. In the Ganga valley, the 6th century BCE was an age of exceptionally intense and varied philosophical inquiry, as well as one of significant political, social, and economic changes. These changes were the culmination of processes outlined in Chapter 5.

While *c.* 600 BCE has been taken to mark the beginning of the early historic period in North India, this date should be understood as an approximate point along a much longer historical continuum stretching across many centuries. The continuing debate on the date of the Buddha's death—an event known in Buddhist tradition as the ***parinibbana***—is central to the chronologies of early historical dynasties, post-Vedic texts, and the historical processes reflected in these texts. According to the *Dipavamsa* and *Mahavamsa*, 218 years elapsed between the *parinibbana* and Ashoka's consecration. On this basis, it has been argued that the Buddha died in 544/543 BCE. Scholars refer to this as the 'uncorrected long chronology'. Theravada communities in South and Southeast Asia accept this date as the beginning of the Buddhasasana or Buddhist era. The 'uncorrected long chronology' was subsequently modified by advancing the date of Ashoka's consecration to give the 'corrected long chronology', according to which the demise of the Buddha occurred some time between 486 and 477 BCE. (Ashoka's consecration is placed in 268/267 BCE.) Another hypothesis, known as the 'short chronology', is based on Sanskrit and Chinese sources, which state that 100 or 116 years elapsed between the Buddha's death and Ashoka's consecration. Accordingly, the *parinibbana* has been dated *c.* 368 BCE or 383 BCE. According to another view, largely on the basis of the 'lists of Elders' in the Pali chronicles, it has been suggested that the *parinibbana* should be dated somewhere between *c.* 400 and 350 BCE (Bechert, [1991] 1995).

The Buddha is supposed to have lived for about 80 years, so depending on which date we accept for his death, we would get a date falling in the 7th, 6th, or 5th century BCE for his birth. Most Indian scholars still favour *c.* 480 BCE for the *parinibbana*, while most Western scholars are inclined to accept more recent dates.

According to A. K. Narain (1993), the Ahraura version of Ashoka's minor rock edict 1 suggests that 256 years had elapsed between the death of the Buddha and the issuing of the edict. If the latest possible dates for the events are taken, i.e., if Ashoka's consecration is dated 264 BCE and the edict belongs to the last year of his reign, i.e., 227 BCE (although the minor rock edicts are generally assigned to the early part of the reign), the *parinibbana* would have to be placed in 483 BCE (256 + 227 BCE) or earlier.

In the context of the debate on the date of the Buddha, excavations at Lumbini in Nepal, a major Buddhist place of pilgrim age, regarded as the birthplace of the Buddha, are significant (Coningham et al., 2013). These excavations were part of a UNESCO project geared towards strengthening the conservation and management of the site and to assess the early archaeological sequence within the Maya Devi temple. Previous excavations had identified various structural phases of the temple, the oldest belonging to Ashoka's time. The 2011–12 excavations, led by Robin Coningham and Kosh Prasad Acharya, dug under the foundations of the Ashokan temple. This led to the discovery of pavements of a pre-Ashokan brick structure. Below this structure were a series of post-holes that appear to represent an older wooden structure. The post-holes suggest the presence of a wooden fence around an open space. The excavators interpret the evidence as indicating the presence of a tree shrine here. Radiocarbon samples from two post-hole fills gave date ranges of 799–546 BCE and 801–548 BCE, indicating that the delineation of sacred space here goes back to a very early date. This has been cited as the first archaeological evidence for the date of the Buddha and suggests that the long chronology, which locates the Buddha in the 6th century BCE, may be correct.

The historic period is usually defined in terms of three diagnostic features—cities, states, and writing. The transition to the early historic took place at different points of time in different parts of the subcontinent. In this chapter, we will mainly discuss developments in North India, where the 6th century BCE marks the beginning of the early historic phase, marked by cities and states. The archaeological marker of early historic urbanism in North India is the Northern Black Polished Ware (NBPW). Writing on stone made its appearance later, in the Maurya period. It is likely that it existed in earlier times, but has not survived as it was on perishable material.

Till recently, with the possible exception of the Mahasthan and Sohgaura inscriptions (discussed in Chapter 7), the early history of the Brahmi script has only been inferred. Evidence from Sri Lanka and Tamil Nadu have added a new dimension to the story. Many years ago, potsherds with Tamil-Brahmi letters were found at Anuradhapura in Sri Lanka and were assigned to the 4th century BCE on the basis of radiocarbon dating (Coningham et al., 1996). Subsequently, sites such as Porunthal, Kodumanal, and Keezhadi in Tamil Nadu have suggested early evidence of Tamil-Brahmi in South India (Rajan et al., 2021). The dates and evidence from these sites (discussed later in this chapter), continue to be the subject of lively debate. But they do tie in with the Anuradhapura dates, and at the very least, indicate the use of writing in South India in the pre-Maurya period. They also suggest that we may need to rethink the issue of transition to the early historic in the subcontinent in a major way.

While the transition to the early historic in North India is dated to the 6th century BCE, and in South India somewhat later, the picture in other parts of the subcontinent is quite different. For instance, in the Northeast, the transition to the historic period took place much later, in about the 4th century CE (Sarma and Hazarika, 2014: 47–49). This reminds us of the need to think of 'Indian' history as a complex mosaic of cultures with different chronologies and trajectories.

Discussions of early Indian history are often framed within an evolutionary scheme of a transition from tribe to territorial state. As discussed in Chapters 4 and 5, the terms 'tribe' and 'state' are difficult to define in universal terms. In this book, the term 'tribe' is being used for the sake of convenience to refer to non-monarchical political formations which have a comparatively less rigid structure of social and political hierarchy and control. The relationship between tribe and state has often been seen in terms of an evolution from a less complex to a more complex political system, but it can also be seen in terms of coexistence and conflict. Over time, some tribal chieftains acquired enough control over resources to establish kingdoms. Others resisted and challenged the attempts of kings to acquire control over the forest tracts, which were rich in resources of many kinds, especially elephants, which were an important part of ancient Indian armies.

While the emergence of agrarian states, cities, and writing are important developments, we must be aware of the people who lived outside their orbit or on their peripheries. Hunting, gathering, and pastoralism did not fade away with the advent of agriculture. Cities existed in the multitude of villages. And for centuries after the emergence of states, forest tribes continued to be an important part of the political map. Due to the inherent imbalances in the sources of history, their presence and importance has to be largely inferred.

If conclusive evidence or argument proves a later date for the Buddha, chronologies for early historic texts and events will have to be re-adjusted. Till then, *c.* 480 can be retained as the date for the *parinibbana*.

The Sources: Textual and Archaeological

For the period *c.* 600–200 BCE, there is for the first time the possibility of comparing evidence from different kinds of textual sources. The dates of some of these texts remain the subject of debate. How they are arranged chronologically has direct impact on the historical reconstructions made on their basis.

As explained in Chapter 1, the Pali canon is not a homogeneous source of history. The first four books of the *Sutta Pitaka* (the *Digha*, *Majjhima*, *Samyutta*, and *Anguttara Nikayas*) and the entire *Vinaya Pitaka* are usually considered to have been composed between the 5th and 3rd centuries BCE. The *Sutta Nipata* also belongs to this period. The *Khuddaka Nikaya* (the fifth book of the *Sutta Pitaka*) and the *Abhidhamma Pitaka* are later works. The geographical context of the composition of the canon corresponds roughly to the middle Ganga valley (modern Bihar and eastern UP).

Historians often use the Jatakas (one of the 15 books of the *Khuddaka Nikaya*) indiscriminately as a source for the 6th century BCE and the Maurya, and post-Maurya periods. Although they may contain older legends, in their present textual form, the Jatakas belong to the 3rd centuries BCE–2nd century CE and should not, therefore, be used as a source for the earlier period. In this chapter, they are cited only occasionally, to fill gaps in the details of political narrative, confirm points emerging from contemporary sources, or to provide a long-term perspective on specific issues.

According to the traditional account, the Pali canon was transmitted to Sri Lanka in 3rd century BCE and initially preserved orally; it was written down in Alu Vihara during the reign of Vattagamini in the 1st century BCE. As pointed out by Steve Collins (1990), we do not know whether this was the Tipitaka as we know it and whether it was a canon in the sense of an exclusivist scripture. Further, the historical background is significant. The Pali canon in the sense of a closed list of scriptures with an authoritative claim to be a faithful record of the Buddha's teaching was a product of the rivalry between the monks of the Mahavihara and Abhayagiri monasteries in Sri Lanka. It was produced by the Mahavihara monks in order to legitimize and define themselves at a time when their Abhayagiri rivals enjoyed political support. The complex compositional history of Tipitaka needs to be kept in mind.

Religious textual sources for ancient India are often classified as Brahmanical, Buddhist, and Jaina. These terms, used for the sake of convenience, actually refer to traditions that evolved and changed over time. The term 'Brahmanical' refers to a social ideology which gives primacy and authority to Brahmanas and religious ideas and practices approved of by Brahmanas; this was not something fixed but changed over time. Johannes Bronkhorst (2007, 2011, 2016) has discussed the eastward movement of Brahmanical culture into the culturally distinct eastern region of Greater Magadha

PRIMARY SOURCES | **Panini and his *Ashtadhyayi***

Panini (this seems to have been his **gotra** name) was a grammarian who lived in the 5th or 4th century BCE. His *Ashtadhyayi*, the oldest surviving Sanskrit grammar, represents a brilliant intellectual achievement. It sums up the rules of Sanskrit grammar in 3,996 aphorisms (*sutras*)—short, highly compressed, and condensed statements—combining brevity with clarity and comprehensive coverage.

Panini mapped out the grammatical rules of Sanskrit as it existed in his time. His work became a landmark in the history of the Sanskrit language and literature, marking the transition from Vedic Sanskrit to classical Sanskrit. There must have been earlier Sanskrit grammarians, but by founding his own school of grammar and becoming a widely acknowledged authority on the subject, Panini surpassed and eclipsed them completely. Panini's grammar was handed down over the centuries from teachers to students, to a large extent through oral instruction.

Panini was the precursor of other Sanskrit grammarians such as Katyayana (4th century BCE) and Patanjali (2nd century BCE). Both acknowledge their respect for him by giving him the honorific *bhagavan*. Patanjali describes Panini as a great teacher and the *Ashtadhyayi* as a vast ocean of learning. He states that students had become careless and indifferent towards the study of grammar, and that Panini wrote in order to change this attitude. His work is said to have become very popular among young students. Some scholars suggest that Panini was also a poet, but the evidence for this is inconclusive.

Little is known about Panini's life. He was a Brahmana, and seems to have belonged to a place called Shalatura in Gandhara country in the north-west. The Chinese pilgrim Xuanzang visited Shalatura in the 7th century CE. He mentions a statue of Panini standing in the town, and tells us that its children pursued the study of grammar and held the great grammarian in high esteem. The 19th century archaeologist Alexander Cunningham suggested the identification of ancient Shalatura with Lahur, a town four miles north-west of Ohind, close to the confluence of the Kabul and Indus rivers.

There are many later legends about Panini. According to one of these, recorded by Xuanzang, it was said that when Panini completed his work, he offered it to the king, who treasured it greatly, ordered everyone in the land to study the book, and offered a reward of a thousand coins to anyone who could recite it fluently. The 9th century *Manjushrimulakalpa* refers to Panini's association with the court of the Nanda king at Pataliputra. The 10th century writer Rajashekhara refers to the institution of a board of examiners at Pataliputra, before whom great grammarians such as Panini and many others appeared. Eleventh-century texts such as Somadeva's *Kathasaritsagara* and Kshemendra's *Brihatkathamanjari* preserve some legendary stories about the great grammarian, based on the earlier *Brihatkatha* of Gunadhya. They tell us that Panini was a student of a teacher named Varsha. The story goes that he was a slow learner and lagged behind his friends in studies. At some point of time, he went off to meditate in the Himalayas. Pleased with his efforts, the god Shiva revealed a new system of grammar to him.

The *Ashtadhyayi* is a work on language. But in order to illustrate the rules of grammar, Panini referred incidentally to many aspects of his time—to places, people, customs, institutions, coins, weights and measures, and peoples' beliefs and practices. This is why historians use the *Ashtadhyayi* as a source of information on the 5th/4th century BCE.

Panini's work was part of a long intellectual tradition in India that considered the study of language as an important part of learning. Patronage of grammarians and the understanding of grammatical works was also considered an important aspect of kingship. As pointed out by Sheldon Pollock, the close relationship between grammar and political power was an important feature of the Sanskrit cosmopolitan order.

Source Agrawala, 1953; Pollock, (2006) 2007: 166–184

(the area to the east of the confluence of the Ganga and Yamuna) and has tried to reconstruct how Brahmanism engaged with that culture.

The Sanskrit Kalpasutras form part of the Vedanga corpus, and include the Shrautasutras, Grihyasutras, and Dharmasutras. The Shrautasutras describe the more elaborate sacrificial rituals; the Grihyasutras deal with domestic rituals; and the Dharmasutras deal with *dharma*. These texts reflect important changes that were taking place within the Brahmanical tradition.

The early Grihyasutras can be dated to roughly 600 to 400 BCE. The changes they reflect include a Brahmanical attempt to standardize domestic ceremonies by using and adapting Vedic *mantras* and rituals. They describe a sequence of *samskaras* (life cycle rituals) beginning with the *upanayana* and attempt to bring diverse customs and folk practices into the Brahmanical fold (Lubin, 2005).

The Dharmasutras are the earliest part of the Dharmashastra corpus. Patrick Olivelle (2009) argues that the Buddha took over the concept of *dharma* with its strong royal associations from the Vedic tradition and injected it with strong ethical content. Later, Ashoka highlighted *dhamma* as an ethical code in his edicts. This raised *dharma* to the status of a central cultural concept with which the Brahmanas were forced to engage. Their response was the invention of an authoritative corpus of texts that dealt specifically with dharma, namely Dharmashastra. This hypothesis hinges on the dates assigned to early Dharmashastra texts. Kane ([1941b] 1974: xi–xii) dates the Dharmasutras of *Gautama*, *Apastamba*, *Baudhayana*, and *Vasishtha* between *c.* 600 and 300 BCE. Olivelle ([2000] 2003: 10; 2010) suggests later dates—3rd century BCE for Apastamba, early 2nd century BCE for Gautama, mid-to late 2nd century BCE for Baudhayana, and 1st century BCE for Vasishtha. Of course, these dates are approximations. The early Dharmasutras and Grihyasutras will be discussed in this chapter. There is an overlap in the discussion of social history in Chapters 6, 7, and 8. It is difficult to ascertain the precise region where the Dharmashastra texts were composed; they seem to broadly belong to North India, although it is possible that Apastamba belonged to some area in the south. All these texts are normative and cannot be treated as straightforward reflections of prevailing social practices. Nor do they reflect identical points of view. They have to be read as attempts of Brahmana *dharma* experts to engage with and regulate widely divergent practices

Due to the complex compositional history of the *Ramayana* and *Mahabharata*—extending roughly from 400 BCE to 400 CE—it is difficult to use these epics as sources for any specific period. They are, however, important for the history of ideas and perspectives on religious and cultural practices. In their multiple tellings and forms, the influence and impact of the *Ramayana* and the *Mahabharata* traditions can be traced across the centuries in various regions of South and Southeast Asia.

The Sanskrit Puranas provide information on dynastic history. The later sections of the Puranic king-lists clearly have a historical basis, but they present several problems. The Puranas contradict each other in places. Rulers of different lines are sometimes mixed up and presented as members of the same dynasty. Contemporary rulers may be described as successors, collateral rulers as direct descendants. Certain kings known from other sources are not mentioned. Although their composition may have ranged over several previous centuries, the major Puranas were compiled in the 4th/5th centuries CE.

Jaina texts represent the third major religious tradition that can be used as historical source material for this period. They include the canonical texts and other works such as the *Bhagavati Sutra* and the *Parishishtaparvan*. Compared with Buddhist tests, Jaina texts have not been used as extensively as historical sources for ancient India, partly due to the problems of assigning dates, and partly due to inadequate attention and study.

A comparison of Buddhist, Puranic, and Jaina texts on details of dynastic history often reveals more disagreement than agreement. This may be due to incomplete or incorrect information available to their composers, or the fact that they were compiled at different times, but it also has to do with their different perspectives.

Apart from indigenous textual sources, there are a number of Greek and Latin narratives of the military career of Alexander of Macdedon by writers such as Arrian, Curtius Rufus, Diodorus Sicilus, Plutarch, and Justin. Written several centuries after the events they describe, they recount Alexander's invasion of India (327–26 BCE) and the political situation prevailing in the north-west at the time. Alexander's life and career became the stuff of legend in the Graeco-Roman world.

Archaeology continues to be an important source for the history of the subcontinent in *c.* 600–200 BCE. In North India, the focus is on the culture associated with a pottery called Northern Black Polished Ware (NBPW). The NBPW phase is generally dated between the 7th century BCE and 2nd/1st centuries BCE, and can be sub-divided into at least two phases—early (7th–3rd centuries BCE) and late (3rd–1st centuries BCE). In this chapter, we are concerned with the former. (As mentioned in Chapter 1, radiocarbon dates from Ayodhya suggest that the NBPW phase at this site could go back to *c.* 1000 BCE, but this is an exception.) The evidence from NBPW sites includes an

PRIMARY SOURCES | Northern Black Polished Ware

This pottery's name is misleading, because it is not only found in North India, it is not always black, nor is it necessarily polished. The NBPW is a well-fired, wheel-made deluxe pottery made of well-levigated clay. It is a fine ware, sometimes as thin as 1.5 mm. Apart from black, it is also found in other shades and colours. The shapes include bowls with straight, convex, tapering, and corrugated sides, dishes with incurved rims and convex sides, dishes with straight sides, knobbed lids, sharply carinated *handis*, and miniature vases.

The pottery has a glossy surface. How exactly this was achieved is not certain. One theory is that some ferruginous compound was applied to pots before they were fired, and that the black colour was the result of firing the pots in a reducing condition. Another view is that the shiny surface was achieved by applying some material, such as oil or plant juice, on the pots after they were fired, but while they were still hot. Yet another study suggests that magnetic iron oxide gave the pottery its black glassy look, while the shine was the result of the application of liquid clay, perhaps containing haematite, along with a natural alkaline substance before firing the pots under reducing conditions. The NBPW is usually unpainted, but there are some instances of designs (bands, wavy lines, dots, concentric and intersecting circles, semi-circles, etc.) painted on in yellow and light vermillion.

Pottery matching NBPW was first found at various sites in the 19th century and at Taxila in 1913. It was subsequently reported at many sites in the Ganga valley and beyond. This pottery has been identified at over 1,500 sites stretching from Taxila and Charsada in the north-west to Amaravati in Andhra Pradesh, and from Prabhas Patan in Gujarat to Tamluk in Bengal. There is a concentration of sites in the Punjab, Haryana, north Rajasthan, Uttar Pradesh, Bihar, and West Bengal. The main excavated sites are Rupar in the Punjab; Raja Karna ka Qila and Daulatpur in Haryana; Bairat, Noh, and Jodhpura in Rajasthan; Hastinapur, Atranjikhera, Kaushambi, and Shravasti in Uttar Pradesh; and Vaishali, Patna, and Sonepur in Bihar. At sites in the Punjab, Haryana, Rajasthan, and western Uttar Pradesh, the NBPW phase is preceded by the PGW phase, with an overlap between them. In eastern UP and Bihar, it is preceded by the Black and Red Ware (BRW) phase.

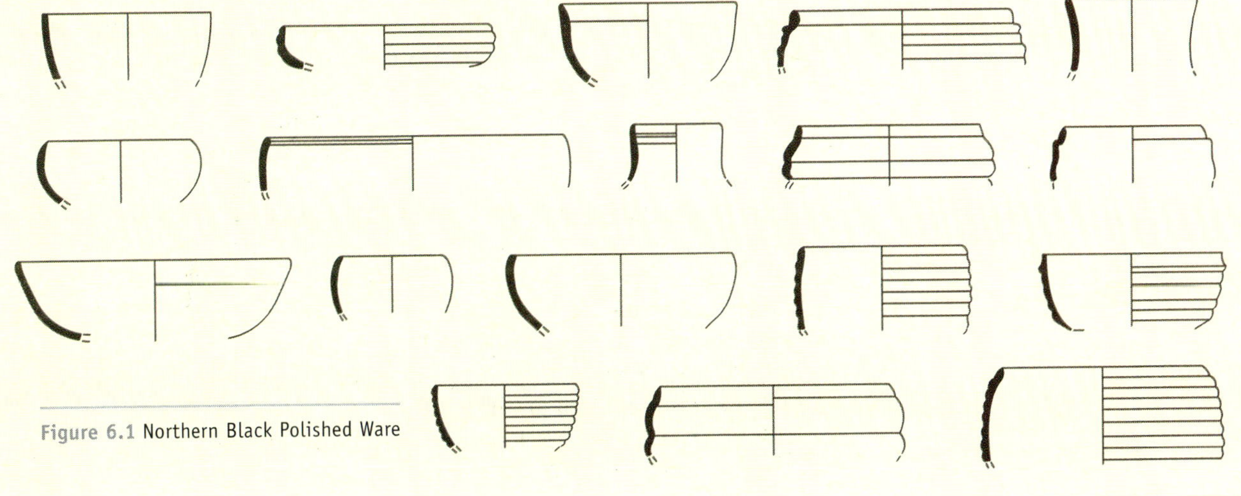

Figure 6.1 Northern Black Polished Ware

early series of punch-marked coins, which mark the beginning of the use of coinage in the subcontinent. Hoards of coins including punch-marked coins have been found at Bhir mound (Taxila), Chaman Huzuri (in Kabul), and Narhan (Gorakhpur district, UP). Unfinished silver blanks (strips of metal without punch marks) have been found in Gandhara and at Narhan.

The 16 Great States

Political history does not only consist of dynastic history. Apart from the details of the rise and the fall of kingdoms and empires, it is important to understand variations and changes in the structure of polities and the ways in which political processes were connected with social and economic history. Changes in political ideology and expressions of power are also integral parts of political history. Apart from rulers, the political sphere included other members of the ruling or governing elite and members of the royal household.

Northern Black Polished Ware from various sites

Monarchy ultimately emerged as the dominant and most successful form of political system, but during the early historic period, there were also oligarchies, where power was in the hands of a group of elite men rather than a single individual. Forest tribes and chieftains were important parts of political history, but we know much less about them, mainly from texts and inscriptions produced in states.

Later Vedic texts, the epics, and the Puranas name many ancient kings and dynasties of early historic North India. It is difficult to assess the historicity of the earliest rulers. From the 6th century BCE onwards, the outlines of the political history of North India becomes clearer, and kings and religious teachers mentioned in different textual traditions can be identified as historical figures.

State polities and societies emerged in the 6th/5th century BCE in a belt stretching from Gandhara in the north-west to Anga in Eastern India, also extending into the Malwa region. The inclusion of Assaka (Ashmaka) in the upper Godavari valley in lists of the great states of the time suggests that similar processes were underway in parts of trans-Vindhyan India as well. The beginning of the early historic phase in South India is usually placed in about the 3rd century BCE. However, in recent years, it has been argued that the evidence for writing in the far south goes back to the 4th century BCE, if not earlier. Further evidence may change the picture. In this book, the early historic culture of South India will be discussed in Chapter 8.

Buddhist and Jaina texts list 16 powerful states (*solasa-mahajanapada*) that flourished in the early 6th century BCE. (Janapada also meant a region consisting of urban and rural settlements, along with its inhabitants.) Apart from these, there must have been smaller states, chiefdoms, and tribal principalities. The *Anguttara Nikaya*'s list of the ***mahajanapadas*** is as follows: Kasi (Kashi), Kosala (Koshala), Anga, Magadha, Vajji (Vrijji), Malla, Chetiya (Chedi), Vamsa (Vatsa), Kuru, Panchala, Machchha (Matsya), Shurasena, Assaka (Ashmaka), Avanti, Gandhara, and Kamboja. The *Mahavastu* has a similar list, but substitutes Shibi (in the Punjab) and Dasharna (in Central India) for the north-western states of Gandhara and Kamboja.[1] The *Bhagavati Sutra* gives a somewhat different list: Anga, Banga (Vanga), Magaha (Magadha), Malaya, Malava, Achchha, Vachchha (Vatsa), Kochchha, Ladha (Lata or Radha), Padha (Pandya or Paundra), Bajji (Vajji), Moli (Malla), Kasi (Kashi), Kosala, Avaha, and Sambhuttara.[2] While some of the names in the two lists are common, the *Bhagavati Sutra* list seems to be later and less reliable.

[1] The names in this list are in Pali; their Sanskrit form is given in brackets. In some cases, the Pali and the Sanskrit forms are the same.

[2] In this list, the Prakrit names are given first, followed by their Sanskrit equivalents in brackets wherever the two differ.

NEW DIRECTIONS IN RESEARCH | **The state and violence**

Violence has been a feature of all human societies, including pre-state and non-state societies. However, the advent of the state ushered significant changes in the institutional structures for both its control and perpetration.

It is not a coincidence that the time when states emerged in the Ganga valley was also the time when ***ahimsa***-oriented religions (religions emphasizing non-violence) came to the fore. These represented powerful responses to certain perennial human problems, as well as to certain specific aspects of their age. In the early historic period, warfare became based on larger and more efficient levels of military organization and deployment than before. The hereditary warrior elites, allied troops, and mercenaries were supplemented (at least to some extent) by a recruited and salaried class of soldiers paid by the state. Military power was essential for defence, territorial expansion, and empire-building. War and political and matrimonial alliances were key factors in the relationships between states.

All states are dependent on control over economic and human resources. The generation and appropriation of the agricultural surplus—essential prerequisites for cities and states—involved the use or threat of coercive force. The emergence of early historic states was accompanied by the beginning of theorizing about kingship, and about the relationship between the state's use of force and the maintenance of the social order. Texts such as the *Mahabharata*, *Manu Smriti* and various Buddhist and Jaina works discuss the origins of kingship and the duties of the king. They described taxation as the king's wages for protecting his subjects, the king's punishment as necessary for the maintenance of order, and military force as a necessary part of rulership.

These theories concealed the coercive aspect of kingship by introducing the fiction of a voluntary social contract between the king and his subjects, which involved their voluntarily giving him taxes for their own benefit. They also assert the necessity of the king's force in discussions of justice. The king's punishment is said to prevent a descent into *matsya-nyaya* (the law of the fish), a terrible anarchy in which the mighty devour the weak. In their projection of the state as the prime wielder of coercive power, these theories of kingship anticipate modern theories of the state that define it in terms of a monopoly or near-monopoly over force.

Over the centuries, the growth and systemization of state violence was accompanied by increasingly sophisticated attempts to mask, invisibilize, justify, and aestheticize this violence. All traditions, including the religions of nonviolence such as Jainism and Buddhism, acknowledged that a certain amount of violence was necessary for kings. Political theorists, poets, and religious thinkers played important roles in creating and disseminating ideologies that transformed political violence into something acceptable, positive, and necessary for the well-being of subjects and maintenance of the social order. At the same time, ancient Indian political discourse made a distinction between force that was necessary, proportionate, and legitimate, and force that was unnecessary, excessive, and illegitimate, thereby leaving open a window for questioning the state's coercive power.

Source Upinder Singh, 2017

Two kinds of states are included in the list of *mahajanapadas*—monarchies (*rajyas*) and non-monarchical states known as *ganas* or *sanghas*. The latter two terms are used synonymously in the political sense in the *Ashtadhyayi* and *Majjhima Nikaya*, and are used interchangeably in this chapter. The translation of *gana* and *sangha* as 'republic' can be misleading. These were oligarchies, where power was exercised by a group of clansmen. The most powerful states in the 6th century BCE were Magadha, Kosala, Vatsa, and Avanti. The relations among the states fluctuated over time and included warfare, truce, and military alliances. Marriage alliances were an important aspect of inter-state relations, but often became irrelevant when it came to realizing political ambitions. Outlines of political history can be reconstructed by using the various textual sources of this as well as later periods (Raychaudhuri, [1923] 2000: 85–210; Majumdar. [Gen. Ed.], [1951] 1968: 1–17).

The kingdom of Kashi was bounded by the Varuna and Asi rivers to the north and south respectively. It is from the names of these two rivers that its capital city Varanasi (modern Benaras), on the banks of the Ganga, got its name. The Jatakas indicate that several Kashi kings aspired to the status of political paramountcy. They refer to a long-standing rivalry between the kingdoms of Kashi and Kosala. Kashi was also involved in occasional conflicts with Anga and Magadha. At one time, one of the most powerful states of North India, Kashi was eventually absorbed into the Kosalan kingdom.

Silver punch-marked coins (obverse and reverse) of Kashi, Kosala, and Magadha

The powerful kingdom of Kosala was bounded by the Sadanira (Gandak) on the east, the Gomati on the west, the Sarpika or Syandika (Sai) on the south, and the Nepal hills to the north. The Sarayu river divided it into a northern and a southern part. Shravasti (identified with modern Saheth-Maheth) was the capital of north Kosala, and Kushavati the capital of south Kosala. Saketa and Ayodhya were two other important cities (in later sources, these were treated as names of the same place). Kosala succeeded in conquering Kashi. It extended its power over the Sakyas of Kapilavastu, and also probably over the Kalamas of Kesaputta and other states in the vicinity. Pasenadi (Prasenajit), king of Kosala, was the Buddha's contemporary and is frequently mentioned in Pali texts. Kosala and Magadha were linked through matrimonial ties during the time of Prasenajit and the Magadhan king Bimbisara, but a bitter struggle between the two kingdoms ensued after the latter's death.

Anga corresponded roughly to the Bhagalpur and Monghyr districts of Bihar. The Ganga bordered it on the north. The Champa river (which can probably be identified with the Chandan) was its boundary with Magadha, which lay to its west. Its capital Champa was one of the greatest cities of the 6th century BCE. Located at the confluence of the Ganga and Champa rivers, it has been identified with modern Champanagara or Champapura village near Bhagalpur. Champa was also an important commercial centre on the trade routes of the time. Merchants are described as sailing overseas from here to Suvarnabhumi (in Southeast Asia).

The kingdom of Magadha roughly covered the modern Patna and Gaya districts of Bihar. It was bounded by the Ganga, Son, and Champa rivers on the north, west, and east respectively and the Vindhyan spurs on the south. Its capital was initially Girivraja or Rajagriha, near modern Rajgir. The Puranas give lists of Magadhan kings, starting with Brihadratha. This dynasty came to an end in the 6th century BCE, making way for the Haryankas. The detailed history of Magadha is given later in this chapter.

The principality of the Vajji (Vrijji) was in Eastern India, north of the Ganga, extending up to the Nepal hills. Most historians consider the Vajji a confederacy of eight or nine clans. The most important members of the confederacy were the Vajjis, Lichchhavis, Videhas, and Nayas/Jnatrikas. Vaishali was both the capital of the Lichchhavis and of the Vajji confederacy, and is identified with modern Basarh in north Bihar. The Lichchhavis are mentioned often in Buddhist texts. They were on good terms with Kosala and the Mallas, but were embroiled in conflict with Magadha. Jaina tradition states that the nine Lichchhavis formed a league with the nine Mallas and 18 clan lords of Kashi and Kosala. The Videhas had their capital at Mithila, identified with modern Janakpur in Nepal. The Jnatrikas were based in Kundapura (or Kundagrama) and Kollaga, suburbs of Vaishali. Mahavira belonged to this clan. The Vajji confederacy is said to have been led by Chetaka, who was the brother of Trishala (mother of Mahavira) and father of Chellana, wife of the Magadhan king Bimbisara.

The Malla principality was located to the west of the Vajjis and consisted of a confederacy of nine clans. There were two political centres—at Kusinara and Pava. Kusinara has been identified with Kasia on the smaller Gandak, about 77 km east of Gorakhpur, and Pava with Padaraona village, about 26 km north-east of Kasia. The Mallas are said to have originally been a monarchy. The Vajjis and Mallas seem to have been allies, although there were some episodes of conflict between them.

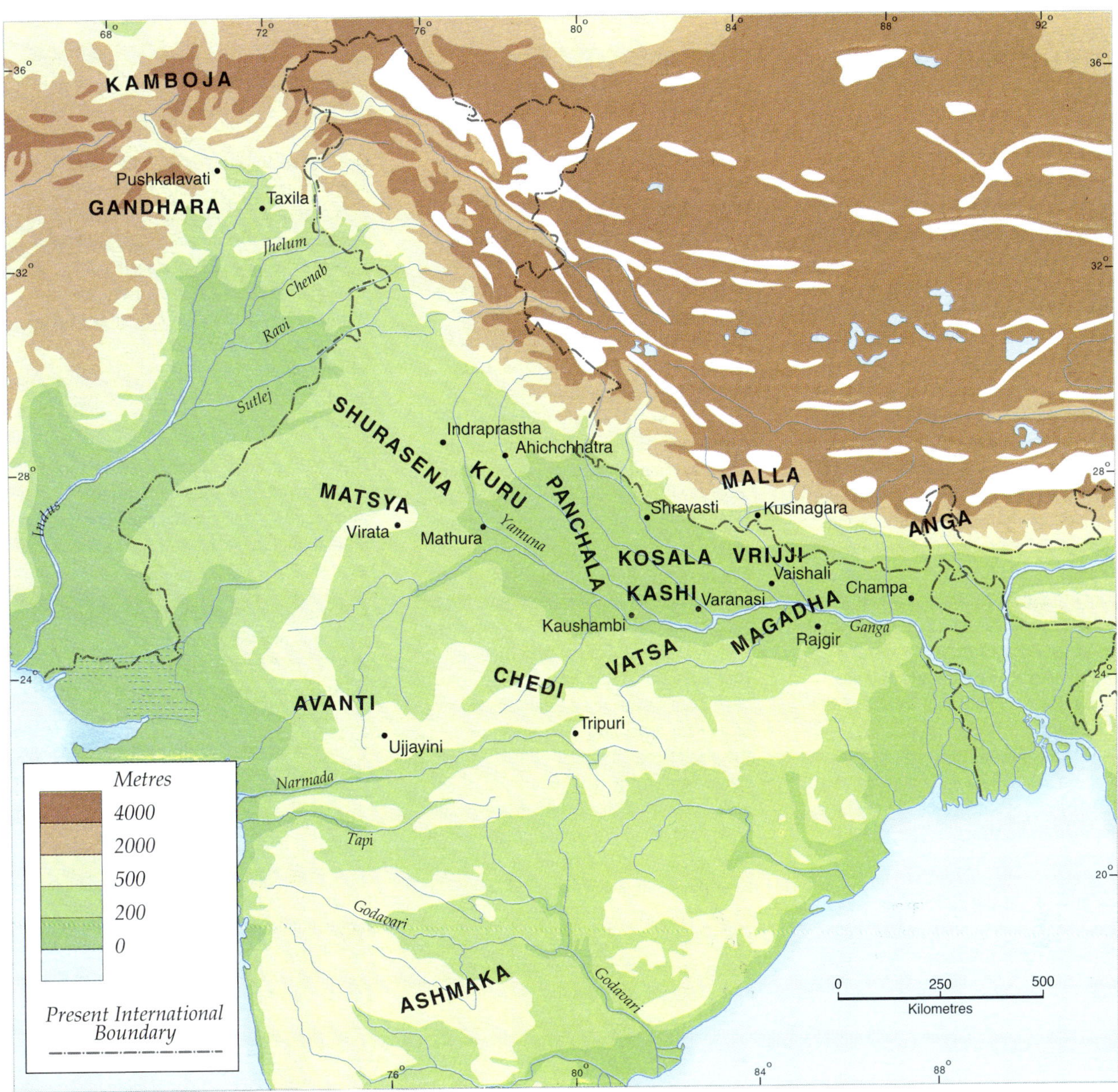

Map 6.1 The 16 *mahajanapadas*

The Chedi kingdom was situated in the eastern part of Bundelkhand in Central India. Its capital was Sotthivatinagara, probably the same as the Shukti or Shuktimati or Shukti-sahvaya of the *Mahabharata*.

Vatsa or (Vamsa), south of the Ganga, was noted for its fine cotton textiles. Its capital was Kaushambi, identified with Kosam village on the right bank of the Yamuna. Legends recount the rivalry between kings Udayana of Vatsa and Pradyota of Avanti, and refer to a love affair and marriage between Udayana and Vasavadatta, Pradyota's daughter. Udayana seems to have entered into matrimonial alliances with the ruling families of Anga and Magadha.

According to Buddhist tradition, the Kuru kingdom was ruled by kings belonging to the Yuddhitthila *gotta*, i.e., the family of Yudhishthira, from their capital at Indapatta (Indraprastha). In the Buddha's time, Kuru was a minor state ruled by a chieftain named Koravya. The Jaina *Uttaradhyayana Sutra* refers to a Kuru king named Isukara who ruled from the town of Isukara. The Kurus established matrimonial relations with the Yadavas, Bhojas, and Panchalas. Up to the time of the Buddha, the Kurus were a monarchy; subsequently, they became a *sangha*.

FURTHER DISCUSSION | **The identification of Taxila**

Many of the major cities mentioned in ancient Indian texts were identified in the 19th century. One of the men who made a major contribution in this field was Alexander Cunningham, an archaeologist who went on to become the first Director General of the Archaeological Survey of India in 1871. Like others, Cunningham pieced together valuable clues to the location of ancient Indian cities from details given in the classical Graeco-Roman accounts and the travelogues of the Chinese pilgrims Xuanzang and Faxian. Unlike others, however, he routinely confirmed his identifications through field surveys. Cunningham counted among his major achievements the identifications of Aornos, Taxila, Sangala, Srughna, Ahichchhatra, Bairat, Sankisa, Shravasti, Kaushambi, Padmavati, Vaishali, and Nalanda. Cunningham had initially identified the site of ancient Taxila (Takshashila) with Manikyala. However, his explorations at Shah-dheri in 1863–64 convinced him that the correct identification lay here. The following extract reveals how he reached this conclusion:

The position of the celebrated city of Taxila has hitherto remained unknown, partly owing to the erroneous distance recorded by Pliny, and partly to the want of information regarding the vast ruins which still exist in the vicinity of Shah-dheri. All the copies of Pliny agree in stating that Taxila was only 60 Roman, or 55 English, miles from Peucolaitis, or Hashtnagar, which would fix its site somewhere on the Haro river, to the west of Hasan Abdal, or just two days' march from the Indus. But the itineraries of the Chinese pilgrims agree in placing it at three days' journey to the east of the Indus, or in the immediate neighbourhood of Kala-ka-sarai, which was the third halting-place of the Mogul emperors, and which is still the third stage from the Indus, both for troops and baggage. Now as Hwen Thsang, on his return to China, was accompanied by laden elephants, his three days' journey from *Takhshasila* [*sic*] to the Indus at *Utakhanda*, or Ohind, must necessarily have been of the same length as those of modern days, and, consequently, the site of the city must be looked for somewhere in the neighbourhood of *Kala-ka-sarai*. This site is found near Shah-dheri, just one mile to the north-east of Kala-ka-sarai, in the extensive ruins of a fortified city, around which I was able to trace no less than 55 *stupas*, of which two are as large as the great Manikyala tope (i.e., *stupa*), 28 monasteries, and nine temples. Now the distance from Shah-dheri to Ohind is 36 miles, and from Ohind to Hashtnagar is 38 more, or altogether 74 miles, which is 19 in excess of the distance recorded by Pliny between Taxila and Peukelaotis [*sic*]. To reconcile these discrepant numbers I would suggest that Pliny's 60 miles or LX, should be read as 80 miles or LXXX, which are equivalent to 73½ English miles, or within half a mile of the actual distance between the two places....

Then follows a discussion of the history of Taxila and a detailed description of the mounds at the site, namely Bhir, Hathial, Sirkap, Kacha-kot, Babar Khana, and Sirsukh.

...In closing my account of the extensive ruins near Shah-dheri, which I have endeavoured to identify with the famous Taxila of the Greeks, I may remark that the identification is most satisfactorily confirmed by the bearings and distances of the next two places visited by Hwen Thsang, both of which will be now described under the names of Hasan Abdal and Baoti Pind. The ruins at these places form, what may be called, the western group of the suburban or outlying remains of Taxila, the ancient capital of the Panjab.

Source Cunningham, 1871: 111–35

The kingdom of Panchala included the Rohilkhand area and part of the central doab region, and was divided into two parts by the Ganga. The capital of Uttara (north) Panchala was Ahichchhatra (identified with modern Ramnagar in Bareilly district, UP), and that of Dakshina (south) Panchala was Kampilya (identified with Kampil in Farukkhabad district, UP). The city of Kanyakubja or Kanauj was located in this kingdom. Several ancient texts mention a king named Chulani Brahmadatta. Going by the testimony of the *Arthashastra*, the Panchalas seem to have later switched to an oligarchic form of government.

The principality of the Matsyas was located in the Jaipur area in Rajasthan, extending into the Alwar and Bharatpur areas as well. Their capital was Viratanagara (modern Bairat), named after Virata, founder of the kingdom. Buddhist texts usually associate the Matsyas with the Shurasenas.

The Shurasenas (or Surasenas) had their capital at Mathura (also known as Madura) on the Yamuna. Buddhist tradition describes Avantiputra, king of the Shurasenas, as a disciple of the Buddha. This king's name (literally, 'son of Avanti') suggests the possibility of a matrimonial alliance between Shurasena and Avanti. The *Mahabharata* and the Puranas refer to rulers of the Mathura region as the Yadu or Yadavas, who included the Vrishnis.

Texts such as the *Ashtadhyayi*, *Markandeya Purana*, *Brihatsamhita*, and the Greek accounts suggest that the Assaka (Ashmaka/Ashvaka) kingdom was situated in the north-west. However, the Assaka of Buddhist texts is located on the Godavari river. Its capital was Potana/Podana or Potali, identified with modern Bodhan. The Godavari separated Assaka from the neighbouring kingdom of Mulaka or Alaka with its capital at Pratishthana (identified with modern Paithan). Jataka stories suggest that Assaka may at some point have come under the sway of Kashi and that it achieved a military victory over Kalinga in Eastern India.

Avanti, in the Malwa region of Central India, was initially divided into a northern and a southern part. The two important towns of this kingdom were Ujjayini (near modern Ujjain) and Mahishmati (identified with modern Maheshwar), both of which are mentioned in ancient texts as its capital. These two cities were important points on trade routes that connected North India, both with the Deccan and with ports on the western coast. Pradyota was a famous king of Avanti, during whose time this kingdom was involved in conflicts with Vatsa, Magadha, and Kosala.

The kingdom of Gandhara comprised modern Peshawar and Rawalpindi districts of Pakistan and the Kashmir valley. Its capital Takshashila (Taxila) was a major centre of trade and learning. King Pukkusati or Pushkarasarin ruled over Gandhara in the mid-6th century BCE. He had cordial relations with Magadha, and waged a successful war against Avanti. The Naqsh-i Rustom inscription of the Achaemenid emperor Darius indicates that the Persians extended their control over Gandhara and the Indus valley in the later part of the 6th century BCE.

Ancient texts and inscriptions usually associate the kingdom of Kamboja with Gandhara. Kamboja included the area around Rajaori, including the Hazara district of the North-West Frontier Province of Pakistan. The Kambojas were a monarchy in the 6th century BCE, but the *Arthashastra* refers to them as a *sangha*.

Gandhara punch-marked coin (obverse and reverse)

The *Ganas* or *Sanghas*

Ancient Indian texts recognize the difference between the political structure and functioning of the *rajyas* and the *ganas* or *sanghas*. Two of the *mahajanapadas*, the Vajji and Malla, were *sanghas*. Buddhist texts mention others as well—the Sakyas of Kapilavastu, Koliyas of Devadaha and Ramagrama, Bulis of Alakappa, Kalamas of Kesaputta, Moriyas of Pipphalivana, and Bhaggas (Bhargas) with their capital on Sumsumara hill. It is interesting to note that most of the *ganas*, especially the politically important ones, were located in or near the Himalayan foothills in Eastern India, while the major kingdoms occupied the fertile alluvial tracts of the Ganga valley.

The *ganas* had greater vestiges of tribal organization than the monarchies. Some may have simply been more complex political forms of older tribal formations. Others may have been created through the subversion of monarchical rule: For instance, the Videhas were apparently originally a monarchy, but had become a *gana* by the 6th century BCE. The Kurus were a monarchy at this time, but became a *gana* a few centuries later. There were two kinds of *ganas*—those that consisted of all or a section of one clan, e.g., the Sakyas and Koliyas; and those that comprised a confederation of several clans, like the Vajjis and Yadavas. The confederacies suggest the existence of a self-conscious political identity among the *ganas*.

The Sakyas claimed to belong to the Ikshvaku family and the solar dynasty. Their principality was bounded on the east by the Rohini river, the Rapti river to the west and south, and the Himalaya mountains to the north. As for the location of its capital, Kapilavastu, some scholars locate it at Tilaurakot, but there is better reason to locate it at Piprahwa-Ganwaria. The amount of detail regarding the Sakyas in Buddhist texts is due to the fact that the Buddha belonged to this clan. The Sakyas were connected through marriage to the royal house of Kosala. Buddhist texts clearly indicate that the Sakya assembly gathered to discuss important business such as forging alliances, embarking on war, and concluding peace.

The principality of the Koliyas of Ramagrama lay to the east of the Sakyas, the Rohini river forming the boundary between the two. Some texts suggest that the two peoples were related to each other. The Bhaggas seem to have been located in the Vindhyan region, between the Yamuna and Son rivers, and were apparently subordinate to the Vatsas. Little is known about the other *ganas*.

Early studies on the *ganas* by Nationalist historians (see, for instance, Jayaswal, 1943) tended to glorify them by exaggerating their democratic features. Comparisons were made with the republics of Greece and Rome and with modern political institutions. A lot of this was no doubt to disprove the assertions of Western scholars that Indians had never known anything other than despotic rule. Later writings (e.g., J. P. Sharma, 1968) adopted a more dispassionate approach.

Governance in these polities was marked by group solidarity among the ruling elite, who formed an oligarchy. The *Arthashastra*, a later text, outlines the special strategies that the would-be conqueror could use to vanquish the *ganas*. Because they were different, the strategies recommended to defeat monarchies would not work, and Kautilya's advice focused on creating dissension among their ranks.

The ancient Indian *ganas* were not like modern democracies. Power was vested in the hands of an aristocracy comprising the heads of leading Kshatriya families. There was no single hereditary monarch. Instead, there was a chief (known variously as *ganapati*, *ganajyestha*, *ganaraja*, or *sanghamukhya*) and an aristocratic council which met in a hall called the *santhagara*. Effective executive power and day-to-day political management must have been in the hands of a smaller group. Even in Athenian democracy where there was an elaborate system of governance involving all citizens, women, slaves, and foreigners did not have political rights. The political system of the *ganas* seems to have been a compromise between government by assembly and by an oligarchy within this assembly.

Later texts offer many details about the Lichchhavis. For instance, the *Ekapanna Jataka* states that in the Lichchhavi capital of Vaishali, there were always 7,707 *rajas* (kings) to govern the kingdom, and a similar number of *uparajas* (subordinate kings), *senapatis* (military commanders), and *bhandagarikas* (treasurers). The preamble to the *Chullakalinga Jataka* refers to the 7,707 ruling families of the Lichchhavis and asserts that they were all given to argument and disputation. The *Mahavastu*, on the other hand, states there were twice 84,000, i.e., 168,000 *rajas* living in Vaishali.

The figures mentioned in these texts cannot be taken literally, but they suggest that the Lichchhavis had a large assembly, consisting of the heads of Kshatriya families who called themselves *raja*. They usually met once a year during the spring festival to transact important public business and elect their leader, who had a fixed tenure. The *uparajas* may have been the eldest sons of the *rajas*. It was at one of the annual meetings of the great assembly that the Lichchhavis honoured the beautiful courtesan Ambapali. It was also at such meetings that the *rajas*, old and new, bathed in the sacred *pokkharani* (tank) mentioned in the *Bhaddasala Jataka*. The Lichchhavi assembly had sovereign power and could pronounce punishments such as death or exile. Day-to-day administrative matters were dealt with by a much smaller council of nine, which carried out business in the name of the larger assembly. The assembly did not include women.

It is possible, even likely, that the procedures of the Buddhist monastic order (*sangha*) were patterned on the *sangha* polities, especially the Lichchhavis. The functioning of the two institutions may have been analogous, though not identical. Meetings at the *santhagara* of the *ganas* were probably announced by the beating of a drum, and there may have been a regulator of seats. Voting was done with pieces of wood known as *salakas*. The collector of votes was the *salaka-gahapaka*, chosen for this job on account of his reputation for honesty and impartiality. The *gana-puraka* was responsible for ensuring the presence of a quorum, which was required for major deliberations.

Buddhist and Jaina texts are more forthcoming than their Brahmanical counterparts on details regarding the *ganas*. This is no doubt because kingship was central to the Brahmanical social and political ideology, which equated kinglessness with anarchy.

FURTHER DISCUSSION | The conflict between the Sakyas and Kosalans

Buddhist tradition narrates the following story of how relations between the Kosalans and Sakyas soured due to a trick played by the latter on Prasenajit:

Prasenajit, king of Kosala, was an admirer of the Buddha, and hit upon the idea of marrying into the Sakya clan, to which the Buddha belonged. He requested the Sakyas for one of their princesses as a wife. The Sakyas were too proud of their lineage to hand over one of their women, but given the power of Prasenajit, were afraid to refuse. So they resorted to a strategem. They passed on a slave girl Vasabhakkhattiya, daughter of a Sakya chief Mahanaman by a slave woman, concealing her low parentage on her mother's side. Vidudabha and Vajira were the son and daughter born of this marriage.

At some point of time, Vidudabha paid a visit to his maternal grandfather's home and learnt of his mother's background. The news reached Prasenajit as well. When the king realized that he had been tricked, he immediately disowned his wife and son. The Buddha mollified him by telling him that it was the father's social status that counted, not the mother's. Vidudabha and his mother were restored to favour due to this intercession. Vidudabha eventually succeeded his father as king, and massacred the Sakyas as revenge for their trickery.

It is impossible to know for sure whether there is any historical basis to this story. But the Kosalan massacre of the Sakyas became one of many episodes remembered in later Buddhist tradition, and it is depicted vividly in relief sculpture at many *stupa* sites.

Monarchies and oligarchies had different internal power equations (Ruben, [1966] 1969). In the *ganas*, Brahmanas and *purohitas* may not have enjoyed the prestige they did in the *rajyas*. There are hardly any references to *purohitas* or gifts of land to Brahmanas in the *ganas*. And in the *Ambattha Sutta* of the *Digha Nikaya*, when the Brahmana Ambattha visited Kapilavastu, members of the Sakya assembly are said to have laughed at him, treating him with scant respect.

The *ganas* were closely associated with the Kshatriyas and were named after the ruling Kshatriya clan; members were linked to each other through real or claimed kinship ties. However, apart from this hereditary elite, various other groups—Brahmanas, farmers, artisans, wage labourers, slaves, etc.—lived in these principalities and had a subordinate status, politically, and probably also economically and socially. They were not entitled to use the clan name and did not have rights of political participation. For instance, Upali, the barber who lived in Sakya territory, and Chunda, the metal smith who lived in Malla territory, were not part of the ruling elite and did not attend the assembly.

The powerful monarchies of the time eventually developed a standing army—a permanent corps of troops recruited and maintained by the state. Such an organization does not seem to have existed in the *ganas*. The Lichchhavis had a strong army, but when not engaged in combat, the soldiers probably retired to their lands.

There may also have been differences in patterns of land ownership. The Kshatriya political elite were probably also the largest landowners in the *ganas*. Walter Ruben ([1966] 1969) suggests that the clan exercised rights over land, and private property may have been absent. Although conclusive evidence is lacking on this point, a custom supposedly practised by the Lichchhavis is suggestive. The story goes that among the Lichchhavis, an exceptionally beautiful woman (e.g., Ambapali) was not allowed to marry, but was to belong (i.e., be available) to all the Lichcchavi men. This may have been an extension of clan rights over other resources such as land.

The *ganas*' greatest asset—governance through discussion among the ruling elite—was also their greatest weakness. They were vulnerable to internal dissension, especially when faced with aggressive monarchies. In the *Lalitavistara*, the future Buddha is described as sitting in heaven, thinking of his impending birth. One of the questions raised is: Which family should he be born in? The other *bodhisattvas* and gods discuss and reject the candidature of the Lichchhavis of Vaishali. They say that these people do not speak to each other in the proper manner, do not follow the *dharma*, do not preserve the ranks of social status and age, do not become anybody's disciples, and each one

PRIMARY SOURCES | Vassakara seeks the Buddha's advice on how to defeat the Vajjis

The *Mahaparinibbana Sutta* begins with the following episode, which reflects the *ganas*' points of vulnerability:

Thus have I heard. The Exalted One [the Buddha] was once dwelling in Rajagaha, on the hill called Vulture's Peak. Now at that time, Vedehiputta Ajatasattu, the king of Magadha, had made up his mind to attack the Vajjians; and he said to himself, 'I will strike at these Vajjians, mighty and powerful though they be, I will root out these Vajjians, I will bring these Vajjians to utter ruin!'

So he said to his Brahmana minister Vassakara, 'Go to the Exalted One, bow down in adoration at his feet on my behalf, and inquire on my behalf whether he is free from illness and suffering, enjoying ease and comfort and good health. Then tell him that I want to attack and destroy the Vajjians. And listen carefully and remember whatever he may predict, and come back and repeat it to me. For the Buddhas speak nothing untrue!'

Vassakara and his cavalcade of chariots drove up as close as possible to Vulture's Peak and walked the remaining distance. Vassakara approached the Buddha, exchanged greetings and compliments of politeness and courtesy, sat down respectfully by his side, and gave him the king's message.

Now at that time, the venerable Ananda was standing behind the Exalted One, fanning him. The Buddha asked him whether he had heard that the Vajjians frequently called public meetings of their clan. Ananda replied he had heard that this was so.

The Buddha said, 'So long, Ananda, as the Vajjians meet together in concord and rise in concord and carry out their undertakings in concord—so long as they enact nothing not already established, abrogate nothing that has been already enacted, and act in accordance with the ancient institutions of the Vajjians as established in former days—so long as they honour and esteem and revere and support the Vajjian elders and consider it a duty to be attentive to their words, so long as no women or girls belonging to their clans are detained among them by force or abduction, so long as they honour and esteem and revere and support the Vajjian shrines in town and country, and do not allow the proper offerings and rites as formerly established and performed to fall into disuse, so long as the rightful protection, defence, and support shall be fully provided for the Arahants [monks who had attained enlightenment] among them, so that Arahants from a distance may enter their realm and live there in ease—as long as they do all these things, the Vajjians can be expected not to decline, but to prosper.'

Then the Buddha said to Vassakara: 'When I was once staying, Oh Brahmana, at Vesali at the Sarandada shrine, I taught the Vajjians these conditions of welfare; and as long as these conditions shall continue to exist among them, we may expect them not to decline, but to prosper.'

'We may expect then,' answered the Brahmana, 'the welfare and not the decline of the Vajjians when they are possessed of any one of these conditions of welfare, how much more so when they are possessed of all the seven. So, Gotama, the Vajjians cannot be overcome by the king of Magadha; that is not in battle, without diplomacy or breaking up their alliance. And now, Gotama, we must go; we are busy and have much to do.'

'Whatever you think most fitting, Oh Brahmana,' replied the Buddha. And Vassakara, delighted and pleased with the words of the Exalted One, rose from his seat and went his way.

Vassakara had picked up on an important hint and was keen to start working out a strategy to overpower the Vajjis.

Source Rhys Davids, (1910) 1951: 78–81

thinks 'I am king! I am king!' The *Arthashastra* asserts that *sanghas* were unassailable and advises the king to win over friendly ones. It suggests that the head of a *sangha* should remain self-controlled and just towards other members, and should do what is beneficial and agreeable to them all.

The *Ashtadhyayi* mentions several *ganas* such as the Kshudrakas, Malavas, Ambashthas, Hastinayanas, Prakanvas, Madras, Madhumantas, Apritas, Vasatis, Bhaggas, Shibis, Ashvayanas, and Ashvakayanas. Slightly later references suggest that the Vrishnis, Andhakas, and other allied tribes living in the Mathura region were part of a *sangha*. Vasudeva Krishna of the Vrishni clan is described as a *sangha-mukhya* (the head of a *sangha*). Non-monarchical states are also mentioned in the *Mahabharata*, Megathenes' *Indica*, and in Greek accounts of Alexander's invasion.

Names of *ganas* (e.g., the Yaudheyas, Malavas, Uddehikas, and Arjunayanas) occur on coins of the early centuries CE, and some are also mentioned in inscriptions. In the 4th century CE, Chandragupta I is known to have married a Lichchhavi princess, Kumaradevi, and this marriage was commemorated on gold coins. Samudragupta is known as *Lichchhavi-dauhitra* (grandson of the Lichchhavis) in inscriptions. Clearly, the Lichchhavis were still a political force worth making an alliance with. However, it was probably Samudragupta's military campaigns that wiped out the *ganas*, or at least reduced them to a position of political insignificance.

The history of the *ganas* of ancient India thus spans at least a thousand years, if not more. Their military defeats at the hands of monarchical states can be seen as a result of the inability of their system of governance and military organization to meet the challenges of empire building. The ambitions of monarchical states were reflected in the political vocabulary of the time, in terms such as *chakravartin*, *samrat*, and *sarvabhauma*. These signified a 'world victor', an emperor who had established his rule over the entire subcontinent. Several centuries later, the rulers of Magadha succeeded in translating the idea of empire into reality.

The Forest Tribes

Beyond the kingdoms and the oligarchies were masses of stateless people, whose histories have to be inferred because they did not leave any written records. The forest was home to many of them. Violence was inherent in the interactions between early states and the forest people. 'Forest' can be understood a shorthand for a variety of ecological zones including mountainous, littoral, and pastoral tracts, all those areas inhabited by what can be loosely described as stateless people, whose political and economic modes of being were different from those associated with agrarian states.

The conflict between the state and the forest is one of the most important and most underestimated aspects of the political history of ancient and early medieval India. The expansion of agriculture, cities, and states involved the steady clearance of forests, but the really massive forest clearance in the subcontinent took place in the middle of the 19th century as a cumulative result of population increase, commercial farming, and the expansion of the railways. Till then, states were always cheek by jowl with the forest tribes. That is why it is not surprising that ancient Indian sources have a great deal to say about the forest and forest people (see Upinder Singh, 2017: 367–459).

The idea of the *mleccha*, with its pejorative view of tribals and foreigners, is found in later Vedic texts. It sought to distinguish the civilized from the barbarian (see Parasher, 1991). With the expansion of agriculture, cities, and states, and the emergence and growth of empires, the forest became an important object of the exploitation and violence of the state. But it was also a constant source of violent challenge to the state. Exploiting, extracting, and controlling valuable economic and military resources like wood, ivory, and elephants involved a steady encroachment on forest habitats and constant conflicts between states and forest people.

Political Conflicts and the Growth of the Magadhan Empire

The outlines of the rise of Magadha to political supremacy can be reconstructed by comparing the information in the Puranic, Buddhist, and Jaina texts (Raychaudhuri, [1923] 2000: 161–210; Majumdar. [Gen. Ed.]., [1951] 1968: 18–36). There are several differences in the dynastic sequences in these sources. Buddhist and Jaina traditions compete with each other in trying to establish their claims to the great kings of the time, while the Puranas disparage those who favoured these traditions. The details given in these texts cannot be taken at face value, but they do indicate that the composers of religious texts were very interested in politics. The political narrative is one of bitter political rivalries, struggles for succession, plots, murders, blood, and gore. Behind the keenly fought political conflicts of the time lay struggles for power over people, land, and resources. The states that won were those that had larger, stronger, better armies, and this in turn was the result of the effective harnessing of economic and human resources, and successful political strategies of administration and control.

Magadha's gradual rise to political supremacy began with the reign of Bimbisara *c*. 545–493 BCE. The statement in the *Mahavamsa* that he was anointed king by his father at the age of 15 suggests that he was not the founder of his dynasty. There is a view that the title Seniya (or Shrenika) given to him in Buddhist texts indicates that he was initially a *senapati* (commander-in-chief), probably of the Vajjis. However, the *Mahavamsa* reference does not support such an inference. According to Ashvaghosha's *Buddhacharita*, Bimbisara belonged to the Haryanka *kula* (family).

Bimbisara entered into a number of matrimonial alliances that helped strengthen Magadha's position. He married Mahakosala, sister of king Prasenajit of Kosala. This marriage brought him a village in Kashi as dowry. He also married a Videhan princess and Khema, daughter of the Madra ruler of central Punjab.

Bimbisara's first capital was at Girivraja (identified with Rajagriha). He led a military campaign against Anga, perhaps to avenge his father's earlier defeat at the hands of its king, Brahmadatta. The campaign was successful, Anga was annexed, and prince Kunika (Ajatashatru) was appointed governor at Champa. A story of Bimbisara sending his physician Jivaka to attend to Pradyota, king of Avanti, in a time of illness suggests cordial relations between the two.

The Buddhist *Mahavagga* states that Bimbisara had a very large kingdom consisting of thousands of prosperous villages. Buddhist texts refer to villages governed by assemblies under village headmen (*gramakas*). They also talk of high-ranking officials known as *mahamatras*, who probably had executive, judicial, and military functions. The king's title 'Seniya' can be taken as indicative that he recruited a standing army maintained on a regular basis through state revenues, and did not rely exclusively on mercenaries.

Jaina texts claim Bimbisara was a follower of Mahavira. According to the *Uttaradhyayana Sutra*, he visited Mahavira along with a retinue of wives, relatives, and servants and became a devoted follower. Buddhist texts, on the other hand, claim that he was a follower of the Buddha. According to the *Sutta Nipata*, Bimbisara first met Gautama about seven years before the latter's enlightenment. The second meeting is described as having taken place at Rajagriha, when the Buddha visited the Magadhan capital with a large group of his disciples. Bimbisara is said to have embraced his teaching, hosted meals for the monks at the palace, and gifted a park called Veluvana to the *sangha*. On another occasion, Bimbisara is supposed to have deputed his physician, Jivaka, to attend to the Buddha and other monks. The king's wife, Khema, is described as well versed in the Buddha's teaching.

Several rules in the *Vinaya Pitaka*—for instance, those dealing with monks eating fruits, the observance of the monsoon retreat, and soldiers joining the army—are stated to have been promulgated by the Buddha in response to issues raised by Bimbisara. After an incident wherein the Buddha did not have money to pay a ferryman who took him across the Ganga, the king is said to have announced a remission of ferry charges for all ascetics. It is impossible to say whether there is any historical basis for such stories; what they do indicate is that Bimbisara was considered an important figure in the early Buddhist tradition.

According to Buddhist tradition, Bimbisara was killed by his son Kunika, also known as Ajatashatru, at the instance of the Buddha's wicked cousin Devadatta. Ajatashatru is said to have later confessed his crime to the Buddha. Jaina tradition, on the other hand, states that Ajatashatru imprisoned his father in order to become king. It states that queen Chellana displayed such devotion towards her husband in prison that Ajatashatru was filled with remorse for what he had done, and rushed forward with an iron club to break his father's chains. Thinking that his son was advancing to kill him, Bimbisara is said to have consumed poison and ended his own life.

The steady expansion of Magadha continued under Ajatashatru (*c.* 493–462 BCE). The conflict with Kosala was an important part of this process. Prasenajit, king of Kosala, was furious at Ajatashatru's patricide. His anger was compounded by the fact that Mahakoshala, one of Bimbisara's wives and Prasenajit's sister, died of grief soon thereafter. Prasenajit rescinded the gift of Kashi village that had been part of his sister's dowry. This was followed by a war between Kosala and Magadha. On one occasion, Prasenajit was defeated and had to flee to his capital. On another, Ajatashatru was captured, but his life spared. According to the terms of the peace that was eventually concluded, Kashi was returned to Ajatashatru, and he also received a Kosalan princess named Vajira in marriage. Prasenajit himself was soon thereafter deposed in a palace coup. He set out towards Rajagriha to seek Ajatashatru's help, but died outside the city gates.

A major success for Ajatashatru was his victory over the Lichchhavis. It seems that the Lichchhavis were supported by various other *ganas*, and also by Kosala. The Lichchhavis were at the height of their power at the time. Ajatashatru realized that he would not be able to defeat them in direct combat. So, he is said to have sent his minister Vassakara on an undercover mission to sow the seeds of dissension within their ranks. The strategy succeeded. According to Buddhist tradition, when Ajatashatru finally attacked, the Lichchhavis were so busy quarrelling among themselves about how they should conduct their defence that Ajatashatru was able to defeat them. Jaina texts state that Ajatashatru used two unique weapons in the war—one was a catapult capable of hurling huge pieces of stone, and the other a chariot with an attached mace, which created havoc in enemy ranks. To conduct the operations against the Lichchhavis more effectively, Ajatashatru ordered fortifications constructed at Pataligrama on the Ganga. This later became the famous metropolis of Pataliputra. The conflict between Ajatashatru and the Lichchhavis was a protracted one and may have lasted 16 years. Ultimately, victory went to Magadha. Ajatashatru also defeated Chanda Pradyota of Avanti.

PRIMARY SOURCES | Ajatashatru's visit to the Buddha

Royal patronage was an important source of prestige for ancient religious sects. Ajatashatru's visit to the Buddha was considered an important event in the Buddhist tradition. It is depicted in a 2nd century BCE relief panel on one of the railing pillars of the western gateway that originally stood at the Central Indian Buddhist site of Bharhut.

The first part of the scene is carved on the lower left side of the panel. It shows a royal procession, headed by a king riding an elephant, followed by his queens, also on elephants. To the right, the king has dismounted from the elephant and stands before two mango trees with his right hand raised, as if to speak. In the third scene, which is on the rear left, the king and queens stand with hands folded reverentially. In the last scene, on the top right, the king performs obeisance before the footprint-bearing throne symbolizing the Buddha.

We know that this scene represents Ajatashatru's visit to the Buddha because a Prakrit inscription on the side reads: *Ajatasatu Bhagavato vandate* (Ajatashatru worships the Lord [Buddha]).

As is the case with Bimbisara, Ajatashatru too is presented as a follower of Mahavira in the Jaina tradition and of the Buddha in the Buddhist. Jaina texts describe the king's frequent visits to Mahavira, his conversations with him at Vaishali and Champa, and his strong adherence to Mahavira's teaching. Buddhist texts describe Ajatashatru as approaching the Buddha to express remorse for his patricide.

On the Buddha's demise, Ajatashatru is said to have gone to Kusinara to claim a portion of his relics on the grounds that he, like the Buddha, was a Kshatriya. He is also credited with building many relic stupas around Rajagriha and repairing many monasteries in and around the city. Buddhist tradition describes him as hosting the first Buddhist council at Rajagriha. This important event, which saw a grand assembly of eminent monks, took place soon after the Buddha's death.

Buddhist tradition describes the four kings who succeeded Ajatashatru as patricides who ruled for a total of 56 years. Buddhist texts refer to the immediate successor as Udayibhadda, Jaina texts as Udayabhadra or Udayin. The Puranas insert a ruler named Darshaka before him. Far from depicting Udayin as a patricide, Jaina tradition describes him as a devoted son, who served as his father's viceroy at Champa before being elevated to kingship, later founding the city of Pataliputra. He is described as a devout Jaina, given to frequent fasting. In fact, he is said to have been killed by an assassin hired by the king of Avanti, while piously listening to a religious discourse. According to the Puranas, Udayin was succeeded by Nandivardhana and Mahanandin. Buddhist tradition, on the other hand, lists Anuruddha, Munda, and Nagadarshaka as Udayibhadda's successors.

The people of Magadha are said to have driven out the ruling family and elected an *amatya* (a high-ranking official) named Shishunaga as king. Shishunaga seems to have had a second capital at Vaishali (according to the *Mahavamsatika*, he was the son of a Lichchhavi *raja* of Vaishali). He succeeded in destroying the power of the Pradyota dynasty of Avanti. The kingdoms of Vatsa and Kosala may also have been annexed by him. Kalashoka (probably the Kakavarna of the Puranas) was Shishunaga's son and successor. His reign saw the shifting of the capital to Pataliputra and the convening of the second Buddhist council at Vaishali. The Shaishunaga dynasty (*c.* 430/413–364/345 BCE) came to a bloody end. The king and his sons were murdered, making way for the Nanda dynasty (*c.* 364/345–324 BCE).

The Puranas call the founder of the Nanda dynasty Mahapadma, while Buddhist tradition calls him Ugrasena. The Jaina *Parishishtaparvan* states that the first Nanda king was the son of a barber by a *ganika* (courtesan). The Greek writer Curtius tells us that he was a barber who became a lover of one of the queens and killed the king at her instigation. The Puranas describe Mahapadma as the son of a king of the Shaishunaga dynasty by a Shudra woman, and express their disapproval by describing the Nanda kings as *adharmika* (those who do not follow the norms of *dharma*). Buddhist texts describe the Nandas as 'of unknown lineage' (*annatakula*). According to the *Mahavamsatika*, Ugrasena was a man of the frontier who fell into the clutches of a gang of robbers, became their leader, and led them to many military successes.

Puranic, Buddhist, and Jaina traditions agree that there were nine Nanda kings. However, the Puranas describe the first king as the father and the later eight as his sons, while Buddhist texts describe all eight as brothers. The Puranas name only Mahapadma and one of his sons, Sukalpa. The *Mahabodhivamsa* gives the following list of nine kings: Ugrasena, Panduka, Pandugati, Bhutapala, Rashtrapala, Govishanaka, Dashasiddhaka, Kaivarta, and Dhana.

The Puranas refer to Mahapadma as one who attained sole sovereignty (*ekarat*) and as an uprooter of the Kshatriyas (*sarva-kshatrantaka*). A possible indication of Nanda military victories in Kalinga is suggested by the 1st century BCE Hathigumpha inscription of Kharavela, which mentions a king named Nanda invading Kalinga, building a canal there, and taking away a Jaina image. The existence of a place called Nau Nand Dehra (Nanded) on the Godavari is taken by some scholars as reflecting Nanda rule over the Deccan. The evidence for the extension of Nanda rule into trans-Vindhyan India is not, however, strong.

Dhana Nanda was ruling Magadha at the time of Alexander's invasion. The Greek accounts call him Agrammes or Xandrames (probably a corruption of Augrasenya, son of Ugrasena). He is described as a powerful king who ruled over the Prasii (Prachya, i.e., the eastern people) and the Gangaridae (the people of the lower Ganga valley). Curtius states that he had an army consisting of 20,000 cavalry, 200,000 infantry, 2,000 chariots, and 3,000 elephants. Other Greek accounts give the number of elephants as 4,000 or 6,000. Although these figures cannot be taken as precise statistics, they do suggest that the Greeks had heard reports of the large and formidable army maintained by the Nandas. Later indigenous sources refer to the fabulous riches of Dhana Nanda, his greed, his exploitation of his people, and his consequent unpopularity.

According to Jaina tradition, the Nandas had several ministers with Jaina leanings. Kalpaka was a minister of the first Nanda king. He is said to have been reluctant to assume office, but once he took on the post, he encouraged the king towards an aggressive expansionist policy. Jaina texts suggest that ministerial office was hereditary. They state that on the death of Shakatala, a minister of the ninth Nanda king, the position was offered to his son Sthulabhadra, who refused it and became a Jaina monk. The post was then accepted by Sthulabhadra's brother, Shriyaka.

The Nanda kings built on the foundations laid by their Haryanka and Shaishunaga predecessors to create the first great empire of North India. Much has been written about the factors that led to Magadha's political success. Its geographical position was certainly favourable. The old capital Rajagriha was surrounded by a perimeter of five easily defended hills and the new capital Pataliputra was protected due to its location at the junction of the Ganga and Son. Moreover, the Ganga and its tributaries—the Son on the south and the Gandak and Gogra on the north—connected this kingdom with the important trade routes. Some historians have mentioned Magadha's comparative freedom from Brahmanical orthodoxy as an asset, but it is difficult to assess the political impact of such a factor.

Kosambi ([1956] 1998: 155) suggested that a monopoly over iron ore mines was a major factor responsible for Magadha's imperialist expansion. As pointed out in Chapter 5, Magadha did not in fact have a monopoly of iron ores, and the exploitation of the ores of south Bihar seem to have started much later. In terms of resources, the kingdom did have advantages of fertile soil and access to timber and elephants in the adjoining forests. The nearby Chota Nagpur plateau was rich in many kinds of minerals and raw materials, and access to these must also have been an important asset.

Resourceful rulers who launched and led successful military campaigns and devised strategic matrimonial alliances played a crucial role in the process of empire building. Ultimately, the basis of Magadha's military success over the centuries was based on effective extraction and deployment of resources by the state and the creation of a strong military force on this foundation. Unfortunately, we do not have details of the administrative, revenue, or military organization of the early Magadhan dynasties.

The Persian and Macedonian Invasions

Kurush or Cyrus I was the first king of the Persian empire, but Cyrus II, 'Cyrus the Great' (*c.* 559–530 BCE) is regarded as its real founder because it was his successful military campaigns that created the empire. Darayavaush or Darius I (522–486 BCE) claimed to be a descendant of Cyrus but was probably a usurper. As he traced his ancestry back to a Persian named Achaemenes, his dynasty is known as the Achaemenid dynasty. Darius was responsible for the eastward extension of the empire and led a campaign into India in *c.* 518 BCE. He despatched an expedition down the Indus under Scylax to explore the mouth of the Indus and the maritime route to the west.

The Persian empire was marked by great political, cultural, and religious diversity and its vastness was unprecedented in the ancient world (for overviews of Persian/Iranian history, see Brosius, 2006: 1–75; Daryaee. [Ed.], 2012). The Greek historian Herodotus tells us that Darius I subdued the 'Indians' (Indus valley) and that 'India' (i.e., the Indus valley) was the twentieth and most prosperous satrapy (province) of the

Persian empire, and reports that the tribute from this province amounted to 360 talents of gold dust, more than that from all other provinces put together. The Old Persian word for the lands/people of the empire is *dahyava* (singular, *dahyu*). The Bisitun inscription of Darius I mentions the people of Gandara (Gandhara) and Maka (the Makran coast of Baluchistan) among the subjects of the Persian empire. Darius' Naqsh-i Rustom inscription includes the Hidus and Gandharians among his subjects. These people are represented in relief carvings of subject people supporting the dais on which stands the throne of the Persian king at Persepolis and Naqsh-i Rustom. They also figure among delegations of subject people bringing gifts depicted on the staircase leading up to the Apadana or throne hall in Persepolis. Persian administrative records known as the Persepolis Fortification Texts contain a reference to a traveller named Abbetema who travelled from Hidu to Susa, but details are lacking.

Darius was succeeded by his son Khshayarsha or Xerxes (486–465 BCE), who maintained his hold on the provinces of Gandhara and Hidu. His army is supposed to have included soldiers from Gandhara and 'India'. There is reference to Xerxes destroying the sanctuary of the Daivas in a troublesome province of his empire; this may allude to events in Gandhara. The Persian empire declined after Xerxes' death, but the Gandharians and 'Indians' continue to be mentioned as subjects of the Persian empire under Artakhsasa or Artaxerxes II (404–359 BCE). The army of Darius III (336–330 BCE) included 'Indian' troops, perhaps mercenaries.

The fact that architectural remains of the Achaemenid period have not been found so far in the subcontinent suggests a nominal control over the Indian provinces. Daric and sigloi coins showing archers in the Tchaman-i-Hazouri hoard found near Kabul, the Oxus treasure, and the Bhir mound indicate the circulation of Achaemenid coins in these areas. But the 'bent bar' punch marked coins found south of the Hindu Kush seem to be a local currency issued by Indian satraps (governors) in this area, suggesting a loose level of control and autonomy (Bopearachchi, 2020a: 7–9).

Apart from its political aspect, the most apparent and direct Persian impact on India was the introduction of the Kharoshthi script, which was derived from Aramaic, a script used in the western part of the Persian empire. Some historians have suggested Persian influence on the Mauryas and on their administration and art, but this seems to have been greatly exaggerated.

By the time of the Alexander's invasion (327–326 BCE), the Persian hold over their Indian provinces must have been nominal or non-existent. Much of what we know about Alexander comes from much later sources that helped create his image as a legendary king. (For a biography of Alexander, see Green, 1991; for accounts of the Indian campaigns, see Stoneman, 2019: 36–78.) The Greek historians give a detailed, though idealized, account of Alexander's Indian campaign. After decisively defeating the Persian army led by Darius, the Macedonian conqueror turned towards the eastern provinces of the erstwhile Persian empire. He established a series of outposts in Afghanistan before venturing further into the subcontinent. According to the Greeks, at that time, the north-west was peppered with a number of principalities. There was some especially long and bitter fighting, for instance, at the walled city of Astes, the stronghold of the Assakenoi, whose army was led by their late king's mother. The Greek historians make a great deal of Alexander's siege of the hill fort of Aornos, because of a tradition that even the god Herakles had been unable to take it.

In 326 BCE, Alexander's army crossed the Indus. Ambhi, the ruler of Taxila, extended support to the Greeks. Porus (Puru or Paurava), who ruled the area between the Jhelum and Chenab, offered resistance, but was overpowered. The obverse of a silver decadrachm depicts a Macedonian on horseback chasing a man on an elephant; this seems to be a depiction of an encounter between Alexander and Porus. The reverse shows Alexander being crowned by Nike, with a sceptre in his left hand and thunderbolt in his right, suggesting that he was the god Zeus. Although Alexander and Porus never had a one-on-one fight, the medallion commemorates an important Macedonian victory and reflects Alexander's political ideology. From the Jhelum, Alexander moved onwards

Alexander medallions (obverse and reverse): silver, Alexander and Porus type; gold, Alexander with elephant scalp headdress

PRIMARY SOURCES | The storming of the Malla citadel

The Greek historians have left several vivid and detailed accounts of Alexander's life and military career. Arrian's *Anabasis of Alexander*, written in the 1st–2nd century CE, gives an account of Alexander's life from his accession to his death. This includes a description of the Indian campaigns. Arrian states that he had derived his information from the writings of Aristobulus of Cassandreia, and Ptolemy, son of Lagus, who went on to become king of Egypt. Both these men had accompanied Alexander on his expeditions. Given below is Arrian's description of the storming of the citadel of the Mallas:

When the citadel was seen to be still in the possession of the army, and many of them were observed drawn up in front as if to repel attacks, some of the Macedonians tried to force an entry by undermining the wall, and others by placing scaling ladders against it, wherever it was practicable to do so. Alexander, thinking that the men who carried the ladders were too slow, snatched one from a man who was carrying it, placed it against the wall himself, and began to mount it, crouching under his shield. After him mounted Peucestas, the man who carried the sacred shield which Alexander took from the temple of the Trojan Athena and used to keep with him and have carried before him in all his battles. After Peucestas, by the same ladder ascended Leonnatus, the confidential bodyguard; and up another ladder went Abreas, one of the soldiers who received double pay for distinguished service.

The king was now near the battlement of the wall, and leaning his shield against it, was pushing some of the Indians within the fort and had cleared that part of the wall by killing others with his sword. The shield-bearing guards, becoming very anxious for the king's safety, pushed each other with ardour up the same ladder and broke it; so that those who were already mounted fell down and made the ascent impossible for the rest. Alexander then, standing upon the wall, was being attacked from all around from the adjacent towers; for none of the Indians dared approach him. He was also being attacked by the men in the city, who were throwing darts at him from no great distance; for a mound of earth happened to have been heaped up there opposite the wall. Alexander was conspicuous both by the brilliance of his weapons and by his extraordinary display of audacity. He perceived that if he remained where he was, he would be incurring danger without being able to perform anything at all worthy of consideration. But if he leapt down within the fort, he might perhaps by this very act strike the Indians with terror, and if he did not, but should only thereby be incurring danger, at any rate he would die not ignobly after performing great deeds of valour worth hearing about by men of later times. Forming this resolution, he leapt down from the wall into the citadel....

Source E. I. Robson cited in Majumdar. (Ed.)., (1960) 1981: 68–69

and captured the area between the Chenab and Ravi. A gold medallion with a portrait of Alexander wearing an elephant scalp headdress on the obverse and an elephant on the reverse, commemorates his Indian victories. However, movement beyond the Beas was prevented by the resistance of his own soldiers, who were weary after many years of fighting and yearned to go home. Alexander retreated to the Jhelum and began his journey towards the Indus delta, leaving the territories he had so recently conquered in the hands of Porus, Ambhi, and Abhisara. The areas lying to the west of the Punjab were entrusted to satraps (governors) and Macedonian garrisons. On the way back, there were military encounters with *ganas* such as the Malloi (Malavas), Oxydrakai (Kshudrakas), Sibae (Shibi), and Agalassoi. Alexander finally reached the Indus delta, from where he took the land route towards Babylon through Gedrosia. He died In 326 BCE.

Alexander's invasion is generally seen as having briefly grazed the north-western rim of the subcontinent, not leading to any major or long-term impact. One of its results, however, was the creation of a Seleucid principality in the north-west and the establishment in the area of several Greek settlements including Boukephala, Nikaia, and several Alexandrias. Recent re-assessments of Alexander's invasion have critically examined both the Alexander legend as well as the historiography of the invasion (Ray and Potts, 2007). The Macedonian invasion represents the first important direct Greek contact with India and Greek writers becoming more familiar with the country. The northwest was also exposed to Hellenistic influence after Alexander's death, when a number of Hellenistic successor states were established by generals from Egypt to the northwestern part of the Indian subcontinent.

Land and Agrarian Expansion

Textual references and evidence from early NBPW sites reflect an expansion in the number and size of village settlements and a process of population growth in the Ganga valley during *c.* 600–200 BCE. For instance, Makkhan Lal's (1984) study of the Kanpur district lists 99 NBPW sites, compared to 46 PGW and 9 BRW ones.

Early Buddhist texts mention different kinds of rural settlements (Wagle, 1966: 13–16). The *Vinaya Pitaka* suggests that one, two, three, or four *kutis* could form a village. *Kuti* probably meant a hamlet consisting of a large house and smaller houses around it. The word *gama* (Pali for *grama*) could refer to a hamlet, village, part of a settlement, temporary settlement, or even a caravan of traders camping in one place for over four months. Pali texts refer to *gamas* of park attendants (*aramika-gama*), carpenters (*vaddhaki-gama*), reed makers (*nalakara-gama*), and salt makers (*lonakara-gama*). People following these professions may have constituted a majority in such villages. *Gamas* of Brahmanas and of Chandalas are also mentioned. Terms such as *gama-gamani* and *gamika* refer to village headmen and overseers.

The basis of the agricultural economy of the various regions had been laid down in the preceding centuries. The importance of agriculture in the Ganga valley is reflected in the many agricultural similes used in Buddhist texts. Several *Vinaya* rules are described as having been made in response to the needs of farmers. For instance, the rule that monks were to stay in one place during the monsoon is said to have been made because farmers complained to the Buddha that monks were walking through their fields during the rains and destroying seedlings. People also practised animal rearing, especially cattle rearing. But land had clearly emerged as the most important basis and form of wealth. The emergence of urban centres suggests increasing yields and agricultural surplus. Rice cultivation continued to be an important aspect of agriculture in the Ganga valley.

As mentioned in Chapter 5, the assessment of the role of iron in agricultural expansion, the generation of an agricultural surplus, and the emergence of urban centres has been debated for long by historians and archaeologists. Iron technology was one of several agents of historical change in the 1st millennium BCE. Iron was certainly being used in agriculture in the Ganga valley by this time. Compared to the preceding PGW phase, there is a marked increase in the number and range of iron artefacts at NBPW levels.

The size of landholdings varied. Small farmers must have used household labour to till their modest plots of land. On the other hand, there were owners of large landed estates. For instance, the Brahmana Kasibharadvaja of Ekanala village is described as employing 500 ploughs on his land. There are references to Brahmana *gamas* in Magadha and Kosala, where Brahmanas were the dominant landowners. Some of these villages may have originally been ***brahmadeyas*** (land gifted by kings to Brahmanas). The only place where the Buddha is described (in the *Samyutta Nikaya*) as having been refused food on his begging rounds is in a Brahmana *gama* named Panchasala.

The emergence of the idea of private property in land is evident from references to the gift and sale of land. For example, Anathapindika, a wealthy *gahapati* of Shravasti, bought Jetavana from prince Jeta Kumara in order to gift it to the *sangha*. Land gifted to the *sangha* was generally orchard land or wooded land. The *Vinaya Pitaka* defines an *arama* (land gifted to the *sangha*) as a flower garden (*puppharamo*) or orchard (*phalaramo*). The *Anguttara Nikaya* in fact explicitly prohibits the *sangha* from possessing agricultural land. It is interesting to note that the *Agganna Sutta* in the *Digha Nikaya* connects the origin of kingship to disputes arising over rice fields.

References in the *Digha* and *Majjhima Nikayas* to Bimbisara and Pasenadi giving land to Brahmanas and the *sangha* indicate that kings had control over some tracts of land. Wastelands, forests, and mines probably also fell within their purview. From the point of view of the state, land was the most important source of revenue. Taxes on land must have varied a great deal. The Dharmashastra texts generally stipulate 1/6th of the subjects' produce as the king's share. However, the *Gautama Dharmasutra* (10.24) states that cultivators must pay the king a tax amounting to 1/10th, 1/8th, or 1/6th of their produce.

Buddhist texts refer to *dasas*, *dasis*, *kammakaras*, and *porisas* working in households and on land. The words *dasa* and *dasi* for male and female slaves are known in earlier sources. But *kammakara* is new and refers to someone who hired out his labour in return for wages. Household labour was no doubt inadequate for owners of large landholdings, and herein lies the origin of the practice of employing wage labour. The compound word *dasa-kammakara* is also sometimes used for labourers. The *Ashtadhyayi* refers to *vetan* (wage) and *vaitanika* (wage earner).

Archaeological and Textual Profiles of Early Historic Cities

In 6th century BCE North India, urban settlements with a distinct urban morphology and architecture gradually emerged in the midst of teeming villages and surrounding forests.

Cities had different kinds of functions and identities, as centres of political control, craft production, or trade; some combined all these. The foundations of this urbanization—the second phase in the north—were laid in the earlier centuries, with the establishment of a firm agricultural base that ensured sustained food surpluses. Settlements grew in population, number, and size. Increasing craft specialization, trade, and the beginning of the use of money led to higher degress of social complexity. Political leadership lent an important element of central direction and control.

The Pali canon refers to different kinds of urban settlements (Wagle, 1966: 23–29; Sarao, [1990] 2007). *Pura* meant a town or city, often associated with fortifications. *Nagara* was a fortress or town. *Nigama* refered to a market town, midway between a *gama* and *nagara* in terms of size and social complexity, and was frequently associated with commercial activities. *Rajadhani* was a capital city. *Nagaraka* was a small town, *mahanagara* a big city. Champa, Rajagriha, Shravasti, Saketa, Kaushambi, and Varanasi were *mahanagaras*. The texts often refer to the walls, gates, and watchtowers of cities and the hustle and bustle of urban life.

There is much less archaeological data about early historical cities compared to the protohistoric Harappan ones. Many areas such as Kashmir, Punjab, Sindh, and the north-eastern states have not been adequately explored. Apart from a few sites such as Taxila and Bhita, there have been very few large-scale excavations. Many early historical urban sites were continuously occupied over many centuries. In some cases, they are occupied even today, which makes it difficult to study their earliest levels. Published details of the smaller scale excavations are incomplete and inadequate, and few radiocarbon dates are available. Most archaeological reports do not distinguish between the early, middle, and late NBPW phases; they offer a consolidated picture of *c.* 700–100 BCE and give comparatively less information on the earlier phases within this time bracket. Although there is much that remains to be known about early historical urbanism, the new urban morphology is clear from textual as well as archaeological evidence.

While many of the major cities mentioned in texts have been identified, some remain unidentified. It is interesting to note that archaeology confirms the importance of the great cities of literature. The details may not match, due to inadequate excavations, lack of full published reports, and the embellishments of the literary tradition. Nevertheless, the profiles of early historic cities can be constructed by putting together the available textual and archaeological evidence (Dilip K. Chakrabarti, 2001: 171–262; 2006: 322–48). These cities were linked to each other through the trade routes of the time.

The city was not only a certain type of settlement. It was also a political, social, and economic space. Literature is often eloquent about these aspects, but the idea of the city

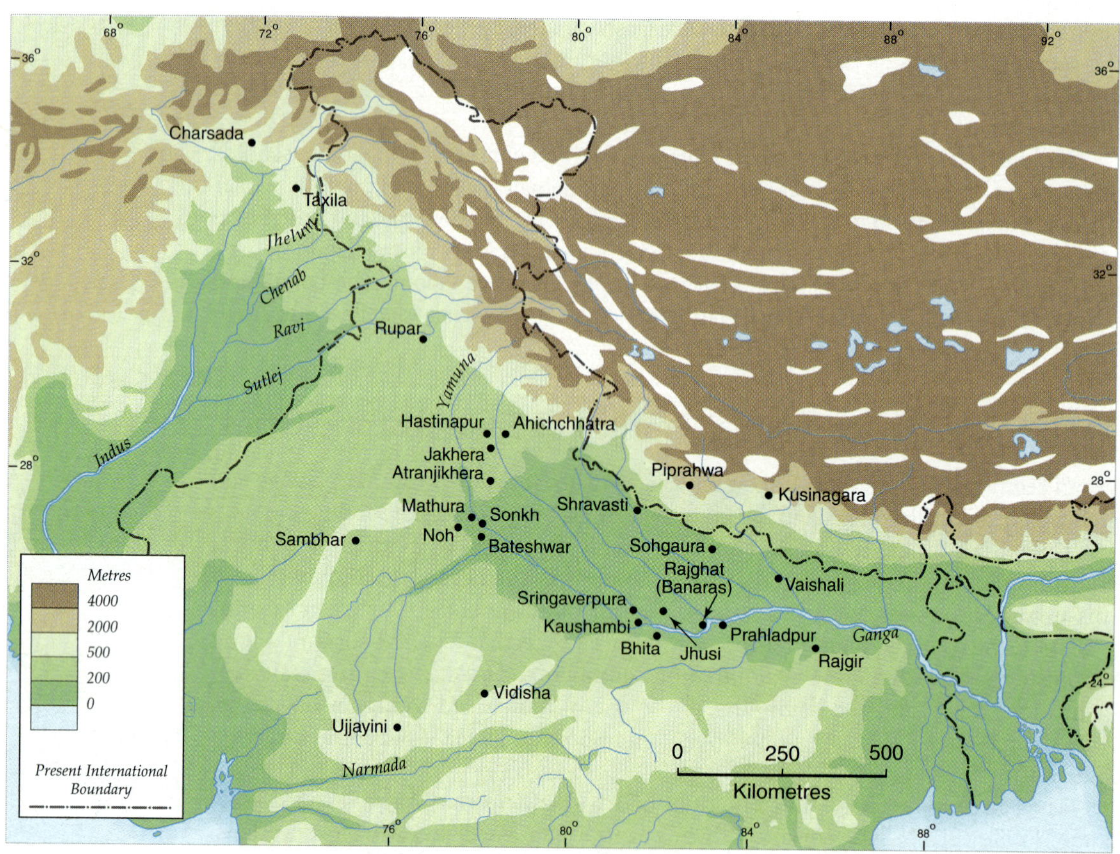

Map 6.2 Some early historic cities of North and Central India

in various texts is by no means uniform (Chattopadhyaya, [1997] 2003). The city meant different things to writers belonging to different places, ages, and social groups. It was sometimes presented as an idealized structuring of space, corresponding to notions of a moral or social order, one in which the king was central. Other texts underlined the socially heterogeneous nature of cities, suggesting that they were considered 'points of convergence'. It is possible to pluck out specific details about cities from texts of this period, but what these texts really do is paint in vivid, verbal colours what Chattopadhyaya describes as the 'citiness of the city'. The city was not just a certain kind of settlement. It was associated with certain sights, sounds, experiences, and values (see Ramanujan, 1999b). A comparison of the images of city life often tells us as much, or more, about the imagination and perspectives of authors than about the urban centres they describe. It is not surprising that archaeological and literary images of ancient cities do not usually match.

The North and North-west

The two great cities of the north-west—Charsada and Taxila—were strategically located at points where the trade routes crossed the Hindu Kush. Apart from the Khyber pass, there were other routes, such as the one running along the Kabul valley. An important route linked Taxila to Kashmir, and further on, to Central Asia. In the 5th century BCE, a part of the north-west came under the sway of the Achaemenids and was subsequently brushed past by Alexander. Charsada represents the ancient city of Pushkalavati. Legend describes it as having been founded by Pushkara, son of Bharata, the brother of Rama. It is mentioned as Peucelaotis and Proclais in classical accounts. Arrian states that the people of the city revolted against Alexander and that a Macedonian garrison was placed here after Hephaestion subdued the revolt. Excavations at the mound of Bala Hisar at Charsada indicate occupation beginning in *c.* 600 BCE. By the early 4th century BCE, the city was protected by a ditch and mud rampart.

NEW DIRECTIONS IN RESEARCH | Site catchment analysis of Semthan

In archaeology, the catchment area of a site refers to the boundaries within which it procured basic resources. The technique of site catchment analysis consists of drawing concentric circles around a site within two, three, and four hours' walking from the centre; analyzing the potential for resource use within each of them, focusing on geology, topography, soil, water, vegetation, climate, flora, and fauna; calculating the proportion of different types of resources in each segment; and integrating this data with the archaeological evidence from the site. Abdul Rashid Lone's site catchment analysis of Semthan is the first such analysis in Kashmir and has yielded valuable information regarding this important settlement on the banks of the Jhelum. It also shows how a single researcher can make an important contribution towards broadening the understanding of a site.

Lone's analysis involved demarcating an arbitrary catchment of 5 km radius around Semthan. The total area consisted of 7880 ha within a perimeter of 31.04 km. This area was subdivided into 16 transacts by a series of lines radiating from the centre. Three concentric circles were drawn at 1, 2.5, and 5 km radius from the centre; these covered an area of 314, 1,649, and 5,917 ha, respectively. The study involved walking from the centre to the periphery in each transact and comprehensively documenting the details of the landscape, including land use, land cover, terrain, water, plants, animals, stone, metals, and minerals. This formed the basis of a mapping of the site using Geographical Information System (GIS). Archaeological remains on the surface of the site were also recorded. Satellite settlements around the site were identified. Modern economic activities in these areas were used to make inferences about past land use. The provenance of materials, especially metals and minerals, found at the excavated site was sought to be identified, extending the explored area from 5 km to 10 km.

The first catchment area within 1 km of the centre of the site consists of about 65% arable land, rich in phosphorous and nitrogen. These days, it is mainly used for apple orchards, and double cropping with rice as a *kharif* crop and rapeseed and barley as *rabi* crops. The evidence for early historic times suggests that rice, which had been introduced at the end of the neolithic period at Gufkral, had become the most important crop, followed by wheat and barley. The clay for the large amounts of pottery found at the site could have been obtained from this catchment area.

The second catchment area was from 1 to 2.5 km from the centre. Today, about 47% of this area is under paddy cultivation, followed by maize. A considerable amount of land (350 ha) is under natural vegetation. The Jhelum, which flows through this area, provides abundant water for irrigation. Lone identified several small archaeological mounds in the area, with linkages to the Kushana, early medieval, and medieval periods. The third catchment area (from 2.5 to 5 km from the centre) covered an area of 5,917 ha. Today, 40% of this is under paddy cultivation and 31% under orchards. Wheat and maize are also grown. About 700 ha is covered with natural vegetation, and 177 ha of land is under water bodies. In early historic times, this area must have been thickly forested and a source of pasture, wild plants, game, and wood. Traces of old habitation were found in this ring.

The analysis of the data yielded the following conclusions: The basic resource needs of the people of early historic Semthan were fulfilled within the settlement. Clay, water, and kitchen garden produce were available within the 1 km radius, within a 10-12 minute walk. For foodgrains, pasture, and fodder for domesticated animals, the inhabitants may have walked upto 2.5 km, a 12-30 minutes' walk. The catchment area of 5 km radius was probably divided into two zones—one to the north and northeast of the site beyond the Jhelum, and the other to the south and southwest. The former could have been used for forest produce, game, and pasture land; the latter for agriculture and clay. The area between 2.5 and 5 km and beyond could have been tapped for hunting large and small game, forest produce, pastureland, and some mineral resources. The catchment area of 5 km around the site is devoid of metal and mineral resources, except for limestone; these would have been obtained from further afield.

Based on the size of the archaeological mound and the explorations, Lone estimated that the population of early historic Semthan may have been approximately 3,271 people.

Source Lone, 2019

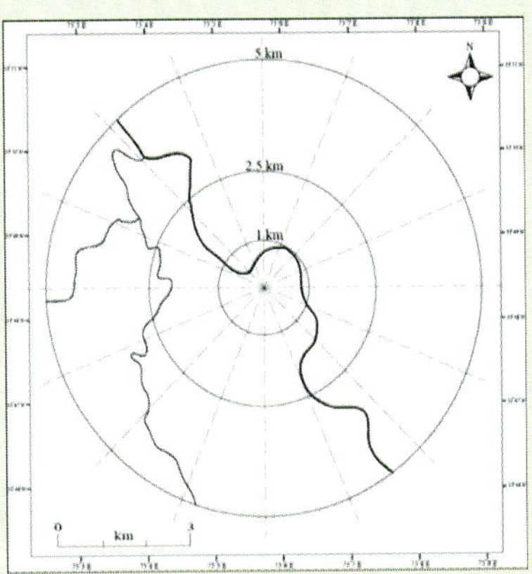

Semthan coordinates

Rashid Lone at the site

Ancient Takshashila (Taxila) was an important city, connected to the overland routes into Afghanistan and Central Asia and to the maritime routes of the Arabian Sea via the Indus. According to epic tradition, this was the place where king Janamejaya performed his great *naga-yajna* (snake sacrifice). The city is also mentioned in Buddhist, Jaina, and Greek accounts. Extensive excavations at Taxila revealed three major settlements at the Bhir mound, Sirkap, and Sirsukh. The Bhir mound represents the site of the oldest city, with occupational levels belonging to the 6th/5th century BCE up to the 2nd century BCE. The earliest levels of this mound (Period IV) showed a burnished red ware, which is known in this region from an earlier period. There was also a new, fine grey or black ware in shapes such as shallow and deep bowls, which seem to be local imitations of the NBPW. Silver punch-marked bar coins and other coin types were found. Comparatively more information is available about the post-3rd century BCE levels at the Bhir mound.

Semthan is an important excavated urban site located in Bijbihara tehsil of Anantnag district of south Kashmir, on the banks of the Jhelum river (see Gaur, 1987; Shali, 1993). It is located on a *karewa*, the local word used for loess deposits formed by ancient lakes. It can be identified with the city of Chakradhara mentioned in the *Rajatarangini*. Archaeological excavations indicate that the occupation of the site goes back to the early historic period. So far, this is the only site in the Kashmir valley that has yielded NBPW. Six periods of occupation were identified here: Period I was labelled 'pre-Northern Black Ware' phase (dated *c.* 700–500 BCE); Period II, the NBPW phase (*c.* 500–200 BCE); Period III, the Indo-Greek phase (*c.* 200 BCE–1st century CE); Period IV, the 'Kushana–Huna' phase (dated *c.* 1st century CE to 500 CE); Period V, the 'Hindu period' (*c.* 500–1300 CE); and Period VI, the 'late medieval' (1300 CE onwards). Period I yielded beads made of terracotta and bone; pieces of copper; and iron arrowhead and iron slag. Period II yielded NBPW along with red ware and a distinctive grey ware; punch marked coins of copper and silver; beads made of terracotta and semi-precious stone; terracotta balls; bone points; a bone stylus and artefacts made of iron objects. Cast copper coins were found in the upper levels of Period II. Palaeobotanical remains of different periods were obtained and analyzed from the site.

The Indo-Gangetic divide, the upper Ganga valley, and the doab

In the Kumaon region of Uttarakhand, NBPW was found at Kashipur in Nainital district, but hardly any details are available. In the Indo-Gangetic divide, Period III at Ropar, at the foot of the Shivaliks, yielded NBPW and is dated *c.* 600–200 BCE. Pottery of this type has also been found at Agroha in Hissar district and at Karna-ka-Qila near Kurukshetra in Haryana.

Excavations at the Purana Qila in Delhi revealed NBPW levels belonging to the 4th–3rd centuries BCE. (More recent excavations may have reached earlier occupational levels.) People lived in houses of mud-brick and burnt brick. A burnt wattle-and-daub structure and several hearths were found. Houses had drains made of both rectangular and wedge-shaped bricks. Terracotta ring wells—about 75 cm in diameter—which may have functioned as soak-pits for waste water, were also discovered. Terracotta figurines of humans and animals, a fragment of a sculpted ring stone, a terracotta piece depicting a horse and armoured rider, a clay sealing, small rings, and an agate disc were among the other artefacts found at NBPW levels. One of the NBPW dishes had the figure of an elephant stamped on the inner side of its base. Two terracotta seals, bearing the names of two individuals, Svatirakhita and Seyankara, were also found.

In the upper Ganga valley, Hastinapura in Meerut district is an important site for which there is a full, published report (Lal, 1954–55). In epic–Puranic tradition, the Kuru capital was located at Hastinapura until a flood led to its being shifted to Kaushambi. Jaina tradition describes Hastinapura as the place where Rishabha, the first *tirthankara*, lived and which Mahavira often visited. Period III at Hastinapura is the NBPW phase and is dated c. 600–200 BCE. It is marked by an element of planning, burnt-brick structures, and terracotta ring wells.

Excavated section showing strata of Periods II, III, IV with embedded jar, Hastinapura

Excavations at Atranjikhera (Etah district, UP) on the banks of the Kali Nadi, a tributary of the Ganga, have provided valuable information on the transition from village to town and the everyday life of the people living here (Gaur, 1983). The site has been tentatively identified with the Vairanja or Veranja of early Buddhist texts, but this identification is far from certain. The excavations showed an overlap between the PGW phase (Period III) and the succeeding NBPW phase (Period IV), which was divided into four phases: Period IVA—c. 600–500 BCE; Period IVB—c. 500–350 BCE; Period IVC—c. 350–200 BCE; and Period IVD—c. 200–50 BCE. In Period IV, the size of the settlement increased significantly and there was a gradual transition from mud houses to structures made of mud-brick and burnt brick. The wide range of artefacts included a rich range of terracotta artefacts including figurines, discs, and beads; beads of semi-precious stones such as agate and carnelian; stone objects such as a pestle, grinder, and balls; and bone and ivory objects. In the upper levels of Period IVB, two coins were found—one silver punch-marked coin and one uninscribed copper coin.

A total of 38 copper objects were found from different phases of the NBPW level—13 from Phase A, 21 from Phase B, 25 from Phase C, and 29 from Phase D. The copper artefacts found in the early phases included antimony rods, nail parer, rods/bars, pins, bangles, an ear ornament, bead, socket, weight, and tubes, apart from some indeterminate objects. A total of 338 iron objects, including 37 indeterminate pieces, were found in all the NBPW levels taken together. Most of the types of Period III continued, but there were 16 new artefact types. Agricultural tools made of iron appeared for the first time in the NBPW phase. Iron plumb bobs were used for the alignment of walls of buildings. Iron weapons suggest the importance of hunting or warfare. Blacksmiths' and carpenters' tools indicate the importance of these crafts. S. K. Chowdhury's analysis of the plant remains found in the Atranjikhera excavations reveals some important details (Gaur, 1983). The OCP and BRW phases yielded a few remains of rice, barley, gram, and khesari. The PGW level gave evidence of wheat, and the manner in which plant remains were scattered about and found in heaps suggested more abundant grain production than before. The NBPW phase showed the cultivation of rice, wheat, and barley, with the addition of a new pulse (*Phaseolus mungo*). The wood remains included laurel, *farash*, bamboo, *deodar*, and Himalayan cypress. As cedar and Himalayan cypress grow in the northern mountains, these finds suggest contact with these regions. Almost a thousand pieces of bone fragments from the site were analyzed. Those belonging to the NBPW phase included bones of domesticated humped cattle, buffalo, goat, sheep, pig, and dog. Horse remains occurred in the PGW and post-PGW phases. Many animal bones were split or cut with sharp tools and charred—clear evidence that the animals were killed for food. The bones of cattle vastly outnumbered those of other animals, indicating that beef was an important part of the diet, apart from venison, mutton, and pork.

Mathura was an important city of early historical India. The *Mahabharata* and the Puranas associate it with the Yadava clan, which included the Vrishnis, among whom Krishna was born. This city was situated at the entrance of the fertile Ganga plains, at the junction of the northern trade route and the one going southwards into Malwa, and on to the western coast. Period I of the Mathura cultural sequence has been identified at the Ambarish Tila, close to the Yamuna, north of Mathura city. It is marked by PGW and shows the gradual growth of a village settlement. At Sonkh, 25 km south-west of Mathura, Period I has PGW, along with a BRW and a coarse grey ware, and is dated c. 800–400 BCE. No structural remains were unearthed, but there were post-holes and a double ditch, which might have enclosed the settlement (Hartel, 1993).

The site of Kampilya, capital of south Panchala, has been identified with Kampil in Farukhabad district (UP). Small-scale excavations here indicated occupation from the

Period I (pre-1200 BCE)
OCP

Period II (c. 1100–800 BCE)
PGW and associated red ware

Period III (6th–3rd century BCE)
NBP and associated ware

Period IV (2nd century BCE to 3rd century BCE)
stamped and incised red ware

Period V (11th–15th centuries)
glazed ware

0 2 cm

Pottery of different periods, Hastinapura

Excavated eastern fortifications, Kaushambi

PGW phase onwards. Ahichchhatra in Bareilly district also has NBPW levels, but most of the details of structures relate to the post-2nd century BCE period.

The archaeological remains at Ayodhya, described in the *Ramayana* as capital of Kosala in the time of Rama, cover a circuit of 4–5 km. Earlier excavations revealed an occupation beginning with the early NBPW phase. Apart from very fine NBPW in different shades, there was a grey ware with linear designs painted on in black. There were remains of houses made of mud or wattle and daub; no baked brick structures were found. Artefacts made of iron and copper were discovered. The 2002–03 excavations at the site revealed many artefacts belonging to the NBPW phase. Terracotta objects comprised broken votive tanks, weights, ear studs, discs, hopscotches, a wheel made on a disc, and a broken animal figurine. Other artefacts included a broken iron knife, glass beads, and a bone point. One of the most interesting objects was a button-shaped light-blue glass object (perhaps originally set in a ring) found in two pieces, with the legend *shidhe* inscribed on it in 3rd century BCE Brahmi letters. As mentioned earlier, calibrated radiocarbon dates from Period I suggest that the NBPW phase at this site may go back to as early as *c.* 1000 BCE.

The city of Kaushambi was the capital of the kingdom of Vatsa and was also an important point on the trade routes connecting the Deccan, the Ganga valley, and the north-west. It has been identified with Kosam village. Excavations here associated Period I with PGW, Period II with BRW, and Period III with NBPW. It has been argued that the imposing defences at the site were built as early as 1025 BCE, but it is more likely that they belong to a later period, perhaps *c.* 600 BCE. Pali texts locate the Ghoshitarama monastery at Kaushambi. Monastic seals of a much later period, bearing the name 'Ghoshitarama', confirmed the identification of the city.

Excavations at Sringaverapura in Allahabad district have indicated that the NBPW phase here goes back to *c.* 700 BCE. The excavations mainly concentrated on a tank complex belonging to the early centuries CE, and there is little information about the earlier occupational phases. The *Ramayana* mentions Sringaverapura as a place where the sage Rishyashringa had his hermitage, and where Rama crossed the Ganga during his journey into exile.

The middle and lower Ganga valley

The site of ancient Shravasti, capital of Kosala, has been identified with the ruins at Saheth and Maheth, on the boundary of Gonda and Bahreich districts (UP). This city too was an important point on the northern trade routes. Maheth represents the city and Saheth the site of the ancient monastery of Jetavana. According to Buddhist tradition, Jetavana was gifted by Anathapindika to the *sangha*. Ramparts around the site probably belong to the 3rd century BCE.

The discoveries at the adjacent sites of Ganwaria and Piprahwa in Basti district (north UP), excavated by an Archaeological Survey of India team led by K. M. Srivastava, should settle the long-standing debate about the location of ancient Kapilavastu (Srivastava, 1996). A large number of sealings and a pot lid bearing the name of the Kapilavastu monastery were found in excavations at Piprahwa. Apart from the ruins of monasteries and shrines, remains of what may represent the original *stupa* built by the Sakyas over the relics of the Buddha have also been identified. Ganwaria represents the town of Kapilavastu. The 7 m thick occupational deposit was divided into four periods—Period I (*c.* 800–600 BCE) is marked by fine grey, black polished, and red wares, Period II (*c.* 600–200 BCE) by the NBPW, and Periods III and IV range from *c.* 200 BCE to 200 CE. The people of Period I lived in mud houses with roofs supported by wood. Burnt-brick structures appeared in Period II. The remains at the nearby site of Tilaurakot in the Nepal terai were long held to represent ancient Kapilavastu. Period I here yielded NBPW and terracotta ring wells.

Rajghat, to the north-east of Benaras, is identified as the site of ancient Varanasi. This city was famed for its fine textiles and was an important point on the northern trade routes. The site shows a five- or six-fold cultural sequence. Period I has been dated *c.* 800–200 BCE and is divided into three sub-periods. The remains of Period IA included iron objects, BRW, and red-slipped and coarse gritty red wares. Period IB saw the beginning of NBPW. There were remains of burnt clay floors and pits lined with terracotta rings. The settlement seems to have been surrounded by a rampart from the middle or early NBPW phase.

The ruins in and around the village of Basarh in Muzaffarpur district of Bihar have been identified with ancient Vaishali, capital of the Lichchhavis and the Vajji confederacy. Vaishali lay along the route from Magadha into the Nepal terai. Buddhist texts have a great deal to say about this city, Jaina tradition describes it as the birthplace of Mahavira, and Puranic tradition connects it with a legendary king named Visala. The mound known as Raja Visal ka Garh shows traces of old fortifications, and a tank known as Khorana Pokhar may represent the coronation tank of the Lichchhavis. Many antiquities and structural remains were found here, some of which may go back to the 5th/4th century BCE. A mud stupa, later encased in brick, was located to the north-west of the tank. It is possible that its mud core represents the stupa built by the Lichchhavis over the Buddha's relics.

The ruins of Shravasti

Rajgir, about 40 miles south-east of Patna, is the site of ancient Rajagriha, the first capital of Magadha. An important trade route from Paithan to the middle Ganga valley terminated here. The city was closely associated with the lives of both the Buddha and Mahavira. Archaeological explorations at Rajgir mainly concentrated on identifying places mentioned in Buddhist texts and Xuanzang's account. There are two cities here—Old Rajagriha and New Rajagriha. Old Rajagriha, nestled between five hills, was surrounded by two stone fortification walls. New Rajagriha, also surrounded by stone fortifications,

lay in the plain to the north. The massive Old Rajagriha outer fortifications ran through the hills, perhaps for 25–30 miles. They have not been dated, but textual sources suggest that they may date to the time of Bimbisara, i.e., the 6th century BCE. The two sets of walls around New Rajagriha probably belong to the time of Ajatashatru, i.e., the 5th century BCE.

In the *Vinaya Pitaka*, the Buddha prophecies the future greatness of Pataliputra and the dangers posed to it by fire, water, and internal discord. The discovery of NBPW at Kumrahar and Bulandibagh in Patna suggests the existence of an early historical settlement in the area, one that can be identified with ancient Pataliputra. But hardly anything is known about the earliest occupation at this site.

Ancient Champa, capital of Anga, has been identified with Champanagar and Champapur villages, 5 km west of Bhagalpur in south Bihar. In the NBPW phase, the site was surrounded by defensive fortifications, surrounded by a moat.

There are a number of important sites in the lower Ganga valley such as Chandraketugarh and Tamluk. However, there is little information about their earliest phase of occupation. NBPW levels at Wari Bateshwar have given a calibrated C-14 date of *c.* 500 BCE. The antiquity of Mahasthangarh may also go back to this period. This suggests that the NBPW in Bengal dates back to the period of the *mahajanapadas* (Chakrabarti, 2006: 324).

Apart from the textual and archaeological profiles of individual sites, important information is provided by settlement studies of certain areas. Erdosy's study (1988) of the Allahabad district (UP) corresponds to an area that would have fallen within the Vatsa kingdom. Erdosy initially dated Period II of the archaeological sequence here to *c.* 600–350 BCE. Subsequently, he went on to distinguish between an early and a late NBPW phase, and taking into account the available C-14 dates, suggested that the early NBPW phase be dated *c.* 550–400 BCE and the mid- and late NBPW phase *c.* 400–100 BCE. In the early NBPW phase, there was a great increase in the size of settlements, suggesting a corresponding increase in population. A four-level hierarchy of settlements was identified. Kaushambi (capital of Vatsa) was already the largest settlement in the area in the PGW phase. In the early NBPW phase, it grew to 50 ha and was surrounded by a mud fortification wall. The second tier of NBPW settlements in the area includes Kara and Sringaverapura, both 12 ha. These were towns associated with various sorts of manufacturing activity. Two sites represent the third level of settlements, around 6–7 ha. These were relatively small settlements, with evidence of some craft activity and iron smelting. The fourth and smallest tier of sites was represented by 16 sites between 0.42 and 2 ha. These were villages of farmers and herders. Over the next few centuries, a fifth hierarchy of settlements (3–5 ha) emerged. There was an increase in the number of large, secondary centres, such as Bhita (19 ha) and Jhusi (over 30 ha). The general long-term trend was towards an increase in the number of village settlements, which were no longer concentrated along water resources such as riverbanks and lakes.

S. B. Singh's study (1979) of the Panchala area in the upper Ganga valley reveals a four-tier settlement structure, but does not distinguish between the early, middle, and late NBPW phases. Ahichchhatra, capital of Panchala, was the largest site. By the 3rd century BCE, it was a huge fortified city, measuring about 180 ha. Atranjikhera was a fortified secondary centre, about 64 ha in size, with evidence of a diverse agriculture base, craft activity, and trade. Jakhera was 8 ha, while the rest of the sites were villages less than 4 ha.

Piprahwa (from top): excavations in progress; steatite relic casket with Brahmi inscription

Pottery of different periods, Ahichchhatra

The Kanpur district (UP) presents a different pattern. Makkhan Lal's study (1984: 66–80) shows a significantly higher number of NBPW sites (99) compared to those of the preceding PGW phase (46). There was a two-level site hierarchy here and no really huge sites. The largest site measured 8.75 ha, and 98 sites were between 0.5 and 5 ha. The mean settlement size went up marginally, from 1.16 ha (PGW phase) to 1.41 ha (NBPW phase). Using modern settlement data and average household size, Lal gave the following population estimates for the entire Ganga–Yamuna doab: OCP phase—52,000; PGW phase—16,300; NBPW phase—426,000; and 2nd century BCE–2nd century CE—900,000. The general picture generated by archaeology is one of rural stability and steady population growth.

Rupendra Kumar Chattopadhyay's study (2018) of the archaeology of coastal Bengal has woven together the evidence from explored and excavated sites to reconstruct the settlement history of this area from Black and Red Ware associated levels of the early historic phase, when the archaeological data is very patchy, to the Gupta and post-Gupta periods, when it becomes more substantial and can be corroborated with epigraphic and textual sources. The study emphasizes the importance of looking at the history of coastal communities beyond their involvement in trade, and discusses the relationship between coastal settlements and their natural landscape, hinterland, and contact zones.

Central India and the Deccan

Although North India is the prime focus of this chapter, reference may also be made here to the evidence of urban developments in some other areas during *c.* 600–200 BCE. In Central India, the ancient cities of Tripuri in the Narmada valley near Jabalpur and Airakina (Eran) near Sagar were probably part of the Chedi kingdom. The occupation of Tripuri goes back to the 2nd millennium BCE, but it is not clear exactly when it assumed an urban status. The settlement at Eran too goes back to the 2nd millennium BCE; it seems to have become a city by the Maurya period.

Ujjayini (modern Ujjain), on the banks of the Sipra river, a tributary of the Chambal, was the capital of Avanti. It was also a major commercial centre, a point from where routes from Northern India bifurcated southwards and westwards. Four occupational phases have been identified at the site. Period I had BRW and a few PGW sherds, and is dated *c.* 750–500 BCE. Other artefacts included terracotta spindle whorls, bone styli and arrowheads, spearheads, crowbars, spades, choppers, and knives made of iron. The settlement was surrounded by an imposing mud fortification wall, outside which was a moat. In Period II, the pottery included black-slipped ware, BRW, and NBPW. There were structures made of mud, mud-brick, stone rubble in clay, and burnt brick. There was a massive burnt-brick tank for water storage, and several terracotta ring wells. The remains of an iron-smelting furnace and a workshop for the manufacture of stone beads and bone arrowheads were identified. The artefacts of Period II included punch-marked coins, large numbers of iron objects, as well as objects made of terracotta, copper, and ivory.

Section showing excavated brick structures of different periods, Ujjain

The remains of ancient Vidisha are located at Besnagar in Raisen district of Madhya Pradesh. This was an important point on the trade routes that traversed the Malwa region. Although the rampart at this site seems to have been built in the 2nd century BCE, the early NBPW phase shows BRW, iron objects, punch-marked coins, and ring wells.

In the Deccan, the kingdom of Ashmaka on the Godavari was one of the 16 *mahajanapadas*. Paithan (ancient Pratishthana), one of the most important early historical sites in this area, has not yet been properly explored. The beginning of the early historical occupation at Nashik goes back to *c.* 400 BCE. The mud core of a *stupa* found at Pauni in the Wainganga valley also appears to belong to this period. Tagara, an important market town, is identified with Ter on the Terna river. Period I here has NBPW. Adam in Nagpur district has given evidence of a 10 ha site with an earthen rampart with gateways on the east. The rampart and associated moat belong to Period III, dated *c.* 1000–500 BCE. The former was subsequently reinforced by a stone battlement. The site of Nagal is located on the south bank of the Narmada, opposite the more famous but less explored site of Broach (ancient Bharukachchha). It yielded evidence of a settlement that may go back to at least the 6th century BCE. The remains included pottery, and bone and iron artefacts.

Sri Lanka and South India

The archaeological profile of Sri Lanka emerges in what is known as the PHEH (Protohistoric–Early Historic) transition, which extends for about 500 years from *c.* 500 BCE onwards. The evidence comes from early Buddhist monastic sites and megalithic sites.

The site of the ancient city of Anuradhapura consists of a central citadel mound and a peripheral zone which included monastic complexes and several irrigation works (Coningham and Allchin, 1995: 159–69; Coningham et al., 1996). The earliest occupation goes back to the mesolithic phase, which continued to the early 2nd millennium BCE. This was followed by the Iron Age levels (600–400 BCE), which gave evidence of rudimentary structures, black and red burnished ware, potsherds with scratched graffiti, iron artefacts and slag, and cattle bones. Coningham and Allchin divided the early historic phase at Anuradhapura into four phases—Early Historic 1 (450–350 BCE), Early Historic 2 (350–275 BCE), Early Historic 3 (275–225 BCE), and Early Historic 4 (225–150 BCE), leading up to the Anuradhapura period (3rd to 6th century CE). (In some of the more recent writings, the Early Historic Period I is divided into several structural sub-phase.) The settlement increased in size to about 26 ha. There were circular huts with large timber posts and deeply dug post-holes. A burial with an iron arrowhead, an object made of copper alloy, a polished rubbing stone, three black and red ware cups, and three other vessels with graffiti were found. The assemblage is described as strongly similar to the megalithic burials of South India. Black and red burnished ware is the main pottery type, but there is also some fine grey ware. Iron, copper and slag, disc beads made of paste, horse bones, and styli/arrowheads made of bone and ivory were found. Artefacts and waste material of conch shell, iron ore, amethyst, and quartz suggest an increase in specialized crafts and trade. Four potsherds with Brahmi letters scratched on them were found. On the basis of his earlier excavations, Deraniyagala had dated the inscribed potsherd bearing level to 600–500 BCE. The radiometric dates obtained by Coningham and Allchin suggest a range between 450 BCE to 350 BCE.

The early dates assigned to Brahmi at Anuradhapura have been the subject of much debate and have been questioned by several scholars. Apart from questioning the reliability of the Anuradhapura C-14 dates, Harry Falk (2014) has stated that Brahmi could not have travelled northwards from Sri Lanka to the mainland long before the time of Ashoka because the Ashokan script shows primary features and the South Indian and Sri Lankan scripts were based on it. He also refers to Tissamaharama in southern Sri Lanka, which has yielded a large number of potsherds, over a hundred of which have Brahmi letters. The radiocarbon dates for the levels where the Brahmi writing has been found range from the 4th century BCE to the 2nd century CE. But on the grounds of comparative palaeography, Falk states that the earliest inscribed sherds from Tissamaharama cannot be dated before the mid-3rd century BCE.

In Tamil Nadu, important sites include Kodumanal on the northern bank of the Noyyal, tributary of the Kaveri, in Erode district (Rajan, 2015). It has been identified with the city of Kotumanam in Sangam texts, famous for gem and jewellery work. The site was excavated over seven seasons between 1985 and 2014. In the course of the excavations, 17 megatlithic graves were opened. Almost 598 potsherds with graffiti marks and 551 with Tamil-Brahmi letters were found. (As discussed in Chapter 1, Tamil-Brahmi was a southern adaptation of Brahmi.) According to Rajan, five AMS dates from various strata and a comparative study of the Tamil-Brahmi and graffiti on the potsherds suggest that occupation at the site goes back to the 6th century BCE. Most of the potsherds have only one or two letters; the longest one has 13 letters. Most consist of one word. Almost all of them seem to be parts of male personal names, probably indicating the person who possessed the pots and/or their contents. The language of the writing is described as Tamil, but there are also many Prakrit and hybrid Tamil-Prakrit names. Apart from the graves and inscribed potsherds, the excavations yielded evidence of punch marked coins, and gemstone, iron and steel, and conch shell industries. Initially, the stratigraphic context of the potsherds was dated between the mid-3rd century BCE and 3rd century CE. Rajan revised the earlier dated to the 4th century BCE. He pointed out that the AMS date range for the inscribed potsherd-bearing levels was between 408 BCE and 200 BCE, and that there was still a 65 cm thick deposit below this. Therefore, according to him, it is possible to date the beginning of writing at the site to the 6th/5th century BCE (Rajan, 2015: 405).

The implications are that the early historic phase in South India began, as in the North, in the 6th century BCE. Recently, 45 radiometric dates from 79 early historic sites in Tamil Nadu have been tabulated and analyzed (Rajan et al., 2021). The sites include Porunthal, Kodumanal, Keeladi, Alangkulam, Achichanallur, and Thelunganur. Out of the 45 radiometric dates, 39 (4 of which were contaminated) belong to early historic sites and 6 are from iron age sites. Of the 35 samples belonging to the early historic phase, 14 are pre-Ashokan (i.e., earlier than *c.* 268 BCE) and one goes back to the 6th century BCE. On this basis, Rajan et al., argue that the early historic phase in South India can be placed in about the 6th century BCE.

Kodumanal: Black and red ware bowl with graffiti; potsherd inscribed with 'nikama'

While the dates for writing from Anuradhapura and the Tamil Nadu sites are consistent, they go against the widely prevalent view that the Brahmi script emerged in North India and spread to various parts of the subcontinent due to Maurya impact. Y. Subbarayalu has questioned the early dates given to writing in the Tamil Nadu sites. With respect to Kodumanal (in Rajan, 2015, vi), he points out that so far there is no evidence of Brahmi in North India before the Maurya period, and that Tamil-Brahmi was not invented for writing Tamil in the beginning; it was adopted and adapted from elsewhere. He suggests that the AMS dates need to be examined. He also points out (personal communication) that of the various AMS samples from Kodumanal, only one has given an early date range of 731–651 BCE; and from Keezhadi, only one sample has given an earlier date range of 764–597 BCE. The rest of the samples give a range from the 4th century BCE to 2nd century BCE. Subbarayalu also points to the fact that a large number of label inscriptions on the Kodumanal potsherds are in Prakrit or influenced by Prakrit. He also argues that Kodumanal and Keezhadi cannot be described as urban settlements. Kodumanal was a flourishing craft centre, but so far the remains of structures or streets have not been found. Keezhadi too yielded a few brick structures associated with industrial activities.

These issues are likely to be debated for some time to come. In the absence of scholarly consensus at the present point of time, the issue can be considered an open one. However, it is likely that new discoveries and excavations at other sites may radically change our understanding of the beginning of the early historic in the Indian subcontinent.

Urban Occupations, Crafts, Guilds, and Money

Early Buddhist texts mention a wide range of occupations (*sippa*, *kamma*), both rural and urban (Wagle, 1966: 134–58). Apart from farmers, cattle rearers, and traders, those employed in the service industry included washermen, barbers, tailors, painters, and cooks. The king employed many different kinds of specialists, including soldiers (*yodhajivas*) of various kinds—foot soldiers, archers, members of the cavalry, elephant corps, and chariot wing. Others in the king's service (*rajaporisas*) included ministers (*mahamachchas*), governors (*ratthikas*), estate managers (*pettanikas*), the royal chamberlain (*thapati*), elephant trainers (*hattirohas*), policemen (*raja-bhatas*), jailors (*bandhanagarikas*), slaves (*dasas* and *dasis*), and wage-workers (*kammakaras*).

Urban occupations included those of the physician (*vejja*, *bhisakka*), surgeon (*sallakata*), and scribe (*lekha*). Accounting (*ganana*) and money changing were other urban professions. Types of entertainers include the actor (*nata*), dancer (*nataka*), magician (*sokajjayika*), acrobat (*langhika*), drummer (*kumbhathunika*), and woman fortune-teller (*ikkhanika*). Some of them performed in festivities known as *samajas*, apart from other occasions. There are also references to the accomplished courtesan (*ganika*) and the ordinary prostitute (*vesi*).

The Pali canon refers to many different kinds of artisans, some of whom must have lived and worked in or near cities, supplying goods for an urban clientele. These included the vehicle maker (*yanakara*), ivory worker (*dantakara*), metal smith (*kammara*), goldsmith (*suvannakara*), silk weaver (*kosiyakara*), carpenter (*palaganda*), needle maker (*suchikara*), reed worker (*nalakara*), garland maker (*malakara*), and potter (*kumbhakara*). Some craft specialists may have lived in their own settlements on the margins of cities. The later evidence of the Jatakas more clearly indicates the localization of certain industries, the association of villages with specific artisan groups, and the hereditary nature of crafts. These processes must already have been underway in *c.* 600–200 BCE.

The *Gautama Dharmasutra* mentions agriculture, trade, cattle rearing, and lending money on interest as occupations of the Vaishyas. It also states that farmers, traders, herdsmen, money-lenders, and artisans had the authority to lay down rules for their respective professions, and that the king should make legal decisions after listening to those who had authority within these professions. This suggests an element of corporate organization. Buddhist texts offer more direct evidence of the emergence of guilds. Terms such as *shreni*, *nigama*, *puga*, *vrata*, and *sangha* are used in ancient Indian texts to refer to various kinds of corporate organizations, including guilds. The *Vinaya Pitaka* mentions the guilds (*puga*) of Shravasti providing a regular supply of food for monks and nuns. More details about guild organization and activities are available in the Jatakas, which list 18 guilds and suggest the close association of heads of guilds with kings.

An important aspect of urbanism was the emergence of coinage. Pali texts contain the first definite references to coins, e.g., *kahapana*, *nikkha*, *kamsa*, *pada*, *masaka*, and *kakanika*. The textual evidence is corroborated by archaeological evidence of punch-marked coins from many sites, most of them made of silver. The beginning of money did not mean the end of barter, but it did mark a qualitative change in economic transactions, with long-term implications for trade. It also ushered in usury (money-lending). Pali texts contain many references to this profession, instruments of credit, people pawning their possessions, the occasional pledging of wife or children by debtors, and bankruptcy. Debtors were in fact debarred from joining the Buddhist *sangha* until they had paid their debts.

It is interesting to note that the increasing range of material goods available for consumption—at least for those who had the requisite resources—was paralleled by the emergence of doctrines that advocated the renunciation of material possessions.

The New Social Elites: the *gahapati* and *setthi*

The social vocabulary of early Pali texts reflects the economic and social changes that took place in North India in *c.* 600–200 BCE. New terminology emerged and old words were endowed with new meaning. Textual evidence indicates the emergence of socio-economic classes, with significant differences in wealth, status, and control over productive resources.

The term *grihapati* occurs in Vedic texts in the sense of the head of a household. The Pali texts tend to use terms such as *gihi*, *gahattha*, and *ajjhavasati* in this sense, and *gahapati* (the Pali form of *grihapati*) in a broader sense (see Uma Chakravarti, 1987: 65–93). Uma Chakravarti points out that apart from being the head of a household, the *gahapati* was also a wealthy property-owner and producer of wealth, associated especially with land and agriculture. Society is often described as consisting of three strata—Khattiya, Brahmana, and *gahapati*—associated with three different domains. According to the *Anguttara Nikaya*, the Khattiya aspires for power and territory, and dominion is his ideal; the Brahmana is associated with *mantra* and *yanna* (*yajna*), and *brahmaloka* is his ideal; the *gahapati* is associated with *kamma* (work) and *sippa* (craft), and the completion or fruit of work is his ideal. There are references to Brahmana *gahapati*s living in Brahmana villages. The *gahapati*'s political importance is suggested in his inclusion among the seven treasures of the *chakkavatti* or universal ruler.

The ***setthi*** (this is the Pali form of Sanskrit *sreshthin*) of the Pali canon was a high-level businessman, associated with trade and money-lending. There are many references to extremely wealthy *setthi*s living in style in cities such as Rajagriha and Varanasi. The *setthi* of the Buddhist texts was a prominent and influential member of the urban community with access to and connections with kings.

Gahapati and *setthi* have specific meanings in early Pali texts and are never used interchangeably. For instance, Anathapindika is consistently referred to as a *gahapati*; it is only in the Jatakas that he is described as a *setthi*. Therefore, the occurrence of the compound word *setthi-gahapati* does not suggest a muddle-headed mixing up of categories. It refers to a person with a rural as well as urban base, one with control over land and business enterprise. The wealth and affluence of *setthi*s and *setthi-gahapati*s can be gauged from the fact that along with kings, they figure among the clientele of the famous physician Jivaka, and are described as paying thousands of *kahapana*s in medical bills.

Trade and Traders

In Buddhist texts, people on the move include the Buddha and his disciples, renunciants belonging to other orders, teachers, students, professionals, kings, soldiers, and traders. All these different kinds of people must have travelled along broadly similar routes and the accounts of their journeys give an idea of the routes of travel, communication, and trade. Archaeological evidence also helps identify trade routes and interactions. The two major trans-regional routes of the time were known as the **Uttarapatha** and **Dakshinapatha** (these terms were also sometimes used to refer to regions). These routes had a long and enduring history extending over many centuries.

The Uttarapatha was the major trans-regional trade route of Northern India. It stretched from the north-west, across the Indo-Gangetic plains, up to the port of Tamralipti on the

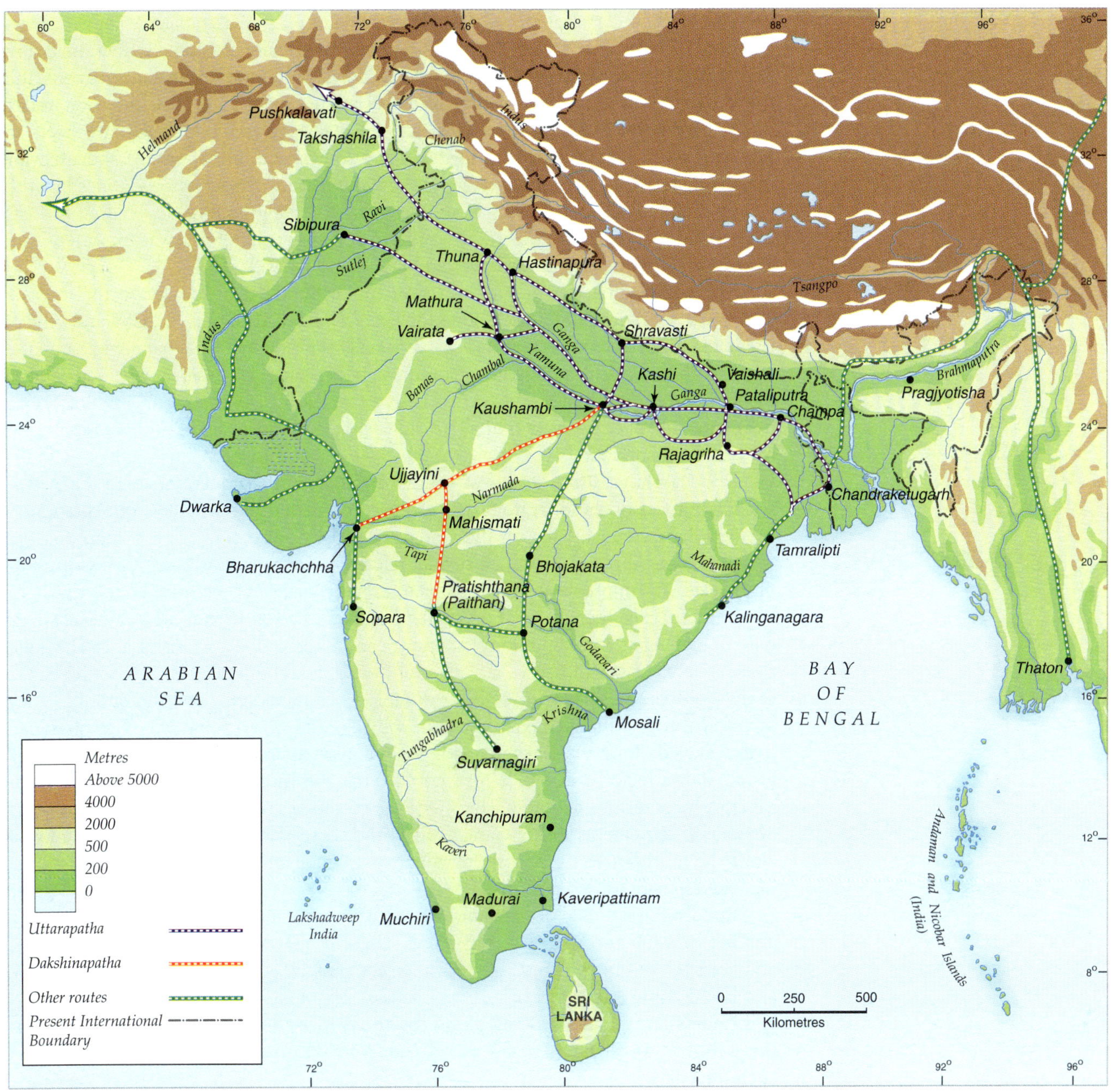

Map 6.3 Major trade routes of early historic India

Bay of Bengal. The *Ashtadhyayi* mentions various kingdoms located along it. Details of the route can be worked out on the basis of references in the *Vinaya Pitaka* and Jatakas. The Uttarapatha had a northern and a southern sector (Lahiri, 1992: 367–77). The northern sector ran through Lahore, Jalandhar, Saharanpur, along the Gangetic plains to Bijnor, and then through Gorakhpur, towards Bihar and Bengal. The southern sector connected Lahore, Raiwind, Bhatinda, Delhi, Hastinapura, Kanpur, Lucknow, Varanasi, and Allahabad, and then moved on towards Pataliputra and Rajagriha. There were many feeder routes connected to the main artery of the Uttarapatha. For instance, one connected it with Rajasthan (an important source of metals and minerals), another with Sindh, and yet another to the Odisha coast.

Nayanjot Lahiri's analysis (1992: 370–71) indicates that archaeological evidence corroborates the textual sources. The distribution of PGW settlements suggests a broad similarity of material culture and cultural interaction across many regions of North India, stretching from Cholistan to the upper Ganga plains. By the NBPW phase, there is archaeological corroboration for the entire stretch of the Uttarapatha. The wide distribution of NBPW itself suggests wide-ranging inter-regional contacts. Raw materials and finished goods were also moving up and down the route. For instance, lapis lazuli from Afghanistan and Central Asia are found at sites extending from the Swat valley in the north-west to the Burdwan district of Bengal. Silver, which may have been an import from the same region (though it was also available in Rajasthan) and used for making coins, has been found all along the Uttarapatha. Semi-precious stones such as amethyst and topaz were moving from the Rajamahal, Singhbhum, and Dhalbhum areas of Eastern India to sites in the middle and upper Ganga valley. Shell was imported from the eastern coast to sites in the lower and middle Ganga valley.

The Uttarapatha was a land-cum-river route. Buddhist texts refer to the riverine movement of traders and goods along the Ganga. The distribution of PGW and NBPW sites along this river and its tributaries—especially the Yamuna, Ghaghara, and Sarayu—suggests that rivers formed major communication routes. The *Ashtadhyayi* and Jatakas mention ferries. But movements across land were clearly also important. Buddhist texts frequently talk of caravans of traders moving along land routes, and Buddhist monks too moved mainly on foot.

The Dakshinapatha—the great southern trade route—is mentioned in the *Arthashastra*, but was operational from the early historic period. It stretched from Pataliputra in Magadha to Pratishthana on the Godavari, and was also connected to ports on the western coast. Although there are several references to trans-Vindhyan regions in Buddhist texts, and more so in the *Mahabharata* and *Ramayana*, because of the northern bias of these texts, there is a certain vagueness about the southern routes. Buddhist texts refer to merchants travelling from Pataliputra and Kaushambi to Pratishthana. The *Sutta Nipata* tells the story of Bavari, a teacher of Kosala, who built a hermitage on the banks of the Godavari in Assaka and sent his disciples on a mission to meet the Buddha. They travelled through Pratishthana, Ujjayini, Vidisha, and on to Shravasti. The physician Jivaka moved along the Dakshinapatha on his way to Avanti. The discovery of PGW in the Malwa region and NBPW in Central India and the Deccan provide archaeological corroboration of this route. The Vindhyas provided iron, copper, and various types of stone to settlements in the Ganga valley, and these raw materials must have moved along the northern sector of the Dakshinapatha. Trade and interaction along this route increased in subsequent centuries.

Buddhist texts talk of caravans with 1,000 carts moving from one *janapada* to another, passing through deserted areas. There is mention of caravans paying tolls and taxes to the king's men. Customs officials (*kammikas*) levied taxes on merchandise and could confiscate the goods of tax evaders. There are stories of robbers who waylaid traders and monks moving along the roads that connected the big cities. It was the job of royal officials known as *rajabhata*s to safeguard the lives and property of such travellers.

The internal trade routes joined the external routes, which linked the subcontinent with other areas. Overland routes connecting Taxila with north Afghanistan and Iran were important for obtaining raw materials such as silver, gold, lapis lazuli, and jade. There may have been a long-distance trade in fine wood between India and Mesopotamia. The Central Asia route had been important from neolithic times onwards. The route via the Bolan pass and through north Afghanistan was also important. Cities such as Taxila and Charsada were major commercial centres. The routes into India from the north-west were followed not only by traders but also by invading Persian and Macedonian armies. The route from Bengal to Myanmar was also probably important, and jade may have been an import from the latter region.

Sea travel and trade are mentioned in the Pali canon. The *Anguttara Nikaya* refers to sea merchants who had a bird aboard their ship to sight land. There is mention of the maritime route to West Asia. The Jatakas contain many accounts of sea voyages. Commodities such as sandalwood and pearls were probably exported from sites along the eastern and western coasts to West Asia and the Mediterranean. Maritime trade with

Southeast Asia also began in the early historical period. Chinese texts are a rich source of information about Southeast Asia.

The earliest archaeological evidence of contacts between South and Southeast Asia comes from the burial site of Ban Don Ta Phet (in west-central Thailand). Thousands of beads were found in the burials here; these included over 50 etched carnelian and agate beads of Indian manufacture. The evidence from Ban Don Ta Phet and from the settlement and industrial site of Khao Sam Keo (on the east coast of the Kra Isthmus) suggest that the contacts with various parts of the Indian subcontinent can be dated to the 4th–2nd centuries BCE.

The expansion of internal and long-distance trade made traders an important urban group. It was no doubt because of their economic affluence that Buddhist texts describe *vanijja* (trade) as one of the high occupations.

Class, Kinship, *Varna*, and *Jati*

From the 6th century BCE, there is evidence of the emergence of socio-economic classes in North India. Buddhist texts refer to disparities in wealth and status. There are references to very poor (*dalidda*) people. Contrasts are drawn between fortunate wealthy people and unfortunate poor people (*mahabhoga kula*, *dalidda kula*; *sadhana*, *adhana*; *sugata*, *dugata*). The roots of such disparities lay in differences in control over productive resources, especially land. A variety of texts throw light on the social history of the times. However, we must remember that the world outside the texts was much more complex and diverse.

Despite the emergence of socio-economic classes, kinship ties continued to be extremely important, and were eventually incorporated into the framework of caste. *Nati* and *nati-kulani* are terms that refer to the extended kin group, beyond the immediate family. *Natakas* included relatives on both the mother and father's side. Kula denotes an extended patrilineal family. The importance of kinship is shown by the fact that although Buddhist monks were supposed to renounce family ties, monastic rules were bent to make allowances for them. For example, monks were ordinarily forbidden to travel during the ***vassavasa*** (the monsoon retreat), but some contact with members of the family could be maintained during this period. They were not generally supposed to go to the battlefield, but could do so to visit a sick or dying relative. We can also note the influence of kinsfolk such as Mahapajapati Gotami and Ananda on the Buddha himself, for instance, on the issue of admitting women to the *sangha*. To a certain extent, the Buddhist monastic order offered an alternative bonding of brotherhood (sisterhood, in the case of nuns) replacing the worldly mesh of kinship relationships. However, the fact that it did not try to completely replace or obliterate conventional kinship bonds shows just how strong these were at the time.

As mentioned earlier, the Grihyasutras represent an important stage in the evolution of the Brahmanical tradition. They offered a model of piety for ordinary householders that was based on a substitution of the older Vedic sacrifices which involved three sacrificial fires by a set of simpler rituals which used one fire, and offered the same rewards. The Grihyasutras describe study of the Veda as the duty of Brahmanas, Kshatriyas, and Vaishyas. They introduce various *vratas* (disciplinary regimens, often translated as 'vows'), which, along with textual study, became markers of Arya status. According to Timothy Lubin (2015), through such innovations, the Grihyasutras (and Dharmasutras) tried to create the idea of a unified trans-regional Arya culture.

The four-fold order of *varnas* (hereditary classes) was central to the social discourse of the Brahmanical tradition. The *varnas* were ideally supposed to be endogamous, i.e., marriage was supposed to take place within the group. But Dharmashastra accepted certain types of inter-*varna* marriages between a man of a higher *varna* and a woman of a lower *varna*. Such hypergamous marriages were known as *anuloma* marriages. On the other hand, marriages between a woman of a higher *varna* and a man of a lower *varna* (hypogamy) were referred to as *pratiloma* unions, and were not approved of. The worst sort of *pratiloma* union was between a Brahmana woman and a Shudra man. The fact that these texts discuss and grade inter-*varna* marriages suggests that such marriages did take place and that *varnas* were not strictly endogamous.

Dharmashastra texts also reveal the gap between theory and practice in the relationship between *varna* and occupation in their theory of *apad-dharma* (*dharma* in times of distress or emergency). In ideal circumstances, people of the four *varnas* must follow the vocations prescribed for them: The ideal activities of the Brahmana are studying and teaching the Veda, performing sacrifices for himself and others, and giving and receiving gifts. Those of the Kshatriya are studying, performing sacrifices for himself, bestowing gifts, and more especially, protecting people. The Vaishya shares the first three activities, but his ideal occupations are agriculture, cattle rearing, trade, and money-lending. The Shudra was supposed to obtain his livelihood by serving the higher *varnas*.

However, in times of emergency, adversity, or distress, a person could be forced to pursue vocations that would normally be considered inappropriate for members of his *varna*. This, according to the Dharmashastra, was perfectly all right. The fact that they had to stretch their ideal scheme in relation to the two important issues of marriage and occupation shows that people were in fact not following the regular norms of *varna-dharma*.

Buddhist and Jaina texts also mention the *varna* order, but for them, the powerful religious sanction associated with it in the Brahmanical tradition was lacking. It was considered an institution created by people, based on natural inclinations and aptitudes. Further, both these traditions placed the Kshatriya above the Brahmana in the *varna* hierarchy.

Gotra (clan affiliation) was an important basis of Brahmana identity. In Buddhist texts, the Buddha invariably addresses Brahmanas by their *gotra*. We can also note the use of the *gotra* name by non-Brahmanas. The Buddha himself is frequently referred to as 'Gotama' (the Pali form of Gautama) which is a *gotra* name, and Mahavira is supposed to have had the Kashyapa *gotra*. This may have had to do with the position of parity that the Buddhist and Jaina traditions tried to maintain between Brahmanas and their own preceptors. Or it is possible that non-Brahmanas took on the *gotra* of the Brahmana preceptor associated with their families.

Varna was not irrelevant as a basis of social identity, but was now competing with another social institution—*jati* (caste). The English word 'caste' comes from the

PRIMARY SOURCES | Activities in times of adversity

The *Gautama Dharmasutra* (7) explains how *varna* duties can be transgressed in times of adversity, within certain limits. Note that the main focus is on the Brahmana:

These are the rules for times of adversity. A Brahmana may receive Vedic instruction from a non-Brahmana, walk behind him, and obey him. Once the study is completed, however, the Brahmana becomes the more honourable of the two.

One may teach, officiate at the sacrifices of, and receive gifts from people of all classes, each preceding occupation being more honourable. When these occupations are unavailable, one may live by the occupations of a Kshatriya, and when even these are unavailable, by the occupations of a Vaishya.

One may not trade in the following goods: perfumes, seasonings, prepared foods, sesame seeds, hemp or linen cloth, skins, garments that are dyed red or washed, milk and milk products, roots, fruits, flowers, medicines, honey, meat, grass, water, poisons, and animals for slaughter; and, under any circumstance, human beings, barren cows, heifers, and pregnant cows. According to some, one may also not trade in land, rice, barley, goats, sheep, horses, bulls, milch-cows, and oxen. One is restricted to bartering seasonings for seasonings and animals for animals; but not salt, prepared food, or sesame seeds. One may, however, exchange uncooked food for an equal amount of cooked food for immediate use.

When none of this is possible, however, one may sustain oneself by any occupation except that of a Shudra; some permit even that when one's life is at stake. Even then, however, one is not allowed to mix with that class or eat forbidden food. When his life is at stake, even a Brahmana may live by the use of arms and a Kshatriya may resort to the occupations of a Vaishya.

Source Olivelle, (2000) 2003: 137

KEY CONCEPTS | *Varna* and *jati*

One of the great triumphs of the Brahmanical tradition is that even today, many people persist in thinking that ancient Indian society was for centuries together divided into four groups—Brahmanas, Kshatriyas, Vaishyas, and Shudras—and consider *varna* to be the basis of *jati*. This was not so. *Varna* and *jati* are both hereditary social classifications and the two did come to be related, but they are not the same thing. There are many differences between them, and the nature of these differences themselves has changed over time:

1. The number of *varnas* is four (or five, if those outside the *varna* fold are considered a category), while the number of *jatis* (including castes and sub-castes) are so numerous that they cannot be counted, and their numbers continue to grow even today.
2. Both *varna* and *jati* are hierarchical orderings. However, the ranking among the four *varnas* is fixed, while the *jatis* have an element of fluidity within particular ranges. In the Brahmanical tradition, the Brahmana stands at the top and the Shudra at the bottom. In the Buddhist tradition, the Kshatriya comes first and the Brahmana second, but the order is still fixed. It is impossible to rank the *jatis* on a single scale of highest to lowest. Although the Brahmanas usually stand at the top of the caste hierarchy and the so-called 'untouchable' groups represented the lowest boundary, the rank of the castes in between the two could be fluid. The relative ranking of castes in fact varies across regions and localities, and depends on a number of factors including control over land, wealth, and political and military power. Caste ranking can be a matter of dispute, even among Brahmanas and 'outcastes'. In recent times, castes have often tried to 'upgrade' themselves (this process is often referred to as **Sanskritization**), and sometimes get 'downgraded'. Upgrading usually involves adopting practices associated with higher castes, e.g., vegetarianism, withdrawal of women into the home, and change in occupation.
3. While there were rules that discouraged social interaction and the acceptance of certain kinds of food by higher *varnas* from certain types of Shudras, the rules of commensality were more clearly defined and established with reference to the *jatis*. These were based on ideas of purity and pollution.
4. The *varnas* were not really endogamous units, since a number of inter-*varna* marriages (the *anuloma* ones) were considered permissible. The *jatis*, on the other hand, were supposed to be endogamous, although certain hypergamous unions may always have been accepted.
5. The *varnas* are associated with a range of occupations, while the *jatis* (at least in the beginning) were associated with specific occupations, even while there were certain occupations that were open to all. It has been argued that function is more important than birth in the *varna* system.

The reason why *varna* and *jati* got connected is because members of a caste often *claim* to belong to a certain *varna* category. The anchoring of the *jati* system to the *varna* system was no doubt in order to give the former the legitimacy of the Brahmanical tradition. For many centuries, lineages that managed to achieve political power often *claimed* to be Kshatriyas. This shows that the *varnas* may have swiftly become normative categories, but at the same time, they retained an important social function as a key reference point for the caste system. Nevertheless, the real, effective basis of a person's social identity, the basis of rules of inter-dining, social interaction, marriage, and occupation in early historical North India was *jati* and not *varna*.

In order to maintain the distinction between *varna* and *jati*, it is better to leave the former untranslated. *Jati*, on the other hand, can be translated as caste (including sub-caste). It is also important to remember that social institutions constantly evolve and change. The function and significance of the categories of *varna* and *jati*, too, have changed over time. Therefore, the precise nature of the *jati* system in ancient times cannot be considered identical to present-day configurations.

Portuguese *castas*, which refers to animal and plant species or breeds; as well as to tribes, clans, races or lineages within human societies. It was first used in the context of Indian society by Portuguese traders operating on the western coast in the 16th and 17th centuries. Sociologists have offered many different definitions of caste in its 20th century form. Enumerations of its key features include hierarchy, hereditary occupations, and attempts of caste groups to separate themselves from others through endogamy and commensality. There are, however, exceptions to the rule of endogamy, and endogamy is often a feature of sub-castes rather than castes. Interpretations of caste are extremely varied, but can be divided into two basic types (Quigley, [1999] 2002: 2–3). On the one hand, there is the materialist interpretation, which sees caste as something that rationalizes and camouflages material inequalities through an idiom of purity and pollution. On the other hand, there is the idealist explanation, which views caste as essentially the product of religious and cultural ideas related to purity and pollution. Another interpretation emphasizes the connection between caste and the political domain, specifically the emergence of kingship and kingdoms. In this book, *varna* is used for the four-fold division of society, and *jati* is used for caste.

The Dharmasutras explain the origins of *jati*s through the ingenious but fictitious theory of the mixture of *varna*s (*varna-samkara*). According to this, *jati*s were the outcome of various kinds of inter-*varna* marriages. In this manner, the Dharmashastra tradition was able to stand by the *varna* theory but acknowledge and explain the existence of *jati*s. Although there is uncertainty about the extent to which endogamy and, more so, commensality were fully established at the time, the beginnings of the caste system can be traced to the 6th century BCE.

The terms *varna*, *jati*, and *kula* are sometimes used interchangeably in ancient texts, while in other places they have a more specific meaning. The *varna* order was still an important reference point, and the terms Brahmana and Kshatriya had significance. However, while many people in the Pali canon are identified as Brahmanas and Kshatriyas, few are identified as Vaishyas or Shudras. Those who would theoretically have belonged to these two categories are generally described with reference to their specific occupation, which was in turn tied up with *kula* and *jati*. This suggests that *varna* was more a theoretical construct tied to the upper categories and that a person's identity in the society of the time was based more on occupation, *kula* (lineage), and *jati* (caste). (The frequency of references to Brahmanas and Kshatriyas in early Buddhist texts could also indicate that these texts were greatly interested in settling the issue of their relative status.) Halbfass (1991: 350–52) suggests that the *varna* system was the prototype of the *jati* system; the two were never sharply distinguished in ancient Indian classical literature, and their relationship was marked by a partial overlap, interaction and 'osmosis'.

It is not easy to identify how *jati*s emerged in the first place. They may have been the result of a combination of factors—the hereditary nature of crafts and occupations, the assimilation of tribal groups into the larger Brahmanical fold, and a social system that privileged birth and regulated hierarchy through marriage rules and endogamy (Jaiswal, [1998] 2000: 13–14). Territorial and occupational differences also played important roles in the emergence of segmented identities.

The Dharmasutra theory of *varna-samkara* was no doubt necessary in order to accommodate and 'place' different groups within the larger social framework. Pali texts refer to high *jati*s (*ukkatta jati*) and low *jati*s (*hina jati*). While Brahmanas and Kshatriyas are included among the former, the latter included the Chandalas, basket makers (*vena jati*), hunters (*nesada jati*), charioteers (*rathakara jati*), and sweepers (*pukkusa jati*). The texts clearly connect *jati* with occupation and convey the idea that the social status of the various *jati*s varied considerably. Much remains to be understood about the early history of caste (see Upinder Singh, 2014a).

The earliest occurrence of the term *asprishya* in the sense of a social group that was condemned by virtue of birth to be regarded by the higher-ups as permanently 'untouchable' occurs for the first time in a later work—the *Vishnu Smriti*. But the practice of untouchability, an extreme form of social subordination, marginalization, and oppression, clearly existed from earlier times and was strengthened over time (Vivekanand Jha, 2004). In early Dharmashastra texts, Chandalas were sometimes categorized as Shudras, but a distinction between the two was established very soon. There were differences among the *smritikaras* (law givers) about just which groups should be included in the category of untouchables, but there is near unanimity about the inclusion of the Chandalas. The *Apastamba Dharmasutra* explains the birth of a Chandala as the result of evil deeds committed in a previous life. It states that a Brahmana guilty of stealing gold or the murder of another Brahmana is reborn as a Chandala. The *Gautama*, *Baudhayana*, and *Vasishtha Dharmasutra*s, on the other hand, describe the Chandala as the offspring of a Shudra man and Brahmana woman, the most degraded of the *pratiloma* unions. All these instances emphasize the low origin of the Chandala.

The Dharmasutras reflect an attitude of extreme prejudice against the Chandalas, often equating them with dogs and crows. They clearly allude to the idea that contact, even accidental, with the Chandala was polluting. According to the *Apastamba Dharmasutra* (2.1.2.8–9), if one touches a Chandala, one should immediately plunge in water; if one talks to a Chandala, one should immediately talk to a Brahmana; if one sees him, one should immediately look at luminous bodies in the heavens (the sun, moon, or stars). Contact with other groups considered lowly, collectively known as *antyajas*, did not require such drastic purification techniques—simply washing the part of the body that had come into contact or sipping water were adequate. Gautama (16, 23, 19) states that a person should not recite the Veda while a corpse or Chandala are in the village. The Dharmasutras lay down severe penances and punishments for men who had sexual relations with Chandala women.

The texts of this period contain many references to the existence of male and female slaves (Chanana, [1960] 1990). The *Digha Nikaya* states that a *dasa* is not master of himself, depends on another, and cannot go where he likes. The *Vinaya Pitaka* speaks of three kinds of slaves—the *antojatako*, *dhanakkito*, and *kara-mara-anito*. The *antojatako* seems to refer to the offspring of a woman slave. A slave who is bought is known as *dhanakkito*. One brought from another country and enslaved is the *kara-mara-anito*. The *Digha Nikaya* mentions a fourth type of slave—*samam dasavayam upagato*, one who has himself accepted enslavement. There are a few references to the manumission of slaves. In fact one of the rules of the Buddhist *sangha* was that slaves could not join until and unless they were freed by their masters.

Given the elitist bias of the textual sources, it is not easy to reconstruct the ways in which groups such as the Chandalas and slaves may have reacted to their subordination and oppression. Chanana ([1960] 1990: 56–57) has identified two instances of resistance in the Buddhist canon. One is a reference in the *Vinaya Pitaka* to the *dasa-kammakaras* of the Sakyas attacking the womenfolk of their masters in the woods as an act of vengeance. The second is the story of the *dasi* Kali and her mistress, the *gahapatni* Vaidehi, in the *Majjhima Nikaya*. Vaidehi had a reputation of being extremely gentle and even-tempered. Kali was submissive and hard-working, and came to the conclusion that her mistress' even temper was the result of her own exemplary conduct. She decided to subject Vaidehi to a test. She started waking up late and did not respond to her mistress' calls three days in a row. Vaidehi couldn't take it. She got more and more angry and finally attacked Kali in fury. Kali was proved right.

While it is indeed possible to identify such reflections of social tension and conflict in ancient Indian texts, it is much more difficult to uncover the textures of the lives, voices, and ideas of subordinated and marginalized groups. This is because subordination and marginalization generally involved an exclusion from the production of knowledge and written texts. One of the challenges for historians is to carefully and creatively read between the lines of the available texts, in order to retrieve the histories of people who lived beyond the margins of elite society.

Gender, Family, and Household

The macro-level political, economic, and social changes of the time were connected to developments at the level of the family and the household. Changing times demanded new ethics. Strict control over women's sexuality and reproductive potential was essential for the patrilineal transmission of property and for the maintenance and perpetuation of the endogamous caste structure. The strengthening of patriarchal authority within the household and the emphasis on certain norms related to marriage and the chastity of women were the means of effecting such control.

Buddhist and Jaina texts prescribe the ideal conduct for members of the monastic community as well as for householders. However, it is the Brahmanical Dharmasutras and Grihyasutras that reflect the most systematic and comprehensive attempts to authoritatively define and regulate a variety of social values and practices in a changing milieu.

Whether we look at Brahmanical or Buddhist texts, it is necessary to distinguish between the ideal situation projected in them and the actual situation that prevailed in their time. This requires reading between the lines and against the grain.

Apart from the married couple, the household could include their unmarried children, married sons and their families, the husband's parents, slaves, and servants. Terms used for the household unit are *kutumba* (this is rare), *ghara,* and the more frequent *kula*. The *kulapati* was the head of the family, *kulaputa* refers to junior males. While the household continued to be the basic unit of agricultural labour, household labour was now often supplemented by wage labourers and, to a lesser extent, by slaves.

The institution of marriage was central to the life of the householder. In Buddhist texts, the type of marriage most approved of is one arranged by parents and where the bride and groom are young and chaste. There is reference to *ahava* (literally, 'the leading', i.e., of the bride by her family) and *vivaha* (literally, 'leading away', i.e., of the bride by the groom's family). It is not certain whether *ahava* and *vivaha* were two different ceremonies or the same one. The *Vinaya Pitaka* mentions 10 kinds of unions between a man and woman: (1) When a woman is bought by money (*dhanakkhita*); (2) when she stays of her own accord with a man (*chhandavasini*); (3) when a man gives her money (*bhogavasin*); (4) when a man gives her clothes (*patavasini*); (5) when an ablution of water is performed (*odapattakani*); (6) when she removes her headgear (*obhatachumbata*); (7) when she is also a female slave (*dasinama*); (8) when she is also a servant (*kammakari*); (9) when she is temporarily with a man (*muhuttika*); and (10) when she is captured in a raid (*dhajahata*). Except for the *chhandavasini* union, all the others involve either some sort of economic exchange or the already subordinate position of the woman. The references to unions where the ablution of water is performed and where the woman removes her headgear suggest the performance of some ceremony (Wagle, 1966: 96, 98).

The Dharmasutras classify marriages into eight types: Brahma, Daiva, Arsha, Prajapatya, Gandharva, Asura, Rakshasa, and Paishacha. This idea is elaborated on in the Smritis. The Brahma marriage is one in which a father adorns and honours his daughter with garments and ornaments, and gifts her to a man who is learned in the Veda and of good conduct. The Daiva marriage is when a father adorns and honours his daughter with garments and ornaments, and gives her in marriage to an officiating priest in the course of the performance of a sacrifice. This form only applies to Brahmanas. The Arsha form involves the gift of a daughter after taking a pair of cattle (a cow and bull) or two pairs, in order to fulfil customary law, not as a sale of the daughter. The Prajapatya marriage is one in which the father gifts the daughter after saying to the couple, 'May both of you perform your religious duties together', and after he has honoured the groom with the appropriate ceremonies such as the *madhuparka*. The Asura marriage is one in which a girl is given away by the father after the bridegroom hands over as much wealth as he can afford to the bride and her relatives. The Gandharva type is a union between a man and woman through mutual love and consent. The Rakshasa type is when a woman is forcibly abducted from her home, her relatives often being beaten or killed. The Paishacha form is when a man has sex with a girl while she is asleep, intoxicated, unconscious, or mentally disordered. The types of marriages were arranged in a descending scale of propriety, and not all of them were approved of by the *smritikaras*. The *Brahma* was considered the best and the Paishacha the lowest. In fact, the last three types are not so much marriages as unions in which women were acquired in different ways, and which were supposed to be followed by marriage rites. The Dharmasutra classification of marriages into various types suggests the prevalence of variations in marriage practices, including dowry and bride-price.

The early Dharmasutras suggest that girls should be married off as soon as they attained puberty. The *Gautama Dharmasutra* (18.20–23) states that a father incurs sin if he does not ensure this, and that a girl should wait for three months after she has started menstruating, after which she should find her own husband. The *Baudhayana Dharmasutra* (4.1.12) recommends that a father should marry his daughter off to a man devoid of good qualities rather than keep her at home after she attains puberty.

Verses of the *vivaha-sukta*, a late hymn from the *Rig Veda*, are rearranged, and not all of them are used (Roy, 1994a). The marriage rituals expressed many important relationships, not only between husband and wife, but also among their larger kin group. Ceremonies such as mounting the stone, the groom grasping the bride's hand, and his pointing to the pole star—are imbued with multiple meanings. The priest now dominated the central ceremony, which was performed in the girl's parental home. The relationship between husband and wife had many different aspects, including mutual support and friendship, sexual and procreative activity, and the subordination of the wife to the husband. In connection with the marriage ceremonies, *Apastamba Grihyasutra* 1.2.15 states that practices devised by women could be adopted. These customary practices are not specified, but were clearly important enough to be acknowledged.

Apart from marriage, the Grihyasutras describe several other domestic rites of passage as well, systematizing them and giving them a firm Brahmanical mooring by underlining the importance of Brahmana priests and the close relationship between the *grihapati* and the domestic fire.

The early Dharmasutras do not approve of widow remarriage. However, they specify the number of years an abandoned woman must wait for her husband before she re-marries. Both Gautama and Baudhayana refer to the *paunarbhava* (son of a woman who has married again) in the list of sons. The early *smritikaras* had an ambivalent attitude towards *niyoga*, the ancient custom of a widow cohabiting with her brother-in-law or another man in order to produce sons. Gautama discusses various views on the matter and acknowledges sons born of *niyoga* as legal heirs to property. On the other hand, Baudhayana (2.2.40) states that the son belongs to the one who sows the seed (the male), and women must therefore be guarded against having sexual relations with men other than their husbands. This text considered *niyoga* unions and their offspring sinful.

The process of defining and redefining rituals was reflected in the emphasis on the *pancha-mahayajnas* (Kane, [1941] 1974: 696–704). These are mentioned in later Vedic texts, but become more important and are now described as obligatory for Brahmanas. The five *mahayajnas* were *brahmayajna* (the study and teaching of the Veda), *pitriyajna* (offerings to the ancestors), *daivayajna* (offerings made into the fire), *bhutayajna* (offerings made to all beings), and *manushyayajna* (honouring guests). Unlike the *shrauta* sacrifices, they were to be performed by the householder himself, without the intercession of priests. Initially, they seem to have been considered a way of discharging a man's duties to the various beings in the universe. Later Dharmashastra texts explain them as atonement for injury or death caused to various beings as part of daily household activities, e.g., in the hearth, grinding mill, broomstick, winnowing basket, mortar and pestle, and water jar. It is interesting to note that these *mahayajnas* were actually simple ceremonies performed by the householder, and were *yajnas* only metaphorically speaking.

Sapinda relationships were central to the Dharmashastra discussion on rules of marriage, inheritance, and rules of purity and impurity to be observed among relatives when a person died. Brahmanical texts prohibit marriage among *sapindas*. This prohibition was supposed to apply to all *varnas*, including Shudras. As explained by Kane ([1941] 1974: 452–58), later Dharmashastra texts give different interpretations of the term *sapinda*. According to one view, the *sapindas* are connected by virtue of their sharing particles of the same body. Father, son, and grandson are *sapindas* because the particles of the body of the father are transmitted to the son and, further on, to the son's son. The son also has *sapinda* relations with his mother, because the mother's body particles continue in him. Extending the same reasoning further, a person has *sapinda* relations with his mother's father, sister, and brother. Husband and wife are *sapindas* because they produce a son through their bodies. The wives of brothers are *sapindas* because they produce sons from their husbands, who are produced from the same body (i.e., their father). Marriages are not supposed to take place between people who fall within the *sapinda* circuit up to a certain specified number of generations. Law-givers such as Yajnavalkya count five ascending and descending generations on the mother's side and seven ascending and descending relations on the father's side as defining the *sapinda* circuit. But other

FURTHER DISCUSSION | **Marriage, according to the Grihyasutras**

There are several variations in the details and sequence of events and ceremonies leading up to marriage in the Grihyasutras. However, the following basic framework can be identified:

1. The time for the marriage should be fixed during the northern movement of the sun along its course, in the period of the waxing moon and on an auspicious day.
2. The groom-to-be sends learned Brahmanas as messengers to the girl's house to convey his acceptance of the marriage. Relatives from both sides accept the alliance.
3. The bride-to-be is specially bathed, her hair washed.
4. The prospective groom kindles the fire and makes a number of offerings.
5. *Kanyadana* (giving away the daughter): The participants sit around the fire. The father gives his final, oral acceptance of the union. Gifts are exchanged.
6. *Madhuparka*: The bridegroom is honoured by offering him a seat, washing his feet, and offering him a honey mixture. He is then offered meat of a cow, goat, fish or some vegetarian fare.
7. *Hastagrabha/Panigrahana*: After the fire is established and the appropriate offerings made into it, the husband grasps the bride's hand saying, 'I take hold of your hand for happiness.' Different ways of grasping the hand are supposed to determine the sex of future progeny.
8. *Lajahoma*: The bride makes three offerings of *lajas* (roasted grain) mixed with *shami* leaves, while the bridegroom recites certain formulae.
9. The bride or the couple step on a stone to attain stability.
10. *Agniparinayana*: The groom takes the bride around the fire, saying, 'I am this, you are she, you are she, I am this; I am heaven, you are the earth; I am the *Saman*, you are the *Rik*. Let us both marry here. Let us beget offspring. Dear to each other, bright, having well-disposed minds, may we live for a hundred years.'
(Steps 8, 9, and 10 are supposed to be performed one after the other and repeated three times.)
11. *Saptapadi*: This consists of walking seven steps together. The seven steps are marked with rice placed to the north of the fire, and the groom makes the bride step on these, starting with the right foot every time. The groom says, 'May you take one step for sap; a second step for juice (or vigour); a third step for the thriving of wealth; a fourth step for comfort; a fifth step for offspring; a sixth step for seasons; may you be my friend with your seventh step. May you be devoted to me; let us have many sons, may they reach old age.' Water is sprinkled on the heads of the bride and groom. The spectators depart; the groom gives gifts to the Brahmanas and the bride's father. The couple leaves for the groom's house, carrying their householder's fire along with them.

According to most texts, the marriage rite ends with the *saptapadi*. There are a number of other rites when the couple arrives at the groom's house. These include the *dhruvarundhatidarshana*, in which the husband points to the pole star and urges his wife to be as stable and firm. According to some authorities, it is this ritual that marks the end of the marriage rite.

Source Apte, 1978: 117–28; Kane, (1941b) 1974: 527–40

law-givers had different opinions about the number of degrees of relationship and the precise point at which the dividing line between permissible and unpermissible marriages was to be drawn.

The *Apastamba Dharmasutra* (1.7.21.8) categorically states that sexual relations with the uterine relations (mothers and sisters) of one's parents and their children are a sin. This would rule out marriage between a man and the daughter of his maternal uncle or paternal aunt. However, the same text (1.19–26) goes on to say that marrying one's maternal uncle's daughter or paternal aunt's daughter is one of the customary practices of the south. Baudhayana states that those who follow these practices in *other* areas (i.e., in North India), incur sin, thereby extending tacit approval to the practice in the South. However, other *smritikaras* forbade cross-cousin marriages, regardless of the geographical or customary context. This suggests that marriage customs varied in different regions and the *smritikaras* were divided on whether or not to sanction them.

Texts refer to monogamous and polygynous marriages. The *Vasishtha Dharmasutra* (1.24) states that a Brahmana can have three wives, a Kshatriya two, and a Vaishya and Shudra only one. The possibility of divorce and remarriage in some circumstances is suggested by the story (*Digha Nikaya* 2) of Mahagovinda, who, when he decided to renounce the world, offered to give his 40 wives to another man, if they so desired. They declined and decided to follow him on to the path of renunciation. Severe consequences were laid down for women who committed adultery. In the *Vinaya Pitaka* (4), a Lichchhavi man consults other members of his clan to get their consent to kill his wife for committing adultery.

The early Grihyasutras have a great deal to say regarding the ideal relationships between members of the household. The *grihapati* (householder) was the centre and master of the household unit. The *griha* (household) was not only seen as a space within which people bound to each other through kinship lived together. Its members were bound to each other through the performance of rituals and activities related to production, reproduction, and social linkages (Tyagi, 2008). The household was considered essential for progeny and to fulfil the debt the householder owed his ancestors. The word used most often for the wife is *jaya*, which refers to her as bearer of her husband's progeny, among whom great importance was attached to sons. The wife was considered as having destructive as well as constructive potential within the household. In laying down the various life-cycle rituals, and extending their formal approval to custom, the Grihyasutras sought to extend Brahmanical control over the variety of social practices, including rites performed by women.

Some Grihyasutras state that a woman could perform rites such as the morning and evening offerings in the domestic fire. But she could not act independently as a *yajamana* in the bigger sacrifices. On the death of the wife, the widower was supposed to cremate her with flames kindled from their domestic fire. He was to establish a new fire when he remarried. Texts such as the *Ashvalayana Grihyasutra* state that when a woman's husband died, she was to lie on the pyre, but should be drawn away from it by a brother-in-law or certain other designated males before it was lit. This symbolized her willingness to accompany her husband to the other world (there is a similar reference), but her place was among the living.

The emergence of private property in land had important implications for the structure and function of the family. The inheritance of property became an important issue. Inheritance was patrilineal. Buddhist texts suggest that the property of both mother and father was generally divided among sons. Where there were no sons, the property went to the next of kin or was taken over by the state. The *Samyutta Nikaya* refers to the property of a *setthi-gahapati*, who died without male heirs, being taken over by king Prasenajit. Wives and daughters seem to have been excluded from the deceased man's inheritance. Certain Buddhist texts refer to a father sometimes transferring his property in favour of his son or some other close male relative during his lifetime.

The Dharmashastra views on inheritance rights, especially those of women, have been summarized and analyzed by Kane ([1946] 1973: 700–36). In general, male heirs, especially sons, took precedence over all others. The *Baudhayana Dharmasutra* includes a man's brothers, his son, grandson, and great grandson from a wife of the same *varna* as the core group of inheritors of his property. The *Apastamba Dharmasutra* (2.6.14.2) states that if a son cannot inherit the property, it should go to the nearest *sapinda*; although it mentions the daughter, it does not mention the wife as a possible heir. Gautama (28.19) states that the wealth of a person who dies heirless should go to his *sapindas*, *sagotras*, or wife. Generally, the claims of the daughter came after those of the wife. Later Dharmashastras often excluded the wife from inheriting her husband's property or set preconditions of chastity before she could claim such a right.

There was, however, a category of property—the ***stri-dhana***—over which the *smritikaras* conceded that a woman did have rights. The first full definition of *stri-dhana* is given in the *Manu Smriti*, but the idea goes back to earlier times. *Stri-dhana* came to mean 'women's property', and referred specifically to certain special kinds of moveable property given to a woman on various occasions during her lifetime. These included presents (jewellery, clothes, household articles, etc.) given by her parents at the time of marriage and by her relatives (father, brothers, etc.) on other occasions. While the Dharmashastra texts disagreed about the extent to which *stri-dhana* was to be considered the permanent property of a woman, they generally agreed that it was to be passed on from mother to daughter (Kane, [1946] 1973: 770–802).

Given the increasingly patriarchal nature of the household, it is not surprising that the preference for sons over daughters continued. The son was considered necessary for the performance of the father's funerary rites, the propitiation of the ancestors, and the continuation of the lineage. The *Digha Nikaya* refers to parents desiring sons because they add to family possessions, continue the family line, inherit the father's property, and pay homage to his ancestors. The *Vinaya Pitaka* refers to people accusing the Buddha of destroying families by making them sonless (by encouraging men to renounce the world). In the *Samyutta Nikaya* (1), the Buddha is presented as consoling Prasenajit, king of Kosala, who was upset at the birth of a daughter: 'A female child,' he tells the king, 'may prove an even better offspring than a male one. For she may grow up wise and virtuous. She will honour her mother-in-law and be faithful to her husband (*patibbata*). The boy she may bear may do great deeds.' These words sum up the ideals associated with womanhood. At the same time, we must note that the renunciant orders, including Buddhism, created an alternative to the householder life for both men and women.

It is important to remember that social customs must have varied considerably depending on social group, region, and locality. As mentioned in Chapter 1, Dharmashastra acknowledged three sources of *dharma*—*shruti*, *smriti*, and *sadachara* or *shishtachara* (custom). The *Baudhayana Dharmasutra* (1.1.1.2) in fact refers to certain customs that are peculiar to the south and north. It must also be remembered that texts tend to tell us about practices and norms for the upper classes of society. The *samskaras* of the Dharmashastra texts, for instance, explicitly exclude the Shudras.

The Renunciatory Tradition

This age of urban affluence, of communities marked by distinctions of class and caste, was also an age of renunciants who advocated giving up attachment to all material things and social relationships. The renunciants were referred to by various terms including ***paribbajaka*** (Sanskrit—*parivrajaka*, 'wanderer'), ***samana*** (Sanskrit—*shramana*, 'one who strives', i.e., to realize the truth), and ***bhikkhu*** (Sanskrit—*bhikshu*, 'one who lives by begging alms'). These were people who had left their homes and lived as wanderers, dependent on food and alms offered by sympathetic or generous householders.

Renunciation and asceticism were not entirely new ideas. Although the householder was central to the Vedic tradition, Vedic texts contain words such as *vanaprasthi*, *tapasi*, *yogi*, *yati*, *vairagi*, *muni*, *vaikhanasa*, and *sannyasi*—all of which have elements of ascetic or renunciatory connotations (Bhagat, 1976). Furthermore, the married householder, though central to the cult of the sacrifice, was irrelevant to the Upanishadic quest for knowledge. However, in the 6th century BCE, due to the strong impact of groups of wandering renouncers, renunciation became a central religious and cultural issue.

The 6th–5th centuries BCE are often known as the age of the Buddha and Mahavira. While these two men were certainly among the most influential thinkers of their time and left their mark in the long term, there were many other renunciant teachers who provided different answers to the mysteries and travails of existence. However, neither the schools not the texts associated with them have survived. They are only known through fleeting and generally unflattering portrayals in texts of their more successful Buddhist and Jaina rivals. The similarities between some of the *shramana* doctrines and practices and the stories of encounters and conversations between their leaders suggest an element of interaction between their proponents. But the competition for adherents also generated tension, if not hostility.

According to Buddhist texts, Purana Kassapa was a teacher who rejected the distinction between moral and immoral and denied that actions had consequences. He taught that good actions (like liberality, self-control, and honesty) did not lead to the accumulation of any merit and that deeds like killing, stealing, and lying were not sinful. Ajita Keshakambalin taught a materialist doctrine. According to him, actions earned neither merit nor demerit, the body returned to the elements after death, and there was no rebirth. The materialist aspect of his doctrine connects him to the later Charvaka school. Pakudha Kachchayana taught that the elements such as earth, water, fire, and air, as well as happiness, sorrow, and life are fixed and unchanging, and do not affect each other. Human action affects nothing—even if a man were to cut off someone's head with a sharp knife, he would not take his life, because the thrust of the sword would simply pass between the seven elements. Sanjaya Belatthiputta is described as someone who refused to say anything definite about anything, earning the label of a person who wriggled about like an eel. His typical response to any question is described in the *Digha Nikaya* as follows: 'If you asked me, "Is there another world?" and if I believed that there was, I should tell you so. But that is not what I say. I do not say that it is so; I do not say that it is otherwise; I do not say that it is not so; nor do I say that it is not so.'

The importance of renunciation in shramanic circles had an impact on the Brahmanical tradition. A significant change visible in the Dharmasutras is the introduction of the concept of *grihastha*. The word *grihapati* (head of the household) is present in Vedic texts and the Grihyasutras. The Dharmasutras, on the other hand, contain the word *grihastha*, which does not have the same meaning. *Grihastha* refers to the stay-at-home householder in contrast to the wandering renunciant (see Jamison, 2019). This suggests that the idea of the *grihastha* was a Brahmanical response to the centrality of renunciation in Buddhism and Jainism (see Olivelle. [Ed.]., 2019 for a discussion of this important word).

Renunciation also had a place in the idea of the *ashramas*. The early Dharmasutras contain the first detailed references to the four *ashramas*—*brahmacharya* (celibate studenthood), *grihastha* (the householder stage), *vanaprastha* (partial renunciation), and *sannyasa* (total renunciation). Olivelle's study of the *ashrama* system (1993) indicates that initially, the four *ashramas* were considered four alternative ways of life that a *snataka* (a young man who had completed his course of Vedic study) could choose from. The authors of this scheme may have been part of a stream of thought represented in some of the early Upanishads against ritualism, and in favour of celibacy and individual choice.

There were differences of opinion among the early Dharmasutras about the legitimacy and relative merits of the *ashramas*. The *Gautama* and *Baudhayana Dharmasutras* are critical of the *ashrama* scheme. Gautama presents the idea of the *ashramas* as a view held by others. He asserts that a young man who had completed his period of study must enter the *grihastha* stage, and that this requirement was based on the authority of the Veda. The *Baudhayana Dharmasutra* describes the idea of the four *ashramas* as the invention of a devil named Kapila and asserts that marriage, procreation, and the performance of sacrifices are essential. The *Apastamba Dharmasutra* accepts the *ashrama* scheme, denies that the celibate *ashramas* are superior to the householder stage, and describes all *ashramas* as of equal value. The appropriate time for entering the third and fourth *ashramas* was also an issue of debate.

The Smritis put the *ashramas* together as an ideal package of four consecutive stages in the life of a *dvija* male. The term *dvija* (twice-born) was initially used only for Brahmanas. Its connotations were later broadened to include Kshatriyas and Vaishyas as well. The three upper *varnas* were considered *dvija* or 'twice-born' as they were eligible for the performance of the *upanayana* (sacred thread) ceremony, which was considered a second birth. Although complete renunciation was ultimately incorporated into the *ashrama* scheme in the *sannyasa* stage, the renunciation advocated by Buddhist and Jaina traditions was different. It could extend over an entire adult life span, and entry into it had a special urgency because it was considered the only way to attain knowledge and liberation. It was open to all, regardless of class, caste, or gender. And by renouncing the world, the renunciant did not walk his own solitary path, but entered a community of renunciants.

The householder and renunciant represented two extremes of the social and a-social worlds. In Buddhist and Jaina traditions, their relationship was one of inter-dependence. Renunciants were dependent on the generosity of householders for food and material sustenance. Householders, for their part, turned to renunciants for instruction and wisdom. The worlds of the renunciant and householder were thus two very different but connected worlds.

FURTHER DISCUSSION | **The *Samannaphala Sutta***

The term *anna titthiya* is used in Buddhist texts to refer to sects other than their own. The word *titthiya* comes from *tirthankara* (literally, 'ford maker', the term also used by Jainas for their teachers). The *Samannaphala Sutta* of the *Digha Nikaya*, a dialogue on the fruits of becoming a renunciant, lists the influential contemporaries of the Buddha.

According to this Sutta, Ajatashatru, king of Magadha, was once sitting on the terrace of his palace, surrounded by his ministers, admiring the beauty of the moonlit night. He asked his ministers which renunciant or Brahmana they should call on to satisfy their hearts with a discourse. The ministers suggested various names—Purana Kassapa, Makkhali Gosala, Ajita Keshakambalin, Pakudha Kachchayana, Sanjaya Belatthiputta, and Nigantha Nataputta (Mahavira). These six are described as homeless wanderers of long standing (*chira-pabbajito*), founders of sects (*titthakaro*), and leaders of their orders (*ganachariyo*). The king was neither impressed nor interested in these suggestions.

At that time, the Buddha, accompanied by hundreds of *bhikkhus*, was staying at Jivaka's mango grove near Rajagriha. Ajatashatru's physician Jivaka suggested that they call on him. The king accepted this suggestion and they all went to the Buddha. Ajatashatru posed the question that was bothering him: 'The fruits of various worldly trades and professions are obvious, but are there any appreciable benefits derived from leading the life of a renunciant?' He told the Buddha that he had asked this question of many others, but had not received a convincing answer.

The Buddha asked Ajatashatru to repeat the replies he had received, and the king did so. It is in Ajatashatru's account of his conversations with the six leading thinkers of the time that we get valuable information about their ideas. The Buddha listened to Ajatashatru's account and then gave him a discourse on the subject, one that left him completely satisfied.

Certain other Buddhist Suttas refer to philosophical ideas current at the time. The *Brahmajala Sutta* refers to 62 different philosophical positions concerning the world, the *atman*, causality, existence, and death. Its conclusion is that all these positions were mere opinions based on sensations and were untenable. A Jaina text, the *Sthananga*, also refers to other doctrines.

The element of competition among thinkers and their doctrines is evident from the accounts. The debates that are recounted are fierce contests, in which the one who lost conceded defeat and had to go over to the other side. There are many examples of Buddhist monks who were originally followers of other teachers. For instance, the famous monks Sariputta and Mahamoggallana were followers of Sanjaya Belatthiputta before they joined the Buddhist *sangha*.

Source Rhys Davids, 1899: 65–95

The Ajivikas

The **Ajivika** sect seems to have been quite old, as there are allusions to predecessors of Makkhali Gosala, its most important leader. Apart from Gosala, Buddhist tradition also connects the Ajivika doctrines with Purana Kassapa and Pakudha Kachchayana. A. L. Basham ([1951] 2003) has put together and analyzed the many scattered references to this sect.

Jaina and Buddhist traditions give accounts of the birth and parentage of Makkhali Gosala, but these seem aimed at giving an etymology for his name and ascribing a low social origin to him, and may therefore have no historical basis whatsoever. The Jaina *Bhagavati Sutra* tells us that his father was a *mankha* (probably an exhibitor of religious pictures and a singer of religious songs) named Mankhali. His mother was Bhadda (a name given to mothers in many mythological Jaina stories). His parents are said to have named him Gosala because he was born in a cowshed in Saravana village, as his parents could find no other place to stay. Buddhaghosha's commentary on the *Samannaphala Sutta* also gives the story of Makkhali's birth in a cowshed, but adds that he was a slave. The *Bhagavati Sutra* states that Makkhali initially followed his father's profession of a *mankha*, moving around with a picture board in his hand. Jaina texts refer to his long association with Mahavira as a disciple who wandered around with him for many years. The stories present Makkhali in a poor light, as a ludicrous figure who constantly gets beaten up, far inferior to Mahivira in terms of knowledge.

A central Ajivika idea was that of *niyati* (fate), the principle that ultimately determined and controlled everything. Human effort was of no consequence in this strictly deterministic doctrine. *Karma* and transmigration existed, but human effort played no role in it, as the paths for souls over thousands of years had already been mapped out.

The Ajivikas had regular places (known as *sabhas*) where meetings were held and important ceremonies performed. This suggests that they had a corporate organization. They had canonical texts, and Buddhist and Jaina texts contain quotations or paraphrases from them. The Ajivikas practised severe asceticism, often eating very little food (though the Buddhists accused them of eating secretly). They seem to have practised ***ahimsa*** (non-violence), but apparently not as strictly as the Jainas, since the *Bhagavati Sutra* mentions that they were allowed to eat meat. They practised complete nudity. Jaina texts criticize them for not observing celibacy.

The Ajivika sect did not practice discrimination on the basis of caste or class, and its ascetics and laity came from various sections of society. Some, for instance, a certain relative of king Bimbisara, were Kshatriyas. The ascetic Panduputta was the son of a wagon-maker (considered low in the social hierarchy). Makkhali Gosala used the workshop of a woman potter Halahala as his headquarters at Shravasti. Prasenajit, king of Kosala, seems to have been a patron of the Ajivika order. Apart from royalty, urban and trading groups were prominent members of the laity.

The severe criticism of the Ajivikas in Buddhist and Jaina texts indicates that they were considered worthy rivals. In the *Anguttara Nikaya*, the Buddha describes Makkhali Gosala as a foolish man who had, more than anyone else, brought grief and sorrow to gods and men. He is likened to a fisherman who casts his net at the mouth of a river to catch and destroy many fish. Clearly, the Buddhists considered his doctrine the worst and most dangerous of *samana* doctrines. Jaina texts too reflect bitter rivalry and conflict with the Ajivikas. The *Bhagavati Sutra* describes a violent quarrel between Makkhali Gosala and Mahavira, in which the former cursed the *tirthankara* and tried to destroy him with his great powers, of course unsuccessfully.

The Ajivika sect continued to be influential during later centuries as well. The *Mahavamsa* suggests that its influence had spread as far south as Sri Lanka. The *Divyavadana* tells the story of an Ajivika fortune-teller in the Maurya king Bindusara's court, who prophesied the future greatness of Ashoka. Inscriptions in the Barabar hills record Ashoka's dedication of some caves to Ajivika ascetics. In the nearby Nagarjuni hills, inscriptions record the dedication of three caves to them by Ashoka's successor, Dasharatha. Ashoka's seventh pillar edict urges officers known as the *dhamma-mahamatas* to busy themselves with the affairs of sects, including the Ajivikas. The Maurya period may have been the heyday of the Ajivika sect, but references to it continue in various sources till the early medieval period.

Early Buddhism

The life of the Buddha

In the Pali canon, the Buddha is presented as a man, but an extraordinary one, whose body bore the 32 signs of a *mahapurusha* (great man). He is the Tathagata, one who has come thus (*tatha*) and gone (*gata*) thus, and has liberated himself from the cycle of rebirth. As mentioned in the beginning of this chapter, the dates of the Buddha's life are a subject of debate. Some elements of his hagiography (sacred biography) are contained in the *Sutta* and *Vinaya Pitakas*, but more detailed and connected accounts are given in later texts such as the *Lalitavistara*, *Mahavastu*, *Buddhacharita*, and *Nidanakatha*—all of which belong to the early centuries CE. It is difficult to extract a historical life-story out of the hagiographies because they have moulded the Buddha's life into a narrative aimed at conveying a series of significant meanings to his followers, designed to have a powerful impact. While some of the episodes may have had a historical basis, others are legendary, and still others may be of a semi-historical and semi-legendary nature.

The Buddha was born as Siddhartha, son of Suddhodana, chief of the Sakya clan, who ruled from Kapilavastu. His mother Maya gave birth to him in a grove at Lumbini, while travelling towards her parents' home, and died within a few days. The story goes that soon after he was born, certain Brahmanas saw the 32 marks of a great man on his body. According to Buddhist tradition, a *mahapurusha* can be of two kinds—a world victor or world renouncer. Suddhodana did not want his son to turn his back on the world and hence took great pains to shield him from its sorrows, bringing him up in a highly artificial atmosphere, surrounded by luxury and pleasant things. Siddhartha married a young woman named Yashodhara and they had a son named Rahula.

The hagiography tells us that when he was 29 years old, Siddhartha saw four things that shattered his composure—an old man, a sick man, a corpse, and a renunciant. The first three scenes brought home to him the harsh realities and inevitabilities of old age, sickness, and death, while the fourth pointed to the way of dealing with these inevitabilities. Siddhartha left his home and family and wandered around for six years, seeking the truth. He attached himself to teachers, but was not satisfied by their instruction. Accompanied by five wandering ascetics, he practised severe austerities until his body was emaciated. He then realized that he must nourish his body and try to attain peace of mind. His companions abandoned him, thinking he had compromised his ascetism. A young woman named Sujata offered him a bowl of milk-rice. Nourished with food, he once again sat under the *pipal* tree, resolving not to get up until he had attained enlightenment. Some texts describe his rising to progressively higher and higher states of knowledge through meditation. Others describe how a wicked being, Mara, tried to tempt and taunt him out of his meditative state, all in vain. Siddhartha ultimately attained enlightenment and became known as the Buddha, the enlightened one.

He sat for seven weeks near this spot, tempted to keep his extraordinary experience to himself. According to Buddhist tradition, the god Brahma had to implore him three times to go forth and spread his insight. The Buddha gave his first sermon on deliverance from suffering to his five former companions in a deer park near Benaras. This event is known as ***dhammachakka-pavattana*** (turning the wheel of *dhamma*). His first five disciples soon themselves realized the truth and became *arhats*. The Buddha wandered about teaching his doctrine for over four decades. He established an order of monks and nuns known as the *sangha*. He died at the age of 80 at Kusinara (identified with modern Kasia).

The Buddha's teachings

Were Buddhism and Jainism philosophical systems or religions? While the term 'religion' can be used retrospectively to refer to them, they were—at least to start off with—not religions in the sense in which the term is often used and understood. They were a path, a way of life that was believed to have the potential to transform a person. The fact that this path was linked to salvation (defined as deliverance from the cycle of birth, death, and rebirth) makes it more than the usual philosophy.

The Buddha addressed his teaching to the monastic order as well as the laity, and there were differences and overlaps between the teachings directed to the two audiences (see Gethin, 1998; Harvey, [1990] 2012). The core of his doctrine is expressed in the *Ariya-sachchani* (**Four Noble Truths**): there is suffering (*dukkha*); it has a cause (*samudaya*); it can be removed (*nirodha*); and the way to achieve this is following the *Atthanga-magga* (**Eight-fold Path**). This path consists of a number of interconnected activities related to knowledge, conduct, and meditative practices. It consists of right view, intention, speech, action, livelihood, effort, mindfulness, and concentration. Meditation is very important in Buddhism and is the key to achieving mental calm and insight. However, a detailed treatment of meditative techniques appears in later Buddhist texts. The path taught by the Buddha is often referred to as the Middle Path—one between extreme indulgence and extreme asceticism.

Dukkha and its extinction are central to the Buddha's doctrine. The Buddha taught that everything is suffering (*sabbam dukkham*). This can be seen as either an extremely pessimistic or an extremely realistic teaching. Suffering refers not only to the actual pain and sorrow experienced by an individual, but also to the potential to experience these

PRIMARY SOURCES | **The analogy of the raft**

In the *Majjhima Nikaya* (1.134–35), the Buddha uses the analogy of the raft to explain that the *dhamma* he taught was a means to attaining an end. Once this end had been achieved, there was no point clinging to it:

It is as if there were a man who had set out on a long journey. He might see a great river in flood, the near shore fearful and dangerous, the far shore safe and free of danger, but there might be no ferry or bridge for crossing from one side to the other. And this man might think, 'This is a great river in flood. The near shore is fearful and dangerous; the far shore safe and free of danger, but there is no ferry or bridge to cross from one side to the other. What if I were to gather together grass, sticks, branches, and foliage and bind together a raft, and then using that raft, striving with my hands and feet, safely cross over to the further shore?' Thereupon that man might gather together grass, sticks, branches, and foliage and bind together a raft, and then using that raft, striving with his hands and feet, he might safely cross over to the further shore. Once he had crossed over, it might occur to him, 'This raft is very useful to me. Using this raft, striving with my hands and feet, I have safely crossed over to the further shore. What if I were to now lift it on to my head or raise it on my back and set off as I pleased?' What do you think of this, monks? If the man did this with the raft, would he be doing what is appropriate?

'Not at all, lord.'

So what might this man do with the raft in order to do what is appropriate? In this case once he had crossed over, it might occur to him, 'This raft is very useful to me. Using this raft, striving with my hands and feet, I have safely crossed over to the further shore. What if I were now to beach this raft on the shore or sink it in the water and go on my way as I pleased?' The man who did this with the raft would be doing what is appropriate. Even so, monks, as being like a raft, I have taught you how *dhamma* is for the purpose of crossing over, and not for the purpose of holding on to. Those who understand the similarity to a raft will let go even of the teachings and practices (*dhamma*), let alone what are not the teachings and practices (*adhamma*).

Source Bhikkhu Nanamoli and Bhikkhu Bodhi, cited in Gethin, 1998: 71–72

things. States of happiness or pleasure are unstable and temporary, as they are dependent on the gratification of the senses through certain objects or experiences. The reasons for suffering include human propensities such as desire, attachment, greed, pride, aversion, and ignorance. Desire (*trishna*) is central to the cause and removal of suffering.

All this is connected with another aspect of existence emphasized in the Buddha's teaching—impermanence (*anichcha*). Impermanence has many facets. In relation to an individual's life, there is no being or power in the universe that can prevent old age, sickness, and death. At a more basic level, what we think of as the 'I' or 'me' is actually an ever-changing compound of a succession of instants of experiences and consciousness. The simile of the river helps explain this—the river seems the same, but the drops of water that constitute it are changing every instant. A later text, the *Milindapanha*, describes the name of a person as a convenient label for a complex, connected cluster of ever-changing elements, similar to a chariot, which consists of many different parts such as pole, axle, frame, and wheels. The idea of a permanent, unchanging 'I' or 'me' is thus the result of misperception and ignorance.

The emphasis on impermanence involved the rejection of any unchanging, permanent, eternal elements or essences such as the *atman*. The elements of conscious existence were divided into the two broad categories of *nama* (mind, the mental factor) and *rupa* (form, body, the physical factor). The former was further sub-divided into four—*vedana* (feelings) arising out of contact with objects of the senses; *sanna* (perception); the *sankharas* (a complex group including knowledge arising out of feeling and perception, and *chetana*—will); and *vinnana* (cognition or conscious awareness). These four elements of *nama*, along with *rupa*, constituted the *panchakhanda* (five aggregates). These mental and physical states together make up what we think of as 'I' or 'me'.

Another important aspect of the Buddha's teaching was ***patichcha-samuppada***—the law of dependent origination. This was both an explanation of all phenomena as well as an explanation of *dukkha*. The elements of this law were presented as a wheel consisting of 12 *nidanas*, one leading to the next: ignorance (*avijja*), formations (*sankhara*), consciousness (*vinnana*), mind and body (*nama-rupa*), the six senses (*salayatana*), sense contact (*phassa*), feeling (*vedana*), craving (*tanha*), attachment (*upadana*), becoming (*bhava*), birth (*jati*), and old age and death (*jara-marana*). The *nidanas* were later divided into three groups pertaining to the past, present, and future lives, and *patichcha-samuppada* therefore also became an explanation of how the origins of rebirth lay in ignorance.

The ultimate goal of the Buddha's teaching was the attainment of *nibbana*. This was not a place but an experience, and could be attained in this life. The Buddha is supposed to have experienced *nibbana*, as did some of his disciples. *Nibbana* literally means blowing out, dying out, or extinction—the dying out or extinction of desire, attachment, greed, hatred, ignorance, and the sense of I-ness. Other words such as *vimokha*, *vimutti*, and *arahatta* are sometimes also used. They all have connotations of freedom, self-mastery, and emancipation, and mean breaking out of the cycle of birth, death, and rebirth. *Nibbana* does not mean physical death. The term *parinibbana* (complete or final dying out) is used for the death of an enlightened being such as the Buddha.

The Buddha's teaching accepts the idea of transmigration (*samsara*) but rejects the idea of the *atman*. What then is it that transmigrates? One interpretation is that Buddhism teaches the transmigration of character or personality. Another possibility is that what is being suggested is the transmission of a life impulse, similar to the transmission of a flame from one candle to another. What the teaching suggests is that the elements of conscious existence do not disappear into thin air on death—they reappear in some other combination and form in another time, at another place. The *Milindapanha* (1st century CE) gives an analogy which explains the whole thing rather well: Just as milk turns into curds, butter, and ghee, a being transmigrates, neither as the same, nor as another.

In the Buddhist universe, there are many worlds and many different kinds of beings, and one can be born as any one of them. The connection between different lives is established by *karma*. *Karma* refers to intentions which lead to actions of body, speech, or mind. Rebirth is governed by the cumulative results of the *karma* of a particular life. Ethics are important in Buddhism. The Buddha laid down an ethical code of conduct both for members of the monastic order and the laity. Monks and nuns were supposed to strictly avoid the following: destruction of life, taking what is not given (theft), sexual activity, lying, the use of intoxicants that cause heedlessness, eating after mid-day, attending entertainments, using perfumes and jewellery, using luxurious beds, and handling gold and silver (including money). The first five rules were supposed to apply to the laity as well, except that celibacy was replaced by chastity. Chastity was important and was defined not just with regard to sexual activity but also sexual desire and thoughts. It was part of the general emphasis on breaking away from desires and sensual pleasures.

The Buddhist emphasis on *ahimsa* involved a critique of Brahmanical animal sacrifices. Monks and nuns were not to kill animals. They were not to drink water in which small creatures lived. However, the emphasis on *ahimsa* did not necessarily entail vegetarianism and monks were not forbidden from eating meat. (See Sahni, 2008 for a discussion of Buddhist environmental ethics.) The Buddha's own last meal—offered to him by a blacksmith named Chunda—is supposed to have included some kind of meat (*sukara-maddava*). The Buddha is said to have refused to make vegetarianism mandatory when urged to do so by his cousin Devadatta. Monks and nuns were to accept all food offered to them on their begging rounds, without showing any desire or preference. They could eat meat or fish given to them, provided certain conditions were met—they should not see, hear, or suspect that the animal in question was killed specifically for their eating. Refusing meat would also deprive the donor of the merit arising from the offering. There were, however, certain exceptions. Monastics could not accept meat that was raw or not thoroughly cooked. The flesh of a human, elephant, snake, dog, horse, lion, tiger, leopard, hyena, or bear was not to be eaten under any circumstances. Ethics were important in Buddhism. But righteous actions could get a person only so far and no further; they were necessary but insufficient conditions for attaining *nibbana*. The ultimate state lay beyond ordinary experiences and distinctions, including those of the moral and immoral.

Buddhism is often seen as an extremely rational doctrine. It must be noted, however, that the Buddha is presented as the fount of knowledge, and the possibility of others equalling him is considered remote, if not impossible. He sometimes performs miracles, usually to convince particularly stubborn adversaries. Gods and heavens exist in Buddhism. Brahma and Sakka (Indra) appear at various junctures, ever reverential towards the Buddha. But the gods cannot help humans in attaining *nibbana*. Only following the path laid down by the Buddha can lead to this goal.

The Buddhist *sangha* and the laity

The monastic order of monks, and ultimately also of nuns, was created within the Buddha's lifetime. Its establishment meant that followers of the Buddha carved out a distinct identity for themselves within the larger community of renunciants. The Buddhist *sangha* became a core institution and a major factor in the dissemination of the Buddha's doctrine. The *Vinaya Pitaka* gives an account (not one that we would consider strictly historical) of the establishment of the *sangha* and the rules that governed it. As mentioned earlier, the order may have been modelled on the *sangha* polities.

The *Vinaya Pitaka* has two main sections—the *Sutta Vibhanga* and *Khandaka*—and an appendix known as the *Parivara*. The *Sutta Vibhanga* contains the *Patimokkha*, a set of monastic rules, 227 for monks and 311 for nuns. The rules are framed by a narrative indicating when and why a particular rule was promulgated by the Buddha and are accompanied by a commentary. The *Patimokkha* was recited by congregations of monks in the fortnightly *uposatha* ceremony held on the full moon and new moon days. The *Khandaka* consists of the *Mahavagga* and *Chullavagga*, which include monastic rules and accounts of episodes in the Buddha's life, the founding of the order of nuns, and the two councils. The *Vinaya* rules deal with all kinds of details in the life of individual monks and nuns—what and how they should eat, walk, talk, what they should wear, and how they should behave. There are also rules governing the corporate life of the *sangha*, including, for instance, ways in which disputes were to be settled. Taken together, these rules aimed at regulating the conduct of a monk/nun, preserving the unity and integrity of the *sangha* as a corporate body, and defining the relations between the *sangha* and laity.

Sukumar Dutt ([1924] 1984) argued that in the early days of the Buddhist *sangha*, monks were wanderers, moving from place to place, and that they gradually settled down at a later stage. The *Vinaya Pitaka* in fact gives this impression. Dutt traced the origin of the settling down to the institution of the monsoon retreat (*vassavasa*). This custom was followed by the Jainas and other ascetic orders as well. It meant that monks were to stay in one place and not move around during the rainy season. The temporary retreats of monks may have gradually become the nucleus of more permanent monastic establishments known as *viharas*. However, Mohan Wijayaratne (1990) argues that the life of members of the Buddhist *sangha* was partly itinerant and partly sedentary right from the beginning. Even during the lifetime of the Buddha, wealthy and generous lay followers made gifts of land to the order and built monasteries. Permanent monastic establishments (known as *vihara*s or *aramas*) must have emerged fairly early, and rules and regulations to govern these communities would have become a necessity.

The *pravrajya* ceremony marked a person's going forth from home into homelessness and his/her becoming a novice under a preceptor. It involved shaving the head and donning ochre robes. The novice recited the formula of taking refuge in the Buddha, *dhamma*, and *sangha*, and then took the 10 vows (these were listed earlier). The *upasampada* was the ordination ceremony when the novice became a full-fledged member of the monastic community. The eight personal possessions allowed to a monk comprised three robes, an alms bowl, razor, needle, belt, and water strainer.

Senior monks held authority within a monastic community. Members of the *sangha* living in a locality were supposed to gather every fortnight on the new moon and full moon (*uposatha*) days to recite the *Patimokkha* rules and confess if they had broken any.

The *Patimokkha* of the *Vinaya Pitaka* identifies more and less serious breaches of monastic discipline. There are a number of other offences which merit consequences ranging from confession of guilt to expulsion. The four most serious offences (known as *parajika*, i.e., defeat) involving expulsion from the *sangha* were: sexual intercourse, taking what is not given, killing someone, and making false claims of spiritual attainment.

The Buddha's followers had a choice—to join the *sangha* or remain outside it. The *sangha* and laity were closely connected. Members of the *sangha* taught the *dhamma* to the laity and were supposed to be examples of righteous living. The monastic community depended on the laity for food and other forms of patronage. For the laity, *dana* (giving) was one of the activities that was supposed to lead to the accumulation of *punya* (merit). It was considered important and meritorious because it involved generosity and letting go of attachment to material things. Interaction between monks and the laity took place in several different contexts. The most frequent one was when monks went to households on their begging rounds for food. If invited, monks were expected to give discourses to the laity and attend important functions in their lives. Permanent monastic establishments must have strengthened the bonds between them. However, their interactions were not supposed to be too close and a certain distance always had to be maintained.

According to tradition, the first lay followers of the Buddha were two merchants, Tapassu and Bhallika. Thereafter, the ranks of the laity expanded swiftly. The laity included male followers (***upasaka*s**) and female followers (***upasika*s**). An *upasaka/upasika* was a person who had declared that he/she had taken refuge in the Buddha, *dhamma*, and *sangha*, but who had not taken monastic vows. For the laity, good conduct consisted in taking the five vows—not to harm living things, not to take that which has not been given, to avoid sexual misconduct, not to indulge in false speech, and not to consume intoxicants. On certain occasions such as the full moon days, or for longer periods of time, a layperson could move a step further by replacing the vow of avoiding sexual misconduct with sexual abstinence, and by taking the additional vows of not eating after mid-day, not attending entertainments, not using jewellery or perfumes, and not using luxurious beds. By following these modified eight vows, the layperson narrowed the gap between herself and the monastic discipline. Buddhist texts give several instances of learned lay-persons. There are also a few instances of a layperson (e.g., the Buddha's father) becoming an ***arhat*** without joining the *sangha*, on simply hearing the doctrine.

The duties for the laity were laid down in the *Sigalavada Sutta*. This emphasized the importance of fulfilling the duties that are implied in certain key reciprocal social relationships—between parents and children, teachers and pupils, husbands and wives, friends and companions, masters and servants and slaves, and *shramanas* and Brahmanas. A man's duties towards his parents, wife, and children are emphasized in the *Mahamangala Sutta* in the *Samyutta Nikaya*. This asserts that a man must be faithful to his wife, must respect her, and not make her unhappy. The Buddha's discourse to Anathapindika's difficult daughter-in-law, recounted in the *Anguttara Nikaya*, describes what was considered appropriate and inappropriate behaviour in a wife.

For later centuries, apart from textual evidence, there is archaeological and epigraphic evidence for the history of the *sangha* and laity. In course of time, pilgrimage to stupas and other sacred places also brought the laity into contact with the *sangha*. A problem is that much more is known about the *sangha* of monks (*bhikkhu sangha*) than about the *sangha* of nuns (*bhikkhuni sangha*).

The social implications of the Buddha's teachings

The Buddha has often been projected as a social reformer, even as a revolutionary, who stood against social discrimination and favoured equality for all. A close reading of the Pali texts reveals a different, more complex picture. The Buddha's doctrine was certainly more socially inclusive than the Brahmanical tradition, but it did not aim at abolishing social differences. Buddhist texts reveal biases of their own and these biases were reflected even in the supposedly a-social world of the *sangha*. The key point is that the

Buddha and Mahavira saw all social relationships as fetters and a source of suffering. It was only by breaking away from these fetters that a person could attain liberation (see Upinder Singh, 2021: 22–32).

The creation of the monastic order had the potential for creating great social upheaval by providing a haven for social dropouts. However, the Buddhist tradition reflects a desire to maintain the status quo and specifies a number of conditions for entry. For instance, soldiers could not join without the permission of the king, slaves could not join until freed by their masters, and debtors could not join until they had paid off their debts.

The Buddhist tradition considered *varna* a man-made ordering, unlike the divine sanction conferred on it by the Brahmanical tradition. In the *Anguttara Nikaya*, the Buddha describes a dream in which four birds of different *varnas* (kinds, colours) came from the four directions and sat at his feet. Similarly, he asserted, monks from the four *varnas*—Khattiya, Brahmana, Vessa, and Sudda—came within his fold. The same text declares that when a person joins the *sangha*, he becomes without *varna* (*vevanniyanti*).

Varna and *jati* were supposed to be irrelevant for aspirants to the *sangha*. However, a close look at its actual composition indicates a significant proportion of upper class members (Uma Chakravarti, 1987: 124–31). A large section of the monks were Brahmanas or Kshatriyas (including, interestingly, Kshatriyas from the *ganas*) or belonged to families enjoying a high status (*uchcha kulas*). Members who came from other backgrounds (*gahapatis*, *setthis*, members of *nicha kulas*) were comparatively few. Brahmanas (e.g., Sariputta, Mahamoggallana, and Mahakassapa) figure prominently among the famous *bhikkhus*. The prominent Kshatriya monks included the Buddha himself and others such as Ananda and Aniruddha. On the other hand, the distinguished monk Upali was originally a barber of the Sakyas.

The Pali canon reverses the Brahmanical order of rank and places the Kshatriya higher than the Brahmana. While the Buddha is frequently portrayed as rejecting the Brahmanical claim to innate superiority, the term 'Brahmana' is used in two senses in Buddhist texts. On the one hand, it is used in the conventional sense as a social category; on the other, it is also used as an ideal category to refer to a wise person who led an exemplary life. In places, the Buddha himself is addressed as 'Brahmana'. The *Sonadanda Sutta* asserts that Brahmanahood was not a matter of birth—a true Brahmana was not one who muttered Vedic verses, but one who had true knowledge. When it came to a description of real Brahmanas, however, the Buddhist texts did not restrain their criticism. And when wealthy, influential Brahmanas with substantial followings of their own accepted the Buddha's teaching, the Pali texts make a rather ostentatious display of such episodes, as they added to the *sangha*'s prestige.

How do we explain the large-scale participation of Brahmanas as monks and lay-followers of the Buddha, especially in view of his criticism of Brahmanical ritual and claims to social pre-eminence? It is possible that the teaching struck a chord because there was debate and discussion of such issues within the Brahmana intelligentsia itself. Further, not all Brahmanas were ritual specialists, and they would therefore not have been offended by the critique of sacrifice. At the same time, Brahmanas joining the *sangha* were evidently looked upon with disapproval by other Brahmanas. This is evident from the response of Vasettha and Bharadvaja to the Buddha's question of how members of the Brahmana community had reacted to their joining the order, narrated in the *Agganna Sutta*.

The fact that *bhikkhus* were supposed to accept food from everyone, regardless of class or caste, suggests a deliberate disregard for current social practices. The Buddha himself did not maintain any restrictions about accepting food. He enjoyed the hospitality of wealthy *gahapatis* and *setthis*, but he also dined with people lower in the social hierarchy. His last meal is supposed to have been at the home of a blacksmith named Chunda.

However, a close reading of the Pali texts shows that they too had a notion of high and low status. The *Vinaya Pitaka* talks about high and low *sippas* (here the word means occupation, not craft). The high *sippas* included money changing, accounting, and

PRIMARY SOURCES | The *Ambattha Sutta*

The Buddha was once on a tour through Kosala country, accompanied by 500 monks. They arrived at a Brahmana village called Ichchanakala and set up camp in the nearby woods. A Brahmana named Pokkharasadi lived in the village on *brahmadeya* land granted to him by Prasenajit. He told his pupil Ambattha to visit the Buddha and see if he bore the 32 bodily signs of a great man. Ambattha went to meet the monks; he wasn't courteous enough, fidgeted about, and was admonished by the Buddha for doing so. Ambattha asserted that the Brahmanas were superior to everyone else. He scoffed at the Buddha's descent and said that the Sakyas were lowly people. As proof, he reported that he had gone to Kapilavastu and had not been properly honoured by the Sakya assembly; in fact its members had made fun of him.

This gave the Buddha an opening to discuss this important issue. He asked Ambattha which family he belonged to, and Ambattha replied that he belonged to the Kanhayana *gotra*.

The Buddha then narrated the following account of the origin of the Sakyas and Kanhayanas: Long ago, a king named Okkaka, wanting to divert the succession in favour of a son born of his favourite queen, banished his older children. They went to the Himalayas and lived on the borders of a lake and married their sisters in order to preserve the purity of their line. This was the origin of the Sakyas. Now king Okkaka had a slave girl named Disa, who gave birth to a baby. The Kanhayanas were the descendants of this child. The Buddha had driven home the point that his lineage was superior to that of Ambattha, and the latter was forced to acknowledge that this was so.

The Buddha then softened the blow by pointing out that Kanha, Ambattha's ancestor, was a great sage. He went on to quote a supposed verse of Sanatkumara (according to legend, one of the five mind-born sons of god Brahma):

> The Kshatriya is the best of those among the fold who put their trust in lineage.
>
> But he who is perfect in wisdom and righteousness, he is the best among gods and men.

The Buddha went on to explain:

> In the supreme perfection in wisdom and righteousness, Ambattha, there is no reference to the question either of birth or of lineage or of pride which says, 'You are held as worthy as I am,' or 'You are not held as worthy as I am.' It is where the talk is of marrying or giving in marriage that reference is made to such things as that. For whosoever, Ambattha, are in bondage to the notions of birth or of lineage, or to the pride of social position, or of connection by marriage, they are far from the best wisdom and righteousness. It is only by having got rid of all such bondage that one can realize for himself that supreme perfection in wisdom and conduct.

The Buddha told Ambattha that howsoever great the Brahmana Pokkharasadi might think himself to be, he was nothing before king Prasenajit who had given him his land. While Brahmanas chanted and memorized verses composed by the *rishis*, their opulent lifestyle was in stark contrast to that of the ancient sages. Ambattha saw the 32 bodily signs of a great man on the Buddha and reported this to Pokkharasadi. Pokkharasadi decided to go see for himself. He too saw the signs and invited the Buddha and his entourage for a meal. On that occasion, the Buddha delivered a discourse that so impressed Pokkharasadi that he declared himself, his family, and his disciples as the Buddha's followers.

Source Rhys Davids, 1899: 112–33

writing; the low ones included the professions of the leather maker, reed worker, potter, tailor, painter, weaver, and barber. Farming, cattle rearing, and trade were considered high occupations. The Buddhist laity was not supposed to engage in trading in weapons, meat, intoxicants, or poisons.

Birth and family were important in worldly matters, but there is a parallel refrain that deeds were more important. In the *Samyutta Nikaya*, when asked about his origins by the Brahmana Sundarika, the Buddha replies, 'Do not ask of the origin (*jati*), ask of the behaviour. Just as fire can be born out of any wood, so can a saint be born in a *kula* of low status.' To this can be added the statement that a person does not become a Brahmana by birth, but by deed. Birth in a high or low family is often explained as the result of actions in previous lives, but the potential for achieving *nibbana* is there in all. The Buddhist position on *varna* and birth emerges clearly in many places, especially in the *Ambattha Sutta* in the *Digha Nikaya*: The Kshatriya is considered superior to the Brahmana when it comes to worldly social status, but the one who has attained *nibbana* is superior to all. But the assertion that *nibbana* was open to all, irrespective of birth and status, was a powerful statement for the time.

The Buddha's *dhamma* must have appealed to the laity because it offered them a coherent code of conduct, one that was in consonance with the times. The positive outlook on emergent affluent groups acknowledged their status and importance. The laity, especially those who gave lavish gifts, included Brahmanas, Kshatriyas, *gahapati*s, members of the so-called *uchcha kula*s and *nicha kula*s. The Kshatriya patrons include powerful kings such as Bimbisara, Ajatashatru, and Prasenajit. Buddhist texts assigned the *gahapati* an especially high social standing. *Gahapati*s were also among the most important lay supporters of the *sangha*. Their importance was acknowledged by the fact that some of them are described as being visited on their deathbed by the Buddha or by other prominent monks, an honour generally reserved for members of the *sangha*.

Buddhism and women

Two important features of early Buddhism were the assertion that the highest goal—*nibbana*—was possible for women, and the creation of a *bhikkhuni sangha*. On the other hand, Buddhist texts reflect stereotyped ideals of the submissive and obedient woman, whose life was supposed to revolve around her husband and sons. They also contain many negative images of women as temptresses and creatures of passion. Comparisons with poisonous black snakes and fire (the message is: stay away from them) are not surprising in a tradition that set such store on celibacy and which therefore perceived women as a threat. Just as monks were warned against women, nuns were warned against men.

Buddhist tradition suggests that the Buddha was not initially keen to establish a *bhikkhuni sangha* but ultimately gave in to the persistent pressure of his disciple Ananda and his aunt and foster-mother Mahapajapati Gotami. The *Vinaya Pitaka* describes him as making the gloomy prediction that the doctrine would decline in 500 instead of 1,000 years because women had been admitted into the *sangha*.

The *sangha* was not open to pregnant women, mothers of unweaned children, rebellious women who associated with young men, and those who did not have their parents' or husbands' permission to join. The rules for nuns were basically the same as those for monks, but there were more rules. The Buddha is also described as having laid down eight special rules subordinating the order of nuns to that of monks. However, it has been suggested that this was a later interpolation. While women could attain salvation, their capability for attaining Buddhahood directly (without first being born as a man) was not initially accepted.

Buddhist texts contain several references to learned nuns. The *Samyutta Nikaya* refers to Khema, whose discourse to king Pasenadi so impressed him that he stood up and bowed before her when she had finished. The *Anguttara Nikaya* tells us that when the Buddha heard the answers Dhammadinna Theri had given to questions posed by

PRIMARY SOURCES | Patachara's song

Patachara was born in a Shravasti banker's family. She got married and had two children, both of whom died. Thereafter, she became a wanderer and joined the *sangha*. The first two verses of her song express her longing for *nibbana*, building up to a description of the moment she experienced it.

When they plough their fields
and sow seeds in the earth,
when they care for their wives
and children,
young Brahmanas find riches.

But I've done everything right
and followed the rule of my teacher.
I'm not lazy or proud
Why haven't I found peace?

Bathing my feet
I watched the bathwater
spill down the slope.

I concentrated my mind
the way you train a good horse.

Then I took a lamp
and went into my cell,
checked the bed,
and sat down on it.
I took a needle
and pushed the wick down.

When the lamp went out
my mind was freed.

Source Murcott, 1991: 33–34

FURTHER DISCUSSION | **The eight conditions imposed on nuns**

According to the *Vinaya Pitaka*, nuns who entered the Buddhist order were supposed to observe 'eight important conditions' for their entire life:

1. A nun, even if ordained for a hundred years, must greet a monk with deference, even if he has been ordained that very day. She must rise up from her seat, salute him with joined hands, and show him respect.
2. A nun must not spend the monsoon retreat in a district where there is no monk.
3. Every fortnight, a nun is to ask the monks two things—the date of the *uposatha* ceremony and to preach the doctrine.
4. At the end of the monsoon retreat, a nun must address the 'triple invitation' to both the order of monks and the order of nuns. She must ask whether anyone has seen, heard, or suspected anything against her.
5. A nun who has committed a serious offence must undergo the *manatta* discipline (a sort of temporary probation) before both orders.
6. It is only after a postulant has followed the six precepts (the five lay vows plus the additional vow of not eating after noon) for two years that she could seek ordination from both orders. (Monks could be ordained at any time they were ready, provided they were at least 20 years old.)
7. A nun is under no circumstances to revile or abuse a monk.
8. Monks can give admonition and advice to nuns, but nuns cannot give either of these to monks.

Source Wijayaratne, 1990: 135–36, 159–60

the laywoman Visakha, he said, 'Visakha, the nun Dhammadinna is truly wise, she is very learned; if you had put these questions to me, I would have given you the same answers.'

The *Therigatha* (Verses of Elder Nuns) is a collection of 73 poems consisting of 522 verses, supposed to have been composed by 72 nuns who had reached a high level of spiritual attainment. Many of these nuns are described as possessing *tevijja* (the three kinds of knowlege), an attribute of *arhats*. Some of the poems express the nuns' experience of *nibbana*. They also tell of the experiences which preceded their joining the *sangha*. These range from unhappy marriages to tragedies such as the death of a child. One of the stories is that of Chanda, a young girl from a Brahmana family, who found herself destitute when her parents died in an epidemic. A nun named Patachara gave her some food to eat, taught her the doctrine, and initiated her into the order.

Monks and nuns were bound to have had some amount of interaction. In fact, nuns were not supposed to live too far away from monks during regular times as well as during the monsoon retreat. They had to consult the latter for the date of the *uposatha* ceremony. If a nun broke certain rules, she had to answer to a mixed gathering of monks and nuns. However, contact and interaction were carefully regulated and restricted. For instance, a monk was not supposed to be alone with a nun in a closed room, and was not allowed to preach to a woman in private without the presence of a third person who could understand what was being said. However, a monk could accompany a nun on a road that was considered dangerous.

A tradition's progressiveness has to be judged by the standards of its own time. By the standards of the 6th/5th century BCE, the Buddha opened up a significant space for women's spiritual aspirations. Similarly, compared to texts of other religious traditions, women are strikingly visible in Buddhist texts. In subsequent centuries, women—both *bhikkhunis* and *upasikas*—were very visible as donors at Buddhist *stupa*-monastery sites. Nevertheless, after its inception, the *bhikkhuni sangha* seems to be a shadowy entity in the available sources.

Can we talk of 'Buddhism' and 'Buddhists' in this early period? We can certainly talk of a Buddhist *sangha*, a monastic order which had a distinct identity of its own among renunciants and within society. But when it came to the laity, the Buddha basically offered a code of conduct. There were no specific outward markers of a follower of his teaching. There were no distinctive Buddhist rites of passage for the laity, and it can be inferred that people who were 'followers' of the Buddha continued their customary

PRIMARY SOURCES | **The seven kinds of wives**

The *Anguttara Nikaya* (3) tells the following story: One day, the Buddha visited the home of Anathapindika, the famous *gahapati* of Shravasti. He found the house very noisy. On making enquiries about the source of the noise, he was told it was Sujata, daughter-in-law of the house. She was rich and came from a wealthy family. She was wilful and unruly, and wouldn't listen to her husband, parents-in-law, nor anyone else. Anathapindika requested the Buddha to counsel her.

The Buddha told Sujata that there were seven kinds of wives, some approved of and others not so:

1. The *vadhaka* (slayer) wife, who is cruel, pitiless, murderous, who neglects her husband at night, passes her time with others, and is bought with money.
2. The *chorasama* (thief-like) wife, who takes the husband's money and longs to ruin and impoverish him.
3. The *ayyasama* (mistress-like) wife, who is lazy, fond of luxuries, expensive to maintain, loves to gossip, and talks in a loud, strident voice. She diminishes her husband's zeal and industry.
4. The *matusama* (mother-like) wife, who takes care of her husband and his property as would a mother her only son's.
5. The *bhaginisama* (sister-like) wife, who treats her husband with respect similar to that of a younger sister towards her older brother.
6. The companion-like wife, who is of good birth, faithful to her husband, and is filled with joy on meeting him, like one meeting a friend after a long time.
7. The *dasisama* (slave-like) wife, who is calm, patient, and obedient, and meekly accepts her husband's beating.

The first three types of wives are said to go to hell after they die, while the other four go to heaven. After listening to this discourse, Sujata decided to become a slave-like wife.

Whether this incident actually happened or not is immaterial. It describes a range of various possible relationships between husband and wife. The fact that Sujata was not initially an ideal wife suggests that there may have been other women like her. The fact that she chooses the most abject, subordinate form of wifehood at the end perhaps reflects the kind of wife who was considered the best by the men who composed these texts. But it is interesting that other sorts of husband–wife relationships are actually envisaged.

Source Wagle, 1966: 91

life-cycle rituals, which for some, must have meant the Brahmanical rituals. This is why it is a bit of a misnomer to talk of a 'conversion' to Buddhism during this period. Becoming a lay follower of the Buddha simply involved a declaration of taking refuge in the Buddha, *dhamma*, and *sangha*, and trying to follow the teaching prescribed for the householder.

Early Jainism

The Jaina *tirthankaras*, Vardhamana Mahavira

The Jaina doctrine is much older than the Buddhist one, but it is difficult to say precisely how old it is. The Buddha and Mahavira were contemporaries and there are some similarities between their teachings, for instance in their rejection of the authority of the Veda, their non-theistic doctrine, emphasis on renunciation and human effort as a means to attaining salvation, and establishment of a monastic order for men and women. However, there are also several marked differences in their philosophical ideas.

The word Jaina means follower of a *jina*, which means victor, a person who has attained infinite knowledge and teaches others how to attain ***moksha***, i.e., liberation from the cycle of rebirth. *Tirthankara* is another word for *jina* and means 'ford builder,' i.e., one who builds fords that help people across the ocean of suffering. The Jaina conception of time consists of an endless sequence of half-cycles called *utsarpinis* and *avasarpinis* (respectively progressive and regressive in terms of degrees of happiness), lasting vast spans of time, and further divided into six stages known as *kalas*. There are supposed to be 24 *tirthankaras* in each half-cycle of time. In our current half-cycle, which is an *avasarpini*, i.e., a period of regressive happiness, the first *tirthankara* was Rishabhadeva. The historicity of all the *tirthankaras* is not easy to ascertain. Neminatha, the 22nd one, may have belonged to the Saurashtra region of Gujarat. The 23rd was Parshvanatha, who lived in Benaras. Vardhamana was the 24th *tirthankara* and came to be known as Mahavira (great hero). All the *jinas* are supposed to have taught the same doctrine.

The *jina* is considered a human being endowed with superhuman insight and knowledge. According to Jaina tradition, he is born with certain unusual characteristics that mark him out for his future destiny. For instance, he has an adamantine body, one that is extremely hard and brilliant, like a diamond. He possesses *avadhijnana*—super-human cognition or psychic power, through which he can perceive distant objects and forsee future events.

At some point in its early history, perhaps in around 300 CE, the Jaina *sangha* came to be divided into two sects—the Digambara (sky-clad) and the Shvetambara (white-clad) sects. There are two different hagiographies of Vardhamana Mahavira—a Digambara and a Shvetambara version, which agree on some points, but disagree on others. Extracting a historical biography of Mahavira out of the hagiographical material is as difficult as in the case of the Buddha.

Vardhamana, the future Mahavira, was born in *c.* 599 BCE at Kundagrama, a city near Vaishali, capital of Videha. Like the Buddha, Mahavira had an aristocratic Kshatriya background. His father Siddhartha was chief of the Jnatri clan, his mother Trishala the Videha king's sister. The Kshatriya bias of the Jaina tradition is stronger than its Buddhist counterpart. According to Shvetambara tradition, Vardhamana was conceived by a Brahmana named Rishabhadatta in the womb of his wife Devananda, but Shakra (Indra) transferred the embryo to the womb of Trishala because a Brahmana woman or one from a low family was not worthy of giving birth to the future *tirthankara*.

Vardhamana is described as displaying extraordinary concern for *ahimsa* (non-injury) even before birth. He lay absolutely still in Trishala's womb so as not to cause her discomfort, and moved slightly to reassure her when he realized through his super-human powers that she feared him dead. According to Shvetambara tradition, having realized how easy it was to cause parents pain and anxiety, Vardhamana vowed there and then not to renounce the world as long as his parents were alive.

The *Acharanga Sutra* describes Vardhamana's parents as followers of the *jina* Parshvanatha. Shvetambara tradition states that Vardhamana entered the householder stage by marrying Yashoda and had a daughter named Priyadarshana. According to Digambara tradition, he never got married. Vardhamana is supposed to have renounced the world when he was 30 years old. The Shvetambara hagiography asserts that he did so after his parents' death. Digambara tradition tells us that he did so while his parents were alive, after taking their permission.

Digambara and Shvetambara traditions both describe Vardhamana as wandering about for about 12 years, practising severe austerities, including meditation and fasting. He is supposed to have attained *kevalajnana* (infinite knowledge, omniscience) outside the town of Jrimbhikagrama, on the banks of the Rijupalika river, in the field of a householder named Samaga.

According to Digambara tradition, on attaining enlightenment, Mahavira was freed from the defects of ordinary human existence such as hunger, thirst, sleep, fear, and disease. He no longer engaged in mundane activities and sat fixed and omniscient in the lotus posture in an assembly hall created by the gods. A divine sound (*divyadhvani*) emanated from his body, and the gods, demi-gods, humans, and animals listened carefully to it. The task of disseminating the teaching was that of the *ganadharas* (chief disciples), the first of whom were the Brahmana Indrabhuti Gautama and his two brothers, who also became the first members of the *sangha*. The number of *ganadharas* soon expanded to 11, all of them Brahmanas. Thus the *tirthankara* created the order of monks, nuns, and laity indirectly. Shvetambara tradition, on the other hand, describes Mahavira as travelling widely and teaching his doctrine himself. Both traditions agree that he died at Papa, i.e., in Pava (identified with modern Pavapuri near Patna) at the age of 72 and became a *siddha*—fully liberated and forever free of embodiment. The traditional date of his passing away is 527 BCE, which marks the beginning of the Vira-nirvana era.

The Jaina understanding of reality

The Jaina criticism of other philosophical systems is that their pronouncements about reality—for instance, on whether reality is eternal or non-eternal, changing or unchanging—represent a single (*ekanta*), partial, and extreme view of things. The views of other schools are not condemned as absolutely invalid but as partially true statements (*nayas*), which cannot lay claim to absolute validity. Jaina doctrine insists that reality is manifold (*anekanta*) (see Jaini, [1979] 2001 and Dundas, 1992 for details of Jaina doctrines). Everything that exists (*sat*, i.e., being) has three aspects—substance (*dravya*), quality (*guna*), and mode (*paryaya*). The Jaina doctrine of ***anekantavada*** (doctrine of the manifold nature of reality) holds that reality is very complex and has multiple aspects.

The doctrines of *anekantavada* and ***syadavada*** (the doctrine of maybe) emphasize the relativity of all knowledge. According to *syadavada*, every judgement we make is relative to the particular aspect of the object we are judging and the point of view from which we judge it. No judgement is true without qualification. The essential point behind *syadavada* and *anekantavada* is that reality cannot be grasped in its entirety and complexity. All that is possible are a number of partially true statements about it. Every statement about reality should be prefixed with the word *syat* ('maybe', or more appropriately in this context, 'in some respect'). Another word that is added to all such statements is *eva* (in fact). Together, the words *syat* and *eva*, added to all statements, emphasize that such statements refer only to a particular aspect of reality from a particular perspective. So, with the addition of '*syat eva*', the statement that the ***jiva*** (soul) is eternal would be accepted as partially true from a certain point of view. But the statement that the *jiva* is not eternal, preceded with the words *syat eva*, would also be accepted as partially true from another point of view. Every statement about any aspect of reality is conditional on four factors—the specific being (*sva-dravya*), specific location (*sva-kshetra*), specific time (*sva-kala*), and the specific state (*sva-bhava*) of the thing that is being spoken of. These ideas are further developed to construct the theory of *sapta-bhangi-naya* (the seven-fold *nayas*).

It has been argued that the Jainas practised something that can be described as intellectual non-violence. The basic argument is as follows: Jaina doctrine recognizes that there are many different perspectives on truth; this translates into toleration and an acceptance of other religious viewpoints. This tolerance is rooted in the emphasis on *ahimsa*: just as all living beings are treated with respect, all perspectives must be treated with respect. According to John Cort (2000), this is not the case. Jaina texts accept that other points of view on the way to *moksha* are partially correct, but for the most part, are incorrect. Only the Jaina doctrine, rooted in the omniscience of the *jinas*, is based on correct perception and correct knowledge.

Existent reality, as understood in Jainism, consists of three basic categories—sentient (i.e., that which has consciousness), material, and neither sentient nor material. The sentient category is represented by the *jiva* (variously translated as sentient essence, life monad, or soul). Matter is the second category and is made of aggregates of atoms (*pudgala*), which have form, colour, taste, and smell, and can be touched and felt. The third category is known as *arupi-ajiva*. It includes four substances (*dravya*)—space (*akasha*), the principle of motion (*dharma*), the principle of rest (*adharma*), and time (*kala*).

Jaina philosophy conceives of an infinite number of *jivas*. The *jiva* does not have a form of its own. In the way in which light from a lamp fills up a room, it acquires the size and form of the body it inhabits and becomes co-extensive with it. The *jiva* has three main qualities—consciousness (*chaitanya*), bliss (*sukha*), and energy (*virya*). Jaina doctrine holds that *jivas* transmigrate due to *karma*, but its ideas of transmigration and *karma* are unique. *Karma* is understood as consisting of material particles floating about in space. Karmic matter is of different kinds; some have a directly negative effect on the *jiva*, others do not. The major culprits are the *mohaniya* (delusion-causing) *karmas*. The *karma* particles obscure and obstruct the consciousness, bliss, and energy of the *jiva*, in the way in which dust mars the reflective power of a mirror. The *karma* particles are attracted towards the *jiva* due to its association with the passions, desire, and hatred. The state when the *karma* particles actually begin to flow towards the *jiva* to bind it is known as *asrava* (flow). A *jiva* associated with *karma* particles is considered to be a *jiva* in bondage (*bandha*).

Some *jivas* have an important quality known as *bhavyatva*—the capability of becoming free—that does not get affected or overwhelmed by the *karma* particles. By exertion and right knowledge, the influx of fresh *karma* can be stopped (*samvara*). The next stage is that of *nirjara* (wearing out). In successive stages, though a transformation of consciousness and behaviour, the *jiva* can move from bondage to liberation. When the last *karma* particle has moved away from the *jiva*, ignorance disappears, and it is restored to its omniscient, ideal state. The cycle of *samsara* is broken and *moksha* is attained. The ladder leading from ignorance to omniscience is visualized as having 14 rungs or stages of purification called *gunasthanas*. One who has entered the 13th stage of *kevalajnana* is known as an *arhat*. An *arhat* who has also already acquired the capability of teaching the doctrine is known as a *tirthankara*. The 14th stage is achieved by an *arhat* immediately before his death, when he is liberated from all activity and from the last few remaining *karma* particles. The final abode of liberated souls is a world called *siddha-loka*.

The Jaina discipline

The ***triratna*** (three gems) of Jainism consists of right faith (*samyag-darshana*), right knowledge (*samyag-jnana*), and right conduct (*samyag-charitra*). There are five great vows (*pancha-mahavrata*) for monks and nuns—not to injure any living being (*ahimsa*); not to utter any falsehood (*satya/sunrita*); not to take what is not given, i.e., not to steal (*asteya*); to lead a celibate life (*brahmacharya*); and non-possession, to call nothing one's own (*aparigraha*). The aim of these vows is to bring about inner purification.

Ahimsa is central to Jainism, and it is the first vow for renunciants as well as the laity. The extent to which Jainas carry this principle is connected to their idea of different forms of life. Jaina doctrine recognizes four main forms of existence—of gods (*deva*), humans (*manushya*), hell beings (*naraki*), and animals and plants (*tiryancha*). The animal and plant category is further sub-divided into smaller sub-categories on the basis of their sense faculties. The lowest category comprises the single-sense bodies (*ekendriya*). The lowest of these are the *nigodas*, tiny organisms that only have one sense, that of touch. These are born together in clusters and their life lasts a fraction of a second. The *nigodas* are supposed to be all over the place, and they also inhabit the bodies of plants, animals, and people. Above the *nigodas*, slightly higher in the scale, are single-sense organisms that inhabit the various elements (*sthavara*). They are known as the earth bodies, water bodies, fire bodies, and air bodies. Plant beings are higher in the scale—although they only have one sense, that of touch, they have a more complex structure and a longer life. Animals are still higher, as they have two to five senses. Those that have all five senses are classified into ones that are totally dependent on instinct and ones that have powers of reasoning.

Injuring living beings is seen as detrimental from two points of view—it causes the victim to suffer and it harms the person who causes the injury. It is not only actions but the emotions and intentions behind actions that count. As injuring others draws on negative emotions and passions, it is detrimental to the achievement of salvation. Strict vegetarianism is thus the most important dietary rule for Jainas. Because it is believed that *nigodas* are especially found in sweet and fermented substances, figs, honey, and alcohol are also forbidden. Even if an animal has not been killed for food but has died a natural death, its meat is not to be eaten, because dead flesh is considered a breeding ground for the *nigodas*. The Shvetambaras made some exceptions—for instance, meat could be eaten if there was a famine or to cure an illness.

The renunciant is supposed to take the observation of *ahimsa* to a higher level in his daily living. Laypersons are supposed to avoid harming beings with two or more senses, but the renunciant is supposed to refrain from harming even single-sense beings

PRIMARY SOURCES | **The liberated man**

The liberated man conquers wrath, pride, deceit, and greed. This is the doctrine of the seer who does not injure living beings and has put an end to acts and to *samsara*. Preventing propensity to sin destroys former actions. He who knows one thing knows all things; and he who knows all things knows one thing. He who is careless in all respects is in danger; he who is not careless in all respects is free from danger.

He who conquers one passion conquers many; and he who conquers many, conquers one. Knowing the misery of the world, rejecting the connection with the world, the heroes go on the great journey; they rise gradually, they do not desire life.

He who avoids one passion avoids them all severally; and he who avoids them severally avoids one. Faithful according to the commandment of the *tirthankaras*, wise, and understanding the world according to the commandment—such a man is without danger from anywhere. There are degrees in injurious acts, but there are no degrees in control.

He who knows wrath, knows pride; he who knows pride knows deceit; he who knows deceit knows greed; he who knows greed knows love; he who knows love, knows hate; he who knows hate knows delusion; he who knows delusion knows conception; he who knows conception knows birth; he who knows birth knows death; he who knows death knows hell; he who knows hell knows animal existence; he who knows animal existence knows pain.

Therefore, a wise man should avoid wrath, pride, deceit, greed, love, hate, delusion, conception, birth, death, hell, animal existence, and pain.

This is the doctrine of the seer who does not injure living beings and has put an end to acts and to *samsara*. Preventing the propensity to sin destroys former actions. Is there any worldly weakness in the seer? There exists none, there is none. Thus I say.

Source *Acharanga Sutta*, 1.3.4; Jacobi, (1884) 1968: 33–35

(*ekendriya*) and element bodies (*sthavara*). Monks and nuns must not dig the earth, lest they kill earth bodies. They must avoid bathing, swimming, or walking in the rain, lest they kill water bodies. They must not light or extinguish flames, to avoid harming fire bodies. They must not fan themselves, to avoid harming air bodies. They must try not to walk on greenery nor touch living plants, to avoid harming vegetable bodies.

Of the differences in daily practices between Digambara and Shvetambara monks, the most important relates to clothing. Both traditions agree that Mahavira and his early disciples had moved around naked. The Digambaras follow that tradition strictly. According to them, a monk must renounce all possessions, including clothes. The only things a monk can carry are a small broom (*rajoharana*) for brushing insects away before sitting down and a water gourd (*kamandalu*) for toilet hygiene. The Shvetambaras, on the other hand, wear white robes; they view nudity as a practice that had fallen into abeyance and was now unnecessary.

For the laity, the basic discipline consists of the *anuvratas*, which are a modified form of the *mahavratas* of monks and nuns. The first three vows are the same as those enjoined on members of the *sangha*, but the last two are replaced by chastity and limiting one's wants. Theoretically, the lay path cannot lead to salvation. But Jainism managed to negotiate the tightrope between monasticism and the householder's life quite well. There was close integration of the monastic and lay community, right from the earliest times.

Although Jaina doctrine distinguishes between acceptable and unacceptable injury to living beings, certain occupations that necessarily involve killing—such as hunting and animal husbandry—are ruled out. The texts list six occupations—governing (*asi*), writing (*mashi*), farming (*krishi*), the arts (*vidya*), trade (*vanijya*), and the practice of various crafts (*shilpa*). Of these, governing and agriculture potentially involve injuring life (insects are destroyed while tilling the soil, while governing can involve warfare) and therefore tend to get ruled out. Trade is likely to cause less injury and it remains a preferred occupation for Jainas even today. The teaching for the laity also emphasized *dana*—giving alms to renunciants and other worthy recipients. The highest form of death for a person, whether renunciant or layperson, involved voluntarily embracing death by fasting and meditating in a prescribed manner.

PRIMARY SOURCES | **On not killing earth bodies**

The living world is afflicted, miserable, difficult to instruct, and without discrimination. In this world full of pain, suffering by their different acts, see the ignorant ones cause great pain. See! There are beings individually embodied in earth. See! There are men who control themselves, while others only pretend to be homeless [i.e., the Buddhist monks whose conduct does not differ from that of householders]. One destroys this earth body by bad and injurious doings, and many other beings besides, which one hurts by means of earth, through doing acts related to earth. About this the Revered One [Mahavira] has taught the truth: for the sake of the splendour, honour, and glory of this life, for the sake of birth, death, and final liberation, for the removal of pain, man acts sinfully towards earth, or causes others to act so, or allows others to act so. This deprives him of happiness and perfect wisdom. About this he is informed when he has understood or heard, either from the Revered One or from the monks, the faith to be coveted. There are some who truly know this injuring to be the bondage, the delusion, the death, the hell. For this man is longing when he destroys this earth body by bad, injurious doings, and many other beings besides which he hurts by means of earth, through his doing acts related to earth. Thus I say.

As somebody may cut or strike a blind man who cannot see the wound, as someone may cut or strike the foot, the ankle, the knee, the thigh, the hip, the navel, the belly, the flank, the back, the bosom, the heart, the breast, the neck, the arm, the finger, the nail, the eye, the brow, the forehead, the head, as some kill openly, as some kill secretly, thus the earth bodies are cut, struck, and killed though they cannot express their feelings.

He who injures these earth bodies does not comprehend and renounce the sinful acts; he who does not injure these, comprehends and renounces the sinful acts. Knowing them, a wise man should not act sinfully towards earth, nor cause others to act so, nor allow others to act so. He who knows these causes of sin relating to earth is called a reward-knowing sage. Thus I say.

Source *Acharanga Sutta* 1.3.4; Jacobi, (1884) 1968: 3–5

The social composition of the Jaina *sangha* and laity

Jaina texts reflect the idea of the superiority of the Kshatriya *varna* over all others. The early medieval *Adi Purana* attributes the creation of the Kshatriya, Vaishya, and Shudra *varnas* to the first *tirthankara* Rishabha, who assumed the powers of a king before he attained *jina*-hood. The Brahmana *varna* is described as having been instituted by Rishabha's son Bharata, the first *chakravarti* ruler. Like the Buddhist texts, Jaina texts criticize the Brahmanas, their sacrifices, way of life, and arrogance. But they also talk of the 'true' or ideal Brahmana, giving the word new content, shifting the emphasis from birth to conduct. Thus re-defined, only a Jaina monk was worthy of being called a Brahmana.

People of all *varnas* and social backgrounds could enter the Jaina *sangha*. The *Uttaradhyayana Sutra* narrates the story of a monk named Harikeshiya who came from a *shvapaka* (Chandala) family. In search of food after concluding a long, arduous fast, he arrived at an enclosure where Brahmanas were performing a sacrifice. The arrogant Brahmanas reviled him and refused to give him food. When Harikeshiya stood his ground and tried to reason with them, the Brahmanas are described as attacking him viciously with sticks, canes, and whips, drawing back only due to the intercession of a ***yaksha*** (demi-god). The Brahmanas realized that they had done wrong, and asked Harikeshiya's pardon. He graciously forgave them, and proceeded to lecture them on the uselessness of performing sacrifices to the gods and how true sacrifice consisted in practising the discipline of the Jaina monk.

Notwithstanding the theoretical position and such episodes, all the chief disciples (*ganadharas*) of Mahavira were Brahmanas belonging to Magadha area, described as having entered the *sangha* with hundreds of their disciples. There was also a strong Brahmana representation among the Jaina *acharyas* (Bhadrabahu, Siddhasena Divakara, Pujyapada, Haribhadra, and Jinasena). Among the laity, Jainism especially enjoyed the allegiance and patronage of the affluent urban merchant class.

Like Buddhist texts, Jaina texts too present women as a danger to the celibacy of monks. Warning monks of women's wiles, they urge them to avoid their friendship and company. At the same time, Jainism did establish a monastic order for women. The

PRIMARY SOURCES | The true Brahmana

The *Uttaradhyayana Sutra* (25) tells the story of a famous Brahmana named Jayaghosha, who had taken the Jaina vows and had subdued all his senses. In the course of his wanderings, he reached the outskirts of Benaras. Here, after fasting for a month, he arrived at the home of a Brahmana named Vijayaghosha, learned in the Vedas. A sacrifice was being performed and, rudely refusing to give him any alms on the grounds that he was not a worthy recipient, Vijayaghosha told him to go beg somewhere else. The monk was unperturbed and struck up a conversation. Not surprisingly, he held forth on Brahmanahood, sacrifice, and *varna*:

The ignorant priests who pretend to know the sacrifice, those whose Brahmanical excellence consists in false science; they shroud themselves in study and penance, being like fire covered by the ashes.

He who is called by people a Brahmana and is worshipped like fire is no true Brahmana. But him we call a true Brahmana, whom the wise point out as such.

He who has no worldly attachment after entering the order, who does not repent of having become a monk, and who takes delight in noble words, him we call a Brahmana.

He who is exempt from love, hatred, and fear, and who shines forth like burnished gold purified in fire, him we call a Brahmana.

A lean, self-subdued ascetic, who reduces his flesh and blood, who is pious and has reached *Nirvana*, him we call a Brahmana.

He who thoroughly knows living beings, whether they move or not, and does not injure them by thoughts, words, or deeds, him we call a Brahmana.

He who does not speak untruth from anger or for fun, from greed or from fear, him we call a Brahmana.

He who does not take anything that is not given to him, be it sentient or not sentient, small or large, him we call a Brahmana.

He who does not carnally love divine, human, or animal beings in thoughts, words, or deeds, him we call a Brahmana.

He who is not defiled by pleasures, as a lotus growing in the water is not wetted by it, him we call a Brahmana.

He who is not greedy, who lives unknown, who has no house and no property, and who has no friendship with householders, him we call a Brahmana.

He who has given up his former connections with his kinsfolk and relations, and who is not given to pleasure, him we call a Brahmana.

The binding of animals to the sacrificial pole, all the Vedas and sacrifices, being causes of sin, cannot save the sinner; for his works are very powerful.

One does not become a *shramana* by shaving one's head, nor a Brahmana by the sacred syllable 'Om', nor a *muni* by living in the woods, nor a *tapasa* by wearing clothes of *kusha* grass and bark.

One becomes a *shramana* by equanimity, a Brahmana by chastity, a *muni* by knowledge, and a *tapasa* by penance.

By one's actions one becomes a Brahmana, or a Kshatriya, or a Vaishya, or a Shudra.

Source Jacobi, (1884) 1968: 136–38

traditional Jaina account of the growth of the *sangha* during the lifetime of Mahavira in fact gives greater prominence to women. According to the *Kalpa Sutra*, when Mahavira died, there were 14,000 monks and 36,000 nuns, 159,000 laymen, and 318,000 laywomen. A total of 1,400 women as opposed to 700 men are described as having attained salvation during his lifetime. Nuns must have played an important role in spreading the Jaina teaching among laywomen.

The issue of clothing was central to the Jaina debate on gender and salvation (Jaini, [1991] 1992). As mentioned earlier, *Digambaras* emphasized the necessity of nudity for members of the order. For them, clothes counted as possessions and were associated with passion, sexual desire, and shame. However, they seem to have shared the social disapproval of women moving around naked in public. A woman's body was thus the obstacle to her attaining salvation. Women mendicants associated with their order, respectfully addressed as *aryika* or *sadhvi* (noble or venerable women), were regarded more like celibate laywomen who had achieved a significant amount of spiritual progress.

According to the Shvetambaras, on the other hand, wearing or not wearing clothes was optional. Women could attain *moksha* in their lifetime. Monks and nuns of this order took the same vows and in theory were considered on par with each other. In practice, however, there was an element of inequality, similar to that which existed within the Buddhist *sangha*. No matter how senior a nun and howsoever junior a monk, the nun

FURTHER DISCUSSION | **Malli or Mallinatha?**

According to Shvetambara tradition, in a previous life, the soul of Malli was born in a king named Mahabala. This king renounced the world along with his seven friends, and all of them became Jaina monks. The eight monks made an agreement to undertake the same number of fasts as part of their ascetic regimen. Mahabala, who was deceitful and sly by nature, found ways of skipping meals by making excuses, and ended up with a greater tally of fasts than had been agreed on. However, apart from this, his conduct was above reproach. As a result of his exertions in following the Jaina path, he became worthy of becoming a *jina*. But because of his one devious act, after spending a long period in heaven, he was born not as a male but as a female, as a beautiful princess named Malli (jasmine flower). The other seven monks were born as Kshatriya warriors of neighbouring kingdoms. They all wanted to marry Malli and battled over her. She was so disgusted by this that she renounced the world and instantly attained *kevalajnana* (omniscience), becoming the 19th *tirthankara*. In the Shvetambara tradition, Malli is the sole exception to the rule that a *jina* must be male.

The Digambaras reject this tradition completely. The 19th *tirthankara* in their tradition was a man named Mallinatha, born into a royal family as a prince, not a princess. After taking the vows of a Digambara monk, he eventually became a *tirthankara*.

Source Jaini, (1991) 1992: 14–15

had to offer respectful salutation first. Nuns could confess their misdemeanors to monks and be censured by them, but the reverse did not happen.

Was it possible for a woman to become a *tirthankara*? Digambara tradition holds that a woman has to be reborn as a man before she can attain salvation. The Shvetambaras, however, acknowledge the possibility of women becoming *jinas*. Malli, their 19th *tirthankara*, was a woman. Both traditions hold that women are not capable of experiencing the worst forms of undesirable volitions, so they can never be born in the seventh and lowest hell. But they also consider misdeeds and negative propensities such as cheating, greed, unpredictability, and cunning to be responsible for rebirth as a woman. Even the Shvetambara tradition about Malli ascribes her birth as a woman to cheating in a previous birth. And Malli never became a popular focus of worship; only one 9th century image, with breasts and a long braid of hair, has so far been found.

According to Jaini ([1991] 1992: 26–27), the denial of the possibility of salvation seems to have been a factor inhibiting women's association with a particular order, as is suggested by the declining number of Digambara nuns. However, the offer of salvation was not in itself an assurance of the long-term survival of a women's monastic order, as is clear from the virtual disappearance of the Buddhist *bhikkhuni sangha* among Theravada communities of Sri Lanka and Southeast Asia. Clearly, there were other factors at work as well.

CONCLUSIONS

The period *c.* 600–200 BCE marks the early historic period in North India. It was an age when the increasing social, economic, and political complexities of the previous centuries manifested themselves in the emergence of cities. The vast majority of people, however, continued to live in villages. Urbanism created new socio-economic divisions and elites. The institution of *jati* (caste) started taking shape. The strengthening of patriarchal control within the household led to the increasing subordination of women. These centuries were marked by a remarkable prominence of the ideal of renunciation and an intense level of philosophical debate and questioning. Buddhism and Jainism were two among many philosophical schools and established long-enduring monastic institutions closely connected with their laity. They questioned the foundations of Brahmanical social ideology. Their creation of monastic orders gave an institutional basis to the principle of renunciation. The social ethics they put forward were in tune with the changing times and appealed to the aspirations of upcoming urban social groups. Although they offered salvation to all and questioned the status quo, Buddhism and Jainism accepted certain elements of social inequality. At the political level, there were two competing types of polities—the oligarchies and monarchies. The growth of the Magadhan empire was underway and involved the defeat and marginalization of other states. It was a short step from the Nanda to the Maurya empire.

FURTHER READINGS

Basham, A. L. (1951) 2003. *History and Doctrines of the Ajivikas: A Vanished Religion*. Indian Edn. London: Luzac & Co.

Bronkhorst, Johannes. 2007. *Greater Magadha: Studies in the Culture of Early India*. Leiden, Boston: Brill.

_______. 2011. *Buddhism in the Shadow of Brahmanism*. Leiden, Boston: Brill.

Chakrabarti, Dilip K. 2001. *The Archaeology of Ancient Indian Cities*. Delhi: Oxford University Press. Chapters 5, 6.

———. 2006. *The Oxford Companion to Indian Archaeology: The Archaeological Foundations of Ancient India, Stone Age to AD 13th Century*. Delhi: Oxford University Press. Chapters 15–18.

Chakravarti, Uma. 1987. *The Social Dimensions of Early Buddhism*. Delhi: Oxford University Press.

_______. 2003. *Gendering Caste through a Feminist Lens*. Calcutta: Stree.

Chanana, Dev Raj. (1960) 1990. *Slavery in Ancient India*, New Delhi: People's Publishing House.

Collins, Steve. 1990. 'On the very idea of the Pali canon.' *Journal of the Pali Text Society* 15: 89–126.

Coningham, R. A. E. and F. R. Allchin. 1995. 'The rise of cities in Sri Lanka.' In F. R. Allchin, *The Archaeology of Early Historic South Asia*. Cambridge: Cambridge University Press, pp. 152–83 (chap. 9).

Dundas, Paul. 1992. *The Jainas*. London and New York: Routledge. Dutt, Sukumar. (1924) 1984. *Early Buddhist Monachism*. New Delhi: Munshiram Manoharlal.

Dutt, Sukumar. (1962) 1988. *Buddhist Monks and Monasteries of India: Their History and their Contribution to Indian Culture*. Rep. Edn. Part I. Delhi: Motilal Banarsidass.

Erdosy, George. 1988. *Urbanization in Early Historic India*. BAR International Series 430. Oxford.

Gethin, Rupert. 1998. *The Foundations of Buddhism*. Oxford and New York: Oxford University Press.

Gupta, Dipankar. (Ed.). 1992. *Social Stratification*. Delhi: Oxford University Press. Especially M. N. Srinivas, '*Varna* and Caste', pp. 28 34, and G. S. Ghurye, 'Features of the Caste System'. pp. 35–48. Stratification

Jha, Vivekanand. (1986–87) 2004. 'Candala and the Origin of Untouchability.' In Aloka Parasher-Sen. (Ed.). *Subordinate and Marginal Groups in Early India*. Delhi: Oxford University Press, pp. 157–209.

Jaini, Padmanabh S. (1979) 2001. *The Jaina Path of Purification*. Berkeley: University of California Press.

Jaiswal, Suvira. (1998) 2000. *Caste: Origin, Function and Dimensions of Change*. Delhi: Manohar.

Kane, P. V. (1941) 1974. *History of Dharmasastra*. Vol. 2, Part 1. 2nd Edn. Poona: Bhandarkar Oriental Research Institute.

———. (1946) 1973. *History of Dharmasastra*. Vol. 3. 2nd Edn. Poona. Bhandarkar Oriental Research Institute.

Lahiri, Nayanjot. 1992. *The Archaeology of Indian Trade Routes up to c. 200 BC: Resource Use, Resource Access and Lines of Communication*. Delhi: Oxford University Press, pp. 367–87.

Lal, B. B. (1954) 1955. 'Excavation at Hastinapura and Other Explorations in the Upper Ganga and Sutlej Basins, 1950–52.' *Ancient India* 10, 11: 5–151.

Lal, Makkhan. 1984. *Settlement History and Rise of Civilization in Ganga-Yamuna Doab (from 1500 BC to 300 AD)*. Delhi: B. R. Publishing Corporation.

Olivelle. (Ed.). 2009. *Dharma: Studies in Its Semantic, Cultural and Religious History*. Delhi: Motilal Banarsidass, pp. 69–89.

_______. (Ed.). 2019. *Gṛhastha: The Householder in Ancient Indian Religious Culture*. New Delhi: Oxford University Press.

Quigley, Declan. (1999) 2002. *The Interpretation of Caste*. Oxford Studies in Social and Cultural Anthropology. 4th rep. New Delhi: Oxford University Press.

Rajan, K., V. P. Yathees Kumar, M. Rajesh, R. Sivanantham, J. Ranjith, and J. Bhaskar. 2021 'Recent Radiometric Dates and Their Implications in Understanding the Early Writing System and Early Archaeology of Tamil Nadu. *Man and Environment* 46, 1: 57–86.

Ray, Himanshu Prabha and Daniel T. Potts. (Eds.). 2007. *Memory as History: The Legacy of Alexander in Asia*. New Delhi: Aryan Books International.

Sarao, K. T. S. (1990) 2007. *Urban Centres and Urbanization as Relected in the Pali Vinaya and Sutta Pitaka*. 2nd Rev. Edn. Delhi: Department of Buddhist Studies, University of Delhi.

Sarma, Pranab Jyoti and Manjil, Hazarika. 2014. 'Situation Northeast Indian Archaeology in Chronological Perspective: Fresh Observations.' In Tiatoshi Jamir and Manjil Hazarika. (Eds.). *50 Years After Daojali-Hading: Emerging Perspectives in the Archaeology of Northeast India. Essays in Honour of Tarun Chandra Sarma*. New Delhi, Research India Press. Chap. 4: pp. 37–59.

Sharma, J. P. 1968. *Republics in Ancient India c. 1500 B.C.–500 B.C.* Lei- den: E. J. Brill.

Sharma, R. S. (1958) 1980. *Sudras in Ancient India: A Social History of the Lower Order Down to circa AD 600*. 2nd Rev. Edn. Delhi: Motilal Banarsidass. Chapter 4.

Sircar, D. C. 1956. *Inscriptions of Aśoka*. New Delhi: Publications Division.

Thaplyal, K. K. 1996. *Guilds in Ancient India: A Study of Guild Organization in Northern India and Western Deccan from circa 600 BC to circa 600 AD*. New Delhi: New Age International Ltd. Publishers.

Wagle, Narendra. 1963. *Society at the Time of the Buddha*. Bombay: Popular Prakashan.

Wijayaratne, Mohan. 1990. *Buddhist Monastic Life According to the Texts of the Theravada Tradition*. Claude Grangier and Steven Collins (Trans. from French). Cambridge: Cambridge University Press.

———. 2001. *Buddhist Nuns: The Birth and Development of a Woman's Monastic Order*. Colombo: Wisdom.

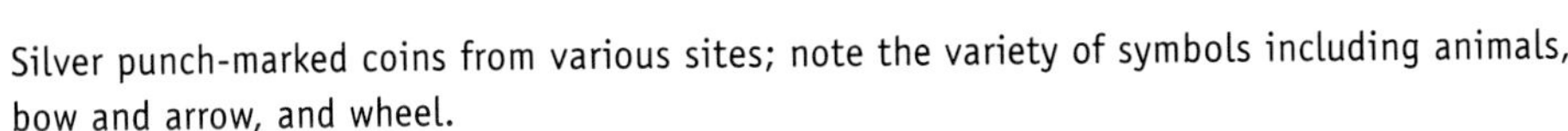

Silver punch-marked coins from various sites; note the variety of symbols including animals, bow and arrow, and wheel.

CHAPTER 7

Power and Piety: The Maurya Empire

c. 324–187 BCE

Ashoka's thirteenth rock edict describes a great war against Kalinga that was fought in the ninth year after his *abhisheka* (consecration). We are told that 150,000 men were captured and deported, 100,000 were killed, and many times that number died. Ashoka's army was victorious but the king took no pride in the victory. Instead, he felt a deep remorse and decided to renounce war and devote himself to practising and spreading *dhamma* (goodness, virtue). Ashoka goes on to give a series of arguments against war in general. He states that the suffering caused by war extends far beyond those who suffer directly, physically. It includes the emotional pain suffered by those who love them. It is especially regrettable that good people, including Brahmanas and *shramanas* (renunciants) suffer. Implicit in Ashoka's reflections and arguments are the ideas that war causes incalculable suffering for the victors, the vanquished, and countless others.

The inscription is autobiographical, philosophical, and political. It describes a transformative event in the life of an emperor and how that event made him confront the problems of war and violence. What explains this powerful reaction to the Kalinga war? Was it because Ashoka was an active participant in the campaign? Was there something unprecedented about the scale of violence in the Kalinga war? Did Ashoka suffer a personal loss—that of a beloved son or friend—which forced him to reflect on how the impact of war extends far the immediate casualties? Was he already becoming more sensitive to violence due to drawing closer to the Buddha's teaching? Does the use of the first person in the inscription mask more hard-headed political calculations? We can only speculate about what lay behind Ashoka's powerful anti-war proclamation.

The Mauryas (*c.* 324–187 BCE) established an empire that extended over almost the entire subcontinent and even beyond it in the north-west. Dynastic history provides an essential framework for political history, but not for understanding other aspects such as social, economic, or religious history. Therefore, this chapter will focus on issues specifically related to the Maurya empire, referring to other aspects only briefly. The discussion of broader historical patterns that stretch across and beyond these centuries will be taken up in Chapter 8. The discussion of social and economic processes discussed in Chapters 6, 7, and 8 should be read as a continuum.

The sources for the Maurya period are more varied than for earlier periods. The king-lists in the Puranas refer to the Mauryas, but there are inconsistencies in detail. One set of texts speaks of 13 Maurya kings who ruled for a total of 137 years, while another set speaks of only 9 kings. Jaina works such as Hemachandra's *Parishishtaparvan* allude to Chandragupta's connections with Jainism. The plot of the *Mudrarakshasa*, a 5th/6th century historical drama written by Vishakhadatta, revolves around the clever machinations of Chanakya, a minister of Chandragupta, against Rakshasa, a minister of the former Nanda king. It is, however, uncertain whether this story has any historical basis. Buddhist versions of the Chanakya–Chandragupta legend are preserved in the *Mahavamsa* and its 10th century commentary, the *Vamsatthapakasini*. Some information on Chandragupta is also available in the *Milindapanha* and *Mahabhashya*. There is a possible reference to the southward expansion of the Mauryas in a poem by the Tamil poet Mamulanar.

In the Buddhist tradition, Ashoka is the focus of much attention and adulation. Texts such as the *Dipavamsa*, *Mahavamsa*, *Ashokavadana*, *Divyavadana*, and *Vamsatthapakasini* contain information about this king. The 17th century history of Indian Buddhism written by the Tibetan monk Taranatha has some even later, mostly legendary, accounts of the Mauryas. The accounts of Ashoka in these Buddhist works should not be considered biographical in the factual sense. They represent the recasting of his life into legend. Due to his association with Buddhism, during the centuries after his death, Ashoka acquired the reputation of being a great king and extraordinary patron of the *sangha* across the Asian Buddhist world.

Apart from Ashoka's inscriptions, the major sources for the history of the Mauryas and their age have traditionally included Kautilya's *Arthashastra* and Megasthenes' *Indica*. Graeco-Roman sources, often referred to as 'classical sources,' are useful for some points on early Maurya political history. These days, most experts on Kautilya's *Arthashastra* consider it a post-Maurya text. The debate on the date of the *Arthashastra* is summarized below, followed by a discussion of Ashoka's inscriptions, Megasthenes' *Indica*, and archaeological and numismatic evidence.

The date of the *Arthashastra*

The *Arthashastra* of Kautilya is an extremely sophisticated and detailed treatise on statecraft. The text and its author are mentioned in many ancient texts, but modern scholars did not have any manuscript of the work till 1905. In that year, a pandit of the Tanjore district handed a manuscript of the *Arthashastra* to R. Shamashastry, librarian of the Mysore Government Oriental Library. Shamashastry published the entire text in 1909 and an English translation in 1915. The publication of the *Arthashastra* created a sensation in the scholarly world because its contents reflected a hard-headed political realism that was in stark contrast to other ancient Indian texts. Kautilya came to be described as the Indian Machiavelli. The *Arthashastra* was translated into many Indian and European languages. A critical edition, based on several manuscripts and early medieval commentaries, and an English translation of that critical edition, were published by R. P. Kangle in 1960–63. Patrick Olivelle's new translation of the critical edition was published in 2013.

Ever since the discovery of the *Arthashastra*, there have been radical differences of opinion about its age and authorship. The name Chanakya does not occur in the *Arthashastra*, but Kautilya does. *Arthashastra* 1.1.19 states that this work, easy to learn and understand, precise in doctrine, sense, and word, and free from wordiness, has been composed by Kautilya. *Arthashastra* 15.1.73 states that this *shastra* was composed by the person who, in resentment, quickly regenerated the *shastra,* weapon, and earth that was under the control of the Nanda kings. These two verses are generally considered later interpolations. On many topics of discussion, the *Arthashastra* cites other authorities' views, followed by that of Kautilya. Kautilya's name also occurs in the colophons at the end of each book.

The *Arthashastra* does not contain any references to the Mauryas, their empire, Chandragupta, or Pataliputra. This is not in itself surprising as it is a theoretical, not a descriptive, work. What is clear is that the connection between this text, Chandragupta Maurya, and the names of Kautilya, Chanakya, and Vishnugupta emerged through a conflation of different traditions after about the 4th century CE (for instance, in the *Panchatantra*, *Jatakamala*, *Mudrarakshasa*, *Dashakumaracharita*, and *Nitisara*), that is, beginning about seven centuries after Chandragupta's time.

Over the years, scholars have sought to compare the *Arthashastra*, Megasthenes' *Indica*, and Ashokan inscriptions, some pointing to their congruence, others to their divergences (see Kangle, 1960–65, Part 3: 78-109). Of course, divergences in themselves are not conclusive as these three sources are of a qualitatively different nature.

Some scholars think that the *Arthashastra* is essentially a Maurya period work. R. P. Kangle (1965: 78–109) has cited various reasons for supporting the 'traditional view' that Kautilya can be identified with Chanakya, who was the mastermind of Chandragupta's defeat of the Nandas and the establishment of the Maurya dynasty. He suggests that Vishnugupta may have been the personal name of the author, Kautilya his *gotra* name, and Chanakya (son of Chanaka) a patronym. As for the date of the text, according to Kangle, on stylistic grounds, the work seems to be earlier that Vatsyayana's *Kamasutra* and was probably earlier than the *Yajnavalkya Smriti* and *Manu Smriti*. The mention of the Ajivikas as an important sect fits in with the Maurya period, as do the references to *sangha* polities and the discussion of the large-scale establishment of agricultural settlements. Kangle suggests that Kautilya may have written the book after having been insulted by the Nanda king, before joining Chandragupta. According to this view, the *Arthashastra* is basically a Maurya period text, although interpolations were added to it during later centuries.

Thomas Trautmann (1971) asserts that the *Arthashastra*, although compiled by a single person, has multiple authors. The basis of the argument is a computer-aided statistical analysis of the *Arthashastra*, focusing on differences in the frequencies of ordinary, frequently occurring words such as *cha* (and) and *va* (or) in the different books of the work. Trautmann argues that different word frequencies point to different authors. He suggests that three or four authors contributed to the composition of the *Arthashastra*—Book 2 may have been completed by *c.* 150 CE, and the final compilation of the text may have happened by *c.* 250 CE.

Trautmann's methodology has been questioned by S. N. Mital (2000). Mital has pointed out that there are differences in the frequencies of *cha* and *va* within different chapters of the same books of the *Arthashastra*. He also points out that differences in the frequency of the use of these particles depended to some extent on the subject matter of that particular section. In sections where there was a greater need to discuss various policy alternatives in the context of different situations (e.g., in the discussion of inter-state relations), there is naturally a greater use of the word *va*. In those sections which required a regular enumeration of details, as in discussions of salaries of government officials or how a courtier should behave, there is a greater frequency of *cha*.

In his Introduction to his translation of the critical edition of the *Arthashastra*, Patrick Olivelle (2013) has suggested a timeline for the evolution of the text. Stage 1 is the period of the 'prehistory' of the work, when the text did not exist, but some of the ideas that later made their way into it were around. This may go back to the mid-1st century BCE or possibly earlier. According to him, the actual composition of the *Arthashastra* went through two stages (Stages 2 and 3). Stage 2 was when the first major redaction, which he terms 'the Kautilya redaction', was composed by a person named Kautilya sometime during *c.* 50–125 CE. Stage 3 was when a person well-versed in Dharmashastra reworked the text and brought it close in line with Brahmanical social ideology to produce what Olivelle terms 'the Shastric Redaction', during *c.* 175–300 CE. According to this view, the *Arthashastra* is a post-Maurya work belonging to the early centuries CE.

In his dating of the 'Kautilya recension,' Olivelle attaches significance to the occurrence of the word *pravala* (coral), which he thinks must refer to Mediterranean coral, which the Indians became aware of during the period of Indo-Mediterranean trade. Coral has been found at Harappa and at various neolithic-chalcolithic and early historic sites in India, but Olivelle's argument is that the *Arthashastra* was aware of ornamental Mediterranean coral in particular. Pliny (1st century CE) mentions that Indians greatly prized Mediterranean coral. *Arthashastra* 2.11.42 refers to two kinds of coral (*pravala*) which are red and lotus-coloured—*alakandaka* and *vaivarnika*. Alakanda can be identified with Alexandria in Egypt. Vivarna may have been a place located somewhere in the Mediterranean region. This suggests that the *Arthashastra* belongs to the period of flourishing maritime trade between India and the Mediterranean. Olivelle also points out that the Kautilya recension of the *Arthashastra* knows silver coins (*pana* seems to be a silver coin), but not gold ones, which were introduced by the Kushanas towards the end of the 1st century CE. According to his hypothesis, while it is theoretically possible that the *sources* used in the *Arthashastra* existed in or around the Maurya period, the text itself did not.

In his recent detailed study of the *Arthashastra*, Mark McClish (2019) too has argued against a Maurya period date for the text on similar lines. He suggests that the *Arthashastra* began as a prose work called *Dandaniti* which was composed in the 1st century BCE or perhaps a bit earlier. We do not know the name of the composer, but he must have drawn on pre-existing ideas of political theorists, and his work was divided into *prakaranas* (topics). The reference to *alakandaka* (Alexandrian coral) and the absence of references to gold coins help date this version of the text. A few centuries later, the text was worked over by a person named Kautilya who brought it more in line with Brahmanical orthodoxy and the idea of *varnashrama dharma*. In the course of this later redaction, the text was divided into *adhikaranas* (books) and *adhyayas* (chapters). The chapter ending verses and some in-chapter ones, including 1.1.19 and 15.1.73, were inserted and the whole text was reworked to make it more consonant with Brahmanical ideology, including several special privileges to be accorded to Brahmanas. It is in this stage that the redactor added his name (Kautilya) to the text, along with citations of his views, as well as verses 1.1.9 and 2.10.63, which attribute the work to Kautilya. This text was called the *Arthashastra*. McClish reiterates the point that leaving aside the verses that are later interpolations, there is nothing in the *Arthashastra* that connects it with Chandragupta or the Mauryas; and that the earliest references to such connections appear many centuries after the Maurya period, perhaps to lend additional authority to the work.

There is no doubt that the *discipline* of *arthashastra* existed before Kautilya's *Arthashastra*. Kautilya himself refers to earlier works on the subject. He also often cites the opinions of specific authorities as well as the experts (*acharyas*) collectively and positions himself vis-à-vis their ideas, very often through disagreement. The topics where many authorities are frequently cited, and which were evidently subjects of debate before his time include crime and punishment, the appointment of counsellors and ministers, the calamities (*vyasanas*) of the state, the powers (*shaktis*) of the king, and war. But there are many sections in the *Arthashastra* where few or no authorities are cited. These include the discussion of the training and protection of the king, the responsibilities of the heads of administrative departments, state control over and participation in the economy, the suppression of criminals, and inter-state policy. These probably contain Kautilya's original contributions. The *Arthashastra*'s reputation and authority may have been based on its introduction of a new perspective, one that was meticulous, methodical, rigorous, and logical. So, while some of the ideas and conceptual vocabulary used by Kautilya must have existed well before his time, his achievement was to create a new synthesis which included many new elements, offering a bold, novel vision of a potential state (Upinder Singh, 2017: 98–101).

While a post-Maurya date for the *Arthashastra* is now accepted by many scholars, some still consider it a Maurya period work, although they recognize that interpolations and changes were made to the text during later centuries. There is, however, general agreement on the fact that the *Arthashastra* is a theoretical work on statecraft and does not describe the Maurya state. Perhaps out of force of habit, some historians continue to use the *Arthashastra* in discussions of Maurya state and administration. This practice was followed in the first edition of this book but has been abandoned in the present edition. It should be emphasized that the *Arthashastra* is a technical treatise on statecraft that speaks in universal terms, as a *shastra* was expected to do. It describes a potential, not actual, monarchical state. It cannot be taken as a description of the Mauryan state, nor, for that matter, of any other historical state. However, it is an exceptionally sophisticated and rich source for ancient Indian political ideas at the cusp of the millennium and will be discussed as such in Chapter 8.

The Major Sources for the Maurya Period

Ashoka's inscriptions

Reference was made in Chapter 6 to the evidence of the Brahmi script in early contexts at Anuradhapura in Sri Lanka and at sites such as Kodumanal, Porunthal, and Keezhadi in Tamil Nadu. According to some historians, the Piprahwa casket inscription and the

PRIMARY SOURCES | **The Mahasthan and Sohgaura inscriptions**

In 1893, a small, inscribed bronze plaque, 1.6 mm thick and measuring 6.4 × 2.9 cm, was found by an inhabitant of Sohgaura village, presently located in Gorakhpur district of Uttar Pradesh. Its surface was rough and uneven and there were holes in the four corners, no doubt in order to attach it to a surface, perhaps a wall. The inscription consisted of four lines in the Prakrit language and Brahmi script, with seven symbols arranged at the top. It recorded an order issued from Manavasiti by the *mahamatras* (a cadre of officials) of Shravasti. It stated that in case of the outbreak of drought, the contents of the storehouses of Triveni, Mathura, Chanchu, Modama, and Bhadra were to be distributed and not withheld.

K. P. Jayaswal interpreted the crescent on the top as an emblem of the Maurya king Chandragupta and connected the contents of the inscription with the Jaina legend of a great famine during the reign of this king. These suggestions are rather speculative.

Many years later, in 1931, Baru Faqir, a resident of Mahasthangarh village in Bagura district of Bangladesh, made an exciting discovery near a tank close to a high mound. Engraved on a small 8.9 × 5.7 cm piece of hard limestone was a fragmentary 7-line inscription, its first part missing and its last line defaced. Its script and language were similar to those of Ashokan inscriptions, but scholars were divided over whether it belonged to the pre-Ashokan, Ashokan, or post-Ashokan period.

The Mahasthan inscription appears to record an order issued by a ruler to the *mahamatra* stationed at Pundranagara (the site of which is represented by Mahasthangarh village), in order to relieve the distress caused on account of famine to some people known as the Samvamgiyas, who apparently lived in and around this town. The measures undertaken may have included the advancing of a loan in coins known as *gandakas* to a person named Galadana, who was perhaps leader of this group. A second step was the distribution of *dhanya* (paddy) from the granary. The inscription goes on to express the hope that the people would be able to tide over the calamity as a result of these measures, and that the treasury would be replenished with paddy and *gandaka* coins. The last line may refer to people having to pay back the coins and paddy to the treasury once they had recovered from the famine.

The dates of the Sohgaura and Mahasthan inscriptions have been debated. While some earlier scholars thought they were pre-Maurya, most now consider them to be contemporary to or later than the Maurya period.

Source Jayaswal, 1933–34; Hazra, 2002: 43–60; Salomon, 1998: 12

Sohgaura and Mahasthan inscriptions may be pre-Maurya or early Maurya; others consider them contemporary to or after Ashoka's time. A fragmentary Sanchi inscription which mentions the name Bindusara may belong to the reign of the Maurya king of this name. While there is some evidence of the Brahmi script before the time of Ashoka, this king's practice of inscribing imperial proclamations on stone marked a major innovation in royal practice.

When James Prinsep succeeded in reading Ashoka's Brahmi edicts in 1837, it was not clear which king's inscriptions they were. This is because most of them refer to Ashoka by the epithets Devanampiya and Piyadasi. The mystery was solved thanks to George Turnour, a British civil servant and scholar in Ceylon, who pointed out that the *Dipavamsa* and *Mahavamsa* used these epithets for the Maurya emperor Ashoka. In later decades, versions of minor rock edict 1 were found at Maski, and later at Udegolam, Nittur, and Gujjara. These contained what is usually considered the personal name of the king—Asoka ('without sorrow'), the Prakrit equivalent of Sanskrit 'Ashoka.' As for the epithets, Devanampiya means 'dear to the gods' or 'beloved of the gods'. Piyadasi can be understood in various ways, including 'one who looks at auspiciousness,' or 'of gracious mien'.

Most of Ashoka's inscriptions are written in the Brahmi script and in the dialects of Prakrit/Middle Indic. The main dialect is the eastern one, which is not surprising given the core area of the Maurya empire. The Girnar inscriptions are in a western dialect. Those at Mansehra and Shahbazgarhi are in a northwestern dialect of Prakrit (sometimes known as Gandhari) and Kharoshthi script (Salomon, 1998: 136). There are a few inscriptions in Greek and Aramaic as well. A bilingual Greek–Aramaic inscription was found at Shar-i-Kuna near Kandahar in south-east Afghanistan. Two Aramaic inscriptions were found at Laghman (in east Afghanistan) and one at Taxila. A bilingual Prakrit–Aramaic inscription was found at Lampaka and another one at Kandahar. (For details of the Ashokan sites and inscriptions see Falk, 2006.)

PRIMARY SOURCES | **The categories of Ashokan inscriptions and their location**

The set of 14 major rock edicts (or portions thereof) occur at:

1. Kandahar (in Kandahar district, south Afghanistan) (only portions of rock edicts 12 and 13)
2. Shahbazgarhi (Peshawar district, North-West Frontier Province [NWFP], Pakistan)
3. Mansehra (Hazara district, NWFP, Pakistan)
4. Kalsi (Dehradun district, Uttarakhand)
5. Girnar (Junagadh district, Gujarat)
6. Bombay-Sopara (originally at Sopara in Thana district, Maharashtra; now in the Chhatrapati Shivaji Maharaj Vastu Sangrahalaya, Mumbai only fragments of rock edicts 8 and 9)
7. Dhauli (Puri district, Odisha; separate rock edicts 1 and 2 replace major rock edicts 11–13)
8. Jaugada (Ganjam district, Odisha; separate rock edicts 1 and 2 replace major rock edicts 11–13)
9. Erragudi (Kurnool district, AP)
10. Sannati (Gulbarga district, Karnataka; portions of rock edicts 13 and 14 and separate rock edicts 1 and 2 were found on a granite slab in a medieval goddess temple)

The set of six (and in one case seven) pillar edicts, or portions thereof, occur at:

1. Kandahar (Kandahar district, south Afghanistan) (only portions of pillar edict 7)
2. Delhi. The Delhi–Topra pillar originally stood in Topra (Ambala district, Haryana). This pillar has seven edicts.
3. Delhi. The Delhi–Meerut pillar originally stood in Meerut (Meerut district, UP).
4. Prayagraj. The Allahabad–Kosam pillar was probably originally located in Kosam, i.e., Kaushambi (Prayagraj district, UP).
5. Lauriya-Araraj (Champaran district, Bihar)
6. Lauriya-Nandangarh (Champaran district, Bihar)
7. Rampurva (Champaran district, Bihar)

The minor rock edicts (MREs) occur at:

1. Bahapur/Srinivasapuri in New Delhi (MRE 1)
2. Bairat (Jaipur district, Rajasthan) (MRE 3)
3. Ahraura (Mirzapur district, UP) (MRE 1)
4. Sahasram (Rohtas district, Bihar) (MRE 1)
5. Gujjara (Datia district, MP) (MRE 1)
6. Rupnath (Jabalpur district, MP) (MRE 1)
7. Panguraria (Sehore district, MP) (MRE 1)
8. Maski (Raichur district, Karnataka) (MRE 1)
9. Gavimath (Raichur district, Karnataka) (MRE 1)
10. Palkigundu (Raichur district, Karnataka) (MRE 1)
11. Nittur (Bellary district, Karnataka) (MRE 1 and 2)
12. Udegolam (Bellary district, Karnataka) (MRE 1 and 2)
13. Rajula-Mandagiri (Kurnool district, AP) (MRE 1 and 2)
14. Erragudi (Kurnool district, AP) (MRE 1 and 2)
15. Brahmagiri (Chitradurga district, Karnataka) (MRE 1 and 2)
16. Siddapura (Chitradurga district, Karnataka) (MRE 1 and 2)
17. Jatinga-Rameshvara (Chitradurga district, Karnataka) (MRE 1 and 2)

As for the minor pillar inscriptions, versions of the schism edict have been found at Sanchi (Raisen district, MP), Sarnath (Varanasi district, Bihar), and Kaushambi (Prayagraj district, UP). Commemorative inscriptions occur at Nigali Sagar and Rummindei (both in Bhairwa district, Nepal). A fragmentary inscription, which may be Ashokan, has been found at Amaravati (Guntur district, AP). Three cave inscriptions of Ashoka's time have been found in the caves in the Barabar hills (Gaya district, Bihar). A donative edict of one of Ashoka's queens is inscribed on the Allahabad-Kosam pillar.

In 2009, a version of Ashoka's minor rock edict 1 was discovered at Ratanpurwa in Bihar.

Source Salomon, 1998: 136–40; Falk, 2006; Thaplyal 2009

Scholars have divided Ashoka's inscriptions into various categories. The two main categories are the 14 major rock edicts, and the 6 (in one case 7) pillar edicts. The rock and pillar edicts are sets of inscriptions that occur, with minor variations, in different places. There are also several minor rock edicts, minor pillar edicts, and cave inscriptions. The minor rock edicts are considered among the earliest inscriptions, the major rock edicts later than them, and the pillar edicts still later. Some inscriptions refer to events with reference to the number of years that had expired since Ashoka's *abhisheka* (consecration). What makes Ashoka's edicts unique is that unlike royal inscriptions of later times, which follow a conventional pattern and phraseology, they reveal the voice and ideas of the king.

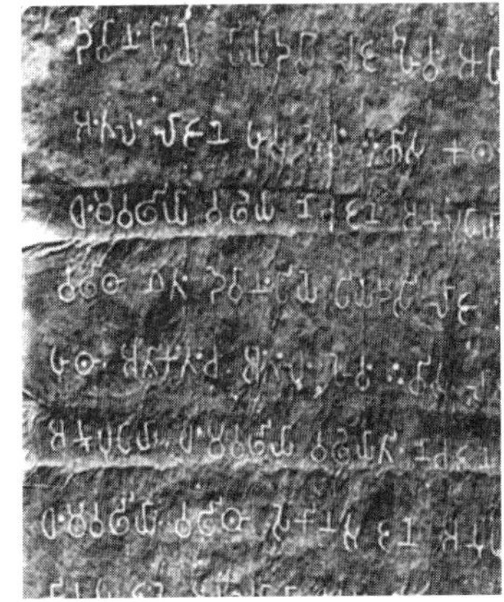

Inscription on Delhi–Topra pillar

We do not know just how many inscriptions Ashoka had inscribed in various parts of his empire. Faxian and Xuanzang mention seeing pillars at places where today there are none. The extant major rock edicts are mostly located along the borders of the empire. The major pillar edicts are concentrated in North India (with the possible exception of the Amaravati fragment). The minor rock edicts have the widest distribution, with

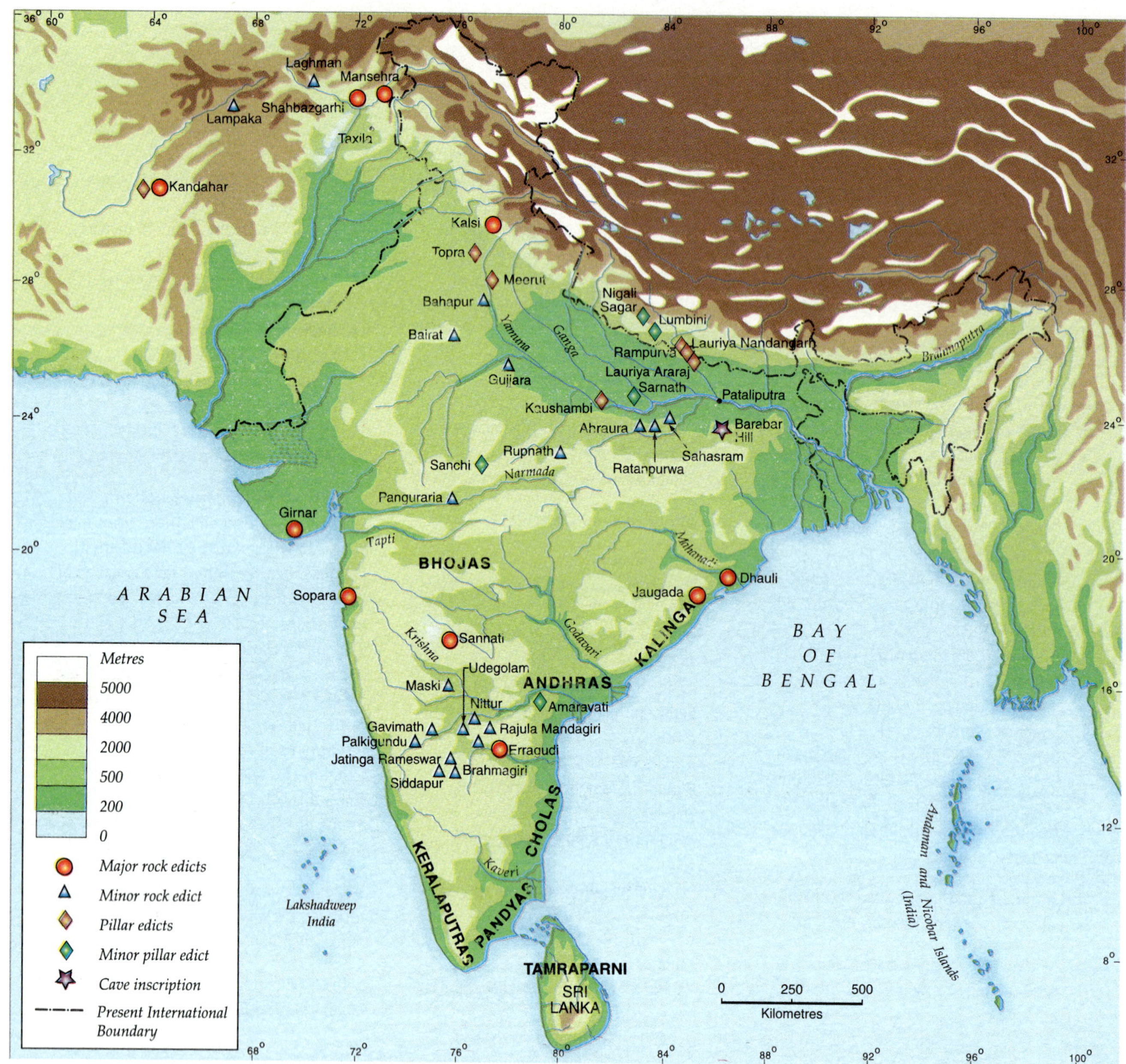

Map 7.1 Find-spots of Ashokan inscriptions

a noticeable clustering in the Andhra–Karnataka area. They are generally found in more remote hilly areas, at sites which may have had an older cultic significance. Ashoka's inscriptions were located along ancient trade and pilgrimage routes. Some of them, such as the ones at Sanchi and Sarnath, were situated at important Buddhist monastic sites. The locations of Ashoka's inscriptions have often been taken as indicative of the extent of the Maurya empire. It is a bit simplistic to think that the Maurya king's effective political control extended over the entire area. This issue will be discussed further on in the section on Maurya state and administration.

Ashoka's inscriptions mostly contain explanations of *dhamma* (the content and nature of *dhamma* will be discussed further on), the king's efforts to propagate it, and his own assessment of his success in doing so. Some of them directly indicate his allegiance to the Buddha's teaching and his close relationship with the *sangha*. They offer a unique insight into Ashoka's ideas, but specific references to other aspects such as his administration or social and economic aspects of the Maurya period are few and indirect.

The frequent use of the first person in the Prakrit inscriptions and the strong personal tone leave no doubt that they were not composed by an inspired ghost-writer but represent the emperor's ideas, desires, and commands, tempered occasionally by honesty and reflectiveness that mitigates their increasingly authoritarian tone. Ashoka must have had an important role in designing the content of his inscriptions. Therefore, they give us a unique insight into the emperor's mind. We can follow his thoughts as he reflects on and agonizes over issues related to kingship and morality over his long, thirty-six-year reign.

References to a few later inscriptions can also be cited here. The Junagadh/Girnar inscription of Rudradaman of 150 CE records that the construction of a water reservoir known as the Sudarshana lake was begun during the time of Chandragupta Maurya and completed during Ashoka's reign. Inscriptions ranging between the 5th and 15th centuries CE in and around Sravana Belagola in Karnataka mention a *muni* (ascetic) named Chandragupta and the Jaina saint Bhadrabahu. A connection with the Maurya king Chandragupta has been suggested, but this is a matter of debate.

Megasthenes' *Indica*

The Maurya period saw a steady expansion of trade with the Western world and the exchange of emissaries between Maurya and Hellenistic kings. It is hence not surprising that Graeco-Roman accounts mention kings Sandrocottus (Chandragupta) and Amitrochates (Amitraghata, i.e., Bindusara), and their capital Palimbothra (Pataliputra). Generally considered an envoy of the Seleucus to the court of the Chandragupta Maurya, Megasthenes may actually have been, at least initially, associated with Sibyrtius, the Macedonian satrap of Arachosia (Bosworth, 1996). Arrian refers to his visiting king Porus as well. As an ambassador, Megasthenes' exposure to Indian society must have been socially and geographically restricted. Information regarding the frequency and duration of his visits to the Maurya court is unavailable. (For the details of Greek interactions with and perspectives on India, see Karttunen, 1989, [1997] 2017; and Stoneman, 2019.)

Megasthenes wrote a book called the *Indica* based on his travels and experiences in India. The book has not survived, but fragments are preserved in later Greek and Latin works, the earliest and most important of which are those of Diodorus, Strabo, Arrian, and Pliny. Diodorus Sicilus was a historian born in Agyrium in Sicily and lived in the second half of the 1st century BCE. Of the 40 books of his work, *Bibliotheca Historica* ('Historical Library'), only Books 1–5 and 11–20 survive; the rest exist in the form of fragments cited in later works. The surviving books describe Alexander's Indian campaign and contain a general description of India based on sources such as Megasthenes' *Indica*. Strabo was a geographer and historian, born in about 63 BCE at Amasia in Pontus in West Asia. His *Geography* consists of 17 books, of which the fifteenth deals with India and Persia. Arrian (Flavius Arrianus) (*c.* 96–180 CE) was a statesman, soldier, philosopher, and historian, born in Nikomedia in Bithynia. He wrote the *Anabasis*, an account of the Asian campaigns of Alexander and his *Indica* was a continuation of this work. The first part describes India, mainly on the basis of the accounts of Megasthenes and Eratosthenes; the second gives an account of the voyage of Nearchus (he had been commissioned to make this voyage by Alexander) down the Indus, along the coast to the Persian Gulf, and up the Euphrates river to Babylon; the third tries to prove that the southern parts of the world were uninhabitable due to great heat. Gaius Plinius Secundus (*c.* 23–79 CE), better known as Pliny the elder, was a Roman scholar. His book *Naturalis Historia* (Natural History) consists of 37 books dealing with diverse subjects such as geography, ethnography, physiology, and zoology. Megasthenes' observations are also cited by a Roman scholar, Claudius Aelianus (2nd–3rd century CE), author of a book on zoology titled *On the Peculiarities of Animals*.

All the references to Megasthenes occur in texts that have a wider canvas than India. Arrian, for instance, is quite frank in the closing sentence of his *Indica*: 'And since my design in drawing up the present narrative was not to describe the manners and customs of the Indians, but to relate how Alexander conveyed his army from India

PRIMARY SOURCES | **The Greeks on Megasthenes**

Later Graeco-Roman writers differed in their opinion of Megasthenes' accuracy and reliability. Strabo and Pliny were scathing in their criticism, Arrian was more trusting. Diodorus did not make any disparaging remarks about Megasthenes, but he left out some of the latter's strange and unbelievable stories about India and Indians.

Strabo:

But it is necessary for us to hear accounts of this country with indulgence, for not only is it farthest away from us, but not many of our people have seen it; and even those who have seen it, have seen only parts of it, and the greater part of what they say is from hearsay; and even what they saw they learned on a hasty passage with an army through the country. Wherefore they do not give out the same accounts of the same things, even though they have written these accounts as though their statements had been carefully confirmed. And some of them were both on the same expedition together and made their sojourns together, like those who helped Alexander to subdue Asia; yet they all frequently contradict one another. But if they differ thus about what was seen, what must we think of what they report from hearsay?

Strabo again:

Generally speaking, the men who have hitherto written on the affairs of India were a set of liars—Deimachus holds the first place in the list, Megasthenes comes next; while Onesicritus and Nearchus, with others of the same class, manage to stammer out a few words [of truth]. Of this we become more convinced while writing the history of Alexander. No faith whatever can be placed in Deimachus and Megasthenes. They coined the fables concerning men with ears large enough to sleep in, men without any mouths, without noses, with only one eye, with spider legs, and with fingers bent backward. They renewed Homer's fables concerning the battles of the cranes and the pygmies, and asserted the latter to be three spans high. They told of ants digging for gold, and Pans [horned demi-gods] with wedge-shaped heads, of serpents swallowing down oxen and stags, horns and all—meantime, as Eratosthenes has observed, accusing each other of falsehood. Both of these men were sent as ambassadors to Palimbothra—Megasthenes to Sandrocottus, Deimachus to Amitrochades his son—and such are the notes of their residence abroad, which, I know not why, they thought fit to leave.

Arrian:

But even Megasthenes, so far as it appears, did not travel over much of India, though no doubt he saw more of it than those who came with Alexander, the son of Philip, for, as he tells us, he resided at the court of Sandrocottus, the greatest king in India, and also at the court of Porus, who was still greater than he....Let this be said by way of a digression to discredit the accounts which some writers have given of the Indians beyond the Hyphasis (Beas), for those writers who were in Alexander's expedition are not altogether unworthy of our faith when they describe India as far as the Hyphasis. Beyond that limit, we have no real knowledge of the country: since this is the sort of account which Megasthenes gives us of an Indian river: Its name is the Silas; it flows from a fountain, called after the river, through the dominions of the Silaeans, who again are called after the river and the fountain; the water of the river manifests this singular property—that there is nothing which it cannot buoy up, nor anything which can swim or float in it, but everything sinks down to the bottom, so that there is nothing in the world so thin and unsubstantial as this water....

Pliny:

India was opened up to our knowledge...by other Greek writers, who, having resided with Indian kings—as for instance Megasthenes and Dionysius—made known the strength of the peoples of the country. It is not, however, worthwhile to study their accounts with care, so conflicting are they, and incredible.

Source H. L. Jones, cited in Majumdar, (1960) 1981: 244; McGrindle, 1877: 20–21, 194, 196–97, 21

to Persia, let this be taken as a mere episode.' For these writers, 'India' was the land beyond the Indus. We do not know whether they had direct access to Megasthenes' work or whether they relied on some secondary account of what he wrote. Nor were all their statements necessarily based on Megasthenes' *Indica* alone. The views of other writers such as Eratosthenes, Ktesius, Onesicritus, and Deimachus are also mentioned. This may help explain the many discrepancies in detail in the accounts of Strabo, Diodorus, and Arrian.

All these writers were part of an older Greek tradition of writing about other lands and people. They wrote for an educated Greek audience and their aim was not only to inform but also to entertain. Later writers selected from Megasthenes' book the bits they thought would interest their audience the most, and left out what they considered were the boring parts (which might have been of great use to historians). They highlighted things about India that were similar to Greece, as well as those that were curious and different. They ended up choosing more or less the same parts, but their narration was not identical. The references to the contents of the *Indica* are separated from each other by time and by the interest, interpretation, and style of the later writers.

Megasthenes' *Indica* described the country, its size and shape, rivers, soil, climate, plants, animals, produce, administration, society, and legends. The Greeks were especially captivated by India's animals and their accounts contain lengthy descriptions of elephants, monkeys, horse training, and elephant hunting. Similarities with their own land were commented on; it was noted that legends indicated that India too was originally inhabited by primitive tribes, and that the arts and other things that improve human life were invented gradually. The Greeks referred to the Indians' worship of Dionysus and Herakles (the names they gave Vasudeva Krishna). They cited similarities between the views of the 'Brachmanes' (i.e., Brahmanas) and Greek ideas relating to the nature of the world and soul. They idealized India when they stated that farmers were never touched in war, that there was no slavery, and that theft was rare. They also erred on several points. For instance, Aelian cites Megasthenes and asserts that Indians did not borrow or lend money on interest. Similarly, Strabo states that Indians were ignorant of the arts of writing and fusing metals, and never drank wine, except at sacrifices.

There were comparisons with Egypt and Europe. For example, the Ganga and Indus were compared with the Nile and Danube, and it was observed that most animals that were tame in the Greek lands were wild in India. There are also fantastic stories, such as those about one-horned horses with heads like those of deer, of huge snakes, and of the river Silas in which nothing would float. Strange customs were recounted. Pliny cites Megasthenes' description of the men living on a mountain called Nulo—we are told that their feet turned backward and that they had eight toes on each foot. He also states that on other mountains, there was a breed of men with heads like dogs, who lived by hunting and fowling, and communicated by barking. Gold-digging ants were said to live in the north-western mountains. Diodorus left out many of these fantastic accounts.

The Greek references to Megasthenes' *Indica* represent India seen through a double filter—the first is Megasthenes' interpretation of what he saw or heard; the second is later Graeco-Roman writers' interpretations of Megasthenes' account. Megasthenes seems to have got some things right and some things wrong (see Thapar, 1984; Stoneman, 2019). The citations from the *Indica* seem to tell us more about ancient Greek perspectives on India than about the history of the subcontinent in the 4th century BCE.

Archaeological and numismatic evidence

Archaeological investigations for this period are rather inadequate and reliable dates are few and far between. As a result, there is very sketchy information about the middle and late NBPW phases in the Ganga valley, both of which broadly correspond to the Maurya period, and even less information about sites elsewhere. Archaeological evidence does not follow the timelines of political history, so as mentioned earlier, this section should be read in conjunction with the contents of Chapters 6 and 8.

Archaeological remains from Kumrahar and Bulandibagh are associated with Pataliputra, the Maurya capital. Other important sites include Taxila, Mathura, and Bhita. Compared to earlier levels, Maurya levels display a greater diversity of artefacts and a heightening of urban features. The material evidence of the Maurya period also exists in the form of Ashoka's pillars and other sculptural and architectural elements, many of them direct products of royal patronage. There are also a number of stone sculptures and terracotta images that appear to be part of a popular, urban milieu.

Punch-marked coins, mostly of silver, continued to be issued and used in the Maurya period. Certain symbols such as the crescent-on-arches, tree-in-railing, and peacock-on-arches have been associated with the Maurya kings. The specific symbolism and

PRIMARY SOURCES | **The message in the landscape**

Nayanjot Lahiri draws on a variety of sources to create a biography of Ashoka woven out of the kings' inscriptions and the ways in which he was remembered in later Buddhist legends. One of the important aspects of her work is the way in which she imaginatively grounds the sites of Ashoka's experiences and inscriptions in the archaeological landscape. As she points out, how his epigraphic message was understood depended not only on his words, but also on the larger context.

At Junagadh, also known as Girnar, Ashoka's 14 rock edicts were neatly inscribed on the eastern side of a large granite rock located in the suburbs of Junagadh city. Each edict was enclosed in etched compartments.

The rock stood near an artificial lake called Sudarshana lake. We know about this lake from a 2nd century CE inscription of the time of the Shaka Kshatrapa ruler Rudradaman. It was inscribed on the same rock as the Ashokan edicts, and gives us the history of this reservoir across several centuries, beginning with its construction during the time of Chandragupta Maurya by his provincial governor Vaishya Pushyagupta and its completion by the Yavana Tushaspha, who was governor of the area during Ashoka's reign (see Chapter 8 for details of the inscription). These references to the construction of a massive water reservoir indicate that the Maurya state had an administrative presence in Junagadh.

The forested tract of Junagadh was surrounded by hills (Girnar is the highest mountain in Gujarat) that offered natural defences. It had access to the coast, which was less than 80 km away. The port of Prabahas Patan was occupied in the Maurya period. The Sudarshana reservoir provided water, probably for agriculture and for drinking.

The location of the Sudarshana lake was identified in the 19th century by Khan Bahadur Ardeseer Jamsedjee, the Naib Dewan of the Junagadh princely state. The blocks of masonry in the Sonarekha river are the remains of the Maurya period embankment. There were mounds near the site. The site of the Maurya town at Junagadh has not been identified. Lahiri suggests that it could have been in the Chamunda area of the modern city, where a mound-like formation is visible, and on the outer edge of the Uparkot fortifications. This is not far from the water reservoir; current inhabitants of the area report that pottery and other ancient remains are found here from time to time.

Lahiri points out the Ashoka's message inscribed on the Junagadh rock would have been understood in conjunction with the impressive waterwork that must have improved the lives of the people of the area. She also points to the remains of Buddhist structures in the Junagadh area, for instance the Bhoria *stupa*, also known as the Lakha Medi *stupa* in the Girnar Reserve Sanctuary. This *stupa* may have been built in Ashoka's time. Remains of structures made of large burnt bricks have also been found in and around the Girnar hills. There are four small valleys between the Girnar range and the surrounding hills at Bhavnath, Hasnapur, Surajkund, and Bhordevi. These are the very places where pilgrims halt these days in the course of the sacred Girnar pilgrimage circuit. These four places have early historial ruins, including the remains of Buddhist *stupas*. This suggests the possibility that before Girnar became a religious centre for Jainas and Hindus, it was a Buddhist centre. Ashoka may have had something to do with this, given the fact that a provincial centre of the Maurya empire was located here.

Lahiri uses this 'zooming out' to the larger landscape of the Girnar area in order to emphasize the point that it is necessary to rethink the idea of a 'standard' Ashokan message conveyed across regions of the Maurya empire. Local interpretations and reception of the emperor's message would have been mediated by many factors, including the perception of political authority and the ground realities, of which the material remains are the surviving markers.

Source Lahiri, 2015: 202–14

significance of the motifs is often difficult to ascertain. Some of them seem to be part of a large, common pool of cultural symbols; others (such as the sun) may have been symbols of royalty. Still others may have had a religious significance. For instance, it has been suggested that the tree-in-railing symbol represents the Buddha's enlightenment and that the symbols consisting of a number of arches represent a *stupa*. However, these interpretations are speculative. The use of a symbol on coins issued by the state would certainly have endowed it with a political significance.

The Maurya Dynasty

The Maurya empire was built on the foundations laid by the Nandas. The first three rulers of the dynasty were Chandragupta (*c*. 324/321–300/297 BCE), Bindusara (*c*. 300/297–273 BCE), and Ashoka (268–232 BCE) (see Majumdar et al., [1951] 1968: 54–94; Raychaudhuri, [1923] 2000: 234–326; Thapar, [1963] 1987: 12–54). The rule of the later Mauryas continued till *c*. 187 BCE.

In Buddhist texts such as the *Digha Nikaya*, *Mahavamsa*, and *Divyavadana*, the Mauryas are described as belonging to a Kshatriya clan called the Moriyas, who ruled at Pipphalivana. The *Parishishtaparvan*, on the other hand, describes Chandragupta as the son of the daughter of a chief of a village of peacock tamers (*mayura-poshakas*). The *Mudrarakshasa* refers to Chandragupta as being of low social origin. The early medieval writers Kshemendra and Somadeva call him *Purva-Nanda-suta* (son of the genuine Nanda). Dhundiraja, a commentator on the *Vishnu Purana*, states that Chandragupta was the eldest son of Maurya, son of the Nanda king Sarvarthasiddhi, by Mura, daughter of a *vrishala* (hunter).

Chandragupta may have first established himself in the Punjab and then moved eastwards until he gained control over the Magadha region. Several texts such as the Puranas, *Milindapanha*, *Mudrarakshasa*, *Mahavamshatika*, and *Parishishtaparvan* refer to his conflict with the Nandas. There is also a tradition referring to Chandragupta overthrowing the Nandas with the help of a Brahmana of Taxila named Chanakya. There are many legends about Chanakya, and he was probably a historical figure. These suggest that he was insulted by the Nanda king and vowed to exterminate the entire lineage. As discussed earlier, Chanakya's connection with the *Arthashastra*, however, was a much later development and post-dated Chandragupta's time by many centuries. The aim may have been to add prestige to the text.

The background to Chandragupta's political rise was the invasion of Alexander of Macedon (327–26 BCE) in the north-west. Greek sources in fact suggest a meeting between Chandragupta and Alexander. They also refer to the conflict between Chandragupta and Seleucus Nikator, who had inherited the eastern provinces of Alexander's empire. This may have occurred in about 301 BCE and was resolved by a treaty. According to its terms, Chandragupta obtained the territories of Arachosia (the Kandahar area of south-east Afghanistan), Gedrosia (south Baluchistan), and Paropomisadai (the area between Afghanistan and the Indian subcontinent) and handed over 500 elephants in return. It is not certain whether a matrimonial alliance was concluded between the two rulers or whether the treaty recognized more general rights of inter-marriage between the Greeks and the Indians.

The only definite inscriptional reference to Chandragupta is in the 2nd century CE Junagadh inscription of Rudradaman, which attributes the beginning of the construction of a water reservoir known as the Sudarshana lake to Chandragupta's reign. By the time of Ashoka, the Maurya presence had extended into the Karnataka region; it is very likely that the major conquests had been made many years earlier by Chandragupta. A poem in the *Akananuru* (*Akam* 251) composed by the Sangam poet Mamulanar refers to the following incident: The Koshar achieved many successes against their enemies. However, the Mokur did not submit to them, and so the Moriyar, who had a huge army, sent an expedition to assist them. The poet describes the Moriyar chariots rolling across a swathe cut in the mountain for their onward march. Another poem by Mamulanar

Rocks bearing the Bahapur/Srinivasapuri edict in East of Kailash, New Delhi; the Delhi–Meerut pillar, near Bara Hindu Rao Hospital, Delhi (from top)

Figure 7.1 Some symbols on Magadhan punch-marked coins

(*Akam* 281) states that the war-like Vadugar formed the vanguard of the Moriyar army as it marched southwards. Vadugar means 'northerners', and refers to the people living in the Andhra–Karnataka region, immediately to the north of Tamil country. If there is any historical basis to these references, they suggest that the Mauryas interfered in the politics of the south, that they had an alliance with a southern power called the Koshar (probably located in north Karnataka), and that troops from the Deccan formed part of the Maurya army.

Some later inscriptions and Jaina texts suggest a connection between Chandragupta, Jainism, and Karnataka. A number of places in the Sravana Belagola hills have the word 'Chandra' as their suffix. Jaina tradition speaks of the relationship between Chandragupta and the Jaina saint Bhadrabahu. The Maurya king is said to have accompanied Bhadrabahu to Karnataka in the wake of the saint's prophecy of the impending outbreak of a 12-year famine in Magadha. The king is also described as having committed *sallekhana* (ritual death by starvation). Later texts such as the 10th century *Brihatkathakosha* of Harishena narrate this story, as does the 19th century *Rajavali-kathe*. Inscriptions in the Sravana Belagola hills, dating between the 5th and 15th centuries CE, mention a person named Chandragupta and Bhadrabahu. It is possible, but not certain, that there is a historical basis to the strong Jaina tradition that connects Chandragupta with Karnataka.

Chandragupta's trans-Vindhyan conquests are suggested by Graeco-Roman sources. Plutarch states that Sandrocottus (Chandragupta) over-ran and subdued the whole of 'India' with an army of 600,000. Justin too describes Chandragupta as in possession of 'India'. It is not certain what exactly these writers meant by 'India'. The Junagadh inscription of Rudradaman indicates that Chandragupta's conquests extended up to Saurashtra in Gujarat. In view of such indirect references, it seems that Chandragupta was the chief architect of the Maurya empire.

Chandragupta was succeeded by his son Bindusara, who ruled between 297 and 273 BCE. According to Jaina tradition, Chandragupta abdicated the throne in favour of his son Simhasena. The *Mahabhashya* refers to Chandragupta's successor as Amitraghata, while the Greek accounts call him Amitrochates or Allitrochates. The *Divyavadana* refers to Ashoka putting down a revolt in Taxila due to the activities of wicked ministers. This may have been an incident that occurred in Bindusara's reign. Taranatha's account states that Chanakya, one of Bindusara's great lords, destroyed the nobles and kings of 16 towns and made him master of all the territory between the eastern and western seas. Some historians consider this an indication of Bindusara's conquest of the Deccan, while others interpret it as a reference to the suppression of a revolt.

Buddhist sources are relatively silent on Bindusara. There is a story of an Ajivika fortune-teller prophesying his son Ashoka's future greatness, which may suggest that the king favoured the Ajivikas. Greek sources refer to his diplomatic relations with western kings. According to Strabo, Antiochus, king of Syria, sent an ambassador named Deimachus to his court. Pliny mentions that Ptolemy II Philadelphus, ruler of Egypt, sent an ambassador named Dionysius. There is a story that Bindusara requested Antiochus to buy and send him some sweet wine, dried figs, and a sophist (a philosopher who specialized in philosophical debate and argumentation). Antiochus is supposed to have replied that while he would certainly send the wine and figs, Greek laws did not permit a sophist to be bought. A fragmentary inscription at Sanchi perhaps refers to Bindusara.

Bindusara's death was followed by a four-year succession conflict. According to the *Divyavadana*, Bindusara wanted his son Susima to succeed him, but Ashoka was supported by his father's ministers. A minister named Radhagupta seems to have played an especially important role. The *Dipavamsa* and *Mahavamsa* refer to Ashoka killing 99 brothers, sparing only one named Tissa.

Although Buddhist texts have a great deal to say about Ashoka (*c.* 268–232 BCE), we cannot take what they say at face value. Because of his close association with Buddhism, Ashoka is presented as a great, ideal king in the Buddhist tradition, and the

FURTHER DISCUSSION | **Legends of Ashoka**

Until the discovery and decipherment of his inscriptions, Ashoka's fame rested on the legendary accounts of his life, preserved in Buddhist texts such as the *Ashokavadana*. The *Ashokavadana* is part of a large collection of legends in the *Divyavadana*, and may originally have existed as an independent text. Although it belongs to the 2nd century CE, it contains many legends of an earlier time. J. Przyluski argues that the basic text was composed by monks of the Mathura region (the text heaps special praise on the city of Mathura, its monks, and monasteries). Mathura was an important centre of Buddhism, especially the Sarvastivada school.

One of the stories in the *Ashokavadana* relates an event of great significance that is described as having happened in Ashoka's previous birth, when he was a small boy named Jaya: One day, Jaya was playing by the roadside, when the Buddha came by. The little boy spontaneously put a handful of dirt into his begging bowl. As he did so, he made a *pranidhana* (resolute wish) that with this meritorious gift, he should become a king and a follower of the Buddha. The Buddha responded to the child's gift with a smile that illuminated the universe with its rays of light. These rays re-entered the Buddha's left palm, signifying that this child would become a great emperor in his next life. The Buddha then turned to his disciple Ananda, and made a prediction that 100 years after the *parinibbana*, this boy who threw a fistful of dirt into his bowl, would become a great, righteous *chakravarti* king, who would rule his empire from his capital at Pataliputra.

Another story in the *Ashokavadana* narrates that Ashoka was disliked by his father Bindusara because of his ugly appearance. Ashoka managed to become king after getting rid of the legitimate heir, by tricking him into entering a pit filled with live coals. He became notorious as 'Ashoka the Fierce' because of his wicked nature and bad temper. He submitted his ministers to a test of loyalty and had 500 of them killed because he found them wanting. When certain women of his harem insulted him, he had the whole lot of them burnt to death. He was so given to sadistic pleasure that he built a hell on earth—an elaborate and horrific torture chamber, where he amused himself by watching the agony of his unfortunate victims. It was as a result of an encounter with a pious Buddhist monk that he was transformed into 'Ashoka the Pious'. Xuanzang, who travelled in India in the 7th century CE, tells us that he visited the site where the torture chamber once stood.

The *Ashokavadana* gives a poignant account of Ashoka's last days. We are told that the king started gifting away state resources to the *sangha*. Fearing that he would empty out the entire treasury, his ministers denied him access to it. Ashoka then started giving away his own personal possessions. Finally, he was left with only one *anwala* (*myrobalan* fruit), which too he gifted. Having given everything he owned to the Order, the king died peacefully.

John S. Strong points out that a number of things have to be kept in mind when analyzing such legends. The authors reworked old legends and traditions, some of which had till then circulated in oral form. Their aim was to confirm the faith of the faithful and to win new adherents to the Buddhist fold. The legends aimed at conveying certain important ideas such as the nature of suffering and how to overcome it and the importance of the laws of *karma* and rebirth. They tried to inculcate devotion to the Buddha and emphasized the merits that would accrue to those who gave generously to the *sangha*. They also highlighted the role that kingship could play in supporting the Buddhist faith.

Buddhist legends in texts such as the *Ashokavadana* were responsible for Ashoka acquiring the reputation of an exemplary Buddhist king who deserved both admiration and emulation, not only in the Indian subcontinent, but in East and Southeast Asia as well.

Source Przyluski, 1967; Strong, 1983

account of his reign and personality in these texts is neither objective nor dispassionate. (For a discussion of Ashoka's life in history and legend, see Lahiri, 2015, 2022; for Ashoka's political ideas, see Upinder Singh, 2017; for the evolution of his thought, see Olivelle, 2023.)

The *Ashokavadana* states that Ashoka's mother was a queen named Subhadrangi, daughter of a Brahmana of Champa. A palace intrigue kept her away from the king. This eventually ended, and she bore him a son. It is from her exclamation—'I am now without sorrow'—that the child is supposed to have got his name. The *Divyavadana* tells a similar story, but in one version, gives the name of the queen as Janapadakalyani. The *Vamsatthapakasini* calls her Dharma. During his father's reign, Ashoka was stationed as governor at Ujjayini, and before that, possibly at Taxila (or he may have just gone there to put down a revolt). The *Dipavamsa* and *Mahavamsa* tell the love story of Ashoka and Devi, daughter of a merchant of Vidisha. Devi went on to become the mother of Ashoka's celebrated children, Mahinda and Sanghamitta, both of whom eventually joined the Buddhist *sangha*. Texts refer to other queens such as Asandhimitta, Tissarakhita,

and Padmavati. An inscription on the Allahabad–Kosam pillar mentions gifts made by queen Karuvaki.

Ashoka preferred to have his words rather than his portrait inscribed in stone. As he made his way into Buddhist legend, his image started to appear at Buddhist sites. Three scenes at Sanchi have been identified as representing Ashoka. A scene carved on the southern gateway of Stupa 1 seems to depict his visit to the Ramagrama Stupa. We see the king with the royal insignia of turban, ewer, and fly-whisk riding in procession in a horse-drawn chariot, accompanied by an entourage that includes infantry, cavalry, elephants, and chariots. The procession is moving toward a *stupa*, on the other side of which four serpent deities (*nagas*) and their families bear offerings in their hands. Another scene, carved on the western pillar of the southern gateway of Stupa 1, may represent Ashoka's visit to the bodhi tree. A Stupa 2 railing relief shows a king—probably Ashoka—supported by or with his arms on the shoulders of two queens, flanked by three attendants. But the most dramatic evidence of royal representations come from Kanaganahalli in the Gulbarga district of Karnataka

While the distribution of Ashoka's inscriptions is usually taken to suggest the extent of the Maurya empire, there must have been differences in the level of control within this area. In the north-west, it extended up to Kandahar in Afghanistan, with the kingdom of

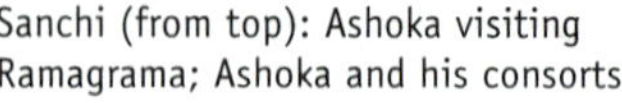

Sanchi (from top): Ashoka visiting Ramagrama; Ashoka and his consorts

RECENT DISCOVERIES | **Stone portraits of Ashoka at Kanaganahalli**

In the autumn of 1993, a team of archaeologists was surveying the area around Sannati in the Chitapur taluk of Gulbarga district, Karnataka. A dam was to be built across the river Bhima near this place, and the survey was necessary for the mandatory environmental clearance. Several sites were discovered in the course of the survey, but the most dramatic evidence came from Kanaganahalli.

This site is situated on the left bank of the Bhima river, 3 km east of the Chandralamba temple at Sannati. Here, some irregular stones arranged in an arc in the midst of agricultural fields attracted the attention of the archaeologists. The excavations began in 1994–95 and the Archaeological Survey of India team unearthed remains of a large brick *stupa* encased with sculpted limestone slabs. Apart from the slabs with reliefs, there were pillars, railings, capitals, and sculptures. Lead coins bearing the names of Satavahana kings, and over 170 donative and label inscriptions were identified. Inscriptions indicate that a *stupa* called the Adhalaka *mahachaitya* existed at Kanaganahalli between the 3rd century BCE and 3rd century CE.

The beautiful relief carvings on limestone slabs that once adorned this *stupa* belong to the 2nd and 3rd centuries CE. They include kings who can be identified by label inscriptions. The representations are highly stylized, without any significant differences in physique or facial features. But there are variations in the composition and in the details of ornaments, headdresses, and clothing. Ashoka figures in two scenes. In one, he appears along with his queen, with three women attendants, two bearing flywhisks and one an umbrella. He wears an elaborate headdress, armlets, and earrings, and interestingly, the sacred thread, worn across the torso. The queen, wearing a necklace, girdle, and heavy anklets, plays with her earring with her right hand. The king's and queen's bodies tilt toward each other at the waist in an affectionate pose. The inscription reads 'Raya Asoko' (king Ashoka).

The second relief sculpture too bears a similar inscription. Here, the king stands with folded hands to the left of the *bodhi* tree, which is preceded by a pair of footprints. A man (perhaps a prince?) stands to the right. In the upper part of the scene are two women, one holding flowers and the other a bowl with some offerings. It has been suggested that this scene represents Ashoka venerating the *bodhi* tree along with his son Mahinda and daughter Sanghamitta. Taken together, these two scenes reflect the iconic status that Ashoka had achieved not long after his death in the Indian Buddhist world.

Of course, we do not know what Ashoka actually looked like, as the Sanchi and Kanaganahalli sculptors lived long after he had died and portrayed him according to prevailing artistic styles and their imagination.

Source Poonacha, 2011; Zin, 2018

Antiochus II of Syria lying to the west. Its eastern frontier extended to Odisha. It included almost the entire subcontinent, except the southernmost parts, which, according to rock edict 13, were ruled by the Cholas and Pandyas, and according to rock edict 2, by the Keralaputras and Satiyaputras. Ashoka's fame is based on his association with Buddhism and his pacifism, which are proclaimed in Buddhist texts and in his own inscriptions.

The Maurya empire declined rapidly after Ashoka. The Puranas mention the names of later Maurya rulers and give the number of years of their rule. The details vary, but it is clear that they had relatively short reigns. The empire became weak and fragmented and seems to have suffered an invasion by the Bactrian Greeks. The Maurya dynasty came to an end when the last king, Brihadratha, was killed by his military commander Pushyamitra, who founded the Shunga dynasty in *c*. 187 BCE.

Textual and Archaeological Profiles of Settlements

Given the dynamics and slow-moving nature of social and economic processes, it is best to read the details in this section along with those in Chapters 6 and 8. The 3rd and 2nd centuries BCE saw a continuation of the processes of agrarian and urban expansion that were underway during the preceding centuries. Cities expanded in size and complexity, and urbanism spread to many new areas such as Kashmir, the Punjab plains, lower Ganga valley, Brahmaputra valley, and Odisha. Urban growth in the far south can also be identified in this period. The connection between the expansion of the Maurya empire and urban development in various parts of the subcontinent is a complex issue. The Maurya impact cannot be ignored, but it should not be exaggerated.

Megasthenes divided the Indian people into seven strata. Diodorus and Strabo use the Greek word *mere* and Arrian *genea* for these divisions. If we combine the descriptions, the seven groups were as follows: philosophers, farmers, herdsmen and hunters, artisans and traders, soldiers, overseers, and the kings' counsellors. This collection of occupational groups and administrative ranks corresponds neither to the *varnas* nor the *jatis*. It seems to have been Megasthenes' own invention, although it is possible that it was modelled on Herodotus' classification of Egyptian society into seven similar, though not identical, classes. According to Megasthenes, no one in India could marry outside their *genos* (this is a Greek word used to refer to clan or other relationships based on descent), nor could they follow another's occupation. Thapar (1984) points out that it is important to understand the nuances of the Greek words Megasthenes used and that although he got the numbers wrong, he did identify two of the important aspects of the caste system—hereditary occupation and endogamy. The *philosophoi* (literally, 'philosophers') are described as being held in high esteem in India. Strabo divides them into the *brachmanes* (Brahmanas) and *garmanes* (*shramanas*). Diodorus refers to nomadic tribes of herdsmen and shepherds. He also states that the artisans (*technitai*) were exempt from taxes and maintained by the state. According to Strabo, no one other than the king could own a horse or elephant. He writes that apart from the independent artisans, armourers and shipbuilders were employed by the state and paid a *misthos* (wage). Megasthenes lauds Indian society for not having any slaves. This was an incorrect statement. The existence of slavery across the centuries is known from various sources. Ashoka's rock edict 9 mentions courteous behaviour towards *dasas* and *bhatakas* (slaves and servants) as part of *dhamma*.

Urban growth was accompanied by an expansion of specialized crafts, trade, and guild organization. Money was increasingly used as a medium of exchange. Megasthenes was wrong in stating that Indians did not borrow or lend money on interest, for we know of money-lending from earlier times. Although there is evidence of earlier writing from Anuradhapura and Kodumanal, the Maurya period saw the earliest royal inscriptions on stone. Writing may have been used in other activities as well, especially to record business transactions. Some of these developments are directly reflected in evidence from middle and late NBPW levels at various sites.

Greek sources describe Pataliputra, the Magadhan capital. One would expect this to be the most accurate part of Megasthenes' account, and as we shall see, archaeological evidence does in fact support it on some important points. Megasthenes describes the city as surrounded by a wooden wall with towers and openings for shooting arrows, beyond which was a moat.

The precise location and extent of the ancient city of Pataliputra has been an issue of debate among archaeologists for a long time, and is connected with the identification of the old course of the Son and Ganga. Ancient ruins that can be connected to the Maurya phase of Pataliputra's history have been identified at several places in modern Patna. The most important of these are at Kumrahar and Bulandibagh. At Kumrahar,

PRIMARY SOURCES | Pataliputra and the palace, according to Arrian and Aelian

But of their [i.e., the Indians'] cities, it is said that the number is so great that it cannot be stated with precision, but that such cities as are situated on the banks of rivers or on the sea coast are built of wood, for were they built of brick, they would not last long—so destructive are the rains, and also the rivers when they overflow their banks and inundate the plains. Those cities, however, which stand on commanding situations and lofty eminences are built of brick and mud. The greatest city in India is that which is called Palimbothra, in the dominions of the Prasians, where the streams of the Erannoboas [Son] and the Ganges unite—the Ganges being the greatest of all rivers, and the Erannoboas being perhaps the third largest of Indian rivers, though greater than the rivers elsewhere; but it is smaller than the Ganges where it falls into it. Megasthenes says further of this city that the inhabited part of it stretched on either side to an extreme length of eighty stadia [over 9 miles], and that its breadth was fifteen stadia [1¼ mile], and that a ditch encompassed it all round, which was six plethora in breadth and thirty cubits in depth, and that the wall was crowned with five hundred and seventy towers and had four-and-sixty gates.

(Arrian, *Indica*, 10)

In the Indian royal palace where the greatest of all the kings of the country resides, besides much else which is calculated to excite admiration, and with which neither Memnomian Susa with all its costly splendour, nor Ekbatana with all its magnificence can vie (for I think only the vanity of the Persians would prompt such a comparison), there are other wonders besides, which I cannot undertake to describe in this treatise. In the parks tame peacocks are kept, and pheasants which have been domesticated; and among cultivated plants there are some to which the king's servants attend with special care, for there are shady groves and pasture grounds covered with trees, and branches of trees which the art of woodmen has deftly interwoven. And these very trees, from the unusual benignness of climate, are always in bloom, and, untouched by age, never shed their leaves; and while some are native to the soil, others are with circumspect care brought from other parts, and with their beauty enhance the charms of the landscape. The olive is not among them, this being a tree that is neither indigenous to India, nor thrives when transported there. Birds and animals that wander at freedom and have never been tamed resort on their own to India and there build their nests and form their lairs. Parrots are natives of the country, and keep hovering about the king and wheeling around him, and vast though their numbers be, no Indian ever eats a parrot. The reason for all this is that they are believed to be sacred and that the Brachmans [Brahmanas] honour them highly above all other birds. They assign a specious enough reason for doing so—namely, that the parrot alone, from the admirable configuration of its vocal organs, can imitate human speech. Within the palace ground, there are also artificial ponds of great beauty, in which they keep fish of enormous size but quite tame. No one has permission to fish for these except the king's sons while yet in their boyhood. These youngsters amuse themselves without the least risk of being drowned while fishing in the unruffled sheet of water, and learning how to sail their boats.

(Aelian, *On the Peculiarities of Animals*, 13.18)

Source McGrindle, quoted in Majumdar, (1960) 1981: 223–24; 414–15

there are remains of pillars, supposedly part of a pillared hall consisting of 10 rows of 8 pillars each. To the north-west of Kumrahar, at Bulandibagh, are the remains of a wooden palisade (fortification), consisting of two parallel walls made of wooden uprights, separated by a width of about 3.75 m (details of the pillared hall and wooden palisade are discussed further on in the section on architecture). Although their stratigraphy is not clearly defined, these may represent remains of the wooden fortifications of Pataliputra described by Megasthenes.

Several other sites give more detailed evidence of life in the cities of the Maurya empire. Excavations at Stratum II at Bhir mound at Taxila (Marshall, 1951) revealed an occupation belonging to the 3rd century BCE. The plan of the settlement was haphazard. Four streets and five lanes associated with blocks of houses were identified. There was a broad 6.70 m wide street (named First Street by the excavators), which did not run straight. Other streets ranged between 3 and 5 m in width, and were often winding rather than straight. The lanes leading off from the streets were narrower but had a more regular alignment. There were traces of covered drains in some places, but none in the main street. Some amount of civic planning is suggested by round refuse bins in the open squares and streets. Rough stone pillars (about 0.91 m high) at the corners of houses guarded them against damage from wheels of passing chariots or carts. The houses consisted of rooms arranged around an open courtyard, usually paved with stone.

Purana Qila: ring wells; storage jar

Some of the larger ones had two courtyards. Bathing areas and open passages were also paved with stone. Sewage from houses was carried by stone surface drains and smaller earthenware drain-pipes into soak-pits. Some of the excavated rooms may have been shops. One of these, which contained many cut pieces of shell and mother-of-pearl, was evidently a shell worker's working area or shop. John Marshall identified a 60 × 23 m complex as a religious structure. A lane divided this into a larger northern block and smaller southern block. The northern block consisted of about 30 rooms, 2 courtyards, and a large pillared hall. The debris from the hall and nearby area included many terracotta reliefs representing a male and a female figure—perhaps deities—holding hands. According to Marshall, they may have been cult images meant to be sold to devotees.

In the Indo-Gangetic divide, Ropar reflects a transition from village to town. Period III at this site is dated *c.* 600–200 BCE, and yielded NBPW and punch-marked and uninscribed cast copper coins. There is also a seal with an inscription in Maurya Brahmi. Houses were made of stone set in mud mortar, although some were of mud-brick and burnt brick. There were remains of a 12 ft wide wall of burnt brick, perhaps leading into a tank for storing rainwater. The upper levels of Period III revealed soak-pits lined with terracotta rings. Maurya period levels have also been found at the Purana Qila in Delhi.

In the upper Ganga valley, remains of a fortified settlement of the Maurya period were discovered at Bhita (Marshall, 1915). John Marshall's excavations were concentrated in the south-east corner of the site, where he uncovered two streets, which he named High Street and Bastion Street. The former was about 9.14 m wide, and probably led to a series of gates with attached guardrooms. The narrower Bastion Street lay to the north-east of this. The fortifications consisted of a 3.40 m thick mud rampart with a circular bastion and a gateway that was blocked at some point. One of the interesting discoveries was a house, which Marshall named 'House of the Guild' due to the discovery of a seal with the word *nigama*. Consisting of 12 rooms arranged around a rectangular courtyard, it may have been double-storyed, and was rebuilt several times. The remains of other similar houses were also unearthed. On the side facing the road, there were often rows of rooms with a platform or verandah in front. Cunningham identified Bhita with a place called Bitbhaya-pattana, mentioned in Jaina texts. On the other hand, Marshall identified it with a place called Vichhi or Vicchigrama, whose name occurred on a seal found at the site. Whether these identifications are correct or not, going by the large number of seals found here, Bhita seems to have been an important trade centre.

In the doab region, Mathura and Sonkh have given evidence of occupation during the Maurya period. At Mathura, the beginnings of urbanization are discernable in Period II, dated between the late 4th century BCE and 2nd century BCE. The pottery assemblage was marked by NBPW. The size of the settlement increased to about 3.9 sq km, a mud fortification wall flanking it on three sides and the Yamuna to its east. Coins made their appearance, and there was prolific evidence of specialized crafts such as the manufacture of terracotta figurines, copper and iron working, and bead making. At nearby Sonkh, the earliest levels of Period II yielded NBPW, terracotta figurines, uninscribed cast and die-struck coins, and silver punch-marked coins.

More detailed evidence is available from Atranjikhera (Gaur, 1983) in the Etah district, where the NBPW sub-phase IVC was dated *c.* 350–200 BCE. This phase was marked by an increase in structural activities. The defences, consisting of a mud rampart topped by a brick parapet, seem to belong to this period. There was a development of terracotta art, coinage, and the first evidence of writing. Five structural phases were identified in

The Bhita mound (UP)

Period IVC. An inscribed terracotta sealing had a partially legible Brahmi legend. There were many terracotta artefacts and beads of terracotta and semi-precious stones (agate, carnelian, quartz, and jasper). Stone objects included a small pestle, grinder, and a broken quern (?). Bone and ivory objects comprised arrowheads, stylii, one ivory bead, and an ivory ear stud. Iron artefacts found in Period IVC (70) were a little less in number compared with Period IVB (79). Copper objects numbered 25, as opposed to 21 in Period IVB. Coins included one defaced copper punch-marked coin and one defaced uninscribed copper coin. A small bone sealing with a legible Brahmi letter and a *svastika* symbol were also found.

In the middle Ganga valley, the defences at Shravasti are dated *c.* 250 BCE, while those of Vaishali and Tilaura-kot belong to the 2nd century BCE. In the lower Ganga valley, the fortified city of Mahasthangarh (ancient Pundravardhana, in Bagura district of Bangladesh) has yielded a Brahmi inscription. The brick rampart at Bangarh (identified with ancient Kotivarsha) can be assigned to the 2nd century BCE. The mud ramparts of Chandraketugarh probably also belong to this period. This site, which dates from the pre-Maurya period, has yielded rich antiquities, especially exquisite terracottas, but its archaeological image still remains hazy. Tamluk was the eastern terminal point of the Uttarapatha and was an important early historical port. NBPW, terracottas and other antiquities connect the occupation here to mid-NBPW levels elsewhere in the Ganga valley.

In Odisha, Dhauli could represent Tosali, while Jaugada could represent Samapa, mentioned in the edicts as Maurya administrative centres. Alternatively, Sisupalgarh could represent Tosali or Kharavela's capital Kalinganagari. Another identification suggested for Tosali is Radhanagar. The mud fortification at Sisupalgarh, built in the early 2nd century BCE, was roughly square shaped, about 3/4 mile on each side and enclosed a large, planned city. At Jaugada on the Rishikulya, Period I, which revealed post-holes and portions of floors made of rammed earth or gravel and evidence of bead making, may date to at least the 3rd century BCE.

In Rajasthan, early urban growth is reflected at sites such as Bairat, Rairh, and Sambhar. Bairat is identified as the site of ancient Viratanagara, capital of the Matsya kingdom. The ruins at the site cover 2½ miles. Excavations in a small 400 × 190 ft area led to the unearthing of many remains of the Maurya and post-Maurya periods, such as pillars, structures including a Buddhist monastery, and many antiquities. The remains at Rairh ranged from the 3rd/2nd century BCE to beyond the 2nd century CE. The structural remains consisted of parallel walls and soak-pits made of terracotta rings. The occupation of the site of Sambhar seems to have begun in the 3rd/2nd century BCE, but little information is available.

The beginning of the early historical phase in Gujarat can be seen in the presence of NBPW at sites such as Broach, Nagal, Prabhas Patan, and Amreli, which can be dated to about the early 3rd century BCE, but detailed information is lacking. Limited excavations on the outer fringes of Broach on the banks of the Narmada revealed a 25 ft thick deposit. Period I was marked by BRW, with NBPW in the upper levels. There was a mud

rampart with a moat, and five terracotta ring wells were found on its inner side. The discovery of many finished and unfinished beads of semi-precious stones are indicative of bead manufacture. The importance of the Gujarat coastal sites vis-à-vis trade increased in the succeeding centuries.

Ujjayini (Ujjain) in Central India was the headquarters of one of the Maurya provinces. Period II had NBPW, copper coins, bone and ivory points, and terracotta ring wells. Two small ivory seals with their owners' names inscribed in early Brahmi letters were also found. This phase probably belongs to the Maurya period. At Besnagar, which represents the site of ancient Vidisha, the rampart, built in 2nd century BCE, enclosed an area of about 240 ha.

In Maharashtra, there are signs of the beginnings of urbanism. At Tagara (Ter), the earliest level had NBPW and a black-and-red burnished pottery, and seems to date to the 3rd–2nd centuries BCE. The fact that a set of Ashokan rock edicts were found at Sopara suggests that it was an important port in Maurya times; however, it has not been properly explored.

Further south, the occupation of sites such as Sannati, Kondapur, and Madhavpur seems to have begun in the Maurya period. Ashokan edicts have been found at Maski and Brahmagiri. Amaravati (ancient Dharanikota) on the banks of the river Krishna has yielded a fragmentary inscription in Maurya Brahmi. Period I at Amaravati goes back at least to the 4th century BCE. Period Ia was marked by BRW and NBPW. Potsherds with Brahmi inscriptions, similar to those found at Anuradhapura in Sri Lanka, were found. Similar pottery continued into Period Ib, and the beginning of the *stupa* complex dates to this period, as does an inscribed stone slab. The settlement of Uraiyur may go back to the 3rd century BCE.

The Nature and Structure of the Maurya Empire

The problems posed by the major sources for the Maurya period have implications for our understanding of the nature and structure of the empire. As mentioned earlier, given the current views on its date, the *Arthashastra* cannot be used as a source for the Maurya period. Megasthenes' *Indica* is replete with several discrepancies and inaccuracies. Ashoka's inscriptions, have the advantage that they are securely dated to his reign, but they mostly deal with Ashoka's *dhamma* and they offer only incidental references to administration. However, they are a rich source for Ashoka's political ideas.

The vastness of the Maurya state qualifies it as an empire, but what sort of empire was it? What did it mean for a territory or people to be absorbed into its fold? What were the strategies and degrees of control over different areas? How effective was this control?

The idea of a highly centralized Maurya empire was based partly on an earlier assumption that empires and centralization go together and on the all-controlling state described in the *Arthashastra*. Later writings questioned this view. Gerard Fussman

Panoramic view of Kaushambi (UP)

(1987–88) argues that given the extent of the empire and the communication networks of the time, the Maurya empire could not possibly have been centralized. Maurya rule was superimposed over a number of existing political units, which must have been allowed to continue to exercise varying degrees of autonomy. Ashoka's personal supervision applied only to the propagation of *dhamma*, not to details of routine administration. Initiatives at the provincial and local administrative level are evident in the script, language, content, and location of the inscriptions. For instance, the fact that the Greek and Aramaic inscriptions in the north-west are not literal translations of the standard edicts suggests that considerable initiative was left in the hands of local officials.

Romila Thapar ([1963] 1987) initially presented the Maurya empire as a new form of government marked by centralized control and planning. Her subsequent reconsideration of the issue (Thapar, 1984) suggests that the Maurya empire was not a homogeneous whole, and that it subsumed different sorts of economies, polities, and life-ways. Using the framework of world systems theory, Thapar suggests that the empire should be considered as consisting of metropolitan, core, and peripheral areas. Magadha was the metropolitan state. The core areas included existing states, areas of incipient state formation, and centres of trade. The peripheral areas included a number of pre-state societies. The relationship between the metropolitan state and the core and peripheral areas varied, but the nature of the relationship did not—it basically involved exploitation.

The Maurya period coincided with a period of steady agrarian and urban expansion, but the precise role of the Maurya state in this development can be debated. For instance, in the case of the southern Deccan, Namita Sugandhi (2003) points to the absence of distinct ceramic types such as NBPW, punch-marked coins, and Maurya art forms of the kind found in the north. On this basis, she suggests that the edicts should be understood as expressions of claims to authority rather than a reflection of actual control. The point is that the presence of Ashokan edicts at various sites indicates Maurya contact, but the precise *nature* of that contact must have varied considerably across different regions and can only be ascertained by carefully examining the larger archaeological context.

While the Maurya period shows continuity with the preceding period in terms of political, social, and economic processes, there are also some new features. The Nandas had a large empire, but the Maurya empire was larger, covering practically the entire subcontinent and extending beyond it in the north-west. Within this vast area, there was a multi-tiered administrative system, and the intensity and nature of control must have varied considerably. The empire was accompanied by manifestations of an imperial ideology and vision, expressed in sophisticated monumental stone sculpture and architecture. The edict-bearing Ashokan pillars stand as imperial monuments bearing the king's unique message to his people. Another significant difference from earlier regimes was that the Maurya emperors were not insular; they looked beyond the limits of the subcontinent. The Mauryan state had a multi-tiered administrative hierarchy in the capital with several provincial centres. The level of actual political and economic control exercised by the central and the provincial administrations must have varied considerably. This is in spite of the fact that Ashoka's style of governance had a significant peripatetic quality—the king, his various officials and inspection teams were constantly on the move.

Ashoka saw himself not as an inheritor but as an innovator, as a king who had inaugurated a new kind of kingship, one that would be a model for his successors. His inscriptions do not contain any genealogy or specific reference to his predecessors. As mentioned earlier, he is frequently referred to by the epithets Devanampiya and Piyadasi. Ashoka describes himself as 'king of Magadha' (*laja Magadhe* in the Bairat-Calcutta minor rock edict) and mentions his capital city Pataliputra (rock edict 4). He boasts of the vast extent of his political dominion. Certain versions of minor rock edict 1 refer to the Jambudvipa, which could refer to the whole earth or to a landmass of which the subcontinent was a part. The inscriptions reflect an awareness that there were Greeks and other ethnic groups within his multi-ethnic empire.

Ashoka distinguished his political domain from those of bordering (*pachanta*) kings. In the south, these included the principalities of the Cholas, Pandyas, Satiyaputras, Keralaputras, and Tamraparni (Sri Lanka). The king claims to have achieved *dhamma-vijaya* over the Yavanas, Kambojas, Nabhakas, Nabhapanktis, Bhojas, Pitinikas, Andhras, Pulindas, Cholas, and Pandyas. The Yonas and Kambojas can be placed in the north-west; the Bhojas, Andhras, and Pulindas can be located in trans-Vindhyan India and the Cholas in the far south.

The geopolitical world with which Ashoka was familiar extended beyond the Indian subcontinent to northern Africa and the Mediterranean. Outside the subcontinent, he claims to have attained *dhamma-vijaya* in the dominions of Antiyoka, Turamaya, Antikini, Maka, and Alikasudara. Antiyoka has been identified with Antiochus II Theos of Syria; Turamaya with Ptolemy II Philadelphus of Egypt; Antikini with Antigonus Gonatas of Macedonia; Maka with Magas of Cyrene in north Africa; and Alikasudara with Alexander of Epirus or Alexander of Corinth. We know the Mauryas entertained diplomats from various Hellenistic kingdoms. Deimachus was the ambassador of Antiochus, king of Syria. Megasthenes was an envoy of Seleucus Nikator or Sibyrtios.

With regard to Maurya administration, Patanjali's *Mahabhashya* refers to the *sabha* of Chandragupta, which may have been the larger council. The *sumbouloi* of Megasthenes also appears to refer to such a body. Ashoka's rock edict 3 states that the *palisa/parisa* (i.e., *parishad*) is to direct the officers known as *yutas* (*yuktas*) in the discharge of certain duties. In rock edict 6, the king states that he should be informed immediately if any dispute arises among members of the *parishad* in the course of their deliberations. This seems to be a reference to a smaller, select body. It can be connected to Megasthenes' *sunedroi* (literally, 'those who sit together', similar in meaning to *parishad*) (Bongard-Levin, 1971).

The political role of high-ranking officials is apparent in the fact that Radhagupta, one of Bindusara's *mantrins* (ministers) seems to have played a key role in Ashoka's successful bid for power. Megasthenes observes that the king was always available for consultation even when being massaged. Ashoka's rock edict 6 also emphasizes the king's accessibility to his officials.

Apart from the king and his consultative bodies, there were a number of high officers in charge of important portfolios. Ashoka's inscriptions mention many kinds of *mahamatas*. Specific types of *mahamatas* mentioned in the inscriptions include the *anta-mahamatas* (*mahamatas* in charge of the frontier areas) and *itthijhakka-mahamatas* (*mahamatas* in charge of women's welfare). The ***dhamma-mahamatas*** were a new cadre of officials created by Ashoka when he had been consecrated 13 years. Their job was to spread *dhamma* all over the empire.

The inscriptions suggest that the Maurya empire was divided into provinces under governors. There seem to have been at least four provinces—a southern one with its centre at Suvarnagiri, a northern one with its headquarters at Taxila, a western one with its headquarters at Ujjayini, and an eastern one with its centre at Tosali. The Girnar

PRIMARY SOURCES | **The life of a king, according to Megasthenes (via Strabo)**

Now the care of the king's person is committed to women, who also are purchased from their fathers; and the bodyguards and the rest of the military force are stationed outside the gates. And a woman who kills a king when he is drunk receives as her reward the privilege of consorting with his successor; and their children succeed to the throne. Again, the king does not sleep in the daytime; and even at night he is forced to change his bed from time to time because of the plots against him. Among the non-military departures he makes from his palace, one is that to the courts, where he spends the whole day hearing cases to the end, even if the hour comes for the care of his person. This care of his person consists of his being rubbed with sticks of wood, for while he is hearing the cases through, he is also rubbed by four men who stand around him and rub him. A second departure is to the sacrifices. A third is that to a kind of Bacchic chase wherein he is surrounded by women, and, beyond them, by the spear-bearers. The road is lined with ropes; and death is the penalty for anyone who passes inside the ropes to the women; and they are preceded by drum-beaters and gong-carriers. The king hunts in the fenced enclosures, shooting arrows from a platform in his chariot (two or three armed women stand beside him), and also in the unfenced hunting-grounds from an elephant; and the women ride partly in chariots, partly on horses, and partly on elephants, and they are equipped with all kinds of weapons, as they are when they go on military expeditions with men.

It is interesting to note that both Kautilya and Megasthenes mention the king's women bodyguards. Equally interesting is Megasthenes' reference to the king changing his bed several times in the night to guard himself against assassins. This fits in well with Kautilya's precautions against assassination.

Source Majumdar, (1960) 1981: 271–72

inscription of Rudradaman mentions Pushyagupta, who was the *rashtriya* (governor) of Saurashtra in Chandragupta's time. Ashoka is supposed to have been stationed as governor at Ujjayini during Bindusara's reign, and the fact that his inscriptions address the governors as *kumara* (or *aryaputra*) suggest a tradition of appointing royal princes to these important posts.

The pattern of the languages and scripts of the edicts suggests that the official cadres in most parts of the subcontinent were familiar with both the Prakrit language and Brahmi script, while those posted in the northwest were not. This suggests the recruitment of officials from among the local communities and the existence of a multi-lingual administration in those areas. The later Junagadh/Girnar inscription of Rudradaman (*c.* 150 CE), which refers to a Yavana (Greek or westerner) named Tushaspha who completed the construction of the Sudarshana lake during the time of Ashoka, suggests that Greek or Persian officials were appointed even in areas other than the northwest.

Ashokan inscriptions suggest that the *pradeshika*, *rajuka*, and *yukta* were important officers at the district level. Rock edict 3 refers to these officers going on tours every five years in order to instruct people in *dhamma* and for other purposes. Bongard-Levin (1971: 115) suggests that the *rajuka*s of the inscriptions can be identified with the *agronomoi* of Megasthenes, who seem to have been connected with the measurement of land for purposes of revenue assessment. The term *rajuka* may come from *rajju*, meaning rope, and the reference may be to the measurement of land using ropes. Though land measurement may have been their main or original duty, in Ashoka's time, the *rajukas* seem to have been high-ranking officers who were also associated with public welfare measures. Ashoka added judicial functions and *dhamma* propagation to their duties.

Sanchi: Ashoka on chariot

Ashoka's inscriptions refer to the *pativedaka*s and *pulisani*, who were responsible for keeping the king informed of public opinion. The former seem to have been spies or reporters, while the latter had a higher rank and wider mandate. The *pulisani* can be connected with Megasthenes' *episcopoi* (Diodorus) or *ephoroi* (Arrian, Strabo).

Megasthenes' account of city administration probably applied specifically to Pataliputra. It mentions six committees of five members each,

PRIMARY SOURCES | **Rock edict 6 (Girnar version)**

Thus, speaks king Devanampiya Piyadasi:

In times past, the transaction of state business and submission of reports did not take place at all hours. But I have now made the following arrangement—reporters (*pativedakas*) are posted everywhere, with instructions to report to me the affairs of the people at any time and place—whether I am eating or in the harem or in the inner apartment or even in the cowpen, in the palanquin, or in the parks. And I am now attending to people's affairs everywhere. And, if there is a dispute, or argumentation arises in the council regarding any donation or proclamation I have made verbally, or in connection with an emergent matter which has been delegated to the *mahamatras*, it must be reported to me immediately, anywhere, at any time. Thus, have I ordered.

For I am never content in exerting myself and in despatching business. For I consider it my duty to promote the welfare of all men. But the root of that is exertion and prompt dispatch of business. Truly, there is no duty more important than promoting the welfare of all men. And whatever effort I make is made in order that I may discharge the debt which I owe to all living beings, that I may make them happy in this world, and that they may attain heaven in the next world.

For the following purpose has this edict on *dhamma* been caused to be written—that it may last long and that my sons, grandsons, and great-grandsons may conform to this for the welfare of all men. But, this is difficult to accomplish without great effort.

Source Hultzsch, (1925) 1969: 12–13

in charge of the following aspects: industrial arts; the entertainment and surveillance of foreigners; maintaining records of births and deaths; trade and commerce (inspecting weights and measures, etc.); supervising the public sale of goods; and the collection of taxes on merchandise sold in the market. The *nagalaviyohalaka-mahamatas* of Ashokan inscriptions were no doubt associated with city administration.

Land was the most important resource and source of revenue for the state. Later writers who cite Megasthenes make conflicting statements about taxation. Some suggest that all land was owned by the king, which is incorrect. Diodorus states that farmers paid a *misthos* (rent? wage?) to the king because all land was owned by him, and that they also paid an additional 1/4th share of the produce to the state. Strabo states that farmers tilled the land for a *misthos* and that they gave 1/4th of their produce to the king. Arrian states that farmers paid *phoros* to the king and the self-governing cities, and that herdsmen, pastoralists, artisans, and traders did likewise. Ancient Indian texts generally place the king's share of the produce (known as *bhaga*) at 1/6th. Ashoka's Rummindei pillar inscription refers to the villagers of Lumbini being exempted from *bali* (this may have been a tax on the area of land) and the *bhaga* being reduced to 1/8th (from 1/6th?). The actual rate and realization of land taxes must have varied over the Maurya empire.

There are no references to land grants in Megasthenes' account, although it does seem to suggest (at least according to Strabo) that Brahmanas were free from taxes. If this was so, it would presumably also apply to land taxes. There are no records of gifts of land made by Ashoka, but pillar edict 7 refers to gifts of an unspecified nature made by him and members of the royal family. Minor pillar edict 3 on the Allahabad–Kosam pillar refers to gifts of mango groves, gardens, and alms houses by queen Karuvaki, while inscriptions in the Barabar and Nagarjuni hills record gifts of caves by Ashoka and his successor Dasharatha to Ajivika ascetics.

Megasthenes mentions six committees of five members each (this seems suspiciously similar to what he says about the framework of urban administration). These were in charge of the navy, supervision of equipment and transport, the infantry, cavalry, chariots, and elephants. Ashoka's inscriptions, not surprisingly, do not give details regarding army administration. But they do indicate an important change in policy that must have had important implications for the Maurya army. Rock edict 13 tells us that after the Kalinga war—the only war he is known to have fought—Ashoka was appalled at the grievous results of warfare, and initiated a policy of *dhamma-vijaya* (victory through *dhamma*). Some historians have pointed out that there was little else (in the subcontinent at least) left to conquer. It has been suggested that Ashoka's pacifism has been exaggerated as there is no indication that he disbanded the army. In fact, he speaks quite sternly to forest tribes in the 13th rock edict, warning them against intransigence. As will be discussed further on, Ashoka's renunciation of warfare seems to have been an important moral choice. And while it is true that he did not disband the army, the wheels of the military machine must have got rusty due to lack of use during his long reign.

As for judicial administration, Ashoka's separate rock edict 1 refers to the judicial functions of the city *mahamatas*. It urges them to be impartial and sympathetic and to ensure that no one was imprisoned or tortured without good reason. It states that every five years, the king would despatch a gentle officer, neither fierce nor harsh, on a tour of inspection to ensure that this was being done. It also states that the prince (governor) at Ujjayini should dispatch an inspection team at least every three years, and that *mahamatas* sent on tours from Taxila should also look into this matter, along with their other duties. Pillar edict 4 refers to the judicial functions of the *rajukas* (in addition to their other duties). The fifth pillar edict states that the king had released a number of prisoners annually, as many as 25 times. Pillar edict 4 contains Ashoka's claim that he had introduced *samata* in judicial procedure. This has been interpreted as uniformity all over the empire or as equality based on ignoring social hierarchies. The best interpretation of *samata* in this context is fairness. The same edict refers to a three-day respite for those condemned to death, in order to give relatives time to appeal the decision, console the condemned man, and to fast and offer gifts on his behalf for his happiness in the next life. This indicates that Ashoka did not abolish the death penalty.

Ashoka's inscriptions refer to certain practical problems of governing a vast and variegated empire. These include the problem of incomplete pacification of conquered territory, the need to create confidence among the borderers, and inadequacies in the justice delivery system. In order to deal with these problems, Ashoka adopted a dual policy of persuasion and surveillance. He announced that quinquennial and triennial surveillance tours would be launched by the king and by the provincial governors to ensure that the officials concerned were behaving in the prescribed manner.

Ashoka's inscriptions are eloquent about his political and moral philosophy (Upinder Singh, 2017: 40–54). The emperor had two ideas of empire—one political, the other moral, the latter encompassing the former. He considered his constituency as extending beyond humans to all living beings (*panas*, *jivas*, *bhutas*); this is why he announced measures undertaken for the welfare of both humans (*manusa*) and animals (*pasu*) (rock edict 2). He apparently thought that it was his duty as king to promote the benefit/welfare (*hita*) and happiness (*sukha*) of all beings in this world and the next and/or their attainment of heaven through instruction in *dhamma*. A paternalistic ideal is reflected in rock edicts 1 and 2, which state: 'All men are my children. Just as with regard to my own children, I desire that they may be provided with all kinds of welfare and happiness in this world and the next, I desire the same for all men.' Ashoka speaks of the debt he owes to all living beings (rock edict 6), and his concern for people who lived beyond the borders of his kingdom (separate rock edict 2). He sought to promote peoples' welfare by planting trees along roads, digging wells, providing medical care for men and animals, and above all, by instructing people in *dhamma*, which, as he pointed out repeatedly, would lead to their happiness in this life and the next. His paternalism was also imbued with authority and sternness.

Ashoka saw himself as the centre of his moral empire, as a model of exemplary behaviour, and as a prophet of *dhamma*. *Dhamma* in Ashoka's inscriptions can be translated as goodness or virtue (the details will be discussed further on). The inscriptions talk of two kinds of interconnected governance—of the self and of the state. The ultimate declared aim of Ashoka's political theory and practice was neither the expansion of territorial power nor the maintenance of the social order, but an extremely radical and intrusive one—the moulding and transformation of the mental and emotional dispositions, attitudes as well as behaviour of human beings.

Ashoka and Buddhism

Ashoka's connection with Buddhism is reflected in Buddhist texts and in his inscriptions. Buddhist tradition considers him an exemplary king and a devout *upasaka*. He had a close connection with the *sangha* and with leading monks of his time such as Upagupta. His generosity as a patron of the *sangha* is reflected in many legends. He is credited with redistributing the relics of the Buddha and enshrining them in *stupas* in every important town. He is supposed to have built 84,000 *stupas* and *viharas*. He is described as having undertaken pilgrimages to all the major places connected with the Buddha's life, and having had them marked with signs for the benefit of future pilgrims. He is also supposed to have exerted himself in spreading the teaching of the Buddha far and wide. In fact, as we shall see further on, Ashoka does seem to have played an important role in building Buddhist establishments in many parts of the subcontinent. Ashoka was an ardent follower of the Buddha's teaching, and had a position of authority vis-à-vis the *sangha*, although he doesn't seem to have become a member of the order.

Ashoka proclaims his faith in the Buddha's teaching in certain inscriptions. In minor rock edict 1, he states that he has been a lay follower for a little over two-and-a-half years. He goes on to admit that for the first year, he did not exert himself much in the cause of *dhamma*, but that for over a year, he had drawn closer to the *sangha* and had been exerting himself vigorously. Minor rock edict 3 has only been found at Bairat (also known as Bhabru). In this inscription, Ashoka greets the *sangha*, professes his deep faith in the Buddha, *dhamma*, and *sangha*, and recommends six texts of *dhamma* that he desires monks, nuns, and laypersons to frequently listen to and reflect on. These six texts are all Buddhist texts. Ashoka's close relationship with the *sangha* is also evident from the so-called 'schism edict', in which he warns members of the order against causing any division in its ranks.

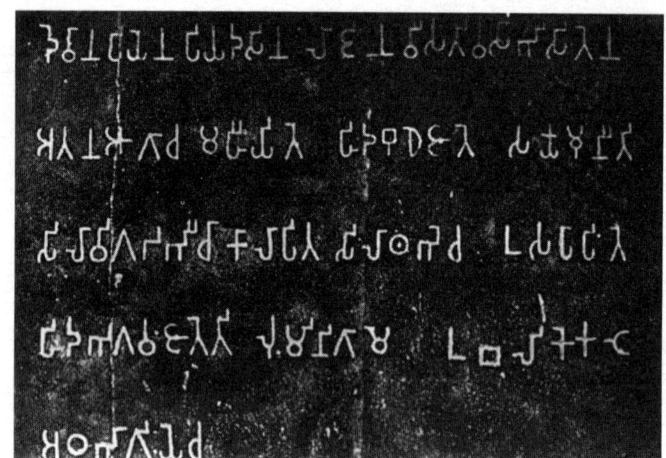

Text: *Devanapiyena Piyadasina lajina visati-vasabhisitena*
atana agacha mahiyite hida Budhe jate Sakyamuni ti
sila vigadabhi cha kalapita sila-thabhe cha usapapite
hida Bhagavam jate ti Lummini-game ubalike kate
atha-bhagiye cha

Translation: When king Devanampiya Piyadasi had been anointed twenty years, he came himself and worshipped (this spot), because the Buddha Sakyamuni was born here. He caused both a stone enclosure and stone pillar to be set up, in order to show that the Blessed one was born here. He made the village of Lummini free of *bali* and paying only 1/8th share of *bhaga*.

The Rummindei pillar inscription (after Hultzsch, [1925] 1969: 164–65)

Buddhist texts present Ashoka as a vile and evil man until he came under the influence of the Buddha's *dhamma* and present Ashoka's 'conversion' to Buddhism as a sudden, transformative event. The reason why 'conversion' has been put in quotation marks here is because in this period, the fixed and mutually exclusive religious identities, boundaries, and 'isms' of the kind that we are used to thinking in terms of were absent. The *Mahavamsa* and *Dipavamsa* tell us that Ashoka turned to the Buddha's *dhamma* when his nephew Nigrodha, who had become a monk at the tender age of 7, preached the doctrine to him. On the other hand, the *Divyavadana* (Xuanzang supports this account) ascribes his being drawn to the Buddha's teaching to the influence of Samudra, a merchant-turned-monk who remained unaffected and unperturbed by the tortures to which he was subjected in Ashoka's torture chamber. The *Ashokavadana* mixes up the two stories and speaks of Samudra, the 12-year-old son of a merchant, as the key figure in Ashoka's coming under the influence of the Buddhist *dhamma*.

Ashoka's inscriptions do not mention any such incidents. The 13th major rock edict speaks feelingly of the Kalinga war (an event the Buddhist texts do not mention), which occurred in the ninth year after Ashoka's consecration, and suggests that this event had an important role to play in his belief in a new kind of pacifism and non-military victory. Minor rock edict 1 indicates very clearly that Ashoka turned towards the Buddha's teaching gradually, not suddenly. The king's own candid confession must be given weightage over the stories given in Buddhist texts.

Further evidence of Ashoka's personal faith in Buddhism comes from the Rummindei and Nigali Sagar inscriptions. The former states that 20 years after his consecration (i.e., in the 21st year), Ashoka visited Lumbini and worshipped here. He had a stone wall built around the place, installed this pillar to commemorate his visit, and announced some tax concessions for the villagers. The Nigali Sagar pillar inscription states that 14 years after his consecration, Ashoka enlarged the *stupa* enshrining the relics of Buddha Konagamana (Kanakamuni, a mythical Buddha) to double its size, and 20 years after his consecration, he came in person to this place and had this stone pillar erected.

The Pali chronicles assert that Ashoka convened a great Buddhist council at Pataliputra, presided over by Moggaliputta Tissa, in order to purge the *sangha* of certain unacceptable practices. The first Buddhist council had been held at Rajagriha immediately after the Buddha's death, and the second one at Vaishali a hundred years thereafter. The Pataliputra council was the third council. However, Ashoka's inscriptions do not mention any such event. There are several possible explanations. One is that no council was convened during Ashoka's reign and the information given in the Pali chronicles is incorrect. A second is that there was a small-scale local affair under the direction of Moggaliputta Tissa, with which Ashoka had little or no connection. A third possibility is that there were actually two councils, which the Buddhist tradition confused and merged into one. The 'schism edict' of Ashoka may be indirect evidence of some kind of council having been held. Heinz Bechert (1982) has argued that Ashoka's intervention in the affairs of the *sangha* had to do with expelling monks and nuns who had violated monastic discipline, not of countering some sort of doctrinal schism.

The *Mahavamsa* mentions a number of Buddhist missions despatched by Ashoka at the conclusion of the third council. Majjhima, Kassapagota, Dhundibissara, Sahadeva, and Mulakadeva were sent on missions to the Himalayan region, and it can be noted that two of these names appear on the relic casket found in Stupa no. 2 at the central Indian monastic site of Sanchi. Maharakkhita was sent to Yona (in the north-west); Majjhantika to Kashmir and Gandhara; Mahadeva to Mahishamandala (in Central India); Yona Dhammarikhita to Aparantaka in western Malwa; Rakkhita to Vanavasi and Mahadharmmarakkhita to Maharrattha (in the western Deccan); Sona and Uttara to Suvarnabhumi (perhaps in Myanmar or Southeast Asia); and Mahinda to Lanka (Sri Lanka).

PRIMARY SOURCES | Minor rock edict 1 (Rupnath version)

Thus, speaks Devanampiya:

A little over two-and-a half years have passed since I have avowedly become a Sakya [a lay follower of the Buddha]. But I was not initially very zealous. But for a little more than a year, I have drawn close to the *sangha* and have been very zealous. Those gods, who during that time were unmingled with the people of Jambudvipa, have now been made to mingle with them by me. For this is the result of my exertions.

And this result cannot be achieved only by persons of high rank alone; even a poor man can attain heaven if he is zealous.

And this proclamation has been issued for the following purpose—that both the poor and rich may be zealous, that even the people residing in the territories outside the borders of my dominions may realize this, and that this same zeal may be of long duration. For this cause will be made by me to progress by at least one and a half times.

And you (my officers) must cause this matter to be engraved on stone whenever an opportunity presents itself. And, wherever there are stone pillars here in my dominions, this should be caused to be engraved on those stone pillars.

And, according to the letter of this proclamation, you must despatch an officer to go everywhere, as far as your district extends.

This proclamation is issued by me when on tour. Two hundred and fifty-six nights have been spent on tour.

The terms used in different versions of this inscription for the king as lay follower of the Buddha are 'Sakya', 'Buddha-Sakya', and *upasaka*. The phrase *sangham upete* in the inscription has been interpreted as indicating that Ashoka visited or joined the *sangha*, but it is best to understand it as referring to his having drawn closer to the order. The last line of the inscription is very interesting. The Ahraura version of the edict has an additional intriguing phrase: *am mamche Budhasa salile alodhe*. Some scholars interpret this as indicating that Ashoka had spent 256 nights on tour after enshrining the relics of the Buddha on some sort of platform (*stupa*?). However, as mentioned at the beginning of this chapter, another interpretation is that this is a reference to the number of *years* that had elapsed since the *parinibbana* of the Buddha.

Source Hutzsch, (1925) 1969: 167–69; Sircar, 1966b

Ashoka's *Dhamma*

Dhamma/dharma is a widely pervasive idea in Indian thought, but its meaning is not identical in all contexts. Most of Ashoka's inscriptions are discourses on *dhamma* (the Prakrit form of *dharma*). Pillar edict 6 reveals that the practice of having inscriptions on *dhamma* (*dhamma lipi*) inscribed in various parts of the empire began 12 (expired) years after the *abhisheka*. From this time onwards, until the end of his long reign, Ashoka seems to have been obsessed with explaining and propagating *dhamma*. His inscriptions are a rich source of information on his ideas about the relationship between political power, goodness, and non-violence. We can imagine that Ashoka's obsession with propogating *dhamma* must have been detrimental to attending to his routine royal duties. While the inscriptions are quite eloquent and precise about what *dhamma* consisted of, historians have different assessments of its nature, especially its relationship with Ashoka's personal faith in the Buddha's teaching.

According to the inscriptions, *dhamma* includes what is good (*sadhu*); because one should practice goodness, *dhamma* also has the sense of duty. The reasons why one should be good have to do with the idea of *kamma/karma*, which is not specifically mentioned, but is definitely implied. Goodness yields merit (*punya*) and beneficial fruits in the next life, and can lead to heaven (*svaga*).The specific virtues that are part of *dhamma* include self-control, purity of thought, liberality, gratitude, firm devotion, truthfulness, and purity. The conduct towards all living beings should be marked by compassion, gentleness, and abstention from injuring and killing. The theme of *ahimsa* (non-injury) is an important aspect of Ashoka's *dhamma* and is frequently mentioned and emphasized. Rock edict 1 announces bans on animal sacrifices (at some or all places?) and on certain kinds of festive gatherings that probably included the killing of animals, and also reports a reduction in the killing of animals for food in the royal kitchens. Pillar edict 5 refers to more sweeping prohibitions promulgated by Ashoka, 26 years after his consecration. Clearly, it would have been impossible to implement such prohibitions over the vast Maurya empire.

The good conduct and social responsibilities that were part of *dhamma* were anchored to certain key relationships. Rock edict 9 begins with a criticism of ceremonies performed by people, especially women, on occasions such as illness, marriage, birth, and setting forth on journeys. Such rituals are described as producing uncertain and meagre results. Ashoka contrasts these with the ceremony of *dhamma*, which is bound to yield results in this world (i.e., this life) and the next. The ceremony of *dhamma* is described as consisting in proper courtesy to slaves and servants, respectful behaviour towards elders, restraint in one's dealings with all living beings, and liberality to *shramanas* and Brahmanas. Rock edict 11 refers to the gift of *dhamma* being the best of all gifts. It is said to comprise the following: proper courtesy to slaves and servants, obedience to mother and father, liberality (i.e., generosity) towards friends, acquaintances, and relatives as well as to Brahmanas and *shramanas*, and abstaining from killing living beings.

Another important aspect of Ashoka's *dhamma* was the inculcation of mutual respect and concord among people belonging to different religious sects or religious communities. This clearly indicates that *dhamma* did not consist in the promotion of a particular sect, Buddhist or otherwise. This aspect of *dhamma* has often been referred to as 'religious toleration', which does not capture its full meaning or intention. Rock edict 12 makes it clear that the king expected people to exercise restraint in criticizing other sects and in praising their own. But he was also asking for something much more positive. He was urging people to honour and try to understand the *dhamma* of others. He wanted to promote the essentials (*sara-vadhi*) of all religions. His was an earnest appeal for religious dialogue and concord.

One of the most remarkable and innovative aspects of Ashoka's idea of his own *dhamma* and the *dhamma* of a king was his renunciation of warfare and his re-definition of righteous conquest. Ashoka's goals and activities correspond in many ways to

PRIMARY SOURCES | **The 5th pillar edict (Delhi–Topra pillar)**

Thus, speaks king Devanampiya Piyadasi:

When I had been anointed twenty-six years, the following animals were declared by me to be inviolable—parrots, *mynahs*, the *aruna*, ruddy geese, wild geese, the *nandimukha*, the gelate, bats, queen ants, terrapins, boneless fish, *vedavayakas*, *puputakas* of the Ganga, skat-fish, tortoises and porcupines, squirrels [?], the *srimara*, bulls set at liberty, iguanas [?], the rhinoceros, white doves, domestic doves, and all quadrapeds which are neither useful nor edible.

Those she-goats, ewes, and sows that are either with young or in milk are inviolable, and also those of their young ones which are less than six months old. Cocks must not be castrated. Husk containing living animals must not be burnt. Forests must not be burnt either uselessly or in order to destroy living beings. Living animals must not be fed with other living animals. Fish are inviolable, and must not be sold on the three Chaturmasis and on the Tishya full-moon during three days, namely—the fourteenth, the fifteenth, and the first *tithi*, and invariably on every fast-day. And during these same days also, no other classes of animals which are in the elephant park and in the fishermen's preserves must be killed.

On the eighth *tithi* of every fortnight, on the fourteenth, on the fifteenth, on Tishya, on Punarvasu, on the three Chaturmasis, and on festivals, bulls must not be castrated, and he-goats, rams, boars, and whatever other animals are castrated must not be castrated on these days. On Tishya, on Punarvasu, on the Chaturmasis, and during the fortnight of every Chaturmasi, horses and bullocks must not be branded.

Until I had been anointed twenty-six years, in this period I ordered the release of prisoners twenty-five times.

Source Hultzsch, (1925) 1969: 127–28

the image of the ideal king—the *chakkavatti dhammiko dhammaraja* (righteous universal ruler)—of the Buddhist tradition. This king establishes his control over the four quarters through righteousness, not through violence or force. Rival kings do not resist, and happily accept his sovereignty, which in any case is not about territorial conquest but spreading *dhamma*. At the same time, in the *Mahasuddasana Sutta* in the *Digha Nikaya*, the shadow of force is present, as the wheel of the exemplary king Sudassana moves forward, accompanied by the four-fold army.

Ashoka seems to have taken the Buddhist idea of *dhamma-vijaya* one step further, with *dhamma* missionaries replacing the king and his army. This is explicated in the 13th major rock edict. As discussed earlier, this inscription gives Ashoka's account of the war against Kalinga, eight years after his *abhisheka*, and his consequent feeling of profound remorse. This is followed by a reasoned critique of war, pointing out that it led, directly or indirectly, to suffering for all. *Dhamma-vijaya* is described as the best kind of conquest, and the king claims to have achieved it over the Yavanas, Kambojas, Nabhakas, Nabhapanktis, Bhojas, Pitinikas, Andhras, Pulindas, Cholas, and Pandyas. Outside the subcontinent, he claims to have attained *dhamma-vijaya* in the dominions of Antiochus II, Ptolemy II Philadelphus of Egypt, Magas of Cyrene (in north Africa), Antigonus Gonatas of Macedonia, and Alexander of Epirus or Corinth. The edict ends with Ashoka expressing the hope that his successors would not embark on any fresh conquest by arms, and that if they could not avoid it, they should at least not be harsh to conquered people. However, tucked away in this pacifist manifesto is a stern warning issued to the forest people. A similar sentiment is expressed in separate rock edict 2 at Dhauli and Jaugada.

The epigraphic form of Ashoka's *dhamma* message coexisted with documentary forms maintained in administrative offices, and the message was also circulated orally by various officials and by the king himself. While Ashoka's inscriptions represent a new and powerful attempt at imperial communication, he was not really trying to speak directly to his people. Most people in his empire would not have known how to read or write, and the location of some of the inscriptions would have made them difficult to read, even for a literate person. The audience of the edicts consisted of three parts—the direct audience consisted of high-ranking administrative officials; the indirect audience were Ashoka's subjects, who were supposed to receive his message through various intermediaries, largely in oral form; and the future audience was posterity.

PRIMARY SOURCES | **The 13th rock edict (Shahbazgarhi version)**

When king Devanampriya Priyadrashi had been anointed eight years, the country of the Kalingas was conquered by him. One hundred and fifty thousand in number were the men who were deported thence; one hundred thousand in number were those who were slain there; and many times as many those who died. After that, now that the country of the Kalingas has been taken, Devanampriya is devoted to the pursuit of *dhamma*, the love of *dhamma*, and to instructing the people in *dhamma*. This is the repentance of Devanampriya on account of his conquest of the country of the Kalingas. For the slaughter, death, and deportation of people that take place in the course of conquering an unconquered country is considered very painful and deplorable by Devanampriya.

But the following is considered even more deplorable than this by Devanampriya—that Brahmanas and *shramanas*, members of other sects or householders who are living there, and who practice obedience and firm devotion to superior persons, obedience to mother and father, obedience to elders, proper courtesy to friends, acquaintances, companions, and relatives, to slaves and servants—all these suffer injury or slaughter or deportation of their loved ones. And if misfortune befalls the friends, acquaintances, companions, and relatives of persons who are full of devotion towards them, even though they themselves be well provided for, this misfortune too becomes an injury to their own selves. This [suffering] is shared by all and is considered deplorable by Devanampriya.

And there is no place where men are not indeed attached to some sect. Therefore, even the hundredth part or the thousandth part of all those people who were slain, who died, and who were deported at that time in Kalinga, would now be considered very deplorable by Devanampriya. And Devanampriya thinks that even to one who should wrong him, what can be forgiven is to be forgiven. And even the inhabitants of the forests which are included in the dominions of Devanampriya, even those he pacifies and conciliates. And they are told of the power to punish them which Devanampriya possesses in spite of his repentance, in order that they may be ashamed of their crimes and may not be killed. For Devanampriya desires towards all beings abstention from hurting, self-control, and impartiality in case of violence. And this conquest is considered the greatest one by Devanampriya—the conquest by *dhamma*.

Source Hultzsch, (1925) 1969: 68–70

Due to limited literacy among his subjects and the difficulty of reading the inscriptions, Ashoka made elaborate arrangements for the oral propagation of his message. Even in the inscriptions, the king is 'speaking' to his subjects—many of the edicts begin with the phrase, 'Thus, speaks Devanampiya Piyadasi.' The separate rock edicts suggest that the edicts were read out and that people listened to them on certain auspicious days such as the full moon days of the months of Ashadha, Karttika, and Phalguna, and the day of the Tishya constellation. Ashoka's message of *dhamma* was also orally propagated by officials such as the *kumaras*, *yutas*, *rajukas*, *mahamatas*, *anta-mahamatas*, *pulisani*, and members of the *parishad*. Rock edict 3 states that the *rajukas* and *pradeshikas* were to go on tours of inspection every five years as part of their other duties, as well as for preaching *dhamma*.

Ashoka created a special cadre of *dhamma mahamatas* 13 years after his consecration. Rock edict 5 enjoins them to spread *dhamma* within the kingdom and among border people such as the Yonas, Kambojas, Gandharas, Rishtikas, and Pitinikas. They were to move around among members of all sects and were to promote the welfare and happiness of servants, masters, traders, farmers, Brahmanas, prisoners, the aged, the destitute, and the king's relatives.

The chief disseminator of the *dhamma* message was, however, Ashoka himself. In major rock edict 8, he states that earlier kings used to go on pleasure tours consisting of hunts and other pastimes. Ten years after his *abhisheka*, he made a pilgrimage to Bodh Gaya. Thenceforth, the royal pleasure tours (*vihara-yatas*) were replaced by *dhamma* tours (*dhamma-yatas*). The latter involved visiting Brahmanas and *shramanas* and giving them gifts, visiting aged folk and distributing gold to them, meeting people of the countryside, instructing them in *dhamma*, and questioning them about *dhamma*. Ashoka asserts that he derived more pleasure from these *dhamma* tours than from anything else. Minor rock edict 1 tells us that he had spent 256 nights (or days) on tour, no doubt busy spreading *dhamma*. The time he must have spent roaming around his empire, giving *dhamma* lectures, and his steadily increasing obsession with making his subjects—indeed the whole world—good must have made Ashoka impatient with the routine affairs of governance.

The word for *dhamma* in Ashoka's Greek inscriptions is *eusebeia* (piety), while the Aramaic inscriptions use *qsyt* (truth) and *data* (law). The Greek and Aramaic inscriptions are not literal translations of the Ashokan edicts. B. N. Mukherjee (1984) points out that although there is a basic conformity in the elements of *dhamma* (non-injury towards living beings, restraint, truthfulness, liberality, compassion, respect towards parents, etc.), the Greek and Aramaic inscriptions also display some interesting differences. For instance, the Kandahar Greek inscription refers to the subjects' devotion to the king's interest as being an important part of *dhamma*. Further, none of the Greek or Aramaic inscriptions refer to the attainment of heaven as a goal or consequence of following *dhamma*, something which the Prakrit inscriptions mention frequently.

As his reign progressed, Ashoka seems to have become increasingly obsessed with propagating *dhamma*. Some of the Greek and Aramaic inscriptions and the later pillar edicts reflect his highly exaggerated idea of the transformation that he had brought about in the conduct and lives of his people.

Historians hold different views about the nature of the *dhamma* of Ashoka's inscriptions. It has been seen as a sort of 'universal religion', containing certain common elements in many religious traditions. It has been interpreted as a form of *raja-dharma* (the *dharma* of a king), consisting of the political and moral principles emphasized in the Brahmanical and Buddhist traditions. It has been understood as a form of the Buddhist *upasaka dhamma* (the Buddha's teaching for the laity). It has also been seen as all these things rolled into one.

Thapar ([1963] 1987: 136–81) has underlined the political rationale behind the propagation of *dhamma*. She minimizes the Buddhist element in Ashoka's *dhamma* and asserts that there need be no connection between the personal beliefs of a statesman and his public proclamations. *Dhamma* was an ideological tool used by Ashoka to weld and consolidate his far-flung empire. Due to lack of support in the early years of his reign, he sought the support of non-orthodox elements and saw the practical advantages of adopting and propagating *dhamma*, which was basically an ethical concept that focused on the relationship between the individual and society. However, it failed as a unifying strategy (Thapar, 1984: 22).

Ashoka's *dhamma* has been compared with the ethics embodied in various textual traditions. However, it should be remembered that religious traditions and identities were very fluid at the time, and that there was an overlap in their ideas and practices. The ideas underlying Ashoka's *dhamma*—rebirth, *karma*, merit, heaven—and the emphasis on social ethics were not confined to Buddhism. Ashoka's *dhamma* was rooted in his faith in Buddhism, but was not identical to it. It bore his personal, idiosyncratic stamp. The inscriptions do not contain certain key ideas associated with the Buddha's teaching, such as the explanation of *dukkha*, the Eight-fold Path, the doctrine of impermanence, or the goal of *nibbana*. Nevertheless, there is a Buddhist core. In 3rd century BCE, Buddhism (along with Jainism) was one of the prominent sects that emphasized *ahimsa* both for the monastic and lay communities.

There is also a striking similarity between the duty-oriented ethics of the inscriptions and the Buddhist *upasaka dhamma* reflected, for instance, in the *Sigalavada Sutta*. The fact that the minor rock edict at Bhabru lists six Buddhist texts as texts on *dhamma* is significant. Buddhist resonances can be seen in the king's assertion of the debt he owes all beings and his concern for the whole world (rock edict 6), and virtues such as self-control and purity of mind that he prescribes in rock edict 7. We can also take note of the fact that according to rock edict 8, Ashoka started the *dhamma* tours after a pilgrimage to Bodh Gaya.

An understanding of Ashoka's *dhamma* has to move beyond textual analysis (Singh, 1997–98). The Buddhist element in Ashoka's *dhamma* can also be seen in the sculptural

The Vaishali pillar

PRIMARY SOURCES | **Ashoka's assessment of his success: the Shar-i-Kuna Greek–Aramaic inscription**

The Greek portion:

Ten years since the consecration having been completed, King Piodosses made known the doctrine of piety to men; and from this moment he made men more pious, and everything thrives throughout the whole world. And the king abstains from killing living beings, and other men and those who are huntsmen and fishermen of the king have desisted from hunting. And if some were intemperate, they have ceased from their intemperance as was in their power; and having become obedient to their father and mother and to their elders, contrary to what happened in the past, they will, also in the future, by so acting on every occasion, live better and more happily.

The Aramaic portion:

Ten years having passed (since the consecration), our lord Prydrs the king promoted truth (*qsyt*). Since then evil has diminished for all men, and he has caused all hostile things to disappear, and joy has arisen throughout the whole earth. And moreover, there is this—for the feeding of our lord the king, little is killed. Seeing this, all men have given up killing animals. And those who caught fish have given up doing so. Similarly, those without restraint have ceased to be without restraint. And there is good obedience to one's mother and father and to the old people, as destiny has laid down on everyone. And there is no judgement for all men who are pious. This has benefited all men and will continue to benefit them.

Source G. P. Carratelli et al., cited in Mukherjee, 1984: 33

motifs associated with the pillars. All of them have a very wide symbolic appeal, but all of them have a special Buddhist significance as well. It is interesting to note that the Girnar rock has a fragmentary inscription referring to the white elephant that brings happiness to the whole world. The Kalsi rock has a small carving of an elephant and an inscription *gajatame* (the best elephant). The elephant appears at Dhauli as well, along with the word *seto* (the white one). Given Ashoka's personal belief in Buddhism, the elephant at Girnar, Dhauli, and Kalsi can be seen as a Buddhist symbol, symbolizing the Buddha-to-be, who is supposed to have entered his mother's womb in the form of a white elephant. The fact that Buddhist remains have been found in the vicinity of many Ashokan pillars (Ghosh, 1967) suggests the possibility that many of them marked sites of *stupas* or monasteries established by the king, again suggesting a link between the *dhamma* of the edicts and Buddhism.

Although Ashoka's *dhamma* was clearly inspired by the Buddhist *upasaka dhamma*, it was not identical to it. Ashoka was an innovator. His *dhamma* was a set of teachings that could not be identified with narrow sectarian belief. Ashoka's statement that all sects have in common an emphasis on self-control and purity of mind (rock edict 7) indicates that he did not consider *dhamma* to be the preserve of any specific religious group. The *dhamma mahamatas* were to occupy themselves with all sects (*pasandas*). It is even more evident in Ashoka's statements (in rock edict 12) that he honours all sects and that people should respect one another's *dhamma*. Inscriptions in the Barabar hills indicate that Ashoka extended his patronage to ascetics of the Ajivika sect. His idea of *dhamma-vijaya* also took the ideal reflected in Buddhist texts a step further. In rock edict 12, Ashoka's expression of a desire for a growth of the essentials of all sects and an atmosphere of concord (*samavaya*), went far beyond the espousal of any particular religious doctrine. It was a passionate plea for genuine inter-religious dialogue and harmony.

Ashoka's edicts express his imperial vision, which emerged from his personal reflections and convictions, his faith in Buddhism, and the realities and problems of governing a large, culturally and economically highly variegated, 3rd-century BCE Indian empire. While the cultivation of virtues and self-control are emphasized in many early Indian traditions, Ashoka made this the cornerstone of his political philosophy and propagated it passionately through his long reign. Although Buddhist legend heralds him as a paradigmatic Buddhist king, his inscriptions tell a more complex story. Ashoka did not seek to create a Buddhist state but a dhammic, moral, state.

Sculpture and Architecture

The discoveries at the site of Dholavira indicate that the origins of monumental stone sculpture and architecture in the Indian subcontinent go back to the Harappan civilization. However, after the decline of that civilization, there is a long gap, and it is only in the Maurya period that monumental stone sculpture and architecture appear on the scene again. This can be linked to higher levels of political complexity in the form of the emergence of an empire, the concentration of wealth in the hands of urban elites, and increased institutionalization of religious activity. The most imposing art of the Maurya period is linked to political ideology and religious practice. This is evident both in the form and patronage of artistic activity.

Many of the surviving remains of art and architecture were the direct result of the patronage of the Maurya kings, especially Ashoka, and fall within the category of 'court art'. However, there are also stone sculptures and terracotta figurines, ring stones, and disc stones, which represent what may be called 'popular art', one connected to the lives, activities, and patronage of ordinary people. A number of questions have been posed with regard to the artistic activity of the Maurya period: How are the origins of stone sculpture and architecture in this period to be understood? Did Western, especially Persian, influence play a key role? And how do we explain the short-lived nature and evident lack of legacy of Maurya court art? What do we know about the artists and artisans? S. Settar (2003) has drawn attention to the inferences that can be made about the artisans who inscribed the Ashokan edicts. One of these artisans, Chapada, left his signature on the rocks at Brahmagiri, Jatinga Ramesvara, and Siddapur.

Sections of a wooden wall had been noticed in the course of sporadic explorations and excavations in the city of Patna over many decades. D. B. Spooner's more systematic excavations at Bulandibagh in 1915–17 gave a better picture of the fortifications. At a depth of 6.6 m, there were two parallel walls of rectangular wooden uprights (38 × 55 cm) separated by a 3.7 m wide tunnel-like gap. The uprights extended 1.5 m below floor level and rested on a bed of *kankar*. Their height above ground level was at least 2.7 m. The floor was paved with long, squared lengths of timber, their ends fitted into sockets made in the vertical uprights. The excavations traced 7.2 m of the walls and about 105 m of the floor. Manoranjan Ghosh's excavations in 1926–27 traced a further 250 m stretch of the wall at the western end and brought to light certain other features. The gap between the two parallel walls may have been a tunnel or it may have been packed with mud. The wooden wall was originally covered with mud upto a certain height and had a roof of wooden beams. The remains of what may have been a gateway were also found. About 200 ft from the western end, a large wooden drain, 40 ft long and 1'8"– 2' 4" wide, 32 ft below the present ground level, crossed the wall at right angles. The sides and base of the drain were made of wooden beams; 60 cm long iron nails were used to connect the beams to each other, and the joints between the planks were made watertight by 7 cm wide strips of iron. Traces of the wooden fortification wall have also been found at sites such as Gasain Khanda, Rampur, and Bahadurpur, not far from Bulandibagh. The remains of a large drain were also reported from some of these sites. Another interesting discovery at Bulandibagh was a large spoked wooden chariot wheel with an iron rim. Waddell's excavations (1892–99) at several places led, among other things, to the discovery of what may have been the foundation of a wooden jetty projecting into the old course of the Son river at Rampur.

A pillar fragment was discovered by Waddell at Kumrahar in Patna in 1903. In 1912–13, D. B. Spooner (1912–13) claimed to have discovered traces of 72 pillars arranged in a neat chessboard pattern. The sites of 8 pillars were later discovered by A. S. Altekar and V. K. Misra. Altekar and Misra (1959) also excavated a number of brick structures in the area, but all of these belonged to the post-Maurya period. The pillar fragments were made of buff-coloured sandstone and had a smooth, polished surface. As no complete pillar was found, their dimensions can only be estimated. Their slightly tapering shafts may have been about 9.91 m long and the diameter of their circular cross-section probably ranged from 75 cm near the base to 55 cm near the top. Although they were made of the same

The Sarnath capital

stone as the free-standing Ashokan pillars, they were thinner and shorter. All of them had a hole on top, clearly for metal dowels that connected the shaft to a capital, which in turn supported the roof. Some of them had masons' marks on their base, including the crescent-on-hill, a symbol which occurs on many punch-marked coins of the time. The pillars were originally fixed on square wooden basements which were laid on a compact layer of clay. The discovery of a large quantity of ash and pieces of burnt wood indicated that the floor and roof were made of wood and that the structure had been subjected to fire. The wooden roof may have been covered by brick and lime plaster, pieces of which were found at the site. There were no traces of walls, and the hall seems to have been open on all sides. About 5 m to the south-east of the hall, seven wooden platforms made of *sal* wood were excavated. These may have supported a wooden staircase leading up to the pillared hall. It has also been suggested that a canal may have connected this spot to the Son river. Spooner suggested a similarity between the vestiges of the pillared hall at Kumrahar and Darius' Hall of Public Audience at Persepolis in Iran, but the Maurya structure that once stood at Kumrahar seems much less elaborate than the Persian palaces.

The majestic free-standing Ashokan pillars may symbolize the axis of the world (*axis mundi*) that separated heaven and earth. Some of the pillars have a set of six (in the case of the Delhi–Topra pillar, seven) edicts, while a few are inscribed with other types of inscriptions, e.g., the commemorative inscriptions at Rummindei and Nigali Sagar and the schism edict at Sanchi. There are also pillars without inscriptions—the one with a bull capital at Rampurva, the pillar with the lion capital at Vaishali, and the Kosam pillar without a capital. It is possible that some of Ashoka's edicts may have been carved on pre-existing pillars. Many pillar fragments found in various parts of the country in different contexts may once have been parts of Ashokan pillars.

The Ashokan pillars are quite similar to each other in form and dimensions. They are made of sandstone that seems to have been quarried at Chunar (in Mirzapur district, UP) or Pabhosa (Prayagraj district, UP). They are considered to be monoliths, i.e., carved out of a single piece of stone (though Jayaswal, 1998, has suggested that a few were not). The pillars have a lustrous, polished surface, which is not visible in the case of those that have had a tumultuous history, such as the Delhi–Meerut pillar. They do not have a base, and the plain, smooth circular shaft tapers slightly upwards to a height of 12–14 m. A cylindrical bolt joins the top of the shaft to the 'capital'—a stone carved in the shape of an inverted lotus (often referred to as the 'bell capital'). On top of this is the abacus (platform) which supports the crowning animal or animals. The abacus is square and plain in earlier pillars, and circular and carved in later ones. All parts of the pillars are carved in the round, i.e., on all sides, and were clearly meant to be viewed from all around.

The motifs associated with the Ashokan pillars have a rich and varied symbolism with resonances in many different Indian religious traditions. Apart from floral designs

The Delhi–Topra pillar, Firoz Shah Kotla, New Delhi

FURTHER DISCUSSION | **Ancient and modern quarries at Chunar**

In 1990, a team of archaeologists of Banaras Hindu University, led by P. C. Pant and Vidula Jayaswal, was exploring megalithic structures near Baragaon (on the boundary between the Mirzapur and Varanasi districts of eastern UP) when they noticed evidence of ancient stone quarries, including many large cylindrical blocks of stone, in the nearby Chunar hills.

Jayaswal went on to conduct a detailed study of stone quarrying and stone use in the Chunar and Sarnath–Varanasi areas, testing a number of hypotheses. Her analysis of the lithic (stone) material and inscriptions found in the area indicated that the hillsides of Chunar had been quarried for sandstone from the 3rd century BCE to the medieval period. Her study revealed a number of other interesting and important results:

1. The low-lying hill near Baragaon village was the main quarrying area in ancient times. Over 450 ancient quarry sites were identified in an area of some 15 sq km. This was done on the basis of marks of extraction of stone blocks, chiselling debris, cylindrical blocks in various degrees of preparedness, and count-marks of the number of finished blocks. Inscriptions, ranging from those written in Brahmi and Kharoshthi of Maurya or early post-Maurya times to Nagari epigraph of the 13th/14th century, gave an idea of the time frame of the quarrying activities.
2. The quarried blocks of stone were chiselled and dressed into cylindrical shape at Chunar itself. Many such blocks were found at the site. This was done in order to roll them down the gently sloping hillside or down the small streams to the Ganga river and further on to sites where there was a demand for the sandstone.
3. The ultimate destination of the Chunar stone included sites such as Sarnath, one of the major sandstone-consuming settlements in ancient times. Varanasi did not give as much evidence of the use of this stone.
4. Stone-carving workshops were situated on the navigational route connecting Chunar and Sarnath. Kotwa, on the bank of the Rajapur nala, a tributary of the Ganga, was one such site which gave positive evidence of stone working. Excavations here revealed an occupational deposit containing a large quantity of chiselling debris, broken fragments of carved stone, and a chisel tester. A large cylindrical block of stone was also found here before the excavations began. On the basis of the style of pottery and stone carving, the stone carving activities at Kotwa were placed between the 2nd/1st century BCE and the 11th/12th centuries CE. The location of such sites along water routes facilitated both the movement of the heavy blocks of stone and the finished products.
5. The reason why Chunar was preferred as a quarry site to other areas such as the Pabosa hills near Prayagraj or Dehri-on-Son in Bihar was the good quality of its stone and its convenient geographical location near the river, which made transportation easier.
6. The fact that the average length of the Chunar blocks ranged from less than 1 m to over 2½ m made Jayaswal look more closely at the Ashokan pillars to check whether they were really monoliths. She examined the Vaishali, Lauriya-Araraj, and Lauriya-Nandangarh pillars, and found that they were in fact made of several pieces of stone. Five blocks of stone could be counted in the latter two pillars. At Lauriya-Nandangarh, a weathered part indicated that the surface of the stone was chiselled, but not polished. Over this surface was a thick (about 1 cm) coat made of crushed pink sandstone mixed with haematite pellets. The lower surface of this coat was rough, but its upper surface had a polished, lustrous appearance.

Chunar was clearly the main resource area for sandstone used for sculpture and architecture in the Ganga valley in ancient and early medieval times. Jayaswal reports that the present-day inhabitants of Baragaon village are mostly stone cutters. Although stone quarrying still goes on in the Chunar hills, modern stone cutters do not extract stone from the old quarries. Their reason is that due to prolonged exposure to the elements, stone from such quarries is not considered suitable for working. They refer to blocks of stone from the old quarries as *mara patthar* (dead stone) as opposed to that from more recent ones, which they call *jinda patthar* (living stone).

Source Jayaswal, 1998

such as the lotus and honeysuckle/palmette, the capitals have other, mostly animal, motifs. The lion appears on the capitals of the Vaishali, Lauriya–Nandangarh, and one of the Rampurva pillars, quadruple lions on the Sanchi and Sarnath capitals, and a bull on one of the Rampurva pillars. An elephant capital (minus the pillar) was found at Sankissa. The Sanchi and Sarnath capitals were surmounted by a spoked wheel. The abacus of the Sanchi pillar has pecking geese, whereas that of the Sarnath pillar has a bull, elephant, horse, and lion, separated by wheels.

The sculptural motifs must have been chosen with great care, possibly by Ashoka himself, and must have been considered to be in harmony with the *dhamma* message. They also have a rich resonance in the Indian cultural tradition. The lotus is a symbol of

Elephant capital, Sankissa

purity and fecundity. Later Buddhist texts tell us that lotus flowers sprang up where Siddhartha took seven steps soon after he was born. Although the wheel occurs in Vedic texts as a symbol of creation and time, on Ashokan capitals it is generally interpreted as the *dharmachakra*—the wheel of *dharma*, representing the Buddha's first sermon. The *chakra* is also associated with imperial power and is mentioned (along with the wheel, elephant, and horse) as one of the seven treasures of the *chakravarti* king in the *Mahasudassana Sutta*. The lion is a solar symbol in many ancient traditions, but it can be noted that the Buddha is referred to as Sakya-simha (lion among the Sakyas) in Buddhist tradition. As for the elephant, the future Buddha is said to have entered his mother's womb in the form of a white elephant, which appeared to Maya in a dream. Jaina tradition also includes the white elephant, a white bull, and a lion among the 14 significant dreams that Mahavira's mother Trishala had when he was conceived. The elephant appears in the Brahmanical tradition as the vehicle of the god Indra and is associated with the goddess Lakshmi in her Gaja-Lakshmi form. The bull is a fertility symbol in many ancient cultures, and can also be taken to represent the asterism of Rishabha, under which the Buddha was born. In later Buddhist sculpture, the horse symbolizes the departure of Siddhartha from his home. Buddhist tradition refers to a mythical Anotatta lake situated in the Himalayas, with rocks in the shape of a horse, bull, lion, and elephant. Taken together, all the symbols associated with the Ashokan pillars had a special Buddhist significance, but they were also part of wider fabric of cultural meaning. It can be noted that many of these symbols occur on ring stones, disc stones, and punch-marked coins of early historic India.

The importance of animals in art can be seen as part of the history of human–animal interactions in history. Divyabhanusinh ([2005] 2008) has pointed out that rise of the status of the lion coincided with the rise of large, powerful kingdoms, and that this magnificent animal had royal connections in ancient Egypt, Mesopotamia, Persia, and India. The features of the lion that set it apart were its majestic size and appearance, its mane, and its powerful roar. The animal prefers the grasslands and allows himself to be seen as king of the animal world, in contrast to the tiger who moves around in thick forests. The elephant has greater importance than the lion in ancient Indian history. The close relationship between kings and elephants was not only due to the animal's size and unusual appearance. As discussed in an earlier chapter, it was due to the fact that elephants became the backbone of ancient Indian armies. It was, therefore, in the interests of kings to protect the forest habitat of these valuable animals (see Trautmann, 2015).

Some art historians have emphasized foreign influence, especially Persian influence, on the court art of the Maurya empire. It has been suggested that Ashoka got the idea of inscribing proclamations on pillars from the Achaemenids. It has been pointed out that the words *dipi* and *lipi* occur in the inscriptions of Darius as well as Ashoka. Inscriptions of both kings begin in the third person and then move to the first person. Distinct Greek influence, and even greater Persian influence, has been identified in the polished surface of the Ashokan pillars and the animal capitals. The stiff, heraldic pose of the lions is seen as further evidence of Western influence. Over the centuries, there was plenty of interaction between ancient India and ancient Iran, whether in the form of trade or the conquest of Gandhara by the Persian emperors. The use of the Aramaic script in certain Ashokan inscriptions in the north-west and the emergence of Kharoshthi from this script were direct results of the interactions between India and West Asia.

At the same time, Niharranjan Ray (1975: 24–26) has drawn attention to the many differences between the Maurya and Persian pillars. The pillars of the Kumrahar hall do not have capitals, whereas those at Persepolis have elaborate ones. The Persian pillars stand on bases, either shaped like a 'bell' (i.e., inverted lotus), or a plain rectangular or circular block. In the Maurya pillars, on the other hand, the inverted lotus appears at the top of the shaft. The shape and ornamentation of the Maurya lotus is different from the Persian ones, the bulge typical of the former being absent in the latter. Most of the

FURTHER DISCUSSION | The medieval and modern histories of Ashokan pillars

Ancient artefacts and monuments often have interesting later life-histories. The two Ashokan pillars that today stand in Delhi are good examples of this:

The 14th century *Tarikh-i-Firuz Shahi* by Shams Siraj Afif gives an account of the columns today known as the Delhi–Topra and Delhi–Meerut pillars. Afif tells us that Sultan Firuz Shah Tughluq noticed the pillars at Topra (in modern Haryana) and Meerut (in modern UP) in the course of his military campaigns, and that he was so impressed by them that he decided to transport them to Delhi. Afif describes the moving of the Topra pillar as follows: Orders were issued to the people living in and around Topra village and to soldiers, directing them to assemble at the pillar, and to bring along with them various tools and lots of silk cotton from the silk cotton tree. When the earth around the column had been carefully removed, it fell on the bed of silk cotton that had been prepared for it. The pillar was encased in reeds and hides and carefully moved onto a specially made carriage with 42 wheels. Men pulled at the ropes attached to the wheels, and the cart was dragged to the Yamuna, where the Sultan appeared to personally direct further operations. The pillar was heaved on to several boats tied together and taken by river to its new home in Delhi. At Firuzabad, it was hoisted onto its present position in the palace complex with great ingenuity, skill, and labour. Nobody could read Ashokan Brahmi by this time, but Afif tells us that some Brahmanas claimed they could. They announced that the inscription contained a prophecy that no one would be able to remove the pillar from its original place till the time of a great king named Sultan Firuz.

The pillar installed in the Sultan's palace at Firuzabad (modern Firoz Shah Kotla) came to be known as the Minar-i-Zarin or the Golden Column. A manuscript of an anonymous work called the *Sirat-i-Firuz Shahi* has painted illustrations of

Drawing in the *Sirat-i-Firuz Shahi* showing how the Ashokan pillar was moved from Topra to Delhi in the 14th century (Page, 1937)

the moving of the Topra pillar and its installation in its new home in Delhi. The Meerut pillar was installed in Firuz Shah's Kushk-i-Shikar or hunting palace (located opposite Bara Hindu Rao hospital, on the northern Ridge, near the University of Delhi).

Several Ashokan pillars have later inscriptions. Many of them record people's names, indicating that the phenomenon of tourists scratching their names onto monuments is not a new one. The Delhi–Topra pillar has three 12th century inscriptions of the Chauhan king Vigraharaja IV. These show that a pillar which had a thousand years earlier proclaimed the *dhamma* of Ashoka and the majesty of the Maurya empire was used to proclaim the victories and greatness of a medieval Rajput king. There are also several later inscriptions in Sanskrit and Persian belonging to the 13th–16th centuries. The Delhi–Meerut pillar has three short early medieval Sanskrit inscriptions. Similarly, the Lauriya–Nandangarh inscription has a Persian inscription of the time of Aurangzeb, and an English inscription which reads: 'Reuben Burrow, 1792.' Reuben Burrow was a surveyor who apparently visited the site in the 18th century.

The fact that the Allahabad–Kosam pillar refers to the *mahamatas* of Kaushambi suggests it was brought to Allahabad from that place at some point of time. Apart from the schism edict of Ashoka, it has the famous Allahabad *prashasti* of the Gupta emperor Samudragupta. It also has an inscription giving the genealogy of the Mughal emperor Jahangir. This pillar, carrying three emperors' inscriptions, ranging across some 2,000 years, is unique. It also has names of various people, scratched onto its surface at different points of time.

Two fragments of Ashokan pillars have been identified at Hissar and Fatehabad in Haryana. The Hissar fragment is located in front of a mosque built by Firuz Shah Tughluq and forms the lowest part of a composite pillar. The Fatehabad fragment, which stands in the middle of a prayer ground associated with a late Mughal wall, is also part of a composite pillar, and bears a long inscription giving genealogical information about Firuz Shah. In fact, it seems that the Hissar and Fatehabad fragments were probably originally parts of the same Ashokan pillar.

There are some recorded instances of Ashokan pillars or their fragments being worshipped as Shiva *lingas*. It is interesting to note that in many places, Ashokan pillars and their fragments are associated in popular local tradition with the Pandava brothers, especially Bhima, and are often known as *Bhim-ki-lat* or *Bhim-ka-danda* (Bhima's pillar or stick).

All this shows how the 'original' meaning and significance of a historical artefact or monument can be radically altered in later times.

Source Upinder Singh, (1999) 2006: xxx–xxxii, 58–62; Singh, 1997–98

Bull Capital, Rampurva

Persian pillars have a fluted surface, while the Maurya pillars are smooth. The capitals of the Persian columns are crowned with a cluster of stylized palm leaves and have two semi-bulls, lions, or unicorns seated back to back, or an upright or inverted cup, with double volutes on the top. The Maurya-type abacus and independent animals carved in the round crowning the pillars are absent in the Persian context. While there may be some similarities in specific features, the effect of the whole is completely different. Moreover, by having pillars inscribed with his messages on *dhamma*, Ashoka transformed them into epigraphic monuments of unique cultural meaning.

The issue of artistic 'influence' is a complex one. There is no doubt that artists and artistic motifs, designs, and styles did and do travel—often over vast distances. In some instances, a particular motif is so strikingly similar to another that one seems to be inspired by the other. In other cases, there is some stylistic similarity, but also certain striking differences and innovations. Sometimes, similar designs can be associated with different meanings. And at still other times, there is similarity in the choice of motifs, but not in the style in which they are executed, pointing to the existence of a shared pool of symbols that were considered to have meaning and significance across different cultures. If the Ashokan pillars cannot in their entirety be attributed to Persian influence, they must have had an undocumented prehistory within the subcontinent, perhaps a tradition of wooden carving. But the transition from stone to wood was made in one magnificent leap, no doubt spurred by the imperial tastes, ambitions, and patronage of the Maurya emperors.

There are a few other samples of sculptures associated with the Maurya court. A polished fragment of a monolithic railing at Sarnath is usually assigned to the Maurya period. The *vajrasana* (throne of meditation) at the Mahabodhi temple at Bodh Gaya is a large stone slab under the *bodhi* tree (this *pipal* tree is supposed to be a descendent of the tree under which the Buddha attained enlightenment). Its original place and purpose are not known for sure. The 16.5 cm thick *vajrasana* is made of sandstone. Its top surface is decorated with a carved geometric pattern that looks like intersecting circles. On the sides are carved floral palmette designs and geese (*hamsas*), in a style similar to that of the carving on the Ashokan capitals.

At Dhauli (Bhubaneswar district, Odisha), on top of the rock which bears Ashoka's edicts is the sculpture of the front part of an elephant. His heavy trunk curls gracefully inwards. His right front leg is slightly tilted, and the left one slightly bent, suggesting forward movement. It is a very naturalistic, powerful portrayal of the animal, and the whole effect is such that it looks as if the elephant is walking out of the rock.

The Maurya period saw the beginning of rock-cut architecture. The Barabar and Nagarjuni hills to the north of Bodh Gaya contain several caves that were inhabited by ascetics in ancient times. Three caves in the Barabar hills have dedicative inscriptions of Ashoka, and three in the Nagarjuni hills have inscriptions of his son Dasharatha. The caves are simple in plan, with plain but highly polished interiors. The longer side of the cave runs parallel to the rock face. The only sculptural ornamentation is a relief carving on the doorway of a cave known as the Lomash Rishi cave. The doorway is modelled after wooden ones. Over the entrance, framed within the earliest example of what art historians call the *chaitya* or *gavaksha* arch with a carved finial, are two bands of relief carving. The upper one has a latticework design; the lower one has a finely carved frieze showing elephants approaching some oblong objects. At both ends of the frieze is a *makara* (a mythical crocodile). The interior of the Lomash Rishi cave consists of two connected chambers. The rectangular one leads into a round, unfinished room which resembles a thatched hut. There is no inscription here, but the cave next door, with an identical interior but lacking the ornamented doorway, has an inscription stating that it was dedicated by Ashoka to the Ajivikas 12 years after his *abhisheka*. This suggests that the Lomash Rishi cave probably also belongs to roughly the same time.

The tradition of making *stupas*—originally funerary mounds—may be pre-Buddhist, and *stupas* did not have an exclusively Buddhist significance. The *Mahaparinibbana Sutta* tells us that eight *stupas* were built over the cremated remains of the Buddha and two

others over the cremation vessel and embers of the funeral pyre. Some archaeologists have suggested that the mud *stupas* at Piprahwa and Vaishali may represent these early *stupas*. Initially, relics of the Buddha were enshrined in the solid core of *stupas*, which became places of veneration and pilgrimage. Soon, relics of the Buddha's disciples and famous monks were similarly enshrined. Veneration and worship were transferred from the relics to the *stupa* itself, whether or not it contained relics. The *stupa* swiftly became an emblem of the Buddha's *dhamma* and an important part of Buddhist monasteries. According to the Avadana texts, Ashoka re-distributed portions of the Buddha's relics to every important town in the land and ordered the construction of *stupas* over them. The Nigali Sagar inscription records this king's enlargement of the *stupa* of a Buddha named Kanakamuni when he had been consecrated 14 years and commemorates his visit to this site. There is, thus, quite a bit of evidence to show that Ashoka played an important role in popularizing veneration of *stupas*.

Ashoka's reign marked an important stage in the history of Buddhist *stupa* architecture. Old mud *stupas* were rebuilt or enlarged with bricks, as evident from excavations at Vaishali and Piprahwa. A fragment of what may be an Ashokan inscription at Amaravati suggests the possibility that the *stupa*-monastery complex located here dates to Ashoka's time. There is an Ashokan pillar at Sarnath, and the Dharmarajika and Dhamekh *stupas* at this place seem to have originated in the Maurya period. At Rajgir, Maurya-type bricks were found at the western part of the mound, marking the site of a *stupa*. The origins of the Dharmarajika *stupa* at Taxila in the north-west may also go back to this period.

Dhauli elephant; façade of Lomash Rishi cave (from top)

Stupa no. 1, Sanchi

An important *stupa* site that definitely dates to Ashoka's time is Sanchi (in Raisen district, MP). This was situated on the outskirts of ancient Vidisha (represented by the site of Besnagar), one of the great cities of Ashoka's empire and also, according to Buddhist legend, the birthplace of his wife, Devi. The remains on the Sanchi hillside include many *stupas*, shrines, and monasteries. The brick core of the largest *stupa*, known as Stupa no. 1 or the Great Stupa, was built in Ashoka's time. We know this because it springs from the same floor level as the pillar that bears Ashoka's schism edict. The *stupa* was about 60 ft in diameter at the base, and was a low dome (less than a full hemisphere) mounted on a low cylindrical drum. It was probably surrounded by a wooden fence and had entrances at the four cardinal points. In the 2nd century BCE, this *stupa* was encased in stone; other additions were made over the next few centuries (these will be discussed in Chapter 8). Stupa no. 1 did not yield any relics.

Several large stone sculptures of what look like human figures have been found at various sites in and around Patna, Mathura, and other places. Many of them represent *yakshas* and *yakshis*, deities whose worship was part of popular religion in many parts of the subcontinent from an early time right down to the present. Most of these images do not bear inscriptions, nor were they found in the course of an archaeological excavation. They were initially ascribed to the Maurya period due to the fact that some or all of their surface was polished. More recent assessments have pointed out that a polished surface is insufficient ground to assign a Maurya date to a piece of sculpture, since the so-called 'Maurya polish' continued into the early centuries CE. Stylistic considerations are, therefore, also very important. The *yaksha* sculpture found at Parkham was initially associated with the Maurya period. Later, some scholars assigned it to the 1st century BCE on stylistic grounds. Its base has an inscription in 3rd/2nd century BCE Brahmi.

Didarganj *yakshi*

Other important examples of stone sculptures include the torso of a nude male figure found at Lohanipur in Patna. It is carved out of sandstone and has a polished surface. Antiquities of the Maurya type, including two polished sandstone pillar fragments, were excavated near the place where the sculpture was found. It is possible, but by no means certain, that this figure depicts a Jaina *tirthankara*. Much of ancient Indian art is characterized by a celebration of the beauty of the human body. In the Jaina tradition, however, nudity reflects a *tirthankara*'s complete renunciation. The 'Didarganj *yakshi*' was found at

FURTHER DISCUSSION | An Ashokan *stupa* at Deorkothar?

In 1982, Phani Kanta Mishra was scouring the Tons valley in Rewa district (MP) for early Buddhist sites. At Paira village, on the right bank of the Tons, he noticed some ancient potsherds, ruined walls, and a small brick *stupa*. The villagers told him about some more brick mounds about 3 km south-east of Paira. The *sarpanch* Ajit Singh led the team of explorers to Deorkothar, a picturesque site overlooking the river. Popular legend associates the brick mound here with an ancient king who wanted to build a magnificent palace. But he died suddenly and the piled-up bricks were all that remained of his dream. Investigations and excavations during 1999–2000 showed Deorkothar to be a site rich in archaeological remains, including a *stupa* of the Maurya period.

The remains at Deorkothar include rock shelters, rock paintings, several *stupas*, monasteries, and inscriptions. The initial explorations identified four brick *stupas* and 29 stone ones, many containing NBPW sherds. Out of the 63 rock shelters, six were found to have paintings, mostly of the early historical period. One of them has a painting of a *stupa* and tree enclosed in a railing.

The most imposing structure was Stupa 1 (over 9 m high). The three other brick stupas were of varying height and dimensions. Stupa 2, located about 400 m south-south-west of Stupa 1, was made out of four different brick sizes. The remains of a colossal pillar with a polished surface suggest a Maurya connection. A six-line inscription in Brahmi letters on it confirms a 3rd century BCE date. The inscription seems to suggest that a monk and his disciples were responsible for setting up the pillar.

Remains of a fallen stone railing were found close to Stupa 1. Some of the fragments had simple, shallow carvings, including half lotuses, full lotuses, and partially open lotus buds. The carvings seem to represent an earlier stage than those at Sanchi or Bharhut, and it is therefore, possible that the stone railing around Stupa 1 at Deorkothar belonged to the Maurya period. The *stupa* seems to have suffered deliberate damage some time before the mid-2nd century BCE.

Source P. K. Mishra, 2001

Didarganj village in Patna. The figure actually seems to be an attendant and not a *yakshi*. Some scholars think that its style, refinement, and polished surface indicate a Maurya association, while others (on the basis of the treatment of the body and the ornamentation) think it belongs to the 2nd century CE. Two headless male sculptures found at Patna bear striking stylistic similarities to the Didarganj figure. They may represent *yakshas*, but more probably attendant figures. If some of these sculptures indeed belong to the Maurya period, this suggests the existence of several centres of stone carving, serving royal and perhaps other patrons as well. Susan Huntington (1985: 52) points out that these sculptures represent an important phase in the portrayal of the human figure in Indian art, and that while certain features such as the polished surface do not have a long-term legacy, other aspects—such as the treatment of the human body, features of the costumes, and objects held in the hands—do. However, some art historians argue that these sculptures belong to the post-Maurya period, to the early centuries CE (Asher and Spink, 1989).

A large number of carved ring stones and disc stones found at various sites in North India have been dated to the 3rd/2nd century BCE (Joshi, 1987). They occur at sites such as Patna, Taxila, Mathura, the Purana Qila in Delhi, Kaushambi, Rajghat, and Vaishali. They generally have a diameter of 5–6 cm, with different sorts of carvings arranged within two or more concentric circles—animals such as the lion, horse, deer, birds, and the crocodile (*makara*); female figures that may represent goddesses; trees and floral designs; and geometric patterns. These ring stones and disc stones may have had a religious or ritualistic significance.

Terracotta art flourished with the expansion of urban centres. The terracottas of this period vary a great deal in terms of theme, style, and possible significance, but they do give an important insight into popular practices, beliefs, and aesthetics. They include male and female figurines, animals, and carts. Some of them may have been toys, but others, especially certain female figurines, may represent religious icons. As mentioned in an earlier chapter, it is not always apparent whether a figurine had a religious/ritualistic significance or not. A great deal depends on the context in which it was found. There is a problem in dating terracottas, and those pieces that are found in stratified contexts in the course of archaeological excavations are, therefore, of special value.

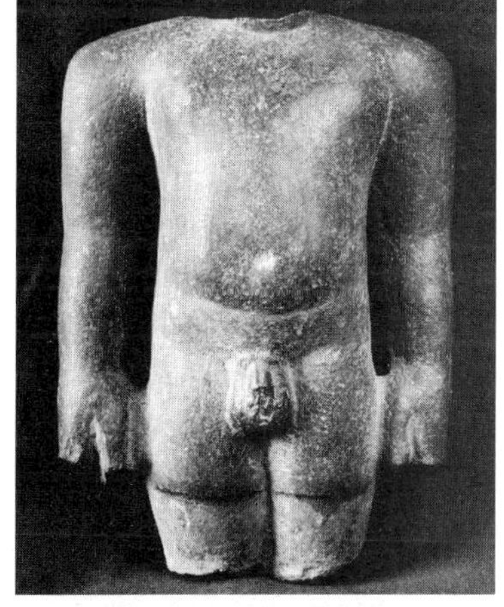

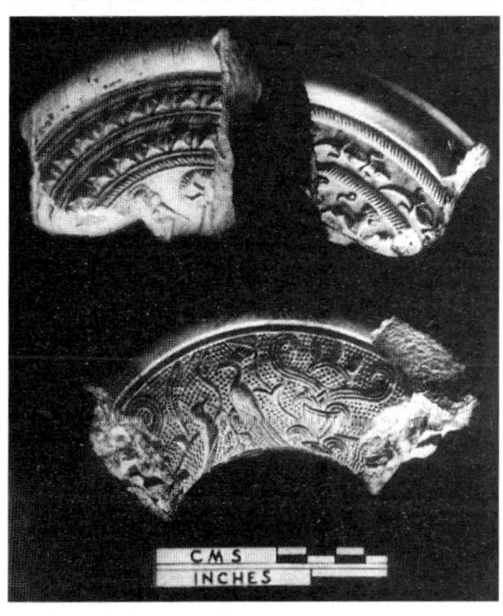

Lohanipur torso; carved ring stones (from top)

FURTHER DISCUSSION | The Parkham *yaksha*, then and now

*Yaksha*s were deities connected with water, fertility, trees, the forest, and the wilderness. *Yakshi*s were their female counterparts and were originally benign deities connected with fertility. *Yaksha* and *yakshi* images of stone and terracotta have been found at many sites in the subcontinent, indicating that their worship was an important part of popular religion in ancient India.

Many *yaksha* images have been found in the Mathura area. The most celebrated of these is a colossal grey sandstone figure (2.59 m high) discovered next to a tank at Parkham village, south of Mathura city. According to some art historians, on stylistic grounds, this image should be assigned to the 2nd/1st century BCE. However, the Brahmi inscription on its pedestal suggests a 3rd century BCE date. The inscription states that this stone image was made by Gomitaka, a pupil of Kunika, and that it was set up by eight brothers who were members of the Manibhadra *puga* (congregation). The inscription clearly indicates that this was an image of the *yaksha* Manibhadra, mentioned in various texts and inscriptions as a tutelary deity of merchants and travellers, and especially worshipped in important trading centres.

The colossal image of the *yaksha* Manibhadra was removed from Parkham village to the Mathura Museum many years ago. But these days, in the month of Magh (January), a Jakhaiya *mela* (i.e., *yaksha* fair) is held in the village. Hundreds of people from surrounding villages converge at Parkham to worship the Jakhaiya (i.e., *yaksha*). On this occasion, a small *yaksha* image—a poor substitute for the original—is brought out, placed in a makeshift enclosure next to the tank, and worshipped.

The colossal *yaksha* suggests gravity and massive strength, and his broken right hand was probably raised in the protection-granting *abhaya-mudra*. His diminutive modern counterpart has a cheerful grin, and raises his left hand in what looks like a friendly wave. Nevertheless, on three consecutive Sundays in January, the *yaksha* regains some of the importance he once enjoyed in the Mathura area over 2,000 years ago.

Source Upinder Singh, 2004a

The Decline, Legacy, and Memory of the Maurya Empire

Since the Maurya empire was the first virtually subcontinental empire, all its aspects have attracted scholarly attention, including its decline. The long reigns of the first three Maurya rulers were followed by many weak rulers with short reigns. Only one of the later Mauryas—Dasharatha—is known to have issued inscriptions. Others are known only from Puranic, Buddhist, and Jaina accounts. An invasion by the Bactrian Greeks further weakened the empire.

Ashoka has been both blamed and exonerated for the decline of the empire. Haraprasad Sastri suggested that Pushyamitra Shunga's coup represented a Brahmanical revolution, instigated by the anti-Brahmana policies of Ashoka and the patronage extended to the heterodox sects by the Mauryas. It is possible that Ashoka's ban on animal sacrifices may have annoyed those Brahmanas whose livelihood depended on performing sacrifices. It is also possible that the appointment of *dhamma-mahamatas* may have struck at the Brahmanas' prestige as custodians of social morality. However, Sastri wrongly interprets a sentence in rock edict 1 as a boast made by Ashoka that he had revealed the Brahmanas to be false gods. The sentence actually states that due to Ashoka's efforts, gods and men had come to mingle, figuratively speaking. In fact, Ashoka's inscriptions contain frequent exhortations to his people to respect *shramanas* and Brahmanas. It is quite evident that the end of the Maurya dynasty was *not* the result of a revolution of any kind.

Ashoka's pacifist policy has also been seen as responsible for the decline of the Maurya empire. As mentioned earlier, Ashoka's pragmatism is reflected in the fact that he did not disband the army, that he did not abolish capital punishment, and that he was quite capable of giving stern warnings to tribal communities. However, a long reign marked by only one military campaign in the early years may have adversely affected the preparedness of the army, and this may have been a factor responsible for the success of the Greek invasion.

As long as the Maurya empire was considered a centralized political system, a weak ruler at the centre could be held responsible for its decline. However, if the empire was not as centralized as once believed, then this argument becomes irrelevant. It has also been suggested that the Maurya state faced some kind of financial crisis, or that there was a more widespread economic crisis in the empire, but there is no evidence for either of these things.

Some of the arguments put forward to explain the decline of the Maurya empire (e.g., in Thapar, [1963] 1987) are anachronistic—they point to things that we should not generally expect to find in ancient states. These include the absence of nationalism, absence of the idea of loyalty to the state rather than to a particular king, and the lack of popular representative institutions. Similarly, although it is true that personal selec-tion must have been important in the appointment of officials and that a Chinese-type examination system did not exist in Maurya India, this is not very helpful in explaining the decline of the Maurya empire. The Maurya empire was vast, diverse, and difficult to hold together. But to attribute its decline to the fact that the Mauryas were unable to restructure the economies of the core and peripheral areas seems to refer to strategies and interventions that are more characteristic of modern nation states.

Given the nature of the evidence, explanations of the decline of the Maurya empire have to be very general. All empires rely on mechanisms of integration and control over territory, resources, and people. These mechanisms include military force, administrative infrastructure, and ideology. In the case of the Mauryas, given the vast contours of the empire, all three must have been strained to their utmost. It was just a matter of time before the distant provinces broke away from the centre.

Historians have debated the impact of the Maurya empire on the history of the subcontinent, especially in the spheres of political and socio-economic developments. The general consensus is that while the Maurya empire did have an impact, this should not be exaggerated.

Ashoka stands apart in the candid confessional style he chose for his edicts, his obsession with explaining and propagating *dhamma*, and his rejection of war. But in several respects, he represents the starting point of mainstream classical Indian political thought. He plucked *dhamma/dharma* out of religious discourse and made it a central political and social issue. He made a bold attempt to assert and emphasize the moral foundations of royal authority and empire, connecting it with the good, happiness, and heaven. He seriously engaged with the problem of violence and conflict in the political and social spheres.

Ashoka can also be seen as foundational with respect to ancient Indian royal religious policy. He recognized the problem of religious conflict and dealt with it through persuasion, exhortation, and action, projecting himself as a king who stood above religious divides. His religious patronage was multidirectional and not limited by his personal religious beliefs. Women of the royal household had the freedom and authority to make pious gifts. In all these respects, Ashoka's political thought and practice can be seen as foundational to the Indian political tradition. But his denunciation and renunciation of war and his massive piety propaganda campaign were radical by the standards of not only his, but any, age.

Patrick Olivelle (2009) argues that the Buddha took over the concept of *dharma* with its strong royal associations (along with other royal symbols) from the Brahmanical tradition and gave it new ethical content, also using it to refer to his doctrine. Then, Ashoka came along and talked extensively about *dhamma* in his edicts. It was his appropriation of the word and his injection of new ethical content into it that transformed it into a central cultural concept, which the Brahmanas were forced to take note of by inventing the disciple of Dharmashastra. For the Buddhists, *dhamma* stood for the word and the teaching of the Buddha, who was its authoritative source. The Brahmanas had to come up with their own version of *dharma* and to identify its source. They did this by creating an enormous authoritative corpus of texts that dealt specifically with the subject—Dharmashastra. Of course, this hypothesis hinges on placing the beginning of the Dharmashastra tradition after Ashoka.

The image of Ashoka as a remarkable, cosmopolitan, peace-loving king survives into our own time. The power and influence of this image can be vividly seen in the selection of Ashoka's Sarnath capital as the emblem of the Indian republic. Along with the Buddha, Mahavira, and Gandhi, Ashoka has become an icon of nonviolence. These icons stand tall in the midst of the layers of violence that have marked Indian history (indeed, all human history), and represent some of the ways in which the problem of violence has been addressed in Indian thought and practice across the centuries.

CONCLUSIONS

The Maurya period saw the establishment of the first virtually subcontinental empire. Such a large empire required new strategies of governance. The Maurya period is known as much for empire-building as for king Ashoka, who renounced all military ambition and exerted himself relentlessly to promote the cause of *dhamma*. Although rooted in his personal faith in the Buddha's teaching for the laity, this *dhamma* was an imperial ideology that bore his strong personal stamp. The imperial power of the Mauryas was visible in monumental stone sculpture and structures, and important beginnings were made in rock-cut and *stupa* architecture. There are also many artefacts that reflect popular aesthetics and religious beliefs. The social and economic processes of agrarian expansion and urbanization of the preceding centuries continued under Maurya rule, and there was a further growth in cities, trade, and the money economy. Although a few specific aspects of these processes have been touched on in this chapter, the broad patterns of social and economic processes that were underway are best discussed outside the framework of political history and will be taken up in the next chapter.

FURTHER READINGS

Chakrabarti, Dilip K. 1995. *The Archaeology of Ancient Indian Cities*. Delhi: Oxford University Press. Chapter 5.

Falk, Harry. 2006. *Aśokan Sites and Artefacts*. Mains am Rheim: Verlag Philipp Zabern.

Fussman, Gerard. 1987–88. 'Central and Provincial Administration in Ancient India: The Problem of the Mauryan Empire.' *Indian Historical Review* 14(1–2): 43–72.

Ghosh, A. 1967. 'The Pillars of Asoka: Their Purpose.' *East and West*, n.s., 17(3–4): 273–75.

Gupta, S. P. 1980. *The Roots of Indian Art (A Detailed Study of the Formative Period of Art and Architecture: Third and Second centuries B.C.–Maurya and Late Maurya*. Delhi: B. R. Publishing Corpn.

Hultzsch, E. (1925) 1969. *Corpus Inscriptionum Indicarum*, Vol. 1, *Inscriptions of Asoka*. Rep. Edn. Delhi: Indological Book House.

Huntington, Susan. 1985. *The Art of Ancient India: Buddhist, Hindu, Jain*. New York, Tokyo: Weather Hill. Chapter 4.

Joshi, M. C. 1987. 'Aspects of Mauryan and Early Post-Mauryan Art.' *Journal of the Indian Society of Oriental Art*, n.s., 16, 17: 15–22.

Lahiri, Nayanjot. 2015. *Ashoka in Ancient India*. Raniket: Permanent Black in association with Ashoka University.

Mukherjee, B. N. 1984. *Studies in Aramaic Edicts of Asoka*. Calcutta: Indian Museum.

Norman, K. R. 1985. 'Guide to the Asokan Inscriptions.' *South Asian Studies* 1: 43–49.

Olivelle, Patrick. 2023. *Ashoka: Portrait of a Philosopher King*. Gurugram: Harper Collins.

Olivelle, Patrick, Janice Leoshko, and Himanshu Prabha Ray. (Eds.). 2012. *Reimagining Aśoka: Memory and History*. New Delhi: Oxford University Press.

Ray, Niharranjan. 1975. *Maurya and Post-Maurya Art: A Study in Social and Formal Contacts*. New Delhi: Indian Council of Historical Research.

Singh, Upinder. 2017. *Political Violence in Ancient India*. Cambridge, MA: Harvard University Press.

Sircar, D. C. 1956. *Inscriptions of Aśoka*. New Delhi: Publications Division.

Stoneman, Richard. 2019. *The Greek Experience of India: From Alexander to the Indo-Greeks*. Princeton and Oxford: Princeton University Press. Chaps. 5–10.

Thapar, Romila. (1963) 2012. *Asoka and the Decline of the Mauryas*. 3rd Edn. New Delhi: Oxford University Press.

———. 1984. *The Mauryas Revisited*. Sakharam Ganesh Deuskar Lectures on Indian History. Centre for Studies in Social Science. Kolkata: K. P. Bagchi & Co.

Detail of a relief sculpture of Ashoka at Kanaganahalli (Karnataka); he wears ornaments and perhaps a sacred thread. The umbrella is an insignia of royalty.

CHAPTER 8

Interaction and Innovation

c. 200 BCE–300 CE

Godawaya lies on the southern coast of Sri Lanka, close to the estuary of the Walawe Ganga. Excavations conducted here from 1994 onwards revealed the remains of a 2nd century CE Buddhist *stupa*, monastery, shrine, and quarry. An inscription states that various duties in the port of Godapavata were transferred by king Gamini Abhaya (Gajabahu) to the monastery. The discovery of various types of pottery, beads, and other artefacts indicated the importance of the site. In 1998, while diving for shells and lobsters, fishermen found an underwater site with lots of pottery about 5 km off the coast from Godawaya. Explorations and excavations by an international team of marine archaeologists led to the discovery of the oldest shipwreck known in South Asia.

The remains included grinding stones or ceremonial benches, various types of ceramics (including black and red ware), purified glass ingots, and iron and copper bars. Decayed wood, possibly part of a ship's hull, were found. Artefact analysis and radiocarbon dating of two wood samples gave a broad range of 2nd century BCE to 2nd century CE. The ship may have been coming from South India and heading towards Godawaya or vice versa (Muthucumarana et al., 2014; Bopearachchi et al., 2016). It belongs to a period when the Indian subcontinent was increasingly drawn into the overland and maritime trade networks connecting various parts of Asia, Africa, and Europe. Due to its central location on the international maritime trade routes, Sri Lanka, known in Graeco-Roman accounts as Taprobane, played a very important role in this trans-continental trade.

The period *c*. 200 BCE–300 CE was historically significant from several points of view. In North India, several invasions from the north-west led to a westward shift in the focus of political power away from the Magadha region. State formation took shape in the Deccan and far south. City life spread to many regions of the subcontinent. Craftspersons produced larger quantities and more varied goods than before, trade within the subcontinent and between its regions and other lands flourished, and money was increasingly used as a medium of exchange. New cultural winds blew into the subcontinent in the wake of the invasions and expanding trade, and the north-west in particular became a major cultural crossroads. The devotional worship of images in shrines became a cornerstone of religious life, cutting across sectarian and cultic boundaries. The increasing institutionalization of religious activity was reflected in religious texts, permanent religious structures, images, and inscriptions. Sophisticated styles of stone sculpture co-existed with vibrant traditions of terracotta art.

The sources for the history of these centuries are many and diverse. The texts composed during this period should be considered not only as sources but also important products of the period, reflecting literary creativity and the history of ideas.

The Jatakas contain many stories of ordinary people, traders, and travellers. Incidental historical references occur in other Buddhist works such as the *Milindapanha* and *Lalitavistara*. Jaina texts throw light on the history of Jainism and provide incidental references of historical value. The Puranas give details on political history, although they often contradict each other on a number of points. The Puranas and epics are a rich source of information on the emergence of early Hindu sects and religious practices.

The later Dharmasutras and Smritis such as the *Manava Dharmashastra* (generally referred to as the *Manu Smriti*), represent Brahmanical discourses, through which we can get glimmers of the intersection between social theory and practice. According to Patrick

Marine archaeologists at Godawaya

Olivelle, the *Manu Smriti's* structure suggests that the original work was composed in the 2nd–3rd centuries CE by a single author—a learned Brahmana who lived somewhere in North India, or at the most by a small group of people. He argues that the text aimed to defend Brahmanical privilege against enemies personified as Shudras and *mlechchhas* and sought to re-establish and strengthen the old alliance between kings and Brahmanas (Olivelle, [2005] 2006: 5–41).

As discussed in Chapter 6, although the prehistory of the *Arthashastra* goes back to the Maurya period, the text is now usually considered a work composed in the early centuries CE. Written in compact Sanskrit prose interspersed with some verses, the *Arthashastra* consists of fifteen books *(adhikaranas)*, divided into 150 sections *(adhyayas)* and 180 topics *(prakaranas)*. The first five deal with internal administration *(tantra)*, the next eight with inter-state relations *(avapa)*, and the last two with miscellaneous topics. The *Arthashastra* refers to several previous works on the subject, none of which have survived. As one of the *purusharthas* (the legitimate goals of human existence), *artha* stands for material gain. The *Arthashastra* states very categorically that *artha* is superior to *dharma* and *kama*, because the latter two are dependent on it. The *Arthashastra* is addressed to kings and other members of the political elite. It gives pragmatic advice on how an ambitious king can maintain and enhance his power. Although Kautilya sees the kingdom *(rajya)* as the norm, he also refers to oligarchies *(sanghas)* and has a chapter on how the *vijigishu* (the king desirous of victory) should get the better of them. The *Arthashastra* does not deal explicitly with theoretical issues such as the origins of the state or kingship, but has a complex and sophisticated conceptualization of the state and governance.

The *Arthashastra* is often associated with an organic theory of the state consisting of seven elements (*prakritis*)—the king (*svami*), minister (*amatya*), territory plus people (*janapada*), fort (*durga*), treasury (*kosha*), force/justice (*danda*), and ally (*mitra*). But the text is not explicitly structured around these seven elements. (The listing of the elements occurs for the first time in the sixth book and is repeated in Book 8.) As mentioned in Chapter 7, some of the conceptual vocabulary used by Kautilya must have existed before him. His achievement was to weave together various elements to construct a comprehensive, detailed political discourse from the perspective of economic and political gain, and to introduce a new vision of a potential state. The *Arthashastra* is an important and highly influential work on statecraft and a rich source of political ideas.

PRIMARY SOURCES | **The Kautilyan state**

Kautilya explains *artha* as the sustenance or livelihood of men, of which the source is the earth inhabited by people. Thus, *arthashastra* is a branch of learning that deals with the means of the acquisition and protection of the earth, which is the source of people's livelihood (*Arthashastra* 1.1–2). Since it is the king who acquires and protects the earth, *arthashastra* is in effect a discipline that deals with statecraft.

The king is central to Kautilya's discussion of politics. He is expected to be of high birth but also educated, well-trained, and endowed with virtues, including self-control (*vinaya*). The ideal king makes careful choices after consulting others and weighs different options, keeping his political interests paramount. The king's duties include safeguarding the *dharma* of the *varnas* and *ashramas* and maintaining order by dispensing justice. One of Kautilya's achievements was to demonstrate through reason that it was in the king's self-interest to ensure the welfare of his subjects.

One of the remarkable aspects of the Kautilyan state is a high level of state surveillance and regulation. Kautilya visualized a highly intrusive state that regulated various aspects of economic and social life. His section on *shunyanivesha* discusses how the state should reclaim land and establish settlements. The state also appears as an entrepreneur involved in the manufacture of commodities such as textiles. Spies in various disguises were to fan out to keep careful watch over officials and subjects, alert to the slightest whiff of rebellion.

The discussion of inter-state relations uses the theory of the *raja-mandala* (circle of kings) and the idea of natural enemies and allies. The four principal states in the circle of kings are the *vijigishu* (the king desirous of victory), *ari* (enemy, whose territory is next to that of the *vijigishu*), *madhyama* (the 'middle' king, located between the *vijigishu* and *ari*, and stronger than both), and the *udasina* (the indifferent, neutral king, who is more powerful than the other three). While the idea of the circle of kings suggests that Kautilya had a small or medium-sized state in mind, in the *Arthashastra*, the idea of empire is reflected in the person of the *vijigishu*, the ambitious king who desires extensive conquest. It is also reflected in Kautilya's description of the *chakravarti-kshetra* (the field of conquest of the emperor) as the region between the Himavat and the sea, 1000 *yojanas* across in extent.

The *Arthashastra* contains the first detailed law code in India. Kautilya did not consider everyone equal before the law. The discussion of civil and criminal law was based on the idea of natural inequality, especially that based on *varna*. Of course, as the *Arthashastra* is a normative text, we do not know to what extent its recommendations were followed in actual legal disputes. Among other things, the text discusses torture, accepts capital punishment, and also provides for the commutation of punishments to fines.

Kautilya is usually seen as a political thinker with a realist, pragmatic approach towards politics, as one who justified all sorts of violence, subterfuge, and deceit for the king's attainment of his political ends. However, the text also advises careful weighing of options before making decisions. Of the three powers of the king—*mantra-shakti* (the power of counsel), *prabhu-shakti* (the power of lordship, i.e. military might), and *utsaha-shakti* (the power of energy)—Kautilya asserts the primacy of the first, recommending that the king should listen to the wise counsel of others. In the discussion of the four *upayas* (expedients)—*sama* (conciliation), *dana* (liberality), *danda* (force), and *bheda* (creating dissension)—he recommends that force should only be used as a last resort.

If the *Arthashastra* is read against the grain, in its description of the king as a constant target of assassination, rebellion, and in its idea of *prakriti-kopa* (the anger of the people, i.e., a popular uprising), it reflects the anxieties and insecurities of those who wielded political power.

Source Upinder Singh, 2017: 96–123

An important aspect of the textual production of this period is the beginning of Sanskrit *kavya*, which includes poetry, prose, and drama (for details, see Warder, 1972–2004, Vol. 2; Leinhard, 1984). Sheldon Pollock ([2006] 2007) has pointed to the connections between *kavya* and *rajya* (kingdoms), and between *kavya* and epigraphic *prashasti* (panegyric).

The works of Bhasa and Ashvaghosha represent the earliest surviving Sanskrit *kavya*. Ashvaghosha was a learned Buddhist scholar and poet who lived in the 1st or 2nd century CE. His two extant works are the *Saundarananda* and *Buddhacharita* (Life of the Buddha). A few passages of his play, *Shariputraprakarana*, also survive. The *Buddhacharita* describes itself as a *mahakayva*. While telling the story of the Buddha's life, it weaves together ideas from various traditions, including the epics and Dharmashastra, and gives detailed rejoinders to Brahmanical ideas connected with kingship, renunciation, and *dharma*.

Bhasa probably lived in the late 2nd century. Several of his plays are based on themes from the *Ramayana* and *Mahabharata*, but he moulded the events and characters in his own way. The *Balacharita* is based on Krishna's boyhood days in Vrindavana. The six

PRIMARY SOURCES | The *Natyashastra*

The *Natyashastra* is the oldest Indian work on dramaturgy, i.e., the theory of drama, but since drama is considered a form of *kavya*, its principles had a wider literary application.

The *Natyashastra* tells us that *natya* (drama) was created as a play-thing (*kridaniyaka*) to give pleasure and divert minds weary of the problems, conflicts, and miseries of daily life. The first chapter of the work describes the gods requesting Brahma for something playful or pleasant. The first play is said to have been performed in heaven in front of the gods and demons on the occasion of the Indra festival. The text tells us that the *Natyashastra* was passed on by Brahma to a sage named Bharata as a fifth Veda in order to save the world from evil passions by a means which, unlike the four Vedas, was accessible to all people. This origin myth clearly aimed at giving legitimacy to the text.

The *Natyashastra* is a composite work reflecting the codification and compilation of earlier material which may have been current among actors over many centuries. This may have initially existed in the form of oral traditions, and later in the form of prose *sutras*, to which verses and commentary were subsequently added. Abhinavagupta's commentary on the *Natyashastra* mentions three recensions of the text, of which only one has survived in the form of two versions.

The *Natyashastra* deals with all aspects of dramatic performances. It discusses *abhinaya*, i.e., the ways in which actors can communicate a dramatic experience to the audience through speech, expressions, various movements of the body, props, costumes, and ornaments. It also discusses topics such as the construction of the theatre, types of plays, the plot and structure of plays, characters, dialogues, the ideal time of performances, and the ideal qualities of actors and audiences. Elaborate props and a drop curtain are noticeably absent. Song and dance were important elements of plays and there are references to street plays.

One of the central concepts discussed in the *Natyashastra* is *rasa* (discussed specially in Chapter 6 of the work). The text uses the analogy of cooking to explain the art and effect of drama. The combination of various foodstuffs, vegetables, sweetners, and spices gives food a taste and flavour, which in turn produces delight and satisfaction. Similarly, in drama, the combination of the causes and effects of emotions give rise to a particular *rasa* or aesthetic experience in the audience, leading to pleasure and satisfaction. The text lists eight *rasa*s associated with eight corresponding basic emotions:

1. the sensitive *shringara rasa* associated with love
2. the comic *hasya rasa* associated with humour
3. the compassionate *karuna rasa* associated with grief
4. the furious *raudra rasa* associated with anger
5. the heroic *vira rasa* associated with energy
6. the apprehensive *bhayanaka rasa* associated with fear
7. the horrific *bibhatsa rasa* associated with disgust
8. the marvellous *adbhuta rasa* associated with astonishment

Rasa is different from *bhava* (feeling). The actors depict certain emotions (*bhava*); the audience experiences corresponding aesthetic experience (*rasa*). The actors imagine and represent the emotions of the characters they portray; the audience reacts to their portrayal. For instance, when the actors act as though they were in love, the audience does not experience the pangs or joys of love, but the sensitive *shringara rasa*. Similarly, when the actors act out grief, the audience does not experience grief but compassion.

According to the *Natyashastra*, death should never be portrayed on stage, nor should it be reported. Other activities generally not to be shown on stage include eating, fighting, kissing, and bathing. The hero was supposed to triumph at the end of the play. Unlike Greek drama, Sanskrit drama does not have a tradition of tragedy (Bhasa is an exception). There may be plenty of sorrow and suffering in the course of the play, but it usually ends on a positive note.

Source Bhat, 1975; Warder, 1972–2004, Vol. 1: 21–24

Mahabharata-related plays are *Madhyamavyayoga, Pancharatra, Dutavakya, Dutaghatotkacha, Karnabhara*, and *Urubhanga*. The two *Ramayana*-related plays are *Pratima* and *Abhisheka*. The *Pratigyayaugandharayana* and *Svapnavasavadatta* are based on the legendary king Udayana. *Charudatta* (which is incomplete), the only play that is not connected directly with political issues or characters, tells the love story of a poor Brahmana named Charudatta and a courtesan named Vasantasena.

Poetry was also written in Prakrit (also known as Middle Indic). The *Gatha Sattasai* (700 Verses in the Gatha Form) composed in Maharashtri Prakrit is an anthology of poems divided into seven sections, each consisting of about 100 couplets. The poems were mostly composed during the 1st to 4th centuries CE, with later interpolations added till at least the 8th century. References to the Vindhya mountains and the Tapi, Reva, and Godavari rivers indicate that the poets lived in western India. Most of the *Gatha* poems are love poems.

PRIMARY SOURCES | **The *Gatha Sattasai***

Many of the *Gatha Sattasai* poems have rural settings and characters, but this is not folk poetry. It is poetry created by city poets for an audience of urban connoisseurs, including members of the royal court. The first and last poems in the *Gatha* are in praise of Shiva, but the rest are, by and large, non-religious. The Satavahana king Hala is supposed to have composed some of the poems and compiled the anthology. Apart from Hala, there are other poets belonging to royal families. The handful of women poets included Anulakshmi, Madhavi, Andhralakshmi, and Reva.

The themes of the poems include kings and nature, but most—especially the most memorable ones—are about lovers eager to get to their rendezvous. As in the Sangam poems, the natural landscape—riverbank, rice fields, village pond—plays a prominent role. The wide cast of characters includes young girls, wives, mature women, prostitutes, farmers, hunters, monks, and travellers. As in the Sangam poems, the poets speak through characters such as the lover, beloved, female messenger, and the beloved's friend. Most speak through a woman's voice. The poems talk of awkward young love, experienced mature love, and the love shared by old couples. They deal with the anticipation of union as well as the pain of separation.

The poets used a variety of poetic devices such as similes, metaphors, and double entendre. But their favourite device was something that the later Sanskrit experts on poetics called *dhvani*—suggestion or implied meaning. Martha Ann Selby has referred to the unique ambiguity of the *Gatha* poems as the 'poetics of anteriority'—that is, the meaning of the poem lies outside the words. The meaning is often not immediately apparent; it has to be prised out. Sometimes it is elusive and opaque; sometimes a poem can be interpreted in many different ways. Later commentaries can help, but their explanations sometimes seem rather contrived.

The *Gatha* poems are like puzzles that invite readers to decipher them by giving free rein to the imagination. Consider the following poem. It is short and simple, erotic in its extreme understatement, creating the image of a brief but intense encounter:

As the traveler, eyes raised,
Cupped hands filled with water, spreads
His fingers and lets it run through,
She pouring it reduces the trickle.

(Trans. Arvind Krishna Mehrotra)

The poems of the *Gatha Sattasai* circulated widely all over the subcontinent. Experts on Sanskrit poetics knew them well and considered them models of refined lyric poetry. Some of the Sanskrit poems of the 7th century *Amaru-shataka* were directly based on them.

Source Selby, 2000; Mehrotra, 1991: 13

Sangam poetry, the oldest surviving literature in the Tamil language, is an important part of the repertoire of available literary sources. (For details, see Shulman, 2016: 43–106; Zvelebil, 1974.) As mentioned in Chapter 1, the term 'Sangam literature' is based on a later tradition of three literary academies, the historicity of which is not certain. The Sangam corpus includes six of the eight anthologies of poems of the *Ettutokai*, nine of the ten *pattus* or songs included in the *Pattupattu*, and the earliest parts of the first two books of the *Tolkappiyam*. The poems are of two types—*akam* (love poems) and *puram* (heroic poems). The poets had diverse social backgrounds and their poems, modelled on the songs of the humble bards and drummers of earlier times, are a rich and evocative source for the society of Tamilakam (the Tamil land) roughly between the 3rd century BCE and the 3rd century CE.

Hardly any scientific treatises of the period *c.* 200 BCE–300 CE survive, with the possible exception of the Sanskrit medical works of Charaka and Sushruta, the origins of which may go back to this period. However, on the basis of later texts, traditions of learning in subjects such as astronomy, mathematics, and medicine can be inferred. Varahamihira's *Panchasiddhantika* (6th century) summarizes the astronomical works and ideas of the preceding centuries.

Graeco-Roman texts (collectively known as 'classical accounts') are among the other important historical sources for the period. They include the works of Arrian, Strabo, and Pliny the Elder. There is also the anonymous *Periplus Maris Erythraei*, whose author seems to have been an Egyptian Greek involved in trade, who travelled from the head of the Red Sea to India and wrote a book based on his experiences and observations. The details in such texts are particularly important for the history of trade. Chinese texts such as the *Qian Hanshu* (*Ch'ien Han-shu*) and the *Hou Hanshu* provide information on the movement and migrations of people in Central Asia, which had a direct impact on the political situation in North India.

Archaeology continues to offer information on settlement patterns, specialized crafts, and trade. The details of urban sites are often scanty, but their broad profiles are clear. In North India, the evidence from late NBPW and post-NBPW levels reveals a significant expansion of urban centres. In archaeological literature, the cultural levels belonging to these centuries are often labelled 'Shunga–Kushana'. The settlements are often fortified and show elements of planning and a considerable use of burnt brick. The pottery includes wheel-turned red ware of medium fabric, frequently with stamped and incised designs. The shapes include bowls with flared or incurved rims, button-knobbed lids, basins with spouts, long bottle-necked 'sprinklers', and miniature vases. The rich range of artefacts includes coins, seals, and terracottas of fine workmanship. In the Deccan and South India, certain sites reveal an overlap between the later megalithic and early historic phase. On the other hand, several urban settlements have neither neolithic–chalcolithic nor megalithic antecedents. There is comparatively less information regarding rural settlements.

During the period *c.* 200 BCE–300 CE, the range, type, and number of inscriptions increased dramatically. In North India, royal inscriptions reflect a transition from Prakrit towards Sanskrit. In the south, the earliest Tamil inscriptions made their appearance. The hundreds of inscriptions available from different parts of the subcontinent include royal inscriptions, which provide details regarding dynastic history. But these are greatly outnumbered by records of pious donations made by ordinary men and women from diverse social backgrounds. These form a valuable source of information on social history and the patronage of religious establishments.

The expansion of state polities and the spread of urban centres and trade led to important developments in coinage. The Indo-Greeks introduced bilingual and bi-script legends on their die-struck coins, and almost all our information on these kings comes from their coinage. The Kushanas minted large quantities of gold coins, as well as copper coins of low denominational value. In the Deccan, the Satavahanas issued coins of silver, copper, lead, and potin. Roman gold coins flowed into peninsular India in large quantities in the course of flourishing Indo-Mediterranean trade interactions. Locally made imitations of Roman gold coins were also made and used. Some of the punch-marked coins found in the far south can be tentatively identified as dynastic issues on the basis of their motifs. There are also definite dynastic issues of the Chola, Chera, and Pandya kings.

A number of interesting coins (mostly made of copper or bronze) throw light on political and economic institutions of the time. These include those issued by non-monarchical states such as the Arjunayanas, Uddehikas, Malavas, and Yaudheyas. A number of 'city coins' were presumably issued by the urban administration of cities such as Tripuri, Ujjayini, Kaushambi, Vidisha, Airikina, Mahishmati, Madhyamika, Varanasi, and Taxila. A handful of negama (nigama) coins reflect the power and authority of merchant guilds.

Visual sources in the form of religious icons and relief sculptures at various sites are a rich source of information. Apart from reflecting developments in the artistic sphere, when analyzed along with donative inscriptions, they offer important perspectives on religious ideas and practice.

Copper coins (obverse and reverse) of the Yaudheyas, Ayodhya, and Kunindas (from top right)

The Political History of North India

The Shungas

According to the *Harshacharita*, Pushyamitra, commander-in-chief of the Maurya army, killed the Maurya king Brihadratha while the latter was inspecting his troops (for details of the political history of North India, see Raychaudhuri, [1923] 2000; Majumdar. [Gen Ed.]., [1951] 1968). This coup brought an end to Maurya rule in 187 BCE. The Puranas describe Pushyamitra as belonging to the Shunga family. There are several references to Shunga teachers in Vedic texts, and the *Brihadaranyaka Upanishad* mentions a teacher named Shaungiputra. Panini connects the Shungas with the Brahmana Bharadvaja *gotra*. Kalidasa's *Malavikagnimitra* describes Agnimitra, son of Pushyamitra, as belonging to the Baimbika *kula* (family/lineage) and Kashyapa *gotra*. While they differ in detail, all these sources indicate that the Shungas were Brahmanas.

Pushyamitra's empire extended over only part of the erstwhile Maurya empire. It included Pataliputra (which was still the capital), Ayodhya, and Vidisha. According to the *Divyavadana* and Taranatha's account, it also included Jalandhara and Shakala in the Punjab. Pushyamitra placed viceroys in at least some parts of his empire. In the *Malavikagnimitra*, Agnimitra is the viceroy at Vidisha. This drama also refers to the conflict between Pushyamitra and Yajnasena, king of Vidarbha (the eastern Maharashtra area) and the victory of the Shungas.

The Shungas also clashed with the Bactrian Greeks. Giving an example of an event belonging to the recent past, the 2nd century BCE grammarian Patanjali refers to the *yavanas* coming up to Saketa (in or around Ayodhya in Ayodhya district, UP) and Madhyamika (near Chittoor in Rajasthan). During this period, Yavana was a general term used in Indian texts for foreigners from the West, including the Greeks. In this case,

PRIMARY SOURCES | **The Besnagar pillar inscription of Heliodorus**

An interesting inscription of the Shunga period is inscribed on a pillar at Besnagar, the site of ancient Vidisha. The inscription is in Prakrit (with a few Sanskritic spellings) and is written in the Brahmi script. It consists of six lines that can be translated as follows:

This *garuda*-pillar of Vasudeva, the god of gods
was constructed here by Heliodora [Heliodorus], the Bhagavata,
son of Diya [Dion], of Takhkhasila [Taxila],
the Greek ambassador who came from the Great King
Amtalakita [Antialkidas] to king Kasiputra [Kashiputra] Bhagabhadra, the Saviour,
Prospering in [his] fourteenth year.

The other side of the pillar has a short inscription, translated as follows:

[These?] three steps to immortality, when correctly followed, lead to heaven: control, generosity, and attention.

The Besnagar pillar inscription indicates that the Shungas continued the Maurya tradition of entertaining ambassadors from Greek courts. Kasiputa Bhagabhadra is identified either as the fifth Shunga king Bhadraka or the ninth king Bhagavata. Amtalakita was the Indo-Greek ruler Antialkidas, known from coins.

What is even more interesting is that Heliodorus, the Greek ambassador, describes himself as a Bhagavata—i.e., a worshipper of the god Vasudeva Krishna, and that he set up this pillar in honour of this god. The *garuda* is a fantastic bird, the vehicle of Vishnu. The foundations of a structure near the pillar no doubt represent remains of the ancient temple in front of which the Greek ambassador left an inscribed record of his devotion.

Source Salomon, 1998: 265–67

it refers to the Bactrian Greeks. Patanjali also mentions sacrifices performed for Pushyamitra. Kalidasa's *Malavikagnimitra* narrates the story of a military encounter between prince Vasumitra (son of Agnimitra) and a Yavana army on the banks of the Sindhu. Whether this was the Indus or a river in Central India is a matter of debate. The conflict apparently took place when, in the course of Pushyamitra's *ashvamedha* sacrifice, the Yavanas challenged the horse which was accompanied by the young prince and his soldiers. In the play the Yavanas are defeated and the horse brought safely home. It is not certain who the leader of the Bactrian Greek army was. Menander, Demetrius, and Eucratides have been suggested as possible candidates; it was probably Demetrius. The Ayodhya stone inscription of king Dhana refers to Pushyamitra as a performer of two *ashvamedha* sacrifices. The *Divyavadana* gives stories of Pushyamitra's cruelty and his animosity towards Buddhism.

Ten Shunga kings are supposed to have ruled for a total of 112 years. According to the Puranas, the last ruler of this line was Devabhuti or Devabhumi. The *Harshacharita* narrates that he became the victim of a conspiracy masterminded by his Brahmana minister Vasudeva, who went on to found the Kanva dynasty. The remnants of Shunga rule probably survived in Central India for some time, till the rise of the Satavahanas. In Magadha, the Kanvas made way for the Mitras in *c.* 30 BCE. The Mitras were, in turn, eventually dislodged by the Shakas.

Map 8.1 Dynasties of India and Central Asia, *c.* 200 BCE–300 CE

The Indo-Greeks

The connected political histories of the Indian subcontinent, Afghanistan, and Central Asia emerge strongly during the period *c.* 200 BCE–300 CE. Northern India witnessed a series of invasions which were qualitatively different from the Persian and Macedonian invasions of earlier centuries. Several waves of warriors crossed the Hindu Kush and made their way into the subcontinent. The invaders succeeded in establishing political principalities and some of them had a strong cultural impact.

Bactria is the ancient name of the area lying to the south of the Amu Daria (Oxus) river and north-west of the Hindu Kush mountains, and corresponds to the northern part of modern Afghanistan, along with adjoining parts of Uzbekistan and Tajikistan. This area was extremely important on the long-distance trade routes of the time. The Greeks of Bactria were originally satraps (governors or subordinate rulers) of the Seleucid empire of West Asia (for details, see Bopearachchi, 2015: Vol. 1, Chaps. 5, 27). In about the mid-3rd century BCE, Diodotus I revolted against the Seleucids and established an independent Graeco-Bactrian kingdom. The Bactrians extended their control into other areas as well. By the early 2nd century BCE, they had moved into the area south of the Hindu Kush. In *c.* 145 BCE, they lost their hold over Bactria, but continued to rule in the north-western part of the subcontinent for a few decades. The Bactrian Greeks who ruled north of the Hindu Kush are known as the Graeco-Bactrians. Those who ruled the south of the Hindu Kush between the 2nd century BCE and the early 1st century CE are known as the Indo-Greeks or Indo-Bactrians. The term Bactro-Indo-Greeks is also used for these two groups.

Bactro-Indo-Greek rule left archaeological markers. The site of Sirkap at Taxila was occupied from the Indo-Greek period onwards, but most of the available evidence relates to the subsequent Shaka–Parthian phase. Excavations at Aï-Khanoum, located at the confluence of the Amu Daria and Kokcha rivers in Afghanistan, revealed a great city of the time of the Bactrian Greeks, which was destroyed by nomadic invaders in *c.* 145 BCE. The architecture of the city and some of the artefacts found here have an unmistakable Greek stamp. Hellenistic influence can be seen in several sites in the north-western part of the Indian subcontinent (see Suchandra Ghosh, 2017).

Numismatic evidence is crucial for the reconstruction of the history of the Bactro-Indo-Greeks, and many rulers are known only from their coins. Large numbers of coins of these rulers (along with those of the Indo-Scythian, Indo-Parthians, and Kushanas) have been found as stray finds, in hoards, in the course of excavations, and in the markets of Pakistan and Afghanistan. However, the details of the reigns, their sequence and chronology, and the extent of their political control remain rather nebulous. The large number of kings within a relatively short period of time suggests that some of them ruled concurrently. Over-struck coins indicate either hostile relations between the two rulers in question or the fact that one of them succeeded the other. Recently, some inscriptions have come to light in Kandahar in Afghanistan and Kuliab in Tajakistan. There is also a tax receipt on leather, whose date includes the names of king Antimachos Theos, and two others named Eumenes and Antimachos.

According to Osmund Bopearachchi, the history of the Greeks of Bactria is a story of rebels, usurpers, and assassins, but only the bare outlines of this story are known (Bopearachchi, 2015 Vol. 1: 66–69, 74). Demetrios I was the first Bactrian Greek ruler to cross the Hindu Kush. A coin type that depicts him with an elephant scalp head-dress announces his conquests in India. Other Bactro-Indo-Greek kings include Euthydemos II; Agathocles, and Pantaleon, who were contemporaneous and issued their own coins; Eucratides I (*c.* 170–145 BCE) who was the last Bactrian Greek ruler to have sway over the area north and south of the Hindu Kush; Heliocles; and Antialcidas (Antialkidas). A faience head, probably from Aï-Khanoum, seems to represent an Indo-Greek king; a comparison with the royal portraits on coins suggests that it may be Demetrios I (Bopearachchi, 2020, Vol. 1, p. 53). The Besnagar pillar inscription suggests that the rule of Antialkidas extended up to Taxila, as his ambassador Heliodorus is described as a native of that city.

PRIMARY SOURCES | Coins of the Indo-Greeks

The coins of the Graeco-Bactrians which circulated to the north of the Hindu Kush were made of gold, silver, copper, and nickel. They followed the Attic weight standard and had Greek legends. The coins have royal portraits on the obverse, while the reverse generally depicts Greek deities (such as Zeus, Apollo, and Athena) along with the name and title of the king.

The Indo-Greek coins, which circulated to the south of the Hindu Kush, were made of silver and copper, and were often square in shape. They had bilingual inscriptions in Greek and Kharoshthi (more rarely, Brahmi) and followed an Indian weight standard. Royal portraits occur on the obverse, but the motifs on the reverse include religious symbols that were Indian rather than Greek in inspiration. An interesting coin series was that of king Agathocles, which depicted the god Samkarshana Balarama on the obverse and Vasudeva Krishna on the reverse.

Graeco-Bactrian and Indo-Greek coins discovered in Afghanistan include three major finds—the Mir Zakah hoard found near Gardez, a hoard found at Khisht Tepe near Qunduz, and coins found in hoards or in the course of excavations at Aï-Khanoum. The Mir Zakah hoard comprised 13,083 coins. Of these, 2,757 were Graeco-Bactrian and Indo-Greek. The rest included Indian bent-bar and punch-marked coins, and Indo-Scythian, Indo-Parthian, and Kushana coins. The Qunduz hoard consisted of 627 silver coins. Of these, 624 were Graeco-Bactrian and three Seleucid. Many coins—including pre-Seleucid, Seleucid, Graeco-Bactrian, Indo-Greek, Indian punch-marked coins, and a few Kushana coins—were discovered in the course of excavations at this site. A smaller hoard at Aï-Khanoum included six coins of the Indo-Greek king Agathocles and 677 Indian punch-marked coins found in the palace area, which seems to have been buried when the city was abandoned. Another hoard, comprising 63 Greek and Graeco-Bactrian coins, was found in the kitchen of a large house outside the north wall of the city. The Aï-Khanoum coins included some coin types that had not hitherto been found anywhere else. The discovery of 10 unstruck bronze flans at Aï-Khanoum indicates that a mint was located here.

The problems in understanding the Indo-Greek coins include interpreting the significance of the monograms and additional letters and numbers on some coins. Monograms are generally identified as marks of a mint or moneyer. But when different monograms occur on coins which were made with the same obverse die, they do not seem to be mint marks. As for the numbers, it is unlikely that they were either dates or ordinal numbers identifying different issues. There is a slim possibility that the additional letters represent the engraver's signature.

The meaning of the monograms on Indo-Greek coins are the subject of debate. Many coins have overstrikes—these may have been because of political reasons, when one ruler defeated another; or reuse of older coins prompted by a shortage of precious metals. Overstrikes on the coins help give information on the sequence of rulers.

Written sources mention only eight Bactro-Indo-Greek kings, but we know of 45 rulers from coins. The coins of the Shakas, Indo-Parthians, and Kshatrapas followed the basic features of Indo-Greek coinage, including bilingual and bi-script legends.

Source Guillaume, 1991; Bopearachchi, 2015

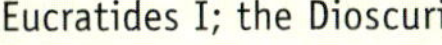
Eucratides I; the Dioscuri

Hippostratus; king on horse

Hermaeus with wife Calliope; king on horse

Menander; goddess Pallas

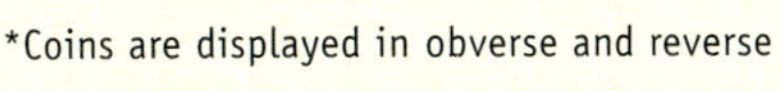
*Coins are displayed in obverse and reverse

FURTHER DISCUSSION | Aï Khanoum: A Hellenistic city in Afghanistan

Aï-Khanoum is located at the confluence of Amu Darya (Oxus) and Kokcha in Bactria in north Afghanistan. The site was excavated from 1964 to 1978 by the French Archaeological Delegation in Afghanistan (DAFA) led by Paul Bernard. The city dates from the late 4th/early 3rd century BCE to *c.* 145 CE and was especially prosperous during the rule of the Bactrian Greeks.

The site is situated in a fertile plain, close to mountains which provided its residents with summer pasture and minerals and stone such as lapis lazuli. A natural acropolis on elevated ground guarded the eastern approach and the city was surrounded by a massive mud-brick masonry wall. The residential area and most of the public buildings were located in the lower part of the site. Remains of bronze coin blanks suggest that a royal mint was located here. Coins of Eucratides I (*c.* 170–145 BCE) suggest that he was probably the last king who ruled from here. Perhaps this was the city that he renamed Eucratidia.

The excavated remains included a large structural complex covering an area of almost 90,000 sq m. This was identified as a palace complex with three functions—as an administrative structure, a residence of rulers, and a treasury. The palace complex had Graeco-Bactrian architectural features. The walls were mostly made of mud-brick, plastered with a layer of clay and whitewashed. The flat roofs added an eastern touch but an edging of terracotta tiles gave them a Greek appearance. There were three types of pillars—Doric, Ionic, and Corinthian.

Other structural remains include a gymnasium, the main part of which was 100 sq m in plan. The building was basically Greek in plan with some Graeco-Bactrian innovations. Its function was identified on basis of an inscription dedicated to Hermes and Herakles. Also found were the remains of a theatre with 35 tiers enclosing a semi-circular area with a 42 m radius. It has been estimated that it could have seated about 6,000 people.

Gymnasium

Palace ruins

Three special seating areas for wealthy or powerful people were identified. Another important structure at the site was located on the city's main street. It was 140 m x 100 m, and had several long storerooms that opened into a large central courtyard. This was identified as an arsenal.

The houses of affluent people were located above the junction of the Amu Darya and Kokcha, and were built along parallel streets running east to west. They had a columned porch, a front courtyard, and a large living room. The bathrooms were very elaborate and consisted of two or three areas (for disrobing, bathing, and storing the bath water) with red-painted stucco walls and floors made of stone or cement-and-pebble mosaic.

Near the entrance to the palace were two tombs. One of them was that of Kineas, who was one of the city's founders. A stone pillar (no longer extant) once stood in front of its porch. Around the base on which the pillar once stood were engraved the last five of the famous Delphic maxims, which describe the virtues of an ideal Greek: 'In childhood learn good manners; in youth control your passions; in middle age, learn to be just; in old age be of wise counsel; die without regret.' The rest of the maxims may have been inscribed on the missing pillar.

Several Greek inscriptions were found at Aï-Khanoum. These include Greek labels on vases in the palace complex. One of the rooms in the palace complex seems to have been a library. The inked letters from decayed papyrus manuscripts could still be seen, making it possible to identify some of the texts that must have been housed here. They included part of an Aristotelian text and part of a poem.

Specimens of stylistically Greek sculptures included an ivory plaque with a representation of the goddess Aphrodite. A gold covered silver plate depicts the Cybele, the Greek goddess of nature, riding on a lion-drawn chariot and driven by Nike, the winged goddess of victory.

In many respects, Aï-Khanoum seems to be a Hellenistic city. But apart from the Greek elements, there are also Persian, Mesopotamian, and local elements. The three temples, for instance, were not built in the Greek fashion. The largest one on the main street near the palace is a huge square structure standing on a three-step platform and showed Persian and Central Asian architectural influences. It is not possible to identify which deity this temple was dedicated to, but libation vessels found buried at the base of the platform indicate that the rituals performed here were not Greek. A broken marble foot encased in a Greek sandal found here was once part of a statue that must have been Greek in appearance, but the type of worship here does not seem to have been Greek. Another temple outside the city wall near the north gate was basically similar to this one. The third temple, located in the south-west corner of the acropolis, consisted of a large stepped platform, perhaps modelled after a Persian fire temple. A bone figurine found at Aï-Khanoum represents what must have been a local goddess. All this is not surprising because Afghanistan was a melting pot of cultural confluence in ancient times.

Source Bernard, 1982

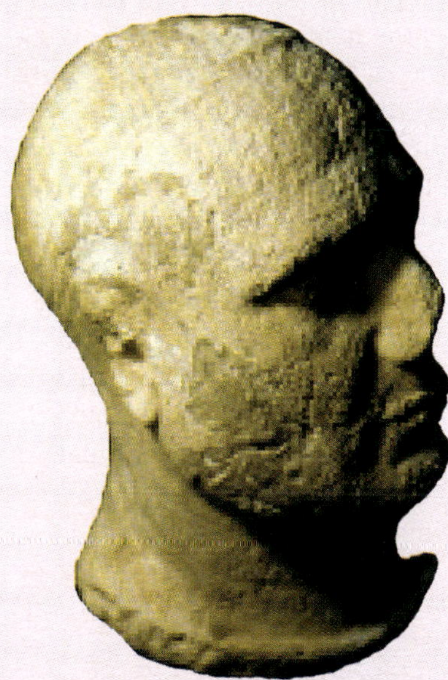

Faience head; sculptural fragment; plaque depicted goddess Cybele (from left)

Silver coin of Appollodotus I (obverse and reverse)

One of the most important Indo-Greek rulers was Menander, whose coins have been found in greater numbers than those of any other Indo-Greek king. He is also the only Indo-Greek king mentioned in Indian sources. King Milinda, who poses a number of questions to monk Nagasena in the Buddhist text *Milindapanha*, is none other than Menander. This king seems to have been born in Begram and had his political centre at Sagala, which can be identified with Sialkot. Plutarch tells us that after Menander's death, there was a conflict over the king's ashes. The Yuezhi (Yueh Chi) tribe wrested Bactria from the hands of the Greeks in the mid-2nd century BCE. Indo-Greek rule over the Gandhara region came to an end due to conflicts with the Indo-Parthians (Pahlavas) and Indo-Scythians (Shakas). Their control over the area to the east of the Jhelum ended in the early 1st century CE when Rajuvula, the Shaka Kshatrapa of the Mathura area, defeated the Indo-Greek king Strato III and captured Sagala (Sialkot). A significant impact of Indo-Greek rule at the cultural level was the Gandhara school of art, which will be discussed further on.

The Indo-Scythians (Shakas) and Indo-Parthians (Pahlavas)

The Scythians or Shakas were a nomadic people who inhabited the Eurasian steppes, a massive swathe of temperate grassland stretching over some 8,000 km from the Hungarian plains in the west to Manchuria in the east (see Cunliffe, 2019). The inhabitants of this world lived a life on the move. Greek sources describe them as uncivilized barbarians, but archaeological evidence from their graves known as kurgans reveals a rich material culture and close interactions with the sedentary Greek and Persian worlds.

In the 2nd century BCE, the consolidation of the Han empire in China by the emperor Qin Shi Huang led to a displacement of the nomadic tribes on the borders of the empire and triggered series of tribal movements in Central Asia. In the course of the 2nd century BCE, the Great Yuezhi tribe displaced the Shakas, who moved southwards into Afghanistan and thence into north-western India.

The history of Scythian and Parthian rule in India is known largely through inscriptions and coins (see Bopearachchi, 2020a: Vol. 1, Chap. 31). In *c.* 85 BCE, a Scythian named Maues took control over Taxila. An inscription found at Taxila mentions a Shaka king named Moga and his *kshatrapa* (governor) Patika. Moga is identified with Maues or Moa, whose name appears on several copper and silver coins, which are similar to those issued by the Indo-Greeks. One series of silver coins show the Greek god Zeus with a sceptre in his left hand, with Nike, goddess of victory, on his right palm. It is likely that Maues conquered the Gandhara region from the Indo-Greeks, but the latter (under Apollodotus II) temporarily recovered some of their lost ground.

In *c.* 55 BCE, another Scythian, Azes I, brought an end to Indo-Greek rule by defeating Hippostratus. He extended his control into the north-western part of the Indian subcontinent. A later ruler, Azilises, seems to have pushed further east, into the Mathura area.

The sequence of Indo-Scythian rulers known from coins are: Vonones/Spalahores, Vonones/Spalagadames, Spalyrises/Spalalgadames, Spalirises, Spalirises/Azes I, Azilises, and Azes II. Some coins suggest the practice of conjoint rule. The Vikrama era of 58/57 BCE, still used in India, is generally thought to mark the accession of Azes I. The Malavas (who originally lived in the Punjab, within the dominion of the Shakas) may have carried its use from the north-west into Rajasthan and adjacent areas when they migrated there. However, recently, the Azes–Vikrama era connection has been questioned (see Falk and Bennett, 2009). The Indo-Scythians or Shakas ruled through governors or subordinate rulers known as *kshatrapas* and *mahakshatrapas* (the term *kshatrapa* goes back to ancient Iran, and was used by the Achaemenids) who played an important role in the expansion of the empire and ultimately became independent. The political career of these Shaka *kshatrapas* was longer than that of their overlords. Rajuvula initially had the title *kshatrapa*, and later *mahakshatrapa*, but for all practical purposes became an independent ruler in the Mathura area, and was succeeded by his son Sodasha. A western line of Kshatrapa rulers, known through coins and inscriptions, held sway in western India (they will be discussed further on).

The land known as Parthia corresponded to Khurasan and the adjoining area south-east of the Caspian Sea (in north-eastern Iran). This area was initially a satrapy of the Achaemenid empire, and then of the Seleucids. In the 3rd century BCE, a nomadic tribe called the Parni or Aparni (who were part of the Dahae confederacy) moved southwards from their home in the Aral Sea area into Parthia, ultimately displacing the Seleucids. They adopted the name of the province and came to be known to outsiders as Parthians or Arcasids (after the founder of the dynasty, Arsases, who ruled in *c.* 238–210 BCE). The Parthians created a vast, multi-ethnic, multi-lingual empire which at its height, extended from Asia Minor to Afghanistan. The details of Parthian history are hazy due to the lack of textual and archaeological evidence. The Parthians had a long-standing conflict with the Romans over control over Armenia and Asia Minor. They are largely known from coins and very unflattering portrayals in Roman sources, where they are described as barbarians and enemies.

In the early 1st century CE, a Parthian named Gondophares established himself as an independent ruler in the eastern parts of the Parthian empire, in the regions of modern Afghanistan. He moved into Gandhara and surrounding areas, defeated the Indo-Scythians, and founded the Indo-Parthian kingdom (for details of Indo-Parthian coins and history, see Bopearachchi, 2020a: Vol. 1, Chap. 31). On his coins, Gondophares has Greek titles which translate as 'Great Kings of Kings' and 'Autocrat' or 'Self-appointed.' He is identified with king Guduhvara, mentioned in an inscription found at Takht-i-Bahi, on the basis of which the beginning of his rule is placed in 20 CE. His reign seems to have continued till *c.* 50 CE. The successors of Gondophares included Abdagases, Aspavarman, Sarpedanes, Sases, and Ubouzanes. The Indo-Parthians were ultimately ousted from north-western India by the Kushana king Kujula Kadphises some time in the 1st century CE. Some coins of Gondophares have overstrikes of Kujula Kadphises.

The Kushanas

The *Qian Hanshu* (*Ch'ien Han-shu*) and *Hou Hanshu* describe the ripple effects of a series of tribal movements in Central Asia from the 3rd century BCE, when the Qing dynasty (221–206 BCE) started expanding and consolidating its power under emperor Qin Shihuang. The Yuezhi were a powerful nomadic tribe based in the Gansu area (in north-west China), who had for years been carrying on a very profitable trade in horses with the Chinese empire. The Xiongnu (Hsiung-nu), who were located on the northern border of the Yuezhi, defeated the latter twice and forced them to move westwards. At this point, the Yuezhi split into two. A small section, which came to be known as the Little Yuezhi, moved south and settled in north Tibet. The Da Yuezhi or Great Yuezhi moved further west, and reached the land occupied by two confederacies of nomadic Scythian tribes, one settled in the area around lake Issyk and the other in the area of lower Syr Darya (Jaxartes). The Yuezhi defeated both and forced the latter to move southwards into the Graeco-Bactrian domain. They were also involved in conflicts with the Parthians. For some time, the Great Yuezhi settled in the area north

Gold coin of Huvishka (obverse and reverse)

of the Amu Darya. Excavations at the sites of Khalchayan and Takht-e-Sangin have revealed archaeological remains of their presence. From here, they gradually moved southwards into Bactria, the area between the Amu Darya and the Hindu Kush mountains (Bivar, 2014).

There were five Great Yuezhi principalities ruled by chiefs known as *yabghus*. One of these five principalities was the Guishuang/Kuei-shang (i.e. Kushana, also spelt Kushan). We know of a Guishang chief named Heraus. In the early 1st century CE, the Guishang *yabghu* Kujula Kadphises (also known as Kadphises I) defeated the other chiefs, amalgamated the five Great Yuezhi principalities, and laid the foundations of a unified Kushana empire. The fact that his coins have been found south of the Hindu Kush suggests that Kushana movement into the Indian subcontinent began in his time (For a summary of Kushana political history, see Bivar, 2014; Bopearachchi, 2015: Vol. 2, Chap. 7).

Kujula Kadphises established his control over the areas of Afghanistan, Gandhara, and Kashmir. His coins (almost of them are in copper) refer to him as a Kushana, and have legends in the Greek language and script on the obverse and Prakrit and Kharoshthi script on the reverse. His epithets include 'maharaja-rajatiraja' (King, King of Kings) and 'sacha-dharmathita' (steadfast in the true *dharma*). The reign of Kujula Kadphises can be placed in *c*. 50–90 CE according to Joe Cribb and in *c*. 30–85/90 CE according to Osmund Bopearachchi.

There are differences of opinion about Kushana chronology and dynastic sequence after the end of the rule of Kujula Kadphises and the coming to power of Vima Kadphises. The Rabatak inscription brought to light a new Kushana ruler named Vima Takto (this reading was disputed by B. N. Mukherjee, who reads the name of the ruler as Saddaskana). The legends on the obverse of two coins of the Kushana ruler Vima Kadphises, found in the Pipal Mandi hoard in Peshwar, describe Vima Takto as the son of Kujula Kadphises and father of Vima Kadphises. Cribb identifies Vima Takto with the unnamed ruler titled Soter Megas ('Great Saviour') of various coins. Bopearachchi asserts that Soter Megas does not form part of the lineage at all—he was a usurper, an isolated, independent ruler who was partly contemporaneous with Vima Kadphises.

Vima Kadphises ruled in the early 2nd century CE and introduced a bi-metallic currency in bronze and gold. His gold coins are exceptional in style and execution. In these, he appears in various poses including seated on a throne, elephant, or chariot, or emerging from a mountain. Sometimes flames are shown emanating from his shoulders. The coins of Vima suggest his allegiance to Shiva worship. But the nature of the representations of this god on his coin types show syncretic images with an amalgam of attributes of Shiva (trident, bull) with those of other gods such as Vishnu (the wheel), Indra (the thunderbolt), and Agni (flaming hair).

Vima Kadphises was succeeded by Kanishka I. There has been an over one century long debate on Kushana chronology, focusing especially on the date of Kanishka. The earlier view was that Kanishka's reign began in 78 CE and that his accession marked the beginning of an era that later came to be known as the Shaka era. Various other dates have been suggested for Kanishka's accession, including 144 CE and 125 CE. As pointed by Harry Falk (2001), the *Yavanajataka* of Sphujiddhvaja, a 2nd century work on astronomy and astrology, mentions the Kushana era and Shaka era as two separate ones. The text suggests that the accession of Kanishka, which marked the beginning of a Kushana era, began 149 years after the beginning of the Shaka era. This would place the accession of Kanishka at 149+78 = 227 CE. There is an older theory (referred to as the theory of the omitted hundreds), according to which, in or around year 100 of the Kanishka era, the counting was rewound and started afresh from year 1. Accordingly, 227 CE should actually be understood as 127 CE. Most scholars now accept 127 CE as the date of Kanishka's accession, but some historians continue to adhere to the earlier date of 78 CE.

PRIMARY SOURCES | The Rabatak inscription

In 1993, an inscribed stone slab was discovered along with pieces of a lion sculpture and ruins of a temple on a hill called Kafir's Castle in Rabatak in Baghlan province, Afghanistan. Sayyid Jafar, governor of the province, invited Tim Porter, a British citizen working for a charity organization, to photograph the remains, and urged him to send one of the photographs to the British Museum. The photograph that Porter sent off was of an inscribed rectangular piece of whitish stone, 90 cm wide, 50 cm high, and 25 cm thick.

The 23-line inscription, written in the Bactrian language and Greek script, proved to be a valuable record belonging to Kanishka's reign. It describes Kanishka as 'the great deliverer, the righteous, the just, the autocrat, the god, one who is worthy of worship, who has obtained kingship from Nana [a West Asian goddess] and all the gods...' He is also referred to as a king of kings and a son of the gods. Kanishka is said to have replaced the use of the Ionian (Greek) language with the noble (*arya*) Bactrian language.

According to the Rabatak inscription, Kanishka commanded an officer named Shaphara to construct a *bago-laggo* (temple) wherein images of the goddess Nana and several other deities were to be installed. The king also commanded this officer to make images of his (i.e., Kanishka's) great-grandfather Kujula Kadphises, his grandfather Saddashkana, his father Vima Kadphises, and of Kanishka himself. Saphara built the temple, and a person named Nokonzoka led worship there, according to the royal command. The inscription invokes several deities to ensure Kanishka's health and victory. It states that the great king worshipped the deities enshrined in the temple. It also suggests that Kanishka started a new era from the year of his accession.

The Rabatak inscription throws important light on Kushana genealogy. N. Sims-Williams and Joe Cribb thought that line 13 referred to a hitherto unknown Kushana king named Vima Takto, son of Kujula Kadphises. However, B. N. Mukherjee argues that the correct reading of the name is Saddaskana (Sadashkana), who was a son of Kujula Kadphises. The inscription also clearly indicates that Vima Kadphises and Kanishka were father and son.

The inscription states that Kanishka's empire included Kaundinya, Ujjayini, Saketa, Kaushambi, Pataliputra, and Champa, and makes the exaggerated claim that his rule extended over the whole of India. It suggests that the empire extended up to Pataliputra and Champa in the east. Kaundinya or Kundina has been identified with Kaundinyapura on the Wardha river in the Amaravati district of Maharashtra, and this may have marked the southern border of the empire.

The inscription also throws important light on the Kushana conception of kingship. Kanishka claims to have obtained kingship through the agency of a number of mostly Zoroastrian deities, headed by the goddess Nana. There is also mention of images of the reigning king and his predecessors in connection with the temple that had been built.

Stone statues of Kushana kings have been found in temples at Surkh Kotal in Afghanistan and Mat near Mathura, and it is possible that similar images may yet be discovered at Rabatak. The crucial question is: Were the kings's statues attendant figures in temples dedicated to various gods, or were the royal images worshipped in these temples? Did the Kushana kings lay claim to a close connection with the gods, or did they claim to be gods themselves?

Source Mukherjee, 1995; Sims-Williams and Cribb, 1995–96

What about the Shaka era? If Kanishka did not found it, who did? Many scholars now think that the Shaka era of 78 CE was founded by one of the Western Kshatrapa rulers, perhaps Chashtana. Another alternative is suggested by Falk (2001). According to him, the Shaka era may have marked a rare astronomical event: on 1st April 78 CE, the sun and moon met jointly in Aries, and with them was Jupiter.

The Kushana empire reached its zenith during the reign of Kanishka (*c.* 127–50 CE). The empire expanded further east into the Ganga valley and southwards into the Malwa region. Kushana influence was felt in Western and Central India as well, where the Shaka Kshatrapas may have acknowledged their overlordship. Kanishka seems to have founded a magnificent *stupa*-monastery complex at Shah ji ki Dhari near Peshawar. A cylindrical gilded bronze reliquary (known as the Kanishka reliquary) was found here. The lid of the box bears three figures—a Buddha sitting on a lotus, flanked by Indra and Brahma. The casket has images of seated Buddhas flanked by Indra and Brahma and a standing figure that may represent Kanishka. Kanishka's name is inscribed on it. The discovery of Kushana coins as far east as Bengal and Odisha does not necessarily indicate that their political control extended this far in the east.

Kanishka image from Mat, Mathura

B. N. Mukherjee (1970) suggested that the presence of diamond mines in Akara (eastern Malwa) and the trade potential of the lower Indus country led to Kushana expansion into these areas. The *Hou Hanshu* states that the Kushanas became wealthy and powerful due to their conquest of Shen-tu (the lower Indus region). This was no doubt due to ports on the Makran coast becoming important in Indian Ocean trade networks. Mukherjee further argues that there was a connection between the decline of this trade and the decline of the Kushana empire. Kanishka's empire extended from Central Asia to the Ganga valley, and included parts of Xingiang in north-western China. The incorporation of this vast area into a single political unit was a major stimulus to trade.

Kanishka is celebrated in Buddhist texts and legends as a great patron of Buddhism. He is supposed to have enshrined the Buddha's relics in a *stupa* at Purushapura, which became the centre of a major monastery. According to Xuanzang, a Buddhist conclave was held during his reign—it is not certain whether in Kashmir, Gandhara, or Jalandhara. Kanishka is said to have patronized Buddhist scholars such as Ashvaghosha and Vasumitra. Missionaries were sent to Kashgar, Yunan, and China. On the other hand, this king's coinage (like that of Huvishka) depicts motifs drawn from a great variety of Indian, Greek, and West Asian religious traditions. Apart from the Buddha and Shiva, they include representations of Persian gods such as Atash (a fire god) and Mithra (a sun god), and Greek deities such as Helios (a sun god) and Selene (a moon goddess).

The Kushana empire began as a Central Asian kingdom, and expanded into Afghanistan and then into north-western and northern India. Chinese sources refer to Kanishka subduing some of the cities of Xinjiang. The centre of this huge empire was Bactria. Kanishka's early coins are in the Greek language and script; his later coins use the Bactrian language and Greek script. The *Hou Hanshu* indicates that the Kushana capital was located at Lan-shih in eastern Bactria. In India, the two important political centres of Kushana power were Purushapura (Peshawar) and Mathura. Excavations at many sites in North India, at Central Asian sites such as Kara tepe and Dalverzin tepe, and at Surkh Kotal in Afghanistan have added to our information about this period.

Huvishka seems to have succeeded Kanishka in *c*. 150 CE. Although a profusion of gold coins of his reign have been found, the great variation in workmanship has been seen as reflecting a period of financial crisis. A massive rock at Hunza, between the Karakoram highway and the Hunza river, has a number of Kharoshthi inscriptions mentioning the names of Kadphises, Kanishka, Huvishka, and various *kshatrapas* and *mahakshatrapas*. According to Bivar (2009), during Huvishka's reign, the Kushana empire was probably affected by a terrible smallpox pandemic that spread between China and the Roman empire, and that this is reflected in the many representations of the smallpox goddess Hariti in Gandhara art.

The Kushana empire started declining from the time of Vasudeva I, in about the mid-2nd century CE, due to the rise of the Sasanids of Iran, who deprived the Kushanas of their western territories. Vasudeva I seems to have been succeeded by Kanishka II, Vasishka, and Kanishka III. Vasudeva II is the last Kushana emperor known by name and his rule seems to have ended in the last quarter of the 3rd century. Some remnants of Kushana rule seem to have lingered on till as late as the 4th century.

The Kushana kings used titles such as *devaputra* (son of a god/the gods) and *bagopouro* (son of god), and *bagoshao* (god king). Some Kushana coins depict the king with a halo around his head and flames emanating from his shoulders; kings are also shown sitting or emerging from clouds or mountains. Some of Kanishka's coins show him like the god Mithra, breaking through the rocks, and as a sort of Wes (a wind god, also connected with military victory, known in Bactria). Historians have understood such representations as exalting the position of the king to the extent of projecting him as divine, an idea quite common in other ancient empires. It has been suggested that the shrine at Mat near Mathura may have been a sanctuary where images of these kings were worshipped. However, this has not been established beyond all doubt.

Copper coin of Soter Megas; gold coin of Kanishka III (obverse and reverse)

The remarkable syncretism in Kushana coinage and sculpture has been discussed by many scholars (see Bopearachchi, 2015: Vol. 2). Vima Kadphises' coins have some of the earliest anthropomorphic representations of the god Shiva. In some of his early coins, we see the head of Siva, but a body that looks like that of Herakles, with the club replaced by a trident and water pot, retaining the lion skin draped over the left arm. Gradually, Siva lost his Greek elements. Kanishka is said to have enshrined Buddha relics in a *stupa* in Purushapura and a major Buddhist conclave was held during his reign. The Kharoshthi inscription on a bronze relic casket found in ruins of the *stupa* at Shah-ji-ki-dheri near Peshawar refers to a *vihara* built by Kanishka and a slave (*dasa*) named Agisala who was the overseer of works there. Kanishka's coins show representations of the Buddha and Maitreya, but also of deities from other pantheons. This variety of religious motifs is usually taken as reflecting the king's personal religious eclecticism or his attitude of religious 'tolerance'. At the level of royal policy, it can be seen as an acknowledgement of the religious diversity within the empire and the attempts of the Kushana kings to connect themselves with the deities worshipped in and around their realm.

The Kushana empire consisted of various tiers of control. Some areas were under the direct control of the kings and others under subordinate rulers with the title *kshatrapa* or *mahakshatrapa*. Some of the subordinate rulers acknowledged Kushana paramountcy and paid tribute. Others, such as the Kshatrapa Chashtana, may have recognized the suzerainty of the Kushana emperor but were more or less autonomous.

The history of the Kushanas is tied to the larger history of West, Central, and East Asia. Chinese sources refer to a Kushana king or viceroy being beaten back by general Ban Chao west of Kucha (in *c.* 90 CE). This seems to have been before Kanishka's time, perhaps during the time of Kujula Kadphises. They also refer to Kanishka's various conquests, including his subduing some of the cities of Xinjiang. There is mention of the Kushanas sending envoys to the Sasanian king Ardashir, to an embassy (perhaps during the time of Vasudeva II) to the Chinese court, and to the Kushanas being among those who sent tribute to the Chinese emperor (Falk. [Ed.], 2015: 98, 125–26).

The decline of the Kushanas led to the resurfacing of several polities which had been temporarily subdued by them.

Coins, seals, sealings, and inscriptions give evidence of several monarchies and *ganas* in different parts of North India. These included the Arjunayanas, who were located in the Bharatpur and Alwar area. Their coins bear the legend *Arjunayananam jayah* (victory to the Arjunayanas) in late 1st century BCE Brahmi. The Malavas were originally located in the Punjab; from here, a large section of them migrated to Rajasthan. Their capital was Malavanagara, identified with modern Nagar. Large numbers of coins referring to the Malava *janapada* have been found in and around this place. Some bear the legend *jayo Malavanam* or *Malavanam jayah*. A lead seal found at Rairh has a legend referring to the Malava *janapada* in Brahmi letters of the 2nd century BCE. The Yaudheya *gana* lived in eastern Punjab and the adjoining areas of Uttar Pradesh and Rajasthan. Their coins have been found in the area from Multan to Saharanpur. A clay sealing found at Sunet near Ludhiana has a bull motif and the legend *Yaudheyanam jaya-mantradharanam* (of the Yaudheyas, the possessors of the secret charm of winning victories). Coins and coin moulds of the Yaudheyas at this site suggest that Karttikeya was the tutelary deity of these people.

The monarchies of this period included a number of kings ruling over parts of North and Central India, who are referred to collectively as Naga kings due to the 'naga' suffix in their names. Their names, taken together with the evidence of texts and sculpture, indicate the popularity of the worship of *nagas* (snake deities) in these areas. Several Naga kings are known from inscriptions, coins, seals and sealings. The Puranas mention the rule of a line of nine Naga kings ruling from Padmavati (identified with modern Pawaya in Gwalior district, MP). Some coins bearing the name of a ruler (*maharaja*) named Ganendra or Ganapa have been found at Padmavati (as well as at Mathura and Vidisha); others found in the same area name other Naga rulers as well. The Puranas also refer to seven Naga kings ruling from Mathura. Most of the coins of this period from the Mathura area give names of rulers ending in the suffix 'mitra' or 'datta'. Inscriptions and coins also name various local dynasties ruling from Ahichchhatra, Ayodhya, and Kaushambi.

Copper coin of the Yaudheyas; local coin of Ujjain (obverse and reverse)

The Shaka Kshatrapas of Western India

As mentioned earlier, the Indo-Scythians/Shakas ruled through their *kshatrapas* (viceroys or subordinate rulers). Some of them continued to have a hold over parts of western India during the Kushana period. An early Kshatrapa line of western India was represented by Mambarus, who is mentioned in the *Periplus*. In the early centuries CE, there were two important lines of Kshatrapa rulers in western India—the Kshaharatas and Kardamakas.

The Kshaharata dynasty included rulers such as Bhumaka and Nahapana. Bhumaka's copper coins, with legends in Brahmi and Kharoshthi, have been found in coastal Gujarat; some also occur in Malwa and the Ajmer area. Nahapana is known through his coins and the inscriptions of his son-in-law, Ushavadata. In the earlier inscriptions, he has the title *kshatrapa*, and in the later ones, *mahakshatrapa* and *rajan*. On his gold and silver coins, he is simply styled *rajan*. He seems to have been ruling more or less independently. Nahapana's coins have been found in the Ajmer area of Rajasthan and the Nashik area in Maharashtra. An inscription of one of his *amatyas* named Aryaman has been found at Junnar in Pune district. At its height, the kingdom seems to have included Malwa, Gujarat, Saurashtra, northern Maharashtra, and parts of Rajasthan and the lower Indus valley. The capital Minnagara can perhaps be identified with Doha, midway between Ujjain and Broach. Nahapana's son-in-law Ushavadata was viceroy of the southern part of the kingdom. Several of his donative inscriptions have been found in the Nashik and Karle caves. These refer to Nahapana; some of them are dated in the Nahapana's regnal years.

The Shaka Kshatrapas were involved in prolonged conflict with the Satavahanas, a powerful dynasty with its stronghold in the Deccan. Control over certain areas, especially those that gave access to the western seaboard, seems to have frequently changed hands. The Nashik and Pune areas, for instance, seem to have been conquered from the Satavahanas either by Nahapana or one of his predecessors. However, Nahapana was apparently defeated by the Satavahana ruler Gautamiputra Satakarni, who wrested the southern territories of the Kshaharata kingdom. This is evident from the discovery of Gautamiputra's inscriptions in the Nashik and Pune districts, his re-striking Nahapana's coins, and certain statements made in an inscription of Gautamiputra's mother, Gautami Balashri.

At about the time that the Kshaharata dynasty came to an end, another line of Shaka Kshatrapas known as the Kardamakas came to the fore in western India. The founder of this dynasty was Chashtana. He is styled *kshatrapa* on his earlier coins and *mahakshatrapa* on his later ones, the additional title of *rajan* occurring throughout. Chashtana may have originally ruled in the Sind area as a subordinate of the Kushanas. After Nahapana's death, he seems to have been a viceroy of the south-western provinces of the Kushana empire. As mentioned earlier, according to many scholars, the era of 78 CE, which later came to be known as the Shaka or Shalivahana-Shaka era, may have been founded by the Kardamaka ruler Chashtana. It may either represent the date of his accession or the year in which he claimed the position of *mahakshatrapa* after Nahapana was defeated, and probably killed, by the Satavahana king Gautamiputa Satakani. The Kardamakas had a practice of senior and junior rulers, who had the titles *mahakshatrapa* and *kshatrapa* respectively. For instance, during the lifetime of *mahakshatrapa* Chashtana, his son Jayadaman, and later his grandson Rudradaman I, were *kshatrapas*. Chashtana was succeeded as *mahakshatrapa* by Rudradaman I some time after 130–31 CE. Both these rulers were successful in winning back some of the territories conquered by Gautamiputra Satakarni from Nahapana.

Silver coins (obverse and reverse) of Nahapana; of Rudrasimha I (from top)

The Kardamaka ruler Rudradaman I is known from his coins, but more so from his Junagarh inscription, dated in the Shaka year 72, i.e., 150–51 CE. This inscription proclaims his wide conquests over areas including Malwa, Saurashtra, Gujarat, northern Konkan, and the Maheshwar area on the Narmada. It states that he twice defeated Satakarni, lord of the Dakshinapatha, but did not destroy him since he was a close relative. The Satakarni mentioned here seems to be none other than Gautamiputra Satakarni. Rudradaman's daughter seems to have been married to Gautamiputra's son, Vasishthiputra Pulumavi. Rudradaman's empire included all the territories of the erstwhile Kshaharata kingdom, except the Nashik and Pune areas.

PRIMARY SOURCES | A lake, a storm, and a king

A rock at Junagadh in Gujarat bears a set of Ashokan edicts, an inscription of the Kardamaka ruler Rudradaman, and an inscription of the Gupta king Skandagupta. While Ashoka's inscriptions contain his discourses on *dhamma*, the other two tell a unique story of the construction, maintenance, and repair of a water reservoir over about 1,000 years. Rudradaman's inscription, consisting of 20 lines of writing, is inscribed near the top of the rock. Several portions of the text are too damaged to read. The script is Brahmi, the language Sanskrit, and the style elegant and literary. In fact, this is the first long inscription in Sanskrit in the subcontinent.

The purpose of the inscription is to record the restoration of a reservoir called Sudarshana lake by the *mahakshatrapa* Rudradaman. The construction of this reservoir was started by Vaishya Pushyagupta, the provincial governor of Chandragupta Maurya. It was completed by the Yavana Tushaspha, governor of the area during Ashoka's reign. The inscription goes on to tell us that many years later, during the reign of Rudradaman, in the winter of the year 72 (no doubt, of the Shaka era, i.e., 150 CE), there was a terrible storm. We are told (line 6) that 'the clouds, pouring with rain, had converted the earth, as it were, into one ocean, by the excessively swollen floods of the Suvarnasikata, Palashini and other streams of mount Urjayat [Girnar]'. The storm, which was 'of a most tremendous fury befitting the end of a *yuga*, tore down hill tops, trees, banks, turrets, upper stories, gates, and raised palaces of shelter.' Stones, trees, bushes, and creepers lay scattered all over. Although precautions had been taken, the storm tore a breach 420 cubits long and wide, and 75 cubits deep into the lake's embankments. All its water flowed out, and the lake came to resemble a sandy desert. The Sudarshana (literally, 'beautiful to look at') lake became *durdarshana* (ugly to look at).

People lamented the terrible event. So great was the damage that Rudradaman's counsellors and executive officers thought the lake was beyond repair. But Rudradaman went right ahead and ordered the job done. The work was supervised by the provincial governor of the province of Anarta and Surashtra—the *amatya* Suvishakha. Suvishakha was a Pahlava and the son of Kulaipa. He is praised as an exemplary officer—able, patient, self-controlled, upright, honest, and not given to arrogance. The lake was reinforced and made three times as strong in length and breadth on all sides in a very short time, without oppressing the inhabitants of towns and villages by taxes, forced labour, or any other impositions. The inscription tells us that Rudradaman had all this done in order to benefit cows and Brahmanas for a thousand years, and for the sake of righteousness (*dharma*) and fame (*kirti*).

The inscription also contains an eloquent eulogy (*prashasti*) of Rudradaman. The genealogy includes his father Jayadaman and grandfather Chashtana. He is described as having become the lord of Akara, Avanti, the Anupa country, Anarta, Surashtra, Svabhra, Maru, Kachchha, Sindhu, Sauvira, Kukura, Aparanta, Nishada, and other countires by dint of his own valour. He is said to have destroyed the Yaudheyas, who had become arrogant and were claiming to be heroes by defeating all the Kshatriyas. He is described as having defeated Satakarni, lord of Dakshinapatha, twice in fair fight, sparing his life only because he was a close relative. We are told that the towns, villages, and markets of this king were never troubled by robbers, snakes, wild beasts, or diseases. His subjects were attached to him, and as a result of his prowess, attained the goals of dharma, *artha*, and *kama*.

The elaborate, poetic description of Rudradaman describes him as one who was distinguished by royal fortune right from the time he was in his mother's womb; who had been chosen by all *varnas* as their lord to protect them; who had made a vow never to kill men except in battle; who was moved by compassion; who reinstated deposed kings; who by raising his hand had earned the strong attachment of *dharma*; who had earned wide fame by his knowledge and practice of grammar, music, logic, and other great sciences; who was skilled in the control of horses, elephants, and chariots, in the use of sword and shield, and in face-to-face combat; who was generous and in the habit of bestowing gifts and honours on others; who showed respect to others and avoided disrespect; whose treasury was overflowing with gold, silver, diamonds, lapis lazuli, and other precious things through rightfully obtained tribute, tolls, and shares; who was a composer of Sanskrit *kavyas* in prose and verse, embellished with figures and the proper use of words, and possessing lucidity, sweetness, vividness, and brilliance; whose body was marked by the most excellent marks and signs such as auspicious length, dimension, height, voice, gait, complexion, vigour, and strength; and who had been wreathed with many garlands at the *svayamvaras* of many kings' daughters. To what extent Rudradaman actually possessed these qualities is anybody's guess. The inscription offers a portrait of an ideal king, according to the standards and in the idiom of the time.

As for Sudarshana lake, Skandagupta's inscription tells us that it burst its banks again in 455–56 CE during the reign of this Gupta king, and that he too had it repaired.

Source Kielhorn, 1905–06

During the late 2nd century CE, the Satavahana king Yajna Satakarni won some of the southern territories of the Kardamakas. In the course of the next century, the latter lost their northern dominions to the Malavas and Abhiras. The last Kshatrapa ruler who definitely belonged to the line of Chashtana was Vishvasena, who ruled at the end of the 3rd century CE. Thereafter, a new line of Kshatrapa rulers was established by Rudrasimha II.

The Mahameghavahanas in Eastern India

The nuclear area of the earliest post-Maurya state in Odisha was located in the lower Mahanadi valley and delta. Its chief monumental markers were located in the Udayagiri and Khandagiri hills (in Khordha district). Here, there are over 30 excavated caves in the sandstone hillsides, the earliest of which belong to the time of the Mahameghavahana family and Chedi lineage. An inscription in Cave 14 on Udayagiri hill, known as the Hathigumpha, describes the achievements of a king named Kharavela who ruled in the 1st century BCE (Jayaswal and Banerji, 1929–30). The inscription is the only piece of evidence about this ruler.

The composer of the 17-line royal inscription in fine Prakrit/Middle Indic literary prose in the Hathigumpha displays masterful powers of compression. After an invocation to the Jaina *arhats* and *siddhas*, and an introduction to the lineage and greatness of the king, one single line describes his childhood, education and training as a prince, and his nine-year stint as *yuvaraja* leading up to his royal consecration at the age of 25. This is followed by a succinct but vigorous annual report of his achievements over 13 years of his reign. The text focuses on three main themes—the king's military accomplishments, his benevolent activities, and his being an ardent follower and patron of Jainism.

The account of Kharavela's military victories begins with his second year when, disregarding the Satavahana king Satakarni, he despatched his army to the western regions. A *yavana* king, a Pandya king, as well as the Musikas (or Asikas), Rathikas, Bhojakas, and an Ava king of Pithumda are those over whom Kharavela claims to have scored victories. There is reference to Kharavela, in his fifth regnal year, extending into his capital a canal that had been excavated 300 years previously by king Nanda. There are also references to two attacks against Magadha, in his eighth and twelfth regnal years. In the second attack, he is said to have caused great terror among the people of Magadha, made king Bahasatimita bow at his feet, brought back the riches of Anga and Magadha, and retrieved and installed an image of a Kalinga *jina* which had long ago been taken away by king Nanda.

There is mention of Kharavela's victorious expedition against Bharadhavasa (i.e. Bharatavarsha, which here seems to be used as a generic term for North India), his breaking up a confederacy of the Tramira (Dramira) country, and terrifying the kings of Uttarapatha.

The Hathigumpha inscription also highlights the king's benevolence towards his subjects in its description of his furthering their material prosperity by spending a large sum of money on various activities in the capital Kalinganagari—repairing gates, walls, and structures which had been damaged by a storm; building the embankments of a lake, tanks, and cisterns; and restoring gardens. The activities of year 13, when Kharavela engaged in a number of activities connected with the Jaina *sangha*, are presented as the climax of his reign. This was when he convened a huge conclave on the Kumari hill (Udayagiri), which attracted wise monks and ascetics from a hundred quarters; built a lavish structure; and had the seven-fold Angas swiftly compiled. Kharavela is described as a layman (*upasaka*) devoted to worship. At the same time, he respected all religious sects (*pasandas*).

The Udayagiri–Khandagiri complex is located just over 16 km from Dhauli and a little over 10 km from Sisupalgarh. Dhauli could represent Tosali, while Jaugada could represent Samapa, mentioned in Ashoka's edicts as Maurya administrative centres. Other identifications suggested for Tosali are Radhanagar and Sisupalgarh. Excavations at the latter site here revealed remains of a large 1 sq km large planned city enclosed by a rampart, gateways, and moat; a monumental pillared structure and stone-lined ponds in the centre; and several residential buildings. Sisupalgarh could represent Tosali or Kharavela's capital Kalinganagari.

PRIMARY SOURCES | Epigraphic dialogue in the Hathigumpha inscription

The Hathigumpha inscription can be seen as an epigraphic chronicle with a long historical memory. In Rock Edict 13, Ashoka described his war against the Kalingas as a terrible event that turned him away from war to the propagation of *dhamma*. The Maurya victory over Kalinga was marked on the landscape by major rock edicts inscribed at Jaugada and Dhauli, which deliberately omitted Rock Edict 13. The Hathigumpha inscription ignored the Maurya invasion. But it is clear that the composer of the Hathigumpha inscription had read Ashoka's edicts, probably those at Dhauli and Jaugada, and that Kharavela's inscription is in direct dialogue with Ashoka's edicts, whose script could still have been read.

There are several marked differences between the contents of Kharavela and Ashoka's inscriptions, especially in their attitude towards war, but there are several interesting connections. Ashoka is a *raja* Kharavela is a *maharaja*. Both mention the *abhisheka* as an important event. Both emphasize the kings' personal virtues. Both use hyperbole—Ashoka for the casualties in the Kalinga war and for the number of years that *dhamma* had been declining before he came along; Kharavela for the huge sums of money he had spent on various benevolent activities. Both mention subduing the Rathikas and Bhojas. Ashoka hits out at popular festivals known as *samajas*; Kharavela entertains the capital city with *samajas* and *utsavas*. Ashoka boasts of spreading *dhamma* among the Yavanas, Kharavela of defeating them. Ashoka talks of his many benefactions to his people, especially through teaching them about *dhamma* and helping them attain happiness and heaven. Kharavela shows a more materialistic bent of mind, making gifts of money and promoting their material prosperity. Ashoka projected himself as an emperor and a prophet of piety, possessing vast political power and a universal moral authority. Kharavela's power and authority were based on military victories, benevolence towards his subjects, and religious patronage. Both kings made their personal religious leanings (Buddhist/Jaina) clear but extended their benevolence towards Brahmanas and declared their respect for all religious sects (*pasandas*). Ashoka announced a general reduction of taxes at Lumbini. Kharavela bestowed *pariharas* (tax exemptions) on Brahmanas. The frequent occurrence of the word *sava* (all) in the description of Kharavela's power can be seen as an echo of the frequent occurrence of the word in Ashoka's inscriptions. The references to *dhamma* and peace in the Hathigumpha inscription can be traced to a Jaina influence but could just as well been an echo of Ashoka's obsession. Ashoka set up pillars inscribed with his *dhamma* message; Kharavela refers to setting up pillars inlaid with beryl for some grand structure.

Ashoka's words and actions reflect austerity and restraint, Kharavela's reflect wealth and opulence. But the anonymous composer of the Hathigumpha inscription seems to have used the edicts as a reference point and sought to establish Kharavela's reputation and superiority in relation to Ashoka. The Jaina centre at Udayagiri-Khandagiri may have been aimed at surpassing anything created by Ashoka. Writing almost a century ago, Jayaswal and Banerji reported traces of polish in the Hathigumpha, which suggest a failed attempt to imitate the polished granite finish of the Maurya-period caves in the Barabar-Nagarjuni hills. But the Udayagiri-Khandagiri complex surpassed the Barabar-Nagarjuni complex in a different way, via sculptural embellishment, especially in the Ranigumpha and Manchapuri caves, which seem to include scenes from Kharavela's life, executed in a fine, distinctive artistic style.

In its balancing and advertising of the many facets of royal power in a royally-sponsored religious establishment, the Hathigumpha inscription has great importance in the history of ancient Indian political ideology.

Source Upinder Singh, 2022b

The Satavahanas in the Deccan

Ashokan inscriptions suggest Maurya contact with the Deccan, especially the southern Deccan. B. D. Chattopadhyaya, ([1987] 2003) has emphasized the importance of numismatic evidence which indicates the existence of numerous small political principalities (he calls them 'localities') that surfaced in various parts of the Deccan after the decline of the Maurya empire and before the advent of the Satavahanas. Coins of local rulers, often bearing the title *maharathi* have been found in stratigraphic contexts at sites such as Verrapuram at pre-Satavahana and Satavahana levels. At Brahmapuri, coins of Kura rulers have been found at pre-Satavahana levels. Unstratified coin finds at Kotalingala give the names of several local rulers such as Gobhadra, Samigopa, Chimuka, Kamvaya, and Narana. A *raja* named Khubiraka is mentioned in a late 2nd century BCE inscription found on a relic casket at Bhattiprolu. All this suggests a significant increase in the power and status of local elites during the 2nd–1st centuries BCE. The Rathikas and Bhojas mentioned in Ashoka's inscriptions were transformed into the *maharathis* and *mahabhojas* of pre-Satavahana times.

The Satavahanas are identified with the Andhras of the Puranas. The *Matsya* and *Brahmanda Puranas* list 30 kings who ruled for a total of 460 years, while the *Vayu Purana* lists 17 kings who ruled for 300 years. Some rulers known from coins and inscriptions are not mentioned in the Puranic lists. There is disagreement among historians about the chronology of the dynasty. There is a long chronology consisting of 30 kings who ruled for about 460 years, and a short chronology which consists of 19 kings ruling for about 260 years. Satavahana rule seems to have begun in the early or middle of the 2nd century BCE. The dates suggested include 150 BCE and 120 BCE.

There is also debate on whether the Satavahanas initially came to power in the eastern or western Deccan. The fact that the Puranas call them Andhras suggests that they were originally based in the Andhra region or that they belonged to the Andhra tribe. The term *Andhra-bhritya* in the Puranas is taken by some historians to indicate that the ancestors of the Satavahanas were subordinates of the Mauryas (*bhritya* means servant or subordinate). However, *Andhra-bhritya* could also mean 'servants of the Andhras', and further, it may apply not to the Satavahanas but to their successors. Apart from the name 'Andhra', the discovery of early Satavahana coins at Kotalingala and Sangareddy (in Telangana) has been used to support the hypothesis that the Satavahanas began their rule in the eastern Deccan. On the other hand, inscriptions in the Naneghat and Nashik caves point to the western Deccan as their original locus. Accordingly, some historians argue that the Satavahanas initially established their hold over the area around Pratishthana (modern Paithan) in the western Deccan, and expanded from there into the eastern Deccan, Andhra, and the western coast.

The Satavahanas kingdom eventually came to cover modern Andhra Pradesh and Maharashtra; at times it also included northern Karnataka, eastern and southern Madhya Pradesh, and Saurashtra. Pliny mentions the Andhra country as including many villages and 30 walled towns, and states that its rulers had a large army of 100,000 infantry, 2,000 cavalry, and 1,000 elephants.

Given the controversy over the date of the beginning of Satavahana rule, it is difficult to give absolute dates for the various rulers of this dynasty. However, the sequence of rulers is fairly certain. The founder Simuka was succeeded by his brother Kanha, who extended the empire westward at least as far as Nashik. The third king of the dynasty was Satakarni I, who enjoyed a long reign of about 56 years. Kharavela, the king of Kalinga, claims in his Hathigumpha inscription to have defied a king named Satakarni in his second regnal year. He also claims that two years later, he defeated the Rathikas of the Maratha country and the Bhojas of Vidarbha, who seem to have been subordinates of the Satavahanas. Later Satavahana kings included Hala, 17th in the line, a poet who is supposed to have compiled the *Gatha Sattasai*, a collection of 700 erotic poems in the Maharashtri Prakrit dialect. Satavahana kings were patrons of Prakrit literature and experimented with language use in their inscriptions (see Ollett, 2017).

PRIMARY SOURCES | The royal portrait gallery in the Naneghat cave

Naneghat (in Pune district, Maharashtra) is one of the important passes connecting the western coastal strip with the Deccan plateau. The plateau dips sharply between two hills into a steep descent consisting of uneven basalt slabs revealing a stunning view on a clear day.

There are three groups of excavated caves here. Unlike other cave sites of the time, these were not monastic habitations. Cave 11 is the most important. On the back wall of the 2.7 m high and 8.7 sq m hall, the undulating rock surface and traces of feet are the ghostly remnants of what was once an imposing Satavahana group portrait consisting of eight life-size figures standing in relief. Label inscriptions over the heads give their names (left to right) as follows:

1. the illustrious king (*raya si*) Simuka Satavahana
2,3. queen (*sirimato devi*) Nayanika and the illustrious king (*rano*) Satakarni
4. prince (*kumara*) Bhayala
5. (the name of the 5th person is lost)
6. *maharathi* Tranakayira
7. prince (*kumara*) Haku-shri
8. prince (*kumara*) Satavahana

This group portrait is flanked by a 20-line inscription, the first 10 lines of which are engraved on the left side wall and lines 11–20 on the right wall. This long Prakrit/Middle Indic inscription is that of a Satavahana queen, whose name has not survived, but can be inferred to be Nayanika (or Naganika) of the label inscription. She was wife of the third Satavahana king Satakarni I, who seems to have been deceased by the time the inscription was engraved; and the mother of king Vedishri.

The inscription is badly damaged, so many details are obscure. The invocation at the beginning is to *dharma*, [Prajapati], Indra, Samkarshana, Vasudeva, Chandra, Surya, the lokapalas—Yama, Varuna, Kubera and Vasava (Indra)—and Kumara (Karttikeya). Various individuals are eulogized, including the queen's son Vedishri; a Dakshinapathapati (perhaps Simuka, father-in-law of Nayanika); and a *maharathi*. This is followed by a eulogy of the queen who is described as leading a life befitting a pious royal widow ascetic. Then there is a very long list of sacrifices, some which seem to have been performed by the queen's husband along with her; and others performed by her on her own. The former include the *rajasuya* and two *ashvamedhas*. Apart from the long list of sacrifices, what is striking is the specification of the lavish *dakshina* (sacrificial fees) given on these occasions, including huge sums of money (silver *karshapanas*), cows, horses, chariots, and villages. The dominant emphasis is on the performance of *yajnas*, but there are references to the gods, the queen performing *vratas*, and king Vedishri performing *purta* activities, bestowing wealth and boons on supplicants, and fulfilling their desires. The inscription has a strong Brahmanical stamp.

The labelled royal reliefs and the long inscription at Naneghat must have been planned as inter-related elements of a powerful assertion of Satavahana power. Perhaps the Satavahanas were responsible for opening out the route via Naneghat or promoting trade along it. Outside the cave, there are rows of cisterns to the left and right. Trade caravans and enemy armies that took this route would have stopped and marveled at the images and words that proclaimed the greatness of the Satavahanas.

Source Mirashi, 1981: 5–16, 20

Naneghat cave (left); Traces of feet of Satavahana royalty; Inscription on side wall (from top right)

Copper coins (obverse and reverse) of Satakarni I (top and centre); of Vasishthiputra Pulumavi

The Satavahanas and Shakas were involved in prolonged conflict. Control over the premier ports such as Bhrigukachcha (Broach), Kalyan, and Suparaka (Sopara) was an important issue in this conflict. The initial expansion of the Kshaharata Kshatrapas was at the expense of the Satavahanas. The fortunes of the Satavahanas were revived in the second half of the 1st century by Gautamiputra Satakarni, during whose reign the empire seems to have reached its peak. Gautamiputra defeated Nahapana and recovered many of the territories that the Shakas had earlier wrested from the Satavahanas. A Nashik inscription, dated in the 18th year of Gautamiputra's reign, records the grant to Buddhist monks of a piece of land that was earlier in the possession of Ushavadata, son-in-law of Nahapana. A hoard of Nahapana's coins found at Jogalthambi in Nashik district includes coins that were re-struck by Gautamiputra. Gautamiputra's coins have been found in the eastern Deccan as well.

The achievements of Gautamiputra Satakarni are described and eulogized in an inscription of his mother Gautami Balashri at Nashik, engraved after his death, during the reign of his son Pulumavi II. He is described as an exterminator of the Kshaharata lineage and restorer of the glory of the Satavahana family. His political domain is described with great specificity as consisting of many lands across Central and Southern India. He was king of Rishika, Ashmaka, Mulaka, Surashtra, Kukura, Aparanta, Anupa, Vidarbha, and Akaravanti. He had succeeded in destroying his enemies—the Shakas, Yavanas, and Pahlavas. His horses are said to have drunk the waters of the three oceans; his commands were obeyed and his feet worshipped by all the princes of the circle of kings. These martial achievements are punctuated by references to other attributes including his physical beauty; his obedience to his mother; his pursuit of the three goals of human existence; his being the abode of the sacred texts and the refuge of royal fortune. His commitment to nonviolence is reflected in the statement that he was averse to hurting even an enemy who had done him offence. The king's relationship with his people is highlighted in the statements that he shared in their joys and sorrows, levied and used taxes fairly, and organized festivals (*samajas*). Gautamiputra is described as a destroyer of the arrogance of the Kshatriyas and a peerless Brahmana (*eka-bamhana*). Simultaneously, the fact that he embodied all the necessary Kshatriya qualities for a great king is proclaimed through his prowess and lustre being compared with that of several Kshatriya heroes. Apart from extending his benevolence to Brahmanas, he is said to have prevented the mixture of *varnas*. Gautamiputra's eulogy is thoroughly permeated with epic–Puranic elements.

The coins of Vasishthiputra Pulumavi, the successor of Gautamiputra Satakarni, have been found in various parts of Andhra Pradesh. Due to his engagements in the east, the Shakas may have got a chance to recover some of their territory. Yajnashri Satakarni was another important Satavahana king. His coins depict ships, some single masted, others double masted. He seems to have revived the struggle against the Shakas, and was probably the last king of his dynasty to control the eastern and western Deccan. The successors of Yajna Shri Satakarni included Gautamiputra Vijaya Satakarni, Chanda Satakarni, Vasishthiputra Vijaya Satakarni, and Pulumavi. Some of the later Satavahana rulers are not mentioned in the Puranic king-lists and are only known through their coins. The Satavahana dynasty came to an end in the mid-3rd century CE.

The Satavahanas claimed Brahmana descent and anchored themselves to the Brahmanical tradition. As mentioned above, the Nashik inscription of Gautami Balashri describes Gautamiputra Satakarni as a peerless Brahmana. References to the performance of a large number of *shrauta* sacrifices by Satakarni I in the inscription of Naganika at Naneghat suggest that this was an important means of acquiring political legitimacy. At the same time, they patronized Buddhist establishments. The use of matronyms by the Satavahana kings is significant. When seen along with the Naneghat inscriptions of Naganika and the Nashik inscription of Gautami Balashri, it is evident that women of the royal household wielded considerable power and authority in the Satavahana kingdom.

Chattopadhyaya ([1987] 2003) points out that in spite of their grand title of 'Lord of Dakshinapatha', it is unlikely that the Satavahanas managed to administratively integrate the entire Deccan. Like the Shakas and Kushanas, they too had a number of subordinate chiefs or rulers who acknowledged their political paramountcy. The *maharathis* and *mahabhojas*—local rulers who had emerged in the pre-Satavahana period—were encapsulated and integrated into the Satavahana polity, and continued to be important even after the establishment of Satavahana rule. Coins indicate the sway of families such as the Kuras, Anandas, and the *maharathi* Hasti in various parts of the Deccan. The *maharathis* and *mahabhojas* mentioned in Satavahana inscriptions appear as donors at Buddhist cave sites in the western Deccan; they had matrimonial ties with the Satavahanas and among themselves. The Sada dynasty ruled in the lower Krishna valley. The Satavahana kingdom was divided into a number of large administrative divisions known as *aharas*. We hear of different sorts of officials such as *amatyas*, *mahamatras*, *mahasenapatis*, and of scribes and record keepers. Villages were governed by village headmen (*gramikas*).

The earliest inscriptions recording royal grants of land, including those associated with tax exemptions, belong to the Satavahana and Kshatrapa periods. The Naneghat inscription of Naganika (1st century BCE) mentions that villages were among the items offered as *dakshina* to officiating priests when certain *shrauta* sacrifices, including the *ashvamedha*, were performed by her husband Satakarni I. A 2nd century CE Nashik cave inscription of Ushavadata describes the donor as one who has given 16 villages to the gods and Brahmanas. The inscription also records the grant of a field by Ushavadata to provide food for the Buddhist monks dwelling in the cave. The earliest reference to the technical term *akhaya-nivi* (*akshaya-nivi*) occurs in one of Ushavadata's Nashik inscriptions (see Visvanathan, 2021). This refers to a grant made in perpetuity, which does not however, permit the alienation or destruction of the principal. An inscription of Gautamiputra Satakarni in one of the Nashik caves records the grant to Buddhist monks of a field located in a village that previously fell within the jurisdiction of Ushavadata. This is the first inscription that associates certain specific privileges and exemptions with a gift of land. It states that the land was not to be entered by agents or soldiers of the king (*apavesa*); not to be interfered with (*anomasa*); not to be dug for salt (*alonakhadaka*); not to be interfered with by the district officers (*arathasavinayika*); and was to enjoy all kinds of immunities (*savajatapariharika*).

Western India was the nuclear area for the creation of an important template of royal political ideology and religious policy (see Upinder Singh, 2022b). The central ideas of a royal land grant, including its political underpinnings, eternal nature, fiscal and other privileges, and legal status, were now in place. All the basic elements of the land grant charter, starting with the auspicious symbols and invocation, are present in inscriptions of the Satavahanas, except for the imprecatory verses at the end. This was an addition made by their Ikshvaku and Vakataka successors. Another change in post-Satavahana times was that copper plates swiftly replaced stone as the favoured surface for recording royal land grants.

Punch-marked coin from Andhra (obverse and reverse)

Kings and Chieftains in the Far South: the Cheras, Cholas, and Pandyas

The early kingdoms of Tamilakam—the land between the Tirupati hills (Vengadam) and the southernmost tip of the peninsula—emerged in rice-growing areas of rich agricultural potential. The principality of the Cholas in the lower Kaveri valley had its capital at Uraiyur. The kingdom of the Pandyas in the valleys of the Tamraparni and Vaigai and had its capital at Madurai. The Cheras on the Kerala coast had their capital at Karuvur, also known as Vanji. All these areas participated in the flourishing trade networks of the time. The premier Chola port was Puhar (also known as Kaveripumpattinam), the

major Pandya port was Korkai, while Tondi and Muchiri were the important ports in the Chera kingdom.

The major sources of information on the political history of the time are laudatory poems, which often exaggerate the achievements and virtues of rulers. Tamil-Brahmi inscriptions corroborate the historicity and rough dates of some of the rulers mentioned in texts. The Chera, Chola, and Pandya kings were the *vendar* (crowned kings). These great kings had their special insignia of royalty such as the staff, drum, and umbrella. They also had specific emblems of power—the tiger, bow, and fish were the emblems of the Cholas, Cheras, and Pandyas respectively. Apart from the *vendar*, there were a number of chieftains known as *velir*. Internecine conflict was a feature of the politics of the time. The kings and chieftains also often fought against each other by forming alliances. The lesser rulers no doubt had to pay tribute to their more powerful counterparts. (For the details of the political history of early historic South India, see Sastri, [1955] 1975: 118–29; Subbarayalu in Karashima. [Ed.]., 2014: 47–55.)

Udiyanjeral is the earliest known Chera king. His son was Nedunjeral Adan, described as having defeated seven crowned kings and winning the exalted rank of *adhiraja*. Poetic exaggeration credits him with extending his conquests upto the Himalaya mountains and carving the Chera bow emblem on them. He defeated an enemy on the Malabar coast and captured several Yavana traders, later releasing them for ransom. He fought a war against a Chola king, an encounter in which both the principal adversaries lost their lives. Kuttuvan, the younger brother of Nedunjeral Adan, is supposed to have conquered Kongu and extended the power of the Cheras up to the eastern and western oceans. One of Adan's sons is described as an *adhiraja* who wore a garland of seven crowns. He achieved military successes against Anji, a chieftain of Tagadur, and led an expedition against a ruler named Nannan, who held sway in the area to the north of Malabar.

Senguttuvan was another of Adan's sons. He won a war against the Mokur chieftain. The *Silappadikaram*, a post-Sangam work, tells us that he attacked Viyalur in the land of Nannan and took the Kodukur fortress in Kongu country. He seems to have successfully backed one of the claimants in a Chola succession conflict, leading to the death of nine other contenders. He is also credited with fighting against an *arya* chieftain in order to obtain stone for an image of Kannaki (the heroine of the *Silappadikaram*) and bathing in the Ganga before bringing the stone back to his country. Kudakko Ilanjeral Irumporai is one of the last Chera kings mentioned in the Sangam poems. He is said to have fought victorious wars against the Cholas and Pandyas. Another Chera monarch, Mandaranjeral Irumporai, ruled in the early 3rd century CE. On one occasion, he was captured by the Pandyas, but managed to regain his freedom and return home.

Two almost identical 2nd century CE inscriptions at Pugalur mention three generations of Chera princes of the Irumporai line. They record the construction of a rock shelter for a Jaina monk on the occasion of the investiture ceremony of the heir apparent Ilankatunko, son of Perunkatunkon, and grandson of king Adan Cher Irumporai. The last mentioned ruler can be identified with king Ilanjeral Irumporai mentioned above. The names of another branch of Chera kings have been found in two short inscriptions at Edakal in Kerala, dated on palaeographic grounds to the 3rd century CE.

Coins (obverse and reverse) of Pandyas (left); of Cheras (right) and Cholas (extreme right)

The Chola king Karikala is associated with many heroic exploits. A poem in the *Pattuppattu* describes how he was deposed and imprisoned early in his reign, but succeeded in escaping and re-establishing himself as king. Karikala is credited with having defeated a confederacy including the Pandyas, Cheras, and their allies at the battle of Venni. We are told that 11 rulers lost their drums in the field (the royal drum was an important symbol of royal power) and that the Chera king, who suffered a wound in the back, committed ritual suicide by starvation. Karikala is credited with another major victory at Vahaipparandalai. This time, we are told that several chieftains lost their umbrellas (the umbrella was one of the insignias of royal power). These and other victories suggest that Karikala succeeded in impressing his might over many contemporary kings and chieftains. Another important Chola ruler mentioned in the poems is Tondaiman Ilandiraiyan. He ruled from Kanchi, either as an independent ruler or as a subordinate of Karikala. He was a poet; of his four songs that have survived, one emphasizes that the personal character of a king was important for him to rule well. In later times, the Chola kingdom was racked by a protracted and bitter war between two contenders for the throne—Nalangilli and Nedungilli.

The early Pandya kings included Nediyon, Palshalai Mudukudumi, and Nedunjeliyan. The death of Kovalan, hero of the *Silappadikaram*, is supposed to have taken place during the reign of the last-mentioned ruler who is said to have died of remorse because of his role in the tragic turn of events. This Nedunjeliyan was followed by another king of the same name. He is credited with many major military victories. It is said that he defeated a confederacy of Cholas, Cheras, and five chieftains at a battle at Talaiyalanganam while he was still very young. (It is in this battle that the Chera king was taken prisoner.) He is also described as having conquered territory from other chieftains. Two early 2nd century BCE Tamil-Brahmi inscriptions from Mangulam record gifts made to Jaina monks by a subordinate and a relative of Nedunjeliyan. Mahadevan suggests that this Nedunjeliyan should probably be placed earlier than the two kings of this name mentioned in Sangam poems. A *c.* 1st century BCE inscription from Alagarmalai mentions a person called Kalu(Katu)mara Natan, who, from his name, seems to have been a Pandya prince or subordinate.

PRIMARY SOURCES | The royal drum

Before they returned from bathing the
awe-inspiring drum
which hungers for blood and is decorated
with golden shoots
of balloon vine and a garland the colour
of sapphire, fashioned
of long dense peacock feathers, their
bright spots shining,
lending a glow to the dark wood of the
drum's sides
where thongs cut lengthwise are tied
without flaw, I
climbed up on its bed, all covered with
flowers and as soft
as if a froth of sesame oil had been
spread over it.
You turned away the edge of your sword
that would have,
had you been enraged, cut me in two!
That was enough in itself
for all the fine Tamil people to know!
But you did even more!
You approached me and raised your
strong arm
big around as a concert drum and fanned
me to keep me cool!
Is it because you have clearly heard that
only for those
who gain fame in this world, making it
spread far and wide,
can there be a place there, in the world
of exalted existence, victorious hero?
Is that why you just did this?

This is one of many Sangam poems that bring out the close relationship between kings and poets. The royal drum (*murahu*) was beaten in the morning to awaken the king, during battle, and on other special occasions. It was made from a special tree and special skin, and was associated with sacred power. The desecration of the drum was considered a very serious offence. In this poem, Mochikirnarin praises Cheraman Takaturerinta Peruncheralirumporai. The poet tells us that he climbed on to the drum by mistake and fell asleep on it. When the king arrived, he did not kill him in fury, but instead fanned him tenderly till he awoke.

Source *Purananuru* 50; poet: Mocikiranar; Hart and Heifetz. (Trans.)., 1999: 278

The Sangam poets also eulogize various chieftains such as Ay, Andiran, and Pari for their bravery and generosity. Pari seems to have held sway in the Pandya country near the hill known as Kodungunram or Piranmalai. Kapilar, who wrote many poems in praise of Pari, seems to have been a loyal camp-follower. He moved to the court of the Chera king Shelvakkadungo Vali Adan only after Pari's death. Other rulers of the time included Adigaiman (also known as Neduman Anji), ruler of Tagadur, who is praised in the poems of the poetess Auvaiyar. Although assisted by the Pandya and Chola kings, he was defeated by Chera Perunjeral Irumporai, whose suzerainty he had to subsequently acknowledge. He died fighting on behalf of the Cheras in an expedition against Pali, the capital of Nannan. This famous chieftain is mentioned in a 1st century CE inscription at Jambai. Tamil-Brahmi inscriptions from Pugalur and Kaniman mention other chieftains as well.

In the Tamil-Brahmi inscriptions found at several places in South India, kings are addressed as *ko* and the chieftains as *ko* or *kon*. Princes have the suffixes 'ko' or 'kon' in their name. The reference in the Pugalur inscription to an investiture ceremony for the heir apparent is significant. The mention of a subordinate ruler or functionary of the Pandya king in a Mangulam inscription is also noteworthy. A *kalatika* (superintendent of pearls, i.e., an officer who supervised pearl fisheries) is mentioned in a 2nd century BCE Mangulam inscription; this person was also a member of a merchant guild. A 1st century BCE inscription from Alagarmalai refers to the *kanatikan* (chief of scribes). Such inscriptions give glimpses into the administrative organization of the Pandyas.

The most important basis of legitimation of political power in early historic South India was the eulogy of the poets. The relationship between poet and patron in ancient Tamilakam was a reciprocal one (Kailasapathy, [1968] 2002, 55–93; Shulman, 2001: 74–75). The poet was dependent on his patron for material support and well-being. But the king too was dependent on the poet. It was only the poet's praise of his generosity and heroism that could lead to his attaining lasting fame. Conversely, the poet's anger could prove costly for his patron and lead to his ruin. In some poems, poor bards

PRIMARY SOURCES | Tamil-Brahmi inscriptions

The script of the earliest known Tamil inscriptions is referred to as Tamil-Brahmi. It is an adaptation of Brahmi for writing the Tamil language. Out of the 26 Tamil-Brahmi letters, 22 are almost identical to the Brahmi ones and have the same phonetic values. There is an omission of letters for sounds not found in Tamil and an addition of letters to represent sounds in Tamil. A dot known as the *pulli* is introduced over consonants which do not have an inherent 'a' attached to them. The language of the Tamil-Brahmi inscriptions is basically Tamil with the addition of Prakrit elements. Iravatham Mahadevan has divided the evolution of Tamil-Brahmi into two phases: Early Tamil-Brahmi (2nd century BCE–1st century CE) and Late Tamil-Brahmi (2nd–4th century CE).

Tamil-Brahmi inscriptions have been found at many sites in Tamil Nadu and Kerala. There is a concentration of the inscriptions in the southern part of Tamil Nadu, and almost all the sites in this region are clustered near Madurai. This seems to have been the area where the script originated, and from where it spread to other parts of South India.

Early Tamil-Brahmi inscriptions are mostly short, and are found in natural rock shelters or caves, on overhanging brows, or on stone beds inside the caves. These were places where Jaina monks and nuns lived. Most of the inscriptions record the donation of the shelters/caves and stone beds, giving the names of the donors, and occasionally the names of the monks or nuns who occupied them. In a few rare cases, the names of the masons are given.

Tamil-Brahmi was not only used for recording religious donations. It has also been found on pottery at many sites—for instance at Arikamedu, Uraiyur, Kodumanal, and Alangulam. It has also been found in Jaffna in Sri Lanka and the ports of Berenike and Quseiral-Qadim on the Red Sea coast. A goldsmith's polished touch-stone (used for testing the purity of gold) found at Khuan Luk Pat in southwest Thailand has Tamil-Brahmi writing belonging to the 3rd/4th century. The inscription reads: 'perum patan kal,' 'the (touch)-stone of Perumpattan.' A few coins, seals, and rings with Tamil-Brahmi have also been found.

Source Mahadevan, 2003

Map 8.2 Tamil-Brahmi and early Vatteluttu inscriptions (after Mahadevan, 2003)

beseech their patrons for favours and gifts. Others indicate that kings would give generously, even if it meant going out on a looting expedition. The relationship between ruler and poet was often very close and intense, based on strong bonds of loyalty, even friendship.

However, Sangam poems also reflect the emergence of new bases of royal prestige and legitimacy—the performance of Brahmanical sacrifices, establishing links with the northern epic tradition, the worship and patronage of certain deities, and the patronage of Jaina ascetics. Several poems refer to the king's performance of Vedic sacrifices. The Pandya ruler Mudukudumi had the title *Palshalai* which means 'one who

Transliteration in Roman script:
kani-i nata-siri-y kuvan...
vel-arai-y nikamatu
kaviti-iy kalitika antai
asutan pina-u kotupiton

TRANSLATION:
To Nanta-siri Kuvan, the ***Kani***. Antai Assutan, the superintendent of pearls and ***kaviti*** of the merchant guild of Vellarai, caused to give the cave (?).

['Kani' is the title of a senior Jaina monk. 'Kaviti' is an honorific title bestowed by kings on ministers, nobles, and merchants.]

Mahadevan, 2003: 318–19

A Tamil-Brahmi inscription at Mangulam

has many halls', presumably sacrificial halls. Certain chiefs claimed to have emerged from the sacrificial fire pit of a northern sage, and connected themselves both with the sage Agastya and the god Vishnu. The chieftain Adigaiman is described as having been born in a family which honoured the gods by performing worship and sacrifices. Later tradition credits the Chera king Senguttuvan as having played an important role in establishing the cult of the goddess Pattini (Kannaki, deified as the epitome of the chaste wife). The Chola king Senganan is described in legend as devoted to Shiva and as having fed the two warring armies on the eve of the Mahabharata war. Tamil-Brahmi inscriptions record the excavation of caves for Jaina monks and nuns by kings, chieftains, and many others.

Coins of the Chola, Chera, and Pandya kings have been identified (see Subbarayalu, 2018). These are mostly of copper (a few are made of silver). They are square or round, and are either cast or die-struck. The obverse symbols include the elephant, tortoise, pair of fish, and tree. The symbols on the reverse—bow and arrow, fish, and tiger—help identify them as Chera, Pandya or Chola coins. Twenty-nine coins have Tamil legends written in the Tamil-Brahmi script. The Cheras also counter-struck silver Roman coins. The dynastic issues circulated in South India along with the silver punch-marked coins and gold and silver Roman coins.

Champakalakshmi (1996: 92–93) has argued that the urbanization of the Sangam age did not take place in a context of a state polity, and that this was an age of tribal chiefdoms or at the most 'potential monarchies'. She asserts that the *vendar* exercised limited control over agricultural tracts and depended on tribute and plunder for their sustenance. However, the evidence of writing, a sophisticated literature, urban centres, specialized crafts, and long-distance trade suggest otherwise. The references in poems to these kings making gifts of gold, gems, muslin, and even horses and elephants suggest a differential access to and control over resources. Kings were involved in long-distance maritime trade as consumers of luxury goods and by developing ports of trade and levying tolls and customs. There is also clear evidence of dynastic coin issues. The existence of at least a rudimentary state structure cannot be denied in the case of the Chola, Chera, and Pandya monarchies, even if these rulers did not have full control over the agrarian plains, a regular or extensive system of taxation, or a centralized coercive machinery.

Sri Lanka

The *Mahavamsa* gives a legendary history of the early history of Sri Lanka, beginning with the arrival of Vijaya and his companions from the kingdom of Sihapura in North India. This arrival is said to have coincided with the Buddha's *parinibbana*. The historical element behind this legend are the migrations that must have taken place from early times from various parts of the mainland to Sri Lanka.

In recent years, several Sri Lankan historians have highlighted the need to question the *Mahavamsa* view of Sri Lanka's early history (see, for instance, Gunawardana, 2000). The monks who composed the chronicles had their own agendas, including presenting the island as a major bastion of the faith. The *Mahavamsa* describes Devanampiya Tissa as ruler who ruled over the whole island, while it is clear that there were several political principalities of which his was one. Dutthagamini was the ruler who seems to have established his rule over the whole island in the 2nd century BCE. The 15 year struggle waged by Dutthagamini against the Tamil invader Elara is described in the *Mahavamsa* as a religious conflict, ignoring the political complexities of the conflict. In Sri Lankan political history, the period from the 2nd century BCE to the 8th century is referred to as the early Anuradhapura period. This was marked by various political contests and conflicts, in which South Indian mercenary troops played a significant role.

Villages and Cities

More is known about cities of *c.* 200 BCE–300 CE than about villages and agriculture. The Jatakas speak of *gamas* ranging from 30–1,000 *kulas* (extended families). There are references to *gamas* associated with particular occupational groups such as reed workers (*nalakaras*) and salt makers (*lonakaras*). There is also mention of villages of potters, carpenters, smiths, forest folk, hunters, fowlers, and fishermen. Some of these villages seem to have been located close to cities.

Early Tamil-Brahmi inscriptions offer brief glimpses into aspects of village life in Tamilakam. A 2nd century BCE inscription at Varichiyur records the gift of 100 *kalams* of rice. A 1st century BCE inscription at Alagarmalai refers to a *koluvanikan* (trader in ploughshares). The *kolu* is the hard iron tip fixed to a wooden ploughshare. A 2nd century BCE inscription found at Mudalaikulam seems to refer to the construction of a tank by the assembly (*ur*) of Vempil village (Mahadevan, 2003: 140, 125). If Mahadevan's interpretation is correct, this is the earliest inscriptional reference to a village assembly in the Indian subcontinent.

The period *c.* 200 BCE–300 CE was marked by urban prosperity all over the subcontinent. Unfortunately, the archaeological details of most early historical sites are rather meagre and tend to be confined to a few details about fortifications. Some sites

FURTHER DISCUSSION | Plant remains from Sanghol

Compared to earlier periods, there is very little archaeological data about the agricultural economy of settlements in different parts of the subcontinent during the early historical period. There are, however, a few exceptions.

A. K. Pokharia and K. S. Saraswat collected over 300 plant samples from 28 trenches of 'Kushana' habitational levels (*c.* 100–300 CE) at the site of Sanghol (Ludhiana district, Punjab). They identified carbonized remains of 17 crop plants, four spices and condiments, 11 wild and cultivated fruits, and one dye-plant:

Cereals

Rice (*Oryza sativa*), two kinds of barley (*Hordeum vulgare* emend. Bowden; *Hordeum vulgare* Bowden var. *nudum*) wheat (*Triticum*, jowar millet (*Sorghum bicolor* Moench).

Pulses

Chickpea (*Cicer arietinum*), field pea (*Pisum arvense*), lentil (*Lens culinaris* Medik), grass pea (*Lathyrus sativus*), green gram (*Vigna radiata* Wilczek), black gram (*Vigna mungo* Hepper), cowpea (*Vigna unguiculata* Walp.), horse gram (*Dolichos biflorus*).

Oil seeds

Field Brassica (*Brassica juncea* Czern and Coss.), sesame (*Sesamum indicum, til*).

Fibre-crops

Cotton (*Gossypium arboreum* G. *herbaceum*).

Spices and condiments

Fenugreek (*Trigonella foenum-graecum*), coriander (*Coriandrum sativum*), cumin (*Cuminum cyminum*), black pepper (*Piper nigrum*).

Fruits

Date (*Phoenix* sp.), *anwala* (*Emblica officinalis*), *jharberi* (*Zizyphus nummularia*), custard apple (*Annona squamosa*, sitaphal), walnut (*Juglans regia*), almond (*Prunus amygdalus* Batsch), grape/raisin (*Vitis vinifera*), *jamun* (*Syzygium cumini*), *phalsa* (*Grewia*), *reetha* (*Sapindus* cf. *emarginatus* Vahl./*trifoliatus*/ *laurifolius* Vahl.), *harra* (*Terminalia chebula* Retz).

Dye plant

Henna (*Lawsonia inermis, mehndi*)

Various weeds and wild plant species (28 types) were also identified. The results of this study give interesting details about the agricultural economy and food habits of the people who lived at Sanghol in the early centuries CE. Several of the plants are known from earlier cultural contexts in the area, showing a broad continuity in agricultural practices from protohistoric times. However, there are also some new additions. People were using spices in their food. It can only be speculated what henna was used for. The discovery of seeds of custard apple in such an early context is especially intriguing, as it is generally believed this fruit was introduced into India from South America by the Portuguese in the 16th century.

Source Saraswat and Pokharia, 1997–98

have been excavated vertically, giving a tiny glimpse of what they hold; a much greater number have not been excavated at all. The archaeological literature often identifies the periods or levels of occupation at sites according to dynastic labels, e.g., Indo-Greek, Shunga, Kushana, or Satavahana. This should at most be understood as a convenient shorthand for broad chronological phases, but can be misleading. For instance, the term 'Shunga' is often used for levels at a site where Shunga rule never prevailed. (For a collation of the archaeological data, see Chakrabarti, 1995: 170–262; 2006: 322–48.)

Certain questions link the subject of this chapter with the discussion in Chapter 7. What was the impact of Maurya rule and to what extent was interaction with the Maurya state an impetus to 'secondary state formation' in these areas? Secondary state formation is the emergence of states which have the model of already existing states before them, and which emerge as a result of interaction with already existent ('pristine') states. While the Maurya impact cannot be discounted, neither should it be given undue emphasis. The long-term development of urban centres required and involved an expansion in agricultural production, developments in specialized crafts, and wider and more intensive and extensive trade networks.

Cities of the north-west

The site of Pushkalavati, one of the important cities of this period, is identified with the mounds at Charsada, spread out over some 4 sq miles. Pushkalavati is known as Peucelaotis or Proclais in Graeco-Roman accounts. Arrian mentions it as a place where Philip had to station a Macedonian garrison due to its revolt against Alexander. The city seems to have been important in the Indo-Greek period, but declined somewhat in the Kushana period due to the increasing eminence of Purushapura (modern Peshawar). Nevertheless, it continued to be a major centre of trade. The occupation at Bala Hisar mound at Charsada goes back to the 6th century BCE. By the 4th century BCE, the settlement had grown and was protected by mud fortifications and a ditch.

Aerial photography at the Shaikhan mound at Charsada revealed a city with a rectangular plan, parallel streets, and blocks of houses, dominated by a large circular structure, probably a Buddhist *stupa*. Excavations indicated occupation from the mid-2nd century BCE to the mid-3rd century CE. Drains, refuse pits, and cesspools of a wide street were identified. While the earlier houses were made of stone diaper masonry (a style of

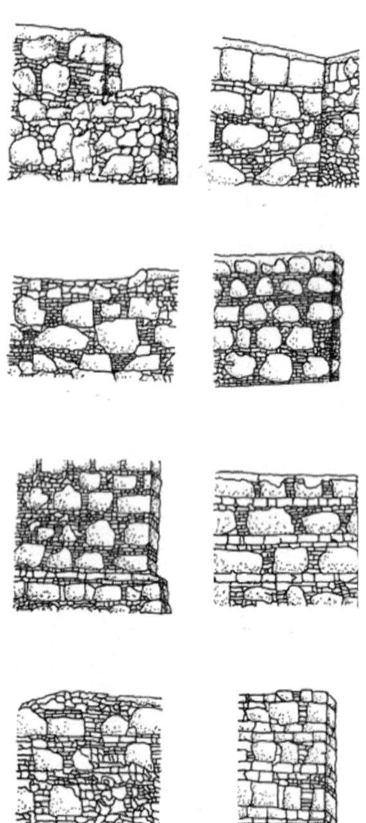

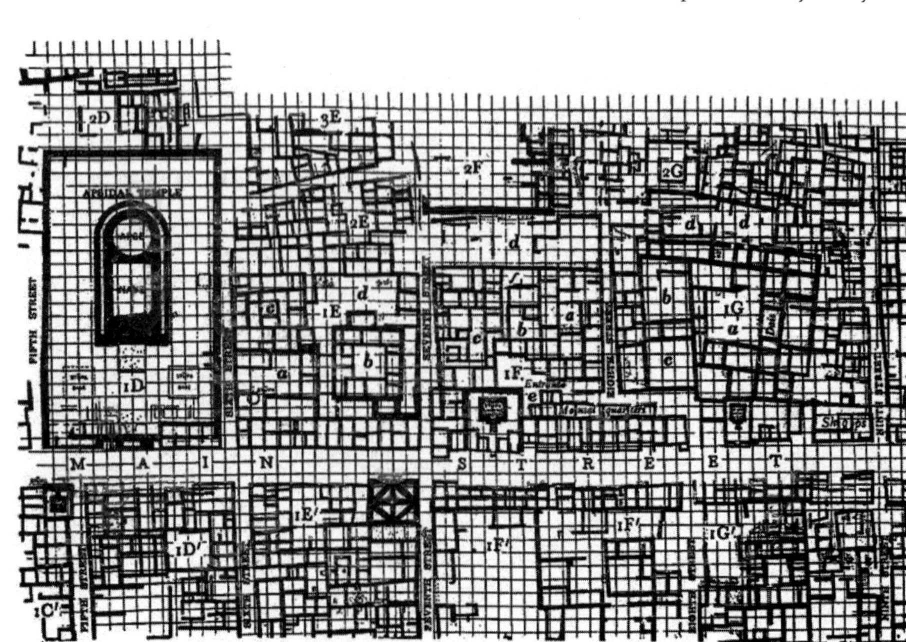

Figure 8.1 Sirkap: stone masonry ranging from the 1st century BCE to the medieval period (left); plan of the apsidal temple and neighbouring block (right) (after Marshall, 1951)

masonry in which spaces between large stone blocks are separated by flat, thin pieces of stone), those of the Kushana phase were made of mud-brick. A room with a fireplace in the middle was identified. A house consisting of a courtyard with rooms built on three sides was also unearthed. The name 'Haradakha' was engraved on the pedestal of a relic casket found in this house; perhaps this was the name of its current or past owner. The courtyard had a bathing area connected to the street by a stone drain. The house was renovated many times, and a shrine with a Buddha figure was added in the last phase of renovation.

The political upheavals and cultural influences of the time were more than evident at Taxila (Marshall, 1951). Here, a new city was laid out in the early 2nd century BCE at the site of Sirkap, to the north-east of the Bhir mound. Although the basic layout of the site seems to have remained more or less the same throughout, little is known about the Indo-Greek phase at Sirkap and most of the remains unearthed in the course of excavations belong to the subsequent Shaka–Parthian phase. The city was marked by grid planning, with streets and structures laid out in an orderly chessboard pattern. Excavations revealed seven occupational levels, ranging from the pre-Indo-Greek to the Shaka–Parthian phase. In the 2nd century BCE, the settlement was located entirely in the plains, and had a mud fortification wall. In the 1st century BCE, it seems to have shifted southwards to incorporate the spurs of the Hathial hills. In this phase, the periphery of the city was almost 5 km long, the entire distance being lined by a stone wall with bastions at regular intervals. The northern gateway was massive and probably two-storeyed. It had four guardrooms on the outer face and was associated with two wells.

The main street divided the city of Sirkap into two parts. The structures included houses, occasionally with a few small *stupas* in between; at least two shrines were also identified. The houses were made of rubble masonry plastered with mud. Most of them were quite spacious (an average of 1,395 sq m) and consisted of rooms arranged around one or more courtyards. One especially large house had 4 courtyards and over 30 rooms. Jewellery and metal artefacts suggest that rich people lived in this section of the city. Rooms opening out onto the main street may have been shops. Marshall identified a structural complex in the south-eastern part of the excavated area at Sirkap as a palace.

Towards the end of the 1st century CE, the Kushanas established a new city at Taxila at the site of Sirsukh, about a mile north-east of Sirkap. Very little excavation work has been carried out here. A section of the stone rubble fortification wall has been identified, with semi-circular bastions at regular intervals. Inside the fortified area, there were two open courts with attached rooms, apparently part of a large building.

Other cities mentioned in texts include Sagala or Sakala (identified with modern Sialkot) in the Punjab plains. This was the capital of the Indo-Greek king Menander and an important city on the trade routes. There is little archaeological data on the settlement of Purushapura (identified with Peshawar), apart from the excavation of the relic *stupa* at Shah-ji-ki-dheri, attributed to the reign of Kanishka. Greek historians refer to an important port called Patala in the Sindh delta, but although it has tentatively been identified with Bahmanabad, this is far from certain.

The Indo-Gangetic divide and the upper Ganga valley

Remains belonging to *c*. 200 BCE–300 CE have been found at many sites in the Indo-Gangetic divide and the upper Ganga valley. Sunet (ancient Sunetra) in Ludhiana district in Punjab has given evidence of occupation from the late Harappan phase onwards. Period IV at this site belonged to *c*. 200 BCE–300 CE. This revealed a burnt-brick house of this period with a courtyard in the middle, two rooms at the back, and what seem to be a kitchen, bathroom, and a room for storing grain. Traces of stairs suggest it was

Hastinapura: Ring wells

two-storeyed, and there were elaborate provisions for drainage. On three sides of this house, there were remains of mud huts, which may have been servants' quarters. Sunet has also yielded a hoard of 30,000 Yaudheya coin moulds, and lots of seals and sealings. Another site in the Punjab which has remains of this period is Sanghol in Ludhiana district. Here, a *stupa* belonging to the early centuries CE and 117 sculptures belonging to the Mathura school of art were discovered.

Agroha in Hissar district (Haryana) had an early historical occupation, and some brick structures described as belonging to the 3rd–4th centuries have been found here. At Karna-ka-Qila, Period I belonged to the NBPW phase, while Period II showed several structural phases belonging to the early centuries CE.

At Hastinapura (in Meerut district, UP), Period IV belonged to the *c.* 2nd century BCE–late 3rd century CE. The pottery consisted of wheel-turned red ware, sometimes with a slip. There were bowls with incurved rims, spouted basins, button-knobbed lids, ink-pot-type lids, bottle-necked sprinklers, and miniature vases. Much of the pottery had stamped and incised designs such as fish, leaves, flowers, *svastikas*, *triratnas*, loops, circles, and other geometric patterns. Some of the pots found in the upper levels had designs painted on in black. The settlement showed an element of planning. Seven structural sub-phases were identified. The houses were all made of burnt brick. One ring well was excavated. The large number of artefacts included iron objects (nails, axes/adzes, sickle, pan, etc.), copper objects (including antimony rods, pins, and a bell), a stone rotary quern, carved ivory handle, and fine handmade and moulded terracotta figurines. The humped bull occurred frequently among the terracotta figurines; there were also wheels, carts, and votive tanks. A terracotta torso of the *bodhisattva* Maitreya was found in the upper levels. The rings and beads (of carnelian, jasper, and terracotta) showed a high quality of workmanship. Two inscribed potsherds and a seal were found. Coins included those of the rulers of Mathura and the Yaudheyas, and there were also imitations of coins of the Kushana king Vasudeva.

In the cultural sequence at the Purana Qila in Delhi, Periods II and III are dated the 2nd–1st centuries BCE and 1st–3rd centuries CE respectively, and reflect urban prosperity. Initially, houses were made of quartzite rubble set in mud mortar. Later houses were made of mud-brick and burnt brick. House floors were generally made of rammed earth and were sometimes paved with mud-bricks. The rich range of artefacts included incised and stamped red ware. Compared to earlier levels, the quantity, quality, and range of

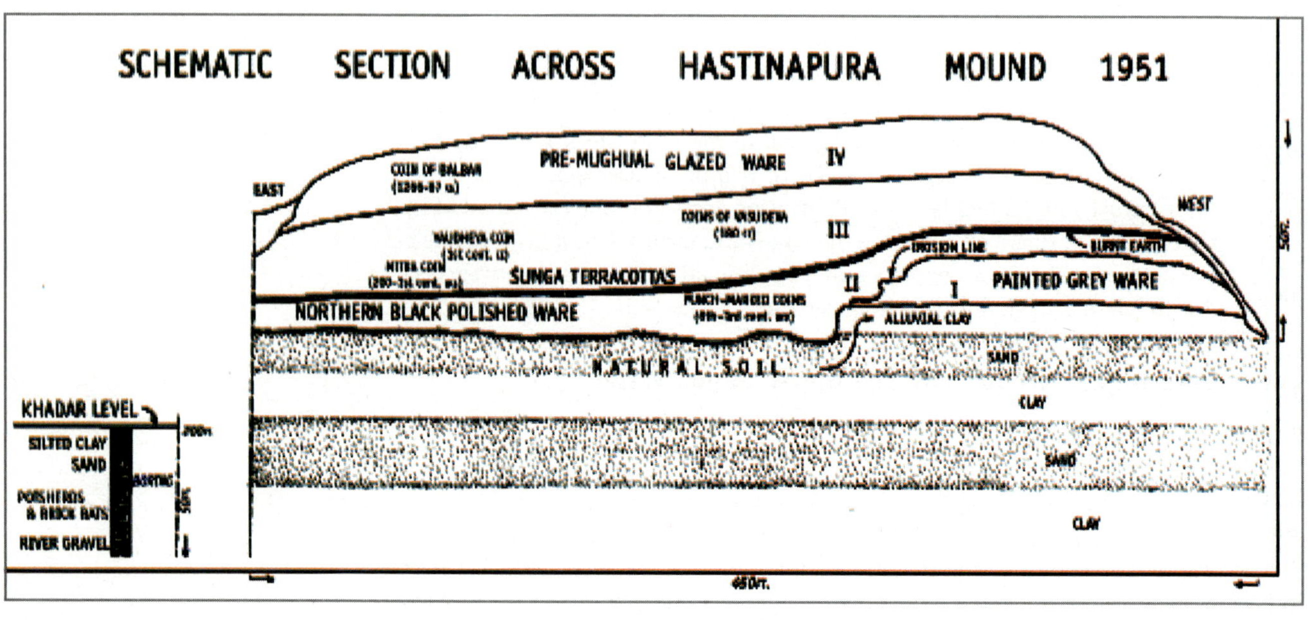

Drawing of excavated section of the mound. (after B. B. Lal, [1954–54]: 12)

terracottas was exceptionally rich. There were animal and human figurines, beads, skin rubbers, fragments of a votive tank, and crucibles. Several terracotta plaques depicted couples, *yaksha–yakshi* pairs, female figures, a female lute player, and elephant riders. Other discoveries included bone points and a small piece of an ivory handle. A seal and several sealings bore the names of various individuals (e.g., Patihaka, Svatiguta, Usasena, and Thiya) in the Brahmi script. A few copper coins of the Kushanas and Yaudheyas were also discovered. Occupational levels and artefacts belonging to the period *c.* 200 BCE–300 CE were found at Mandoli and Bhorgarh in Delhi as well.

As mentioned in an earlier chapter, the NBPW Period IV at Atranjikhera is divided into four sub-phases—IVA, IVB, IVC, and IVD. In Periods IVC (*c.* 350–200 BCE) and IVD (*c.* 200–50 BCE), the settlement grew into a town. There was an increase in building activity and the use of burnt brick. The remains of brick walls, floors and drains, barns, a granary, and terracotta ring wells were discovered. The fortifications seem to have been constructed in Period IVC and underwent four stages of strengthening and renovation. The important structural remains of Period IVD included an apsidal temple associated with a broken Gaja-Lakshmi (the goddess Lakshmi flanked by elephants) plaque. The site seems to have been exposed to flooding several times.

Mathura was an important centre of craft activity (especially textiles) and trade, and was also a religious centre associated with Buddhism, Jainism, and early Hinduism. It also seems to have been a political centre. Period III in the Mathura sequence, dated 2nd–late 1st century BCE, shows an accentuation of urban features. The ceramic assemblage was dominated by a red ware, with some grey ware as well. There was a beginning and a gradual increase in the number of burnt brick structures. The terracottas and other craft items were marked by stylistic sophistication. There were many inscribed coins, seals, and sealings. In Period IV, dated the 1st–3rd centuries CE, the fortification wall, which had fallen into disuse in the previous period, was strengthened, enlarged, and supplemented with an inner fortification. The red wares of this period included pots with painted and stamped designs. There was a more limited quantity of fine red polished ware, including sprinklers. A similar picture of increasing urban complexity and sophistication comes from nearby Sonkh.

Excavations at Ayodhya (Ayodhya district, UP) yielded structural remains and antiquities of this period. In the late NBPW phase, there were houses made of burnt brick and terracotta ring wells. A grey terracotta figure of a Jaina saint, assigned to the 4th/3rd century BCE, is among the earliest Jaina images found so far. In later levels, there were punch-marked coins, uninscribed cast coins, inscribed copper coins, and a number of terracotta sealings. The discovery of rouletted ware suggests trade links with eastern India, where this type of pottery occurs in large quantities. The report of the 2002–03 excavations at Ayodhya lists a number of artefacts found at *c.* 2nd–1st centuries BCE (Period II) levels, including black-slipped, red, and grey ware. Terracotta objects included human and animal figurines, a bangle fragment, ball, wheel, and a broken sealing with only the Brahmi letter *sa* readable, a stone saddle quern and lid fragment, a glass bead, a bone hairpin, an engraver, and ivory dice. A stone-and-brick structure was also identified. The levels belonging to the 1st–3rd centuries CE (Period III) yielded red ware, human and animal terracotta figurines, a fragment of a bangle, a terracotta votive tank, a glass bead, and copper antimony rod. Stone and brick structures were found in this and later periods. A massive brick structure running into 22 courses was identified.

Purana Qila: walls of different period; terracotta plaque

Purana Qila: Stamped and incised pot-sherds; anthropomorphic pot

At Sringaverapura (Prayagraj district, UP), the settlement reached its maximum size in the 2nd century BCE. An elaborate brick tank complex belonging to the late centuries BCE was excavated. B. B. Lal (1993) suggests that the tank, which shows remarkable engineering skill, was probably geared towards providing potable water for the expanding settlement, the eastern part of which was no longer close to the Ganga. Water was brought into the tank from the river by means of a channel. There is also a late Kushana period structural complex, consisting of two sections separated by a corridor. One of the rooms yielded a small copper bowl with remains of seeds and pulses.

Reference was made in an earlier chapter to Erdosy's study (1988) of settlements in the Allahabad (now Prayagraj) district (UP) and to the features of Periods I and II. Here we will look at Periods III and IV, which were initially dated *c.* 350–100 BCE and *c.* 100–300 CE respectively. Subsequently, Erdosy revised the dates for Period III to 400–100 BCE, which he thought corresponded more closely to available radiocarbon dates for the mid- and late NBPW phase and to the later date for the *parinibbana* of the Buddha suggested by Bechert. In Period III, there was a continuation of trends visible in Period II. The new features included the spread of settlements to the forested upland areas located far away from the riverbanks, and the appearance of a new (fifth) tier of settlements, represented by four sites ranging in size from 3.46 to 5.15 ha. A network of towns emerged, at least two of which are known from Period II. Kaushambi was the largest site and there were seven other towns in the 19–50 ha range. These included Kara, Sringaverapura, Jhusi, Bhita, Reh, Lachchhagiri, and Tusaran Bihar. Major settlements were located along rivers, separated by an average distance of 31 km. The general pattern is of a rapid expansion of rural and urban centres, with a clear settlement hierarchy. Kaushambi developed into a major fortified city in this period. It is estimated that the occupied area of 150 ha within the defence walls may have supported a population of about 24,000 people. There were also mounds marking settlements just outside the defence walls, covering about 50 ha, and it has been estimated that the population, including these areas, may have been about 32,000.

In Prayagraj district, Period IV (100 BCE–300 CE) saw a continuation of the five-fold settlement hierarchy and a peak of urban prosperity. There was a steady expansion of the occupied area and population of Kaushambi. Some 200 ha were occupied within the fortified area, supporting a population of about 32,000 people. The defences were strengthened and the occupation outside the walls seems to have declined. Nevertheless, the total occupied area grew to about 226 ha and the population to about 36,000. Arrowheads and skeletons found at *c.* 2nd century BCE levels point to war and destruction. Outside the eastern gate, the remains of a brick altar in the shape of an eagle flying to the south-east, associated with animal and human bones, including a skull, were found. G. R. Sharma (1960) suggested that this was an altar where the *purushamedha* (human sacrifice) was performed. The trend of expanding settlements in the upland areas continued. While the population of Kaushambi grew, in Kanpur district as a whole, there was a drastic slowing down of population growth and a deepening of the divide between cities and villages.

Indor Khera is a site in Bulandshahr district (UP), between the Kali Nadi and Ganga. Here, there is a mound 285 × 428, rising to a maximum height of 17 m (Menon and Verma, 2010a), where excavations revealed material remains from the early historic to the early medieval period. Among the important discoveries is a craft quarter in the north-western part of the site. The excavations shed valuable light on the technological, spatial, and social organization of crafts. At levels dated *c.* 200 BCE–500 CE, firing areas and artefacts such as anvils, socket stones, pottery stamps, bone engravers, and stone polishers were found. Also found were materials such as lumps, rolls, and pellets of clay and terracotta; sand deposits which may have been used for tempering pots; unbaked artefacts; waste or over-fired material; and defective objects. The discovery of all this within four adjacent houses suggests household workshops.

NEW DIRECTIONS IN RESEARCH | **Finding children in the archaeological record**

Children tend to remain invisible in history and archaeology. They appear fleetingly in descriptions of child burials and certain small objects interpreted as toys. Is it possible to recover the experiences and activities of children in ancient times through material remains? Archaeologists working on other parts of the world have tried to answer these questions. However, in India, the archaeology of childhood is a relatively new area. Against this background, Jaya Menon and Supriya Verma's attempt to find evidence of children playing and learning at the site of Indor Khera is significant.

In traditional societies, craft skills tend to be passed on within the family through oral instruction, demonstration, and training in practice. Ethnographic evidence indicates that while men tend to be the makers of pottery, their family members, including women and children, help in various ways, for instance, in procuring and preparing the clay and decorating and moving the vessels. The work of child novices who are learning the craft can be identified through features such as errors and finger marks.

The 2007 excavations in the north=-western part of Indor Khera revealed a craft quarter and a potter's house belonging to the period *c.* 200 BCE to 300 CE. Certain artefacts (44 in number) found in this house suggest the presence and activities of children learning the craft. These include miniature vessels made from poorly-kneaded clay. Most of these were hand-modelled and used the pinching technique, which is one of the simplest techniques used by children when they are starting to learn clay modelling. Many of the vessels were simple bowls, the easiest form to make, which children would have been taught to make first. These vessels were asymmetrical in shape, with clumsily made rims and uneven edges. Crack marks were the result of inadequate drying. The vessels do not seem to have been carefully fired; some of them were left unfired. (Children would not have done the firing; this would have been done by adults.) The miniature vessels show different levels of skill, indicating the handiwork of children at different learning levels. They may have been made by children between 5 and 8 years old whose hands were small, whose motor skills were not fully developed, and who were being taught the craft by elders in the family.

Also found were small lumps of clay (19 in number), some flattened, others with depressions in them. These seem to have been pieces given to younger boys and girls to play with while they watched the older children learning and the adults working.

This study indicates the potential of using material evidence to identify children as producers of material culture.

Source Menon and Verma, 2010b

Indor Khera: archaeologists at work; miniature vessels (from top)

Red spouted vessel and sprinkler from 'Kushana–Gupta' levels, Sarnath

The middle and lower Ganga valley and Eastern India

At Saheth-Maheth (ancient Shravasti), Period II belonged to the late centuries CE. The mud-and-brick rampart belonged to this period. At the site of what is believed to be the Jetavana monastery, excavations revealed *stupas*, monasteries, and shrines going back to the Maurya period. One of the *stupas* revealed a relic casket containing pieces of bone, gold leaf, and a silver punch-marked coin. A rectangular tank and a monastic complex belonging to the Kushana period were also identified.

Period II at Rajghat is dated *c.* 200 BCE–1st centuries CE. In the earlier structural phase of this period, there was a house consisting of two rooms, a vestibule, bathroom, and a well. A terracotta ring well was found in the later phase. Period III, dated from the 1st to the end of the 3rd century CE, represents the most prosperous phase of the site.

Khairadih is a site on the Sarayu river in Ballia district (eastern UP). It yielded remains of the early centuries CE, such as a street, lanes, and structures including a two-roomed house and an underground structure. At Ganwaria in Basti district (eastern UP), Periods III and IV have been labelled as belonging to the Shunga and Kushana periods respectively.

At Basarh (ancient Vaishali) in Muzaffarpur district Bihar, the excavated sections included fortifications. Period I belonged to the 2nd century BCE, Period II to about the 1st century BCE, and Period III was labelled 'Kushana–Gupta' (3rd–4th centuries CE). A tank, generally identified as the coronation tank of the Lichchhavis, was identified. The coins and terracottas found in association with the tank suggest that it was built in the 2nd century BCE. At Katragarh, also in Muzaffarpur district, there is a 'Shunga period' fortification, in which three structural phases were identified—the ramparts were made of burnt brick in the first and third phases, while in the second phase, the walls had a massive mud core and a moat.

Lauriya-Nandangarh in Champaran district of Bihar has a large, terraced *stupa* dated between the 1st century BCE and 2nd century CE. There are also indications of fortifications. Balirajgarh in Darbhanga district has remains of a large, fortified settlement. The excavations here concentrated on the defence wall made of mud-brick, which seems to belong to the 2nd century BCE.

In Bhagalpur district, at the site of ancient Champa, the fortification was strengthened by a brick wall. Brick houses and a drain have been assigned to the Kushana–Gupta phase. At Patna, there are remains of an apsidal shrine belonging to *c.* 100–300 CE.

A 3rd century BCE inscription identifies Mahasthangarh (in Bogra/Bagura district, Bangladesh) with Pundranagara, capital of ancient Pundravardhana. The site is about 185 ha and reveals occupation from the NBPW phase to the 12th/13 century CE. The early historical city consisted of an oblong area (5000 × 4500 ft) enclosed by massive fortifications, which in turn were bordered by a deep moat on three sides, the Karatoya river skirting the western and part of the northern edge. NBPW, and punch-marked and cast copper coins were among the artefacts found. Chakrabarti (2006: 324) draws attention to the trade connections between Wari Bateshwar and South-east Asia. He also suggests that the location of Mahasthan on the western bank of the Karatoya indicates multiple linkages via trade routes with the Barind and Bhagirathi sectors of West Bengal, the Bihar plains, Tibet, and the Brahmaputra valley of Assam. Assam may have been connected to south China via Myanmar.

The site of Bangarh in South Dinajpur district (West Bengal), on the banks of the Purnabhava river, has revealed a 1800 × 1000 ft settlement enclosed by fortifications and a moat on three sides. The five cultural phases range from the Maurya to the medieval period. The *c.* 200 BCE–300 CE phase was marked by urban prosperity. The earlier mud fortifications were replaced by brick ramparts. Houses made of burnt brick, and drains and cesspits were found. Bangarh is identified with Kotivarsha, an important administrative centre.

Other early historical sites in Bengal include Tamluk and Chandraketugarh. Tamluk (ancient Tamralipti) in Midnapur district, on the banks of the Rupnarayan river, was an

FURTHER DISCUSSION | **Chandraketugarh**

Panchachuda

Chandraketugarh, located in the Ganga delta, actually consists of a cluster of villages in 24 Parganas district of West Bengal, about 25 miles north-east of Kolkata. The villages include Berachampa (Dheuliya), Ranakhola, Ghorapota, Dhanpota, Chuprijhara, Singerati, Shanpukur, Jhikra, Mathbari, Hadipur, and Ghazitala. Artefacts similar to those found here occur in many other neighbouring villages as well. The name 'Chandraketugarh' comes from a local legend of a medieval king of this name.

In early historic times, Chandraketugarh was connected to the Ganga by the Vidyadhari river, and must have been an important centre of trade, and possibly also a political centre. It can perhaps be identified with the Gangaridae of Graeco-Roman accounts.

Due to the frequent chance discoveries of antiquities on or below the surface, Chandraketugarh was known to be an exceptionally rich archaeological site from the beginning of the 20th century. However, it has still not been adequately explored or excavated. In 1906, Tarak Nath Das and some other inhabitants of the area petitioned the government to explore the site. A. H. Longhurst of the Archaeological Survey of India visited the place in 1907 and described it as of little interest. R. D. Banerji made a visit in 1909 and reported on some of the finds. Between 1956–57 and 1967–68, the Ashutosh Museum of the University of Calcutta carried out excavations at five different sites at Chandraketugarh. The excavations revealed the remains of a mud rampart, probably going back to the 2nd century BCE, and some other structural remains.

A detailed report of the findings was never published. Some surface explorations were conducted at the site in 1967–68 and 1972–73.

The brief preliminary reports of the excavations do not give a clear or consistent stratigraphy of Chandraketugarh. The broad sequence, however, seems to be as follows (using broad dynastic labels for convenience):

Period I: pre-Maurya—*c*. 600–300 BCE
Period II: Maurya—*c*. 300–185 BCE
Period III: Shunga—*c*. 185 BCE–50 CE
Period IV: Kushana—*c*. 50–300 CE
Period V: Gupta—*c*. 300–500 CE
Period VI: post-Gupta—*c*. 500–750 CE
Period VII: Pala-Chandra-Sena—*c*. 750–1250 CE.

Various kinds of artefacts have been found at the site over the years, including coins, pottery, seals and sealings, and figurines made of ivory, wood, and bronze. There are some interesting inscriptions in a combination of Brahmi and Kharoshthi, mostly on pots, seals, and plaques. However, the site is best known for its large number of remarkable terracotta objects, most of which can be assigned to *c*. 200 BCE–300 CE. Chandraketugarh was obviously a major centre of terracotta craft.

Inamul Haque has given a detailed account and catalogue of 963 terracottas found at Chandraketugarh, including figurines and plaques. There were a great variety of representations of women, many of them ornamented with elaborate jewellery and associated with foliage and flowers. Some of them may have been *yakshi*s or goddesses. One of the recurring types is known as the *panchachuda*—a woman with emblematic hairpins, usually in the form of five weapons (sword, arrow, battleaxe, trident, and elephant goad) radiating out of her hair. These intriguing sets of hair ornaments sometimes appear on one side of the head, sometimes on both. Other figurines depict male figures, animals, winged human figures, fat dwarfs, carts, and rattles. Some plaques depict erotic scenes.

The terracottas are mostly brick red or reddish brown in colour, though a few are buff or grey. The early figurines are hand moulded, while later ones show the use of single and double moulds, which would have been convenient for mass production. It is not easy to assign precise dates to the terracottas. Few were found in the course of the excavations, and very few have been dated by the thermoluminescence method. They are often dated on the basis of style, but this can be problematic as the co-existence of different styles cannot be ruled out.

These beautiful, mass-produced terracottas were not the work of rural craftspersons making images for a village market. They were products of an urban milieu, catering to an urban clientele. They are not only important representatives of the crafts and aesthetics of their time, but also offer useful information on aspects of social life and religious practice.

Source Haque, 2001

Chandraketugarh terracottas

important port mentioned in Indian, Graeco-Roman, and Chinese sources. Here, the remains of Period II (3rd/2nd century BCE) and Period III (1st–2nd centuries CE) included a brick tank and some terracotta ring wells. Remains of the early centuries CE included burnt-brick structures, rouletted ware, fine terracotta figurines, coins, seals and sealings, beads, and evidence of writing in Brahmi, Kharoshthi, and possibly a mixture of the two scripts.

Other sites in Bengal include Kotasur (Birbhum district) on the banks of the Mayurakshi, which has revealed a fortified settlement. Pokhanna (Bankura disctrict) on the banks of the Damodar is another possible urban centre. Mangalkot (Burdwan district), at the confluence of the Kunur and Ajay rivers, seems to have been a large urban centre and has yielded a rich range of antiquities. Wari Bateshwar, located on an old course of the Brahmaputra, has given evidence of NBPW, rouletted ware, black-slipped ware, knobbed ware, and an ordinary dull red ware. Iron slag indicates iron smelting in the area. Certain types of beads are of special significance. Sandwiched glass beads were imported from Egypt and the Mediterranean, and the gold-foil glass beads may have come from Rome. The Indo-Pacific monochrome drawn glass beads were manufactured in the Tamil Nadu area and traded to various parts of South and South-east Asia.

In Odisha, excavations at Jaugada on the Rishikulya river revealed remains of an early historical settlement going back to at least the 3rd century BCE. It was surrounded by mud fortifications, beyond which was a ditch. Remains of bead making were found at the site. There is greater amount of information from the site of Sisupalgarh, which may represent the Tosali mentioned in Ashoka's inscriptions, or Kalinganagari, the capital of Kharavela's kingdom. Excavations indicate occupation from the 3rd century BCE to the 4th century CE. Excavations here revealed remains of a large, 1 sq km large planned city enclosed by a rampart, gateways, and moat; a monumental pillared structure and stone-lined ponds in the centre; and several residential buildings (Mohanty and Smith, 2009). No structural remains were found in Period I; there was only simple, plain pottery, mostly grey or red. The early part of Period II (*c.* 200 BCE–100 CE) was the most prosperous. Huge mud walls, a little over 10 m wide at the base and over 8 m high, punctuated with impressive gateways, guardrooms, passages, and watchtowers, were built in the beginning of the 2nd century BCE. Later, the mud walls were strengthened by adding a layer of stone gravel on top. Still later, two brick walls were built on top of this and the space in between was filled with mud and stone. The town was well planned, measuring 1 km on each side, and was more or less square shaped in plan. Houses were made of stone or brick, with two or three rooms and a large verandah in front. Streets were laid out systematically, crossing each other at right angles. The remains of a large pillared hall were found in the middle of the town. Artefacts of this phase included red ware, some with a bright polished surface, and BRW. Terracotta earrings, iron implements, and weapons (including nails, spikes, sickles, and daggers) and beads of semi-precious stone, were also found. In the later part of Period II (*c.* 100 CE), the town showed signs of decline. The pottery of this phase was less impressive and consisted mostly of a coarse and dull-looking red ware with crude decorations. Other finds included glass bangles, a silver and copper coin, and several terracotta earrings. Clay bullae (medallions) with designs of animals with human heads suggested Roman contact. Period III (*c.* 200–350 CE) reflected a further decline. The pottery was red or yellowish-red, coarse, and not too well made. Coins and terracotta ear ornaments were also found. The discovery of two coin moulds suggests that coins were minted here. Radhanagar is another important early historic site in Odisha.

Central and Western India

The site of Rairh in Rajasthan has yielded remains ranging from the 3rd/2nd century BCE to the 2nd century CE (and later times as well). Terracotta ring wells and walls of structures were excavated. Remains going back to the 3rd/2nd century BCE have also been found at Sambhar. Nagari has given evidence of occupation dating from *c.* 400 BCE.

In Central India, Besnagar, located at the confluence of the Bes and Betwa rivers, represents the western capital of the Shungas. It was also an important point on the trade routes connecting North India with the Deccan and the western ports. The pillar with the inscription of Heliodorus was found here; excavations in the vicinity revealed the remains of what must have been a Vasudeva temple.

At Ujjain, Period IIIA was dated *c.* 200 BCE–500 CE. The pottery was mostly a red ware of medium fabric. There were lots of beads of semi-precious stones, terracotta, bone, and ivory; bangles of terracotta, glass, shell, and copper; pendants of stone and terracotta; ear ornaments of terracotta, glass, and shell; terracotta gamesmen and skin rubbers; antimony rods made of copper and ivory; ivory combs and hairpins; and clay bullae moulded from Greek or Roman coins. Dice made of terracotta and ivory were found. There were terracotta figurines of humans and animals, votive tanks, and stone images of deities. Coins of the Kshatrapas, Kushanas, and later dynasties were found, as was a coin mould of the Roman emperor Augustus Hadrianus (117–34 CE). There is evidence of bead manufacture at the site, especially of those made of chalcedony. There was also a sealing engraved on the flat, circular knob of a terracotta casket with a Prakrit inscription in Brahmi letters of the 1st century CE.

Remains of the early centuries CE have been found at Pawaya (ancient Padmavati), at the confluence of the Sindhu and Parvati rivers. This site is well known for its variety of terracottas and fine stone sculptures, including images of the *yaksha* Manibhadra and a *naga* figure. A few capitals, including a palm capital of the 1st century BCE associated with the deity Samkarshana, have also been found.

P. K. Basant (2012) has analyzed the remains from the Buddhist site of Sanchi in the larger context of the settlement history of the Malwa region. This includes longer-term interactions between hunter-gatherers, pastoral nomadists, and farmers; the emergence and expansion of city life; and the networks connecting Malwa with other parts of the subcontinent.

Cities and Towns of the Deccan and Andhra

In the Deccan, the transition to the early historical urban phase has to be reconstructed on the basis of archaeology alone, as textual evidence is unavailable. Aloka Parasher (1992) has pointed out that historians often treat the Deccan as a passage between North and South India and explain cultural developments in this region in terms of the diffusion of civilizational traits from elsewhere. The impact of Maurya rule and Indo-Roman trade on urbanization in the Deccan have been over-emphasized, and insufficient attention has been paid to the internal processes of cultural change. Further, within the Deccan, there has been an undue focus on certain areas, especially places where Ashoka's inscriptions or Buddhist structures have been found, and a neglect of other areas that have been treated as marginal or peripheral.

The Deccan can be broken up into various sub-regions—northern, central, eastern, and southern. Parasher highlights the diversity of cultural processes and cultural sequences between the southern and central Deccan, and among sites within these regions. It is interesting to note that in the southern Deccan (with a few exceptions such as Brahmagiri), sites with prominent neolithic–chalcolithic or early iron age megalithic occupation do not have impressive early historical remains. Hallur is a good example of this. Conversely too, a significant number of large early historical sites do not have any significant prior occupation, either of the neolithic–chalcolithic or the early iron age. Examples of this from the southern Deccan are Chandravalli, Banavasi, Vadagaon-Madhavpur, and Sannati.

In the central Deccan, there is no direct evidence of Maurya presence, but early historical sites such as Peddabankur, Kotalingala, Dhulikatta, Polakonda, and Kadambapur have given evidence of pre-Satavahana period occupation, not always associated with megalithic remains. Kotalingala is a 50 ha mound located at the confluence of the Paddavagu and Godavari rivers. The ancient settlement was surrounded by a mud fort. There were four occupational levels, the second of which belonged to the early centuries CE. Many pre-Satavahana and Satavahana coins were found at the site. The mound at Dhulikatta (in Peddapalli district, Telangana) on the right bank of the Hussanivagu river was about 18 ha. Here, there was a fortified town enclosed by a mud fortification wall with gateways. A palace complex was identified in the middle of the mound. There were also regular residential structures and granaries. A Buddhist *stupa* situated nearby belonged to the 3rd century BCE. Peddabankur is a 30 ha mound, 10 km east of Dhulikatta. The site was not fortified. Several residential structures made of brick and mud-over-stone-rubble foundations were found here. There were cisterns, wells, soak pits, and drains. Two structural phases were identified—Period I was dated *c.* 250–100 BCE and Period II *c.* 50 BCE–200 CE. The discovery of several thousand Satavahana coins suggests that a mint was located here. A gold coin of Augustus was also found. Some 22 wells and the remains of a blacksmith's workshop were the other major finds. The site of Kondapur was unfortified, with houses made of brick or rubble. This seems to have been a bead and terracotta making centre. The religious structures included a *stupa*, *vihara*, and two *chaityas* (shrines).

The discovery of a large number of Roman coins and imitation bullae at all these sites indicates that the economy of the Deccan was heavily dependent on trade. Another important feature is that all these sites have yielded plenty of iron artefacts and evidence of iron working. At Dhulikatta, a crucible of iron (15 cm in diameter) was found along with charred wood, leafy material, mud, and large terracotta cakes. This paraphernalia seems to have been connected with iron smelting. At Peddabankur, there was evidence of a terracotta forge, about 20 cm in diameter. The working floor of the forge was embedded with pieces of iron slag and finished iron artefacts such as nails, a sickle, knife, and ring. This seems to have been a blacksmith's workshop.

Bhokardan in Aurangabad district, Maharashtra, has been identified with ancient Bhogavardhana. This city was located on the ancient route from Ujjayini to Pratishthana, and its inhabitants are mentioned in donative inscriptions at Central Indian Buddhist sites such as Sanchi and Bharhut. Two periods of occupation were identified in the course of excavations (Deo, 1974). Period Ia belonged to the pre-Satavahana or early Satavahana phase and Period Ib to the late Satavahana phase. Period II was associated with the post-Satavahana period. The habitation remains of Period Ia included ash pits, a hearth, bathing area, and lime and stone floors rammed with earth. Period Ib saw the most intensive building activity at the site and improvements in the quality of structures. Traces of foundations, brick walls, floors, post-holes, fallen roofs, and a ring well were discovered. There were community hearths; a regular hearth and the remains of a kitchen were also identified.

The artefacts discovered in the Bhokardan excavations included punch-marked coins, Satavahana and Kshatrapa coins made of copper, and a few terracotta seals and sealings. The pottery of Period Ia included black and red burnished ware, coarse black and red ware, coarse red ware, red-slipped ware, and crude handmade red wares. The pottery of Period Ib included coarse red ware, a ware with a red wash, red-slipped ware, red polished ware, tan-slipped ware, drab black ware, black burnished ware, BRW, unburnished BRW, and micaceous red-slipped ware. Almost 2,000 beads of various materials were found. A large proportion were made of terracotta, followed by glass, shell, and faience. Agate, carnelian, chalcedony, crystal, and jasper were some of the semi-precious stones used. There were a few jade, lapis, and ivory beads. Nodules of semi-precious stones, unfinished beads, and bead moulds indicate a thriving bead industry. Other important crafts included the making of shell bangles and ivory work. Hundreds of terracotta objects, including human and animal figurines, were found at the site. Lots of iron and copper artefacts and a few lead ones were discovered. The iron objects included kitchen utensils and equipment, tools, weapons, and carpentry items. Copper objects included ornaments, pots, fish hooks, and antimony rods. Clay bullae, two pieces of **amphorae**, and a piece of red ware that seems to be an imitation of red polished ware reflect a connection with Indo-Mediterranean contacts. The analysis of the plant remains at the site revealed a variety of cereals and legumes. The bone remains were of 17 species, including human bones and those of wild and domesticated animals.

Important information on the material culture of the people living in the Deccan during this period comes from the site of Adam in Nagpur district, Maharashtra (Nath, 1999). A hoard of Roman gold coins was found here, and subsequent explorations revealed an ancient fortified settlement and a mud *stupa*. The 1988–92 excavations revealed a five-fold cultural sequence, ranging from the mesolithic phase to *c*. 300 CE. A large proportion of the antiquities belonged to the early centuries CE. Six thousand coins of the Satavahana period were found, including 86 lead portrait coins. The discovery of coin moulds suggests that this was a mint town. A large number of seals and sealings were also discovered, some with inscriptions giving the names, titles, and offices of individuals. One of the sealings bore the name of the Assaka (Ashmaka) *janapada*. An interesting discovery was a hoard of over 70 sealings with an hour-glass-shaped design, found stacked on the floor of a house, surrounded by an ash deposit. These sealings were fired but never used.

The large number of terracotta objects found at Adam included representations of humans and animals, votive tanks, spindles, wheels, and skin rubbers. Bone objects included points, engravers, dice, and a beautifully carved comb. Ivory objects included pendants with incised designs. Thousands of beads of clay, glass, stone, faience, and metal were found. The stones used included carnelian, agate, chert, quartz, jasper, chalcedony, and amethyst. The discovery of bead polishers and many beads in different designs and in different stages of preparation shows that bead manufacturing was an important craft. Metal artefacts included those made of iron, copper, silver, and lead. The repertoire of iron objects included types such as spearhead, arrowhead, sword, dagger, hoe, ploughshare, axe, sickle, knife, nail, and ring. The discovery of a few gold beads and pendants and the stone moulds of a goldsmith point to another important craft. Cubical stone weights, querns, mullers, and a sculpted fragment of a human face have also been found. The rich range and quantity of the artefacts found at Adam is striking.

In Andhra, one of the most important sites is Nagarjunakonda (Guntur district, AP) in the Krishna valley, surrounded by offshoots of the Nallamalai hills (Sarkar and Misra, 1972; Soundararajan et al., 2006). This was the capital of the Ikshvaku dynasty. Remains of a fortified citadel were identified on the summit of the Peddakundelagutta hill. Near the eastern gateway, there were some barracks, stables, and a stone cistern. Close to the western gateway were what appear to be some ritualistic structures, including a four-tiered stepped tank connected with drains and passages. The discovery of bones (perhaps of a horse and goat) outside the tank led to it being labelled an *ashvamedha* tank. To the south of this was a smaller two-tiered tank, shaped roughly like a tortoise. Located nearby were remains of structures that may have been palace buildings. The residential area of ordinary people lay to the east of the citadel, where the remains of streets, lanes, and houses were found. Houses had large storage jars arranged in rows. The paraphernalia (including terracotta crucibles, a touchstone, and oblong moulds for designs for ornaments) found in one of the houses suggested that it was the house or workshop of a goldsmith. A stadium-like complex associated with steps leading up to it on all sides and a pavilion to the west was another important discovery. The site also yielded remains of a canal. On the river side, there was a cremation ground, a stepped *ghat*, and several temples (about 18), including one dedicated to the god Karttikeya. Most of the published information about Nagarjunakonda concerns the various Buddhist *stupas*, shrines, and monasteries found scattered over the site.

Amaravati is another major site in the same district. It is supposed to mark the site of ancient Dharanikota. A large Buddhist establishment was located here (see Shimada, 2013). The six occupational periods ranged from the 2nd century BCE to the 2nd/3rd century CE. Epigraphic evidence suggests that the origins of the monastic establishment may date to the Maurya period. The citadel was surrounded by a massive mud fortification. Soak-pits and drains were identified. There were remains of a navigational channel and a huge wharf, both of which underwent strengthening and embellishment in the various structural phases. The artefacts included a goldsmith's mould, glass bangles, and ear-rings of great variety, probably imports. Rouletted ware and terra sigillata were also found.

See p. 490 for details of rouletted ware and terra sigillata

Cities of the far south

The first phase of urbanism in South India is generally associated with the period *c.* 300 BCE–300 CE, although recent evidence suggests earlier beginnings. Graeco-Roman sources mention many towns and cities and use the term *emporium* for coastal towns associated with foreign trade. The Tamil word *pattinam* means port, as in Kaverippumpattinam (also known as Puhar). Sangam poems describe the urban centres of early historical South India. However, archaeological evidence does not match the literary descriptions of cities. This is partly due to inadequate excavations. Some sites such as Madurai and Kanchipuram have been continuously occupied till the present, and this has made horizontal excavations impossible. Champakalakshmi (1996: 117–40) has given a comprehensive account of the urban centres of early historical South India. A few of these centres are discussed below.

Vanji or Kuravur/Karur was the capital of the Chera dynasty. As many as 11 Sangam poets hailed from this place. It can be identified with Karur on the banks of

Map 8.3 Cities of early historical South India (after Champakalakshmi, 1996)

the Amaravati river (a tributary of the Kaveri), in Tiruchirapalli district. Literary, archaeological, numismatic, and epigraphic evidence confirm the status of Vanji/Kuruvur as a political centre as well as an important centre of crafts and trade. Excavations at the site yielded BRW (some with graffiti marks), pieces of Roman amphorae, and locally made rouletted ware. A Roman copper coin belonging to the reign of Claudius, was also found. Roman coins have been found in larger quantities at other places nearby, such as Vellavur and in the bed of the Amaravati river. The discovery of hundreds of copper coins with Chera symbols such as the bow and arrow, as well as several silver portrait coins, indicate that a Chera mint may have been located here. Literary sources refer to jewel making as an important craft of Karuvur. This is confirmed by the discovery of finger rings with various motifs carved on them (including those in the Graeco-Roman style) and legends giving the names of various individuals. Not far from Karur, there are early Tamil-Brahmi donative inscriptions at Pugalur and Arachchalur, recording donations made by Chera rulers as well as craftspeople and merchants; one of the merchants is specifically associated with Karur.

Muchiri—the Muziris of classical accounts—was the foremost port in the Chera kingdom. The *Periplus* speaks of cargo-laden ships landing here from Arabia and Egypt, and gives long lists of imports and exports. Pliny, on the other hand, states that due to the danger of pirates, ships had to anchor some distance away. An interesting 2nd century document known as the Vienna Papyrus records an agreement concerning the transportation of goods between two merchants—one based in Alexandria, the other in Muchiri. (The excavations at Pattanam are discussed further on, in the section on long-distance trade.)

Madurai (in Madurai district, TN), capital of the Pandya kingdom, is celebrated in Tamil tradition as the place where the third Sangam was held. There is a description of Madurai in the *Maduraikkanchi*, which is part of the *Pattuppattu*. It describes it as a large, grand city, enclosed by walls on three sides and the Vaigai river on the fourth. There is mention of its palace, temples, large houses, and two markets. Literary sources describe Madurai as a major centre of crafts such as the making of gold ornaments, ivory work, inlay work, chank cutting, and bangle making. There are references to its traders selling pearls and precious stones. The *Arthashastra* mentions Madurai as a centre of fine cotton textiles. The neighbouring area has yielded many coins, including Pandya issues. Early Tamil-Brahmi inscriptions have been found at many sites nearby; inscriptions at Alagarmalai record endowments made by merchants from Madurai.

Korkai was an important Pandya port, celebrated for its pearls in Sangam poems and Greek accounts. The *Arthashastra* also refers to the pearl fisheries of Pandya country. Today, Korkai village (in Tirunelveli district), near the mouth of the Vaigai, is about 6 km inland, but during early historical times it was no doubt right on the sea coast. Excavations here revealed BRW and locally made rouletted ware. There were potsherds inscribed with Brahmi letters belonging to *c.* 200 BCE–200 CE. There are reports of NBPW sherds from the site, and a radiocarbon date takes the beginning of the settlement to as early as the 8th century BCE. Pearl oysters found at various levels in the excavations confirm the literary references to Korkai as an important centre of pearl fishing.

Uraiyur, capital of the early Cholas, is identified with a site that is today part of the town of Tiruchirapalli. Sangam poems describe it as a great fortified city with magnificent buildings. It is interesting to note that the poems also mention burial grounds full of stones on its outskirts, a description strongly reminiscent of megaliths. The fine textiles of Uraiyur are mentioned in Tamil and Graeco Roman texts. Excavations revealed three phases of occupation at the site. The pottery of Period I included BRW, russet-coated painted ware, rouletted ware, and arretine ware. Some potsherds had graffiti and inscriptions in Brahmi of the 1st and 2nd centuries CE. In Period II, the BRW was gradually replaced by red-slipped ware. A rectangular cistern found at this level was identified as a dying vat. Period III at Uraiyur belonged to the early medieval period.

PRIMARY SOURCES | Madurai in the *Maduraikkanchi*

The *Maduraikkanchi* contains a long, poetic description of Madurai. Here is a small part of that description:

The city walls are sky-high and contain strong sally-ports and gateways old and strong
on whose door posts is carved great Lakshmi's form.
Their strong-built doors are blackened by the *ghee*
poured as libation. And above the gates
are rooms that look as high as cloud-capped hills,
through which pass streams of men like the Vaigai's flow.
The houses there have rooms of diverse kinds
that seem to reach the skies and windows broad
through which the south wind blows.
In wide long streets
that are as broad as rivers, crowds of folk
of various professions and speech create a noise
in the morning market-place while buying things.
The loudly-beating drum which makes a noise
like the wind-swept ocean's roar announces loud
to all a festival. When instruments
are played with ease, as one runs one's hands
in water, those who hear their music dance
with glee and shout, in streets where morn and eve
the people buy and sell.
The streets present a very charming scene.
There one may see the various pennons used
at festivals; those flags of victory great
with various names, presented to the chiefs
who took day after day fort after fort....

Source Chelliah, 1962: 251

Kaveripumpattinam (also known as Pumpuhar or Puhar) was the premier Chola port in early historical times. Classical accounts refer to it as Khaberis or Camara. An entire Sangam collection—the *Pattinappalai*—is devoted to a description of this place. There are references to its two bustling markets laid out between the two sectors of the city, guarded by officers of the king, and to its inhabitants who spoke different languages. Kaveripumpattinam has been identified with Kaveripattinam, a small fishing village on the Tamil Nadu coast, located at the point where the Kaveri river flows into the Bay of Bengal. Excavations at the site (Soundararajan, 1994) reconstructed its history from the 3rd century BCE to the 12th century CE, and documented the growth of the settlement from a small village port with a simple dockyard made of wood and poles to a large and impressive port city. Ancient remains have been found in many villages nearby as well. At Vanagiri, there are remains of an artificial channel that drew water from the Kaveri into a reservoir for irrigation purposes, probably built in the early centuries CE. Brick platforms for landing boats were found at Kilayur. Pallavanesvaram has a Buddhist temple and monastery dated to about the 3rd century. The large number of early medieval Chola coins found at Kaveripattinam indicates that it continued to be an important port in later times as well.

Kachchi (Kanchi) of the Sangam texts went on to become the famous temple city and Pallava capital of Kanchipuram in later centuries. Remains of the early historical period have been excavated in the area of the Shankara *matha*. Here, the lower levels of Period IA yielded BRW, while the upper levels had black-slipped ware and rouletted ware, conical jars, terracotta figurines, and a Satavahana coin of the 2nd century CE. Excavations near the Kamakshi temple revealed three broad periods of occupation. Period IA had BRW in the lower levels, while Period IB showed BRW, rouletted ware, terra sigillata, beads, terracottas, and iron artefacts. A structure was identified as a Buddhist shrine. Roman coins have not been discovered so far at Kanchi, but they have been found at many places in its vicinity. Vasavasamudram (in Chingleput district), at the mouth of the Palar river, was probably the port connecting Kanchi to the sea. Excavations here yielded amphorae sherds, rouletted ware, and beads. There are remains of brick structures, terracotta double ring wells, and heaps of shell lime and beads. However, no BRW was reported. It is possible that Vasavasamudram may represent Nirppeyarru, a port mentioned in texts.

There are a large number of megalithic sites in the Krishna and Kaveri valleys, especially along the major trade routes. One of the most important of these is Kodumanal (Rajan, 1990, 1991), on the northern bank of the Noyyal, a tributary of the Kaveri. It can be identified with the ancient city of Kotumanam, famed in Sangam texts for gem and jewellery work. The site is located in the Kongu area, which is rich in beryls, other semi-precious stones, and iron ore. It is a habitation-cum-burial site and dates from the 3rd century BCE to the 3rd century CE. As discussed in Chapter 6, according to Rajan, the beginning of writing at Kodumanal, and therefore, the beginng of the early historic phase in South India, can be dated to the 6th/5th century BCE (Rajan, 2015: 405). The evidence of iron-and-steel making (two furnaces and iron slag have been found), gemstone cutting, spinning, weaving, and the manufacture of shell bangles, suggest that it was a major industrial centre. Potsherds with Tamil-Brahmi writing have also been found.

Kodumanal: bead-making factory, megalithic burial (1st row); copper objects (extreme left); spindle whorls, pot with Tamil-Brahmi inscription 'Campan-sumanan' (2nd row); potsherd with Tamil-Brahmi inscription 'Nikama', russet coated ware (3nd row); black and red ware bowl with graffiti, agate beads (4th row)

There are over 150 burials to the east and north-east of the habitation area at Kodumanal. The earlier ones were secondary burials in which disarticulated remains were interred inside a cist. In the later period, there were pit burials in the houses, close to floor levels. The burials contained a large number of bowls and cups with post-firing graffiti, some resembling Brahmi letters. Over 100 inscribed pieces of pottery were also found in the excavations. Most of these were in the Tamil language and Tamil-Brahmi script. There are Tamilized Prakrit names too. Palaeo-magnetic dating of these potsherds has given a range of *c.* 300 BCE to 200 CE. The writing on the pots includes the names of people, some Tamil, others Sanskritic. One of the words in the inscriptions was *nikama* or *nigama*, which means guild. Kodumanal gives important evidence of the transition to the early historical phase in South India, especially with reference to the beginnings of literacy and the development of centres of craft production.

Champakalakshmi argues (1996: 92) that the early historical urbanism of the far south was not induced by deep-rooted socio-economic change, but was stimulated by Indo-Roman trade, inter-regional trade (largely coastal trade between the Ganga valley, Andhra, and the Tamil regions), and later, by trade with South-east Asia. She argues that trade activity led to the emergence of a few urban enclaves, which declined in the 3rd century along with the trade. This hypothesis is difficult to accept as trade cannot be considered an independent variable unrelated to deeper social and economic processes. In fact, the literary and archaeological evidence of specialized crafts such as metal working, bead making, and weaving; the descriptions in the poems of the markets of Puhar and Madurai; the references to wealthy traders and their lavish gifts; the beginnings of the use of money—all these things suggest that certain fundamental transformations in social and economic life were going on in South India.

In Sri Lanka, early Brahmi inscriptions are found in two broad zones—the north-western and south-eastern—in the upper and mid-levels of the river basins and on the coastal south-east. Texts such as the *Mahavamsa* describe the city of Anuradhapura (Silva, 2000). However, it is necessary to use archaeological and epigraphic evidence to get a clear picture of what was happening on the ground.

While the focus has usually been on the features of the Sri Lankan Buddhist sites, as pointed out by Senake Bandaranayake (2000), these sites have to be seen as part of the larger settlement history of the island. They were the culmination of agrarian developments based on wet rice cultivation, tank irrigation, and the use of iron technology. The large-scale irrigation works, the earliest of which go back to the 1st century CE, are a notable feature. For instance, the Alahara canal carried the water of the Ambanganga (a tributary of the Mahavali) across a distance of over 48 km to the Anuradhapura area. These developments eventually led to the emergence of urban centres. Excavations at the megalithic site of Ibbankatuva revealed a burial site with cists containing large terracotta urns with funerary remains and grave goods. There is a similarity between the symbols found on the large capstones of the cists and graffiti marks on early pottery, suggesting an overlap between the megalithic–early historic phase.

Crafts and Guilds

The archaeological evidence cited in the previous sections includes very specific information on craft activity in the various regions of the subcontinent. As for textual sources, in the context of North India, Buddhist texts such as the *Angavijja*, *Lalitavistara*, *Milindapanha*, and *Mahavastu* refer to many professions, crafts, and guilds of craftspersons and traders. The *Milindapanha* alone mentions some 60 types of crafts. The localization of crafts is evident from Jataka stories which mention villages named after the main profession of their inhabitants—e.g., potters, carpenters, metal smiths, foresters, hunters, fowlers, fishermen, and salt makers. Within towns, houses of specific types of craftspersons were often concentrated in certain streets and quarters. In the context of South India, Sangam literature indicates the existence of many specialized crafts such as weaving, gem working, shell working, and metal working.

The Jataka stories often attach the suffix *kula* (family) or *putta* (son of) to various craft terms, indicating that sons tended to follow their father's profession. Thus, there are references to a *satthavahakula* (family of caravan traders), *kumbhakarakula* (potters' family), *setthikula* (family of merchant-cum-bankers), *kammarakula* (metal smiths' family), *atavirakkhikakula* (family of forest guards), *dhannavanijakula* (grain merchants' family), *pannikakula* (greengrocers' family), and *pasanakottakakula* (stone grinders' family). Terms ending in *putta* include *satthavahaputta* (son of a caravan trader), *nisadaputta* (son of a hunter), and *vaddhakiputta* (son of a carpenter). An inscription from Jamalpur in Mathura records the setting up of a stone slab, part of a *naga* shrine, by the Chhandaka brothers, all of whom were stone masons (*shailalakas*), probably following in their father's footsteps. Although the hereditary principle operated in occupations, there must also have been a certain amount of flexibility and social mobility.

The variety of craft specialization is also evident from inscriptions from different parts of the subcontinent. Tamil-Brahmi inscriptions mention a mason, master mason, carpenter, and goldsmith. Donative inscriptions from sites such as Sanchi, Bharhut, and Mathura record the pious gifts of various kinds of artisans—potters, weavers, masons, goldsmiths, carpenters, sculptors, and ivory workers. Those from the western Deccan mention occupational groups such as jewellers (*manikara*), goldsmiths (*suvanakara*), blacksmiths (*kamara*), ironmongers (*loha-vanij*), perfumers (*gadhika*), and stone masons (*selavadhaki*). Such inscriptions reflect the prosperity of craftspersons, their social standing, and their connections with burgeoning religious centres.

During the period c. 200 BCE–300 CE, there was a significant increase in the number of guilds, as well as in their scale of activities. The works of Moti Chandra (1977), H. P. Ray (1986), and K. K. Thaplyal (1996) have collated much of the data regarding this issue. The Jatakas refer to 18 guilds, but mention only four by name—those of wood workers (*vaddhakis*), smiths (*kammaras*), leather workers (*chammakaras*), and painters (*chittakaras*). Eighteen seems to be a conventional figure, and the actual number of guilds must have varied in different places at different times. The *Mahavastu* mentions many guilds of Kapilavastu, including those of gold workers, workers in chank shell, ivory carvers, lapidaries, stone carvers, perfumers, silk and wool weavers, oil pressers, curd sellers, sugar manufacturers, sweetmeat makers, flour makers, fruit sellers, and wine makers.

Guilds are also mentioned in inscriptions. For instance, inscriptions of the western Deccan mention guilds of weavers, potters, flour makers, oil millers, bamboo workers, and merchants. An inscription at Junnar records the gift of a cave consisting of seven cells and a cistern by a guild of corn dealers (*dhanika seni*). A 3rd century Nashik inscription of the time of the Abhira king Ishvarasena mentions several guilds of crafts and trades in this city. An early 2nd century CE inscription from Nashik refers to two guilds of weavers at Govardhana (modern Nashik).

Two Tamil-Brahmi inscriptions from Mangulam near Madurai, referred to earlier in this chapter, mention the merchant guild (*nikama*) of Vellarai (Mahadevan, 2003: 319, 323). One of these indicates that members of this guild collectively contributed towards the carving of stone beds for Jaina ascetics in one of the caves. Vellarai is identified with the modern village of Vellarippatti near Mangulam. The high status enjoyed by members of merchant guilds is indicated by the title *kaviti* given to Antai Assutan, a member of the same guild, who appears as a donor in another Mangulam inscription. *Kaviti* was an honorific title bestowed by kings on ministers, nobles, and merchants. It is even more noteworthy that this guild member seems to have been the superintendent of pearls in the Pandya administration. The occurrence of the word *nikama* on a potsherd from Kodumanal is another important piece of evidence.

The Jatakas refer to the head of a craftspersons' guild as *jetthaka* or *pamukkha*. There are references to heads of guilds of garland makers (*malakara-jetthaka*), metal workers (*kammara-jetthaka*), carpenters (*vaddhaki-jetthaka*), and caravan traders (*vaha-jetthaka*). There are many references to *sarthavahas*—heads of caravan merchants. The head of a merchant guild was also referred to as a *setthi*. The *Manu Smriti* reflects a more elaborate and complex organization of guilds than the Jatakas. Inscriptions indicate that guilds functioned as bankers.

Guilds appear to have had a close relationship with kings. The *Mugapakkha Jataka* refers to the heads of the 18 guilds being part of the official entourage of a king. In the *Suchi Jataka*, the head of a blacksmiths' village is described as a favourite of the king (*raja-vallabha*). The *Nigrodha Jataka* suggests that the royal officer known as the *bhandagarika* had some authority over guilds. The *Uraga Jataka* refers to the head of a guild being appointed a *mahamatra*. The *Arthashastra* recommends that officials keep a record of the transactions and conventions of guilds. It also suggests that guilds be provided with specially designated areas in towns for pursuing their crafts and work. The term *shreni-bala* in the *Arthashastra* seems to refer to a guild or corporate organization of warriors, and not to troops maintained by regular guilds.

Dharmashastra texts give the king the right to interfere in the affairs of guilds in certain situations. The *Manu Smriti* states that if a guild member broke an agreement out of greed, the king should banish him.

The importance of guilds is evident from coins and seals issued by them. Some coins found at Taxila have the legend *negama* on the reverse in Brahmi letters of the 3rd/2nd

PRIMARY SOURCES | Guilds as bankers

Several inscriptions of this period refer to people investing money with guilds as a pious endowment, the interest from which was to be given over to Brahmanas, Buddhist monks, or earmarked for some other pious activity. Guilds may have functioned as bankers in more mundane transactions as well, but records of these have not survived.

A Mathura inscription, dated in the 28th regnal year of the Kushana king Huvishka (106 CE) refers to a permanent (*akshaya-nivi*) investment of 550 *puranas* with a guild of *samitakaras* (perhaps flour-makers) and 500 *puranas* with another guild, the name of which is not clear. The donor, Kanasarukamana, seems to have been a subordinate of the Kushanas. The interest from these investments was to provide food for 100 Brahmanas in an open hall every month and for the distribution of food to the destitute, hungry, and thirsty on a daily basis.

An inscription from Junnar refers to an investment of the income of two agricultural fields at Vadalika by one Aduthuma with a guild at Konachika for the purpose of planting *karanja* and banyan trees. Another Junnar inscription records the investment of some money with guilds of bamboo workers and braziers.

A Nashik inscription belonging to the reign of the Kshatrapa ruler Nahapana records a permanent investment of 3,000 *karshapanas* made by the king's son-in-law, Ushavadata. Two thousand *karshapanas* were invested by him with a weaver's guild of Govardhana (Nashik) at 1 per cent rate of interest, and 1000 *karshapanas* were invested with another weaver's guild of the place at the interest rate of ¾ per cent per month. The interest of the first investment was to be used to provide cloth worth 12 *karshapanas* for each of the 20 monks who lived in the monastery, while that from the second was to provide them with light meals. These investments were proclaimed in the guild assembly (*nigama-sabha*) and inscribed on stone as a permanent record. Thaplyal points out that this is the only ancient Indian inscription that clearly specifies the rates of interest on monetary investments, and that the monthly and annual interest rates work out to 12 and 9 per cent respectively. He also notes that these rates of interest are lower than the standard 1¼ per cent per month mentioned in the *Arthashastra* and the Smritis. Further, it is interesting to note that two weavers' guilds of the same town were offering different interest rates. Thaplyal suggests that ¾ per cent per month may have been the usual rate of interest in the Nashik area. The guild that was supposed to provide cloth for the monks may have offered a higher rate of interest because (*a*) since the cloth was supposed to be provided annually, there was the possibility of compounding the monthly interest, which was not possible in the case of the guild that was supposed to provide meals to monks on a daily basis; (*b*) it had the advantage of directly supplying in kind the very item it was manufacturing—i.e., cloth.

A 258–59 CE Nashik inscription of the reign of the Abhira ruler Ishvarasena mentions an endowment made in perpetuity by a woman named Vishnudatta with four different guilds of the town, in order to provide medicines for Buddhist monks living in the monastery on the Trirashmi hill. A thousand *karshapanas* were invested with a guild of *kularikas* (potters), 2,000 with a guild of *odayamtrikas* (workers who made hydraulic engines, water clocks. etc.), some amount (the part of the inscription specifying the amount is damaged and cannot be read) with the guild of *tilapishakas* (oil-millers), and 5,000 *karshapanas* with another guild, whose name cannot be read.

People may have spread out their investments in different guilds to be on the safe side, in case one of the guilds went bankrupt.

Source Thaplyal, 1996: 90–92, 176–79

century BCE. On the obverse are what may have been names of localities—Ta(Ra)limata, Dujaka, Dojaka, A(taka?)taka, and Kadare. The legends *pamchanekame* and *hiranasame* also appear on certain coins. Some scholars consider them to be coins issued by city administrations, while others think they were issued by guilds. The term *pamchanekame* may refer to a corporation of five guilds. *Hiranasame* can be understood as the Prakrit form of *hiranyasvami*, which may mean an issuer of coined money. The coins in question may have been issued by a guild of traders responsible for issuing coins. Two copper coins from Kaushambi bearing the legend *gadhikanam* in letters of about the 2nd century BCE were probably issued by a guild of perfumers. Also belonging to about the same period are a number of coins bearing the names of cities such as Varanasi, Kaushambi, Vidisha, Erakina (Eran), Ujjayini, and Mahishmati. These may have been issued by city administrations or guilds that may have been influential in the city administration.

Seals and sealings with the terms *nigama*, *nigamasya*, or variants of these words have been found at sites such as Rajghat, Bhita, Hargaon, Jhusi, and Ahichchhatra. The script ranges from the 3rd century BCE to the early centuries CE. Some of the coins have symbols and a few also seem to bear personal names. A sealing found at Rajghat has a *svastika* symbol and the legend *gavayaka* (guild of milkmen) in Brahmi letters of the 1st century BCE. A Bhita sealing has the legend *shulaphalayikanam* in 2nd century BCE letters. This could be a reference to a guild of makers of arrowheads or spearheads. A seal from Ahichchhatra has the legend *kumhakara seniya* ('of the guild of potters') in writing that belongs to the 1st century CE.

Trade and Traders

The period *c.* 200 BCE–300 CE saw a significant expansion of trade activity, both within the subcontinent and between the subcontinent and other lands. Trade was facilitated by the expansion of the money economy, and the issuing of small denominational coins by the Kushanas and Satavahanas paved the way for the use of coins for small-scale transactions. Texts of this period refer to coins known as *dinara*, *purana*, and *karshapana*. In the far south, apart from northern coins and locally made punch-marked coins and Roman *denarii*, there is evidence of die-struck coins issued by the Chera, Chola, and Pandya kings. Most coins in ancient India were issued by the state, but as mentioned above, there are a few examples of city coins and guild coins. Barter and the use of cowrie shells (the shell of the gastropod *Cypraea moneta*, found in the waters off the Maldive islands) as a unit of exchange continued along with money-based transactions.

The Dharmashastra texts lay down various prescriptions concerning taxes, profit, and rates of interest on loans. However, they need not necessarily be reflective of the way trade and markets actually functioned. The *Manu Smriti* suggests that traders should be taxed on their profit, not on their capital outlay, and suggests a 5 per cent tax rate. The texts lay down punishments for adulteration, cheating, and fraudulent measures. The interest rates prescribed are high. The *Manu Smriti* states that interest rates should vary according to the risk factor, and also according to the *varna* of the borrower.

The Jatakas give accounts of long caravan journeys. They mention people travelling on foot and bullock carts, and rich people travelling in chariots and palanquins. They refer to wells and tanks along roads, and rest houses where weary traders and travellers halted for rest and refreshment. They talk of city gates being closed at night. There are Jataka stories of *bodhisattvas* who were *sarthavahas*, who led their caravans with calm and wise judgement. Ports were often important manufacturing centres themselves or were connected to such centres in their hinterlands. Texts such as the Jatakas refer to partnerships among merchants.

Sangam texts give vivid literary sketches of the markets and traders of Tamilakam. They describe the markets of Puhar and Madurai and their sellers of flowers, garlands, aromatic powders, betel leaf, shell bangles, jewellery, cloth, garments, wine, and bronze. The poems mention caravans (*chattu*) of itinerant traders, who carried goods such as

FURTHER DISCUSSION | **Ancient travellers**

In ancient times, as today, people travelled for many different reasons. Apart from traders, travellers included students, teachers, professionals, ascetics, and entertainers. People travelled to see new places, meet friends and relatives, start a new life, or just for the adventure and fun of it. Moti Chandra has put together many of the interesting Jataka stories about travel and travellers. Here are a few:

There is a Jataka story of a horse trader who came to Varanasi from Uttarapatha with 500 horses. A *bodhisattva* allowed him to put a price on his horses. The king hoped to make some money for himself and, out of greed, sent one of his own horses for the sale. Unfortunately, the king's horse bit the others and brought the price of all of them down drastically.

The *Darimukha Jataka* tells the story of prince Darimukha who finished his education in Taxila and then set out on a series of travels to study the manners and customs of people in various parts of the country. He took a friend—the son of a royal priest—along for company.

A Jataka narrates the story of four sisters who, after the death of their father, travelled to many cities for the purpose of philosophical debate. They carried along with them the branches of a jamboline tree. Arriving at Shravasti, they planted the branches outside the city gates and announced that if anybody dared to uproot them, they would have to engage them in public debate.

Another Jataka speaks of 500 travelling acrobats who arrived in Rajagriha every year and earned much money from their performances. One of the female acrobats performed such amazing acrobatic manoeuvres that a banker's son fell in love with her and proposed marriage. She agreed, on condition that he too become an acrobat and join the troupe. The besotted suitor accepted her terms.

The *Shankha Jataka* tells the story of a Brahmana named Shankha, who was financially ruined due to his extravagant habits. Deciding to revive his sunken fortunes through trade enterprise, he built a ship and loaded it with cargo. He then bade farewell to his relatives, headed for the port along with his servants and set sail for Suvarnadvipa (South-east Asia).

The *Samuddavanija Jataka* tells of 1,000 families of carpenters living near Varanasi who took an advance for making a large order of furniture which they could not make on time. Hounded by disgruntled clients and fearing the consequences, they decided to migrate. They swiftly built some ships and sailed off along with their families to a wonderful island, endowed with fruit trees and fields of rice and sugarcane. Here, they met a passenger from a shipwreck, who was happily living a life of ease and contentment.

Such incidents in the Jataka stories need not necessarily represent 'historical facts'. Nevertheless, the characters and situations woven into the stories do tell us about travel and travellers in early historical India.

Source Chandra, 1977: 56–57, 61, 64

paddy, salt, and sometimes pepper to the interior regions, and perhaps also brought goods from the interior regions to the ports. There are descriptions of difficult journeys made by caravans of salt traders (*umanachchattu*), their goods laden on bullock carts, equipped both with plenty of provisions for sustenance and bows and spears for protection. The *paravatar* were inhabitants of the sea coasts who were initially involved in fishing and making salt and toddy. They gradually diversified into pearl diving as well as long-distance trade in pearls, chank bangles, tamarind, fish, precious stones, and horses, and became quite prosperous in the process. Tamil-Brahmi inscriptions mention merchants dealing in cloth, salt, oil, ploughshares, *gur* (unrefined sugar), and gold.

Trade continued to ply along the Uttarapatha and Dakshinapatha (for details, see Chapter 5). The Uttarapatha connected Taxila in the north-west with Tamralipti in the Ganga delta. Other important routes included the sea route connecting Sindh and Gujarat. The route from Rajasthan to the Deccan followed the western foothills of the Aravalli hills. From Mathura, an important route followed the Chambal valley to Ujjain in the Malwa region, and from there to Mahishmati in the Narmada valley. From Mahishmati, after crossing the Satpura hills and the Tapi river, one route crossed the Western Ghats to Surat, while another went into the Deccan. Routes connected Ujjayini in Malwa with Bharukachchha and Supparaka on the western coast. Another route connected Kaushambi with Vidisha in eastern Malwa. The long-used routes of South India followed the rivers, and included those connecting Manmad and Masulipatam, Pune and Kanchipuram, Goa and Tanjavur–Nagapattinam, and Kerala and Cholamandala.

Important trade termini in northern India included Pushkalavati in the north-west, Patala and Bhrigukachchha in the west, and Tamralipti in the east. The *Periplus* refers to market towns of western India such as Paithana (Paithan), Tagara (Ter), Suppara (Sopara), and Calliena (Kalyan). Strabo talks of boats from the sea sailing up the Ganga to Pataliputra. Further south, the port of Muziris (Muchiri) was important. There was active coastal trade as well. The ports on the eastern coast gradually emerged as a significant factor in India–Mediterranean maritime trade in the late 1st or early 2nd century CE.

Textual sources mention various items involved in trade between different regions of the subcontinent—cotton textiles from the east, west, and far south; steel weapons from Aparanta in the west as well as from the eastern regions; horses and camels from the north-west; and elephants from the eastern and southern regions. The Jatakas mention the merchandise for which certain cities were famous—e.g., the silk, fine muslin, and sandalwood of Varanasi; the red blankets of Gandhara; the woollen textiles of the Punjab; and the cotton textiles of Kashi. The *Arthashastra* refers to textiles of the south. Kanchi and Madurai were renowned for their fine cotton cloth. The *Pattinappalai* tells us that horses were imported from the north. Pepper was another important commodity of trade. Archaeological evidence from sites in different parts of the subcontinent helps to construct a more detailed and specific inventory of goods that were involved in the trade of the times.

Long-distance trade

The flourishing long-distance trade of the period *c.* 200 BCE–300 CE comes alive in many texts and is also documented in archaeology. Marine archaeology has brought to light important evidence of ancient coastal cities that have been swallowed up by the sea. Excavations at Dwarka and Bet Dwarka off the Gujarat coast (these sites have yielded much earlier remains as well) have revealed remains of structures, stone images, objects made of copper, bronze and brass, iron anchors, and a wrecked boat belonging to the period *c.* 200 BCE–200 CE. These sites were clearly oriented towards maritime trade.

The Jatakas mention long-distance journeys over land, river, and sea. Indian traders are described as venturing into Suvarnadvipa (South-east Asia), Ratnadvipa (Sri Lanka), and Baveru (Babylon?). There is also reference to ports on the western coast such as Bharukachchha, Supparaka, and Suvara and those on the eastern coast such as Karambiya, Gambhira, and Seriva. There are stories of voyages, difficult journeys, and shipwrecks. The Jatakas refer to sailors organized in guilds, the head of which was known as the *niyamakjettha*.

Sangam poems talk of *yavanas* bringing goods by ship into the ports of South India. The ports on the Coromandel coast were especially important for trade with South-east Asia. There is mention of merchants speaking many different languages at Kaveripattinam. Another port that is mentioned is Perimula (or Perimuda). This has been tentatively identified as located at the mouth of the Vaigai, near Rameswaram. Excavations here revealed Roman pottery and coins, as well as locally made imitations of Roman pottery and local coins.

The demand for Chinese silk in the Mediterranean region was a major stimulus to trans-regional and trans-continental trade in this period. The existence of the Kushana empire was a stimulus to trade as it included a section of both silk routes and also because it probably provided a modicum of safety for traders and a reduction of tariff posts. The maritime route from the western coast of India to the Persian Gulf was known from protohistoric times. It became increasingly important in the early centuries CE after traders started taking advantage of the south-west monsoon winds to sail across the Indian Ocean.

What did the Indian boats of the time look like? The Jatakas talk of ships made of planks of wood, equipped with three masts, rigging, sails, planks, and oars. The crew of a big ship included the captain (*shasaka*), pilot (*niryamaka*), a person in charge of manipulating the cutter and ropes, and a bailer of water. Greek and Roman texts mention the stitched tradition of Indian boats—instead of using nails, the planks of wood were stitched together by strong fibres. Like other ancient mariners such as the Phoenecians

PRIMARY SOURCES | **Kaveripattinam in the *Pattinapalai***

Here is part of the vivid description of Kaveripattinam in the *Pattinapalai*, which is part of the *Pattuppattu*. Note the idealized description of the *vanigar* (merchants):

...The good and worthy gods protect
the city's limits. Here are brought
swift, prancing steeds by sea in ships,
and bales of pepper black, by carts.
The Himalayas send gems and gold,
while the Kudda hills send sweet san-
dal-wood and *akhil*; pearls from the south
sea come, red coral from the eastern sea.
The Ganga and the Kaveri bring
their yield. Sri Lanka provides its food,
and Myanmar manufactures rare.
With other rare and rich imports
this wealth lies close and thickly piled,
confused along the spacious streets.
Where merchants live the fish is safe
in the sea, and the cattle on the land.
Quite free and happy are their lives
Amidst their multiplying kin
They know no foes; the fish play
near the fishers' quarters unafraid,
and cattle multiply untouched
in butchers' haunts. The merchants thus,
condemn the taking of these lives.
They tolerate not thieving vile.
They do their duties by the gods,
oblations offer, tend with care fine bulls
and cows, exalt the priests, that teach
the Vedas four; they give their guests
food cooked and uncooked too.
Unstintingly they dispense alms,
and live a life of gracious love.
The long yoke of their curved plough
is balanced with a central pin—
even so their hearts are poised and just.
They speak the truth and deem it shame
to lie. For others' goods they have
the same regard as for their own
in trade. Nor do they try to get too
much in selling their own goods,
nor give too little when they buy.
They set a fair price on all things.
Their ancient wealth was thus acquired.
It's here the merchants crowded live.

Source Chelliah, 1962: 39–40

and Babylonians, Indian sailors used special birds to identify land. When released from the ship, these would fly towards land if it was nearby, but would otherwise return to the ship. The ancient Greeks often remarked on the differences between Indian boats and those of the Mediterranean lands. Onesicritis (who is supposed to have sailed to the mouth of the Indus in the course of Alexander's campaign) is cited in Strabo's account as stating that the Indian boats' peculiar construction and the inferior quality of their sails were responsible for their poor sea worthiness. Pliny also mentions the peculiar construction of Indian boats, but describes them as suited to the seas they sailed on. The distinctive feature of these boats was that their planks were not held together with nails, but were stitched together with coir rope made especially for the purpose. Sewn boats were probably considered better suited to withstanding the impact of strong waves and hitting the shore.

Apart from Chinese silk, other commodities were involved in the vibrant trade interactions and networks connecting the Indian subcontinent, Central Asia, West Asia, China, South-east Asia, and Mediterranean Europe. Given the enormous distances involved in the transport of some of the goods, it is not surprising that these trade networks involved many groups of traders from different lands. Apart from abundant textual material, archaeological evidence from port sites in various parts of India, the Red Sea, Persian Gulf, and east Africa has added considerably to our understanding of long-distance trade across these regions (see Boussac et al., [Eds.]., 2016).

Trade with East and South-east Asia

The period *c.* 200 BCE–300 CE saw an intensification of trade contacts between the Indian subcontinent and East and South-east Asia. Given its proximity to Central Asia and the Chinese military garrisons in the Pamirs, the area around Gandhara was of special interest to the Han emperors of China. The initial military and political interests were, however, soon overtaken by trade and religious exchanges with the Indian subcontinent. The commercial exchanges were dominated by silk.

The history of the early trade interactions between ancient India and ancient China have been discussed by Xinriu Liu (1988). The great Chinese Silk Route connected India with Central Asia, West Asia, and Europe. This route stretched some 4,350 miles from Loyang on the Yellow river (also known as the Huang He) in China to Ctesiphon on the Tigris river in West Asia. From Loyang it went on to Ch'ang and Tunhuang, near the source of the Yellow river. From there, the route bifurcated into a northern and a southern segment. The northern route went through the oases that lay between the northern edge of the Takla Makan desert and the Tienshan mountains. The southern one went along the southern edge of the desert and the Kunlun mountains. The two routes met at Kashgar, only to again split into two. The northern route, which ran through Kokand and Samarkand in Tajikistan and Uzbekistan and went on to the Caspian Sea, was the main route to Persia. The southern route went through Bactria (northern Afghanistan) and joined up with the northern route at Merv in Turkmenistan. From Afghanistan, a route ran through Kapisi and the Kabul valley to the north-western cities of the subcontinent such as Purushapura, Pushkalavati, and Taxila, and to the cities further inland. Another route from Kashgar ran through Gilgit in Kashmir. North-west India became an important junction for the trade between China and the Roman empire. As pointed out by Liu, the cost and risks of overland and overseas transportation across long distances must have added significantly to the cost of Chinese silk.

Coral and glass were valued commodities in China in the early centuries CE, but there is not a great deal of archaeological evidence of Roman glassware reaching China. In fact, very few Roman items have been found there, perhaps due to inadequate archaeological excavations. Frankincense and styrax were two fragrances that were obtained by the Chinese from Central Asia and then exported westwards. These and other Chinese and Central Asian items were imported into India and then shipped to the west from ports such as Barygaza (near the mouth of the Narmada) and Barbaricon (at the mouth of the Indus). Superior animal hides were among the Central Asian products. The important items transported from or through India to China during this period were pearls, coral, glass, and fragrances. Silk was the major Chinese export to India.

Trade between China and the West was disturbed in the 3rd and 4th centuries due to political factors. After the end of the Han dynasty in 220 CE, China remained divided, except for a brief period of unification under the Qin dynasty. This was also the time when the Byzantine empire broke away from Rome and when the Kushana empire collapsed. Some of the cities along the Oxus seem to have become deserted in this period. However, trade between China and India did not come to an end, although there were some changes in routes.

The history of mainland and maritime South-east Asia is an exciting field of study (for overviews, see Tarling, [1992] 1999; Miksic and Goh, 2017). For a long time, historians tended to view India's relations with this region through the perspectives of Greater India, Indianization, or Hinduization, which visualized the creation of a larger sphere of Indian influence in South-east Asia through a process of cultural colonization. In recent decades, perspectives on the history of South-east Asia have changed a great deal.

As pointed out by O. W. Wolters (1982), there are certain general factors that apply across South-east Asia. For instance, the ocean has played an important part in South-east Asian history; many societies in this region are marked by cognatic kinship systems; and there was a prevalence of an idea of leadership in which men of prowess were believed to have superior spiritual qualities. At the same time, South-east Asia has always been a region of great cultural diversity and cannot be treated as a single, homogeneous region. Further, although Indian influence (and Chinese influence) on this region cannot be denied, "Indian materials tended to be fractured and restated and therefore, drained of their original significance," through a process of "localization" (Wolters, 1982, p. 52). This means that when Indian influences travelled to South-east Asia, they got transformed into something new through their interactions with local cultures. There is an urgent need to further explore the nature, networks, and agents of the interactions between South and South-east Asia (see Manguin et al. [Eds.], 2011; Singh and Dhar. [Eds.], 2014).

Map 8.4 Major routes connecting Asia, Europe, and Africa

Map 8.5 India and South-east Asia

Ancient Sanskrit and Pali texts refer to a land known as Suvarnadvipa or Suvarnabhumi—the land of gold, associated with riches. This is usually identified with South-east Asia. This identification is more certain in the *Arthashastra*, which refers to incense called *kaleyaka* from Suvarna-bhumi, and aloeswood that came from beyond the sea. The *Milindapanha* also refers to Suvarnabhumi in the context of shipping ports. The Jatakas mention sea voyages from Varanasi and Bharukachchha to this land.

There is archaeological evidence of maritime links between India and both coastal and inland South-east Asia from *c.* 500/400 BCE onwards (Ray, 1994, 2021; Manguin et al., 2011). The most prolific Indian artefacts found in South-east Asia are beads of coloured glass, faceted carnelian, and etched agate. Reference was made in Chapter 6 to the burial site of Ban Don Ta Phet (west-central Thailand). Evidence of Indian contact came from over 50 etched carnelian and agate beads of Indian origin. A carnelian leaping lion (perhaps representing the Buddha as Sakya-simha or lion of the Sakyas) is of Indian origin. The evidence from Ban Don Ta Phet and from Khao Sam Keo (on the east coast of the Kra Isthmus) suggests that the contacts with various parts of the Indian subcontinent can be dated to the 4th–2nd centuries BCE. Indian bead-making technologies used to suit regional styles could reflect the presence of Indian craftspersons in the area (Glover, [1996] 2012; Glover and Bellina, 2011). Etched carnelian beads have also been discovered as surface finds at sites such as U Thong and Krabi in Thailand. A few have been found in the course of excavations at Kuala Selinsing in Malaysia. Glass beads in different shapes and colours—some of South Indian origin—have been found at several South-east Asian sites in contexts ranging from *c.* 300 BCE to the 17th century CE.

In the 1st century CE, there was an increase in the quantity and variety of Indian items exported from India to South-east Asia. The background to this change was the emergence of kingdoms in mainland South-east Asia, an increasingly ranked society, expansion of craft production, and greater inter-regional trade. Khuan Lukpad (in the Malay peninsula) yielded beads made of glass and semi-precious stones and seals with Brahmi inscriptions ranging from the 1st to 7th centuries. Indian artefacts have been discovered in emerging urban centres in the valleys of the Chao Phraya, Irrawaddy, and Mekong rivers. The site of Beikthano in Myanmar has yielded sherds of rouletted ware and a piece of clay with an impression in Brahmi letters reading 'Sangha siri'. Chinese sources talk about the kingdom of Funan in present-day Vietnam. The site of Oc-Eo in the Mekong delta (in Vietnam) was an important centre of maritime trade between east and west. Since coinage was absent in South-east Asia till the middle of the 1st millennium BCE, the early trade activity must have been via barter or the use of cowrie shells.

On the basis of textual and archaeological evidence, the following list of exports from South-east Asia to India can be compiled: gold, spices such as cinnamon and cloves, aromatics, sandalwood, and camphor. Some of these items were shipped on to Western markets from India, as there was a demand for them in the Mediterranean region as well. It is also possible that tin was exported to the subcontinent from the Malay peninsula. Exports from India to South-east Asia included cotton cloth, sugar, beads, and certain kinds of pottery. The trade was clearly not confined to luxury goods.

H. P. Ray (1994: 7) argues that there were a number of changes in international trade patterns in the 3rd and 4th centuries. These included the splitting up of long-distance trade networks into regional and local circuits. There was a southward shift in Roman trade interests. There was also an expansion of India's trade with West Asia.

Sri Lanka played an increasingly important role in long-distance trade networks (see Bopearachchi, 2015, Vol. 1: 76–77; Vol. 2, chaps. 11–18). The style and workmanship of two gold rings found at Aï-Khanoum is Greek, but they are studded with a sapphire and a star ruby, which seem to be from Sri Lanka. This suggests that by the 3rd century BCE, Sri Lankan traders were interacting with the Greeks of Bactria and with Indians as intermediaries. Many Indo-Greek, Indo-Scythian, and Kushana coins have been found at sites in Sri Lanka, and lapis lazuli must have reached the island from the Kokcha mines in Bactria. Sri Lanka came to play an increasingly important role in Indian Ocean trade networks. Greek and Latin texts refer to the island as Taprobane. They refer to the products of the island, including ivory, tortoise shell, precious stones, muslin, rice, honey, and spices. Explorations and excavations at sites such as Tissamaharama, Nariyagama, Panirendawa, Kelaniya, and Ridiyagama have thrown valuable light on craft production and trade. Some of the beads found at these sites are also found at Indian coastal sites. Kelaniya yielded rouletted ware made in India as well as fragments of Mediterranean pottery. The evidence indicates that from the 4th century onwards, traders were circumnavigating Sri Lanka, and the island was increasingly drawn into trade networks across the Indian Ocean.

The relationship between the regions of South and South-east Asia was not confined to trade. It extended to the cultural sphere and is especially visible in the travels of Hinduism and Buddhism as also of artistic styles. Portable religious icons, including mass-produced clay images made from seals or moulds, that circulated with expanding Buddhist pilgrim circuits, were part of the circulation of religious ideas and rituals (Skilling, 2011). But South-east Asian cultures were never passive recipients. The processes of selection and localization meant that Indian influences were often transformed when they settled into their new cultural niches.

The cross-cultural exchange that is visible seems asymmetrical. However, in recent years, historians have tried to identify 'reverse flows', that is, South-east Asian influences travelling westwards to South Asia, for instance in ceramic and ship-building techniques (Selvakumar, 2011) and musical instruments (Nicolas, 2011). The old 'Indianization' theory has been replaced by the recognition of the complexities involved in South and South-east Asian interactions. There is still a great deal to be discovered about the networks and agents of cultural interactions between South and South-east Asia.

Trade with the Mediterranean region

As mentioned earlier, the term Yavana was initially used in ancient Indian texts to refer to the Greeks, but soon came to refer to all foreigners who came from the regions lying to the west of the subcontinent. In Ashoka's inscriptions, the *yavanas* appear as a people who lived on the north-western borders of the Maurya empire. During *c.* 200 BCE–300 CE, they appear as 'westerners' involved in trade. Early Tamil literature frequently refers to them. Sangam poems mention their large ships sailing on the Periyar river, bringing in gold and wine and sailing away with cargoes of black pepper. A poem in the *Pattuppattu* compares the noise made by the weavers of Madurai with that made by workers who loaded and unloaded merchandise onto *yavana* ships at midnight. A poem by Nakkirar refers to the Pandya king Nanmaran drinking perfumed and cold wine brought by the *yavanas*.

During the period between the 2nd century BCE and 3rd century CE, Indian traders were increasingly drawn into a vast web of trade interactions involving China, the Red Sea, Persian Gulf, east Africa, and the Mediterranean. Many groups of traders were involved in the trade between India and the Mediterranean, often referred to as Indo-Roman trade (see Tomber, [2008] 2012; H. P. Ray, 2014; Ranabir Chakravarti, [2002] 2020). Apart from the export of Indian goods to the Mediterranean, India also played an important role in the Chinese silk trade. The annexation of Egypt by the Roman emperor Augustus in 30 BCE had important implications for the expansion of trade via the Red Sea route. A part of the overland trade across Central Asia was diverted to India and goods moved onwards from the Indian ports to the Roman empire via the sea route. Trade between India and the Roman empire declined after the time of Marcus Aurelius in the late 2nd century CE, partly as a result of the internal vicissitudes of the Roman empire; however, it did not come to an end. After a lull, it revived in the 4th century and continued to the 7th century.

Egypt played an important role in the trade between the Indian Ocean and the Mediterranean world, and Alexandria, Myos Hormos, and Berenike were important ports. The monsoon winds (referred to as Hippalus in western sources) were known to Indians, Arabs, Persians, and Greeks, but were now increasing used for oceanic travel. This meant that sailors could use the open sea route rather than the coastal route from Arabia to the ports of western India. The winds could be dangerous when at their height, but once they had settled down, they made ocean crossing swifter. Sailors seem to have started the voyage from the Red Sea ports in late July. It took them 30 days to reach the port of Ocelis in Arabia, and from here, using the monsoon winds, it was a 20-day journey to Muziris on the Kerala coast, where ships would have been able to dock in about late September. Ports such as Barbaricum on the Indus delta and Barygaza on the mouth of the Narmada became less important than the south-eastern ports. Sailors used the north-east monsoon winds (October to February) to return to the Red Sea.

The *Periplus* gives a list of goods exported to the Roman empire from ports on the Indus delta and the Gujarat coast. Pliny and Dio Chrysostom refer to the drain of Roman gold into India. The Vienna Papyrus, which records the terms of a business deal between two shippers of Alexandria and Muchiri, seems to refer to a loan for the acquisition of goods including nard (aromatic balsam), ivory, and textiles. This important document records the loading of cargo on a ship called the Hermapollon, docked at Muziris. The cargo was to be shipped to one of the Red Sea ports, from where it was to be taken overland and by river boat to Alexandria in Egypt. Excavations at Sumhuram in the Arabian peninsula revealed rouletted ware and paddle impressed ware made in the Indian subcontinent. These pottery types have also been found at Arikamedu, Pattanam, and Berenike, and suggest maritime links between Tamilakam and the Arabian peninsula. Potsherds with Tamil personal names inscribed in the Tamil-Brahmi script have been found on the Red Sea coast. All this shows the active role of Tamil traders in Indian Ocean trade. Pepper from South India was in great demand in the Mediterranean. Ports on the Coromandel coast of eastern India also participated in long-distance trade. Inscriptions and drawings found on the island of Socotra (Strauch. [Ed.], 2012) in the

Indian Ocean, between the southern coast of Arabia and the Horn of Africa, have given valuable information about the active participation of Indian traders in maritime networks of the early centuries CE.

An ivory statuette, perhaps representing the goddess Lakshmi or a *yakshi*, found in Pompeii, reflects the cross-cultural interactions during this period. More recently, a 3rd century CE Sanskrit Buddhist dedicatory inscription dated in the sixth regnal year of the Roman emperor Phillip and a 71 cm high Buddha statue were found at Berenike.

The large number of Roman coins discovered in India comprise almost 170 finds from about 130 sites (Suresh, 2004: 27–88, 153–59). Most of the coins belong to the reigns of emperors Augustus (31 BCE–14 CE) and Tiberius (14–37 CE), and there are also imitations of these coins. There are silver coins known as *denarii* and gold ones known as *aurei*. The silver coins are more numerous, both in Rome and India. There is a concentration of finds in the Coimbatore area of Tamil Nadu and the Krishna valley in Andhra Pradesh. Although some Roman coins have been found at sites in western India, for example, near Sholapur, Waghoda, Vadgaon-Madhavpur, and Kondapur, they are relatively few in number. Apart from a handful of finds at sites such as Taxila, Manikyala, and Mathura, scarcely any Roman coins have been found in North India. While the Kushanas may well have melted down and re-minted Roman gold coins, this does not explain the virtual absence of silver coins in the north.

In areas where well-established systems of currency already existed—for instance in the Kushana and Satavahana kingdoms—Roman coins may have been melted down for bullion, whereas in the eastern Deccan, where indigenous currency systems were weaker, they may have been used as currency. Roman coins made their way to India well after the reigns of the kings in whose reigns they were issued. P. Berghaus (1991) also points to Roman copper coins in Gujarat from the 2nd half of the 3rd century CE. Roman bronze coins are found at several places in India, mostly in Tamil Nadu, in contexts dating from the latter half of the 4th century CE. Thousands of them have also been found in Sri Lanka. This clearly shows the southward shift of maritime networks.

PRIMARY SOURCES | *Periplus Maris Erythraei* (The Periplus of the Erythraean Sea)

Ancient Greek and Roman geographers referred to the Indian Ocean, Red Sea, and the Persian Gulf as the Erythraean Sea. The *Periplus Maris Erythraei* is a unique handbook, written in Greek for traders involved in mercantile activity between Egypt, east Africa, southern Arabia, and India. The book must have been useful for traders in ancient times; it also offers historians a very useful source of detailed information on trade in the Indian Ocean.

The text survives in the form of a 10th century manuscript preserved in Heidelberg (of which there is a copy in the British Museum). The manuscript is full of errors and omissions, and apart from the hand of the original copyist, there are changes, corrections, and mistakes inserted by another hand. Lionel Casson, who has published a recent edition, translation, and commentary, points out that this must be partly because of errors in the original manuscript that the copyist was copying from and partly because the *Periplus* mentioned many places and things that were unfamiliar to him.

Although some scholars place the *Periplus* as late as the 3rd century CE, it seems to belong to the mid-1st century CE. It is clearly the work of one author, whose name we do not know. We can tell, however, that he must have been a Greek who lived in Egypt, because he mentions 'the trees we have in Egypt' and also gives the Egyptian equivalents of Roman months. Certain references in the text and the level of detail indicate that the author wrote from personal experience, not from hearsay. He had the interests and writing style of a businessman, rarely betraying any literary flourish. He was evidently a merchant writing for the benefit of other merchants. His book gives details of sailing schedules, routes, trade, ports, and merchandise. The author also threw in information about rulers whose control extended over the ports. He was a curious and observant man, and added many remarks on flora and fauna and on the appearance, life, and customs of people of different lands. One thing that he does not say much about is religion.

The *Periplus* describes trade conducted along two main routes starting from the Red Sea ports of Egypt. One route went along the African coast, the other to India. There are references to other routes as well. The wealth of detail in the book has enabled historians to draw up an inventory of items traded at various ports involved in Indian Ocean trade networks in the early centuries CE.

Source Casson, 1989

Map 8.6 Distribution of Roman coins in India (after Suresh, 2004)

RECENT DISCOVERIES | Dramatic discoveries in Hoq cave, Socotra

Socotra is the main island of an archipelago (part of the Republic of Yemen) located at the entrance to the Gulf of Aden. In 2000, Belgian speleologists (scholars who study caves) made some exciting discoveries in Hoq Cave in the limestone plateau located at on the north-east coast of the island, at a height of about 350 m above sea level. The cave is like a long, narrow corridor that stretches for about 2.5 km, and is up to 100 m wide and 30 m high. It yielded a large, exciting corpus of inscriptions and drawings left by visitors from India, Africa, and West Asia. The inscriptions and artefacts (which included ceramic jars and incense burners with remains of coal and incense), were found towards the rear of the cave, starting almost 1 km from the entrance.

The interior of the cave is dramatic, with stalactites and stalagmites of different sizes all along. The ancient writing usually occurs in clusters at 18 different places in the cave—on the walls, floor, or on the stalagmites and stalactites. Some of it is inscribed using the sharp end of a broken stalagmite, some is written using mud from the floor. One text is written using charcoal. The cave is very dark and torches (remains of these have been found) would have been used by the ancient visitors. The darkness of the cave and careless or superimposed writing make it difficult to read some of the inscriptions.

Ingo Strauch identified a total of 193 Indian inscriptions written by 117 people in Hoq Cave. A man named Ravahaka inscribed his names 10 times at 5 different spots. The Indian texts are in places accompanied by South Arabian, Aksumite, Greek, and Bactrian texts. A wooden tablet with a 3rd century CE Palmyrene inscription was also found. On palaeographic grounds, the Indian inscriptions can be dated from the 2nd to 5th centuries CE.

The inscriptions are very short. Almost all are written in a western variety of the Brahmi script that was being used in Gujarat and adjacent areas from the 2nd to the 5th centuries CE. There is one Kharoshthi inscription. The language can be described as Sanskrit, Middle Indic (Prakrit), or Sanskrit with Middle Indic features. The epigraphs mostly record the names of men who came here, along with additional information such as their father's name, occupation, and native place. Three writers refer to themselves *navikas* and one calls himself *niryamaka* (sailor or helmsman). There are also some drawings of Indian ships with multiple masts, a very curved stern, and two rudders. Several visitors came from the ports of Bhrigukachcha (Bharuch) and Hastakavapra (Hatab) in Gujarat. Many inscribed sealings bearing personal names have also been found in Hoq Cave. All this is valuable evidence of the activities of Indian traders in western Indian Ocean trade.

The cave may have had some religious significance, perhaps associated with a cave deity. However, none of the Indian inscriptions refer to such a deity. Seven inscriptions are religious in character. Some of the names of the people mentioned have Buddhist, Vaishnava, or Shaiva affiliation. Drawings of tridents (a Shaiva symbol), *stupas*, wheels, and auspicious symbols such as the vase of plenty (*purnaghata*) have been found in various places in the cave.

The *Periplus* refers to Socotra as Dioskourides. It mentions tortoise and 'dragon-blood' (*Dracaena Cinnabari*, a tree resin) as products of the island, and states that Arabs, Indians, and Greeks lived here. As pointed by Strauch, Socotra was not a major hub of international trade networks but was located on the edge of these networks. This was no doubt the reason why the dramatic evidence in Hoq Cave remained unseen and intact for almost 1500 years.

Source Strauch, 2016; Strauch. (Ed.)., 2012

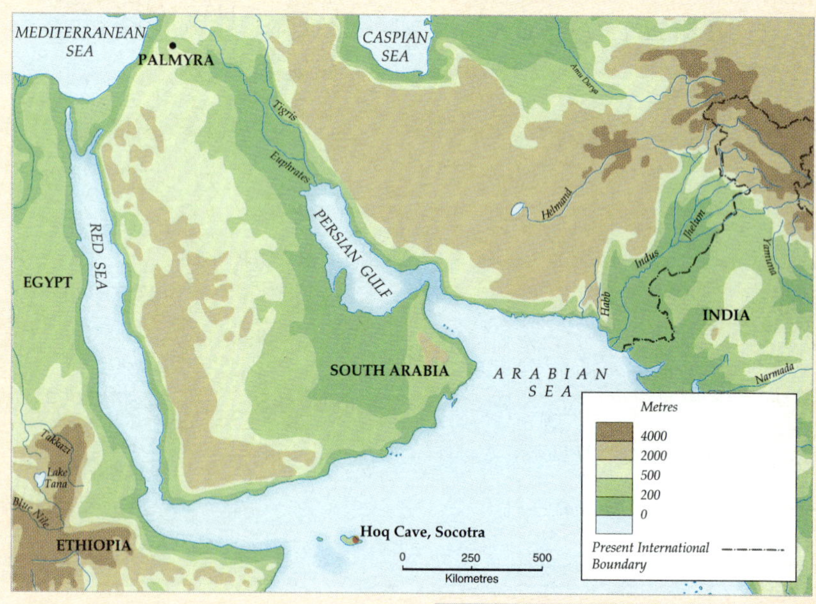

Map of Socotra

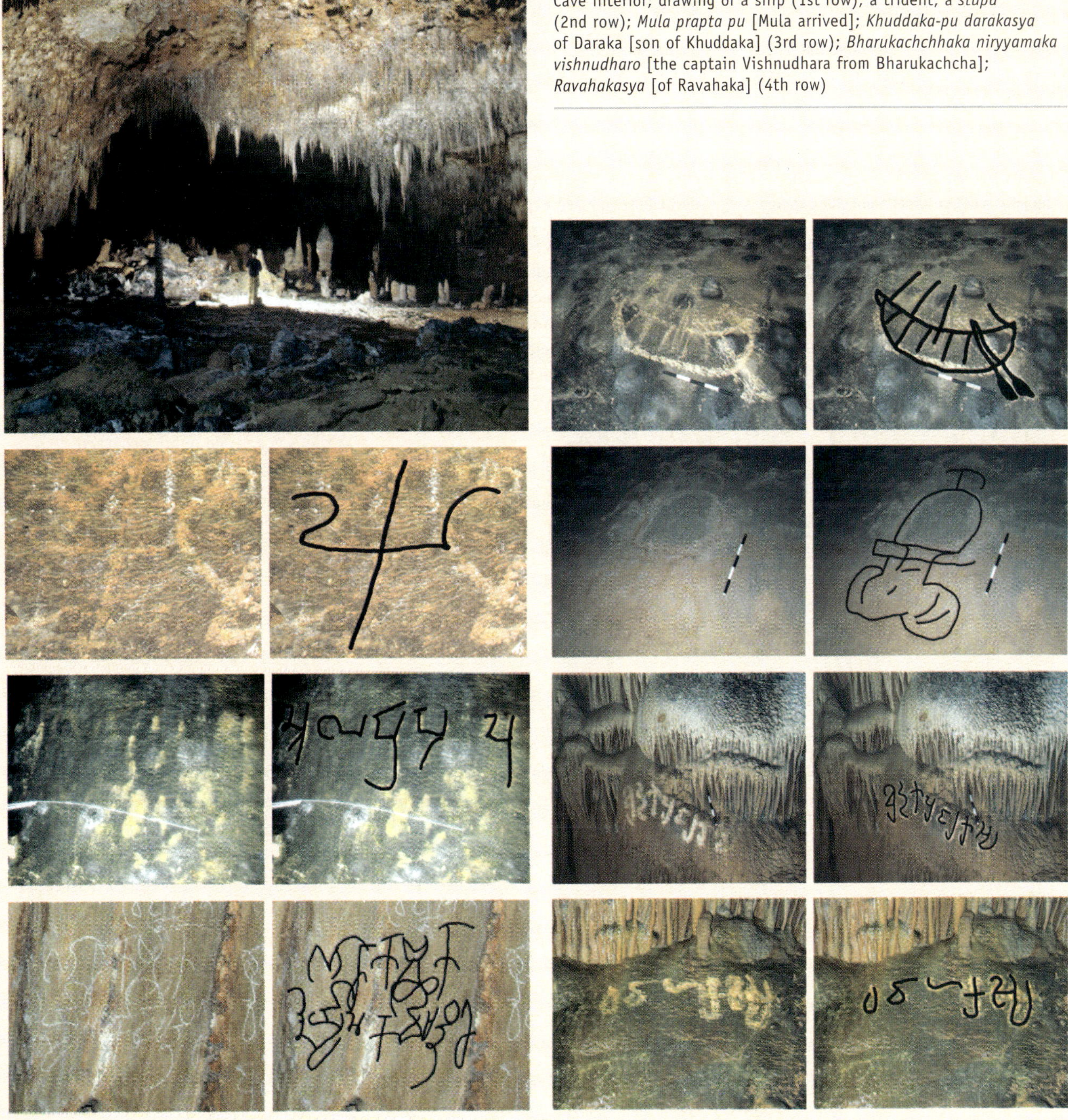

Cave interior; drawing of a ship (1st row); a trident; a *stupa* (2nd row); *Mula prapta pu* [Mula arrived]; *Khuddaka-pu darakasya* of Daraka [son of Khuddaka] (3rd row); *Bharukachchhaka niryyamaka vishnudharo* [the captain Vishnudhara from Bharukachcha]; *Ravahakasya* [of Ravahaka] (4th row)

*In the paired images, the left image shows the drawings and inscriptions as they appear in the cave; the image on the right has superimposed lines for clarity.

PRIMARY SOURCES | **A Greek play set on the Malabar coast**

The fragment of a 2nd century CE papyrus found among a pile of manuscripts at Oxyrhynchus in Egypt carries the script of a Greek comedy, the *Charition*. The play is in mixed prose and verse and is based on Euripides' *Iphygenia in Tauris*. It seems to be a performance script, which mentions cues for the actors and gives musical notations and sound effects. It is a copy, so the play must be older than the papyrus.

The play is set near a temple dedicated to a goddess on the Malabar coast of western India. A Greek princess named Charition has fallen into the hands of the Indians, who are described as barbarians; perhaps she has been sold to them by pirates or has been shipwrecked. She has sought sanctuary in a temple of a goddess. Her brother arrives with others to rescue her but he too is captured. He manages to escape, but barbarian warrior women appear on the scene, having returned from hunting, armed with bows and arrows. They run away terrified when the fool, who is part of the princess' entourage, passes wind loudly. The fool suggests to Charition that she should steal some objects from the goddess's temple. She refuses to do something so improper and tells him to prepare some wine to offer to the Indians. As they are unaccustomed to drinking, they will not know that it has to be diluted with water; they will get drunk and the Greeks will be able to make a quick getaway.

The 'Indian' king appears along with his retinue, all fresh from having bathed. They speak among themselves in 'Indian', and proceed to drink the wine without diluting it, get quite maudlin, and start to sing and dance. The fool goes on asking, 'What are they saying?' and tries to imitate the 'barbarian' speech. In the end, the king suddenly breaks into Greek, along with the chorus. The fool trips the Indian king and the Greeks tie him up. Indian women warriors appear carrying bows, but Charition and her companions manage to escape and sail off home on their ship.

Although unintelligible speech is a feature of the Greek idea of the barbarian, the representation of foreign speech in a Greek play is unusual. The lines spoken by the Indians seem like unintelligible gibberish, but they appear to be an imitation of a real Indian language. Scholars have variously suggested that it was Kannada, Tulu, or a mixture of old Sanskrit and Old Kannada but this is not clear.

As this is a performance script, it can be inferred that it was for the use of the director or the prompter. The play must have been performed in a theatre here, at Oxyrhynchus. Of course, it may have been performed elsewhere as well.

The setting of the play is appropriate as this was a period of brisk contact between the Mediterranean region and the Malabar coast. The audience may also have been aware of this larger context.

Source Tsitsiridis, 2011

Apart from coins, valuable information regarding Indo-Mediterranean contacts comes from pottery. The two types of Roman pottery found in India are amphorae jars and terra sigillata. Amphorae are jars with a large oval body, narrow cylindrical neck, and two handles. Terra sigillata is a red glazed pottery, decorated by being pressed into a mould. Scholars used to call it 'arretine ware', after Arezzo, an important centre for the production of such pottery. However, not all pottery of this type found at Arikamedu in fact came from Arezzo. Hence, the use of the more appropriate term terra sigillata, which includes moulded, decorated wares as well as undecorated, wheel-made ones made in Italy or imitations thereof. Rouletted ware is a pottery with a smooth surface and usually a metallic lustre, with concentric bands of rouletted designs. Pottery of this type found at several Indian sites, especially in eastern and south-eastern India (both on the coast and in the interiors) was once thought to be a foreign ware; however, it is now considered to be locally produced. Red polished ware, which is found at many sites in Gujarat, was also once considered a foreign ware, but is now considered to have been locally made.

Valuable evidence of India's maritime trade links comes from the site of Arikamedu on the Coromandel coast, 4 km from Puducherry, on the right bank of the Ariyankuppam river, just where it enters the Bay of Bengal. Excavations conducted in 1945 revealed an occupation stretching from the end of the 1st century BCE to the 1st and 2nd centuries CE. Northern and southern sectors of the settlement were identified. A brick structure in the northern sector was identified as a warehouse. In the southern sector, two walled courtyards associated with tanks and drains were tentatively identified as dying vats

FURTHER DISCUSSION | **Excavations at Arikamedu**

Arikamedu was excavated by Mortimer Wheeler in 1945 and by Jean-Marie Casal during 1947–50. It was re-excavated in 1989–92. The 1989–92 excavations resulted in new discoveries and a re-assessment of some of the old evidence and conclusions.

1. Earlier, it was thought that the settlement at Arikamedu was established in the 1st century BCE with the beginning of Indo-Roman trade. Recent excavations brought to light the fact that a fairly well-established settlement was already in place at the site before the advent of this trade.
2. The earlier excavations had identified the northern sector as a port area and the southern one as an industrial area specializing in bead and textile manufacture. However, it seems that activities were not so neatly divided. It also seems that some people—probably merchants and sailors—lived in both sectors.
3. More foreign pottery was found in the northernmost part of the settlement, so it is possible that some foreigners may have lived here.
4. The tank-like structures in the southern sector do not appear to be connected with dying cloth at all. They may have been enclosures for storing food or other sorts of goods.
5. Earlier, it was thought that Indo-Roman trade ended in the 2nd century CE and that Arikamedu was abandoned thereafter. The recent excavations indicate that although the trade did decline, it did not come to an end. Some amount of trade seems to have continued till the 7th century.
6. Coins of the Chola kings, medieval clay lamps, and remains of still later periods indicate that Arikamedu was occupied—with some breaks—till modern times. East Asian pottery at the site suggests a re-orientation of trade networks.

Other questions to which there are yet no definite answers include: What did the Roman amphorae jars hold? Was it wine, sauce, or olive oil? Who were the consumers of the merchandise—foreign traders, wealthy Indians, or both? Did traders from the Roman empire actually live at Arikamedu in large numbers? The textual and archaeological evidence was initially understood as indicating the existence of Roman settlements in South India. Recent studies have questioned this. The amphorae may have contained wine for local elites rather than for Roman traders living at Indian sites. And it is also clear that the Indo-Roman trade was not a direct trade between the Indians and Romans, but involved the participation of middlemen from many regions, including the Arabs and Greeks of Egypt.

Source Begley, 1996

where muslin cloth was dyed and prepared for export. Locally produced pottery was found, but there were also some Mediterranean wares—amphorae and arretine ware (which, as mentioned earlier, is now usually referred to as terra sigillata). The amphorae were jars with a pink body, yellow slip, and two handles. There was also a rouletted black ware which showed some foreign influence. Other finds included over 200 beads of shell, bone, gold, terracotta, and semi-precious stones. A Graeco-Roman gem bore what could be an intaglio carving of the emperor Augustus. A fragment of a Roman lamp made of a fine red ware was also found. On the basis of these discoveries, Mortimer Wheeler concluded that Arikamedu was Poduke, one of the *yavana* emporia (trading stations) mentioned in classical accounts. Recent excavations at Arikamedu have led to the revision of some of these ideas.

Apart from Arikamedu, Mediterranean amphorae and terra sigillata have been found at other southern sites such as Uraiyur, Kanchipuram, and Vasavasamudram (both in Chingleput district). They have also been found at sites in Gujarat and western India—such as Dwarka, Prabhas Patan, Ajabpura, Sathod, Jalat, and Nagara. Other sorts of objects that may possibly be of Roman origin have also been reported—e.g., terracotta objects, glassware, metal artefacts, and jewellery. However, many of these seem to be imitations of Roman objects. Clay bullae made in clay moulds imitating Roman coins are quite common all over the subcontinent. The bullae have a loop or perforation suggesting that they were worn around the neck. Brahmapuri, in the western part of Kolhapur town (in Maharashtra), yielded a large hoard of 'Roman' bronzes, including a statuette of Poseidon, the Roman sea god. Suresh (2004: 153–55) points out that the distribution pattern of Roman artefacts in India indicates that while the trade was initially concentrated on the western coast, the Coromanadel coast soon became more important.

RECENT DISCOVERIES | Pattanam: the ancient Muziris?

From 2007 to 2015, the Kerala Council for Historical Research conducted nine seasons of explorations and excavations at Pattanam, a site in Vadekkekara village in Ernakulam district. The site is now about 4 km away from the Arabian Sea coast but in ancient times, it was a sea port. The Periyar river flows 5 km flows north and its tributary, the Paravur Thodu, flows about 1 km south of the site. The mound extended over about 111 acres. Sixty one trenches were excavated; these comprise less than 1 percent of the total area of the site. The excavations revealed a large volume and variety of remains that throw valuable light on interaction of the Kerala coast with the Mediterranean, West Asia, South-east Asia, and China.

The following phases of occupation were identified:
Iron Age (1000 BCE–500 BCE)
Iron Age - Early Historic Transition (500 BCE–300 BCE)
Early Historic (300 BCE–500 BCE)
Early Medieval (500 CE–1000 CE)
Medieval (1000 CE to 1600 CE)
Modern (1600 CE to the present)

Most of the excavated objects belong to the Early Historic period (3rd century BCE to 5th century CE). Local and Indian pottery types constituted about 99% of the total pottery finds. These included Black and Red Ware (BRW), Russet Coated Painted Ware (RCP), Indian Rouletted Ware (IRW), and 'Type 10' fine grey ware.

There was also a large variety of foreign pottery, indicating maritime trade connections from the early historic period with the Mediterranean region, north Afghanistan, west Asia, and China. Amphorae, terra sigillata, intaglios, and Roman glass fragments point to trade with the Mediterranean. Most amphorae sherds found at Pattanam were containers for transporting wine. There was Turquoise Glazed Pottery (TGP) from southern Iran and torpedo jars (pots with a body resembling a torpedo) of Mesopotamian origin. Chinese ceramics, including blue and white, white glaze, and brown glaze porcelain, point to a flourishing trade with East Asia during 1500–1900 CE.

The rich repertoire of artefacts found at Pattanam included beads of many different stones, grinding stones (granite), stone weights, and terracottas. Artefacts made of iron, copper, lead, and gold were also found. A miniature axe made of gold may have been a pendant or ornament. Among the interesting finds from a level belonging to the early centuries CE was a thin oval-shaped carnelian piece (about 1.5 x 1.0 cm) with a human figure carved in intaglio. It seems to represent the Greek Goddess Tyche or the Roman Goddess Fortuna.

Remnants of a wharf, with remnants of a wooden canoe, were identified at the site. The wharf was made of laterite granules, lime, and clay and had a brick lining.

The botanical remains recovered from the site included rice, black pepper, cardamom, frankincense, peat, bark, charcoal, leaves, roots, seeds, wood, and pulses. The faunal remains included bone fragments and teeth.

The Pattanam project involved experts from different countries, promises to reveal more details about India's maritime trade with the rest of the world. The material is still being analyzed. It has been suggested that Pattanam may represent the ancient port of Muchiri, the Muziris of classical Greek and Latin sources. Whether or not the identification is accepted, the site was clearly an important, busy port in ancient times.

Source Pattanam Excavation Field Report, 2011

Carnelian intaglio with Greek or Roman goddess, carnelian intaglio with leaping lion, terra sigillata (1st column); Chinese porcelain, turquoise glazed pottery, south Arabian ovoid jar fragments, glass beads, torpedo jar fragments (2nd column); amphorae sherds, stone beads, gold objects (3rd column)

Map 8.7 The Erythraean Sea, according to the *Periplus* (after Huntington, 1980)

The wider roles of trade and traders

Merchants appear as donors in inscriptions from different parts of the subcontinent in this period. The increasing affluence of sections of the merchant community coincided with religious institutions getting more institutionalized and organized. Patronizing such institutions by extending financial support was simultaneously an expression of devotion and piety as well as a quest for the validation of social status. (this aspect will be discussed later in this chapter)

Seafaring merchants can be identified in sculptures at several religious establishments. For instance, a railing medallion from Bharhut depicts a huge sea monster on the verge of swallowing a boat and its crew. An inscription suggests that this was a scene depicting the Jataka story of the merchant Vasugupta, who was saved from disaster by meditating on the Buddha. A Mathura sculpture depicts a *bodhisattva* in the form of a horse saving shipwrecked sailors from ravenous *yakshis*. A more graphic reflection of the perils faced by mortal seafarers are the hero stones found on the Konkan coast, sculpted with scenes of sea battles, set up by survivors in honour of those who had lost their lives.

It has been argued that a close relationship soon developed between Buddhist monasteries, traders, and guilds. Liu (1988: 122–23) has argued that as monasteries expanded and received more gifts, they were forced to get involved in various kinds of financial activities, and this led to the forging of a reciprocal relationship between monks and traders. Passing traders provided donations to monasteries, and monasteries in turn provided services for traders. Liu gives two examples to substantiate this point. The residue of what may be wine sedimentation (alternatively, it could be the residue of some sort of medicine) was found in amphorae sherds at the monastic site of Devnimori in Gujarat. The second example comes from Shaikhan Dheri, the site of ancient Pushkalavati. Here, a workshop or storeroom of what appears to be a liquor distillation apparatus was found in a Buddhist monastery. Liu argues that the evidence from these two sites shows that Buddhist monks were engaged in liquor trade. They may also have traded in items such as incense and precious stones, which may have been used for liturgical purposes. Although the evidence for direct links between Buddhist monasteries and trade is not very substantial, Buddhism did flourish in the midst of expanding urbanism and trade.

Other important issues relate to the cultural impact of trade and trade as a vehicle of cultural transmission. Liu has demonstrated the connections between long-distance trade, urbanization, developments in Buddhist theology, and the spread of Buddhism in China. She shows how the demand for relics, images, and ceremonial objects played an important sustaining role in Sino-Indian trade. Ray (1994) too argues for links between Buddhism and trade in this period, directing attention to possible Buddhist symbols and legends on coinage, seals, and pottery, and to the emergence of the idea of the *bodhisattva* Avalokiteshvara as the saviour of travellers and seafarers. She argues that trade networks between the Indian subcontinent and South-east Asia were initially dominated by trading groups owing allegiance to Buddhism and that Buddhism spread to South-east Asia through trading channels. However, while trade was an important vehicle of cultural transmission, there were other agents as well. The activities of Chinese and Indian monks are an important part of the story of the spread of Buddhism to China. And the fact that rituals in South-east Asian courts were dominated (as in India) by Brahmanical practices points to the presence of Brahmana ritual specialists in those courts.

More recently, Jason Neelis (2011) has argued that trade networks were catalysts for Buddhist transmission, and that the *sangha's* ability to adapt to changing conditions of support and its ability to appeal to diverse audiences were important factors in its spread. Further, patterns of transmission overlapped with cultural and commercial exchanges due to a symbiotic relationship that developed between monastic communities and donor networks in a 'moral economy' of merit, where donations to the monastic order were perceived as having the potential to result in even more valuable rewards.

Aspects of Social Change in North India and the Deccan

All the developments discussed thus, far in this chapter had social implications. However, there are a few aspects of social history that require further, separate discussion. The four *varnas* and *ashramas* remained the pillars of Brahmanical ideology, represented in the Dharmashastra texts of this period. The earlier idea of *ashramas* as alternative paths was, however, replaced by the idea of their being consecutive stages. Outsiders such as the *yavanas* were absorbed into the *varna* scheme and were accounted for through the theory of *varna-samkara* (mixture of *varnas*). In the early Dharmasutras, the *yavanas* were described as the offspring of Kshatriya men and Shudra women. The *Mahabharata* variously describes them as the sons of Yayati; as born from the sage Vasishtha's cow (along with others such as the Pahlavas, Dravidas, and Shakas) to destroy Vishvamitra's army; or as Shudras. The *Manu Smriti* refers to them as *vratya-kshatriyas*—Kshatriyas who were degraded due to their non-performance of the sacrificial rituals. Such references indicate a tension between social incorporation and exclusion.

Jati, lineage, and occupation continued to be important bases of social identity. The texts do not give detailed evidence regarding the functioning of caste. They do, however, reflect a preference for endogamy and a hereditary element in occupations. There are also references to people of the same profession living in separate settlements or in distinct parts of settlements. As for restrictions regarding giving and accepting food, texts tend to talk mostly about those at the top of the caste hierarchy—the Brahmanas—and those considered outside the pale of caste society—the Chandalas.

The *Manu Smriti* contains a more detailed discussion of Chandalas than earlier texts. Some of its statements are a continuation of what earlier law givers had to say, but what stands out is the complete segregation of this group. The Chandala was to live outside the village (10.51). He could enter a village or town for performing functions assigned to him, but is to be distinguished by marks at the king's command (10.55). Several Jataka stories suggest that the injunctions regarding untouchability in the *Manu Smriti* were close to prevailing social practice. In these stories, the Chandalas are portrayed as a despised people living in separate settlements, whose sight and touch were considered polluting by others. They included corpse removers, cremators, executioners of thieves, sweepers, public performers, hunters, and fruit sellers. The extreme prejudices against Chandalas are echoed in Jaina texts as well.

The existence of *jati* or caste distinctions and hierarchies did not mean that the system always operated with complete rigidity. There are indications of an element of social flexibility, reflected, for instance, in the recognition extended to the offspring of unequal unions. The *Bhaddasala Jataka* tells the story of how Prasenajit, king of Kosala, was furious when he found out that the Sakyas had tricked him into marrying the daughter of a Sakya prince by a slave woman. The king repudiated his wife and son, but took them back when the Buddha told him that the family of the mother did not matter; it was the father's family that counted. There is a Jataka story of a prince who, in the course of a love affair, apprenticed himself successively to a potter, basket maker, florist, and cook. Other stories tell of a prince becoming a trader, and a young man from a noble family becoming employed as an archer. Brahmanas are portrayed as taking to trade, living as hunters and trappers, farming, hiring themselves out as cowherds, etc. Of course, all these are instances of a person of a higher social station adopting vocations of the lower orders. Stories of successful upward mobility of lower-status groups are few.

As emphasized in an earlier chapter, there was a close connection between caste and roles and relations within the household, especially those between men and women. The strengthening of the patriarchal nature of the family and the increasing subordination of women is reflected in various ways in Dharmashastra works. Texts of this period contain many apparently contradictory statements about women. For instance, the *Manu Smriti* both praises and reviles women. Olivelle ([2005] 2006: 29–36) suggests that the contradictions can be partly explained by the specific context of the statements. For instance, where the discussion is about how men must guard their wives (9.14–16), women are described as lustful, fickle, hard-hearted, and completely untrustworthy. On the other hand, where the discussion is about how men should respect women (9.26–28), the latter are described as bearers of many blessings and as none less than Shri (the goddess of fortune) within the home. Where the discussion is about how men must not abuse women (3.56–58), Manu states that the gods rejoice where women are revered; where they are not, no rite bears fruit. The *Manu Smriti* emphasizes the husband's control over his wife and her property; but it also states that the wife cannot be sold or repudiated, and that she cannot be treated as chattel, since she is obtained from the gods and not received like cattle and gold in the market (9.95). The husband is also supposed to support the wife in all circumstances, provided she is faithful (9.95).

Vijay Nath (1993–94) has examined the changing relationships between women and property in Brahmanical texts from the time of the *Rig Veda* to the 5th–6th centuries CE. She argues that by the time of the Smritis and Puranas, women were relegated to a position of almost complete subordination and subservience, and were treated as items of property, on par with Shudras. Women had a low priority among claimants to inherited property in the early Dharmasutras. But, according to Nath, from about the 2nd century BCE, the law givers recognized and gave prescriptions regarding women's right to inheritance. It should be noted, however, that this only applies to *stri-dhana*. According to the *Manu Smriti* (9.194), *stri-dhana* includes six types of gifts—those received before the nuptial fire, in the bridal procession, those given or taken as a token of love (by her father-in-law or mother-in-law), and those received from her brother, mother, or father. However, it did not include inherited property or even property acquired by a woman through her own labour. Regular property rights continued to be essentially governed by rules of patrilineal inheritance. Nath extends her argument to assert that women's rights to inherit immoveable property were significantly acknowledged and expanded in the later centuries (Gupta and post-Gupta periods) in order to maintain the family's control over property and to prevent it from escheating to (i.e., being taken over by) the state.

The preference for sons over daughters was accentuated and women were increasingly relegated to the domestic sphere. The anxiety to marry girls off as early as possible was connected to the great importance attached to maintaining female chastity and producing children. Unlike the earlier Dharmasutras, which stated that girls should be married on attaining puberty, later texts advocated pre-puberty marriages for them.

Like other Dharmashastra works, the *Manu Smriti* prefers marriages to take place within the *varna*, but acknowledges the existence of inter-*varna* unions and extends approval to *anuloma* (hypergamous) ones. However, the mixture of *varnas* that arose though *pratiloma* marriages is condemned as leading to chaos and ruin, and the king was enjoined to prevent them.

There are references to polygyny in the Dharmashastra, such as in the discussion of the property rights of a man's sons born of various wives. For women, on the other hand, lifelong monogamy is presented as the ideal. The *Manu Smriti* disapproves of widow remarriage. It asserts (9.47) that a daughter should only be given away in marriage once. On the other hand, it refers elsewhere (9.175) to the *paunarbhava* as the son of a woman who has remarried because she has been widowed, abandoned, or because she wants to do so. In the *Manu Smriti*, the idea of temporary self-denial and celibacy for widows in the earlier Dharmasutras is replaced by lifelong strictures. In an interesting argument, Stephanie Jamison has argued (2006: 191–214) that the hardening of attitudes towards women in texts like the *Manu Smriti* and negative statements about their inherent nature, reflect a realization that women have mental agency and the capacity to act independently. The reason for this anxiety was the rise of a new female type—the woman ascetic.

Sati—the immolation of a woman on her husband's funeral pyre—is an extreme, violent practice connected with the idea of a woman's chastity and fidelity to her husband in a highly patriarchal society. The earliest eyewitness account of the practice

FURTHER DISCUSSION | **The Jatakas as a source of social history**

The Jatakas can be used to reveal aspects of the everyday lives of ordinary people. They reflect a society marked by deep differences based on class and caste. The themes of hierarchy and pollution taboos occur frequently in the stories. Uma Chakravarti points out that while the popular narrative format ruled out a direct discussion of Buddhist philosophical themes, the stories were moulded in order to convey certain unambiguous messages emphasizing Buddhist ethics. The Buddhist monks must have drawn on a pool of existent folklore, and given it a Buddhist tinge.

The Jatakas consist of stories within stories. Each tale has four parts. There is an introductory story set in the age of the Buddha. Then comes the main story, set in a mythical past, wherein the Buddha appears as the protagonist or witness. The third part is a verse that summarizes the crux of the story, and the fourth and final part links the story of the past with the present. As is the case with other folk tales, the Jatakas deal with real concerns and issues of human society, even when the stories apparently deal with animals. Animals, like humans, are described as living in an unequal world. Sometimes, an inferior animal is made to realize his inferiority vis-à-vis superior ones. At other times, weaker animals are shown as getting the better of stronger ones through cunning. For instance, there is the story of the boar who was challenged to a contest by a lion. The boar dreaded the encounter because he knew he was no match for the lion. His fellow boars thought of a strategy—they suggested that he roll about in dung for seven days, and that the clean and finicky lion would refuse to fight him. They were proved right; the lion could not stand the stink and conceded defeat.

In the *Setaketu Jataka*, a Chandala is shown subverting the Brahmanical notion of pollution: A well-known teacher had a Brahmana student who thought a great deal of his high caste. One day, the student happened to come near a Chandala. The Brahmana was horrified at the thought that the wind might strike the Chandala's body and then strike him, thereby polluting him. He therefore, ordered the Chandala to move to the leeward side of the road so that he did not stand in the wind's path. He himself moved to the windward side. However, the Chandala did not oblige. He stood his ground on the windward side of the Brahmana and said that he would obey the Brahmana only if the latter could answer his question. The Brahmana accepted the challenge, but was unable to answer the question. As a result, he had to put up with public humiliation at the hands of the Chandala.

Several Jataka stories project prejudices against women, similar to those present in the Buddhist canonical texts. Women of the upper classes are frequently described as innately fickle, untrustworthy, and adulterous. The *Bandana Mokkha Jataka* tells the story of a queen who extracted a promise of fidelity from the king. She herself, on the other hand, committed adultery with every single messenger the king solicitously sent to ask about her welfare. On the other hand, there are stories of women from humble families, who, along with their menfolk, are shown seeking moments of pleasure in the midst of a life of hardship and poverty.

Source Uma Chakravarti, 2006: 198–221

occurs in a Greek source, the *Bibliotheca Historica* of Diodorus Sicilus (1st century BCE). Vedic texts and the *Manu Smriti* do not mention *sati*. Early textual references occur in the Sanskrit epics. The Uttarakanda of the *Ramayana* (generally considered a later addition to the text) refers to the mother of the female ascetic Vedavati committing *sati* on her husband's death. In the *Mahabharata*, the four wives of Vasudeva (Krishna's father) are said to have killed themselves on his death as do five wives of Krishna. Madri, one of Pandu's wives, commits *sati* when he dies, but Kunti does not. In the Stri Parva of the *Mahabharata*, the widows of the heroes who die at Kurukshetra mourn and lament; they do not commit *sati*. However, Sanskrit *kavya*, Puranas, and later Dharmashastra texts contain several references to the practice of *sati*.

While the Dharmashastra texts contain various prescriptions about the ideal roles of women belonging to the upper echelons of society, other texts introduce us to women from different backgrounds, associated with different vocations. In the Pali Jatakas, apart from queens, nuns, and courtesans, we encounter women associated with various occupations such as basket making, weaving, and dying.

Our window into gender relations expands still further when we look at non-textual evidence, especially inscriptions from various parts of the subcontinent (see Shah, 2001). Some record the activities of royal women. For instance, royal women of the Satavahana family are prominent in the epigraphic record and exercised initiative in making donations in their own right. We can also note the use of matronyms by some Satavahana kings; names like Gautamiputra and Vasishthiputra suggest the king took on his mother's *gotra*. In the Brahmanical system, *gotra* is inherited from the father, not the mother. The evidence of kings named with reference to their mother is therefore significant, but on its own it does not necessarily constitute evidence of matriarchy or even matriliny. Matronyms may have been a way of identifying parentage in a polygynous situation. The use of the same matronym by more than one king also suggests the practice of cross-cousin marriage among the Satavahanas and Ikshvakus.

However, the issue is not just one of matronyms. As mentioned earlier, the inscriptions of the Satavahana queens Naganika and Gautamiputra Balashri indicate that women of the royal household wielded considerable authority. Mekhola Gomes's (2021) study of Ikshvaku inscriptions demonstrates the convergence of kinship networks and political power in the Ikshvaku kingdom. References to natal families in women's donative inscriptions at Nagarjunakonda are common (both among royal and non-royal women), as are statements that the merit of their pious gifts should accrue to both sides of their family. While Chamtisiri was the most prominent royal patron at Nagarjunakonda, Bodhisiri stands out as a non-royal donor whose benefactions were extensively spread over many monastic establishments. Royal women were married to high-ranking officials (or their husbands were elevated to such rank). We can also note a Nashik inscription which describes the composer as a woman *pratiharakshi* (doorkeeper) named Lota.

As will be discussed later, women appear in large numbers as donors at Buddhist and Jaina sites. This suggests that certain women had some degree of control over the economic resources of their households. Finally, if we want to look for women of this period, we have to move beyond the words found in texts and inscriptions into the realm of images. As we shall see further on, various aspects of women and femininity are represented in the sculpture of this period.

Society in Early Historic South India

Ancient Tamil texts reflect processes of interaction between the northern Sanskritic and the southern Tamil cultures. The Sangam poets were familiar with the *Mahabharata* and *Ramayana* legends. In fact, the Chola, Chera, and Pandya kings claim to have fed the warring armies on the eve of the war. This should be understood as an attempt on the part of these dynasties to connect themselves with the epic tradition. The *Tolkappiyam* states that marriage rituals were introduced into Tamil country by the Aryas. We know that Buddhism, Jainism, and the worship of the gods Vishnu and Shiva also travelled from north to south. Reciprocal exchange between Sanskrit and the Dravidian languages is also evident in early texts.

The epic–Puranic tradition contains several legends about Agastya and Parashurama, connecting these sages with trans-Vindhyan India (Sastri, [1955] 1975: 70–74). Historians interpret them as allegorical stories, a symbolic reflection of the spread of Brahmanical cultural influences to South India. The *Rig Veda* refers to the *rishi* Agastya's curious birth from a *kumbha* (jar). The epics have more to say about him. The *Mahabharata* tells the following story: Agastya was married to a princess of Vidarbha named Lopamudra. Lopamudra wanted him to provide her with all sorts of luxuries without compromising his asceticism. Agastya went to three Arya kings for help, but in vain. Accompanied by these kings, he then approached Ilvala, king of Manimati, for help. Ilvala was a wicked demon who hated Brahmanas because long ago, a Brahmana had refused to grant him a boon making him equal to Indra. He had devised a devious ploy to avenge himself. He would transform his younger brother Vatapi into a ram and offer its meat to a Brahmana. Then, using his special powers, he would recall Vatapi to life and the latter would rip open the Brahmana's stomach and emerge laughing. In this way, the duo had killed many a hapless Brahmana. When Agastya turned up at his court with the three Arya kings, Ilvala turned his brother into a ram and offered the meat to the sage. Agastya ate it, but when Ilvala called his brother to come forth, only air emerged.

Due to Agastya's remarkable metabolism, Vatapi had already been digested. Ilvala ended up giving Agastya the riches he needed to satisfy Lopamudra.

In another *Mahabharata* story, Agastya travels south and tells the Vindhyas to stop growing till he returns, which he never does. In the *Ramayana*, Rama tells his brother Lakshmana on the way to Agastya's hermitage that this sage had fought the *asuras* (demons) and had made the Dandaka forest fit for the habitation of Aryas. Agastya is mentioned as an important sage in Tamil tradition. The *Manimekalai* mentions his miraculous birth from a jar and connects him with two Chola kings. Early medieval tradition lists him as a member of the first and second Sangams. A work on grammar called the *Agattiyam* is said to have been composed by him in the first Sangam.

The main thread of the legend connecting Parashurama with South India is as follows: Jamadagni was suspicious of his wife Renuka's fidelity and ordered his son Parashurama to kill her. Parashurama complied and had to expiate his sin of matricide by exterminating the Kshatriyas, enemies of the Brahmanas. He did this and then, on Vishvamitra's instructions, gifted the entire earth to the Brahmanas. Having no place to call his own, he performed a rigorous penance, as a result of which the god Varuna granted him a boon. Parashurama was to stand at Kanyakumari at the southernmost tip of the peninsula. He was to throw his *parashu* (axe) northwards, and could have all the land that fell within the throw. Parashurama did this; his axe landed at Gokarman, and all the land upto that point became his. He brought in Brahmanas from the north and settled them in villages, providing law codes for them and for others.

It must be emphasized that although ancient texts indicate various kinds of interactions between northern and peninsular India, this interaction was a reciprocal one. The history of South India cannot be seen simplistically as a story of 'Aryanization', with northern Sanskritic influences operating on a passive south. In earlier chapters, we traced the development of neolithic–chalcolithic and early iron age cultures in South India. Here, we will explore the evidence from Sangam poetry. This can be combined with the archaeological evidence of the later megalithic phase in the far south cited in both in this chapter and in Chapter 5.

Sangam literature reflects a society with its distinctive cultural traditions, one which celebrated war and love. Mention was made earlier of the close relationship between kings and bards, and of the *puram* poems that praised the valour and generosity of kings. There are also the beautiful love (*akam*) poems that speak of the love between man and woman. The poet does not speak through his or her own persona, but uses various characters such as the heroine, her friend, her foster mother, or the hero as his mouthpiece. The love poems use an interesting convention of associating themes with different landscapes known as *tinai*, each named after a flower. The *kurinchi* or mountain landscape was associated with the union of lovers, the *palai* (arid terrain) with separation, the *mullai* (pastoral region) with patient waiting, the *neytal* (seashore) with pining, and the *marutam* (riverine tracts) with sulking. The poems use vivid imagery and often rely on understatement and suggestion to convey deep emotion.

Sangam poems contain several incidental references to material culture, often as part of the poem's setting or in similes and allusions. There are references to farming (rice and barley are mentioned), cattle rearing, and fishing. There are also several references to iron. *Kuruntokai* 16 refers to iron-tipped arrows. *Akananuru* 72 compares a bear digging out the comb from a termite mound, the front of which is swarming with fireflies glimmering like sparks from beaten metal, to a blacksmith forging iron. *Purananuru* 116 refers to the proud horses and iron weapons of the kings who came to fight Pari. *Purananuru* 21 talks of a mighty fortress called Kanapper which disappeared like water vapourized by iron heated in a glowing fire by a black-handed smith.

The social classification of *varna* was known to Sangam poets. There is mention of the *Arashar* (kings), *Vaishiyar* (traders), and *Velalar* (farmers). The Brahmanas are also mentioned, some of them closely associated with the courts of kings and patronized by ruling elites. They are described as performing *yajnas*, including ones on the battlefield, to ensure victory. In the *Padirrapattu*, the sage Kapila advises kings that they should give

PRIMARY SOURCES | **An ancient Tamil love poem**

If mother knows, let her, and if our lovely,
kind street with its loud mouths hears, let it.
I'm telling you nothing else happened—
you can be sure of it.
I swear it by the god at Pukār with its curved eddies.
We were playing with our garlanded friends
in an ocean grove making little houses,
heaping up play rice, and as we were resting a bit
because we were exhausted, a man came.
"Beautiful ones with round, soft, bamboo-like arms,
the light is going and I am very tired.
Would there be anything wrong if I ate a guest's food
on a soft leaf and stayed in your noisy village?"
he said. Turning our faces downward,
we each tried to hide behind the other,
and we said,
"Our food isn't fit for you, it's *kolumin* fish,
which only low people eat," and then
at that instant we said, "Isn't that the boats
returning with their tall, waving banners?"
and we kicked over our sand houses with our feet.
As we were leaving, of all of us,
fixing his gaze on me he said, "O you with a lovely forehead,
may I go?" making me almost die of shame. I said,
"You may leave," and he stood there
holding the support of his high chariot
and looking at me—still it seems to be before my eyes.

Source *Akananuru 110*; poet: Pontaip Pacalaiyar; Hart (Trans.), 2015: 121

important jobs such as those of advisers to Brahmanas. However, the four-fold *varna* classification had little application to ancient Tamil society. The *jati* system was not a feature of this society either.

The more relevant basis of social classification was *kuti*. The *kuti* were clan-based descent groups and were central to the early Tamil system of agricultural production. Although associated with lineage and hereditary occupation, there were no real restrictions on inter-dining and social interaction among the *kuti* groups. The process whereby caste took root in South India is not adequately understood. Some scholars see it as a further development of the *kuti* organization. Rajan Gurukkal (2010: 244–50) suggests that Brahmana landholdings played a key role in eventually breaking down the kin-based system of agrarian organization and the emergence of a new agrarian order and social relationships based, among other things, on caste.

Sangam literature reflects a belief in sacred or magical forces called *ananku* that were supposed to inhabit various objects. The job of carrying out rites and rituals to control the *ananku* was that of groups such as the Pariyans, Tutiyans, Panans, and Velans. They were associated with ritualistic singing, dancing, and trances, and with lighting the cremation fire and worshipping memorial stones. On this basis, George L. Hart (1976: 43) argues that the association of low castes with pollution is of southern origin. *Ananku* was also believed to cling to women. If a woman was chaste, her *ananku* would be under control and had auspicious potential. Women were considered impure during menstruation and for a number of days after childbirth. Widows were considered extremely inauspicious and dangerous, and were supposed to lead a very austere life.

Sangam poems are pervaded with a warrior ethic. The goal of the hero of the *puram* poems was *pukal* (glory, fame) and a heroic death was greatly valued. It was believed that the spirit of a warrior who died in battle dwelt in paradise. A poem in the *Purananuru* suggests that the bodies of warriors who did not die in battle were cut with swords before the funerary rites, to simulate death in battle. The practice of *vattakirutal* was one in which a defeated king committed ritual suicide by starving himself to death, accompanied by those who had been close to him during his lifetime. The worship of memorial stones (*natukal*) was a corollary of the importance of the heroic ideal. Memorial stones were erected in honour of heroes who died fighting valiantly in battle; the spirit of the fallen hero was believed to reside in these stones.

Different kinds of funerary practices are mentioned in the poems. In *Purananuru* 228, the poet addresses a potter who must make urns for the dead Valavan. There are

PRIMARY SOURCES | **A heroic death**

When she heard the many voices saying, "That aged woman with dry,
veined arms where the soft flesh hangs down, she whose belly
is wrinkled like a lotus leaf—her son was afraid of the enemy army
and he showed them his back and ran!"
then rage overcame her and she said,
"If he fled in the furious battle,
I will cut off the breast
at which he sucked!" and she snatched up a sword and she
turned over every body lying there on the blood-soaked field.
And when she found her son who was scattered
in pieces, she felt happier than she had been the day she bore him.

Purananuru 278: The song of Kakkaipatiniyar Nachchellaiyar. Note that this poem, with its graphic and startling glorification of a heroic death, was composed by a woman.

Source *Purananuru* 278; poet: Kakkaipatiniyar Naccellaiyar; Hart and Heifetz. [Trans.]., 1999: 165

several references to cremation. In *Kuruntokai* 231, the heroine laments that her lover avoids her as though she were a burning ground for strangers. *Purananuru* 356 gives a fearsome description of a burning ground. In *Purananuru* 363, the poet speaks of the finality of death and of the cremation ground as the final home of great, good kings. There are also references to the exposure of the dead in *Akananuru* 77 and *Purananuru* 231.

Sangam poems suggest the practice of widow immolation in early historic South India. There is also evidence of memorial stones commemorating women who committed *sati*. These *sati* stones vary in composition and complexity, but can be identified by their representation of an outstretched right arm, bent at the elbow, adorned with bangles, the palm of the hand facing outwards. Bangles signify that the woman is not to be considered a widow. The additional motifs of the sun and the moon indicate a belief that her fame would last forever.

Vijaya Ramaswamy ([1989] 1999) has drawn attention to the many references to women and work in Sangam poems and slightly later works, more so in rural than urban contexts. The poems mention women engaged in agricultural activities such as planting paddy seeds and weeding. Tasks such as the husking and winnowing of paddy were performed entirely by women. Young girls kept watch over the agricultural fields and drove away birds and animals. Women were involved in cattle rearing and dairy farming. The terms *ayichchiyar*, *kovichchiyar*, and *idaichchiyar* were used for shepherdesses. As today, so also in early historical times, spinning was done almost entirely by women. Sangam texts refer to women spinners as *parutti pentukal*. However, there are no references to women weavers. Bleaching and washing cloth were other activities in which women were involved. There is an interesting reference in the *Purananuru* to a potter woman of Venni (Vennikuyattiyar); she was also a poetess who composed a poem on the victory of Karikala at the battle of Venni. Women were engaged in basket making and pith work. Fisherwomen were involved in catching and selling fish and the extraction and selling of fish oil. Men and women living in coastal areas made and sold salt. The *Akananuru* mentions beautiful women of the seashore exchanging salt for paddy with peasant women. Women are also mentioned in connection with the making and selling of toddy made out of fermented rice. Garland making and flower selling were other occupations associated with women. Sangam poems often mention the *chevilittai*—foster mothers or wet nurses, who seem to have been closely associated with family members. The *viraliyar* were women bards and dancers belonging to the *panar* community of wandering minstrels. There are also references to kings employing women bodyguards.

Sangam poetry shows the existence of a vibrant and sophisticated literary culture in ancient Tamilakam. A 2nd century CE inscription from Mannarkoil mentions the *katikai*. This term, derived from the Sanskrit *ghatika*, may refer to an assembly of learned persons, an institution of higher learning, or a place where such an assembly or institution was located.

Champakalakshmi (1975–76) identifies the 'Sangam age' with the last phase of the megalithic culture in the Tamil region. She further identifies the megalithic communities and their large agricultural settlements with the *velir* (chieftains) and the *velala* (peasantry) of the Sangam poems. She substantiates her argument with a correlation of the *velir* settlements known from literature with the megalithic sites. Apart from identifying such specific correlations, there is a broad correspondence between some of the cultural features reflected in Sangam poetry and that of megalithic sites of the far south. This includes a subsistence base consisting of agriculture, cattle rearing, and fishing; the use of iron; and a milieu in which warfare and weapons were important. The poems, like the megaliths, reflect a variety of modes of disposal of the dead. The hero stones of the poems can similarly be connected with the memorial stones of the megalithic tradition.

Philosophical Developments

The modern distinction between philosophy and religion is difficult to maintain in the context of ancient cultures. Indian philosophical traditions offered different explanations about the nature of reality and knowledge, but they usually also had a soteriological aspect (soteriology means a path to salvation or liberation) and many of them came to be eventually connected with one or other religious tradition. The indigenous term for philosophy is *darshana*, which literally means 'view'. Another important term is *anvikshiki*, which literally means 'looking at', and eventually came to mean logical reasoning.

The Charvaka school was also known as Lokayata (literally 'that which is found among people'). The tenets of the school are supposed to have been contained in a *sutra* composed by Brihaspati, but no such text has survived. Whatever we know about Charvaka is through references in texts of rival schools. Its followers rejected the authority of the Vedas and the Brahmanas. They questioned the efficacy of sacrifice. They argued, for instance, that if food offered to deceased ancestors could reach them, it should also be possible to transfer food long-distance in a similar manner to hungry travellers. Charvaka was an atheist school. It also rejected the ideas of an eternal soul, rebirth, and the laws of *karma* and *punya* (merit). Its materialist doctrine asserted that the body and consciousness were products of combinations of matter. Charvaka accepted only one basis of knowledge—that which is perceived by the senses. Rejecting the distinction between good and bad actions, the followers of Charvaka philosophy urged that the pleasures of life should be enjoyed—at least this is how their rival schools present their ideas.

Later texts refer to two Charvaka schools—Dhurtta and Sushikshita, but details are lacking. The former apparently held that only the four elements—earth, water, air, and fire—existed. They understood the body as composed of a combination of atoms and rejected the idea of a soul. Sushikshita Charvaka, on the other hand, accepted the idea of a soul that was distinct from the body. However, this soul was not eternal—it was destroyed when the body was destroyed.

In the early medieval period, several texts listing and discussing different philosophical views (these are known as doxographies) were written. These intersected with an older binary division into *astika* and *nastika* (see Nicholson, [2010] 2011: 166–84, 191–92). *Astika* means 'one who says it is' and *nastika* means 'one who says 'it is not.' The terms could therefore, be given varying content. The dividing lines between *astika* and *nastika* are a good indicator of how proponents of different philosophical schools and religious traditions saw themselves in relation to others. While there were different views on what exactly made someone or a philosophical school or a religious group *nastika*, in all cases, the term had negative connotations. *Nastikas* were not only criticized; their views were condemned, and they were supposed to be shunned. The *Mahabharata* talks about *nastikas* who deny the authority of the Veda; their views cannot be accepted or be condoned. They should be avoided at all cost and kings are advised to go all out to eliminate them (see Dayal, 2019). The *Manu Smriti* criticizes Brahmanas who use *hetu* (logic) to question the *shruti* or *smriti*, which are the sources of *dharma*, and states that such *nastika* denigrators of the Veda should be ostracized.

The terms *astika* and *nastika* were also used in non-Brahmanical texts but were given different content. The 4th century Buddhist text *Bodhisattvabhumi* criticizes various types of Buddhists but reserves its strongest condemnation for those who hold a position of universal negation and say that nothing exists. Later texts identify them with Buddhists of the Madhyamika school. The Jaina scholar Haribhadra's *Shaddarshanasamuchchaya* (8th century) describes six schools—Buddhism, Nyaya, Samkhya, Jainism, Vaisheshika, and Mimamsa—as the *astika* schools which affirm the existence of the other world, transmigration, virtue, and vice. Of these, he asserts that Jainism is the best. He gives the *nastika* label to the materialist Lokayata school (Nicholson, [2010] 2011).

The idea of the 'six systems of orthodox philosophy' emerged fairly late. The 14th century *Sarvadarshana-samgraha* lists six *astika* schools of philosophy. This work is ascribed to the Advaita Vedantin scholar Madhava, who was a minister in the Vijayanangara empire and later became the head of the Shringeri matha. This text juxtaposes the *astika* schools (Samkhya, Yoga, Nyaya, Vaisheshika, Purva Mimamsa or Vedanta, and Uttara Mimamsa) against the *nastika* schools (which include the Buddhists, Jainas, and Charvaka materialists). All the schools—*astika* and *nastika*—are shown to be inferior to Advaita Vedanta. The point to note is that the idea of the 'six systems' of the *astika* tradition is something that emerged much later, in the medieval period. These schools are often treated as three inter-related pairs—**Purva Mimamsa** and **Uttara Mimamsa** (or Vedanta), **Nyaya** and **Vaisheshika**, and **Samkhya** and **Yoga**.

Although the idea of the six systems forming a group is late, these philosophical systems themselves are very old, just how old is difficult to say. The cryptic *sutra* style of their early texts paved the way for many different interpretations and commentaries. These philosophical traditions refer to each other, often in order to refute rival claims. They reflect a context of philosophical debate among a small intelligentsia. The names of some of the authorities are known, but there is much that remains unknown about the debaters, their audience, and their patrons.

Mimamsa means exegesis, i.e., explanation, and the school of this name was devoted to Vedic exegesis. It aimed at explaining Vedic texts from the point of view of the nature and goals of sacrificial rituals. Its earliest known important thinker was Jaimini, author of the *Mimamsa Sutra*, who lived in the 2nd century BCE. The Mimamsa school held the Vedas to be eternal and the authority on *dharma*. Jaimini understood Vedic ritual texts as embodiments of *dharma* in which sacrifice was central. He used the rules of language framed by grammarians in order to explain how statements in the Vedas were to be interpreted as injunctions related to sacrifice. This school came to be known as Purva Mimamsa in order to distinguish it from another school rooted in the Vedic tradition—Uttara Mimamsa or Vedanta. In early Mimamsa doctrine, the gods were irrelevant; it was the sacrifice that was central. Later Mimamsakas acknowledged the existence of a supreme god.

While Purva Mimamsa focused on sacrificial acts, Vedanta focused on knowledge and was based on an interpretation of the Upanishads. A key text was Badarayana's *Brahma Sutra* or *Vedanta Sutra*, which belongs to about the same time as the *Mimamsa Sutra*. The aim of the *Vedanta Sutra* is to inquire into *brahman*, the central concept of the Upanishads. The text emphasized that all things were part of *brahman*. Both Mimamsa and Vedanta saw the Vedas as a valid source of knowledge whose authority could not be questioned. They laid the ground work of various views on the issues of the *pramanas*, i.e., the grounds of knowledge.

In self-conscious contrast to Mimamsa, Vedanta emphasized the path of knowledge (*jnana*) as opposed to that of works or sacrifice (*karma*). Arguing that the results of sacrifice were impermanent, while the object of knowledge (*brahman*) was eternal and unchanging, Vedantic schools, of which there are three principal variants (and many sub-variants), gave an account of *brahman*, the world, and the relation between the two. Vedantic cosmology is largely incorporated from the earlier Samkhya system. Because its principal and most influential variant, sometimes called 'Shankara Vedanta' after its founder, affirms the exclusive reality of *brahman* and relegates everything else to illusion, Vedanta texts had much to say about the nature of error. Like the other philosophical systems, Vedanta too was framed within a liberation theology; the ultimate aim of knowledge was *moksha*, i.e., liberation from *samsara*

The *Vaisheshika Sutra* of Uluka Kanada was written some time between the 2nd century BCE and 1st century CE. This text claimed to be concerned primarily with *dharma*. Describing *dharma* as that from which the highest good was achieved, it ascribed the authority of the Veda to the fact that it dealt with *dharma*. The philosophy of the *Vaisheshika Sutra* can be described as pluralistic realism. Vaisheshika comes from the word *vishesha* which means particularity, and the aim of the school was to investigate the particularities of the pluralities of things that exist in the world. This school identified seven fundamental categories (*padarthas*) of things that exist—substance, quality, action, universality, particularity, a relation of inherence, and absence or negation. The category of substance was further divided into nine types of atoms—earth, water, fire, air, ether, space, time, self, and mind. The first four are material and the rest are immaterial. In each individual, there is only one mind atom associated with a single self atom. All atoms, whether material or immaterial, are considered eternal and indestructible. These atoms join together in different combinations to produce the various things we see in the world around us. The Vaisheshika explanation of reality also identifies 17–24 kinds of qualities and five kinds of actions that are associated with substances. Qualities and substances are considered inseparable. An example is that of a red rose—just as the rose cannot exist without its quality of redness, its redness cannot exist independent of the rose.

Vaisheshika was closely associated with Nyaya, a school concerned primarily with logic and epistemology (a theory concerning the nature and bases of knowledge). Nyaya ascribes its own origins to a person named Akshapada Gotama, who is supposed to have lived in the 3rd century BCE. However, the *Nyaya Sutra* ascribed to him does not seem to be older than the 1st century CE. Nyaya took over many of the Vaisheshika ideas and added to them. It laid down a formal method of reasoning to establish the correctness of the Vaisheshika pluralistic explanation of reality. It also claimed that true knowledge gained through Vaisheshika could lead to liberation.

According to the Nyaya system, something should be inquired into only if there was some doubt about it, if there was some possibility of arriving at a definite conclusion, and if such an inquiry contributed to liberation from the cycle of rebirth. It also stipulated that there should be some observable data that could be used in the investigation. There are five stages in the Nyaya method of argument—a statement of the thesis that is to be proved; a statement of the reason for the thesis; an example that acts as a rule that can be used to support the thesis; connecting this rule to the thesis; and a restatement of the thesis which has been proved. An example of these five stages given in the *Nyaya Sutra* is as follows: (*a*) There is fire on the hill; (*b*) We can say this because there is smoke there; (*c*) Where there is smoke, there is fire; (*d*) There is smoke, which is associated with fire, on the hill; (*e*) Therefore, there is fire on the hill. The Nyaya system of logic attached importance to perception, reasoning, and inference.

The *Samkhya Karika* ascribed to Ishvarakrishna belongs to the mid-4th or mid-5th century CE. However, Samkhya was a very old philosophical system that went back at least to the time of the Upanishads. Kapila is described as the legendary founder of the school. Samkhya has a detailed ontology (a theory of being) and epistemology. It holds that the world we see around us really exists. Two fundamental categories in Samkhya thought are *purusha* (the spiritual principle) and *prakriti* (matter or nature). There are supposed to be many *purushas*, all of them eternal, unchanging, passive, and conscious witnesses. *Prakriti*, on the other hand, is eternal and unchanging, but also active and unconscious. It has three *gunas* or qualities—*sattva* (goodness), *rajas* (energy or passion), and *tamas* (darkness or inertia). The relationship between *purusha* and *prakriti* is described as similar to a passive observer watching a dancer. Liberation consists of the

PRIMARY SOURCES | **The *Bhagavad Gita***

The *Bhagavad Gita* (The Song of the Lord) is an important philosophical and religious text of this period. The *Gita* forms the third episode in the Bhishma Parva of the *Mahabharata* and presents itself as the revelation made by the god Krishna to Arjuna on the eve of the Mahabharata battle. It is generally seen as a later interpolation into the *Mahabharata* and assigned to *c.* 200 BCE.

This text reflects a new age looking back at an older time. The celebration of war has turned to a sombre reflection on its meaning and consequences. There is also a new notion of god—an all-powerful being, who can lead those who take refuge in him to liberation from the cycle of rebirth, one who descends to earth when people need him, and one with whom *bhaktas* (devotees) can bond in a close, personal relationship.

The *Gita* is a philosophically very rich and complex text. It draws on and reflects strands of many different philosophical ideas—such as *yoga*, *moksha*, *karma*, and renunciation—and casts them into something new. It emphasizes the importance of fulfilling *varnashrama dharma*. It talks of the imperishable *atman* and the irrelevance of death. Its exhortation of *karma yoga* advocates the renunciation not of acts but of their fruits; i.e., actions should be performed with no regard to their fruits or consequences. Given below is an excerpt from Krishna's discourse to Arjuna:

The Lord said:

You sorrow over men you should not be sorry for, and yet you speak to sage issues. The wise are not sorry for either the living or the dead. Never was there a time when I did not exist, or you, or those kings, nor shall any of us cease to exist hereafter. Just as creatures with bodies pass through childhood, youth, and old age in their bodies, so there is a passage to another body, and a wise man is not confused about it. The contacts of the senses with their objects, which produce sensations of cold and heat, comfort and discomfort, come and go without staying, Kaunteya. Endure them, Bharata. The wise man whom they do not trouble, for whom happiness and unhappiness are the same, is fit for immortality.

There is no becoming of what does not already exist, there is no unbecoming of what does exist: those who see the principles see the boundary between the two. But know that on which all this world is strung is imperishable: no one can bring about the destruction of this indestructible. What ends of this unending embodied, indestructible, and immeasurable being is just its bodies—therefore, fight, Bharata! He who thinks that this being is a killer and he who imagines that it is killed do neither of them know. It is not killed nor does it kill.

It is never born nor does it die;
Nor once that it is will it ever not be;
Unborn, unending, eternal, and ancient
It is not killed when the body is killed.

The man who knows him for what he is—indestructible, eternal, unborn, and without end—how does he kill whom or have whom killed, Partha?

As a man discards his worn-out clothes
And puts on different ones that are new,
So the one in the body discards aged bodies
And joins with other ones that are new.

Swords do not cut him, fire does not burn him, water does not wet him, wind does not parch him. He cannot be cut, he cannot be burned, wetted, or parched, for he is eternal, ubiquitous, stable, unmoving, and forever. He is the unmanifest, beyond thought, he is said to be beyond transformation; therefore, if you know him as such, you have no cause for grief.

Source *Bhagavad Gita* 24[2].10–25; van Buitenen. (Trans.)., 1981: 75–77

purusha realizing its distinction from *prakriti*. The Samkhya system also talks of other categories such as *buddhi* (will and the discriminating faculty), *ahamkara* (I-ness, the ego), and mind. Samkhya considers perception and reliable testimony as valid bases of knowledge, and attaches a great deal of importance to inference.

Yoga was another ancient system of thought and practice. The author of the *Yoga Sutras* is unknown, though this text came to be attributed to Patanjali. The *Yoga Sutras* are a manual of yogic practice. They describe the eight stages of *yoga*, five of which deal with training the body and the rest with perfecting the self, leading to the acquisition of *siddhis* (signs of success). At the very outset, the *Yoga Sutras* state that their aim is cessation of the activities of the mind (*chitta-vritti-nirodha*). These activities include valid cognition, misconception, conceptualization, sleep, and memory. The aim is to focus the mind in such a way as to achieve complete tranquility and control. This is expressed in terms of distinguishing the 'seer' or higher self, known as *purusha*, from that which is seen or manifest, which is known as *prakriti*.

The philosophical ideas of Buddhism and Jainism were discussed in earlier chapters; subsequent developments will be discussed further on in this chapter.

Looking at the History of Religions beyond the Framework of 'isms'

In the realms of religious doctrines and practices, the period *c.* 200 BCE to 300 CE reflects several continuities with the earlier centuries, but also some striking new developments. One of the most important of these was the beginning of new devotional practices within Buddhism and Jainism and the emergence of what can be termed early Hinduism or Puranic Hinduism. New forms of worship were accompanied by new liturgies and mythologies. Religious teachers, saints, gods, and goddesses were worshipped or venerated in the form of images within the context of religious shrines. A shrine is basically a demarcated sacred space, and such demarcations must have existed in much earlier times. In this period, however, the construction of stone shrines gave such structures greater permanence and prominence than their earlier counterparts. A shrine was not only a sacred space, it was also an important social space within which people participated in community worship or veneration and interacted with each other. Patronage of shrines was an act of piety as well as a validation of social, and sometimes political, status.

The history of religions is usually constructed on the basis of frameworks provided by religious texts, which are not always accurately reflective of popular practice. Apart from their elite authorship and normative nature, some of these texts are difficult to date. The beliefs and practices they mention often have earlier beginnings. Further, dominant religious traditions usually try to marginalize or ignore other traditions and therefore, often give a distorted idea of their significance. We have already seen this in the case of the Ajivika sect, which, notwithstanding all the criticism of its ideas and leaders in Buddhist and Jaina texts, was clearly influential in many parts of the subcontinent across many centuries.

Further, religious texts do not always clearly reflect regional or local variations in practices, and there are some widely prevalent practices that they do not mention at all. For all these reasons, although texts are extremely valuable sources for the history of religions, they have to be looked at along with evidence from archaeology, inscriptions, and coins. Religions are best studied by carefully taking into account all the available evidence. Apart from remains of structures and images found at various sites, it is necessary to understand how these sites were integrated into their hinterland and with larger religious networks.

Religious traditions did not exist in isolation, but in interaction with each other. The connections and interactions can be seen at the level of shared ideas such as *karma* and rebirth (even though the details of these conceptions varied). They also emerge clearly when we look at the archaeological evidence from specific sites, areas, and regions. Sacred places belonging to different religious traditions are often found in close proximity to each other. The sculptural motifs associated with ancient religious establishments reveal the existence of a shared pool of auspicious symbols. Their shrines reflect shared architectural styles that cut across sectarian differences. All this is not surprising, as these traditions and their adherents shared a common cultural space. We will also see that there are several religious practices that were not specifically associated with a specific religious tradition but were an enduring feature of popular religion over many centuries. At the same time, the relationship between different religions or cults could also take the form of competition and conflict.

A few examples of the multiple interlocking religious layers at many places can be given here. The Mathura region, which is strongly associated with the legend and worship of Krishna, had a very variegated religious landscape between *c.* 200 BCE and 300 CE (Upinder Singh, 2004a). This is evident from the great variety of sculptures, structural remains, and inscriptions that have been found here. For instance, the Katra was the site of a Buddhist *vihara*, the Jamalpur mound was the site of a Buddhist establishment and of a shrine of the *naga* deity Dadhikarna, while a Jaina establishment stood on the Kankali Tila. (For a description of Buddhist remains in the Mathura area, see Vinay Gupta, 2009.) Kanika Kishore Saxena (2021) has documented the varied and changing religious landscape of Mathura from the 3rd century BCE to the 12th century CE, focusing on Jainism, Buddhism, the worship of Vasudeva Krishna and other Hindu deities, *yakshas* and *nagas*, and the patronage of Brahmanas. In South India, the site of Nagarjunakonda in Guntur district, Andhra Pradesh, which today lies submerged in the waters of the Nagarjunasagar lake, offers another dramatic example of the heterogeneity of the religious landscape. Here, there were over 30 ancient Buddhist establishments and 19 Hindu temples, as well as some medieval Jaina shrines. Rima Hooja's study (2004) of early Hinduism in Rajasthan highlights that sites such as Bairat, Nagari, Rairh, Nagar, Sambhar, and Rang Mahal show the co-existence of various belief systems and sects in the region during this as well as later periods. Snigdha Singh (2022) has compared the donative inscriptions from Bharhut, Sanchi, the Western Ghats, and Mathura between the 2nd century BCE and 2nd century CE, and has analyzed the identity markers of monastic and lay donors from a gendered perspective.

The worship of *yakshas* and *yakshis*, *nagas* and *nagis*

Ananda K. Coomaraswamy ([1928–31] 1980: 36) argued persuasively that the worship of *yakshas*, *yakshis*, *nagas*, *nagis*, and goddesses was the natural source of the devotional (*bhakti*) elements that became so pervasive in Indian religions. He also argued that the worship of *yakshas* and *yakshis* implied temples, *puja* (devotional worship with offerings), and a cult. *Yakshas* were deities connected with water, fertility, trees, the forest, and the wilderness. The evidence of literature and sculpture graphically illustrates the metamorphosis of the *yaksha* from a benevolent, powerful deity who was the focus of exclusive worship to a terrifying, demonic creature, reduced to the position of a subsidiary attendant figure associated more with fertility than with wealth (see Sutherland, 1992; Misra, [1979] 1981). *Yakshis* or *yakshinis*, the female counterpart of *yakshas*, were originally benign deities connected with fertility. Many of the *shalabhanjikas*—a generic term for sensuous sculptural representations of women grasping the branch of a tree—found in diverse religious establishments across the subcontinent, were actually *yakshis*. *Yakshas* and *yakshis* appear often in Brahmanical, Buddhist, and Jaina texts, generally as demonic and frightening creatures. Their worship was eventually absorbed into and marginalized by the dominant religious traditions, but the frequent references to them shows just how popular and widespread this worship once was.

Sanghol *yakshi*

It is difficult to estimate the antiquity of the cults of the *yakshas* and *yakshis*. However, during *c.* 300 BCE–200 CE, they were still an important part of the religious landscape. These cults are often described as minor, rural folk cults, but the evidence indicates otherwise. The many imposing stone images of *yakshas* and *yakshis* from Mathura and elsewhere were evidently products of urban workshops produced for urban clients. They reflect the existence of iconographic conventions and community worship in shrines. *Yaksha* figures found at Besnagar and Pawaya in Madhya Pradesh hold a money bag in their left hand, indicating their connection with wealth. Mention was made in the previous chapter to the colossal figure of *yaksha* Manibhadra found at Parkham near Mathura. Literary and epigraphic evidence indicates that Manibhadra was a tutelary deity of merchants and travellers, especially worshipped in important trading centres.

The worship of female deities associated with fertility and childbirth, considered protectresses of children with the power to ward off disease, is an important aspect of popular religious practice all over India today. In the early historical period, such functions were associated with *yakshis*. Collossal stone images of *yakshis* of this period have been found at many places. While the large stone statues of *yakshas* and *yakshis* indicate the prevalence of community worship in the public domain, the many smaller stone and terracotta images indicate that they were worshipped in a private, domestic context as well. In the Mathura area, colossal images of *yakshas* and *yakshis* disappear around the turn of the millennium, but the small statues are still found in large numbers, indicating their continuing importance as objects of worship in the domestic sphere.

The worship of serpents—*nagas* and *nagis* (or *naginis*)—was another important aspect of religious worship that cut across religious boundaries. The *nagas* and *nagis* were associated with water and fertility. Like the *yakshas* and *yakshis*, they too were originally the focus of exclusive worship, but were in course of time absorbed into the dominant religions. Colossal *naga* figures belonging to the early centuries CE have been found in many places. Their imposing nature and the technical finesse of their carving make it amply clear that they do not represent a simple folk or village cult. One of the most impressive of these is a seven-hooded *naga* image found at Mathura with an inscription that places it in the early 2nd century CE. An inscription found at the Jamalpur mound at Mathura indicates that a shrine dedicated to Dadhikarna, lord of the *nagas*, once stood here, and records a gift made in its favour by the Chhandaka brothers who belonged to a family of stone masons of Mathura.

Evidence of the importance of the *naga* cult comes from the remains of an elaborate brick and stone *naga* temple (Apsidal temple no. 2) at Sonkh near Mathura. The structural phases of this temple ranged from the beginnings of the 1st century BCE to the 2nd century CE.

Remains of a *naga* temple, the earliest structural phase of which seems to belong to the 2nd/1st century BCE, were also found at Maniyar Math near Rajagriha. Large numbers of *naga* images occur everywhere in the subcontinent. For instance, in the central Deccan, Peddabankur and Kotalingala have not given any evidence of Hindu/Brahmanical temples or sculptures, but have yielded many *yaksha* and *naga* figurines as well as female figurines of possible cultic significance. Special reference may be made to an iron figurine of a snake found at Peddabankur. We can also note the fact that many people and villages mentioned in inscriptions were named after *nagas* and *yakshas*.

Like the *yakshas* and *yakshis*, the *nagas* and *nagis* were gradually dethroned from their position of importance as major foci of worship in the urban, public domain, but their worship continued to be important, as is evident from small stone and terracotta statuettes found at various sites, as well as large images found in the environs of sites such as Sanchi. The story of Krishna subduing Kaliya *naga* can be interpreted as an allegorical reference to the ultimate victory of Vishnuism over the once very popular *naga* cult.

Mathura (from top): sandstone Nagaraja from Chhargaon; terracotta 'goddess' figurine

Goddesses, 'votive' tanks, and shrines

The discovery of female terracotta images from various sites from prehistoric times onwards has been discussed in earlier chapters. Whether or not these had a cultic or religious significance involves subjective judgement, and apart from their appearance and attributes, the context in which they are found is crucial. Where cultic significance is suggested, the context may help explain whether such images were objects of worship, votive offerings, or part of the paraphernalia of domestic rituals. As mentioned in an earlier chapter, the label 'goddess' or 'mother goddess' shelters a number of distinct and different goddesses, most of whose names we do not know. Not all of them necessarily had maternal attributes. Ancient goddesses were variously invoked for fertility, prosperity, childbirth, the safeguarding of children, and protection against disease.

The worship of goddesses during *c.* 200 BCE–300 CE is evident from archaeological evidence from many sites. For instance, in the Mathura area, a number of goddess figurines have been found in stratigraphic contexts in the course of excavations. These first appear in Period II (late 4th–2nd centuries BCE). The 'goddess' figurines of the succeeding centuries display greater stylistic refinement, technical innovations, and an increase in number and variety. They usually have prominent breasts and broad hips,

Terracotta tank

and wear ornaments such as appliqué necklaces, bracelets, earrings, and girdles. Some are crowned by a profusion of rosettes, while others have more elaborate headdresses consisting of a mass of conical sprouts or grass blades encircled by a cluster of cactus-like plants.

Female figurines are sometimes associated with terracotta artefacts that are referred to in archaeological literature as votive tanks and votive shrines. ('Votive' means an offering made on completion of a vow. Since it is not clear whether these artefacts were connected with vows, the word 'votive' has been placed in inverted commas.) These have been reported from many sites in the subcontinent, from Taxila in the north-west to Chirand in the east and Kolhapur in the south, in contexts ranging from the 3rd century BCE to the 3rd century CE. At Sonkh near Mathura, on the other hand, they were found from 3rd century BCE levels right up to medieval levels, showing that such objects were part of the paraphernalia of domestic rituals for over 1,000 years. The Sonkh excavations yielded 266 fragments of such tanks or shrines (Hartel, 1993: 195 *ff*.). The majority belonged to Period III (late 2nd–late 1st centuries BCE). These artefacts vary in shape and size, and are associated with one or more of the following features: lamp-cups and/or birds and lamps on their rim; houses built around a courtyard structure, or a structure (probably a shrine) raised on a platform supported with pillars and approached by a staircase or ladder; a lotus plant standing upright in the tank; figures of a snake, frog, or fish at the base of the 'tank'; female figures seated along the wall, carrying a child in their arm and a bowl in their lap. Most of the terracotta tanks and shrines were evidently supposed to be filled with water. The votive shrines can also be seen as miniature representations of popular shrines, apparently connected with the worship of goddesses and *nagas*.

Vedic Rituals

During *c*. 200 BCE–300 CE, there are several indications of the continuing importance of Vedic rituals. Rulers like Pushyamitra Shunga and certain Satavahana and Ikshvaku kings claimed to have performed Vedic sacrifices. Sacrificial posts (*yupas*) are depicted on some coins. A Yaudheya coin found in excavations at Sambhar has on its obverse a bull standing in front of a *yupa* enclosed in a railing. Copper coins of the Arjunayanas depict a similar scene. A clay seal from Sambhar shows a *yupa* in a railing, with the name of a person written in Brahmi letters of the 2nd century BCE. From the 3rd century CE onwards, there are a number of Sanskrit inscriptions inscribed on stone *yupas* (stone representations of wooden sacrificial posts) from various parts of Rajasthan. An early inscription from Nagari refers to the *ashvamedha yajna* performed at this place by a person named Sarvatata of the Parashara *gotra*.

Excavations at Mathura revealed pits containing ash, animal bones, and pottery in some residential structures, which may represent remains of the performance of sacrifices. More definite and dramatic evidence comes from Isapur (in Mathura) on the left bank of the Yamuna. Here, two stone *yupas* were discovered, both carved with a girdle rope with a noose at the end, representing the rope to which the sacrificial animal was tied. A Sanskrit inscription on one of the pillars (dated in year 24 of the reign of the Kushana king Vasishka) states that the pillar was set up by a Brahmana named Dronala while performing a 12-night *sattra* (sacrifice). They are suggestive of a grand sacrifice and a *yajamana* who had considerable resources.

As mentioned earlier, excavations outside the eastern gate of Kaushambi yielded remains of a brick altar in the shape of an eagle flying to the south-east, along with animal and human bones, including a skull. G. R. Sharma (1960) suggested that these were the remains of a performance of the *purushamedha* (human sacrifice). At Purola in Uttarkashi district of Uttarakhand, archaeologists discovered a burnt brick structure in the shape of a *garuda* with its head towards the east and tail towards the west. This may have been an altar for Vedic rituals, belonging to the 2nd century BCE–1st century CE. Jagatgrama near Kalsi in Uttarakhand revealed inscriptions mentioning the performance of several *ashvamedha* sacrifices by a king named Shilavarman. The remains of brick altars used in the course of these sacrifices were also found.

A very interesting discovery comes from the site of Sanghol in Ludhiana district, Punjab. Excavations in the south-eastern part of a large mound in the village revealed a religious complex containing a number of fire altars (*havan-kundas*), belonging to the early centuries CE. The complex consisted of about a dozen rectangular and squarish cistern-like pits built close together next to a rectangular platform of burnt brick. The material found inside these pits included ash, loose soil, wood charcoal, charred grains, seeds, and fruit remains. Several seals and sealings inscribed with motifs and Brahmi inscriptions were also found in the area. K. S. Saraswat and A. K. Pokharia (1997–98) analysed the botanical remains. Their analysis revealed seven types of grains including rice, barley, wheat, *moong*, *urad*, *masoor*, and *til*. The remains of wild and cultivated fruits were also found—jujube, date, almond, raisin, *chilgoza*, pistachio-nut, and *gular* fig. Remains of plants with medicinal properties—*anwala*, *haritaki*, *jaiphal*, holy basil (*tulsi*), black pepper, and *phok* (*Ephedra*) were also found. There were also a few nuts of *Cyperus* sedge, which is considered sacred in rituals. The wood of *pipal*, *gular*, *palash*, *kaith*, *tamal*, *deodar*, and *chandan* were identified. These were evidently used as fuel in the sacrifice.

Clearly, Vedic sacrifices continued to have an importance during the period *c.* 200 BCE–200 CE. Among other things, they formed one of several bases of political legitimation for rulers. However, at the level of popular practice, there was a marked shift away from a sacrifice-centred religion.

Puranic Hinduism

The English word 'Hinduism' was first used by Raja Ram Mohun Roy in 1816–17. As mentioned in the Introduction, the word 'Hindu' is much older and is derived from the Sindhu (Indus) river. It was originally a geographical term, variants of which were used in ancient Persian, Greek, and Chinese sources to refer to the lands along or beyond the Sindhu river. In the course of the medieval period, the term came to acquire a religious meaning.

Modern-day Hinduism differs from other major world religions in many important respects, in that it has no founder, no fixed canon which embodies its major beliefs and practices, and no organized priesthood. It is also marked by a great variety in beliefs, practices, sects, and traditions. Some scholars argue that Hinduism is not so much a religion as a set of socio-cultural practices; others argue that it is inextricably linked to the existence of caste, and still others hold that we should talk of Hindu religions in the plural rather than the singular. The relative newness of the word, the problems of definition, and the existence of much internal diversity, are not sufficient reasons to avoid the use of the term Hinduism. The term can be also used with retrospective effect to refer to a long and complex religious process, whose roots lie in the Vedic tradition, whose forms of religious practice are visible in the Puranas, and which include a great deal of diversity.

For the purpose of historical analysis, historians often make a distinction between Vedic religion and Puranic Hinduism, even though the latter anchored itself in the former. As discussed in Chapter 5, the religious practice of the *Rig Veda* is centred around the performance of *yajnas*, and there are no references to the worship of deities in temples.

The beginning of the theistic trends that came to the fore in this period can be traced to the later Upanishads. However, the process is more clearly visible in the *Mahabharata* and *Ramayana*. The new religiosity of devotion is also reflected in the *Bhagavad Gita* and the Puranas. The Puranas, many of which were compiled during the 4th/5th centuries, reflect features of religious practice such as the worship of deities in a temple context, the performance of *vratas* (vows), and pilgrimage. It can be inferred from texts, archaeological evidence, sculptures, inscriptions, and coins that these practices go back to an earlier time and that the Puranas reflect a Brahmanical approval of practices that were already in vogue. The period *c.* 200 BCE–300 CE can be seen as the formative phase in the evolution of Hindu pantheons.

Certain early textual references to devotional practices include the mention in the *Baudhayana Grihyasutra* (2.3.13) of the worship of images of deities in connection with the ceremony of the first outing of a newborn child from the house. The *Gautama Dharmasutra* (9. 12–13, 45) alludes to images of the gods in the context of rules for a person who has just entered the householder stage. Patanjali's *Mahabhashya* mentions images of the deities Shiva, Skanda, and Vishakha. The *Arthashastra* (2.4.17, II.4.19) recommends that the temple dedicated to the guardian deity and the family deity of the king should be located in the centre of the city. It also advocates the building of temples dedicated to the deities of the four quarters at the four city gates. This text mentions shrines for the tutelary gods of various groups of people (2.5.6, II.4.18) as well as in storehouses. There is also mention (4.10.16) of temple property, including images, crops, cattle, slaves, fields, houses, money, gold, and coins.

The earliest inscriptional references to and archaeological remains of Hindu temples belong to *c.* 200 BCE–300 CE. Reference was made earlier to the Besnagar pillar inscription of Heliodorus, which records the installation of a pillar associated with a Vishnu temple and the remains of the foundations of a temple nearby. A 2nd century Nagari inscription mentions a temple of Samkarshana and Vasudeva. The remains of a temple dedicated to the Matrikas (the Seven Mothers) or Durga at Sonkh, a Lakshmi temple at Atranjikhera, a Shaiva temple at Gudimallam, and temples dedicated to Vishnu and Shiva at Nagarjunakonda can be considered to be among the earliest vestiges of Hindu temples in the subcontinent.

Stone and terracotta sculptures from sites such as Mathura clearly indicate that the popular cults of the *yakshas* and *yakshis*, *nagas* and *nagis* were gradually being pushed to the margins by the gods and goddesses of the Brahmanical tradition. The most influential of the newly emerging cults were associated with the worship of the gods Shiva and Vishnu and the goddess Durga.

Although the period *c.* 200 BCE–300 CE witnessed the development of sectarian cults that revolved around the worship of a particular god or goddess as a supreme deity, there was also a parallel process which visualized the Hindu gods as closely related and performing complementary functions. This is evident, for instance, in the idea of the triad of Brahma, Vishnu, and Shiva, present in the *Mahabharata* and more clearly developed in the Puranas. In this triad, Brahma is associated with the creation of the world, Vishnu with its preservation, and Shiva its destruction. The three gods are also associated with different principles, from which arises their division of labour—Brahma is associated with *rajas* (the creative, active principle), Vishnu with *sattva* (the unattached, passive principle), and Shiva with *tamas* (the dark, fierce principle). In some places in the Puranas, the gods operate in their respective spheres according to this division of labour, in others they are described as manifestations of the same divine being.

The acknowledgement of other gods and their being considered worthy of respect is also evident from the fact that shrines dedicated to one deity often have sculptural representations of other deities as well. Polytheism simply refers to a belief in many gods; monolatory means the belief in a supreme god without denying the existence of other gods. It is the latter term that best describes emergent Hinduism.

SHAIVISM

It has been suggested on the basis of the so-called Pashupati seal that the roots of Shiva worship may go back to the Harappan civilization. In the *Rig Veda*, the word *shiva* (auspicious) occurs, but not as the name of a god. On the other hand, there is a god named Rudra, who is mentioned infrequently and whose description as a fierce and feared god bears striking resemblance to that of Shiva of the Puranas. Later Vedic literature contains many references to a god known variously as Shiva, Rudra, Ishana, Mahadeva,

Maheshvara, Bhava, Pashupati, and Sharva. The Shatarudriya hymn in the *Vajasaneyi Samhita* addressed to Rudra-Shiva, describes him as a powerful but fierce god. Elsewhere in later Vedic texts, he is associated with snakes, poison, and cremation grounds. The *Shvetashvatara Upanishad* hails him as lord of all gods, the god of destruction, and as one who grants ultimate release. Several names of Shiva are mentioned in the *Astadhayayi*.

Some historians have suggested that the Sibae, who are described in Graeco-Roman accounts as living in the Punjab during the time of Alexander's invasion, may have been worshippers of Shiva. The *Mahabhashya* mentions Rudra-Shiva as a deity connected with medicinal herbs and one who is offered animal sacrifices. It also refers to the *Shiva-bhagavatas* who carried iron lances and wore animal hides. The Pashupata sect seems to have been the earliest Shaiva sect and had ascetic and mystic associations. The *Linga Purana* and later inscriptions attribute the establishment of this sect to Lakulin or Nakulin. However, other texts attribute the founding of the sect to Shrikantha.

The multiplicity of Shiva's forms and his various aspects and exploits are encapsulated in some of his Puranic epithets. To mention just a few, Shiva is Chandrashekhara (the god who has the crescent moon in his hair), Gangadhara (supporter of the Ganga), Vaidyanatha (lord of physicians), Kalasamhara (the destroyer of time), Pashupati (lord of animals), and Shankara (the beneficent). One of the most interesting manifestations of Shiva is as Ardhanarishvara—the god who is half woman. These various forms of the deity are described in the Puranas and are depicted in sculpture.

Shiva is today most popularly worshipped in temples in his *linga* form which represents male procreative energy and power. The origins of *linga* worship in the Indian subcontinent seem to go back to Harappan times. The *Rig Veda* refers disapprovingly to people who worship the phallus (*shishnadevas*). During *c.* 200 BCE–200 CE, the cult came to be connected with the worship of Shiva. The worship of the female creative aspect, represented by the *yoni*, was amalgamated into the *linga* cult. The Puranas give the story of the origin of the *linga* (*lingodbhava*). The *Ramayana* refers to Ravana worshipping Rudra in the *linga* form. The *Mahabharata* states that the sages and gods have always worshipped the *linga*.

Sculptural representations of stone Shiva *lingas* appear in the 2nd century BCE. One of the earliest representations is a *c.* 2nd century BCE architectural fragment found at Bhuteshwar in Mathura. This shows a *linga* on a platform under a pipal tree encircled by a railing, being worshipped by two winged creatures. *Mukha-lingas*—*lingas* with one or more faces of the god carved on them—also became popular in this period. The combination of the anthropomorphic and *linga* form (*mukha-lingas* and *vigraha-lingas*) also appeared. A 2nd/1st century BCE *linga* found at Gudimallam village in Andhra Pradesh has the figure of Shiva carved on it. Anthropomorphic Shiva images of the 1st and 2nd centuries CE indicate an already diverse iconographic base.

Phallic emblems occur on certain coins of Taxila and Ujjain. Some Ujjain coins have Shiva and a bull on the obverse and the *linga* in front of a tree on the reverse. Coins of the Kushana king Vima Kadphises have representations of Shiva, the bull, and the trident. The popularity of the worship of Karttikeya, the son of Shiva, is reflected in his depiction on punch-marked coins and on coins of the Yaudheyas. Mention may also be made of a gold piece of about this period, depicting the Shaiva bull emblem on the obverse; the reverse shows the god's consort Amba holding a flower, with a legend describing her as the deity of the city of Pushkalavati.

The fierce and strange nature of Shiva is described in the story of Daksha's sacrifice, narrated in the epics and the *Bhagavata Purana*: Shiva's father-in-law Daksha invited the gods to attend a great sacrifice but did not include Shiva in the guest list on account of his unconventional appearance and behaviour. Sati, Shiva's wife, attended the sacrifice but killed herself in grief when her father reviled her husband. Shiva was enraged, and destroyed the sacrifice. The *Bhagavata Purana* gives Daksha's description of Shiva to Sati—as roaming in the cremation grounds with ghouls as his attendants, wearing bones and garlands of skulls, and bathing in the ashes of funeral pyres (Banerjea, 1966: 84).

Shiva is a god who combined in himself the aspects of asceticism and fertility (see O'Flaherty, 1973). The god's *tapas* is described as generating great heat that threatens the world, as does his amorous activity. On the one hand, there are Puranic stories which describe how the gods sent down Parvati and Kama in order to move Shiva from chastity to fertility. On the other hand, there are myths which narrate how Agni had to intervene to interrupt Shiva and Parvati's love making in order to move the god from fertility to chastity. Mythology allows for the combination of extremes and contradictions.

The northern gods Shiva and Vishnu are known to the Sangam literature of Tamilakam. The *Akananuru* refers to Shiva as the three-eyed god who wears the *konrai* flowers, bears the cresecent moon on his matted locks, and has Uma as his consort. The poet Nakkirar compares a Pandya king with Shiva, Vishnu, Balarama, and Subrahmanya (Karttikeya). He refers to Shiva as Kurram, god of death and destruction. Murugan, an important god of South India, became part of Shiva's family and was identified with his son Skanda-Karttikeya. One of the temples at Nagarjunakonda was evidently dedicated to Karttikeya.

Relief showing winged creatures worshipping *linga*, Mathura

THE FORMATION OF THE VAISHNAVA PANTHEON

The *Rig Veda* contains five hymns addressed to Vishnu. He is grouped with the solar deities and described as a powerful god living in the mountains. The Vedas mention his three great strides whereby he encompassed the universe. Later Vedic texts such as the *Taittiriya Samhita* and *Shatapatha Brahmana* connect him with the dwarf (the dwarf is associated with extraordinary cleverness and spiritual attainment) and the earth.

The history of Vaishnavism involved the gradual coming together of the initially independent cults of various deities such as Narayana, Vasudeva Krishna, Shri, and Lakshmi (Jaiswal, [1967] 1981). The importance given to Vishnu seems to have been a later development that took place at the stage when the Brahmanization of these cults was established. The details of the historical processes underlying these associations, amalgamations, and hierarchies are not entirely clear. The term 'Vaishnava' as an epithet of a worshipper of Vishnu occurs in the later portions of the *Mahabharata*.

The worship of Narayana was one of the important elements eventually absorbed into Vishnuism. Some scholars have suggested that Narayana was originally a non-Vedic god. He is mentioned in the *Rig Veda* and *Shatapatha Brahmana*. He is associated with a five-day sacrifice called the *pancharatra sattra*, through the performance of which he is supposed to have attained superiority over all beings and identity with them. This god also seems to have been associated with asceticism. The *Mahabharata* calls him a great *yogi* and identifies him with Vishnu. This text in fact refers to the god more often as Narayana than Vishnu. One of the impressive early images of Narayana is a colossal image found at Mathura.

The worship of Vasudeva Krishna seems to have originated in the Mathura region. The *Ashtadhayayi* explains the word *Vasudevaka* as one whose object of *bhakti* is Vasudeva. This is the earliest reference to devotion to Vasudeva, although the precise meaning of *bhakti* in this context is uncertain. Megasthenes states that the Sourasenoi, who lived in the Mathura region, worshipped Herakles, by which he must have meant Vasudeva Krishna, who was the Indian god bearing the closest resemblance to the Greek god Herakles.

The complex character and varied associations of Vasudeva Krishna suggest that his legends include an amalgamation of originally separate strands and traditions. The *Chhandogya Upanishad* mentions a sage named Krishna Devakiputra (son of Devaki), pupil of *rishi* Ghora Angirasa. In the *Mahabharata*, Vasudeva Krishna is the ally and adviser of the Pandavas. In the *Bhagavad Gita*, he drives Arjuna's chariot, convinces him that it is his *dharma* to fight the battle, and reveals himself as an *avatara* (incarnation) of Vishnu. The first detailed account of Krishna's life story occurs in the *Harivamsha*, an appendix to the *Mahabharata*. This narrates Krishna's birth, his life with his foster parents Nanda and Yashoda in Vrindavana, and his conflict with his wicked uncle Kamsa. Puranas such as the *Vishnu*, *Padma*, *Brahmavaivarta*, and *Bhagavata* provide further details of Krishna's life in Vrindavana. Krishna's association with Radha came to the fore much later, in the 11th–12th centuries. Radha is not mentioned in the 10th century *Bhagavata Purana*. On the other hand, the 12th century *Gita Govinda* of Jayadeva celebrates the love of Radha and Krishna.

It is possible that the core of the legends that were eventually associated with Vasudeva Krishna grew around a historical figure belonging to the Vrishni clan, living in the Mathura area. Vasudeva Krishna was one of five heroes (*pancha-vira*) worshipped by the Vrishnis of the Mathura area—Samkarshana (also known as Baladeva or Balarama, son of Vasudeva by Rohini), Vasudeva (son of Vasudeva by Devaki), Pradyumna (son of Vasudeva by Rukmini), Samba (son of Vasudeva by Jambavati), and Aniruddha (son of Pradyumna). Many 'kinship triads' depicting Vasudeva Krishna, his brother Baladeva, and their sister Ekanamsha, stylistically dated to the early centuries CE, have been found in the Mathura area. The relative size of the figures shows that Baladeva was initially considered more important than Krishna. An inscription found at Mora in Mathura district refers to the installation of images of the five heroes by a woman named Tosha during the reign of Shodasa (i.e., the late 1st century BCE–early 1st century CE). Fragmentary sculptures of two male figures discovered at the site may represent two of the images mentioned in the inscription. Another image, possibly originally from Mora, inscribed on a door jamb and belonging to the reign of Shodasa, refers to a *torana* (gateway) and *vedika* (railing) which formed part of a *maha-sthana* (large temple) of Vasudeva.

The fact that the worship of Vasudeva Krishna swiftly spread beyond the Mathura region is indicated by epigraphic evidence. The Besnagar pillar inscription describes Heliodorus, Greek ambassador to the Shunga court, as a *bhagavata*, i.e., a worshipper of lord Vasudeva Krishna. A 2nd century BCE inscription found at Nagari in Rajasthan mentions a temple of Samkarshana and Vasudeva. A 1st century BCE inscription from Gosundi in Chittorgarh district of Rajasthan records the construction of a stone enclosure for the place of worship (*puja-shila-prakara*) in honour of Samkarshana and Balarama by a person who is described as a *bhagavata* and a performer of the *ashvamedha* sacrifice.

In the early centuries CE, there was a dramatic increase in the number and variety of Vaishnava images produced in the Mathura area. Representations of Vasudeva Krishna are the most numerous, but there are also a large number of small stone statuettes of Vishnu (usually four-armed), Vishnu on *garuda*, and Vishnu in the form of a partly anthropomorphic Varaha (boar) form. We may also note the fact that 2nd century BCE coins of the Indo-Greek king Agathocles found at Aï-Khanoum in Afghanistan depict Krishna and Balarama.

PRIMARY SOURCES | **Krishna and Balarama on Agathocles' coins**

The coins found at Aï-Khanoum included 6 drachms of a coin type of the Indo-Greek king Agathocles. The die-struck silver coins have an irregular square shape. Their weight range (between 2.328 and 3.305 gm) is similar to that of Indian punch-marked coins.

The obverse and reverse of these coins bear images of male figures. The figures on both sides have a long oval face and large round eyes. They stand in an identical pose—in a frontal position with their legs slightly apart, their feet turning outwards on a horizontal plane. They wear what looks like a thick pleated skirt. An upper garment or shawl falls from their shoulders, covering the waist and leaving the chest bare. They wear large hooped earrings. A large scabbard is attached to the left side of their waist. Their heavy shoes have long pointed toes that curl backwards. Their helmet-shaped headdress has a stem with a plume billowing out like a wide canopy on top, and two ends of a ribbon billowing out below. This seems to have been a Greek engraver's misinterpretation of the chhatra or parasol.

What is most striking about these figures are the attributes that differentiate them. The figure on the obverse holds a miniature plough in his left hand, identifying him as Balarama, who is also known as Haladhara (wielder of the plough). In his right hand, he holds up a pestle (*musala*). The figure on the reverse holds a large, eight-spoked wheel in his left hand against his left flank, which makes it look like a shield. This wheel (*chakra*) is the symbol of Vasudeva Krishna. In his right hand, he holds up something which may be a conch shell, though it looks more like a vase. The figure on the obverse stands between the two lines of a vertical legend in Greek, giving the name of king Agathocles. The legend on the reverse gives the king's name in the Prakrit language and Brahmi script.

These coins are extremely important for the early history of the worship of Balarama and Vasudeva Krishna. For one thing, this evidence can be dated with precision to the reign of Agathocles, i.e., *c.* 180–170 BCE. Secondly, the iconographic details make the identification of the two figures certain, not ambiguous as is the case with certain figures on punch-marked coins. These are among the earliest images of these deities found so far. Third, these coins indicate that the worship of these gods had spread far beyond the Mathura region, where the cult of the five heroes, including Samkarshana and Vasudeva Krishna, had originated. While the clothes the figures wear could pass for Indian attire, the helmet, scabbard, and boots are not typically Indian, and seem to be Greek elements. And finally, the fact that these gods appear on the coins of an Indo-Greek king indicates that their cults were important enough to receive royal recognition.

It may be noted that rock carvings at Chilas in Kashmir, along a major trade route in the Gilgit valley, include a pair of figures, holding what seem to be a plough and disc, wearing wide open coats similar to that of the Kushana period. Their identification as Balarama and Krishna is confirmed by Kharoshthi inscriptions found in the area.

Source R. Audouin and P. Bernard, in Guillaume, 1991: 81–116

The pastoral setting of the stories about Krishna's childhood may have originated in legends of a god worshipped by the Abhira tribe. The Abhiras appear to have been a tribe that came into India from the north-west in about the 1st century BCE. Originally settled in the Punjab, they later moved into the lower Indus valley, and further to Saurashtra and the western Deccan. In the *Padma Purana*, Vishnu states that he will be born among the Abhiras in his eighth incarnation. The amorous stories about Krishna and the *gopis* (cowherd girls), narrated in texts such as the *Harivamsha* and *Vishnu Purana* may have originated from the same source.

The worship of Samkarshana Balarama, initially very popular in the Mathura region and beyond, was eventually overshadowed by the cult revolving around his younger brother Vasudeva Krishna. The *Mahabhashya* mentions temples of Balarama. The *Arthashastra* refers to Samkarshana's taste for alcohol and suggests that his devotees engaged in ritual drinking. The Puranas too mention this aspect of Samkarshana's personality. This deity also seems to have been connected with snake worship. Images show a snake canopy over his head and the *Mahabharata* refers to his being an incarnation of Sheshanaga (the great snake on whose coils Vishnu rests). He is connected with agricultural operations, as is clear from his very name (*samkarshana* means ploughing), and his epithets 'Haladhara' (wielder of the plough) and 'Musalin' (one who wields the pestle). Several Puranas such as the *Vishnu*, *Harivamsha*, and *Bhagavata* tell the story of how Samkarshana Balarama forced the Yamuna to change its course by pulling it with his ploughshare.

The Vaishnava pantheon also came to include the goddess Shri Lakshmi. The *Shri Sukta*, a supplement to the *Rig Veda*, describes Shri as a moon-like golden-coloured deer decorated with ornaments made of gold and silver, and also invokes her as Lakshmi. But certain references in later Vedic texts such as the *Vajasaneyi Samhita* and *Taittiriya Aranyaka* suggest that Shri and Lakshmi were initially two different goddesses. 'Shri' means well-being or prosperity, and the goddess of this name may have originally been a fertility goddess. 'Lakshmi' means sign, token, or mark, and the goddess of this name seems originally to have been associated with the signs of prosperity and luck. By extension, she also became a goddess of wealth. By about the 3rd/4th century CE, Shri Lakshmi was absorbed into the Vaishnava pantheon as the consort of Vishnu. The *Mahabharata* and *Ramayana* know her in this role and the Puranas further elaborate on her association with Vishnu.

One of the frequent representations of Shri Lakshmi in sculpture is in her Gaja-Lakshmi form: the goddess sits or stands on a lotus; she is flanked by two elephants who pour water over her from pitchers held in their upraised trunks. At Sonkh, a relief carving of Lakshmi on an architectural fragment was found at pre-Kushana levels and seems to be the oldest stone sculpture found at the site. Lakshmi is represented on a large number of stone images of this period. She is also depicted on a terracotta plaque found at late NBPW levels in an apsidal temple at Atranjikhera, Period IVD (*c.* 200–50 BCE).

Gaja-Lakshmi is also frequently represented on coins. She appears on coins of the Shunga king Jyesthamitra and on those of the Indo-Scythian kings Azes II and Azilises. She also appears on 1st century BCE coins of kings of Ayodhya—Vayudeva, Vishakhadeva, and Shivadatta. In the Mathura area, coins of Rajuvula, Shodasa, and Toranadasa have the Gaja-Lakshmi motif. The goddess is also clearly visible on a 1st century BCE Ujjain coin. A female figure seated on a lotus is a recurring sculptural motif at Buddhist sites such as Sanchi, Bharhut, and Bodh Gaya. She is sometimes interpreted as Maya giving birth to the Buddha, but the iconography is so specific that it seems to be the goddess Lakshmi. References to Lakshmi's form carved on doors in the Sangam text *Pattuppattu* indicate that this goddess had come to be associated with auspiciousness in South India as well.

See p. 533 (middle, left) for a photograph of Maya on lotus at Sanchi

The idea of the *avataras* is an important Vaishnava doctrine. The word *avatara* comes from the root *avatri* which means to descend. In the *Rig Veda*, gods such as Indra have the ability to assume different forms. The Vaishnava idea of the *avataras* does not, however, simply refer to Vishnu's ability to assume various forms at different points of time. The *Gita* states explicitly that he does so with a specific purpose—in order to destroy evil and to protect *dharma*.

The number of Vishnu's *avataras* is conventionally reckoned as 10, but some of the names vary in different texts. The *Vayu Purana* lists Narayana, Narasimha, Vamana, Dattatreya, Mandhata, Jamadagnya, Rama, Vedavyasa, Krishna, and Kalki. Sculptures from the Mathura area suggest that the *avatara* concept was in its infancy. The *chatur-vyuha* concept (that of the four emanations of Vishnu) becomes visible towards the end of the Kushana period.

SHAKTI WORSHIP

As we have seen earlier, the worship of goddesses associated with fertility is one of the oldest and most enduring features of religious practice in the subcontinent. In the course of the 1st millennium, the Puranas tried to bring some of these goddesses together, presenting them as different manifestations of the female principle—*shakti* (Banerjea, 1966: 115–23). The Durga-Gayatri in the *Taittiriya Aranyaka* (10.1) is the first place where we find the names of some of the goddesses who later came to be associated with the worship of Shakti—Katyayani, Kanyakumari, and Durga. Durga is described as an impetuous, energetic goddess. She is the daughter of the sun (or fire), she has the colour of fire, she burns with austerities and is sought after for the reward of the performance of rites. The *Shatarudriya* section of the *Maitrayaniya Samhita* of the Black *Yajur Veda* refers to the Gayatri-*mantras* of several Puranic deities, including Girisuta-Gauri, the goddess who is daughter of the mountains. The *Mundaka Upanishad* mentions the goddesses Kali and Karali as two of the seven tongues of Agni. In the Puranas, these goddesses are described as the terrifying forms of Durga. Later Vedic texts also refer to Bhavani (the female form of Bhava, i.e., Shiva) and Bhadrakali (the auspicious and peaceful form of Kali). The *Periplus* refers to a place called Comari associated with the worship of a goddess; this may be a reference to Kanyakumari.

In the *Mahabharata*, Yudhishthira and Arjuna recite a Durga *stotra* on two separate occasions (Virata Parva 4.6; Bhishma Parva 6.23). The *Harivamsha* (Vishnu Parva, Chapter 3) contains the *Arya-stava*, a hymn in praise of Durga. This begins by addressing the goddess by various names—Arya, Narayani, Tribhuvaneshvari, Shri, Ratri, Katyayani, and Kaushiki. She is also called Aparna and Nagna-Shabari. It goes on to refer to her association with the hills (especially the Vindhyas), rivers, caves, forests, gardens, and animals, both wild and domesticated. It speaks of tribes such as the Shabaras, Barbaras, and Pulindas worshipping her. She is described as the daughter of Nandagopa and the sister of Baladeva. She is said to personify death, and is fond of wine, meat, and sacrifice. She is the mother of *mantras* and the *gayatri* of the gods. She personifies the virginity of young girls and the good fortune of married women. She pervades the universe and is a saviour in all kinds of dangers such as those arising out of war, fire, riverbanks, thieves, vast uncharted fields, life away from home, imprisonment due to royal disfavour, and the striking of enemies.

The growing popularity of the worship of Durga is reflected in the epics. The *Devi-Mahatmya*, which was incorporated into the *Markandeya Purana* by about the 7th century BCE, contains verses in praise of the Devi (Great Goddess) and gives many accounts of her exploits and greatness. These stories tell of how the gods, harassed by various demons, approached her for help, and how she succeeded in destroying the demons. One of these stories concerns the demon Mahishasura (a demon in the form of a buffalo) who had vanquished the gods. The goddess is described as having emerged out of the combined and concentrated energy of all the gods, defeating the demon after a fierce battle.

Although the *Devi-Mahatmya* is a relatively late text, the sculptural evidence from many early historical sites indicates the popularity of the worship of Durga Mahishasuramardini from much earlier times. For instance, the Mathura area has yielded a large number of stone Durga images, including those of Mahishasuramardini, belonging to the period *c.* 200 BCE–300 CE. At Sonkh, a stone plaque found in late 1st century BCE–early 1st century CE levels possibly depicts Durga as Mahishasuramardini; Durga images occur in large numbers in levels of the subsequent period. A stone Matrika plaque may have been the central cult image in Apsidal temple no. 1 at Sonkh, and a large number of terracotta plaques depicting Durga as Mahishasuramardini were found in and around this temple.

The emergence of Mahayana Buddhism

In the history of Indian Buddhism, the period *c.* 200 BCE–300 CE is associated with the emergence of Mahayana. The terms 'Mahayana' (the greater vehicle) and 'Hinayana' (the lesser vehicle) were coined by the Mahayanists. Needless to say, non-Mahayanists would not have considered or described themselves as the followers of a lesser, i.e., inferior path. The origins of Mahayana have often been traced to the older Mahasanghika school. It is not clear in exactly which part of the subcontinent Mahayana ideas first developed. Till recently, the emergence of Mahayana was earlier thought of as leading to a major schism (split) in the *sangha*. More recent writings have suggested that the issue has to be reconsidered. To begin with, there is the question of what a schism means in the Buddhist tradition. Heinz Bechert (1982) has argued that *sangha-bheda* (a split in the *sangha*) has implications that are very different from the notion of schism in the history of Christianity. In the Buddhist tradition, schism was associated with issues concerning monastic discipline, not doctrinal issues. Further, it is evident that emergence of Mahayana did not, in fact, lead to a split in the *sangha*.

Treating the early history of Indian Buddhism as a neat unilinear process of Hinayana followed by Mahayana (and the latter followed by Tantric Vajrayana) is problematic and oversimplifies a much more complex reality (see Skilling, 2012). As mentioned in Chapter 1, the Pali *Tipitaka* was given the status of a canon of Sri Lanka in the 5th century CE by the Mahavihara monks at a time when the Abhayagiri monks were in the ascendant. So the canonization of the *Tipitaka* actually post-dates the emergence of Mahayana. In the history of Buddhism, it is useful to distinguish *nikayas* (sects) from *vadas* (schools based on doctrines). Mahayana was neither a *nikaya* nor a *vada*. It can be understood as a series of tendencies that cut across these.

Far from being a movement instigated by the devotional practices of the laity, Mahayana seems to have been a set of ideas and teachings that originated among a group of monks within the *sangha* (Gethin, 1998: 225). Given the centrality of the *Vinaya* rules, there was nothing to prevent monks who had different views on matters of doctrine and practice from living together as part of a monastic community. This is confirmed by Faxian and Xuanzang who visited India in the 4th/5th and 7th century respectively, and described Mahayana and non-Mahayana monks living together in the same monasteries. The difference was that the former venerated and worshipped images of the *bodhisattvas*, whereas the latter did not. Thus seen, Mahayana was not initially a sectarian movement, nor did it did cause a schism in the *sangha*.

Several Mahayana Sutras were translated into Chinese in the late 2nd century CE. The composition of the earliest Sutras can be placed in the 2nd century BCE. These Sutras claim to contain the teaching of the Buddha and do not project themselves as representing a radical break with the older tradition; in fact, they directly draw on this tradition. For instance, the *Lalitavistara* contains many passages from the Pali canon. There was an increasing use of Sanskrit in Mahayana texts. The important Mahayana Sutras include the *Prajnaparamita Sutras*, of which the *Ashtasahasrika* seems to be the oldest. Mahayana received its classic exposition in the writings of thinkers such as Nagarjuna, Aryadeva, Asanga, and Vasubandhu. The accounts of the Chinese pilgrims also throw light on the history of Mahayana in India. Further evidence is provided by inscriptions and archaeological evidence from Buddhist monastic sites.

The idea of the *bodhisattva* (Wisdom Being; also spelt *bodhisatva*) is known to earlier Buddhism. Gotama himself is said to have been born as an ascetic named Megha or Sumedha in an earlier birth. He is described as having taken a vow to tread the path of Buddhahood in the presence of an earlier Buddha named Dipankara, only to postpone his own enlightenment out of compassion for others. However, the idea of the *bodhisattva* assumed greater importance in Mahayana. The highest goal in the older Buddhism was the attainment of *nibbana* and becoming an *arhat*. Mahayana considered this a lesser goal; the higher one consisted in following the path of a *bodhisattva* and attaining Buddhahood. There is a crucial difference between the *arhat* and *bodhisattva*. The *arhat* is one who strives to attain *nibbana*, and having achieved this goal for himself, disappears from the cycle of *samsara*. The *bodhisattva*, on the other hand, is one who has attained great wisdom, but decides to refrain from taking the final step into *nibbana*, choosing to actively engage with the world for aeons on end in order to help others achieve this goal. Great compassion (*maha-karuna*) for others is a key element in the Mahayana ideal of the *bodhisattva*.

The conduct and practices that formed part of the path leading to Buddhahood were not very different from those recommended in the earlier tradition. The several stages along the *bodhisattva* path involved the attainment of a number of perfections known as *paramitas*. These were originally listed as six and later expanded to ten. They consisted of generosity (*dana*), good conduct (*shila*), patient forbearance (*kshanti*), mental strength (*virya*), meditation (*dhyana*), wisdom (*prajna*), skilfulness in means (*upaya-kaushalya*), determination (*pranidhana*), power (*bala*), and knowledge (*jnana*).

Nagarjunakonda reliefs (from left): subjugation of Naga Apalala; the elephant Nalagiri

In the early Buddhist tradition, represented in the *Tipitaka*, the Buddha was considered a man, one among several beings who had attained enlightenment and become an *arhat*. However, he was definitely a superior man (*mahapurusha*), the unequalled teacher par excellence of the path to salvation. At any given time, there could be only one Buddha, the next one appearing only when the teaching of the previous one had died out. What exactly happened to a Buddha after death was left somewhat hazy, but he definitely disappeared from the cycle of *samsara*. Mahayana had a different perspective on such issues. It increased the gulf between the attainments of an *arhat* and a Buddha. It also introduced the idea of transcendent Buddhas and *bodhisattvas*, who stood between *nibbana* and *samsara*. It conceived of many Buddhas and *bodhisattvas* such as Maitreya, Avalokiteshvara, and Manjushri, all of whom simultaneously worked for the deliverance of sentient beings in their respective 'Buddha-fields' (*Buddha-kshetra*).

Mahayana philosophical ideas were represented in the texts of two major Buddhist schools—**Madhyamaka** and **Yogachara**. The founder of the Madhyamaka school was Nagarjuna (2nd century CE). His most important work was the *Mula-Madhyamaka-Karika* (Root Verses on the Middle). The idea of *shunyata* (emptiness) is an important feature of this work. *Shunyata* does not mean that nothing exists. It means that appearances are misleading, and that permanent selves and substances do not exist. The *Abhidharma* texts spoke of *dharmas*—here, the word stands for the basic elements of mind and matter which comprised the universe. According to Nagarjuna's analysis, the ultimate truth, seen in the light of the entire teaching of the Buddha, is that the *dharmas* are empty, i.e., they do not exist *per se*. Later important thinkers of the Madhayamaka school included Aryadeva, Buddhapalita, Bhavaviveka, Chandrakirti, and Shantideva.

The ideas associated with the Yogachara school are contained in Sutra texts such as the *Samdhinirmochana* and the *Lankavatara*. This school is known as Yogachara because of the importance it attaches to meditation as a means of attaining the highest goal. Yogachara gives a detailed account of consciousness. As in earlier Buddhist thought, it talks of six types of consciousness which consist of the inputs a person gets from his senses plus his conscious thought. Yogachara, however, identifies these as as part of the *active* level of consciousness. It identifies two other levels—the first is the level of the defiled mind (*klishta-manas*) which is defiled with things such as the idea of I-ness and delusion. The other level of consciousness is the store consciousness (*alaya-vijnana*), which contains the store of all the seeds sown by the defilements of the active consciousness. A person's ordinary experience is based on how his consciousness processes the world. By following the path of a *bodhisattva*, defilement and illusion melt away and perfect clarity and knowledge is attained. Yogachara attaches great importance to the analysis of consciousness and asserts that mundane experiences are fundamentally constructs of the mind. This school is supposed to have been founded by a monk named

Maitreyanatha. Its important exponents included Asanga, Vasubandhu (both belonging to the 4th century), Sthiramati (6th century), and Dharmakirti (7th century).

The most direct implication of Mahayana ideas at the level of popular practice was the worship of Buddhas and *bodhisattvas* through images in shrines. The older Buddhism had considered the veneration of *stupas* and relics meritorious, but not essential. Mahayana, on the other hand, attached great importance to devotion to the Buddhas and *bodhisattvas*. There was also a gradual shift from the veneration of symbols of Buddha Sakyamuni to the worship of images of many Buddhas and *bodhisattvas*. This shift can be seen in the sculptures at various Buddhist sites.

As mentioned earlier, archaeology has much to offer for the history of religions. Lars Fogelin's study (2006) of the architecture and landscape of the monastic site of Thotlakonda in northern coastal Andhra analyses the material remains of religious practice within a larger social context. On the one hand, the location of the monastery on a hilltop, the inwardly focused cloister, and the concealed location of the refectory suggests monastic isolation. On the other hand, links with the laity are visible in the donative inscriptions, the creation of a public worship space within the monastery, and small *stupas* (referred to as 'votive' stupas in some works) memorializing important monks within the public worship area. A noteworthy feature of the archaeological landscape of Thotlakonda are the large numbers (231) of memorial cairns (made of piled-up stones) outside the monastic complex, most of them commanding a view of the monastery. These probably marked the places where ashes of less prominent monks and devout laypeople were buried.

What was the place and role of women in Buddhism during these centuries? Diana Y. Paul (1979) points out that like earlier Buddhist texts, Mahayana texts too reflect negative as well as positive images of women and femininity. These texts reveal how men perceived themselves in relation to women. In some places, women are portrayed as mysterious, elusive, sensual, dangerous, and weak in body and in mind. In other places, they are portrayed as wise, maternal, gentle, compassionate, and creative. Women's sexuality is seen as threatening to others and to their own spiritual aspirations, and there are several stories of women tempting and destroying monks. Although the path of renunciation was open to women, the texts frequently focus on women within the household and display an anxiety about the impact of women leaving their household to become nuns. Mahayana texts were divided in their opinion regarding women's potential to follow the path leading to *bodhisattva*-hood. Although a few do suggest that maleness and femaleness were illusory and irrelevant categories, most of them present two alternative paths to attaining *bodhisattva*-hood for women. Some Sutras declare that a woman could not enter this path until she was re-born as a man. Others contain stories of miraculous sex changes. For instance, the *Saddharmapundarika Sutra* tells the story of an 8-year-old *bodhisattva* girl, daughter of a *naga* king Sagara, whose sex changed as soon as the prophecy of her impending Buddhahood was made.

It should be noted that all the available information about the *sangha* during these centuries is about the *sangha* of monks. Evidence regarding the *bhikkhuni sangha* is largely confined to references to nuns as donors in inscriptions. Nuns made gifts individually and collectively, and the places mentioned in connection with collective gifts no doubt mark the places where *bhikkhuni sanghas* were located. Monastic centres of nuns did exist, but they are not known by name or fame. All the great monastic centres known from texts and inscriptions were centres of male monasticism. Further, although nuns (along with other women) appear very often as donors at male monastic centres, there is not a single inscription of this period recording a donation to the *bhikkhuni sangha*. There seems to have been a gross disparity between the patronage enjoyed by the male and female monastic orders. The decline of the latter was inevitable in such a situation.

The period *c*. 200 BCE–300 CE saw the expansion and spread of Buddhist *stupa*-monastery complexes in various parts of the subcontinent. Details of some of these will be discussed later on in this chapter, in the sections on architecture and sculpture.

FURTHER DISCUSSION | **Monastic and lay practices in texts versus inscriptions**

Archaeological and epigraphic evidence are vital sources for the history of Buddhism. Gregory Schopen emphasizes the dangers of an overly text-based understanding and points out that scholars who rely exclusively on textual sources assume that these texts were widely known and important. It is in fact quite possible that at least some of them may not have been known to the majority of Buddhist monks or lay persons. Schopen directs attention to many points on which texts lay down a position that did not reflect what people were actually doing. There are also several widespread practices that are either not mentioned or not discussed in any detail in texts. A few examples of the 'mismatch' between the literary and epigraphic evidence are given below:

The texts tell us little about the burial practices of monastic communities. *Stupas*, with or without relics, on the other hand, indicate the development of an elaborate *stupa* cult.

Stupas were set up not only to enshrine relics of the Buddha, but also those of important monks. Small votive *stupas* in the vicinity of larger ones contained the funerary remains of devout members of the laity. We know about these and other mortuary practices of early Buddhists almost entirely from archaeology and inscriptions.

Buddhist texts tell us that a monk left everything, including his property, behind him when he joined the *sangha*. On the other hand, there are plenty of inscriptions which specifically mention monks and nuns making donations to *stupa*-monastery complexes. This clearly indicates that members of the order retained some control over their property—which was often quite substantial—even after joining the *sangha*.

The texts tell us that members of the *sangha* were not supposed to handle money. However, sites such as Sanchi have yielded not only coins but semi-precious stones under the floors of monastic cells. Even more interesting is the discovery of lead coins in a monastery at Nagarjunakonda, found along with earthenware die for making such coins. Monks were evidently making coins; whether legally or illegally, is not certain.

Karma and *dana* (gift giving) are important in the Buddhist textual tradition. But the hundreds of donative inscriptions from various early Buddhist sites indicate the wide prevalence of an idea that is found nowhere in the early texts—the idea of the transference of merit. This is the idea that the meritorious results of the actions of one person can be transferred to another person. Donative records at sites such as Sanchi and Bharhut often state specifically that the donor had made the gift for the benefit of his or her parents or for the welfare of all beings. Such an idea is found even in inscriptions representing the Hinayana stream.

The epigraphic evidence suggests that the distinctions between monastic and lay practices were not as sharp as earlier believed. Gift-giving was an important activity not only for the laity but also for the monastic community. Similarly, monks and nuns participated actively in the *stupa* cult along with the laity.

Source Schopen, 1997

Buddhism in Sri Lanka

According to the 4th/5th century Pali chronicles, the *Dipamvamsa* and *Mahavamsa*, the introduction of Buddhism to Sri Lanka took place during the time of the Maurya emperor Ashoka, when Devanampiya Tissa (*c.* 250–210 BCE) ruled over the island. Ashoka's son and daughter, Mahinda and Sanghamitta, are assigned important roles in this process; the latter is said to have brought across branches of the sacred *bodhi* tree. The earliest Buddhist donative inscriptions in Sri Lanka go back to the 3rd century BCE. S. Paranavitana (1970) mentions 1276 inscriptions found at 269 sites across different parts of the island. Some of the important sites are Hatthikuchchi, the various sites at Anuradhapura, Mihintale, Ritigala, Dimbulagala, and Situlpawa.

The early inscriptions are found in monastic dwellings, which are mostly natural caves, enlarged and improved for human habitation. The major intervention was the drip-line carved on the cave brow to prevent rain water from entering the cave. The inscriptions are usually found below this drip line. They are in the Brahmi script and a variety of Prakrit which has often been referred to as Sinhala-Prakrit, Early Sinhala, or Proto-Sinhala, but which shows significant affinities with the Prakrits found in North India. There are a few Tamil words.

Although no donative inscription of Devanampiya Tissa was found among these Brahmi inscriptions, one inscription records a donation that may have been made by one of his consorts, and another by the sister of one of his consorts. Three donations by Uttiya, Devanampiya Tissa's brother and successor, have also been found. The donative inscriptions indicate that the sources of patronage of the *sangha* included members of the ruling elite, local rulers, chieftains (*parumakas*), village headmen (*gamikas*), *gapatis* (*gahapatis*, i.e., land-owners), craftsmen, and family members of these people (Coningham, 1995). Brahmanas, monks, and nuns also figure as donors. Buddhism was evidently well-integrated into the political and social fabric of Sri Lanka during this period.

Hatthikuchchi

The Buddhist *sangha* in Sri Lanka was divided into various rival groups which competed with each other for royal patronage. The relationship between the state and *sangha* was not only one of mutual inter-dependence, but also one of conflict, as monks got involved in succession disputes. The rivalry between the Abhayagiri and Mahavihara reached a crisis point in the last quarter of the 3rd century CE during the reign of Mahasena, when according to the *Mahavamsa*, at the instigation of a monk named Sanghamitta from Chola country, the Mahavihara was destroyed and its monks forced to abandon their monastery and flee (Liyanagamage, 2000). A new *vihara* called Jetavana was built within the boundaries of the Mahavihara. The Mahavihara suffered a blow but survived. Rivalry, persecution, and violence continued to mark the history of the Buddhist *sangha* in Sri Lanka in later centuries as well.

Over time, the size and complexity of Buddhist monasteries in Sri Lanka increased steadily, large *stupa*-monastery complexes were built, and the connection between state and *sangha*, based on reciprocal interests, was strengthened (see Dias, 2001). Grants of land, tanks, and canals led to monastic communities becoming involved in land management. The large size and scale of monasteries at sites such as Anuradhapura indicate the great wealth and influence of the monastic order. Kings such as Mahasena (276–303) sought to interfere in the *sangha* by issuing *dhamma-kammas*—royal orders regulating monastic affairs, including financial affairs—ostensibly to purify it and remove corrupt practices.

Although Sri Lanka is considered a land of Theravada Buddhism, ancient inscriptions and sculptures at various sites reveal the increasing impact of Mahayana. The island also had a strong, continuing tradition of 'forest monks,' who lived in remote areas in the wilderness.

The Digambara–Shvetambara schism in Jainism

In an earlier chapter, mention was made of the Digambara–Shvetambara schism within the Jaina *sangha*. It is difficult to date this development; it may have taken place in *c.* 300 CE. Digambara tradition explains the schism by referring to a southward migration of Jaina monks in the wake of an impending famine. According to some accounts, the leader of the migrant group was Bhadrabahu and the monks spent 12 years in the Karnataka region. Bhadrabahu died, but his followers finally made their way back to Pataliputra in Magadha. When they arrived there, they found that much had changed. The northern monks, led by Sthulabhadra, had codified the canon. They had also started wearing clothes, which the southerners thought unacceptable, as to them this represented retention of shame and ran counter to the ascetic requirement of renouncing all possessions. The recently-returned group later came to be known as the Digambaras, while the northerners, who wore white clothes, came to be known as the Shvetambaras. The Digambaras completely rejected the canon compiled by Sthulabhadra and denounced the northerners as false Jainas.

The Shvetambaras, on the other hand, ascribe the origin of the Digambara sect to a self-initiated monk named Shivabhuti. We are told that Shivabhuti, hearing of the older practice of monastic nudity that had died out after the time of Mahavira, decided to re-institute it and became the founder of the Digambara sect. Both these Digambara and

Shvetambara accounts of the split are late and are considered of dubious historical value, although it is possible that a southward migration of monks did actually take place, possibly in the 4th century BCE.

The archaeological and inscriptional evidence suggests a gradual move among Jaina monks from the practice of total nudity towards wearing clothes, rather than an abrupt split of the kind suggested by the Digambara and Shvetambara traditions (Dundas, 1992: 42–43). All the early *tirthankara* images from Mathura are naked; it is only in the 5th century CE that there is an image of Rishabha wearing a lower garment. Clothed images became common among Shvetambaras several centuries later. Also notable is the fact that an inscription recording a land grant to Jaina sects by a late 5th century CE king from South India refers to the Shvetambaras but uses the old term 'Nirgrantha' (bondless) to refer to naked monks, suggesting that the term Digambara had not yet become all that common. The council of Valabhi in the 5th century may have been a decisive event in the hardening of the divide between the Shvetambaras and Digambaras. This was an exclusively Shvetambara gathering with no Digambara monks present. The early medieval Yapaniya sect may reflect an intermediate position, wherein monks generally moved around naked, but covered their private parts with a piece of cloth when begging for alms or when they were in the presence of the laity. Eventually, the Shvetambaras came to predominate in western India and the Digambaras in the south.

A number of tracts (over 40) on *shravakachara* laid down the conduct for the Jaina laity. These began with the 2nd century *Charitraprabhrita* of Kundakunda down to the 17th century *Dharmasangrahatika* of Yashovijaya. These texts narrate stories and give detailed instructions on the importance of keeping various vows and what to do for expiation if the vows were broken. They also lay down the *shravaka-pratima*—steps whereby a lay person could systematically and progressively prepare himself for complete renunciation. The only comparable Theravada Buddhist text is the 12th century *Upasakajanalamkara* of Ananda. Like the Buddhists, Jainas too may also have followed the Brahmanical *samskaras* (life-cycle rituals) for a long time. The earliest attempt to codify the *samskaras* for the Jaina laity was made in the early medieval period by Jinasena, who gave a new Jaina interpretation of what were still basically the Brahmanical *samskaras*.

An important development in the early centuries CE at the level of Jaina lay practice was the development of temple worship and religious rituals for the laity. A naked and headless stone torso found at Lohanipur (near Patna), belonging to the Maurya or post-Maurya period, has been tentatively identified as a Jaina *tirthankara*. If the identification is correct, this represents the earliest Jaina image found so far. There is plenty of evidence of Jaina images from various sites from *c.* 200 BCE onwards. The Jaina idea of *puja* is different from its Hindu counterpart. The *tirthankaras* are believed to be aloof and cannot be moved by making offerings. Offerings to them are given *up* by devotees; they are not offered *to* the *tirthankaras*. Folkert (1993) points out that Jaina temple worship developed outside the influence and control of the monastic order. This is in contrast to Buddhism, where monks came to control the shrines. *Puja* in Digambara Jaina shrines is today generally carried out by a priest, while in Shvetambara temples, lay people play a major role in this activity.

Several important centres of Jainism of this period can be identified. The 1st century BCE Hathigumpha inscription of the Kalinga king Kharavela refers to his retrieving an image of a *jina*. This is the earliest epigraphic reference to image worship in Jainism. The Udayagiri and Khandagiri caves in Odisha are among the oldest long-standing centres of Jaina monasticism. The large number of Jaina images and inscriptions from the Mathura area indicates the popularity of Jainism here (Kishore Saxena, 2021). We can note the discovery of the vestiges of a Jaina *stupa* at the Kankali Tila at Mathura, indicating that the veneration of *stupas* was not exclusively a Buddhist practice. Inscriptional and later textual evidence suggests that this *stupa* came to be known as the Devanirmita Stupa (the *stupa* made by the gods). Other Jaina finds at Mathura include stone tablets known as *ayagapatas* and *shilapatas* carved in relief, lots of *Jaina tirthankara* images (some with representations of monastics and laity on the pedestals), and donative inscriptions.

The donative inscriptions indicate that the Jaina *sangha* was organized into units known as *gana, kula, shakha,* and *sambhoga*. Members of the *sangha* played an important role in inducing the laity to make donations. Women donors are very prominent.

The early spread of Jainism to South India and Sri Lanka is indicated by the reference in the *Mahavamsa* to the building of houses and temples for the Nigantha (Jaina) ascetics at Anuradhapura in Sri Lanka by the 4th century BCE king Pandukabhaya. The *Maduraikkanchi* describes a magnificent temple of the Nirgranthas (Jainas) at Madurai. In Tamil Nadu and Kerala, there are 28 Jaina cave sites with 84 inscriptions (Mahadevan, 2003). These are mostly short, donative records in old Tamil (with some Prakrit words and some old Kannada influence), inscribed in the Tamil-Brahmi script. The donors came from a variety of backgrounds and included royalty, guilds, and artisans. Although the inscriptions continue into later centuries, the maximum belong to the 2nd–1st century BC. They clearly indicate that Jainism had made a strong impact in South India.

Religious Architecture and Sculpture

The historiography of the art and architecture of ancient and early medieval India reveals a variety of different perspectives (see Chandra, 1975; Mitter, 1977; Pandya Dhar, 2008). Modern academic inquiry into ancient Indian architecture and sculpture began in the 19th century and was rooted in colonial power equations. These were reflected, for instance, in the tendency of Western scholars to exaggerate the element of foreign influence on Indian art and architecture and their presentation of the history of this art as a story of decay. Subsequently, apart from the descriptive approach, focusing on the evolution and details of artistic features and styles, another approach, reflected in the writings of scholars such as Ananda Coomaraswamy and Stella Kramrisch, attempted to grasp the deeper, spiritual, symbolic underpinnings of Indian artistic creativity. Subsequently, art historians have raised many new questions, including those related to spectatorship, the relationship between textual and visual sources, and gender issues in Indian art (see Dehejia. [Ed.], 1997).

As mentioned earlier, a shrine is basically a demarcated sacred space within which worship or veneration takes place. The earliest shrines in the subcontinent simply consisted of a fenced-in space or tree. Some of them were associated with the worship of *yakshas* and *yakshis*, and *nagas* and *nagis*. The Buddhist *Mahaparinibbana Sutta* refers to many *chetiyas* (*chaityas*) or shrines in the city of Vaishali. Two fragmentary carved columns from the site of Amaravati are interesting in this context. One of them has a relief carving of a tree enclosed by a railing and an inscription in 2nd century BCE Brahmi, which indicates that this was a representation of the Bahuputta *chetiya*. The second one shows the worship of a tree and the Buddha's footprints, the inscription below identifying this as the Chapala *chetiya*.

During *c.* 200 BCE–300 CE, the increasing institutionalization of religious activity and its ability to elicit patronage from different sections of society led to the beginnings of traditions of more permanent and elaborate religious structures. Most of the surviving sculpture and architecture of these centuries is in fact religious in nature. This evidence is important not only for the history of art and architecture but for the history of religion as well. Inscriptions from these sites give information regarding the identity of the people who financed the building of these religious establishments.

The religious monuments of ancient India usually throng with images reflecting beauty and exuberance. As mentioned in Chapter 1, ancient Indian art—most of which is found in religious contexts—accepts and celebrates the sensuous bodily form. The idealized human body in ancient sculpture, as pointed out by Vidya Dehejia (2009), is the body adorned with clothes and ornaments. Physical beauty was seen as a concomitant of political power as well as spiritual power. Viewers of ancient Indian art often think that many of the human figures—especially the voluptuous women—are nude. Actually, their diaphanous robes often give an *illusion* of nudity. (As mentioned earlier, nudity in Jainism has a different meaning; the nakedness of the *tirthankaras* reflects their complete renunciation.) The icons of deities that were enshrined in the sanctum of temples would have been embellished with clothing and ornaments as part of temple rituals. But there is no doubt that many of the bodies depicted in ancient art—of ordinary men and women, gods and goddesses, demi-gods, and saints—are beautiful and sensuous, i.e., they appeal aesthetically to the senses.

Early Buddhist sites such as Sanchi, Amaravati, and Nagarjunakonda have many relief sculptures of amorous couples, referred to by art historians as *mithuna* figures. *Mithuna* couples are depicted on the doorways of shrines of all religious denominations. These images are not connected specifically with any specific religion; rather, they were part of a larger stratum of Indian ideas associated with auspiciousness and beauty. Apart from amorous couples, there are sensuous female figures, identified as *yakshis* or *shalabhanjikas*, entwining their slender limbs around the sinuous trunks of trees and grasping their branches. They are connected with the idea of *dohada*, which literally refers to the cravings of a pregnant woman, except in this context, the idea is that the tree longs for the touch of a beautiful woman which will enable it to flower. The woman-and-tree motif connects the feminine with nature, beauty, and fertility. Relief sculptures of men and women drinking and having a good time (referred to as Bacchanalian scenes) are found in Gandhara and Mathura art. There are also depictions of sex (*maithuna*) in terracotta plaques found at sites such as Chandraketugarh, Tamluk, and Kaushambi. The function of these plaques is not certain.

The sculpture and architecture of *c.* 200 BCE–300 CE can be discussed within smaller chronological or dynastic units of time and of region. The following sections offer, however, only a very general overview of some of the important developments. It can be noted that the varieties of architectural styles and sculptural ornamentation cut across religious and sectarian boundaries.

Early Hindu temples and sculpture

The evidence of Hindu temples of this period consists mostly of ground plans revealed by archaeological excavations; the superstructures have not survived (for detailed discussion, see Meister, Dhaky, and Deva. [Eds.], 1989). Among the earliest are vestiges of what must have been a Vishnu temple in the vicinity of the 2nd century BCE Heliodorus pillar at Vidisha in Madhya Pradesh. The remains of this temple are dated to the 3rd century BCE. The shrine consisted of an inner ellipse (8.10 × 3 m) separated by a 2.5 m gap from the outer ellipse. The latter had a rectangular projection (7 × 4.85 m) to the east, where the entrance was located. The temple had a brick plinth; its superstructure must have been made of wood, thatch, and mud. It was raised higher on a mud platform after it was damaged by floods.

Two elliptical structures of about the same period have also been found at Dangwada in Central India. One of these had a plinth of boulders. An inscribed clay seal indicated that it was a Shiva temple. The other temple had a mud plinth; an inscribed clay seal indicated that it was a Vishnu temple.

Nagari in Chittorgarh district of Rajasthan represents the site of the ancient city of Madhyamika. Here, a 1st century BCE inscription refers to the building of a stone enclosure for a Vishnu shrine. The remains of an older structure, which can be dated to the 3rd century BCE, were found below the level of the enclosure. The structure consisted of two ellipses—the inner one was 10 m long and 3.5 m wide, while the outer one was 14 m long. The 1.8 m space in between functioned as a circumambulatory path. The structure was made of mud and wood, and had a rammed floor of broken bricks and lime.

Archaeologists excavating one of the small mounds outside the main mound at Atranjikhera in Etah district (UP), found remains of an apsidal temple belonging to the late NBPW phase, Period IVD (*c.* 200–50 BCE) (Gaur, 1983: 256–57). The temple faced east and had a raised platform around which was a circumambulatory path. The discovery of a broken, corroded upper part of a Gaja-Lakshmi plaque, showing two elephants sprinkling water over the head of the goddess from their upraised trunks, suggests that this temple was dedicated to Lakshmi.

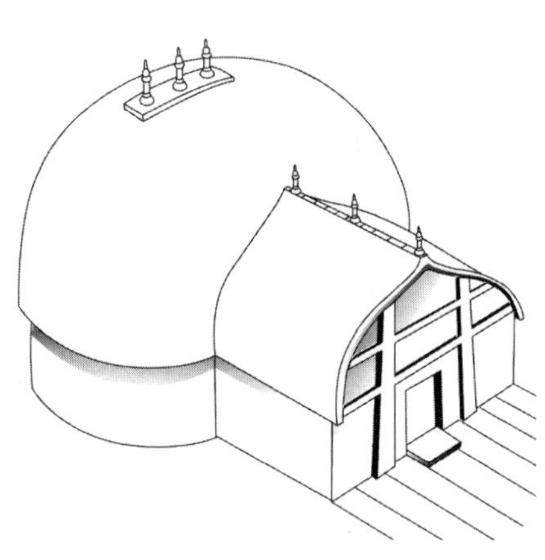

Figure 8.2 Reconstruction of what the Vidisha temple may have looked like (after Khare, 1967)

The site of Sonkh near Mathura gave evidence of a multi-temple urban complex (Hartel, 1993). Apsidal temple no. 1 was the central focus of the residential structures and streets around it. The temple, oriented roughly in an east–west direction, was initially a small structure, and was renovated and enlarged over time. Roughly nine structural phases belonging to the 1st and 2nd centuries CE were identified. The temple began as a small squarish structure, about 3.05 × 3.30 m. It developed into an apsidal structure, about 9.70 × 8.85 m, standing on a raised platform. This was enclosed by a thick wall on three sides, with a room-like structure in the entrance area on the eastern side. On the floor of the apse was a 60 cm high plinth covered with a slab, probably used as an altar for an image. A Matrika plaque carved on mottled red sandstone was found on the floor at its base, and may have been the central cult image which was probably reinstalled in successive structural phases. A large number of plaques depicting Durga as Mahishasuramardini were found in or around this temple. In its last structural phase, just before it fell into disuse, the apsidal shrine seems to have reverted to its squarish shape.

Remains of the much more elaborate Apsidal temple no. 2 were discovered 400 m north of the main excavated area at Sonkh. In its most developed form, the temple can be visualized standing high above surrounding buildings on a 15 × 11.50 m high brick platform, with a pond to its east. The apsidal sanctum had a vaulted roof with pinnacles, which were probably green glazed. The entrance was decorated with an arch-shaped carved stone tympanum above the doorway. To the north of the temple was a row of cells arranged on three sides of a courtyard. The temple complex was enclosed by a stone railing, most of it carved on both sides. The beautifully carved remains of a stone gateway, consisting of two pillars supporting a superstructure of three architraves with voluted ends, were found on the southern side of the railing. An architectural fragment belonging to the bottom lintel of the gateway bore a relief carving of a *naga* and a *nagi* seated on thrones, surrounded by attendants and people with hands folded in obeisance. This carving, a number of stone sculptures and reliefs, terracotta figurines and moulds, inscriptions, and the top half of a four-sided, seven-headed stone *naga* image leave no doubt that Apsidal temple no. 2 was a magnificent *naga* temple.

Excavations in the Parashurameshwara temple at Gudimallam (Chittoor district, AP) have revealed the history of this Shiva temple from the 2nd century BCE onwards (Sarma, 1994). In the earliest stage, the stone Shiva *linga* carved with the image of the god

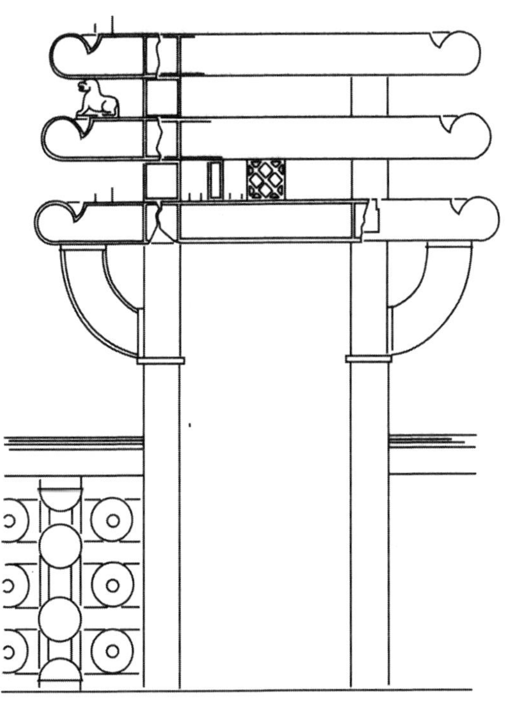

Naga temple and its southern gate, Sonkh (after Hartel, 1993)

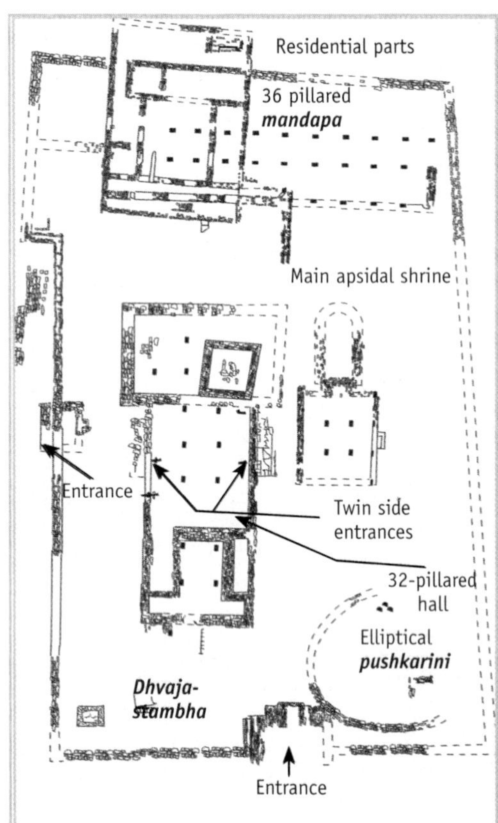

Figure 8.3 Plan of the Ashtabhujasvamin temple, Nagarjunakonda (after Soundararajan et al., 2006)

was placed within a 1.25 m square stone railing. The temple was hypaethral (open-air, roofless). Bones of domesticated sheep with cut marks on them suggest animal sacrifice. Phase II in the structural history of the temple is dated from the 1st to the 3rd centuries CE. An apsidal temple was built around the Shiva *linga* in this period. Considerable architectural elaboration took place in early medieval times. However, it is interesting to note that the same Shiva *linga* remained the object of worship in the sanctum throughout.

Nagarjunakonda represents the ancient site of Vijayapuri, capital of the Ikshvaku dynasty (*c.* 225–325 CE). Here, nestled in a valley surrounded by offshoots of the Nallamalai hills and the river Krishna, was a magnificent royal city replete with royal residences, bathing *ghats*, tanks, memorial stones, Hindu temples, Buddhist *stupas*, shrines, and monasteries (Sarkar and Misra, 1972; Soundararajan et al., 2006). Unfortunately, most of these structures were destroyed when the site was submerged due to the building of the Nagarjunasagar dam. The remains of 9 Hindu temples were identified near the citadel and 10 were located further upstream along the banks of the Krishna. The temples were dedicated to a *yaksha*, Karttikeya, Ashtabhujasvamin (Vishnu), and Shiva as Sarvadeva and Pushpabhadrasvamin. The Hindu temples are fewer than the Buddhist remains, but are significant in terms of their structural features and their likely role in the urban landscape and Ikshvaku political practice.

The temple complexes at Nagarjunakonda did not have a uniform architectural plan. Brick was the main construction material, with stone used for the pillared *mandapas*. Wood was also used. The temples shared some features with Buddhist monasteries at Nagarjunakonda—the apsidal form, pillared halls, moonstones at the entrance, and the use mostly of brick (often plastered), stucco, some stone, and wood. As pointed out by Soundararajan (Soundararajan. [Ed.]., 2006: 200–01), the important features of the Nagarjunakonda temples include pillared halls, a single pillar in front of the shrine (*dhvaja-stambha*); tanks; and a variety of plans including apsidal and square.

Buddhist architecture and sculpture

The period *c.* 200 BCE–300 CE saw an expansion in the number and scale of Buddhist monastic complexes (known variously as *sangharama*, *vihara*, or *lena*) which included dwellings for monks, *stupas*, and shrines. The term *chaitya* means a sacred space, but is more specifically used to refer to Buddhist shrines. Many of the early Buddhist cave shrines contained a *stupa* as the object of veneration, and large, independent *stupas* soon came to form an integral part of Buddhist monasteries.

Debala Mitra, Director General of the Archaeological Survey of India (1975–83), who explored and excavated several Buddhist sites

The *stupa* represented many things in the Buddhist tradition. It stood for the *axis mundi* (the centre of the universe); it symbolized the *parinibbana* of the Buddha; it was a repository of relics of the Buddha and other monks; it was a place of veneration, worship, and pilgrimage for monks and laity. The *Mahaparinibbana Sutta* suggests that the practice of erecting funerary mounds over the bodily remains of kings pre-dated Buddhism. However, there are no references to such a practice in Vedic literature, and the earliest surviving *stupas* are in fact associated with Buddhism. These include the mud *stupas* at Piprahwa and Vaishali.

In an earlier chapter, mention was made of the important role played by Ashoka in popularizing the *stupa* cult. Initially, relics of the Buddha were embedded in the core of *stupas*. In the next stage, relics of the Buddha's disciples and companions were similarly enshrined. Worship was soon transferred from the relics to the *stupa* itself. The veneration of relics remained important in the Theravada Buddhist world, both for lay and monastic communities (see Trainor, 1997; Strong, 2004). Relics could be of various kinds, for instance, corporeal relics (*sharirika*); relics of use (*paribhogika*, for instance, bowl or robe); and relics of commemoration (*uddeshika*, for instance, the *bodhi* tree).

FURTHER DISCUSSION | The modern histories of ancient Buddhist relics

Ancient Buddhist relics and reliquaries were greatly sought after by 19th century European archaeologists, explorers, and treasure hunters, and many reliquaries and relics found their way into European museums. However, they soon came to be recognized as special type of artefacts. This is because for devout Buddhists, relics of the Buddha or Buddhist monks were seen as possessing enormous sacred power and potency.

Apart from their religious importance, relics often played a political role in Sri Lanka and mainland South-east Asia (Blackburn, 2010).

The acquisition and enshrinement of relics and control over ancient Buddhist sites in India became an important part of the Buddhist revival launched by Anagarika Dharmapala and his establishment of the Maha Bodhi Society in 1891. Many relics found by the Archaeological Survey at sites such as Bhattiprolu, Taxila, Nagarjunakonda, and Mirpur Khas were handed over to the Maha Bodhi Society and were enshrined in *viharas* built by the Society. Relics had an important role in the evolution of Buddhist devotional practices, rituals, and evolution of subcontinental and Asian Buddhist pilgrimage networks. As Asian Buddhist elites and religious groups got interested in acquiring them, some of them became part of prolonged negotiations and ended up travelling long distances, acquiring new cultural and political meanings.

In 1897, a civil engineer named W. C. Peppé discovered relics in caskets at Piprahwa (in modern Basti District, UP; generally identified with ancient Kapilavastu). These were widely believed to be Buddha relics. (The discoveries were soon enveloped in a scandal surrounding the archaeologist Führer, who had been inventing details while documenting the finds.) The Piprahwa relics were sought by the ruler of Siam, Chulalongkorn. The British saw this as a good opportunity to secure their Burmese frontiers and to advance their interests in Siam by appealing to the religious sentiments of the court. The Piprahwa relics were transferred to the government of Siam in an elaborate ceremony held on 14th February, 1899. The king of Siam in turn distributed some of the relics to Burma (now Myanmar), Sri Lanka, and Japan (Sraman Mukherjee, 2017).

The bone relic discovered by A. H. Longhurst in the *mahachaitya* at Nagarjunakonda (believed to be a relic of the Buddha), became the focus of rival claims in the 1930s. Monks from a monastery at Kelaniya near Colombo and the Maha Bodhi Society were among the claimants. This led to a debate about the special nature of religious relics and the appropriate place for their custody or display. Ultimately, the relics were presented to the Mulagandhakuti Vihara built by the Maha Bodhi Society at Sarnath on the occasion of the celebration of its first anniversary in December 1932. The relic was handed over by Daya Ram Sahni, Director General of the Archaeological Survey, on behalf of the Viceroy of India, to a Sinhalese high priests, in the midst of elaborate ceremonials, and a large international audience, that included an ailing Anagarika Dharmapala (Upinder Singh, 2016: 84–107).

The reliquaries and relics excavated by Alexander Cunningham and F. C. Maisey at Sanchi and other *stupas* in Central India ultimately found their way into the British Museum and Victoria and Albert Museum. The Begum of Bhopal made an unsuccessful attempt to have them brought back to Bhopal in around 1919. In the 1930s, Buddhist societies including the Maha Bodhi Society, petitioned the Indian Government to work for the return of the relics of the monks Sariputta and Mahamogallana from the Victoria and Albert Museum. The relics finally left England in 1947, after making ceremonial stops in Ceylon, Burma, and Nepal. They were brought to Sanchi and handed over to the Maha Bodhi Society in 1952 by Prime Minister Jawahar Lal Nehru in a grand ceremony, in the presence of the premier of Burma, and many prominent international figures. It is another matter that the relics that were transferred were later found to be from Satdhara and not Sanchi (Lahiri, 2016: 70–75)!

In 1955, Prime Minister Nehru presented some of the Sanchi relics to Ceylon, expressing the hope that the gift would cement the cultural ties between India and that country. The Indian Government was not the only one initiating relic diplomacy. In 1957, Nehru received relics of the Chinese pilgrim Xuanzang, along with some books about him from the Dalai Lama on behalf of the Chinese government. The relic, supposedly a fragment of the skull cap of the Chinese pilgrim, is now enshrined in a memorial hall at Nalanda.

The continuing important of relic diplomacy is reflected in the Indian government's 11-day loan of Buddha relics to Mongolia in 2022, for display and veneration during the Buddha Purnima celebrations in the Ganden Tegchenling monastery in the Mongolian capital, Ul.

Source Blackburn, 2010; Sraman Mukherjee, 2017; Upinder Singh, [2016] 2023c; Lahiri, 2016

Special importance was attached to relics that were believed to be the Buddha's corporeal remains. These were supposed to be located at certain sites in India and were coveted all over the Asian Buddhist world. The *Mahavamsa* assigns a special role to Ashoka, his son Mahinda and daughter Sanghamitta in the spread of Buddhism to the island of Sri Lanka. The text describes the arrival of Buddha relics to Anuradhapura, thanks to Ashoka and the god Sakka (Indra), during the time of king Devanampiyatissa. The relics are said to have included the Buddha's post-cremation remains, his right collar bone, and his alms bowl. Later traditions talk about the travels of the Buddha's tooth relic from Dantapura in Kalinga to Sri Lanka. It was initially kept in Anuradhapura and moved around as the political centre moved, finally ending up in Kandy, where the Temple of the Tooth continues to be a major centre of Buddhist worship.

During *c.* 200 BCE–300 CE, *stupas*—with or without relics—became an important part of Buddhist monasteries. The *stupa*-monastery complexes were located close to urban centres and along major trade and pilgrimage routes. Some marked places connected with important events in the life of the Buddha. Most of the major *stupa*-monastery complexes were located on the outskirts of the great cities of the time—Mrigadava outside Kashi, the Dharmarajika *stupa* outside Taxila, Sanchi outside Vidisha, Amaravati outside Dharanikota (the Satavahana capital), and Nagarjunakonda outside Vijayapuri (the Ikshvaku capital). Bharhut was also evidently located on the outskirts of a city which has not so far been identified with any site mentioned in ancient texts.

Most Buddhist *stupa*-monastery sites were built over many centuries, and reveal the gradual evolution of sculptural and architectural style as well as of religious thought and practice (see Hawkes and Shimada. [Eds.]., 2009). The architectural and sculptural features of *stupas* of this period shared certain common features, but there were also some distinct regional traditions. The architectural and sculptural features of a few important sites are discussed below. It should be noted that an understanding of these sites should not only focus on the archaeological, epigraphic, and sculptural evidence found there, but also on how these sites were integrated into their larger hinterland. It should also be noted that ancient Buddhist sites in India have an eventful long-term history and have been central to Dalit Buddhist identity, the Buddhist revival in Asia, and the creation of modern Buddhist pilgrimage circuits (see Upinder Singh, 2010).

STUPA-MONASTERIES OF THE NORTH-WEST

In the Gandhara region, Indian and Hellenistic features coalesced (Huntington, 1985: 130–33). There was a significant expansion of Buddhist monasteries in Gandhara and northern Afghanistan in the early centuries CE, but very little evidence of their architectural form survives. Takht-i-Bahi in Pakistan and Guldara in Afghanistan are two important sites. Excavations at Takht-i-Bahi revealed a large monastic complex that included several connected clusters of cells arranged around courtyards, *stupas*, and sculptures. A *stupa* once stood in one of the courtyards, but only its square base survives.

Extensive evidence of early Buddhist shrines and *stupas* comes from Taxila. The city of Sirkap at this site was founded by the Indo-Greeks and continued to be occupied during Shaka and Parthian rule. The excavated remains mostly belong to the latter phase. The largest structure is a ruined Buddhist apsidal temple, located in Block D. This has a screen between the apse and area for assembly. A number of stone heads showing Indian and Greek features and styles were found here; some may represent *bodhisattvas*. In front of the shrine, on both sides of the entrance, were the square bases of *stupas*. This structure can be dated to the first half of the 1st century CE.

Another important structure at Sirkap was the so-called 'shrine of the double eagle' in Block F, probably built in the late 1st century BCE. Its only surviving portion is the square base of what was obviously a *stupa*. This has relief carvings of pillars and pilasters with acanthus leaf capitals in between. The carvings represent three different types of gateways: a *torana* (gateway) with two architraves, similar in general form and shape to those found at Sanchi; a doorway with a *chaitya* arch (also known as the ogee arch), and a classic Hellenistic pedimented façade. The *chaitya* arches have representations of double-headed eagles, while the *toranas* have single-headed eagles. It is interesting to note that over half a dozen small *stupas* were found within the regular residential area of Sirkap. The laity must have offered worship here.

Several *stupa*-monastery complexes outside the city of Taxila have structural phases belonging the early centuries CE. The largest of these include the Dharmarajika (locally known as the Chir tope), probably belonging to the Maurya period. As at other

Gandhara sites such as Manikyala and Jamalgarhi, this *stupa* consisted of a low circular plinth surmounted by a hemispherical dome. The monastic area lay to its north. In the 1st century BCE, the Dharmarajika *stupa* came to be surrounded by a ring of miniature *stupas*. These were later replaced by miniature shrines. In the 1st century CE, the *stupa* was rebuilt, and its solid core was replaced by a wheel-shaped plan. In the 2nd century CE, flights of stairs were built at the four cardinal points. (Almost all the other *stupas* at Taxila have only one flight of stairs). Shrines with images appeared from the 1st century CE in the vicinity of the Dharmarajika as well as in some of the other Taxila monastic complexes.

In contrast to the *stupas* of Central India, those of the north-west had a tower-like appearance with sculptural decoration on the base and dome. The modest-sized Guldara *stupa* (2nd century CE) rises from a high square base, with stairs leading up to it from the east. The outer façade of the structure consists of thin, flat slabs of sedimentary rock, carefully arranged one on top of the other (this is known as the diaper masonry technique and was introduced to this region by the Parthians), the interior filled with stone rubble. The *stupa's* base and dome were decorated with pilasters, niches, and different kinds of arches. The capitals of the pilasters framing the niches seem to have been inspired by Corinthian capitals, while the *chaitya* arches that they frame reflect an Indian feature. Large stucco images must have once adorned these niches.

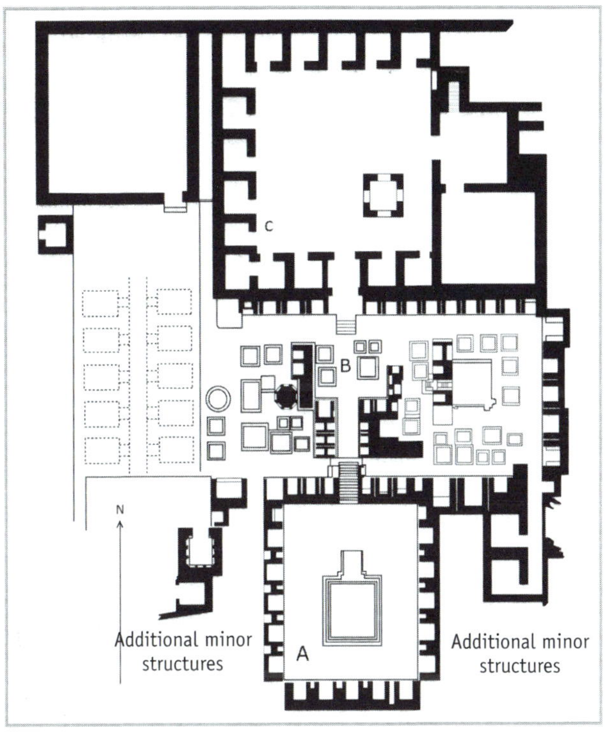

Figure 8.4 Plan of monastic complex, Takht-i-Bahi (after Huntington, 1985)

CENTRAL INDIAN *STUPAS*—SANCHI AND BHARHUT

The many Buddhist monastic sites in Central India include Bharhut, Sanchi, Satdhara, Andher, Sonari, and Bhojpur. Of these, those of Bharhut and Sanchi have been best studied. The sculptures at Bharhut range from the 3rd century BCE to the end of the 2nd century BCE, while its inscriptions have been dated to the 2nd–1st centuries BCE. The Bharhut *stupa* has been completely destroyed over time and its parts are scattered in various museums, with a major collection housed in the Indian Museum in Kolkata. Sanchi has the advantage of being in a better state of preservation than many other early Buddhist *stupa*-monastery sites, and we will therefore, focus on it.

Sanchi (in Raisen district, MP) is referred to as Kakanava or Kakanaya in early Brahmi inscriptions found at the site (Singh, 1996). In the 4th century CE, it was known as Kakanadabota, while an inscription of the late 7th century refers to it as Bota-Shriparvata. The site is not associated with any event in the Buddha's life. It was located near Vidisha, one of the greatest cities of the Maurya empire. This was also the birthplace of Devi, with whom, according to legend, Ashoka had a serious romance. The remains at Sanchi include *stupas*, pillars, shrines, and sculptures ranging from the 3rd century BCE to the 12th century CE. These provide a remarkable history of Buddhism in stone, spanning some 15 centuries.

There are several *stupas* at Sanchi. As mentioned in an earlier chapter, the brick core of Stupa no. 1 belongs to Ashoka's time. In the 2nd century BCE, this *stupa* was encased in stone, using dark purple-grey sandstone which was available locally. Many other *stupas*, shrines, and monasteries were built over the next few centuries. The *stupas* had a stone circumambulatory path (*pradakshina-patha*); two flights of stairs (*sopanas*) at the base; stone railings (*vedikas*) at the ground, berm (the ledge located between the base and the dome), and summit level; and a stone umbrella (*chhatra*) on the summit. Stone railings and four gateways (*toranas*) at the cardinal points enclosed the entire sacred space. While no relics were found in Stupa no. 1, Stupa no. 2 contained a relic box with bone fragments of 10 Buddhist monks. Stupa no. 3 had the relics (bone fragments, beads) of the famous monks Sariputta and Mahamogalana.

Yakshi on pillar, Bharhut

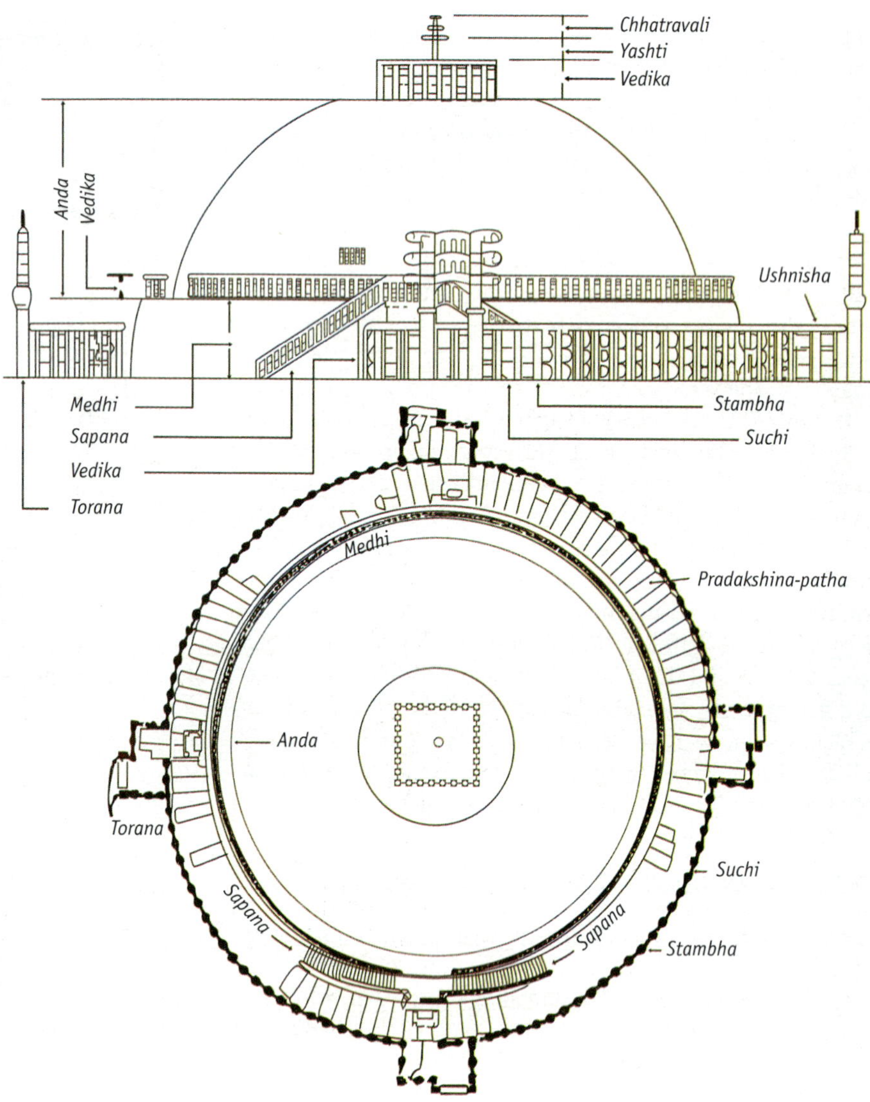

Figure 8.5 Plan of Sanchi Stupa no. 1 (after Mitra, 1971)

Bharhut railing medallion

In Central India, the surface of a *stupa* was not embellished with sculptures. Sculptural decoration—if any—was reserved for the railings and gateways. The shape of the gateways suggests that they were stone renditions of wooden prototypes. Traces of plaster and red paint at a few places on Stupa no. 1 indicate that the Sanchi *stupas* were probably covered with a layer of plaster and red paint. This and the garlands decorating the *stupas* represented in reliefs indicate that the *stupas* of ancient times did not look as austere as they do today.

The other structural remains at Sanchi belonging to *c.* 200 BCE–200 CE include pillars, a pillared hall, and shrines, including an apsidal one. A study of approximately 750 sq km around Sanchi has documented many different kinds of archaeological remains, including evidence of settlement, Buddhist structures, sculptures, and irrigation works (Shaw, 2004). Many of these belong to the period between the 1st century BCE and 5th century CE. Sanchi has many ancient dams made of mud, faced with dressed blocks of stone. These created reservoirs for storing rainwater, suggesting that the monks were involved in water harvesting, not only for providing drinking water, but also for irrigating the surrounding fields. Till recently, there was a question about their dates. However, Optically Stimulated Luminescence (OLS) dates from some of these dams confirm that they were constructed during the late centuries BCE, contemporaneous to the early Buddhist monasteries at the site (Shaw et al., 2007). This is important evidence for the involvement of Buddhist monasteries in the construction and management of irrigation works that would have enhanced agricultural production in the area. Most of

Sanchi Stupa no. 1 (from top): *Stupa*; gateway; details of railing and gateway sculptures

the *naga* sculptures in the Sanchi area were situated on top of or close to ancient dams, indicating the importance of the worship of *nagas* (associated with water and agricultural fertility), long after the establishment of the Buddhist monastery. Understanding Sanchi in the context of its wider archaeological landscape offers insights into the interface between Buddhism, Vaishnavism, and the *naga* cult.

STUPAS OF SOUTH INDIA AND SRI LANKA

Nagarjunakonda: Buddha image

The large number of important Buddhist monastic establishments located in Andhra Pradesh include Amaravati, Jaggayyapeta, and Nagarjunakonda. The first two of these are in a ruinous state and the third was submerged by the waters of the Nagarjunasagar dam. However, we get an idea about their basic structure and features from their surviving remains. The Buddhist monastery at Amaravati was located next to Dharanikota, capital of the later Satavahanas (for details, see Shimada, 2013). The discovery of what may be an Ashokan inscription at this place suggests that the beginning of the monastic establishment may be dated to the Maurya period. The Amaravati *stupa* was the largest in the Andhra country and is referred to in ancient inscriptions as a *mahachaitya*. As a result of indiscriminate excavation and removal of sculpted stones from the site from the late 18th century onwards, the drum of the brick *stupa*, the circumambulatory path, and a few railing uprights are all that survive at the site (for the story of how this happened, see Upinder Singh, 2004: 249–89).

Nagarjunakonda contained over 30 Buddhist establishments belonging to the 3rd–4th centuries CE. The inscriptions mention at least four different sects—the Mahaviharavasin, Mahishasaka, Bahushrutiya, and Aparamahavinaseliya (the last one is mentioned in the maximum number of inscriptions). There is great variety in the architecture and arrangement of the Buddhist complexes here. Some of them consisted of a *stupa* and monastery, others of a *stupa*, monastery, and *chaitya*, and still others of a monastery and *chaitya*. There are several isolated *stupas* and also small votive *stupas*. H. Sarkar (1966) has estimated that going by the size and number of dwelling spaces, the monastic community of Nagarjunakonda may have numbered about 450.

Some of the *stupas* of the Andhra region had a solid brick or stone construction. The body of others consisted of a spoked-wheel plan made of bricks, the spaces in between filled with mud. This spoked-wheel plan translated a key Buddhist symbol—the *chakra*—into an architectural feature, also endowing the structure with greater strength. While the spoked-wheel plan appears at many sites, the Amaravati *stupa* had a solid brick core. The Bhattiprolu *stupa* (2nd century BCE) may represent an intermediate stage—it had a mostly solid core, with a wheel plan in the central portion. (It may be noted that the wheel-shaped plan also occurs outside the Andhra region—for instance, in the Dharmarajika *stupa* at Taxila, at Shah-ji-ki-Dheri, and in Mathura.) At Nagarjunakonda, most of the *stupas* were made of brick, a few were made of stone rubble, and one had a brick rim enclosing a rubble and earth packing. Most of the Nagarjunakonda *stupas* had wheel-shaped bases. The number of spokes in the wheel ranged from 4 to 10 and usually varied according to the size of the *stupa*—the larger the *stupa*, the more spokes in the wheel. A few *stupas* had a *svastika* instead of a wheel inset into their base.

Another notable feature of some of the Andhra *stupas* was that raised on a platform at the four cardinal points were five tall free-standing pillars known as *ayaka* pillars. One interpretation is that they represent five important events in the Buddha's life—his birth, renunciation, enlightenment, first sermon, and death. *Ayaka* platforms and pillars are, however, absent at Salihundam and Ramatirtham, and even at some of the *stupas* at Nagarjunakonda. Outside Andhra, such platforms have been reported at Vaishali.

Stupa with spoked-wheel plan, Nagarjunakonda

The base and a part of the dome of some of the great *stupas* of this region were faced with sculpted limestone slabs in the early centuries CE. For example, the dome, railings, and gateways of the Amaravati *stupa* were profusely ornamented with beautiful relief carvings. At Nagarjunakonda, on the other hand, although the relief sculptures depict *stupas* with railings, very few actual railing fragments have been found, and they are all plain and uninscribed.

Map 8.8 Early historic monasteries in Andhra Pradesh and Telangana

Nagarjunakonda stadium, *mahachaitya*

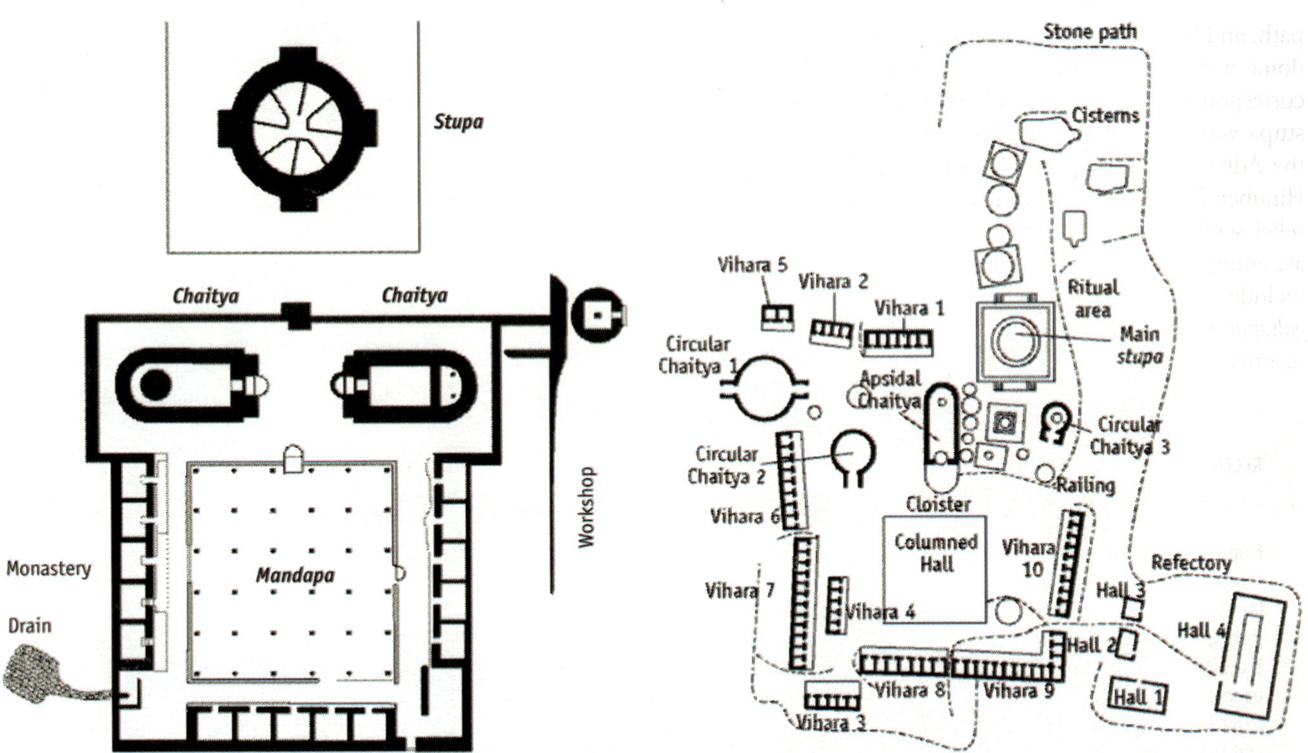

Figure 8.6 Plan of a *stupa*-monastery complex, Nagarjunakonda (after Soundararajan et al., 2006); Thotlakonda monastery (after Fogelin, 2006)

There are a large number of early historical Buddhist sites in north coastal Andhra Pradesh, for instance at Thotlakonda, Bavikonda, Pavuralakonda, Sankaram, and Dharapalem. The first three of these were excavated recently. Thotlakonda (see Sastry, Subrahmanyam, and Rao, 1992) yielded remains of several *viharas*, *chaityas*, and *stupas*; the occupation of the site was dated between the 3rd/2nd century BCE and the 2nd/3rd century CE.

The site of Phanigiri (in Telangana) revealed the ruins of a Buddhist complex dating between the 1st century BCE and 3rd century CE, located on a granite hill-top near the banks of the Aleru river, a tributary of the Musi (for details, see Ahuja. [Ed.], 2021). These included a *stupa* (18 m in diameter) with four platforms in the cardinal directions, which must have supported *ayaka* pillars. The *stupa* contained a terracotta relic pot containing a silver casket, within which were bits of silver and gold foil and beads. The *stupa* was not faced with carved slabs, but had limestone friezes of lotus petals along the base of the drum. A unique feature, not found so far in any other *stupa* in the region, was a finely carved stone gateway (*torana*) with three architraves. There were also remains of two large and two small apsidal halls, three *viharas* consisting of nine cells each, the base of an octagonal structure (perhaps a *stupa* or a shrine), and two water cisterns. Many finely carved architectural elements and reliefs carved on stone slabs were found, along with stucco sculptures. The donors included the chief physician of the Ikshvaku king Rudrapurushadatta (his inscription was carved on an octagonal pillar), and a monk named Dhammasena. A Phanigiri inscription praises the superiority of the Buddha over Shiva and Krishna, revealing competition, if not conflict, between their worshippers. Broken images at Phanigiri suggest a violent end to this Buddhist complex (Skilling, 2008).

Turban relic sculpture, Phanigiri

Excavations at Kanaganahalli in Gulbarga district (Karnataka) yielded remains of a Buddhist establishment that can be dated between the 3rd century BCE and 3rd century CE. It included a *stupa*, monastic complex, a small apsidal temple, several small *stupas*, and paved platforms (see Poonacha, 2011). The *stupa* was about 26 m in diameter and had four *ayaka* platforms in the cardinal directions. The eastern platform supported four columns. Buddhapadas and four Buddha statues once stood on the *ayakas* and eight Buddha images were located in the circumambulatory passage. *Yaksha* statues were placed on the sides of the *ayakas*. The *stupa* was surrounded by a rail which created a circumambulatory path, and had four entrances facing the *ayakas*. The drum and the lower part of the *stupa* dome were paneled with stone slabs carved with beautiful narrative reliefs. The style corresponds to the early and later Amaravati style. The excavations indicated that the stupa was enlarged at least three times. Inscriptions indicate that the *stupa* was called the Adhalaka *mahachaitya*. The site yielded over 170 inscriptions (Nakanishi and von Hinüber, 2014), including donative and label inscriptions. Buddhist monks shown in the relief sculptures and donative inscriptions accompanied by relief sculptures of donors are among the other striking features of this important site. The donors at Kanaganahalli include monks and nuns, *upasakas* and *upasikas*, *vanijas*, sons of *vanijas*, *gahapatis*, *gahapati-vanijas*, *amacas* (ministers), and *manikaras* (jewelers). There are two donative records of caravan traders (*sarthavahas*) from the north.

RECENT DISCOVERIES | Satavahana kings in Kanaganahalli sculptures

Monika Zin's reconstruction of the sculptures associated with the Adhalaka mahachaitya helps understand its iconographic programme. The drum and the lower part of the stupa dome were paneled with stone slabs carved with narrative reliefs. The style of the sculptures and the inscriptions indicate that they were carved over several generations, and ranged from the 1st century BCE to the early 2nd century CE.

Although there are no Satavahana donative inscriptions here, kings of this dynasty are mentioned in 56 inscriptions and several are represented in the relief sculptures. They can be identified from label inscriptions. The kings mentioned in the label inscriptions are Matalaka, Sundara, Satakarni, and Pulumavi. These sculptures were probably made during the reign of Vasishtiputra Pulumavi in the 2nd century CE. It is very likely that the set of slabs was commissioned either by Pulumavi or by a high-ranking Satavahana noble or official on his behalf.

A slab showing a king making a gift by pouring water from spouted vessel has the inscription: *raya satakani mahachetiyasa rupamayani* (King Satakarni donates silver lotus flowers to the mahachetiya). This seems to represent Gautamiputra Satakarni.

Another relief shows a king pouring water into the right palm of another king, with the accompanying inscription: *raya pulumavi ajayatasa ujeni deti* (King Pulumavi gives Ujeni to Ajayata). Oskar von Hinüber suggests that this seems to be a visual record of a political event—Vasishthiputra Pulumavi handing over the city of Ujjayini to his Kshatrapa rival Chashtana, a political setback being presented as an act of magnanimity. Both reliefs depict Satavahana kings in attitudes of extraordinary generosity.

The importance of the Satavahana reliefs at Kanaganahalli emerges from Zin's reconstruction of their original arrangement on the dome near the northern *ayaka*, next to scenes from the life of the Buddha and representations of Ashoka. Scenes representing Ashoka are flanked on both sides by scenes from the Buddha's life or places connected with his life; and the latter are flanked by the depictions of the Satavahana rulers. Zin suggests that the images of Satavahana kings at Kanaganahalli could reflect the association of kings with prosperity. She adds that placing the Satavahana kings around Ashoka and Buddhist symbols endowed them with prestige and also implicitly represents them as Buddhist rulers.

At Kanaganahalli, the Satavahanas do not appear directly as ordinary donors. They are depicted as great kings, along and on par with Ashoka.

Source Zin, 2018a, 2018b; von Hinuber, 2016

Inscribed reliefs: 'King Pulumavi gives Ujeni to Ajayata' (left); 'King Satakarni donates silver lotus flowers to the *mahachaitya*' (right)

Due to many centuries of religious patronage and the close ties between the state and *sangha*, the Buddhist sites of Sri Lanka are much more extensive and elaborate than those known in India. Ancient texts refer to three categories of *viharas* – *rajavihara, mahavihara,* and *vihara*. The first of these were associated with kings. Many Buddhist sites in Sri Lanka were occupied over a long period of time, so it is difficult to give specific dates to them. While structural embellishment may have gone on over the centuries, some have yielded early inscriptions and sculptures. The early Buddhist *stupa*-monastery sites at Anuradhapura include Mahavihara, Ruvanvali, Mirisavatiya, Dakkhina, Abhayagiri, Lankaramaya, and Jetavana vihara. Mihintale near Anuradhapura, Sithulpawa, and Tissamaharama are other important early sites.

The Sri Lankan *stupas* are quite different from their Indian counterparts. They stand on a cylindrical, sometimes multi-tier, base. The domes are of varying shapes and were made of burnt bricks. The exterior was lined with plaster and painted. The height of the dome varied and could be quite imposing. (For instance, the Jetavana *stupa* was originally 400 ft high.) A small square structure on the summit of the dome supported an attenuated spire. The ornamented railings and gateways found at early historic Buddhist *stupa* sites in India are absent in Sri Lanka. The only sculptural embellishment is found on the *vahalkadas* or *ayakas*—projecting front pieces joined to the *stupa*—located at the four cardinal points. Apart from the residential buildings (*parivena*), there was an image house (a shrine with a Buddha image), chapter house (*uposatha-ghara*), a Bodhi shrine (*bodhi-ghara*), and refectory (*mahapaka* or *bojana-hala*). Carved moonstones at the foot of flights of steps leading to religious structures are distinctive features of the Anuradhapura monasteries. Some of the Sri Lankan monasteries had large tanks and elaborate water management systems. A great deal more work needs to be done by scholars on the Buddhist sites of Sri Lanka.

The close relationship between the monastic communities in Andhra and Sri Lanka and the expanding Buddhist networks are evident from Nagarjunakonda inscriptions. An inscription on the floor of the apsidal temple to the east of the *mahachaitya* refers to the great community of Buddhist monks (*mahabhikhu-sangha*) who had renounced the world and who had assembled from various countries (*nana-desa-samanagata*). Inscriptions found at the pillared hall associated with the *mahachaitya* refer to the *mahavihara* and the *mahabhikhu-samgha* who had assembled from various lands. The apsidal temple associated with the Chula-Dhammagiri Vihara (Site 43) at Nagarjunakonda was endowed by an *upasika* named Bodhisiri. It is described as having been constructed for the benefit of the Tamraparni *acharyas*, who had gladdened many lands (Kashmir, Gandhara, China, Chilata, Tosali, Avaranta, Vanga, Vanavasi, Yavana, Damila, Palura, and the island of Tambapanni) through their teaching. It is possible that the Tamriparni *acharyas* were not monks from Sri Lanka but a group of Indian monks with close ties to Sri Lankan communities. Vincent Tournier (2018) suggests that such statements should be understood as part of a rhetoric of widespread spiritual conquest or conversion, rather than be taken literally. However, they do seem to suggest the idea of an expanding Asian Buddhist world.

Jetavana stupa, Anuradhapura (left); Abhayagiri moonstone (right)

Mihintale: Kanthaka chetiya (1st row, left); stone rice bowl (1st row, right); alms hall (2nd row, left); 'hospital' (3rd row, left), medicinal bath (3rd row, right)

Abhayagiri guard-stone (left); Sandagiri Buddha (right)

EARLY RELIEF SCULPTURE AT BUDDHIST SITES

Art historian Niharranjan Ray (1975: 58–66) pointed to a sharp contrast between Maurya and post-Maurya art. The art of the Maurya period was essentially a dignified and aristocratic court art. It was art in the round, to be seen from all sides, in which animals figured prominently. Post-Maurya art, on the other hand, reflected popular tastes and patronage. It was largely relief art (where the carving is done on one surface and is meant to be seen from the front alone) and was by and large narrative in character. The human figure emerged as an important part of the composition. Except for Udayagiri and Khandagiri, which had Jaina associations, the relief art of the period *c.* 200 BCE–300 CE was mainly Buddhist in affiliation.

Although there were differences in the stone used by the artist-artisans who produced the relief sculpture at these sites, there is a broad similarity in theme and sculptural vocabulary. However, distinctive styles emerged. The intricate and elaborate surface decoration and the shallowness of the relief carvings at sites such as Sanchi, Bharhut, and Amaravati suggest that these represented a translation of the woodcarver's art into stone. The artists were adept at showing the human body from a frontal perspective, but had some difficulty showing side views. On the scale of sculptural maturity, the reliefs of Sanchi, Bharhut, Amaravati, and Nagarjunakonda show progressive development. The sculptures of Amaravati are a bit more mature than those at the Central Indian sites—the relief scenes are less crowded and the frontality of the figures is less pronounced. The carving at the Andhra sites is deeper and stylistically more developed. The scenes are still crowded, but the human figures are more natural and graceful than in earlier sculpture. As pointed out by Stella Kramrisch ([1921] 1994: 127), in early Buddhist relief art, the landscape does not form the background of action, but takes part in it and constitutes it.

These sites offer the earliest sculptural representations of important episodes in the Buddha's life and of the Jataka stories. The reliefs represent two kinds of narration—monoscenic and continuous (Dehejia, 1997a: 4–6). Mono-scenic narration depicts a single major episode, which reminds the viewer of the entire story. In continuous narration, several different scenes of the story were depicted in sequence, usually without any break or partition in between, one scene simply merging into the next. The size of the figures represented in the scenes was not based on realistic dimensions but according to their relative importance in the story that was being told. At Bharhut, Pauni, and Amaravati, the Jataka scenes are labelled. This is of great help in identifying the meaning of the sculptures.

Many of the sculptural reliefs represent important scenes from the life of the Buddha (see Marshall, Foucher, and Majumdar, [1940] 1982). In the early stages, the artists depicted these scenes without showing the Buddha in bodily form. There were four key episodes from his life that were most frequently represented, especially at important places of honour on the gateways—*jati* (birth), *sambodhi* (enlightenment), *dharmachakra-pravartana* (the first sermon), and *mahaparinibbana* (death). To this list can be added two others—*avakranti* (the descent, i.e., conception) and the *mahabhinishkramana* (the great departure). At Sanchi, the Gaja-Lakshmi depiction is sometimes interpreted as Maya seated on a lotus. The Buddha's enlightenment is represented by the *bodhi* tree, variously combined with an umbrella over it, a throne in front of it, or a railing around it. The first sermon at Sarnath is represented by the wheel. The *stupa* symbolized the Buddha's death. The conception is represented in scenes showing Maya asleep on a couch with a white elephant at the top of the panel. Siddhartha's departure into homelessness is represented by a bridled horse and a groom holding an umbrella over the head of the invisible rider.

'Scythian figure', Nagarjunakonda

Many of the relief carvings at early Buddhist sites drew from a larger pool of cultural symbols and ornamentation that had nothing specifically Buddhist about them.

For instance, Sanchi sculptures depicted *yakshas*, *yakshis*, *nagas*, and *nagis*. Animals included (in order of frequency and importance) the lion, elephant, horse, and bull. Other animals that occur are the deer, stag, camel, buffalo, rhinoceros, boar, bear, squirrel, and rodents. Monkeys are conspicuous by their absence at Sanchi, but occur at other sites. There are some hybrid or fantastic animals—e.g., an elephant-headed stag, winged lion, lion with an eagle's head, lion with a human face, centaurs, and sea monsters. Some of these show West Asian influence. Among birds, *hamsas* (geese) occur very often, usually in pairs. There are a few representations of cranes, peacocks, and parrots. Fish, tortoises, and snakes are also depicted. Among trees, the *pipal* appears very often. Other trees that can be identified are the mango tree and possibly one palm tree. Floral designs include the full-blown or half-blown lotus, suspended garlands, creepers, and a floral pattern known as the honeysuckle ornament. Human figures are not as realistically depicted as some of the animals and have a certain stiffness about them. Some of them may represent donors.

Some frequently occurring sculptural symbols have uncertain origins and meanings. One of these is the three-pronged symbol often referred to by art historians as a 'taurine' (because it resembles the horns of a bull) or *nandi-pada* (a misnomer based on the coincidence that hoof marks and the words *nandi-paam* were found next to this symbol on Padana hill near Mumbai). This has been variously interpreted as a fire symbol, the Vedic *vajra* (thunderbolt), or Shiva's trident. At Buddhist sites, this symbol is usually interpreted as the *triratna*, standing for the Buddha, *dhamma,* and *sangha*. Another frequently occurring symbol is the *shrivatsa*, the meaning of which too is uncertain. It may be noted that there is a resemblance between this symbol and the anthropomorph of the copper hoards.

The Buddha image starts appearing both in relief and free-standing sculpture at Buddhist sites in around the 1st century BCE/1st century CE. The Andhra Buddha images have massive bodies and wear robes with accentuated folds. The representation of the Buddha in anthropomorphic form did not, however, completely replace the older convention of depicting him in symbolic form. For instance, at Nagarjunakonda, relief panels depicting the Buddha in symbolic and anthropomorphic form occur side by side.

The close relationship between Andhra and Sri Lanka is visible in the Andhra influence on Buddha images found on the island A few portable marble reliefs found on the island are in the Amaravati–Nagarjunakonda style and must have been brought here by traders or pilgrims. Bopearachchi argues that the large white marble Buddha image found at Tissamaharama, not far from Sandagiri vihara, was made in Andhra in the Amaravati style (Bopearachchi, 2015, Vol. 2, pp. 225–45; Bopearachchi, 2020). Apart from images made in Andhra, there were many others made by artists in Sri Lanka trained in the Andhra style.

And yet, in spite of the Andhra influence, as mentioned earlier, Sri Lankan *stupas* are quite different from their Andhra counterparts, indeed from *stupas* anywhere in India. The ornamented railings and gateways found at early historic Buddhist *stupa* sites in India are absent in Sri Lanka. The carved limestone slabs that ornamented the dome of the Amaravati and Nagarjunakonda *stupas*, and the *ayaka* pillars that are found at the cardinal points, are not found here. The narrative reliefs (including Jataka scenes) that are a ubiquitous feature of early Buddhist sites in India are virtually absent in Sri Lanka. The sculptural embellishment of *stupas* in Sri Lanka is sometimes found on the *vahalkadas/ayakas*, on the moonstones at the base of staircases leading up to the structures, and on 'guard-stones' flanking the base of the staircases. Interestingly, the animals that adorn Ashokan pillars—lotus, geese, and a procession of lion, bull, horse, and elephant—are the very ones found on the moonstones. A distinctive feature of the free standing Sri Lankan Buddha images is that the forehead is marked by a prominent *urna* – a circular protuberance on the forehead.

Maya's dream (the conception), Amaravati; the Buddha's birth, Nagarjunakonda (1st row); Gandhara school; Nagarjunakonda: Great Departure (2nd row); first sermon; ornamented *stupa* (3rd row)

BUDDHIST CAVES IN THE WESTERN GHATS

The rock-cut Buddhist monasteries in the Western Ghats can be dated between *c.* 100 BCE and 200 CE. Vidya Dehejia (1972) has identified two distinct phases of architectural activity—the first one belonging to *c.* 100 BCE–20 BCE and the second one to *c.* 50–200 CE. The early phase is represented at sites such as Kondivte, Nadsur, Bhaja, Tulja, Pitalkhora, Kondane, Ajanta, Nashik, and Bedsa. The second phase is represented by additions made at Nashik and Junnar, and the excavation of caves at new places such as Karle, Kuda, Mahad, Karadh, Shelarvadi, and Kanheri. The monasteries consist of *viharas* and *chaityas*.

Kanheri caves

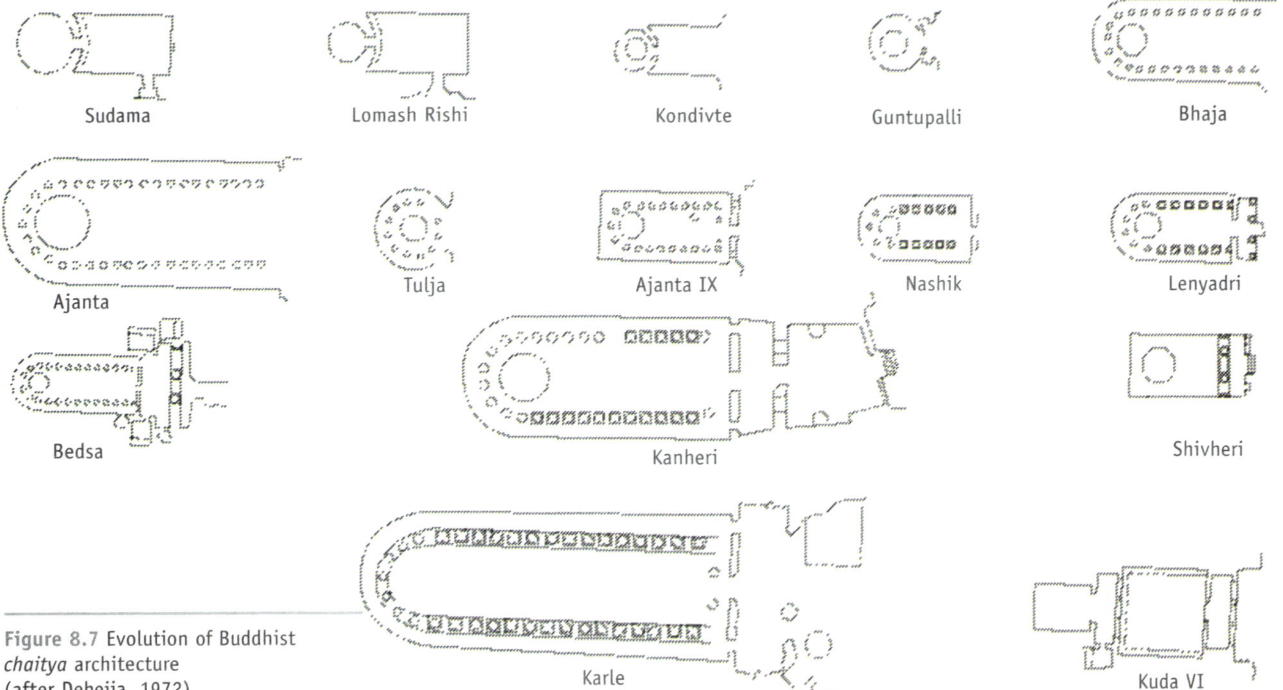

Figure 8.7 Evolution of Buddhist *chaitya* architecture (after Dehejia, 1972)

Map 8.9 Buddhist caves in the Western Ghats

The development of early cave architecture in India can be traced from the early reference point of the Lomash Rishi and Sudama caves in the Barabar hills (certain aspects of which were discussed in Chapter 7). At that stage, the *chaitya* was cut parallel to the rock face and consisted of a rectangular chamber leading into a small circular room. Both the Lomash Rishi and Sudama caves were clearly modelled on wooden architectural prototypes.

The plan of the Kondivte cave (*c.* 100 BCE) in the Western Ghats represents the next stage. Here too there was a rectangular hall leading into a round *stupa* chamber, with a narrow circumambulatory passage around the *stupa*. But the *chaitya* was now excavated perpendicular to the entrance. This meant that the worshipper would face the object of worship as he/she entered the *chaitya*. The light from outside would also illuminate the entire chamber, including the *stupa*.

The next stage in the evolution of Buddhist cave architecture was when two rows of pillars were introduced, following the line of the walls and extending into the apse. This created a path for walking down an aisle, circumambulating the rock-cut *stupa* in the apse, and walking back through the other aisle. This is the typical Buddhist *chaitya* of western India. An example of this is the large *chaitya* hall at Bhaja (100–70 BCE), with its impressive horseshoe-shaped entrance arch. The central hall has a high barrel-vaulted roof, while the side aisles have lower half-vaulted ceilings. Wooden ribs were added to the ceilings. This and the slightly leaning stone pillars show the continuing imprint of wooden architecture. Cave 3 at Pitalkhora is another example of a typical *chaitya* of western India. At Bedsa, apart from an apsidal *chaitya* with pillars, there is an apsidal structure without pillars that connects into cells on three sides, which were apparently living quarters for monks.

The early *viharas* in the Western Ghats were simple, and usually consisted of cells arranged around a central hall with an open verandah in front. A few were two-storeyed. Inside the monastic cell, there was a rock-cut bed and sometimes a rock-cut pillow. Monks may have placed a lamp in the small wall niches. A few caves give evidence of relief carving. The richly carved reliefs in the verandah and flanking the entrance of Vihara 19 at Bhaja are among the earliest of these. Some of the narrative reliefs may represent Jataka stories, while the gods Surya and Indra flank the entrance into the central chamber. The *viharas* at Pitalkhora are also associated with impressive relief sculpture.

The next major phase of Buddhist cave architecture in this area belongs to the 2nd and 3rd centuries CE. Some caves were directly connected with the patronage of Satavahana and Kshatrapa kings. There is basic continuity with the features of earlier caves such as those at Bedsa, but an increase in the scale of the construction. There was also greater sculptural ornamentation on the outer walls, including a profusion and variety of *mithuna* couples (a male and female, supposed to represent auspiciousness). The interior of the *chaitya* has a *stupa* as the object of veneration. The pillars have elaborate capitals. The roof over the central nave is still ribbed and vaulted, while that over the side aisles is flat.

Vihara 3 at Nashik is a little later. It is known as the 'Gautamiputra cave', as it has inscriptions belonging to the time of this Satavahana king. It consists of a central hall surrounded by monastic cells. The rich sculptural decoration of the outer walls and the doorway are noteworthy. Another unusual feature is that the back wall of the central hall has a relief carving of a *stupa* flanked by two female worshippers and two celestial creatures. The smaller *chaitya* hall at Kanheri belongs to the reign of Yajnashri Satakarni, the last powerful Satavahana king. *Mithuna* figures flank the entrance to the hall, but they are thick and stiff compared to the voluptuous and graceful ones at Karle.

The earliest Ajanta murals in Chaityas 9 and 10 also belong to this period. The mural in Chaitya 10 shows a king accompanied by his retinue venerating a *bodhi* tree and then a *stupa*, and then passing through a gateway. There are also paintings of the *Shyama Jataka* and *Chaddanta Jataka*. There are two sets of early paintings in Chaitya 9—one represents a scene with herdsmen and animals, while the other shows *nagas* approaching a *stupa*.

Chaitya halls: Karle; Bedsa (1st row); Kanheri; Bhaja *chaitya* hall entrance (2nd row); view of Bhaja caves; Nashik Cave 18 (3rd row)

Jaina and Buddhist remains in Eastern India

The Udayagiri and Khandagiri hills in Puri district, Odisha, are located about 6 km west from Bhubaneswar, not far from the site of Shishupalgarh. This is one of the oldest groups of Jaina rock-cut caves. The sandstone rocks of these hills are easy to excavate but not very suitable for intricate carving. The stone is brittle and the caves have suffered much damage due to weathering. The Hathigumpha inscription, carved over an overhanging rock in front of Cave 14, connects these caves with the Mahameghavahana or Chedi dynasty of Kalinga, and dates them to *c.* 1st century BCE. Two other kings of this dynasty—Kudepasiri and Vaduka—appear as donors of two chambers in Cave 9 (also known as the Manchapuri cave). These hills continued to be occupied by Jaina ascetics, with a few breaks, right up to the present.

Unlike the Buddhist caves in the Western Ghats, the caves of Udayagiri and Khandagiri have no congregation halls or rock-cut shrines (Mitra, 1992). In a later period, however, some of the cells were enlarged and converted into shrines. The cells were excavated where the rock permitted, and were not laid out according to any plan. Rock-cut steps connected some of them to each other. The tiny cells graphically reflect the hard ascetic regimen of the monks who lived here. With a few exceptions, they are not high enough to permit a man to stand up. They are also very narrow, so that a person lying down would not have been able to stretch out fully. The low doorways would have required monks to bend low in order to enter. Some caves had rudimentary shelves cut into the wall. The only other luxury was an upward slope of the floor, which may have served as a pillow, but might equally have been geared towards preventing the accumulation of water in the cell. The interior of the cells was stark and plain, but the outer façade and brackets sometimes had carved ornamentation.

There are two main types of caves in these hills—those with and without pillared verandahs. In the latter case, cells were arranged along one, two, or three sides of the verandah. The pillars and pilasters are generally square shaped below and above, and octagonal in the middle. The corners of the squares are chamfered into half-medallions at the points where they meet the octagonal section. Some caves are two storeyed. The Ranigumpha (the queen's cave), the largest and best preserved of these, is two storeyed and consists of a large rectangular courtyard with cells on three sides. A small chamber, flanked by the relief of a guardian figure and rich sculptural decoration on the outer walls, projects into the courtyard on either side.

Mitra (1992: 9–10) points out that there are several striking similarities between the arched and convex ceilings of these caves and the ceilings of mud huts in Eastern India. The verandah roofs were supported by non-functional architraves and rested on pillars, similar to the bamboo or wooden posts of a hut. The roofs also project outwards in the form of eaves, the inner side of which curves in a manner similar to that found in thatched or tiled huts to break the flow of rainwater. Traces of lime plaster indicate that the cave walls were once plastered. Reservoirs (some with steps) cut into the rock would have held rainwater and provided a water supply for the monks. There is an apsidal structural temple made out of large blocks of laterite on the crest of Udayagiri hill. This is one of the oldest apsidal structures found in Eastern India.

Udayagiri–Khandagiri (from top): Cave 1, Ranigumpha; verandah of Cave 10

The sculptural decoration of the Udayagiri and Khandagiri caves shares some features with the ornamentation at early Buddhist sites, including the honeysuckle design, and winged animals. Symbols such as the *nandipada*, *srivatsa*, and *svastika*

Kayama elephant (left); Langudi (right)

occur often, as do trees, lotuses, and snakes. Animals such as the horse, lion, elephant, and perhaps bull occur in places on pilasters. None of the reliefs can be conclusively interpreted as depicting scenes from the lives of the *tirthankaras* or from Jaina mythology. The verandah walls of the Ranigumpha and Manchapuri caves have some relief scenes that seem to be connected with royalty. A scene in the verandah of the Manchapuri cave may represent a king who may perhaps be none other than Kharavela retrieving the Kalinga *jina*.

Early historic Buddhist remains have been found at the site of Langudi (Jajpur district), which has given evidence of a large *stupa*, relief carvings of *stupas*, images, and inscriptions. Remains of a *stupa* at Tarapur and a rock-cut elephant at Kayama are among the early historic Buddhist remains in Odisha (see Patnaik, [2020] 2021: 200–08).

The Gandhara school of sculpture

The north-west was an area of cultural confluence and the inter-mixture of sculptural styles, especially under the Shakas, Indo-Parthians, and Kushanas (Huntington, 1985: 133–49; Bopearachchi, 2020; Ahuja. [Ed.], 2019). Begram represents the site of the ancient city of Kapisha. Located at the crossroads between the subcontinent and regions lying to the east and west, it has yielded a great deal of important archaeological evidence. This includes a fabulous hoard of treasure that long ago must have belonged to a very rich person of excellent taste. The objects include Hellenistic plaster casts of metal-work designs, glass-ware from Syria, Roman and Alexandrian sculptures, Chinese lacquer work, and over 1,000 carved ivory and bone objects that are clearly of Indian origin. The 'Begram ivories' reflect different styles and can be dated between the late 1st century BCE/early 1st century CE to around the 3rd century CE. Some carved panels show a pair of women standing under a *torana* (gateway) with three architraves similar in construction to the Sanchi gateways. Another large ivory sculpture may perhaps represent the goddess Ganga. The ivory objects include some hunting scenes carved in the Parthian double-line style. An intricately carved coffer top, assigned to the 2nd century CE, reflects an interesting amalgam of Graeco-Roman floral designs on the borders with a depiction of the female form that is very Indian. There seem to be some similarities between the carvings on the Begram ivories and the later sculptures of Amaravati and Nagarjunakonda. Even more interesting are similarities with some of the bone and ivory objects found amidst a buried treasure at the 2nd century BCE–3rd century CE Jetavana *stupa* at Anuradhapura in Sri Lanka.

Gandhara sculpture

Other important artefacts found in the Kapisha region of Afghanistan include a gold reliquary set with rubies found at Bimaran, which seems to belong to the late 1st century BCE. The representations on the reliquary include two sets of three figures—a standing Buddha flanked by the gods Indra and Brahma. This is one of the earliest examples of the Buddha image.

Gandhara style: Buddha; standing figure

The Swat valley of Pakistan has yielded a number of Buddhist sculptures stylistically linked to the Parthian art of Iran, rather than the Graeco-Roman influences so typical of the contemporary art of Gandhara. One of the important objects is a relief carving of a seated haloed Buddha figure flanked by a standing Brahma and Indra, belonging to the early 1st century CE. The facial features of the figures, the deeply incised lines, and the style bear an unmistakable Parthian stamp. Huntington (1985: 120–21) points out that images such as these indicate that the earliest stone Buddha images pre-dated the Kushana period and that certain iconographic conventions were already well established in the pre-Kushana times.

During the Kushana period (late 1st century–3rd century CE), the Afghanistan–Gandhara region and Mathura emerged as two major centres of artistic activity. The stone sculptures include some royal portraits, but most of them have religious themes. There are stylistic similarities as well as variations, reflecting the hands of different ateliers. While some art historians hold that the Gandhara school (according to Huntington, it should properly be referred to as the Bactro-Gandhara school) shows very little evidence of stylistic change over time, it is possible that such changes did exist but have not yet been properly studied.

The Gandhara school flourished between the 1st and 5th centuries CE; it continued till the 7th century in parts of Kashmir and Afghanistan. The initial impetus probably came during the Indo-Greek period, but the peak of activity was in the first two centuries CE. Most of the Gandhara sculptures are made of stone. In the beginning, blue schist and green phyllite were the main materials used by sculptors. Stucco (lime plaster) began to be used in the 1st century CE, and it had almost completely replaced stone by the 3rd century.

The Gandhara school, like the Kushana coinage, shows a marked syncretism. Its themes were Indian but its style Graeco-Roman. Images of Buddhas and *bodhisattvas* were favourite themes; hence it is sometimes referred to as Graeco-Buddhist art. The Graeco-

Roman influence is clear in the facial features and curly or wavy hair, the muscular body, and the fine, deeply delineated folds of the robes. Standing Buddha images are very common and usually have the following features: The Buddha stands barefoot, with one leg slightly bent. His heavy robe covers both shoulders. His left hand is by his side and seems to be holding his robe, while the right one is bent and has the palm raised in the protection-granting *abhaya mudra*. His curly hair is piled on top of his head in a knot (known as the *ushnisha*). His elongated earlobes recall his earlier life as a prince, when they were weighed down by ear ornaments. A halo encircles his head. There are also seated Buddha images. The *mudras* include the *dharmachakra mudra* (the teaching pose) and the *dhyana mudra* (the meditative pose). Some of the Buddha figures have a moustache. The Gandhara school also produced many images of the Buddha seated in meditation.

Apart from Buddha figures, the Gandhara artists also carved *bodhisattva* images. Although it is not possible to identify them all, Maitreya seems to have been portrayed most often. Avalokiteshvara (Padmapani) was another popular figure. Maitreya can be identified by the vase he holds in his left hand, while Padmapani holds a lotus. Unlike the Buddha figures, the *bodhisattvas* are often heavily ornamented, have elaborate hairdos and/or turbans, and wear sandals. Many of them have moustaches.

Sculptures and relief panels depict scenes from the life of Gautama Buddha as well as Jataka scenes. While the Gandhara artists carved many of the scenes that had engaged the artists of the early Buddhist sites of Central India and Andhra, they tackled these themes in different ways. For instance, in the Gandhara reliefs, the scene of the Buddha's birth is represented by Maya grasping the boughs of a *sal* tree, the child emerging from her right side or standing near her foot. The god Indra stands ready to receive the baby and many attendants are present. Other frequently depicted sculptural themes include the king of the *yakshas*, Panchika, and his consort Hariti. Panchika was associated with wealth and Hariti was a *yakshi* who, according to Buddhist tradition, was transformed from a child devourer to a protectress of children due to the Buddha's intervention.

Fasting Siddhartha, Gandhara school

The few metal sculptures of the Gandhara school include a metal reliquary found at Shah-ji-ki-dheri (near Peshawar), the site of Kanishka's capital Kanishkapura, mentioned above. The lid of the box bears three figures—a Buddha sitting on a lotus, flanked by Indra and Brahma. The casket has images of seated Buddhas flanked by Indra and Brahma and a standing figure that may perhaps represent Kanishka, whose name occurs on it.

The Gandhara artists filled out the biography of the Buddha, adding events described in texts such as the *Lalitavistara*, such as Siddhartha going to school, Brahma and Indra bathing the newborn Siddhartha with scented water, his marriage to Yashodhara, the Buddha gazing at the *bodhi* tree with unblinking eyes, and the *bhikkhuni* Utpalavarna transforming herself into a *chakravarti* king to be the first to worship the Buddha on his descent from the Trayatrimsha heaven. While the Hindu gods usually appear as subordinate figures in the Buddhist scenes at Gandhara, there are also interesting representations of Vishnu as *varaha*, and Hari-Hara. The syncretic deities that were produced by the Gandhara artists include a stone image known as the Pontecorvo Shiva (now in the Museo Nazionale d'Arte Orientale in Rome) that was found in Taxila. At first glance, he looks like Shiva. He has with three heads—the middle one human (with a third eye in the forehead), flanked by a boar head and a bovine head. He is standing and ithyphallic, and wears a *dhoti* and an upper garment over his left shoulder. He holds a trident in his back right hand, a rosary in the front right hand, a *chakra* in the back left hand, and a flask in the front left hand. The third eye, trident, and the ithyphallic aspects connect him with Shiva; the boar head and *chakra* are associated with Vishnu; the flask and chaplet can be associated with Shiva or Brahma (For details and illustrations of this and other Gandhara images, see Bopearachchi, 2020a, Vols. 1, 2).

Early stone sculptures from Vidisha and Mathura

Vidisha and Mathura were among the important centres of high sculptural art in this period (see Huntington, 1985: 150–62). The Vidisha remains include the stone pillar bearing the 2nd century BCE inscription of Heliodorus found at Besnagar. This pillar is quite different from earlier Maurya pillars. It is not as tall, nor does it have a polished surface. The shaft is also very different and consists of four parts of unequal length—the lowest part is faceted into 8 sides, the portion above this into 16 sides, and the portion above this into 32 sides. The topmost section is round. A garland is carved in relief between the second and third sections. The shaft supports a capital in the form of an inverted lotus, decorated with leaves at the top. Going by the inscription, the square block (carved with geese and the honeysuckle design) on top of the lotus must have been crowned by a *garuda* emblem.

Buddha image from Govind Nagar, Mathura

A few other sculptures from Vidisha are assigned to the 'Shunga' period, i.e., 2nd century BCE–1st century CE. These include a pillar capital in the form of a banyan tree, which may represent the wish-fulfilling *kalpa-vriksha*. Representations of large-sized figures include an over 3 m high sandstone image of Kubera (king of the *yakshas* and god of wealth) holding a money bag in his left hand. There is also a stylistically similar but smaller female figure, with a bunch of flowers or fruits hanging down from her left hand and an unidentifiable object in her right hand.

Mathura was one of the pre-eminent cities of North India. It was the southern capital of the Kushanas and an important centre of crafts and trade, religious activity, and artistic production. The sculptors of this area used red sandstone quarried at Sikri, not far away. Their sculptures share iconographic similarities with those of the north-west, but the style is very different. It is completely indigenous and shows no trace of foreign influence. The Mathura style can be seen as a further development of the traditions of sculpture of sites such as Besnagar, Sanchi, and Bharhut. The themes were varied, including *yakshas*, *yakshis*, *nagas*, *nagis*, Buddhas and *bodhisattvas*, Jaina *tirthankaras*, and Hindu deities.

Extant specimens of the Mathura school include several seated Buddha images. Although there are variations, the Buddha usually sits cross-legged on a throne (in some cases a *simhasana*, i.e., lion throne), with his right hand raised in the *abhaya mudra*. His head is shaved or has curly hair, and he has a coiled *ushnisha* (a protuberance or a topknot of hair) which looks like a seashell. He wears a transparent *dhoti*, one end of which is draped across his chest and goes over his left shoulder. His head is surrounded by a halo with scalloped edges, above which is the carving of a *pipal* tree. He is flanked either by two small *bodhisattvas* or by the gods Indra and Brahma. There are separate images of the *bodhisattvas*, especially Maitreya, Vajrapani, and Avalokiteshvara. The Mathura artists also carved reliefs of scenes from the Buddha's life. A colossal Buddha image found at Sarnath is also considered to be typical of the Mathura style.

The earliest representations of the *jinas* appear on Mathura *ayagapatas* from the 1st century BCE onwards. These were followed by a large number of Jaina images found especially at Kankali Tila. These included a pillar fragment with four standing *tirthankaras* with long arms carved on the four sides. There was a seated *tirthankara* image, its head broken. The *tirthankara* images share some similarities with the Buddha images. Like the Buddhas, they have long ear-lobes and some of them share an auspicious mark known

as an *urna* between the brows. A difference lies in their nudity. The early images do not have the *lanchanas* (cognizance or symbols on their chest) which help identify the individual *tirthankaras* (see Kishore Saxena, 2021: 69–70).

The iconographic conventions of images of many Hindu deities were established in the early centuries CE. The many stone sculptures discovered in the Mathura area include images of Shiva, Vishnu, Surya, Durga, and Lakshmi. A seated Surya image found at Kankali Tila shows West Asian influence in his moustache, tunic, boots, and ringed crown. Shaiva images represent the god in anthropomorphic or *linga* form, as well as in *mukha-lingas* and *vigraha-lingas*. Mention was made earlier of an architectural fragment found at Bhuteshvara near Mathura, which shows a Shiva *linga* under a tree, surrounded by a railing and worshipped by winged creatures. The early Shiva images from the area already show a diverse, though formative, iconographic base. They show Shiva alone or with the Nandi bull, Shiva with his consort Parvati, and in various forms including the Chaturvyuha Shiva (Shiva with his three emanations), Ardhanarishvara (the god who is half woman), and Harihara (a combination of Vishnu and Shiva).

The early centuries CE marked an explosion in the number and variety of Vaishnava images produced in the Mathura area. Doris M. Srinivasan (1989) points out that during this period, Mathura became the premier centre of the dissemination of Vaishnava sculptural art. The sculptures included kinship triads depicting Vasudeva Krishna, his brother Baladeva, and their sister Ekanamsha. There are many independent images of Vasudeva Krishna, but also some of Vishnu (four-armed), Vishnu on *garuda*, and in anthropomorphic boar form. The *avatara* concept was clearly in its infancy and the idea of the *chaturvyuha* (the four emanations of Vishnu) became evident in the late Kushana period. Mention may also be made of a colossal Narayana image found at Mathura.

Among the goddesses at Mathura, apart from anonymous female deities, Matrikas, and *yakshis*, it is Lakshmi and Durga who stand out. Mention may be made of a beautiful image, identified by some as Shri Lakshmi. The figure stands on two lotus buds that emerge out of a vase of plenty (*purna-ghata*). She holds a fruit in her right hand and seems to gently press her right breast with her left hand, as if offering milk. Whether or not she represents Lakshmi, she clearly evokes beauty, fecundity, and nourishment.

Mathura was an important pacesetter of artistic style in North India, and images made in this area were exported to other cities such as Kaushambi, Ahichchhatra, and Sarnath, right upto Mahasthangarh in the east.

Mathura (from top): Nagaraja; seated *tirthankara*; Surya; Karttikeya

Terracotta art

Terracotta female figurine, Mathura

Terracottas are sometimes wrongly considered simple rural crafts, not worthy of the attention of scholars. As pointed out by Devangana Desai (1978), terracotta art really came into its own with the advent of city life, and the mass production of terracottas of fine aesthetic quality and skill was clearly associated with an urban milieu. A great volume and variety of fine terracottas were produced in *c.* 200 BCE–300 CE; in fact, this is the high point in the history of ancient Indian terracotta sculpture. Huntington (1985: 88–89) suggests the possibility that terracotta art may have provided a stylistic model for early stone sculpture, although the wealth of surface decoration that marks many of the terracottas of this period is absent in early stone sculpture.

A profusion of exquisite terracottas of this period have been found at sites such as Chandraketugarh, Mathura, Kaushambi, and Ahichchhatra. They reflect the existence of a number of regional styles and techniques and a great variety of decorative motifs. In some areas, the use of moulds became popular and facilitated mass production. The round figures of earlier centuries made way for flat moulded plaques. Female figures appear very often. The terracotta plaques of Eastern India show women with round faces and well-defined features; they wear diaphanous clothes and a profusion of heavy but finely detailed ornaments. They often have elaborate headdresses. The figures known as *panchachuda* have five hairpins in the form of weapons. These seem to represent a goddess whose name we do not know, but whose worship seems to have been popular all over North India. Female figurines associated with plants, flowers, fish, etc. may have been goddesses associated with fertility and prosperity. *Yakshas*, *yakshi*s, *nagas*, and *nagis* occur in profusion. Lakshmi is prominent among the identifiable goddesses depicted in terracotta art. Another important deity is Vasudhara, a goddess associated with fertility and auspiciousness. Not all terracottas represented religious themes. There were other themes, such as amorous couples, animal fights, wrestlers, and children playing with toys.

The variety in subjects and iconography grew, as did distinctions of regional styles. Sites such as Mathura, Kaushambi, Chandraketugarh, and Tamluk give evidence of a

Terracotta plaques, Chandraketugarh

further refinement of terracotta art. The reliefs became deeper than before. Terracottas from the north-west reflect the new cultural influences in the area and include artefacts made by double moulds, along with the hand-moulded variety. Many terracotta heads found in the Ganga valley and the Gandhara area show great skill in detailed human portraiture with nuanced facial expressions. In the late Kushana period, monumental hollow terracottas started being made in moulds. With the further development of devotional cults, the variety of deities depicted in terracottas also grew. Life-size figures of Lakshmi and Hariti and a head of Kubera have been found at Kaushambi.

In the Deccan, many terracottas belonging to the early centuries CE have been found at sites such as Kondapur, Nagarjunakonda, Yelleswaram, Sannati, Ter, Paithan, and Nevasa. Some of them are made of refined whitish clay known as kaolin. They include many human and animal figures made in double moulds. The Deccan terracottas are stylistically different from those of northern and Eastern India in their distinctively delicate portrayal of the human figure. Animal figurines include elephants, bulls, and rams. Horses occur most frequently and are often replete with ornaments, bridles, reins, and saddle. There are urbane, well-dressed couples wearing rich ornaments, people riding horses, and children. The terracottas that clearly seem to have a cultic significance include plaques depicting a nude fertility goddess with her legs spread out, found at sites such as Nevasa, Nagarjunakonda, Ter, and Yellesvaram.

Two terracotta and one stone plaque of the goddess known as Lajja-Gauri have been found in a 1st century BCE–1st century CE context at Padri in Gujarat, associated with a structure that may represent a temple (Shinde, 1994).

The patronage of religious establishments

The increasing visibility and architectural elaboration of religious establishments were based on increasing and sustained sources of patronage. Inscriptions at many sites give the names and often also the social and political status of the patrons. Expressions of religious piety were linked to other issues such as quests for the affirmation of political and social status and legitimacy. While texts give an idea of the social background of the patrons of various religious traditions, inscriptions offer more direct and reliable information on this issue.

What were people donating? In the case of Hindu temples, they gifted images and financed the building of shrines and associated structures such as tanks and halls. In the case of Buddhist establishments, they gave money to finance *stupas*, shrines, monastic residences, miniature (votive) *stupas* and *chaityas*, and the carving of images. They made monetary investments, the interest from which could be used for running the establishment, and they also gifted land. Donations made in favour of Jaina establishments were mostly channelized into excavating caves for Jaina ascetics. Donative inscriptions sometimes give the names of various religious sects of the time. It is interesting to note that there is some degree of overlap in the ways in which pious sentiments are expressed. For instance, the Buddhist donative inscriptions at Mathura frequently express the idea that the aim of the gift was the welfare and happiness of all sentient beings—reflecting the idea that merit (*punya*) can be transferred from one person to another. A similar sentiment is expressed in some of the Jaina donative inscriptions at Mathura. For instance, an inscription on a pillar fragment with *tirthankaras* carved on all four sides dedicates the gift of this pillar to the happiness and welfare of all creatures. A Mathura inscription associated with a shrine dedicated to the *naga* deity Dadhikarna also expresses a similar sentiment.

Some of the patronage to religious establishments came from political elites. The social background of ruling lineages varied greatly. There were Brahmana kings or

RECENT DISCOVERIES | Gifts of water pots from ancient Gandhara

Apart from inscriptions, material remains often provide important insights into the patronage of ancient religious establishments and on aspects of monastic and lay practice regarding which the texts are silent. An example are the interesting discoveries of fragments of ancient texts written on birch bark associated with a number of pots and pot fragments with writing on them. The palaeography, linguistic and stylistic features of the writing on the manuscripts and pots, and the stylistic features of the pots themselves suggest a date falling in the 1st–2nd centuries CE. Richard Salomon has given a preliminary account of these discoveries, which originally seem to have belonged to eastern Afghanistan.

In the early centuries CE, Gandhara had emerged as a major centre of Buddhism in the subcontinent and as an important centre for the dissemination of Buddhism to other lands such as China. The manuscripts in question consist of writing in black ink on joined strips of birch bark. All of them had suffered varying degrees of damage. Most of them were incomplete fragments of Buddhist religious texts in the Gandhari language and Kharoshthi script. The exception was a Sanskrit medical text written in the Brahmi script. The manuscripts seem to have been texts discarded from a Buddhist monastic library, probably after a copyist had made fresh copies.

F. R. Allchin's analysis of the pots and inscriptions reveals the following details: Four pots were complete and one had lost its neck and rim. They were wheel thrown and were made out of finely sorted clay. They had a smoothened or lightly burnished surface and a light cream/buff wash or slip. The pots were globular or near-globular in shape, basically the kind of vessels used for storing water or other household commodities. Three of them were decorated with stamped impressions of rosettes. The writing in black ink was added onto the shoulder of the pot after firing. Allchin's reading of the inscriptions on the pots is given below:

Pot A: 'This waterpot is the pious gift of Vasavadata, wife of Susoma, for the benefit of her own health. May it be for a proper share on the part of [her] husband Suhasoma, for a proper share on the part of [her] mother and father, for a proper share on the part of [all beings], for a proper share on the part of her friends, kinsemen, and blood relatives.'

Pot B: 'This waterpot [is a gift] to the universal community, in the possession of the Sarvastivadin teachers in the Purnaga grove.'

Pot C: 'This waterpot [is] the pious gift of Viratata, wife of Srvahiama; [she] presents [it] to the universal community at Rayagaha in the possession of the Sarvastivadin teachers, who teach actions, who teach energy, who teach causation [who teach karma].

Pot D: '[Given] to the universal community, in the possession of the Dharmaguptakas.'

Pot E: 'This waterpot is the pious gift of Hastadata, wife of Teyavarman, to the universal community, for the benefit of her own health. May it be for the principal share (?) of the monastery attendant (?) Tevarman, of the nun ?, of Sudasna, of Guhadata, of ?, of ?, of ?, of ?, in short (?), of all beings (?); and in honour of [her] brother.'

The writing on the pots clearly represents donative records. The writing on the potsherds is also donative in nature. Taken together, the evidence suggests that people commonly gifted such water pots to the monastic community. In some cases, a pot was gifted to a particular monk, whose name was written on the pot. Compared to gifts inscribed on the stone elements of ***stupa***s and monasteries, these were comparatively small, humble gifts. Evidence from the site of Hadda in Afghanistan shows that such water pots were later used to inter the funerary remains of monks. The collection of manuscripts and pots in the British Museum collection indicates that similar pots were also used for the ritual burial of discarded monastic manuscripts.

* [] = an unclear or partially preserved syllable (***akshara***), whose reading is not certain.

? = a visible but illegible syllable.

Source Salomon, 1999

those claiming Brahmana descent, e.g., the Shungas, Kanvas, Mitras, and Satavahanas. There were lineages that originated outside the subcontinent such as the Indo-Greeks, Indo-Parthians, Shakas, and Kushanas. No matter what the geographical or social background of the dynasties, there were some similarities in their policies vis-à-vis religious patronage. In their quest for legitimacy and building alliances they generally patronized a variety of religious establishments.

As mentioned earlier, the Kushanas are well known for exalting the status of the king. Their epithet *devaputra* has been interpreted as a claim to divinity or at least an assertion of a close relationship with divinity. In the Kushana period, there was a tradition of royal portraiture and royal shrines. Important evidence of both comes from the site of Mat near Mathura. Archaeological excavations here revealed the outlines of a large rectangular structure with a round sanctum at its western end. Several damaged statues were found, none of them *in situ*, but none within the circular sanctum. These

See p. 442 photograph of the Kanishka statue

included the headless statue of Kanishka, mentioned in the beginning of this chapter. Near the centre of the circular structure was a headless figure wearing a tunic and boots, seated on a throne with lion-shaped supports. The inscription on the base refers to the construction of a *devakula* (temple), garden, tank, well, assembly hall, and gateway during the reign of a Kushana king whose name cannot be read with certainty. A later Sanskrit inscription on the pedestal of a broken image (probably representing a Kushana prince), inscribed during the reign of king Huvishka, seems to record the repair of this temple. The last line of the inscription refers to some provision made for Brahmanas, who were regular guests at this place. The question is: was the *devakula* a shrine where deified dead kings were worshipped—similar to the *devakula* mentioned in the dramatist Bhasa's *Pratima-nataka*? Or was it a royal temple dedicated to some other deity or deities, also housing images of Kushana royalty? Images of Kushana kings were also found at Surkh Kotal in Afghanistan, *in situ* and not in the cella. V. S. Agrawala (1949: 126–27, 152) suggested that the Mat shrine may have been a Shiva temple on the basis of his identification of two life-size fragmentary sculptures found at the site as Shiva and Durga. Whether the Kushanas built royally endowed monumental temples where deified kings or gods or both were worshipped, this was a striking innovation in the theory and practice of kingship.

Kanishka is known as a patron of Buddhism. However, his coins depict various deities associated with different cultural traditions—Indian, Graeco-Roman, and Iranian. The coins of the Indo-Parthians, Shakas, and more so of the Kushanas, are often seen as a reflection of the religious eclecticism and 'tolerance' of these kings. They can perhaps be better interpreted as representing royal policy in an age when the north-west had become a melting pot for different religious and cultural traditions. For newcomers, it made eminent sense to connect themselves with and proclaim their allegiance to important religious traditions or cults of the time. They also simultaneously patronized Brahmanas and promoted the use of the Sanskrit language. Under the Kshatrapas and early Kushanas, Sanskrit increasingly became the language of inscriptions, and the use of Sanskrit gradually spread to private donative records as well.

The Satavahanas were one among many dynasties to proclaim their performance of the *shrauta* sacrifices such as the *ashvamedha*. Like the Kshatrapas, they extended patronage both to Brahmanas as well as to Buddhist monks. As mentioned earlier, the earliest surviving land grant recording a grant of land with fiscal exemptions belongs to the Satavahana period. This was the beginning of a long-standing tradition that was to become increasingly prevalent over the succeeding centuries, with far-reaching implications. It is interesting to note that in the case of the Satavahanas (as well as the Ikshvakus), there was a trend of royal women making donations to Buddhist establishments, while royal men concentrated on patronizing Brahmanas and Hindu temples.

The site of Nagarjunakonda gives a unique, graphic architectural representation of the close relationship between the Ikshvaku kings and religious establishments. Here there is a royal complex including a citadel, royal residences, Buddhist monasteries, Hindu temples, and 22 *chhaya stambhas*. *Chhaya stambhas* were memorial pillars, most of them carved with scenes from the life of the deceased person. One of these pillars commemorated the Ikshvaku king Chantamula and was set up by 30 women members of his family. Apart from rulers and nobles, such pillars also commemorated dead soldiers, a military commander, an artisan, and religious people. The Nagarjunakonda inscriptions record gifts made by Ikshvaku royalty to Hindu temples and Buddhist monks. These kings are also described as performers of *shrauta* sacrifices. The oldest known copper plate grant in India belongs to the Ikshvaku period. This is the Patagandigudam grant of king Ehavala Chantamula which records the building of a four-hall compound and the grant of land in favour of a Buddhist monastery.

At Nagarjunakonda, women of the royal family, high-ranking military commanders and affluent non-royal people appear as donors. Among donors at the *mahachaitya*, the most prominent is Chamtisiri, sister of the deceased first king Chantamula, and aunt and mother-in-law of the reigning second king Siri Virapurisadata. The most prominent non-royal female patron was Bodhisiri, who financed the building of an apsidal temple, and made gifts to various *viharas* in the area.

The major part of the finances for religious establishments in various parts of the subcontinent during this period, in fact, came from non-royal people. H. Luders' (1963) study of the Bharhut inscriptions lists a total of 222 inscriptions dating *c.* 125–75 BCE. These mention monks, nuns, laywomen, and laymen as donors. The donors included only four royals and a profusion of ordinary individuals. Their names indicate the practice of naming people after *nakshatras* (asterisms), Brahmanical gods, *yakshas*, *bhutas* (spirits), and *nagas*. The donors came from places ranging from Pataliputra in the east to Nashik in the west, indicating that Bharhut attracted pilgrims and patrons not only from Central India but from further away as well.

Over 800 inscriptions were found at Sanchi (Upinder Singh, [1996] 2023a). They range from the 'schism edict' of Ashoka to inscriptions of the 9th century CE. The vast majority are votive inscriptions belonging to the 2nd century BCE–2nd century CE. The Sanchi monastery seems to have been established in Ashoka's time, but royal patronage did not play an especially important role in its subsequent growth. The inscriptions identify donors on various bases such as name, kinship relations, occupation, native place, and as members of the monastic order or the laity. Female and male donors occur in almost equal proportions. This in fact suggests a much higher level of female patronage than suggested by textual sources. The occupation of donors is specified in a few inscriptions as *gahapati* (4 inscriptions), *setthi* (12), *lekhaka* (scribe; 4), *vanija* (trader; 6), *kamika* (artisan; 2), *avesani* (foreman of artisans; 1), *dantakarehi* (ivory-workers; 1), *vadhaki* (mason; 2), *pavarika* (cloak seller; 1), *sotika* (weaver; 1), and *rajuka* (1). *Setthis* and *gahapatis* are mentioned less often than the texts would lead us to expect. The fact that a large number of donors were monks and nuns indicates that members of the monastic community continued to have some access to and control over financial resources. Particularly interesting are collective gifts made by kin groups, and more strikingly, by the entire laity (*upasakas* or *upasikas*) of a particular place. Entire villages also made gifts. Most of the donors mentioned in the Sanchi inscriptions came from Central India, but some came from places in Rajasthan, Maharashtra, and North India as well. In the early centuries CE, there is an appearance of the first inscriptions recording gifts of Buddha or *bodhisattva* images.

Jaina inscriptions from Mathura also reveal a significant participation of women donors (see Kishore Saxena, 2021). They indicate that *tirthankara* images were gifted by the wives of a merchant, householder, jeweller, banker, and village headman. Many of these gifts were made at the request of Jaina nuns. Early Tamil-Brahmi inscriptions in Tamil Nadu and Kerala record donations made by men and women of varied social backgrounds for the excavation of caves for Jaina monks and nuns. The donors included members of the Chera and Pandya royal families, but there are also specialized craftspeople and traders, e.g., salt merchants (*uppu vanikam*), a toddy merchant (*panita vanikam*), ironmonger (*kolu vanikam*), cloth merchant (*aruvai vanikam*), and gold merchant (*pon vanikam*). Early Brahmi inscriptions in Sri Lanka record donations made by Tamil merchants in favour of Buddhist establishments.

Inscriptions from various sites interestingly indicate the participation of *yavanas* in the networks of pious donations. Heliodorus, the Yavana worshipper of Vasudeva, has already been mentioned several times in this chapter. Inscriptions at Buddhist sites such as Sanchi and those in the Western Ghats (Nashik, Junnar, Karle) refer to *yavanas* as donors. Many Yavana donors, mostly residents of Dhenukakata, are mentioned at Karle.

NEW DIRECTIONS IN RESEARCH | **The archaeology of forests**

The Bandhavgarh National Park and Tiger Reserve, in Umaria district of Madhya Pradesh, is a well-known wildlife sanctuary in India which boasts the highest density of tiger populations in India. The richness of its wildlife is accompanied by a rich historical heritage.

Many ancient rock-cut caves are located in the Bandhavgarh forests. Unlike other early historic cave and rock shelter sites, these caves were not the abode of monks or nuns. This is evident from the 24 inscriptions which were documented many years ago by N. P. Chakravarti. The inscriptions are mainly in the Prakrit language and the Brahmi script and have been assigned to the 2nd century CE on the basis of palaeography and references to the kings of Kaushambi and the Magha dynasty.

A recent study by Nayanjot Lahiri, M. B. Rajani, Debdutta Sanyal, and Samayita Banerjee connects the early archaeological evidence from Bandhavgarh with its forest landscape. It presents the first results of a 2021–22 exploration of the 109 sq km of the Tala range and a small part of Magdhi in the Reserve. The survey involved ground-level survey using GPS devices as well as satellite imagery of the site. However, while satellite imagery was useful in understanding the topography and water resources of the site, it did not give a clear picture of the location of ancient structures, many of which were covered by silt and dense vegetation. Ground survey, in the accompaniment of forest guards, was the only way to map the remains. The study resulted in a thorough documentation of the cartographic locations and elevations of the caves in the study area. Inscriptions were juxtaposed with the archaeological survey.

The survey located 81 rock-cut shelters, some of which had not been previously documented. These included the caves mentioned by Chakravarti, where the inscriptions have now become very faint. The cave shelters were interwoven with water channels, reservoirs, and wells, which seem to have been contemporary to them. They were clustered on the north side of Bandhavgarh hill and on smaller hillsides facing the same direction. The choice of location was probably due to the availability of perennial water with shady forests, which would have provided plentiful game. Another factor was that the north face of the hill lay directly on a trade route coming in from the north, from sites such as Kaushambi and Mathura.

The caves show considerable architectural variety. Some consist of a small room, just enough for one person to sit in. Others were bigger and had stone benches or beds. Some others consisted of 2 rooms with separate entrances and open verandahs. Cave 2 (called Badi Gupha) had one entrance which led into a large pillared space flanked by nine rooms. Cave CA 16 (known as Rani ki Jhiriya) had 6 small rooms around a central pool (the water had dried up) which had rock-cut pillars on three sides.

While there are a few religious symbols, the donative inscriptions at Bandhavgarh indicate that these caves did not have a religious purpose. They were used by traders and travelers who rested here in the course of their journeys. The donors included members of a *goshthi* (some sort of committee), traders, merchants belonging to a *negama* (guild), a gold-smith, wood-worker, and blacksmith, a minister, and a king (Vaisravana of Kausambi). A merchant named Pusa had a tank, cave, and exercise hall made. Round cup-marks on some of the cave floors may have been used for pounding grain. There must have been a support staff to maintain these resting places and to provide for the needs of the weary traders and travelers who stopped to rest in the Bandhavgarh forest in the course of their long journeys.

The Bandhavgarh study shows how the natural and historical landscapes intersected in this forest.

Source Lahiri et al., 2022

Tiger striding out of Bandhavgarh cave; Cave 4 (left), carvings of animals and hunters (right)

CONCLUSIONS

During c. 200 BCE–300 CE, state formation and urbanization spread to many more parts of the subcontinent. The series of invasions from the North-west had political and cultural impact. Political structures and chains of command are more visible now than for the preceding Maurya period. New expressions of political ideology emerged. In this period of political flux, the different bases of royal legitimation included the patronage of Brahmanas and diverse religious establishments, and the performance of Vedic rituals. There was a significant expansion of city life, specialized crafts, and trade networks within and beyond the subcontinent. In the religious sphere, doctrinal debates and devotional worship were key features, and the increasing institutionalization of religious sects is clearly reflected in permanent religious structures. The rich, varied textual production and sophisticated sculptural and architectural styles reflect the cultural vitality and versatility of these centuries. Patronage came from pious donations by various groups of people whose access to financial resources was accompanied by a desire for validation of their political or social status.

FURTHER READINGS

Bacus, Elizabeth A. and Nayanjot Lahiri. (Eds.). 2004. *The Archaeology of Hinduism: World Archaeology* 36(3).

Banerjea, J. N. 1966. *Pauranic and Tantric Religion (Early Phase)*. Calcutta: University of Calcutta.

Bhandarkar, R. G. (1913) 1982. *Vaisnavism, Saivism and MinorReligious Systems*. Poona: Bhandarkar Oriental Research Institute.

Bivar, A. D. H. 2014. 'Kushan Dynasty i. Dynastic History.' *Encyclopaedia Iranica, online edition*, available at http://www.iranicaonline.org (accessed on 19.9.22).

Bopearachchi, Osmund. 2015. *From Bactria to Taprobane: Selected Works of Osmund Bopearachchi*. 2 Vols. Vol. 1: *Central Asian and Indian Numismatics*; Vol. 2: *Art History and Maritime Trade*. New Delhi: Manohar.

____. 2020. *When West Met East: Gandharan Art Revisited*. 2 Vols. New Delhi: Manohar.

Boussac, Marie-Françoise and Jean-François Salles. 1995. *Athens, Aden, Arikamedu: Essays on the Interrelations Between India, Arabia and the Eastern Mediterranean*. New Delhi: Manohar, Centre de Sciences Humaines.

Boussac, Marie-Françoise, Jean-François Salles, and Jean-Baptiste Yon. (Eds.). 2016. *Ports of the Indian Ocean*. Delhi: Primus Books.

Chakrabarti, Dilip K. 2006. *The Oxford Companion to Indian Archaeology: The Archaeological Foundations of Ancient India, Stone Age to AD 13th Century*. New Delhi: Oxford University Press. Chapters 17, 18.

Chakravarti, Ranabir. (2002) 2020. *Trade and Traders in Early IndianSociety*. New Delhi: Manohar.

Champakalakshmi, R. 1996. *Trade, Ideology and Urbanization: South India 300 BC to AD 1300*. Delhi: Oxford University Press.

Coomaraswamy, Anand K. (1928–31) 1980. *Yakshas*. 2nd Edn. New Delhi: Munshiram Manoharlal.

Dehejia, Vidya. 1972. *Early Buddhist Rock Temples: A Chronological Study*. London: Thames and Hudson.

Gethin, Rupert. 1998. *The Foundations of Buddhism*. Oxford and New York: Oxford University Press. Chapter 9.

Ghosh, Suchandra. 2017. *From the Oxus to the Indus: A Political and Cultural Study c. 300 BCE to c. 100 BCE*. Delhi: Primus.

Gurukkal, Rajan. 2010. *Social Formations of Early South India*. New Delhi, Oxford University Press.

Hart, George L. 1979. *Poets of the Tamil Anthologies: Ancient Poems ofLove and War*. Princeton: Princeton University Press.

Hawkes, Jason, and Akira Shimada. (Eds.). 2009. *Buddhist Stupas in South Asia: Recent Archaeological, Art-Historical, and Historical Perspectives*. New Delhi: Oxford University Press.

Huntington, Susan. 1985. *The Art of Ancient India: Buddhist, Hindu, Jain*. New York and Tokyo: John Weatherhill Inc. Chapters 5–9.

Jaiswal, Suvira. 1981. *The Origin and Development of Vaisnavism: Vaisnavism from 200 BC to AD 500*. New Delhi: Munshiram Manoharlal.

Kane, P. V. (1946) 1993. *History of Dharmasastra*. Ancient and Mediaeval Religious and Civil Law. Vol. 3. Poona: Bhandarkar OrientalResearch Institute.

Liu, Xinriu. 1988. *Ancient India and Ancient China: Trade and Religious Exchanges*. Delhi: Oxford University Press.

Manguin, Pierre-Yves, A. Mani, and Geoff Wade. (Eds.). 2011. *Early Interactions between South and Southeast Asia*. Singapore, Institute of South-east Asian Studies and New Delhi, Manohar.

Mahadevan, Iravatham. 2003. *Early Tamil Epigraphy: From the Earliest Times to the Sixth Century AD*. Chennai: Cre-A and the Department of Sanskrit and Indian Studies, Harvard University.

Marshall, John, Alfred Foucher, and N. G Majumdar. (1940) 1982. *Monuments of Sanchi*. Vol. 1. Rep. Edn. Delhi: Swati Publications. Misra, Ram Nath. 1981. *Yaksha Cult and Iconography*. New Delhi: Munshiram Manoharlal.

Mirashi, V. V. 1981. *The History and Inscriptions of the Satavahanas and the Western Kshatrapas*. Bombay: Maharashtra Board for Literature and Culture.

Mukherjee, B. N. 1995. 'The Great Kushana Testament.' *Indian Museum Bulletin*. On the Rabatak inscription.

———. 2004. *Kushana Studies: New Perspectives*. Kolkata: Firma KLM.

Neelis, Jason. 2011. *Early Buddhist Transmission and Trade Networks: Mobility and Exchange within and beyond the North-western Borderlands of South Asia*. Leiden, Boston: Brill.

Olivelle, Patrick. (Ed.). 2006. *Between the Empires: Society in India 300 BCE to 400 CE*. Oxford and New York: Oxford University Press.

Ollett, Andrew. 2017. *Language of the Snakes: Prakrit, Sanskrit, and the Language Order of Premodern India*. California, University of California Press.

Ramanujan, A. K. (1985) 2006. *Poems of Love and War: From the Eight Anthologies and the Ten Long Poem of Classical Tamil*. Delhi: Oxford University Press.

Ray, Himanshu Prabha. 1986. *Monastery and Guild: Commerce Under the Satavahanas*. Delhi: Oxford University Press.

Ray, Niharranjan. 1975. *Maurya and Post-Maurya Art: A Study in Social and Formal Contacts*. New Delhi: Indian Council of Historical Research.

Sarkar, H. 1966. *Studies in Early Buddhist Architecture of India*. NewDelhi: Munshiram Manoharlal.

Shastri, Ajay Mitra. (Ed.). 1999. *The Age of the Satavahanas*. Great Ages of Indian History. 2 Vols. New Delhi: Aryan Books International.

Shulman, David. 2016. *Tamil: A Biography*. Cambridge, MA: The Belknap Press of Harvard University Press.

Suresh, R. 2004. *Symbols of Trade: Roman and Pseudo-Roman Objects Found in India*. New Delhi: Manohar.

Thaplyal, K. K. 1972. *Studies in Ancient Indian Seals: A Study of North Indian Seals and Sealings from Circa Third Century CE to Mid-Seventh Century AD*. Lucknow: Akhila Bharatiya Sanskrit Parishad.

———. 1996. *Guilds in Ancient India: A Study of Guild Organization in Northern India and Western Deccan from Circa 600 BC to Circa 600 AD*. New Delhi: New Age International Ltd. Especially see Appendices 4, 5, and 6.

Terracotta plaque depicting a heavily ornamented female figure with weapons radiating from her hair; referred to by art historians as *pancha-chuda*.

CHAPTER 9

Aesthetics and Empire

c. 300–600 CE

A little over 1,500 years ago, a guild of silk weavers of Lata (in Gujarat) set out on a long journey along with their families. It is not clear what compelled them to move from their homes, but they ultimately reached and settled down in a town called Dashapura in Central India. During the reign of emperor Kumaragupta I, at a time when Bandhuvarman governed the town, the guild financed the building of a temple dedicated to the sun god, Surya. It was a magnificent temple with broad and lofty spires, and its consecration ceremonies were performed in the winter of 437–38 CE. As the years passed, a part of the temple was damaged, possibly by lightning. The guild decided to intervene and finance repairs and renovation. The work began in the spring of 473–74 CE. All these details are given in an inscription discovered at Mandasor, which corresponds to the Dashapura of the inscription. The text of the inscription was composed by Vatsabhatti, a devotee of Surya. He was also the very person whom the guild had entrusted with building and repairing the temple.

The Mandasor inscription is one of many epigraphs of the period *c.* 300–600 CE, which is often referred to as the Gupta period. Dynastic labels have fallen into disfavour among historians. Even if they are used, in this case, it must be remembered that although the political history of North India during these centuries was dominated by the Guptas, the Vakatakas carved out a large kingdom in the western Deccan and were a dominant political force at the time. It is also necessary to take into account political developments in other parts of the subcontinent.

Indian historians who lived and wrote during the period of Nationalist resistance to colonial rule portrayed the Gupta period as a 'golden age'. The glorification of the Gupta period can be viewed as a reaction of Nationalist historians to Imperialist historiography. The features that were highlighted included the political unification of a large part of the subcontinent under what was presumed to be a centralized government, the production of exceptionally fine works of Sanskrit literature, significant developments in the spheres of stone sculpture and architecture, and a presumption that all this was based on economic prosperity and social harmony.

The traditional understanding of the Gupta period underwent a radical revision in the 1960s and 1970s. This was part of an attempt to rectify the biases inherent in Nationalist historiography. It was also part of a larger historiographical shift dominated by left-oriented historians, a shift away from political narrative towards the study of political and socio-economic structures. Even earlier, Marxist scholars such as B. N. Datta and D. D. Kosambi had written about a feudal stage in Indian history. The idea was taken further by R. S. Sharma ([1965] 1980), who argued that the main features of feudalism existed in the Gupta period and were intensified in subsequent centuries. According to Sharma, the political essence of feudalism lay in the administrative organization of kingdoms being based on land. Its political essence lay in the institution of serfdom. Peasants were tied to the land owned by intermediaries, to whom they paid rent in kind and labour. The economy was essentially self-sufficient, and goods were produced mainly for local use and not for the market. Several feudal features were listed by Sharma: royal grants of land; the transfer of fiscal and judicial rights to the beneficiaries; the grant of rights over peasants, artisans, and merchants; an increased incidence of forced labour; a decline in trade and coinage; payment of officials through land revenue assignments; and the growth of the obligations of the *samantas* (subordinate or feudatory rulers). From this perspective, the seven centuries from *c.* 300 CE onwards were marked by political fragmentation and a collapse of the urban economy. In spite of critiques of the feudalism hypothesis, for many years it remained the dominant perspective on the period *c.* 300–1200 CE.

During the 1970s and 1980s, scholars such as B. D. Chattopadhyaya ([1983] 1997) and Hermann Kulke (1982) put forward an alternative historical paradigm. They argued that far from being a period of political breakdown, the early medieval period was marked by the beginning of an intensive process of state formation at the regional and sub-regional levels. Land grants were one of several strategies adopted by rulers to legitimize their power, and played an integrative role in the politics and societies of the time. Several detailed studies of the epigraphic data from various regions of the subcontinent (see, for instance, Upinder Singh, 1994; Sinha Kapur, 2002) have substantiated this hypothesis.[1] Some of these will be discussed in Chapter 10.

The sources for the period *c.* 300–600 CE (see Gupta, [1974] 1979, Vol. 1: 1–166; Chakrabarti and Sinha. [Eds.], 2018) include inscriptions—mostly on stone, some on copper plates—of the imperial Guptas and those of contemporary dynasties such as the Vakatakas, early Kadambas, Varmans, and Hunas. The *prashastis* (panegyric) of royal inscriptions can be understood as message-bearing media, offering details on royal genealogies and political events. However, they generally report political successes rather than reverses, and the inscriptions of different dynasties sometimes make conflicting claims. The epithets and descriptions of kings reflect prevailing hierarchies of power and ideals of kingship. Royal land grant inscriptions represent important socio-economic processes of their time and provide information regarding administrative structures and agrarian relations. Donative inscriptions of private individuals offer glimpses into social history and the sources of patronage of religious establishments.

Coins and seals too were public message-bearing media, apart from being media of exchange or authentication respectively. Gupta kings issued large numbers of gold coins known as *dinaras* (after the Roman *denarius*). These bore the names and epithets of kings, including metrical legends. The obverse generally had a representation of the king and the reverse an image of a deity. Rulers such as Chandragupta II, Kumaragupta I, Skandagupta, and Budhagupta also issued silver coins, similar in weight and fabric to those of the western Kshatrapas. The obverse had the king's portrait, sometimes accompanied by a date; the reverse had a motif (e.g., a *garuda* or a peacock), surrounded by a circular legend. Copper coins of the Guptas are rare. The coins of contemporary dynasties include those of the early Kadambas, Ikshvakus, Vishnukundins, and 'Nagas'. A number of Vakataka coins made of base metal with a high proportion of copper have been found in the Wardha area. They are irregular in size and have a light weight standard. Similar coins were found in excavations at Mansar near Ramtek in Nagpur district. Large numbers of seals and sealings have been found at sites such as Basarh (ancient Vaishali), Bhita, and Nalanda. The Hunas initially issued coins made of copper and silver. The early ones follow Sasanian prototypes, while those issued after their Indian conquests follow Kushana and Gupta styles. Mihirakula's copper coins have the Shaiva bull emblem on the reverse.

Important developments took place in the sphere of Sanskrit literature during *c.* 300–600 CE. The epics and major Puranas were given final shape, and these texts form important sources for religious and cultural processes of the time. The *Yajnavalkya*, *Narada*, *Vishnu*, and *Brihaspati Smritis* also belong to this period. Kamandaka's *Nitisara*, a work on polity addressed to kings, was composed some time between *c.* 500–700 CE. The *Manjushri-mulakalpa*, a Buddhist Mahayana text, has a chapter on the history of India and of Gauda and Magadha in particular from the early centuries CE to the early medieval period. The Jaina *Harivamsha Purana* (8th century) and *Tiloya Pannati* give some details concerning political chronology. Fragments of the *Devi-Chandragupta*, a lost drama written by Vishakhadatta, were found preserved in a manuscript of Bhoja's

Copper plates found in a pot; copper plate seals (from top)

[1] There are various edited volumes containing important contributions to the debate on the nature of the historical processes in early medieval India. See, for instance, Mukhia. (Ed.), 1999; Jha. (Ed.), 2000; Upinder Singh. (Ed.), 2011; Kulke and Sahu. (Ed.), 2022. For an expansion of the range of historical questions, see Bisschop and Cecil. (Ed.), 2021.

Shringara-Prakasha, and are relevant for Gupta political history. Sanskrit *kavya* constitutes an important source for the social history of the period. Works on medicine and astronomy are important sources for intellectual history. Along with other technical treatises such as the *Kamasutra* (on pleasure) and the *Amarakosha* (a lexicon, the dates for which range between the 6th and 9th century), they offer information on other aspects as well. The Tamil epics—the *Silappadikaram* and *Manimekalai*—belong to the 5th/6th century and are a rich source of information on the history of South India. Another important Tamil text of about the same period is the *Tirukkural* or *Kural*. The author

PRIMARY SOURCES | Faxian's *Fuguo ji*

Faxian's *Fuguo ji* (*A Record of Buddhist Countries*) is much more than a riveting personal memoir or travelogue. Faxian left Xian (Chang'an) in 399 CE and returned about 14 years later. He clearly states his aim several times—the Vinaya in China was incomplete; so, he had come to India to acquire Vinaya texts.

But his work sought to accomplish much more than what he states explicitly. Faxian sought to recreate for Chinese readers the sacred geography of India at the time of the Buddha, weaving into it the Buddha's life story, and describing the various places associated with the Sakyamuni (as well as other Buddhas), the miracles performed by him, the objects used by him, his bodily relics, the *stupa*s and monasteries that marked the sacred spots, and the nature and numerical strength of the Buddhist community in various places. Faxian's description of Indian monks often emphasizes their sense of decorum and proper behaviour, indicating that he wanted to present them as a role model to their Chinese counterparts. His account of his travels also perhaps aimed at inspiring others to undertake the journey to India, and if they were not able to do so, to read the account of the marvellous lands and places he had visited.

It was an emotional journey for Faxian. While visiting the sacred places associated with the Buddha's life, he was aware that he came from a far-away country where the Buddha had never set foot. In Rajagriha, Faxian bought incense, flowers, and oil for lamps. He asked two local monks to guide him to Mount Gridhrakuta, where he offered flowers and incense and refilled the lamps to keep the flames burning. He cried in deep sorry at the place where the Buddha had taught the *Shuramgama-samadhi-sutra*. Then he said, "Faxian, who was not yet born at the time of the Buddha, was able to see nothing more than the ruins and monuments left by him."

Upon arriving at the Jetavana *vihara*, Faxian and his companion Daozheng reflected that this was the place where the Buddha had lived for two years. They felt sad that they and their friends had been born in a far-off country. They had travelled together through many lands, and some of them had passed away. As they gazed at the place where the Buddha had once lived, they were deeply moved, and their hearts were filled with sorrow.

When they arrived in Central India, they were impressed by the conduct and decorum of the monks. Daozheng lamented the incompleteness of the Vinaya rules observed by the monks in China. He swore not to be reborn in a far-off country until he achieved Buddhahood. So Daozheng remained in India, but Faxian's intention in undertaking the journey was to propagate the Vinaya in China, so he went on.

Faxian does not mention a single contemporary Indian ruler by name. There is no mention whatsoever of the Guptas or any other ruling house of the time. He mentions many kings of the past, namely Kanishka, Bimbisara, Ajatashatru, and Prasenajit. But the king who is given the most importance is Ashoka. He is clearly the model king as Buddhist patron that Faxian wanted to project.

He gives an idealized picture of the 'Middle Kingdom' (Madhyadesha). He states that the climate was temperate and pleasant. The people were well off and happy and were not placed under requirements for household registration or any official restrictions. Those who tilled the king's lands were asked only to pay land rent and were free to stay or leave as they pleased. Kings ruled without recourse to capital punishment. Offenders were only obliged to pay a penalty according to the nature of the offence. Those who plotted high treason were not killed; their right hand was cut off as punishment.

The fact that Faxian stayed on in Sri Lanka for two years indicates its importance as a centre of Buddhism. He talks about the Abhayagiri and Mahavihara monasteries, states that the king and the citizens had deep respect for Buddhism, describes the royal patronage extended to Buddhism, the great wealth of the monasteries, and their close relationship with kings. Here, he obtained various texts "all of which were unknown in China." They were obviously texts that Faxian had not seen in the places he had visited in India. Faxian's account describes Buddhism in Sri Lanka as a strong and vibrant living tradition with powerful political patronage.

After Faxian's return to China, he said to his fellow monks, "When I look back on what I have been through, my heart begins to pound, and I start sweating. I bravely undertook a perilous journey, not sparing my body, because I had a purpose, and I foolishly and single-mindedly devoted my life to it. That was why I cast my life into the journey in which death seemed almost certain, in the hope that I might have one chance out of ten thousand of surviving."

Faxian's *Fuguo ji* was the first detailed Chinese account of the sacred Buddhist sites of India. The text played an extremely influential role in expanding and moulding the Chinese awareness of India.

Source Li, (2002) 2014

Tiruvalluvar may have belonged to a community of weavers or drummers. The text is divided into three parts, on *aram* (virtue), *porul* (wealth), and *kamam* (pleasure). The author was aware of the ideas of Dharmashastra, Nitishastra, and Arthashastra, possibly also with the *Kamasutra*. The *Kural* contains didactic poems which offer advice on many matters, including virtue, love, friendship, kingship, honour, and nonviolence. Some scholars see a Jaina influence on the work. Other important texts belonging to this period will be discussed in the course of the chapter.

Between the late 3rd and 8th centuries, many Chinese monks travelled to India in order to collect Buddhist texts, visit important places of Buddhist pilgrimage, and interact with Indian monks. The stream of Chinese monk-scholars reached its peak in the 5th century. Some monks recorded their observations, but only three records have survived in their entirety—those of Faxian, Xuanzang, and Yijing. The travels of Faxian in India lasted about a decade (*c.* 337–422 CE) and took him from the north-west into the Ganga valley, right down to the eastern seaport of Tamralipti in the Bay of Bengal. From here, he took the sea route to Simhala (Sri Lanka) and further on to South-east Asia, whence he headed back to China. Faxian spent the rest of his life translating the enormous number of texts he had collected. He also wrote an account of his travels called the *Fuguo ji* (A Record of Buddhist Kingdoms). Although the book does not mention the name of the reigning king (who must have been Chandragupta II), it contains several observations about the life of the people, some erroneous. Instead of reading the accounts of Faxian and Xuanzang as a series of statements (sometimes erroneous) about India in the 5th and 7th centuries respectively, there is a need to problematize them by taking into account their perspective, purpose, and audience (see Deeg, 2007). Numerous Indian monks went to China as well, but there are no accounts of their travels or experiences.

There are also a few Western accounts of India in this period. An example is Cosmas Indicopleustes' *Christian Topography*, written in the 6th century. The author was a merchant who travelled widely to areas including India, before becoming a monk. The writings of Procopious of Caesarea throw light on India's trade relations with the Byzantine empire.

Although there are many sculptural and architectural remains of this period, most of them religious in nature, there is little documentation of archaeological evidence from sites revealing the details and textures of everyday life. Nevertheless, sites such as the Purana Qila, Ahichchhatra, Basarh, Bhita, and Kaveripattinam do provide important data.

Political History

The Gupta dynasty

There are no specific details about the origins or social background of the Guptas (for details of political history, see Gupta, [1974] 1979; Goyal, 2005). Their original home may have been located in Magadha, north Bengal, or more probably, the lower doab. The idea that they were Vaishyas is based on the recommendation in texts such as the *Manu Smriti* and *Vishnu Purana* that the name suffix 'gupta' was appropriate for members of this *varna*. On the other hand, some scholars have argued that the Guptas were Kshatriyas. This is largely based on their matrimonial alliances with the Lichchhavis (who were Kshatriyas) and Nagas (who are presumed to have been Kshatriyas), and the fact that the marriage of Prabhavatigupta (daughter of Chandragupta II) into the Brahmana Vakataka dynasty would have fallen within the Dharmashastra norms of hypergamous *anuloma* marriages. However, the alliance with the Vakatakas and the possibility that a princess of the Brahmana Kadamba family may have been married to a Gupta king have been used to argue that the Guptas were Brahmanas. Furthermore, inscriptions of Prabhavatigupta, the Gupta princess who was married to the Vakataka ruler Rudrasena II, describe her as belonging to the Dharana *gotra*. Since the Vakatakas are known to have belonged to the Vishnuvriddha *gotra*, Dharana seems to be the *gotra* of the Guptas. According to S. R. Goyal (2005: 84), this was not simply a case of rulers taking on the *gotra* of their preceptors but a clear indication that the Guptas were Brahmanas.

'King and queen type' coin, Chandragupta I; Lakshmi/Durga seated on lion on reverse

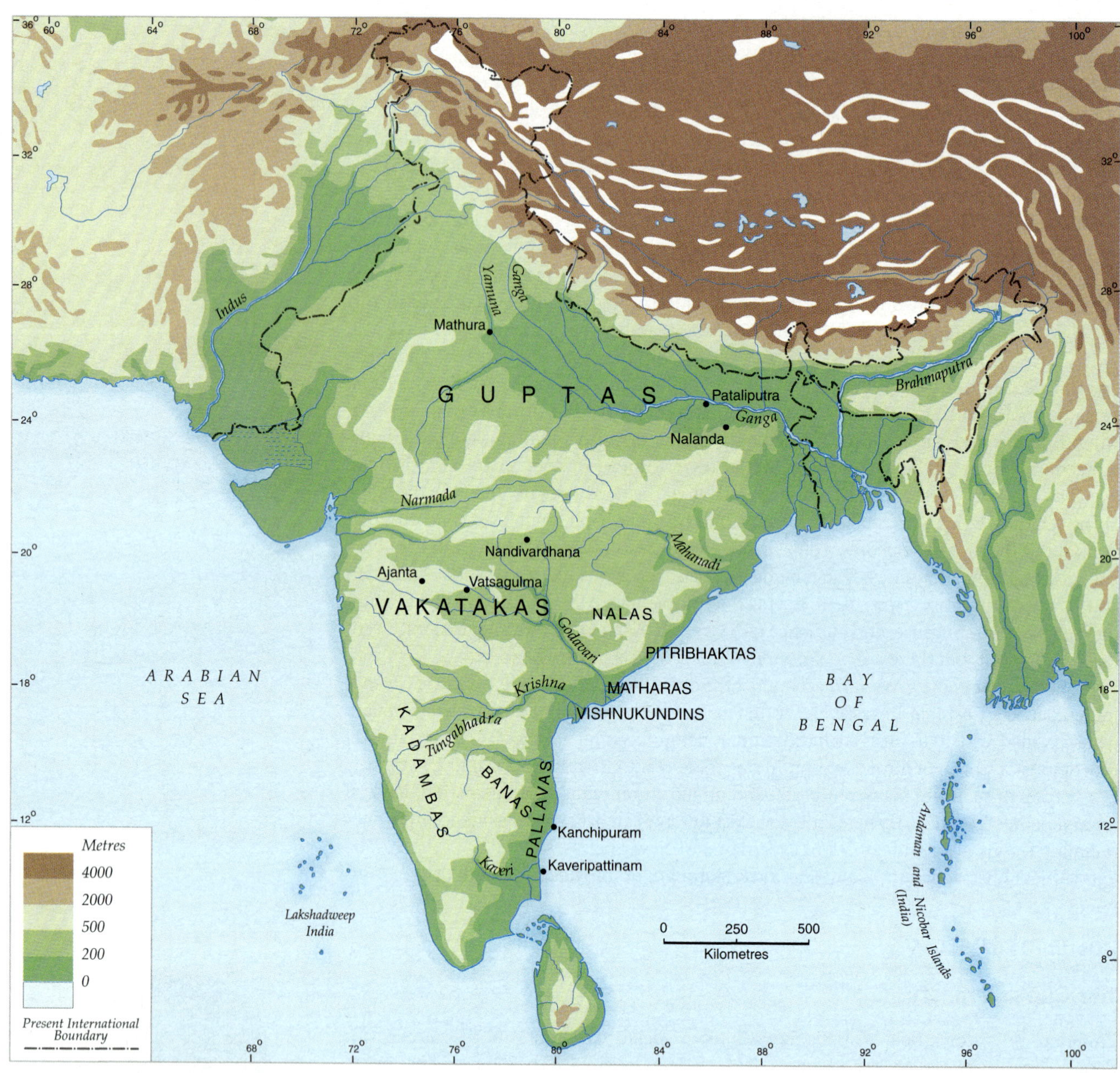

Map 9.1 The kingdoms of the Guptas, Vakatakas, and some contemporary dynasties

The genealogical accounts of the Guptas mention *maharaja* Gupta and *maharaja* Ghatotkacha as the first two rulers of the line. It is not clear whether they were independent rulers or subordinates of some other king. Gupta inscriptions are dated in an era which, according to the testimony of Al-Biruni's *Tahqiq-i-Hind*, began in 319–320 CE. This must mark the accession of the third Gupta ruler Chandragupta I (319–335/36 CE), who seems to have laid the foundations of the empire. In inscriptions, he has the title *maharajadhiraja* (great king of kings), and such titles, henceforth, became signifiers of imperial power and status.

The only known event of this king's reign is his marriage to Kumaradevi, a Lichchhavi princess. The marriage was commemorated on coins issued either during the reign of Chandragupta or his son Samudragupta. They have the figures and names of the king and queen on the obverse; the reverse has a goddess seated on a lion and the legend *Lichchhavayah*. Samudragupta is referred to as *Lichchhavi-dauhitra* (grandson of the Lichchhavis) in his Allahabad *prashasti*. The Lichchhavis were based in the Nepal terai. The fact that the Guptas entered into a matrimonial alliance with them and advertised this in inscriptions and on coins indicates their political importance at the time.

A passage in the *Vishnu Purana* refers to the Guptas enjoying all the territories along the Ganga upto Prayaga (Prayagraj, Allahabad), as well as Saketa and Magadha. A variant in some manuscripts predicts that all the territories along the Ganga up to Prayaga would be enjoyed by the people of Magadha and the Guptas. As both versions mention the Guptas in the plural, they cannot be considered references to the conquests of Chandragupta I. The empire of Chandragupta I may have included the areas of modern Bihar and parts of Uttar Pradesh and Bengal.

Chandragupta I's death was followed by a fratricidal struggle between his sons Kachagupta and Samudragupta. Kachagupta seems to have been a successor or rival of Samudragupta. His coins, found along with those of other Gupta kings in the Bayana, Tanda, and Balia hoards, refer to him as a performer of good deeds and exterminator of all kings.

Brahmi script, Allahabad *prashasti*

Information regarding Samudragupta (*c.* 350–370 CE) is based on his inscriptions and coins. A fragmentary *prashasti* of this king is carved on a block of red sandstone at Eran. Two copper plate inscriptions found at Gaya and Nalanda, dated in the reign of Samudragupta, are considered spurious by many historians. The most important epigraph of Samudragupta's reign is the *prashasti* on the unique Allahabad (now Prayagraj) pillar, whose surface also carries inscriptions of Ashoka and the Mughal emperor Jahangir. The Gupta inscription, in prose and verse, eulogizes the achievements, conquests, and personality of Samudragupta. The composer was a man named Harishena, whose titles—*sandhivigrahika* (minister for peace and war), *kumaramatya* (a high-ranking cadre of officials), and *mahadandanayaka* (an important judicial or military officer)—indicate his high rank in court circles. That he was also a skilled writer is evident from the *prashasti*. The inscription weaves an image of Samudragupta as an exceptional individual and ideal king, and simultaneously offers very specific details regarding his military achievements and conquests. Although there are problems in identifying some of the rulers and places it mentions (see Gupta, [1974] 1979, Vol. 1: 258–82), the Allahabad *prashasti* clearly presents the Gupta empire as the epicentre of a complex web of varied political relationships.

Samudragupta must have inherited an empire that included the Magadha area of Bihar and adjoining areas of Uttar Pradesh and Bengal, stretching to the Himalayan foothills in the north. His initial military campaigns were directed towards extending his control over territories lying immediately beyond this area. Line 14 of the inscription refers to his capturing a king of the Kota family while the latter was playing in the city of Pushpa (identified variously with Pataliputra or Kanauj); this may have been a ruler of the upper Ganga valley. Line 21 refers to Samudragupta violently exterminating a number of kings of Aryavarta and making all the kings of the forest his servants, i.e., subordinates. The kings of Aryavarta mentioned are Rudradeva, Matila, Nagadatta, Chandravarman, Ganapatinaga, Nagasena, Achyuta, Nandin, and Balavarman. Rudradeva may be identified with the Vakataka king Rudrasena I, the western Kshatrapa ruler Rudradaman II, or his son Rudrasena III. Or he may be the same as the Rudra whose coin has been found at Kaushambi. Matila is mentioned on a seal from Bulandshahr district (UP), but the name is not accompanied by any epithet suggesting royal status. Chandravarman may have been a local ruler of Bengal, whose inscription has been found at Susuniya near Bankura. Alternatively, he may be the Chandravarman mentioned in an inscription found at Mandasor in Central India. The coins of a Ganapatinaga have been found at Pawaya in Central India. A king named Nagasena is mentioned in the *Harshacharita* as ruling from Padmavati. Coins of a king named Achyuta have been found at Ramnagar (ancient Ahichchhatra) in Bareilly district (UP). The territories of the various kings mentioned in Lines 14 and 21 seem to have been annexed, leading to an extension of the Gupta empire over the Ganga–Yamuna valley up to Mathura and Padmavati in the west.

'Tiger slayer type' coin, Samudragupta; on reverse, goddess Ganga standing on *makara*, holding lotus

Other areas were subordinated in a different manner. Line 22 of the *prashasti* refers to rulers offering tribute, obeying the orders of the Gupta king, and coming to perform

'Ashvamedha type' coin, Samudragupta; queen/goddess(?) standing on lotus on reverse

obeisance before him. They included the frontier kings of Samatata, Davaka, Kamarupa, Nepala, and Kartripura. Samatata corresponds to south-east Bengal. Davaka refers to the area around Daboka in Nagaon district and Kamarupa the Guwahati region, both in Assam. Nepala corresponds roughly to modern Nepal. Kartripura may have comprised Kartarpur in Jalandhar district and the erstwhile Katuria raj of Kumaon, Garhwal, and Rohilkhand. The polities subordinated in this manner also included a number of *ganas*, namely the Malavas, Arjunayanas, Yaudheyas, Madrakas, Abhiras, Prarjunas, Sanakanikas, Kakas, and Kharaparikas. At this time, the Malavas were based in south-east Rajasthan, the Arjunayanas in the Bharatpur–Alwar areas of Rajasthan, while the Yaudheyas held sway in parts of Punjab and Rajputana. The Sanakanikas were located in eastern Malwa or somewhere in the north-western part of the subcontinent. The Kakas may have been connected with Kakanadabota, the ancient name for Sanchi in the Raisen district of Madhya Pradesh; or they may have been located in the north-west. The Madrakas originally had their capital in modern Sialkot in the Punjab. The Abhiras may at this point of time have been located in the northern Konkan. The Prarjunas were probably located in the north-west. The relationship between the Gupta emperor and all these groups had certain elements of a feudatory relationship, although there is no direct mention of their having provided troops. Perhaps this was subsumed within the phrase *ajna-karana* (obeying the orders) of their overlord.

Lines 19 and 20 of the Allahabad *prashasti* refer to Samudragupta having captured and then released several southern kings. These included Mahendra of Kosala, Vyaghraraja of Mahakantara, Mantaraja of Kairala or Kaurala, Mahendra of Pishtapura, Svamidatta of Kottura on the hill, Damana of Erandapalla, Vishnugopa of Kanchi, Nilaraja of Avamukta, Hastivarman of Vengi, Ugrasena of Palakka, Kubera of Devarashtra, Dhananjaya of Kusthalapura, and all the other kings of Dakshinapatha. Kosala corresponds to the modern Raipur, Bilaspur, and Sambalpur areas of eastern Madhya Pradesh and western Odisha. The forested kingdom of Mahakantara may have been located in the Vindhyas, the Kosala area, Central India, or Odisha. Kairala corresponds to the Kerala region, but if the correct reading is Kaurala, this may have been located on the eastern coast of Andhra Pradesh. Kottura may be Kothoor, near Mahendragiri in Ganjam district of Odisha. Pishtapura is identified with modern Pithapuram in Godavari district, Andhra Pradesh. Erandapalla was located in Ganjam district of Odisha or Visakhapatnam district of Andhra Pradesh. Vishnugopa was a Pallava king of Kanchi, ruling the area of the Chingleput district. Hastivarman was a king of the Shalankayana dynasty of Vengi, located between the Krishna and Godavari rivers in Andhra. Devarashtra is identified with the Yellamanchili region of Visakhapatnam district. Kusthalapura may correspond to Kuttalur in north Arcot district of Tamil Nadu, but this is far from certain.

Line 23 of the inscription refers to some rulers rendering all kinds of service to Samudragupta, seeking the use of the Gupta *garuda* seal and entering into matrimonial alliances with the Guptas of their own accord. These included rulers with the epithets *Daivaputra*, *Shahi*, and *Shahanushahi*, probably representing the last vestiges of Kushana rule. The Shakas and Murundas (the phrase 'Shaka-Murunda' can, alternatively, be interpreted as the Shaka lords) are also mentioned in this context. There is further mention of the people of Simhala, i.e., Sri Lanka, and all the other island dwellers. A Chinese text refers to king Meghavarna of Sri Lanka sending a mission accompanied with gifts to Samudragupta, asking his permission to build a monastery and rest house for Sri Lankan pilgrims at Bodh Gaya. Permission was evidently granted and the monastery built, as its magnificence was described by Xuanzang in the 7th century.

At the end of his reign, Samudragupta's empire seems to have comprised much of Northern India, with the exception of Kashmir, western Punjab, Rajasthan, Sindh, and Gujarat. It included the highlands of Central India to the east of Jabalpur, Chhattisgarh, Odisha, and the area on the eastern coast at least up to Chingleput. This inner core of directly annexed territories was rimmed by a large number of subordinate states. Beyond these, to the north-west, lay the last vestiges of the Shakas and Kushanas, over whom Samudragupta claims to have impressed his might. To the south were the kings of Dakshinapatha, who were humbled, but who suffered neither annexation nor a reduction to feudatory status. Still further south lay the island of Sri Lanka, which, we are told, also acknowledged Gupta suzerainty. The Guptas did not create an all-India empire under their direct control. But through their successful military campaigns, they established a network of political relationships of paramountcy and subordination that extended beyond the area under their direct rule.

Samudragupta emerges from the Allahabad *prashasti* as a restless conqueror. But military success is just one aspect of Harishena's portrait of the king. He is also described as an able and compassionate ruler, concerned about the welfare of his subjects. Apart from such conventional characterizations that appear often enough in *prashastis* of ancient kings, there are some non-standard elements that may have been based on talents Samudragupta actually possessed. For instance, he is described as having put Brihaspati (the preceptor of the gods) to shame by his sharp and polished intellect, and likewise Tumburu and Narada with his fine musical performances. He is described as a *kaviraja* (king among poets), whose poetry surpassed the glory of the genius of poets.

'Lyrist type' coin, Samudragupta; seated Lakshmi on reverse

The Samudragupta of Harishena's inscription is not a man; he is a superman. His extraordinary qualities are emphasized through hyperbole and analogies with the gods. In tune with references in the *Manu Smriti* and the *Mahabharata*, he is described as the equal of the gods Kubera, Varuna, Indra, and Yama. Harishena also uses double entendre (*shlesha*) to compare Samudragupta with the god Vishnu: He is inscrutable (Achintya); he is Purusha, the cause of the prosperity of the good and the destruction of the bad. Like Vishnu's, his heart can be won through devotion (*bhakti*). He is a human being in his performance of the rites and conventions of the world; otherwise, he is a god (*deva*) who resides in this world.

Sheldon Pollock ([2006] 2007: 240) has pointed out that the Allahabad inscription heralds a new imperial idea that was both quasi-universal and projected within a specified geopolitical space. When considered as part of a continuing process of the evolution of the ideology of kingship that goes back to earlier centuries, although it has certain important novel features, the Allahabad inscription reflects an exceptionally sophisticated synthesis of various elements of kingship drawn from earlier times, expressed in superior Sanskrit verse and prose. It is interesting to note that Samudragupta's inscription is inscribed on a pillar that also bears several Ashokan inscriptions (the six pillar edicts and minor pillar edicts 1 and 3). This pillar also bears an inscription of the 16th century Mughal emperor Jahangir.

Samudragupta's coins represent him in various poses suggestive of prowess and martial skills—as an archer holding a bow in his left hand and an arrow in his right; standing with a battleaxe in his left hand with a dwarf looking up at him; or trampling and killing a tiger. The '*ashvamedha* type' shows a sacrificial horse standing before a decorated *yupa*. In the 'standard type', which is the most frequent, he holds a long staff (this may actually represent a spear, javelin, or sceptre) in his left hand and offers oblations into a fire altar with his right; the *garuda* standard appears to the left. A coin depicting Chandragupta I and his queen standing face to face is attributed either to Chandragupta I or Samudragupta. One of Samudragupta's coin types shows him sitting on a couch, playing the *vina* (lyre). The obverse of this king's coins sometimes depict a goddess identified as Ardoksho or Lakshmi. In the *ashvamedha* type coins, there is a standing female figure (perhaps a queen, Laksmi, or Rajya-Lakshmi, i.e. the goddess of royal fortune) holding a fly whisk. Legends on Samudragupta's coins include epithets such as *parakramah* (brave), *apratirathah* (invincible), *ashvamedha-parakramah* (powerful enough to perform the *ashvamedha*), and *vyaghra-parakramah* (brave as a tiger). The longer metrical legends expand such images—e.g., 'one who has won victories on a hundred battlefields and conquered the enemies wins heaven' or 'the king of kings who performed the horse sacrifice, having protected the earth, wins heaven'.

Gupta genealogies list Chandragupta II as Samudragupta's successor. But evidence indicates that a king named Ramagupta ruled in between, from *c.* 370 to 375 CE.

The peak of the territorial expansion of the Gupta empire was reached during the reign of Chandragupta II (*c.* 376–413/15 CE), son of Samudragupta and Dattadevi.

FURTHER DISCUSSION | **Ramagupta—did he exist?**

Many years ago, three passages of a lost play, the *Devi-Chandragupta* of Vishakhadeva (generally identified with the playwright Vishakhadatta), were found in a manuscript of Bhoja's *Shringara-prakasha*, while six passages were found in a manuscript of Ramachandra and Gunachandra's *Natya-darpana*. Taken together, these passages tell the following story:

There was a king named Ramagupta, whose kingdom was invaded by a powerful Shaka king. On the advice of his minister, instead of facing the invader, Ramagupta bought peace by agreeing to hand over his queen Dhruvadevi to the enemy. The king's younger brother Kumara was incensed at this dishonourable capitulation. He entered the Shaka camp disguised as Dhruvadevi and killed the enemy king. Later, he killed his brother as well and married his sister-in-law. There are reverberations of these dramatic events in later texts such as Bana Bhatta's *Harshacharita* and Shankararya's commentary on this text. An 11th century Persian work called the *Majmat-ul-Tawarikh* by Abul Hasan Ali offers the additional information that Chandragupta's killing of the Shaka king increased his popularity among his subjects. This made Ramagupta jealous, and Chandragupta pretended to be insane prior to killing his brother. Allusions to these sensational events in 9th/10th century Rashtrakuta inscriptions indicate that their memory lingered for a very long time.

Copper coins that can be assigned to Ramagupta were found at Bhilsa in Central India. These bore the *garuda* emblem and were similar to Chandragupta's coins in style, fabric, and weight standard. Further, three images of Jaina *tirthankaras* found at Durjanpura near Vidisha in Central India have inscriptions recording their installation by *maharajadhiraja* Ramagupta. There is a view that this represents a later Gupta king, but many historians see this as clinching evidence of the historicity of a brother of Chandragupta II named Ramagupta. Coins and inscriptions thus, seem to support the story of the *Devi-Chandragupta*.

Gupta inscriptions indicate that Chandragupta had a wife named Dhruvadevi and had children by her, but do not mention Ramagupta. This is not all that surprising, as the genealogies mention only those kings who came in the direct line of succession. Since the succession passed to Chandragupta and *his* sons, Ramagupta is ignored. Another example of this is the case of the later king Skandagupta, after whose reign the succession passed to the descendants of his brother Purugupta. Hence, Skandagupta is not mentioned in the genealogies in his successors' inscriptions.

Source Goyal, 2005: 261–74

This king had the epithets *parama-bhagavata* and *Vikramaditya*. A Sanskrit inscription on an iron pillar in the Mehrauli area of Delhi refers to a king named Chandra, who has been variously identified with the Maurya king Chandragupta, the Gupta kings Chandragupta I or Samudragupta, the Naga king Chandramsha, Chandravarman of Malwa, or a king mentioned in an inscription found at Susuniya (see Joshi. [Ed.], 1989). But there are several good reasons for identifying him with Chandragupta II: Chandragupta II is referred to as Chandra on his coins; the Udayagiri cave inscription states that he went on a *digvijaya* (victory over the quarters); the Delhi region seems to have formed part of his empire; and he was a Vaishnava. Another issue that has been debated is whether the Mehrauli inscription was posthumous or not. D. R. Bhandarkar suggested that the king was alive when it was engraved. But according to D. C. Sircar, the pillar was probably erected by Chandragupta II towards the end of his life, while the record was engraved after his death, during the reign of his successor Kumaragupta.

The Mehrauli inscription suggests that Chandragupta fought against a confederacy of enemies in Bengal and also led a campaign into the Punjab. His coins and inscriptions indicate that his rule extended into Malwa and Western India. This must have been at the expense of the Shakas. The last Shaka inscription found in Western India is dated in year 310 of the Shaka era, i.e., 388 CE; Gupta rule must have prevailed thereafter. The empire of Chandragupta II thus, seems to have extended from Bengal to the north-west and from the Himalayan terai to the Narmada. The Guptas entered into a matrimonial alliance with the Vakatakas of the Deccan—Prabhavatigupta, daughter of Chandragupta by queen Kuberanaga, was married to the Vakataka king Rudrasena II. This alliance united the ruling houses of the two major kingdoms of the subcontinent. Legends about a great king named Vikramaditya may have been partially based on Chandragupta II, to which various elements were added (Sircar, 1969b).

PRIMARY SOURCES | **The inscription of Chandra and the legend of the unsteady pillar**

On whose arm fame was inscribed by the sword, when in battle in the Vanga country, he repulsed with his breast the enemies who, joining together, had advanced against him; by whom, crossing the seven mouths of the Sindhu, the Vahlikas were conquered in battle; by the breeze of whose valour the southern ocean is still perfumed.

He, the lord of men, whose body, as though weary, has departed from this earth to another world [heaven] won by his deeds, but who remains on this earth in his fame; whose great glory, the result of his destruction of his enemies, does not yet leave this earth—like the heat [from the smouldering embers] of a now quiet fire in a great forest.

By that king, who acquired supreme sovereignty on earth for a very long time by his own prowess [and] who, having the name Chandra and a beauty of countenance resembling the full moon, having fixed his mind with devotion on Vishnu, this lofty standard of the lord Vishnu was set up on Vishnupada hill.

The Sanskrit inscription translated here is inscribed on an iron pillar which stands in the Jami Masjid in the Qutb complex in Delhi. The pillar with its solid, slightly tapering shaft stands 7.16 m tall. It is surmounted by an inverted lotus emblem, over which there are three fluted discs (*amalakas*) supporting a square pedestal. The pillar must have been crowned by a Vaishnava emblem, perhaps a *garuda*. It is considered remarkable because of the metallurgical skill required to forge such a long piece of iron, the clarity of its inscriptions after so many centuries, and the fact that it has remained comparatively rust-free, even after so many centuries.

Chemical analysis has shown that it is made of pure wrought iron, containing 99.7 per cent iron with a very low sulphur and very high phosphorus content. There is, in fact, evidence of rusting on those parts of the pillar where it has been exposed to prolonged contact with water—the underground and topmost portions, where water could accumulate in the grooves.

It is not certain where the pillar originally stood. Most historians believe it is not *in situ*. The inscription refers to a hill named Vishnupada, but today there is nothing resembling a hill nearby (of course it is possible that the area was hilly many centuries ago). D. R. Bhandarkar located Vishnupada in the Himalayas, close to the source of the Beas river. On the other hand, Fleet pointed out that the underground supports of the column included several small pieces of metal

that seem to have been part of its original underpinnings, not the sort of things that would have been brought along if the pillar had indeed been transported here from elsewhere. Therefore, it is possible that the pillar was located here or nearby, right from the beginning.

At some point of time, the Gupta iron pillar got entangled in legend and folklore with the naming of Delhi. One version of the story, recounted in the *Prithviraja Raso* is as follows: A learned Brahmana told the Rajput king Bilan Deo or Anangapala Tomara that the pillar was immoveable, that its base rested on the hood of the serpent king Vasuki, and that Anangapala's rule would last as long as the pillar stood. Anangapala was curious. He had the pillar dug out, but its lower part was found smeared with the blood of the serpent. Realizing he had made a mistake, the king ordered the pillar to be re-installed. But in spite of all attempts, the pillar remained loose (*dhili*). And, the story concludes, in the looseness of the pillar lies the origin of the name of Dilli, i.e., Delhi.

We may note that the iron pillar bears several other short inscriptions. These include an 11th century inscription which seems to refer to Anangapala establishing Delhi.

Source Upinder Singh, (1999) 2006: 76–83

A rock at Hunza (in Gilgit district in Kashmir) bears some Kharoshthi inscriptions of the early centuries CE and some short Sanskrit inscriptions in the Brahmi script of the Gupta period. Some of the latter mention a person named Chandra, in one case with the additional epithet of *Vikramaditya*. A few inscriptions also mention a person named Harishena. Some historians have identifed these two individuals with the Gupta king Chandragupta II and Harishena, composer of the Allahabad *prashasti*, and suggest that these inscriptions were inscribed in the course of a Gupta military campaign in the area. However, the Chandra of the Hunza inscriptions could well have been a local ruler.

Chandragupta II was succeeded by Kumaragupta (*c.* 415–454), who performed the *ashvamedha* sacrifice. His coins have representations of the god Karttikeya. Towards the end of Kumaragupta's reign, there seems to have been an invasion from the north-west (the identity of this enemy is not known), which was suppressed by prince Skandagupta. The reign of Skandagupta (*c.* 454–467 CE) saw the Gupta army repulse a Huna invasion. An inscription on the Girnar rock mentions the repair of the Sudarshana lake by Skandagupta's provincial governor Parnadatta.

After the imperial Guptas, the political history of North India saw the rule of various lines such as the Later Guptas, Maukharis, Pushyabhutis, and Maitrakas (see Bakker, 2014). Later Gupta kings included Purugupta, Kumaragupta II, Budhagupta, Narasimhagupta, Kumaragupta III, and Vishnugupta. Gupta suzerainty was recognized by the Parivrajaka *maharajas* and perhaps also by the *maharajas* of Uchchakalpa in Central India. As the empire weakened, subordinate rulers became increasingly independent. The Gupta empire declined due to a variety of factors including competition from the Vakatakas, the rise of Yashodharman of Malwa, and Huna invasions.

In the 4th century, various Hunnic people rose to power in Central Asia. In the 5th century, they threatened the Roman, Sasanid, and Gupta empires. The Huns/Hunas crossed the Hindu Kush mountains and occupied Gandhara; their further movement was repulsed by Skandagupta's army. However, in the late 5th century or early 6th century CE, the Huna chief Toramana managed to conquer Punjab, large parts of Western India and the area around Eran in Central India. The evidence suggests that the Huna sway may have extended over parts of Uttar Pradesh, Rajasthan, Punjab, and Kashmir. The *Kuvalayamala*, an 8th century Jaina text, refers to Toramana adopting the Jaina faith and living on the banks of the Chenab at Pavvaiya.

Mihirakula was the son and successor of Toramana. An inscription of his was found at Gwalior. Xuanzang locates his capital at Sakala (Sialkot). The *Rajatarangini* refers to Mihirakula's cruelty and suggests that he ruled over Kashmir and Gandhara, but clearly exaggerates when it refers to his conquest over South India and Sri Lanka. Although he over-ran much of North India, Mihirakula suffered defeat at the hands of Yashodharman of Malwa, Narasimhagupta, and the Maukharis. The power of the Hunas declined thereafter.

The Vakatakas of the Deccan

The history of the Vakatakas (Mirashi, 1963; Shastri, 1997; Bakker, 1997) is known from inscriptions, archaeology, and from texts such as the Puranas. The location of their original home is a subject of debate. Some scholars place it in South India. This is based on the mention of 'Vakataka' in a fragmentary inscription at Amaravati in Andhra Pradesh and certain similarities between some technical terms in Vakataka inscriptions and the Hirehadagalli and Mayidavolu grants of the Pallava king Shivaskandavarman. Further, the Basim plates of Vindhyashakti II use the title *Haritiputra* for Pravarasena I and *Dharmamaharaja* for Sarvasena I and the reigning king. These titles also occur in inscriptions of southern dynasties such as the Pallavas, early Kadambas, and Chalukyas of Badami. Certain inscriptions of the time of Harishena (the last known king of the Vakataka line of Vatsagulma), describe the family of one of his ministers as hailing from Vallura, which Mirashi identifies with Velur, about 30 miles from Hyderabad in Andhra Pradesh. This reference too has been used to support the hypothesis that the Vakatakas were originally based in South India.

'Lion slayer type' coin, Chandragupta II (obverse); goddess seated on lion (reverse); 'Archer type' coin, Kumaragupta I (obverse); Lakshmi seated on lotus (reverse)

Ajay Mitra Shastri (1997) has pointed out that none of the above arguments are conclusive, and that inscriptions and the Puranas indicate that this dynasty initially established its base in the Vindhyan region, north of the Narmada. The Puranas refer to the dynasty as the Vindhyakas. The town of Kanchanaka, mentioned in the Puranas in connection with one of the early kings, Pravarasena I, can be identified with Nachna or Nachna-ki-talai village in Panna district of Madhya Pradesh. Several early Vakataka inscriptions and structural remains of the period have been found here. This clearly indicates that the Vakatakas first established themselves in the Vindhyan region, which included a large part of the Bundelkhand and Baghelkhand tracts. From here they extended their power southwards, eventually becoming a major political power in the Deccan. Vakataka rule lasted from the mid-3rd to the early 6th century CE. The dynasty had matrimonial ties with the imperial Guptas, Nagas of Padmavati, Kadambas of Karnataka, and Vishnukundins of Andhra.

Vindhyashakti I was the founder of the dynasty. The Ajanta inscription of the time of Harishena alludes in poetic terms to his military achievements. The sun is said to have been obscured by the masses of dust raised by his horses' hoofs in many battle. He is said to have won the whole world by the prowess of his arms. His majesty is compared to that of the gods Puramdara (Indra) and Upendra (Vishnu).

The second king of the line was Pravarasena (the Pravira of the Puranas),who seems to have extended the empire southwards into Vidarbha and the adjoining areas of the Deccan. His capital was Kanchanaka (modern Nachna). The marriage between his son Gautamiputra and the daughter of the Naga king Bhavanaga cemented an important political alliance. The Puranas mention Pravira as performing several *vajapeya* and *vajimedha* sacrifices, accompanied by the distribution of many lavish gifts. Later inscriptions refer to his belonging to the Vishnuvriddha *gotra*, and mention his performing four *ashvamedhas*, one *vajapeya*, and several other sacrifices. Pravarasena I was the only Vakataka king with the imperial title *samrat*; the others had the relatively modest title *maharaja*.

The successors of Pravarasena I were divided into two branches (the Puranas suggest four), which, on the basis of their political centres, can be referred to as the Padmapura–Nandivardhana–Pravarapura line (also known as the eastern or main branch) and the Vatsagulma line. This division may have originated in a partition of the empire within Pravarasena's lifetime. The Padmapura–Nandivardhana–Pravarapura line was represented by Rudrasena I, the successor of Pravarasena I. Later Vakataka inscriptions describe him as grandson of Bhavanaga and a devotee of Mahabhairava (the fierce form of Shiva). Even if the identification of Rudrasena with the Rudradeva of Samudragupta's Allahabad *prashasti* is problematic, this Vakataka king could not have remained unaffected by the sweep of the Gupta monarch's military campaigns and may have had to acknowledge his paramountcy.

Prithvishena I, the successor of Rudrasena I, is described in later Vakataka incriptions as a righteous conqueror. Much is made of his qualities of truthfulness, straightforwardness, compassion, humility, and purity of mind, and he is compared to the epic hero Yudhishthira. His authority was recognized by Vyaghraraja of the Nachna and Ganj inscriptions. Padmapura seems to have been an important administrative centre during the time. During the later part of Prithvishena I's reign, his son Rudrasena II was married to Prabhavatigupta, daughter of the Gupta emperor Chandragupta II. This was an important alliance for both houses. When Rudrasena died, his sons Divakarasena, Damodarasena, and Pravarasena were minors, and Prabhavatigupta held the reins of government as regent between *c.* 402–419.

Prabhavatigupta's inscriptions give her natal genealogy and emphasize her natal connections. Her *gotra* is given as Dharana, not Vishnuvriddha, the *gotra* of the family into which she had married. Nandivardhana (identified with Nandardhan or Nagardhan village, about 28 miles from Nagpur) seems to have become the capital during this period. The seal of Prabhavatigupta's Miregaon plates describes her as 'mother of two kings'. Crown prince Divakarasena did not live long enough to ascend the throne, but his younger brothers Damodarasena and Pravarasena II did.

The largest number of Vakataka inscriptions belong to the reign of Pravarasena II. The earlier ones were issued from Nandivardhana and the later ones from Pravarapura (once identified with Paunar in Wardha district, now with Mansar in Nagpur district). Prabhavatigupta continued to issue inscriptions in her own right and died during the later part of her son's reign. Apart from wielding political authority, Prabhavatigupta brought Vaishnava influence into the Vakataka court. The Kevala Narasimha temple

PRIMARY SOURCES | A queen's grant

The set of inscribed copper plates that came to be known as the Poona plates of Prabhavatigupta were preserved as an heirloom in the family of Balwant Bhau Nagarkar, a coppersmith of Poona, who originally lived in Ahmadnagar in Maharashtra. The two plates, each 9 ¼″ long and 5 ¾″ broad, are joined by a ring bearing an oval seal. The inscription is in Brahmi of the nail-headed type (i.e., the letters are topped with a triangle with its apex pointing downwards) and shows a mixture of northern and southern features. It is different from the usual script of the Vakataka inscriptions, which are written in box-headed Brahmi letters. The language is Sanskrit and the text is mostly in prose, except for the verse on the seal and the imprecatory verse at the end. The translation of the legend on the seal reads: '[This is] the enemy-chastising command of the mother of the *yuvaraja*, the ornament of the Vakatakas, who has attained fortune by inheritance.' The translation of the inscription is as follows:

Seen. Success! Victory has been attained by the Bhagavat! Hail! From Nandivardhana—

There was the *maharaja*, the illustrious Ghatotkacha, the first king of the Guptas. His excellent son [was] the *maharaja*, the illustrious Chandragupta I. His excellent son [was] the *maharajadhiraja*, the illustrious Samudragupta, [who was] born of the *mahadevi Kumaradevi*, [who was] the daughter's son of the Lichchhavi [chief], [and] who performed several sacrifices. His excellent son [is] the *maharajadhiraja*, the illustrious Chandragupta II, graciously favoured by him [i.e., Samudragupta], who is a fervent devotee of the Bhagavat [Vasudeva Krishna], who is a matchless warrior on the earth, who has exterminated all kings, whose fame has tasted the waters of the four oceans, [and] who has donated many thousands of crores of cows and gold [coins].

His daughter, the illustrious Prabhavatigupta of the Dharana *gotra*, born of the illustrious *mahadevi* Kuberanaga, who was [herself] born in the Naga family;—who is the ornament of both families [Guptas and Vakatakas, or Guptas and Nagas]; who is a fervent devotee of the Bhagavat; who was the chief queen of the illustrious Rudrasena II, the *maharaja* of the Vakatakas; who is the mother of the *yuvaraja*, the illustrious Divakarasena;—having announced [her] good health, commands the householders of the village, Brahmanas, and others [residing] in the village of Danduna [situated], in the *ahara* of Supratishtha, to the east of Vilavanaka, to the south of Shirshagrama, to the west of Kadapinjana, and to the north of Sidivivaraka, as follows—

Be it known to you that on the twelfth [lunar] day of the bright [fortnight] of Karttika, we have, for augmenting our own religious merit, donated this village, with libations of water, to the *acharya* Chanalasvamin, who is a devotee of the Bhagavat, as a gift not previously made, after having offered it to the footprints of the Bhagavat. Therefore, you should obey all [his, i.e., the donee's] commands, with proper respect.

And we confer here on [the donee] the following exemptions associated with an *agrahara* granted to *chaturvidya* [Brahmanas], as approved by former kings—[This village is] not to be entered by soldiers and policemen; [it is] exempt from (the obligation to provide) grass, hides as seats, and charcoal [to touring officers]; exempt from [the royal prerogative of] purchasing fermented liquors and digging [salt]; exempt from the [right to] mines and *khadira* trees; exempt from [the obligation to supply] flowers and milk; [it is donated] together with [the right to] hidden treasures and deposits [and] together with major and minor taxes.

Wherefore, this [grant] should be maintained and augmented by future kings. Whoever, disregarding our order, will [himself] cause or make [others] cause the slightest obstruction upon him, when complained against by the Brahmanas, we will inflict punishment, together with a fine.

And there is, on this point [the following] verse sung by Vyasa—'To him who takes away land given by himself or by another, accrues the demerit arising from killing 100,000 cows.'

This charter has been written in the thirteenth [regnal] year. [It has been] engraved by Chakradasa.

Legend on seal:

[This is] the enemy-chastising command of the mother of the *yuvaraja*, the ornament of the Vakatakas, who has attained royal fortune by inheritance.

Source Mirashi, 1963: 8–9

inscription indicates that she gave her daughter Atibhavati in marriage to Ghatotkachagupta (Prabhavatigupta's brother by her Naga mother), who may have ruled briefly after Kumaragupta I.

Pravarasena II is considered author of the *Setubandha*, a Prakrit *kavya* about Rama's conflict with Ravana. Ravana's younger brother Vibhishana has a prominent role in the work and is given several dramatic lines expressing his grief at Ravana's death. Pravarasena was not his father's eldest son, and his two older brothers, Divakarasena and Damodarasena, evidently did not ascend the throne. Hans T. Bakker (2008: 12–14) makes the interesting suggestion that Pravarasena may have put into Vibhishana's mouth sentiments that he might have himself experienced after his success in a violent fratricidal struggle for the throne.

FURTHER DISCUSSION | **Mansar**

During the later part of the reign of Pravarasena II, the Vakataka capital was moved to Pravarapura, which can be identified with Mansar, about 6 km west of Ramagiri. Here, excavations on a mound known as Hidimba Tekdi revealed the remains of what may have been a palace complex.

The site was first noticed and described by T.A. Wellsted in 1934. It was excavated from 1997–98 onwards and excavation reports were published by Amarendra Nath (1994–95), and J.P. Joshi and A.K. Sharma (2001). The discoveries shed valuable light on the Vakataka period.

Three seal were found with the legend 'Pravareshvara.' This refers to the Shiva temple at the site (MNS 3), probably named Pravareshvara after the king. As pointed out by Martine Kropman, these sealings—and for that matter all other sealings found at Mansar—are different from those accompanying the copper plate charters issued by Pravarasena and Prabhavatigupta. The sealings of the copper plate characters use more elaborate formulae stating that the charter represents an order of the king. Here, however, there is simply the name of the temple. All seals and sealings are in the box-headed Vakataka Brahmi script and can be dated to the 5th century. Seal dies with the legends 'pravarasya,' 'shri jaya-vriddhi', and 'shri-prabhaka' were found. There are some fragmentary inscriptions on walls and rocks at the site, mostly found the south side of the Pravareshvara temple. According to the excavators, they are mostly prayer hymns in Sanskrit.

The 'Man of Mansar'

A startling discovery in the foundations of the temple complex was a large clay figure of a man with a hole in his breast. This 'Man of Mansar' seems to represent a novel construction ritual embodying ideas of human sacrifice to ward off evil spirits.

Six Shiva *lingas* on square platforms were found half-way down the southern and western slopes of the hill.

Many broken images, including a Shiva image and a fragment of an Uma-Mahesvara image were found at Mansar. However, it is difficult to identify the rest of the sculptures, partly due to their fragmentary condition and partly because they were not central cult images. A few may represent episodes from the *Ramayana*.

The site also revealed a brick shaft (65 sq.cm). In the upper part, which was filled with earth, a small snake image made of greenish soapstone and some pottery were found. Below this was a false floor, under which was a large pot containing ashes, as well as several small pots. According to Hans Bakker, the location of this shaft between two royal temples and the similarity of this stone snake with the stone snake guarding the entrance to the Kevala Narasimha temple indicate that this may have been a royal funerary monument of the powerful Vakataka queen Prabhavatigupta.

Mansar was an integrated royal residential, ceremonial, and religious centre displaying a complex level of conceptualization, planning, and execution.

Source Bakker, 2004; Kropman in Bakker. (Ed.)., 2008; Bakker in Bakker. (Ed.)., 2008

The death of Pravarasena II may have also been followed by a succession struggle. Narendrasena ultimately emerged successful. His epithet *parama-maheshvara* indicates that the Vaishnava influence, ushered into the Vakataka court by Prabhavatigupta, had waned. The political alliance between the Guptas and Vakatakas became strained during the later part of his reign. The claim made in his son Prithvishena II's inscriptions that Narendrasena's commands were obeyed by the kings of Kosala, Mekala, and Malava seems to be an exaggeration. In fact, his position may have been challenged by his own relatives, perhaps those of the Vatsagulma branch. Narendrasena married a princess of Kuntala, probably a Kadamba princess. Two copper coins that can perhaps be attributed to this king have been found at Paunar.

The last known king of this line was Prithivishena II, whose inscriptions refer to his having twice rescued the sunken fortunes of his family. A copper coin from Paunar seems to belong to his reign. The end of the rule of the Nandivardhana branch of the Vakatakas may have been a result of competition with the Vatsagulma branch or with the Nalas of Dakshina Kosala.

The Sudarshana lake at Junagadh has been mentioned earlier in this book. This lake seems to have acquired a celebrity status, for the name Sudarshana became popular for lakes and reservoirs in the northern Deccan. A reservoir built by Prabhavatigupta's children in their mother's memory was known as Sudarshana. And the Hisse-Borala stone inscription records the making of a tank called Sudarshana by Svamilladeva, an officer of king Devasena.

Archaeological evidence for the Vakatakas includes the remains of a royal ritual center at Ramagiri (Ramtek hill), not far from Nandivardhana. This consisted of seven temples dedicated to Vishnu in his various incarnations, including the Kevala Narasimha temple, which may have been a memorial shrine built in memory of queen Prabhavatigupta by her daughter and son. Relief panels found in the area depict scenes from the life of the epic hero Rama, including the encounter between Sugriva and Vali. The site of Mansar represents Pravarapura.

Vatsagulma, capital of the western Vakataka line, has been identified with modern Washim in Akola district. Sarvasena I (son of Pravarasena I), founder of the Vatsagulma branch, had the title *Dharma-maharaja*. The fact that his lost work, *Hariivijaya*, is lauded by later writers suggests that he was a renowned Prakrit poet. Some of his verses were incorporated into the *Gathasattasai*. The kingdom of Vindhyashakti II, the successor of Sarvasena I, seems to have included the Marathwada region. The Ajanta inscription of the time of Harishena refers to Vindhyashakti II's victory over the Kadambas of Vanavasi who ruled over Kuntala, i.e., north Karnataka. Vakataka interference in the Kadamba kingdom increased during the reigns of subsequent rulers such as Sarvasena II and Devasena. Devasena's daughter was married to the Vishnukundin king Madhavavarman II Janashraya.

The last known king of the Vatsagulma line was Harishena, whose Thalner plates were issued in his third regnal year. He expanded Vakataka power southwards towards Ashmaka in the Godavari valley and northwards towards the borders of Avanti. Many of the Ajanta caves were executed during his reign, although none of his own inscriptions have been found there. The inscriptions in Cave 16 and the nearby Ghatotkacha cave were inscribed at the behest of his minister Varahadeva, and the one in Cave 17 apparently by one of his vassals. The Ajanta cave inscription of Varahadeva credits Harishena with defeating or surpassing the rulers of Kuntala, Avanti, Kalinga, Kosala, Trikuta, Lata, and Andhra. These inscriptions provide several details about the political history of the Vatsagulma branch.

Other contemporary dynasties

The political history of *c.* 300–600 CE includes conflict and war as well as political and matrimonial alliances. Several polities that emerged in different parts of the subcontinent were absorbed into multiple hierarchies of power consisting of paramount and subordinate rulers.

The historical phase in the North-east began in the 4th century CE (see Sarma and Hazarika, 2014: 50–51). In the Brahmaputra valley, the kingdom of Kamarupa emerged in lower Assam and the Davaka kingdom in central Assam. Both are mentioned in Samudragupta's Allahabad pillar inscription. Kamarupa gradually expanded up to the Bay of Bengal. Other small principalities emerged in the Dhansiri-Doyang valley and the Sadiya area.

During the period of Gupta and Vakataka ascendency and decline, areas like Odisha and Andhra saw the beginnings of a sustained process of state formation. In the 4th century CE, Odisha was divided into several small principalities, some of which owed allegiance to the Guptas. Dynasties such as the Pitribhaktas, Matharas, and Vasishthas rose to power in southern Odisha. The 5th century saw the rise of the Eastern Gangas in south Kalinga. These kings were probably a branch of the Western Gangas and were migrants from Karnataka. Their capital was Kalinganagara, identified with Mukhalingam in Ganjam district. In northern and central Odisha, inscriptions refer to the rule of dynasties such as the Vigrahas and Mudgalas/Manas and feudatories of Shashanka (a king of Bengal) such as Shubhakirti and the Dattas. The Nala, Sharabhapuriya, and Panduvamshi lineages established themselves successively in the area of Dakshina Kosala, which included western Odisha and eastern Madhya Pradesh.

In the Deccan, coins and inscriptions mention various rulers and chieftains. A few inscriptions found at Banavasi mention the Chutu kings, who are held to represent the Kuntala branch of the Satavahanas. The Bhojas were probably originally based in the Berar region. A branch of this family seems to have migrated to the Goa region in the Konkan, as several Bhoja copper plate grants, dated the 7th century CE on palaeographic grounds, have been found in this area. The Traikutakas were located on the western coast between Kanheri and Surat and adjacent areas, which were previously under the control of Abhira rulers. Inscriptions and coins reveal the names of three Traikutaka kings who can be assigned to the 5th century. The Kalachuris came into prominence in the second half of the 6th century in northern Maharashtra, Gujarat, and parts of Malwa.

The dynasties of the western Deccan included the early Kadambas, Banas, and Alupas. The Kadambas replaced the Chutus in the Banavasi area. The Kadamba king Mayurasharman is said to have been a Brahmana who became a Kshatriya and took the name Mayuravarman. In the Mysore region, the western Gangas came to the fore from the later half of the 4th century CE. The founder of the line was Konkanivarman, with his capital at Kolar. The middle of the 6th century saw the Chalukyas of Badami rise to power in the Karnataka area.

In the eastern Deccan, in the Guntur area of Andhra Pradesh, there is evidence of the rule of a lineage that traced its descent from an eponymous ancestor named Ananda. The Shalankayanas had their stronghold between the Krishna and Godavari deltas, with their capital at Vengi. The Ikshvakus (discussed in Chapter 8) were based in Vijayapuri in the lower Krishna valley. The Vishnukundins seem to have originally been based in the Kurnool area south of the Krishna and ruled in Vengi between *c.* 440 and 600 CE.

The Pallavas seem to have been initially based in the Krishna valley and gradually moved southwards, extending their rule over Tondaimandalam, the area between the north Penner and Vellar. They established their capital at Kanchipuram. Some Prakrit and Sanskrit stone and copper plate inscriptions of kings of this dynasty have been assigned on palaeographic grounds to the period between the 3rd and 7th centuries CE. The Prakrit inscriptions mention several kings including Shivaskandavarman, who seems to have ruled in the early 4th century. Vishnugopa was one of the kings of Dakshinapatha defeated by Samudragupta. The Sanskrit inscriptions mention several other kings such as Virakurcha, Skandashishya, Simhavarman I, and Simhavarman II. From the mid-6th century, Tamil started being used in Pallava inscriptions. The Pallankoyil grant of Simhavarman is the oldest known copper plate grant which uses Sanskrit for the *prashasti* portion and Tamil for the details of the grant. Towards the end of the 6th century, Simhavarman inaugurated the age of the great political expansion of the Pallavas.

Inscriptions of the Pandyas, Pallavas, and Chalukyas refer to a period of political and social dislocation caused by a people called the Kalabhras. The Kalabhras have been variously identified with the Muttaraiyar rulers of Kodumbalur, a people of Karnata, Kalappalars belonging to the Vellala community, or Kalavar chieftains mentioned in Sangam literature. The Kalabhras seem to have been a war-like clan that dominated the political scene of the Tamil country for a few centuries, but were defeated in the later 6th century by the Pandyas and Pallavas. Various aspects of the Pallava period will be discussed in Chapter 10.

The Royal Ideology and Administration of the Gupta and Vakataka Kingdoms

From *c.* 300 CE onwards, political hierarchies can be identified by the titles of rulers, which reflect relations of paramountcy and subordination. Gupta inscriptions reflect changes in the vocabulary of political relationships and the emergence of certain epithets and expressions that remained fairly stable over the next few centuries. From Kumaragupta's reign onwards, the three titles that expressed the claim to political paramountcy were *parama-daivata* (supreme worshipper of a god or the gods), *parama-bhattaraka* (supreme lord), and *maharajadhiraja* (great king of kings). References to subordinate kings bowing their heads at the lotus feet of their overlord became commonplace. The pecking order was fluid. Further, 'subordinate kings' were often powerful in their own realms; although they acknowledged their overlords, in their *prashsastis*, they made grand statements about their own power and achievements.

Some historians have suggested that the Gupta kings claimed divine status. However, what we see is an attempt to exalt the king's status by comparing and connecting him with the gods, rather than an assertion of the king's divinity. Inscriptions associate kings with the gods in various ways. Chandragupta II and Kumaragupta have the epithet *parama-bhagavata*, announcing them as the greatest worshippers of Vasudeva-Krishna. Double entendre, associating a great king with a great god, is expressed visually at Udayagiri, and was also favored in inscriptions and texts. In the Gupta empire, coins functioned as an eloquent medium of royal communication, whose outreach was much greater than that of the royal *prashastis*. We often see the king with a halo around his head, in three-quarter or profile view. He is shown either with a slender figure or with pronounced musculature, the latter often found on coins where he is portrayed as a warrior or shown killing a powerful animal. The obverse of the coins usually bears the name of the king, and the reverse his *biruda* or epithet. Numismatic portrayals match the epigraphic descriptions of Gupta kings as all-rounders, advertising them as great warriors with extraordinary physical strength and prowess, hunters and killers of powerful animals, performers of great sacrifices, ones who had achieved great fame, favoured by the goddess Shri, wielders of the rod of justice, and devotees of deities. The *garuda* banner (the emblem of the god Vishnu) appears on many coins. The goddess Lakshmi unites ideas of fertility, wealth, and kingship. She appears standing, sitting, walking, and holding a lotus, cornucopia, and/or diadem; in some cases, she sprinkles coins. A coin of Skandagupta has an interesting variation: The king stands with a female figure next to him; the fact that she is holding a lotus suggests that she is Lakshmi herself.

Vakataka kings usually have the epithet *maharaja* (great king), and on occasion, *samrat* (emperor). Several Vakataka kings are given the title Dharma-maharaja (great king of *dharma*). Kings are eulogized as having established the Krita *yuga* (the most perfect age) on earth. Apart from describing themselves as Brahmanas, the Brahmanical stamp in Vakataka inscriptions can be seen in references to their performance of grand Vedic sacrifices, often more than once. Pravarasena I is described as having performed four horse sacrifices, seven Soma sacrifices, as well as others such as the *agnishtoma*, *aptoryama*, *ukthya*, *shodasin*, *brihaspatisava*, and *vajapeya*. The Puranas refer to his having made liberal gifts to Brahmanas at his performance of the *vajapeya* sacrifice.

There is also a declaration of sectarian affiliation, Shaiva or Vaishnava. The king is projected as the foremost devotee of a particular god—*parama-maheshvara* (foremost devotee of Shiva) or *parama-bhagavata* (foremost devotee of *Vasudeva-Krishna*). This is

FURTHER DISCUSSION | **The Varaha relief at Udayagiri**

A group of caves in the Udayagiri hills near Vidisha in Madhya Pradesh represent a religious complex created during the reign of the Gupta king Chandragupta II (*c*. 376–413/415 CE). While the centre of the Gupta empire was located far away, perhaps at Pataliputra (Patna) or Prayaga (Prayagraj), military campaigns brought the Guptas to Central India.

An imposing scene carved in relief in a shallow cave represents the god Vishnu in his Varaha (boar) incarnation. In the central part of the niche, we see Varaha rescuing the earth goddess Prithvi from the waters. The god is shown with the broad, muscular body of a man and the head of a boar. He exudes strength and masculine power. His right hand is placed on his hip and his left one on his bent knee. A massive garland is flung around his body. The tiny Prithvi clings to his tusks. Vishnu-Varaha's left foot rests on the hoods of a *naga* (snake deity), who gazes up at him with his hands folded in obeisance. Behind the *naga* is the broken torso of a human figure. The god is flanked by rows of sages and celestial beings, and the river goddesses Ganga and Yamuna.

In the 5th century, water cascading down from a cistern on top of the rocky outcrop and made its way through a central path cut into the rock cluster all the way down to the cave floor, where it lapped the base of the magnificent image of Vishnu-Varaha raising the earth up from the ocean.

There are many different interpretations of the Udayagiri relief. Does the human figure at the bottom of the scene represent the Gupta king Samudragupta or Chandragupta II, or a feudatory ruler, presented as a devotee of the great god? Or does the powerful Varaha represent the king? Or is there deliberate ambiguity, with Varaha representing both god and king?

Although Vishnu in his various forms dominates Udayagiri, other Hindu deities (Shiva, Durga Mahishasuramardini, Ganesha) are also represented, and there is a Jaina shrine as well. An inscription refers to the excavation of a shrine of Vishnu by a feudatory of Chandragupta II. Another records the gift of a cave dedicated to Shiva by Virasena, a resident of Pataliputra and a minister of the king. Not far from Udayagiri, traces of the Guptas are found at the Buddhist monastery complex at Sanchi, where Chandragupta II made a grant of land and money along with his military commander Amrakardava.

The Udayagiri caves display the crafting of a powerful, carefully conceptualized, and executed statement in image and word, expressing the arrival of a bold new vision of kingship entwined with a new kind of religiosity. The Gupta inscription at Sanchi indicates that in spite of these developments, the donative policy of political elites continued to be multidirectional.

Source Upinder Singh, 2017: 177–79

accompanied by the idea that the king had won royal fortune through the grace of that particular god.

As mentioned earlier, Pravarasena built a Shiva temple which was named Pravareshvara after himself. This practice of naming Shiva *lingas* and temples after donors took off in this period and continued thereafter. Nevertheless, although most of the Vakataka kings were worshippers of Shiva, the remains from Vakataka sites such as Ramagiri and Mansar reveal Vaishnava elements as well.

In the Vakataka kingdom too, inscriptions reflect a vocabulary of political hierarchy, and a subordinate king or feudatory is routinely described as one who meditates at the feet of his overlord. But hierarchies were not rigid or immutable. While the Vakataka king stood at the apex of his kingdom, the *prashastis* of subordinate rulers often imitate the phraseology of their overlords and sometimes outdo them. For instance, in the Bamhani plates of the feudatory Bharatabala, Bharatabala is given much more elaborate and copious praise than his Vakataka overlord. At Ajanta and in the Ghatotkacha cave nearby, wealthy, and powerful ministers such as Varahadeva made lavish religious endowments. In fact, while the Vakataka rulers directed their patronage toward Brahmanas and temples, other members of the political elite patronized Buddhist monasteries.

The imagery and remains at Udayagiri and Mansar articulate a new vision of political power, in which kingship and sectarian religion were united. But the sectarianism that emerged in the political sphere accommodated a variety of elements—a situation that is often referred to as one of 'tolerance', but which should rather be described as an inclusive sectarianism which acknowledged the diversity of religious beliefs within the kingdom.

Gupta seals and inscriptions mention official ranks and designations, whose precise meaning is often uncertain. The term *kumaramatya* occurs on six Vaishali seals, which suggests that this title represented a high-ranking officer associated with an office (*adhikarana*) of his own. The designation '*amatya*' occurs on several Bhita seals, and the *kumaramatya* seems to have been pre-eminent among *amatya*s and equivalent in status to princes of royal blood. *Kumaramatyas* were variously attached to the king, crown prince, revenue department, or a province. One of the Vaishali seals refers to a *kumaramatya* who seems to have been in charge of the maintenance of the sacred coronation tank of the Lichchhavis.

Individuals of the rank of *kumaramatya* sometimes had additional designations as well, and such ranks could be hereditary. For example, Harishena, composer of the Allahabad *prashasti*, was a *kumaramatya*, *sandhivigrahika*, and *mahadandanayaka*, and was the son of *mahadandanayaka* Dhruvabhuti. The Karamdanda stone inscription of Kumaragupta mentions two generations of *mantri-kumaramatyas* who served two generations of kings—Shikharasvamin who served Chandragupta II, and Shikharasvamin's son Prithivishena, who served Kumaragupta I. Prithivishena is subsequently described as *mahabaladhikrita*.

The Gupta empire was divided into provinces known as *deshas* or *bhukti*s, administered by governors who were usually designated as *uparikas*. The *uparika* was directly appointed by the king and, in turn, frequently appointed the head of the district administration and the district town board. A Vaishali seal refers to the office of the *uparika* of Tirabhukti. One of the Damodarpur copper plates (which refers to Gupta era years 124 and 129) describes Chiratadatta, the *uparika* of Pundravardhana *bhukti*, as appointed by the king (Kumaragupta I). It further states that Chiratadatta appointed *kumaramatya* Vetravarman as head of the *adhishthana adhikarana* (district office) of Kotivarsha. Another Damodarpur plate (of unknown date) tells us that Kumaragupta I appointed *maharaja* Jayadatta as *uparika* of the same province, and that Jayadatta in turn appointed the *ayuktaka* Bhandaka as head of the *adhisthana adhikarana* of Kotivarsha. The Damodarpur plate of the reign of Vishnugupta, dated in year 224 of the Gupta era, mentions an *uparika* whose name is lost, but who has the epithets *maharaja*, *bhattaraka*, and *rajaputra* and who appointed Svayambhudeva as *vishayapati*. It also refers to the *uparika* as carrying on the administration 'with the enjoyment of [the rule] consisting of elephants, horses, and soldiers', indicating his control over the military machinery as well. The fact that the *uparika* had the title *maharaja* in three of the Damodarpur plates indicates his high status and rank in the administrative hierarchy. The Eran pillar inscription of Budhagupta, dated Gupta year 165, refers to *maharaja* Surashmichandra as a *lokapala* governing the land between the Kalindi and Narmada rivers. *Lokapala* here seems to refer to a provincial governor.

Saurashtra was an important province of the Gupta empire. Skandagupta's Junagadh inscription provides details about the Sudarshana lake that had been built during the Maurya period and repaired in Rudradaman's time. It states that Skandagupta appointed Parnadatta as *goptri* (governor) of Surashtra (Saurashtra). Parnadatta in turn appointed his son Chakrapalita to govern the city where this inscription was inscribed. In Gupta

PRIMARY SOURCES | **An ancient panchayat?**

Eight inscriptions at the Buddhist monastic site of Sanchi in Central India belong to the period *c.* 300–600 CE. Of these, one is an 11-line prose epigraph inscribed on the outer side of the eastern gateway of Stupa 1. The inscription is damaged in places and there are disagreements among scholars regarding its reading and interpretation. It is dated in year 93 (of the Gupta era), i.e., 412–13 CE, and refers to the reign of *maharajadhiraja* Chandragupta, mentioned in Line 7 as 'Devaraja'. This king was no doubt Chandragupta II.

The inscription opens with a eulogy of the *sangha* of the *mahavihara* of Kakanadabota. It goes on to introduce Amrakarddava, son of Undana, who belonged to the Sukuli country and was apparently a military commander of Chandragupta II. The incription records the gift of a piece of land (perhaps a village) named Ishvaravasaka and 25 *dinaras*. The gift was made in perpetuity. Half of the endowment—this seems to refer to the income from the land—was to support the feeding of five monks and the maintenance of a lamp in the *ratnagriha* (literally, jewel house, apparently a shrine), on behalf of Chandragupta. The other half of the income—this appears to refer to the interest on the monetary gift—was to support the feeding of five monks and the maintenance of a lamp in the *ratnagriha* on behalf of Amrakarddava himself.

There is disagreement concerning the interpretation of Lines 5 and 6. According to N. G. Majumdar, these indicate that the land was bought from certain members of the royal household or family (*rajakula*) named Maja, Sharabhanga, and Amrarata. Fleet thought likewise. On the other hand, Chhabra and Gai understood '*rajakula*' as a palace and interpret Maja, Sharabhanga, and Amrarata as names of palaces occupied by Chandragupta II during his military campaigns. According to this interpretation, Ishvaravasaka was bought from the proceeds of the sale of these palaces. D. C. Sircar accepted the standard meaning of *rajakula* as royal family, but added that it seems as though one half of the money and the price of the *vasaka* (which he tentatively translated as 'house-site') was paid by Amrakarddava and the other half by his friends. Chhabra and Gai suggested that since the income from the land and the interest on the money were supposed to support identical activities, the two gifts must have been of similar value.

Line 6 also contains the phrase *pancha-mandalya pranipatya*. Fleet ammended *mandalya* to *mandalyam* and saw herein a reference to Amrakarddava having prostrated himself before the village panchayat before making the gift. N. G. Majumdar retained the phrase *pancha-mandalya pranipatya*, and translated it as 'having prostrated himself together with the group of five', adding that he was not sure about the meaning. According to D. R. Bhandarkar and G. S. Gai, Fleet's amended reading and interpretation of this line do not make sense, because if the *pancha-mandali* was indeed a village body, one would expect this word to appear in the accusative and not in the locative case. They suggest that the phrase in question refers to Amrakarddava prostrating himself (prior to making the gift) so that five parts of his body—forehead, elbows, waist, knees, and feet—rested on the ground.

What is to be made of these controversies? The interpretation of *pancha-mandali* as referrring to a panchayat-type village body consisting of five individuals seems more plausible that the other suggestions. The reference to Amrakarddava prostrating himself before or saluting this body before making this gift fits in well with the details of several other land grant inscriptions of this period, which reflect the role of local-level administrative departments and functionaries in land transactions. Likewise, the reference to the land being bought—either from or by certain members of a royal family, prior to being gifted—is also in tune with several land grant charters. Perhaps the emperor Chandragupta was associated with the grant of land and Amrakarddava with the monetary gift. On the other hand, while Chandragupta may have taken direct initiative in making the gift, it is also possible that Amrakarddava was simply indicating his devotion to his king by expressing a desire that the latter should share in the religious merit that would accrue from this pious gift.

Although the interpretation of crucial parts of this inscription remains problematic, it should be noted that this is the only known record of a land grant made in favour of the Sanchi establishment.

Source Chhabra and Gai. (Eds.)., 1981: 251

year 136 (i.e., 455–56 CE), the Sudarshana lake burst its embankments due to torrential rain and Chakrapalita had the breach repaired after two years' work in the year 137 (i.e., 456–57 CE). The inscription thus, reflects the practice of the delegation of official responsibilities from father to son, and the role of the provincial government in initiating the repair of waterworks.

The provinces of the Gupta empire were divided into districts known as *vishayas*, under officers known as *vishayapatis*. The *vishayapati* seems to have been generally appointed by the provincial governor. However, the Indore copper plate inscription dated in Gupta year 146, during the reign of king Skandagupta, suggests that this was not always the case. It describes the *vishayapati* Sharvanaga who was governing Antaravedi (which referred either to the area around Indore or Kanauj) as being favoured by the king, which suggests that he owed his appointment to him. It may be noted that the Eran pillar inscription of the time of the Huna ruler Toramana refers to Airakina *vishaya*, indicating an element of continuity in administrative divisions in post-Gupta times.

Significant details of district-level administration in Bengal are reflected in the Damodarpur copper plates dated in Gupta year 124 during the reign of Kumaragupta I. These record orders regarding certain land transactions issued to village officials by the *adhikarana* of Kotivarsha *vishaya*. The *adhishthana adhikarana* of Kotivarsha had five members—the *uparika* or *vishayapati* (who was the head), the *nagara-sreshthin* (chief merchant/banker), *sarthavaha* (chief caravan trader), *prathama-kulika* (chief artisan or merchant), and *prathama-kayastha* (chief scribe or an officer in charge of revenue collection). This indicates that the *vishayapati* was assisted in his administrative duties by certain prominent members of the town.

Administrative units below district level included clusters of settlements known variously as *vithi*, *patta*, *bhumi*, *pathaka*, and *petha*. There are references to officials known as *ayuktakas* and *vithi-mahattaras*. At the village level, villagers chose functionaries such as the *gramika* and *gramadhyaksha*, and village elders also had an important role to play in various matters. The Damodarpur copper plate of the reign of Budhagupta (of Gupta year 163) mentions an *ashtakula-adhikarana* (a board of eight members) headed by the *mahattara*. *Mahattara* has a range of meanings including village elder, village headman, and head of a family or community. The Sanchi inscription of the time of Chandragupta II mentions the *pancha-mandali*, which may have been a corporate village body.

The Gupta king was assisted by a council of *mantrins* (ministers). The Allahabad *prashasti* refers to an assembly or council, presumably of ministers—known as the *sabha*. The various high-ranking functionaries included the *sandhivigrahika* or *mahasandhivigrahika* (minister for peace and war), who seems to have been a high-ranking officer in charge of the conduct of relations with other states, including initiating war and concluding alliances and treaties. Harishena, composer of the Allahabad *prashasti*, was (among other things) a *sandhivigrahika*. An Udayagiri inscription describes Virasena Shaba, a *sandhivigrahika* of Chandragupta II, as a poet. These two inscriptions indicate that officers who discharged the job of drafting treaties had much more than just basic skills of drafting and composition.

Several seals and inscriptions of *c*. 300–600 CE mention the names of *dandanayakas* and *mahadandanayakas*, who were high-ranking judicial or military officers. One of the Vaishali seals mentions a *mahadandanayaka* named Agnigupta. The Allahabad *prashasti* refers to three *mahadandanayakas*. The fact that the composer of the *prashasti*, Harishena, a *mahadandanayaka* (with the additional titles of *sandhivigrahika* and *kumaramatya*), was the son of *mahadandanayaka* and *khadyatapakita* Dhruvabhuti, suggests the hereditary nature of such important administrative posts. The inscription also mentions *mahadandanayaka* Tilakabhatta as the executor of the inscription. A Bhita seal mentions a *mahadandanayaka* named Vishnurakshita. This official also had the designation *mahashvapati* (commander of the cavalry), clearly indicating military functions, and he is said to have appointed the *kumaramatya*.

Seals and inscriptions mention other military designations such as *baladhikrita* and *mahabaladhikrita* (commander-in-chief of the army). A Vaishali seal mentions Yakshavatsa, a *bhatashvapati* (commander of infantry and cavalry). The standard term *senapati* does not occur in Gupta inscriptions, but is mentioned in some Vakataka epigraphs. A Vaishali seal mentions the *ranabhandagaradhikarana*—office of the military storehouse. Another Vaishali seal mentions the *adhikarana* (office) of the *dandapashika*, which may have been a district-level police office.

The officials connected specifically with the royal establishment included the *mahapratihara* (chief of the palace guards) and the *khadyatapakita* (superintendent of the royal kitchen). A Vaishali seal mentions a person named Vinayashura, described as both a *mahapratihara* and a *taravara*. The top layer of the administrative structure also included *amatyas* and *sachivas*, who were executive officers in charge of various departments. The system of espionage included spies known as *dutakas*.

The *ayuktakas* were another cadre of high-ranking officers. It is possible that there is some similarity between their functions and those of the *yuktas* of the Ashokan inscriptions and *Arthashastra*. The Allahabad *prashasti* describes Samudragupta's *ayuktakas* as ceaselessly engaged in restoring wealth to the many conquered kings. One of the Damodarpur plates mentions an *ayuktaka* who was also a *bhandaka* and head of the district town administration of Kotivarsha *vishaya*. A Vaishali seal mentions the *adhikarana* of the *vinayashitisthapaka* of Tirabhukti. The term *vinayashitisthapaka* has been translated as 'one who maintains moral and social discipline', but the precise functions of this officer are unclear.

Vakataka inscriptions offer comparatively less information regarding administrative structure. The Vakataka empire was divided into provinces called *rashtras* or *rajyas*. For instance, the Pakkana *rashtra* is mentioned in the Belora plates, the Bhojakata *rashtra* in the Chammaka plates, the Varuchha *rajya* in the Pandhurna plates, and the Arammi *rajya* in the Dudia and Padhurna plates (all these inscriptions belong to the reign of Pravarasena II). The *rajyas* were administered by governors known as *rajyadhikritas*. Provinces were further subdivided into *vishayas*, which were in turn divided into *aharas* and *bhogas* or *bhuktis*. Vakataka grants refer to an officer called the *sarvadhyaksha*, who appointed and directed subordinate officers known as *kulaputras*. The duties of the latter included the maintenance of law and order. The *chhatras* and *bhatas*, usually understood as referring to irregular and regular troops, represented the coercive arm of the state. They wandered about the countryside, extracting taxes due to the state, and may have also been responsible for maintaining law and order. The *rajuka*, known in Maurya sources as an officer connected with revenue assessment, is mentioned in the Indore plates of Pravarasena II as the writer of the land grant charter. The *senapati* and *dandanayaka* were military officers. Interestingly, the Vakataka charters are described as drafted in the *senapati*'s office. Inscriptions belonging to various years of the reign of Pravarasena II mention different persons as *senapati*. This either indicates changes in the occupancy of the post, or that several individuals had this designation.

An inscription outside Cave 16 at Ajanta records the gift of the cave to the Buddhist *sangha* by Varahadeva, a minister of the Vatsagulma branch of the Vakatakas. The first 20 verses give the genealogy of the reigning king Harishena. The inscription also describes Varahadeva and his father Hastibhoja who served as minister under Harishena and his father Devasena respectively. Hastibhoja is described as an abode of merit, as having a broad and stout chest, obliging, loving, affable, and as one who destroyed the allies of his enemies. He is said to have ruled his people well, being as dear to them as their father, mother, and friend. King Devasena is said to have entrusted the care of government to him and devoted himself to the enjoyment of pleasures. Varahadeva is said to have ruled the land well, possessing the virtues of liberality, forgiveness, and generosity. An inscription in the Ghatotkacha cave at Guwada, 11 miles west of Ajanta, records the dedication of the cave by a person whose name is lost, but who, going by other details, seems none other than Varahadeva. The inscription describes members of his family as excellent Brahmanas known as Valluras, after their native home. Vallura has been tentatively identified with a village called Velur in Karimnagar district of Karnataka. There is a long genealogy and eulogy of the family, and it seems that as many as nine generations served as ministers under the Vakatakas.

The inscriptions of feudatories of the Vakatakas refer to some additional administrative terms. The *rahasika*, mentioned in the Bamhani plates of Bharatabala, a ruler of Mekala, seems to have been a confidential officer attached to the king. The same inscription mentions the *gramakuta* or village headman. The *devavarika* (perhaps the same as *dauvarika*) may have been the head of the village police, while the *gandakas* may have been the equivalents of the *bhatas* of Vakataka grants. The *dronagrakanayaka* may have been in charge of the administrative unit known as the *dronagraka* or *dronamukha*.

Revenue Resources of States

The *Narada Smriti* (18.48) asserts that subjects owe the king revenue as a reward for the protection he provides them. Kamandaka's *Nitisara* 5.84–85 advises the king to be like a florist or milkman in matters of taxation. Just as cows have to be tended at certain times and milked at others, and just as a florist takes care of his plants and sprinkles water on them, besides cutting them—similarly the king should help his subjects with money and provisions at certain times and tax them at others. However, Kamandaka warns sternly that royal officials who become rich through ill-gotten gains should be bled like a surgeon bleeds a swelling abcess.[2]

The *Nitisara*, like the *Arthashastra* before it, emphasizes the importance of the royal treasury and mentions various sources of revenue. The many ambitious military campaigns of kings like Samudragupta must have been financed through revenue surpluses. Gupta inscriptions reveal some details about the revenue department. The *akshapataladhikrita* was the keeper of royal records. The spurious Gaya copper plate inscription refers to Gopasvamin, the *akshapataladhikrita* of Samudragupta, as having ordered the copper plate to be inscribed. A number of *pustapalas* or record keepers maintained records of land transfers. Gupta inscriptions mention fiscal terms such as *kara*, *bali*, *udranga*, *uparikara*, and *hiranya*. Vakataka inscriptions mention the terms *klipta* and *upaklipta*; they also refer to *vishti* or forced labour.

There is a problem in interpreting the precise meaning of some of the fiscal terms mentioned in inscriptions (see Jha, 1967; Maity, [1957] 1970: 74–95; Sircar, 1966a). *Bhaga* was a term used for the king's grain share, which the *Narada Smriti* describes as 1/6th of the agricultural produce. This is supported indirectly by the Paharpur and Baigram plates, which state that 1/6th of the merit accruing from a donation, probably the equivalent of his standard grain share, would go to the king. But as mentioned earlier, 1/6th was a conventional figure, and there is no information regarding the actual amount realized by ancient states from farmers.

Inscriptions of the Guptas and other contemporary dynasties often mention the *bhoga* and *kara* along with *bhaga*. *Bhoga* may have referred to the periodical supplies of fruit, firewood, flowers, etc. that villagers were obliged to give to the king. *Kara* was a generic term for taxes. However, it has also been variously interpreted as a specific tax—a property tax, an emergency tax levied on traders, artisans, and others, an agrarian tax over and above the king's customary share, or a periodical tax levied on villagers. *Bali* is known from earlier times. It has been interpreted as a generic term for taxes, the king's grain share (i.e., the same as *bhaga*), a tax on the area of land, or a religious cess. The *uparikara* may have been a tax imposed on farmers without any proprietory rights in the soil, a tax on termporary tenants, or an additional cess. The meaning of *udranga* is similarly uncertain. It may have been a tax on permanent tenants, or it may have been related to *dranga*, which, according to the *Rajatarangini*, was a watch station. By extension, the *udranga* may have been a sort of police tax levied on a district for the maintenance of the local police station. Yet another interpretation connects *udranga* to *udaka*, suggesting it may have been a water tax. *Hiranya* is generally understood as the king's share of the agricultural produce in cash. It may have been a levy in addition to the standard tax realized in grain or its cash equivalent.

Apart from these frequently occurring terms, there are certain others whose meaning is even less certain. These include *vata-bhuta*, which, it has been suggested, may refer to cesses for the maintenance of rites performed for the winds and spirits. The term *halirakara* has been interpreted as a plough tax, or alternatively as an extra tax imposed on the area that could be cultivated by one plough in a single season.

Urban sources of revenue included *shulka* or tolls. The Bihar stone pillar inscription of Skandagupta refers to an official called the *shaulkika*—collector of *shulka*. Vakataka

---

[2] In the discussion in this and following sections, although the main focus is on the sources of the period *c*. 300–600 CE, there is occasional reference to earlier and later sources, in order to provide a longer term perspective on certain issues.

inscriptions mention the terms *klipta* and *upaklipta*. According to D. C. Sircar, the former may have meant a purchase tax or a sale tax, while Maity suggests it may not refer to a tax at all but to some royal right over land. The *upaklipta* may have referred to some additional or minor taxes.

Sources of state income included royal monopolies on treasure trove, deposits, mines, and salt reserves. Villagers were obliged to provide royal officers on tour with grass for animals, hides for seats, and charcoal for cooking. Villages made into *agraharas* were exempted from such obligations.

Land Ownership

The debate regarding the ownership of land in ancient and early medieval India has focused on assessing the evidence for communal/corporate ownership (i.e., ownership in the hands of the village community), royal ownership, and private ownership (Maity, [1967] 1970: 19–33). Although the Dharmashastra texts have a great deal to say about property, their opinions on land rights vary considerably, and contradictory statements are sometimes made within the same text. Certain texts suggest that the village community had an important say in land-related matters, even if this did not amount to full-fledged ownership.

A few earlier sources assert the indivisibility of landed property, i.e., that it could not be divided. The *Mimamsa Sutra* of Jaimini (6.7.3) states that the earth is common to all and even an emperor cannot give away all his land. This opinion was confirmed several centuries later by Shabarasvamin (4th century CE) in his commentary on the *Mimamsa Sutra*. A few inscriptions can also be cited to support the idea that in ancient India, land was considered the property of the village community.

However, much more evidence can be cited to support royal ownership. For the earlier period, there are the references in Greek texts that quote Megasthenes as saying that all land in India was owned by the king, and Kautilya's reference to some land (known as *sita* land) owned by the king. While the intimate connection between the king and the earth is frequently invoked in ancient Indian texts, there are several more specific statements in the Dharmashastra that can be used to argue that the king owned the land and that this was considered the justification for taxation. The law books of the Gupta period reflect the growth of royal power and authority, and make a stronger assertion of the king's ownership of the soil, but also reveal some ambivalence. The *Katyayana Smriti* (verse 16) states that the king is the owner of the soil (*bhu-svamin*) and hence can claim 1/4th of the farmers' produce. However, the very next verse states that because they dwell on the land, human beings are declared to be its owners. The *Narada Smriti* (11.27, 42) gives the king the right to divest the peasant of his field and house, but at the same time, advises him not to resort to such drastic measures as these are the householder's means of subsistence. An unequivocal assertion of the royal ownership of land is found in certain later sources such as a commentary on the *Narasimha Purana*, which states that land belonged to the king and not to the cultivators, and in Bhattasvamin's 12th century commentary on the *Arthashastra*, which seems to justify taxation on the grounds of royal ownership of land. On the other hand, from early times, there was a school of thought that rejected the idea of the king's ownership of land and declared taxation to be the king's wages for the protection he provided to his subjects. Jaimini and Shabara were the strongest proponents of this view.

Inscriptions, especially land grants, have also been cited as proof of the royal ownership of land. However, although land grants indicate that the state or the king owned *some* land, they do not necessarily indicate that this applied to *all* land. That the king was not the absolute owner of all land is also indicated by inscriptions recording the purchase of land by kings for the purpose of pious donation.

As pointed out in Chapter 6, in North India, the institution of private property in land emerged in about the 6th century BCE. This institution was well entrenched by *c.* 300–600 CE. The law books of this period discuss and distinguish between the issues of possession, ownership, and legal title to property in general and land in particular. Laws regarding the partition, sale, and mortgage of land are laid down. Literary references to various types of private land transactions are matched by those from inscriptions. Numerous inscriptions record the purchase of land by individuals for the purpose of donations to Brahmanas or religious institutions.

How can all this evidence be reconciled? Epigraphic references suggesting corporate or communal ownership are very few and belong to an early period. And although the village community—or at least its dominant section—may have had a say in land-related matters, this did not amount to corporate or communal ownership. Sources from *c*. 300 CE onwards suggest that the king was considered the lord of all the land in a general sense, but not the 'owner' in the legal sense. Private property in land existed under the umbrella of a somewhat vague or largely theoretical notion of ultimate royal control, and the king's claims did not preclude the rights of private individuals. Some tracts of land were under direct royal control. Private ownership prevailed outside these tracts.

It should also be remembered that notions of ownership in ancient and early medieval India were not necessarily identical to modern Western ones, and the sources sometimes suggest a hierarchy of land rights rather than exclusive or absolute ownership rights. For instance, one of the Ashrafpur plates (7th/8th century CE) from Bangladesh speaks of a plot of land that was enjoyed by a person named Sharvantara, cultivated by Shikhara and others, and donated by the king to a Buddhist monk named Sanghamitra.

The Dharmashastra views on property-related issues have been discussed in detail by Maity ([1957] 1970). The *Brihaspati Smriti* (7.23) mentions seven ways of acquiring immovable property—through learning, purchase, mortgage, valour, marriage, inheritance, and succession to the property of an heirless kinsman. The *Narada Smriti* (1.51) lists inheritance, gifts made through love, and gifts brought into the home by the wife as the three sorts of wealth for all, but goes on to distinguish (1.52–54) between different ways in which members of the four *varnas* acquire wealth through their pursuit of their specific vocations. Both the *Narada* and *Brihaspati Smriti*s state that long and uninterrupted possession is a ground for claiming ownership of property. The *Narada Smriti* (11.24) states that if the owner of a piece of land is unavailable, dead, or unable to cultivate his land, a stranger who tills the land without being opposed by the owner should be allowed to keep the produce. According to the *Brihaspati Smriti* (7.27–28), if a person has enjoyed unopposed and uninterrupted possession of land for 30 years, it cannot be taken away from him and the ownership rights of the original owner stand null and void. However, this does not apply if the person who is enjoying the property is a friend or relative of the original owner. Nor does a king, minister, or learned Brahmana become legal owner of property simply due to long-term possession (Brihaspati 7.44-46). According to both the *Narada Smriti* (1.91) and *Brihaspati Smriti* (7. 54), if property has been enjoyed by three generations and has passed into the fourth, legal title becomes unnecessary and it cannot be taken away.

However, these very texts contain statements to the effect that long-term possession does not give a person legal rights over property. The *Yajnavalkya* and *Brihaspati Smriti*s distinguish between mere possession of land and legal title. According to the *Brihaspati Smriti* (7.24–25) and *Narada Smriti* (1.84), mere possession does not create proprietary rights; legal title is necessary to validate possession. The latter text (*Narada Smriti* 1.84–87) lays down rules about illegal possession, and states that a person who cannot produce evidence of legal title to property has to be considered a thief, even if he has enjoyed possession for a hundred years.

Types of Land, Land Measures, and Land Tenure

The *Nitisara* (2.20) describes cattle-rearing, farming, and trade as the three sources of livelihood (*varta*) of the Vaishya and urges the king to ensure that those proficient in these activities are free from want. Texts and inscriptions give details about types of land, land tenure, and land measures. The *Amarakosha* lists 12 types of land—*urvara* (fertile), *ushara* (barren), *maru* (desert), *aprahata* (fallow), *shadvala* (grassy), *pankila* (muddy), *jalaprayamanupam* (wet), *kachcha* (adjacent to water), *sharkara* (full of pebbles and pieces of limestone), *sharkavati* (sandy), *nadimatrika* (watered by a river), and *devamatrika* (watered by rain). In inscriptions, the term *kshetra* is used for a field, especially a cultivated field. *Khila* means untilled land or cultivable wasteland. *Aprahata* too means cultivable wasteland. The term *aprada* refers to unsettled land. *Vastu* was habitat land. There is also mention of pasture land. Texts such as the *Amarakosha* mention various types of cereals. Varahamihira's *Brihatsamhita* mentions the astrological portents of bad harvests and famine. Various types of waterworks for providing drinking water and irrigation, e.g., wells, canals, tanks, and embankments are mentioned in texts. The role of the state in building and maintaining some of these is indicated by the Junagadh inscription.

Several inscriptions, e.g., the Gunaigarh grant of Vainyagupta, and the Damodarpur, Paharpur, and Baigram copper plates refer to potential donees applying for wasteland. It is not clear whether this was because of increasing pressure on arable land, the relative cheapness of such land, or the easy availability of tax concessions for reclaiming wasteland.

Texts and inscriptions mention various land measure terms (Maity, [1957] 1970: 48–61). The *angula* (probably ¾ inch) was the smallest measure. The *hasta* (cubit) was the standardized distance between the tip of the elbow and the middle finger (18 inches). Larger units of measure included the *dhanu/danda* and *nala*. The land measures used in Eastern India included the *adhavapa* (3/8–1/2 acre), *dronavapa* (1½–2 acres), and *kulyavapa* (12–16 acres). These were the areas required to sow one *adhaka*, *drona*, and *kulya* of grain respectively. *Pataka* was another land measure, and seems to have been equivalent to 60–80 acres. Other terms included *pravartavapa* (this was much smaller than a *kulyavapa*), *padavarta* (over 1 ft), and *bhumi*. The large number of land measure terms indicate that there was no single standard set of measurement and that different measures were current in different regions.

The *Brihaspati* and *Narada Smriti*s emphasize that boundaries of landed property should be clearly demarcated. Inscriptions suggest that this was in fact done, no doubt to prevent property disputes. Boundaries were demarcated using trenches or pillars or with reference to natural features such as trees, tanks, and anthills. The *Brihaspati Smriti* (19.20–22) suggests that dry cow dung, bones, charcoal, chaff, pottery pieces, bricks, cows' tails, stones, cotton seeds, and ashes should be put in pots and buried at the boundaries. These boundary-markers should be pointed out to children and young people, who should in turn point them out to children and young people when they grew old. In this manner, boundaries of landed property would become part of common knowledge, transmitted from one generation to the next.

Inscriptions mention several technical terms pertaining to land tenure in the context of the rights given to donees over gifted land (Maity, [1957] 1970: 36–45). A gift made according to the *nivi-dharma* seems to have meant the grant of permanent usufructuary rights (the right to enjoy the fruits of the land). The terms *akshaya-nivi* and *aprada-dharma* seem to have meant that the gift was inalienable (i.e., it could not be given away, gifted, sold, etc.). On the other hand, *nivi-dharma-kshaya* appears to have meant that the donee was given full rights over the land, along with the powers of transfer and sale. Another important technical term is *bhumichhidranyaya*. This has been interpreted as non-agricultural land or land fit to be cultivated. D. C. Sircar (1965: 367–98) on the other hand, suggested that it alluded to the ancient custom whereby a person who brought fallow land under cultivation for the first time was entitled to its tax-free enjoyment. In course of time, he suggests, *bhumichhidra-nyaya* came to mean uncultivable land. The frequent mention of this term in land grant inscriptions does not, however, support such an interpretation. It may have been a term that emphasized the permanent and comprehensive rights over the land bestowed on the donees.

The fact that there are no secular sale deeds of this period may be because such records were maintained on perishable material and were not inscribed on stone or metal. However, 11 inscriptions, all from Eastern India, record the purchase of land for pious donations and reflect the involvement of local governments in the process. The basic procedure was as follows: The potential buyer applied to the district office and city council, giving the details of the land he wanted to buy, the reasons why he wanted to do so, and his willingness to pay the prevailing price. The city council consulted the office of the record keepers. The applicant paid the price for the land to the district office. The local government inspected the land and demarcated its boundaries according to the standard measure. The city council then recorded and announced the sale in the presence of the royal officials, village headman, Brahmanas, and householders. The price of land within an area could vary. For instance, one of the Damodarpur copper plates records that in 443–44 CE, one *kulyavapa* of *aprada* and *aprahata* land in Pundravardhana *bhukti* was bought at the rate of 3 *dinaras* per *kulyavapa*. On the other hand, the Paharpur copper plate states that in 479 CE, Nathasharma and his wife Rami bought 1½ *kulyavapa* of *khila* land in the same *bhukti* at the rate of 2 *dinaras* per *kulyavapa*.

Royal Land Grants

As mentioned in an earlier chapter, the earliest mention of royal gifts of land to Brahmanas occur in later Vedic texts. The ambivalence of the early texts eventually made way for wholehearted approval and the *Mahabharata*, for instance, makes repeated exhortations to kings to gift land to Brahmanas. In a perceptive statement in the *Danadharma* section (33.17) of the *Anushasana Parva* of this text, Bhishma tells Yudhishthira that Brahmanas can deify those who are not gods and can dethrone existing gods; they are the king makers, and a king can hope to retain his position only as long as he enjoys their favour. The *Danadharma Parva* refers to three major types of gifts—the gift of gold (*hiranya-dana*), cattle (*go-dana*), and land (*prithvi-dana*). The gift of land is considered the best, as it is the source of jewels, animals, and grain. The Dharmashastra and Puranas likewise extol the gift of land to Brahmanas and promise that those who bestow appropriate gifts on worthy Brahmanas will attain fame in this world and happiness in the world to come.

The earliest textual references to kings granting land associated with tax exemptions and privileges occur in the *Arthashastra*. Dharmashastra includes Brahmanas among those who should be exempt from taxes and also extol the merit of royal gifts of land to them. But it is only in the *Brihaspati Smriti* that these two things are explicitly connected, and there is a clear assertion that land gifted by kings to Brahmanas should be tax-free.

Such references indicate that prescriptive texts of the Brahmanical tradition, which were composed, maintained, and transmitted by Brahmanas, not surprisingly, considered such gifts a good thing. The question is: Were the repeated injunctions reflective of prevailing practice or where they an attempt to further such a practice? Evidence from other sources suggests that it was probably a bit of both. For instance, the Pali canon of the Buddhists refers to kings such as Bimbisara of Magadha and Prasenajit of Kosala gifting land to Brahmanas.

A set of copper plates, with ring and seal

As mentioned in Chapter 8, the earliest inscriptions recording royal land grants, as well as land grants associated with privileges and exemptions, are found at Naneghat and Nashik in the western Deccan, and were made by the Satavahanas and Shaka Kshatrapas of the Kshaharata line. Various technical terms associated with land grants are also found in these inscriptions. There was an increase in royal land grants from the 4th century. From the 5th/6th century, kings virtually all over the Indian subcontinent were making such gifts, the details of which were generally inscribed on copper plates. Villages granted to Brahmanas were known as *agraharas*, *brahmadeyas*, or *shasanas*. A more neutral term for a Brahmana village, and one that does not indicate whether or not it was the result of a royal endowment, is *bhatta-grama*. Although there are records of royal grants to other sorts of beneficiaries, including Buddhist and Jaina monasteries, Vaishnava and Shaiva temples, and a much smaller number of 'secular grants', until about the 10th century CE, the majority of royal land grants were made to Brahmanas.

The imperial Guptas were not, however, involved in a big way in this development. There is only one bonafide inscription recording a land grant made by a Gupta king. This is the Bhitari stone pillar inscription of Skandagupta, which records the gift of a village in favour of a Vishnu temple, but does not make any stipulations regarding the terms of the gift. Apart from this, there are the spurious Gaya and Nalanda copper plates of Samudragupta. The Gaya plate records the grant of Revatika village in Gaya *vishaya* to a Brahmana named Gopasvamin. The Nalanda plate of Samudragupta records the gift of Bhadrapushkaraka village in Kramila *vishaya,* and Purnanaga village in Krivila *vishaya* to a Brahmana named Jayabhattasvami. Both grants are described as having been made along with the due known as the *uparikara*. The villagers were instructed to obey the donees and to give them all the taxes such as the *meya* and *hiranya*. The inscriptions also state that henceforth, tax-paying cultivators and artisans of other villages should not enter this *agrahara*. Some scholars consider the Gaya and Nalanda inscriptions as spurious due to the spellings of some words, certain ungrammatical portions, and the epithets used for Samudragupta. It has also been suggested that they may have been later copies of genuine grants. However, Chhabra and Gai (1981: 225–26, 229–30) point out that while the palaeography of the Gaya plates can be assigned to the early 8th century, that of the Nalanda plates definitely belongs to the Gupta period. They also argue that grammatical lapses occur in many inscriptions, especially where there are long compound words, and that this cannot be a ground for considering an inscription a forgery.

The Bihar stone inscription, which seems to belong either to the reign of Budhagupta or Purugupta, records the erection of a sacrificial post (*yupa*) by a minister who also happened to be a brother-in-law of king Kumaragupta. This minister built some temples dedicated to the god Skanda and the Sapta-Matrikas (the seven Divine Mothers). The inscription mentions the gift of certain shares in two villages, probably for the maintenance of these temples. The inscription is fragmentary; if the gift carried specific terms, they no longer survive.

While the imperial Guptas were not apparently great donors of land to Brahmanas, the Vakatakas were. The tally of the gifted villages mentioned in Vakataka inscriptions is 35. A large number of these gifts were made during the reign of Pravarasena II—his 18 or 19 inscriptions record the gift of 20 villages in all. A wide range of technical terms are mentioned in the grants, indicating the exemptions and privileges that were bestowed on the gifted land and the donees. Thirteen inscriptions mention the area of land, ranging from 20 to 8000 *nivartanas* by the royal measure. There are also a few instances of villages being donated in exchange for previous gifts. The Yavatmal plates of Pravarasena II record the renewal of an earlier grant. From the time of Pravarasena II, there seems to have been a shift in the location of gifted villages from the eastern to the western part of the Vakataka kingdom, particularly to the Tapi valley (Shrimali, 1987: 25). Land grants were also made by subordinate rulers of the Guptas and Vakatakas. These included, for instance, the Parivrajaka *maharajas* who ruled over the Baghelkhand area and acknowledged the suzerainty of the Guptas, and Bharatabala, a ruler of the Mekala country, who was a subordinate of the Vakatakas.

Land grants to Brahmanas in the Karnataka area may have begun in the 2nd century, but their number increased after the 7th century. The earliest Pallava royal land grants are recorded in the 3rd/4th century Mayidavolu plates and the Hirehadagalli plates (both in Prakrit). The Pulankurichi inscription of about the 5th century CE records the creation of a *brahmadeya* settlement and mentions the superior rights (*miyatchi*) of the donees and the subordinate rights (*karan-kilamai*) of the cultivators.

While kings were the prime donors of land, others contributed as well. Inscriptions from Bengal include records of land grants to Brahmanas by private individuals, grants made to Brahmanas at their own request, and grants made by kings at the request of other people. For instance, the Dhanaidaha copper plate inscription of Gupta year 113 (432–33 CE) states that a royal officer (*ayuktaka*) bought some land and gifted it to a Brahmana named Varahasvamin. One of the Damodarpur copper plates (dated in Gupta year 124) states that a Brahmana named Karppatika applied for the grant of a piece of land to the administration of Pundravardhana *bhukti* stationed in the headquarters at Kotivarsha *vishaya*. Another example of a Brahmana applying for the grant of land is that of Supratikasvamin of the Ghugrahati copper plate of the reign of Samacharadeva. The Tippera copper plate of Lokanatha records a grant to over 100 *chaturvedi* Brahmanas at the request of a *mahasamanta*.

Royal land grants are central to hypotheses relating to historical processes in early medieval times, an elastic term that can be used to refer to some or all of the period from *c.* 400–1200/1300 CE. In this book, the term 'early medieval' is used for the period *c.* 600–1200 BCE. The full implications and impact of the phenomenon of royal land grants and details of the larger debate that they form part of will be discussed in the next chapter. It should be noted that royal land grants to religious beneficiaries are also found in Sri Lanka. This will be discussed further in Chapter 10.

PRIMARY SOURCES | The terms of the Vakataka grants

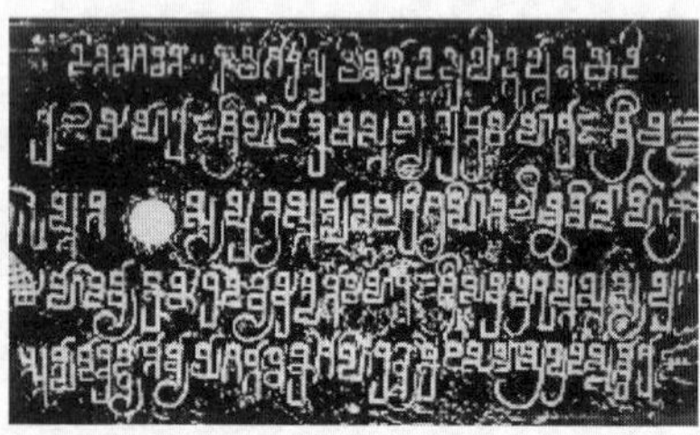

The Vakataka grants bestowed many exemptions and privileges on the gifted land. The meaning of some of the technical terms is not certain. The Basim plates of Vindhyashakti II of the Vatsagulma branch record the king's grant of Akasapadda village to certain *Atharva Veda* Brahmanas. The following exemptions and privileges were associated with the grant (the language is a mixture of Prakrit and Sanskrit):

a-chand-adichcha-kalo: to last as long as the moon and the sun [i.e., forever]

a-rattha-samvvinayika: not to be entered by the district police;

a-lavana-kenna-kkhanaka: exempt from [the royal prerogative] of digging salt and purchasing fermented liquor;

a-hiranna-dhanna-ppanayapa-deya: exempt from the obligations to gift grain and gold [to the king];

a-puppha-kkhira-ggahana: exempt from the obligation to supply flowers and milk;

a-parampara-go-bali-vardda: exempt from the obligation to supply [to the state] customary cows and bulls;

a-chara-siddhika, a-chammangalika: exempt from providing pastures, hides, and charcoal [to touring officials];

a-bhada-ppavesa: not to be entered by [royal] soldiers;

a-khatta-chollaka-venasika: not to provide sleeping cots, water pots, and slaves (perhaps to touring officers);

a-karada: not to pay taxes;

a-vaha: not to provide draught cattle (for the transport of officials);

sa-nidhi, s-opanidhi: along with the right to hidden treasures and deposits;

s-ukutuppanta: along with major and minor taxes;

sa-mancha-maha-karana: along with the right to platforms and large fields;

savva-jati-parihara-parihita: exempted with all kinds of immunities.

The Poona plates of Prabhavatigupta also refer to the donees being granted the right to mines and *khadira* trees. The term *sarvva-vishti-parihara-parihritah* in the Jamb, Siwani, and Pauni plates of Pravarasena II, the Riddhapur plates of Prabhavatigupta, and the Mahurjhari plates of Prithivishena II indicates that the gifted land was free from forced labour. The Siwani and Patna Museum plates have the term *sa-panchasha-takah*, the meaning of which is not clear. The Siwani plates have *sa-koratah*, which has been variously translated as 'together with coconut plantations', 'together with the right to bulls', or 'along with undulating wastelands'. The Riddhapur plates of Prabhavatigupta state that the field was granted along with a farmhouse and four farmers' huts (*abhyantara-niveshena-saha karsha-ka-niveshanani cha*). The Pauni grant of Pravarasena II records the gift of a village along with the habitations (*saha-niveshana*). Some of the grants contain the phrase *a-bhata-chchhatra-praveshya*, which means 'not to be entered by regular and irregular troops' or, alternatively, 'not to be entered by soldiers and policemen'.

The Chammak plates of Pravarasena II have a curious stipulation. The donees—1,000 Brahmanas—were to enjoy the gifted land as long as they did not commit treason against the kingdom, as long as they were not found guilty of the murder of a Brahmana, or of theft, adultery, and high treason, etc.; as long as they did not wage war and did not harm other villages. It was declared that if they indulged in or assented to any such acts, the king would be justified in taking the land away from them. The inscription suggests the apprehension that Brahmanas patronized by the king were capable of presenting a violent threat to society and to the king.

Source Mirashi, 1963

Patterns of Urban History

R. S. Sharma (1987) has argued that the peak of early historical urbanism in the subcontinent occurred between *c.* 200 BCE and 300 CE. This was followed by two phases of urban decay—the first in the later half of the 3rd or in the 4th century CE, and the second after the 6th century CE. According to Sharma, archaeological evidence from all over the subcontinent reflects the phenomenon of urban decline. He also points to a decrease in references to artisans and merchants in inscriptions. Sharma admits the literary evidence for urban decay is not strong, but cites the gloomy prophecy made in Varahamihira's *Brihatsamhita* that various towns will either be destroyed or will fall on evil days, the Valmiki *Ramayana*'s description of Ayodhya after Rama's exile, and the picture of the city's desolation in Kalidasa's *Raghuvamsha*. He explains the urban decay as the result of a decline in long-distance trade and asserts that it lasted for at least seven centuries. A mild urban renewal occurred in some parts of the subcontinent in the 11th century, and by the 14th century, urbanism became a recognizable process.

With specific reference to the Vakataka kingdom, Shrimali (1987: 30) argues for a decline in trade, traders, and the urban economy, and asserts that the inscriptions convey a picture of a non-monetary, small-scale village economy, an expansion of rural settlements, a contraction of urbanism, and an early onset of feudalism. There are scarcely any references to urban centres (this is actually not surprising, given that they are grants of rural land). Only about 16 settlements can be tentatively identified as having some sort of urbanness—on the basis of suffixes such as 'pura', 'puraka', and 'nagara'.

The hypothesis that there was a subcontinental urban decay during *c.* 300–600 CE, can be questioned on several grounds.[3] Texts of the time abound in lengthy, poetic descriptions of cities and city life that need not be taken literally, but certainly reflect an idea and awareness of flourishing urban centres. Sanskrit *kavya* was an urban phenomenon and catered to an urbane, sophisticated urban audience. The characters and action largely took place in an urban setting. Daud Ali (2006) has reconstructed various aspects of urban courtly culture using a wide range of Sanskrit texts. Shonaleeka Kaul (2010) argues that representations of city life in Sanskrit kavya should be seen not as stereotypes but as complex archetypes rich in symbolic meaning, and that its descriptions and characters (such as the *nagaraka*, *ganika*, and *kulastri*) captured the universalized essence of the urban experience. One of the challenges in reconstructing patterns of urban life in the period *c.* 300–600 CE is to explore the literary images of city life in texts with sensitivity to the conventions of their genre, keeping in mind their chronology and historical context, factoring in the experiences, imagination, and perspectives of their authors. Another challenge is to seek more data from archaeology.

The *Brihatsamhita* mentions the opulent paraphernalia of kings and courts and mansions of kings, officials, and other wealthy people. The *Mrichchhakatika* gives a vivid description of the heroine Vasantasena's magnificent house in Ujjayini, its lofty portal and gold doors studded with diamonds, and its lavishly decorated rooms. The *Amarakosha* offers lists of words for various kinds of ornaments and elaborate articles of clothing. The descriptions of the wealthy, educated, refined, and sophisticated man-about-town—referred to in the *Kamasutra* as the *nagaraka*—are similarly connected with an urban milieu. And the very production of a sophisticated range of literature of various genres, as well as the architectural and sculptural products of this period, point to an urban milieu and urban sources of patronage.

The vivid descriptions of cities and city life in the Tamil epics clearly indicate that urbanism was an ongoing process in the far south. The *Silappadikaram* describes the busy and bustling markets of Puhar and Madurai, with sellers of flowers, garlands, aromatic powder, betel nut, shell bangles, wines, cloth, and garments. There were also shopkeepers, gem workers, and various kinds of skilled workers. Puhar is described as having

[3] The problems in accepting this theory for the subsequent centuries will be discussed in Chapter 10.

PRIMARY SOURCES | **The lifestyle of the *nagaraka***

When a man has become educated, he enters the householder stage of life and begins the lifestyle of a *nagaraka*, using money that he has inherited, on the one hand, or obtained from gifts, conquest, trade, or wages, on the other, or from both. He settles down in a city, a capital city, a market town, or some large gathering where there are good people, or wherever he has to stay to make a living. And there he makes his home in a house near water, with an orchard, separate servant quarters, and two bedrooms. This is how the house is furnished: In the outer bedrooms there is a bed, low in the middle and very soft, with pillows on both sides and a white top sheet. [There is also a couch.] At the head of the bed there is a grass mat and an altar, on which are placed the oils and garlands left over from the night, a pot of beeswax, a vial of perfume, some bark from a lemon tree, and betel. On the floor, a spitoon. A lute, hanging from an ivory tusk, a board to draw or paint on, and a box of pencils. Some book or other, and garlands of amaranth flowers. On the floor, not too far away, a round bed with a pillow for the head. A board for dice and a board for gambling. Outside, cages of pet birds. And, set aside, a place for carpentry or woodworking and for other games. In the orchard, a well-padded swing in the shade, and a bench made of baked clay and covered with flowers.

He gets up in the morning, relieves himself, cleans his teeth, applies fragrant oils in small quantities, as well as incense, garlands, beeswax, and red lac, looks at his face in the mirror, takes some mouthwash and betel, and attends to the things that need to be done. He bathes every day, has his limbs rubbed with oil every second day, a foam bath every third day, his face shaved every fourth day, and his body hair removed every fifth or tenth day. All of this is done without fail. And he continually cleans the sweat from his armpits. In the morning and afternoon he eats.... After eating, he passes the time teaching his parrots and mynah birds to speak; goes to quail-fights; engages in various arts and games; and passes the time with his libertine [*pithamarda*, the hero's sidekick], pander [*vita*, an educated but parasitic courtier], and clown [*vidushaka*, usually a Brahmana who teases the king]. And he takes a nap. In the late afternoon, he gets up and goes to salons to amuse himself.

And in the evening, there is music and singing. After that, on the bed in a bedroom carefully decorated and perfumed by sweet-smelling incense, he and his friends await the women who are slipping out for a rendezvous with them....

He amuses himself by going to festivals, salons, drinking parties, picnics, and group games.

On a specified day at half moon or full moon, there is always an assembly of invited guests at the temple of the goddess Sarasvati. Visiting players also come and give an audition for them, and on the second day they are rewarded with a fixed fee....

A salon [*goshthi*] takes place when people of similar knowledge, intelligence, character, wealth, and age sit together in the house of a courtesan, or in a place of assembly, or in the dwelling-place of some man, and engage in appropriate conversation with courtesans. There they exchange thoughts about poems or works of art, and in the course of that they praise brilliant women whom everyone likes, and they bring in women who love all men equally. They have drinking parties at one another's houses. There the courtesans get the men to drink, and drink after them, wine made from honey, grapes, other fruits, or sugar, with various sorts of salt, fruit, greens, vegetables, and bitter, spicy, and sour foods.

Picnics can be described in this same way. Early in the morning, men dress with care and go out on horseback, attended by servants and accompanied by courtesans. They enjoy the daytime events there and spend the time at cockfights, gambling, theatrical spectacles, and then in the afternoon they go back again in the same way, taking with them souvenirs of the pleasures of the picnic. And in the same way, in the summer, people enjoy water sports, in pools built to keep out crocodiles.

Source *Kamasutra* 1.4.5–1.4.26; Doniger and Kakar. (Trans.)., 2002: 18–20

two parts—the *pattinappakkam* or *akanagar* (residential area) and the *maruvurpakkam* (coastal port area). The residential area had houses of rich people, feeding houses, gardens, meeting places, tanks, public baths, and temples. The cemetery and burial grounds were located outside the city. The epics talk of Hindu temples and Buddhist and Jaina establishments in the cities. The *Manimekalai* mentions a *vihara* and *chaitya* at Vanji.

The archaeological data on cities of this period is rather meagre but does not point to a material decline (see Dikshit, [1971] 2018). At Purana Qila in Delhi, there were remains of structures made of reused bricks. There was moulded pottery, including a lid with a *kinnara* motif (half man, half horse) and a damaged terracotta female figurine. A terracotta seal bore the outline of a conch above and the legend *Gopasya* (of or belonging to Gopa) below. Another seal read *jitam bhagavata* (victory to *bhagavata*, i.e., Vasudeva Krishna), while a third bore the legend *Sri traividya* in Brahmi letters of the Gupta period. The 1970–71 excavations revealed a building of this period which had undergone three or four stages of construction. Initially the structure was oblong in plan with a partition wall. Subsequently, a verandah or room with a rounded corner was added in front. Still later, the floor levels were raised, steps added, and two partition walls constructed inside. A 60 cm high brick pedestal with a stepped base was built against one of the walls beside the entrance. In the last phase, another verandah was built in front, the floor levels raised even further, and more steps added. A sealing inscribed with Brahmi letters of the Gupta period and a gold-plated coin of the archer type with the legend *Shri Vikrama* were found embedded in the debris of the last structural phase. Other antiquities included a few human terracottas, a piece of carved shell bangle, a small damaged sandstone *mukha-linga*, and painted pots. There were also some sealings with names inscribed on them.

Sarnath: 'Kushana-Gupta' red ware pot, bowl, and lids

In the upper Ganga valley, a terraced temple belonging to the early Gupta period was reported at Ahichchhatra (Bareilly district, UP). At Hulaskhera (Lucknow district), there are remains of a Gupta period citadel. Among the sites in the middle Ganga valley, a seal of the city administration of Varanasi in Brahmi of the Gupta period was found at Rajghat. In Patna, the remains of a Buddhist monastery were identified at a distance from the Maurya remains at Kumrahar. An inscribed terracotta sealing, assigned on palaeographic grounds to the Gupta period, indicated that it was called Arogya-vihara. In the lower Ganga valley, burnt brick fortifications of this period were found at Mahasthangarh (in Bagura district of Bangladesh).

The evidence from Basarh (ancient Vaishali) requires special attention. This site yielded hundreds of seals and sealings. In the 1903–04 excavations (Bloch, 1903–04) structural remains unearthed in the Basarh fort (known as Raja Bisal-ka-garh) were assigned to the Gupta and post-Gupta periods on the basis of the palaeography of the seals. In one of the trenches, a large number of inscribed seals and sealings of the early Gupta kings were found in a square room, along with pottery and burnt wood. According to Bloch, the room seems to have been an underground chamber used to store important letters and other documents, to which the seals were fixed. Bloch discovered about 720 seals and sealings and over 1,100 seal impressions at the site, most of them from this chamber. The language was basically Sanskrit, and the script an eastern variety of 4th/5th century Brahmi. The legends included mention of the *adhikarana* of the *kumaramatya*, the *yuvaraja* (prince or heir apparent), *mahapratihara*, *dandapashika*, *mahadandanayaka*, *ashvapati*, *taravara*, the *adhikarana* of the *uparika* of Tirabhukti, and the *adhishthana-adhikarana* of Vaishali. There were references to individuals described as *kulika* (artisan or merchant), *sreshthi* (banker), and *sarthavaha* (caravan trader). One seal referred to the *shreshthi-kulika-nigama* (the guild of bankers and artisans/merchants). Another referred to the *shreshthi-sarthavaha-kulika-nigama* (the guild of bankers, caravan traders, and artisans/merchants). The large number of seals and sealings discovered by Spooner in the 1911–12 excavations (Spooner, 1913–14) included 16 sealings with the legend *shreshthi-nigamasya* (of the guild of merchants/bankers).

The excavations conducted in 1950 (Deva and Mishra, 1961) established a four-fold cultural sequence for Vaishali, ranging from *c.* 500 BCE to 500 CE: Period Ia (*c.* 500–300 BCE), Period Ib (*c.* 300–150 BCE), Period II (*c.* 150 BCE–100 CE), Period III (*c.* 100–300 CE), and Period IV (*c.* 300–500 CE). The remains of Period IV (which concern us here) included structures made of re-used bricks, and terracottas and sealings inscribed in Brahmi letters of the Gupta period. The 1958–62 excavations (Sinha and Roy, 1969) focused mainly on the pre-Maurya phase, the identification of the *abhisheka* tank, and the establishment of the relic *stupa*. The excavators suggested the following cultural sequence for the site: Period I (pre-NBPW, i.e., pre-600 BCE); Period II (NBPW, *c.* 600–200 BCE); Period III (*c.* 200 BCE–200 CE); Period IV (*c.* 200–600 CE); and Period V (post-600 CE; post-Gupta, pre-Mughal). Very few structures of Period II were found but the structural remains belonging to Periods III and IV were quite substantial. Several ring wells were found. Periods IV and V yielded several fragile structures. In the Baniya village area, ruins of a more or less rectangular brick shrine, associated with a platform-like structure, were assigned to Period IV. The excavators commented that the structures of the Gupta period, though fairly large, were made of broken bricks, unlike those of the Shunga and Kushana periods, which were made of substantial bricks. The excavations revealed 98 sealings, tokens, etc. While some of these belonged to the Maurya, Shunga, and Kushana periods, the largest number belonged to the Gupta period, and a few to the early medieval period. They included a sealing with the legend *shreshthi-sarthavaha-prathamakulika-nigamah* in Brahmi of the Gupta period. The site yielded many terracottas belonging to various occupational phases and a large number (157) of coins. Of the recognizable specimens, the most numerous (68) were cast copper coins, followed by punch-marked coins (15). There were a few Kushana copper coins (9) and two medieval coins, but not a single coin belonging to *c.* 300–600 CE was found. Nevertheless, the seals and sealings indicate that Vaishali was an important administrative headquarters and a flourishing commercial centre during this period. The prolific seals and sealings of high-ranking functionaries and leading merchants, bankers, and merchants are suggestive of close interactions and connections among them.

Bhita near Prayagraj revealed structures of various periods, including those of *c.* 300–600 CE, mostly made of re-used or broken bricks (Marshall, 1915). Various artefacts were unearthed, the most numerous and interesting of which were seals and sealings. The excavations conducted by Marshall in 1911–12 revealed 210 of these, comprising 120 varieties and 67 duplicates. The rest, 23 in number, were very worn out. The seals and sealings ranged from the 4th/3rd century BCE to the 9th/10th century CE, and included those of royalty, officials, and other urban elites. The majority belonged to the period *c.* 300–600 CE; only two belonged to the 9th/10th century. The legends included mention of a *shreshthi* named Jayavasuda (in 4th/5th century CE letters). One of the sealings of this period referred to a guild (*nigama*).

The 4th century saw the beginning of the historical period in the North-east. Important excavated sites are Ambari in Assam, the Sekta burial site in Manipur, and Vadagokugiri/Bhaitbari in Meghalaya (see Sarma and Hazarika, 2014: 50–51). Ambari has been identified with the Pragjyotisha, the capital of the Barman dynasty, and has given evidence of a neolithic and historical phase, the latter yielding pottery and stone and terracotta sculptures. Sekta has yielded burials associated with pots. The material found here shows contact with the mid-Ganga valley as well as with South China and Myanmar. Vadagokuri or Bhaitbari revealed material affinities with Mahasthangarh in Bangladesh. Epigraphic and archaeological evidence from the Dhansiri-Doyang valley suggests the existence of an independent kingdom here from the 5th century.

While archaeological evidence indicates the decline of certain Buddhist monastic establishments (such as those at Pauni in Western India), it also shows the growth of several others. In Central India, several *viharas*, shrines, and sculptures at Sanchi belong to this period. In Eastern India, Sarnath witnessed building activity and the monastery of Nalanda achieved international renown. The monastic community of Ajanta flourished in Western India. In South India, while Nagarjunakonda seems to have declined after the end of the Ikshvaku dynasty, the *mahachaitya* at Amaravati continued to thrive. Buddhism continued to flourish in Sri Lanka. The existence of major monastic centres in various parts of the subcontinent points to urban centres with which the monasteries had a symbiotic relationship.

Craft Production, Guilds, and Trade

The abundant inscriptions and seals mentioning artisans, merchants, and guilds suggest thriving urban crafts and trade. There are several references to artisans, traders, and occupational groups in Vakataka inscriptions. The Indore plates of Pravarasena II mention a merchant (*vanijaka*) named Chandra, who bought half a village and donated it to some Brahmanas. The gifted village Charmanka in the Chammak copper plates of Pravarasena II may have been a settlement of leather workers. The Thalner copper plates record the gift of Kamsakaraka and Suvarnakara, which, from their names, seem to have been villages of bronze workers and goldsmiths. A goldsmith named Ishvaradatta is mentioned as the engraver of the Pattan plates. Kallara, mentioned in the Pandhurna plates, and Madhukajjhari, mentioned in the Patna Museum plates, may have been villages of alcohol distillers. The inhabitants of Ishtakapalli of the Mandhal plates may have specialized in brickmaking. Places such as Ishtakapalli, Hiranyapura, Lavanatailaka, and Lohanagara seem to have been connected with brickmaking, goldwork, salt manufacture, and iron working respectively (Shrimali, 1987: 29). All this goes against the hypothesis of urban decline.

Metal working is listed in the *Kamasutra* as one of the 64 arts (*kala*). The *Amarakosha* lists various metals such as gold, silver, iron, copper, brass, and lead. The *Brihaspati Smriti* mentions metal workers working with gold, silver, and base metals. Apart from the many iron objects found at archaeological sites, the iron pillar at Mehrauli reflects the high level of metallurgical skill of the time. Coin casting, metal engraving, pottery making, terracotta work, and wood carving were other specialized crafts. Artistic remains indicate the existence of architects, builders, stone masons, sculptors, mural painters, and labourers. The Ajanta paintings abound in representations of royal palaces and mansions of the wealthy.

The *Amarakosha* mentions several words connected with cotton textiles—weaver, loom, thread, coarse, and fine fabric. We can note the evidence of stitched clothes in Indian sculpture from the early centuries CE. The Ajanta paintings depict elaborate garments and imply skilled tailors and embroiderers. Beautiful ornaments are described in literature and depicted both in sculptures and in Ajanta paintings. The *Amarakosha* lists many types of precious and semi-precious stones. Varahamihira's *Brihatsamhita* deals with the qualities of diamonds, rubies, and pearls. Ornaments were also made out of coral and conch shell. The descriptions of the life of the *nagaraka* in the *Kamasutra* and in *kavya* literature suggest the existence of garland makers and makers of cosmetics, unguents, and perfumes.

The Mandasor inscription, which refers to the migration and activities of a prosperous guild of silk weavers, has been mentioned earlier. Verse 20 of the inscription talks of silk—'Womankind, though saturated with youth and complexion (and) decorated with golden necklaces, betel leaves and flower dressing, does not attain to transcendent beauty until she has put on a pair of silken garments.' It is interesting to note that the Indore copper plate of the time of Skandagupta also states that the guild of oil men was supposed to provide oil for the Surya temple even if it moved to some other place. This suggests that the migration of craft guilds was a reality.

Dharmashastra texts refer to partnerships in craft production and trade. They mention the apprenticeship of novices with master craftsmen. The Faridpur plate of Gopachandra seems to refer to big traders (*pradhana-vyaparinah*). Texts mention rules for hiring conveyance such as bullock carts, boats, and beasts of burden. They refer to various aspects of business activities such as the return of sold goods. Rules for the protection of the interests of traders and consumers, and punishments for adulteration and the non-delivery of goods are also laid down.

The *Narada* and *Brihaspati Smriti*s describe the organization and activities of guilds. They mention the guild chief and two, three, or five executive officers. Guild laws were apparently laid down in written documents. The *Brihaspati Smriti* refers to guilds meting out justice to their members and suggests that these decisions should, by and large, be approved by the king. There is also mention of the philanthropic activities of guilds, for instance, providing shelter for travellers and building assembly houses, temples, and gardens. As mentioned earlier, certain inscriptions indicate the important role of the chief of the guilds of artisans and traders in district-level administrative bodies. Also noted were seals mentioning joint corporate bodies of merchant-bankers, caravan merchants, and artisans.

Apart from the Mandasor inscription, the flourishing condition of guilds is indicated by inscriptions which refer to guilds as donors and bankers. The Indore plates of the Vakataka king Pravarasena mention a merchant (*vanijaka*) named Chandra, who bought half of the village that was gifted by the king to certain Brahmanas. The Gadhwa inscription (dated in Gupta year 88, i.e., 407 CE) of the time of Chandragupta II mentions the investment of 20 *dinaras* in a guild headed by Matridasa, for the benefit of Brahmanas. Two other inscriptions from Gadhwa, belonging to the reign of Kumaragupta I, record the investment of 13 and 2 *dinaras* with two guilds for the maintenance of *sattras* (alms-houses).[4] The Indore inscription of Skandagupta (of Gupta year 146, i.e., 465 CE) records an endowment made by a Brahmana Devavishnu for maintaining a perpetual lamp in a Surya temple at Indrapura (i.e., Indore). It states that the temple was built by two merchants of this place—Achalavarman and Bhrikunthasimha—and that the money was invested with a guild of oil-manufacturers headed by Jivanta. The guild was to ensure a regular supply of oil for the lamps in the temple, even if it migrated elsewhere.

R. S. Sharma ([1965] 1980) has argued that the Gupta and post-Gupta periods saw a decline in the money economy. He points out that the Guptas issued many gold coins, but comparatively few silver and copper coins. Till recently, it was believed that the Vakatakas did not issue any coins, but this misconception has been dispelled. Although no gold or silver coins have been found so far, several copper coins can be associated with this dynasty. They vary considerably in size, shape, and weight. They usually have the short-form of the king's name or title on the obverse, and a geometric or linear symbol or an animal motif on the reverse (Raven, 2004). We can also note the discussion of money-lending in texts. For instance, the *Narada Smriti* (1.46–47) refers to money gained through usury as 'spotted wealth' and 'black wealth', but the Dharmashastra texts of the time do lay down detailed rules concerning usury, including the drawing up of contracts, the role of local custom in fixing rates of interest, and various kinds of pledges that could be accepted as security for loans. A general rate of 15 per cent per annum interest is advocated for secured loans. The rates of interest for unsecured loans are much higher and vary with the *varna* of the borrower, members of the lower *varnas* being required to pay higher interest rates. The *Brihaspati Smriti* (10.67) states that when a piece of immoveable property such land has been enjoyed and has yielded more than the principal, the debtor should automatically recover the pledge. The effects of defaulting on a loan are said to pursue the debtor in his next life. The *Narada Smriti* (1.7–8) asserts that a person will be born as a slave in the house of his creditor, in order to pay off the debt through his labour. The detailed discussion of money-lending (including the mention of joint money-lending enterprises) clearly points to a context in which money was being used, borrowed, and loaned for profit.

The account of Cosmas mentions various ports on the western coast of India such as Calliena (Kalyan), Sibor (Chaul), and the markets of Male (Malabar), Parti, Mangarouth (Mangalor), Solapatana, Nalopatana (Necynda), and Pandopatana. Faxian refers to Tamralipti in Bengal as an important centre of trade on the eastern coast. These ports and towns were connected with those of Persia, Arabia, and Byzantium on the one hand and Sri Lanka, China, and South-east Asia on the other. Faxian describes the perils of the sea route between India and China. Monks moving from India to China along the land route via Central Asia must have followed the routes of caravan traders.

Chinese sources mention items from India such as rare gems, pearls, fine textiles (probably muslin), saffron, spices including pepper, and aromatics. Xinru Liu (1996: 50–56) points out that in spite of the indigenous manufacture of silk, India continued to import silk yarn and cloth from China and played an important role in

---

[4] The word *sattra* refers to a certain kind of sacrifice performed by Brahmanas, but is also used for various meritorious acts such as setting up almshouses or charitable feeding houses.

Map 9.2 Important ports in Indian Ocean trade networks, *c.* 300–600 CE (after Horton and Middleton, 2000)

trade networks that transported Chinese silk to the Mediterranean world. The reason for the continuing demand for Chinese silk in India was that Indian artisans made silk out of the cocoons of wild silkworms. They collected the cocoons after the worms had gnawed through them, and spun the yarn from floss made from the broken cocoons. The techniques of raising mulberry silk cocoons and unravelling the thread from boiled cocoons were unknown in India till they were introduced by Central Asian immigrants in the 13th century. Indian silk was, therefore, not as soft or shiny as Chinese silk, and although Indian cotton textiles were exported to other lands, its silk was never a major article of export in ancient times. The silk that left Indian shores for export was probably imported Chinese silk. In fact, even after the technical innovations in Indian silk production in the medieval period, Chinese silk remained a luxury item that was much in demand. It figured among the gifts given by Chinese emperors to foreign embassies. Kalidasa refers to rich people wearing garments made of *chinamshuka* (Chinese silk).

As mentioned in Chapter 8, fresh perspectives emerge when the Indian subcontinent is located in its larger Asian context. Kingdoms emerged in the 1st millennium CE in various parts of South-east Asia (for useful overviews, see Guy. [Ed.]., 2014; Tarling. [Ed.]., [1992] 1999; Miksic and Goh, 2017; Stark, 2021; Stargardt, 2021). The genealogies of early kings often traced their ancestry to India. For instance, according to traditional histories of Myanmar, the earliest kingdom in the Irrawaddy valley was founded by a dispossessed prince from India. Cambodian tradition tells of a Brahmana named Kaundinya who married a Cambodian princess. A 9th century inscription from Dong Duong claims that the rulers of this area were descendants of sage Bhrigu of the *Mahabharata*.

Knowledge of the Indian languages and scripts started making its way to South-east Asia during the early centuries CE. Sanskrit and Pali were used in inscriptions for several centuries before the transition to indigenous South-east Asian languages. Sanskrit inscriptions appeared in South-east Asia around the 4th century CE (see Griffiths, 2014) and were written in scripts evolved from Indian Brahmi. The earliest were in a variety of box-headed Brahmi (4th–5th centuries), followed by a script that can be described as late southern Brahmi (5th–8th centuries). After the 8th century, there was the emergence of South-east Asian scripts such as the Kawi script in Java. Scripts derived from northern Brahmi and Siddhamatrika are found in Arakan and Java. The Pyu script found at sites in the Irrawaddy valley of Myanmar, written in a language called Pyu that has not been properly understood, displays elements of both northern and southern Brahmi.

The most spectacular evidence of the travels of Hindu and Buddhist influences from India to South-east Asia comes from sculpture and architecture (for a fine, illustrated discussion, see Guy. [Ed.], 2014, also available online), which display the influences emanating from different parts of the subcontinent, in all cases remoulded according to local style and idiom. This becomes very visible from the 4th century onwards and built on the earlier contacts between South and South-east Asia, which were discussed in Chapter 8. South-east Asian cultures were also influenced by each other's artistic styles.

The ports of South India played a pivotal role in trade with South-east Asia and China. The stories of the Tamil epics are set in the cities of Madurai, Kaveripumpattinam/Kaveripattinam, Vanji, and Kanchipuram. In the *Silappadikaram*, Manaikan, Kannaki's father, was a ship's captain living in the great river port of Puhar. Kovalan was the son of a caravan trader. The *Silappadikaram* mentions a street of cloth merchants at Madurai, where piles of cloth woven out of cotton, hair, or silk were stocked. Weavers (*karukas*) brought fine silk and various kinds of cotton and woollen textiles to the markets of Kaveripattinam. The *Manimekalai* has stories of merchants making sea voyages

PRIMARY SOURCES | Sanskrit inscriptions at Vo-canh and Kutei

An inscription on a block of granite was found near the village of Vo-canh in the Khanh Hoa province of central Vietnam. It consists of 15 lines on one face and seven lines on the second face. The writing on the first face is too fragmentary to be read. The first seven lines of writing on the second face are lost; the remaining lines seem to be in continuation of lines 8–14 of the writing on the first face. The language of the inscription is Sanskrit. There are two verses in the Vasantatilaka metre, and the rest of the inscription is in prose. The date of the inscription is much debated; it is usually placed between the 2nd and 4th century CE on palaeographic grounds.

The epigraph records a donation made by a king belonging to the lineage of Shri Mara. The translation is as follows:

> Mercy for the people...
>
> First conquest...
>
> Ordered by the excellent king in the assembly on the full-moon day (?)
>
> Let them drink the nectar of the words of kings.
>
> Royal family of Shri Mara...He who is the delight of the family of Shri Mara, and conversant with the ways of the world, being seated on the throne, said (the following) words, beneficial to the people, in the midst of his own kinsmen, after having satisfied his sons, brothers, and kinsmen (?) by enjoying wealth in common with them: "Whatever silver, gold, movable and immovable property and stores (of grain?) that I possess, all that I consecrate to those who are near and dear to me. This is my commandment, and future kings also should approve of it. Be it known to my heroic servant (or servant called Vira).

Four inscriptions were found inscribed on stone *yupas* (sacrificial posts) at Kutei in East Kalimantan province of Indonesia on the island of Borneo. The language is Sanskrit, the script was derived from southern Brahmi. The inscriptions belong to about the 5th century. One of them is translated as follows:

> The illustrious lord of men, the mighty Kundunga, had a famous son, Ashvavarman, who, like unto Anshuman, was the founder of a noble lineage. His were three eminent sons resembling the three sacrificial fires. Foremost amongst these three and distinguished by austerity, strength, and self-restraint, was the illustrious Mulavarman, the lord of kings, who had performed a Bahusuvarnaka sacrifice. For that sacrifice this sacrificial post has been established by the eminent Brahmanas.

Source Golzio. [Ed.], 2004: 1; Chhabra, 1965: 85–86; Griffiths, 2014

to Sri Lanka and Java. In the Jatakas, Manimekalai is in fact the name of a goddess who protects and saves seamen. The *Silappadikaram* refers to *yavana* craftsmen in cities, *yavanas* living in their separate quarters in Puhar, and Tamil kings hiring *yavana* guards to protect the gates of their fortresses. The epics also describe the lavish lifestyle of Indian merchants.

Spices such as pepper and cardamom continued to be produced and exported from the Kerala region. But with increased demand, these were also imported from South-east Asia and then sent on westwards. Cotton cloth was another important southern export and the *Silappadikaram* mentions 32 varieties of cotton fabric. It refers to kings despatching vessels loaded with eaglewood, silk, sandalwood, spices, and camphor in the early cool season. Tamil texts refer to silk as *pattu*.

Excavations at Kaveripattinam (Soundararajan, 1994) revealed remains stretching from the 3rd century BCE to the 12th century CE. At nearby Pallavaneswaram, there are remains of a brick Buddhist *vihara* and a large, multi-storeyed temple. The temple belonged to *c*. 6th century and the *vihara* to the 4th century. Two bronze Buddha images were found within the precincts. The evidence of coastal trade can be connected with the flourishing settlements off the coast of Sri Lanka such as Mantai in the north and Kirinda and Godavaya in the south.

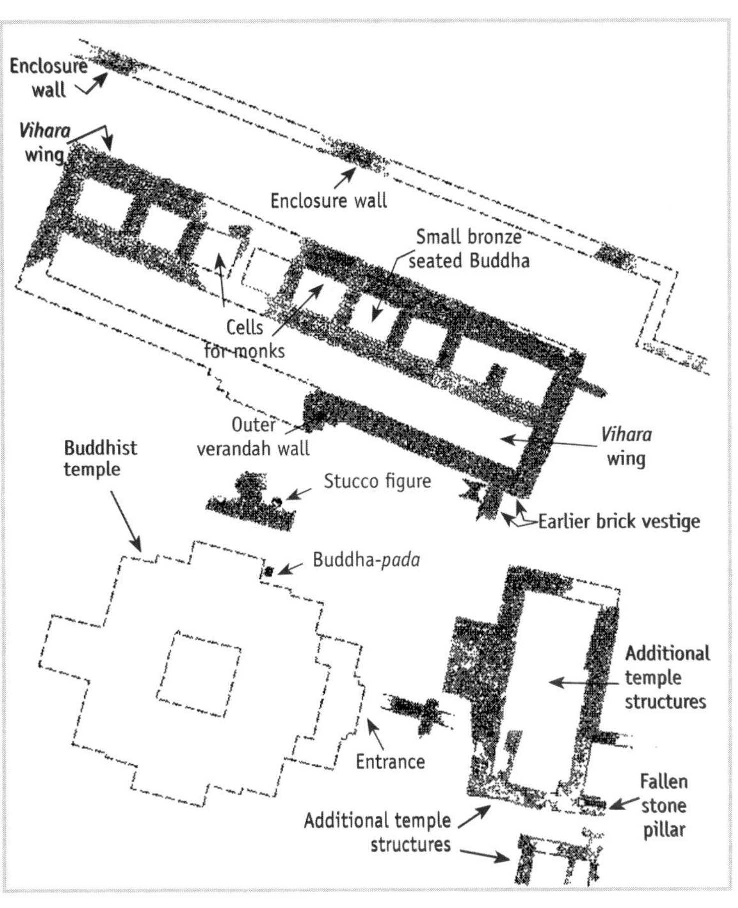

Figure 9.1 Buddhist complex, Pallavaneswaram, Kaveripattinam; the *vihara* belongs to the 4th century, the temple to the 6th century

Aspects of Social Structure: Gender, Forms of Labour, Slavery, and Untouchability

The main aim of pilgrims such as Faxian was to provide pious Buddhists in China with an opportunity to visualize places and events connected with the Buddha's life (see Tansen Sen, 2006: 33). Their accounts have to be problematized by taking into account their aims and audience (Deeg, 2007). It is, therefore, not surprising that references to mundane details concerning the lifestyle of Indians are few and cursory. Faxian presents an idealized picture of Indian society in the 5th century for his Chinese audience. He describes a happy and contented people enjoying a life of peace and prosperity. They did not have to register their households or appear before magistrates. Farmers who worked on royal land had to give a certain portion of their produce to the king.

More specific and accurate information about social life during the period can be obtained from other sources. Royal women are visible on coins and seals. Mention was earlier made of the 'king and queen type' of coins, such as that depicting Chandragupta I and his wife Kumaradevi. Queens also appear on the reverse of certain coins. A queen sitting on a couch, with a flower in her right hand appears on the reverse of coins of Kumaragupta I and Chandragupta II. A standing female figure holding a fly whisk in her right hand, appears on the reverse of the *ashvamedha* type coins of Samudragupta and Kumaragupta I. As the queen was supposed to fan and bathe the horse in the *ashvamedha* sacrifice, this may represent a queen. (Alternatively, she may represent a goddess.) The discoveries at Basarh (ancient Vaishali) include three oval sealings of Dhruvasvamini (wife of Chandragupta II), with a seated lion and an inscription.

Matrimonial alliances were an important part of the politics of the time. This is indicated by the mention of queens in Gupta inscriptions such as the Allahabad *prashasti* of Samudragupta and the Bhitari pillar inscription of Skandagupta. The Vakataka genealogies do not generally mention queens. However, Vakataka inscriptions reveal the exercise of political power by queen Prabhavatigupta during the reigns of three consecutive Vakataka rulers. Some royal women took the initiative in gift-giving. Prabhavatigupta made grants in her own right; we can also note the Masoda plates of Pravarasena II, which record a grant made at the request of an unnamed chief queen. A fragmentary inscription found on the walls of the Kevala-Narasimha temple in Ramtek (Nagpur district) records the construction of this temple (given the name Prabhavatisvamin) in memory of the deceased queen Prabhavatigupta by her daughter, possibly in conjunction with her brother Pravarasena II.

The multiple matrimonial alliances of kings are well known. Sanskrit *kavya* reveals the complex relationships within polygynous royal households (see Daud Ali, 2007). The *Kamasutra* suggests that polygyny was also prevalent among sections of the non-royal elite. The Ghatotkacha cave inscription of Varahadeva gives a long genealogy of the donor's family. This includes mention of a person named Soma, who is described as having taken Kshatriya as well as Brahmana wives. He is said to have obtained a son named Ravi with marks of royalty on his person from the Kshatriya wife, and sons learned in the Veda from the Brahmana wives.

While such inscriptions give glimmers of information about royal and elite households, Dharmashastra texts such as the *Narada* and *Brihaspati Smriti* throw light on household and gender relations from the point of view of Brahmanical social ideology. The *Kamasutra* of Vatsyayana consists of seven sections on the following topics—general practices and precepts; sex between men and women; obtaining a bride; the duties of a wife; relations with wives of other men; courtesans; and secret formulae to ensure sexual success (see Roy, 1998). The social ideology reflected in the *Kamasutra* intersects in many ways with that of the Dharmashastra texts, but there were also major differences of opinion between the experts on *dharma* and *kama*.

According to the *Kamasutra*, a good wife serves her husband diligently, keeps the house clean and well-decorated, and manages the servants and household finances efficiently. She is dutiful and submissive. She waits on her husband, attends social and other occasions only with his permission, entertains his friends, and serves her in-laws and obeys their orders. She worships every day at the household shrine. When her husband is away, she leads a restrained life, wears only the minimum ornaments, and performs religious rituals and fasts, going out of the house only when essential. She grows different sorts of plants and trees in the garden. She has knowledge of agriculture, cattle rearing, spinning, and weaving, and knows how to take care of her husband's pets. When her husband is away, she ensures that his finances do not suffer. If she has a co-wife, she is supposed to look upon her as a sister or mother, depending on their relative age.

The *Kamasutra* visualizes the *nagaraka* (urban connoisseur) and the *ganika* (courtesans) as experts in *kama*. Sanskrit *kavya* literature too refers to *ganikas*. For instance, the heroine of the *Mrichchhakatika* is a courtesan named Vasantasena. *Kavya* texts display an ambivalent attitude towards the *ganika*. On the one hand, she is admired and celebrated for her beauty, wit, and other accomplishments. On the other hand, the fact that her sexual favours could be bought by anyone for money meant that she could never hope to attain social respectability. There are also textual references to the ordinary prostitute, whose life was devoid of the glamour and wealth associated with the *ganika*.

Although much of the *Kamasutra* is addressed to men, Vatsyayana recognizes the possibility of women reading his work. He considers women as active agents with desires and needs that must be understood by men. He describes the *gandharva* marriage—one based on mutual love—as the best. Although the *Kamasutra*'s main focus is on heterosexual relationships, it does discuss homosexuality. Apart from men and women, Vatsyayana refers to the 'third nature' (*tritiya prakriti*).

The *Kamasutra* deals in a pragmatic, matter-of-fact way with sexual relations between men and married women. However, Dharmashastra texts considered adultery by women as a sin for which penances were prescribed. Some texts held penance to be unnecessary and asserted that an adulterous woman regained her purity after her menstrual period. The *Narada Smriti* (*stripumsa*, verse 91) states that if a woman was found to have committed adultery, her head should be shaved, she should lie on a low bed, be given poor food and clothes, and should devote herself to removing the sweepings from her husband's house. A great deal hinged on the social status of the individuals involved. For instance, if a woman committed adultery with a Shudra or a low-caste man, the Smritis suggest that her husband abandon her. A virtuous wife, on the other hand, was to be cherished.

Dharmashastra texts continue to advocate that a widow should lead a celibate and austere life. The *Brihaspati Smriti* (verses 483–84) offers the alternative that she burn herself on her husband's funeral pyre. There are instances of the practice (known as *sahamarana* or *sahagamana*) in the *Mahabharata*—e.g., Madri, wife of Pandu, burns herself on his funeral pyre and some of Vasudeva and Vasudeva Krishna's wives are described as having done likewise. Widow remarriage seems to have been considered with disfavour. That it did, however, happen is suggested by the *Amarakosha*, which gives synonyms for a *punarbhu* (remarried widow), her husband, and for a *dvija* who has a *punarbhu* as his principal wife. Vatsyayana mentions widows who took lovers.

While the subordinate and dependent position of women is increasingly emphasized in texts of the time, the law books reflect an increase in the scope of *stri-dhana*. A later text, the *Katyayana Smriti* (7th/8th century) lists the various types of *stri-dhana* as follows: That which is given to women at the time of marriage before the nuptial fire is known as *adhyagni stri-dhana*. That which a woman obtains when being taken in a procession from her father's house to the groom's house is known as *adhyavahanika stri-dhana*. That which is given out of affection to a woman by her father-in-law or mother-in-law and that which is received by her at the time of performing obeisance at the feet of elders is known as *pritidatta stri-dhana*. That which is obtained as the price of household vessels, beasts of burden, milch cows, ornaments, and slaves is said to be *shulka* (bride's fee). That which is obtained after marriage from members of her husband's family and from the family of her father's kinsmen is described as *anvadheya* (subsequent gift). That which is obtained by a married woman in her husband's or father's house or an unmarried girl from her parents or brothers is known as *saudayika*. It is notable that Katyayana's description of the categories of *adhyagni* and *adhyavahanika* is quite wide and can include gifts from non-kinfolk and strangers, as well as those received by a woman on a number of special occasions other than marriage.

As far as forms of labour are concerned, the texts mention hired labour used in farming, watching fields, harvesting, tending cattle, craft production, and household work. The *Brihaspati* and *Narada Smriti*s lay down rates and rules for the payment of wages in cash or kind. Payment in kind could take the form of a share of the item, such as grain, milk, or domesticated animals. The *Narada Smriti* states that the employer must pay wages to the worker at a fixed time as per agreement, at the beginning, middle, or end of the work. If wages had not been fixed in advance, the worker was entitled to 1/10th of the profit (*Narada Smriti* 6.2–3). The *Brihaspati Smriti* (16.1–2) states that the servant of a farmer was entitled to 1/5th of the crop along with food and clothing or to only 1/3rd of the crop. Of course, these are all prescriptions, not descriptions of prevailing practice.

Forced labour (*vishti*) became more common than before in this period. The fact that it is mentioned along with taxes in land grant inscriptions suggests that it was considered a source of income for the state, a sort of tax paid by the people. The fact that most of the inscriptions referring to *vishti* come from the Madhya Pradesh and Kathiawar regions may suggest that this practice was more prevalent in these areas.

The *Narada Smriti* has a detailed discussion of slavery and lists 15 types of slaves. This enumeration is more detailed that in the *Arthashastra* and *Manu Smriti*, but basically consists of elaborations or sub-divisions of already known types. These include war captives reduced to slavery, debt enslavement, and voluntary enslavement. Slaves could be handed down to descendants of their erstwhile owners along with other items of property. Slaves are generally mentioned as domestic servants or personal attendants. A child born of a woman slave in a master's house was considered his slave as well. The *Narada Smriti* (5. 26) asserts that a slave can be pledged or mortgaged, and that the master could hire out his services to another. The *Narada Smriti* prescribes the amputation of the foot of a person found guilty of abducting a slave woman. It also discusses the manumission of slaves—a slave born in the house, bought, obtained, or inherited could be freed only when the master desired to do so. The ceremony of manumission is described—the master was supposed to remove a jar of water from the shoulder of the slave and break it. He was then supposed to sprinkle some parched grain and flowers over his head and say three times: 'You are no longer a *dasa*.'

According to Faxian, Chandalas had to live outside towns and marketplaces, and were expected to strike a piece of wood when they approached so that others could get out of their way to avoid their touch. In South India, the notion of untouchability seems to have emerged in the late Sangam period. A work called the *Acharakkovai* refers to water touched by a *pulaiya* being considered defiled and unfit for consumption by higher caste people, and states that even glancing at a *pulaiya* was polluting. The Tamil epics also allude to the practice of untouchability. In the *Manimekalai*, Brahmanas are exhorted not to touch Aputtiran, the son of a Brahmana woman and Shudra male, lest they be polluted. (For a discussion of the practice of untouchability in South India, see Hanumanthan, 2004.)

The epics and Puranas wax eloquent on the evils of the Kali age. The idea of a pristine *Krita* age followed by a progressive dharmic decline, can be traced to fairly early times, and it can be questioned whether the idea reflects a specific historical crisis occurring in the post-300 CE period. The many evils of the Kali age that are enumerated in the epics and Puranas include, for instance, that people will be liars; members of the four *varnas* will not follow their prescribed duties; *yajnas*, gifts, and *vratas* will be substituted by other practices; *mlechchha* kings will rule the earth; lands will be depopulated and filled with wild animals, snakes, and insects; women will be unchaste; cows will yield little milk; the rains will not come in the proper season; traders will practise various kinds of fraud; people will not live long and will grow bald early in life. The descriptions of the Kali age in Brahmanical texts suggest fears about the fragility of the social fabric and its vulnerability to chaos. While prescribing the exemplary social and political order, these texts were clearly aware of the fact that reality differed considerably. The idea of the four *yugas* also justified differences in norms of behaviour over time, as the Dharmashastra tradition held the view that different *dharmas* were prescribed for different *yugas*.

Patterns of Religious Developments

The period *c*. 300–600 CE is often seen as a phase of 'Brahmanical revival' or a consolidation of Brahmanical ideology. This is reflected in the firm establishment of Sanskrit as the language of royal inscriptions and the increasing popularity of temple-based sectarian cults. Actually, 'Brahmanism' was being transformed into a new sort of synthesis that can be described as Puranic Hinduism. The origins of this process lay in the preceding centuries, and its post-6th century history will be traced in the next chapter.

The developments of Hindu religious ideas and practices can be tracked down through the Puranas, religious sculpture and architecture, and inscriptions. The Puranas show the expansion of the Brahmanical tradition by engaging with diverse religious traditions in the subcontinent (Kunal Chakrabarti, 2001) and by accommodating women and lower castes to some extent in religious practices such as *vratas* (Monika Saxena, 2019). The Puranas refer to various rites, *vratas* (vows), and *tirthas* (pilgrimage) as part of religious practice. Sectarian symbols appeared on seals. For instance, the Bhita seals have many Shaiva and Vaishnava legends, and symbols such as the *linga*, *trishula*, bull, Gaja-Lakshmi, *shankha* (conch), and *chakra* (wheel). Royal *prashastis*, coins, and seals proclaimed the sectarian affiliations of kings. Some of the Gupta kings proclaimed themselves as *Bhagavatas*, i.e., worshippers of Vasudeva Krishna. Most of the Vakatakas described themselves as devotees of Shiva, and two as devotees of Vishnu. The major Hindu sects that became increasingly popular during these centuries focused on the worship of Vishnu, Shiva, and Shakti.

Textual and archaeological evidence testifies to the growth of Jaina establishments in areas such as Karnataka, while Buddhist monastic centres can be identified in different parts of the subcontinent. Royal and non-royal donative inscriptions, provide an idea of the social groups who were patronizing religious establishments.

Although they had their unique features and doctrines, the various religious traditions and sects were part of an interactive cultural milieu. It is therefore, not surprising to note that their trajectories overlapped and intersected to some extent. At the level of popular religious practice, iconic worship in shrines was a feature of the Hindu cults as well as Jainism and Buddhism. We can note the close juxtaposition of Hindu and Jaina caves at Badami, and of Hindu, Jaina, and Buddhist shrines, at Ellora and Aihole. Architectural forms and sculptural ornamentation frequently cut across sectarian boundaries. There are broad similarities between Hindu, Buddhist, and Jaina cave shrines and between Jaina and Hindu structural temples. Shrines of various religious traditions shared a common pool of auspicious symbols and ornamentation, often over vast stretches of time. A striking example is the similarity of medallion-type and other ornamentation (for instance, the motif of garland bearers) at the Buddhist site of Amaravati and the much later Hindu shrines at Aihole and Pattadakal. One of the important factors responsible for this shared pool of symbols and expressions was the fact that they were conceptualized and executed by a common pool of architects and artisans.

The links and associations between different Hindu deities emerge clearly in the sculptural programme of many temples, where the presiding deity is naturally most prominent, but where a plethora of other gods and goddesses are also represented. The links are also reflected in the formation of pantheons and the emergence of composite deities such as Hari-Hara, who is part Vishnu and part Shiva. The incorporation of the Buddha into the list of Vishnu's *avataras* is often cited as an instance of the religious syncretism of the time. There are other examples as well. For instance, Indra, Vishnu, Rama, Hara, and Kama are mentioned in a donative inscription of Varahadeva, minister of the Vakataka king Harishena, in one of the Buddhist caves at Ajanta. Another example is the *Silappadikaram*'s description of a Jaina *arhat* using epithets of Shiva and Brahma such as Shankara, Chaturmukha, Ishana, and Svayambhu.

There were, however, limits to accommodation and syncretism, and relations between religious communities were not always harmonious. Although the Buddha is included in the list of Vishnu's *avataras* in some Puranas, he appears very infrequently in Vishnu temples, and never as the main object of worship. Philosophical texts give evidence of fierce debate and contestation. Competition and conflict no doubt revolved not only over doctrinal issues but also over patronage. The competitive relationship between various cults were sometimes expressed graphically in iconic form, for instance, in representations of the Devi trampling on other Hindu gods, or Buddhist deities trampling Hindu ones (usually Shiva).

The 'great traditions' interfaced not only with each other, but also with a myriad of local beliefs and practices. Stone and terracotta images of various gods, goddesses, demi-gods, and demi-goddesses such as *yakshas*, *yakshis*, *nagas*, *nagis*, *gandharvas*, *vidyadharas*, and *apsaras* indicate other foci of popular devotional worship. The independent worship of *yakshas* and *nagas* continued during these centuries. For instance, there was a *yaksha* temple at Padmavati near Gwalior and a temple of the *yaksha* Maninaga at Rajgir. At Ajanta, a *naga* shrine is associated with Cave 16, while Cave 2 has a shrine dedicated

FURTHER DISCUSSION | **Hari-Hara in the Badami caves**

Hari-Hara is a composite god, half Hari (Vishnu) and half Hara (Shiva). One of the earliest sculptural depictions of Hari-Hara is carved in the Badami caves (late 6th century). Shiva forms the right side of this composite deity and Vishnu the left. The god is shown with four arms. His rear right hand holds a battleaxe entwined with a snake (an attribute of Shiva), while his rear left hand holds a conch shell (a symbol of Vishnu). His front right hand is broken, and the front left is in the *katihasta* position, the arm slightly bent and resting on the thigh.

The right part of the crown shows Shiva's matted locks (*jata-mukuta*) and the left part the *kirita-mukuta* of Vishnu. The ear-rings are also different. The right ear is adorned with Shiva's *sarpa-kundala*, and the left ear with Vishnu's *nakra-kundala* (or *makara-kundala*). The Nandi bull and Parvati stand on the right, while a pot-bellied *garuda* and Lakshmi stand on the left.

The lower section of the panel is enlivened by dwarfish figures of members of Shiva's *gana* or entourage. Some of them are dancing, while others play on musical instruments.

to the *yakshi* Hariti and her consort Panchika. However, the colossal sculptures of the type found in earlier times disappear, and *yakshas*, *nagas*, and their consorts now appear more often as *dvarapalas* (gatekeepers) of the great gods or as subsidiary figures. This phenomenon reflects the attempts of the dominant religious traditions to establish links with the popular cults as well to appropriate and subordinate them.

An interesting feature of donative inscriptions of this period are gifts for the maintenance of *sattras* or charitable feeding houses, which seem to have been associated with religious establishments. For instance, a fragmentary stone inscription found at Gadhwa (in Prayagraj district, UP) appears to record a gift of 10 *dinaras* and another gift of uncertain value for the maintenance of a *sattra*. The donors included some people headed by Matridasa and a woman of Pataliputra. Another inscription from Gadhwa, dated in Gupta year 98, records a gift of 12 *dinaras*, probably for maintaining a *sattra*.

Although devotional forms of religious practice were becoming increasingly prevalent, the fact that kings of many dynasties performed Vedic *yajnas* indicates that these continued to be an important basis of royal legitimation. Samudragupta and Kumaragupta, Vijayadevavarman of the Shalankayana dynasty, Dharasena of the Traikutaka dynasty, and Krishnavarman of the Kadamba dynasty claim to have performed the *ashvamedha*. The Vakataka king Pravarasena I is described in inscriptions as having performed many elaborate *yajnas*. Inscriptions of the Bharashivas and Pallavas boast of their performance of various *shrauta* sacrifices. There are also some *yupa* inscriptions. As mentioned earlier, the Bihar stone pillar inscription refers to the setting up of a sacrificial post by the brother-in-law of a Gupta king. While maintaining their connections with the *shrauta* sacrificial tradition, kings simultaneously connected themselves with the increasingly popular sectarian cults, as is evident from their sectarian epithets and their patronage of temples.

The varied invocations and religious imagery of royal *prashastis* and the diverse beneficiaries of royal gifts indicate that royal patronage was not necessarily channelized exclusively in one particular direction. This has often been interpreted as a reflection of a sort of 'religious toleration' that was supposedly fashionable among ruling elites in ancient and early medieval India. When seen from the perspective of royal policy, the dispersal of patronage across a wide spectrum of beneficiaries made good political sense, as it permitted the forging of ties and alliances with a variety of social groups and religious communities.

The emergence of Tantra

Tantra is extremely complex and difficult to define. It is not a religion, but a set of diverse ideas and practices represented in sects belonging to different religious traditions; it had a powerful impact not only in India but across Asia (see Padoux, 2017; Davidson, 2002). Some general features of Tantra include the importance attached to energy, rituals, yogic practices, fierce deities, and sexual rites. During this and succeeding periods, the impact of Tantra was felt not only in Shaiva and Shakta sects, but also within the Buddhist fold, although to a much less extent in Jainism. Hindu and Buddhist Tantra share some broad similarities, but have many philosophical differences.

The Tantric path was supposed to be a secret one, divulged by preceptors to select initiates. It involved the cultivation of beliefs and practices that were believed to lead to the attainment of supernatural powers and a state of liberation. The Tantra of early medieval India drew on diverse sources of inspiration including the Veda, Mimamsa, Sankhya, Yoga, and Vedanta, but it developed its own unique characteristics. Evidence for the worship of Tantric deities goes back to the 5th century, and some of the texts may also have been composed in this period. The early medieval period saw a further development of Tantric cults and practices.

Tantra considers Godhead as involving the union of a masculine and feminine aspect. Energy (*shakti*) is conceived of as feminine and is central to the Tantric view of the universe and liberation. Tantric practice is usually called *sadhana*. Initiation (*diksha*) into a sect involves ritual initiation, an important part of which is the imparting of a secret *mantra* by the guru to the initiate. *Mantras* (prayers and formulae) and *bijas* (syllables associated with various deities, believed to have a mystic potency) have an important role. Diagrams known as *yantras*, *mandalas*, or *chakras*, and symbolic gestures known as *mudras* play an important role in rituals. Hathayoga postures and meditation (*dhyana*) are also important. All these are supposed to be harnessed towards awakening the *kundalini* energy that lies coiled like a serpent in the body, drawing it upwards towards union with the supreme. Sexual symbolism and magic are other aspects of Tantra. The notion of *puja* (worship) in Tantra involves transforming the worshipper into the deity. It is often associated with five elements (*panchatattva*)—namely *mada* (alcohol), *mamsa* (meat), *matsya* (fish), *mudra* (generally parched grain), and *maithuna* (sexual intercourse).

Tantrism was divided into a number of sects, the principal ones associated with the worship of Shiva, Shakti, and Vishnu. The various sects had their own texts, most of the important ones being in Sanskrit. There was a close relationship between the Shaiva and Shakta cults as the deities Shiva and Shakti were considered closely related. The most important early Tantric sect among the Vaishnavas was the Pancharatra. The Sahajiyas of Bengal were a later sect belonging to the Tantric variety of Vaishnavism. The Shaiva Tantric sects such as the Kapalikas, Kalamukhas, and Nathas came to the fore in the early medieval period. Apart from the existence of probably small groups of Tantric practitioners, there was the larger phenomenon of a widespread impact of Tantrism on non-Tantric cults and traditions. While the groups of Tantric adepts and practitioners may have been small, they acquired a large following, including in royal courts. This made Tantra a powerful presence in religious, social, and political life in early medieval India. Tantra will be discussed further in Chapter 10.

The evolution of the Vaishnava pantheon

The worship of the gods and goddesses that ultimately came to be absorbed into the Vaishnava pantheon was visible in the period *c.* 200 BCE–300 CE. During the subsequent centuries, this pantheon became more clearly identifiable. The cults of Narayana, Vasudeva Krishna, and Samkarshana Balarama were absorbed into the Vaishnava fold, and Shri Lakshmi was recognized as the consort of Vishnu. However, in spite of the increasing importance of the Vishnu element, the cults of these various deities still retained their individual identity. This is evident from the fact that although the term

'Vaishnava' occurs frequently in the Puranas, it is rare in the *Mahabharata*. It is also not all that frequent in inscriptions of this period, while the term *parama-bhagavata* occurs often.

The worship of the *avataras* of Vishnu became increasingly popular. As mentioned in Chapter 8, the *avataras* eventually came to be conventionally reckoned as 10, but some of the names vary in different texts. The *Matsya Purana* lists 10 *avataras*. Three—Narayana, Narasimha, and Vamana—were divine, and seven—Dattatreya, Mandhatri, Rama (son of Jamadagni), Rama (son of Dasharatha), Vedavyasa, Buddha, and Kalki—were human. The *Vayu Purana* replaces the Buddha with Krishna. The *Bhagavata Purana*, which is a much later text (probably belonging to the 10th century), gives three different lists of the *avataras*. The assimilative potential of the *avatara* doctrine is indicated by the fact that some Puranas incorporate the Buddha in the list. The later *Bhagavata Purana* (10th century) does this, but changes the Buddha's parentage—it describes him as the son of Ajana and states that he was born in Magadha. However, it should be noted that the Buddha incarnation was supposed to delude demons and lead them to hell.

The *garuda* became the emblem of the Gupta emperors, and from the time of Chandragupta II, Gupta kings had the title *parama-bhagavata* in their inscriptions. The early Chalukyas adopted the boar as their emblem. Most Chalukya inscriptions—and those of their feudatories as well—start with an invocation to and praise of Vishnu's boar incarnation. Some of the early Pallava and Ganga kings proclaimed themselves as worshippers of Vasudeva Krishna. Kings ruling in other parts of the country also described themselves as *bhagavatas*. Some inscriptions suggest that there was no contradiction between the worship of Vasudeva Krishna and the performance of Vedic sacrifices. The *Brihatsamhita* of Varahamihira states that the installation of an image of Vishnu should be performed by the *bhagavatas* according to their own rule, and that during such an installation, the twice-born priest should offer sacrifice into the fire with corresponding *mantras*. Lakshmi continued to be a prominent goddess associated with good fortune, including that of kings and cities, apart from being recognized as the consort of Vishnu. Her Gaja-Lakshmi form is depicted on many Gupta coins.

We have seen in Chapter 6 how *ahimsa* was initially associated with renunciants, especially Jainism and Buddhism. However, it gradually seeped into other traditions as well. *Ahimsa* was an important aspect of the Vaishnava sects. The Narayaniya section of the *Mahabharata* states that in the horse sacrifice performed by king Vasu Uparichara (a devotee of Vishnu) no animals were slaughtered; the only offerings were products of the wilderness. The *Vishnu Purana* states that a devotee of Vishnu does not indulge in any sort of violence.

Early Pancharatra and Vaikhanasa were important Vaishnava traditions which combined devotionalism towards Vishnu with ascetic and yogic elements. Non-injury was an important part of the Pancharatra understanding of ritual. The Narayaniya Parva of the *Mahabharata*, although not a specifically Pancharatra text, contains several Pancharatra elements. It advocates devotion to Narayana, who is also referred to as Vasudeva, Vishnu, and Hari. It does not reject Vedic sacrifice, but rather emphasizes renunciation and non-injury, and prescribes rituals that do not involve animal sacrifice. Yogic practices are also emphasized. The text mentions two concepts that were to become important in Pancharatra—the idea of the four emanations of Vishnu and the five observances of the day (*panchakala*). The four emanations were named after the Vrishni heroes—Vasudeva Krishna, Samkarshana, Pradyumna, and Aniruddha. These four emanations are interpreted in a cosmological way—Vasudeva representing the supreme reality, Samkarshana matter (*prakriti*), Pradyumna cosmic mind (*manas*), and Aniruddha cosmic self-consciousness (*ahamkara*). The Narayaniya Parva uses the term *murti* for them, while later texts use the term *vyuha*. The Pancharatra concept of *panchakala* consists of the following: *abhigamana* (approaching the god, i.e., morning prayers, etc.), *upadana* (collection of material for worship), *ijya* (sacrifice, i.e., worship), *svadhyaya* (studying the texts), and *yoga* (meditation).

The *Vaikhanasa Shrautasutra* and *Vaikhanasa Smartasutra* (composed sometime between the 4th and the 8th centuries) emphasize devotion towards Vishnu or Narayana. The *Smartasutra* refers to the installation of an image of Vishnu in a home, temple, or sacrificial arena, accompanied by Vaishnava *mantras*. It also refers to various disciplines and virtues to be practised by hermits devoted to Vishnu. Yoga is considered extremely important in the stage of complete renunciation, where the goal is union with the Supreme Self.

The sculptures and inscriptions of the period allude to many aspects of Vishnu. They variously describe him as associated with the *garuda*; resting on the waters of the four oceans; supporter of the three worlds; slayer of demons such as Madhu, Mura, and Punyajana; and as bearer of the discus, club, the bow made of horn, and the sword known as Nandaka. Although there is epigraphic and sculptural evidence of the worship of various *avataras* of Vishnu, four incarnations were especially prominent—the Varaha (boar), Narasimha (man-lion), Vamana (dwarf), and Manusha, i.e., Vasudeva Krishna. These are depicted repeatedly in relief carvings on the walls of cave shrines and structural temples.

The many Vaishnava sculptures found at Mathura include images of the *avataras* such as the boar, dwarf, man-lion and Vasudeva Krishna. The Dashavatara temple at Deogarh in Jhansi district contains relief panels depicting many scenes associated with Vasudeva Krishna and the Nrisimha and Vamana *avataras*. One of the most impressive sculptures of these centuries is a colossal figure of Krishna effortlessly lifting up Govardhana mountain, originally found at Varanasi. This is the largest known free-standing stone image of the period. The full, round face is much damaged, so the features cannot be made out clearly. Krishna's locks of hair hang over his shoulders. He wears ornaments around his arms (the arms are not original; they were added later) and neck and a low crown. Vaishnava emblems and legends have been found on seals and sealings at sites such as Sunet, Bhita, and Basarh. Lakshmi also appears on some of the Bhita seals.

Krishna lifting Govardhana from Varanasi; Vishnu resting on Sheshanaga, Deogarh

Gaja-Lakshmi

The popularity of Vaishnavism in South India became more pronounced in the hymns of the Alvar saints, which will be discussed in the next chapter. However, the *Silappadikaram* mentions temples of Krishna and Baladeva at Madurai, Kaveripattinam, and other places. This is also the period when Vaishnavism started travelling outside the Indian subcontinent to Cambodia, Malaya, Java, and Bali in South-east Asia.

Inscriptions indicate the diverse sources of patronage enjoyed by Vaishnava establishments. Several inscriptions recording gifts to temples of Vasudeva Krishna and Vishnu have been found at Tusham in Haryana, Nagari in Rajasthan, Bhitari and Gadhwa in Uttar Pradesh, and Eran, Mandasor, and Khoh in Madhya Pradesh. The Mehrauli iron pillar inscription of Chandra (mentioned earlier) refers to the setting up of a standard of the god Vishnu at a place called Vishnupada. An inscription in the Udayagiri caves near Vidisha, inscribed over two sculpted panels depicting Vishnu and a goddess, refers to the dedication of the panels of the cave by a *maharaja*, who was probably a feudatory of Chandragupta II. An inscription on a stone pillar belonging to the reign of Skandagupta at Bhitari records the installation of an image of Vishnu as Sharngin (wielder of the bow or horn called Sharnga) and the allotment of the village in which the pillar stood. The Junagadh inscription of the reign of Skandagupta tells us that in Gupta year 138 (i.e., 457–58 CE), Chakrapalita had built a temple dedicated to the god Vishnu under the name Chakrabhrit (wielder of the *chakra*). The Eran inscription of the first regnal year of the Huna king Toramana refers to Dhanyavishnu, brother of a high-ranking notable of Airakina *vishaya*, who erected a shrine over the boar image on whose chest the inscription is inscribed.

Shaivism

The worship of Shiva also increased in popularity during the period *c.* 300–600 CE. Shiva came to be associated with Ganesha, Karttikeya, and the river goddess Ganga. The Shaiva Puranas describe the various forms of the god and the installation of Shiva *lingas* in temples and indicate the existence of various Shaiva sects. Although they present Shiva's worship as part of the mainstream *smarta* tradition, it is clear that some sects existed on its margins, while others were clearly outside it. This issue will be discussed further in Chapter 10.

The Pashupatas seem to be one of the oldest and most important Shaiva sects. Their philosophical underpinnings consisted of a distinction between the individual soul (*pashu*), god (*pati*), and worldly fetters (*pasha*). Liberation, conceived of as a state in which the soul and Shiva come to be closely associated, could be obtained through the grace of the god. The Pashupatas were associated with yogic practices and are often described as ascetics with ashes (*bhasma*) smeared on their bodies. Sculptures and inscriptions indicate the popularity of the Pashupata sect in Mathura and several other areas. The frequency of the depiction of Lakulisha in the Lakshmaneshvara, Bharateshvara, and Shatrughneshvara temples—the earliest extant temples in Odisha—suggests that they were associated with the Pashupata sect.

Remains of Shiva temples have been found at Bhumara and Khoh in Central India. Sculptures and inscriptions bear indirect testimony to the existence of many more that have not survived. The god is mentioned and invoked in numerous inscriptions, and certain kings (e.g., the Maitrakas of Valabhi) described themselves as *parama-maheshvara* (supreme worshipper of Maheshvara, i.e., Shiva). The Karamadanda inscription of the time of Kumaragupta I refers to the installation of a *linga* named Prithvishvara by a person named Prithivishena, a *mantrin* and *kumaramatya*. An inscription on the back wall of one of the Udayagiri caves (MP) refers to the gift of the cave as a temple of Shambhu (Shiva) by Virasena, a resident of Pataliputra and a minister of Chandragupta II, who had come to this place along with the king in the course of a military expedition. The Mathura pillar inscription, dated in the Gupta year 61, records the building of a temple-cum-residence by a teacher named Uditacharya for his teacher and his teacher's teacher, and for the installation of two Shaiva images. The practice of naming a Shiva *linga* or temple after preceptors or patrons is evident in this period.

Ekamukhalinga from Khoh (MP)

FURTHER DISCUSSION | **Mahadeva in the Elephanta cave**

The small island of Elephanta, off the coast of Mumbai, was given this name by the Portuguese after a large elephant sculpture once located here. Several caves are scattered over the island. The most famous of these is Cave 1, dated to the mid-6th century CE. This large cave, measuring about 40 m north–south, consists of a spacious pillared hall, at the western end of which is a square shrine containing a *linga* and *yoni*. Imposing *dvarapalas* (doorkeepers) flank its four entrances. The niches in the walls of the large hall frame several fine relief carvings. One of these depicts Lakulisha, and this suggests that the caves were associated with the Pashupata sect.

The most spectacular carving in the hall is an over 5 m high relief carving of Maheshvara (Shiva) with three faces. The faces in the centre and to the right have a tranquil expression, while the one on the left is angry, with bulging eyes. Some scholars suggest that a fourth (at the back) and perhaps even a fifth (on top, facing the ceiling) face are implied. This is because the *Vishnudharmottara Purana* describes the five faces of Shiva. According to one interpretation, the three faces represent Aghora-Bhairava (a fierce form of the god), Shiva, and Parvati. Stella Kramrisch identified the three faces as those of Shiva as Sadyojata, Aghora, and Vamadeva. Here is an excerpt from Kramrisch's description—detailed, inspired, and evocative:

> The great sculpture of Mahadeva is an image of the fully manifest Supreme Shiva. In the middle is the face of Sadyojata; the faces of Aghora and Vamadeva are collateral. The breadth of the shoulders belongs to the central face; the chest, showing but the slightest modeling, is smooth and young. It is as if breathing and holding the breath, as is shown by the ebbing curves of the necklace laid on its raised surface. It is hemmed in on the right and the left by the hands; the right hand is raised—it is damaged; the left rests on the base and holds a ripe fruit with its point up. The shoulders are also those of the lateral faces. These are turned against them, and it is on their backs that their hands come to rest. The one on the spectator's left, belonging to the wrathful face, has a serpent rearing its head from between its fingers, while the one on the right, belonging to the blissful face, holds a lotus flower and is delicately poised on the shoulder. Thus, beset with emblems and hands, their fingers pointing upwards in the middle of the bust, closing in where they rest upon the shoulders, the broad body fills the width of the recess like an altar beset with offerings.
>
> The middle boldly projecting, the frontal image surges upwards straight and strong as a pillar, with silence on its face and radiance on its crown. The heads on the right and the left repeat the ascent of the central pillar, clinging to it collaterally with their high curving crowns, and forming with it the outline of a strong triple arch which firmly binds together the outline of the triple image.
>
> Each of the three faces is steeped in its own mood, a closed world, each silent, unseeing, each turned away from the other, but each blossoming in generous curves round the stem whence they originate and derive their stability. They are carved in widely sweeping surfaces which bind the crowned triune head in depth just as the triple 'arch' binds it vertically. Hands and flowers, serpent, hair, and jewels are laid against the smoothness of face and body. Each face has its own physiognomy, each crown correspondingly its own ornaments, the hands their respective symbols; but they are upheld and comprised by the power and unity of the total image.

Source Kramrisch, [1946] 1994: 142–44

The worship of the great goddess

The importance of the worship of Durga, reflected in the epics and Puranas, was mentioned in Chapter 8. The *Ramayana* describes Uma as the daughter of Himavat and the sister of Ganga. The *Harivamsha* refers to the goddess as the sister of Vishnu and Indra. She also appears in mythology as Ekanamsha or Bhadra, sister of Vasudeva Krishna. The *Mahabharata* refers to her as the wife of Narayana and Shiva. Eventually, she came to be especially associated with Shiva. Shiva is Girisha (lord of the mountains); she is Girija, Shailaputri, Uma Haimavati, and later, Parvati. Shiva is Umapati (husband of Uma); as his consort, she is Maheshvari, Ishani, Mahadevi, Mahakali, and Shivani. The various aspects of the goddess reflect the different facets of her personality. In her destructive aspect, she was known as Kali (Destruction), Karali (The Terrible), Bhima (the Frightful), and Chandi/Chandika/Chamunda (the Wrathful). The *Markandeya Purana* refers to her as destroyer of many demons such as Mahishasura, Raktavija, Shumbha and Nishumbha, Chanda, and Munda. On the other hand, the goddess had a pacific aspect, reflected, for instance, in her manifestation as Sarasvati. Perhaps the fact that both Shiva and Shakti combined benevolent and terrifying forms was an important factor in the merging of their cults.

The epic-Puranic tradition is replete with stories reflecting the close connection between Shivaism and Shaktism. The *Mahabharata* mentions three Shakta *pithas* (places considered sacred by virtue of their association with the goddess Shakti). It connects the location of the *pithas* with the dismembering of the body of Sati which Shiva carried away on his shoulder after her death. Legends describe the resurrection of Sati as Uma and the difficult penances she performed to regain her husband. There are descriptions of the marriage of Shiva and Parvati, accounts of their life of conjugal bliss on mount Kailasha, and the terrible fate that befalls those who disturb their love-making. Through the centuries, sculptors delighted in depicting the majestic, loving couple on temple walls.

The worship of Shakti was especially popular in Eastern India, but was not confined to this area. This is evident from the many Durga images found in different parts of the country. These images can be categorized as *ugra* (fierce) or *saumya* (pacific). Durga Mahishasuramardini was the most popular representation of the fierce aspect of the goddess. Many Mahishasuramardini images of this period have been found, including at Udayagiri and Bhumara in Central India. A relief of Durga Mahishasuramardini is carved outside Cave 6 at Udayagiri in Madhya Pradesh. The carving is quite damaged, but the basic features are clear enough. The goddess has 12 arms and she holds in her many hands the weapons given to her by various gods. She presses down on the buffalo with one of her legs and holds its tail in one of her hands as she drives the trident into its neck with another.

Durga was also worshipped as one of the Sapta-Matrikas or Seven Mothers. The seven mothers were Brahmani, Maheshvari, Kaumari, Vaishnavi, Varahi, Indrani, and Yami (Chamunda). The Puranas describe them as energies of various gods who assisted the Devi in fighting the demons. Inscriptional references to the Matrikas include the mention of the building of a temple dedicated to them by Kumaraksha, a minister of Vishvavarman, ruler of Dashapura. The Bihar stone inscription mentions Skanda and the divine mothers. Relief sculptures of the Matrikas in association with Shiva have been found at Badoh-Pathari, not far from Besnagar. A badly damaged group of Matrika sculptures, perhaps originally from Besnagar, are now lodged in the Gwalior Archaeological Museum. Matrika figures were also found at Shamalaji in Gujarat. The figure of a female figure associated with a lion on Gupta coins may represent Durga.

The worship of other deities

The god Brahma is eulogized in the *Brahma Purana*, and the *Brihatsamhita* and *Vishnudharmottara Purana* describe how his images were to be made. Brahma sculptures have been found at many places, although they are not as numerous as those of the more popular deities. He is generally shown with three faces (the fourth face does not appear in relief sculptures) and is potbellied and four armed. He holds a *shruk* (a large wooden ladle used in sacrifices), *shruva* (a small wooden ladle used in sacrifices), *akshamala* (string of beads), and *pustaka* (book) in his hands. His vehicle is the *hamsa* (goose). Although he was part of the Puranic idea of a trinity of gods mentioned in the Puranas, and although *tirthas* such as Prayaga and Pushkara were associated with him, Brahma never became as important a focus of worship as Shiva, Vishnu, or Durga. He eventually became a subsidiary deity, whose images were housed in niches of temples dedicated to other gods.

The *Bhavishya*, *Shamba*, *Varaha*, and other Puranas describe the origin of the worship of Surya and the priests and festivals associated with him. The *Kurma Purana* states that kings should worship Vishnu and Indra, and that Brahmanas should especially worship Agni, Aditya (i.e., Surya), Brahma, and Shiva. The *Surya-hridaya* hymn in this Purana praises Surya as the greatest god who includes all other gods within him. The priests of solar temples are referred to as Bhojakas, Magas, and Somakas, and the Brahmanas of Shakadvipa were especially connected with Surya worship. The Magas seem to have priests of Iranian descent who worshipped the fire and the sun. The Western influence on the Surya cult is indicated by the iconography of the early images. The northern images of the period under review—such as in a relief carving in the Shiva temple at Bhumara—depict him with a high cylindrical headdress, a long coat with a scarf tied at the waist, holding two lotus buds, his feet encased in boots. He is often associated with a horse-drawn chariot.

Remains of Surya temples have been found in Western India, especially Gujarat. Inscriptional evidence testifies to the patronage extended to such temples in Gwalior, Indore, and Ashramaka in Central India. We have already noted the Mandasor inscription which records the building and renovation of a Surya temple at Dashapura by a guild of silk weavers. An Indore copper plate belonging to the reign of Skandagupta records a grant made by one Devavishnu for the maintenance of a lamp in a Surya temple. Maharaja Sarvvanaga of Uchchhakalpa made a gift in favour of a Surya temple located at Ashramaka. A Gwalior inscription belonging to the reign of Mihirakula records the building of a temple dedicated to this deity. Surya images have been found in Bengal. Chitraratha (i.e., the sun god) was one of the tutelary deities of the Shalankayana dynasty of the Andhra region.

The earliest representations of Karttikeya occur on punch-marked coins of earlier centuries. This god was also an object of popular worship during the period *c.* 300–600 CE, and came to be absorbed into the family of Shiva as his son. The Bilsad stone pillar inscription (UP) records the building of a gateway with a flight of steps, the establishment of a *sattra*, and the erection of the column on which the inscription is inscribed at a temple of the god Mahasena, i.e., Karttikeya, by a person named Dhruvasharman. Kings of the Kadamba dynasty were devotees of this god. The Gupta emperor Kumaragupta I (Kumara is in fact another name of Karttikeya) used the peacock—the vehicle of Karttikeya—as his symbol. The worship of this deity was also popular in South India, where he was known as Subrahmanya. Northern images of Karttikeya usually show him two-armed and riding on the peacock, holding a spear. At times, he is shown with his consorts Devasena and Valli. There is a relief carving of a standing Karttikeya in Cave 3 at Udayagiri.

Ganesha or Ganapati, the god with the potbelly and elephant head, also became increasingly important during this period. Texts describe him as the leader of the *ganas*, the unruly followers of Rudra-Shiva. Ganesha was considered a god who bestowed success and removed obstacles from the path of his devotees. In Gupta and post-Gupta sculpture, he is depicted sitting, standing, or dancing. A terracotta plaque in the Bhitargaon temple (UP) shows him in an unusual pose—flying through the air, his trunk dipping into a pot of sweets (*modaka*), which he holds in one of his four hands. In other sculptures, he holds various other things—e.g., a manuscript, pen, broken tusk, or hatchet. His vehicle is the mouse, which is sometimes depicted at the bottom of his sculptural representations.

The Tamil epics reveal a society with multiple religious layers. In the *Silappadikaram*, Kovalan and Kannaki are inclined towards the Jaina path. They are accompanied to Madurai by a Jaina nun named Kavundi. Kovalan's father and mother become Buddhist renunciants. Kannaki's parents are associated with the Ajivikas. The *Silappadikaram* refers to Vedic rituals and also mentions various gods such as Indra, Shiva, Vishnu, and Murugan and several goddesses including Durga. Both Tamil epics describe the Indra festival. The Indra cult seems to have been closely associated with the court and connected with the prosperity of the king and kingdom. At one point in the story, Shiva, who is said to be consorting with Parvati on mount Kailasha, comes down to observe the celebration of the Indra festival at Puhar. Elsewhere, Vishnu is described as the saviour of the world, and the Brahmana whom Kovalan and Kannaki meet on their way to Madurai gives a eulogistic speech about the god. At Madurai, the cowherd girls are described as performing the *rasa-lila* and singing songs about Krishna and Pinnai (Radha). It is interesting to note that towards the end of the epic, Kannaki includes Brahmanas among those who should be spared by the fire god when Madurai is engulfed in flames.

Kannaki, the heroine of the *Silappadikaram*, was regarded as an incarnation of the goddess Pattini, who is today one of the most popular deities among the Buddhists of Sri Lanka and the Hindus who live on the eastern coast of the island. Obeyesekere ([1984] 1987) argues that Pattini was originally a deity worshipped by adherents of the heterodox sects (Buddhists, Jainas, and perhaps also Ajivikas), especially merchants, of South India. The reference to the construction of a Pattini shrine by the Chera king Senguttavan should not be interpreted as a historical fact but as an attempt to legitimize the antiquity of a central Pattini shrine that existed at Vanji at the time when the Tamil epics were written. The Pattini cult must have been well established in the far south before this period. In later times, the goddess was 'Hinduized' and assimilated into the Kali cult. Pattini was an angry deity, whose anger was directed at evil people, and she was also associated with rational justice. When she was assimilated into the Kali cult, her anger became punitive and irrational.

Buddhism

Several Yogachara and Madhyamaka thinkers can be placed in or close to this period. Prominent among the Yogacharins were Asanga and Vasubandhu (late 4th/early 5th century). The famous Madhyamaka scholars included Buddhapalita (6th century), Bhavaviveka (6th century), and Chandrakirti (7th century). There was a notable growth of certain monasteries in size, scale, and ornamentation. Literature, inscriptions, sculpture, and the architectural remains of monastic establishments indicate that Mathura, Kaushambi, Sarnath, Bodhgaya, and Kasia were among the important centres of Buddhism in North India. Other important Buddhist centres included Mrigashikhavana in Bengal, Valabhi and Devnimori in Gujarat, Ajanta in Western India, Sanchi in Central India, Amaravati and Nagarjunakonda in the Andhra country, and Kanchipuram in the Tamil Nadu area.

Kanheri: Buddha

The element of *bhakti* made its impact on Buddhism with rites of worship similar to those practised in Hindu shrines. The philosophical basis of the pantheon of Buddhas and *bodhisattvas* that became objects of popular worship was the Mahayana doctrine of the *Tri-kaya* (Three bodies). According to this, Buddhahood had three aspects—the *Nirmana-kaya*, *Sambhoga-kaya*, and *Dharma-kaya*. The *Nirmana-kaya* (Transformation body) refers to the different forms assumed by the Buddha on the earth out of compassion for people, in order to teach them. The *Sambhoga-kaya* (Enjoyment Body) comprised the limitless forms that could be adopted by a Buddha to appear before and teach the *bodhisattvas* for their enjoyment. Each Sambhoga Buddha was supposed to preside over his own Buddha land (*Buddha kshetra*). The *Dharma-kaya* (Dharma-body) included the *Jnana-kaya* (Knowledge body) and *Svabhavika-kaya* (Self-existent body). The former consisted of perfect wisdom and spiritual attainments through which a *bodhisattva* became a Buddha. The *Svabhava-kaya* consisted of the ultimate and essential Buddhaness.

Among the countless Buddhas and *bodhisattvas*, a few became the especial focus of monastic and lay worship. These included the heavenly Buddha named Amitabha (infinite radiance). The heavenly *bodhisattvas* included Maitreya (the kind one). The *bodhisattva* Avalokiteshvara (the lord who looks down, i.e., with compassion) was supposed to be one of Amitabha's assistants and was considered the epitome of compassion. This aspect is best reflected in the fact that he is supposed to have refused to take the final step into Buddhahood because he wanted to help all beings attain this state. In his fully evolved iconography in later sculpture and painting, Avalokiteshvara wears royal clothes and a crown in which is embedded an image of Amitabha; the lotus bud he holds in one of his hands symbolizes the beauty of his compassion. Sometimes his hands are cupped around a *chintamani* (wish-granting jewel). Manjushri (sweet glory) was supposed to be an assistant of the heavenly Buddha Shakyamuni and was associated closely with wisdom. His images show him holding a lotus on which there is a copy of the *Prajnaparamita Sutra*; he also wields a flaming sword, which stands for the wisdom with which he cuts through delusion. Vajrapani was a *bodhisattva* whose symbol was the *vajra* (thunderbolt); he was considered a protector of snakes and a guardian of the elixir of life. The goddess Tara was the feminine personification of compassion. Tradition describes her either as born out of Avalokiteshvara's teardrop (he was shedding tears of despair at the enormous task of liberating all sentient beings) or from a lotus that grew in his tears. Tara was supposed to save people from eight great fears—lions, elephants, fires, serpents, robbers, water, imprisonment, and demons (these can also be interpreted metaphorically).

Kanheri: colossal Buddha; Buddha and *bodhisattva* figures

Numerous Buddhas and *bodhisattvas* are represented in the sculpture and paintings at Ajanta. The Sanchi sculptures likewise depict various Buddhas and the *bodhisattva* Vajrapani. At Bagh in Central India, the side and rear walls of Cave 2 have sculptures of Buddhas and *bodhisattvas*. At Kanheri, the largest cave site in India, Avalokiteshvara is depicted in Cave 90, which also has a Buddha *mandala* (an arrangement of Buddhas associated with the various directions) representing the *Tri-kaya* carved on one of the walls. Cave 41 at Bagh has an 11-headed Avalokiteshvara flanked by his consorts Tara and Bhrikuti. At Aurangabad, the verandah of Cave 6 has a relief carving of Avalokiteshvara, while Cave 7 has a beautiful representation of Tara.

Faxian mentions the flourishing condition and property holdings of monasteries in North India. He indicates that Hinayana doctrines were popular in the Gandhara, Bannu, Kanauj, and Kaushambi areas. Hinayana and Mahayana schools both flourished in Afghanistan, the Punjab, Mathura, and Pataliputra. In Khotan, on the other hand, he says there were only Mahayana monks. The Chinese pilgrim also reports many monasteries that were deserted or in ruins. These include empty monasteries at Gaya and Kapilavastu.

The Chinese pilgrim talks of *stupas* built in memory of monks such as Sariputra, Mahamoggalana, Ananda, and other great teachers. He states that nuns made offerings at the *stupa* of Ananda as he was instrumental in setting up the *bhikkhuni sangha*, and that monks associated with the Abhidhamma and Vinaya venerated the *stupa* of Rahula. Those following the Mahayana path worshipped Prajnaparamita (i.e., Prajna Devi), Tara, Manjushri, and Avalokiteshvara. Faxian mentions many *stupas* dedicated to various monks at Mathura, including three built by Ashoka. These included the relic *stupas* of Sariputra, Mudgalaputra, Purna Maitrayaniputra, Upali, Ananda, and Rahula, apart from *stupas* dedicated to various *bodhisattvas*.

Faxian mentions a ceremony involving a procession of images at Khotan and Pataliputra. In Khotan, where the ceremony lasted two weeks, the chariots carrying the images were decorated with precious stones, silken streamers, and canopies, and were led by Mahayana monks. The king bowed low before the chief image and

Kanheri: 11-headed Avalokiteshvara

the queen and other women scattered flowers. A similar ceremony was held at Pataliputra every year on the eighth day of the month of Jyaishtha, but it lasted only two days. Images of the Buddha flanked by those of various deities and *bodhisattvas* were placed and carried forth on four-wheeled chariots shaped like *stupas*. The local Brahmanas participated in the festivities and the Vaishyas distributed gifts and medicines. Faxian also tells us that wealthy *setthi*s built monasteries and endowed them with agricultural land, gardens, orchards, cattle, and agricultural workers.

The *Silappadikaram* and *Manimekalai* indicate that Buddhism and Jainism were well-established in cities of South India such as Puhar, Vanji, and Madurai, especially among merchants and artisans. The composition of the *Manimekalai* is attributed to Sattanar, described in the preface of the text as a wealthy grain merchant. The epic opens by introducing a courtesan named Madhavi and her daughter Manimekalai, who lived in a Buddhist convent. The latter is the heroine of the story and ultimately enters the Buddhist order. The Buddhism portrayed in the epic is of the Mahayana variety. The Buddha is deified; there are references to many Buddhas, and to the concept of the *Tri-kaya*. The epic speaks of the worship of the Buddha in shrines at Puhar. The story has an emphasis on renunciation tempered with compassion and charity. This is reflected, for instance, in the episode where Manimekalai feeds the famine-struck people of Kanchi with her magic almsbowl. There are many references to *bodhisattvas* in the epic. Two chapters deal with philosophical issues, specifically with inferential logic and the Buddhist doctrine of causation. The author seems to have been well-versed in various aspects of Buddhist philosophy, including the intricacies of Buddhist logic and the ideas of scholars such as Buddhaghosha and the Yogachara school of Asanga and Vasubandhu. There are numerous philosophical discourses in the text. The frequent recourse to miracles and spells in the story may reflect elements of Buddhist Tantra. Overall, the epic portrays and emphasizes Buddhist values and ethics.

The fact that the *Manimekalai* was a text that emerged in a context of religious competition is evident in its criticism of the beliefs and practices of other religious communities. A drunkard makes fun of a Jaina monk right at the beginning of the epic. At another place, Sattanar contrasts the hard-heartedness of a Jaina monk with the kindness of his Buddhist counterpart. The critique of Brahmanical animal sacrifice is evident in the story of how, in one of his previous births, a person named Aputra saved a cow from imminent slaughter at a sacrifice. Manimekalai seeks instruction in various philosophical doctrines including Vedic, Shaiva, Vaishnava, Ajivika, Samkhya, Vaisheshika, and Lokayata, but ultimately takes refuge in the Buddha and the *sangha*.

Map 9.3 Faxian's route (after Sen, 2006)

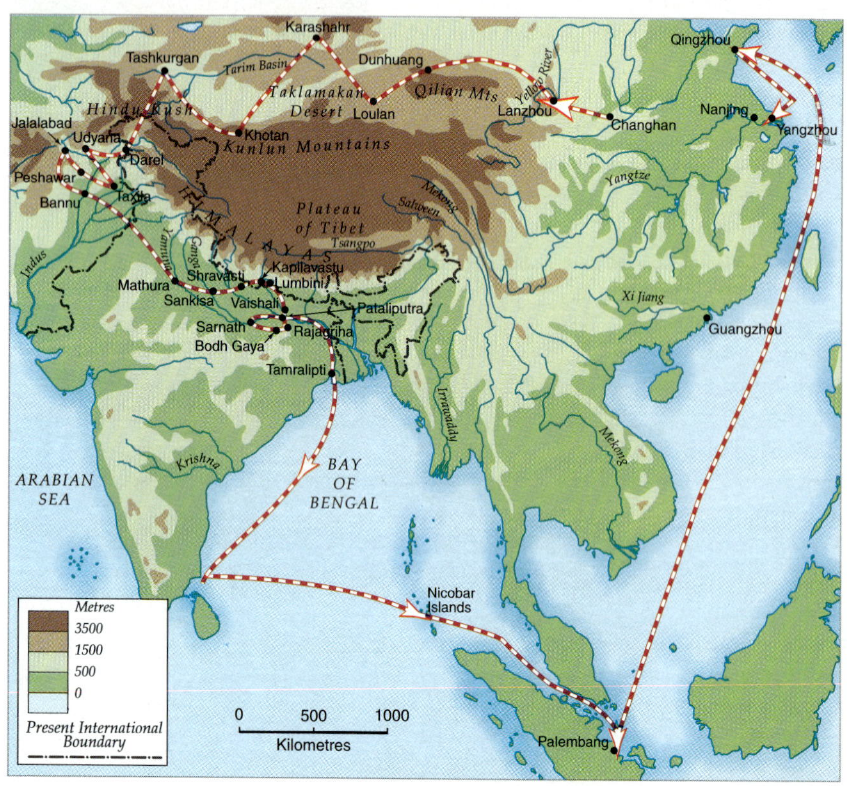

The *Manimekalai* is deeply imbued with Mahayana ideas. According to Anne Monius (2001), the text indicates the existence of a substantial body of lost Buddhist texts in Tamil. She suggests that the audience of the text must have consisted of a sophisticated, multi-lingual community, rooted in a multi-religious cultural milieu, within which Buddhist views were articulated. She also points out that the geographical horizons of the Buddhist world imagined in the epic minimizes its northern connections and relocates and plants it firmly in South India, Sri Lanka, China, and South-east Asia.

The *Manimekalai* minimizes the northern connections and emphasizes connections with Sri Lanka (which it refers to as Ratnadvipa) and South-east Asia, especially with Java (which it refers to as Chavakam). Monius argues that this is the only Tamil text to visualize a larger Buddhist world, defined by Buddhist values and events.

Remains of monasteries have been unearthed at Kaveripattinam and 4th century iconographic representations of the Buddha's footprints have been found at this place. There are also some images, including a life-size sculpture of the Buddha, stylistically dated to the 4th–6th centuries, found in a goddess temple at Kanchipuram. A 3rd/4th century image was found by a fisherman in the sea, a few kilometres south of Kaveripattinam. Literary traditions connect famous Buddhist monks such as Buddhaghosha, Buddhadatta, and Dhammapala with South India. This too suggests the existence of thriving monasteries in this area.

While the Gupta kings are generally linked with the promotion of Brahmanical cults, some of them extended patronage to Buddhism as well. Paramartha, a Buddhist scholar of the period, states that king Vikramaditya sent his queen and prince Baladitya to study under the tutelage of the famous Buddhist monk and scholar Vasubandhu. It is possible that this refers to Skandagupta and Narasimhagupta I Baladitya (son of Purugupta). The *Manjushrimulakalpa* (*c.* 800 CE) praises Skandagupta as a wise and virtuous king, and tells us that Narasimhagupta became a Buddhist monk and gave up his life through *dhyana* (meditation). Xuanzang suggests that some Gupta kings patronized the Nalanda monastic establishment. Seals of the later Gupta kings Budhagupta, Narasimhagupta, Kumaragupta III, and Vainyagupta have been found at the site and suggest a connection.

The aesthetically most striking Buddhist images of the period *c.* 300–600 CE come from Sarnath and Mathura, which were important centres of Buddhism. Buddhist sculptures have been found at cave sites such as Bagh in Central India and Kanheri and Aurangabad in Western India. Archaeological evidence shows the existence of large monastic establishments at Sarnath, Ajanta, Sanchi, Amaravati and Nagarjunakonda. Faxian does not mention Nalanda, but Xuanzang does, and states that he stayed there for quite some time. Therefore, it was thought that the monastery may have been built during the late Gupta period. Excavations at the site have, however, revealed some pre-Gupta remains. Nalanda enjoyed royal patronage in post-Gupta times too, during the reigns of Harshavardhana and the Palas.

Buddhism continued to spread into many lands of Asia during this period. While this can be understood as a part of larger processes of cultural interaction, especially trade, a key role was played by monks. We know a little bit about some of them, but there must have been countless men whose commitment to the Buddhist path gave them the courage and determination to persevere in the face of the long, hard journey to India and back.

There were thriving Buddhist communities in Sri Lanka and interactions between monks of India and Sri Lanka increased. In the 5th century, the monk Buddhaghosha travelled to Sri Lanka. He translated several scriptural commentaries into Pali and wrote a work called the *Visuddhimagga* (Path of Purification), which soon attained the status of a classic work on Theravada doctrine and meditation. Monasteries in Sri Lanka continued to receive grants of land and money and some of them became very wealthy. Merchants invested grain or money in guilds, the interest from which was to be used for the maintenance of monks. The interdependence between state and *sangha* furthered factionalism within the Order. Mahayana ideas continued to make an impact. In donative inscriptions, apart from transferring merit, donors expressed the desire to attain Buddhahood. Some inscriptions of the 6th/7th century record people paying sums of money to release themselves or their families from *veherala/vaharala*. This word has been interpreted in various ways, including as slavery or compulsory work for monasteries (Dias, 2001: 101).

The importance of Sri Lanka in the Asian Buddhist networks steadily increased. It is significant that the account of the formal inauguration of the *bhikshuni sangha* in China in the 5th century is connected not only with India but also with Sri Lanka. According to Baochang's *Biographies of Buddhist Nuns* (5th century), the first proper ordination ceremony of Chinese nuns was only possible when nuns from Sri Lanka arrived in China. In 433, the Sri Lankan nun Devasara arrived in the capital and she and her fellow *bhikshunis* are said to have organized the first proper dual ordination ceremony, in which a group of monks from India also took part. This tradition too reflects the expanding Asian networks and the significant place of India and Sri Lanka in these networks.

In China, thousands of Buddhist shrines and monasteries were built as Buddhism rapidly acquired both a popular following as well as royal patronage under the Sui and T'ang dynasties. Several Buddhist schools known as *tsungs* (clans) emerged, each tracing its history to a different founder. These schools specialized in different aspects of Buddhist doctrine and practice, but monks and nuns could be associated with several of them. Although the doctrines of some schools had almost direct parallels with their Indian counterparts, as Buddhism developed in China, it interacted with Chinese thought to produce a uniquely Chinese synthesis and manifestation as well. The Ching-t'u (Pure Land) soon emerged as the most popular Buddhist school in China. India was acknowledged as having an especially important place in the Buddhist world, leading to what has been described as a 'borderland complex' in China, arising from the fact that China did not figure in the Buddhist universe (Sen, 2003:10–13, 55–57).

Many Indian monks who travelled to China during these centuries belonged to Kashmir (Dutt, [1962] 1988: 294–310). They included Sanghabhuti, author of a commentary on the *Sarvastivada Vinaya*, who was in China in 381–84 CE. The monk Punyatrata travelled to Central Asia along with his student Dharmayashas and translated several Sarvastivadin texts between 397 and 401 CE. From here, he made his way to China, where he lived and worked during 424–453. Buddhayashas travelled to Kashgar and thereon to Kucha. Gunavarman, a Kashmir prince, took another route to the east. He travelled to Sri Lanka, on to Java, from where he sailed to China, arriving in Nanking in 431 CE.

The best known among the Indian monks or monks of Indian origin who travelled to China are Kumarajiva (5th century), Paramartha (6th century), and Bodhidharma (6th century). Paramartha belonged to Ujjayini. He was sent along with various Buddhist texts to China as part of a return mission sent by a Gupta king to the Chinese emperor in the mid-6th century. He travelled extensively, lived in various monasteries, translated many texts into Chinese, and also composed some original works. He ended up spending some 23 years in China, and never came back to India. Several works translated and written by Paramartha came to be included in the Chinese *Tripitaka*. Bodhidharma travelled to China by sea. Some accounts state that he came from India, others from Iran. He was a staunch believer in the doctrine of *shunyatavada* (nothingness). An apocryphal story presents him in conversation with the Chinese emperor, refusing to acknowledge any contribution made by the latter towards spreading the Buddhist *dharma* and asserting that where all was emptiness, nothing could be called holy. The emperor angrily demanded, 'Who is he who speaks to me thus?' Bodhidharma's reply was, 'I don't know.' Bodhidharma did not write any books, but his disciple Hui-ke went on to found the Chan (Zen in Japanese) school of Buddhism.

The spread of Buddhism to different parts of Asia during these centuries was part of complex socio-political and cultural interactions. Apart from China, Buddhist (and Hindu) influences also made their way into South-east Asia. Sarvastivada and Mahayana Buddhism were evident in north Myanmar from the 3rd century CE. In Cambodia, Buddhist and Hindu (especially Shaiva) influences, already visible from the early centuries CE, had taken firm root by the 6th century. Similar processes were underway in the Malay peninsula, Java, and Sumatra. Mahayana and Shravakayana Buddhism arrived in Vietnam via India and China by the 3rd century. Buddhism was transmitted to Korea from China, and by the 6th century, had made an impact all over the Korean peninsula. In 538 CE, a Korean embassy arrived in Japan, armed with a Buddha image, Buddhist monks, and texts. Buddhism had officially arrived in Japan and was soon declared a state religion during the reign of regent prince Shotoku (573–622).

FURTHER DISCUSSION | **Kumarajiva (343–413 CE)**

It is difficult to disentangle myth from historical fact in the life stories of monks scattered through many Chinese texts. Kumarajiva's father, Kumarayana, was a scholar belonging to Kashmir who migrated to Kiue-tsa, a town in Kucha, a prosperous principality located on the edge of the Gobi desert, not far from the Tsunling mountains in north Central Asia. Kucha was a cultural crossroads, with both Iranian and Indian influences making a strong impact. Kumarayana became a minister of the king of Kucha and married a princess named Jiva. Their son was named Kumarajiva, a name which makes perfect sense in itself but which also consists of an amalgam of part of both his parents' names.

Kumarajiva's father died early. When the child was 9 years old, he was taken by his mother to Kashmir to be educated. At that time, the Sarvastivadin sect was influential in this region. Kumarajiva studied Buddhist texts and doctrines under the tutelage of Bandhudatta. On their way homewards, mother and son spent some time in Kashgar, where Kumarajiva continued to absorb himself in study. According to tradition, it was here that he changed from a Hinayanist to a Mahayanist. After arriving in Kucha, Kumarajiva swiftly built up a reputation as a formidable scholar, a reputation that spread beyond the confines of the small Central Asian principality.

In 384 CE, the Chinese invaded and annexed Kucha. The story goes that the general who led the invading forces had been instructed by none other than the emperor, who had heard of Kumarajiva's great scholarship, to bring Kumarajiva back to China. So the monk was taken away along with other spoils of war. It is said that the emperor himself came to receive him when he arrived in the capital Chang'an (Xian).

Kumarajiva spent 12 years ensconced in the great monastery of Chang'an. Legend has it that the emperor visited him from time to time, to listen to his discourses. An ambitious project of translating Buddhist texts into Chinese had been underway for over three centuries in the White Horse monastery in Loyang in northern China. Kumarajiva was placed at the head of a similar translation project at Chang'an.

The Chang'an monastery soon emerged as a major competitor of the White Horse Monastery as a translation bureau. Kumarajiva found many of the existing translations unsatisfactory. Assisted by a large contingent of Chinese monks and a secretarial staff reportedly running into hundreds, he embarked on a new translation of the *Prajnaparamita Sutra*. He then turned to the translation of many other Sanskrit texts, assisted by hundreds of Chinese monk-scholars. The texts translated in this manner are said to have eventually totalled 300. Some of them were incorporated into the Chinese *Tripitaka*. Vimalaksha, a well-known monk of Kashmir, is also supposed to have worked along with Kumarajiva between 406 and 413. Kumarajiva was not only a skilled and learned translator. He also authored texts in Chinese, including an account of the life of Ashvaghosha.

Apart from being an immensely learned and industrious Buddhist scholar, what kind of person was Kumarajiva? There are some legends, such as the one narrated in the official history of the Qin dynasty: The emperor sent 10 beautiful women to Kumarajiva to choose one as a bride. Kumarajiva succumbed to temptation, abandoning his monk's life for that of a householder. However, he soon repented and rejoined the order. It is said that from that point onwards, he always began his discourse by saying, 'Follow my work, but not my life, which is far from ideal. But the lotus grows out of mud. Love the lotus; do not love the mud.'

Kumarajiva died at Chang'an and his last rites were apparently performed according to Indian customs. His life's work was carried forward by his students.

Source Dutt, (1962) 1988: 303–306

Jainism

During the 4th–5th centuries, councils of the Shvetambaras were convened at Mathura and Valabhi and the canon was codified. The Mathura council was presided over by Khandila (or Skandila), while the Valabhi council was presided over by Nagarjuna. Another council was later held at Valabhi. The Shvetambaras and Digambaras came to be sub-divided into various groups known as *sangha*s and *gana*s in the south, and *kula*s, *shakha*s, and *gachchha*s in the north.

As far as Jaina philosophy is concerned, the period *c.* 300–600 CE saw major contributions to logic. Many commentaries (*niryuktis* and *churnis*) were also written. Major monk-scholars of the time included Kundakunda, Samantabhadra, Siddhasena Divakara, and Pujyapada (also known as Devanandi). Kundakunda was a Digambara scholar who seems to have lived in the early 4th century. It is possible that the modern village of Kondakunde in Anantapur district of Andhra Pradesh represents his native home. All the texts attributed to him are in Prakrit. His most important works include the *Samayasara* and *Pravachanasara*. Samantabhadra, another major Digambara thinker, probably lived in the last quarter of the 4th century. His major philosophical works include the *Aptamimamsa* and *Yuktanushasana*. His *Svayambhustotra* and *Jinastutishataka* are in praise of the *tirthankaras*, while the *Ratnakarandakashravakachara* is a treatise on ethics for the Jaina laity. Siddhasena Divakara was a skilled logician, and his important works include the *Nyayavatara* and *Sammatitarkasutra*. The latter explains the doctrine of *anekantavada* on the basis of logic. The Digambaras and Shvetambaras both claim him as one of their own. Pujyapada (5th century) was the author of a grammatical work, the *Jainendra*. His skill as a logician is evident from his *Sarvarthasiddhi*, a commentary on the *Tattvarthadhigamasutra*. A gradual shift from Prakrit to Sanskrit was underway in Jaina texts during this period.

Asim Kumar Chatterjee (2000) has collated the evidence relating to the history of Jainism in different parts of the subcontinent during this period. The evidence of texts, inscriptions, sculptures, and structural remains indicates that Mathura was an important stronghold of Shvetambara Jainism. A Mathura inscription dated in Gupta year 113 (433 CE), belonging to the reign of Kumaragupta, mentions a Jaina monk named Datilacharya, belonging to the Vidyadhari *shakha* and Koliya *gana*. Samadhya, a disciple of this monk, gifted a Jaina image at the direction of his preceptor. Another inscription from Mathura, dated in year 299 of an uncertain era, mentions the erection of a temple (*devakula*) and the gift of an image of Mahavira by three people named Okha, Sarika, and Shivadina.These are just a few of the many inscriptions recording grants to Jaina establishments at Mathura.

Many Jaina images of the 4th–6th centuries have been discovered in Central India, including at Panna and Sira Pahari. The *Vasudevahindi*, a Jaina text that probably belongs to the 5th century CE, mentions a temple of Jiyantasvamin Mahavira at Ujjayini. Jaina tradition also mentions Dashapura (modern Mandasor), and describes several Shvetambara monks, especially those associated with the Kaushambika *shakha*, as being connected with this place in the early centuries CE. An inscription found at Udayagiri near Vidisha, belonging to the reign of Kumaragupta and dated in Gupta year 106 (426 CE), records the setting up of an image of Parshvanatha by Shankara, a former warrior and a disciple of Gosharman, who himself was a disciple of Bhadracharya.

Tirthankara, Kankali Tila, Mathura

In the middle Ganga valley, an inscription on a pillar found at Kahaum (Gorakhpur district, UP), belonging to the reign of Skandagupta and dated in year 141 of the Gupta era (461 CE), speaks of the setting up of five *tirthankara* images at this place by a person named Madra, who is described as having equal respect for *dvija*, *guru*, and *yati*. Vestiges of some shrines have been found in the area.

In Eastern India, important inscriptional evidence comes from Rajgir. An inscription near the Son Bhandar cave mentions a renowned Jaina ascetic (*muni*) named Vairadeva who is described as an *acharya-ratna* (jewel among *acharyas*). A fragmentary inscription is inscribed on a black basalt image of Neminatha found in the ruins of a small shrine at Rajgir. It refers to *maharajadhiraja* Chandra, who must be one of the two Gupta kings of this name. Metal images of the *tirthankaras* have been found at Chausa (Bhojpur district, Bihar).

Digambara establishments were also located in Bengal. A copper plate inscription found at Paharpur in Bangladesh records a gift made by a Brahmana couple—Nathasharman and his wife Rami—to a *vihara* in Vatagaoli for the worship of the *arhats*. The *vihara* was presided over by the disciples of the Nirgrantha *acharya* Guhanandin of Kashi, who is described as associated with the *Panchastupanikaya*.[5] Harishena's *Brihatkathakosha* decribes the founding of the five *stupas* at Mathura. The term 'Panchastupanikaya' refers to a sect that initially developed its base in Varanasi and Mathura, and spread to other areas, including Bengal. Jinasena, famous author of the *Adipurana*, belonged to this sect.

The convening of two councils at Valabhi indicates that Gujarat was an important centre of Jainism. Jaina tradition asserts that the *Kalpa Sutra*

[5] As pointed out in the previous chapter, the veneration of the *stupas* was not confined to Buddhism.

was recited during the reign of Dhruvasena, a Maitraka king of Valabhi. The *Visheshavashyakabhashya* of Jinabhadragani seems to have been composed in the early 7th century in Valabhi during the reign of a king named Shiladitya. The *Kuvalayamala* and *Vividhatirthakalpa* refer to Jaina temples adorning Gurjaradesha. Several Shvetambara images have been found at Valabhi. The *Harivamsha* (8th century) refers to a temple of Parshvanatha built by king Nanna; this was probably a Digambara temple. Jinasena mentions a Digambara temple of Shantinatha at Doshtatika near Girnar. Literary references and sculptural remains also indicate the spread of Jainism to the Rajasthan and Maharashtra areas.

In South India, the Digambara sect was strong in the Karnataka area. A Jaina council (*sangam*) was convened in the late 5th century at Madurai under Vajranandi. Kanchi was another important Jaina centre. Influential Jaina teachers such as Kundakunda are described as southerners, and certain traditions also describe Siddhasena Divakara and Samantabhadra as hailing from the south.

Mention was made in Chapter 1 of the Jaina elements in the Tamil epic, the *Silappadikaram*. Kavundi, a Jaina nun, plays an important role in the story. Jaina philosophical discourses are scattered throughout the text. For instance, at Shrirangam, Kovalan, Kannaki, and Kavundi meet a Jaina monk who gives them a short sermon. At Madurai, Kavundi gives another discourse, touching on issues such as rebirth and attachment, and foretells that something terrible will soon befall Kovalan and Kannaki, because the merit they had stored in their past lives was now exhausted. The epic refers to Jaina ascetics and to temples and charitable institutions of the Jainas at Puhar. It describes the magnificent temple of the Nirgranthas (Jainas) at Kaveripattinam and mentions wandering Jaina ascetics known as Charanars coming to this shrine on various occasions, including the *ratha* festival. This festival must have involved images of the *jina*s being taken out on carts in a procession. There are also descriptions of Jaina shrines at other places such as Vanji, Uraiyur, and Madurai. The *Manimekalai*, on the other hand, with its strong Buddhist overtones, opens with a drunkard making fun of a Jaina ascetic, especially of his dirty, unwashed body. This is suggestive of an element of tension or rivalry between Buddhists and Jainas.

Inscriptions of the 5th–6th centuries CE in the early Vatteluttu script have been found in many parts of South India. Some of these throw light on the history of Jainism. A cave at Sittannavasal (in Pudukkottai district, TN) contains seven inscriptions, apparently recording the names of donors who gifted this cave shelter to Jaina ascetics. The longest one refers to a collective gift made by members of a village. There are also several memorial inscriptions in the region. For instance, an inscription at Tirunatharkunru records the death of a Jaina monk named Chantirananti after fasting for 57 days.

Jainism attracted royal patronage from various quarters. An 8th century text called the *Kuvalayamala* by Udyotanasuri suggests that the Huna ruler Toramana extended patronage to Jainism. It describes this king as a follower of an *acharya* named Harigupta who was born in the Gupta family. Inscriptions of Ramagupta on three *tirthankara* images found near Vidisha in Central India not only throw light on the issue of Ramagupta but also on the history of Jainism. One of these records the making of the image on behalf of Ramagupta on the advice of *acharya* Sarppasena Kshamana, grand-pupil of Chandra Kshamacharya, who is described as a *panipatrika* (one who uses the hollows of his palms as an alms bowl and drinking bowl). This suggests that Chandra Kshamacharya belonged to the Digambara sect.

The early Pallavas extended patronage to both Hindu and Jaina religious establishments. A mid-6th century inscription belonging to the reign of Simhavarman II records the gift of a village to a Jaina saint named Vajranandin for the worship of the *jina*. The donee is described as belonging to the Nandi-*sangha* at Vardhamaneshvara *tirtha*. This suggests the location of a Jaina *tirtha* near Kanchi. An inscription of about the same period at Hoskote (in Bengaluru district, Karnataka) refers to the construction of a temple (*devayatana*) dedicated to the *arhat*s, by the mother of the Pallava king Simhavishnu at Pulligere village in the Korikunda division. The monks of the Yavanika (i.e., Yapaniya) *sangha* were associated with this shrine.

The Western Gangas, who were based in the south Karnataka area, were enthusiastic patrons of Jainism. A tradition recorded in later inscriptions suggests that Konakanivarman, the founder of the dynasty, was assisted in his rise to power by a Jaina saint named *acharya* Simhanandi. A late 5th century inscription found at Nonamangala records a land grant made by king Madhava III to a Jaina temple established by monks belonging to the Mula-*sangha*. Three inscriptions (one of which is considered a forgery) of the reign of Avinita Konkanivarman record grants made in favour of Jaina establishments. One of them (from Nonamangala) states that the king made the grant on the advice of his preceptor (*upadhayaya*), the great *arhat* Vijayakirti.

The early Kadambas, another dynasty based in the Karnataka area, also patronized Jainism. Their inscriptions refer to various Jaina sects such as the Nirgranthas, Shvetapatas, Yapaniyas, and Kurchakas. The Halsi grant of king Kakutsthavarman begins with an invocation to Jinendra (lord of the *jinas*), and suggests the presence of a Jaina temple at this place. Several grants in favour of Jaina establishments were also made by king Mrigeshavarman. The Banavasi inscription, dated in the third regnal year of the same king, records the grant of black-soil land in Brihat-Paralura village in favour of a Jaina shrine to provide for the following activities—sweeping the temple; anointing the image with ghee; and for worship and repairs. It also records the grant of an additional piece of land for decorating the image with flowers. Another Banavasi grant, dated in this king's fourth regnal year, records a grant in favour of three beneficiaries—a temple of Jinendra at Paramapushkala, the *sangha* of the Shvetapata-*mahashramanas* and the Nirgrantha-*mahashramanas*. It is interesting to note that the Jinendra temple seems to have been the joint property of the Digambaras and Shvetambaras. An undated inscription of the reign of Ravivarman mentions that part of the grant was to meet the expenses of the eight-day festival of the lord *jina* at Palashika, in which the king also participated.

A Classical Age of Art?

The age of the Guptas is often described as a classical age in the sphere of cultural developments. The basis of such a description is the fact that during *c.* 300–600 CE, an exceptionally fine aesthetic ideal is apparent in many parts of the subcontinent. Art and literature both reveal parallels in their ideals of beauty, displaying a fine balance between the sensual and spiritual. While appreciating the artistic production of these centuries, we can, at the same time, question whether it indeed represents 'the best' of Indian literature, sculpture, and architecture—which is implied in the use of the term 'classical age'—or whether it marks one of several epochs that saw impressive developments in artistic creativity.

Is there such a thing as a 'Gupta style' of art which emerged and flourished during the reign of the Gupta kings and which spread over their realm? Many historians are critical of using dynastic labels, but art historians point out that in some cases, including this one, dynastic labels are appropriate. J. C. Harle ([1986] 1990: 89) points to the remarkable degree of uniformity in temples, stone sculpture, and terracotta art all over the Gupta empire. From the point of view of the history of art, he suggests ([1974] 1996: 6) that the period can be further divided into three phases—the early Gupta period, which in some regions extended into the 5th century CE; the Gupta period proper; and the late Gupta period, which may be said to have begun as early as the 2nd quarter of the 5th century in Western India, but significantly later in the east.

The early Gupta phase has been described by Hermann Goetz (1963) as a successful combination of the paradoxes of earthiness and daintiness, strength and elegance, the sublime and the grotesque. These features were fused into a graceful and harmonious style in the Gupta period proper. In the late Gupta period, the representation of the human body became more slender and the poses of the figures more stylized. According to Harle, the brief period between the early and later Gupta periods produced some of the world's finest art, characterized, among other things, by a unique elegance and an ability to effectively express higher spiritual states. Joanna Williams (1982: 3–4) suggests that the Guptas may have been responsible more for the extent of the spread of a common artistic idiom than its precise form. She describes the art of this period as imbued with a strong intellectual flavour, displaying a fine balance between representational credibility and abstracting tendencies.

Of course we must remember that if we use the term 'Gupta art', it is a convenient shorthand. For not all the specimens of sculpture included in such a discussion were produced within the political domain of the imperial Guptas. Walter Spink (2006:3) points out that the Vakatakas have for far too long been considered the poor relations of the Guptas. The caves at Ajanta, Bagh, Dharashiva, Ghatotkacha, Banoti, and Aurangabad bear testimony to the fact that it was the Vakatakas who were the last sponsors and guardians of the so-called 'golden age'. Spink attributes the Ajanta caves of the period to a single, intense burst of enthusiasm during the reign of the Vakataka king Harishena (*c.* 460–77 CE). It was Harishena's death, he argues, that marked the end of the golden age.

An analysis of the artistic developments of this period has to take into account the patronage of dynasties such as the Guptas and Vakatakas. But it is important to note that other elite groups were also involved in the networks of patronage. The developments in architecture and sculpture in this period reflect the increasing popularity of theistic cults.

Developments in architecture

The period *c.* 300–600 CE represents an important stage in the history of Indian temple architecture. Most of the surviving temples are located in the hilly areas of Madhya Pradesh and are in a ruined state. The stone temples include the Vishnu temple at Tigawa, the Shiva temples at Bhumara and Khoh, the Parvati temple at Nachna-Kuthara, and the Buddhist shrines at Sanchi. Outside Central India, there is the Buddhist temple at Bodh Gaya in Bihar and the Dashavatara temple at Deogarh in Jhansi district (UP). There are also ruins of a temple of this period at Dah Parbatia on the banks of the Brahmaputra in Assam. Apart from these stone temples, there are brick temples at Bhitargaon (Kanpur district, UP), Paharpur (Rajshahi district, Bangladesh), and Sirpur (Raipur district, Chhattisgarh) (see Meister, Dhaky, and Deva. [Eds.]., 1988).

The early temples were small. The square *garbha-griha* (sanctum), about 10 x 10 ft, was just large enough to house the image. There was a small portico and the roof was usually flat. Temple walls tended to be plain, but the doorways were often intricately and profusely carved. Later temples—those of the late 5th and 6th centuries—reveal some changes. The temple was now built on a raised plinth and had a *shikhara* (spire). The Dashavatara temple at Deogarh and the temple at Bhitargaon, both of which probably

Dashavatara temple, Deogarh

Bhumara and Nachna-Kuthara temples (top left); Lakshmana temple, Sirpur (top right); Bhitargaon brick temple; detail of doorway, Nachna-Kuthara

had curvilinear *shikharas*, are examples. The Deogarh temple had four large porches and its *shikhara* was about 40 ft high. The stones that comprised the structure were secured to each other with dowels. The Bhitargaon temple is made of terracotta and brick. Its outer walls are decorated with terracotta panels depicting mythological scenes. This temple provides one of the earliest examples of the true arch in India. The pillars of later temples of this period have capitals in the form of *purna-kalashas* (water pots). Although an elaboration on the earlier temples, they have a very modest appearance compared to temples built in later centuries.

The sculptural decoration on the main doorway of the Deogarh temple includes various kinds of motifs—birds, attendants, *purna-ghatas*, *mithuna* figures (couples), *svastikas*, foliated scrolls, and dwarfish figures. All these, except the birds, are also found on the doorway of the Dah Parbatia temple. Another typical feature of this period is the carving or painting of the conch and lotus on door jambs. This occurs, for instance, on the Deogarh temple.

The many Buddhist *stupas*, *chaityas*, and *viharas* built during this period include those at Jaulian, Charsada, and Taxila in Gandhara. In Eastern India, there is the Dhamekh *stupa* at Sarnath, which was enlarged and encased in stones carved with beautiful scroll work and geometric designs. The 128 ft high *stupa* has four niches at the cardinal points for Buddha images. Several fine Buddhist sculptures of the Gupta period were found at the site.

The cave architecture of this period is almost entirely Buddhist. There are, however, a few exceptions. For instance, the Brahmanical cave at Udayagiri has an inscription belonging to the reign of Chandragupta II. This shrine is partly rock-cut and partly stone-built. It has a pillared portico in the front, a carved doorway, and pillars with *purna-ghata* capitals. There are also the Elephanta caves, the largest one of which, dedicated to Shiva, was mentioned in an earlier section of this chapter.

The most prominent examples of the rock-cut architecture of this period are found at Ajanta and Bagh (Huntington, 1985: 239–74). The spectacular Buddhist site of Ajanta consists of several caves nestled in a curving section of the Sahyadri hills, overlooking the Waghora river. There are 28 caves at Ajanta. There were two phases of

The Ajanta caves

activity at this site—five caves were excavated in the Satavahana period, while 23 belong to the Vakataka period (inscriptional evidence establishes this). Of these, two (Caves 19 and 26) were *chaityas*, the rest *viharas*. The scale and magnificence of the Ajanta caves suggest that they must have housed a prominent monastic community which attracted lavish patronage from the elites of the Vakataka kingdom. Spink (2006: 11) describes Cave 1 as 'the most sumptuous rock-cut *vihara* ever made in India' and attributes its patronage to Harishena. No inscription of this king has, however, been found at Ajanta.

The two *chaityas* at Ajanta—Caves 19 and 26—belong to the late 5th and early 6th centuries. They stand apart from cave shrines of the earlier period on account of their richer sculptural ornamentation, both inside and outside, and the profusion of figures from the Mahayana pantheon. Cave 19 consists of a rectangular hall rounded into an apse at the rear. The hall is divided into a central section and two side aisles by a number of richly carved pillars that go down the entire length of the hall and around the central image of worship—a *stupa* with a high, almost spherical dome within which a standing Buddha is carved in high relief. The roof is vaulted and ribbed, a translation of the old wooden ceilings, now rendered in stone. The cave has an elaborately carved façade, with Buddha figures, attendants, and various ornamental devices. The upper part of the interior has sculpted panels representing Buddhas. The cave must have been originally painted in many different colours.

Cave 26, which belongs to a slightly later period, has more elaborate and detailed sculptural decoration. It enshrines a huge *stupa* with a seated Buddha carved in high relief, adorned with richer ornamentation than its counterpart in Cave 19. The main Buddha figure on this *stupa* sits with legs hanging down from his seat. The inner walls of the cave have many carvings, including a 7 m long Buddha in a reclining pose on the left wall, representing the *parinibbana*, surrounded by figures in mourning.

Ajanta (from top): Cave 19 façade (left), interior (right); Buddha figures

Like the *chaityas*, the Ajanta *viharas* too display a profusion of sculptural ornamentation. They consist of a colonnaded porch and three entrance doors leading into a hall. The hall, with pillars arranged in a square, leads into an antechamber with a pillared portico, which in turn opens into a shrine room. The introduction of a shrine room into the *vihara* is an innovation of this period. Monastic cells are arranged around the central hall, and in some cases, also in the front. The columns and doorways of the *viharas* show great variety. Some are rather plain, others richly decorated with sculptures. Fluted columns make their appearance for the first time.

The exquisite sculptures at Ajanta are complemented by beautiful murals on the walls, ceilings, doorframes, and pillars. Originally, most of the caves had paintings. Today paintings survive in only six—Caves 1, 2, 9, 10, 16, and 17. Out of these, Caves 9 and 10 seem to belong to the 2nd/1st century BCE. The second phase of painting corresponds to the Vakataka period. The technique of painting is known as *fresco secco*. A thick layer of mud, mixed with vegetable material, was applied on the rock surface. A thin coat of plaster was applied on top of this. Paintings were made on this prepared surface, using pigments mixed in a glue or gum medium. This type of fresco is different from true fresco (*fresco buon*), in which powdered pigments are mixed with water and applied on wet lime-plastered walls, and in which the colours dry and set along with the plaster. The artists must have used brushes made of animal hair. They used and blended six colours—white made from lime, kaolin, and gypsum; red and yellow from ochre; black from soot; green from a glauconite (a mineral); and blue from lapis lazuli. All these materials, except for lapis lazuli, were available in the vicinity of Ajanta.

Ajanta paintings: scene of prince's court from *Vessantara Jataka*, Cave 17; Bodhisattva Padmapani (1st row); Buddha (2nd row, left); details of paintings (2nd row, right and 3rd row)

Ajanta: flautists, Cave 1

Apart from narrative scenes connected with the Buddhas, *bodhisattvas*, and Jatakas, the Ajanta frescoes depict *yakshas*, *gandharvas*, and *apsaras*. In addition to the 'religious scenes', there are many scenes of everyday life in cities and villages. The artists' deep and sympathetic understanding of nature is evident in the representations of trees, flowers, and animals such as elephants, monkeys, deer, and hares. There is also a great variety of decorative patterns. In the narrative paintings, episodes flow from and into each other in different directions, without any clear demarcations. Kramrisch observes that the Ajanta paintings are not conceived in terms of depth; rather, they come forward towards the viewer. The artists knew the technique of foreshortening and their paintings are marked by 'multiple perspective'—objects are painted as if seen simultaneously at eye level, from above, as well as from below (Kramrisch, [1937] 1994: 273, 277). The paintings are marked by a fine balance between the material and the spiritual.

The human figures are slender, well-proportioned, and elegant. Women have narrow waists and full breasts, their faces are marked by highly arched eyebrows and elongated, lotiform eyes. There is an intricate range of sophisticated costumes, jewellery, and hairstyles. The artists used shading and highlighting to great effect, giving parts of their compositions a luminous glow. The paintings display some stylistic differences, reflecting the different hands that made them. It can be noted that the *Vishnudharmottara*, a supplement to the *Vishnu Purana*, was composed in about the 7th century CE, the very time when artists were painting the last paintings at Ajanta (Kramrisch, [1928] 1994: 264). This text gives a detailed account of the theory and practice of painting and refers to earlier works on the subject. The beautiful Ajanta murals themselves point to a long tradition of mural painting in India.

Bagh is located about 150 miles north-west of Ajanta. Nine caves at this site belong to *c.* 500–600 CE. Broadly similar in plan and arrangement to those at Ajanta, the Bagh caves are more simple and plain. The end of the hall usually has a *chaitya* instead of a Buddha image. The purpose of a large room attached to one of the larger *viharas* is not certain. Some caves have additional columns in the interior of the central hall to support the roof. The Bagh caves also had paintings, which have practically disappeared. Other major Buddhist cave sites include Kanheri and Aurangabad.

One of the most spectacular examples of the art and architecture of this period in South Asia is at Sigiriya in Sri Lanka. This is not a religious complex but a political one, with distinctive and unique features. Sometimes seen as a capital city, it is better understood as a royal complex. This palace-garden complex is located on a huge rock that rises about 800 metres from the plain, next to a lake called Sigiri Wewa. Evidence of occupation by Buddhist monks has been found in caves and rock shelters at the site, but the most striking remains belong to the time of king Kasyapa (477–95 CE). The complex was carefully planned with moats, walls, ramparts, and gateways and landscaped with terrace gardens, rock gardens, and water gardens. The remains of a colossal brick lion flank the foot of the staircase on the lower terrace. The staircase meanders upwards towards the palace area, which was located on the summit of the hill. The palace area, surrounded by a brick wall and arrangements for drainage of rain water, consisted of various structures, cisterns, and gardens, cut into the rock and finished with brick lined with stucco. Sigiriya is also known for its beautiful paintings. The site displays a high level of conceptualization, technical skill, and aesthetic planning.

Sculpture

Buddha figures on stone slab

The period *c.* 300–600 CE shows a continuation of earlier styles and trends derived from the Mathura and Gandhara schools, but also the introduction of new ones. Much of the sculpture was inspired by themes drawn from Hindu, Buddhist, and Jaina traditions. The iconographic conventions of religious sculpture became elaborated and fixed. The sculpture of this period is rich in ornamental designs such as the foliated scroll.

The Vishnu images are very varied. Some of them combine the anthropomorphic and theriomorphic forms of the Varaha (boar) *avatara*. Another form (found at places such as Mathura and Gadhwa) shows the god in a human form, surrounded with several radiating heads. The deity's attributes such as the *shankha* and *chakra* are often personified as dwarfish attendants known as *ayudha-purushas*. The images of Shiva depict him in a combination of the *linga* and anthropomorphic form. The Buddha images display a greater variety of *mudras* than before. The plain halo of the earlier period makes way for ones decorated with bands of ornamentation, and the Buddha's body is clothed in transparent drapery. Distinct styles—e.g., those of Mathura and Sarnath—are discernable in the Buddha sculptures.

In Central India, at Udayagiri, all the caves except for one Jaina cave, depict Hindu deities. Most of the sculptures are carved outside the caves. These include a four-armed standing Vishnu (Cave 6), Kumara (Cave 3), an *eka-mukha-linga* (Cave 4), *pratiharas* (doorkeepers, Cave 6), and Durga Mahishasuramardini (Caves 4, 6). A particularly powerful relief shows Vishnu in his boar incarnation rescuing the earth from the waters. At Eran, there is a magnificent boar sculpture with an inscription of the time of the Huna ruler Toramana. At Sanchi, numerous Buddha and *bodhisattva* images reveal some similarities with those of Mathura and western Uttar Pradesh. The notable sculptures from Besnagar include a Vishnu head and a representation of the Sapta-Matrikas.

Mathura continued to be a major centre of sculpture. There are seated *tirthankaras*, including a headless one dated in Kumaragupta's reign. The figures are usually carved against the background of a carved throne or are flanked by attendants carrying fly-whisks (*chamaras*). A dated stone image of a seated *tirthankara* belonging to 432–33 CE was found at the Kankali Tila at Mathura and is currently in the State Museum in Lucknow. It differs from the seated *tirthankara* figures of preceding centuries in several ways. This *jina* has a stocky body, with wide hips and high waist, which makes the crossed legs appear as though they are tilting forward and downwards. The Mathura artisans produced many magnificent standing Buddha figures as well. Many Vishnu images and *mukhalingas* have also been found at Mathura.

See p. 620 for photograph of Kankali Tila *tirthankara*

The Buddha images from eastern Uttar Pradesh and Bihar stand out from those of the earlier centuries with their expression of serene spirituality. The Sarnath Buddhas of this period are considered by several art historians as among the greatest works of art produced in the entire history of ancient India. Two standing figures and one seated Buddha figure are especially renowned for their beauty and finesse. The seated Buddha shows him in the meditative *padmasana* pose. His hands are in the *dharmachakra mudra*, the *mudra* of teaching, wherein both hands are held and touch each other at chest level. The halo around his head is beautifully ornamented. Beneath the throne is a *chakra*, flanked with monks with hands folded in veneration.

The Buddha images from Sarnath differ in several ways from those of Mathura. The robes have no folds; only the outline of the transparent robes is indicated. Sarnath has also yielded many *bodhisattva* images and narrative reliefs depicting scenes from the Buddha's life. There are many damaged specimens of standing Buddhas from Mathura; only two are comparatively intact. One is housed in the Mathura Museum, the other in Rashtrapati Bhavan. Both are colossal, standing almost 2 m tall on stiff legs. They have huge, beautifully ornamented haloes around their heads. The pleats of their outer robe (*sanghati*) are clearly outlined, and present a rhythmic flow of lines. They hold up a portion of this robe in their left hand. The right hand is missing, but was probably raised in

Buddha head, Mathura

FURTHER DISCUSSION | **The Sigiriya paintings and the poems on the Mirror Wall**

According to the *Chulavamsa*, Sigiriya was built by Kassapa, who killed his father in order to become king. After the death of king Kasyapa, the Sigiriya complex was abandoned and eventually became covered with forest. It was rediscovered in the 19th century and clearance and excavations were conducted under the direction of H. C. P. Bell, the first Archaeological Commissioner of Ceylon. The work continued in later years, during the time of Senarath Paranavitana, the first Sri Lankan Archaeological Commissioner. Another round of excavations were conducted at the site during the 1980s under the

The Sigiriya rock (top); mirror wall (left); remains of colossal lion (right)

direction of Senaka Bandaranayake as part of the Sri Lanka – UNESCO Cultural Triangle Project

Along the ascent up the Sigiriya rock, over 100 m above ground level, are the remains of paintings that once extended in a band almost 140 m long and up to 40 m high across the western face of the Sigiriya rock. What survives of this gigantic picture gallery are 21 female figures. The figures have been variously interpreted as *apsaras* (celestial nymphs) or women of the royal court. Paranavitana suggested that the complex symbolized the idea of king Kassapa as Kubera, the god of wealth, residing on Alaka mountain. He suggested that the women in the paintings represented Lightning Princesses and Cloud Damsels, the dark-complexioned ones being personifications of clouds and the fair-complexioned ones personifying lightning. While art historians have some seen similarities with the Ajanta murals, the style of the Sigiriya paintings is quite distinctive and unique in terms of their non-religious themes, flowing body lines, and bold colours.

Long after the Sigiriya complex was abandoned, many visitors came to the site and marveled at the paintings. Some of them inscribed graffiti poems on the highly polished wall opposite the paintings (this is known as the Mirror Wall). The hundreds of inscriptions date from the 6th to the early 14th century. About 700 of them were deciphered by Paravitana and some more by Benille Priyanka. These include poems inspired by the paintings. One of them reads in translation as follows:

> Lovely this woman
> excellent the painter!
> And when I look
> at hand and eye
> I do believe she lives.

Source Bandaranayake, 2013; Bopearachchi, 2015, Vol. 2, pp. 165–200

Sigiriya paintings

Buddha seated in the preaching *dharmachakra pravartana mudra*; standing Buddha

See p. 609 for photograph of Krishna lifting Govardhana

the protection-granting *abhaya mudra*. The Hindu sculptures from this area include a lintel depicting Vishnu, Surya, Chandra, a procession of musicians, young girls, and food-bearers. A relief carving of Krishna lifting Govardhana mountain was found at Varanasi.

Apart from the Ajanta caves (some of the sculptural features of which were described in the earlier section), examples of the Buddhist sculpture of these centuries are found at Kanheri and Aurangabad. There are over 100 caves at Kanheri, located in Sanjay Gandhi National Park, Borivili, Mumbai, ranging from the 2nd century BCE to the 11th century. About 25 belong to the time of the Traikutakas. The magnificent site includes many *caityas*, *viharas*, water cisterns, and donative inscriptions. The Kanheri caves of this period are comparatively simple, but their sculptural embellishment includes representations of various Buddhas and *bodhisattvas*, including figures arranged in *mandalas*. At Aurangabad, near Ajanta, several Buddhist caves were excavated in the 5th–6th centuries. Their sculptural decoration includes Buddha and *bodhisattva* figures. Huntington (1985: 267) suggests that the prominence of female imagery, especially the female attendants who frequently flank the *bodhisattvas*, may reflect Tantric or Vajrayana influence. One of the most beautiful relief sculptures in these caves is found to the left of the central door in Cave 7. This shows Tara flanked by two female figures (perhaps aspects of herself) accompanied by dwarfs. On the left wall of the same cave shrine is a fine relief of a woman dancer, flanked by six female musicians.

Dancer and musicians, Aurangabad cave

Among the stone sculptures assigned to the period c. 300–600 CE is a larger-than-life figure of a horse carved out of beige sandstone, found at Khairigarh (UP) and currently in the State Museum, Lucknow. It bears a much damaged Sanskrit inscription, which seems to refer either to Samudragupta or Kumaragupta I. It has been suggested that this horse represents the sacrificial horse in one of the *ashvamedha* sacrifices performed by Samudragupta, but there is no definite evidence to support such an interpretation.

Kanheri cave, sculptures, painting

FURTHER DISCUSSION | **Vakataka sculpture**

While most discussions of the sculptural art of the period *c.* 300-600 CE focus on the Gupta empire, the sculptural production of the Vakataka kingdom too is impressive and stylistically distinct.

Among the most spectacular Vakataka sculptures are two large stone Narasimha images found in small temples close to teach other on Ramtek hill. The two sculptures are almost identical. They are seated in the *maharajalilasana*—with the left leg lying bent on the seat, and the right leg flexed with knee raised. The powerful left arm rests on the left knee. The right arm holds the rim of a small *chakra* that rests on the ground.

The many sculptures found at Mansar include an image that is usually identified as Shiva. This is because of the skull and crescent in his hair, and the snakes that form his anklets. The rosary and matted locks point to his asceticism. However, this Shiva is a dwarfish, cherubic, smiling figure and is very different from that found elsewhere. The sculpture has alternatively been interpreted as one of the *ganas* of Shiva, Kubera, or a *nidhi* (personification of wealth).

Several other sculptures of the Vakataka period were found at Mansar, Paunar, and Mandhal. Robert Brown suggests a possible affinity with the sculpture at Amaravati and Nagarjunakonda. Whatever may be the case, the images reflect a unique artistic style that had evolved in the Vakataka kingdom.

Source Brown, 2004

Mention may also be made here of the developments in the north-west. Sites such as Hadda in Afghanistan show the increasing use of stucco instead of stone. The relief sculptures show elements and modifications of the earlier Gandhara style. Among the most fabulous sculptures in this region were the gigantic figures carved onto a cliff side at Bamiyan. One of these was a Buddha figure standing almost 55 m high. Tragically, the spectacular Bamiyan sculptures were destroyed some years ago by the Taliban.

The dilapidated remains of a Buddhist *stupa* belonging to about 500 CE were excavated at Kahu-jo-daro in Mirpur Khas in Sindh (Sabyasachi Mukherjee, 2022). The *stupa* contained two sets of relics—in an earthenware pot and in a stone casket. A unique feature of the *stupa* is the fact that the high square platform which supported the elongated dome was originally lined with terracotta relief panels depicting seated Buddhas in the niches of the four faces of the platform supporting the dome. A terracotta relief which seems to depict a lay worshipper was also found. All the terracotta reliefs were originally painted. The other finds at the site included decorative moulded bricks and hundreds of 'votive tablets', very similar to those found at Nalanda and Sarnath.

Stucco head from Taxila

Metal images produced during the period *c.* 300–600 CE include a copper image of the Buddha found at Sultanganj (Bihar). This is stylistically similar to the stone Sarnath sculptures, but is now usually thought to belong to a later period. Small images of Buddhas and *bodhisattvas* have been found at Gandhara and at many sites in the Ganga valley as well. A hoard of metal sculptures that seem to stylistically belong to this period was found at Chausa in Bihar. It includes a figure of the Jaina *tirthankara* Rishabhanatha.

The terracotta art of this period includes small figurines and plaques found at many places including Kaushambi, Rajghat, Bhita, and Mathura. These represent animals, ordinary people, and gods and goddesses such as Durga, Karttikeya, and Surya. Many terracotta heads have been found at Akhnur in Kashmir. Terracotta plaques stamped with heads and figures were also found at the site of Harwan in Kashmir. Several finely modelled terracotta reliefs were found at the Buddhist *stupa* site of Devnimori in Gujarat. The seated images were placed in niches all around the lower part of the *stupa*. The *stupa* was also faced with terracotta ornamentation—decorated pilasters, jambs, medallions, *chaitya* arches, vegetal scrolls, grotesque heads, etc.—which have been found at the site. The brick temple at Bhitargaon was faced with terracotta panels and other sorts of ornamentation, only a few traces of which survive. Among the remarkable pieces of monumental terracotta sculpture are the almost life-size images of the goddesses Ganga and Yamuna found at Ahichchhatra. Such images were placed in temple niches.

Mirpur Khas (from left): seated Buddhas; devotee

Terracotta images of Ganga and Yamuna, Ahichchhatra; colossal Aukana Buddha (from top)

The art of South Asia includes many fine sculptures produced in In Sri Lanka, where Buddhism was expanding and receiving lavish patronage. One of the most imposing images is a colossal Buddha image at Aukana (Avukana). It is generally said to have been made during the reign of the 5th CE ruler Dhatusena, but it could belong to the 7th/8th century. The granite image is within the precincts of a brick image house (shrine). It stands on a lotus pedestal and is 11.36 m in height. The image has his right hand raised in the protection-granting *abhaya mudra* and could represent Dipankara Buddha.

Indian religious and artistic influences are very visible in the various kingdoms of South-east Asia from the 4th/5th century CE onwards (for an overview and images, see Guy, 2014a; Guy 2014b; Guy. [Ed.], 2014). They are visible in the Pyu sites in central Myanmar, Cha mpa on the Vietnam coast, Dvaravati in Thailand, Shrivijaya in Sumatra and the Malay peninsula, and the kingdoms referred to in Chinese sources as Funan (in south Vietnam) and Zhenla (central Cambodia). Brahmanas and Buddhist monks were the agents, and must have travelled across the seas on merchant ships. While the influence of the style of the Sarnath Buddha images art can be seen in some of the sculptures in South-east Asia (and China) (Brown, 2011), the influence of Andhra styles is also visible. The circulation of portable images must have been an important factor in the circulation of artistic styles. A royal Shaiva complex was once located at My Son in Vietnam, where an inscription of a ruler named Bhadravarman was found. At Shrikshetra in Myanmar, there are monumental *stupas*, including a relic chamber which contained a 20-page manuscript made of gold leaf and a gilded silver reliquary. Other sites in mainland and maritime South-east Asia give evidence of the impact of Vaishnavism, Shaivism, and Buddhism on the religious ideology and practice of rulers. In all cases, we see the Indic influences interfacing with local traditions to produce a new kind of synthesis.

Textual Production

The period *c.* 300–600 CE is often described as the classical age of Sanskrit literature in that it represented the attainment of a high watermark and set standards for later ages.

There was an increase in the use of prose in Sanskrit literature during this period. This is also the time when the transition from Prakrit to Sanskrit in royal inscriptions became complete. In the mid-1st millennium BCE, the Prakrit dialects underwent a transition from the stage of the intermediate Prakrits (e.g., Maharashtri, Shauraseni, and Magadhi) to the phase of the dialects known as Apabhramsha. The *Natyashastra* prescribes that in Sanskrit drama, the 'high' characters such as kings, ministers, etc. speak in Sanskrit, while the 'low' characters such as women (even queens) and servants generally speak in Prakrit. This sort of convention was in fact followed in Sanskrit dramas.

We know very little about the authors of the literary masterpieces of these centuries. Often, there is confusion about when and where they lived, and legends are more abundant than definite biographical details. For instance, some legends describe Shudraka as a king of Vidisha, others suggest that he may have been a ruler of the Abhira tribe. Kalidasa seems to have been connected with the city of Ujjayini, and is associated in tradition with the court of a king named Vikramaditya, although whether or not this was the Gupta king Chandragupta II is uncertain. (For an overview of the *kavya* texts of this period, see Warder, 1972–2004, Vol. 3.)

Kalidasa is counted among the most brilliant playwrights of this period, although there is uncertainty about exactly when he lived and wrote. His dramas—*Abhijnanashakuntala*, *Malavikagnimitra*, *Vikramorvashiya*, and his lyrical poems—*Raghuvamsha*, *Kumarasambhava*, and *Meghaduta*—are considered masterpieces of Sanskrit literature. Known, among other things, for his beautiful poetic descriptions of love, his works also display an element of humour in some places. His style is considered an example of the Vaidarbhi style, i.e., the style of the Vidarbha region. Banabhatta and Dandin praise the sweetness (*madhurya*) of his writing. However, Kalidasa also invited some criticism from ancient critics. For instance, Mammata in his *Kavyaprakasha* describes the eighth canto of the *Kumarasambhava*, where Kalidasa describes the love making of Shiva and Parvati, as improper. Kalidasa's *Raghuvamsha* is an extremely important and influential poetic work. It tells the story of kings of the Ikshvaku dynasty, including Dilipa, Raghu, and Rama, but it is also political poetry of the highest order and reveals the interersection of the ideals and realities of kingship (see Upinder Singh, 2016c).

Vishakhadatta's *Mudrarakshasa* is a play set in the Nanda–Maurya period. Shudraka's *Mrichchhakatika*, Bharavi's *Kiratarjuniya*, and Subandhu's *Vasavadatta* are among the other prominent literary works of the period. Bhatti's *Ravanavadha* (7th century) illustrates the rules of grammar while telling the story of Rama's life. Other great dramatists of the time such as Mentha, author of a work called *Hayagrivavadha*, are known through references and quotations in the writings of later writers and literary critics.

Apart from *kavya* literature, there were works that laid down the principles of poetics (*kavyakriyakalpa*) and dramaturgy (*natyashastra*). There is considerable overlap in these two subjects. Bhamaha's *Kavyalankara* (late 5th century) and Dandin's *Kavyadarsha* (7th century) deal principally with poetics. The main function of *kavya*, according to these treatises, is to produce delight or joy. There must have been interaction between the writers (*kavis*) and theoreticians.

Warder (1972–2004, Vol. 1: 200–04) points out that apart from select performances for elite audiences consisting of kings and wealthy patrons, *kavya* probably obtained its widest audience in dramas performed in popular festivals. Plays were performed in kings' palaces and some kings were themselves gifted *kavis*. *Nagarakas* were supposed to organize and participate in social gatherings (*goshthis*) and festivals (*samajas*) that included dramas. It is notable that most of the *kavis* we know of seem to have been Brahmanas.

Many important Sanskrit texts were compiled during *c.* 300–600 CE. These include the major Puranas, the *Mahabharata*, and the *Ramayana*. In the field of grammar, Bhartrihari (5th century) wrote a commentary on Patanjali's *Mahabhashya*. As mentioned at the

PRIMARY SOURCES | **The cloud messenger**

In Kalidasa's *Meghaduta*, a lovelorn *yaksha*, banished to Ramagiri mountain by the god Kubera, beseeches a passing cloud to relay his message to his beloved. The poem consists of a little over 100 verses, all in the *mandakranta* metre, which has 17 syllables per line. The *yaksha* gives the cloud directions to Alaka, the place where his beloved lives, and tells him what to convey to her. In the following verses—evocative even when translated from the original Sanskrit into English—the *yaksha* describes to his cloud messenger the condition in which he will find his beloved. We may note that the critic Bhamaha, who lived in about the same period as Kalidasa, is critical of poets introducing messengers such as clouds, birds, the wind, moon, and bees into their works, unless the character concerned is mad with longing. But that was precisely the state of the lovelorn *yaksha*.

[...] Know her to be my second life,
alone, speaking little,
mourning like a *chakravaki*
her companion far away.
With the passing of these long days,
racked by intense longing,
the young girl
would appear so changed I think,
like a lotus-plant struck by the chilling hoar-frost.

Weeping passionately, her eyes would be swollen and her lips withered by burning sighs;
my beloved's face cupped in the palm of her hand,
only glimpsed through loose tresses flowing down
would surely appear like the miserable moon
stricken pale when shadowed by you.

She will come into your view absorbed
in the day's rites of worship or drawing my likeness
imagined wasted by separation or asking
the melodious songster in the cage,
'sweet one, do you remember our lord?
You were a favourite with him.'
Or, clad in a drab garment she may place
the lute on her lap, wishing to sing a melody
set to words signifying my name;
succeeding somehow in tuning the strings
wet with her tears, O gentle friend, she forgets
again and again the sequence of notes
even though she composed it herself.

Or, beginning with the day of our parting
she may count the months remaining,
laying out in order on the floor,
flowers placed at the threshold;
or, savouring imagined pleasures of love
treasured in her heart:
such are the only diversions of women
sorrowing in the absence of their husbands....

Source *Meghaduta*, verses 82–86; Rajan, 1989: 156–57

beginning of this chapter, several Dharmashastra works—the *Yajnavalkya*, *Narada*, *and Brihaspati Smritis*—were composed in this period. No extant works on sculpture survive, but given the universality of art styles, such texts must have existed. The *Vishnudharmottara Purana* has a section on painting.

Kamandaka's *Nitisara* may have been composed time between *c.* 500 and 700 CE. This Sanskrit verse treatise consists of twenty *sargas* (cantos) subdivided into thirty-six *prakaraṇas* (sections). Generally regarded as a derivative, unoriginal thinker who simply repeated Kautilya's ideas, sometimes incorrectly, Kamandaka should be recognized as an important political thinker with a distinct perspective, whose work, like the *Arthashastra*, acquired an authoritative reputation, not only within India but also in South-east Asia (see Upinder Singh, 2016b).

The *Panchatantra* (The Five Books, or The Five Topics) is a political treatise that may have been composed in around the 3rd/4th century. This Sanskrit text is written in elegant prose, interspersed with verses. Vishnusharman, the putative author, is described as having composed this work after having studied all the works on governance. The prelude is followed by stories and stories within stories, arranged in five books on the following topics: creating dissension among allies; securing allies; peace and war; losing what one has gained; and hasty actions. The wit and humour and fact that the characters are animals blunt the rawness of the stories, but political conflict, violence, killing, and avoiding being killed are important parts of the *Panchatantra* tales. The main frame suggests that the author or authors were Brahmanas who were experienced not only in statecraft but also in the art of storytelling.

Vatsyayana's *Kamasutra* has been discussed earlier. The *Kamasutra* is about *kama* (sensual pleasure), in which *samprayoga* (sex) has a central place. Vatsyayana talks about the sixty-four *kalas* (arts) that should be studied along with the *Kamasutra*. The *Kamasutra*

PRIMARY SOURCES | **Teaching politics through animal stories**

The *Panchatantra* describes itself as a treatise on statecraft (*Nitishastra*) of great charm. It starts by paying homage to the experts—Manu, Vachaspati, Shukra, Parashara and his son, and Chanakya—who had composed great works on kingship. The text is aware of the ideas and conceptual vocabulary of *Dharmashastra* and *Arthashastra*. But because it consists of dramatic, witty, and entertaining stories, its flavour is completely different.

Although it describes itself as a political treatise, the stories and lessons of the *Panchatantra* could also apply to every-day life. A lot of the stories are about sheer survival, including political survival. Most of them are quite violent; they are about animals trying to kill and eat other animals or animals trying to escape being killed by other animals. It is said several times that there can be no friendship between meat-eaters and grass-eaters, the eaters and the eaten. This appears to be a metaphor for the natural enmity between the weak and the strong, the predator and his prey. It is invoked in the context of the relationship between king and courtier and between rivals in the court circle. With one notable exception (the crow and the mouse), the eater ends up eating the eaten.

The brilliance of the stories and the universality of their message made them travel across time and region in different languages and forms, making the *Panchatantra* one of the most influential Indian texts of all time.

The oldest translation was a 6th century translation into Pahlavi. In the 8th century, an Arabic translation was written by a scholar named Abdullah Ibn al-Muqaffa. Its title was *Kalilah-wa-Dimnah*. The work reached Europe by the 11th century and by the 16th century, there were versions in English, Greek, Latin, German, Italian, Spanish, Czech, and old Slavonic. Johannes Hertel counted over 200 versions in over 50 languages. The *Panchatantra* had an influence on the Arabian Nights and the fables of La Fontaine, and may have been among the pool of sources for Sufi stories.

The reasons for the extensive travels of the *Panchatantra* and its individual stories include the fact that they are extremely entertaining, they address certain universal political and personal concerns and were highly adaptable to different cultural contexts. Unfamiliar animals could also be changed into familiar ones. For instance, the frame story of Book 5 ('On hasty actions'), has in its cast of characters a Brahmana, mongoose, and snake. In the Arabic version, this became a story of a priest, dog, and snake; and in the Welsh version, it became a story about a knight, dog, and wolf. The stories also lent themselves well to illustrations, and there are many illustrated Persian and Arabic manuscripts.

The *Panchatantra*'s teaching was a pragmatic philosophy that caters both to the political and the personal and every day, especially in the context of dealings between the weak and the strong. Its lessons include: use your wits and strategy; kill rather than be killed; don't be rash; don't trust people; never let enemies get the better of you; outwit others before they outwit you; listen to good advice; don't talk nonsense; have confidence in yourself; never lose heart; think fast when you are cornered; don't build castles in the air; cherish your friends; money isn't everything.

Source Upinder Singh, 2017: 226–237

describes itself as part of a long tradition of scholarship. It contains the ideas of a very specific type of intellectual—an expert on pleasure.

Philosophical texts reflect the debates of the time and refute their rivals' positions. Reference was made in earlier sections of this chapter to the leading exponents of Buddhist and Jaina philosophy. New sections added in this period to the *Brahmasutras*, *Yogasutras*, and *Nyayasutras*, included a refutation of the Buddhist and Jaina schools. The many philosophical texts belonging to this time include the *Samkhya-karika* of Ishvarakrishna, which gives a systematic account of Samkhya philosophy, and seems to belong to the 4th/5th century. Vyasa's commentary on Patanjali's *Yogasutra* may also belong roughly to this period. Pakshilasvamin Vatsyayana, a Nyaya scholar, can be assigned to the mid-4th century CE. Prashastapada's *Padarthadharmasangraha*, a commentary on the *Vaisheshika Sutra* of Kanada, can be assigned to the 5th century. Noted scholars of Mimamsa included Prabhakara and Kumarila Bhatta, who lived a little later, in the 7th century.

Astronomy and Mathematics

The developments in various spheres of the natural sciences need to be investigated and subjected to sober analysis, avoiding exaggerated claims but acknowledging important contributions and breakthroughs. There are problems of interpretation as ideas in the ancient texts are often expressed in a cryptic fashion, and it is sometimes difficult to translate some of the terminology in what was essentially "a verbally expressed mathematical culture" (Divakaran, 2018: 17). As mentioned in Chapter 5, the earliest evidence of ancient Indian astronomical knowledge is contained in the Vedanga texts on *jyotisha* or astrology, the main focus of which was to fix the date of sacrificial rituals. Astronomical science continued to develop in later centuries, as is evident from the discussion of various schools in Varahamihira's *Panchasiddhantika*.

However, in about the 5th century CE, there was a major advance in astronomical and mathematical thinking in India. This advance is associated with Aryabhata (I). Aryabhata wrote at least two works—the *Aryabhatiya*, a text which survives and deals with astronomy and mathematics, and the *Aryabhata-siddhanta*, which is known only through references in later works. He brought together Greek-inspired astronomy and Shulbasutra geometry to create one science, with decimal arithmetic as the binding element. Astronomy and mathematics became joined together. Aryabhata seems to have been a native of Ashmaka country (located either in the north-west or on the Godavari). This is clear from the fact that the 7th century commentator Bhaskara I calls the *Aryabhatiya* the *Ashmaka-tantra* and *Ashmakiya*, and refers to the followers of Aryabhata as *Ashmakiyas*. A statement in the *Aryabhatiya* indicates that Aryabhata lived in Kusumapura, i.e., Pataliputra. He was obviously aware of the ideas and methods of his predecessors, but struck his own course. 'I dived deep in the ocean of astronomical theories, true and false,' he writes, 'and rescued the precious sunken jewel of true knowledge by means of the boat of my own intellect.' (*Aryabhatiya*, 4.49)

The *Aryabhatiya* consists of 121 two-line Sanskrit verses, divided into four parts. This short text contains the many astronomical and mathematical insights of this remarkable scholar (for details, see Divakaran, 2018: 157–67). Aryabhata described the earth as a sphere (*gola*). However, he had an earth-centric view of the universe—he thought that the planets moved around the earth in circular epicycles. Nonetheless, he was the first astronomer to give a scientific explanation of eclipses. He established that eclipses were not caused by the demons Rahu and Ketu, but by the moon coming within the earth's shadow or between the earth and sun. He worked out how to ascertain which part of the moon would be obscured during an eclipse. He understood the concept of relative motion, and discovered that the earth rotated on its axis. He estimated the rate of rotation as 1 minute of arc in 4 seconds. He estimated the diameter of the earth in *yojana* units. Another one of his many achievements was to find out the *sine* functions and use them in astronomy. He worked out the correct equation for calculating the orbit of a planet, and gave an extremely accurate estimate of the length of a year (365.2586805 days). Unfortunately, we do not know about the experiments or methods used by Aryabhata in reaching such momentous conclusions.

Although Aryabhata invoked tradition, he also boldly broke with it in certain ways. He referred to time as being without beginning or end, but described the *yuga* as a fixed, astronomically defined period of time (4,320,000 solar years) applicable to all planets, rather than as elastic and divinely ordained. His assertion that the earth was a sphere (and not a flat disc) was also a break with tradition, So was his idea of a rotating rather than a stationary earth. In fact, this was criticized and rejected by some of his peers, and the verse in the *Aryabhatiya* which talked about the earth's rotation (*Aryabhatiya* 4.10) was changed in later manuscripts of his work. We have here an example of ancient censorship, an attempt of conservative scholars to erase the memory of new scientific discoveries. In spite of some of its controversial aspects, the impact of Aryabhata's work was enormous. This is evident from later citations of his ideas and the many commentaries on the *Aryabhatiya*.

Varahamihira was a 6th century astrologer, astronomer, and mathematician who belonged to Avanti (in western Malwa). Mention has already been made of his *Panchasiddhantika*, wherein he summarized the five astronomical schools prevalent in the time. His *Brihatsamhita* is an encyclopaedic work dealing with diverse topics including how to sharpen swords, how to ascertain the value of precious metals and stones, how to make trees bear fruit out of season, how to distinguish the good breeds of animals, and how to

PRIMARY SOURCES | Ancient mathematical and medical manuscripts

In 1881, a fragmentary manuscript consisting of 70 birch bark leaves was discovered by a farmer in Bakhshali village, about 80 km north-east of Peshawar and 150 km north-west of Taxila. It came to be known as the Bakhshali Manuscript and is currently located in the Bodleian Library of Oxford University. The manuscript is incomplete and the title of the work and the author's name are unknown. The language of the text is Sanskrit influenced by the local language of the area and it is written in the Sharada script, which was used in the north-west. The Bakhshali manuscript is the oldest Sanskrit mathematical manuscript so far discovered. The manuscript seems to belong to sometime between the 8th and 12th century, but the work itself must be older, just how much older is difficult to say. While some scholars place it between 300–500 CE, others suggest it belongs to the 7th century CE. All admit the difficulty in dating the text. As pointed out by Hayashi (1995: 85), the work seems to be a compilation of mathematical rules and examples. So, a distinction needs to be made between the following: the authors of the original rules and examples; the compiler; the commentator/s; the scribe. The commentator identifies himself as the son of Chajaka, as a Brahmana, and as a king of mathematics (*ganaka-raja*).

The Bakhshali manuscript discusses topics such as fractions, square roots, arithmetic and geometric progressions, simple equations, and the rational approximation for the square root of a number which is not a perfect square. It also deals with advanced topics such as the summation of complex series and simultaneous linear equations. The work contains a full-fledged symbolic decimal notation for numbers. There are many symbols for zero, usually represented by a dot.

Source Hayashi, 1995; Plofker, 2009: 157–62; Divakaran, 2018: 167–73

divine the location of water. It also discusses the nature and structure of temples, palaces, and houses. It gives an explanation of seasons and discusses meteorological issues such as the correlation between the clouds, winds, and amount of rainfall.

Brahmagupta, an astronomer and mathematician of the late 6th/7th century, was the author of the *Brahmasputasiddhanta* (628 CE) and the *Khandakhadyaka* (665 CE). These texts became very influential within India, and their Arabic translations and adaptations introduced Indian astronomy to the Arabs. The *Brahmasputasiddhanta* is also the first surviving Indian text containing a systematic discussion of astronomical instruments, as well as methods of computing astronomical elements from readings taken with them (Sarma, 1986). The instruments include accessories, astronomical instruments for measuring time and observing the celestial bodies, instruments that turn automatically for the duration of one day, and ones that rotate perpetually. The accessories (*samsadhana*) comprise water, a pair of compasses (*bhrama*), plumb-line (*avalamba*), hypotenuse (*karna*), shadow (*chhaya*), mid-day (*dinardha*), the sun, and the local latitude (*aksha*). The text mentions nine astronomical instruments—*chakra* (a circular wooden plate graduated into 360°), *dhanus* (a semi-circular plate), *turyagola* (a quarter plate), *yashti* (staff), *shanku* (gnomon), *ghatika* (clepsydra), *kapala* (a horizontally placed circular plate), *kartari* (two semi-circular plates joined together at different levels), and *pitha* (a horizontally placed *chakra*). S. R. Sarma points out that the instruments, made of wood or bamboo, are very simple in design and could not have provided much precision in measurement. This suggests that astronomers probably relied more on their superior computing skills. However, Brahmagupta also referred to complex automatic devices called *svayamvaha yantras*, which reflects an awareness of the idea of perpetual motion.

Among the most important discoveries of ancient Indian mathematicians was the decimal system of notation, based on the place value of the first nine numbers and the use of a symbol known as *bindu* for zero (see Sarma, 1988; Baig and Sarma. [Eds.], 2003). The place value system refers to the idea that the value of a numeral depends on its place or where it stands in a number. (For instance, the value of the numeral 6 is different in numbers such as 160 and 106). A decimal system of notation means counting numbers in units of ten. The zero is a specific number preceding 1. In a place value system, it indicates that that place is empty (as, for instance the 0 in the number 100 or 305).

Although in modern mathematics, the place value system, a decimal place value system (based on units of 10), and the zero go together, in the history of mathematics, this was not necessarily so. For instance, the ancient Babylonians had a place value system without the use of zero, and had a counting system based on 60. Similarly, as we have seen, the Vedic texts are familiar with a decimal system (i.e., counting in units of tens), but there is no evidence that they had the concept of a decimal place value of numbers, or of the zero as a number.

The decimal place-value system occurs in a 3rd century work on astrology called the *Yavanajataka* by Sphujidhvaja (Hayashi, 2003: 366). This work does not, however, mention the zero. The decimal system of notation was used by Varahamihira and was referred to by Aryabhata in his *Aryabhatiya*. Aryabhata's method of extracting the square root and cube root presupposes the decimal place value of numbers. This shows that Indian mathematicians were using the system in the 5th century CE. In Europe, the old cumbersome system was followed till the 12th century, when the Europeans learnt the new system from the Arabs, who had learnt it from India. Arab writers such as Ibn Washiya, Al-Masudi, and Al-Biruni in fact give the credit for the discovery of the system to the 'Hindus,' that is, Indians.

The Bakhshali manuscript uses a dot for zero, but as discussed earlier, the date of this text is much debated. A symbol for zero does not occur in early Brahmi inscriptions. The zero occurs both as a dot and as a small circle in three 7th century Sanskrit inscriptions found in Cambodia and Indonesia (see Divakaran, 2018: 122–29). These are dated in Shaka years 605, 606, and 608, i.e., 683 CE, 684 CE, and 686 CE. In India, the circular symbol for zero first occurs in a Gwalior inscription of 876 CE. But the use of a symbol for the numerical zero must go back to a time long before its appearance in inscriptions in India and South-east Asia.

In the history of the evolution of the concept of zero, discussions among grammarians and philosophers—ideas such as absence, emptiness, absence, loss, infinity—may also have had an influence. But these are different from the idea of zero as a specific number (preceding 1) and as a number that could be used in a place value system indicating that that place was empty. Pingala's *Chandahsutra*, a 3rd/2nd century BCE work on prosody, uses the word *shunya* as a number. There is a reference to the term *shunyabindu* in Subandhu's 4th century play, *Vasavadatta*. Chronograms (known as *bhuta-sankhya*), which use words to represent numbers, are based on the idea of place value. So, the idea of zero as a numeral expressed in the form of a symbol seems to have been around several centuries before it appears in inscriptions.

Aryabhata's *Aryabhatiya* is a work on astronomy and deals only incidentally with problems of mathematics. Along with rules of involution and evolution, it deals with the arithmetical progression of numbers and their squares and cubes. In the field of geometry, Aryabhata describes the various properties of a circle and gives a very accurate value for pi (π) correct to 4 decimal places at 3.1416. Aryabhata is regarded as the father of algebra. His work solves a number of complex simultaneous equations. The use of the *sine* functions in solving problems in astronomy indicates the development of trigonometry. The *Aryabhatiya* gives tables for the trigonometric ratio *sine* (called *jya* in Sanskrit) for angles from 0 to 90 degrees at intervals of 3¾ degrees. The same *sine* tables are also found in the *Surya Siddhanta*. Aryabhata also perfected the methods of solving in integers certain types of indeterminate equations. Later mathematicians such as Brahmagupta and Bhaskara II also made contributions in this sphere. Unlike Greek writers on geometry, ancient Indian mathematicians did not give proofs or demonstrations.

Reference may be made here to some of the developments in later centuries as well. In the 7th century, Indian mathematics came to be divided into two main areas—arithmetic with mensuration and algebra. Bhaskara I (early 7th century) wrote a commentary on the *Aryabhatiya*, where he gave an interesting geometrical treatment for algebraic formulae. Brahmagupta (7th century) made important contributions to geometry. He was the first mathematician to discuss the method of obtaining a cyclic quadrilateral having rational sides and to give the area of a cyclic quadrilateral. He also put forward theories on the circum-diameter of a triangle and for finding the diagonals of a cyclic quadrilateral in terms of its sides. Mahavira (9th century) was a famous mathematician of Karnataka who lived in the court of the Rashtrakuta king Amoghavarsha Nripatunga of Manyakheta. He wrote a book called *Ganitasarasangraha* which dealt with various mathematical problems. He also gave formulae for the area and circumference of an ellipse. The formula he gave for the area of an ellipse was incorrect, but the one for the circumference was correct. Bhaskara II (12th century), author of the *Lilavati* was another important mathematician, whose writings contain some important ideas of calculus.

There are different assessments on the extent of Greek influence on Indian astronomy and mathematics. That there is some influence is clear—whether it is Ptolemaic or pre-Ptolemaic is debated. The Sanskrit names of the signs of the zodiac have Greek origins, and it seems that Greek influence led to the sequence of planets being fixed in the names of the seven days of the week. The late 3rd century Sanskrit text called the *Yavanajataka* reflects the transmission of Hellenistic astronomical ideas into India. At the same time, there are several differences between ancient Greek and Indian astronomy. Indian astronomy had its own unique features, and Indian astronomers appear to have made certain major breakthroughs independently. As pointed out by Divakaran (2018: 385–86), the story of mathematics (as is the case with many other sciences and disciplines) is the story of journeys—journeys of individuals, texts, and ideas. These journeys are part of the circulation of different kinds of knowledge across various parts of the ancient world.

Medical Knowledge

Although there may have been several different systems of medicine in ancient India, the texts and traditions of only one of these—Ayurveda (literally, 'knowledge for longevity')—have come down to us (Wujastyk, [1998] 2001). The *Charaka* and *Sushruta Samhita*s are its earliest surviving texts. There is little evidence to substantiate the claim made by the Ayurveda tradition that its roots lie in the Veda. Although Vedic texts do contain ideas related to healing and medicine, these do not match those of Ayurveda. Neither is there any indication that Ayurveda owed anything to Greek medicine; not a single Greek loan word can be identified in its terminology. Debiprasad Chattopadhyaya ([1977] 1979) argues that the medical literature represents part of a 'secular', i.e., non-religious empirical tradition that, at some point of time, came to be Brahmanized. On the other hand, Kenneth G. Zysk (1991) holds that the roots of Ayurveda lie in the milieu of the Buddhist monasteries of early historical India, and that medical knowledge and the practice of the monks gradually spread beyond the confines of the monasteries. (Direct evidence of this comes from the monasteries of Sri Lanka, where surgical instruments and medicinal baths have been found.) It is interesting to note the interweaving of philosophical ideas, for instance, those of Samkhya, Yoga, and Vaisheshika, in the medical texts.

The *Charaka Samhita* contains several chronological layers. The origins of the work may go back to the 3rd/2nd century BCE. The Bower manuscript contains passages very similar to those in the *Charaka Samhita* and indicates that Charaka was considered a medical authority by the early 5th century CE. The name Charaka occurs in colophons at the end of each chapter of the book. The main body of the text presents itself as containing knowledge received by Agnivesha from his teacher, a sage named Atreya. It seems that the medical system described in the work was known as the system of Agnivesha and that Charaka simply edited Agnivesha's text. In the 4th or 5th century CE, the text seems to have been edited again by a person named Dridhabala.

The *Charaka Samhita* is divided into 120 chapters arranged in 8 sections: The *Sutra* section deals with pharmacology, food, certain diseases and their treatment, doctors and quacks, and various philosophical issues. The second (*Nidana*) section deals with the causes of eight important diseases. The third (*Vimana*) deals with issues such as taste, nutrition, pathology, and medical studies. The fourth (*Sharira*) deals with anatomy, embryology, and philosophy. Then there are sections dealing with diagnosis and prognosis (*Indiriya*), therapy (*Chikitsa*), pharmacy (*Kalpa*), and a further discussion of therapy in general (*Siddhi*).

PRIMARY SOURCES | **The ideal hospital, according to Charaka**

The Chinese pilgrim Faxian refers to houses dispensing charity and medicine in the cities of North India. The *Charaka Samhita* gives details of how a hospital should be equipped:

'Now I shall set forth the chapter which starts with the preparations to be made,' said the Venerable Atreya....

The hospital building:

I shall now point out in brief the various supplies. Thus, an expert in the science of building should first construct a worthy building. It should be strong, out of the wind, and part of it should be open to the air. It should be easy to get about in, and should not be in a depression. It should be out of the path of smoke, sunlight, water, or dust, as well as unwanted noise, feelings, tastes, sights, and smells. It should have a water supply, pestle and mortar, lavatory, a bathing area, and a kitchen.

The Staff:

After that, one should select the staff of soup and rice cooks, bath attendants, masseurs, people to help patients with getting up and sitting down, and herb grinders. They should be good-natured, clean, well-behaved, loyal, practical, and pious. They should be skilled in nursing, and accomplished in all treatments. They should not be reluctant to work. The attendants should be able to sing, play instruments, and perform recitations, as well as being skilled in verses, songs, legends, and ancient lore. They should be pleasant and able to anticipate. They should know the where and when of things, and be generally sociable.

Supplies:

There should be bustard-quails, grey partridges, hares, black-buck, Indian antelope, black-tails, *chinkara*, sheep, and a nice, healthy milk cow with a live calf and good arrangements for grass, shelter, and drinking water.

There should be dishes, cups, water barrels, jugs, pots, pans, saucepans, large and small jars, bowls, platters, spoons, straw mats, buckets, oil pan, churns, leather, cloth, thread, cotton, wool, and so forth. There must be beds and seats, and so on, with vases and receptacles placed near them. Their coverlets, quilts, and pillows should be neatly made, and they should have bolsters. These are to make it easier to apply treatments involving lying down, sitting down, oiling, sweating, massage, balms, showers, massage ointments, vomiting, purges, decoction enemas, oil enemas, purging the head, urine, and faeces. There should be smooth, rough, and medium grinding stones with well irrigated uppers. Knives and their accessories must be supplied, as well as pipes for smoking [i.e., for fumigation of the nose and mouth], tubes for enemas and douches, a brush, a pair of scales, and a measuring instrument.

There must be supplies of ghee, oil, fat, marrow, honey, sugar-cane treacle, salt, kindling, water, mead, molasses rum, liquor, fermented barley-water, fermented bean-husk, blended liquor, spirits, curds, sour cream, watered buttermilk, fermented rice-water, and urine. There must also be supplies of *shali* rice, sixty-day *shali* rice, mung beans, green gram, barley, sesame, poor-man's pulse, cottony jujube, grapes, white teak, *phalsa*, myrobalan, emblic, belleric myrobalan, as well as the various kinds of drubs used during oiling and sweating.

There should be drugs for throwing up, soothing, and those which have both effects, as well as medicines well-known for constipating, for kindling the digestion, digestives, and those which remove wind.

All these supplies, as well as anything else that might be needed in an emergency, should be reckoned up and provided for the purpose of treatment. And items of food over and above the prescribed diets should also be laid on.

Source *Charaka Samhita* 1.15.1–7; Wujastyk, (1998) 2001: 77–78

The *Sushruta Samhita* too has several chronological layers. The original text, which dealt basically with surgery, may have been composed in the late centuries BCE, but it was added to and edited over several centuries till about the 5th century CE. Commentaries on the work mention the name of an editor named Nagarjuna. The text as it has come down to us consists of six sections. The first (*Sutra*) section deals with issues such as the origin and parts of medicine, a doctor's training, therapeutic substances, food, surgery, the treatment of wounds, and the extraction of splinters. The second (*Nidana*) deals with symptoms of diseases, their pathology, prognosis, and surgery. The third (*Sharira*) deals with embryology, anatomy, and philosophy. *Chikitsa* deals with therapy, *Kalpa* with poisons. The *Uttara* section deals with eyes, teeth, children's care, and diseases attributed to demons, etc.

The concepts of *dosha* (humours), *dhatu* (body tissues), and *mala* (waste products) are central to Ayurveda. Three semi-liquid substances or *doshas*—*vata* (wind), *pitta* (bile, choler), and *kapha/shleshman* (phlegm)—are supposed to circulate in the body. The *vata* is supposed to be localized mostly in the large intestine, the *pitta* in the navel, and the *kapha* in the chest. The three *doshas* interact with the seven basic elements of

PRIMARY SOURCES | The Bower Manuscript

In 1890, a British lieutenant named Hamilton Bower was camped at Kucha on the northern fringe of the Gobi desert (in present-day Xinjiang province in north-west China) while hunting down the Afghan assassin of a Scottish trader. He was approached by a man who offered to sell him a bundle of ancient birch bark manuscripts which had been found in a nearby *stupa*. Bower bought them, and they ultimately reached the hands of the epigraphist A. F. Rudolf Hoernle in Calcutta. The collection of manuscripts came to be known as the Bower Manuscript.

It is a collection of fragmentary manuscripts that seem to have originally belonged to a Buddhist monk-physician named Yashomitra living in the monastery of Qum Tura, close to Kucha. The manuscripts were buried in a memorial *stupa* dedicated to this monk when he died. They include seven treatises—three on Ayurveda, two on divination by using dice, and two on incantations to be used against snakebite.

The manuscripts were very difficult to read as they were damaged in many places; their technical vocabulary was obscure and difficult to understand. Hoernle laboured for 20 years and finally published the complete text and translation. The manuscripts belonged to the late 4th or early 5th century CE and proved to be an invaluable source for the history of ancient Indian medicine.

The manuscripts include spells and references to divination and astrology, and describe some formulae supposed to have been revealed to medical practitioners by the gods. They contain a technical medical vocabulary and discuss details of different diseases, their treatment, and the medicinal properties of various plants. There is a classification and discussion of tumours, tastes, secretions, and poisons. Among the interesting subjects of discussion is why baldness afflicts men more than women; the cure recommended involves frequent blood-letting, washing of the head, and the application of certain oils mixed with pepper and myrobalan (*anwala*).

Source Hoernle, 1893–1913

the body—chyle (the pulp to which food is reduced in the stomach), blood, flesh, fat, bone, marrow, and semen and with the waste products produced by the body. Body fluids are visualized as carried around the body through innumerable ducts, pipes, and tubes. Sushruta uses interesting similes to explain the function of the network of ducts—he describes it as similar to veins on a leaf, providing nutrition to all parts of the body through their contraction and dilation, just as a garden or field is irrigated by water-carrying canals. Digestion is seen as the central process of bodily functions.

Diseases are believed to be caused either by an inordinate build-up of one of the *doshas* in its location or by its movement into another area of the body. They are divided into those that can be cured, those that can only be alleviated, and those for which there is no cure. They are linked to other factors including lapses of judgement, the suppression of natural urges, *karma*, and the influence of demons. The discussion of epidemics mentions their connection with bad water, rats, and mosquitoes. Methods of medical diagnosis include direct perception and inference. Sushruta states that touching, looking, and questioning are the three methods that a doctor should use while examining a patient, but adds that he should use all of his five senses. Ayurveda prescribes various kinds of therapies including dietary regulation, massage, enemas, ointments, bloodletting, and surgery. It emphasizes moderation, including in eating, exercise, and medication.

The *Sushruta Samhita* describes surgery as the most useful branch of medical knowledge and gives information on surgical techniques and practices in ancient India. The author discusses the training of a surgeon and gives a detailed description of his tools. There are descriptions of surgical procedures such as the dislodging of the eye lens for the removal of cataract, cutting for a stone in the bladder, removing splinters and arrows, and suturing. The text also refers briefly to plastic surgery—a flap from the skin being grafted to repair a severed nose (rhinoplasty), and the repair of torn earlobes. It also discusses how corpses can be used to study human anatomy.

Other important ancient Ayurveda texts include Vagbhata's *Ashtangahridaya* (Heart of Medicine), a comprehensive and systematic presentation of Ayurvedic medical knowledge, which may belong to *c*. 600 CE. Another important work called the *Ashtangasamgraha*

(Tome on Medicine) is ascribed to the same author. Other ancient Ayurvedic treatises include Kashyapa's compendium, which deals mainly with the diseases of women and children. It may belong to the 7th century, although some parts may be based on older material. The 14th century *Sharngadhara Samhita* offers a brief but succinct account of Ayurveda. Its recipes are still used by the Ayurvedic pharmaceutical industry.

The ideas of Ayurveda had an impact outside the subcontinent as well. The major texts became accessible to other regions and cultures via translations into languages such as Arabic, Persian, and Tibetan, and there is evidence that Ayurvedic ideas influenced botanical science in Europe as well. Ayurveda is an ancient system of Indian medicine which has continued into our own times as one of several traditional alternatives to the allopathic tradition of modern medicine.

Mention may also be made of developments in veterinary science. The *Hastyayurveda* of Palakapya is a work consisting of 160 chapters. It deals with the diagnosis and treatment of the major diseases of elephants through medication and surgery.

CONCLUSIONS

Interpretations of the period *c.* 300–600 CE range from the extremes of a golden age marked by brilliance in all spheres to a feudal age marked by political fragmentation and economic decline. Neither of these extreme views are convincing. While the Gupta and Vakataka empires were not homogenous, centralized polities, inscriptions reveal fairly complex administrative and revenue structures. Land grant inscriptions reflect changes in agrarian relations, which intensified in later centuries. The evidence does not suggest a decline in urban centres, crafts, or trade. The development of complex religious pantheons and a further institutionalization of religious establishments were reflected in sculpture and architecture. The creative production of these centuries, especially in the spheres of Sanskrit literature and stone sculpture, reveals exceptionally fine aesthetic qualities and was based on the patronage of urban elites. The significant advances in the sciences of astronomy, mathematics, and medicine were carried forward in the early medieval period.

FURTHER READINGS

Bakker, Hans. 1997. *The Vakatakas: A Study in Hindu Iconology*. Groningen: Egbert Forsten.

Banerjea, J. N. (1956) 1975. *The Development of Hindu Iconography*. 2nd Rev. Edn. New Delhi: Munshiram Manoharlal.

———. 1966. *Pauranic and Tantric Religion: Early Phase*. Calcutta: University of Calcutta.

Chakrabarti, Kunal and Kanad Sinha. (Eds.). 2018. *State, Power and Legitimacy: The Gupta Kingdom*. Delhi: Primus Books.

Chatterjee, Asim Kumar. 2000. *A Comprehensive History of Jainism. Vol. 1: From the Earliest Beginnings to AD 1000*. New Delhi: Munshiram Manoharlal. Chapters 7, 8.

Chattopadhyaya, B. D. (1994) 1997. *The Making of Early Medieval India*. Delhi: Oxford University Press.

Divakaran, P. P. 2018. *The Mathematics of India: Concepts, Methods, Connections*. New Delhi: Hindustan Book Agency and Singapore: Springer. (Sources and Studies in the History of Mathematics and Physical Sciences series; managing editor Jed Z. Buchwald).

Flood, Gavin. (Ed.). n.d. *The Blackwell Companion to Hinduism*. New Delhi: Blackwell.

Goyal, S. R. 2005. *The Imperial Guptas: A Multidisciplinary Political Study*. Jodhpur: Kusumanjali Book World.

Gupta, P. L. (1974) 1979. *The Imperial Guptas*, 2 Vols. Varanasi: Vishwavidyalaya Prakashan.

Liu, Xinru. 1996. *Silk and Religion: An Exploration of Material Life and the Thought of People, AD 600–1200*. Delhi: Oxford University Press.

Maity, S. K. (1957) 1970. *Economic Life in Northern India in the Gupta period (c. AD 300–550)*. 2nd Rev. Edn. Delhi: Motilal Banarsidass.

Padoux, André. 2017. *The Hindu Tantric World: An Overview*, Chicago and London: University of Chicago Press.

Sen, Tansen. 2003. *Buddhism, Diplomacy, and Trade: The Realignment of Sino-Indian Relations, 600–1400*. Honolulu: Association for Asian Studies and University of Hawaii Press.

Sharma, R. S. (1965) 1980. *Indian Feudalism*. Madras: Macmillan.

Shastri, Ajay Mitra. 1997. *Vakatakas: Sources and History*. Great Ages of Indian History. New Delhi: Aryan Books International.

Shrimali, Krishna Mohan. 1987. *Agrarian Structure in Central India and the Northern Deccan (c. AD 300–500): A Study of Vakataka Inscriptions*. New Delhi: Munshiram Manoharlal.

Singh, Upinder. (Ed.). 2011. *Rethinking Early Medieval India: A Reader*. New Delhi, Oxford University Press.

Spink, Walter M. 2006. *Ajanta: History and Development*. 3 Vols. Leiden, Boston: E. J. Brill.

Thaplyal, K. K. 1996. *Guilds in Ancient India*. New Delhi: New Age International. Especially Chapters 2, 5.

Warder, A. K. 1972. *Indian Kavya Literature*. Vol. 1 and 3. Delhi: Motilal Banarsidass.

Williams, Joanna. 1982. The *Art of Gupta India: Empire and Province*. Princeton, New Jersey: Princeton University Press.

Wujastyk, Dominik. (1998) 2001. *The Roots of Ayurveda: Selections from Sanskrit Medical Writings*. New Delhi: Penguin Books.

Zysk, Kenneth G. 1991. *Asceticism and Healing in Ancient India: Medicine in the Buddhist Monastery*. New York and Bombay: Oxford University Press.

Painting of beautiful woman holding flowers at Sigiriya (Sri Lanka); did she represent a royal woman, goddess, or semi-divine being?

CHAPTER 10

Emerging Regional Configurations

c. 600–1200 CE

- Textual and archaeological sources
- Political structure and political narrative
- Royal land grants
- Rural society
- Urban processes
- Historical processes in South India
- The religious sphere
- Architecture and sculpture
- Conclusions

An inscription on a wall of the Amritaghateshvara temple at Tirukkadaiyur refers to an event that took place in around 1025 CE. It states that in his 15th regnal year, Rajendra I sent many ships across the sea and conquered Kadaram which was protected by the deep sea, captured its king, and took over Srivijaya and the war gate of its city. Srivijaya was a maritime state based in Sumatra. Kadaram is Kedah in the Malay peninsula and was at that time an outpost of Srivijaya. The inscription lists twelve other cities (some in the Malay peninsula) which it says were overrun by the Chola soldiers. Rajendra Chola's invasion of Srivijaya is a unique military event. Indian kings fought many wars but mostly across land. The Gupta ruler Samudragupta claimed in his Allahabad *prashasti* to have sway over Simhala (Sri Lanka) and all the other islands. Rajendra's navy, however, sailed much further across the ocean to South-east Asia. The larger context of the expedition were the high stakes of Indian Ocean trade.

The term 'early medieval' is often used by historians to refer to the period between *c.* 600 and 1200/1300 CE. The term is not new, but it has been used in different ways. The idea of the 'early medieval' that informs most mainstream history writing today goes back to the 1950s and the shift from dynastic history to historical processes. Historians pointed out that the Hindu–Muslim–British periodization was flawed and inconsistent and gave unnecessary importance to the religious affiliations of political elites. Instead, they focused their attention on social, political, and economic structures. It was argued that certain important changes took place in these spheres long before the Turkish invasions and the establishment of the Delhi Sultanate. This use of the term 'early medieval' soon took root among historians working on early Indian history, although there were differences of opinion about its start and end dates. There is, however, another usage of the term. Some scholars refer to the Delhi Sultanate period as early medieval and distinguish it from the Mughal period, which they refer to as late medieval. So, there are currently two ideas of the early medieval. The real breakthrough will come when historians are able to integrate the two. The challenge has to do with the different languages of the primary sources and also the understanding of process of continuity and change in the long-term in precolonial India.

As mentioned in Chapter 9, historians have debated the nature of the society, polity, and economy of early medieval India. This period has often been labelled one of crisis, decline, decay, and decadence. The older histories attributed the decline to the advent of 'Muslim rule'. (This phrase has been put in inverted commas because the term 'Muslim' is a very broad one; is more useful to describe the Ghaznavids and Ghurids more specifically on the basis of their native language as Turks.) Subsequently, the feudalism school described the period as an age marked by political fragmentation, the transformation of peasants into serfs, and a decline of urban centres and the money economy. The feudalism hypothesis has been applied to both north as well as South India. For South India, there is another interpretative framework—the **segmentary state** model, which presents the kings of this age as ritual figures, devoid of the two important props of royal power—a revenue infrastructure and a standing army. A third major interpretative framework for early medieval India suggests that in many parts of the subcontinent, these centuries were marked by the formation and proliferation of states at the regional level. This hypothesis can be connected with the more specific argument that the early medieval period was one of urban change, but not of urban decay.

While most historians supported one or other model, some have remained non-aligned. Much of the older historiography focused on pan-Indian, or at least trans-regional patterns, but the research of the past few decades highlights the regional and sub-regional specificities and variations.

The positive impact of several decades of vigorous debate is that it raised important questions about political, social, and economic processes. The negative fallout was that certain issues remained under-studied (see Upinder Singh, 2011: 5–13). These include the human interface with changing environments, the role of the forest and forest people, gender and the household, the religious and cultural domains, the history of ideas and emotions, and the cultural interactions between India and the wider world.

The political hierarchies and changes in agrarian relations that the feudalism model highlights are an important aspect of the early medieval period, but its understanding of royal land grants can be questioned. These grants can be seen as part of the integrative processes that the integrative/processual model talks about but it is also necessary to focus on changes in agrarian relations, and the elements of conflict and violence in the history of the period cannot be ignored. The challenge is to identify the insights and shortcomings of the various models, and to try to move beyond them.

In recent years, many studies have helped fill the gaps in the earlier historiography. While the heartlands of large kingdoms and empires have always attracted historians' interest, the need to understand the smaller principalities, non-state societies, and forest tribes is now recognized. There is an awareness of the need to develop a better archaeological understanding of early medieval and medieval India. There is continued interest in understanding the historical experiences of subordinated and marginalized social groups. The invisibilization of women in the earlier debates has been challenged by highlighting the role of royal and non-royal women in the formal and informal exercise of power and authority. Explorations of religion, literary cultures, and intellectual history are no longer tied to the old theoretical frameworks. Visual sources are being incorporated into the historical narrative. Exciting new perspectives are opening up with the history of ancient and early medieval India being seen as part of a larger global history.

Instead of attempting a complete or comprehensive account of all the historical aspects of the history of the subcontinent during period *c.* 600–1200 CE, this chapter focuses on a few issues such as the larger historiographical debates and especially on developments in the Deccan and the far south.

Textual and Archaeological Sources

Sheldon Pollock ([2006] 2007: 1) argues that there were two great moments of transformation in culture and power in pre-modern India. The first happened around the beginning of the Common Era, when Sanskrit, which had a long history as a sacred language restricted to religious practice, was 're-invented' as a language for literary and political expression, eventually spilling out far beyond the frontiers of the subcontinent. The second moment of transformation was located in the beginning of the second millennium CE, when vernacular speech forms became literary languages and began to challenge the position of Sanskrit, eventually replacing it. This was part of the emergence of regional configurations in politics and culture during the early medieval period.

The early medieval period was one of great vitality in the intellectual, creative, and artistic fields, and this points to sustained patronage by affluent urban and political elites. As mentioned earlier, the texts produced in a particular period are not only sources, but also important parts of the history of that period. It is not possible to give a detailed listing or discussion of the texts of various kinds in different languages produced between *c.* 600–1200 CE. Some of them have been mentioned in Chapter 1. Therefore, the discussion below is illustrative, not exhaustive. (For good overviews of various textual sources of ancient and early medieval India, see Jan Gonda. [Gen. Ed.], [1973–87] 2022.) Sanskrit had ceased to be a language spoken by ordinary people many centuries earlier, but a great volume and variety of Sanskrit texts were produced in the early medieval period. These include philosophical commentaries and religious texts, *bhanas* (monologue plays), *stotras* (hymn compositions), story literature, and anthologies of poetry. The technical literature includes works on metre, grammar, lexicography, poetics, music, architecture, medicine, and mathematics.

Many important and influential Dharmashastra compilations, digests, and commentaries were written during the early medieval period (see Mathur, 2007). The compilations include the *Chaturvimshatimata*, which put together the teachings of 24 law-givers. Jimutavahana wrote a work on procedural law called the *Vyavaharamatrika* and a digest of laws on inheritance called the *Dayabhaga*, which became extremely influential in Bengal. Major commentaries include those of Medatithi (9th century), Govindaraja (11th/12th century), and Kulluka (12th century) on the *Manu Smriti*. Vijnaneshvara (11th–12th centuries) and Apararka (12th century) wrote commentaries on the *Yajnavalkya Smriti*. Vijnaneshvara's commentary, titled *Mitakshara*, became an authority on various aspects of Hindu law. Other important Dharmashastra works include Lakshmidhara's *Kritya Kalpataru* (12th century) and Devanabhatta's *Smritichandrika* (11th/12th century).

The early medieval Puranas reflect the increasing popularity of theistic elements within Hinduism. They include the *Bhagavata Purana* (*c.* 10th century), the *Brahmavaivarta Purana* (composed sometime between the 10th and 16th centuries), and the *Kalika Purana* (10th/11th century). Sections on *tirthas* (pilgrimage), *vratas* (vows), penances, gifts, and the *dharma* of women were added to the older Puranas during this period. The Upapuranas, many of which were composed in Eastern India, are valuable for the information they provide on popular beliefs, customs, and festivals. They can be used to trace the dialogue between Brahmanical and non-Brahmanical ideas, customs, and practices.

The Sanskrit *kavya* literature of these centuries has sometimes been described as marked by pedantry, ornateness, and artificiality. This description undermines the wide range and virtuosity of the literary production of the period (for details, see Warder, 1972–2004, Vols. 1, 4, 5, 6; Bronner et al. [Eds.], 2014). Many works of Sanskrit prose, poetry, and drama were composed in the early medieval period. These include Dandin's *Dashakumaracharita* (7th century) Banabhatta's *Kadambari* and *Harshacharita* (7th century); Magha's *Shishupalavadha* (7th century); Bhavabhuti's *Malatimadhava*, *Mahaviracharita*, and *Uttararamacharita* (8th century); and Shriharsha's *Naishadhacharita* (12th century). Historical and epic-Puranic themes were popular in *kavya*. Apart from poetry and prose, a mixed style consisting of alternating prose and verse, known as *champu*, made its appearance. This period was extremely productive for Sanskrit texts on literary theory, poetics, and aesthetics. Important works include Dandin's *Kavyadarsha* (7th century); Vamana's *Kavyalamkarasutra* (8th century); Anandavardhana's *Dhvanyaloka* (9th century); Rudrata's *Kavyalamkara* (9th century); Rajashekhara's *Kavyamimamsa* (10th century); Mammata's *Kavyaprakasha* (11th century); Abhinavagupta's *Abhinavabharati* (commentary on Bharata's *Natyashastra*) and *Lochana* (commentary on Anandavardhana's *Dhvanyaloka*); and the Paramara king Bhoja's *Shringaraprakasha* and *Sarasvatikanthabhushana* (11th century).

The growth of regional polities was accompanied by the composition of Sanskrit royal biographies by court poets. Banabhatta's *Harshacharita* is one of the well-known works of this genre. Sandhyakaranandin's *Ramacharita* is written in *shlesha* (with double meaning) and simultaneously tells the story of the epic hero Rama and the Pala king Ramapala. The few works of poetry woven around quasi-historical themes or characters included Padmagupta's *Navasahasankacharita*, which tells the tale of king Sindhuraja Navasahasanka of Malwa, and his winning of the hand of a princess named Shashiprabha. Bilhana wrote the *Vikramankadevacharita*, a eulogistic work about Vikramaditya VI, the Chalukya king of Kalyani. Hemachandra's *Kumarapalacharita* (in Sanskrit and Prakrit) tells the story of Kumarapala, king of Anahilawada, while illustrating the rules of grammar. The *Prithvirajavijaya* of Jayanaka is an incomplete Sanskrit *mahakavya* woven around Prithviraja Chauhan. Chand Bardai's *Prithviraj-raso* (in Brajbhasha, with some

Rajasthani elements) is much later heroic epic eulogizing the personality and exploits of Prithviraja. All these works have to be analyzed carefully taking into account the background and aims of their authors and the contexts in which they were written. Kalhana's *Rajatarangini* is a *kavya* which presents a chronicle of the rulers of Kashmir from the earliest times up to the 12th century CE.

The Buddhist turn towards Sanskrit had taken place many centuries earlier, in about the 2nd century BCE. Pali retained its importance in Sri Lanka and Buddhist cultures in South-east Asia. Most of the Prakrit works of this period are Jaina texts in the Maharashtri Prakrit dialect. Jaina writers and poets wrote in Sanskrit, Prakrit, and Apabhramsha. Apabhramsha represents the last stage of the Prakrit languages, and contains a blend of later Prakrit with elements of the regional languages. The various modern North Indian languages emerged from it. Jaina works included hagiographies of the Jaina saints as well as tellings of the *Ramayana* and *Mahabharata*. Although literary theorists discussed Prakrit and Apabhramsha, these languages were not used in royal inscriptions of this period. Apabhramsha works of this time include Pupphayanta's *Mahapurana*, Kanha and Saraha's *Dohakosha*, and several texts on Jaina doctrines and saints, epic poems, short stories, and *dohas* (couplets).

The early medieval period saw burgeoning of literature in the regional languages, a process that Pollock refers to as vernacularization ([2006] 2007: 283–329). By this, he means the literary and political promotion of local languages, and the choice to write texts in regional languages. This choice is also reflected in inscriptions, where the regional languages were initially used for documentary details and then gradually started being used for politically expressive purposes. This marked a major change from the 1st

PRIMARY SOURCES | **Kshemendra's satires**

Kshemendra was a brilliant intellectual and writer who lived and wrote in Kashmir during the late 10th/early 11th century. He belonged to an affluent family but does not seem to have been part of the court circle. He was well-versed in Vaishnava and Buddhist philosophy and studied literary theory with Abhinavagupta. He wrote in Sanskrit. His surviving works include abridged versions of the *Mahabharata* and *Ramayana*, and verse works on the Buddha's former lives and the ten incarnations of Vishnu. He also wrote several satirical texts—*Samayamatrika* (Little Mother by Compact), *Narmamala* (Garland of Mirth), *Kalavilasa* (A Dalliance with Deceptions), and *Deshopadesha* (Advice from the Countryside).

Kshemendra's satirical descriptions of social life are very different from the sophisticated, cultured world of Sanskrit *kavya*. He makes fun of many people—administrative officials, Brahmanas, ascetics, monks, nuns, doctors, astrologers, gurus, widows, surgeons, merchants, singers and other entertainers, goldsmiths, lawyers, relatives, outcastes, villains, misers, courtesans, procuresses, parasitic libertines, students, old men's wives, poets, alchemists, gamblers, fools, gurus, religious devotees, lute players, doctors, retirees, scholars, scribes, ascetics, even gods. He brings out the greedy, exploitative, and hypocritical nature of many respectable people. However, he does not mock kings.

Kshemendra made fun of people who practised fake religiosity. The protagonist of *Kalavilasa* is a man named Muladeva, a great authority on the arts of deception. Muladeva observes that hordes of swindlers, including yogis, gurus, and chanters of the Veda roam about the world. They offer hope to hundreds of people desirous of magic powers, and lead them to ruin. Kshemendra discusses the intoxication of asceticism and devotion, along with other kinds of intoxication—of wealth, folly, learning, power, lineage, obsession with purity and drinking. He states that the intoxication of asceticism makes one look to the sky without noticing the impediments on the ground. The intoxication of devotion makes one believe in marvels and lose sight of oneself.

In *Deshopadesha*, Kshemendra makes fun of people who practise false piety, including ascetics and priests. The characters in the *Narmamala* include an official who is initially a Buddhist, then pretends to be a worshipper of Vishnu, and then, in order to protect the health of his wife, turns to the Tantric Kaulas. He invites to his house an arrogant, greedy Kaula guru, who is ignorant, unscrupulous, and fond of drinking. The guru is described as an expert in cheating all kinds of people, including prostitutes, lechers, and officials. When he turns up, people line up and offer obeisance. He holds a fake ritual ceremony to fool them.

Kshemendra says that he composed the *Narmamala* for the entertainment of good people, to make them laugh, and to advise them on how to avoid falling into the hands of tricksters and scoundrels. His works represent a vibrant tradition of social and religious satire in ancient India.

Source Haksar. (Trans.)., 2011, 2014a, 2014b

millennium, when Sanskrit played the role of a trans-regional cosmopolitan language in texts and inscriptions, a language associated with power and prestige. The use of Sanskrit did not disappear in the 2nd millennium, but the textual sphere was now marked by the increasing use of regional languages, which were aware of the Sanskrit textual traditions, and developed in conversation with it. This development is first visible in South India.

As discussed in Chapter 8, Tamil has a long literary history which begins in around the 2nd century BCE. Early medieval Tamil texts include the devotional songs of the Alvars and Nayanmars and the hagiographies of the saints. Royal biographies include the anonymous *Nandikkalambakam*, a poem in some 80 stanzas, giving a eulogistic account of the reign of the Pallava king Nandivarman III. Kamban's *Ramayana* was perhaps composed in the 12th century. Important Jaina works in Tamil include the *Chulamani* and *Sivaka-chintamani*. Buddhist Tamil works include grammatical texts such as the *Viracholiyam*. Pallava and Chola inscriptions reveal a division of labour between Sanskrit and Tamil—Sanskrit was used for the politically expressive *prashasti* portions and Tamil for the documentary portions. From the time of Rajendra Chola, Tamil took over both roles. New genres appeared—for instance the Ula poems, which describe the procession of a royal hero as women along his route are overcome with desire for him. Patronage for literature came from the court, but also from other elites, and some of the poems have a strong temple context rather than a courtly one. David Shulman suggests that the Chola period marks a new, 'imperial moment" in the history of Tamil, when new aesthetic sensibility, styles, and genres emerged, and patrons and audiences expanded (Shulman, 2011: 150–94). The geographical spread of Tamil also expanded far beyond its original locale and the language was spoken by far-flung diaspora communities extending from Sri Lanka to south China. These developments were linked to historical developments in the Chola period.

The early medieval period saw the beginning of Kannada literature (Pollock, [2006] 2007: 330–436; Devadevan, 2020: 281–305). Kannada appeared in royal inscriptions in the late 5th century, but its use for creative expression in texts and inscriptions began several centuries later. Several works in this language were composed, some under the patronage of the Rashtrakutas, Hoysalas, and Chalukyas. As in the case of Tamil literature, Kannada literature too developed in conversation with the Sanskrit tradition. The *Kavirajamarga* (Way of the King of Poets), attributed to Shrivijaya, written in the 9th century during the reign of the Rashtrakuta king Amoghavarsha (and perhaps with his collaboration), is considered the first Kannada literary work. It is basically a work on poetics, but also contains some material on language and grammar. Pampa's Kannada telling of the *Mahabharata* (titled *Bharatam* or *Vikramarjunavijayam*) was composed in the 10th century. Major Kannada works on lexicography, poetic metre, and grammar were written between the 10th and 13th centuries.

Telugu appeared in inscriptions by the end of the 6th century, but its literary uses appeared several centuries later. The first Telugu *kavya* was produced in the court of the Eastern Chalukyas in the early 11th century. Marathi appeared in inscriptions in the late 10th/early 11th century and Marathi literature made its appearance several centuries later. Texts and inscriptions in the North Indian regional languages are known after the 13th and 14th centuries.

The world of intellectuals, writers, and poets in early medieval India was a multilingual one. Tamil was Dandin's native language, but he wrote in Sanskrit. His work on poetics, the *Kavyadarsha*, circulated widely and was rendered into many languages including Tamil, Kannada, Sinhala, and Tibetan. The world of early medieval intellectuals was also multi-disciplinary, where knowledge flowed across disciplinary boundaries. Some exceptional individuals made their mark in several areas. A notable example is Abhinavagupta, a leading exponent of Kashmir Shaivism, who also wrote on literary theory and poetics.

Textual sources offer both direct as well as indirect information about their time. An example of a text that gives direct, useful historical information is the anonymous *Lekhapaddhati*, a Sanskrit and Prakrit work composed in Gujarat in about the 13th century, which contains models of various types of legal documents. Another example is

PRIMARY SOURCES | Kamban's *Iramavataram*

The *Iramavataram* is a highly popular and influential Tamil rendering of the story of Rama. 'Iramavataram' means 'Rama's becoming an *avatara*' or 'The Descent of Rama.'

Very little is known about the author, Kampan. The etymology of his name has lent itself to legends, for instance, that he was born near a temple pillar (*kampan stambha*) or was the son of the king of Kampanadu. He may have been named after the god Shiva in Kanchipuram, who is called Kampan in the *Tevaram*. Kampan was born in Tirutaluntur village. According to some accounts, he was an *uvachcha*—a non-Brahmana priest, perhaps at a temple of the goddess Kali. He was patronized by a chieftain named Chataiyappan or Chataiyan who lived in Tiruvenneynallur (in modern Thanjavur district, Tamil Nadu). Kamban refers to this patron in every thousandth verse of his work. He is said to have quarreled with the Chola king and gone off to Andhra for some time, eventually dying in Nattaracankottai (Ramanathapuram district, Tamil Nadu). Several other works are attributed to him, but they are so different from the *Iramavataram* that it is unlikely that Kampan wrote them.

Various dates between the 9th and 12th centuries have been suggested for Kampan. By this time, Rama's story was well-known in the far south. There are references to it in *akam* and *puram* poems, as well as in the *Silappadikaram*. Rama was also well known in Alvar *bhakti* poetry. Once Kamban wrote Rama's story in the *Iramavataram*, no other Tamil poet dared to try to surpass his rendition.

The *Iramavataram* is a sophisticated literary work consisting of over 12,000 stanzas divided into six books (*kantam*), subdivided into cantos (*patalam*). The author was learned in the Sanskrit *kavya* tradition, but he was also steeped in the Tamil cultural, literary, and *bhakti* traditions. Sound, metre, and rhythm are tailored to match events and emotions in his work. Although the *Iramavataram* broadly follows the main story line of the Valmiki *Ramayana*, it is not a literal translation. Unlike the latter, the *Iramavataram* begins with a description of river waters. Kamban wove into his work the idea of the five *tinai* or landscapes of earlier Sangam poetry. His telling of Rama's story is vivid and dramatic. He introduced changes in the details of certain episodes and in the presentation of certain characters. Emotions run high and there are vigorous dialogues. There is lots of action and there are gory descriptions of war. Ravana and Shurpanakha are treated as evil, but are given psychological depth and a somewhat empathetic treatment. The *Iramavataram* ends with Rama's return to Ayodhya after defeating Ravana. There is no equivalent of the *Uttarakanda* in the text.

The *Iramavataram* is a deeply religious work and is imbued with the ethos of Tamil Vaishnava devotion. In the Valmiki *Ramayana*, direct references to Rama's divinity are concentrated in the first and seventh book. In the *Iramavataram*, Rama is frequently recognized as an incarnation of Vishnu by those who he encounters, but he himself seems to be unaware of his divine status. Although Kamban considered Rama a great god and an exemplar of virtues, he gives him human-like vulnerabilities by describing his moments of despair and uncertainty.

Kamban achieved celebrity status as a great Tamil poet and his *Iramavataram* was swiftly recognized as a classic. It had enormous impact on Tamil literature. It came to be very well known in South India beyond the Tamil-speaking areas, as well as in various parts of South-east Asia. If the Valmiki *Ramayana* and Tulsidas's *Ramcharitmanas* are the best known tellings of Rama's story in North India, in the south, it is Kamban's *Iramavataram*.

Source Zvelebil, 1973: 207–17; Shulman, 2016: 166–74; Hart and Heifetz. (Trans.)., 1988: 1–36

the *Krishi-Parashara*, an early medieval text of Bengal, dealing with agriculture. Historical information can also be prised out of story literature. For instance, Jaina folk tales (*dharma-kathas*) of Western India often have merchants as protagonists, and are a useful source of information on trade and traders. The stories in the *Kathasaritsagara* are a source of information on social history. Mathematical texts such as the 9th century *Ganitasarasangraha* of Mahaviracharya and the 12th century *Lilavati* of Bhaskaracharya offer incidental information about prices, weights and measures, wages, and coins.

Apart from texts in Indian languages, Chinese and Arab accounts are useful sources of information for early medieval India. Xuanzang's work was titled *Tang xiyu ji* (earlier spelt *Si-yu-ki*) (The Records of the Western Regions Visited During the Great Tang Dynasty). One of Yijing's works (*Nanhai jigui neifa zhuan*, 'A Record of Inner Dharma Sent Back from the Southern Seas') gives an account of Buddhist doctrines and practices in India, while the other (*Xiyu quifa gaoseng zhuan*, 'Biographies of Eminent Monks Who Went to the Western Regions in Search of Dharma') provides brief biographical sketches of 56 Chinese monks who visited India in the 7th century. In the former work, he wrote: "If you read this record of mine, you may, without moving one step, travel in all the five countries of India." Yijing also wanted to rectify the "errors" in the monastic

FURTHER DISCUSSION | **Wang Xuance's missions to India**

The Chinese travellers who made the arduous journey from China to India and back included monks and diplomats. Wang Xuance was one of several official envoys sent by the Tang emperors to India in the 7th century. According to Bangwei Wang, various sources suggest that he travelled to India three times. A Buddhist encyclopaedia edited by a contemporary monk named Daoshi, who also happened to know Wang Xuance personally, states: 'The Tang ambassador Wang Xuance has been there [India] three times. When I met Xuance, he told me this.' In fact, Daoshi makes a similar statement in two other places in his work. Wang Xuance himself made the following assertion in one of his reports to the emperor: 'Since Buddhism arose in India, I, the servant [of Your Majesty], have been sent there three times, and I saw and heard a lot.'

Wang was first sent to India by emperor Taizong as assistant to the imperial ambassador Li Yibiao. Members of the delegation left China in 643 and travelled to India via Tibet and Nepal. In Magadha, they met king Harsha and visited a number of Buddhist pilgrimage places. This is how Wang Xuance described the experience: 'I had the unexpected good fortune to see the venerable footprints [of the Buddha]. Sometimes sad, sometimes happy, I could not control my feelings.' The delegation returned to China in 645. A year or two later (in 646 or 647), Wang once again started off for India, this time as the head of the delegation. The route was the same as that adopted for the first mission. Chinese sources state that this embassy was attacked by soldiers led by a person named Arunasha, and all except Wang Xuance and his second-in-command Jiang Shiren were either killed or captured. Scholars have different opinions on the date of Wang Xuance's third mission, which must have taken place some time between 657 and 661 CE.

Bangwei Wang draws attention to the discovery of an inscription in Skyid-grong in Tibet, which throws light on this third mission. The inscription on a rock face is seriously damaged, especially in its lower part. The surviving text covers an area 81.5 cm in width and 53 cm in length. It consists of 222 legible characters arranged in 24 lines, many parts too damaged to be read. The main purport of the inscription can, however, be understood. It states that the emperor sent Wang and his companions to India in the sixth month of the third year of Xianqing, i.e., in 658 CE. In the fifth month of the summer of some year (probably in 659 CE), the delegation arrived at a certain place, probably the very spot where the inscription was inscribed. There is also mention of some hitherto unknown members of Wang's delegation. The inscription also indicates that the route taken by the delegation passed through Skyid-grong and Nepal.

Another inscription mentioning Wang Xuance was recently discovered at the Longmen Grotto in Luoyang. This records his gift of a Maitreya image for the southern cell of the Bingyan Grotto in the second year of Lingde (i.e., 665 CE). The diplomat was evidently a pious lay Buddhist.

Wang Xuance wrote a diary of his visits to India called *Zhong Tianzhuguo xing ji* (Records of the Travels to Middle India), which apparently included maps of India and sketches of Buddhist artefacts. Unfortunately, the diary is lost.

Source Wang, 2002; Tansen Sen, 2003: 23, 40, 205, 261

practices in China by comparing them to India. The important Arab works include the 9th–10th century writings of travellers and geographers such as Sulaiman, Al-Masudi, Abu Zaid, Al-Biduri, and Ibn Haukal. Later Arab writers include Al-Biruni, Al-Idrisi, Muhammad Ufi, and Ibn Batuta. Such accounts are especially useful for information on Indian Ocean trade.

With the Ghaznavid and Ghurid invasions, the subcontinent was drawn into the orbit of the Persianate culture, which extended across Iran, Central Asia, and Afghanistan. The eastward spread of Persianate culture into the subcontinent and its interaction with the earlier Sanskrit culture can been seen as a major aspect of Indian history from the 11th to the 18th centuries CE (Eaton, 2019: 3–18). This argument can be expanded to include the regional cultures that were emerging in various parts of the subcontinent.

While much work has been done on the political, economic, and social processes in the various regions of the subcontinent during the early medieval period, the intellectual history of this period needs much more attention. The rich textual production of these centuries is related to the many important developments in the spheres of intellectual history, an aspect that needs much more study (see Devadevan, 2020).

The history of the Turkish invasions and the Delhi Sultanate is often reconstructed on the basis of an uncritical reading of court chronicles and epics of conquest and resistance, which were written against the background of bitter political conflicts. This has led to viewing this period in terms of an antagonistic encounter of a monolithic Hinduism with a monolithic Islam. But neither of these were homogeneous categories. Just as the umbrella term Hinduism includes a great variety of religious ideas and practices, Muslim communities too were divided into different groups such as Sunnis, Shias, Ismailis, and Sufis. A careful analysis of the early medieval sources which is attentive to their genre, authorship, and audience, offers a more nuanced and textured picture of the different ways in which Sanskrit, Persianate, and regional literary cultures interacted with each other to produce a new synthesis marked by cultural interaction and confluence.

As for the previous centuries, inscriptions continue to form a major source of historical information for *c.* 600–1200 CE. The interpretation of the epigraphic data is in fact central to the major debates concerning this period. Royal land grant inscriptions, mostly recording grants to Brahmanas, are especially important. Equally important are epigraphs recording non-royal and royal gifts made to religious establishments.

The assessment of the early medieval numismatic evidence is an issue of debate. As mentioned in the previous chapter, the hypothesis that there was a subcontinental decline in the money economy from *c.* 400 CE onwards can be questioned. Archaeological data on the early medieval period is extremely meagre, and this is a major drawback when it comes to framing and testing hypotheses related to settlement history.

Political Structure and Political Narrative

As discussed in Chapter 9, there are at least three competing theoretical models for understanding the history of early medieval India—the feudalism, integrative/processual, and segmentary state models. The political history of this period is best understood as a series of competing states, the more successful polities consisting of paramount and subordinate rulers. The contours of kingdoms were fluid and are difficult to define. Kingdoms are more easily identified by their nuclear areas and political centres than by their boundaries. The political narrative of these centuries reveals some large, relatively long-lived kingdoms such as those of the Cholas, Rashtrakutas, Palas, and Pratiharas. There were also the more numerous short-lived kingdoms which had a much more modest range of territorial control. The interaction between lineages took the form of war and conflict as well as of military and matrimonial alliances. The details of how different lineages established their political and agrarian resource base in various parts of the subcontinent are obscure. B. D. Chattopadhyaya ([1983] 1997: 205–08) has pointed out that there was no dichotomy between lineages and states in early medieval India, and that lineage ties were in fact central to political formations.

The spread of state society was accompanied by a high level of spatial mobility of political elites and unprecedented levels of military build-up. The incessant warfare during the period indicates the importance of coercive power and military might in the politics of the time. Apart from a centrally hired core, the armies of kings included mercenaries. For instance, many Pala inscriptions from Bengal and Bihar address (among others) military contingents recruited from among the Gaudas, Malavas, Khashas, Kulikas, Hunas, Karnatas, and Latas. Similarly, the *Rajatarangini* mentions that kings of Kashmir recruited mercenaries from other areas. The core and mercenary troops were supplemented, when the need arose, by the military might of allied and subordinate rulers.

In many instances, the expansion of state society involved the displacement or integration of tribal communities. The interactions between tribal and Brahmanical cultures (however, difficult it may be to define both these terms) are reflected indirectly in inscriptions. For instance, the Sanskrit inscriptions of Assam contain a sprinkling of Khasi, Bodo, and other non-Sanskritic words (Lahiri, 1991: 101). In south-east Rajasthan, the expansion of the power of the Guhila dynasty involved the transformation of the Bhils from hunter-gatherers to farmers. The foundation legend of king Guhadatta killing the Bhil chief Mandalika and seizing power suggests a fierce contest between the Guhilas and Bhils (Sinha Kapur, 2002: 38–39). The tribal element surfaces in other ways in Odisha (Upinder Singh, 1994: 287–88). Inscriptions of the imperial Ganga king Anantavarman Chodaganga refer to an ancestor named Kamarnava who defeated Shabaraditya, no doubt a chief of the Shabara tribe. On the other hand, the names of some dynasties, details of their origin myths, and references to their worshipping autochthonous deities such as Stambheshvari suggest that some of these kings were in fact successful tribal chiefs who had enhanced their political power and had also got 'Hinduized'. The importance of the tribal element in the history of Odisha is best reflected in the Jagannatha cult, which clearly had tribal origins.

The *prashasti*s of royal inscriptions reveal prevailing political hierarchies. Inscriptions of subordinate kings frequently refer to their overlord, while those of more powerful rulers sometimes mention their subordinates. Although there are various problems with the feudalism hypothesis as a whole, the term 'feudatory' or 'vassal' can be applied to subordinate rulers who were obliged to offer allegiance and military service to their suzerains. The emergence and development of such chains of command generally had nothing to do with land grants. There are some instances of early medieval kings granting land in return for military service, but this was by no means the general trend.

Claims to political paramountcy were reflected in the use of three titles (these go back to earlier times) that usually occur together in inscriptions—*maharajadhiraja*, *parameshvara*, and *parama-bhattaraka*. Paramount kings were sometimes described as commanding the obeisance of the *samanta*s or of the circle of kings. Titles of subordinate rulers included *maharaja*, *samanta*, *mahasamanta*, *ranaka*, and *mahasamantadhipati*. Such a ruler was often also described as 'one who has obtained the five great sounds' (*samadhigata-pancha-mahashabda*), apparently referring to the privilege of hearing the sound of five musical instruments. Subordinate status was also indicated through the use of the overlord's dynastic era and by the lesser king being described as meditating at the feet of his overlord.

Political ideology is an important part of political history. The royal *prashasti* contains poetic embellishment, conventional rhetoric, and downright flattery. But along with the royal seals and invocations, it allows us to identify certain elements that comprised both the ideals and practice of kingship. The sectarian epithets of kings reflect more than mere religious affiliations or eclecticism, and can be viewed from the perspective of royal policy. The titles and designations in land grant inscriptions suggest the different tiers, ranks, and functionaries in the administrative infrastructure of kingdoms, although it is not always possible to identify their precise meaning. During the early medieval period, the horizontal and vertical linkages of political power are more visible than ever before and the emergent political elites can be connected with alliances with landed groups, some of them created and buttressed by royal grants.

There is also the issue of the political and courtly culture. Daud Ali (2006) has discussed the emergence and efflorescence of courtly culture in Sanskrit texts through an analysis of texts ranging from the 4th to the 12th century, drawing attention to courtly manners, ethics, ideas of love and beauty, situating them within their political and social context. Moving beyond the figure of the king to the royal household and the aristocratic court, he discusses the elaborate and highly formalized protocols of courtly society, including the internal dynamics of sexual love and erotic pleasures in courtly texts. Ali suggests that the activities of the royal harem (*antahpura*) were patterned on the same logic of obligation and favour that governed the relations of the male-oriented assembly hall (*sabha*). The emphasis in political treatises on the cultivation of *vinaya* (self-control, discipline) among kings and other members reflected what was considered an important quality for a successful career in the royal court.

Notwithstanding the patriarchal nature of society, the political history of early medieval India gives several instances of queens succeeding to the throne. Three women rulers—Didda, Yashovati, and Sugandha—are known from Kashmir. Among the Eastern Chalukyas, Vijayamahadevi became ruler after the death of her husband Chandraditya. She is known to have issued a land grant to Brahmanas in the fifth year of her reign. A Kadamba queen named Divabbarasi is known to have ruled till her minor son attained majority. She too made land grants. In Odisha, there are instances of several queens of the Bhauma-Kara dynasty ascending the throne. Prithivimahadevi, also known as Tribhuvanamahadevi, is described as having ascended the throne at the behest of feudatories. Dandimahadevi,

FURTHER DISCUSSION | The image of the ideal king in inscriptions of Odisha

The analysis of kingship in ancient India has traditionally been based on literary sources. However, inscriptions constitute another important source of information on this subject. The *prashastis* of royal inscriptions are especially informative on the ideology of kingship. They offer a good sketch of the image of the ideal king in different times and regions.

The recurrent themes in *prashastis* of kings of early medieval Odisha include their bravery, military exploits, and physical beauty. Comparisons with the heroes of the *Mahabharata*—especially Yudhishthira—are frequent, as are comparisons with legendary kings such as Puru, Dilipa, Nala, Nahusha, Mandhata, Bharata, and Bhagiratha. Kings are also often compared with various deities, sometimes with the very deity whom they worshipped, usually either Shiva or Vishnu. Cultic affiliation is indicated through sectarian epithets such as *parama-maheshvara*, *parama-bhagavata*, and *parama-vaishnava*.

The king is eulogized in some inscriptions as protector of his people, custodian of *dharma*, and maintainer of the order of the *varnas* and *ashramas*. He is frequently eulogized as a remover of the stain of the Kali age. Such references occur in many inscriptions, cutting across sectarian and religious affiliations. They are also present in inscriptions of the Bhauma-Karas, who were Buddhists.

Kingship is associated with the performance of sacrifices in Shailodbhava inscriptions. The *prashasti* of these kings highlights their performance of the *ashvamedha* and *vajapeya* sacrifices, described in some epigraphs as having fallen into abeyance. However, no other dynasty of early medieval Odisha advertised itself in such a manner. This suggests that the performance of Vedic sacrifices was not a significant component in the ideology of kingship in ancient and early medieval Odisha.

Very few *prashastis* eulogize the king as builder of temples, *mathas*, or *viharas*. On the other hand, he is frequently eulogized for his generosity, often being compared with the *kalpa-vriksha* (tree of plenty). Some epigraphs specify the kinds of things he gifted, including land, gold, grain, cows, and elephants. Land grant inscriptions contain a series of benedictory and imprecatory verses eulogizing the gifting of land by kings to Brahmanas. Some describe the king as *parama-brahmanya* (greatly devoted to the Brahmanas). Apart from such references, the sheer evidence of hundreds of records of such grants indicates that *dana* (ritual giving), particularly *bhumi-dana* (the gift of land) to Brahmanas and religious establishments, was considered a pious activity especially appropriate for kings.

Source Upinder Singh, 1994: 114–16

Dharmamahadevi, and Valkulamahadevi were other Bhauma-Kara queens. While these women ascended the throne due to the absence of a male heir, the accession of Prithivimahadevi seems, in addition, to have had something to do with the influence and intervention of her Somavamshi father. Imperial titles were feminized for the Bhauma-Kara queens into *parama-bhattarika*, *maharajadhiraja* (both ending with an elongated 'a') and *parameshvari*. Looking beyond political narrative and normative texts, Tara Sheemar Malhan (2017) has analyzed the stories in the 11th century *Kathasaritsagara* to reconstruct the intersection between political power and society in the early medieval period.

A problem in reconstructing the complex tangle of the political history of early medieval India is that the grandiose claims of political success made by kings of one dynasty may be exaggerated and are, in fact, sometimes contradicted by counter-claims made by rivals. Nevertheless, a basic narrative can be constructed (see Majumdar. [Gen. Ed.], [1955] 1964, [1957] 1966; Majumdar. [Ed.], 1981; Sharma and Shrimali. [Eds.], 1992; Chakrabarti and Lal. [Eds.], 2014, Vol. 5). As it is not possible to give a detailed account, the discussion below gives an outline, focusing on some of the major dynasties that came to the fore during the period *c.* 600–1200. (For a useful compendium of perspectives on the state in different periods of Indian history, including the early medieval, see Kulke and Sahu. [Eds.], 2022.)

The Deccan

The political history of peninsular India during *c.* 600–900 CE was marked by internecine warfare between the Chalukyas of Badami (known as the early Chalukyas), Pallavas of Kanchi, and Pandyas of Madurai. All three rose to power in the 6th century, but in the mid-8th century, the Chalukyas made way for the Rashtrakutas of Manyakheta. Apart

PRIMARY SOURCES | The Aihole inscription of Pulakeshin

The Meguti temple at Aihole (Bagalkot district, Karnataka) stands on top of a hill, commanding a panoramic view of the surrounding countryside, including a large crop of megaliths nearby. Embedded in the eastern wall of this Jaina temple is a 19-line inscription in Sanskrit verse, written in the southern script typical of the 7th century. The inscription is dated in the year 556 (of the Shaka era), i.e., 634–35 CE. The composer, a poet named Ravikirti, was also the one who had the temple built. The inscription is a *prashasti* of the Chalukyas, especially the reigning king Pulakeshin II, who is referred to as Satyashraya (the abode of truth). It contains many details about the history of this dynasty, but its literary merits are also great. These suggest that Ravikirti may not have been making an idle boast when, in verse 37, he describes himself as the equal of Kalidasa and Bharavi. A few translated excerpts from the inscription are given below (pronouns starting with capital letters—He, Him, etc.—refer to Pulakeshin II):

Victorious is the holy Jinendra—he who is exempt from old age, death, and birth—in the sea of whose knowledge the whole world is comprised like an island.

And next, long victorious is the immeasurable, wide ocean of the Chalukya family, which is the birthplace of jewels of men that are ornaments of the diadem of the earth.

And victorious for very long is Satyashraya, who in bestowing gifts and honours on the brave and on the learned, both together on either, observes not the rule of correspondence of number....

An account of the early kings of the Chalukya line follows, upto the reign of Pulakeshin II's uncle Mangalesha.

...Then, on the subversion of that (i.e., Mangalesha's) rule encompassed by the darkness of enemies, the whole world grew light again, invaded as it were by the lustrous rays of His (i.e., Pulakeshin's) irresistible splendour. Or when was it that the sky ceased to be black like a swarm of bees with thundering clouds, in which flashes of lightening were dancing like banners, and the edges of which were crashing in the rushing wind?

When, having found the opportunity, he who was named Appayika, and Govinda approached with their troops of elephants to conquer the country north of the Bhaimarathi, the one in battle through His armies, came to know the taste of fear, while the other at once received the reward of the services rendered by him.

When He was besieging Vanavasi, which for a girdle has the rows of *hamsa* birds that sport on the high waves of the Varada as their play-place, and which by its wealth rivalled the city of the gods, that fortress on land, having the surface of the earth all around covered with the great sea of his army, to the onlooker seemed at once converted into a fortress in the water.

Although in former days they had acquired happiness by renouncing the seven sins, the Ganga and Alupa lords, being subdued by His dignity, were always intoxicated by drinking the nectar of close attendance upon him.

In the Konkanas the impetuous waves of the forces directed by Him speedily swept away the rising wavelets of pools—the Mauryas.

When, radiant like the destroyer of Pura [i.e., Shiva] He besieged Puri, the Fortune of the western sea, with hundreds of

from the Chalukyas of Badami, there were two other branches of the lineage who ruled independently—the Chalukyas of Lata and the Eastern Chalukyas of Vengi. From time to time, the Eastern Gangas of Mysore and the Eastern Chalukyas got embroiled in events by taking sides in the conflicts between the Western Chalukyas, Pallavas, and Pandyas.

The Western Chalukyas claimed Brahmana origin as Haritiputras of the Manavya *gotra*. The king who established the independent power of this dynasty was Pulakeshin I (535–66). He built a strong fortress at Vatapi (Badami) and is described as having performed a number of *shrauta* sacrifices including the *ashvamedha*. The kingdom was further enlarged by Pulakeshin's son Kirtivarman I (566/67–597/98), who fought successful wars against the Kadambas of Banavasi, Mauryas of the Konkan, and Nalas of the Bastar area. He also claimed many other military successes, including against the kings of Vanga, Anga, Kalinga, Magadha, Pandya, and Chola.

The end of Kirtivarman's reign was marked by a war of succession between his brother Mangalesha and nephew Pulakeshin II. Pulakeshin II (610/11–642/43) emerged triumphant and went on to achieve many brilliant military successes, which are described in an inscription at Aihole. These included victories against the Kadambas of Banavasi, Alupas, Gangas of Mysore, and Mauryas of Konkan. He despatched expeditions into Andhra, south Kosala, and Kalinga. One of his most important victories was against Harshavardhana on the banks of the Narmada river. Pulakeshin was involved in a protracted conflict with the Pallava ruler Mahendravarman. Pulakeshin died soon after this event. The conflict

ships in appearance like arrays of rutting elephants, the sky, dark blue as a young lotus and covered with tiers of massive clouds, resembled the sea, and the sea was like the sky.

Subdued by His splendour, the Latas, Malavas, and Gurjaras became as it were teachers of how feudatories, subdued by force, ought to behave.

Harsha, whose lotus feet were arrayed with the rays of jewels of the diadems of hosts of feudatories prosperous with unmeasured might, through Him had his joy [*harsha*] melted away by fear, having become loathsome with his rows of lordly elephants fallen in battle.

While He was ruling the earth with his broad armies, the neighbourhood of the Vindhya, by no means destitute of the lustre of the many sandbanks of the Reva, shone even more brightly by his great personal splendour, having to be avoided by his elephants because, as it seemed, they by their bulk rivalled the mountains.

Almost equal to Indra, He by means of all the three powers, gathered by him according to rule, and by his noble birth and other excellent qualities, acquired the sovereignty over the three Maharashtrakas with their nine and ninety thousand villages.

Through the excellencies of their householders prominent in the pursuit of the three objects of life, and having broken the pride of other rulers of the earth, the Kalingas with the Kosalas by His army were made to evince signs of fear.

Hard pressed [*pishta*] by Him, Pishtapura became a fortress not difficult of access; wonderful (to relate), the ways of the Kali age to Him were quite inaccessible.

Ravaged by Him, the water of Kunala—coloured with the blood of men killed with many weapons, and the land within it overspread with arrays of decorated elephants—was like the cloud-covered sky in which the red evening twilight has risen.

With His six-fold forces, the hereditary troops and the rest, who raised spotless *chauris*, hundreds of flags, umbrellas, and darkness (i.e., dust), and who churned the enemy elated with the sentiments of heroism and energy, He caused the splendour of the lord of the Pallavas, who had opposed the rise of his power, to be obscured by the dust of his army, and to vanish behind the walls of Kanchipura.

When straight away He strove to conquer the Cholas, the Kaveri, who has the darting carps for her tremulous eyes, had her current obstructed by the causeway formed by his elephants whose rutting-juice was dripping down, and avoided the contact with the ocean.

There He caused great prosperity to the Cholas, Keralas, and Pandyas, he being the hot-rayed sun to the hoarfrost—the army of the Pallavas.

While He, Satyashraya, endowed with the powers of energy, mastery, and good counsel—having conquered all the quarters, having dismissed the kings full of honours, having done homage to the gods and Brahmanas, having entered the city of Vatapi—is ruling, like one city, this earth which has the dark-blue waters of the surging sea for its moat....

This stone mansion of Jinendra, a mansion of every kind of greatness, has been caused to be built by the wise Ravikirti, who has obtained the highest favour of that Satyashraya whose rule is bounded by the three oceans.

Source Kielhorn, 1900–01

continued under Mahendravarman's successor Narasimhavarman, who occupied Badami. Pallava control over Badami and the southern areas of the Chalukya empire continued under later rulers, who were involved in conflicts with contemporary powers. In the mid-8th century, the Western Chalukyas were overwhelmed by the Rashtrakutas.

The Chalukyas established themselves in Vengi when Pulakeshin II handed over control of the conquered Andhra territory to his brother Vishnuvardhana I, who established his line known as the Eastern Chalukyas. Vijayaditya II (806–846) was one of the most important rulers of this dynasty. During his reign, initial reverses at the hands of the Rashtrakutas were followed by successful military expeditions against them and the Gangas, and campaigns into Gujarat. Rashtrakuta inscriptions acknowledge the change in the balance of power, when they admit that the glory of their kingdom was 'drowned in the ocean of the Chalukyas'. But the Rashtrakutas soon re-established themselves and the Eastern Chalukyas were forced to acknowledge their paramountcy. A matrimonial alliance was also forged between the two powers.

The power of the Eastern Chalukyas reached its peak under Vijayaditya III (848–891/92), who claimed to have won victories over the Pallavas and Pandyas and to have given shelter to a Chola king. He also claimed to have been victorious over the Gangas, Rashtrakutas, Kalachuris, and a king of south Kosala. Conflict with the Rashtrakutas continued during the reign of the Chalukya king Bhima I (892–922). Bhima was captured by the enemy, but ultimately released. From the reign of Vijayaditya IV, numerous

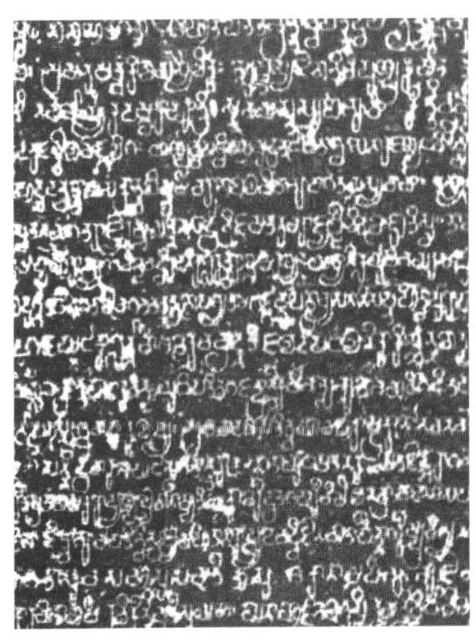

Brahmi script, Aihole inscription

Map 10.1 Major dynasties of peninsular India, *c.* 700–1300

succession disputes erupted and the Rashtrakutas backed contenders in some of these. Some of the rulers of this period had very short reigns—e.g., Vijayaditya IV ruled for six months, Tala for one month, and Vijayaditya V for a mere fortnight. Some amount of political stability was restored during the reigns of Bhima II and Amma II, but the kingdom started crumbling thereafter. In 999 CE, Rajaraja Chola conquered Vengi.

The Rashtrakutas were an important power in the political history of the Deccan between the 8th and 10th centuries. In certain copper plate grants, the Rashtrakutas claim descent from the lineage (*vamsha*) of Yadu. (In the epics, Yadu was the son of Yayati and the brother of Puru and Turvasu; Krishna was supposed to be a descendant of Yadu.) Various inscriptions elaborate on this mythical story of origin, stating that the Rashtrakutas belonged to the Satyaki branch of the Yaduvamsha, mentioning an eponymous ancestor.

'Rashtrakuta' means the chief of a *rashtra* (division or kingdom, depending on the context). The word occurs in inscriptions of several dynasties from about the

NEW DIRECTIONS IN RESEARCH | **Betel-bag bearers in royal courts**

The cultivation and use of betelnut is known from the early centuries CE. The Sanskrit word *tambula* can refer to the betel leaf vine (*Piper betle* L.), as well as to a roll consisting of a leaf of this vine, smeared with slaked lime, enclosing sliced areca nut, and other ingredients. *Tambula* occurs in texts such as the *Kamasutra* and *Brihatsamhita* and appears as a breath freshener, digestive, and something that made the body healthy and attractive. The leaves and flowers of the plant were used for decorating the body. The ritualized use of *tambula* occurs, for instance, in its being offered to the gods as part of *puja*. There are also indications that it had an importance in courtly manners and ritual. Sanskrit terms for the betel-bag bearer include *tambuladayaka*, *tambulavahin*, *tambulika*, and *tambulakarankavahin*. He was a high-ranking functionary who carried a pouch with the ingredients for making the betel rolls.

Betel leaves seem to have been part of the lives of aristocrats and affluent people at least from the Gupta period onwards. During the 9th/10th centuries, the gift and exchange of betel increased in many roles, including rituals of welcome and social and political alliances. The royal betel-bag bearer played a significant role in these rituals. He was responsible for preparing and gifting the rolls to those involved in the rituals.

The 12th century text, *Manasollasa*, mentions the importance of the betel-bag bearer. This is also underscored in inscriptions from the 9th to 16th centuries in the Deccan. In court ritual, being offered betel could be an expression of courtesy and favour. It could also symbolize the acceptance of a position of subordination and loyalty by the recipient. In inscriptions of the Deccan, the betel-bag bearer is referred to by variants of the Kannada word *hadapa* or *adapa*, which refers to the bag in which the ingredients and instruments to make the betel roll were kept. Being made a *hadapa* was considered an honour that was enjoyed by high-ranking elite men.

The court of the Chalukyas of Kalyan (*c*. 970–1200 CE) seems to be the centre from which the political use of betelnut travelled to other courts. The title of *hadapa* was bestowed by the Chalukyas on their military retainers, subordinates, and feudatories. The title appears in the courts of the subordinates of the Chalukyas as well, who sought to imitate the courtly practices of their overlords. The betel-bag bearer became a familiar and important person in the political circle of later dynasties such as the Yadavas, Kakatiyas, and Hoysalas. By the time the Vijayanagara empire emerged in the 14th century, the betel-bag bearer had become an established figure in royal courts of the Deccan and continued as such during the reigns of the Vijayanagara kings.

Source Daud Ali, 2018

4th century, in the sense of a class of provincial officials. It is possible that the Rashtrakutas originally belonged to a group of such officials. The origins of the dynasty can be traced to the Kannada-speaking area. One of the titles used by kings of the main and subordinate lines was *Lattalura-puraveshvara* (lord of the great city of Lattalura); Lattalura has been identified with Latur on the Maharashtra–Karnataka border. The Rashtrakutas achieved spectacular military successes in the north and south. At some point or other, they defeated the great powers of the time such as the Pratiharas, Palas, Eastern Chalukyas, and Cholas. However, they did not manage to hold on to their northern conquests for long.

The Rashtrakutas appear to have migrated from the Latur area to the western part of Amaravati district in *c*. 625 CE. Here, they carved out a principality and ruled for several generations as feudatories of the Chalukyas. They assumed an independent status under Dantidurga ('He whose elephant is his fortress'), who ascended the throne in 733 CE. Dantidurga won many military victories and assumed imperial titles.

The Rashtrakuta empire expanded during the reigns of Dantidurga's successors, especially under Krishna I, Govind III, Dhruva, and Amoghavarsha. There were incursions into the north as well as against rulers of peninsular India. The magnificent Kailasanatha temple at Ellora was built during the reign of the Rashtrakuta king Krishna I. Amoghavarsha (814–878) came to throne as a young boy and enjoyed a long reign. He built a new capital city of Manyakheta (identified with modern Malkhed). He was a patron of literature and a scholar himself. He is supposed to have contributed to the composition of the *Kavirajamarga*, the earliest Kannada work on poetics. Amoghavarsha was involved in conflicts with Vengi, the Gangas, and Palas. He faced many serious rebellions during his reign. Later Rashtrakuta kings achieved some military successes—for instance, Kanauj was captured during the time of Indra III, and there were victories against the Cholas during the time of Krishna III—but there were several reverses as well. Towards

Hero stone, Karnataka

the end of the 10th century, the Paramara ruler, Harsha Siyaka, sacked Manyakheta and this event signalled the decline of the Rashtrakuta dynasty.

The connections between the early Kadambas (4th to 6th century) and later Kadambas (10th to 14th century) are unclear. The two major lines of the latter were the Kadambas of Goa and Hanagal, who were forced to accept the position of subordinates of the Chalukyas and Yadavas. The later Kadambas issued bilingual inscriptions in Sanskrit and Kannada. Prachi Sharma's (2021) study of the Kadamba *prashastis* reveal a strong impact of imagery from the *Ramayana* and *Mahabharata* traditions.

Hundreds of inscribed and uninscribed memorial stones found in various parts of peninsular India (Settar, n.d.) reflect different kinds of violence and conflict in the society of their time. They also represent a widespread and long-standing tradition of memorializing the dead in stone. The large numbers of memorial stones found in Karnataka differ widely in form, style, and content. Chronologically, they range from the 5th to 19th centuries, with a peak during the 10th–13th centuries. A majority of them are *viragals* (memorials for heroes), mostly honouring men who died in the course of cattle raids, either as defenders or attackers. However, an interesting memorial stone found at Kembalu records the death of a queen who led her men in such a raid. There are memorials to those who died while protecting their womenfolk from enemies, those who perished while helping or rescuing friends and relatives, and those who gave their lives defending their lord or their land. Some memorial stones record the bravery of people who died defending their town or village from kings, princes, robbers, and oppressive officers. There are also memorials in memory of those who died while fighting wild animals such as elephants, cows, boars, tigers, and even horses. Sometimes, only the name of the hero is inscribed, with no mention of the circumstances of his/her death.

The far south

In Tamil Nadu, the *viragals* are concentrated in the area adjacent to the southern border of Karnataka and mostly belong to between the 5th/6th and 12th centuries CE, after which they decline in number. Initially, memorial stone inscriptions in this area are in the Tamil language and Vatteluttu script, while the later ones are in the Tamil language and Tamil script. Like those of Karnataka, most of the Tamil Nadu *viragals* record the death of men in cattle raids. Some mention other kinds of violent incidents such as battles, robbers' raids, and attacks by wild animals. The hero stones of this region are simple compared to those of other areas. They generally consist of a single relief panel depicting the hero standing with weapons in his hands. He often holds a sword in his right hand, a bow, arrow, or shield in his left, and a quiver filled with arrows on his shoulder. His face is in profile, but his torso faces the front; his left leg is usually lifted to give the impression of movement and action. A pedestal or memorial shrine is also often shown next to him.

The political history of the far south during this period was dominated by the Pallavas, Pandyas, Cheras, and Cholas (Sastri, [1955] 1975: 146–215; Karashima, [Ed.], 2014). The Pallavas were associated with Tondaimandalam, the land between the north Pennar and north Vellar rivers. Inscriptions refer to early kings of this line such as Shivaskandavarman, who ruled in the early 4th century CE. However, the ruler who played a crucial rule in the Pallavas' rise to power in the last quarter of the 6th century was Simhavishnu. Putting an end to the political disturbances caused by the Kalabhras, he conquered the land upto the Kaveri, coming into conflict with the Pandyas and the ruler of Sri Lanka.

Simhvishnu's successor was Mahendravarman I (590–630), renowned as a great patron of the arts, and apparently a poet and musician in his own right. His reign saw the beginning of a conflict between the Pallavas and Western Chalukyas. The army of Pulakeshin II reached perilously close to the Pallava capital Kanchipuram and annexed the northern part of that kingdom. Subsequently, during the reign of Narasimhavarman I Mahamalla (630–68), the Pallavas managed to settle scores by winning several victories over the Chalukyas with the aid of their ally Manavarman, a Sri Lankan prince, who later became ruler of the island kingdom. The climax of these victories was Narasimhavarman's invasion of the Chalukya kingdom and his capturing Badami. This Pallava king claims to have defeated the Cholas, Cheras, and Kalabhras. Two naval expeditions despatched to help Manavarman were successful, but this Sri Lankan ruler subsequently lost his kingdom and arrived in the Pallava court as a political refugee. Narasimhavarman was an enthusiastic patron of architecture. The port of Mamallapuram, along with its five temples known as the *rathas*, was built during his reign.

The Pallava–Chalukya conflict continued during the subsequent decades, interspersed with some peaceful interludes. The Pallavas also came into conflict with the Pandyas to the south and the Rashtrakutas to the north. In the early 9th century, the Rashtrakuta Govinda III invaded Kanchi during the reign of the Pallava Dantivarman. Dantivarman's son Nandivarman III managed to defeat the Pandyas. The last known imperial Pallava king was Aparajita. Aided by Western Ganga and Chola allies, he defeated the Pandyas at a battle at Shripurambiyam. The Pallavas were ultimately overthrown in *c.* 893 by the Chola king Aditya I, and thereafter, control over Tondaimandalam passed into the hands of the Cholas.

Kings of the Pandya dynasty are known in the early historical period, but their connection, if any, with the Pandyas of early medieval times, is unclear. The first two rulers of the early medieval line were Kadungon (560–90) and his son Maravarman Avanishulamani (590–620). The latter is credited with ending Kalabhra rule in the area and reviving Pandya power. The Pandyas were involved in internecine wars with the Pallavas and other contemporary powers. King Rajasimha I (735–65) had the epithet *Pallava-bhanjana* (breaker of the Pallavas). The empire expanded during his reign and during that of his successors Jatila Parantaka Nedunjadaiyan (756–815) and Shrimara Shrivallabha (815–862). The Pandyas were completely overpowered by the Cholas in the 10th century. Pandya copper plate grants are bilingual, using Tamil and Sanskrit. The Tamil portion also includes a eulogy of the donor.

On the Kerala coast, the Chera Perumals continued to hold sway, in spite of the fact that several Pallava, Pandya, Chalukya, and Rashtrakuta rulers claimed military successes in the area. Few details of Chera history are available (for details, see Narayanan, [1996] 2013). One of the last kings of the line was Cheraman Perumal, regarding whom there are many legends. Different sources describe him variously as a Jaina, Christian, Shaiva, or Muslim, and it is possible that he renounced the world, dividing his kingdom among his kinsmen or vassals. His reign ended in the early 9th century.

Chola kings are known in early historical South India, but their post-Sangam history is unclear, as is their connection with the Cholas of early medieval times. The founder of the early medieval Chola dynasty of Tanjore was Vijayalaya. He established his power in the area around Uraiyur, captured Tanjore from the Muttaraiyar chieftains, and extended his kingdom along the lower Kaveri. Vijayalaya accepted the overlordship of the Pallavas.

Aditya I (871–907), the successor of Vijayalaya, achieved significant military successes and expanded the Chola kingdom. He confederated with the Pallavas to defeat the Pandyas in the battle at Shripurambiyam and obtained some territories in the Tanjore area as recompense. He then went on to defeat and kill his Pallava overlord Aparajita in 893. This victory gave him control over Tondaimandalam. Thereafter, he went on to conquer Kongudesha (corresponding roughly to Coimbatore and Salem districts) from the Pandyas, perhaps with the help of the Cheras. He also claims to have captured Talakad, capital of the Western Gangas. Aditya I entered into a matrimonial alliance with the Pallavas by marrying a Pallava princess.

Copper Pallava coin (obverse and reverse); gold coin of Chola king Kulottunga I (obverse and reverse)

Parantaka I (907–953), who succeeded Aditya I, won several victories with the help of his allies such as the Western Gangas, the Kodumbalur chiefs, and the ruler of Kerala. He succeeded in conquering Madurai, after which he took the title of *Madurantaka* (destroyer of Madura) and *Maduraikonda* (capturer of Madurai). He defeated the combined armies of the Pandyas and the king of Sri Lanka at the battle of Vellur,

and the Pandya territories fell into Chola hands. These victories were, however, followed by a resounding defeat at the hands of the Rashtrakutas in 949. The army of Krishna III defeated the Chola army at the battle of Takkolam. The Rashtrakutas over-ran Tondaimandalam and Krishna III assumed the title of 'Conqueror of Kachchi (Kanchi) and Tanjai (Tanjore)'. The Cholas gradually recovered their power during the reigns of kings such as Sundara Chola Parantaka II (957–73), who defeated a combined Pandya–Sri Lankan army and also launched an invasion of the island kingdom. By the time Uttama Chola came to the throne (973), most of Tondaimandalam had been retrieved from the Rashtrakutas.

The peak of Chola power was reached during the reign of Arumolivarman, who assumed the title of Rajaraja on his accession. From Rajaraja's reign (985–1014) right up to the 13th century, the Cholas remained the major political power in South India. Through a series of successful military campaigns, Rajaraja broke the confederation between the Pandyas and the rulers of Kerala and Sri Lanka. A successful naval expedition to Sri Lanka led to the destruction of Anuradhapura, and a Chola province was established in the northern part of the island. Rajaraja also achieved victories against the Western Chalukyas and Rashtrakutas. The Maldives were captured towards the end of his reign. Rajaraja sent an embassy to the Song court. After a few months' stopover in Srivijaya, it reached its destination in 1015, after Rajaraja's death. Chinese sources describe it as a large embassy consisting of 52 men, bearing gifts including a robe and cap decorated with pearls of different sizes, ivory, and incence.

The process of Chola territorial expansion continued and reached its peak under Rajaraja's son and successor Rajendra I (1012–44). His reign was marked by military victories against the Pandyas, the ruler of Kerala, and the Western Chalukyas. The Chola army established control over Vengi and after defeating the Eastern Gangas, reached the Ganga. In order to commemorate this important achievement, Rajendra assumed the epithet Gangaikondachola ('The Chola king who took the Ganga'). His new capital was given the name Gangaikondacholapuram. The northern part of Sri Lanka was occupied. A successful naval expedition was despatched in 1025 CE to the kingdom of Srivijaya, which had great strategic importance in Indian Ocean trade. Unfortunately, Chola inscriptions give few details about the organization of the army or navy (Subbarayalu, 2009a).

While the Chola interface with Srivijaya was episodic, the relationship between South Indian kingdoms with Sri Lanka was long and complex (see Spencer, 1976; de Silva, 1981: 24–26). South Indian and Sri Lankan kings interfered in each other's succession disputes. Sri Lanka became a refuge for defeated enemies and also a base of attack. Lankan kings relied heavily on Indian mercenaries. In the late 7th century, Manavarman come to power with the assistance of the Pallavas, but once he became king, he tried to curb the power of the Tamil military commanders and courtiers. His successors were less successful in doing so. The Pandyas invaded the island during the reign of Sena I (833–53) and sacked Anuradhapura. Subsequently, Sena II invaded Pandya country with Pallava support, ostensibly in support of a rebel prince, and sacked Madurai. After the rise of the Cholas, Sri Lankan rulers sought to ally themselves with the Pandyas, sending an army to support the Pandya ruler Rajasimha II against the Chola king Parantaka I. Parantaka was victorious, and the Pandya king fled to Sri Lanka.

The initial Chola incursions into Sri Lanka were brief and aimed mainly at plunder. During the time of Rajaraja, they began to aim at territorial conquest. The Cholas established their rule over the northern part of the island known as Rajarata. Mihindu V, who ascended the throne in 982, became the last Sinhala king to rule at Anuradhapura. He was defeated by a Chola army and was taken to the mainland as a prisoner of war. The Chola conquest is described in the *Mahavamsa* as a violent event that involved the destruction of the *viharas* and relic *stupas* of Anuradhapura. Rajendra I launched military expeditions in the south and claimed to have completed the conquest of Sri Lanka. The Cholas moved the capital from Anuradhapura to Polonnaruwa, close to the Mahavali river. While their control over the southern part of the island remained tenuous, Rajarata

Gold coins (obverse and reverse); of Rajaraja Chola and Rajendra Chola (from top)

FURTHER DISCUSSION | The Chola expedition against Srivijaya

Rajendra Chola is credited with having sent several expeditions across the Indian Ocean, to Sri Lanka, the Maldives, and the Andamans. The most adventurous one was against the thalassocracy (ocean state) of Srivijaya, mentioned in the beginning of this chapter. This kingdom was initially based in South-east Sumatra but succeeded in establishing its control over the Malay peninsula and the Straits of Malacca. While the importance of Indian Ocean trade is recognized as the important context for Rajendra Chola's military campaign, many aspects of the expedition remain debated. How many expeditions were there? Was it a raid or a conquest? Was it motivated by Rajendra's desire for glory or was it his way of trying to outshine his father Rajaraja? Did the trade guilds have a direct or indirect role to play in the episode? What was the precise sequence of events that led up to it and what were its consequences?

According to Tansen Sen, there were three Chola attacks against Srivijaya ports—a smaller scale one in 1017, a larger one in 1025 (both during the time of Rajendra), and a third one in the 1070s (during the reign of Kulottunga). The reason for the attacks seems to be that the Srivijayans were interfering in the direct trade between South India and Song China. This argument has been made by other scholars, but Sen uses Chinese sources to identify some specific instances of the Srivijayan interference.

In the 11th century, Chinese markets and ports were important centres of international trade. Earlier dynasties such as the Han and Tang had taken measures to restructure Chinese fiscal, market, and credit structures and promoted the growth and diversification of private trade. A Bureau of Maritime Commerce (Shibos) was established in Guangzhou in 714 and maritime trade was brought under government control. Urban and demographic growth led to an increasing demand for foreign goods in Chinese markets. The Song dynasty continued the policy of actively promoting maritime trade. The traditional tribute system was revamped and turned into a major source of income for the court, which benefitted from taxes and tribute. China was an important part of the increasingly integrated Indian Ocean trade networks in which traders from the Chola, Srivijaya, and Arab kingdoms were key participants.

Srivijaya emerged in the last quarter of the 7th century as an important transit point for ships moving between India and China. Srivijayan embassies to the Song court became very frequent between 960 and 1017 (there were about 16 missions). Chinese sources inform us about the lavish gifts they bore, including frankincense, black pepper, rosewater, aromatics, and medicines.

In the early 11th century, the trade triangle between China, Srivijaya, and the Chola domain became increasingly complex and fraught with potential for conflict, due to the Song dynasty's revamping of the tribute system, the Srivijayans' attempts to dominate trade passing through the Straits of Malacca, and the Chola interests in expanding their commercial and political presence in the Indian Ocean. The Srivijayans saw the Chola measures as a threat to their position. Chinese sources indicate that the Srivijayans were passing on inaccurate information about the Cholas to the Song court, and even convinced the court that the Cholas were Srivijayan vassals. Trade and diplomacy were intimately connected. It was trade competition that led to the Chola attacks on Srivijaya.

The impact of the 1025 Chola attack on Srivijaya was initial shock and disruption—no Srivijayan embassy went to China for three years. But Srivijaya soon regained its position in the Straits of Malacca. Its missions to China resumed in 1028 and the Cholas sent a diplomatic mission to China in 1033.

Religious and cultural exchanges between India, China, and South-east Asia had been ongoing for many centuries. In the 11th century, on certain occasions, trade rivalry led to conflict and war.

Source Tansen Sen, 2009

was a province of the Chola empire for a long time. In the middle of the 11th century, a Sinhala prince named Kitti, who later took the name Vijayabahu I, established his base in Rohana and launched numerous attacks on the north, finally expelling the Cholas from the island in 1070.

Military conflicts marked the reigns of kings after Rajendra I, but the Cholas held their own till the time of Kulottunga I (1070–1120). His reign saw the despatch of an embassy of merchants to China and flourishing trade with the kingdom of Srivijaya. Kulottunga has the title *Shungam-tavirtta* (abolisher of tolls) in inscriptions. Although his long reign was comparatively peaceful, during the second half, the kingdom faced hostility from the Chalukyas and Hoysalas, and its power seems to have diminished. There was some recovery during the rule of Vikrama Chola, who succeeded in re-establishing Chola control over Vengi. Later rulers included Kullotunga II, Rajaraja II, and Kullotunga III. The power of the imperial Cholas declined thereafter, and the dynasty came to an end in the 13th century.

Chola inscriptions generally refer to the king as *ko* (king), *perumal*, or *peruman adigal* (the great one). He was also given more grandiose titles signalling paramountcy

FURTHER DISCUSSION | **Religious and political symbolism in the Thanjavur temple**

Shiva as Tripurantaka

Thanjavur or Tanjai was the political and ceremonial centre of the imperial Cholas. The city was located at the south-western tip of the fertile Kaveri delta, which formed a rich agrarian resource base for the dynasty. The physical and symbolic centre of Thanjavur was the magnificent Brihadishvara temple dedicated to Shiva, built during the reign of Rajaraja. That this was an imperial temple, closely connected with the ruling dynasty, was evident in many ways, for instance in the fact that it was also known as the Rajarajeshvara temple after the king. It was also reflected in some of the sculptures and paintings that adorned the shrine.

The walls of the Brihadishvara temple have representations of Shiva in many forms, including Nataraja, Harihara, Lingodbhava, Ardhanarishvara, and Bhairava. They also depict other deities such as Gaja-Lakshmi, Sarasvati, Durga, Vishnu, and Ganesha. However, one representation—the Tripurantaka form of Shiva—stands out. This form alludes to the Puranic story in which the god destroys the three cities or fortresses of the demons with one arrow.

Shiva Tripurantaka is not prominent in temple sculpture before the Chola period. In the Brihadishvara temple, we see him in all the niches of the upper part of the wall of the *vimana*. He also appears in two sculpted panels and one imposing fresco painting in the inner ambulatory of the temple. A four-armed bronze image which originally belonged to the temple also seems to depict Shiva in this form—the god stands in an archer's pose, although the bow and arrow are not shown.

R. Champakalakshmi points out that the prominence of the Tripurantaka form of Shiva in the Thanjavur temple has to be understood as a part of the temple's larger iconographic programme. Since the temple was a symbol of Rajaraja's power, the Tripurantaka form must have had a special political significance as well. Its association with the theme of victory over evil demons may have had a special appeal for a king who projected himself as a great conqueror.

But there are other angles as well. The Tripurantaka story is one of the most important episodes in the Shaiva *bhakti* work called the *Tevaram*. It is also notable that in this episode, Brahma is described as Shiva's charioteer and Agni as his arrow. The Vedas are described as becoming the wheels of his chariot and the Mandara mountain his bow. Vishnu took the form of Mayamoha and tried to delude the demons who, however, remained steadfast in their devotion to Shiva. After destroying their three cities, Shiva took on two of them as his doorkeepers and the third as his drummer. Like many other Puranic stories, there is a sub-text which, in this case, emphasizes the subordination of other gods to Shiva. The Tripurantaka form of Shiva may therefore, have tied in well with Rajaraja's attempt to raise the Shaiva cult to a position of pre-eminence in his kingdom.

We can also note a mural in the south wall of chamber 5 which seems to represent Rajaraja Chola himself as a prime devotee of Shiva as Dakshinamurti, a form in which the god preaches the highest knowledge to various sages.

Source Champakalakshmi, 1996: 424–41

e.g., *raja-rajadhiraja* and *ko-konmai-kondan*, both of which mean king of kings. Inscriptions portray the ruling king as endowed with an attractive physical appearance, a great warrior and conqueror, a protector of *varnashrama dharma*, a destroyer of the evils of the Kali age, a generous giver of gifts (especially to Brahmanas), and a great patron of the arts. Kings were often compared with the gods, sometimes directly, at other times through the use of double entendre. For example, Rajaraja is referred to as *Ulakalanda Perumal*, (the great one who measured the earth). This could apply to the king, who is known to have ordered a great land survey for revenue purposes. It could equally apply to the god Vishnu who is supposed to have encompassed the universe with his three strides.

The dynasties of early medieval South India, even those that may have been connected in some way with their namesakes of the early historical period, crafted new origin myths for themelves (Veluthat, 1993: 30–50). These were rooted in the epic–Puranic traditions of the Suryavamsha (solar lineage) and Chandravamsha (lunar lineage) The origin myths sometimes combined a Brahmana and Kshatriya ancestry (this is known as a *brahma-kshatra* ancestry), with an emphasis on the latter. Claims to Kshatriya status were reflected in epithets, e.g., Rajaraja's title of *Kshatriya-shikhamani* (crest jewel of the Kshatriyas). Many kings had names ending in 'varman', the name suffix that texts such as the *Manu Smriti* associated with Kshatriyas. The Pandyas linked themselves to the lunar dynasty and the Cholas to the solar dynasty. The Pallavas claimed to be Brahmanas of the Bharadvaja *gotra*, and traced their line back to the god Brahma, going on to list Angiras, Brihaspati, Shamyu, Bharadvaja, Drona, Ashvatthama, and the eponymous Pallava.

Prashasti and genealogy are absent in Chera inscriptions. It has been suggested that this may have been because the Cheras followed a matrilineal system of succession, but this is not entirely convincing. Later textual tradition emphasized the importance of Brahmanas and temples in their accounts of the dynasty's origins. For instance, the *Periyapuranam* mentions king Cheraman Perumal sitting in a temple, and then being brought to the city and crowned king. The 16th century *Keralolpatti* states that the king was invited to accept kingship by representatives of the Brahmanas.

While northern Brahmanical elements seem to have become pan-Indian in early medieval royal inscriptions, the inscriptions of the Pandyas appealed to Tamil traditions as well. For instance, kings of this dynasty claim to have had their twin fish emblem carved on the peak of the Himalayas or Mount Meru. They also claim to have been anointed and taught Tamil by the sage Agastya, and as having built the great city of Madurai and establishing the Sangam there. Another interesting element concerns language. In the copper plate grants of the Pandyas, the Sanskrit *prashasti* portion is followed by the Tamil portion, which includes royal eulogy as well as details of the grant. In Pallava and Chola inscriptions, the royal *prashasti* is usually in Sanskrit and the rest is in Tamil. A difference is that in the Chola period, the Tamil portion of bilingual inscriptions includes verses eulogizing the king known as *meykkirtti* (for an overview of South Indian royal epigraphic practice, see Francis, 2021).

Apart from connecting themselves with the epic–Puranic tradition, South Indian kings also legitimized their power through the performance of sacrifices such as the *ashvamedha* and *rajasuya*. The inscriptions also mention rituals such as the *hiranyagarbha* and *tulapurusha*. The gifting of land to Brahmanas and making gifts of various kinds to temples were other important activities linked to the legitimation of royal power.

The circuit of power in the Chera, Pallava, and Chola kingdoms included several local chieftains. (Such chiefs do not seem to have been particularly important in the Pandya kingdom, where the only ones mentioned are the Ays.) One view is that these chieftains were governors appointed by kings to rule over divisions of their kingdom. However, they actually seem to have been subordinates or feudatories, similar to (and in some cases perhaps descendants of) chieftains who are known from the early historical period. The chiefs provided military back-up when required. It is also likely that they paid tribute to their overlord and attended his court. They were connected to the kings and to each other through matrimonial alliances.

In the Chola kingdom, the Cholas exercised direct control over Cholamandalam, which corresponded roughly to modern Thanjavur and parts of Tiruchirappalli districts. Outside this core area, chiefs such as the Paluvettaraiyar, Vel of Kodumbalur, Miladu, Banas, and Gangas held sway. There is an inverse correlation between the power of kings and the inscriptional references to chieftains. In the early 11th century, at the midpoint of Rajaraja Chola's reign, an increase in centralization led to a corresponding decline in inscriptional references to chiefs. In the late 11th century, especially after the reign of Kulottunga I, there was a rise in the number of such references, indicating an increase in their power as the Chola monarchy declined.

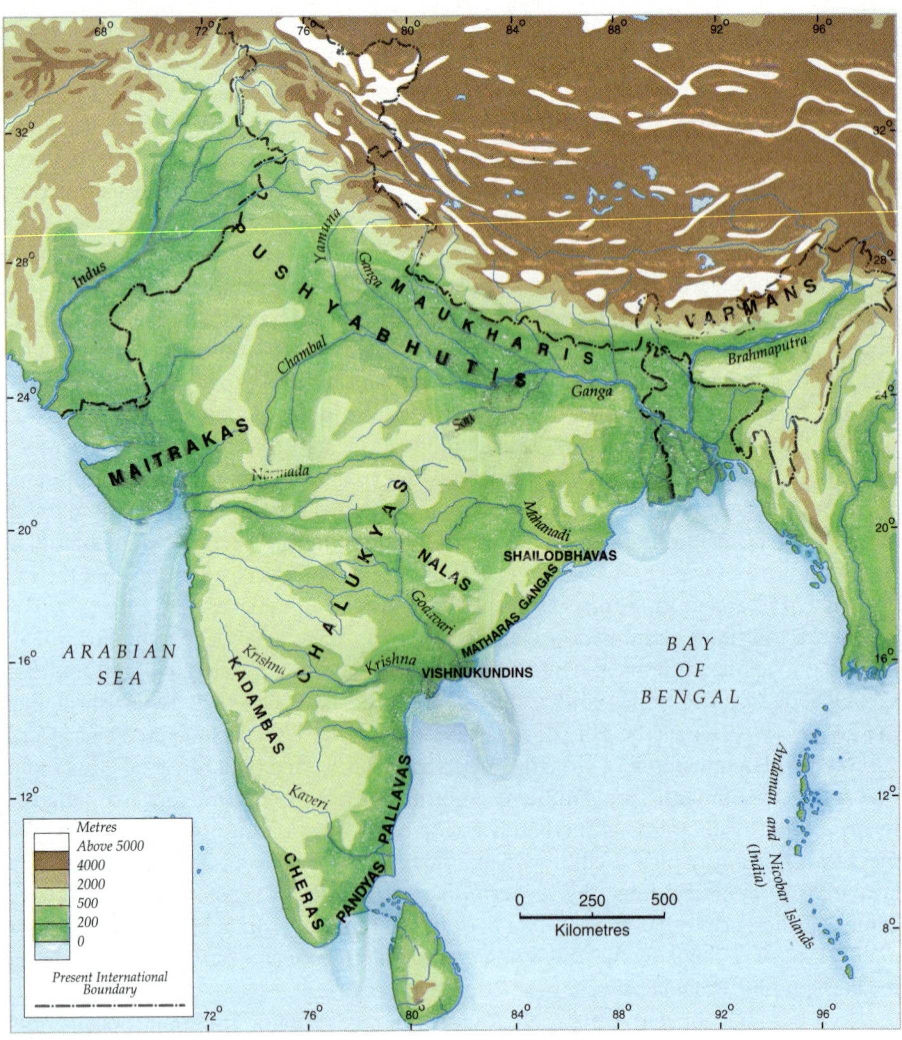

Map 10.2 Some dynasties of India, c. 550–700 CE

North India: the Pushyabhutis, Harshvardhana

Two major sources of information regarding the Pushyabhuti dynasty are the *Harshacharita*, a prose biography written by Banabhatta, court poet of king Harshavardhana, and the account of the Chinese pilgrim Xuanzang. The Pushyabhutis initially had their base in the area around Sthanishvara (modern Thanesar in Ambala district, Punjab). Little is known about the first three kings of the dynasty. The fourth king of the line was Prabhakaravardhana, described in the *Harshacharita* as a great general with many military victories to his credit. With the marriage of princess Rajyashri to the Maukhari ruler Grahavarman, an important marriage alliance was forged between the Pushyabhutis and the Maukharis of Kanyakubja (Kannauj), who were their neighbours to the east.

The dramatic events that subsequently overtook the Pushyabhutis are narrated by Banabhatta. Prabhakaravardhana died and was succeeded by his son Rajyavardhana in *c.* 605 CE. Close on the heels of this event, Grahavarman was killed by the king of Malava, and Rajyashri was imprisoned. Leaving the reigns of governance in the hands of his younger brother Harshavardhana, Rajyavardhana marched towards Kanyakubja, defeating the Malava army along the way. His next encounter was with the army of Shashanka, ruler of Gauda (in Bengal). According to the story given in the *Harshacharita*, Rajyavardhana was killed by Shashanka through a stratagem. Harshavardhana became king. One of his first actions was to rush towards Kanyakubja and rescue his sister, who was on the verge of committing *sati*. Kannauj subsequently passed into the hands of the Pushyabhutis. At some point, Harsha moved his capital from Thaneswar to Kannauj.

Map 10.3 Xuanzang's route (after Sen, 2006)

The reign of Harshavardhana, also known as Harsha, was marked by a number of military engagements. He defeated Shashanka but the latter seems to have soon recovered his lost territories. Harsha is said to have impressed his might on the rulers of Sindh, Valabhi, and Kashmir. According to the Aihole inscription, he received a crushing defeat at the hands of Pulakeshin II. There are differences of opinion on when the battle took place and whether Harsha was defeated or forced to retreat. There are different assessments of the extent of Harsha's empire. In terms of modern landmarks, Harsha inherited a kingdom that extended over Haryana and parts of southern Punjab and eastern Rajasthan. The addition of the Maukhari kingdom brought in Uttar Pradesh and parts of Bihar. His rule also seems to have extended into Odisha. Beyond the areas under his direct control, the rulers of Kamarupa, Kashmir, Valabhi, and Malava may have owed him allegiance. Some of the subordinate rulers, who had titles such as *raja*, *samanta*, and *mahasamanta*, used the Harsha era of 606 CE (the year of accession of this king) in their inscriptions. Embassies were exchanged with China during Harshavardhana's reign; three embassies were sent by each side.

Xuanzang gives a vivid description of the beauty, grandeur, and prosperity of Kannauj, the capital of Harsha's empire. Regarding the king, he tells us that he divided the day into three parts—attending to administrative duties during one, and devoting himself to religious works during the other two. He mentions Harsha making frequent tours of inspection around his kingdom. Periodic assemblies, attended by subordinate kings, reinforced the political hierarchy. Harsha is known to have made religious land grants, and Xuanzang suggests that ministers and officials may also have been paid through such grants.

FURTHER DISCUSSION | **The life and travels of Xuanzang**

Xuanzang was the youngest of the four sons of Hui, a man who had refused high office to devote himself to scholarly pursuits. When he was under 12 years old, he was taken to a Buddhist monastery by one of his brothers, and soon became a probationer. It was a time of political turmoil and of distress caused by famine and urban unrest. Xuanzang travelled around from one monastery to another and was eventually ordained as a monk at Jingtu monastery in Luoyang. After spending a few more years travelling and studying in China, Xuanzang decided to visit India. He left Xian (Chang'an) in 627 CE, and eventually, spent many years travelling around the subcontinent, returning to China in 645 CE. When he returned home, he wrote an account of his travels titled Da-Tang xiyu ji (Si-yu-ki) (The Records of the Western Regions Visited During the Great Tang Dynasty). The audience he had in mind was the Tang emperor and Chinese monks. He wrote:

> Though the Buddha was born in the West, his Dharma has spread to the East. In the course of translation, mistakes may have crept into the texts, and idioms may have been misapplied. When words are wrong, the meaning is lost, and when a phrase is mistaken, the doctrine becomes distorted.

Xuanzang collected hundreds of manuscripts, some of which were unfortunately swept away and lost in the flood waters of the Indus on his homeward journey. He brought back 657 Buddhist texts from India. Xuanzang became part of a massive translation project in China, centred in Xian, patronized by the Tang emperor. He also tried to foster diplomatic exchanges between India and China by lobbying with his patrons, the Tang rulers Taizong and Gaozong. Xuanzang was a keen observer of politics. This may have been in part due to his family background. Some of his ancestors had not only distinguished themselves through their scholarship but had also occupied high posts in administration.

But there are places in the *Da-Tang xiyu ji* where Xuanzang idealizes the Indian situation. For instance, in one place, he states that in India, people who violated filial piety either had their nose and ears or hands and feet cut off, or that they suffered exile or banishment. This sort of observation seems to have been due to his desire to emphasize the virtue of filial piety which was cherished by the Chinese. According to D. Devahuti, Xuanzang was not as biased an observer as he is sometimes held to be. He sometimes praised non-Buddhist kings, and sometimes found fault with Buddhist ones. Devahuti also observes that Xuanzang wrote the account of his Indian travels after arriving home in China, far from the court of Harsha, with little practical inducement for indulging in flattery.

Xuanzang's work is a unique source for the study of cross-cultural perspectives. Apart from the account of the doctrines and practices of Buddhist monks, *stupas*, monasteries, and pilgrimage sites, it offers many other details about 7th century India. These include descriptions of its landscape, climate, produce, cities, the caste system, and various customs of the people. Xuanzang describes Kannauj and king Harsha, whom he presents as a virtuous and brave ruler, favourably inclined towards Buddhism. He describes his audience with this king, which led to the establishment of diplomatic relations between Kannauj and the Tang court. Even after his return to China, Xuanzang continued to play an important role in promoting both religious and diplomatic exchanges between China and India.

There is, however, a need to problematize the accounts of Faxian and Xuanzang instead of reading them as a series of factual statements (sometimes erroneous) about India in the 5th and 7th centuries respectively. Instead of trying to pluck out 'facts' from them, these works have to be understood as part of the genre of Buddhist monk-pilgrim records, with attention to their perspective, purpose, and audience. For instance, Max Deeg points out that Xuanzang did not visit all the places he describes in his book and in some instances, relied on hearsay or on earlier accounts. This is the case, for instance, in his description of Sri Lanka. Deeg suggests that Xuanzang never visited Mathura but based his account on Faxian's description of the 'Middle Country' (Madhyadesha). Further, Xuanzang's account of his conversation with king Shiladitya (Harsha) cannot be treated as a factual description—the Chinese monk wove into his account fulsome praise of the Tang emperor and presented Harsha as a model Buddhist king. Both these features were for the benefit of the Tang emperor.

Source Devahuti, (1970) 1983; Tansen Sen, 2006; Deeg, 2007

Modern Xuanzang statue, Xian

We do not have much detail regarding Harsha's administration, but there seems broad continuity in administrative units and official designations from the Gupta period. The kingdom was divided into *bhuktis*, which were in turn divided into *vishayas*. The Banskhera and Madhuban inscriptions mention various high-level officials associated with the making of the grant. The inscriptions refer to the king's camp of victory containing boats, elephants, and horses. Bana mentions forest guards known as *vanapalas*. There is mention of an official called the *sarva-palli-pati* (chief of all the villages). Xuanzang states that people were taxed lightly and that the king took one-sixth of the farmer's produce as his grain share. Inscriptions mention dues such as *bhaga, bhoga, kara,* and *hiranya*—terms known from earlier inscriptions. Xuanzang gives a stereotyped description of the army as consisting of infantry, cavalry, chariots, and elephants.

Inscriptional evidence suggests that the early Pushyabhuti rulers were worshippers of Surya. Rajyavardhana was a devotee of the Buddha. The *Harshacharita* and the king's inscriptions indicate that Harsha was a devotee of Shiva, but Xuanzang describes him as partial towards Buddhism. According to him, Harsha aggressively demanded of the king of Kashmir a tooth relic buried in a *stupa*. Harsha is said to have convened a great assembly at Kannauj, and quinquennial assemblies at Prayaga. Xuanzang describes one of these, which he personally attended. Many kings, including those of Assam and Valabhi, were present. *Shramanas*, Brahmanas, and adherents of various sects were invited, many religious discourses were delivered, the king distributed lavish gifts and worshipped the Buddha, Shiva, and the Sun on consecutive days.

Harsha was a patron of learning and the arts, and had various talents himself. He is supposed to have written three dramas, a work on grammar, and at least two Sutra works. The three plays attributed to him are the *Ratnavali*, *Priyadarshika*, and *Nagananda*. The *Nagananda* is about the *bodhisattva* Jimutavahana, and the *Ratnavali* and *Priyadarshika* are romances. It is possible that the king himself composed the text of the Banskhera and Madhuban inscriptions. The Banskhera inscription has the king's signature and shows his calligraphic skills. Bana tells us that the king was an accomplished lute player. Bana, Mayura, and Matanga Divakara were among the accomplished writers associated with his court.

Harsha's death in 648 CE was followed by a period of political turmoil until the rise of Yashovarman in *c*. 715–45 CE. Thereafter, a number of lineages vied for control over Kannauj. One of the striking features of the political history of the times was the tripartite struggle between the Rashtrakutas, Palas, and Gurjara-Pratiharas.

Eastern India

The death of king Shashanka in *c*. 637 was followed by over a century of political confusion in Bengal (Majumdar. [Gen. Ed.], [1955] 1964: 44–57). Yashovarman of Kannauj, Lalitaditya of Kashmir, and a Chinese army invaded the area. Much of Bengal passed into the hands of Bhaskaravarman, the ruler of Assam, while territories in Bihar and Odisha were conquered by Harsha. The Khalimpur copper plate of Dharmapala asserts that finally Gopala, founder of the Pala dynasty, was elected by the people, rescuing them from *matsya-nyaya* (chaos).

Gopala's successor Dharmapala (770–810) initially suffered defeats at the hands of the Pratiharas and Rashtrakutas, but went on to conquer large parts of Northern India. He held a *durbar* at Kannauj, installed his puppet ruler Chakrayudha on the throne, and proclaimed his own paramountcy. This *durbar* was attended by many vassal chiefs. The nucleus of Dharmapala's empire was Bengal and Bihar, which came under his direct rule. Beyond this, the kingdom of Kannauj was a dependency. Further to the west and south, the rulers of the Punjab, western hill states, Rajputana, Malwa, and Berar acknowledged his sovereignty. According to a tradition preserved in the *Svayambhu Purana*, Nepal was also a vassal state. Tibetan tradition credits Dharmapala with founding the Buddhist monastery of Vikramashila (identified with Antichak in Bhagalpur district, Bihar) and Somapura (identified with Paharpur in Rajshahi district, Bangladesh).

Map 10.4 Major dynasties of Northern, Central, and Eastern India, *c.* 700–1100 CE

Tibetan tradition ascribes the founding of the Odantapuri monastery (in Bihar) to this king as well, although other sources say it was founded by Devapala or Gopala.

Devapala (810–850), the successor of Dharmapala, extended the empire and claimed to have extracted tribute from the whole of Northern India from the Himalayas to the Vindhyas, from the eastern to the western oceans. His inscriptions claim that his military campaigns led him as far as Kamboja in the west and the Vindhyas in the south and that he exterminated the Utkalas, conquered Pragjyotisha, curbed the pride of the Hunas, and destroyed the haughtiness of the lords of the Dravidas and Gurjaras. Devapala too was a patron of Buddhism.

The power of the Palas declined in the late 9th century, as weak kings suffered defeat at the hands of the Rashtrakutas and Pratiharas. The subordinate rulers of Assam and Odisha assumed independence. The Chandelas and Kalachuris refer to defeats inflicted by their armies on Gauda, Radha, Anga, and Vanga. There was a revival of Pala power in the late 10th century under Mahipala I, another brief period of recovery in the 11th century, followed by a decline in the 12th century.

The Palas exercised power over Assam (known as Kamarupa or Pragjyotisha) for some time during the time of Devapala. Then, in about 800 CE, a local ruler of Kamarupa named Harjaravarman threw off the Pala yoke and asserted his independent status. This is suggested by his imperial titles and the fact that there are no references to the Palas in the inscriptions of his successors. This dynasty, known as the Salamba dynasty, ruled between *c.* 800 and 1000 CE. Their capital was Haruppeshvara, on the banks of the Lauhitya, i.e., Brahmaputra. According to tradition, the Karatoya river was the western boundary of Kamarupa.

In Odisha, the late 6th century saw the Shailodbhavas establish themselves in Kongoda (roughly modern Puri and Ganjam districts). Initially subordinates of Shashanka, they soon asserted their independence. The decline of the Shailodbhavas in the 8th century was paralleled by the rise of the Gangas of Shvetaka. They were migrants from Karnataka, who had established themselves in the north Ganjam area. The Gangas of Kalinganagara were also migrants from Karnataka. They moved into Odisha towards the end of the 5th century and established themselves in the Vamsadhara and Nagavali valleys in south Odisha. They claimed in their inscriptions to have achieved overlordship over all of Kalinga by the quivering edge of their sword. In north Odisha, the Bhauma-Karas exercised power from the 8th/9th century into the 10th century.

FURTHER DISCUSSION | Some origin myths of the dynasties of Odisha

In the Odisha region, royal origin myths became more elaborate after the 7th century. Although the details of these myths obviously cannot be considered as historical 'facts', they do encode significant information about the origin of lineages. Furthermore, as these myths were one of various strategies adopted by ruling lineages to legitimize their power, it is important to carefully analyse them and identify the traditions to which these dynasties anchored themselves.

The origin myth recounted in Shailodbhava inscriptions speaks of a man named Pulindasena, famed among the people of Kalinga. Although endowed with virtue, strength, and greatness, he did not covet sovereignty, but worshipped the god Svayambhu to create a man capable of ruling the earth. The god granted him this boon, and Pulindasena saw a man emerging from the splintering of a rock. This was the lord Shailodbhava, who founded a distinguished lineage that was named after him. One of the Shailodbhava inscriptions adds two verses attributing the miraculous birth of Shailodbhava to Hara or Shambhu (i.e., Shiva). The Pulindas were an ancient tribe mentioned in various ancient texts, and the importance attached to Pulindasena reflects the tribal origins of the Shailodbhava dynasty. The motif of emerging or being born from a rock perhaps points to the rocky terrain in which the dynasty was initially based. The importance attached to Shiva can be connected to the fact that the Shailodbhavas were worshippers of this god. Most of their inscriptions have the Shaiva bull motif on the seal; many of them begin with an invocation to Shiva and describe the king as *parama-maheshvara*. Shailodbhava inscriptions also eulogize the Mahendra mountain, referring to it as a *kula-giri*, i.e., a 'tutelary mountain'.

The Bhanja origin myth is also interesting. The fact that the various groups of Bhanja kings may represent collateral ruling houses or different lineages with a common clan affiliation is suggested by the fact that in their inscriptions, they all claim origin from an egg, although details vary. The early Bhanjas of Khinjali *mandala* claimed to belong to the egg-born lineage (*andajavamshaprabhava*). The outline of this story is elaborated on in the inscriptions of the Adi-Bhanjas. These state that Gandadanda Virabhadra, progenitor of the Adi-Bhanja family, burst out of the egg of a peahen in the great hermitage of Kotyashrama, where he was reared by the sage Vasishtha. The peafowl clearly had an important significance for the Bhanja lineages. However, it is interesting to note that in Adi-Bhanja inscriptions, the miraculous birth of the progenitor of the lineage was set in a respectable Brahmanical locale—a hermitage of the sage Vasishtha. Another version of the story introduces Ramadeva, probably none other than Rama of epic vintage, into the account.

While the Shailodbhava and Bhanja origin myths reflect a mixture of Brahmanical and tribal elements, the Somavamshis and imperial Gangas anchored themselves to the epic–Puranic tradition. The Somavamshis claimed to belong to the lunar dynasty. The Korni and Vizagapatnam plates of the Ganga king Anantavarman Chodaganga give the most grandiose account of all, tracing the ancestry of the dynasty back to the god Vishnu.

Source Upinder Singh, 1994: 120–22

A number of new dynasties came to the fore in Odisha between the 10th and the mid-12th centuries. In north and central Odisha, the several lineages whose names ended with the suffix 'bhanja' included the Bhanjas of Khinjali *mandala*, the Adi Bhanjas of Khijjinga-kotta (in Mayurbhanj and Keonjhar areas), and the Bhanjas of Baudh (in the Kandhamal district area). During the 9th–11th centuries, the Shulkis and Tungas ruled over the Dhenkanal area, while the Nandodbhavas were established in the Dhenkanal and adjoining Cuttack and Puri areas. In the course of the 10th century, the Somavamshis of Dakshina-Kosala expanded their dominion to carve out an empire that included large parts of northern and central Odisha.

The rapid expansion of the Ganga kingdom began in the 10th century and culminated in the unification of north and south Odisha. The Ganga king Anantavarman Chodaganga was responsible for displacing Somavamshi rule in lower Odisha in the early 12th century. The military expansion of the imperial Gangas may have been assisted by their alliance with the Cholas. The mother and one of the queens of Anantavarman were Chola princesses. This did not, however, rule out military conflict—Kulottunga I twice sent armies against Kalinga. Anantavarman made inroads into Bengal as well.

Lineage names and genealogical accounts sometimes throw light on the origins of certain lineages. In some cases, though—e.g., the Shailodbhavas, Kulikas, Shulkis, and Bhauma-Karas—they point to tribal origins. Other kings such as the Tungas, Somavamshis, and imperial Gangas used *gotra* designations, suggesting claims to Brahmana status.

There is also evidence of the migration of lineages. Mention has already been made of the various Gangas lineages who were immigrants from Karnataka. The Bhauma-Karas may have come from Assam, the Somavamshis from south Kosala (in eastern MP and western Odisha), and the Tungas from Rohitagiri (identified with Rohtasgarh in Shahabad district of Bihar).

The Rajput clans

The use of the term *Rajaputra* for specific clans or as a collective term for various clans emerged by the 12th century. The Agnikula myth, which refers to certain clans emerging from the fire of a great sacrifice conducted by sage Vasishtha on Mount Abu, is also a fairly late phenomenon, and had emerged by the 16th century. The 'Agnikula Rajputs' included the Pratiharas, Chaulukyas, Paramaras, and Chahamanas. The medieval bardic traditions of Rajasthan contain lists of 36 Rajput clans. There are some differences in the lists, indicating that the claims to Rajput status remained somewhat fluid.

B. D. Chattopadhyaya ([1976] 1997: 57–80) has pointed out that the emergence of the Rajputs was part of a widespread phenomenon of the proliferation of lineage-based states in early medieval India. The emergence of the clans that eventually came to be considered as Rajputs can be understood against the background of various factors such as the expansion of the agrarian economy, new features in land distribution (including the distribution of land among royal kinsmen), inter-clan collaboration in the form of political and matrimonial alliances, and the construction of fortresses on an unprecedented scale. (For the political history of the Rajput clans, see Majumdar. [Gen. Ed.], [1955] 1964, and Majumdar. [Gen. Ed.], [1957] 1966.)

Silver Gurjara-Pratihara coin (obverse and reverse)

The Gurjara-Pratiharas were among the various dynasties that arose in North India after the break-up of the Gupta empire. The dynasty was founded by a Brahmana named Harichandra, in the area around Jodhpur in Rajputana. Various other Gurjara families, probably collaterals, set up small principalities to the south and east of this area. The antecedents of the Gurjara-Pratihara dynasty are a subject of debate. The word *pratihara* means doorkeeper. Both the early Jodhpur and imperial Pratiharas had a common tradition that their name came from the fact that their ancestor, the epic hero Lakshmana, once served as a doorkeeper to his brother Rama. Some historians think that the Gurjaras were a foreign people who came into India in the wake of the Huna invasions. Another view is that Gurjara is the name of a country (i.e., land), not of the people, though in ancient times people generally gave their name to their land and not vice versa. A few scholars consider the Gurjaras and Pratiharas to be two different families or tribal groups. Others think that the Pratiharas were a clan of the Gurjara tribe. The modern Gujars who inhabit the north-west, western Rajasthan, Gujarat, and Uttar Pradesh may represent their descendants.

The Gurjara-Pratiharas became prominent in the second quarter of the 8th century, when their ruler Nagabhat I offered successful resistance to the Arabs. This king's line soon became the most important powerful Pratihara family, eclipsing the Nandipuri and Jodhpur branch. Nagabhata's control extended over parts of Malwa, Rajputana, and Gujarat. Later Gurjara-Pratihara kings, included Nagabhata II, moved into the Kannauj region. The Gurjara-Pratiharas were involved in constant conflicts with other contemporary powers such as the Palas and Rashtrakutas.

The best known Gurjara-Pratihara king was Bhoja, grandson of Nagabhata II. He ascended the throne in or before 836 CE, and had a long reign of over 46 years. His earliest inscription—the Barah copper plate of this date was issued from the *skandhavara* (royal camp of victory) at Mahodaya. Mahodaya may have been another name for Kannauj. Bhoja was defeated by the Palas, Rashtrakutas, and Kalachuris in the first part of his reign, but subsequently managed to make a comeback. He won victories against the Palas and possibly also against the Rashtrakutas, aided by feudatories such as the Chedis and Guhilas. His kingdom probably included Awadh and Kathiawar and extended up to the Punjab. The Kalachuris of Gorakhpur and Chandellas of Bundelkhand acknowledged his overlordship. A 9th century Arab account of India, attributed to the merchant Sulaiman, refers to the great military power and riches of a king named Juzr, usually identified with Bhoja.

The Gurjara-Pratiharas subsequently suffered several defeats. In the early 10th century, during the time of Mahipala, the Rashtrakuta Indra III completely devastated the city of Kannauj some time between 915 and 918. There was another Rashtrakuta invasion in *c*. 963, this time led by their king Krishna. The feudatory chiefs and provincial governors of the Gurjara-Pratiharas gradually started asserting their independence; the empire disintegrated and was reduced to the area around Kannauj. The Gurjara-Pratiharas had a rather shadowy existence thereafter and were wiped off the political map by the Ghaznavids in the early 11th century.

The inscriptions of the Chandellas, who established themselves in Bundelkhand, trace their descent to a mythical ancestor named Chandratreya, born of the moon. The historical founder of the dynasty was Nannuka, who can be placed in the first quarter of the 9th century. Inscriptions connect the early kings of this dynasty with Kharjjuravahaka (Khajuraho), which was their capital. The Chandellas initially seem to have been vassals of the Pratiharas of Kannauj and were involved in conflicts with them, as well as with the Palas and Kalachuris. The Chandella kingdom expanded steadily under early kings such as Jayashakti and Vijayashakti. Jayashakti was also known as Jejjaka and Jeja, and the Chandella principality came to be known as Jejabhukti after him. The expansion continued under Harsha (900–925 CE), who helped the Pratihara ruler Mahipala recover his throne after it was captured by the Rashtrakuta Indra III in about 914 CE. The Chandella king Yashovarman captured Kalanjar and pushed the northern boundary of the kingdom up to the Yamuna. Successes against the Kalachuris and Paramaras extended the southern boundary of the kingdom up to the borders of Chedi and Malwa. Yashovarman also achieved victories over the Somavamshis, Kambojas, and Palas, though Yashovarman seems to have acknowledged the overlordship of the Pala ruler Devapala. The Chandellas took advantage of the decline of the Pratiharas and Palas to assert their independence. Dhanga, the first independent Chandella king, took the title of *maharajadhiraja*. Several of the Khajuraho temples were built during his reign.

To the south of the Chandella kingdom lay the principality of the Kalachuris of Chedi country, also sometimes referred to as Dahala-mandala. The Chedi capital Tripuri is identified with Tewar, 6 miles west of Jabalpur. Kokkala I, the earliest king of the dynasty, probably ascended the throne in *c*. 845, and fought successful wars against the Pratiharas of Kannauj and their feudatories, the Arab governor of Sindh, Rashtrakutas, Shilaharas of Konkan, and the ruler of Vanga. Later kings included Shankaragana,

Silver coin (obverse and reverse) of Gurjara-Pratihara king Bhoja I; debased gold coin (obverse and reverse) of Chandella king Madanavarman

Yuvaraja, and Lakshmanaraja. The poet Rajashekhara, associated with the court of the Gurjara-Pratihara king Mahendrapala and his son Mahipala, was also closely associated with the Kalachuri court of the time. Rajashekhara's drama, the *Viddhashalabhanjika*, was staged in the court of Yuvaraja in order to celebrate the victory against the Rashtrakutas. Kalachuri power suffered reversal during the reign of Yuvaraja II, with defeats at the hands of the Chalukya Taila II and the Paramara king of Malwa, Munja. This was followed by recovery under Kokkalla II, when expeditions were successfully launched against the Chaulukyas, Chalukyas, and the kingdom of Gauda. A collateral branch of the Kalachuris ruled at the time on the banks of the Sarayu.

The kingdom of the Paramaras of Malwa was adjacent to that of the Kalachuris. This lineage seems to have originally been based in the Mount Abu area of Rajasthan. According to a tradition preserved in certain texts and later Paramara inscriptions. According to this story, the sage Vishvamitra stole Vasishtha's wish-granting cow (*kama-dhenu*). Vasishtha performed a sacrifice on Mount Abu in order to recover his precious cow. A hero sprang out of the sacrificial fire and forcibly seized the cow from Vishvamitra. Vasishtha named this hero Paramara (slayer of the enemy) and made him king. The story goes on to tell us that Upendra, the earliest known king of the Paramara dynasty, was born in the lineage of this hero. However, an early Paramara inscription does not mention this story; it describes kings of this dynasty as having been born in the family of the Rashtrakutas.

The capital of the main branch of the Paramaras was Dhara (identified with modern Dhar, MP). The early Paramaras were vassals of the Rashtrakutas. Upendra, who probably ruled in the first quarter of the 9th century, may have been made ruler of the Deccan by Govinda III after the latter's successful military expedition in Malwa. The Paramaras were temporarily eclipsed when they lost Malwa to the Pratiharas. Their power revived in the mid-10th century during the reigns of Vairasimha II and Siyaka II (also known as Harsha). Siyaka threw off allegiance to the Rashtrakutas in the later part of his reign, and the Rashtrakuta army was defeated at Kalighatta, on the banks of the Narmada. Siyaka chased the Rashtrakuta army right upto their capital Manyakheta, but subsequently withdrew. His successor Munja (also known as Utpala or Vakpatiraja II) extended the empire, achieved military successes against the Kalachuris, and sacked Tripuri. He led many expeditions into Rajputana and defeated the Hunas. He sacked Aghata, the capital of the Guhilas of Medapata, captured some territories of the Chahamanas of Naddula, and annexed Mount Abu and the southern areas of Jodhpur from the Chahamanas, placing his sons and a nephew in charge of the conquered territories. Munja also invaded the Chaulukya kingdom of Anahilapataka and Lata. He was finally defeated by the Chalukya ruler Taila II. Munja was an accomplished military leader, poet, and patron of art and literature. He is also credited with having dug many tanks and built many temples. Sindhuraja, Munja's successor, recovered some of the territories that had been lost to the Chalukyas.

The Chaulukya family (not be confused with the Chalukyas of southern India) had at least three branches. The oldest branch ruled from Mattamayura in Central India and its earliest rulers included Simhavarman, Sadhanva, and Avanivarman. Another branch line was founded by Mularaja I, who established his capital at Anahilapataka (also known as Anahilavada). A third branch was founded by Barappa in Lata, with its political centre at Bhrigukachchha (Broach) in southern Gujarat. Mularaja I of Anahilapataka led military expeditions into Saurashtra and Kutch and against the Abhiras. His power diminished due to invasions of the Chahamanas and the Chaulukyas of Lata. Another defeat at the hands of the Paramaras led Mularaja to take refuge with the Rashtrakuta king Dhavala. He was eventually able to recover his kingdom, but his successors remained embroiled in conflicts with the Kalachuris and Paramaras.

In Mewar in south-east Rajasthan, in the 7th century, two lines of Guhilas ruled from Nagda–Ahada and Kishkindha, and there was a small Guhila principality at Dhavagarta. By the 10th century, the major Guhila families included those of Nagda–Ahada, Chatsu, Unstra, Bagodia, Nadol, and Mangrol. The early inscriptions of the Guhilas of Nagda–Ahada describe them as belonging to the lineage of Guhila. A 10th century inscription

FURTHER DISCUSSION | **The Tomaras and Delhi in legends and inscriptions**

The Tomara Rajputs have a special connection with the Delhi area. Mention was made in the previous chapter of the iron pillar in Mehrauli in Delhi. The pillar, which carries the inscription of king Chandra, bears several other short inscriptions, including an 11th century inscription which seems to refer to Anangapala Tomara establishing Delhi.

The connection between the Tomaras and Delhi is reflected in medieval legends. One of these legends is connected with the iron pillar and is one of several stories that explain how the city of Delhi got its name. According to one version, recounted in the *Prithvirajaraso*, a learned Brahmana told the Rajput king Bilan Deo or Anangapala Tomara that the pillar was immoveable, that its base rested on the hood of Vasuki, the king of serpents, and that Anangapala's rule would last as long as the pillar stood. The king was curious and had the pillar dug out, but the lower part was smeared with the blood of the serpent. Realizing that he had made a grave mistake, he ordered the pillar re-installed. However, in spite of all attempts, it remained loose (*dhili*). And, the story concludes, in the looseness of the pillar lies the origin of the name Dhilli or Dhillika (from where we get Dilli and Delhi).

This is, of course, a myth, but the Tomara connection with the Delhi area is reflected in archaeological evidence. Anangpur (mentioned in Chapter 2 as a major palaeolithic site) in the Badarpur area has remains of early medieval fortifications and structures, and the name of this village connects it with one of the various Tomara kings named Anangapala. The stone masonry dam near the village was probably built by him. Anangapala II was the founder of the citadel of Lal Kot in the Mehrauli area, and probably also built the tank known as Anang Tal. The reservoir of Suraj Kund is attributed to the Tomara king Surajpala. The Tomaras are, thus, associated with the construction of the earliest surviving waterworks in the Delhi area.

Several inscriptions recount later memories of a sequence of rulers over the area. A 12th century inscription found in a small town called Bijholia in Rajasthan describes the Chauhan king Vigraharaja as the conqueror of Dhillika (Delhi). The 13th century Palam Baoli inscription (found in a step well in Palam village) records the construction of a step well by Uddhara, a householder of Dhilli. Line 3 of this inscription speaks of the land of Hariyanaka, which was first enjoyed by the Tomaras, then by the Chauhans, and thereafter by the Shakas. The term 'Shaka' is here used for the Delhi Sultans, and the inscription gives a list of the 'Shaka' rulers from Muhammad of Ghor up to Balban. A 13th century inscription found at Sonepat (known as the Delhi Museum stone inscription) records the construction of a well in Suvarnaprastha village, and states that Dhillika in the Hariyana country was ruled successively by the Tomaras, Chahamanas, and Shakas. A 14th century inscription found in Sarban village (near Raisina road in New Delhi) records the building of a well in Saravala village by two merchants named Khetala and Paitala. Four stanzas narrate the past of Dhilli, giving the same sequence of rulers as the inscriptions mentioned above, except that the term used for the Delhi Sultans is not 'Shaka' but 'Turushka' (Turks).

Source Upinder Singh, (1999) 2006: 81–83, 89–97

The Anangpur dam; Suraj Kund reservoir

names 20 kings, beginning with Guhadatta and ending with Shaktikumara. Guhadatta is described as a Brahmana from Anandapura (identified with Vadnagar in north-east Gujarat). Later inscriptions give another account, describing Bappa Rawal as the founder of the dynasty, combining Brahmana and Kshatriya elements in their origin accounts. These accounts reflect the complex process of the transformation of the Guhilas of the Nagda–Ahada line from a local to a sub-regional state in the 10th century, and to a regional state of Mewar in the 13th century (Sinha Kapur, 2002).

Of the many branch lines of the Chahamanas, the oldest ruled in Lata till the mid-8th century. Another branch was founded by Lakshmana at Naddula in south Marwar. A third, founded by Vasudeva, established itself in the early 7th century in Shakambhari-pradesha with its capital at Shakambhari, which has been identified with Sambhar near Jaipur. The Chahamanas of Shakambhari were originally subordinates of the Pratiharas, with whom they also had matrimonial ties. They assumed independence during the reign of king Simharaja. At the end of the 10th century, their kingdom stretched at least up to Sikar and Jaipur on the east, Pushkar on the south, and Parbatsar in Jodhpur on the west.

The Tomara kingdom was adjacent to that of the Chahamanas of Shakambhari. The Tomaras ruled the Hariyana country from their capital Dhillika (Delhi), initially acknowledging Pratihara paramountcy. In the 10th century, they were involved in conflict with the Chahamanas of Shakambhari. They continued to rule Hariyana country until the mid-12th century, when they were defeated by the Chahamana king Vigraharaja IV. Prithviraja III, also known as Rai Pithora, was one of Vigraharaja's nephews.

The contemporary sources of information on Prithviraja Chauhan consist of a contemporary but incomplete court *mahakavya* titled *Prithviraja-vijaya* composed by Jayanaka and a few inscriptions. Later sources include the Persian chronicles, *Taj al-Ma'asir* and *Tabaqat-i Nasiri*, and the still later epic poem *Prithviraj-raso* by Chand Bardai. Some of the political events in his reign can be reconstructed on their basis (see R. C. Majumdar. [Gen. Ed.], [1957] 1966: 104–15). These include his conflict with a cousin Nagarjuna, who had political ambitions and was defeated. Prithviraja led armies against the Chandellas of Jejabhukti and defeated king Paramardi/Paramal, but the hold over Jejabhukti proved tenuous. He also fought against the Chaulukya ruler Bhima II of Gujarat, a conflict that ultimately led to a treaty between the two. Prithviraja's army achieved victory against the army of Muhammad of Ghur on the battlefield of Tarain in 1191. Ghuri retreated and went back to Ghazni to recoup. He returned in 1192. The armies faced each other on the battlefield of Tarain once again; this time, the Ghurid army was victorious. (For Prithviraja in history, memory and legend, see Talbot, 2016.)

Kashmir and the north-west

The early rulers of the Karkota dynasty, which established its rule in Kashmir in the 8th century, included Lalitaditya. The reign of king Vajraditya witnessed Arab raids into Kashmir. Jayapida, one of the most powerful Karkota kings, launched an ambitious three-year-long expedition against the eastern countries and claims to have defeated five chieftains of Gauda. On his way back from this campaign, he seems to have defeated the ruler of Kanyakubja. The Karkota dynasty came to an end in 855–56 CE. It was followed by the Utpala dynasty, founded by Avantivarman. He is credited with having taken major steps to prevent the flood waters of the Mahapadma (i.e., Wular) lake from damaging crops. Another ruler was Shankaravarman, who led military campaigns into the Punjab and Gujarat. The later years of this dynasty were marked by political intrigues, and power changed hands frequently. The successors of the Utpalas included kings such as Yashakara and Parvagupta.

The political history of early medieval Kashmir indicates the important political role played by the Tantrins (a body of foot soldiers), Ekangas (a body of soldiers who functioned as royal bodyguards), and landed chiefs known as the Damaras. The history of this region also reveals a tradition of powerful queens. The best known is Didda, who dominated Kashmir politics in the second half of the 10th century. Kalhana's *Rajatarangini*

Billon coin (obverse and reverse) of Chahamana king, Prithviraja II; coin (obverse and reverse) of Shahi king Spalapatideva (from top)

FURTHER DISCUSSION | Didda

The invisibilization of women in the earlier debates on early medieval India has been challenged by Devika Rangachari who has highlighted the role of royal and non-royal women in the formal and informal exercise of power and authority. The *Rajatarangini*'s description of the 12th century history of Kashmir mentions three women rulers—Yashovati of the Gonanda dynasty, Sugandha of the Utpala dynasty, and Didda of the Yashaskara dynasty. Of them, Didda (Didda is a respectful term for an elder sister, still used by Kashmiri pandits) had the longest and most eventful stint, exercising political power for almost 50 years. This included the period of her husband Kshemagupta's reign, the time that she was regent for her minor son Abhimanyu, and the years she ruled Kashmir in her own right after ascending the throne in 980–81 CE.

Didda's career is described in the sixth *taranga* of the *Rajatarangini*. Kalhana describes how this queen was aided in her rise to power by a minister, the loyal Naravahana, who 'established the rule of the dowager over the entire kingdom and made her comparable to Indra'. Describing how she managed to create a rift in the ranks of her enemies, Kalhana observes:

> She, whom none believed had the strength to step over a cattle track—the lame lady—traversed, in the manner of the son of the wind, the ocean of the confederate forces. (6.226)

He describes how she ruthlessly killed her son and three grandsons before ascending the throne. Didda had an affair with a courier and herdsman named Tunga, who soon became her trusted confidante. The queen chose her nephew Sangramaraja as her successor, thereby diverting the succession to her maternal family from Lohara. Kalhana refers to Didda founding towns, temples, and monasteries. These included the towns of Diddapura and Kankanapura and a temple called the Diddasvamin temple. This queen is also credited with repairing many temples dedicated to the gods.

Although Kalhana narrated Didda's rise to power and the details of her reign, he clearly disapproved of her. He describes her as deficient in moral character, mercilless by nature, and as one who was easily influenced by others. Further, for Kalhana, her personality reflected the defects of womankind:

> Even in the case of those who are born in high families, alas! the natural bent of women, like that of rivers, is to follow the downward course. (6.316)

As we have seen earlier, women rulers are known from other regions as well. Devika Rangachari points out that a comparison of the women rulers of Kashmir with those of Andhra (notably Rudramadevi) shows some important differences. For instance, in passing power on to the Loharas, Didda managed to divert royal succession from the Yashaskaras to her natal family. Of course it is likely that initially, a woman ruler such as Didda may have been considered a safe bet by those who sought to keep the succession within the ruling family, and that matters took an unexpected turn once the queen had established herself and got used to exercising power.

Rangachari draws attention to the fact that, in spite of his prejudices, Kalhana portrays both royal and non-royal women as historically relevant figures. In the realm of political power, women appear as sovereign rulers as well as powers behind the throne, and some of them played an important role in the founding and destruction of lineages. The *Rajatarangini* also reflects the direct and indirect political influence of courtesans and women of 'low' birth in the harem. In Kashmir, as elsewhere, within the constraints of the prevailing patriarchal power structure, male control over political power was occasionally breached.

Source Pandit. (Trans.)., (1935) 1968: 244–60; Rangachari, 2009, 2020

(River of Kings) gives a connected account of the kings of Kashmir from the early ones of legend to the historical rulers of the 12th century. Kalhana is often described as India's first historian. However, as mentioned in Chapter 1, Kalhana considered himself primarily a great poet (*mahakavi*), one who could make pictures of the past come vividly alive. He described the natural beauty of Kashmir, wove lively character sketches, and gave dramatic descriptions of political events. His work is replete with moralizing, and often explains events by citing *karma* or fate. Kalhana used Sanskrit *kavya* to give literary expression to the distinctive regional and cultural identity of early medieval Kashmir (see Kaul, 2018).

The Turkish Shahiya/Shahi dynasty had its base in the Kabul valley and Gandhara area. In the second half of the 9th century, Kallar, a Brahmana minister of king Lagaturman, overthrew the Shahiya king and staked his claim to power, laying the foundation of a Hindu Shahi dynasty. Kallar is identified with king Lalliya of the *Rajatarangini*. He does not seem to have been able to maintain his control over the Kabul valley for long. After yielding before the Yaqub ibn al-Layth (of the Saffarid dynasty of Iran) in 870 CE, he was forced to move his capital to Udabhanda, modern Und village in Rawalpindi district (Ohind). The Shahi dynasty ultimately collapsed in the wake of the Ghaznavid invasions.

During the 7th and 8th century, the Arabs, united by the new religion of Islam, succeeded in extending their conquests from north Africa and Spain to Central Asia. Sindh was a lucrative area from the point of view of trade routes (see Wink, 1999, Vol. 1: 201–18).Arab inroads into Western India began with a naval expedition to Thana near Mumbai in 637 CE; this was followed by expeditions to Broach and Debal, a port in Sindh. None of these resulted in any decisive territorial gains. The Arabs were subsequently involved in protracted campaigns against the kingdoms of Zabul and Kabul in Afghanistan. They also launched several expeditions resulting in the conquest of Makran. They finally succeeded in getting a foothold in Sindh, when Al-Hajjaj, the Ummayad Caliph's governor of Iraq, despatched an army under his nephew and son-in-law, Muhammad bin Qasim. The capture of Debal was followed by the annexation of Nirun and Sadusan, and there was a decisive victory over king Dahar (or Dahir), ruler of Sindh at Ar-Rur. Alor, Brahmanabad, and Multan were subsequently taken. Bin Qasim was in Sindh for over three years, when he was recalled by the Caliph and killed at the latter's orders. These events are recounted in an early 13th century Persian work, the *Chachnama* which claims to be translation of an older Arabic work. (On the need to understand the political discourse of this text instead of reading it literally, see Asif, 2016.) The Arab hold over Sindh remained precarious after Muhammad bin Qasim's departure. A later governor Al-Junayd made inroads towards Malwa and Gujarat; these were thwarted by the Pratihara Nagabhata I and the Lata Chaulukya ruler Pulakeshin Avani Janashraya. Arab control over Sindh further weakened during the governorship of Al-Junayd's successor Tamim.

Ghaznavid coins (obverse and reverse)

The subsequent Turkish invasions of north-western India are sometimes seen as cataclysmic events that created a major rupture in the Indian fabric, a series of events that eventually led to the spread of Muslim rule in India. This is partly the result of an uncritical reading of texts such as the Persian court chronicles and partly the result of looking back at Indian history through the lens of the two nation theory. The history of this period is much more complex. (On the history of the Turkish invasions and the establishment of the Delhi Sultanate, see Eaton, 2019; Jackson, 1999; Sunil Kumar, 2007; Wink, 1999, Vol. 2.)

To start off with, it is necessary to replace the blanket label of 'Muslim invaders' with more specific identification. The Ghaznavids and Ghurids were Turks in the sense of speakers of dialects of the Turki language. The Ghaznavids were also originally military slaves. The institution of military slavery was initially prevalent in Iraq during the Abbasid Caliphate, and from here, spread to Iran and Afghanistan. Military slaves inducted into the Ghaznavid and Ghurid armies were usually young warriors captured in Central Asia, skilled in archery on horseback. Apart from capture in war, they were also acquired through capture, purchase, or gift. This type of military slavery is very different from other forms of slavery known in the ancient and early medieval world. Military slaves were men whose ties to their kin and native land had been broken. Their primary allegiance was to their owners, on whom their careers and fortunes depended. Another important development in the early 11th century was the decline of the Abbasid Caliphate (which had replaced the Ummayad Caliphate in the mid-8th century). This meant that while Muslim sultans still acknowledged nominal allegiance to the religious authority of the Caliph, they were in effect independent.

In the 9th and 10th centuries, parts of Central Asia and Afghanistan were under the control of the Samanid dynasty. A commander-in-chief and slave of the Samanids named Alptagin shook off allegiance to his overlord and established a semi-independent principality in eastern Afghanistan, with Ghazni as its capital. In *c.* 975, Alptagin was succeeded by his slave and son-in-law Sabuktigin, who consolidated his independent position in Ghazni and went on to launch several raids into Peshawar in the Indus valley. Sabuktigin was succeeded by his son Mahmud. Mahmud (*r.* 997–1030) launched 17 campaigns into the Indian subcontinent over 27 years. These included expeditions against the Shahiyas, Multan, Bhatinda, Narayanpur, Thaneshwar, Kannauj, Mathura, Kalinjar, and Somnath. Mahmud's 1025 invasion of Somnath on the Gujarat coast and his destruction of the Shiva temple here became the stuff of legend (see Davis, [1997] 1999: 186–221; Thapar, [2005] 2008). In spite of his reputation as a religious zealot, Mahmud's invasions and his temple destruction were based not on religious fervour but on the desire for plunder. His army was multi-ethnic and included Turks, Central Asians, Indians, Dailamis, Kurds, and Arabs (Bosworth, [1963] 1992: 110). His incursions into India were primarily aimed at plundering wealth, especially gold and silver. This was needed to finance the maintenance of a large army and bureaucracy, the military expeditions in Iran and Central Asia, and the costs of maintaining an opulent court at Ghazni. The Ghaznavids introduced into the Punjab a bureaucratic system based on revenue assignments, new political ideas with the sultan at the centre, and a tradition of Sufi saints, who were considered spiritually powerful and had a complex relationship with rulers (Eaton, 2019: 35–37).

The Turks succeeded in establishing a firm foothold in north-western India two centuries later, during the reign of Muhammad of Ghur. The house of Ghur started off as a minor principality and a subordinate of the Ghaznavid rulers, and eventually attacked and absorbed Ghazni. The Ghurids were chieftains affiliated to the Karramiya religious sect. The decline of the power of the Ghaznavids and Seljuqs gave them the opportunity to capture Ghazni in 1148 and Herat in 1175 from the Seljuqs. The expanding Ghurid kingdom, which extended across both sides of the Hindu Kush mountains, was ruled by two brothers. The older brother, Ghiyath al-Din Sam, ruled the western part (the Khurasan area) from Firuzkuh. The younger brother, Shihab al-Din bin Sam, also known as Muhammad Ghuri (*r*. 1173–1206), ruled over the eastern part of the kingdom from Ghazni.

With Ghazni as his base, starting in 1175, Muhammad Ghuri made several military inroads into India. Initial victories in Multan, Uchh, and southern Sindh were followed by defeat at the hands of the Solankis of Gujarat. Victories in Multan and northern Gujarat were followed by defeat at the hands of the Chaulukyas. Muhammad Ghuri's later expeditions aimed at territorial conquest. The conquest of the Punjab was followed by the defeat suffered by the Turkish forces at the hands of Prithviraja Chauhan in the first battle of Tarain (1191). The second battle of Tarain (1192) saw the Ghurids defeat a Rajput confederacy. This was followed by a rapid expansion of Ghurid power across North India, spearheaded by armies led by Muhammad Ghuri's slave commanders. Qutb al-Din Aibek, Ghuri's commander-in-chief, swiftly moved into Delhi, Ranthambore, Kannauj, Gwalior, and Kalinjar, while another commander, Bakhtiyar Khalji, annexed Bihar and Bengal. Ghuri's nominal suzerainty, thus, came to extend over almost the whole of North India. But control over these areas was tenuous and the Indian acquisitions were still an appendage to the Ghurid empire. In 1196, Ghuri returned to join his elder brother in the Afghanistan and Khurasan regions and succeeded the latter as ruler on his death in 1203. However, his power was destabilized by his Turkish rivals in Khurasan. Ghuri was killed in 1206. The slave commanders in India were left without a master and were now legally free. From the political rivalries, Aibek ultimately proved successful. During the reigns of Aibek (1206–10) and Iltutmish (1211–36), the Delhi Sultanate became more firmly established as an independent political entity, and eventually broke off its ties of allegiance to Ghazni.

Ghurid coins (obverse and reverse)

While Muhammad Ghuri's military invasions are sometimes presented in religious terms, it should be noted that his initial expeditions were against the Ismailis of Multan and Ghazanvids in Lahore. His Indian campaigns were aimed at establishing an independent kingdom for himself. Ghuri placed his slave commanders as governors of conquered territories or reinstating defeated rulers. The *iqta* system—transferable assignments of revenue in lieu of salary, especially for military service—which was common in the Ghurid realm, was introduced into India. The coinage of the Ghaznavid and Ghurid rulers that circulated in their Indian territories shows continuities with earlier Indian numismatic practices. This included Indian motifs, scripts, and titles. For instance, coins of Muhammad Ghuri issued in the Indian part of his kingdom followed the Indian weight standard. They have the motifs of the bull on the obverse and horseman carrying a spear on the reverse. Muhammad Ghuri's name appears on the obverse in the Devanagari scribe, with the prefix 'Shri'. Some of the Ghurid coins have the goddess Lakshmi on the obverse, and the king's name prefixed by 'Shri' or 'Hammira' (from the Arabic 'amir').

Royal Land Grants

Royal land grants are a major source for the history of early medieval India and are central to debates concerning this period. The incidence of grants by kings to Brahmanas increased significantly during *c.* 600–1200. The phenomenon reveals certain general patterns as well as regional specificities.

Brahmadeyas (land gifted to Brahmanas) had a political dimension. These settlements were created by royal order, and the rights of the Brahmana donees were declared and confirmed by royal decree. The feudalism hypothesis interprets *brahmadeyas* as a cause as well as a symptom of political fragmentation. This interpretation is difficult to accept for various reasons. Why should kings have voluntarily eroded their own power? Furthermore, was this really a period of political fragmentation? The political narrative in the preceding sections in fact clearly indicates that the early medieval period was marked by an unprecedented level of the proliferation of state polities at the regional, sub-regional, and trans-regional levels, within a broader economic context of agrarian expansion. Far from being symptoms of the disintegration of polities or royal disempowerment, land grants to Brahmanas were one of several integrative and legitimizing policies adopted by kings.

From the point of view of fledgling kingdoms struggling to establish their power and legitimacy, the patronage of Brahmanas, a social group that had traditionally enjoyed a privileged socio-religious status, did not amount to an inordinate loss of revenue or control. In fact, kings who 'granted' a piece of land may not have been in a position to realize revenue from that land in the first place. From the point of view of the large, established kingdoms, the making of a few land grants did not significantly deplete state resources. The maximum number of grants and the most lavish grants—both to Brahmanas and to religious establishments—were generally made by the most powerful dynasties and kings. In fact, the increase in royal land grants indicates higher levels of control over productive resources by kings compared to earlier periods. Strategies of control, alliances, and collaboration with prestigious social groups were an important facet of the politics of the time. The increase in the wealth and power of a section of Brahmanas and institutions such as temples did not take place at the expense of royal power (see Upinder Singh, 2006: 203–4).

Leaving aside the Delhi Sultans, inscriptions of other early medieval dynasties bear testimony to the Brahmanization of royal courts all over the subcontinent. Brahmanas emerged as ideologues and legitimizers of political power by crafting royal genealogies and performing prestigious sacrifices and rituals. As pointed out earlier, many royal genealogies linked lineages with the epic–Puranic tradition and assigned kings a respectable *varna* status. Origin myths often indirectly reflected actual relationships between social groups and institutions. For instance, myths enshrined in later literary sources of Kerala assigned an important place to Brahmanas and temples in their explanation of the origins of kingship, reflecting the close relationship that existed between kings, Brahmanas, and temples. The direct political role of Brahmanas in the Chera period is evident in the fact that Brahmanas of the leading Brahmana settlements formed part of the *Nalu Tali* (the king's council) at Mahodayapura.

While royal grants to Brahmanas remained a feature throughout the early medieval period, from about the 10th century, there was a shift towards donations to temples. There were also some 'secular grants'. For instance, Karnataka gives evidence of kings making grants of land in return for military service. In Odisha too, the imperial Gangas made grants to *nayakas* or military chiefs. However, at the subcontinental level, the number of instances of 'service' or military grants were very few compared to those made to Brahmanas and religious establishments.

Brahmana beneficiaries

Although Brahmana landowners existed in earlier centuries, there was a significant acceleration, intensification, and expansion of Brahmana control over land in the early medieval period. In the previous chapter, reference was made to a few instances of land grants made to Brahmanas by private individuals, some grants made to Brahmanas at their own request, and others made by kings at the request of certain people. The complexities revealed by these earlier inscriptions are less apparent in inscriptions of later times. However, there are still some clues which suggest that certain other people had a hand in grants ostensibly made by kings. An example is the 13th century Calcutta Sahitya Parishat copper plate inscription of Vishvarupasena, which records the king's gift to a Brahmana named Halayudha. Five of the eleven plots of land 'gifted' to this Brahmana are described as having been previously purchased by Halayudha himself, and the inscription actually seems to reflect a royal ratification of these purchases. Among the inscriptions of Odisha, some Bhauma-Kara and Ganga grants refer to feudatories or members of their families as the *vijnapti* (the person at whose request the grant was made). Such evidence corroborates D. C. Sircar's (1969a: 7) suggestion that land grant charters often camouflaged the identity of people involved in making the grant and sometimes even the very nature of the transaction.

Common sense might suggest that Brahmanas who were given grants of land were associated with the royal court. Some early medieval inscriptions of Bengal do, in fact, describe the donees as *shantivarikas* or *shantyagarikas*—men in charge of the performance of religious rites for the king. Other inscriptions from the same region describe land as having been gifted as *dakshina* for the performance of certain rites. In Odisha, some Brahmana donees were connected with the royal court as priests (*purohitas*, *punya-vachakas*), astrologers (*jyotishis*), and administrators. Similar instances can be cited from other parts of the country. However, the vast majority of inscriptions do not reveal a court connection for the Brahmana donees.

Brahmana recipients of royal grants are identified in inscriptions by their ancestry, *gotra*, *pravara*, *charana*, *shakha*, and native place. *Gotra* refers to the exogamous clan system of the Brahmanas. The *gotras* are divided into *ganas*, each of which has its own *pravara*. The *pravara* consists of a series of names (1, 2, 3, or 5) of supposed ancestral *rishis*. *Charana* refers to a school of Vedic learning, and *shakha* to a particular recension of a Veda. Inscriptions tend to use *charana* and *shakha* interchangeably. They highlight the Vedic learning of Brahmana donees, for instance by mentioning their titles such as *acharya*, *upadhyaya*, and *pandita*.

The references to native place indicate that some Brahmana donees were recent migrants into the area, and that there was a significant degree of spatial mobility among a section of the Brahmanas. Several phases of Brahmana migrations can be identified in early Indian history. The details of the earliest migrations, which may have begun as early as in *c*. 800 BCE, are shrouded in a mythological haze. The initial eastward movement is reflected in the gradual, though grudging, acknowledgement of the eastern regions in early Brahmanical literature, and the eastward extension of the term Aryavarta. The southward movement is reflected in legends associated with Agastya and Parusharama, which were mentioned in Chapter 8. Another phase of southward migration can be associated with the 'Sangam age', i.e., the early historical period of South India.

The Brahmana migrations of later times are better documented. The 16th century *Keralolpatti* records a tradition of 32 villages as the original Brahmana settlements in Kerala, which seems to reflect developments that occurred in the early medieval period. The late medieval Kulaji texts of Bengal trace the ancestry of the Kulin Brahmanas of Bengal to five Brahmanas from Kanyakubja, who were requisitioned by king Adisura to coach the Bengal Brahmanas in the correct performance of Vedic rites. Although the characters and details of this story cannot be treated as historical, they do suggest a few important things that are corroborated by other sources—namely, that the prestige of the Brahmana in early medieval India was still grounded in his Vedic learning, and that learned Brahmanas were migrating from Madhya-desha (the middle Ganga valley) into eastern lands.

Apart from such textual references, from the 5th century onwards, land grant inscriptions document the influx of Brahmana immigrants from the heartland of Madhya-desha into the areas of Maharashtra, Bengal, Madhya Pradesh, and Odisha. Some migrants came from renowned centres of Brahmanical learning such as Takari, Shravasti, Kolancha, and Hastipada. The phenomenon of migration intensified in the 8th century. The fanning out of Brahmanas into different parts of the subcontinent explains the need to fix the relative ranking of groups belonging to different regions. A broad division that had emerged by the 10th century was that of the Pancha-Gaudas (the northern group) and the Pancha-Dravidas (groups living south of the Vindhyas). The former included the Sarasvata, Gauda, Kanyakubja, Maithila, and Utkala Brahmanas. The Pancha-Dravida group included the Gurjjaras, Maharashtriyas, Karnatakas, Trailingas, and Dravidas.

But why were Brahmanas migrating? Factors such as political instability and pressure on land have been cited as possible reasons (Datta, 1989: 224), but these are not entirely convincing. The migrations can be connected with the search for a better livelihood arising out of specific historical contexts. The earlier phases of eastward and southward migrations may have been related to the decline of sacrifice-oriented religious practice in North India, especially in the early historical period. Members of the Brahmana community who had earned their livelihood by officiating at sacrifices, may have been impelled to leave their homes in search of alternative occupations that offered a more secure and lucrative income. This may also explain why the post-6th century BCE literature displays such diversity in the occupations followed by Brahmanas.

The migrations of the early medieval period coincided with the proliferation of kingdoms in various parts of the subcontinent, and may have had to do with new incentives rather than pressures (see Upinder Singh, 2009). The emerging political elites required legitimation and an administrative infrastructure, and this opened up new opportunities and avenues of employment for learned, literate Brahmanas. By this time, the religious practices of ordinary people had become increasingly oriented towards theistic devotion and had little to do with the Vedas or *shrauta* rituals. Yet, it is interesting to note that during the centuries that saw the virtual eclipse of Vedic religious practice at the popular level, Brahmanas were consistently advertised in inscriptions as Vedic scholars, or at least in terms of their Vedic affiliations, and kings were advertising their patronage of such Brahmanas. The big gulf that existed between the Sanskritic–Vedic tradition on the one hand and the lives of ordinary people on the other may have been the very factor that made this tradition a useful legitimizing basis for elite groups who were keen to highlight their loftiness and aloofness from the masses. Therefore, it is not a coincidence that two major phases of Brahmana migration coincided with major phases of state formation.

Certain inscriptions mention Brahmanas with unusual non-Sanskritic names, and some of them may represent Brahmanized tribal priests. For instance, some Eastern Chalukya inscriptions record grants made to Boya Brahmanas—these were originally priests of the Boya tribe, who got Brahmanized at some point of time. Inscriptions sometimes also mention Brahmanas with unheard-of *gotras*, or whose *gotras* and *pravaras* do not match. These may represent groups which had invented a Brahmana identity for themselves in order to improve their social and economic prospects.

The nature of *brahmadeya* settlements

While discussing the nature of *brahmadeya* settlements, it is difficult to detach the body of 'facts' from the theoretical frameworks in which they are embedded and, as mentioned earlier, the theoretical frameworks contradict one another in crucial respects. Further, although some general features and trends hold good for most of the subcontinent, *brahmadeyas* of different regions, sub-regions, and periods often had their own specificities.

Not all Brahmana settlements were the result of royal land grants. And although we will never have precise statistics, it is important to remember that *brahmadeya* villages must have formed a small proportion of settlements in most areas.

As already mentioned, from the point of view of the state, the creation of *brahmadeyas* generally involved a renunciation of actual or potential sources of revenue. Land grant inscriptions sometimes state that the land was granted along with treasure trove and hidden deposits, forests, and heirless property. Going by textual evidence, the king theoretically had rights over these, and the transfer of such rights to the donees would have affected the state's prerogatives. Inscriptions also indicate that *brahmadeyas* were not to be interfered with by the state, its officers, or its soldiers. In the Chola empire, certain important *brahmadeyas* had *taniyur* status within the *nadu* (locality), i.e., they were independent of the jurisdiction of the *nadu*. All this indicates that for all practical purposes, the *brahmadeyas* were autonomous islands in the rural landscape, where the Brahmana donees were free to do as they pleased, and where the writ of the state did not apply. The apparent independence of the *brahmadeyas* was, however, tempered by their close relationship with the king.

In some cases, land grants involved the establishment of Brahmana settlements outside the margins of settled agricultural tracts, thereby leading to an extension of the margin of cultivation. But the vast majority of grants were made in areas that were already settled and where land was already being tilled. This is quite clear from the description of where the gifted villages were located, as well as from other details. For instance, post-12th century grants of Bengal often mention the annual income of the gifted land and state that the land was granted along with habitat land (*vastu-bhumi*). Evidently, what the grants usually did was to insert Brahmana donees into an already existing social, economic, and cultural web.

Brahmadeya land could vary from a small plot, a single village, or several villages. The number of donees, likewise, varied from a single Brahmana to several hundreds. There are instances of donees receiving multiple gifts. One of several examples of a vast area being granted to a large number of Brahmanas is recorded in the 10th century Pashchimbhag plate of Srichandra (from Bengal). This records a grant to 6,000 Brahmanas, along with several people associated with a *matha* (monastery) of the god Brahma, and a temple of Vishnu. Three *vishayas* (districts) in Shrihatta *mandala* in Pundravardhana *bhukti* were granted and were transformed into a *brahmapura* that was named Shrichandrapura after the king. The boundary details indicate that *brahmadeyas* were sometimes contiguous to each other, reflecting a trend towards an increase in the number and density of Brahmana settlements in certain areas.

The technical vocabulary of the land grant inscriptions is not always easy to unravel. It is clear, however, that the majority of the grants gave the Brahmana settlements a permanent tax-free status. This meant that the land in question was considered tax free from the point of view of the state. The dues which the state may have actually or potentially been entitled to levy on the villagers were now to be paid to the donee. *Brahmadeyas*, thus, had a special revenue status, and the right to collect and retain revenue was vested in the donees.

The permanent nature of the grant was expressed in statements to the effect that the gift was to last as long as the sun, moon, and stars, i.e., forever. This implied (this point was also sometimes stated explicitly) that after the death of the donee, his rights would be inherited by his successors. A few inscriptions indicate the re-gifting of villages to new donees. This shows that there was sometimes a gap between what was prescribed and what actually happened, but it is likely that the vast majority of gifts were at least initially inherited by the heirs of the original beneficiaries.

Royal land grants generally gave the donees fairly comprehensive rights over the resources of the land. However, beyond the general stipulations about the permanent, hereditary, and tax-free nature of the grants, there were significant differences in the terms of the grants across and within regions. The grants of the Palas, who ruled over parts of Bengal and Bihar between the 8th and 12th centuries usually state that the land was

FURTHER DISCUSSION | ***Kara-shasanas* and *kraya-shasanas***

While most land grant inscriptions specify that the gifted land was tax exempt from the point of view of the state, there are a few exceptions. Such tax-paying grants are known as *kara-shasanas*. The few instances of *kara-shasanas* come from Odisha, Bengal, and Andhra Pradesh. Given below are the examples from Odisha.

The Bobbili plates of Chandavarman state that the registration of the amount payable for the village was fixed at 200 *panas* to be paid annually in advance, as in the case of the 36 (i.e., all other) *agraharas*.

The Ningondi plates of Prabhanjanavarman suggest that the dues for the land were fixed at 200 *panas* to be paid in advance.

The Ganjam grant of the Shvetaka Ganga king Prithivivarmadeva states that the land was given subject to the payment of taxes (*sa-karikritya*), and the annual rent is specified as 4 *palas* of silver.

Among the grants of the Gangas of Kalinganagara, the Kalahandi grant of Vajrahasta seems to stipulate the amount of rent to be paid in the month of Phalguna. The Chicacole grant of Anantavarman states that the revenue was fixed at 10 *mashakas* (probably meaning either 10 coins or silver weighing 10 *mashakas*).

The Angul plate of the Bhauma-Kara queen Dharmamahadevi seems to suggest that Shakemva village was given as a revenue-free gift, while 10 *malas* of land in Deshala village were given subject to the annual payment of 3 *palas* of silver.

The Jurada grant of Nettabhanja states that the annual sum levied on the village was fixed at 4 *palas* of silver, and an additional 4 *palas* was to be paid in the form of a tax known as *khandapala-mundamola* (possibly a tax that had to be paid to the officer in charge of the territorial unit known as the *khanda*).

Among the Shulki inscriptions, the Talcher plate of Kulastambha specifies the *trin-odaka* (i.e., tax) as 2 *palas* of silver, even though the conventional phrases referring to the tax-free nature of the endowment are also present. The Puri plate of Kulastambha specifies the tax as 10 *palas* of silver.

The Talcher plate of the Tunga ruler Gayadatunga states that the tax had been fixed at 4 *palas* of silver. The Asiatic Society plate of the same king refers to the land as having been constituted into a *kara-shasana* and specifies the tax as being fixed at 9 *palas* of silver.

The two sets of Patna plates of the Somavamshi king Janamejaya Mahabhavagupta state that the annual tax had been fixed at 8 and 5 *palas* of silver respectively.

The absence of any specific reference to the tax-free status of the land in the grants of the imperial Gangas may suggest that these grants, too, were not tax free.

All this suggests the existence of at least two major categories of land grants—one that was exempt from all revenue claims of the state and another that remained subject to what was perhaps a nominal tax. The overwhelming majority of the grants fell into the former category.

Apart from the *kara-shasanas* (revenue-paying grants), a small number of inscriptions from early medieval India record secular sale deeds. These are known as *kraya-shasanas*. D. C. Sircar has pointed out that both the *kraya-shasanas* and *kraya-shasanas* often carry the very imprecatory and benedictory verses that are a part of the regular land grants.

Source Upinder Singh, 1994: 66, 240; Sircar, 1952

granted up to its boundaries, grass, and pastures (*sva-sima-trinayuti-gochara-paryanta*), along with its ground (*sa-tala*), with the space above the surface of the ground (*s-oddesha*), with mango and *madhuka* trees (*s-amra-madhuka*), with water and dry land (*sa-jala-sthala*), and along with pits and barren spots (*sa-gartt-oshara*). It was exempt from all dues (*a-kinchit-pragrahya*) and was granted along with all the dues such as the *bhaga*, *bhoga*, *kara*, and *hiranya* (*samasta-bhaga-bhoga-kara-hirany-adi-pratyaya-sameta*). Pala inscriptions also have the term *a-chata-bhata-praveshya*, which means that the land was not to be entered by the king's irregular or regular troops, i.e., soldiers of any kind.

The answer to the question of whether or not the Brahmana donees were granted judicial rights hinges on the interpretation of terms such as *sa-dash-aparadha* and *sa-chauroddharana*. These terms or their variants are found in inscriptions of some dynasties, including the Palas. *Sa-dash-aparadha* has been interpreted in three ways. According to one interpretation, it indicates that the donees were given the right to the proceeds of fines imposed on people who had been found guilty of certain criminal offences. A second interpretation is that it referred to immunity from punishment granted to the donees in case they themselves committed such crimes. The third interpretation is that it refers to the right to try people who were accused of certain offences. The term *sa-chauroddharana* can be interpreted either as indicating the right to punish those found guilty of theft or as the right to realize fines from those found guilty of this crime.

Inscriptions from various parts of the country indicate the wide scope of authority vested with the donees. For example, certain inscriptions of Odisha describe the land as having been granted along with the habitat land and forest (*sa-padr-aranya*). This is similar to post-12th century inscriptions of Bengal which transfer rights over the habitat land (*vastu-bhumi*) to the donees. From the 9th century onwards, some inscriptions of Odisha (those of Udayavaraha and the Bhauma-Kara, Shulki, and Tunga dynasties) state that the land was granted along with control over the outposts in the village, landing or bathing places, and ferries (*sa-kheta-ghatta-nadi-tara-sthan-adi-gulmaka*). This can be understood as referring to rights over dues collected at these spots or as rights over military outposts at these places. Another significant stipulation occurs in inscriptions of the Bhauma-Karas, Adi-Bhanjas, Shulkis, and Tungas, where land is said to have been granted 'along with weavers, cowherds, brewers, and other subjects' (*sa-tantravaya-goku-ta-shaundik-adi-prakritika*). Mention can also be made of certain land grants of Karnataka which indicate the transfer of sharecroppers (*addhikas*) along with the land.

At the same time, many donees did *not* have one important right—the right to alienate land, i.e., to transfer, sell, or dispose of it in any way. As mentioned in Chapter 9, the inalienability of gifted land is indicated by the stipulation that it had been granted according to the *nivi-dharma*, *akshaya-nivi-dharma*, or *aprada-dharma*. Similarly, several Odisha inscriptions contain the term *a-lekhani-praveshataya*. This meant that the land could not be made the subject of another document, i.e., it could not be sold. In such cases, the rights of Brahmana donees over the land gifted to them were more than those of a landlord, but less than those of a landowner.

The impact of Brahmana settlements on agrarian relations

Royal patronage strengthened the economic power of a section of the Brahmana community and led to the further growth of a Brahmana landed elite. Members of this elite cannot be described as 'Brahmana feudatories', as this confuses them with other groups such as *samantas* or subordinate rulers who had to provide military service to their overlords. Even the term 'Brahmana intermediaries' is inappropriate, because the Brahmanas were not passing taxes or material resources on to the kings.

Most historians view the early medieval period as one of agrarian expansion, in which land grants played an important role. But there are major differences of opinion regarding the nature of agrarian relations during this time. How exactly did the establishment of *brahmadeyas* affect the rights of various sections of the rural community—large or small peasant proprietors, tenants, sharecroppers, and landless labourers? Do the long lists of *pariharas* (exemptions) that we find in many of the land grant charters indicate an increasing oppression of the peasantry? Varied answers have been given to such questions. The feudalism school argues that land grants led to an increasing subordination and oppression of rural groups by Brahmana donees. Burton Stein (1980: 63–84) speaks of a Brahmana–peasant alliance in early medieval South India. The proponents of the 'integration' or 'processual' model have not directly addressed the issue of agrarian conflict in detail.

The insertion of Brahmana donees into the village community introduced a new element into agrarian relations, eroding the older ones. As mentioned earlier, in the context of early Brahmana settlements in South India, Rajan Gurukkal has argued that such settlements involved the employment of non-family labour and hence eroded the kinship basis of production relations. The fact that most of the land grants carried with them a tax-free status meant that villagers were supposed to hand over various dues to the donees. Sometimes, inscriptions refer to taxes in a very general way. At other times, they specify a long list of tax exemptions —i.e., taxes that the villagers had to pay to the donees instead of to the state. The fact that the donees were also often given rights over water resources, trees, forests, and habitation area would have affected the rights enjoyed by the village community. Most village-level disputes must have been settled by a section of the village community and, therefore, where inscriptions suggest the possibility of the transfer of judicial rights or the right to collect fines for criminal offences, it is the rights of this section that would have been affected.

There seems little doubt that the terms of the *brahmadeya* grants, varied as they were, created a class of Brahmana donees who enjoyed superior rights and control over the resources and inhabitants of the village. In economic terms, the relationship between Brahmana donees and other rural groups was marked by dominance and exploitation. The substitution of state exploitation and control by the more close-at-hand Brahmana exploitation would probably have meant higher levels of subjection of the average farmer. This is not, however, the equivalent of the institution of serfdom in the European manorial system.

Although the general trend was towards increasing levels of social and economic stratification in rural society, the degree and specificities of this stratification varied in different areas. The level of economic dominance achieved by the donees was affected by a number of variables such as ecology, the availability of arable land, the level of organization among the Brahmanas, and the presence or absence of competing social and corporate groups. In Assam, where cultivable land was not in short supply and where large numbers of non-Brahmanas also held land, the extent of social and economic stratification was not as rigid as in other areas. In South India, corporate organizations of Brahmanas known as *sabhas* furthered the power of the donees. In Kerala, the power and influence of the *sabha* was enhanced by the absence of corporate organizations of other social groups. Increasing rural stratification sharpened socio-economic conflicts, although direct references to such conflicts are few and far between. Certain inscriptions of Karnataka, which do give direct instances of such conflicts, will be discussed further on.

Land grants as part of larger social and cultural processes

B. D. Chattopadhyaya ([1994] 1997: 16) has argued persuasively that the major historical processes operative throughout Indian history, including the early medieval period, were the expansion of state society through the process of local state formation, the transformation of tribes into peasants and caste formation, and cult appropriation and interaction.

Land grants strengthened the position of a section of the Brahmanas (the recipients of royal land grants) in rural areas. They backed the Brahmana's traditionally high social status by political support and economic power, and gave him wide-ranging control over land, resources, and people. Brahmanas emerged as a dominant caste in *brahmadeya* villages. In areas where *brahmadeya* villages were situated close to tribal communities, the latter were introduced to plough agriculture. Some tribal groups were absorbed into the fold of caste society; others were given the status of outcastes or untouchables. The phenomenon of land grants was connected to the proliferation of castes in other ways as well. For instance, the need to record large numbers of land transactions was an important factor in the transformation of the *kayasthas* (scribes) from an occupational group into a caste.

The increase in the number and scale of land grants had an important impact on the Brahmanas themselves. Reference was made earlier to the emergence of regional classifications and hierarchies of status among Brahmanas. As they were drawn into new networks of activities and social relations, Brahmanas came to be divided into a number of sub-castes. In the Tamil Nadu and Karnataka areas, the engagement with temple religion led to the emergence of the Shiva Brahmanas—a Brahmana sub-caste associated with Shiva temples.

Integration into local society could also lead to the modification of marriage practices. In Kerala, while most Brahmanas maintained their patrilineal system, the Brahmanas of Payyanur took to matriliny. The Nambudri Brahmanas had a custom (it is not clear when exactly it began) of the eldest son marrying a Brahmana woman, while the other sons had *sambandam* relations with Nair women. This practice must have been geared towards keeping the property of the Brahmana family intact and consolidated. However, it could only have emerged within the context of the Nair matrilineal society.

The early medieval period saw the increasing popularity of temple-based sectarian religion, and from about the 10th century onwards, inscriptions indicate an increase in royal patronage of temples. Was there any connection between the *brahmadeyas* and these developments? Some Brahmanas moulded their activities to the temple milieu by becoming temple managers, others took on the less prestigious vocation of temple priests. Inscriptions of South India testify to the direct participation of Brahmanas and Brahmana *sabhas* in temple management. Brahmana settlements in Kerala seem to have been temple centred right from the time of the earliest inscriptions. We can therefore, assume that the Brahmanas of the *brahmadeyas* must have played an important role in the spread of temple-oriented religion, in spite of the fact that the inscriptions persist in emphasizing their Vedic, rather than their sectarian, affiliations.

Where established in or near tribal areas, *brahmadeyas* functioned as nodes of reciprocal interaction between Brahmanical and tribal religions, and different sorts of religious syntheses resulted. Tribal communities were exposed to Brahmanism and Brahmanism too was transformed in the course of its interaction with regional, local, and tribal traditions. In times of migration, marriages between Brahmanas and local women may have been an additional factor that furthered the interaction between the Brahmanical and tribal worlds. These interactions were reciprocal, but not equal or evenly balanced, as the Brahmanical elements eventually emerged as dominant. The cult of Jagannatha in Odisha is a good example of the Brahmanization of a tribal deity, and has been analyzed in detail by many scholars (Eschmann, et al. eds, [1978] 2014). R. S. Sharma (1974) has suggested that the interaction between Brahmanical and tribal cultures via land grants played an important role in the emergence and development of Tantra.

The fact that the early medieval period with its proliferation of land grants to Brahmanas also saw such an enormous output in the sphere of Sanskrit literature does not seem to be a coincidence. We have seen how these centuries saw the opening out of avenues of employment for literate, learned Brahmanas in the administrative structures of proliferating royal courts. Brahmana scholars, poets, and dramatists were also feted and patronized in these courts. Patronage through land grants may also have played an important role in promoting and sustaining Brahmana scholarship. Wealth based on the control of land, and the emergence of clusters of settlements inhabited by Brahmana specialists in various branches of Sanskrit learning may have provided a section of the Brahmana intelligentsia with the security and wealth necessary for sustained intellectual activity.

Rural Society

From a general discussion of historical processes that affected the lives of villagers in various parts of the subcontinent, we move on to vignettes of the specificities of rural societies and agrarian relations in different regions. Direct textual evidence regarding the details and textures of rural life in this period is meagre. There is, however, a text that deals exclusively with various aspects of agricultural operations. This is the *Krishi-Parashara* (Majumdar and Banerji, 1960), apparently composed in the Bengal area some time between *c.* 950 and 1100 CE. Ascribed to an author named Parashara, it is written in Sanskrit verse, sprinkled with a few prose *mantras*, in simple and straightforward language and style. The *Krishi-Parashara* does not mention any form of irrigation and declares the knowledge of rainfall to be the root of agriculture. Towards this end, it gives a series of maxims concerning the relationship of planetary movements, seasons, wind direction, and rainfall. It recommends the use of weathervanes comprising a flag tied to a post. It advises the farmer about the importance of manure for a luxuriant paddy crop. It gives instructions for the proper procedure of rice cultivation. It offers advice regarding the kind of plough and draught animals that should be used. Eight different parts of the plough are distinguished. A ploughshare measuring 9 cubits, called the *madika*, is declared to be best suited for all operations.

After explaining how seeds should be preserved, the *Krishi-parashara* discusses the sowing procedure. This, it urges, is best done in Vaishakha (April–May), but the sowing of seeds for transplantation is best undertaken in Shuchi (May–July). After sowing the seeds, the *mayika* (probably a ladder-shaped instrument for levelling rice fields) should be used, otherwise the seeds would not grow evenly. The process of transplantation (*ropanabidhi*) is described and the suggestions about the distance at which seedlings should be planted vary according to prevailing planetary conjunctions. Instructions are given for thinning out the paddy (*kattana*), the removal of weeds (*nistrinikaranam*), and the regulation of water. Pausha (December–January) is harvest time, and details are given for planting the *medhi*, a pillar post in the middle of the threshing floor to which the oxen were tied. After harvesting and threshing the grain, states Parashara, the farmer should have it weighed with an *adhaka* (probably a vessel for measuring grain).

Apart from prescriptions related to agricultural processes, especially the cultivation of paddy, the *Krishi-Parashara* also offers information on early medieval agricultural rituals and festivals in Eastern India. The worship of cows in Kartika (October–November), during the *go-parva* (festival of cows), says Parashara, ensures the health of cattle for a year. The fruits of agriculture are denied, he continues, to the farmer who does not perform the *hala-prasarana*, the ceremonial first ploughing. In connection with fertility beliefs, we may note Parashara's injunctions against allowing the collected seeds to come into contact with a menstruating woman or one who is barren, pregnant, or has just borne a child. We are told that during three days of the month of Ashadha, the Ambuvachi takes place—this is when the earth menstruates and seeds must not be sown. The *mantra* prescribed in the *Krishi-Parashara* for the dispersal of birds and animals from fields and to keep paddy fields free from disease consists of mystical syllables used in Tantric texts. On an auspicious day in Pausha, before the harvesting of paddy, Parashara states that a ceremony called the *pushya-yatra* should be performed. This included ceremonial feasting, dancing, music, and prayers to the sun. Deities mentioned in connection with agricultural operations include Prajapati (the text in fact begins with a salutation to him), Shachi, Indra, Marut, and Vasudha. However, it is Lakshmi who is the recipient of the final prayer at the end of agricultural operations, a prayer which Parashara recommends should be inscribed in granaries to ensure prosperity.

Inscriptions are more forthcoming than most texts about village life. The general term for 'village' in the early medieval inscriptions of Bengal and Bihar is *grama* or *pataka*. The *vastu* (homestead land) formed the core of the village settlement. The boundaries of landholdings were marked by rivers, marshy land, tanks, cattle paths, date and banyan trees, and adjoining villages. Villages sometimes had boundary walls or boundary posts. Inscriptions mention various types of trees—mango, jackfruit, betel nut, coconut, and *madhuka*. Rice was the staple crop and some inscriptions mention paddy fields. Almost all of the land grant inscriptions of the Sena dynasty give the dimensions of the gifted land in meticulous detail, using both surface measures (*nala*, *pataka*, *bhu-pataka*, etc.) as well as seed measures (*drona*, *bhu-drona*, *adhavapa*, etc.), which were probably originally calculated in terms of rice output. It is also interesting to note that all the Sena grants specify the annual revenue income of the gifted land in terms of currency units called *puranas*, *kapardaka-puranas*, and *churnis*. This suggests the maintenance of careful revenue records by the state.

Apart from royal functionaries, most of the land grants of Bengal and Bihar address the cultivators (*kshetrakarah*) or inhabitants (*prativasinah*) of the village. The invariable mention of Brahmanas and the chief among Brahmanas (*Brahmanottarah*) indicates their importance at the village level. A few inscriptions mention certain other groups of people as well. For instance, the Irda plate of Nayapala addresses tradesmen and clerks, in addition to cultivators and residents. The Ramganj plate of Ishvaraghosa includes the *karmakaras* (wage labourers) among those addressed. Some of the Pala grants mention the *puroga*—a village leader or chief. The terms *mahattara* or *mahattama* can be understood as referring to village elders or heads. The term *kutumbin* is increasingly used in the sense of a farmer.

PRIMARY SOURCES | Popular agricultural sayings of early medieval Bengal

Although the Bengali language was fully developed by *c.* 1000 CE, there is scarcely any surviving pre-1300 CE literature in this language. The earliest works include the *Dak Tantra*, popularly known as the *Dakar Bachan*, a Buddhist Tantric work containing aphorisms and wise sayings in old Bengali. Another similar work, which has undergone more changes over time, is the *Khanar Bachan*. According to popular belief, Khana was the daughter-in-law of the astronomer Varahamihira. The 'Dak' of the *Dakar Bachan* lives in popular imagination in the more humble form of a milkman. 'Dak goala' often appears as the signature of the sayings.

The sayings contained in these two works are largely concerned with agricultural matters, although they also touch on astrology, medicine, and domestic issues. Consisting of short, rhyming aphorisms, the *Dakar Bachan* and *Khanar Bachan*, are closely related to the soil and climate of Bengal, and even today serve as agricultural manuals for farmers in this region. Given below is a translation of some of the sayings of Dak and Khana:

If it rains in the month of Agrahayan [November–December], the king goes a-begging.

If it rains in the month of Paush [December–January], money may be had even by selling the chaff.

If it rains at the end of Magh [January–February], the king and his country become blessed.

If it rains in Phalgun [February–March], the millet *chinakaon* (*Peanicum miliaceum*) grows abundantly.

Khana says, the paddy thrives in the sun and the betel in the shade.

If the paddy gets profuse sunshine by day and showers by night, it develops rapidly. Khana says, the drizzling rain in the month of Kartik [October–November] does immense good to the paddy.

Hear, O son of ploughman, put some smut of paddy in the bamboo-bush; if you do so near the root of the shrubs, they will soon cover two *kudas* [about 174 square cubits] of land.

O son of ploughman, plant *patol* (*Trichosanthis dioeca*) in a sandy soil; your expectations will be fulfilled.

Sow the seeds of mustard close, but those of rye at some distance from one another. Cotton plants should be put at the distance of a leap from one another, and jute should by no means be planted near them, for cotton plants will perish if they come in contact with water from the jute-field.

If the sky is covered by mist in Chaitra [March–April] and there is plenty of paddy in Bhadra [August–September], the earth is afflicted with plague and other disasters of that sort.

If a southern wind blows in the month of *Ashadh* [June–July], there will be a flood in the year.

If in Paush there is heat in the atmosphere and cold in Vaishakh [April–May], in that year heavy rainfall will commence from the first part of Ashadh.

If the clouds take the form as if cut by spade and axe, and the wind blows off and on, it should be understood that rainfall will commence in a day or two; O my peasant friend, do not waste time in such weather, but busy yourself in constructing a ridge around your field to preserve the water.

If in the night the clouds cover the sky and there be rain throughout the day, O brother farmer, it will be in vain for you to go to your field for work.

Source D. C. Sen, 1954: 17–27

Ryosuke Furui's (2020) analysis of patterns of social change in the different sub-regions of Bengal between the early 5th and mid-13th century, situates these within their political and economic contexts. This study is based on inscriptions (especially copper plate grants) as well as textual sources such as the Puranas, Dharmashastra, and *kavya*. Steady agrarian expansion is a feature across the centuries. In the mid-6th to early 7th century, in Vanga (southern Bengal), Radha (western Bengal), and Pundravardhana (northern Bengal), local bodies called the *adhikaranas*, known from earlier times, continued to be important. Landed magantes called the *mahattaras* came to the fore. The study reveals an increase in state control and social stratification in the early medieval period. In the 7th and 8th centuries, Brahmana settlements increased in number and Buddhist monasteries patronized by political elites came to the fore. Between the 9th and 11th centuries, the kingdom of the Palas emerged in the northern and western sub-regions and the Chandras in the east. There was an increase in state control over the countryside as well as an increase in social stratification. Subordinate rulers (*samantas*) became important. The role and influence of Brahmanas and Buddhist monasteries in rural areas increased. Between the last quarter of the 11th century and the mid-13th century, Eastern India entered a phase of socio-economic changes in a context wherein political elites were closely allied with Brahmanas and the influence of the latter increased greatly.

Nayanjot Lahiri's (1991) study of the early medieval inscription of Assam suggests that in this region, agricultural activity and settlements were concentrated in or near the valleys of the Brahmaputra and other rivers. Such settlements are especially visible in the Tezpur and Guwahati areas. The frequent mention of rivers and streams in the description of village boundaries confirms the connection between the location of agrarian villages and riverine water resources. The hills that fringe the Assam valley (e.g., the Mikir, Khasi, Garo, Singori, Haji, and Sualkuchi hills) are conspicuous by their absence in the inscriptions. Apart from rivers and streams, the boundaries of villages are indicated by features such as agricultural fields, embankments, ponds, trees, roads, and villages. Rice cultivation was the most important activity in the agricultural villages. The habitations (*vastu*) were located in the midst of clumps of bamboo and fruit trees, surrounded by fields. Pasture land was sometimes situated on the borders of agricultural land, and in some cases may have consisted of agricultural land left fallow for a few years. Embankments geared towards controlling and channelizing water are mentioned frequently. Apart from rice, inscriptions mention various kinds of fruit (jackfruit, figs, black berry, mango, walnut, and sweet root) and trees (banyan, *saptaparna*, *jhingani*, *odiamma*, bamboo, and cane). Trees with trade potential included betel nut, sandalwood, and silk cotton. These do not seem to have been grown in plantations.

In Assam, as in many other areas, kings made grants of land to Brahmanas. The ranks of the rural community comprised Brahmanas, tribals, and several other groups. They included the *kaivarttas* (traditionally associated with fishing and boating) as well as other occupational groups such as potters and weavers. This suggests a combination of agricultural activity with craft specialization. Household units formed the core of agricultural labour. After the 9th century, there is a clear pattern of an increase in the number of agricultural settlements based on wet rice cultivation, which must have been accompanied by demographic growth.

Irrigation played an important role in the expansion of agriculture in early medieval Rajasthan (Chattopadhyaya, [1973] 1997). Tanks and wells were the main sources of artificial irrigation, and there are many references to these in 12th–13th century inscriptions, especially in west Rajasthan, where water was most scarce. These mention different types of wells (*dhimada/dhivada*, *vapi*, *araghatta/araghata/arahata*), tanks, and reservoirs (*tadaga*, *tatakini*, *pushkarini*, etc.). Some tanks seem to have been named after people who built them.

Whether the Persian wheel was in use in early medieval Rajasthan is debated, and hinges on the interpretation of the term *araghatta*. The key issue is whether the reference is to the Persian wheel or to the *noria*, and whether the former was being used in India before the 13th–14th centuries. The *noria* is a wheel which has pots or buckets attached to its rim without a chain for carrying the pots, or a gear mechanism to ensure a continuous flow of water. It could only be used to draw water from close to the surface or from a river. The Persian wheel, on the other hand, had gears and a chain to carry the pots and was associated with a well. The *araghatta* seems to have been different from an ordinary well (*dhimada*) or a step well (*vapi*), and the general consensus among many historians is that it does refer to something similar to the Persian wheel, if not exactly identical to it.

A Persian wheel

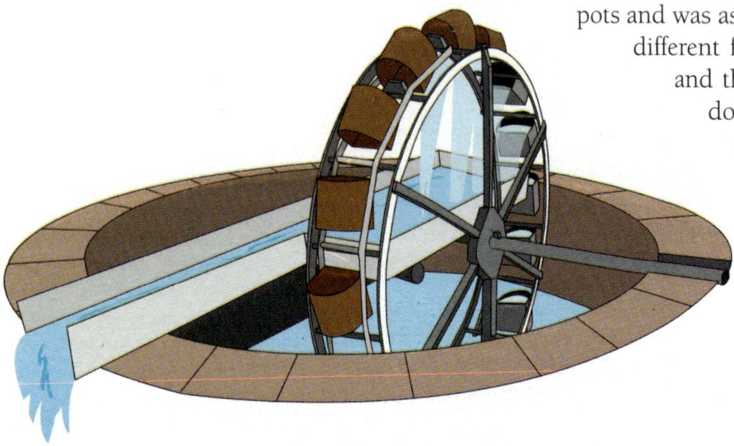

Crops mentioned in the inscriptions of Rajasthan include rice, wheat, barley, *jowar*, millet, and *moong*. Oilseeds such as sesame and sugarcane were cash crops. There are references to crops growing in fields that were irrigated by tanks or wells, and the Dabok inscription of 644 CE suggests the practice of growing two crops a year. The people who controlled irrigation resources included kings, royal officials, corporate bodies such as *goshthis*, and individual cultivators.

There was an expansion of irrigation works in the low rainfall areas of north Gujarat, Saurashtra, Kutch, and south Rajasthan (V. K. Jain, 1990: 24–34). The *Aparajitaprichchha* of Bhuvanadeva, an architectural work composed in Western India in about the 12th century, mentions rivers, lakes, wells, tanks, and *arahatta*s as sources of water for irrigating fields. Inscriptional references to irrigation increased from the 7th–8th centuries to the 11th–13th centuries. Large numbers of tanks, wells, and step wells (*vapi*s) were constructed in the 12th–13th centuries by rulers, nobles, and merchants. The Chaulukyas of Anahilavada took initiatives in building irrigation works and seem to have had an irrigation department. The expansion of irrigation must have facilitated double cropping. Inscriptions of Western India mention irrigated fields of barley, millet, rice, wheat, and pulses. Irrigation played a significant role in the increasing cultivation of cash crops such as sugarcane, oilseeds, cotton, and hemp, which were important items of trade between the 11th and 13th centuries.

The inscriptions of Odisha (Upinder Singh, 1994: 238–39, 241, 196) mention various land measure terms such as *timpira, muraja, nala, hala,* and *mala*. The descriptions of the boundaries of land often contain a mixture of Sanskrit, Oriya, and Telugu words. Village boundaries were indicated by features such as trees, rocks, anthills, trenches, rivers, hills, embankments, tanks, wells, and the boundaries and junctions of adjoining villages. As for water resources, rivers and tanks are mentioned most frequently, while wells occur in fewer inscriptions. The Achyutapuram plates of Indravarman state that no one should cause hindrance to the donee if he opened the sluice of the tank. The reference seems to be to a royal tank (*raja-tataka*), mentioned among the boundaries of the gifted land.

The details of rural life and agrarian relations in South India will be discussed later in this chapter.

One of the questions that arise in the context of agrarian relations and pressures on cultivating groups concerns resistance and rebellion. There are some instances of violent rebellion in the early medieval period, but none of them were 'popular' rebellions. For instance, the Kaivarta rebellion in Eastern India in the late 11th century, which temporarily shook the Pala kingdom, was not a 'popular revolt', nor a 'peasant revolt.' The fact that the Kaivartas were fishermen and boatmen who had turned into landowners suggests a social dimension, but the event was basically a revolt of *samanta*s. The Damara rebellion in early medieval Kashmir involved powerful landlords, not ordinary people. On the other hand, there are epigraphic references to agrarian conflicts, in some cases involving the state, from South India, which will be discussed further on.

Urban Processes

The idea of a decline of cities, urban crafts, trade and money in early medieval times is an important part of the hypothesis of Indian feudalism. In the previous chapter, there was reference to R. S. Sharma's theory of a two-stage urban decay, one beginning in the second half of the 3rd or the 4th century, and the second one starting after the 6th century (Sharma, 1987). Sharma summarized archaeological data from various regions to substantiate his theory. He admits that the Indian literary evidence for urban decay is not strong, but cites the accounts of Xuanzang and Arab writers. His explanation of urban decay centres around a supposed decline in long-distance trade. Urban decline undermined the position of urban-based artisans and traders; artisans were forced to migrate to rural areas; traders were not able to pay taxes; the distinction between town and village became blurred. Urban contraction was, however, accompanied by agrarian expansion. Elsewhere, Sharma, ([1965] 1980: 102–5) cites epigraphic references to the transfer of rights over markets to donees, merchants transferring part of their profits to temples, and the transfer of customs dues from the state to temples. On this basis, he talks of a feudalization of trade and commerce. He argues that a mild urban renewal began in some parts of the subcontinent in the 11th century, and that urban processes were well-established by the 14th century. A revival of foreign trade—linked to an increase in the cultivation of cash crops, better irrigation techniques, increasing demand for commodities, improvements in ship-building and an expansion of internal trade—is cited as a major reason for the urban revival, as well as for the decline of the feudal order.

As mentioned in Chapter 9, the hypothesis of urban decline can be questioned on various grounds. The evidence for this comes from texts, archaeology, and inscriptions. The textual, monumental, and artistic production of the early medieval period would have required substantial urban patronage. Chattopadhyaya ([1986] 1997) argued that in the early medieval period, while some urban centres declined, others continued to flourish, and new ones emerged. Therefore, the early medieval period saw the third phase of urbanism in India. Xuanzang suggests that cities such as Kaushambi, Shravasti, Vaishali, and Kapilavastu were in decline. But he also mentions flourishing ones such as Thaneswar, Varanasi, and Kanyakubja. We know much more about the protohistoric and early historic cities of the subcontinent. The archaeological data on the settlements of the early medieval period is patchy and inadequate. But it is sufficient to show that some early historical cities continued to be inhabited during early medieval times, e.g., Ahichchhatra, Atranjikhera, Rajghat, and Chirand. Chattopadhyaya also marshalls epigraphic evidence from the Indo-Gangetic divide, the upper Ganga basin, and the Malwa plateau, with a special focus on the sites of Prithudaka (modern Pehoa in Karnal district, Haryana), Tattandapura (Ahar, near Bulandshar, UP), Siyadoni (near Lalitpur in Jhansi district, MP), and Gopagiri (Gwalior). While Prithudaka may have been a semi-urban marketing centre, the other three clearly had an urban status in the 9th–10th centuries.

Over the years, the understanding of the urban processes in early medieval India has grown substantially. There is a realization among scholars that the archaeology of early medieval (and medieval) India has been neglected for far too long; there is a greater focus now on redressing this lacuna (see, e.g., Swadhin Sen et al. [Eds.], 2023). There is also greater sensitivity among historians when it comes to exploring textual representations of city life. Due to these two factors, is likely that in the coming years, our understanding of urban processes in early medieval India will further expand significantly. The examination of urban centres cutting across the conventional divides of periodization is also likely to yield useful results (see Mukhopadhyay and Ghosh. [Eds.], 2022). In West Bengal and Bangladesh, archaeological explorations and excavations have revealed several large early medieval sites and settlements (see Chowdhury and Chakravarti. [Eds.], 2018, Vol. 1).

Literary works are important sources of information on city life, reflecting the perspectives of the authors, and moulded according to the literary conventions of the time. However, they involve the literary imagination and should not be read literally. Literature offers representations of city life, not factual descriptions. But these representations were rooted in history. Although they may seem repetitive and stereotypical, they are not identical, and they display changes across time and space. Which cities are mentioned is also a point of interest. As is the case with all sources, it is necessary to read the texts carefully and to read between the lines in order to make historical inferences. Literary representations of cities to be understood in their chronological, spatial, and historical contexts. The challenge is to get glimmers of city life of the time through the apparently conventional, stylized descriptions. Kanad Sinha's (2022) analysis of representations of city life in the *Dashakumaracharita* indicates that although Dandin remained faithful to *kavya* conventions in his descriptions of cities, there is much in these descriptions that is specific to his own time and experiences. Interestingly, Kanchipuram, where Dandin lived, is only mentioned fleetingly in the text, but Sinha argues that its elements may have seeped into descriptions of other cities. Given the fact that the early medieval period was marked by the production of a large and varied range of literary works in several languages, there is great scope for analyzing these works skilfully and carefully in order to understand the nature of urban processes that were unfolding during the time they were written. Much more analysis is required of the textual representations of city life in early medieval texts. Due to the qualitative difference between literary and archaeological evidence, we should not expect them to mirror each other.

With regard to the institutional frameworks of trade operations in market towns, Ranabir Chakravarti (2002: 187–219) has emphasized the importance of *mandapikas* in the trade circuits of early medieval India. These were, for the most part, local centres of exchange that constituted an intermediate level between the small, periodic markets (*hatta, hattika*) and larger trade centres (*pattana*). The *mandapikas* were integrated into their rural hinterlands, and functioned as nodes of exchange of various types for edible staples and cash crops. They were also centres for the collection of commercial tolls and duties. Analogous to these were the *penthas* in the Deccan and the *nagarams* further south. These were centres of trade and administrative units between the village and district levels. Chakravarti also draws attention to the tradition of *raja-shreshtis* (royal merchants). Although the references to such merchants go back to the 4th/3rd century BCE, they are mentioned more frequently in the early medieval period, especially in the Deccan and South India. These royal merchants may have procured luxury items and war animals for rulers. It is not certain whether they also collected revenue at trade centres on the king's behalf. Thus, the information about trade networks in the early medieval period has been steadily increasing. No longer can it be considered as a period marked by a subcontinental decline in internal and long-distance trade.

With regard to monetary history, John S. Deyell (1990: 4–7) has convincingly shown that money was not scarce in early medieval India, nor were states of the time suffering from a financial crisis. There was a reduction of coin types and a decline in the aesthetic quality of coins, but not in the volume of coins in circulation. The main focus of Deyell's work is on the post-1000 CE period, but the roots of the currency systems of that period lay in the preceding centuries. He also points out that the debasement of coinage was not necessarily a signal of financial crisis of the state nor of a general economic crisis. In fact, it could reflect an increasing demand for coins in a situation where the supply of precious metals was restricted. Such shortages occurred for a variety of reasons, from time to time, in different parts of the world. We know that Afghanistan was a major source of silver for the Indian subcontinent. Deyell argues that North India experienced a sustained shortage of silver in 1000 CE (and in some places as early as 750 CE), and that this made it necessary for rulers to dilute the silver content of their coins.

Silver coins known as 'Gadhaiya coins' issued by merchants were circulating in various parts of Gujarat and Western India. The Pratiharas issued silver coins. But evidence of dynastic issues seems lacking in the case of the Palas, Senas, and Rashtrakutas. In recent years, certain coin types have been identified as dynastic issues. For instance, apart from the already known silver coins of Harsha, certain gold coins with the legend 'Pratapa' have been identified as issued by the Pushyabuti king Prabhakaravardhana or Harshavardhana (Deyell, 2017). While silver and gold coins are known from south-east Bengal (Samatata and Harikela coins), it is generally thought that the Pala kings did not issue any coins. However, a gold coin depicting a king hunting a lion or boar on horseback on the obverse, and the depiction of Lakshmi on the reverse, along with the legend 'Sriman Dharmapalah' has been attributed to the Pala king Dharmapala (Tandon, 2006). Its similarities with a few other gold coins may suggest that they too were Pala issues. The Cholas issued coins made of gold, silver, and copper.

Gold coin (obverse and reverse) of Dharmapala

Apart from attributing certain coin types to certain dynasties, there has been major scholarly shift from a focus on coin types to understanding monetary systems. For instance, in the Bay of Bengal region, the monetary system was mainly based on moneys of account, using cowries as a standard of value (see Deyell, 2019; Deyell and Mukherjee. [Eds.], 2019). Most transactions in the Indian Ocean world were done through a combination of moneys of account and cowries. Bengal transitioned from a mixed monetary system to a coin-based one with the establishment of the Bengal Sultanate in the 12th century.

From the 7th century onwards, the Arabs swiftly expanded their political dominion into northern Africa, the Mediterranean region, Central Asia, and Sindh. Their territorial conquests in Egypt, Persia, and Sindh gave them strategic control over Indian Ocean trade. The political success of the Arabs had important implications for the spread of Islam as well as for the expansion of international trade. Arab conquests and the establishment of the Ummayad and later, the Abbasid caliphates, made it possible for Arab traders to emerge as lead players in trade along the overland as well as the maritime routes that connected Europe with East Asia.

Texts such as the 9th century *Ahbar as-Sin wa'l-Hind* describe the long maritime journeys made by Arab traders from ports in Oman to Quilon (Kollam) in Kerala and on to China, via the port of Kalah-bar (probably located north of Singapore) and the Malacca Straits. K. N. Chaudhuri (1985: 37–41) has shown out that by the 11th century, the Indian Ocean trade was divided up into smaller segments—the stretch from the Red Sea and Persian Gulf to Gujarat and Malabar; from the Indian coast to the Indonesian archipelago; and from South-east Asia to East Asia. Great trade emporia emerged at the junction of these three segments, providing merchants with cargo, shipping services, and protection. They included Aden, Hormuz, Cambay, Calicut, Satgaon, Malacca, Guangzhou, and Quanzhou. Chaudhuri highlights the importance of silk, porcelain, sandalwood, and black pepper in the Asian trade of medieval times. These commodities were exchanged for various items such as incense, horses, ivory, cotton textiles, and metal products. India's maritime networks were strongly oriented eastwards, towards China and East Asia. Sri Lanka was an important hub of Indian Ocean trade.

Traders of the subcontinent were part of a wider world of overland and maritime trade interactions that connected Africa, Europe, and various parts of Asia (see Pearson, 2003; Ray, 2003; Alpers, 2014; Beaujard, 2020; Ranabir Chakravarti, 2020). Apart from commodities, people, texts, knowledge, icons, religious traditions, and ideas moved along the routes of trade. The ocean was a vehicle for trade and cultural contact, but it could also be a space for competition, conflict, and violence.

The history of Indian Ocean trade and the role of subcontinental traders in it, can be reconstructed on the basis of a variety of textual, epigraphic, numismatic, and archaeological sources. A vast stretch of water extended from the Red Sea to the Strait of Malacca, and from east Africa to Australia. Shipwrecks bear vivid testimony to the perils of oceanic voyages (Guy, 2019). For instance, the wreck of a ship found at Phanom Surin near Bangkok reveals a vessel made of wooden planks sewn together using coconut coir. The artefacts found on board included pottery of Chinese, Burmese, and Persian Gulf origin, along with ordinary pots used for cooking on board. An inscription found on a jar in the Middle Persian Pahlavi script reads 'Yazd-bozed' (God saves) and has been dated to the 8th century. The remains of a 9th century shipwreck were found near Belitung island in Indonesia (see Flecker, 2001). Excavations indicated that this ship was carrying a large cargo of ceramics, mostly Chinese Changsa Ware. Other items found in the shipwreck included 10 tonnes of lead ingots, cast iron cauldrons (some with tripod legs), copper alloy bowls, and grinding stones. An analysis of the ship's construction indicates that it was an Indian or Arab vessel. It may have been an Indian ship supplying Chinese goods to West Asia, or it could have been an Indian-built ship owned by Arab traders.

The analysis of the literary and epigraphic sources of Western India (*c.* 1000–1300 CE) by V. K. Jain (1990) indicates that traders of this region were carrying on business in luxury goods as well as in staples such as foodgrains, pulses, salt, oil, ghee, jaggery, coconut, betel leaf, arecanut, spices, textiles, pottery, animals, fragrances (e.g., sandalwood, camphor, musk, aloe, and saffron), ivory, and gold. Jain suggests that Indian traders of Western India tended to confine their operations to coastal and internal trade, leaving the operations further afield to the Arabs and others. The main imports into Western India included metals (both base and precious), silk, gems, spices, wine, frankincense, and horses. As far as exports are concerned, there was a change during the 11th–13th centuries. Before this, India's exports mainly comprised luxury goods such as fine textiles, silk, and spices. From the 11th century onwards, although these remained important, there was a significant expansion in the range of exported items, which came to include sugar, cotton and flax cloth, buckram, tanned leather, leather goods, and weapons such as swords and spears. Hoards of *gadahiya/gadhaiya* coins of the 7th–12th centuries have been found in various parts of Western India, indicating the use of money as a medium of exhange. Traders also used *hundikas* or bills of exchange, which facilitated large-scale transactions without the use of money. Inscriptions often mention toll houses (*shulka-mandapikas*), and commercial taxes were an important source of state income.

Merchants played an important role in the administrative organization of the Chaulukyas, occupying important civic and military posts such as those of the *mahamatya* and *dandadhipati*. Many of the traders of Western India were Jainas. Jaina texts such as the *Shatsthanakaprakarana* of Jineshvara Suri (11th century) laid down the ethical code that Jaina merchants should follow. Merchants of Gujarat made their mark not only as patrons of learning but also as writers of works of *kavya*, poetics, philosophy, and grammar. Hemachandra, who wrote several important Jaina texts as well as works on subjects such as grammar, metrics, and philosophy, was the son of a merchant of Dhandhuka. Gujarat merchants made generous grants to support the building of temples, wells, and tanks. The temples at Mount Abu and Girnar reflect such patronage. Inscriptions from this region also refer to tolls and taxes that were due from merchants being transferred to religious establishments for their maintenance and for the celebration of festivals.

India's trade with South-east Asia and China grew in the early medieval period. The trade with South-east Asia will be discussed in the later section on urban processes of South India. Tansen Sen (2003: 236–37) has argued that between the 7th and 15th centuries, there was a major change in the nature of Sino-Indian interactions, from Buddhist-dominated to trade-centred exchanges. By this time, China itself had emerged as a major centre of Buddhism. The increasing Sinification of Chinese Buddhism and the growing importance of indigenous Chinese Buddhist schools and practices had led to a reduction in the importance of cultural transmission from India to China. The stream of Buddhist monks moving between India and China continued in the 10th and 11th centuries, as did the project of translating Indian texts into Chinese. But Indian Buddhism was no longer an essential lifeline for the survival and growth of Chinese Buddhism. Sino-Indian trade links in early medieval times can be divided into three phases. The 7th–9th centuries saw a continuation of the earlier demand for Buddhist ritual items. In the 9th–10th centuries, there was a decline in overland trade between India and China due to disturbed political conditions in Central Asia and Myanmar. In the late 10th century, both tributary and commercial relations were revived, and overland and maritime trade grew significantly.

Xuanzang mentions silk among the most popular materials for clothing in India. One of the Sanskrit words for silk is *kausheya*. This was probably indigenously produced silk, as opposed to *china-patta* or *chinamshuka*, which was either Chinese silk or silk woven from Chinese yarn in India (Liu, 1996: 49–72). As mentioned in Chapter 9, although silk was manufactured in India, it was not as fine as Chinese silk, and the demand for the latter therefore, continued. Silk fabric and garments were important gift items brought to India by Chinese diplomatic missions and monks. However, by the 11th century, Chinese porcelain had overtaken silk as an import into India. Some of the porcelain was carried further westwards by traders to the lands bordering the Persian Gulf and Red Sea, where too it was much in demand. Other Chinese items imported into India included hides, vermilion, fruits (such as pears and peaches), camphor, lacquer, and mercury. There is also mention of metals such as gold, silver, and copper coming from China. As for items imported by China from India, these seem to have increased in range in the 11th century, and included horses, frankincense, sandalwood, *gharu* wood, *sapan* wood, spices, sulphur, camphor, ivory, cinnabar, rose water, rhinoceros horn, and putchuck. Some of these items, such as frankincense and rose water, originated in the Persian Gulf area and moved on eastwards from the Indian ports. Others originated in India. By the end of the 13th century, Indian textiles became one of the most important Indian exports to China (Tansen Sen, 2003: 182–85).

The expanding trade between China and India was accompanied by a re-orientation of routes. From the 8th century onwards, the maritime routes between India and China became more frequently used than the overland ones. One of the sea routes went through the Andaman and Nicobar Islands, while another one passed by the Bay of Bengal ports on to Sumatra and the South China Sea. The increasing preference for the sea routes was partly due to changes in maritime technology, specifically the shift from sewn ships to sturdier ones with nailed hulls.

The diversification of trade commodities and trade links seems to be the general pattern as far as Indian trade in the early medieval period is concerned. Meera Abraham's (1988) analysis of the list of commodities mentioned in inscriptions of the Ayyavole guild indicates a shift away from luxuries towards a greater emphasis on staples and basic goods such as yarn, textiles, dyes, processed iron, pepper, and horses. Abraham also points out that in the mid-12th century, inscriptions started recording the import of large quantities of goods imported into South India from West Asia, South-east Asia, and China. The imports included precious stones, pearls, perfumes, aromatics, myrobalans, honey, wax, textiles including silk, spices, horses, and elephants. Lists of export items handled by members of the South Indian merchant guilds include cotton textiles, spices (e.g., pepper), iron, dyes, ivory, areca, and putchuk. From the 13th century, the west coast became increasingly important. Quilon (Kollam) was an important port and the Chinese Yuan emperors sent missions to this place. The shift in the centre of gravity towards the western ports of South India and Sri Lanka indicates an expansion of Indian trade links with Egypt and West Asia.

While discussions of early medieval maritime trade tend to be dominated by a focus on the ports of Gujarat and South India, the Bay of Bengal ports also had a role to play, even though the activity was not as intense as that off the Malabar, Coromandel, or Gujarat coasts. Till the 8th century, Tamralipti (Tamluk in Medinipur district) was the most important port in Bengal. Samandar, probably located near Chittagong, rose to prominence in the post-8th century CE and is frequently mentioned in the Arab accounts.

There was also active interaction between the Odisha coast, Sri Lanka, South-east Asia, and East Asia. Excavations at Khalakapatna (on the left bank of the Kushbhadra river in Puri district) and Manikapatna (on the channel connecting Chilika lake with the Bay of Bengal) have yielded important evidence. Chinese celadon ware and porcelain, two Chinese copper coins, and some glazed pottery which may have originated from West Asia were found at Khalkatapatna, which seems to have been an important port between the 11th and 14th centuries. Manikapatna has revealed a cultural sequence from the early historical period to the 19th century CE. Chinese pottery, including celadon ware (and possibly also local imitations), and Chinese copper coins have been found here.

There is, thus, substantial evidence of various regions of the subcontinent being involved in overland and maritime trade in the early medieval period. The trade networks were linked with religious networks that connected India with the regions of East Asia and South-east Asia (for the latter, see Ray, 2021). The importance of seafaring in the Indian Ocean world is reflected in the frequent appearance of Avalokiteshvara as savior from the eight *bhayas* (fears) and protector of mariners at many sites in India and Sri Lanka.

Historical Processes in South India

The nature of South Indian states

We now move to a more specific focus on South India. The historiography of early medieval South India has gone through several distinct phases. The writings of pioneering scholars such as Nilakantha Sastri represented a major initiative in weaving together the scattered data from diverse sources into a larger historical narrative. However, this narrative was tinged with nationalist fervour, and there was a tendency to glorify the Chola state, which was presented as a highly centralized empire. This approach came in for severe criticism in the 1960s, when Burton Stein ([1975] 1976) put forward a hard-hitting critique of the 'traditional historiography' represented by scholars like Sastri, T. V. Mahalingam, and A. Appadorai. According to Stein, a major flaw in their interpretation of the early medieval polity of South India was that they did not relate the state to society and economy, especially to the agrarian order. He pointed out that there was an inconsistency between the glorification of the Chola state as a strong, centralized, bureaucratized monarchy, and the simultaneous eulogy of strong local self-governing institutions.

The fault, according to Stein, did not lie in the understanding of the economy, but in the characterization of the state.

Central to Stein's alternative model were the concepts of sacral kingship, segmentary state, peasant society, and peasant state. According to Stein, the theory as well as practice of South Indian kingship reflects a sacred kingship rather than bureaucratic or 'constitutional' kingship. The effective power of kings and their control over people and resources were confined to the core areas around their political centres, outside which kings were basically ritual figures. Land revenue was extracted only from a limited area and states were dependent on looting expeditions for their sustenance. Stein denied the existence of a Chola bureaucratic machinery through which the state could have made its presence and control felt at the local level. He also denied the existence of a Chola standing army, arguing that military power was distributed among various groups including peasants, merchants, and artisans. Deprived of the supports of a bureaucracy, revenue collection machinery of any significant dimension, and standing army, the hypothesis of a centralized Chola state collapses.

While it is true that the omnipotence of the Chola state was exaggerated by earlier scholars, there are many problems in the alternative offered by Stein. It is difficult to accept his description of early medieval South Indian kingship as purely sacral. Such a description ignores the basis of enduring power and military success achieved by dynasties such as the Cholas. Stein emphasizes that looting expeditions were the basis of ancient Indian kingdoms and cites the military expeditions of Samudragupta and the petty cattle raiders of South India as examples. It can be countered that these two examples actually reflect two qualitatively different types of political systems. War and loot were certainly part and parcel of the politics of ancient and early medieval kingdoms, but the formation and persistence of empires such as the Maurya, Gupta, Satavahana, and Chola indicates that they were based on something more than sporadic looting expeditions. Some sort of administrative structure and revenue infrastructure did exist in these polities, and long-term or sustained military success was ultimately based on the state's ability to mobilize and control people and resources. Stein also creates an artificial dichotomy between ritual sovereignty and 'real' power. In fact, he confuses effective political or coercive power with centralized control.

The research of Karashima (1984; Karashima. [Ed.]., 2014, 84–97) indicates that several titles in Chola inscriptions refer to administrative offices, and that the Chola kings made certain attempts to centralize their administration. This is confirmed by the study of tax terms by Subbarayalu (1982) and Shanmugan (1987). Heitzman's analysis of tax terms and functional titles in Chola inscriptions shows that although the early Chola state reveals few hints of an elaborate administrative system, from about 1000 CE, a hierarchy of royal land revenue officials began to reach out in a thorough and systematic fashion to villages throughout Cholamandalam. There was also an increase in the personal involvement of Chola kings in issuing orders aimed at directing and re-organizing land taxation (Heitzman, 1997: 227).

The framework that Stein considers most applicable to early medieval South India is that of the segmentary state. As will be discussed further on, the usefulness of this model and its applicability to early medieval South India can be questioned. Stein's description of the early medieval South Indian state as a peasant state is even more questionable and seems to represent an extreme reaction to the idea of a highly centralized monarchy. The existence of corporate village organizations does not indicate that peasants exercised political power at a higher level.

The feudalism model has been applied to early medieval South India by scholars such as Kesavan Veluthat (1993) and R. N. Nandi (2000). Other scholars prefer to sidestep both the segmentary and feudal models and to focus on specific issues. For instance, Heitzman discusses the mode of production and the links between land, labour, and the state structure. Similarly, while marshalling an impressive range of inscriptional data, Karashima (1984: xxiv–xxvi) holds that there are problems with both the feudal and the segmentary models, and that the Chola period did in fact see the formation of a

KEY CONCEPTS | The segmentary state, according to Southall and Stein

The idea of the segmentary state is based on anthropologist Aidan W. Southall's *Alur Society: A Study in Processes and Types of Domination* (1953). Southall argued that the political system of the African Alur tribe combined lineage segmentation and political specialization. Southall discussed the process whereby this immigrant tribe established its domination over a series of chiefless societies, often without the use of force. According to him, in many parts of the world, at most times in history, the form of political organization has been segmentary rather than unitary.

Southall made a fundamental distinction between a unitary and a segmentary state. The unitary state is a political system in which there is a central monopoly of power exercised by a specialized administrative staff within defined territorial limits. The power structure of a segmentary state is different. In this case (this is somewhat confusing) 'specialized political power is exercised within a pyramidal series of segments tied together at any one level by the oppositions between them at a higher level and ultimately defined by their joint opposition to adjacent unrelated groups' (Southall, 1953: 260). Further:

1. Territorial sovereignty is recognized but limited and relative. Political authority is strongest near the political centre and gets more and more diluted towards the periphery, often shading off into a ritual hegemony.
2. There is a centralized government, but there are also many peripheral foci of administration over which the centre exercises only limited control.
3. There is specialized administrative staff at the centre, but it is repeated on a reduced scale at all the peripheral foci of administration.
4. Monopoly of the use of force is successfully claimed to a limited extent and within a limited range by the central authority, but legitimate force of a more restricted type is associated with the peripheral foci as well.
5. There are several levels of subordinate foci of power. They are organized pyramidally in relation to the central authority. Similar powers are repeated at each level, but with a decreasing range. The peripheral authorities are reduced images of the central authority.
6. The more peripheral a subordinate authority, the greater opportunity it has to change its allegiance from one power pyramid to another. Segmentary states are thus, flexible, fluctuating, and interlocking.

Burton Stein (1980) added some additional points to Southall's description of the segmentary state. He suggested that sovereignty in a segmentary state is dual, consisting of actual political control and ritual sovereignty. There could be a multiplicity of centres, one a source of ritual sovereignty, the others exercising political control over territorial segments. Stein asserted that the specialized administrative staff at the centre may have its counterparts at the level of the lower segments as well. Further, the organization of the segmentary state is pyramidal in two senses—first, the relationship between the centre and the peripheral foci of power is in all cases identical; and second, there is opposition which is complementary among the parts of the state as a whole, as well as within any constituent segment.

The problem is that the segmentary state is a conceptual category that includes within its purview states that have very little in common except a certain 'segmentation' of power—take the contrasts between the Alur tribal system and medieval European feudal states. Southall actually allowed for a whole range of segmentary states, with systems such as the Alur standing at a lower rung, and suggested that it would be a good idea to identify different varieties of segmentary states.

In view of the catch-all nature of the category of the segmentary state, it does not seem to be a very useful theoretical model for understanding state systems. As for early medieval South India, the empirical evidence does not correspond to Southall's or Stein's concept of a segmentary state. The focus on segmentation gives inadequate attention to the processes making for integration. And the abstract discussion of the relations within and among the various segments, as described by both Southall and Stein, is not particularly clear.

centralized state. But he asserts that his aim is to focus on certain specific issues, not to present any overarching theoretical framework.

Early medieval South Indian states were neither highly centralized, nor devoid of real power. The relations between paramount kings and their political subordinates can be described as feudal, but the relationships between kings and the beneficiaries of their land grants do not fit into the feudalism model. Therefore, while all three theoretical frameworks for early medieval India have some perceptive elements, none of them are acceptable in their entirety. As mentioned earlier, a challenge for future research is to move out of the straitjackets of existing models (see Karashima. [Ed.], 2014).

The volume of data on state and society in early medieval South India has been growing steadily. However, much of the scholarship has focused on the Chola state and society. An important issue to be kept in mind is that South India should not be considered as a homogeneous unit for the purposes of analysis, nor should its history in the early medieval period be exclusively equated with the Cholas. There were differences in the historical processes unfolding in the core areas of Cholamandalam in the Kaveri valley and those of other areas such as Kerala, Karnataka, and Andhra. This issue has been factored into the following discussion, wherever possible.

Administrative structures

Early medieval states of South India were clearly not as powerful or centralized as suggested by Sastri, nor as ineffectual as suggested by Stein. The important functionaries associated with the royal court included the king's advisers and priests. Chola inscriptions mention the Brahmana *purohita* and *rajaguru*. The Pallavas and Cheras had a council of ministers and the Pandya inscriptions refer to *mantrins* (ministers) who may have been organized into a council. Other high-ranking functionaries who were closely associated with the king in early medieval courts, but whose functions are not certain, include the *adhikari*, *vayil ketpar*, and *tirumandira-olai* (Veluthat, 1993: 75–86).

Karashima, Subbarayalu, and Matsui's (1978) concordance of personal names, epithets and titles in Tamil inscriptions reveals several functionaries who were associated with the central administration. The larger number of terms for offices and officials in the Chola inscriptions compared to those of the Pallavas, Pandyas, and Cheras, suggest an expansion of the administrative structure, especially from the reign of Rajaraja I (985–1014) onwards. After the reign of Kulottunga I (1070–1120), there is a decline in such references, indicating that a reverse process had set in. The titles of individuals associated with administrative offices include *araiyan*, an honorific for important people. Some functionaries associated with the court had titles such as *udaiyan*, *velan*, and *muvendavelan*, indicating that they were landowners.

Officials at the *nadu* (locality) level included the *nadu-vagai*, *nadu-kakani-nayakam, nadu-kuru*, and *kottam-vagai*. The precise functions of many of these officers are not certain and there seems to have been some overlap in their duties. There are also indications of a hereditary element in official appointments.

The Cholas had a large land revenue department consisting of several rungs, but it was largely concerned with maintaining accounts. The assessment and collection of revenue were undertaken by corporate bodies such as the *ur*, *nadu*, *sabha*, and *nagaram*, and sometimes by local chieftains, who passed the revenue on to the centre. In the early 11th century, during the reign of Rajaraja I, the Chola state initiated a massive project of land survey and assessment, and there was a reorganization of the empire into units known as *valanadus*. Two surveys were also conducted in the reign of Kulottunga I. In the post-Rajaraja period, the revenue department was known as *puravu-vari-tinaikkalam* or the *shri-karanam*.

Certain frequently occurring terms in inscriptions give information about the dues imposed by the state on cultivators. *Eccoru* referred to the obligation of villagers to provide food for state officials. *Muttaiyal* and *vetti* meant the obligation to provide labour services. *Kudimai* was another term for such labour services. In the early Chola period, there were many land revenue terms such as *puravu*, *irai*, *kadan/kanikkadan*, and *opati*. *Kadamai* emerged as the most important land revenue term in the later Chola period. Its precise rate is uncertain (it may have been as high as 40 to 50 per cent of the produce), and it seems to have been collected in kind. The *antarayam* was a rural tax realized in cash. There is a steady rise in the number of revenue terms in inscriptions, peaking during the reign of Rajendra II, and declining from the time of Kulottunga I.

The many military expeditions of the kings of early medieval South India suggest an effective army organization, but details are meagre. The personal bodyguards attached to kings and chieftains were connected to their lords through ties of loyalty. There was a hereditary element in their selection and they seem to have been given assignments of land revenue. There was some sort of standing army, recruited and maintained by the state, and the *senapati* and *dandanayakam* were important military officers.

Chola inscriptions mention several military contingents. Periodical levies of troops from the chieftains supplemented the standing army, when required. The expedition to Sri Lanka during the reign of Rajaraja I and the Srivijaya expedition during the reign of Rajendra I are often cited as evidence of a Chola navy. Whether this was a regular, separately recruited and organized naval force, or whether we are looking at episodes when soldiers were transported across the oceans, is not certain.

Regarding the administration of justice, scholars such as K. A. N. Sastri suggested the existence of a central or royal court of justice called the *dharmasana*. However, this seems more a reflection of the idea that the king was theoretically the highest court of appeal. The day-to-day administration of justice seems to have been actually handled by various local bodies such as the *sabha*.

Rural society

Burton Stein (1980: 67–68) described the society of early medieval South India as a 'peasant society'. By this, he meant the following: most people of the time lived in settled agrarian villages; peasant agriculture and related occupations provided the main means of subsistence and wealth; the structure of social relations corresponded to the characteristics of peasant societies, including asymmetrical power relations with those powerful enough to demand a share of the produce; well-developed corporate organizations existed; and there were effective alliances among various corporate elements. Stein stated that his aim was to describe the agrarian basis of South Indian history during Chola and post-Chola times. But in attempting to redress the balance, and in emphasizing the peasantry as the prime social, economic, political, and cultural element in South Indian history, he ended up sidelining kings, chieftains, merchants, and other urban groups.

Stein acknowledged that caste principles of hierarchy and inequality gave an important specific quality to Indian peasant society, but argued that this feature could not be used to raise serious doubts about whether this was indeed a peasant society. In spite of the existence of segregation, internal hierarchy, and exploitation, in India, as elsewhere in the world, peasant life was marked by social, ritual, and political interdependence and co-operation. Stein also asserted that, typical of peasant societies, the Indian peasant household was multi-dimensional, despite the caste-based division of labour and occupational specialization. Stein's treatment of the peasantry as a virtually undifferentiated mass, at the most divided between lower and dominant sections, is questionable.

Another problematic aspect of Stein's hypothesis is his description of the relationship between Brahmanas and peasants as an alliance. He described Brahmanas as the prime mediators of order and legitimacy and saw their interaction with the peasantry as the primary cultural nexus of South Indian peasant society during the early medieval period. The Brahmana–peasant alliance was a self-consciously worked out one, based on self-interest. Given the popularity of Buddhism and Jainism in the urban centres, Brahmanas realized that they were best off establishing their base in rural areas. As for the peasants, Stein suggested that they were aware of their need to forge some sort of cohesion and ideological unity against their perennial enemies—the hill people. The entire argument is unconvincing.

As far as the specific features of South Indian village life are concerned, it is evident that the basic unit of rural society was the *ur*. This term refers to the villages themselves as well as to the village assemblies. These were non-*brahmadeya* villages, and were also known as *vellanvagai* villages. Inscriptions indicate that apart from agricultural fields, these villages included the habitation area, sources of drinking water, irrigation works, pasture land, and cremation grounds. In the habitation area, the *ur-nattam* or *ur-irukkai* represented the residential quarter of the landowning farmers, the *kammanacheri* was the residential quarter of artisans, and the *paraicheri* the residential quarter of agricultural labourers.

A hierarchy of rights and statuses existed at the village level. These included the socially and spatially segregated groups, also considered as ritually impure—the *paraiyar*. Then, there were the cultivating groups known as the *vellalar*, among whom a distinction can be made between landowning farmers (*kaniyudaiyar*) and tenant farmers (*ulukudi*). The *vellalas* were identified with the Shudra *varna*, but unlike in the north, the Shudra tag did not carry with it connotations of a lowly social status and discrimination. This is because the *vellala* were an economically powerful group; holders of that important basis of wealth—land. This gave them a status that was almost as high as that of the Brahmanas. Service groups such as potters and blacksmiths may have had control over small plots of land. An analysis of land transfers in the late Chola period indicates the emergence of economically powerful and locally influential landlords.

There are a few interesting references in Karnataka inscriptions to villages headed by women (Nandi, 2000: 217). For instance, an inscription belonging to 902 CE mentions the wife of a man named Bittayya as the head of a village named Bharangiyur. An inscription of 1055 refers to a woman named Chandiyabbe as a *gavundi* (village chieftain) and another woman named Jakkiyabbe as her *mantraki* (counsellor). An epigraph from the Shikarpur *taluk* mentions the wife of a district headman succeeding her husband to his office after his death.

The inscriptional evidence of royal land grants to Brahmanas in South India goes back to the 3rd/4th century, and this practice became quite widespread in the early medieval period. Karashima (1984: xx–xxi) suggests that there was an important difference

PRIMARY SOURCES | The history of a Karnataka village

Kanakatte is a village in the Arsikere *taluk* of Hassan district in south Karnataka. B. D. Chattopadhyaya analyzed 15 inscriptions from this place in order to reconstruct the history of this village over about a hundred years. In the inscriptions, the village is called Kalikatti.

The earliest inscription is inscribed on a hero stone at Arakere. Dating to *c.* 890 CE and belonging to the reign of a Ganga king named Satyavakya Permanadi Rachamalla, it records the death of a *samanta* named Shri Muttara. Shri Muttara died heroically fighting a battle against the Nolambas. We are told that he was rewarded posthumously with the award of two villages—Arikere (which can be identified with the find-spot of the inscription) and Kalikatti. The benefit of this endowment must have gone to Shri Muttara's descendants.

Over two centuries later, Kalikatti is mentioned in two inscriptions belonging to the reign of the Hoysala king Vishnuvardhana (1108–42 CE). It had obviously become an important place as it is described as the foremost village in a territorial unit known as 'Magare 300'.

One of the inscriptions is dated 1130 CE, and tells us that *mahasamanta* Singarasa of Arasikere obtained Kalikatti free from all obstructions and governed it. He installed a deity named Singeshvara (named after himself), and made some grants of dry and wet land to the Kalamukha priest for the maintenance of the Shiva shrine. One of the pieces of land was situated near the first ridge of the small sluice of the big tank (*hiriya-kere*) of the village. An inscription of 1132 CE suggests that Singarasa was removed from his headquarters at Arasikere and shifted to Kalikatti. Singarasa went on to install a *linga* named Bettadakalideva in the village, and granted some more gifts of dry and wet land near the big tank of the village, to the temple.

An inscription of 1189, belonging to the reign of the Hoysala king Ballala II, describes Kalikatti as a resplendent village (*ur*) with well-filled tanks, areca palms, rice fields, and fine temples. Several of the Kalikatti inscriptions mention the big tank of the village, and some mention its sluices. Other tanks, including one known as Aduva-gere, are also mentioned. Some tanks—Hariyoja's tank, Mangeya's tank, Boviti's tank, and Bitteya's tank—were named after the people who presumably owned them. The *yoja* suffix in Hariyoja's name suggests that he was an artisan. The references to tanks being set up at different points of time reflect several initiatives to expand the irrigation infrastructure of the village, and this must have increased agricultural productivity.

The 12th century inscriptions give the names of various *samantas* and *mahasamantas* who ruled over Kalikatti. Some of them set up temples and donated lands to them. In early 13th century inscriptions, Kalikatti is referred to as a *sthala* or a *nad*. There is mention of its various *hallis* (hamlets), two new tanks, and two new images of deities enshrined in temples. The *hiriya-kere* of the old days was even now being mentioned. But a big change took place in this period—the settlement became an *agrahara* and was given the name Vijaya-Narasimhapura. The details of the inscriptions also throw light on the social changes that took place in the settlement over time.

Source Chattopadhyaya, 1990

in the patterns of landholding in *brahmadeya* and non-*brahmadeya* villages. While individual holdings existed in the former, communal holding prevailed in non-*brahmadeya* villages. However, there is evidence of individual ownership in non-*brahmadeya* villages. In general, the trends visible through the early medieval period include the strengthening of individual property rights and an increasing disparity in the size of land holdings.

Inscriptions of the Chola period record several instances of land transfers via sale or gift, involving the transfer of *kani* rights. *Kani* signified the rights of possession over land, sometimes also associated with the idea that the possessor of these rights had certain duties and obligations to perform. Chola and Pandya land grants refer to two sorts of land rights—the *karanmai* (the right to cultivate) and the *mitatchi* (a superior possessive right). When these two terms occur together, they refer to the right to cultivate the land and to have it cultivated. There is also mention of *kutimai* (the right of occupancy). The *karanmai* was of two types—*kudi nikki* and *kudi ninga*. *Kudi nikki* suggests a situation in which people previously settled in the village were either removed or deprived of their rights. *Kudi ninga* meant that such people were not to be disturbed. Some land grants state that the land was granted along with the labourers attached to it.

A striking feature of the history of early medieval South India is the existence of a number of strong corporate bodies in the rural and the urban spheres. The *ur* was the corporate body of the *vellanvagai* villages. The members of this corporate body consisted of the tax-paying landowners of the village. Although the number of members was not fixed, it was usually less than 10. The *ur* dealt with various matters related to land management such as land sale, gift, and tax exemptions.

The *sabha* was the Brahmana assembly in *brahmadeya* villages. Membership was governed by criteria such property ownership, family antecedents, learning, and good conduct. The *sabha* was concerned with managing landed property, including property associated with temples. Its duties included collecting revenue and maintaining accounts. It could also supervise religious activities in the temple. Going against the *sabha*'s decision was considered a serious offence, punishable by social ostracism. While the size of Brahmana *sabhas* in the Karnataka area was initially fairly small, some 11th–12th century inscriptions mention very large *sabhas* consisting of 300, 500, 1,000, 2,000, 3,000, and even 12,000 members. This suggests a growing Brahmana population in certain villages.

There were close links between some of the Brahmana *sabhas* and the Chola court. Two inscriptions from Uttaramerur state that the resolution of the *sabha* was made in the presence of an official especially deputed by the king. Even more telling are two Thanjavur inscriptions which indicate that Rajaraja I issued orders to the *sabhas* of Cholamandalam to perform various types of services in the Brihadishvara temple. Important *brahmadeyas* in the Chola empire had *taniyur* status. *Taniyur* means 'separate village'. The villages concerned were considered independent entities within the *nadus* in which they were located.

Several inscriptions from the Karnataka area point to sources of conflict within the rural community (Nandi, 2000: 125–27). Although some of these are post-12th century inscriptions, they are close enough to the chronological frame of this book to be relevant. Conflict could arise over the introduction of Brahmana donees into a village. For instance, a mid-13th century epigraph tells us that the *gaudas* (cultivators) of a village protested against the conversion of their village into a *brahmadeya*, upon which the king sent an army to pillage the village in order to punish them. Conflicts could arise over village resources. A 1230 CE inscription from Hassan *taluk* states that two farmers died while trying to prevent agents of the Brahmanas from cutting down palmyra trees in their village. Water was an especially sensitive issue. A 1080 CE inscription from the same *taluk* refers to a conflict between a Brahmana and a farmer's family over drawing water from a village tank. An early 13th century inscription mentions a conflict between farmers and a chief over an irrigation tank. The chief was killed and the Hoysala king set up a hero stone in his memory and built a new tank.

A 1231 CE inscription from Mannargudi, belonging to the time of Rajaraja III, reveals the burden of compulsory labour levies on farmers. It states that the *nattar* (leading men of the locality) of the *taniyur* village of Rajarajadhiraja-chaturvedimangalam complained to the Brahmana *sabha* and *mahasabha* of the unbearable burden of compulsory labour imposed on them. The problem was not simply a question of the amount that they had to pay, but of various collecting agencies who demanded the same levies. Some of the tax collectors seem to have been armed. The inscription also mentions *nettal* (compulsory labour) imposed on villagers for the repair work to be conducted in the capital city, Rajarajapuram. Subbarayalu (2000: 92–4) points out that this city was located about 35 km away from Mannargudi, and it would have been an arduous task for villagers to trek all the way there to fulfil their labour obligations. The *sabha* and *mahasabha* of the village met to consider the complaints of the leading men of the locality and specified the levies that could hereafter be imposed.

The *nadu*—the 'locality' consisting of several settlements, rural or urban—was a more important unit than the village in early medieval South India. The term *nadu* also referred to the assembly of the locality. *Nadus* were usually named after one of their villages. It is difficult to identify the exact number of *nadus* in the Chola kingdom. Subbarayalu counted 140 in the Cholamandalam area and 65 in the area to its north. Their numbers were not static over time, and there was an increase after the 9th century. The fact that *nadus* varied a great deal in size indicates that they were not artificial administrative divisions created by the state. Clusters of villages similar to the *nadu* existed in the Pallava and Pandya kingdoms as well, though in the Pallava inscriptions, they are referred to as *kottam*. Such units seem to have been absent in the Chera kingdom.

Members of the *nadu* assembly were known as the *nattar*. They formed an influential corporate body that functioned collectively, and they figure among the people addressed in royal inscriptions. The *nadu* was the basic unit of revenue, and the *nattar* played an important role in revenue matters. They were responsible for land assessment and tax collection, passing on taxes to the various *nadu*-level officers of the king. The *nattar* also played an important role in managing irrigation works. They donated land to temples and were custodians of gifts made by others. Although it initially probably consisted mainly of the dominant landowners, in the course of the 12th and 13th centuries, the *nadu* assembly also came to include landowning artisans and merchants.

Agriculture and irrigation

The expansion of the agrarian economy was the result of various factors such as the extension of the margin of agriculture through land reclamation, the spread of irrigation techniques, and an expansion in the range of crops. The increase in the area under cultivation can be inferred from the fact that donees of land grants were sometimes given rights over forested area, references to forests in the vicinity of gifted land, and the mention of the transfer of wasteland to the donee. There is some direct evidence as well. A 6th century inscription of the Kadambas (who ruled over the Goa area) gave the Brahmana donee the right to engage labourers in order to clear a piece of forested area and bring it under cultivation. It also mentions the reclamation of a tract of coastal land, and its conversion to rice fields by damming up seawater.

The use of the *araghatta* (Persian wheel) spread to South India in the early medieval period. Inscriptions mention sluices which distributed the water of rivers and tanks. Nandi (2000: 91–94) has described the various improvements in agricultural technology in the Karnataka region. The first references to tanks with sluice-weir devices in this area belong to the 8th century, and the number of such references increases thereafter. An inscription of 890 CE from the Hiriyur *taluk* states that farmers of a village constructed a large tank provided with four sluices. The practice of building channels connecting tanks with river waters also took off, and there seems to have been a spurt in the building of tanks.

NEW DIRECTIONS IN RESEARCH | **Irrigation devices in early medieval Tamil Nadu**

James Heitzman has analyzed references in Chola inscriptions from five *taluks* in central Tamil Nadu—Kumbakonam, Tiruchirappalli, Tirukkoyilur, Tirutturaipundi, and Pudukkottai—and identified the distribution and changes in irrigation technology during the Chola period. The references to irrigation works—tanks, wells, canals, sluices—often occur in the descriptions of the boundaries of gifted land.

Going by the frequency of the references, Kumbakonam and Tiruchirappalli *taluks* show a strong reliance on canals. Canals constituted as much as 85 per cent and 84 per cent of the irrigation works mentioned in inscriptions from these two areas respectively. We can note that Kumbakonam *taluk* is in the lower Kaveri valley and Tiruchirappalli *taluk* is further upstream. Tanks constituted only 7 per cent of the total references. In Tirutturaippundi *taluk*, canals constituted 79 per cent of the mentioned irrigation works and tanks 15 per cent. In Pudukkottai *taluk*, the frequency of canals was 49 per cent and tanks 38 per cent. In Tirukkoyilur *taluk*, 60 per cent of the references were to canals and 23 per cent to tanks. Sluices constitute only 4.7 per cent of the references, while wells constitute 5.4 per cent of the terms.

The reasons for differences in irrigation technology between various sub-regions were to a large extent ecological, and depended on which type of technology was best suited to a particular terrain. Another interesting point is that inscriptions reveal striking similarities with the general patterns of irrigation prevalent in these areas today.

Canals and tanks were the major types of irrigation works utilized in early medieval Tamil Nadu. However, there were some changes over time. For instance, in both Kumbakonam and Tirukkoyilur *taluks*, over time, there is a systematic increase in references to canals and a reduction in references to tanks. In Pudukkottai *taluk* on the other hand, there is a decline in the frequency of references to canals.

If the data is put together, the picture that we get is as follows: In the Kumbakonam *taluk*, the development of the irrigation network began before the Chola period, and its basic nature remained unchanged through the period of Chola rule. In Tirukkoyilur *taluk*, tanks were initially the most important source of irrigation, but in course of time, river-fed canals became increasingly important. In Pudukkottai *taluk*, canal development may have peaked in the 11th century, after which it plateaued. In Tiruchirappalli *taluk*, investment in canals was relatively low in the 11th century, but went up in the 12th century.

Source Heitzman, 1997: 38–54

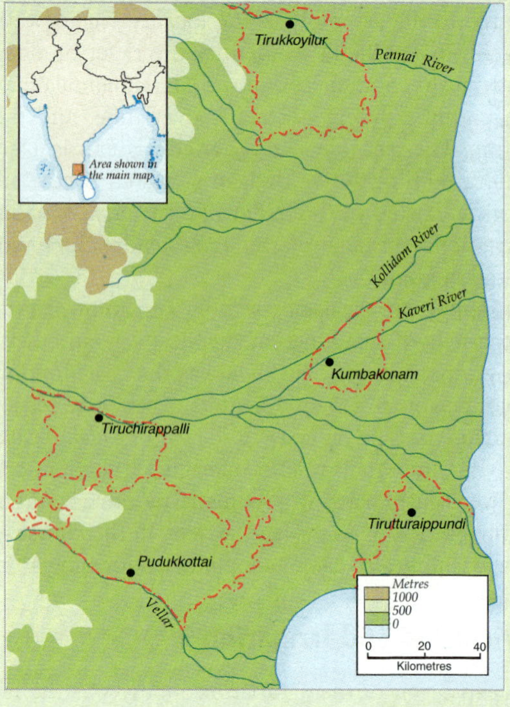

Chola inscriptions mention various types of irrigation works such as tanks, canals, wells, and sluices. Some Chola kings are credited with initiating tank and canal construction. For instance, Rajendra I is supposed to have begun the construction of the Cholaganga tank and canal network. Members of the village community, Brahmanas, kings, and chieftains played a role in the maintenance of irrigation works. However, when it came to the construction and maintenance of the more numerous small-scale irrigation works, members of the village community played a central role. The *nattar* stepped in when several villages were involved or affected. There are epigraphic references to tank maintenance committees (*erivariya*). Farmers were sometimes granted sowing rights over adjacent plots of land in return for taking on the responsibility of dredging tanks.

A steady extension of the margin of cultivation, the spread of irrigation works, and changes in market demand led to changes in patterns of land use. In the Karnataka area, apart from rice, there was an increasing emphasis on various types of millets such as *priyangu* (*panicum italicum*), *ragi* (*eleusine coracana*), *jowar* (*sorghum vulgare*), and *bajra* (bulrush millet). Also increasingly grown were inferior varieties of rice such as *shyamaka*, *nivara*, *kangu*, *kodrava*, and *karadusha*. There was an increase in the cultivation of cash crops such as sugarcane, betel leaves and areca nuts, coconuts, oranges, and spices such as black pepper and ginger.

Urban processes

The early medieval period represents a second major phase of urban growth in South India. The hypothesis of urban decay has no validity whatsoever for this region. Cities played different, often multiple, roles—as political centres, centres of manufacturing and trade, and as sacred or ceremonial centres.

Market or commercial centres were known as *nagarams*. The *nagaram* was an urban space, connected mainly with the production and exchange of commodities, at the local, inter-regional, or international level. Agricultural produce also moved in and out of it. A *nadu* could have one or more *nagarams*. Like some of the important *brahmadeyas*, certain *nagarams* were given *taniyur* status, which made them independent and free of the jurisdiction of the *nadu* they were located in. The *nagaram* had a corporate body consisting of merchants, members of which were known as the *nagarattar*. This group was also involved in land management; it owned and managed land known as *nagarakkani*, from which it collected revenue.

The *nagarams* seem to have become increasingly important in the Chola period, when the *nagarattar* appear often as donors in inscriptions (Champakalakshmi, 1996: 45–46). The number and lavishness of their gifts (mostly money, gold, and silver) peaked in the middle Chola period. At this point, there was also the emergence of corporate organizations associated with specialized groups—e.g., the Saliya *nagaram* and Sattum Parishatta *nagaram*, which were connected with the textile trade; the Shankarappadi *nagaram*, which was a corporate organization of oil and ghee suppliers; the Paraga *nagaram*, which was a corporate organization of seafaring merchants; and the Vaniya *nagaram*, a powerful organization of oil merchants.

There were significant improvements in craft techniques. For instance, the earlier hand oil mills used for oil pressing were replaced by bullock-driven oil mills. Improvements also took place in the textile weaving industry. An 11th century inscription from Challakere *taluk* mentions the grant of a site for setting up a loom.

Various centres of craft production can be identified, some showing a continuous growth from the early historical period. Kanchipuram, located in a major cotton-growing region, was one of the most important centres of the weaving industry from the early historical period onwards. Many other weaving centres mushroomed in the area around the city, and also in the Thanjavur and South Arcot district areas. In the 12th–13th centuries, weavers and merchants started investing in land and became part of the land-owning elite.

There were close connections between cities, kings, and temples in South India. The background to these links included the increasing power of the Chola state, the increasing popularity of Vaishnava and Shaiva *bhakti*, and the emergence of the temple as a prominent religious institution in the urban landscape. In the late Pallava and early Chola periods, there was a significant shift of royal patronage from gifts to Brahmanas towards gifts to temples. Earlier kings of South India had built and patronized temples. But the Cholas constructed a large number of new, architecturally elaborate temples, and also rebuilt some of the old temples in stone. The magnificent temples at Thanjavur and Gangaikondacholapuram were architectural proclamations of the close connection between the political and religious domains.

The city of Thanjavur was located on the southern bank of the Vadavaru river on the south-western edge of the fertile, agriculturally rich Kaveri delta. Gangaikondacholapuram, the other royal city, was located on the northern edge of the delta. A settlement called Tanjai existed in pre-Chola times, but it was transformed into a major royal and temple city during the reign of Rajaraja I (Champakalakshmi, 1996: 62–64). The Brihadishvara temple dominated the city and constituted its centre. The area around the temple formed the city's inner circuit. This was where the political and priestly elites lived. Outside this

Map 10.5 Urban centres in Tondaimandalam, *c.* 1300 CE (after Champakalakshmi, 1996)

was an outer residential circuit, which housed other urban groups such as merchants. There are references to four markets (*angadis*) in the city. The temple generated a demand for material such as milk, ghee and flowers, as well as services of various kinds such as those provided by priests, temple women, musicians, washermen, and watchmen. Special performances were staged in the temple on days marking the birth asterisms of members of the royal family. Apart from the king, members of the royal family made many gifts to the Brihadishvara temple. As mentioned earlier, some of its sculptural ornamentation and paintings were imbued with strong political meaning.

The Brihadishvara temple was a major building project and may have taken 7 to 8 years to build. The temple drew many areas and groups into its economic web. Inscriptions state that over 600 employees were drawn from villages and towns in various parts of the Chola kingdom to serve in the temple. Revenue from many far-flung villages, including some in Sri Lanka, was assigned to it for its maintenance. The management of its financial resources was in the hands of Brahmana *sabha*s of several villages. Farmers, herdsmen, and artisans living around Thanjavur supplied many of its requirements.

Another example of a major urban complex of the period are Kudamukku and Palaiyarai, located adjacent to each other in the most fertile part of the Kaveri delta (Champakalakshmi, 1996: 331–55). Kudamukku represented a sacred centre, while the palace complex of the Cholas was located at Palaiyarai. The history of these twin settlements

FURTHER DISCUSSION | **Weavers and weaving in early medieval Tamil Nadu**

Vijaya Ramaswamy's study of the weavers of South India between the 10th and 17th centuries shows a match between the textile centres of that period and those of present times. The most important weaving communities in early medieval times in the Tamil Nadu area were the Saliyar and Kaikkolar. During the Chola period, the latter seem to have combined the vocations of weavers and soldiers. Weavers had their own residential sector in all towns. This was often located in the temple square, as was the case in Thanjavur.

The varieties of textiles and techniques used in cloth manufacture can be gleaned from literary and epigraphic sources. Muslins (known as *sella*) and chintz (known as *vichitra*) were much in demand. Vegetable dyes such as red safflower, indigo, and madder were used. Block printing seems to have been in vogue in South India from the 12th century onwards. Artisans used both vertical and horizontal looms, and the use of patterned looms seems to have begun in the 11th century.

The industry was well organized and textiles were important commodities both in internal and external trade. Weavers sold their goods at local fairs, but at the higher level, the textile trade was controlled by powerful merchant guilds. There is also evidence of weavers' guilds known variously as *samaya pattagara*, *saliya samayangal*, and *seniya pattagara*. Ramaswamy refers to the mobility of some of the weaver castes within South India. These migrations may have taken place in the Vijayanagara period (15th–16th centuries), which saw a high point in the development of the weaving industry.

The Cholas actively encouraged the weaving industry in their kingdom and derived revenue from it. Inscriptions mention taxes such as the *tari irai* or *tari kadamai* (loom tax). Other dues included *achchu tari* (probably a tax on the patterned loom), *tari pudavai* (probably a tax on cloth), *panjupeeli* (a tax on cotton yarn), *parutti kadamai* (a tax on cotton), *nulayam* (a tax on cotton thread), and *kaibanna* or *bannige* (a tax on dyers). A tax called *pattadai nulayam* was levied on silk thread. On the other hand, there is evidence of the state announcing tax concessions and tax remissions for a specified period to weavers in new settlements in order to attract them. Kulottunga I was given the title *Sungam tavirta Cholan* (remover of customs duties). This alludes to his having abolished customs dues at ports in order to promote trade.

The increase in the socio-economic status of weavers and their involvement in temple honours and activities in early medieval South India are reflected in the many donations they made to temples. These took the form of money, livestock (cows, sheep), and shares of cloth or land. The gifts were aimed at defraying the cost of the building of shrines, making and installing images, the maintenance of perpetual lamps, providing woven cloth, and the celebration of festivals. Some donations were made as expiation for crimes. There is also evidence of weavers being given land by temples or village assemblies for services rendered by them.

Weavers invested money in land and were involved in money-lending as well. The Madras Museum copper plates of Uttama Chola state that the king deposited money with certain groups of weavers for the celebration of a festival at the temple of Uragam at Kanchipuram. Some weavers were also given managerial roles in the temple, including the management of finances and maintenance of accounts. In return for performing these important duties, they were declared exempt from taxes.

Source Ramaswamy, 1985

goes back to earlier times, but they came into prominence during the Chola period. Kudamukku was the site of many temples, and is mentioned in *bhakti* songs of the Alvars and Nayanars. Endowments by members of the royal family, officials, merchants, artisans, and others led to a steady growth of its temple establishments, especially the Nageshvara temple, which became the most prominent shrine. Kudamukku was an important point on the trade routes. It was a centre of betel nut and areca nut cultivation as well as an important centre of crafts such as metal work and textiles. A Chola mint was probably located here. The history of Palaiyarai goes back to the 7th century, but it came into prominence as an important administrative centre and as the residential capital of the Cholas. Both Kudamukku and Palaiyarai were knitted to their rural and coastal hinterlands through intricate ties.

The history of Madurai and Kanchipuram as political centres, centres of commodity production (especially cotton textiles), and religious activity goes back to the early historical period. In early medieval times, both of them grew in size and importance. Kanchipuram, a prominent centre of weaving and commerce, is mentioned in inscriptions and texts as a *managaram* (big city). It was initially connected to the port of Nirppeyyarru on the banks of the Palar river. Subsequently, Mamallapuram emerged as its major port outlet. There was a significant expansion in Kanchipuram's hinterland through land grants and the growing web of the temple economy. Apart from its economic role, Kanchipuram also had an important cultural significance and was an important centre of Buddhism, Jainism, Vaishnavism, and Shaivism.

The urban developments of the early medieval period were reflected in caste organization. In Karnataka (Nandi, 2000: 158–80), there was the emergence of trading castes such as the Garvares. These were northern merchants who migrated southwards in the 10–11th centuries. Other occupational groups of this region that evolved into castes included the *gaudas* and *heggades*. The *gaudas* or *gavundas* were originally cultivators or village headmen, while the *heggades* were initially revenue officials. Apart from the *kayasthas*, another group of professional scribes known as the *karanas* also assumed the form of a caste.

A major development in early medieval South India was the emergence of a supra-caste dichotomy—the *idangai* (left hand) and *valangai* (right hand) caste groupings. The castes that were classified as belonging to the right-hand consisted mostly of agricultural groups. Those of the left hand comprised mostly artisanal and trading groups. Initially, these were not antagonistic groupings, but an element of conflict did emerge in later times.

Trade and traders

Many trade routes intersected at ports on the eastern coast of South India. Mamallapuram developed under the Pallavas, and Nagapattinam became prominent in the Chola period. Kaveripattinam too was important, but less so compared to Nagapattinam from the 11th century onwards. Tiruppalaivanam and Mayilarppil were coastal towns that served the area to the north of Kanchipuram. Kovalam and Tiruvadandai were located to the north of Mamallapuram, while Sadras and Pudupattinam were located to its south. Other important coastal towns included Pallavapattinam, Cuddalore, and Tiruvendipuram. Corporate organizations of merchants played a leading role in fixing customs duties on goods in such port towns. Quilon (Kollam) was an important port town on the western coast, and there is inscriptional evidence of an agreement between the Manigramam guild, foreign traders, and the king regarding various issues such as taxes, warehouses, and the protection of merchants and their merchandise at this port.

The ports and market towns of South India were involved in a flourishing transit trade as well as direct trade with far-flung areas. The goods involved included both staples and luxury goods. Eleventh century inscriptions mention several commodities involved in trade transactions within the subcontinent—rice, pulses, sesame, salt, pepper, oil, cloth, betel leaf, areca nut, and metals. Twelfth century inscriptions mention a larger range of commodities including wheat and other foodgrains, pulses, groundnut, sesamum, jaggery, sugar, cotton, cumin, mustard, coriander, ginger, turmeric, elephants, and gems. A 12th century inscription found at Shikarpur (in Shimoga district, Karnataka) mentions merchants travelling along land and water routes with cargoes consisting of elephants, horses, sandalwood, camphor, musk, saffron, and precious and semi-precious gems such as moonstones, rubies, diamonds, pearls, lapis lazuli, onyx, topaz, and carbuncles. Inscriptions at Piranmalai (Ramanathapuram district, Tamil Nadu) mention imports such as aloeswood, sandalwood, silk, rose water, camphor, oil, perfume, elephants, and horses. Many of these items were imported from South-east Asia. Horses came from Arabia, silk from China, elephants from Myanmar, and rose water from West Asia.

The Chola kings promoted trade in various ways, including by setting up *erivirappattanas*. These were protected mercantile towns, which emerged as important centres of trade. Some of the Chola military expeditions—such as those to Sri Lanka in the 1080s and against ports in the Malaysian peninsula and Indonesian islands in 1025 and the 1070s—were probably more than looting expeditions and aimed at controlling important trade sectors. In the case of expeditions against Sri Lanka, apart from the fact that Mantai (Mannar) was an important entrepôt of maritime trade, an added incentive must have been the desire to control the pearl fisheries of the Gulf of Mannar.

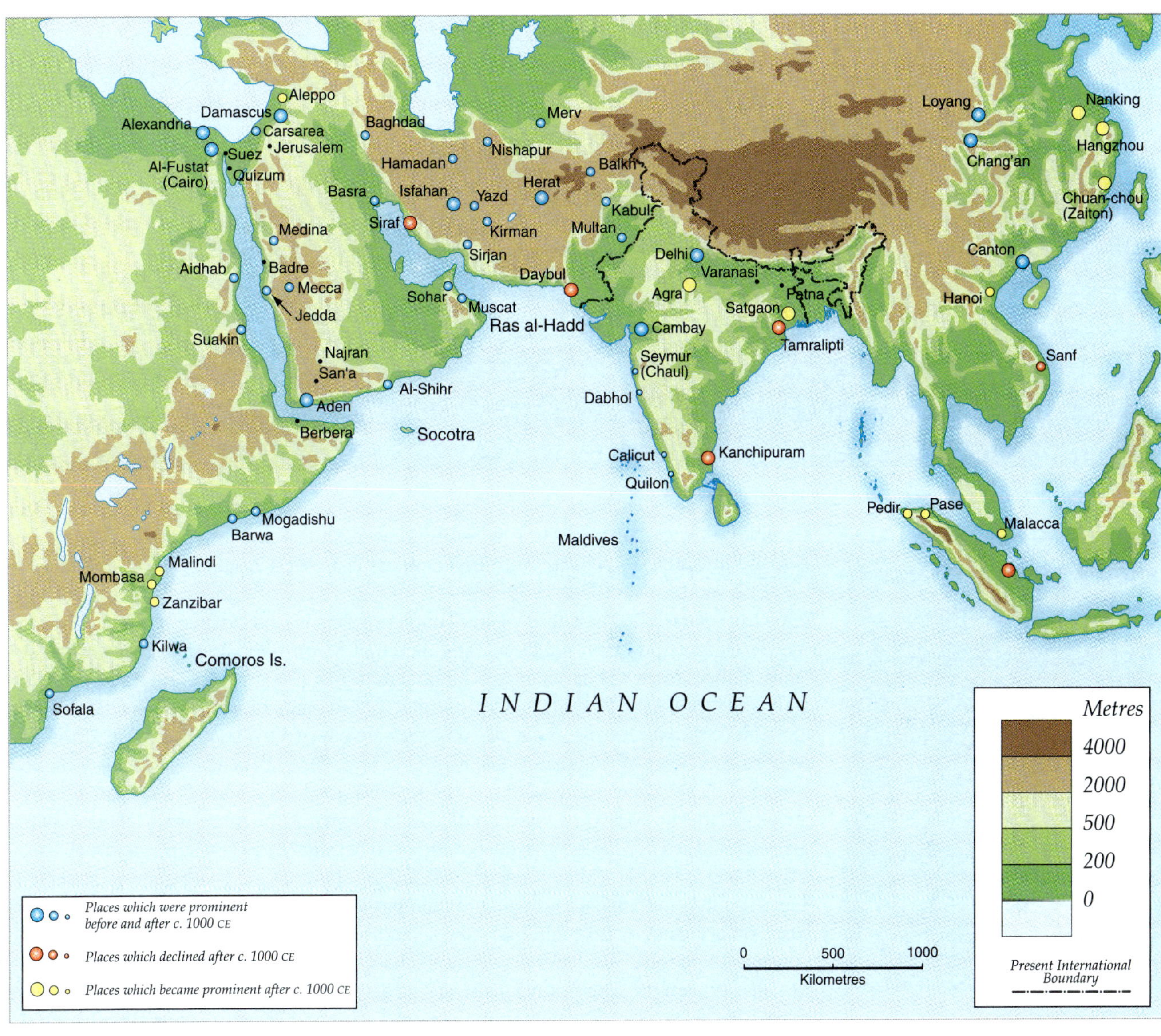

Map 10.6 Ports and cities in Indian Ocean trade networks, c. 600–1500 (after Chaudhuri, 1985)

The expanding contacts between South India and South-east Asia are reflected in inscriptions and sculptures (Abraham, 1988: 29–31; Karashima, 2009; Subbarayalu, 2009b). The Tanjore inscription of Rajendra Chola I mentions a kingdom of Madamalingam, which can probably be identified with Tambralinga, not far from the Kra isthmus (this links Thailand and Malaysia), an important centre of maritime trade. An important route linked Takuapa to the Bay of Bandon. Hindu images dating from the 4th century onwards have been found in this area. Two Chola period images were discovered at Vieng Sra and a Surya image of the Chola style was found at Jaiya. A profusion of pottery and glass remains were discovered at Ko Kao island, situated at the mouth of the Takuapa river. Many were from China, while some may possibly have been of West Asian and Indian origin.

There was reciprocal interaction between the elites of South, South-east, and East Asia. Inscriptions record grants made by South-east Asian kings at Nalanda, Bodh Gaya, and Nagapattinam. Inscriptions mention various gifts in favour of deities enshrined in temples of Nagapattinam on behalf of the kings of Shri Vijaya and Kadaram. The Khmer king sent a gift to Rajendra I. A trade mission was sent by Rajaraja Chola to China in 1015. Chinese sources mention four tribute-bearing missions sent by the Cholas to the court of the Song emperors between 1015 and 1077. They are described as bearing gifts

of elephant tusks, rhinoceros horns, pearls, frankincense, rose water, putchuk, barus camphor, brocade, opaque glass, and plumflower. Out of these items that were in great demand in China, some were from India, others from West Asia.

J. C. van Leur's ([1934] 1955: 133–37, 197–200) theory of the India–South-east Asia trade being largely in the hands of small-time peddlers is contradicted by the evidence of the existence of powerful guilds in early medieval South India and incontrovertible evidence of their involvement not only in internal trade but also long-distance trade, especially with South-east Asia. Corporate organizations of merchants became very prominent from the 10th century onwards. In inscriptions, they are referred to as *samaya*, which means an organization created through an agreement or contract. Members of such associations were governed by a code of conduct known as the *bananju-dharma*. One of the most powerful guilds was the Ayyavole (The Five Hundred), also known as the Ainnurruvar. This was originally established in Aihole in Karnataka and soon became the largest supra-regional association of merchants. The Manigramam was another important merchant guild located in the Tamil country, and was subordinated to the Ayyavole in the 13th century. The guilds were based on occupation and economic interest, and membership cut across lines of caste and religion. There were also links between merchant guilds and associations of craft specialists such as weavers. The Anjuvannam was an association of foreign merchants who were initially involved in trade activities on the Kerala coast and later fanned out to other areas.

Examples of cultural interaction between India and South-east Asia (from top): the *stupa* at Borobudur, Java; Vishnu temple, Angkor Vat, Cambodia: *apsara* reliefs, view of temple, *Mahabharata* relief

FURTHER DISCUSSION | **Gifts by South-east Asian rulers at Nalanda, Nagapattinam, and Bodh Gaya**

The 9th century Nalanda copper plate inscription is inscribed on both sides of a single copper plate. The 66 lines of Sanskrit in the Siddhamatrika script record a grant of five villages by the Pala king Devapala in his 39th regnal year, at the request of *maharaja* Balaputradeva, the Shailendra ruler of Suvarnadvipa/Yavabhumi in favour of a monastery built by the latter at Nalanda. The Shailendra dynasty was based in central Java. The income from the villages was to provide for the various needs of the monks, for the writing of Buddhist texts, and for the maintenance of the monastery. The inscription contains two separate, sequential *prashasti*s of the two kings involved in the transaction, both of whom describe themselves as devotees of the Buddha. Balaputra's mind is described as having been attracted by the many excellences of Nalanda. This indicates the fame and eminence that this monastic centre had achieved in this part of South-east Asia by the 9th century.

The larger Leiden plates consist of 443 lines inscribed on 21 copper plates. Like many Chola inscriptions, the inscription consists of two parts—one in Sanskrit, the other in Tamil. The Sanskrit part is in the Grantha script and gives the invocation, a detailed Chola genealogy, and the purport of the inscription. It tells us that in the 21st year of his reign (i.e. in 1006), Rajaraja Chola gave the village of Anaimangalam to a temple of the Buddha in the Chulamanivarma-vihara, which had been built by the ruler of Shrivishaya (Srivijaya) and Kataha (located in the Malay peninsula) named Maravijayottungavarman, who belonged to the Shailendra family, and who was the son of Chulamanivarman (the temple was obviously built in his name, i.e. memory). It goes on to tell us that after the death of Rajaraja, his son Rajendra (in his 20th year, i.e., in 1032) had a permanent edict issued for the village that had been granted by his father.

The smaller Leiden plates of Kulottunga consist of three plates. Dated in year 20 of the king's reign, i.e., 1090, the inscription records a grant of villages to the same Buddhist establishment at Nagapattinam, described as having been constructed by the Kadaram king. Kadaram was at this time probably under the control of Srivijaya, although it is possible that it enjoyed a certain amount of autonomy. This inscription is entirely in the Tamil language and script (with a few Grantha letters). It tells us that messengers (*dutas*) of the king of Kadaram petitioned Kulottunga to make certain endowments to Chudamanivarma-vihara in Nagapattinam. The document records the details of certain land in several villages assigned to the monastic establishment.

The kings of Burma had a long-standing relationship with Bodh Gaya. A late 13th century epigraph found here (in the Burmese language of the Arakanese type and the Burmese Kyouktsa script) states that one of the 84,000 *chaitya*s built by Siri Dhammasoka (i.e., the Maurya emperor Ashoka), king of Jambudvipa, at the place where the milk-rice offering (Sujata's offering to Siddhartha) had been made, fell into ruin due to the stress of age and time. A senior monk repaired the *chaitya*. Thereafter, it fell into ruin again. The 'King of the Law,' 'Lord of the White Elephant' (a Burmese king) sent his *acharya* Dhammarajaguru to repair it. When the money was found to be insufficient, Putasin Man (i.e., Buddhasena, who seems to have been a local ruler) extended a helping hand. The work was resumed and continued for two years. The inscription gives details of the dedication ceremony that was held when the work was completed. The audience of this inscription was Burmese, as is evident from the Burmese language and script used in it.

These instances of royal patronage of Buddhist establishments by South-east Asian kings mark a new kind of interaction among Asian political elites.

Source Upinder Singh, 2014

Most of the guild inscriptions have been found in South India, but some have also been found in Sri Lanka and East and South-east Asia (Abraham, 1988: 29–33, 60). An inscription mentioning the Ayyavole was found at Padaviya in Sri Lanka. This gives a eulogy of the guild and lists its different component groups. A 1088 CE inscription of the same guild was found at Loboe Toewa in Sumatra. The Manigramam seems to have established a base at Takuapa in Thailand. This is evident from a 9th century inscription found near this place, along with some stone sculptures of Indian manufacture which seem to have been associated with a temple. The fact that the epigraph mentions armed protection extended over a tank suggests that the traders were accompanied by soldiers. The inscription invokes the title of the Pallava king and suggests the existence of an autonomous coastal settlement of Tamil traders here. In China, Quanzhou in Fujian province yielded over 300 Hindu images and artefacts, and a bilingual Tamil–Chinese inscription. This suggests the presence of a colony of Tamil merchants, perhaps members of a guild, in the 13th/14th century.

FURTHER DISCUSSION | **Aihole and Ayyavole**

Inscriptions form a major source of information on the guilds of early medieval South India. Most of them are on stone, a few on copper plates. The stone inscriptions are often associated with temples and usually record donations made by guild members. A few refer to public services performed by them, or agreements between rulers and merchants regarding the setting up of mercantile townships. Guild inscriptions frequently include a *prashasti* of the guild, which throws light on its relationship with the state and other organizations, as well as the religious affiliations of guild members. Lists of commodities involved in trade are also often given.

Aihole, located on the banks of the Malaprabha river in the fertile Raichur doab in Bijapur district, Karnataka, is known for its magnificent Chalukya period temples. The Ayyavole guild seems to have originated in this town. It was probably founded by a group of Brahmana *mahajanas* (traders) of this place in about the 8th century. The earliest inscription referring to this guild is found in the Lad Khan temple at Aihole. Several other Aihole inscriptions, ranging from the 8th to 12th centuries, mention it as well. The town of Aihole was also known by other names such as Ayyavole, Aryapura, and Ahichchhatra. Inscriptions refer to members of the Ayyavole guild as 'ornaments on the brow of that great lady, the city of Ahichchhatra', or as 'the 500 *svamis* [lords] of the illustrious town of Ayyavole'. Inscriptional references to the Ayyavole range from the 8th/9th century to the late 17th century. During the early medieval period, against the background of expanding trade and urban settlements, the activities of this guild expanded.

Given the large area that the Ayyavole operated over (Karnataka, Tamil Nadu, southern Andhra Pradesh, and parts of Kerala), one of the questions that arises is whether it functioned as a loose federation of units or whether it had a centralized organizational structure. Opinions on this issue vary greatly. Meera Abraham suggests that the organization consisted of a sort of federation of units, each operating over fairly large areas.

The Ayyavole had close links with various ruling elites and enjoyed royal patronage. The Cholas had a close relationship with this guild. According to tradition, the Pandya kings invited the Nattukottai Chettiars, members of Ayyavole, to migrate from Kaveripattinam to their territory. The Ayyavole had links with other, smaller merchant associations such as the Valanjiyar, as well as close links with *agraharas* and *agrahara* Brahmanas.

Source Abraham, 1988

As Chola power waned in the 12th century, the merchant guilds of South India became increasingly independent and less dependent on royal support. Trading caravans moved around with armed protection. Merchant guilds jointly fixed tolls and cesses, and made joint donations to temples along with the Chittirameli and Pandinen Vishaya, which were associations of agriculturists controlling the production and exchange of agricultural commodities.

The Religious Sphere

Religious developments in early medieval India show continuities as well as changes compared with the preceding centuries and can be reconstructed on the basis of religious texts, inscriptions, architecture, and sculptural remains. At the level of popular worship, the focus was on devotional worship in temples and on pilgrimage. The Hindu sects, especially those associated with the worship of Vishnu, Shiva, and Shakti, became increasingly popular. The Tantric tradition became stronger and exerted its influence over Hindu, Buddhist and, to a lesser extent, Jaina traditions. While the Hindu sects were fairly widespread throughout the subcontinent, Buddhist and Jaina sects had a more restricted provenance. Jainism held sway in Western India and Karnataka, while the strongholds of Buddhism were located in Eastern India, Kashmir, and the Himalayan regions. The age-old *naga* cults still held their ground, as evident in the importance of the worship of Nilamata *naga* in Kashmir.

The early medieval period saw the advent of Islam on the subcontinent. Reference has been made to Arab merchants settled in various parts of Western India. Epigraphic and textual evidence indicates that by the 13th century, the Muslim population in these ports and towns included not only Arab shipowners and traders, but also local oilmen and masons. Several inscriptions record the building of mosques by wealthy traders.

The centuries after the establishment of the Delhi Sultanate saw a growth in the number of Muslims in the subcontinent.

Christian, Jewish, and Zoroastrian settlers too made their homes in India, especially along the western coast. While the religions of Islam, Christianity, Judaism, and Zoroastrianism originated in other parts of Asia, during the early medieval period, they became part of Indian history. A Jewish community, consisting largely of traders, established itself in the Malabar area. It is difficult to date the advent of Christian communities in India. It is not clear whether there is any historicity to the tradition of St. Thomas' visits to India. Christian communities, especially those linked to the Syrian Christian Church, were well established on the western coast in the early medieval period. In the 8th century, Zoroastrians (later known as Parsis) fleeing from persecution in Iran, too arrived and settled on the western coast.

Religious shrines derived patronage from various sections of society. The political patronage of certain temples, especially after the 10th century, led to the emergence of royal temples. Religious sects were an important aspect of emergent regional cultures. Religious identities also became more clearly defined during these and the subsequent centuries. As it is not possible to detail all the developments in the religious history of various parts of the subcontinent, a few of these developments are summarized below, including a closer look at Vaishnava and Shaiva *bhakti* in South India.

Buddhism in early medieval India

Buddhism rapidly became an Asian religion during these centuries. The places associated with the Buddha played an important role in this process. And yet, the early medieval period is said to have witnessed a decline of Buddhism in this period. The picture that emerges is a complex one, with a decline in some areas but strength and resilience in others. Xuanzang noted many large, flourishing monasteries in the Magadha area, such as those of Nalanda, Tilodaka, and Bodh Gaya, but also mentioned many deserted or ruined monasteries elsewhere. The Chinese pilgrim spent over five years studying the Yogachara doctrine at Nalanda. Yijing visited Bodh Gaya and the monastery of Tilodaka, which he described as housing some 1,000 monks. Xuanzang offers a general description of the monasteries of the time. He mentions their skilful construction and refers to their having a three-storeyed tower at each side, profusely painted doors and windows, and low walls. Buddhism rapidly became an Asian religion during these centuries. The places in India associated with the Buddha had an important place in this process. And yet, the early medieval period is said to have witnessed a decline of Buddhism in India. The picture that emerges is a complex one, with a decline in some areas but strength and resilience in others. The monks' cells were plain outside and ornamented inside. There were large, high assembly halls in the middle of the building, storeyed chambers, and turrets of varying height, with doors facing eastwards. Textual sources and inscriptions indicate the location of monasteries of early medieval times, and archaeological remains of many of these have been identified.

The *Chachnama* refers to Buddhism flourishing in Sindh in the north-west. In Kashmir, the Jayendra monastery at Shrinagara and the Raja *vihara* at Parihasapura declined by the 11th century, but the Ratnagupta monastery and Ratnarashmi monastery at Anupamapura flourished in the 11th and 12th centuries. Several Buddhist *viharas* were built during this period in Nepal, as well as in Ladakh, Lahul, and Spiti. There was active interaction between Tibetan monks and these monasteries. It was the Tantric form of Buddhism that flourished at most of the major monastic centres. The Buddhist monasteries at Sanchi and Amaravati continued to flourish till the 12th–13th centuries.

In Eastern India, monasteries such Nalanda, Odantapura (perhaps located at Bihar Sharif near Nalanda), Vikramashila (sometimes identified with Antichak in Bhagalpur district, Bihar), and Somapura (located at Paharpur in Naogaon district, Bangladesh) flourished in the early medieval period. Clay sealings found at Paharpur bearing the name of Somapura-*vihara* confirm the identification of the site with the ancient monastery (Dikshit [1938] 1999; Swadhin Sen, 2018). The excavated structural remains included a

PRIMARY SOURCES | **A letter from Xuanzang to Prajnadeva**

After Xuanzang returned to China, he busied himself translating Buddhist Sanskrit texts into Chinese in the Tz'u-en monastery at Ch'ang an. During this period, he corresponded with some of the monks he had met in India. One of these was Prajnadeva, a senior monk belonging to the Mahabodhi monastery at Bodh Gaya. Prajnadeva had sent Xuanzang the text of a hymn composed by himself and a present of two rolls of cotton cloth. He had also asked the Chinese monk to let him know if he required any copies of Buddhist texts. This is what Xuanzang wrote in reply, in 654 CE. (As the letter was in Chinese, someone in the Bodh Gaya monastery must have been equipped to translate it for the recipient.):

Bhikshu Xuanzang of the great T'ang empire begs to address this to the venerable Tripitaka-Master Prajnadeva of the Mahabodhi monastery:

Your Reverend, it has been quite long since we parted, which enhances my longing and admiration for you. The non-communication between us all the more leaves the thirst of the yearning unquenched.

Bhikshu Dharmadirgha arrived here with your very kind letter which brought me delight. There were also two rolls of fine cotton cloth and one fascicle of a hymn. I feel rather embarrassed as my want of virtue does not deserve such kindness.

The weather is getting warmer now, and I do not know how you have been keeping since you last wrote.

I can imagine how you have assimilated the theories of all the schools, pondered over all volumes of the scriptures, hoisted the flag of the right *dharma*, led the swerving people to the correct path, and beat back the discordant preachers. You surely maintain your spirit in front of princes and nobles, and compliment or criticize at will in a galaxy of talented people. All this contributes to your highly pleasant demeanour.

As for me, my incapacity is compounded by the decline of vigour. This all the more increases my yearnings when I remember the virtue of Your Reverend.

During my sojourn in your country, I had the honour of meeting Your Reverend. In the convocation at Kanyakubja, we also engaged in a debate and argued our respective view-points in the presence of the princes and thousands of devotees. As one of us expounded the tenets of the Mahayana school, the other advocated the aims of Hinayana. In the course of debate, our arguments unavoidably got heated. In order to defend the truth, there was scant regard for personal feelings. Thus, there were clashes. But, as soon as the debate was over, we did not take each other amiss. Now, you have sent word through the messenger apologizing for the past. How scrupulous you are!

You, holy sir, are profound in scholarship, eloquent in speech, firm in belief, and superb in cultivation. You are [in excellence] greater than the expanse of the water in the Anavatapa lake, and purer than the purest *mani* [jewel]. Your Reverend set an example for emulation by the juniors, among whom Your Reverend stood like a giant.

I wish you all the best in your endeavour in promoting the noble tradition and disseminating the true *dharma*.

Mahayana Buddhism surpasses all other schools in its perfection in reasoning and in its meridian level in argument. It is regrettable that Your Reverend has reservations about it. It is like preferring a sheep-drawn or deer-drawn cart to a bullock-drawn carriage, or preferring crystal to beryl. Enlightened as Your Reverend is, why such persistence in unbelief? Our mundane life is ephemeral. It is advisable that Your Reverend makes an early resolution to embrace *Alamkaraka-saddharma* [the Mahayana path] so that there is no regret at the end of life.

Now, there is a messenger returning to India, I send you my sincere regards and a little memento as a token of my gratitude. It is too inadequate to express my deep feelings for Your Reverend. I hope Your Reverend would appreciate this.

When I was returning from India, I lost a horse-load of scriptures in the river Sindhu. I attach herewith a list and request that they be sent to me. This much for the present.

Yours
Bhikshu Xuanzang

Source Tan Chung, cited in Devahuti, 2001: 282

residential complex consisting of four wings with 177 cells arranged around a courtyard. A shrine in the centre of the courtyard was cruciform in plan; its external walls were ornamented with 63 stone sculptures. Toilets and other remains were found within and outside the courtyard. Structural remains of a temple and *stupa*s were found in an adjacent area called Satyapirer Bhita. A recent study of the landscape around the site has brought to light the relationship between the monastic establishment and the settlements in its hinterland (Swadhin Sen et al., 2014). This has connected the provisional stratigraphy of the site with changes in the fluvial landscape of the area due to shifting river channels and floods. The larger point of the study is that Buddhist monasteries have to be studied within their wider natural and archaeological landscapes and in relation to agrarian processes and settlement history. A large monastic complex was located at Moghalmari (in West Medinipur district, West Bengal) (see Sanyal, 2018d). Excavations at Antichak in

Bhagalpur district of Bihar (Verma, 2011; Sanyal, 2018a) revealed remains of a Buddhist complex dating from the 8th to early 13th century. It included a large *stupa*, 253 monastic cells, lots of Buddhist and Hindu sculptures, small *stupas*, terracotta plaques, and metal sculptures. A large number of iron weapons were among the interesting discoveries. A monastic sealing had the name 'Shri-Jayasenadeva-mahavihara.'

The Mahabodhi temple at Bodh Gaya (see Asher, 2010; Sanyal, 2018b) went through many stages of construction and repair. Apart from the temple itself, a large number of images (some of which are currently in the *mahant*'s complex nearby) belong to the early medieval period. Xuanzang refers to a Sri Lankan monastic community at Bodh Gaya, living in a monastery built by a Sri Lankan king. By the time of Xuanzang, Bodh Gaya had become much more than an important *Indian* Buddhist site; it had become a major *Asian* Buddhist site. Eventually, it became an important symbolic centre and pilgrimage destination for monks and laity from China, Tibet, Myanmar, and Sri Lanka. The attraction of the site increased in later centuries. The great symbolic importance of Mahabodhi in the Asian Buddhist world is also indicated by the various 'recreations' of the Mahabodhi temple in other parts of Asia and its frequent representation on Buddhist plaques and tablets at sites in different lands.

The huge Nalanda complex (Asher, 2015; Sanyal, 2018c) consisted of a large *stupa*, five temples and 9–11 monasteries. A large number of sculptures (stone, bronze, stucco) belonging to the early medieval period were found here, along with many inscribed seals and sealings, including monastic, royal, and administrative ones. About 29 km west of Nalanda is the site of Telhara, which has revealed remains of a large monastic complex. Several other monastic remains have been found in Eastern India (Choudhary, 2016) and no doubt more remain to be found. One of the interesting features of the Buddhist monastic establishments of the early medieval period is the discovery of Hindu images, along with Buddhist ones.

The Pala kings have often been given credit for the continued strong presence of Buddhism in Eastern India. Their seals on their copper plate grants have the emblem of the *dharmachakra* flanked by deer; their inscriptions invoke the Buddha and describe kings as his devout worshippers (*parama-saugata*). However, direct epigraphic evidence of their patronage of Buddhist monasteries in their domain are few. Early Pala kings such as Dharmapala and Devapala are known to have built shrines and made gifts to the Nalanda monastery. Devapala made a joint endowment to Nalanda, along with Balaputradeva, a Shailendra king of Java, an interesting example of trans-regional grants. However, as pointed out by Sanjukta Datta (2017, 2019) there were several other benefactors involved in extending financial support to monasteries. These included subordinate rulers, monks, and 'petitioner-donors' who are the actual donors but sought the Pala king's ratification of the land transfers. Gifts to Brahmanas continued to be favoured by the Pala kings but Buddhism was not in a state of decay or decline in Bihar and Bengal.

Nalanda (from top): monasteries; stucco Buddha; Avalokiteshvara

FURTHER DISCUSSION | **Ratnagiri**

Ratnagiri hill is located on the banks of the Keluo stream, not far from the confluence of the Brahmani and Birupa rivers, in Jajpur district, Odisha. Local tradition connects it with the palace of a mythical king. Debala Mitra's excavations conducted at this site (1958–61) brought to light a huge monastic complex that flourished from at least the 5th to the 12th century, declined by the end of the 13th century, but continued to exist till the 16th century. Several sealings have the name of Shri-Ratnagiri *mahavihara*, indicating that this was the name of the monastery.

The excavations revealed a huge main *stupa*, two monasteries, eight shrines, many small *stupa*s, sculptures, and architectural elements. Several building phases were identified in the main structures.

The main *stupa* (Stupa 1) was located near the south-west corner of the highest point of the hill. The dome was missing. The brick base is about 14 ft high and made of fine brickwork with a plaster of shell-lime. The projections have horizontal reliefs. The inner part of the *stupa* was in the form of a 12-spoked wheel made of brick, the spaces within which were filled with mud. This *stupa* was built before the 9th century over the plinth of an older *stupa* that may have belonged to the Gupta period. The area around the main *stupa* was crowded with small *stupa*s of different sizes and forms, some with decorations carved in relief. Some of them have images of the Buddha, Tara, or various Vajrayana deities carved in niches of their drums. Charred bones, beads, and gold coins were found in some of them. Others contained a stone or terracotta plaque inscribed with Buddhist ritual formulae. Apart from hundreds of portable monolithic *stupa*s, many sculptures and stone and terracotta plaques were found near the main *stupa*. Stupa 2 was located to the east of Stupa 1.

To the north of Stupa 1, and facing it, were two monasteries found side by side, separated by a narrow alley. Monastery

1 was the larger of the two and was initially built in the 7th/8th century and had two structural phases. It was two-storeyed and consisted of 24 cells around a courtyard. The main entrance consists of elaborately carved chlorite stone, with figures in the niches, including those of Vajrapani and Padmapani. A beautifully carved Gaja-Lakshmi is carved on the stone door-frame of the entrance. Monastery 2 is smaller and single-storeyed. Remains of several shrines were also found.

A large number of artefacts were found during the Ratnagiri excavations. These included bronze images of the Buddha, Lokeshvara, Maitreya, Manjushri, and Tara. There were many stone images as well.

A 12th century copper plate inscription found at Ratnagiri belonged to the reign of the Somavamshi king Karna. It records the gift of a village in favour of a woman named Rani Karpurashri who was associated with the Salonapura *mahavihara* in Utkala-desha. She seems to have been a queen or concubine of the king and seems to have been connected with a Buddhist monastery.

Taranatha's early 17th century account states that the Ratnagiri monastery was constructed on the crest of a mountain in the kingdom of Odivisha (Odisha) during the rule of a king named Buddhapaksha. This king has been identified with the Gupta ruler Narasimhagupta Baladitya. Taranatha states that three sets of Mahayana and Hinayana texts were kept here, and that there were 500 monks and 8 schools of *dharma*. The monastery is also mentioned in an 18th century Tibetan text, *Pag Sam Jon Zong*, where is associated with the Tantric Kalachakra *tantra*.

Source Debala Mitra, 1971: 225–32

This is also the case in Odisha. Xuanzang mentions a hundred Mahayana monasteries in this region and describes some of them. In the 8th century, a king of Odisha (perhaps one of the Bhauma-Kara rulers) is said to have sent an autographed copy of a text called the Gandavyuha to the Chinese emperor Te-tsong, through a monk named Prajna. Apart from the textual sources, there are several sprawling Buddhist monasteries in Odisha, some of which give evidence of activity from the early historic to early medieval period (Mitra, 1971: 223–33; Ray, 2013; Patnaik, [2000] 2021). Udayagiri, Lalitagiri, and Ratnagiri are among these.

Buddhist images of the early medieval period show great variety in iconographic forms and testify to the popularity of devotional worship. The *Bodhicharyavatara* of Shantideva (8th century CE) describes the Mahayana rites of worship. These included bathing the image with scented water, offering food, flowers, and clothes, swinging censers, and burning incense, and the performance of vocal and instrumental music. Donative inscriptions of the Maitrakas of Valabhi refer to provisions made to cover the cost of incense, lamps, oil, and flowers (*dhupa-dipa-taila-pushpa*).

Spiti valley (HP) (from top right): Key Monastery; Tabo Monastery, clay statues in assembly hall; Alchi, Ladakh: painting of shrine

The early medieval period saw the ascendency of Tantric Buddhism, also known as Vajrayana (Thunderbolt or Diamond Vehicle) or Mantrayana (Vehicle of the Mantras), which combined ritual, magic, meditation, and a belief in the great efficacy of *mantras* in attaining spiritual perfection. The earliest texts of this tradition are the *Manjushrimulakalpa* and the *Guhyasamaja* (5th–6th centuries). The thunderbolt and diamond both symbolized power and strength, characteristics of a person who had attained *siddhi* (enlightenment). The *vajra*-sceptre and bell were important elements in the ritual paraphernalia of Vajrayana. Mantras were considered an important means to attain spiritual perfection. One of the most important ones was the six-syllable *mantra* described in the tradition as the *hridaya* (heart) of Avalokiteshvara: *Om mani padme hum*. *Om* and *hum* were sacred sounds. *Mani padme* literally means 'jewel in the lotus', or it may refer to a *bodhisattva* named Manipadma. Buddhist Tantra has complex symbolic interpretations of this *mantra*, which was believed to have great potency. Female deities had an important place in the Vajrayana pantheon. The most popular of these was Tara. The exponents of Tantric or esoteric Buddhism were known as Siddhas or Tantra-gurus. The 16th century Tibetan traveller gives an account of famous Siddhas.

The *Hevajra Tantra* advocates the attainment of liberation by using and sublimating sexual energy. Sexual rituals, alcohol, and meat were part of some of the rituals. The path

Tara

Tara, Alchi

Tara was known in earlier centuries, but became increasingly important in the early medieval period when she was recognized as a Buddha. The *Manjushrimulakalpa* lists her various names—Bhrikuti, Mamaki, Lochana, Shveta, Pandaravasini, and Sutara. Later texts speak of her many forms, of which the Green and White were the most popular. These are said to have been born from the tears of Avalokiteshvara when he saw the terrible conditions in hell. Tara represents the feminine personification of transcendent wisdom and extraordinary compassion. She is considered to have a great capacity to relieve people's suffering. She is a saviour who protects people from eight great *bhayas* (fears)—lions, elephants, fires, serpents, robbers, drowning, imprisonment, and demons. She has multiple emanations that help her perform her work for humanity.

The *Mahapratyangira-dharani* refers to her as the greatest deity. She is described as white in colour, wearing a garland of *vajras* around her neck, holding a *vajra* in her hand, and bearing the figure of Vairochana on her crown. Many *Tara-stotras* (Tara hymns) were composed from the 7th century CE. The 8th century *Sragdhara-stotra* describes her as one who gives strength to the weak and succour to those in distress, and as the saviour of all beings from sufferings of all kinds. Early medieval *stotras* elevate Tara to the position of a companion of Avalokiteshvara and mother of all the Buddhas, associating her with *maitri* (love) and *karuna* (compassion). In Tantric Buddhism, Tara came to be considered as the *shakti* (energy) of the Buddha, or as an emanation of one of the various Buddhas, or as a Buddha herself.

One of the most frequent iconic representations of Tara in Northern and Eastern India depicts her in a form known as Khadiravani Tara or Shyama Tara, considered to be an emanation of the Dhyani Buddha Amoghasiddha. She is shown standing or sitting gracefully, with her right hand in the boon-granting *varada-mudra*, and holding a lotus with a long stalk in her left hand. She has two attendants—Ashokakanta Marichi to her right and Ekajata to her left. Eight miniature goddesses or scenes are sometimes shown to the left and right. Another form of Tara is Mahachina Tara or Ugra Tara, an emanation of Akshobhya. This is her terrifying form, in which she appears four armed, standing on a corpse. She holds a sword and chopper in her right hands, and a lotus and skull cap in her left.

Source Miranda Shaw, 2006: 306–58

of Sahajayana, taught by the *mahasiddha* Saraha, on the other hand, advocated neither rituals nor *mantras*. It emphasized instruction by a guru and held that it was possible to attain a liberated state while enjoying a worldly life. The Sahajiyas rejected obtuse philosophy and devotional worship, and attached prime importance to intuition in the attainment of salvation. This sect was especially influential in Bengal.

Some scholars have analyzed the social aspects of Tantric or esoteric Buddhism. Miranda Shaw's (1994) study of women in Tantric Buddhism, suggests that women and men are integral to the Tantric way, and that they are both seen as capable of creating non-exploitative, non-coercive, and mutually enlightening relationships, and as capable of attaining liberation together. This can be seen, for instance, in the image of the union of a male and female Buddha as a symbol of enlightenment, as well as in the powerful iconography of Yoginis in Tantric iconography. Shaw argues that women played an important role in the creation of Tantric Buddhism and that they participated actively and fully in it as teachers, students, practitioners, and innovators. This seems a somewhat idealized view.

Ronald M. Davidson (2002) has tried to relate Tantric Buddhism to the broader patterns of political, social, and economic change in the early medieval period. Although

NEW DIRECTIONS IN RESEARCH | **The Buddhist heritage of the Maldives**

With its coral reefs, beautiful beaches, and biodiversity, the Maldives is well known as a tourist destination. The country, which is part of the Indian subcontinent, consists of 1192 islands in the Indian Ocean. Out of its area of about 90,000 sq. km, only 298 sq km is land.

In 1922, H. C. P. Bell, the first Archaeological Commissioner of Ceylon, excavated the remains of two Buddhist monasteries (one small, one large) and a *stupa* on Gamu Island. A Buddha head and a small, seated Buddha figure were among the finds. He also examined the remains of a *stupa* at Foh Mulah. Bell thought there were some similarities between the Buddhist structures of the Maldives and those at Anuradhapura in Sri Lanka. Subsequently, other Buddhist structural remains, relic caskets, stone and metal images, and a carved Buddha footprint were found on the islands. Some of the antiquities were housed in the National Museum in Male. In 2012, vandals unfortunately destroyed many of them.

Three inscriptions studied by Jost Gippert throw interesting light on the islands' Buddhist heritage. The first inscription was found on Landhoo island. It is inscribed on a rectangular coral block (about 56 x 19 x 21 cm), which is broken into three pieces. About two-thirds of the inscription, which once extended across all four sides of the stone, is preserved. It seems to have been a continuous text, some of which is difficult to read. The language is Prakrit, with some Sanskrit elements. The script resembles the Brahmi script of South Indian inscriptions of the 6th-8th centuries. The inscription refers to smashing of the possession caused by various evil spirits, demons, and beings. Its contents are similar to the *Sitatapatradharani*, a text available in Sanskrit and translations thereof, which has formulae to prevent possession by various beings. Gippet suggests that the coral stone inscribed with *dharani*s may have been located in a shrine.

Two other coral artefacts with multiple carvings of faces and Sanskrit inscriptions belong to the 9th/10th centuries. Both stones have male grimacing faces with bulging eyes carved on them. The inscriptions on both these intriguing stone pieces seem identical. Each begins by paying homage to the *vajra*s of body, speech, and mind and ends with hailing Yamantaka. The inscription is a *mantra* used to invoke Yamantaka, the leader of the 'Wrathful Kings' of Tantric Buddhism. Similarities have been found with the *Guhyasamjatantra* and *Manjushrimulakalpa*, although the inscribed mantra is closer to the former.

Unfortunately, these stone pieces were destroyed in the 2012 vandalism.

The Maldives were a major source of cowrie shells, which were part of a parallel money economy for centuries in various parts of Asia. The Buddhist aspect of the history of these islands has, however, been less well-known. A coral *linga*, found in 1959 on Ariadu island in the vicinity of the remains of three Buddhist *stupa*s, are clues to Hindu influence as well.

The archaeological remains and the Prakrit and Sanskrit inscriptions discussed here point to the fact that Buddhist monks had made their way to the Maldive islands and established monasteries here, and that Tantric Buddhism had a strong impact before the introduction of Islam in these islands.

Source Gippert, 2004, 2013–14; Forbes, 1987

his analysis is limited insofar as it takes the feudal paradigm and all its corollaries as a given, it does raise important issues about the social dimensions of esoteric Buddhism. Davidson suggests a 'samantization' of the gods, in which deities, like kings, came to be organized into a hierarchy of supremacy and subordination. He also sees a political resonance in the fact that Tantric Buddhism had as its defining metaphor the individual achieving kingship and exercising dominion. The newer forms of Buddhism had to grapple with the collapse of old sources of support and patronage and had to forge new social links. The *siddhas* evolved networks of political patronage and engaged with tribal and outcaste groups. Some monasteries grew into *mahavihara*s and became owners of large landed estates. Women's participation—both at the monastic and lay level—declined sharply, something very apparent from the inscriptional silence from all over the subcontinent.

In the long run, there was a decline of Buddhism in India, but it was neither uniform nor absolute. The factors suggested for the decline include Buddhism's failure to maintain a distinct identity; an alleged 'degeneration' brought in by increasing Tantric influence; an aggressive Hinduism; and the Turkish invasions. Giovanni Verardi (2018) argues that Buddhism did not slowly fade away; it was pushed out by an aggressive Brahmanism, and this involved a great deal of violence and persecution. There is much about the history of Buddhism in early medieval India, especially the reasons for the decline in lay support and patronage, which remains unclear. It should also be noted that some of the monasteries that were established in Tibet and in the western Himalayas during early medieval times have a continuous history right down to the present.

Major centres of Jainism

Jainism was popular in parts of Rajasthan, Gujarat, Bengal, Odisha, Madhya Pradesh, Uttar Pradesh, and Karnataka (Chatterjee, 1984). Xuanzang's account suggests that the Digambara sect was more widespread than the Shvetambara sect. Jaina establishments received royal patronage from the Chapas of Gujarat and the Paramara kings.

Details of Dilwara temple, Mount Abu

FURTHER DISCUSSION | **The colossal image of Gommateshvara at Sravana Belagola**

Sravana Belagola, a small town in the Channarayapatna *taluk* of Hassan district in Karnataka is an important Jaina pilgrimage site. Its name derives from *shramana*, which means 'ascetic' in Sanskrit, and *bela-kola* which means 'white tank' in Kannada. The town lies between two rocky hills known as Chandragiri or Chikkabetta and Vindhyagiri or Indragiri (also known as Doddabetta).

The 37 Jaina temples at Sravana Belagola were built between the 8th and 18th centuries. A Jaina monastery here has 17th–18th century mural paintings on its wall. Over 500 inscriptions in this town speak of the history of the place. However, Sravana Belagola is best known for its colossal 17.5 m high monolithic statue of the saint Gommateshvara or Bahubali, which is said to be the tallest free-standing monolithic sculpture in the world.

In Jaina tradition, Gommata or Bahubali is the son of Adinatha, the first *tirthankara*. Tenth century inscriptions in Kannada, Tamil, and Marathi, engraved at the base of the image, tell us that it was made at the orders of Chamunda Raja or Chavunda Raya. Chamunda Raya was a minister of the Ganga king Rachamalla (Rajamalla), who ruled from 974 to 984 CE.

Bahubali's statue, carved out of light-grey granite, can be seen on the top of the hill on which it stands from as far away as 10 km, but cannot be glimpsed from the base of that hill. The nude image is carved in the round up to the knees, at which point it merges into the matrix of the rock. The surface of the figure is highly polished. Bahubali stands erect in the *Kayotsarga* pose, with stiff, unbent arms and legs, the arms not touching the body. His feet are planted on a full-blown lotus. His taut, robust body has high, broad shoulders, a slim waist, and a broad pelvis. His hair is curly, his face broad, and his chin and nose well shaped. His body has the *lakshanas* (signs) of a *mahapurusha* (great man) such as ears with long lobes and unusually long arms. Creepers entwining his arms and legs, and anthills rising up to his thighs, bear testimony to his extraordinary penance. His gaze is calm and resolute, and the subdued smile playing on his lips reflects his inner tranquility. Bahubali is flanked by the carving of a *yaksha* and *yakshi*.

The *mahamastabhisheka* or head anointment of Bahubali is performed every 12 years. On this occasion, devotees pour offerings including milk, flowers, and jewels over the head of the colossal image. The most recent *mahamastabhisheka* was held in 2006.

Source Nagaraj, 1980

In peninsular India, some of the Gangas, Rashtrakutas, Eastern and Western Chalukyas, and Kadambas were patrons of Jaina scholars and establishments.

A large number of Jaina works were written in Sanskrit, Prakrit, Apabhramsha, Kannada, and Tamil during this period. The great Jaina philosophers of the time included Akalanka, Haribhadra, and Vidyananda. Akalanka, author of the *Tattvartharajavarttika*, was a skilled logician, and seems to have lived in the 8th century. Haribhadra was also a logician, and his works include a commentary on Dinnaga's *Nyayapravesha*. His *Anekantajayapataka* contains a refutation of Buddhist and Brahmanical doctrines. Vidyananda lived in the 9th century and belonged to Pataliputra. His works include the *Aptamimamsalamkrita*, which contains a detailed discussion of the principles of logic. The *Adi Purana* (8th century) of Jinasena and Gunabhadra listed and outlined a set of *samskaras* (life-cycle rituals) which were Brahmanical in form, but were endowed with distinct Jaina meaning. Echoing the prejudices of Brahmanical texts, the *Adi Purana* states that Shudras were not to be included in certain higher religious practices, including monkhood.

Jaina shrines of the early medieval period were located at various places in modern Uttar Pradesh including Deogarh and Mathura. The Digambaras were active in Samatata and Pundravardhana in Bengal. Several places of Jaina pilgrimage were located in Rajasthan, including at Chittor. The Dilwara temples of Mount Abu are among the most spectacular Jaina temples of this period. The Jaina centres in Gujarat included Bhrigukachchha, Girnar, and Valabhi, which was famous for its temple of Chandraprabha and a

FURTHER DISCUSSION | Ritual death in the Jaina tradition

Cultural attitudes towards death are connected with ideas about life, the body, and the goal of human existence. In Jainism, the body is seen as perishable and as an abode of misery. The highest goal is to attain liberation from the cycle of birth and death. Jaina texts contain a detailed typology of death. These include special kinds of ritual death. These are not considered as suicide, but as ways of voluntarily embracing death in order to attain heaven, perfection, or liberation.

The various types of ritual death are not to be undertaken without careful thought. They can be performed only in exceptional circumstances, for instance in the face of a serious calamity, severe famine, terminal illness, or insurmountable problems in sustaining a spiritual life. They require extensive preparation. The guidance of a preceptor ensures that the ritual is performed with full awareness and control of the faculties and without any negative thoughts or passions.

Evidence of these practices in early medieval India comes from texts and memorial stones. The term *nisidhi/nishidhi* can refer to the place or posture chosen for mortification; a mental state; or the place where the bodily remains of a person who has performed ritual death are interred. Most often, it refers to the stone memorial of a person who has performed ritual death. These memorial stones may have inscriptions and/or carvings on them.

Nisidhi/Nishidhi stones at Sravana Belagola; *Paduka* at Sravana Belagola (from top)

There are over hundreds of *nisidhi*s in Karnataka. They are concentrated in certain sacred places. The Chandragiri and Vindhyagiri hills at Sravana Belagola ('Sepulchral Hill', 'Hill of Death') in Hassan district, together form an important Digambara Jaina site and place of pilgrimage. According to legend, the ritual death of saint Bhadrabahu and Chandragupta took place here. Inscriptions indicate that in the early medieval period, the performance of ritual death was initially confined to monks and nuns. Later, there are references to its performance by laity as well (including some royalty).

In the Sravana Belagola inscriptions, the word *nisidhi* first occurs at in the 7th/8th century, but it is extensively used only in the 12th century. The inscriptions mention various other technical terms that refer to specific types of ritual death. These include *samadhi*, *sallekhana*, *sanyasana*, *pandita*, *pauggamaṇa*, *panchapada*, and *aradhana*. The frequency of the occurrence of these terms changes over time. In some cases, more than one term occurs. For instance, the 10th century Ganga king Marasimha is said to have attained the *samadhi* death and observed the *aradhana yoga*. Machikabbe, mother of queen Shantala, performed *sanyasana*, and died a *pandita* death, listening to the account of *samadhi*.

In order to understand the meaning of such technical terms, it is necessary to look at the explanations in texts. *Aradhana* emphasizes listening to and understanding the Aradhana texts and their philosophical ideas. *Panchapada* is a type of death that emphasizes the prayer of five phrases to the *pancha-parameshthi*s (five great teachers). This hymn is to be repeatedly chanted/listened to. *Sanyasana* emphasizes renunciation and abstinence from food, etc. *Sallekhana* is a type of ritual death that emphasizes fasting. *Samadhi/Samadhi yoga* emphasizes mental concentration, meditation, and control of the senses. *Pandita-marana* ('wise man's death') emphasizes right knowledge. There are different kinds of *pandita marana* depending on intensity, kind, and period and the type of bodily mortification. *Pauggamana* emphasizes mortification of the body.

Source Settar 2016, 2017

NEW DIRECTIONS IN RESEARCH | **Jainism in the religious landscape of Mathura**

In a comprehensive analysis of the religious landscape of Mathura across fifteen centuries, from the third century BCE to the twelfth century CE, Kanika Kishore Saxena reveals the long, complex, and multi-layered religious history of Mathura before it developed strong associations with Vasudeva Krishna. The main focus of Kishore Saxena's work is *dana* within and across religious traditions—Jainism; Buddhism; the worship of Vasudeva Krishna and other Hindu deities; *yakshas* and *nagas*; and the patronage of Brahmanas. Her data base consists of almost 300 inscriptions, examined in conjunction with the sculptural and archaeological remains. Because of the long period of the study, continuities and changes in the religious landscape can be discerned.

Parshvanatha

The analysis reveals Jainism to be a dominant religious tradition in Mathura across the centuries. In the early period (*c.* 2nd century BCE to 3rd century CE), gifts were associated with temples; images of *tirthankaras* and carved stone tablets of homage known as *ayagapatas* and *shilapatas* were the most frequent items of donation. The most important Jaina site at Mathura is Kankali Tila, which yielded structural remains of a *stupa* and two temples, and 86 inscriptions ranging from the 2nd century BCE to the 11th century CE. The *jina* image appears in Mathura as early as the 1st century BCE. The earliest *jinas* who can be identified here are Rishabhanatha, Mahavira, and Parshvanatha. Kankali Tila gives evidence of *stupa* worship. Apart

Sarvatobhadra *Jina*

from the discovery of a brick *stupa*, *stupas* are carved on an architrave of a *torana* (gateway), *ayagapatas*, and *shilapatas*. *Stupa* worship is usually seen as a Buddhist practice, but it seems to have been practice among Jainas in Mathura. Jaina donative inscriptions have been found at other sites in Mathura as well, such as Katra, Rani ki Mandi, and Isapur. Donors include monks and nuns, whose monastic affiliations are indicated by reference to their belonging to specific

temple dedicated to Mahavira. In Central India, Jaina establishments existed at Sonagiri and Khajuraho. In Western India, there were well-established Jaina centres at Nasik and Pratishthana. There are Jaina caves at Ellora. In Odisha, the Jaina establishments at Udayagiri and Khandagiri continued to flourish in the early medieval period.

Jainism had a strong presence in the Karnataka area. The Aihole inscription of Pulakeshin II begins with an invocation to Jinendra (lord of the *jinas*) and tells us that the poet Ravikirti was responsible for the building of the temple in whose wall the inscription is embedded. Jaina temples are located at Sravana Belagola, Koppana, and Halebeedu. Jaina inscriptions have also been found in various parts of Andhra Pradesh. Donative inscriptions belonging to the reigns of Pallava, Chola, and Pandya kings have been found in various parts of Tamil Nadu, and they contain the names of various Jaina saints. One who is mentioned frequently is Ajjanandi, who seems to have lived in Madurai in the 9th century. Other saints, who were probably his contemporaries or near contemporaries, include Indusena and Mallisena. Jaina inscriptions at places such as Sravana Belagola give long lists of pontifical succession stretching over many centuries. By the end of the early medieval period, Jainism retained a significant presence in Gujarat, Rajasthan, and Karnataka.

ganas, *kulas*, and *shakhas*. Monks and nuns are also referred to in inscriptions as inspiring the laity to make gifts. They are sometimes carved on the pedestal of *jina* images, along with lay followers and children. Women donors outnumber male donors. In inscriptions, male and female lay donors are identified on the basis of their kinship relationships. Additionally, male donors are often identified on the basis of their occupation, while women donors may be identified on the basis of the occupation of their husbands.

Textual, epigraphic, and sculptural evidence indicate that Mathura continued to be an important centre of Jainism after the 4th century. The first Jaina council was held in this city in the 4th century. But the number of Jaina images and donative inscriptions decrease. The *ayagapatas* and *shilapatas* of the earlier period disappeared, and there were stylistic changes in the *jina* images. There are a total of 10 donations belong to the 4th-11th century period. Five of these are from Kankali Tila. After the 6th century, monks and nuns were no longer identified according to their *gana*, *kula*, and *shakha*. The term *gachchha* makes its appearance in the 11th century. Women donors are present but are not as dominant as they were in earlier centuries. Kinship and occupation are mentioned along with native place.

A 10th/11th century inscription records donations by the Shvetambara *sangha* in Mathura. This is the earliest epigraphic reference in Mathura to the schism in the Jaina *sangha*, which took place several centuries earlier, certainly by the 3rd century CE. This suggests that specification of Digambara or Shvetambara affiliation was not considered important for the purpose of donative records. In fact, the element of nudity, which was a major difference in monastic practice between these two sects, was not relevant in the context of *jina* images, as virtually all of them (at least till the 11th century) are depicted naked.

Kishore Saxena raises the issue of the interactions between different religious communities and institutions in a pluralistic religious landscape. Her comparative analysis of patronage, phraseology, and epithets across religious traditions indicates that donors of different religious affiliations were usually introduced in the inscriptions within kinship and occupational frameworks. Royal patronage was of minimal importance. Donations by women show their active participation in religious life (a pattern seen elsewhere too). Over the period of the study, Jaina women donors outnumber their male counterparts by almost three times. Women's prominence was not restricted to Jainism alone. At Mathura, taking all the donative inscriptions across religious traditions over the entire period of the study, women donors outnumbered male donors, two to one.

Jaina goddess Chakreshvari

Source Kishore Saxena, 2021

One of the significant features of Jainism in the early medieval period is the importance of goddesses in popular worship (see Cort, 1987). The *tirthankaras* are considered aloof and do not intercede in human affairs. Devotion to goddesses could not lead to enlightenment, but it could help in attaining worldly goals. So, although goddesses were not the main focus of worship in shrines, they had a strong presence. In many Jaina temples, although the main and subsidiary shrines contain images of the *tirthankaras*, the walls and ceilings are carved with beautiful, sensuous female figures. The goddesses are thought to live in the upper, middle, and lower realms. In the upper realms are goddesses such as Sarasvati and Lakshmi, shared by Hinduism and Jainism. In the middle realm are the 16 Tantric *vidyadevis*, associated with magical or occult powers and practices. In the lower realm are the *yakshis*, attendants of the 24 *tirthankaras*. The dividing lines between *yakshi*, *vidyadevi*, and goddess are difficult to draw. The *yakshis* of the lower realm—Ambika, Padmavati, and Jvalamalini—were the most popular Jaina female divinities. Ambika is associated with childbirth and is shown seated on a lion, accompanied by her two sons. Padmavati seems to have originally been a snake goddess (she is the consort of the *naga* king Dharnendra) who later became the attendant of the 23rd *tirthankara* Parshvanatha. Sarasvati, the goddess of learning, has a place in the Hindu,

Buddhist, and Jaina pantheons. Her earliest sculptural image is in fact found at Kankali Tila, a Jaina site in Mathura. Shri or Lakshmi, goddess of wealth was worshipped by merchants of different religious denominations.

Shankara and Advaita Vedanta

The early medieval period saw a great deal of philosophical writings related to the various *darshanas*. One of the most influential thinkers of the time was Shankara, who lived in the late 8th and early 9th centuries. It is difficult to separate historical detail from legend in Shankara's hagiographies, all of which were composed after the 14th century (Pande, [1994] 1998). One of the most popular of these is the *Shankara-digvijaya* of Madhava. This describes Shankara as travelling all over the country, meeting and debating with philosophical adversaries, defeating them all. Shankara was one of the most influential proponents of Vedanta. His version of Vedanta is known as Advaita Vedanta.

As mentioned in Chapter 8, the Upanishads form the last part—*anta*—of the Vedas. They, and the philosophies based on them, are therefore, called Vedanta (sometimes referred to as Uttara Mimamsa). Mention was made in an earlier chapter of the various Vedanta philosophical systems based on the Upanishads, including Badarayana's *Brahma Sutra* and the *Bhagavad Gita*. The earliest formal exposition of Advaita or non-dualistic Vedanta was put forward by Gaudapada in the 7th or 8th century in his *Mandukyakarika*,

FURTHER DISCUSSION | The Hagiographies of Shankara

Shankara seems to have been a relatively obscure figure during his lifetime and for several centuries thereafter. The view of Shankara as representing an aggressive Hindu assertion in the early medieval period is based on his hagiographies, the earliest of which were written many centuries after his time in the 14th and 15th centuries, during the Vijayanagara period. They reflect the concerns of the hagiographers and their times. The hagiographies present a picture of Shankara's thought that is very different from that contained in his own works. They describe him as an ardent devotee of Shiva and as an incarnation of this god. The best-known hagiography is Madhava's *Shankara-digvijaya*, which written sometime between 1650 and 1800 and collated material from several earlier texts.

The basic facts of Shankara's life are that he was born in a Brahmana family in the Kerala region, left home at an early age to become a *sannyasi*, and became a student of the philosopher Govinda (a student of the Advaita philosopher Gaudapada). Shankara wrote numerous works, the most important of which are commentaries on the Upanishads, *Bhagavad Gita*, and Brahmasutras. He travelled a great deal and engaged in many philosophical debates. Other details that can be extracted from the hagiographies are that his father died early and that Shankara himself died at the early age of 32.

Shankara's hagiographies do not emphasize his debates with Buddhists. They give the credit for defeating the Buddhists and establishing the supremacy of the Veda to Kumarila Bhatta. In spite of Kumarila's victories, he is said to have decided to immolate himself on a slow-burning pyre of chaff to atone for his having deceived his Buddhist teacher. Shankara is said to have been passing by when the fire was blazing, and the two men are said to have had a philosophical conversation. The fact that these are not historical accounts should be clear from the fact that Kumarila lived well before Shankara.

Shankara is said to have travelled all over the country, meeting and debating with other philosophers, defeating them all. The most heated debates took place with the Shaktas, tantric worshippers of Bhagavati, Shaiva dualists, Vaishnava Pancharatras, a Bhedabheda Advaitin, and Jainas. There are hardly any Vaishnava opponents. The tone of the debates varies considerably across texts, ranging from cordiality to insult. The hagiographies make much of Shankara's debates with various great philosophers of his time, but they do not usually give details of their philosophical content. The fact that Shankara's debate with the Mimamsaka Mandanamishra is an important event in all the hagiographies shows that at the time when they were written (14th-16th centuries), Advaita Vedanta philosophers considered Mimamsakas as their most formidable competitors.

The fact that many of Shankara's hagiographies have the word *vijaya* (victory) or *digvijaya* (victory over the quarters) in their title indicates their drawing of a parallel between world victor and world renouncer (an idea also found in early Jainism and Buddhism). The descriptions of Shankara's travels to places from the Himalayas to Rameshvaram, and from Dvaraka to Kamarupa, are reminiscent of the Puranic mapping of places of pilgrimage in various parts of the subcontinent and also of the *digvijayas* of great emperors.

Source Bader, 2000; Clark, 2006

a verse commentary on the *Mandukya Upanishad*. Gaudapada was influenced by Madhyamika and Vijnanavada Buddhism. He held that worldly objects were similar to things seen in a dream. Reality is one (*a-dvaita*), and the idea of plurality is due to *maya* (illusion born out of ignorance).

Gaudapada's ideas were developed further by Shankara, who tried to demonstrate that the Upanishads and Brahmasutras contained a systematic, unified philosophy. His major work is his *bhashya* (commentary) on the *Brahma Sutra*. According to Shankara, the performance of Vedic sacrifices was for people who wanted to attain material, worldly gains, but the Upanishads contained the way to supreme knowledge. In his monistic doctrine, *brahman* is the ultimate reality. It is without qualities (*nirguna*). It is pure consciousness, eternal and unchanging. All change and plurality is only apparent. Shankara identified two levels of reality—conventional reality and absolute reality. An example he gave to illustrate this idea is that of a person looking at a coiled rope and thinking that it is a snake. The rope seems like a real snake, but it is not one. The reason for mistaking conventional reality for absolute reality is ignorance (*avidya*). The goal of Advaita Vedanta is liberation from the cycle of rebirth, which consists of the realization of the oneness of the *atman* with *brahman*.

Shankara's vigorous espousal of a philosophy whose roots lay in the Vedic tradition is seen by some scholars as a key factor in the decline of Buddhism in India. On the other hand, it is interesting to note that his critics referred to him as a 'hidden Buddhist'. This is because his treatment of the world as illusion struck them as rather similar to the ideas of the Mahayana schools. However, it should be noted that while defending his interpretation of the Upanishadic doctrine, Shankara also countered objections that could be raised against it by proponents of other schools, putting forward a strong critique of the viewpoints of Buddhist schools as well as other schools such as Samkhya, Nyaya, and Mimamsa.

Shankara is supposed to have founded the Dashanami sect and to have established four or five monasteries known as the Amanaya *mathas* (see Kulke, [1993] 2001). Although it is clear that some sort of organization for preserving and propagating Shankara's teaching emerged fairly early in the day, many historians have argued that the *mathas* (including those at Shringeri and Kanchi) seem to have been established several centuries later, and were attributed to Shankara in order to endow them with prestige. The Shringeri *matha*, for instance, seems to have been set up in the 14th century, during the Vijayanagara period.

The Hindu Sects

At the level of popular practice, it was theistic worship that prevailed, and along with this, there was the development of a theology of *bhakti*. Within the Hindu tradition, although many deities (e.g., Surya, Ganesha, Karttikeya, and Brahma) formed the focus of devotional worship, Vishnu, Shiva, and Shakti were the most popular. There was an increase in the number and geographical spread of temples during this period. Temple sculptures show great variety in the forms of representation of deities, as well as a pan-Indian systemization of iconic forms. Sectarian epithets became common in royal inscriptions, kings patronized the building of temples, and certain temples became closely identified with their royal patrons. However, royal patronage was neither the only nor the most important source of patronage. As in earlier centuries, there were many groups of non-royal people who offered donations to religious establishments.

Although at one level, deities like Vishnu, Shiva, and Shakti formed the focus of exclusive worship of devotees who considered them supreme deities, at another level, they were also part of a larger community of gods. Monolatry—a belief in a supreme god without denying the existence of other gods—is an important aspect of Hinduism. This is why, apart from representations of the presiding deity, Hindu temples often depict various other deities as well. David Lorenzen ([1999] 2006) has argued that a consciousness of a Hindu identity emerged between 1200 and 1500 during the period of interaction with Islam, and that this is reflected in the works of Kabir, Ekanath, Anantadas, and Vidyapati.

It should be noted that the vast forest tracts were inhabited by tribal communities who had their own distinctive cultural identities and practices. The relationship between Hinduism and tribal religion was marked by reciprocal interaction and a constantly shifting frontier. This can be seen in the incorporation of certain tribal deities into the Hindu pantheon and the Hinduization of tribal deities and communities (see Sontheimer, 2022). The historical context of these 'incorporative processes' must have included a great deal of conflict and violence. In the inscriptions of Odisha, references to the goddess Stambheshvari in the grants of the Shulki dynasty and in some of the grants of the Bhanjas of Khinjali *mandala* suggests that she was a tribal goddess who was initially worshipped in the form of a post or pillar. The most striking example of the Hinduization of a tribal deity is Jagannatha in Odisha (see Eschmann et al. [Eds.], [1978] 2014). The tribal element is evident from the iconography of the images of Jagannatha, Subhadra, and Balabhadra in the Jagannatha temple at Puri, which are very different from classical Hindu icons. According to legend, Jagannatha was first worshipped Vishvavasu, a chief of the Shabara tribe. The Daita priests, who are supposed to be the descendants of the original tribal worshippers, have an important role to play in the temple rituals.

VAISHNAVISM AND SHAIVISM

'Durga' temple, Aihole: Shiva with Nandi bull; Varaha lifting Prithvi

Textual evidence and temple sculpture indicate that the idea of the ten incarnations of Vishnu was more or less standarized in the early medieval period. Pancharatra texts expanded on the idea of the *vyuhas* (emanations) of Vishnu, and the number of *vyuhas* increased from 4 to 24. Some aspects of Vaishnava theology were discussed in Chapter 9, and others will be discussed later on in the section on South Indian *bhakti*.

The divine cowherd Krishna emerged as a major focus of devotional worship within Vishnuism. The *Harivamsha*, a supplement to the *Mahabharata*, describes the many legends associated with Krishna's childhood and youth. The *Bhagavata Purana* is another important Vaishnava text. It seems to have been composed in South India in the 9th–10th centuries. Book 10 of this Purana is the *Krishna-charita*, which gives a detailed account of Krishna's life—his birth and his childhood with his foster-parents Nanda and Yashodha; his cowherd life in Braja and his miraculous exploits such as killing Putana and overcoming the serpent Kaliya; and his relationship with the *gopis* (cowherd girls). The text speaks in particular of one *gopi* whom Krishna especially loves, but does not mention her name. In Krishna *bhakti*, the love of the *gopis* for Krishna, their longing for him, and their grief at their separation from him, is used as a metaphor for the relationship between devotee and god.

There are stray references to a Radha in earlier texts such as the *Matsya*, *Varaha*, and *Linga Puranas*. She is not mentioned directly in the *Harivamsha*, or in the *Vishnu* and *Bhagavata Puranas*. It was Jayadeva's celebrated 12th century lyric poem, the *Gita-Govinda* that brought Radha into the limelight. This work is known for its high literary quality and powerful eroticism. The theme of the love between Radha and Krishna was elaborated on in a later Purana, the *Brahmavaivarta Purana*.

Sculptural representations of the various *avataras* of Vishnu have been found in many parts of the subcontinent. The goddesses Lakshmi, Sarasvati, and Bhudevi are often associated with him. Vaishnava devotionalism acquired a strong expression in South India in the hymns of the Alvars, which will be discussed later. Many Vaishnava temples and sculptures are attributed to the early medieval period. The most important early Tantric sect among the Vaishnavas was the Pancharatra. The Sahajiyas of Bengal were a later sect belonging to the Tantric variety of Vaishnavism.

Alexis Sanderson (2006; 2009: 44–45) has described the early medieval period as the Shaiva Age. This is because during these centuries, Shaivism increasingly attracted political affiliation and patronage across South and South-east Asia. Between the eighth and twelfth centuries, there is evidence of many kings taking *diksha* from Shaiva preceptors, and there is an increase in epigraphic references to Shaiva *mathas* (monasteries). According to Sanderson, Shaivism appealed to a growing body of royal patrons by

FURTHER DISCUSSION | **The 'Durga' temple at Aihole**

The 'Durga temple' at Aihole is named after a nearby fort, and is *not* dedicated to the goddess Durga. It was probably built in about 725–30 CE, during the reign of the Chalukya king Vijayaditya. The temple is apsidal in form and has an ambulatory passage running along the entire outer side of the apse. The *mandapa* (hall) and verandah are basically in the Dravida style, while the *shikhara* is a variety of the Nagara style. The small sanctum with a rounded back has a raised circular altar. The image of the presiding deity was removed at some point, it is not known when.

The Durga temple is an enigmatic structure. The issues that scholars have grappled with include the place of this temple within the larger history of temple architecture, whether the *shikhara* was part of the original structure or whether it was added later to an originally flat-roofed shrine; and whether the sculptures in the circumambulatory passage were original or later additions.

The biggest mystery, however, concerns the deity to whom this temple was dedicated. Over the years, it has been variously connected with Shiva, Vishnu, Brahma, and Aditya (Surya). It has also been argued that it was a Buddhist shrine, taken over at some point by the Shaivas. This view, which is not longer accepted, was based on the erroneous belief that the apsidal architectural form was associated exclusively with Buddhism. In actual fact, this form was used in the religious architecture of the Ajivikas, Jainas, and the Hindu sects.

The *pradakshina-patha* (circumambulatory passage) of the temple consists of a verandah gallery running all around the shrine. The outer rim of this gallery is formed by a parapet and 28 square pillars, letting in plenty of air and light. On the inner wall of this gallery are 11 wall niches, separated by pilasters. These niches frame a series of relief sculptures, only seven of which have survived. These reliefs are considered among the sculptural masterpieces of the Chalukya period. The themes of these sculptures are: Shiva with Nandi; Vishnu in his man-lion Narasimha *avatara*; Vishnu on *garuda*; Vishnu in his boar incarnation; Durga Mahishasuramardini; and Hari-Hara (the combination of Vishnu and Shiva). One of the empty niches once contained an image of Shiva as Bhikshatana.

The sheer variety of the sculptures makes it difficult to identify the cultic affiliations of the temple. Shaiva temples of this region usually depict a variety of deities, but have a Nandi *mandapa* (a pavilion enshrining the Nandi bull), which is absent here. Therefore, it does not seem to be a Shiva temple. As its sculptural programme does not privilege the goddess, it does not seem to be a goddess temple. Vishnu temples of this region and period tend to have exclusively Vaishnava sculptural themes, so this was not a Vishnu temple. The view among many art historians today is that the Durga temple was dedicated to Aditya (Surya). There is an image of this deity above the entrance, and a gateway inscription refers to it as a temple of Aditya. Several representations of the sun god have been found elsewhere on the structure as well. However, even if it can be understood as a Surya temple, in many respects, the form and style of the Durga temple at Aihole remain unique.

Source Tartakov, 1997

extending and adapting itself to include rituals and prescriptions that fitted in well with early medieval kingship. It also succeeded in standardizing its rituals and doctrines and in creating a trans-regional organization. The most important Tantric sects were Shaiva. There was a close relationship between the Shaiva and Shakta sects due to the close connection between the deities Shiva and Shakti.

Shaiva sects with formal initiation rituals belonged to one of two different but overlapping paths—the Ati-marga and Mantra-marga (Sanderson, 2006: 1–3; 2015b: 3–5; Padoux, 2017: 30–31). The Ati-marga (outer path) was restricted to Brahmanas. Initiates

Varaha sculpture from Lalitapur, 10th/11th century

became celibate ascetics, and their goals were purification and liberation. Mantra-marga (*mantra* path) or full-fledged Tantric Shaivism was open to all social groups, and members could opt to be ascetics or householders. Its aims were the acquiring of *siddhis* (supernatural powers), the transformation of the soul, and liberation. Mantra-marga included exoteric and esoteric traditions. In the exoteric Mantra-marga, the forms of worship of Shiva and the offerings made to him were similar to those in Brahmanical rituals. In the esoteric branch of the Mantra-marga, the main deities were fierce gods known as Bhairavas or fierce female deities. Offerings included alcoholic and blood offerings, and rituals included sexual rites. As pointed out by André Padoux, Tantra percolated in a powerful way into mainstream religious life in a way that it was often not recognized as being specifically Tantric.

As mentioned in Chapter 9, in Tantra, godhead is understood as involving the union of a masculine and feminine aspect. *Shakti* (energy) is conceived of as feminine and is central to the Tantric view of the universe and liberation. Tantra has a strong ritualistic and yogic element. There are many deities, male and female, often very fierce. The idea of *puja* in Tantra involves propitiating the deity and, according to the medieval commentaries, transforming the worshipper into the deity. Rituals involving sex are one of the distinctive features of Tantra and were to be performed by qualified initiates according to fixed rules. Texts such as Abhinavagupta's *Tantraloka* (10th century) explain *kama* not as pleasure but as a kind of passion that was a gateway to transcending the self and uniting with God.

Tantra did not challenge the Brahmanical tradition directly. In fact, it attempted a compromise in various ways. Most of the Tantric texts were written in Sanskrit and were composed by Brahmanas. The Shaiva and Vaishnava sects (both the Tantric and non-Tantric ones) recognized the Vedas and *smriti* texts and the idea of the *dharma* of *varnas* and *ashramas*, but they held that true liberation could only be achieved by following the Shaiva or Vaishnava path respectively. This attitude of conditional acceptance was not reciprocated (Sanderson, 2015). Orthodox Vaidika Brahmanas rejected all views that did not rest on the Veda. The 7th century *Tantravarttika* of the Mimamsaka Kumarilabhatta describes followers of Samkhya, Yoga, Pancharatrika Vaishnavas, Pashupata Shaivas, Buddhists, and Jainas as contradicting the Veda and hence unacceptable.

But the increasing popularity of the Shaiva and Vaishnava sects meant that orthodox Vaidika Brahmanas had to coexist with them. A Brahmana who followed the Vaidika traditions and rituals could also worship a supreme deity. The coexistence was especially visible in political circles. Kings who advertised themselves as worshippers of Vishnu, Shiva, a *jina*, or the Buddha gave grants of land to Vaidika Brahmanas. Some also boasted about their performance of Vedic sacrifices.

The increasing popularity of the worship of Shiva was accompanied by the development of various Shaiva philosophical schools, whose ideas show considerable overlap. The Agamas are considered authoritative texts by followers of Shaiva Siddhanta, Kashmir Shivaism, and the Virashaiva tradition. They are considered as containing the words of Shiva himself and are supposed to be taught only to select initiates. These Agamas seem to have been composed in the Tamil-speaking area between *c.* 400 and 800 CE. Although they recognize the importance of knowledge (*jnana*), ritual (*kriya*), and yogic practice and conduct (*charya*), they attach prime importance to *bhakti*. Recognizing the authority of the Vedic tradition, they nevertheless consider Shaiva *bhakti* as superior to the performance of Vedic sacrifices. The rituals prescribed for performance at home and in temples are supposed to be performed with Shaiva mantras, although they also include some Vedic mantras. The texts also discuss the making of religious images and the construction of temples.

Shaiva Siddhanta was a major Shaiva philosophical school in South India. It recognized three eternal principles—God (Shiva), the universe, and souls. Shiva was considered to have created the world through his will and energy (*shakti*). Shaiva Siddhanta accepts the authority of the Vedas, Agamas, and the hymns of the saints, but interprets the Vedic tradition through the perspective of Shaiva *bhakti*.

The influential Kashmir Shaiva school was associated with a monistic or non-dualistic philosophy, according to which the *atman* (individual soul) and the world were identical with Shiva. The universe was considered a manifestation created by Shiva through his creative power, and is compared to a reflection of a city or village in a mirror. Shakti is considered the feminine aspect of the god. The ideas of the Kashmir Shaiva school are contained in the *Shivasutras*, which, according to tradition, were revealed by the god himself to a sage named Vasugupta, who can be placed in the 8th–9th centuries. His pupils Kallata and Somananda further elaborated on the philosophical doctrines. Other leading figures of the school include Abhinavagupta, Utpala, and Ramakantha.

The Kapalikas and Kalamukhas were two important Shaiva sects. No texts of these sects have survived, and their history has to be reconstructed on the basis of inscriptions and highly negative references to them in the texts of their adversaries. These sects had monasteries (*mathas*) and well-organized priesthoods. Lorenzen's ([1972] 1991) study of these orders shows that although they had their distinct monastic groups, they did not have separate laities. The Kapalikas were Tantric Shaivite ascetics who lived in the forest. They carried a skull bowl for begging and were associated with a *mahavrata* or great vow. They are described as performing penances, animal and human sacrifice, and sometimes practising self-mutilation. The Kalamukhas seem to have been an offshoot of the Pashupatas, and were especially active in the Karnataka area between the 11th and 14th centuries. There are many inscriptions recording gifts to temples and *mathas* of this sect. The inscriptional references to various Shaiva sects in early medieval India have been discussed by V. S. Pathak (1960).

Shaiva *bhakti* became extremely popular in South India due to the ideas and activities of the Nayanmar saints, which will be discussed in a later section of this chapter. Aspects of Shaiva sculpture and architecture too are discussed in a later section.

THE WORSHIP OF THE GREAT GODDESS

Mention was made in Chapter 8 to the *Devi-Mahatmya*, which was inserted into the *Markandeya Purana* by about the 7th century. This contains verses in praise of the Devi (goddess) and speaks of her many exploits, including how she vanquished the demon Mahishasura. The stories narrated in the *Devi-Mahatmya* are accompanied by verses in which the gods praise her in various ways. The *Narayani-stuti* speaks of her *Vaishnavi-shakti* sustaining the entire universe. It refers to her nine Matrika forms, and to her other manifestations as Lakshmi, Sarasvati, Narayani, Katyayani, Durga, Bhadrakali, and

FURTHER DISCUSSION | The Goddess as slayer of the demon Mahisha

The 700 verses of the *Durga-saptashati* in the *Markandeya Purana* praise the goddess and narrate her many victories. In one place, the goddess is said to have briskly jumped onto the body of the buffalo demon Mahisha, pressed him down with one leg, and thrust her spear into his neck. In this aspect, she is known as Durga Mahishasuramardini (Durga, slayer of the demon Mahisha). The basic iconography of Durga Mahishasuramardini, which is in fact the most frequently depicted form of the goddess in sculpture, was fixed in the early centuries CE. However, within the broad iconographic parameters, ancient crafts people made choices in terms of detail and portrayal, and their individual creations often carried a distinctive stamp. Some of the most impressive sculptural representations of Durga Mahishasuramardini were made by sculptors of the early medieval period.

Sculptural depictions of the goddess show some variations on the basic theme. The number of arms varies; the lion sometimes appears as her mount, at other times by her side. In some places, the buffalo demon is shown as an animal, in others as part man, part animal. In some representations, the image of the goddess captures and conveys strength and vigour. At other places, the sculptor managed to simultaneously convey gracefulness and femininity.

One of the most impressive representations of Durga Mahishasuramardini is located in a niche in the Virupaksha temple at Aihole. The carving is very deep, almost but not quite in the round, giving it a three-dimensional effect. The demon is depicted as a human with buffalo horns. His head is pressed down under the goddess' left foot. Her arms are arranged in a rhythmic pattern. Her sword effortlessly cleaves the demon's body. The sculptor managed to create an image that is at once exceptionally graceful, realistic, and powerful.

Kamakhya Temple, Guwahati

Ambika. In the last 14 verses of the *Devi-Mahatmya*, the goddess declares her future manifestations in different ages—as Yogamaya (daughter of Nanda and Yashoda), Raktadantika, Shatakshi, Shakambhari, Durga, Bhima, and Bhramari. In the last canto, in a promise reminiscent of the *Bhagavad Gita*, she announces that she will appear from time to time in the world, in order to destroy demons and evil.

Architectural and sculptural remains from various parts of the subcontinent reflect the widespread worship of Durga, as well as the allied cults of the Matrikas (usually mentioned as seven or eight in number) and the Yoginis. Multi-armed Durga images of this period occur in large numbers, especially in Eastern India. They also occur in the Tamil Nadu area, where an iconographic peculiarity is the association of the goddess with a stag. Representations of the goddess as Nishumbhamardini (slayer of the demon Nishumbha) occur among the reliefs at many temples belonging to the Chola period. The worship of the Sapta-Matrikas and Yoginis was also popular in Eastern India. The Matrikas were mentioned in Chapter 9. The Yoginis, eventually reckoned as 64 in number, are described in texts as attendants or manifestations of Durga in her battle against the demons Shumbha and Nishumbha (Bhattacharyya, 1974: 100–05. Anamika Roy, 2015).

Mahishasuramardini: Sivadol temple, Sibsagar; Virupaksha temple, Pattadakal; Nataraja temple, Chidambaram (from left)

Hirapur, Odisha (from top): Chaunsat Yogini temple, Yoginis; Sapta-Matrika sculpture

The principal Yoginis were identified with the Matrikas. In Odisha, several Matrika images have been found in and near Jajpur (among other areas), and hypaethral (roofless) temples of the Yoginis occur at Ranipur Jharial and Hirapur.

The inscriptions of early medieval India refer to many local goddesses. For instance, those of Odisha mention Viraja and Stambheshvari, and those of Assam mention Kamakhya. The Puranic tradition wove the many goddess cults together by developing the idea that the various local goddesses were manifestations of one great Goddess, the great Devi. Kunal Chakrabarti (2001) has demonstrated how in Bengal, the encounter between Brahmanism and a strong tradition of the worship of autonomous goddesses resulted in a regional cultural synthesis which gave primacy to goddess worship. The *Matsya Purana* gives a list of 108 names of the great goddess, while the *Kurma Purana* invokes her with 1,000 names.

The *Kalika Purana* is an important Shakta text belonging to the early medieval period (van Kooij, 1972). Composed in the area of Assam or in some adjoining part of Bengal, it reflects the diverse forms of the worship of Devi. The goddess is described as having both a benign and a terrifying form. In her *shanta* (calm) form, she has a strongly erotic character. In her *raudra* (fierce) manifestation, she is best worshipped in a cremation ground. The *Kalika Purana* describes the *dakshina-bhava* (the right method) and the *vama-bhava* (the left method) of worship. Although both have a Tantric imprint, it is stronger in the latter. The 'right method' consists of various regular rites and rituals. The 'left method' includes rituals involving the use of alcohol, meat, and sexual rites. The Purana also contains details of the performance of the popular festival of Durga Puja.

The Puranas mention various sacred places associated with the different manifestations of Devi (Sircar, 1973, Bhattacharyya, 1974). The *Devi Bhagvata* refers to such places as *pithas*. The *Kalika Purana* mentions seven *pithas*, associated with places where the dismembered pieces of Sati's body are supposed to have fallen. These were located at Purnagiri, Devikuta, Uddiyana, Kamagiri, the eastern point of Kamarupa, the western point of Kamarupa, and Jalandhar. The number of *pithas* increased subsequently and this reflects a dramatic expansion in the sacred geography associated with the goddess. The *Kularnava Tantra* mentions 18 *pithas*, while the *Kubjika Tantra* mentions 42. Pilgrimages to Shakta *pithas* were well established in the early medieval period.

South Indian *bhakti*: the Alvars and Nayanmars

In the early medieval period, the Alvar and Nayanmar (also known as Nayanar) saints of South India gave a new emphasis and expression to Vaishnava and Shaiva devotionalism, one that was deeply rooted in the Tamil land, language, and ethos. As mentioned in an earlier chapter, the Sanskrit word *bhakti* comes from the root *bhaj*, which means to share or participate. By extension, the *bhakta* is one who shares or participates in the divine. The Tamil word that is used by Alvars and Nayanmars to express their devotion to their god was *anbu*, which means love. The use of the term *bhakti*, or its Tamil version *patti*, is fairly late. The relationship between devotee and god was perceived as a reciprocal one, and the term used to refer to the love of the god for his devotee was *arul*.

The roots of South Indian *bhakti* can be traced to certain features in late Sangam poetry, as well as to certain elements in the *Paripatal* and *Pattuppattu*. For instance, a poem called the *Tirumurukarruppatai* (The Guide to Lord Murugan) in the latter text refers to the god Murugan by using epithets that encapsulate important episodes in his mythology. There is also a tendency to describe Murugan as living in specific places, the devotee being urged to visit the shrines there. Zvelebil (1977) has pointed out that from the point of view of formal structure, the ancestry of *bhakti* poetry can be traced to the *tanippatal*, the single bardic stanzas found among both *akam* and *puram* poems. We can also see links with one of the settings of the heroic poems, namely *patan*, which focuses on eulogizing the patron and asking him for gifts. *Patan* poems and *bhakti* songs both have an intense, personal tone. In the context of *bhakti*, however, the focus shifts from the king to the god, praising the latter and beseeching him to bestow deliverance on his devotee.

PRIMARY SOURCES | **Songs of the Nayanmar saint Appar**

On Shiva *bhakti*:

Why bathe in Ganga or in Kaveri?
or take a holy dip at Kumari?
Why bathe where mingle waters of the seas?
One thing alone will to your rescue come—
Seeing everywhere the Lord Supreme.

Why chant the Vedas, follow Vedic *karma*?
Why preach day by day the books of *dharma*?
Why the six Vedangas learn by rote?
One thing alone will to your rescue come—
thinking always of the Lord Supreme.

Why roam the forests, wander through the towns?
perform strict *tapas* as in books laid down?
why fast and starve, sit gazing at the blue?
One thing alone will to your rescue come—
faith in him, Lord of Wisdom True.

Fetching waters from a thousand *tirthas*
of what avail such futile ritual act?
Like it is to mindless fool who water brings
and guards it safely in a leaking pot!
One thing alone will to your rescue come—
Loving at all times our gracious Lord.

Appar on the community of *bhaktas*:

Whoever they be
wherever they be
if they bow to Shiva
Shiva who carries
Ganga in his locks
to me they are as gods—
they may be
lepers foul
with rotting flesh
or outcastes
of the lowest breed
they may even skin the cow
and eat its flesh—
if they but love Shiva
to them I bow
to them
I offer worship.

Source *Tirumurai* 5, Appar's hymn 99, verses 2, 4, 6, 8, and 10; in Dehejia, 1988: 13–14; *Tirumurai* 6, hymn 95, verse 10; in Dehejia, 1988: 38

According to tradition, there were 12 Alvars and 63 Nayanmars. The hymns of these saints are still sung in temples. The saints themselves are worshipped, a practice that goes back to the Chola period. Images or paintings of the Nayanmars are usually found in the hall around the sanctum and are worshipped. Vishnu temples generally have a separate shrine for images of the Alvars. There is uncertainty about the historicity of some of the saints and it is often difficult to disentangle fact from myth in their hagiographies. The male saints were not recluses or ascetics. They lived their lives as a part of society and most of them were married. The case with the female saints was, as we shall see, different.

Alvar and Nayanmar poetry reflects a devotion that is at once intimate, intense, and ecstatic. The poets visualized their god in various ways—as friend, mother, father, master, teacher, and bridegroom. Many male saints took on the feminine voice of a lover or bride when expressing their longing for union with god. For instance, Manikkavachakar spoke of his lord as the eternal bridegroom. Nammalvar spoke of the lord having such an overwhelming maleness that the *bhakta* loses his own maleness. Apart from the fact that the objects of devotion were male, given prevailing gender roles, the female voice was probably considered especially appropriate for the expression of complete love and surrender. (There are a few instances of women saints assuming a male voice.)

Nayanmar is an honorific. The Shaiva saints did not refer to themselves by this name; they described themselves as *atiyar* (servant) or *tontar* (slave), indicating that they considered themselves servants or slaves of Shiva. Out of the 63 Nayanmars, 3 (known as the *muvar*, 'three revered ones')—Sambandar, Appar, and Sundarar—are considered especially important, and their images are sometimes housed in a special separate shrine in temples. They are occasionally accompanied by an image of Manikkavachakar.

The idea of a community of Shaiva poet-saints goes back to the early 8th century, when Sundarar wrote a poem titled *Tiruttondar Tokai* (Assembly of Sacred Slaves), which listed 62 Nayanmars. In the early 10th century, Nambi Andar Nambi wrote a work called the *Tiruttondar Tiruvantai* (Sacred Poem of the Holy Slaves), wherein he gave a short hagiography of these 62, adding Sundarar's name to the list. He also collected the songs of the saints. In the mid-12th century, stories of the saints' lives were put together in a work called the *Periyapuranam*. This forms the 12th and final book of the canon known as the *Tirumurai*. The collection of hymns known as the *Tevaram* is part of this larger work.

Bronze image of Manikkavachakar

In Shaiva *bhakti*, the relationship between the god and his devotee was often expressed as analogous to that between master and slave. The poems of Manikkavachakar frequently refer to the experience of 'melting' before the lord. There is a deprecation of the body and the corporeal state. There are descriptions of ecstatic worship, where the devotee stammers, tears pour out, when he dances and feels as though he is melting. The tone is frenzied and the poet often reviles himself for his shortcomings. He also talks to the god in familiar tones. An example is Manikkavachakar's song in which he threatens to revile the god Shiva as a madman (*pitta*) if he abandons him.

Alvar means 'those who dive deep' or 'those who are absorbed in the divine'. The hymns of the 12 Alvars were collected in the 10th century by Nathamuni in the *Nalayira Divya Prabandham* (Four Thousand Holy Hymns), which constituted the Vaishnava canon. The first major hagiography of the Alvar saints was a 12th century work called the *Divyasuricharitam* by Garudavahana. In Alvar *bhakti*, the relationship between the devotee and Mayon or Mal (Krishna) was often expressed in terms of the lover–beloved relationship. In some instances, the mother–child relationship was also invoked. For a devotee of the lord, the performance of sacrifices or actions conventionally considered as marks of religious piety were meaningless. The focus was entirely and exclusively on love for the god.

Friedhelm Hardy (1983) has analyzed the mythological references in the *Tiruvantatis*, which represent the earliest stage of Alvar religiosity, and highlights the prominence of the Krishna *avatara*. Devotees are described as serving, worshipping, praising, and adorning the god, clearly indicating the ritual worship of the image of Krishna in a temple context. There are also references to the idea of the deity being immanent in the devotee. Hardy identifies a systematic shifting of the geographical context of Alvar activity from the Venkatam–Kanchi area to south Tamil Nadu and south Kerala on to a network of shrines extending all along the coast from Venkatam to Kottiyur, and eventually ending up in a concentration in Shrirangam. The external structure for this *bhakti* was provided by some 95 temples.

Nammalvar's poems used the style of the older *akam* poems with a new symbolism, the relationship between devotee and deity being described as analogous to that between lover and beloved. The mythology of Krishna and his association with the *gopis*, including one named Pinnai, lent itself well to an emphasis that was at once emotional and erotic. The erotic element found its fullest expression in the poems of the woman-saint Kodai, who came to be known as Andal (literally, 'one who rules'). Andal's poems are laced with the pangs of separation and a longing for union with her lord.

The *bhakti* saints came from varied social backgrounds. A significant proportion (about two-thirds) were Brahmanas, as were some of the most important saints. But there were also people from other social backgrounds—kings, minor chieftains, civil and military officials, merchants, and landowners. The saints also included a cowherd, washerman, weaver, potter, toddy fermenter, hunter, fisherman, and highway robber.

PRIMARY SOURCES | **Andal's songs**

[I]

The marriage tent is decorated
The podium is adorned with garlands of pearls
The golden *purnakumba* (auspicious pot) is ready
I see Madhava enter like a handsome young bull.
In the presence of gods he takes my hand
And circumambulates the fire.
This dream, I saw, my friend.

[II]

How fortunate is the conch
which Kannan takes to his lips
Andal enquires of it how they taste
Does it have the flavour of camphor [Karpuram]?
The sweet smell of the lotus?
Does it taste sweet
that handsome mouth of coral hue?
I'm in dead earnest to know
how the mouth of Madhava
who broke the elephant tusk
tastes and smells
O, thou, silvery conch of the sea.

Source *Varanamayiram, Nachchiyar Tirumozhi*, Srivatsan, cited in Ramaswamy, 1997: 125; K. C. Kamalaiah, cited in Ramaswamy, 1997: 126

Two saints—the Shaiva saint Nandanar and the Vaishnava saint Tiruppan Alvar—are described as 'untouchables'. Nandanar earned his living by slaughtering animals for the leather used to make drums and gut for stringed musical instruments. According to his hagiography, Shiva ordered the priests of the Chidambaram temple to light a fire in front of the temple, through which Nandanar passed unscathed. His desire to see his lord being fulfilled, he is said to have disappeared under the foot of the dancing Shiva. Tiruppan Alvar longed to see lord Vishnu at Shrirangam. According to his hagiography, the god appeared to one of the Brahmana temple priests in a dream and instructed him to place Tiruppan on his shoulder and carry him into the inner sanctum. This is how the Alvar saint managed to enter the temple and see his lord. Having done so, he sang a song—his last one—and merged into the image of Vishnu. The stories of Nandanar and Tiruppan Alvar's life can be read in two ways. On the one hand, they suggest that the path of the preeminent *bhakta* was open even to those whom society considered 'untouchable'. On the hand, it is a poignant fact that the entry of these saints into their god's sanctum was not an easy one. It required divine intervention and resulted in death.

13th century copper alloy image of Karaikkal Ammaiyar

The implication of *bhakti* for women is a complex issue. Works such as the Shaiva *Periyapuranam* in places have a negative portrayal of women. There are very few women among the *bhakti* saints. Three women figure among the Nayanmars—Karaikkal Ammaiyar, Mangaiyarkkarasiyar, and Isainaniyar. Andal was the only woman Alvar. The fact that a few women figure among the *bhakti* saints is significant, but on the whole, the leadership was predominantly and overwhelmingly male. As far as larger participation is concerned, it can be noted that the *mathas* did not admit women. And it was only during the time of Ramanuja (11th century) and with the increasing impact of the Virashaiva movement from the 12th century onwards, that women devotees were given a greater participatory role in Shaiva *bhakti*.

As noticed in earlier chapters, the relationship of women and salvation is problematic in all religious traditions. In the case of South Indian *bhakti*, Uma Chakravarti ([1989] 1999) has pointed out that the hagiographies and songs of the *bhaktins* indicate that there was a fundamental difference in the experience of *bhakti* for men and women. In the case of male saints, there was no contradiction between the life of a householder and devotion towards the god. However, the female body directly impinged on the path of the *bhaktin*. Youth and beauty were a burden, and the *bhaktin* could not combine marriage and family with devotion.

PRIMARY SOURCES | **Karaikkal Ammaiyar—her life and songs**

The hagiography of Karaikkal Ammaiyar tells the following story: Young Punitavati's husband was shocked and terrifed when he discovered her unusual powers, which were the result of her extraordinary devotion to Shiva. He abandoned her and married another woman.

Punitavati prayed fervently to Shiva, telling him she did not need her beauty any longer. She beseeched him to transform her into an ugly demoness (*pey*). Shiva granted her desire and transformed her into an ugly, emaciated woman. Thereafter, she became known as Karaikkal Ammayaiyar. She embarked on a pilgrimage to Mount Kailasha. As she did not want to defile the path to Kailasha with her feet, she is said to have walked on her hands into the god's presence. She was welcomed by Shiva, whom she addressed as *appa* (father).

Karaikkal Ammayaiyar also realized her dream of seeing Shiva perform the *tandava* dance in the banyan forest at Tiruvalankatu. This is how she described the scene in one of her songs.

Sagging breasts and swollen veins,
protruding eyes, bare white teeth.
Skeletal legs and knobbly knees
has this female *pey*.
She lingers, weeps, and wails
and wanders aimless in the forest—
There, holding fire but cool of limbs
with matted hair in all directions
Shiva dances his cosmic dance—
this forest
this sacred Alankatu
is the home of our supreme lord.

The songs of Karaikkal were not set to music nor sung in temples. Perhaps they were considered too dark and forbidding. Images of this Nayanmar saint appeared in temples only after the 12th century.

Source *Tiruvalankadu Mutha Tirupadikam*, verse 1, *Tirumurai* 11; Dehejia, 1988: 118

Vijaya Ramaswamy (1997) has also underlined the fact that the claims of women to asceticism, priesthood, and indeed to salvation, have always been bitterly contested. Throughout history, women have usually responded to their spiritual calling only by breaking off ties with their family, and have risked being labelled as rebels and deviants.

In order to assess the social significance and impact of the *bhakti* tradition, it is necessary to look beyond the leadership. The ideas expressed in the *bhakti* songs and the extent to which *bhakti* expanded the social access to sacred space also need to be examined. Although its leadership was dominated by elite groups, especially Brahmanas, and although it did not overturn existing social relations, *bhakti* did create a religious community within which traditional social distinctions could be transcended, at least with regard to the relationship between the *bhakta* and his/her god. Such an idea comes across very strongly in some of the songs of the saints, which recognized the community of *bhaktas*—*bhakta kulam* or *tondai kulam*.

Many years ago, D. D. Kosambi (1962: 31–32) suggested that *bhakti*, with its focus on devotion and loyalty, was an ideology well suited to the needs of the feudal state. This argument was extended subsequently by some historians who argued that the emergence of temples as landed magnates made them part of the entrenched feudal set-up. Because the *bhakti* movement was a temple-based movement, the feudal label was extended to it, and it was argued that the movement in fact not only reflected but legitimized feudal social relations (Jha, 1974; Narayanan and Veluthat, 1978). However, we have seen that there are a number of problems with the characterization of early medieval India in general and the role of temples in particular as 'feudal'. Apart from this fact, it can also be noted that labelling *bhakti* as a feudal ideology conceals the fact that it did, at least to some extent, question prevailing social hierarchies, and it did expand the social contours of sacred space.

The philosophical underpinnings of South Indian *bhakti* and later developments

The Shrivaishnava *acharyas* with sought to integrate the deeply emotional Alvar *bhakti* with the Pancharatra Agamas and the philosophy of Vishistadvaita (qualified non-dualism) (for a detailed discussion, see Jagannathan, 2015). Nathamuni, considered the founder of the Shrivaishnava sect, lived in the late 10th/early 11th century. He was born in Viranarayanapura and lived in Shrirangam. In his *Nyayatattva*, Nathamuni emphasized the idea of *prapatti*—complete surrender to the god. Other influential Srivaishnava *acharyas* were Yamunacharya (10th century), Ramanuja (11th–12th centuries), and Madhva (12th/13th century).

Ramanuja initially lived in Kanchipuram, but later settled down at Shrirangam. He is described as having been persecuted by a Chola king who was a devotee of Shiva, due to which he sought refuge in the court of the Hoysala king. Ramanuja wrote several works such as the *Vedantasara*, *Vedarthasamgraha*, and *Vedantadipa*. He also wrote commentaries on the *Bhagavad Gita* and the *Brahmasutra*. His philosophy, known as Vishishtadvaita (qualified non-dualism), combined Vaishnava *bhakti* with Upanishadic monism. In this doctrine, Brahman is *sa-guna*, i.e., possesses qualities. In his aspect as Ishvara, he can be invoked by his devotees through *bhakti*. The relationship between *brahman* and the individual selves (*atman*) is explained as similar to that between a rose and redness. *Brahman* cannot exist without the atman, just as a red rose cannot exist without redness. *Atman* and *brahman* are not different from each other, nor are they the same thing. They are distinct, but inseparable.

Madhva wrote commentaries on the *Brahmasutra* and Upanishads and also wrote a work called the *Bharatatatparyanirnaya*, based on the Puranas and epics. He rejected the idea that God was the material cause of the creation of the world. He considered God to be completely different from the individual soul and the world. He held that the individual soul is marked by many defects, but can attain near-perfection by serving and worshipping God. The relationship between God and the soul was likened to that between master and servant.

The social implications of Virashaivism were complex (Jagannathan, 2015). The theology of this sect repeatedly asserted that the lowest castes have as much access to salvation as the highest. Although the critique of caste did not amount to a complete rejection, Shrivaishnava bhakti did seek to open its doors and accommodate diverse social groups (including women) into its fold. Shrivaishnavism was strongly connected with specific temples and pilgrimage. The Vishnu temple at Shrirangam became an important early centre, with the early *acharyas* being based here. Relations between the Shrivaishnavas, Buddhists, Jainas, and Shaivas were marked by competition and one-upmanship.

Shaiva Siddhanta (mentioned earlier) was another school of Shiavism that became popular in South India in early medieval times. This school gave an exposition of the philosophical and metaphysical aspects of Shaiva *bhakti*. The most important southern exponents of Shaiva Siddhanta were Meykandadeva, Arulnandi Shivacharya, Marai Jnana Sambandhar, and Umapati Shivacharya. The 13th century *Shivajnanaḍbodham* by Meykanda contains the basic doctrine of the school.

The early medieval period saw the emergence and increasing popularity of the Virashaiva or Lingayat movement. This sect originated in north-western Karnataka in about the 12th century. Although its leadership was largely Brahmana, its main social base comprised artisans, traders, and farmers. It had an anti-caste and anti-Brahmanical orientation. It rejected the Vedic tradition, sacrifices, rituals, caste, and ideas of pollution. The focus was on intense devotion to Shiva and the community of bhaktas was open to all. Although it espoused *ahimsa*, it critiqued Jainism, which was highly influential in the Karnataka area. The sect traced its lineage to five legendary teachers—Renuka, Daruka, Ghantakarna, Dhenukarna, and Vishvakarna. However, the great popularity it achieved in Karnataka was to a large extent the contribution of Basavanna, who lived in the 12th century. He was born in a Brahmana family and at a young age rebelled against Brahmanical ritualism. The core Virashaiva ideas are encapsulated in free verse lyrics in Kannada known as *vachanas*, composed by the saints. Akka-Mahadevi was a 12th century woman saint belonging to Virashaiva tradition. Her *vachanas* express her intense love for Shiva.

PRIMARY SOURCES | The *vachanas* of Basavanna

The rich
will make temples for Shiva.
What shall I,
a poor man,
do

My legs are pillars,
the body the shrine,
the head a cupola
of gold.

Listen, O lord of the meeting rivers,*
things standing shall fall,
but the moving ever shall stay.

Look here, dear fellow:
I wear these men's clothes
only for you.

Sometimes I am man,
sometimes I am woman.

O lord of the meeting rivers
I'll make war for you
but I'll be your devotees' bride.

Don't you take on
this thing called bhakti:

like a saw
it cuts when it goes

and it cuts again
when it comes.

If you risk your hand
with a cobra in a pitcher**
will it let you
pass?

*Kudalasangamadeva (Lord of the meeting rivers) is a name with which Basavanna frequently invokes Shiva. Kudalasangama is a sacred place in north Karnataka, located at the meeting point of two rivers, a place where Basavanna is said to have attained enlightenment.

** Putting the hand in a pitcher containing a snake, like drinking poison or walking on fire, is an ordeal to be performed when a person seeks to prove his/her innocence, chastity, etc.

Source Basavanna 820, 703, and 212; Ramanujan. (Trans.)., 1973: 88, 87, 79

From the Karnataka region, the Virashaiva movement spread to other parts of South India. Male as well as female members of this sect wear a *linga* called the *ishta-linga* on their body, and attach no importance to worshipping the god in temples. While loving kindness towards all was a feature of the teaching of some of the saints, the greatest emphasis was on devotion towards Shiva. The Virashaivas accepted many of the doctrines of other Shaiva schools, but its core ideas are encapsulated in free verse lyrics known as *vachanas*, composed by the saints.

Inter-religious dynamics

The relationship between the religious traditions discussed above was marked by coexistence and confluence as well as rivalry and conflict (Upinder Singh, 2021: 178-227).

The fact that the Buddha is mentioned among the list of Vishnu's *avataras* in some Puranas is sometimes presented as evidence of religious syncretism. However, it should be noted that his portrayal in these texts is not especially positive. He is supposed to delude the wicked in the Kali age and pave the way for the arrival of the Kalki *avatara*. The early Bengal Upapuranas say many negative things about Buddhists, describing them as symbols of evil, defiling, and to be avoided. The later Upapuranas offer a more positive image; they describe the Buddha as an embodiment of peace and beauty, and connect him with the compassionate aim of ending animal sacrifices. In spite of being recognized as an *avatara*, the Buddha was never worshipped in Vishnu temples.

Buddhist texts narrate the Trailokyavijaya episode, where Heruka, an emanation of the *bodhisattva* Vajrapani, gets angry with Shiva Maheshvara and destroys him by crushing him under his left foot. He then resurrects Shiva and his consort as Uma Maheshvara and gives them a new name, Bhairava–Bhairavi, and admits them into the Buddhist fold as his followers. This episode is also represented visually in many Buddhist images. Religious conflict is also reflected in the many images of wrathful Buddhist Tantric deities trampling on Hindu gods and vice versa.

As we have seen, the relationship between the Vaidika Brahmanas and the sects that held Vishnu, Shiva, or Shakti to be a supreme deity was complex. Some of the South Indian *bhakti* saints strongly questioned Brahmanical religious practice and social ideology. The songs of the Shaiva Nayanmar saints contain a great deal of criticism of other religious communities, especially the Jainas. Food habits frequently recur as a basis of criticism (Ulrich, 2007). Jaina texts, on the other hand, concentrate their criticism against the Buddhists, who they evidently considered their strongest rivals.

The complex inter-religious dynamics of the time are also reflected religious satire, such as the *Mattavilasa-prahasana*, *Agamadambara*, and the works of Kshemendra. The 7th century *Mattavilasa-prahasana* of Mahendravarman is a farce that makes fun of the Buddhists, Kapalikas, and Pashupatas. The *Agamadambara* is a Sanskrit play, written in 9th/10th century Kashmir by Jayanta Bhatta, a renowned Nyaya philosopher. The play reveals tensions between different religious and philosophical views current in Kashmir at the time. At the end, persecution and conflict are replaced by a politically pragmatic resolution of conflict. All groups, including the Mimamsakas, Naiyayikas, Shaivas, Vaishnavas, Buddhists, and Jainas (but not the Charvakas) are told that they are welcome to live happily in the kingdom.

In earlier centuries, Buddhist texts refer to persecution by the Pushyamitra Shunga, Shashanka, and the Hunas. There are references to episodes of religious persecution in the early medieval period as well. The Pallava king Mahendravarman I is said to have initially been a Jaina who was converted to Shaivism by the saint Appar, and thereafter persecuted the Jainas. A Pandya king of Madurai who converted from Jainism to Shaivism is said to have impaled 8,000 Jainas in revenge for the latter's attempt to kill the Shaiva saint Sambandar. This scene is depicted in a relief sculpture in the Meenakshi temple at Madurai, and the event is still celebrated in the temple's festivals. According to Shrivaishnava hagiography, Ramanuja fled from the persecution of the Shaiva Chola king. The *Chulavamsa* describes how Pandya and Chola armies plundered the monasteries of Anuradhapura. The Chola army is said to have completely destroyed Anuradhapura, which was both a political and religious centre.

Kalhana's *Rajatarangini* refers to episodes of religious persecution in the history of Kashmir. He refers to Jalauka, a Shaiva successor of Ashoka, who destroyed a Buddhist monastery and later rebuilt it. Tarapida and Jayapida of the Karkota dynasty are said to have oppressed Brahmanas. During the reign of the latter, 99 Brahmanas are said to have protested against the persecution by drowning themselves in the Tulamulya river. Shankaravarman of the Utpala dynasty plundered many temples, rescinded tax-free grants, and imposed taxes on temples. King Kshemagupta destroyed the Jayendravihara monastery in Srinagara and used the material to build a temple. Kalhana states that greedy king Harsha of the Lohara dynasty plundered the wealth of temples and appointed an official for overthrowing images of deities and melting them down for the royal treasury. As mentioned above, there is a hypothesis that the decline of Buddhism in the subcontinent involved a certain amount of violence.

While such accounts may have used hyperbole for the sake of dramatic effect or (in the case of hagiographies) in order to create religious boundaries and identities, they do point to episodes of religious persecution, often driven by economic or political motives.

Patronage to temples

The construction and embellishment of religious establishments was the result of patronage from diverse sources. Hermann Kulke ([1993] 2001) has pointed out that early medieval kings tried to buttress their authority by extending patronage to major pilgrimage places (*tirthas*), large-scale grants to temples, and the construction of imperial temples. Royal patronage was important in the case of specific shrines and reflected the close relationship that kings sought to establish with certain deities and temples. An example is the Brihadishvara temple at Thanjavur (Tanjore), already discussed in various contexts. Such temples were built at the direction of the king, and donations by the king and members of his family and court played an important role in their maintenance. As pilgrimage networks expanded, various *mahatmyas*—texts extolling the greatness of individual *tirthas*—were composed in Sanskrit and the regional languages.

Odisha gives some instances of royally endowed temples. The largest temple at Bhubaneswar is the Lingaraja temple. According to tradition, it took three generations of Somavamshi kings to complete the temple of Krittivasa (as the Lingaraja was then known). Till the 12th century, Odisha was a predominantly Shaiva area. Then, in the 12th century, the worship of the deity Purushottama (later known as Jagannatha) was raised to the status of an imperial cult with the construction of the Purushottama temple at Puri by the Ganga king Anantavarman Chodaganga. According to tradition, Anantavarman's aim was to build a temple more magnificent than the Brihadishvara temple at Thanjavur. In 1230 CE, Anangabhima III dedicated his empire to Purushottama, describing himself as the deputy of the god. But apart from such notable examples, the trajectories of development in temple building and architecture in Odisha were more or less independent of the vicissitudes of political history and political patronage.

In South India, a large number of inscriptions record royal donations to temples, mostly of gold, land, and some of livestock and paddy. The number of such donations went up dramatically from the Pallava to the Chola periods. For instance, among the donative inscriptions at Tirupati, 11 belong to the Pallavas, and 31 to the Cholas. Royal land grants to temples were made in perpetuity and were associated with several tax exemptions and privileges. Temples also leased land out to tenants. For example, an inscription belonging to the reign of Sundara Chola (957–73) states that the temple management gave out 124 *veli* (a land measure) of *devadana* land to a certain person, who was supposed to hand over 2,880 *kalam* (a grain measure) of rice every year to the temple at the rate of 120 *kalam* per *veli*.

Lingaraja Temple, Bhubaneswar (Odisha)

NEW DIRECTIONS IN RESEARCH | **Temple women in Chola inscriptions**

Leslie Orr's study shows that the 'temple women' of the Chola period were very different from the *devadasis* of the 20th century. In fact, although there are a few earlier occurrences, the term *devadasi* seems to have really come into vogue only in the early 20th century.

The words used for temple women in the Chola period inscriptions were *tevaratiyar* (devotee of god), *tevanar makal* (daughter of god), and *taliyilar* or *patiyilar* (woman of the temple). The identity of these women was not based on birth, caste, professional skill, or ritual function. It was based on their connection with a temple, deity, or place.

These women were not generally connected with performing rituals or management roles in the temple. There are a few instances of their performing minor, sometimes menial services, for the temple. There is also an increasing number of temple women who were slaves functioning within the temple context. But by and large, temple women were connected to temples, especially those located in their native villages or towns, through their donations. They appear prominently in this capacity in inscriptions, especially in the 12th and 13th centuries, more so in the northernmost and southernmost parts of Tamil Nadu. Temple women were distributed all over Tamil Nadu, and although they were closely associated with certain towns such as Kanchipuram, they were more often associated with small temple establishments. In the late Chola period, these women acquired certain privileges and honours in exchange for their donations. These included, for instance, the honour of being given a place close to the deity in a procession or the right to sing a certain part of a hymn before the deity. Such honours seem to have gradually become hereditary. Temple women of the Chola period do not seem to have been married.

In the early Chola period, temple women mostly made gifts to defray the cost of maintaining perpetual lamps. In the late Chola period, they also made gifts to support services in the temple on a daily basis or on festive occasions, to support temple personnel, build temples, or make and install images. In these respects, their gifts were similar to those made by other categories of donors, male or female.

Inscriptions indicate that women in the Chola period had access to and control over economic resources of their households. Orr suggests that while women in general become less visible as donors in Chola inscriptions, temple women remain constantly visible.

The modern *devadasi* phenomenon is marked by hereditary transmission, professional skill, and temple dedication. None of these were operative in the case of the temple women of the Chola period. These women were neither temple dancers nor prostitutes. They were not married to the god, nor is there any indication that their sexual activity was exploited or confined to the temple context. Their history in the Chola period cannot be seen as a story of degeneration or decline—in fact their position got strengthened and well-established over time.

Source Orr, 2000a

Many temple establishments underwent a significant enlargement due to lavish royal patronage. The Mukteshvara temple, with 54 employees, was the largest Pallava temple. The Brihadishvara temple at Thanjavur had over 600 employees. These included dancing women, dancing teachers, drummers, tailors, goldsmiths, and accountants. Temple employees were generally paid in kind, specifically in rice. In the Chola period, some of them were also paid in the form of revenue assignments.

Jagannatha temple, Puri (Odisha)

Some scholars, for instance D. N. Jha (1974), argue that the emergence of temples as landed magnates in South India, and the increase in the number of *pariharas*, signify the increasing oppression of the peasantry and the growth of feudal agrarian relations. Jha further asserts that temples became centres of political power, leading to the decentralization of political power. However, it is abundantly clear that the relationship between kings and temples was not one of rivalry but alliance. Patronage to temples was a major means of acquiring, proclaiming, and maintaining political legitimacy.

Temple patrons included chieftains, landowners, merchants, villages, and town assemblies. Merchants generally donated money and livestock, sometimes gold and silver ornaments (Jha, 1976). Many of the gifts were made for the maintenance of perpetual lamps in temples. For example, a Thanjavur inscription records the gift of 30 *kashu* (these were probably copper coins) by a merchant's wife for the maintenance of a perpetual lamp in a temple during the reign of Parantaka I. An inscription belonging to the reign of the same king records the gift of 90 sheep by a merchant to the Vedaranyam temple in Thanjavur district for the maintenance of a perpetual lamp. A 1055–56 CE inscription from Tiruchirappalli district records the installation of an image in a temple and the donation of two gold *kalanju* (a *kalanju* was either a gold coin or its equivalent in weight, about 32 *ratis*) for the maintenance of lamps by merchants. There are also some instances of merchants gifting land to temples. Some inscriptions mention the purchase of the land, prior to it being gifted.

Merchant guilds, too, made donations in the Chola period. For instance, there are inscriptions recording gifts made by the Manigramam of Kodambalur and the Dharmavaniyar and Valanjiyar of Tennilangai. There are also some instances of artisan groups getting involved in temple management. For instance, the Madras Museum plates of Uttama Chola (970–85 CE) indicate that the weavers of Kanchipuram were given the task of managing the financial and other affairs of the local temple.

From the point of view of social history, patterns of donations to religious establishments also tell us something about women's participation in religious life. Leslie Orr (2000b) has analyzed the epigraphic evidence of women's patronage of Hinduism, Jainism, and Buddhism in Tamil Nadu between *c*. 700 and 1700. The evidence of Jaina and Buddhist establishments and inscriptions has to a large extent been erased due to the subsequent decline of these religions in this area; therefore, the amount of information pertaining to Hindu temples is comparatively much greater. Nevertheless, women appear as donors in all three religious traditions. The social background of women who made donations was more or less similar.

Apart from 'religious women' (nuns, temple women, etc.), there were queens, women belonging to the family of chieftains, and wives of landowners, merchants, and Brahmanas. The donations were, for the most part, not so much channelized towards monasteries or *mathas* as towards supporting worship in shrines. They were for the construction of temples, making images, provision of lamps, flowers, and food for the deity, and providing for those associated with temple services. Orr emphasizes that instead of looking for female counterparts of priests, ascetics, and monks (the very roles from which they tended to be excluded), it is necessary to recognize the importance of gift giving as a religious activity. If this is done, the abundance of evidence of women donors in various religious traditions gives a picture of active participation, rather than total marginalization.

Islam and Muslim communities

As discussed earlier, Islam was introduced into the Indian subcontinent in the early medieval period. (For an introduction to the life of Prophet Muhammad, the *Quran*, and ideas and practices within early Islam, see Schimmel, 1992; and Ernst, 2005. For the history of early Islamic polities and cultures, see Hodgson, 1974, Vols. 1, 2; Wink, 1999, Vols. 1, 2; and Crone, 1980.) Muhammad, the founder of Islam, was born in *c*. 570 in the city of Mecca, an important trading city in Arabia. His family belonged to the Hashim clan of the powerful Quraish tribe. His father died before his birth and his mother when he was six years old, and he was brought up by his uncle Abu Talib. After a series of spiritual experiences while meditating in a cave in Mount Hira, he started preaching his ideas which included monotheism, moral responsibility, and the final judgement of God in the afterlife. He gradually acquired a following but also faced much hostility and opposition in Mecca. In 622, he was invited to Yathrib (later known as Medina), and his emigration to this town marks the beginning of the Muslim Hijra era. He eventually returned triumphantly to Mecca, where he died in 632. Abu Bakr, the Prophet's father-in-law, became the first Khalifa/Caliph (successor). The armies of Abu Bakr and his successor Umar I achieved a remarkable series of military successes in Iraq, Syria, Egypt, and Persia.

Islam recognizes earlier Prophets (including Abraham, Moses, and Jesus) but considers Muhammad as the final Prophet, whose revelation completed and corrected the earlier ones. The Arabic *Quran* (literally 'recitation'), believed to be the word of Allah (God) revealed to the Prophet Muhammad, forms the foundation of Islam. The *Quran* consists of 114 sections called *suras* which contain varying number of verses known as *ayas* (literally, 'sign' or 'miracle'). The text invokes Allah by references to his many qualities, especially his beneficence, mercy, and compassion. Occupying a position of authority next to the *Quran* are collections of Hadith (literally 'report'), which are believed to represent the Prophet's sayings and are sources of his exemplary words and actions known as *sunna*.

Certain core beliefs and practices of Islam are referred to as its five pillars. These are systematically presented in the Hadith of Jibril (Gabriel). The first is the profession of faith called the *shahada*, which consists of an assertion that there no God but Allah and the Prophet Muhammad is the messenger of Allah. The *shahada* marks the entry into the Muslim *umma* (community of believers). The other pillars are praying five times a day (*salat* or *namaz*); offering a proportion of earnings in alms (*zakat*); fasting (*sawm*) during Ramadan (the 9th month of the Islamic lunar year); and going on pilgrimage to Mecca (*hajj*).

The social ethics (*akhlaq*) of Islam emphasize virtues such as kindness, honesty, and humility and injunctions against lying, cheating, adultery, using intoxicants, and engaging in wasteful expenditure. *Jihad*, literally 'struggle' or 'striving,' was applied to military conflicts against non-believers, but also to inner struggles against one's baser instincts. Traditions of Islamic law (*sharia*) were based on interpretations of the *Quran*, Hadith, scholarly consensus, and jurists' reasoning based on analogy. These traditions intersected with local custom.

While prayer could be performed in any clean place, during Muhammad's lifetime, a place for congregational prayer, the *masjid* (literally 'the place where one prostrates'), was established. Over time, *masjid*/mosque architecture developed in different ways in different parts of the Islamic world. However, regardless of their architectural features, in all mosques, a niche called the *mihrab* indicates the direction of Mecca, facing which prayers are to be offered.

In Sanskrit *mahakavyas* and inscriptions, generic terms such as Tajika, Turushka, Yavana, Parasika, and *mleccha* are used to refer to Muslim invaders and rulers. In the context of the politics of the time, they are depicted as among many contenders for political power as enemies, allies, or subordinates (Chattopadhyaya, 1998). In the 12th and 13th centuries, Sanskrit sources used two new terms to refer to Muslim rulers—*hammira* (from the Arabic and Persian 'Amir') and *suratrana* (from 'Sultan'). The earliest reference to the term *musalmana* seems to be in a 7th century Buddhist commentary (van der Kuijp, 2006). While most Sanskrit sources tend to be silent or say little about Islam, 11th century Buddhist Vajrayana texts known as the *Kalachakratantra* discuss the religious beliefs and practices of Muslims in detail (Truschke, 2021: 11–18).

Other sources give a much more detailed picture of what was happening on the ground. As mentioned earlier, the early medieval period saw migrations and diasporas of several communities involved in trade. Among the earliest such movements were those of Arab and Persian traders, who settled along the Konkan, Gujarat, and Malabar coasts. An inscription of 875 CE records the king of Madurai granting asylum to a group of Arabs. This is the first instance of an Arab settlement on the Coromandel coast. Accounts of Arab merchants and geographers in Indian Ocean trade refer to the presence of Muslim communities on the western coast of India and Sri Lanka. Rashtrakuta and Shilahara inscriptions are other important sources.

A vibrant culture based on shared economic interests and marked by cultural hybridity and confluence is visible at several coastal sites. The 9th century copper plates found at Kollam (in Kerala), dated in the fifth year of Sthanu Ravi, record certain benefactions made to a Tarisappalli located there. This may have been a Syrian Christian church. Most of the inscription is in Tamil, inscribed in Vatteluttu, with a few words in the Grantha script. The sixth plate, however, contains signatures of witnesses in three languages and scripts—Arabic written in the Kufic script; Pahlavi; and Judaeo-Persian written in the Hebrew script. Arabic inscriptions at Cambay, Prabhasapattana (Somnath), Junagadh, and Anahilavada indicate that Arab shipowners and traders were living in these parts of Gujarat in the 13th century. A Sanskrit inscription found at Sujanagar in Munshiganj district in Bangladesh records some benefactions made during the reign of Bhojavarman (1137–45). It refers to certain provisions made by *mahasamanta* Shri Avudeva, son of the *panchakulika* Hasi (these seem to be Sanskritized versions of the Arabic names Abu and Hashim or Asif), for repairs to a *vihara* protected by Allaha-bhattaraka-svamin, that is, the lord Allah (Furui, 2019). The reference seems to be to a Muslim shrine or institution. In addition to the textual and epigraphic references, the architectural evidence of mosques (discussed further on) indicates the presence of Muslim communities in various regions from the 8th century onwards, long before the Ghurid invasions.

Arab accounts, Rashtrakuta and Shilahara inscriptions, and archaeological evidence reveal the cosmopolitan social composition of the town of Sanjan on the Konkan coast (in Valsad district in southern Gujarat) (Suchandra Ghosh, 2022). Apart from the local people, its inhabitants included Arabs, Parsis, and Jews, making it a striking example of cultural convergence in early medieval India. Arab accounts contain many references to the Konkan coast and Sindan (Sanjan) and praise the Rashtrakuta kings. One of the Chinchani copper plate grants (found 30 km south of Sanjan) of the time of the Rashtrakuta ruler Indra III (915–28) refers to a Tajika named Madhumati Sugatipa, son of Sahariyara (this seems to be the Sanskritized form of Muhammad bin Shahriyar), who had been appointed as a governor of Samyata-pattana (Sanjan port) by Krishna II (878–915) and continued in that position during the reign of Indra III. This governor is said to have established control over the coast and set up free ferries on two streams and a feeding house where free food was given to people from different lands. Another inscription from Chinchani, belonging to the time of the Shilahara king Chittaraja, refers to this king's subordinate Chamundaraja, who was ruling over Samyana-pattana (Sanjan). It records the grant of an oil mill to the Kautuka *mathika* of the goddess Bhagavati. The people addressed in this inscription include merchants named Alliya, Mahara, and Madhumata (these are Sanskritized forms of Arabic names) who seem to have been persons of high standing in the port and may have been involved in administration.

It is important to remember that Islam was and is not a homogenous or monolithic religion. Its history was marked by many theological and doctrinal debates. There were and are differences of belief and practice between Muslim Sunnis, Shias, Sufis, and other groups. The great variety of pre-colonial South Asian Islamic traditions were linked to their specific regional or local cultural contexts as well to the larger global Islamic world (Eaton. [Ed.], 2003). While discussing the impact of Islam, some scholars follow Marshall Hodgson's use of the term "Islamicate" (in distinction to "Islamic," which has direct religious connotations) to refer to cultural practices that have wider currency among Muslims and non-Muslims, and are not directly rooted in scriptural sources, for instance, Islamicate art or literature (Ernst, 2005, 64–65). Regardless of whether or not this term is used, the advent of Islam in the Indian subcontinent is an important part of the continuing story of cultural plurality and confluence that have been part of Indian history over the centuries.

Architecture and Sculpture

The Nagara, Dravida, and Vesara styles of temple architecture

The early medieval period was marked by remarkable developments in the spheres of art and architecture. Distinct regional architectural and sculptural styles emerged in different areas, including Kashmir, Rajasthan, and Odisha. In peninsular India, major edifices were built through the patronage of the Rashtrakutas, early Western Chalukyas, Pallavas, Hoysalas, and Cholas. In contrast to previous centuries, when a great proportion of the major architectural remains were Buddhist, in this period, the remains are dominated by Hindu temples.

A number of architectural texts known as the Shilpashastras were written in early medieval times. These refer to three major styles of temple architecture—Nagara, Dravida, and Vesara. The Nagara style is associated with the land between the Himalayas and Vindhyas, the Dravida style with the land between the Krishna and Kaveri rivers, while the Vesara style is sometimes associated with the area between the Vindhyas and the Krishna river. Temple styles are actually best studied on the basis of extant temple remains. Hardy (1995: 7–9) points out that Nagara and Dravida should be understood as architectural languages, in the sense that they provide a vocabulary, a range of elements, and a family of forms which can be put together in different ways. He also suggests that the term 'Karnata-Dravida' is a better term than 'Vesara' for the Chalukya temples of the Deccan.

The basic plan of the Nagara temple is square, with a number of projections in the middle of each side, giving it a cruciform shape. The temple's elevation is marked by a conical or convex *shikhara* or temple tower, consisting of several layers of carved courses, usually crowned by an *amalaka* (notched ring stone). These two features—the cruciform plan and curvilinear *shikhara*—are visible in northern temples from the 6th century CE (the 'late Gupta' period), for example in the Dashavatara temple at Deogarh and the brick temple at Bhitargaon (both in UP). The beginnings of the typical Nagara *shikhara* can be seen in the Mahadeva temple at Nachna Kuthara (7th century) and the brick Lakshmana temple at Sirpur (both in MP). The fully developed Nagara style is evident by the 8th century.

The most striking feature of the Dravida temple is its pyramidal *shikhara*, which consists of progressively smaller and smaller storeys, culminating in a slender pinnacle surmounted by a small dome (*stupika*). In a later stage, South Indian temples came to be marked by huge gateways known as *gopurams* and by pillared halls and corridors.

Nagara style *shikhara*, Lingaraja temple, Bhubaneswar (left); Dravida style *shikhara*, Brihadishvara temple, Thanjavur (right)

The earliest traces of such features go back to the Gupta period and are not restricted to the far south—e.g., they occur in Northern and Central India and the Deccan. They can be seen in the Parvati temple at Nachna Kuthara and the Lad Khan, Kont Gudi, and Meguti temples at Aihole. In temples built in the Dravida style, the square inner sanctum is set within a large covered enclosure. The external walls are divided into niches by pilasters.

The Vesara style is a hybrid style (*vesara* literally means 'mule') that borrowed from the northern and southern styles. It is difficult to define, as the mixture of northern and southern elements may vary. Temples built in the Deccan under the later Chalukyas of Kalyani and Hoysalas are considered examples of this style. However, looking at the temple architecture of the Deccan simply as a combination of northern and southern elements means missing out on its distinctiveness and variations.

Due to constraints of space, it is not possible to give a comprehensive account of the architectural and sculptural traditions and remains of all the parts of the subcontinent (for a comprehensive discussion, see Huntington, 1985: Chapters 11–22; Meister and Dhaky. [Ed.]., 1989; and Meister, Dhaky, and Deva. [Eds.]., 1989). Therefore, the following sections offer a brief sampling, consisting of an overview of Indian temple architecture in the Deccan and the far south, and the metal sculpture of the Chola period. This is followed by a section on early mosques in the subcontinent.

Khajuraho temple, MP; trefoiled arches of the Martanda temple, Kashmir (from top)

Temples of the early medieval period are marked by exquisite sculptures. Many of them are sensuous and sensual, some are erotic. As mentioned in Chapter 8, the sensuous refers to that which is aesthetically pleasing to the senses, the sensual refers to that which is related to amorous or sexual pleasure, while the erotic has stronger and direct connections with sexual desire. The erotic element is especially prominent in temples of the early medieval period, for instance those at Khajuraho, Konarak, and Bhubaneswar (see Desai, 1975). The Khajuraho temples, built under the patronage of the Chandela kings, include shrines dedicated to Shiva and Vishnu. They contain many *maithuna* reliefs depicting sexual acts. Such scenes are also found in Jaina temples such as the Parshvanatha temple at Khajuraho. Although their appearance in a religious context may surprise modern viewers, this was not the case for the people who designed and built these temples, and the devotees who worshipped here. Sexual images in temples have been interpreted in various ways—as auspicious symbols, as fertility symbols endowed with magico-religious potency, or as devices to ward off the evil eye. They have been variously described as reflecting an increasing decadence in the aesthetic tastes of royalty; an invitation to the beholder to transcend desire and reach a higher spiritual plane; and as representing Tantric sexual rites or influence. The explanation may lie in a combination of some of these factors, especially Tantra.

NEW DIRECTIONS IN RESEARCH | **The sacred geography of Jageshwar**

The central Himalayas (stretching across the northern part of Himachal Pradesh, Uttarakhand, and Western Nepal) constitute a region that has not been studied extensively from the historical and art historical point of view. Nachiket Chachani has reconstructed the evolution in the sacred landscape of the region between *c.* 300 BCE to the 12th century and its emergence as an important area for Hindu pilgrimage. These processes involved interactions between various communities living in the mountains as well as with people living in the plains to the south. Patrons, architects, master masons, and sculptors played important roles. The multiple sacred associations of the physical landscape of the area—above all, the Himalayas, the Ganga, and its tributaries—was key to these processes.

The earliest material remains in the region are the Ashokan edicts at Kalsi and the remains of fire altars at Jagatgram.

Two Mathura sandstone sculptures (one of Shiva, the other possibly of Parvati) have been found at Rishikesh. The brick remains of the earliest temples (5th century onwards) are found at Lakhamandal and Koteshwar villages. These were followed in the 7th century by stone temples constructed at Palethi and Lakhamandal. None of these became major pilgrim centres.

Dandeshvara temple, Almora (left); view of Jageshwar temples (top)

The first major centre of pilgrimage in the central Himalayas sprang up at Jageshwar, located in a forested area, 35 km north-east of Almora in the modern state of Uttarakhand. Today, the Jageshwar valley has 150 stone monuments, almost 200 stone steles, many commemorative monuments, and has yielded a large number of copper alloy statues. There are two clusters of temples—one at Dandeshwar in the middle of the valley, and the other at Jageshwar proper. Most of the Jageshwar temples are dedicated to Shiva. A few are rectangular and are built in the Valabhi mode. The rest have square plans and show the selective influence of the Nagara style. But the artists and craftsmen who designed and made these temples experimented and created something new and different.

The creative process involved many factors, including the unique geographic setting in a thickly forested area, with many *devadara* trees (which have a special association with the god Shiva)

Mrityunjaya temple, Jageshwar

along the north-northeast flowing stream called the Jataganga. The earliest phase of temple building at Jageshwar is dated to the 7th/8th century and is represented by shrines such as the Nava Durga temple. The iconography of the images, representations of Lakulisha, and the many *mukhalinga*s carved with one or five faces of the god Shiva (*eka-mukhalinga*s and *pancha-mukhalinga*s) indicate that the early temples were associated with the Pashupata sect. Evidently, the Pashupatas, who were established in many parts of the subcontinent, were very active in the Jageshwar valley. Several generations of Pashupata ascetics were able to attract enough patronage and support from the local communities in the area for the building of a large number of temples over several centuries.

The Mrityunjaya temple (built between the mid-9th to mid-10th century) reflects changes in architectural form, sculptural style, and an enhancement in the scale of patronage. This is the first temple in the valley which has a large front hall attached to it. Names of pilgrims, inscribed in 8th/9th century letters on the walls, pillars, and pilasters of the congregational hall indicate that the temple was visited by pilgrims from different backgrounds and places. In the 10th century, the Dandeshvara temple became the largest temple built in the Jageshwar valley. A copper-alloy sculpture of a male figure (about half a metre high) once stood in the temple and represents a lamp bearer. The sculpture seems to have been cast between the 9th and late 12th century. Its creator was familiar with the artistic traditions of Spiti, Tibet, and Nepal, but produced an image that was distinctive and unique. It is possible that it was cast in the Almora hills and that it represented a royal patron who financed the building of the temple.

By the twelfth century, the central Himalayas had become a part of larger pilgrimage networks. The sacrality of the region was based both on its multitude of temples as well as a physical landscape believed to be powerfully charged with sacred meaning.

Source Chanchani, 2019: 75-112

Western India and the Deccan

The caves at Ellora (7th–8th centuries) represent the last phase of Buddhist cave architecture in Western India (Huntington, 1985: 268–81). Their architecture and sculpture shows some continuities with earlier centuries (e.g., with Ajanta, Bagh, and Kanheri), but there are also some changes. These include an increase in the size of the side shrines and a double row of stone benches (in Cave 5). Other distinctive features are the larger scale and the richness of sculpture, reflected, for instance, in Cave 12, known as Tin Thal. This consists of three storeys, and represents the climax and the end of the cave excavations at Ellora. The sculptural programme of the Buddhist caves at Ellora includes arrays of Buddhas and *bodhisattvas*. A group of eight *bodhisattvas* are sometimes arranged together in a *mandala* formation (for instance, in Cave 12).

Apart from its magnificent Buddhist and Jaina caves, Ellora is also known for the spectacular Kailasanatha temple. This Shiva temple was excavated out of the rocky hillside in the late 8th century under the patronage of the Rashtrakutas. The temple is actually a complex, comprising a main shrine consisting of a lower and an upper storey, a Nandi pavilion, subsidiary shrines, wall, gateway, and cloisters. The superstructure of the temple corresponds to the Dravida style. Practically all the surfaces of the temple complex are richly ornamented with bold, dramatic, and exceptionally fine sculptures. Most of them are Shaiva, but there are also representations of Vishnu. In fact, the sculptures to the left of the entrance are mostly Shaiva, while those to the right are mostly Vaishnava. A similar logic of sculptural arrangement is found along the back wall of the gallery surrounding the temple. The sculptures include representations of Shiva, Shiva and Parvati, Ravana shaking Mount Kailasha, Durga, the Sapta-Matrikas, Ganesha, and the goddesses Ganga, Yamuna, and Sarasvati. The Kailasanatha temple marks the highest point of rock-cut temple architecture in the subcontinent.

In the Deccan, major examples of early medieval rock-cut shrines and structural shrines are found at several places in Karnataka. The early architectural phase (6th–early 8th centuries) is represented at Badami and Aihole. This was followed by the later and grander 8th century temples at Pattadakal. Badami represents the site of Vatapi, capital of the early Western Chalukyas. The temple architecture of the Deccan shows an amalgam of northern and southern features, but attained a distinctive identity of its own during these centuries.

There are two notable cave shrines at Aihole, one Shaiva and the other Jaina, both with heavily ornamented interiors. The Shaiva cave, known as the Ravanaphadi cave, consists of a central hall, two side shrine sections, and a *garbhagriha* with a *linga* at the back. There are sculptures on the walls and on part of the ceiling as well. These include representations of Shiva as Nataraja and of the Sapta-Matrikas. Compared to the figures at Ellora and Badami, the figures are more slender and have tall crowns. Outside the entrance of the cave, there are carvings of dwarfs and doorkeepers wearing Scythian-type attire.

Kailasanatha temple, Ellora

The rock-cut caves at Badami are carved into the red sandstone hillside overlooking a tank. Of the three major caves, the largest one is Vaishnava, while the others are Shaiva and Jaina in affiliation. The caves have a simple plan, consisting of a verandah and a pillared hall leading into a small square sanctum in the back wall. The walls and ceilings are decorated with carvings. Cave 3 has huge, impressive relief sculptures of the

Ellora (from top right): Kailasanatha temple, Ravanalifting Mount Kailasha; ornamental pillar; JainaTirthankara; goddess Ganga

Ellora: cave interior and shrine;
Manushi Buddhas, Teen Thal cave

various Vishnu incarnations, including Varaha (boar), Narasimha (lion), and Vamana (dwarf). It may be noted that the boar was also the symbol of the Western Chalukyas. The bracket figures in Cave 3, mostly consisting of *mithuna* figures (amorous couples), are exceptional in their variety and finesse.

The structural temples of the period were for the most part built out of large blocks of stone, without the use of mortar. The inner walls and ceilings have sculptural ornamentation. Many of the major temples are located at Aihole. Mention was made earlier of the Meguti temple, which has the famous inscription of Pulakeshin II. Most of the Aihole temples are Hindu shrines and show considerable variation in plan. These include the apsidal 'Durga temple', mentioned earlier. The Lad Khan temple, on the other hand, has a pillared porch, a large square hall with pillars arranged in two concentric squares, at the end of which is a small shrine area. At Mahakuta, not far from Badami, there are

See p. 736 for a photograph of Durga in the Virupaksha temple

Badami (from top): cave exterior ceiling bracket *mithuna* figures; cave interior; dancing Shiva

Pattadakal (from top): Virupaksha temple; Papanatha temple: entrance; Gaja-Lakshmi on ceiling; Rama, Sita, and Lakshmana on outer wall; view of temple

Hoysaleshvara temple, Halebeedu: eastern entrance; ornamental pillar

some 20 temples belonging to the early Western Chalukya period, almost all of them with northern style curvilinear *shikharas*.

Pattadakal is situated some 16 km from Badami. The temples at this place reflect a further development of the Deccan traditions of temple architecture and sculpture. Mention was made at the beginning of this chapter to the Virupaksha temple, the largest and most profusely sculpted shrine at Pattadakal. This was dedicated to Shiva and built at the instance of Lokamahadevi, chief queen of the Chalukya king Vikramaditya II. Similar to temples made in the Dravida style, it consists of a complex of shrines, including a Nandi shrine, within a rectangular walled enclosure. The main temple consists of a pillared hall with three porch extensions, an antechamber, and sanctum with an enclosed passage for circumambulation (this is known as the *sandhara* style). The *shikhara* is in the Dravida style. Niches in the outer walls have fine, deep carvings, mostly of Shiva. The temple's interior is also ornamented with sculptures. The exceptional carving of Durga in one of the niche shrines has been mentioned in an earlier section. The doorway leading into the sanctum which enshrines a *linga* is elaborately carved with *dvarapalas* and other figures.

A later, major phase of temple architecture in the Deccan is associated with the Hoysala dynasty which ruled over southern Karnataka from its capital at Dwarasamudra (modern Halebeedu). Remains of temples of this period are found at Halebeedu, Belur, and Somnathpur. These are noted for their extremely fine, delicate, and detailed carvings executed on smooth chlorite schist on walls and ceilings. The most imposing shrine at Halebid is the 12th century Hoysaleshvara temple. This consists of two separate shrines with a cruciform plan, resting on cruciform-shaped plinths. The two shrines are almost identical to each other and are joined together with a covered passage. Both of them are preceded by a Nandi pavilion, containing profusely ornamented but sympathetically and realistically carved sculptures of Nandi bulls. The *shikharas* of the two temples are missing. The Keshava temple at Belur consists of a complex of shrines in a large courtyard. The main shrine was built in the early 12th century. The pillared *mandapa* is cruciform

FURTHER DISCUSSION | **Artists' signatures at Pattadakal**

Pattadakal is a sleepy village nestled in a bend of the Malaprabha river in the Bagalkot district of Karnataka. Its temples are some of the many examples of the spectacular developments in architecture and sculpture in the early medieval period. These temples were built during the time of the early Western Chalukyas and combine elements of both the Nagara (northern) and Dravida (southern) styles. Their walls bear exquisite sculptures. Monuments are generally associated with the rulers who ordered them to be built. Architects and sculptors did not usually leave their names on their creative work. At Pattadakal, however, some of them did.

The Virupaksha temple is considered the finest among the Pattadakal temples. It was constructed at the behest of the Chalukya queen Lokamahadevi to commemorate the conquest of Kanchipuram by her husband Vikramaditya II in the mid-8th century. However, here we have signatures of the architects who conceived the edifices and the skilled craftspeople who created them. The east porch of the Virupaksha temple has a Kannada inscription eulogizing the master architect who designed the temple. It reads (in translation): 'Gunda, whose conversation is entirely perfect, who has for his jewelled diadem and crest jewel the houses, vehicles, seats, and couches [that he designed], the *sutradhari* [architect] of the southern country.' Another inscription nearby tells us that this architect was given the title of *Tribhuvanacharya* (maker of the three worlds). Several reliefs on the temple walls bear signatures of the sculptors who carved them.

At the south-eastern corner of the village is the Papanatha temple, similar in its basic plan to the Virupaksha temple but with a *shikhara* in the northern style. The outer walls are adorned with panels depicting scenes and characters from the *Ramayana*, accompanied by label inscriptions. Some of the artists carved their names. Two of these names also appear on the panels of the Virupaksha temple, indicating that the two shrines were built around the same time. The northern passage wall of the Papanatha has a Kannada inscription giving the name of Revadi Ovajja, who belonged to the guild of the Sarvasiddhi *acharyas*, the same guild to which the architect of the Virupaksha temple belonged. The inscription tells us that he was the maker of the southern side of the temple. Carved close to the inscription are figures of chisels. The names of sculptors such as Baladeva and Devarya are engraved on the temple walls. In fact, Baladeva's name appears several times.

The sandstone quarry site used to construct the Pattadakal temples was located about 5 km north of the village at Motara Maradi and Shankaralingana Gundu. Here, there are rough drawings in varying sizes of Ganesha, Mahishasuramardini, Shiva *linga*s, and Nandi bulls. Some broad similarities can be seen between the themes of these carvings and those on the Pattadakal temples. The difference is that what we have at the quarry site is clearly 'rough work,' which does not match the finished excellence visible at the temple site. Stylized carvings of animals such as the lion, peacock, and what may be a camel, have also been identified. There are engravings of architectural members such as *chaitya* arches, pillars, and various sculptural motifs such as *purna-ghata*s, conches, a *svastika*, and tridents.

Durga relief, Pattadakal (left); sketch for Durga relief at quarry site (right)

Stones with wedge marks; attendance marks; Motara Maradi inscriptions; rough sketch of Ganesha and trident (from top)

The quarry site also has a set of inscriptions giving what seem to be names of the craftsmen who worked here. Srinivas V. Padikar's readings of the inscriptions on the rock face below are as follows: Shri [Janashrayan]; Shri Gu vikra (an abbreviation for Shri Gunavikraman). Thereafter a *parashu* (axe) is carved. Below these are the following inscriptions: Shri Marucan (the intended reading may be Shri Marutan); Shri Gunavikran (probably meant to be read Shri Gunavikraman).

There are various kinds of masons' marks on some of the rocks. Rows of short, thick strokes, vertical as well as horizontal, have been tentatively identified as 'attendance marks,' notched by the artisans who worked at the site, no doubt taken into account on pay day.

Some of the stones at the quarry site have wedge-marks left by masons who cut the stone blocks for the temples.

Meghana Kuppa and Srikumar M. Menon conducted a study of the wedge marks found at temple and quarry sites at Pattadakal and elsewhere in the Malaprabha valley. The method of stone cutting would have involved scooping out holes along the intended line of fracture of the rock and thereafter inserting and hammering steel wedges into them till the stone fractured along the line of wedge holes. According to Kuppa and Menon, the wedge marks of early Chalukya artisans were different from those left by wedge marks of the late medieval stonecutters of the Vijayanagara empire at Hampi and surrounding areas. The Early Chalukya wedge holes were lenticular in shape and the wedge marks that were left on the stone after splitting them were U-shaped. In contrast, in the Vijayanagara period, the wedge holes are invariably angular, and the wedge holes rectangular. This study, identifying a 'signature' of masons, opens up interesting possibilities and can be extended to other areas and periods, especially for architectural features such as fortifications that may be difficult to date, and can help trace the larger history of masonry practices, guilds, and migrations.

Source S. V. Venkateshaiah (personal communication), Michell, 2002: 36–37, 80–81; Shrinivas V. Padigar (personal communication); Kuppa and Menon, 2018

Hoysaleshvara temple, Halebeedu (from top left): Nandi; Ganesha; Keshava temple, Belur: huntress; Shiva and Parvati (centre); Ravana lifting Kailasha; Hanumana

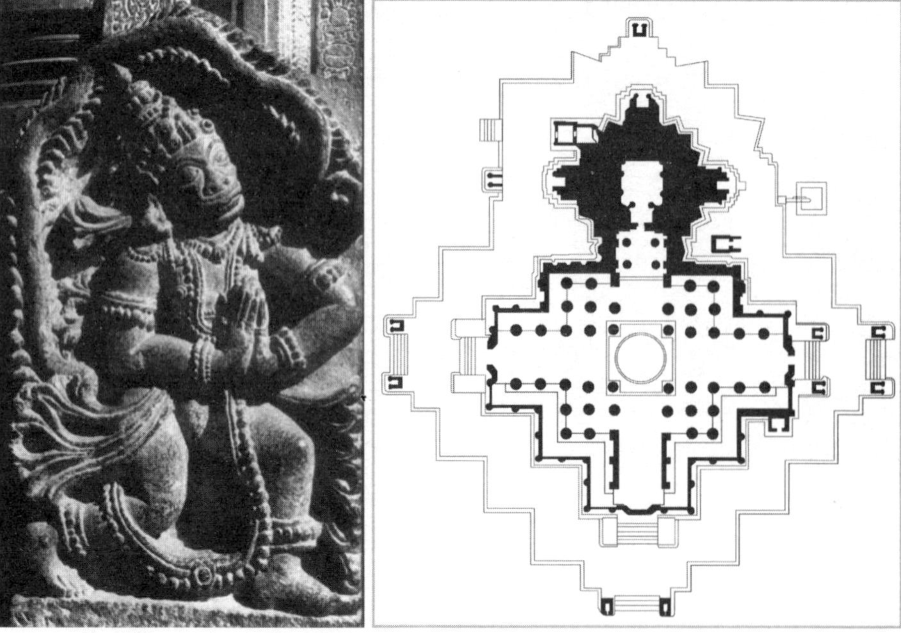

Figure 10.1 Plan of Keshava temple, Belur (right)

in plan and rests on a plinth of the same shape. The *shikhara* of the shrine is no longer extant. The intricate carvings on the outer and inner walls, pillars, screens, and bracket figures are remarkable for their finesse.

The 13th century Keshava temple at Somnathpur represents the high point of temple architecture and sculpture of the Hoysala period. The temple's plan is more complex than that of earlier ones. It is a triple shrine, with the three shrines consisting of star-shaped projections on three sides, the shape of the plinth following the intricate outline of the shrine. The *shikhara* is of moderate height, and stands stylistically midway between the Nagara and Dravida temple towers. The walls and ceilings of the temple are richly carved in the manner of other Hoysala temples, including, however, a number of erotic themes. The three images housed in the three shrines are Keshava (the main image), Krishna as Venugopala (playing the flute), and Janardhana Vishnu.

The Pallava kingdom

Apart from a few earlier specimens, the history of stone architecture in South India begins in the 7th century and can be connected with the increasing popularity of the *bhakti* sects. The Pallava kings, especially Mahendravarman I (600–625 CE), Narasimhavarman I (625–670 CE), and Narasimhavarman II Rajasimha (700–728 CE), were great patrons of the arts. The remains of the architecture of the Pallava period are mostly found at Mamallapuram and Kanchipuram (see Meister and Dhaky. [Eds.]., 1989: 23–80). They comprise cave temples, monolithic temples, and structural temples. Pallava sculpture has a distinctive style that is different from the Gupta period sculptures of North India. The faces of the human figures are oval with high cheekbones, and the bodies slender with tapering limbs.

Pallava cave shrines are smaller and less complex in plan than those at Ajanta and Ellora. The relatively plain caves are represented by the Lakshitayatana temple at Mandgappattu, Lalitankura's cave at Tiruchirappalli, and some of those at Mamallapuram (also known as Mahabalipuram). The massive pillars in these caves are square at the bottom and top, and chamfered into an octagonal shape in between. The cave façade is generally plain, *dvarapalas* usually marking the two ends. The larger caves have columns inside as well, leading into a sanctum guarded by *dvarapalas* and *dvarapalikas*. The sanctum contains a *linga* or images of Shiva, Vishnu, or Brahma. Representations of these and other deities are also carved on the walls of the hall. Some of the relief carving, for instance the scene of Shiva receiving Ganga on his head in the Tiruchirappalli cave, is exceptionally fine.

Vishnu resting on Sheshanaga, Mamallapuram cave

NEW DIRECTIONS IN RESEARCH | Playful ambiguity and political authority in the Mamallapuram relief

Padma Kaimal's analysis of the Mamallapuram relief suggests that it is not necessary to choose between Arjuna's penance and the descent of the Ganga in order to understand it. She suggests that the relief tells both stories, and combines them with many metaphors, comic allusions, and political promises. These various elements, voices, and ambiguities coexist within the carefully and elaborately planned relief scene in a playful way, creating a deciphering game for viewers.

Kaimal's analysis involves a careful examination of the details of the action-packed relief and demonstrates how these details can be used to both support and question whether the intention was to portray Arjuna's penance or the descent of the Ganga. For instance, although it is possible to identify an ascetic who is standing on one leg with his hands joined over his head as Arjuna, and an adjacent figure as Shiva, certain features of the tableau resist this interpretation. Although there are hunters and a boar, they do not seem to be central to the scene. The figures identified as Arjuna and Shiva could just as well be interpreted as Bhagiratha and Shiva. The importance of water in the scene suits the descent of the Ganga story, but the presence of hunters does not fit with that story.

The relief can also be seen as making a political statement, which is not surprising as it was probably patronized by Pallava kings. The themes of the Ganga and Arjuna have to do with a heroic penance leading to protection, themes that had resonance with the qualities of a great king. The heraldic lions carved at the left and right edges of the relief can be seen as royal emblems. Controlling water was also an important aspect of Pallava kingship.

The element of playfulness in the relief comes through in the depiction to the lower right of the cleft of a cat performing austerities, in the same pose at the human ascetic. It brings to mind a story from the *Panchatantra*, about a cat who masquerades as a pious ascetic in order to fool and gobble up gullible mice. The artist/s seem to have introduced humour, even parody here. It is interesting that Pallava king Mahendravarman is supposed to have written two religious satires—the *Bhagavadajjuka* and *Mattvilasa-prahasana*. Rulers of this dynasty may have appreciated humour and satire, not only in literature but also in art.

Kaimal reflects on how 7th century audiences may have responded to the relief. Mamallapuram was the premier Pallava port and looked out to the sea. Visitors from various lands who came to this port must have stood before the relief in awe, musing over it, and talking to each other about the multiple possible meanings that it brought to their minds. What a great location to visually proclaim the greatness of the Pallava kings!

Source Kaimal, 1994

The more elaborate Pallava period caves are located at the port city of Mamallapuram, named after the Pallava king Narasimha I, also known as Mahamalla (great hero). The columns in these caves are comparatively slender. Their shaft is multi-faceted, sometimes fluted or round, with cushion-shaped capitals and seated lions at the base. Some of the caves, such as the Adi-Varaha cave, are preceded by a tank. The rock-cut caves at Mamallapuram contain many striking mythological scenes carved in relief. These include Vishnu rescuing the earth, Vishnu taking three strides, Gaja-Lakshmi and Durga (in the Adi-Varaha cave), Mahishasuramardini in the Durga cave, and Krishna lifting Govardhana mountain (in the Pancha-Pandava cave). The relief carving of the Pallava cave shrines is generally shallower than that in the Deccan. The main figures are slender, delicate, and elegant. Their headdresses and crowns are quite plain, and they wear little or no jewellery.

However, the most dramatic of all the reliefs of this period is the gigantic open- air relief at Mamallapuram carved across two boulders, about 15 m high and 30 m long. On the rock face are a profusion of figures—people, animals including elephants—all in near life-size dimensions. The natural cleft between the two rocks, in which are carved a *naga* and a *nagini* figure, is meant to represent a river. The scene represented in this relief has been interpreted in two different ways—as the descent of the Ganga or as Arjuna's penance. In the story of the descent of the Ganga, which occurs in the *Mahabharata* and *Ramayana*, king Bhagiratha performs great austerities in order to bring the celestial river Ganga to the earth in order to bring an end to a terrible drought. The god Shiva helps by receiving the river on his matted locks to break the power of its descent and the Ganga then flows gently to the earth, purifying it. The story of Arjuna's penance occurs in the *Mahabharata* and forms the theme of the *Kiratarjuniya*. In this story, Arjuna performs a penance to obtain Shiva's weapons. A boar

Mamallapuram (from top): open-air relief; details of ascetic, elephants, monkey pair near relief

Mamallapuram *rathas* (from top): Dharmaraja; Bhima; Arjuna and Draupadi; Nakula-Sahadeva

Shore temple, Mamallapuram

is sent by some *asuras* to kill him. Shiva intervenes to protect Arjuna, disguised as a *kirata* (hunter). Both claim to have shot the boar, and a conflict erupts. Shiva wins and reveals his true self to Arjuna; Arjuna pays him obeisance and receives the divine weapon he desires.

The lower left side of the Mamallapuram relief seems unfinished. (On the widespread occurrence of apparently unfinished sculpture in ancient Indian art, and differences in notions of 'finish,' see Dehejia and Rockwell, 2016.)

The other group of architectural remains at Mamallapuram are nine rock-cut temples, of which five are clustered together. The name of the great Pallava builder king Mamalla was in later times misunderstood as referring to the five Pandava heroes, and the five temples at Mamallapuram came to be known after the legendary Pandavas and their wife Draupadi. The shrines are often referred to as the five *rathas*. *Ratha* means a chariot and the reference to temples as *rathas* may have been based on the idea that they were representations of the celestial chariots that the deities were supposed to move around in. The *rathas* are known as the Dharmaraja, Bhima, Draupadi, Arjuna, and Sahadeva *rathas*. It is interesting to note that although located in close proximity to each other, these shrines display very different architectural features.

The Dharmaraja *ratha* is square in plan. It has open porches and a terraced pyramidal tower. Its pillar shafts are supported by seated lions. The Bhima *ratha* is longitudinal in shape with a barrel-vaulted roof. The Draupadi *ratha* is a very small square structure with a curvilinear roof shaped like the thatched roof of a hut. The Arjuna *ratha* is incomplete; it may have been abandoned due to the rock not being able to withstand the pressure of carving. The Sahadeva *ratha* too is incomplete. The outer walls of the Mamallapuram temples are decorated with scenes from Hindu mythology. The south face of the Dharmaraja *ratha* has a relief sculpture which an inscription identifies as king Narasimhavarman Mamalla I.

During the reign of Narasimhavarman II Rajasimha, the rock-cut technique of temple building was replaced by structural temples. The Shore temple at Mamallapuram is assigned to the reign of Rajasimha, but additions may have been made in later times. This has three shrine areas containing a stone Shiva *linga*, Somaskanda (Shiva with Uma and Skanda, a popular theme in the Pallava period), and Vishnu resting on the serpent Ananta. The two *shikhara*s are terraced and slender. The relief sculptures of the temple are very eroded due to the effects of the sea breeze and sand.

The Rajasimheshvara or Kailasanatha temple at Kanchipuram is also assigned to the reign of Narasimhavarman II Rajasimha. Within a large rectangular enclosure is a complex consisting of a main shrine and over 50 subsidiary shrines. The main temple consists of a square sanctum enshrining a *linga*, with an enclosed circumambulatory passage. It is surrounded by nine small shrines. The *shikhara* is in the typical southern style. The pillared hall and verandah preceding the shrine may have been added later. The enclosure walls of the complex have *gopura*s. The Kailasanatha temple is more heavily ornamented with sculptures than other structures of the Pallava period. Representations of Somaskanda are very frequent, and lions are a recurring motif on the enclosure wall. This temple marks an important stage in the evolution of the South Indian temple.

It has been suggested that Pallava art had an influence on Sri Lankan sculpture. For instance, some similarities have been suggested between the Mamallapuram relief and the treatment of the carvings at Isurumuniya in Anuradhapura (Kavork Dohanian, 1983). However, the relief carving of man and horse found at Isurumunia (perhaps representing Parjanya and Agni or a Hindu village god Aiyanar) is quite enigmatic and does not seem to have any Indian counterpart.

Some scholars argue that the Shaiva temples on the Dieng plateau in central Java, dated between the mid-7th century to 8th century were modelled on the Pallava temples in Mahabalipuram. However, although the *shikhara* is of the Dravida style, there are

Isurumuniya (Sri Lanka): 'man and horse' (left); 'lovers', perhaps Shiva and Parvati, 7th/8th century (right)

Dieng temples, Java

many stylistic differences. One of the temples—the Chandi Bhima—has affinities with the North Indian Nagara style, and the influences may have been from the Chalukyan kindom (Romain, 2011). Further, while multiple Indian influences were making their way to Java, the end product was unlike anything seen in India. It was distinctly Javanese.

The Chola temples

While Pallava temples are mostly located in and around Kanchipuram, Chola temples are concentrated further south, around Tanjore (Huntington, 1985: 509–39; Meister and Dhaky, 1983: 223–64, 289–330). They do not show a simple or straightforward evolution from the earlier Pallava temples and in fact reflect certain new features. Inscriptions indicate that many brick temples of Pallava times were rebuilt in stone during this period. The temple architecture of the Chola period can be divided into at least two phases on the basis of dynastic markers—the early phase (mid-9th to the early 11th centuries) and the late phase (early 11th to the 13th centuries). Some art historians suggest a division into three phases—early (850–985), middle (985–1070), and late (1070–1270)—and divide these into further sub-phases.

The earliest phase is represented by the Shiva temple at Narttamalai, built by the Chola king Vijayalaya or by a Muttarayar chief in the mid-9th century. It consists of a *vimana* (this term refers to the sanctum and its superstructure) joined to an *ardhamandapa* (the hall preceding the sanctum), which has two rows of three pillars. The main shrine is surrounded by six subsidiary shrines (there may originally have been eight) known as *parivaralayas*. The sanctum is circular and contains a *linga* and *yoni*. The outer walls have relatively little sculptural ornamentation, but two *dvarapalas* flank the western entrance. The walls have pilasters, but there are no niches containing images of deities, as is common in later Chola temples.

The next phase is represented by temples built during the reigns of Aditya I (871–907 CE) and Parantaka I (907–55 CE), for instance the Brahmapureshvara temple at Pullamangai, the Nageshvarasvami temple at Kumbakonam, and the Koranganatha temple at Srinivasanallur. The Brahmapureshvara temple consists of an *ardhamandapa* joined to the *vimana*. A *mukhamandapa* (porch) was added subsequently. The temple was built in a shallow stone-lined pit that was once probably filled with water. This ties in with the fact that inverted lotuses are carved along the lower part of the outer walls. The frieze of lions along the base of the temple is a typical feature of Chola temples. Pilasters divide the outer walls into niches known as *devakoshthas*, which contain images of various deities including Ganesha, Durga Mahishasuramardini, and Brahma. The figures are natural

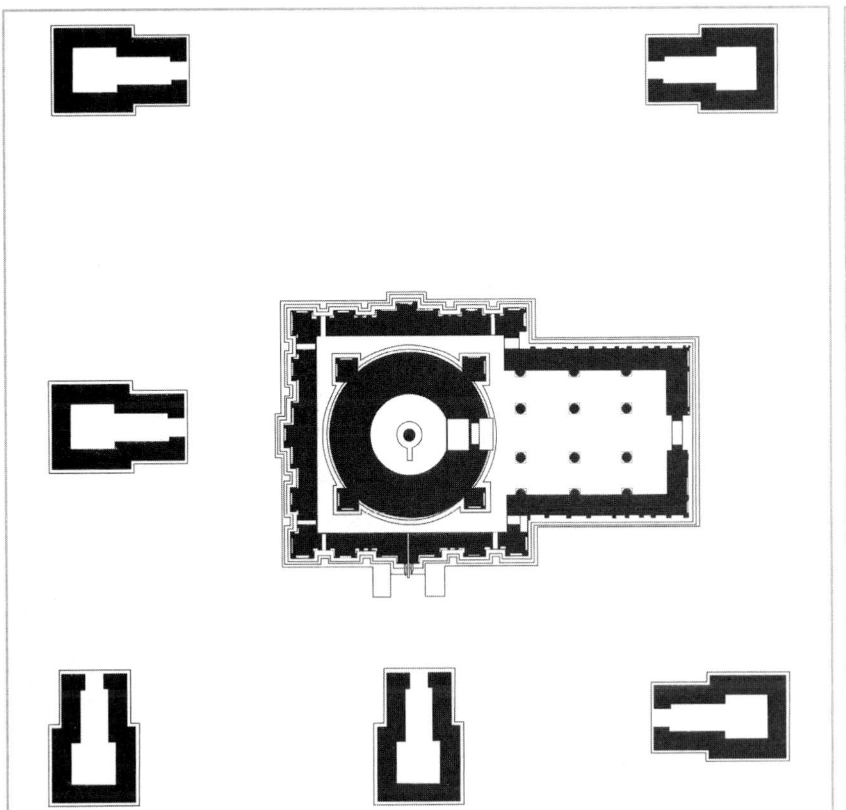

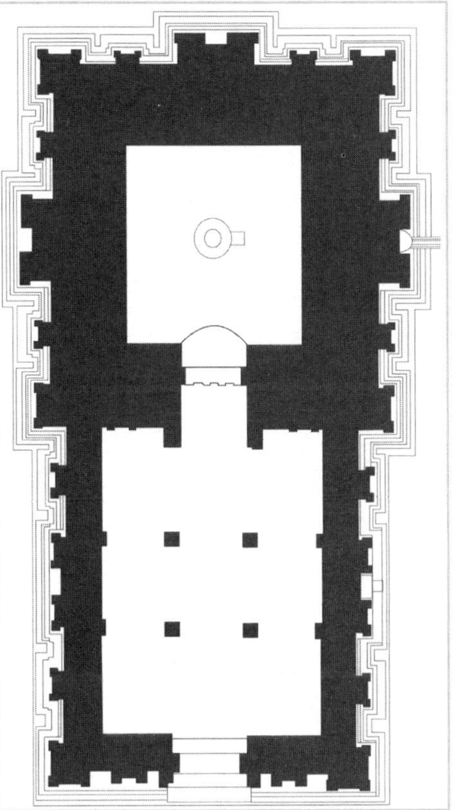

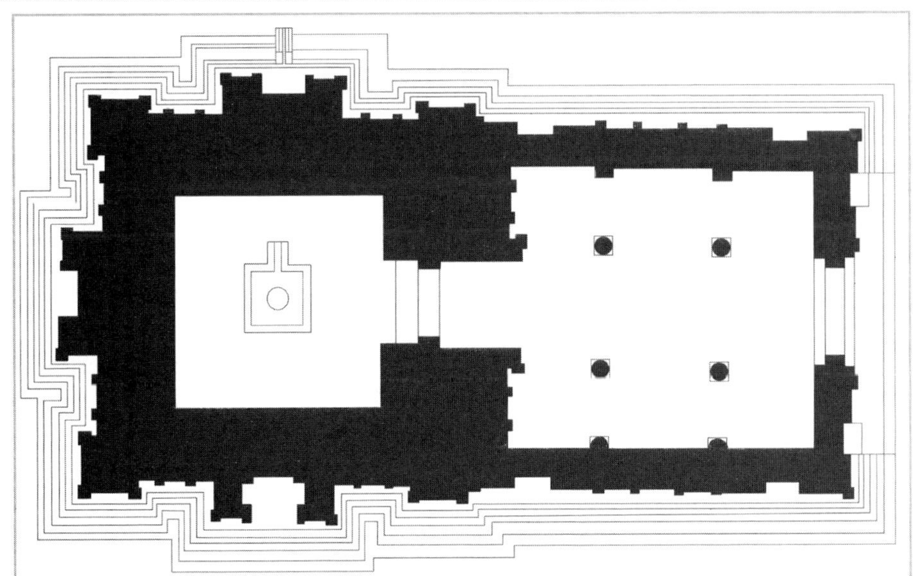

Figure 10.2 (from top) Plans of Shiva temple. Narttamalai; Brahmapureshvara temple, Pullamangai; Nageshvarasvami temple, Kumbakonam (after Huntington, 1985)

Brihadishvara temple, Thanjavur (from top): view of temple; sculptural detail

and slender, with high headdresses. Representations of deities and mythological scenes, including those from the *Ramayana*, appear on the outer walls.

The original structure of the Nageshvarasvami temple consists of a joined *ardhamandapa* and *vimana*. Deeply carved representations of deities appear in the pilastered niches. The Koranganatha temple is similar in basic structure, except for the addition of an *antarala* (vestibule or antechamber) between the *vimana* and *ardhamandapa*. The frieze along the outer base consists of rows of inverted lotuses, and there are also rows of lions and elephants. The sculpted figures are more heavily ornamented than in other temples of this period.

The third phase of Chola temple architecture is associated with Shembiyan Mahadevi, a queen who was a major patron of temple building during the reigns of her husband Gandaraditya (949–57 CE), her son Uttama I (969–85 CE), and in the early part of Rajaraja I's reign. A large number of older brick temples were rebuilt in stone during this period. A major change is noticeable in the nature of sculpted figures, which appear rather stiff and lifeless. An example of a temple built at the instance of Shembiyan Mahadevi is the Agastyeshvara temple at Anangapur.

The culmination of Chola temple architecture is represented by the Brihadishvara (also known as the Rajarajeshvara) temple at Thanjavur. With an approximately 60 m tall *vimana* and a towering, pyramidal *shikhara*, this Shiva temple was one of the largest and most grand structures of its age, displaying certain new architectural features compared to earlier temples. The main shrine consists of a pillared porch, a pillared *mukhamandapa* and *ardhamandapa*, an *antarala*, and the sanctum. The ornamentation of the outer walls is much more profuse than in earlier shrines. The niches are deep and projecting, and the figures they frame are carved in the round. The lower niches mostly contain representations of Shiva in his various manifestations, including Nataraja. One of the upper levels has 30 representations of

Brihadishvara temple, Thanjavur: *Gopura* (left); sculptural detail (right)

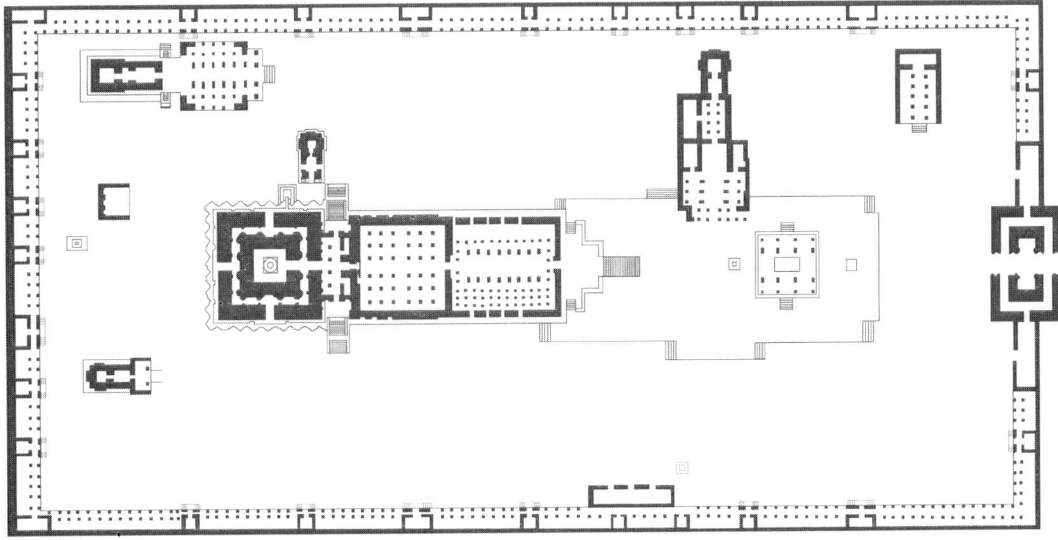

Figure 10.3 Plan of Brihadishvara temple

Relief panels, Brihadishvara temple, Thanjavur

Shiva as Tripurantaka, destroyer of three cities. Three huge Shiva sculptures and many paintings are located in the circumambulatory passage around the sanctum. In front of the temple is an almost 6 m long Nandi bull carved out of a single stone, later enclosed in a pavilion. The temple stands within a huge rectangular enclosure. On the east are two imposing temple gateways (*gopuras*), the lower part of which is made of stone, the upper storeys of brick. The figures carved on the *gopuras* are heavier and more ornamented than in earlier temples.

Rajendra I (Rajaraja's son) built a temple called Brihadishvara in his new capital Gangaikondacholapuram. It was not completed and lies in a ruinous state, but enough survives to show the uneven quality of its workmanship and the fact that it did not compare well with its namesake in Tanjore. The Gangaikondacholapuram temple has a lower *vimana*, its *shikhara* is curved inwards, and its walls are more heavily embellished with sculptures.

The last phase of Chola temple architecture belongs to the 12th–13th centuries. During this period, the *gopura* became more dominant than the *vimana*. This is evident in the Shiva temple at Chidambaram, which was mostly built during the reigns of Kulottunga I (1070–1122 CE) and his successors. Wheels and horses were added to the outer walls of the temple, to give it the appearance of a chariot.

Chola metal sculpture

The Chola period is well known for the aesthetic and technical finesse of its metal sculpture. Thanjavur was a major centre of the production of such images. The metal images of North India tend to be hollow, while those of South India were solid. Both were, however, made through the lost wax method. Traditionally, the northern images are supposed to be made out of an alloy of eight metals (gold, silver, tin, lead, iron, mercury, zinc, and copper) while the southern ones are supposed to be made of an alloy of five metals (copper, silver, gold, tin, and lead). The analysis of actual images indicates that these formulae were not always followed. The iconography and style of metal images were similar to those of their stone counterparts. The images were clothed and ornamented and formed part of temple rituals and ceremonials. Many of the southern images were carried about in processions. The images of Shiva as Nataraja, i.e., Lord of the Dance, appear frequently among Chola metal sculpture. (See Sivaramamurti, [1974] 1994) for a detailed discussion of Nataraja in Indian art and literature.) Other themes include Krishna and the Alvar and Nayanmar saints. There are a few Buddhist images as well.

Many Shiva temples of South India have a separate *natana-sabha*, where the image of Nataraja is placed. This can be seen, for instance, in the temple at Chidambaram. The dancing Shiva was of two types—angry and pacific. Shiva's cosmic dance symbolizes the cyclical creation and destruction of the universe, and its elements have been interpreted in various ways. In his 'dance of bliss' (*ananda tandava*), Shiva usually has four arms. He wears

NEW DIRECTIONS IN RESEARCH | **Archaeometric analysis of Nataraja images**

Ancient Hindu metal images rarely have inscriptions, and scholars tend to date them in relation to the stone sculptures found in temples with datable inscriptions. The oldest three-dimensional stone Nataraja figures are found in temples built by the Chola queen Sembiyan Mahadevi; for instance the image in the mid-10th century Kailasanathaswami temple. According to some scholars, the bronze Natarajas also emerged during this period. However, Sharada Srinivasan's analysis of the archaeometric, iconographic, and literary evidence shows that bronze representations of Shiva's *ananda-tandava* first appeared in the Pallava period, between the 7th and mid-9th centuries.

There is no foolproof method for dating solid metal artefacts. However, lead isotope ratio analysis and trace element analysis can be used to identify similar or different sources of the metals. This can be combined with an analysis of style to indicate which images constitute a group. Srinivasan's analysis of 130 metal images revealed that the metal artefacts of the Pallava and Chola periods show different archaeometric results. On this basis, she argues that two Nataraja bronzes—one found at Kunniyar in Thanjavur district and another currently housed in the British Museum—that have traditionally been described as 'Chola bronzes' were in fact in all likelihood made during the Pallava period.

The early Pallava bronze representations of Nataraja are metal translations of wooden images. The limbs are close set, the sash hangs downwards, and the rim of fire is elliptical. Later, in the Chola period, craftspeople recognized the greater tensile strength of metal in comparison with wood. In the Chola bronzes, the limbs, sash, and locks flare out towards a circular rim.

According to Srinivasan, well-rounded stone Natarajas came to the fore during the reign of Sembiyan Mahadevi, several centuries *after* the earliest metal images of the Pallava period. This may have been due to the poor tensile strength of stone in comparison to metal, which initially made it difficult, for instance, for stone carvers to carve the raised left leg of the dancing Shiva.

Sculptors rendered Shiva's ecstatic and powerful dance in stone and bronze, while poets described it in words of wonder. For instance, Manikkavachakar's *Tiruvachakam* says 'Let us praise the Dancer who in good Tillai's hall dances with fire, who sports, creating, destroying, this heaven and earth and all else.'

Source Srinivasan, 2004

Chola Nataraja bronze

a snake as an ornament. His front left arm is in a pose referred to as *danda-hasta* (staff hand) or *gaja-hasta* (elephant hand). In his rear left hand, he holds a flame, in his rear right hand a drum; his front right hand is in the release-granting *abhaya* pose. The drum symbolizes creation, the fire symbolizes destruction. The hand of the *gaja-hasta* points to his lifted foot, which is the refuge of the world. Shiva's left leg is thrust out across his body. He usually dances on a dwarf, Muyalaka, who signifies ignorance or evil. The god's locks of hair, which cradle the goddess Ganga, radiate out into the surrounding rim of flames. The attributes of the Natarajas of South India are different from the equally impressive images of the dancing Shiva found in other parts of the subcontinent such as at Ellora or Badami. There are differences in the expression, ornamentation, the number of arms, and in the attendant figures.

Early mosques in the subcontinent

The Arab and Ghurid invasions in the north-west and the Arab involvement in Indian Ocean trade led to the construction of the earliest mosques in the subcontinent. Remains of these have been found in lower Sindh and the Swat valley in Pakistan, and in Kutch and Gwalior in India (Alka Patel 2008; 2021). The mosques at Banbhore and Mansura in Sindh can be dated to the 8th century.

Vestiges of early mosques can also be identified at Gwalior in Central India and Bhadreshvar in Kutch in Gujarat (Patel, 2008: 12–14, 16–19). In Gwalior, an architectural

FURTHER DISCUSSION | Mosques in Sindh and the Swat valley

Banbhore in central Sindh may represent the site of ancient Daibul. The mosque here went through four phases of reconstruction between the early 8th century and 12th centuries and showed evidence of reuse of earlier materials in later phases. The mosque was located in the middle of a fortified enclosure. Its perimeter walls, lined with limestone, enclosed a 122 x 128 ft area. A square minaret seems to have been located at the southeastern corner. There was a covered prayer area, an open central courtyard of baked bricks, and roofed double aisles on the northern, southern, and eastern perimeters. It was a hypostyle mosque—this means that its prayer hall had rows of columns. The prayer area was divided into three aisles of ten columns each; the columns were made of wood (the wood had decayed) and stood on stone bases, some of which had carving. The *qibla* wall (the mosque wall which faces the direction of Mecca) was the thickest of the perimeter walls, and the *mihrab* (the niche in the *qibla* wall) may have been carved out and capped by a semi-circular stone that was found within the prayer area. The courtyard had three aisles made by two rows of wooden pillars standing on stone bases. Inscriptions in the Arabic Kufic script were found here. The style of the Bhanbhore mosque has similarities with early Ummayid mosques in Kufa and Wasit and those in North Africa. As pointed out by Alka Patel, in the absence of any local mosque-building traditions, the Arab conquerors fell back on the memories of mosques in their homeland.

The Mansura mosque (also in Sindh) was probably built during the time of Muhammad bin Qasim in *c.* 738. Mansura started off as a cantonment, not far from Brahamanabad, the ancient Rai capital. In the 9th century, during the time of the Habbari Amirs, it grew into a major centre of trade and learning. Excavations at the site revealed a brick fortification wall punctuated by four gates. These enclosed residential structures, two large buildings, one of which seems to have had an administrative/political significance, and the other a mosque. The main mosque probably had a hypostyle plan, which was expanded during the time of the Habbaris in the 9th century. It measured 150 x 250 ft. As in the Banbhore mosque, the central courtyard had cloistered aisles on the north and south. The prayer area was divided into 13 aisles made with 60 wooden columns resting on stone bases. The *mihrab*, carved out of the *qibla* wall, was semi-circular in plan. The lower, inner walls of the building seem to have been made of teak wood.

The remains of a mosque have been found at Udegram in the Swat valley of Pakistan. Like Sindh, this region too was important on the overland routes of the time. The mosque was located in an unfortified residential area. On the basis of an Arabic inscription, it can be dated to 1048-49 CE. The inscription states that the mosque was built by the Amir and Hajib Abu Mansur Nushtegin, who may have been a governor appointed by the Ghaznavid Sultan. The 63 x 84 ft mosque was made of schist and was rectangular in plan. The courtyard and a slightly lower ablution pool are paved with schist. The *mihrab* set into the *qibla* wall was square in plan but arched into a niche on top using the corbelling style. The entire area seems to have been roofed, and there were rows of wooden columns resting on stone bases.

Source Patel, 2008

Remains of mosques at Banbhore, Bhadreshvar, and Udegram; Gwalior *mihrab* (from top)

fragment that looks like an 8th century *mihrab* is built into the wall next to the Hathi Pol entrance of the Man Mandir, the fortified palace at Gwalior, which was constructed between the 15th and 16th century. The *mihrab* seems to have been part of an 8th century mosque, and is made in the local style found in temples in the area. At Bhadreshvar in Kutch, there are remains of two mosques (the Chhoti and Solakhambhi mosques), tombs, a step-well, and some cenotaphs, which seem to belong to the mid-12th century. The plans of the mosques are similar to southern Iranian types, but they were clearly built by local craftsmen. A unique architectural feature of these two mosques, not seen elsewhere, are two parallel *qiblas*, creating two prayer areas. The errors in the Arabic inscriptions in the cenotaphs indicate that they were executed by local carvers who did not know the language and script.

CONCLUSIONS

The political history of the early medieval period was marked by a proliferation and expansion of states in various parts of the subcontinent. Land grants to Brahmanas played an important role in the legitimation of political power and had a significant impact on agrarian relations. There was agrarian expansion in various parts of the subcontinent and rural societies became increasingly stratified. This was not a period of urban decay. This is most evident from South India, where urban crafts, cities, trade, and trade guilds flourished. Trade links between the Indian subcontinent, Central Asia, China, and South-east Asia expanded significantly. Devotional worship was a marked feature of religious thought and practice. Temples functioned not only as sacred spaces, but also as the core of urban centres and as political symbols. The patronage they attracted made them points of convergence of the activities and aspirations of diverse social groups. The advent of Islam was an important feature of the religious history of the subcontinent. Significant developments in the cultural sphere included the production of a wide range of texts in Sanskrit and regional languages such as Tamil and Kannada. There was an efflorescence and refinement in religious architecture and sculpture, and distinct regional styles became apparent. During *c.* 600–1200 CE, the developments at the political, social, economic, and cultural levels crystallized into distinct regional formations and patterns. The early medieval period was truly a period of cultural confluence, when elements of Perso-Islamic, Sanskritic, and regional cultures interacted with each other to create a series of new cultural syntheses.

FURTHER READINGS

Abraham, Meera. 1988. *Two Medieval Merchant Guilds of South India*. New Delhi: Manohar.

Ali, Daud. 2006. *Courtly Culture and Political Life in Early Medieval India*. New Delhi: Cambridge University Press.

Bhattacharyya, N. N. 1974. *History of the Sakta Religion*. New Delhi: Munshiram Manoharlal.

———. (1982) 1999. *History of the Tantric Religion: An Historical, Ritualistic and Philosophical Study*. New Delhi: Manohar.

Chakrabarti, Kunal. 2001. *Religious Process: The Puranas and the Making of a Regional Tradition*. Delhi: Oxford University Press.

Chakravarti, Ranabir. 2020. *The Pull Towards the Coast and Other Essays: The Indian Ocean History and the Subcontinent Before 1500 CE*. Delhi: Primus Books.

Champakalakshmi, R. 1996. *Trade, Ideology and Urbanization: South India 30 BC to AD 1300*. Delhi: Oxford University Press.

Chattopadhyaya, B. D. (1994) 1997. *The Making of Early Medieval India*. Delhi: Oxford University Press.

_______. 1998. *Representing the Other? Sanskrit Sources and the Muslims (Eighth to Fourteenth Century)*. New Delhi: Manohar.

Davidson, Ronald M. 2002. *Indian Esoteric Buddhism: A Social History of the Tantric Movement*. New York: Columbia University Press.

Dehejia, Vidya. 1988. *Slaves of the Lord: The Path of the Tamil Saints*. New Delhi: Munshiram Manoharlal.

Devahuti, D. (1970) 1983. *Harsha: A Political Study*. 2nd Edn. Delhi: Oxford University Press.

Deyell, John S. 1990. *Living Without Silver: The Monetary History of Early Medieval North India*. Delhi: Oxford University Press.

Eaton, Richard M. 2019. *India in the Persianate Age: 1000–1765*. London: Allen Lane. Introduction, Chap. 1.

Eaton, Richard M. (Ed.). (2003) 2006. *India's Islamic Traditions, 711–1750*. Oxford in India Readings, Themes in India History Series. New Delhi: Oxford University Press. Introduction.

Ernst, Carl W. 2005. *Following Muhammad: Rethinking Islam in the Contemporary World*. New Delhi: Yoda Press.

Eschmann, Anncharlott, Hermann Kulke, and Gaya Charan Tripathi. (Eds.). (1978) 2014. Revised and enlarged Edn. *The Cult of Jagannath and the Regional Tradition of Orissa*. New Delhi: Manohar.

Furui, Ryosuke. 2020. *Land and Society in Early South Asia: Eastern India 400–1250 AD*. London and New York: Routledge.

Goyal, S. R. 1986. *Harsha and Buddhism*. Meerut: Kusumanjali Prakashan.
Guy, John. (Ed.). 2014. *Lost Kingdoms: Hindu–Buddhist Sculpture of Early South-east Asia*. New York: Metropolitan Museum of Art. Available online at https://www.metmuseum.org
Hardy, Friedhelm. 1983. *Viraha-bhakti: The Early History of Krsn Devotion in South India*. Delhi: Oxford University Press.
Heitzman, James. 1997. *Gifts of Power: Lordship in an Early Indian State*. Delhi: Oxford University Press.
Huntington, Susan. 1985. *The Art of Ancient India: Buddhist, Hindu, Jain*. New York, Tokyo: John Weatherhill Inc. Chapters 11–22.
Jain, V. K. 1990. *Trade and Traders in Western India*. New Delhi: Munshiram Manoharlal.
Karashima, Noboru. 1984. *South Indian History and Society: Studies from Inscriptions AD 850–1800*. Delhi: Oxford University Press.
Karashima, Noboru. (Ed.). 2014. *A Concise History of South India: Issues and Interpretations*. New Delhi: Oxford University Press.
Kulke, Hermann. (1993) 2001. *Kings and Cults: State Formation and Legitimation in India and South-east Asia*. New Delhi: Manohar.
Kulke, Hermann and Bhairabi Prasad Sahu. (Eds.). 2015. *Interrogating Political Systems: Integrative Processes and States in Pre-Modern India*. New Delhi: Manohar.
_______. (Eds.). 2022. *The Routledge Handbook of the State in Premodern India*. London and New York: Routledge; Indian edition.
Kulke, Hermann, K. Kesavapany, and Vijay Sakhuja. (Eds.). 2009. *Nagapattinam to Suvarnadwipa: Relections on the Chola Naval Expeditions to South-east Asia*. Singapore: Institute of South-east Asian Studies.
Lahiri, Nayanjot. 1991. *Pre-Ahom Assam: Studies in the Inscriptions of Assam between the Fifth and the Thirteenth Centuries AD*. New Delhi: Munshiram Manoharlal.
Liu, Xinru. 1996. *Silk and Religion: An Exploration of Material Life and the Thought of People, AD 600–1200*. Delhi: Oxford University Press.
Lorenzen, David N. (1999) 2006. Who Invented Hinduism? In David Lorenzen, *Who Invented Hinduism?* Essays on Religion in History. New Delhi: Yoda Press, pp. 1–36.
Manguin, Pierre-Yves, A. Mani, and Geoff Wade. (Eds.). 2011. *Early Interactions between South and South-east Asia*. Singapore east Asia. Singapore, Institute of South-east Asian Studies and New Delhi, Manohar.
Nandi, R. N. 2000. *State Formation, Agrarian Growth and Social Change in Feudal South India c. AD 600–1200*. New Delhi: Manohar.
Pollock, Sheldon. (2006) 2007. *The Language of the Gods in the World of Men: Sanskrit, Culture and Power in Premodern India*. Delhi: Permanent Black.
Ramaswamy, Vijaya. 1985. *Textiles and Weavers in Medieval South India*. Delhi: Oxford University Press.
———. 1997. *Walking Naked: Women, Society, Spirituality in South India*. Shimla: Indian Institute of Advanced Studies.
Rangachari, Devika. 2009. *Invisible Women, Visible Histories: Gender, Society and Polity in North India (Seventh to Twelfth Century AD)*. New Delhi: Manohar.
Ray, H. P. 2021. *Coastal Shrines and Transnational Maritime Networks Across India and South-east Asia*. New York and London: Routledge.
Sanderson, Alexis. 2009. 'The Saiva Age—The Rise and Dominance of Saivism during the Early Medieval Period.' In Shingo Einoo. (Ed.). *Genesis and Development of Tantrism*. Tokyo: Institute of Oriental Culture. pp. 41–349.
Sastri, K. A. Nilakanta. (1955) 1975. *A History of South India from Prehistoric Times to the Fall of Vijayanagar*. 4th Edn. Madras: Oxford University Press.
Schimmel, Annemarie. 1992. *Islam: An Introduction*. New York: State University of New York Press.
Sen, Swadhin, Supriya Varma, and Bhairabi Prasad Sahu. (Eds.). *The Archaeology of Early Medieval and Medieval South Asia: Contesting Narratives from the Eastern Ganga-Brahmaputra Basin*. London and New York: Routedge, 2023.
Sen, Tansen. 2018. *India, China and the World: A Connected History*. New Delhi: Oxford University Press.
Sen, Tansen. (Ed.). 2014. *Buddhism Across Asia: Networks of Material, Intellectual and Cultural Exchange*. Singapore: ISEAS and New Delhi: Manohar.
Sharma, R. S. (1965) 1980. *Indian Feudalism*. Madras: Macmillan.
———. 1987. *Urban Decay in India (c. 300–c.1000)*. New Delhi: Munshiram Manoharlal.

Singh, Upinder. 1994. *Kings, Brahmanas and Temples in Orissa: An Epigraphic Study AD 300–1147*. New Delhi: Munshiram Manoharlal.

_______. (Ed.). 2011. *Rethinking Early Medieval India*. Delhi: Oxford University Press.

Sinha Kapur, Nandini. 2002. *State formation in Rajasthan: Mewar during the Seventh–Fifteenth Centuries*. New Delhi: Manohar.

Stein, Burton. 1980. *Peasant State and Society in Medieval South India*. Delhi: Oxford University Press.

Subbarayalu, Y. 1982. 'The Chola State.' *Studies in History* 4(2): 265–306.

Veluthat, Kesavan. 1993. *The Political Structure of Early Mediaeval South India*. New Delhi: Orient Longman.

Wink, André. 1999. *Al-Hind: The Making of the Indo-Islamic World*. Vol. 1: *Early Mediaeval India and the Expansion of Islam 7th–11th Centuries*; Vol. 2: *Al-Hind: The Slave Kings and the Islamic Conquest 11th–13th Centuries*. New Delhi: Oxford University Press: New Delhi: Oxford University Press.

Yadava, B. N. S. 1973. *Society and Culture in Northern India in the Twelfth Century*. Allahabad: Central Book Depot.

Eleventh century copper alloy image of the Shaiva saint Sambandar; such images may have been used in processions during temple festivities.

A Note on Diacritics

Sanskrit

Vowels

अ	आ	इ	ई	उ	ऊ	ऋ	ए	ऐ	ओ	औ	•	ः
a	ā	i	ī	u	ū	ṛ	e	ai	o	au	ṁ	ḥ

Consonants

क	ख	ग	घ	ङ	च	छ	ज	झ	ञ
ka	kha	ga	gha	ṅa	ca	cha	ja	jha	ña
ट	ठ	ड	ढ	ण	त	थ	द	ध	न
ṭa	ṭha	ḍa	ḍha	ṇa	ta	tha	da	dha	na
प	फ	ब	भ	म	य	र	ल	व	
pa	pha	ba	bha	ma	ya	ra	la	va	
श	ष	स	ह						
śa	ṣa	sa	ha						

Tamil

Vowels

அ	ஆ	இ	ஈ	உ	ஊ	எ	ஏ	ஐ	ஒ	ஓ	ஔ
a	ā	i	ī	u	ū	e	ē	ai	o	ō	au
[ʌ]	[a:]	[i]	[i:]	[u,w]	[u:]	[e]	[e:]	[ʌy]	[o]	[o:]	[ʌu]

Consonants

க	k	த	t	ல	l
ங	ṅ [ŋ]	ந	n	வ	v [u]
ச	c	ப	p [p, b]	ழ	ḻ
ஞ	ñ	ம	m	ள	ḷ
ட	ṭ [t,d]	ய	y [j]	ற	ṟ, R
ண	ṇ [ɲ]	ர	r	ன	N

Glossary

Acheulian tools: an assemblage of stone tools marked by advanced and increasingly symmetrical handaxes and cleavers; primarily associated with the lower palaeolithic, they continue into later parts of the stone age as well
***agrahara*:** land or village gifted by a king
***ahimsa*:** non-injury, non-violence
Ajivikas: An ancient religious sect, associated with Makkhali Gosala
***akam*:** Sangam love poems
Alvars: the Vaishnava saint-poets of early medieval South India
***amphorae*:** a type of Roman pottery—jars with a large oval body, narrow cylindrical neck, and two handles
***anekantavada*:** the Jaina doctrine of the manifold nature of reality
animal domestication: the process of selective breeding of animals, which involves removing them from their natural habitat and rearing them under artificial conditions under human control for purposes of human gain
***antarala*:** the vestibule or antechamber of a temple
***anvikshiki*:** literally, 'looking at'; logical reasoning
Apabhramsha: a stage of the later development of the Prakrit language up to the end of the 1st millennium CE
***araghatta*:** the Persian wheel, or a similar contrivance
Aramaic: a language and script. The Aramaic or North Semitic script was the official script of the Assyrian, Babylonian, and Achaemenid empires; Ashokan inscriptions indicate the use of the language and script in the north-western part of the Indian subcontinent
Aranyakas: literally 'forest books'; part of the Vedic corpus
Archaeo-botany: the study of ancient plant remains
archaeological sources: all tangible, material remains
archaeology: the study of the human past through material remains
archaeometry: a range of scientific techniques and analyses involving the use of measurement in order to analyse ancient objects or materials
Ardha-Magadhi: an eastern dialect of Prakrit; the earliest Jaina texts are written in this dialect
***ardhamandapa*:** the hall preceding the sanctum in a temple
***arhat*:** a person who has attained enlightenment
***Ariya-sachchani*:** the Four Noble Truths related to suffering; an important part of the Buddha's teaching
artefact: a portable object made or altered by human hands
***ashrama*(s):** the four stages of life—*brahmacharya* (celibate studenthood), *grihastha* (the householder stage), *vanaprastha* (partial renunciation), and *sannyasa* (complete renunciation); can also mean a hermitage
assemblage: in archaeology, refers collectively to all the industries found at a site
***astika* schools:** philosophical schools that accepted the authority of the Vedas, comprising those that later came to be described as the six classical systems of Hindu philosophy
***atman*:** the imperishable ultimate reality within the self, according to the Upanishads
***Australopithecus*:** a hominid genus
***avatara*:** an incarnation of the god Vishnu
Ayyavole: a powerful merchant guild of early medieval South India
bands: small and usually nomadic communities, usually related to each other through kinship
***bhagavata*:** a worshipper of Vasudeva Krishna
***bhikkhu*:** Pali (Sanskrit *bhikshu*), literally 'one who lives by begging alms'; a Buddhist monk
***bhikkhuni*:** a Buddhist nun
biface: handaxe
Black and Red Ware (BRW): Pottery whose surface is partly black and partly red, found in various different chronological and cultural contexts
blade: a flake tool, the length of which is more than twice its width
***bodhisattva*:** a future Buddha
boustrephedon style: a style of writing in which consecutive lines start in opposite directions
***brahma*:** sacerdotal power
***brahmacharya*:** the stage of celibate studenthood in the *ashrama* scheme
***brahmadeya*:** land gifted to Brahmanas, generally by kings
***brahman*:** the imperishable, ultimate reality in the universe, according to the Upanishads
Brahmanas: Members of the premier *varna* in the Brahmanical *varna* order; prose explanations of the Vedic Samhitas
Brahmi: an ancient Indian script
burin: a small stone tool, made on a blade, with a 'screw-driver' edge
burnished ware: a pottery whose surface is polished with a hard instrument (made of stone, wood, metal, etc.) before firing, in order to produce a shine that remains after the firing process.
cairn stone circle: a type of megalithic burial, marked by a stone circle and a heap of large, piled-up stones
cairn: a type of megalithic burial, marked by a heap of large, piled-up stones
Carbon-14 (C-14)/radiocarbon dating: a scientific dating method used in archaeology, based on the principle of radioactive decay; used to date organic material
carburization: heating iron in association with carbon to make steel
celts: ground and polished handaxes; typical neolithic tools
Cenozoic: 'the age of the mammals'; comprised the Tertiary and Quaternary eras; began about 100 mya
***chaitya*:** a Buddhist shrine
chalcolithic: a culture marked by the use of copper/bronze and stone
chamber tomb: a megalithic grave consisting of a chamber, usually consisting of two or four vertical slabs of stone covered by a horizontal capstone
***charana*:** school of Vedic study
Charvaka: an atheistic materialist philosophical school, also known as Lokayata
chiefdom stage: a transitional stage between a pre-state kinship society and a civil state society
chopper: a large, unifacial tool
chopping tool: a tool made on a core or pebble, flaked alternately on both sides to produce a wavy cutting edge
cist: an underground megalithic chamber tomb made of vertical and horizontal stone slabs
clan: comprises several unilineal descent groups who trace their descent from a common ancestor, either actual or mythical
cleaver: a flattish tool made on a broad rectangular or triangular flake, one end of which has a broad and straight cutting edge
copper hoards: certain specific types of copper objects found in protohistoric contexts in the doab as well as in some other parts of the subcontinent
core tools: stone tools made on cores, usually large in size

cowries: marine shells, once used as currency in many parts of the world; in India cowries from the Maldive islands were used as currency from ancient times till the colonial period
cranial capacity: brain size
cult: religious beliefs and practices associated with the worship of a particular deity
culture: a word with many meanings, associated with patterns of thought and behaviour learnt by an individual from the larger social group; in its narrowest technical sense in archaeology, it refers to a recurring assemblage of material traits
***dakshina*:** sacrifical fee
Dakshinapatha: the great southern trade route
***dana*:** ritual giving
***darshana*:** literally, 'view'; philosophy
***dhamma*:** a Pali word (Sanskrit, *dharma*), referring to the ideal conduct of an individual living in society
***dhammachakka-pavattana*:** Pali, literally 'turning the wheel of *dhamma*'; the Buddha's first sermon in the deer park near Benaras
***dhamma-mahamatas*:** a new cadre of officials created by Ashoka to propagate *dhamma*
***dharma*:** a Sanskrit word that is difficult to translate; the proper, ideal conduct of a person as a member of society; a course of action which leads to the fulfillment of the goals of human life.
Dharmashastra: a group of Sanskrit texts dealing specifically with *dharma*
Dharmasutras: the earliest Dharmashastra texts, written in the *sutra* (aphoristic) style
diffusionist theories: theories which explain cultural innovation and change as a result of stimulus or influence from a point of origin
Digambara: literally 'sky-clad'; a Jaina sect
discoid core technique: a type of prepared core technique used to make stone tools
dolmenoid cist: a megalithic chamber tomb that is partly underground
dolmen: a megalithic chamber tomb that is fully above ground-level
Dravida: the southern style of temple architecture, marked, among other things, by a pyramidal *shikhara* (tower)
Dravidian: a family of languages, including Tamil, Telugu, Malayalam, and Kannada
***dvija*:** literally 'twice born'; those entitled to the performance of the *upanayana* (sacred thread) ceremony, which is considered analogous to a second birth, viz., the upper three *varnas*, namely the Brahmanas, Kshatriyas, and Vaishyas
early Harappan: the early, formative, proto-urban phase of the Harappan culture
Eight-fold Path: the path taught by the Buddha for release from suffering
elementary family: a married couple and their children, who may or may not live together
epigraphy: the study of inscriptions
epi-palaeolithic: a transitional stage of stone tool making, marked by tools that are smaller than those typical of the upper palaeolithic, but smaller than microliths
ethno-archaeology: a branch of archaeology that studies the behaviour and practices of living communities in order to interpret the archaeological evidence related to communities who lived in the past
extended burial: a burial in which the body is laid out in an extended position
extended family: two or more elementary families (or parts of them) joined together
factory site: a place where tools were made
faunal analysis: the analysis of animal bones
feudalism school: with reference to early medieval India, a school that argues that this was a period of political and economic fragmentation
field archaeology: the exploration and excavation of sites
food-producing society: a society which meets at least half its food needs for at least part of the year through the domestication of animals and/or plants, in a context where animals and plants are not tied to their natural habitat
Four Noble Truths (*Ariya-sachchani*): an important part of the Buddha's teaching, viz., there is suffering; it has a cause; it can be eliminated; and the way to eliminate it is to follow the Eight-fold Path
fractional burial: the burial of disaggregated bones
***gahapati*:** Pali for Sanskrit *grihapati*, i.e., householder; a wealthy property-owner
Gaja-Lakshmi: a popular representation of the goddess Lakshmi, flanked by two elephants, sometimes holding jars in their trunks
***gana*:** a word which has many meanings, including an oligarchy
***garbha-griha*:** the inner sanctum of a temple, where the image of the main deity is placed and worshipped
***garuda*:** a fantastic bird, the vehicle of Vishnu
genus: an assemblage of related species
***gotra*:** the clan system of the Brahmanas; sometimes also applicable to non-Brahmanas
Grantha script: a South Indian script used for writing Sanskrit
***grihastha*:** the householder stage in the *ashrama* scheme
hagiography: sacred biography
handaxe: a roughly triangular-shaped stone tool, usually made on cores and flaked on both sides
Henotheism/Kathenotheism: a term used by Max Müller to refer to the phenomenon in the *Rig Veda*, where whichever deity is invoked is spoken of as a supreme god
Hinayana: literally 'the lesser vehicle'; a set of Buddhist schools
historiography: the construction and writing of history
history: the study of the human past; more specifically, the study of literate societies of the past
Holocene/Recent: the seventh, still-continuing epoch of the Cenozoic era; began about 10,000 ya
hominid: a term with wide connotations, used for a group consisting of all modern and extinct Great Apes and humans (that is, modern humans, chimpanzees, gorillas and orangutans plus all their immediate ancestors).
hominin: a narrower group consisting of modern humans, extinct human species, and all our immediate ancestors.
***Homo erectus*:** a hominid species that had a fully erect posture
***Homo habilis*:** literally 'hand-using man'; a hominin species
***Homo sapiens neanderthalis*:** a species of *Homo sapiens* that became extinct
***Homo sapiens*:** 'thinking man'; anatomically modern humans
household: people who share a common residence
***hundikas*:** bills of exchange used by traders in early medieval India
Indo-European: a family of languages that includes Sanskrit, the modern north Indian languages, and many other languages of Asia and Europe
Indo-Aryan: a sub-group of the Indo-Iranian branch of the Indo-European family of languages
Indo-Aryans: speakers of Indo-Aryan languages
***in situ*:** in its original place
industry: comprises similar artefacts made of the same material found at a site
inhumation: burial

janapada: literally, 'foothold of a tribe'; a territorial state; a region consisting of urban and rural settlements, along with its inhabitants
Jatakas: one of the 15 books of the *Khuddaka Nikaya*, containing stories of the previous births of the Buddha
jati: a word with several meanings including caste, birth, and type.
jina: literally 'victor'; a Jaina saint
jiva: a word with many meanings in different traditions; in the context of Jaina philosophy, variously translated as sentient essence, life monad, or soul
***kani* rights**: rights over land in early medieval South India, sometimes also associated with certain duties and obligations
kara-shasanas: tax-paying *agraharas*
karma: the doctrine according to which actions have consequences that manifest themselves in present and future lives
Kharoshthi: an ancient script prevalent in the north-west
kinship society: a pre-state society in which kinship is central
kottam: settlement clusters in the Pallava kingdom, similar to the *nadus*
kraya-shasana: a secular land-sale deed
kshatra: secular power
kshatrapa: a viceroy or subordinate ruler of the Scytho-Parthians; a title assumed by kings of the Kshaharata and Kardamaka dynasties
Kshatriya: the *varna* associated with warfare and rulership
kula: a word with a range of meanings, including an extended patrilineal family
language: spoken symbols of communication
late Harappan: the post-urban phase of the Harappan culture
Levallois technique: an advanced technique of making flake tools by first preparing the core
lineage: a group of unilineal kin
linga: a phallic emblem of the god Shiva
literary sources: texts, written or oral
logo-syllabic script: a script in which each symbol stands for a word or syllable
Lokayata: an atheistic materialist philosophical school, also known as Charvaka
lower palaeolithic: the earliest part of the palaeolithic age, which ranged between about 2 mya to 100,000 ya
Madhayamaka: a major Mahayana school founded by Nagarjuna, in which the idea of *shunyata* (emptiness) is of great importance
mahajanapadas: the great states of the 6th century BCE
mahakshatrapa: viceroy, subordinate ruler; a title assumed by some kings of the Kshaharata and Kardamaka dynasties
Mahayana: literally 'the greater vehicle', a set of Buddhist schools
mandapika: a local centre of exchange, in between small periodic markets and larger trade centres
Manigramam: a powerful merchant guild of early medieval South India
manuscripts: books or documents written by hand
matha: monastery
matriarchy: a social system in which dominant power and authority within the family is vested in women
matrilineal system: a unilineal kinship system recognizing descent though the mother
mature Harappan: the urban phase of the Harappan culture
megalithic cultures: cultural remains found in the megaliths and at the habitation sites associated with them
megaliths: monuments made of large, roughly-dressed slabs of stone
menhir: a type of megalithic burial, marked by a single, large, standing stone
mesolithic: Holocene stone age cultures, marked by the use of microliths, usually with a hunting-gathering subsistence base
metrology: the measurement and arrangement of coins by weight
microliths: tiny stone tools, ranging in length from under 1 cm to 5 cm
microwear analysis: the study of wear marks on tools in order to understand their function
Middle Indic: a term often used these days for Prakrit
middle palaeolithic: the middle part of the palaeolithic age, ranging between about 100,000 to 40,000 ya
mihrab: niche in a mosque's *qibla* wall, which faces the direction of Mecca
***mithuna* figures**: amorous couples that occur often in the sculptural decoration of shrines
moksha: liberation from the cycle of birth and death
monogamy: a system in which a person has one spouse at a time
monolatory: a belief in a supreme god while acknowledging the existence of other gods
monotheism: a belief that there is only one god
mukhamandapa: the porch of a temple
multi-lineal system/cognatic system: a system which recognizes descent both through the mother and the father
nadu: the locality, consisting of several settlements, in early medieval South India
Nagara style: the northern style of temple architecture, marked, among other things, by a curvilinear *shikara* (tower)
nagarakkani: land owned and managed by the *nagaram*
nagarams: market or commercial centres in early medieval South India
nagarattar: the corporate organization of the *nagaram*
nagas: male serpent deities
nagis/naginis: female serpent deities, consorts of the *nagas*
Nalayira Divya Prabandham: a work by Nathamuni, containing the hymns of the Alvar saints
nastika: a term used by proponents of certain philosophical schools/religious groups to refer to those they considered outside the pale
Nataraja: The dancing Shiva
nattar: the leading men of the *nadu* (locality) in early medieval South India
Nayanmars/Nayanars: The Shaiva saint-poets of early medieval South India
negative feedback food procurement systems: food procurement systems which involve a balanced exploitation and use of food resources within an area and which discourage any change
neolithic revolution: a phrase coined by V. Gordon Childe in order to highlight the great significance of the changes ushered in by the neolithic age
neolithic: food-producing stone age cultures, marked by ground and polished stone tools
New Archaeology: a trend that emerged in archaeology in the 1960s; represented by the processual school
nibbana: a term used often in the Buddhist tradition for liberation from the cycle of birth and death
Nitishastra: Sanskrit works on statecraft
niyoga: levirate; the ancient custom of a widow cohabiting with her brother-in-law or another man in order to produce sons
Northern Black Polished Ware (NBP or NBPW): a distinctive type of fine pottery with a glossy surface, made and used between *c.* 700 and 200 BCE
nuclear zones: areas of early plant domestication, which lay within the natural habitat zones of those specific plant types
numismatics: the study of coins
Nyaya: a philosophical school concerned primarily with logic and epistemology
Ochre Coloured Pottery (OCP): a protohistoric pottery type found at several sites in the doab

orthostats: vertical slabs in a megalithic chamber tomb

Painted Grey Ware (PGW): a distinctive type of fine, grey pottery with designs painted on in black, made and used in parts of north India between *c.* 1000 and 500 BCE

palaeo-anthropologists: scholars who study the biological and cultural evolution of early humans

palaeo-botanical studies: the analysis of ancient pollen and other minute plant remains, seeds, charcoal, sediments, and geological strata

palaeo-channel: an old course of a river

palaeolithic: the earliest and longest part of the stone age, corresponding with the Pleistocene geological era

palaeo-magnetic method: a dating method used in archaeology

palaeontology: the study of the remains of dead organisms across enormous spans of time

palaeo-pathology: the study of disease through an analysis of ancient bone remains

Pali: an ancient language belonging to the Indo-European family of languages; the language of the canon of the Theravada school

palynology: the analysis of pollen and spores

***paramitas*:** perfections whose attainment led to the *bodhisattva* path; a Mahayana idea

***paribbajaka*:** Pali, literally, 'wanderer', renunciant

***pariharas*:** exemptions and privileges granted to donees in royal land grants

***parinibbana*:** the passing away of the Buddha

***patichcha-samuppada*:** Pali, the law of dependent origination; a part of the Buddha's teaching

patriarchy: a social system in which males (usually the eldest of them) exercise dominant power and authority within the family

patrilineal/agnatic system: a unilineal kinship system which recognizes descent relationships through the father

pebble tools: tools made on pebbles, in which only the working edge is flaked

***Periyapuranam*:** A 12th century work containing hagiographies of the Nayanmar saints

petroglyph: created when some substance of a rock surface is removed through engraving, bruising, hammering, chiselling, or scooping

pit circle: a type of megalithic burial, marked by a circle of large stones

plant domestication: the process of selective breeding of plants, which involves removing them from their natural habitat and growing them under artificial conditions under human control for purposes of human gain

plate tectonics: the movement of massive tectonic plates embedded within the earth

Pleistocene: the sixth epoch of the Cenozoic age; began about 1.6 mya

polyandry: a system in which a woman can have several husbands

polygamy: a system in which one person can have more than one spouse at the same time

polygyny: a system in which a man can have several wives

polytheism: a belief in many gods

positive feedback food procurement systems: food procurement systems where the productivity of resources increases as a result of human interference and exploitation

post-excarnate burial: the practice where the bones of a dead person are collected and buried after the body is de-fleshed, for instance, by exposing it to the elements

post-processualism: a school of archaeology that challenged many of the assumptions, methods, and goals of processualism, and had a more complex and nuanced understanding of material culture

Prakrit: an ancient language belonging to the Indo-European family of languages, with various dialects such as Maharashtri, Shauraseni, and Magadhi

***pramanas*:** grounds of knowledge

***prashasti*:** panegyric

***pravara*:** the names of one, two, three, or five supposed ancestral *rishis*, connected with the *gotra* system of the Brahmanas

prehistory: the past before the advent of writing; the stone age

prestations: obligatory exchanges between groups of people, involving material as well as non-material items

primary burials: burials in which the body was directly buried in the ground

Primary/Palaeozoic era: the first of the four geological eras

pristine state: a state which emerges from indigenous stimuli, usually with no pre-existing models

processualism/processual archaeology: a school of archaeology which tried to understand cultures and cultural processes holistically and emphasized the importance of explanation, generalization, and theory-building

protohistory: a term used in different senses; a segment of the past that is transitional between prehistory and history

***puram*:** war poems of the Sangam corpus

Purva Mimamsa: a school of Vedic exegesis

Quaternary: the fourth of the four geological eras

qibla: the wall in a mosque which faces the direction of Mecca

rouletted ware: a pottery with a smooth surface and usually a metallic lustre, with concentric bands of rouletted designs, found especially in eastern and south-eastern India; once thought to be a foreign ware, now considered locally produced

rusticated ware: pottery whose surface is roughened with a thick slurry of clay

***sabha*:** a tribal assembly mentioned in Vedic texts; the assembly of a Brahmana village in early medieval South India

salvage archaeology: identifying endangered sites and saving them from destruction

***samana*:** a Pali word (Sanskrit *shramana*); literally, 'one who strives', a renunciant

***samanta*:** subordinate ruler; feudatory

Samhita: a collection of hymns, associated with the Vedas

Samkhya: a very ancient philosophical school which views the world as consisting of two fundamental categories of *purusha* (the spiritual principle) and *prakriti* (matter or nature)

***samskaras*:** literally 'preparation', 'arrangement'; rituals marking important life stages

***sandhara*:** a temple style with an enclosed passage for circumambulation

Sangam literature: texts in old Tamil, comprising the earliest parts of the *Ettutokai*, *Pattuppattu*, and *Tolkappiyam*

***sangha*:** a word with many different meanings including oligarchy, the Buddhist monastic order, and the Jaina monastic order

***sannyasa*:** the stage of complete renunciation in the *ashrama* scheme

Sanskritization: an idea developed by the sociologist M. N. Srinivas, referring to a tendency of lower castes to imitate and adopt norms and practices of the upper castes in order to improve their ranking in the caste hierarchy

***sapindas*:** people who are held to be related to each other, an important category in Dharmashastra discussions on rules of marriage, inheritance, and rules of purity and impurity to be observed among relatives when a person died

sarcophagus burial: a burial in which the funerary remains are placed in a terracotta trough

script: writing; a system of visual communication using signs or symbols associated with specific meanings or sounds, written on some surface

secondary burials: the practice of removing the remains of a corpse from one grave after some time and re-burying them in another grave
secondary state: a state which has the model of an already-existing state before it, and which emerges as a result of interaction with this already-existing ('pristine') state
Secondary/Mesozoic: the second of the four geological eras
segmentary state: a state marked by the segmentation of power; originally put forward by Southall with reference to the African Alur tribe, subsequently applied by Stein to the states of early medieval South India.
setthi: Pali (Sanskrit *sreshthin*); a high-level businessman associated with trade and money-lending
shakha: a recension of a Veda
Shivaism (Shaivism): the worship of Shiva as a supreme god
Shudra: the fourth *varna*, which was supposed to serve the upper three *varnas*
shruti: literally 'that which has been heard', the Veda
Shvetambara: literally 'white-clad', a Jaina sect
Siddhamatrika: an ancient script, known from the 6th century CE; also known as Kutila
site: a place where there are artefacts or any material remains of past human activity
slip: a coating on pottery
smriti: literally 'remembered texts'; a category of Sanskrit texts that includes the Vedangas, Puranas, epics, Dharmashastras, and Nitishastra
species/specie: organisms that are similar in physical structure and behaviour, and which inter-breed with each other, or could do so if they had access to each other
state society: a society which is stratified and whose polity is marked by the existence of a state
stratigraphic context: the precise archaeological level at which an object is found
stri-dhana: 'women's wealth'; various types of moveable property given to a woman on various occasions during her life-time, passed on from mother to daughter
syadavada: literally 'doctrine of maybe'; the Jaina doctrine of the partial nature of all statements about reality
Tamil–Brahmi: an ancient script of South India, consisting of an adaptation of the Brahmi script in order to write the Tamil language
taniyur: a special status given to certain *brahmadeyas* in early medieval South India, making them independent of the *nadu* wherein they were located
terra sigilatta: moulded, decorated wares as well as undecorated, wheel-made ones made in Italy or imitations thereof; earlier referred to as Arretine ware
Tertiary: the third of the four geological eras
Tevaram: a collection of hymns, part of the canon of South Indian Shaiva *bhakti*
thermoluminescence: a scientific method used in archaeology to date inorganic material that has been heated rapidly, e.g., pottery
Tipitaka: Pali, literally 'the three baskets' or 'three collections', Buddhist canonical texts; the Pali Tipitaka is the canon of the Theravada school
tirthankara: literally, 'ford builder'; a Jaina saint
Tirumurai: the canon of South Indian Shaiva *bhakti*
Tiruttondar-Tiruvantai: a work by Nambi Andar Nambi, which gives a short hagiography of the Nayanmar saints
Tiruttondar-Tokai: a work by Sundarar, which lists 62 Nayanmar saints
torana: the gateway of a shrine
transepts: vertical stone slabs that divide a megalithic chamber tomb into sections
tribe: a term that is difficult to define precisely; comprises a number of related clans
triratna: literally, 'the three gems'; in Jainism, refers to the triple path of right faith, knowledge, and conduct
unchambered tomb: a megalithic grave which does not have a chamber
unilineal kinship systems: kinship systems which recognize descent relationships through either the father or the mother
Upanishads: philosophical texts that are part of the Vedic corpus
upasaka: a male lay follower of the Buddha's teaching
upasika: a female lay follower of the Buddha's teaching
upper palaeolithic: the latest part of the palaeolithic age, ranging between about 40,000 to 10,000 ya
Uttara Mimamsa: also known as Vedanta; a philosophical school that emphasized the path of knowledge as opposed to that of works or sacrifice
ur: a non-*brahmadeya* village of South India; the corporate assembly of such a village
Uttarapatha: the major trans-regional trade route of northern India
Vaisheshika: a philosophical school of pluralistic realism
Vaishya: the *varna* associated with agriculture, animal husbandry, and trade
vanaprastha: the stage of partial renunciation in the *ashrama* scheme
varaha: the boar incarnation of the god Vishnu
varna: literally 'colour'; the concept of four hereditary classes—Brahmana, Kshatriya, Vaishya, and Shudra
varna-samkara: the mixture of *varnas* due to inter-*varna* unions
vassavasa: the monsoon retreat of Buddhist monks
Vatteluttu: An ancient South Indian script used for writing Tamil
Vedanga: literally 'limbs of the Veda', auxiliary texts associated with the Vedas
Vedas: four ancient Sanskrit texts, namely the *Rig Veda*, *Yajur Veda*, *Sama Veda*, and *Atharva Veda*
velir: chieftains of South India
vellala/vellalar: cultivating groups of South India
vellanvagai: non-*brahmadeya* villages of early medieval South India; same as *ur*
vendar: the three 'crowned kings' of early historical South India, i.e., the Cholas, Cheras, and Pandyas
Vesara: a style of temple architecture which has a blend of elements associated with the Nagara and Dravida styles; also referred to as Karnata-Dravida
vihara: a Buddhist monastery
vimana: the sanctum of a temple and its superstructure
viragal: the word for a 'hero stone' in the Tamil Nadu area
Vishnuism (Vaishnavism): the worship of Vishnu as a supreme god
yajamana: the person for whom the *yajna* (sacrifice) is performed and who bears its expenses
yajna: sacrificial ritual
yakshas: deities associated with water, fertility, trees, forests, and the wilderness
yakshis: female deities associated with fertility, consorts of *yakshas*
yavana: Greeks, foreigners from the West
Yoga: a philosophical school which aimed at focusing the mind to achieve complete tranquility and control
Yogachara: a major Mahayana school which attached great importance to meditation as a means of attaining the highest goal
yupa: sacrificial post

References

Abraham, Meera. 1988. *Two Medieval Merchant Guilds of South India*. New Delhi: Manohar.

Acri, Andrea. (Ed.). 2016. *Esoteric Buddhism in Mediaeval Maritime Asia: Networks of Masters, Texts, Icons*. Singapore: ISEAS.

Acri, Andea, Roger Blench, and Alexandra Landmann. (Eds.). 2017. *Spirits and Ships: Cultural Transfers in Early Monsoon Asia*. Singapore: ISEAS.

Acri, Andrea and Peter Sharrock. (Eds.). 2022. *The Creative South: Buddhist and Hindu Art in Mediaeval maritime Asia*. Vol. 1. Singapore: ISEAS.

Agrawal, D. P. 1982. *Archaeology of India*. London and Malmo: Curzon Press.

Agrawala, V. S. 1949. 'A Catalogue of the Images of Brahma, Vishnu, and Shiva in Mathura Art.' *Journal of the UP Historical Society* 22: 102–210.

________. 1953. *India as Known to Panini (A Study of the Cultural Material in the* Ashtadhyayi). Lucknow: University of Lucknow.

Ahuja, Naman. 2021. *Phanigiri: Interpreting an Ancient Buddhist Site in Telangana*. Mumbai: Marg Publications and Department of Heritage Telangana.

________. (Ed.). 2019. *Gandhara: A Confluence of Cultures. Marg*, 70, 4. Mumbai: The Marg Foundation.

Akhilesh, Kumar, Shanti Pappu, Haresh M. Rajapara, Yanni Gunnell, Anil D. Shukla, and Ashoka K. Singhvi. 2018. 'Early Middle Palaeolithic Culture in India around 385–172 ka Reframes Out of Agrica Models. *Nature* 554: 97–102.

Ali, S. M. 1966. *Geography of the Puranas*. New Delhi: People's Publishing House.

Allchin, Bridget and Raymond Allchin. 1997. *Origins of a Civilization: ThePrehistory and Early Archaeology of South Asia*. New Delhi: Viking.

Alpers, Edward A. 2014. *The Indian Ocean in World History*. Oxford, New York: Oxford University Press.

Altekar, A. S. (1938) 1991. *The Position of Women in Hindu Civilisation: From Prehistoric Times to the Present Day*. Reprint Edn. Delhi: Motilal Banarsidass.

Altekar, A. S. and V. K. Misra. 1959. *Report on the Kumrahar Excavations, 1951–55*. Patna: K. P. Jayaswal Institute.

Ali, Daud. 2006. *Courtly Culture and Political Life in Early Medieval India*. New Delhi: Cambridge University Press.

________. 2007. 'Courtly Love and the Aristocratic Household in Early Medieval India.' In Fransisca Orsini. (Ed.). *Love in South Asia: A Cultural History*. New Delhi: Cambridge University Press. pp. 43–60.

________. 2018. 'The Betel-Bag Bearer in Medieval South Indian History: A Study from Inscriptions.' In Manu Devadevan. (Ed.). *Clio and her Descendants: Essays for Kesavan Veluthat*. Delhi: Primus Books. pp. 535–57.

Ali, S. M. *Geography of the Puranas*. 1966. New Delhi: People's Publishing House.

Anthony, David W. 2007. *The Horse, the Wheel, and Language: How bronze age riders from the Eurasian steppes shaped the modern world*. Princeton and Oxford: Princeton University Press.

Apte, Usha M. 1978. *The Sacrament of Marriage in Hindu Society from Vedic Period to Dharmashastras*. Delhi: Ajanta Publications.

Ardeleanu-Jansen, Alexandra. 2002. 'The Terracotta Figurines from Mohenjodaro: Considerations on Tradition, Craft and Ideology in the Harappan Civilization (*c.* 2400–1800 BC).' In S. Settar and Ravi Korisettar. (Eds.). *Indian Archaeology in Retrospect, Protohistory: Archaeology of the Harappan Civilization, Vol II*. New Delhi: Indian Council of Historical Research and Manohar. pp. 205–22.

Asher, Frederick M. (1983) 2018. 'Historical and Political Allegory in Gupta Art.' In Kunal Chakrabarti and Kanad Sinha. *State, Power and Legitimacy: The Gupta Kingdom*. Delhi: Primus Books. pp. 812–24.

________. 2010. *Bodhgaya*. New Delhi: Oxford University Press.

________. 2015. *Nalanda: Situating the Great Monastery*. Mumbai: Marg Foundation.

Asher, Frederick M. and Walter Spink. 1989. *Maurya Figural Scultpure Reconsider. (Ed.)*. Ars Orientalis 19: 1–25.

Asif, Manan Ahm. (Ed.). 2016. *A Book of Conquest: The* Chachnama *and Muslim Origins in South Asia*. Cmbridge, MA: Harvard University Press.

Atre, Shubhangana. 1985–86. 'Lady of the Beasts—The Harappan Goddess.' *Puratattva* 16: 7–14.

Bader, Jonathan. 2000. *Conquest of the Quarters: Traditional Accounts of the Life of Śaṅkara*, New Delhi: Aditya Prakashan.

Bagchi, P. C. 1950. *India and China: A Thousand Years of Cultural Relations*. 2nd Edn., Bombay, Hind Kitabs Ltd.

Bakker, Hans T. 1997. *The Vākāṭakas: A Study in Hindu Iconology*. Groningen: Egbert Forsten.

________. 2004. 'Mansar.' In Hans T. Bakker. (Ed.). *The Vākāṭaka Heritage: Indian Culture at the Crossroads*. Groningen: Egbert Forsten. pp. 71–85.

________. 2014. *The World of the Skandapurāṇa: North India in the Sixth and Seventh Centuries*. Leiden, Boston: Brill.

Bakker, Hans T. (Ed.). 2004. *The Vākāṭaka Heritage: Indian Culture at the Crossroads*. Groningen: Egbert Forsten.

________. (Ed.). 2008. *Mansar: The Discovery of Pravareśvara and Pravarapura Temple and Residence of the Vākāṭaka King Pravarasena*. Proceedings of a Symposium at the British Museum (London, 30 June – 1 July, 2008).

Bandaranayake, Senake. 2013. *Sigirya: city, palace, gardens, monasteries, paintings*. Colombo, Central Culture Fund.

________. 2000. 'The Settlement Patterns of the Proto-Historic—Early Historic Interface in Sri Lanka.' In R. A. L. H. Gunawardana, S. Pathmanathan, and M. Rohanadeera. (Eds.). *Reflections on a Heritage: Historical Scholarship in Premodern Sri Lanka*. Colombo: Central Culture Fund. pp. 1–14.

________. 2014. *The World of the Skandapurāṇa: Northern India in the Sixth and Seventh Centuries*. Leiden, Boston: Brill.

Banerjea, J. N. 1966. *Pauranic and Tantric Religion: Early Phase*. Calcutta: University of Calcutta.

Basa, Kishor K., Rabindra K. Mohanty, and Simatri B. Ota. (Eds.). 2015. *Megalithic Traditions in India: Archaeology and Ethnography*. 2 Vols. Bhopal: Indira Gandhi Rashtriya Manav Sangrahalaya and New Delhi: Aryan Books International.

Basant, P. K. 2012. *The City and the Country in Early India: A Study of the Malwa Region*. Delhi: Primus.

Basham, A. L. (1951) 2003. *History and Doctrines of the Ajivikas: A Vanished Religion*. Indian Edn. London: Luzac & Co.

Bates, Jennifer, Kelly Wilcox Black, and Kathleen D. Morrison. 2022. 'Millet Bread and Pulse Dough from Early Iron Age South

India: Charred Food Lumps as culinary Indicators.' *Journal of Archaeological Science* 137: 105531. https://doi.org/10.1016/j/jas.2021.105531

Beaujard, Philippe. 2020. The Worlds of the Indian Ocean: A Global History. 2 Vols. Cambridge: Cambridge University Press.

Bechert, Heinz. 1982. 'The Importance of Asoka's so-called Schism Edict.' In L. A. Hercus, F. B. J. Kuiper, T. Rajapatirana, and E. R. Skrzypczak. (Eds.). *Indological and Buddhist Studies: Volume in Honour of Professor J. W. de Jong on his Sixtieth Birthday. Bibliotheca Indo-Buddhica No. 27*. Delhi: Sri Satguru Publications. pp. 61–68.

_______. (Ed.). (1991) 1995. *When Did the Buddha Live? The Controversy on the Dating of the Historical Buddha*. Selected Papers Based on a Symposium Held Under the Auspices of the Academy ofSciences in Gottingen. Delhi: Sri Satguru Publications.

Bednarik, Robert G. 1997. 'The Archaeological Significance of Beads and Pendants.' *Man and Environment* 23(2), July–Dec: 87–99.

_______. 2001. 'The Oldest Known Rock Art in the World.' *Anthropologie* 39/2–3: 89–97.

_______. 2002. 'The Dating of Rock Art: a Critique.' *Journal of Archaeological Science* 29: 1–20.

Begley, Vimala. 1996. *The Ancient Port of Arikamedu: New Excavations and Researches 1989–1992*. Vol. *I (Memoires Archaeologiques, 22)*. Pondicherry: L'école Française d'Extrème-Orient.

Behera, Pradeep K. 1991–92. 'Sulabhdihi: A Neolithic Celt Manufacturing Centre in Odisha.' *Puratattva* 22: 125–31.

Bellwood, Peter. 2005. *First Farmers: The Origins of Agricultural Societies*. Malden MA: Blackwell

Berghaus, P. 1991. 'Roman Coins from India and Their Imitations.' In A. K. Jha. (Ed.). *Coinage, Trade and Economy*. Nashik: Indian Institute for Research in Numismatic Studies. pp. 108–21.

Bernard, Paul. 1982. 'An Ancient Greek City in Central Asia.' *Scientific American* 246, 1: 148–59.

Beteille, Andre. (1960) 1977. 'The Definition of Tribe.' In Romesh Thapar. (Ed.). 1977, *Tribe, Caste and Religion in India*. Delhi: Macmillan. pp. 7–14.

Bhagat, M. G. 1976. *Ancient Indian Asceticism*. New Delhi: Munshiram Manoharlal.

Bhan, Kuldeep K., and Massimo Vidale. 2014. 'Technology, Craft Production, Raw Material, manufacturing Techniques and Activity Areas.' In Dilip K. Chakrabarti and Makkhan Lal. (Eds.). *History of Ancient India*. Vol. 2: *Protohistoric Roots*. New Delhi: Vivekanand International Foundation and Aryan Books International. pp. 263–308.

Bhandare, Shailendra. 2006. 'A Tale of Two Dynasties: The Kshaharatas and the Satavahanas in the Deccan.' In H. P. Ray. (Ed.). *Coins in India: Power and Communication. Marg* 57(3): 24–32. Mumbai: Marg Publications.

Bhat, G. K. 1975. *Bharata-Natya-Manjari: Bharata on the Theory and Practice of Drama–A Selection from Bharata's Natyasashtrra*. Poona: Bhandarkar Oriental Research Institute.

Bhattacharyya, N. N. 1974. *History of the Sakta Religion*. New Delhi: Munshiram Manoharlal.

Binford, Lewis R. 1968. 'Post-Pleistocene Adaptations.' In Sally R. Binford and Lewis R. Binford. (Eds). *New Perspectives in Archaeology*. Chicago: Aldine.

Bisht, R. S. 2015. *Excavations at Dholavira 1989–90 to 2004–05*. New Delhi: Archaeological Survey of India.

Bisschop, Peter C. and Elizabeth A. Cecil. (Eds.). 2021. *Primary Sources and Asian Pasts*. Berlin/Boston: de Gruyter.

Bivar, A. D. H. 2014. 'Kushan Dynasty i. Dynastic History.' *Encyclopædia Iranica, online edition*, available at http://www.iranicaonline.org/articles/kushan-dynasty-i-history (accessed on 19.9.22).

Blackburn, Anne M. 2010. 'Buddha-Relics in the Lives of Southern Asian Polities.' *Numen* 57: 317–40.

Bloch, T. 1903–04. 'Excavations at Basarh.' *Annual Report of the Archaeological Survey of India*: 81–122.

Boivin, N. 2004. 'Rock Art and Rock Music: Petroglyphs of the South Indian Neolithic.' *Antiquity* 78(229): 38–53.

Bökönyi, Sándor. 1997. 'Horse Remains from the Prehistoric Site of Surkotada, Kutch, Late 3rd Millennium B.C.' *South Asian Studies* 13:297–306.

Bongard-Levin, G. M. 1971. 'Megasthenes' "Indica" and the inscriptions of Asoka.' In *Studies in Ancient India and Central Asia*. Calcutta: Indian Studies Past and Present. pp. 109–22.

Bopearachchi, Osmund. 2015. *From Bactria to Taprobane: Selected Works of Osmund Bopearachchi*. 2 Vols. Vol. 1: *Central Asian and Indian Numismatics*; Vol. 2: *Art History and Maritime Trade*. New Delhi: Manohar.

_______. 2020a. *When West Met East: Gandhāran Art Revisit. (Ed.)*. 2 Vols. New Delhi: Manohar.

_______. 2020b. *Roots of Śrī Laṅkān Art*. Colombo, Department of Archaeology.

_______, Senrath Disanayaka and Nimal Perera. 2016. 'The Oldest Shipwreck in the Indian Ocean. In Marie-Françoise, Jean-François Salles, and Jean-Baptiste Yon. (Eds.). 2016. *Ports of the Indian Ocean*. Delhi: Primus Books. pp. 412–27.

Bose, Shibani. 2020. *Mega Mammals in Ancient India: Rhinos, Tigers, and Elephants*. New Delhi: Oxford University Press.

Bosworth, A. B. 1996. 'The Historical Setting of Megasthenes' Indica,' *Classical Philology* 91, no. 2: 113–127.

Bosworth, Clifford Edmund. (1963) 1992. *The Ghaznavids: Their Empire in Afghanistan and Eastern Iran 994–1040*. New Delhi: Munshiram Manoharlal.

Boussac, Marie-Françoise, Jean-François Salles, and Jean-Baptiste Yon. (Eds.). 2016. *Ports of the Indian Ocean*. Delhi: Primus Books.

Braidwood, Robert J. 1960. 'The Agricultural Revolution.' *Scientific American* 203(3): 130–48.

Brockington, J. L. 1984. *Righteous Rama: The Evolution of an Epic*. Delhi: Oxford University Press.

Bronkhorst, Johannes. 2007. *Greater Magadha: Studies in the Culture of Early India*. Leiden, Boston: Brill.

_______. 2011. *Buddhism in the Shadow of Brahmanism*. Leiden, Boston: Brill.

_______. 2016. *How the Brahmins Won: From Alexander to the Guptas*. Leiden, Boston: Brill.

Bronner, Yigal, David Shulman, and Gary Tubb. (Eds.). 2014. *Innovations and Turning Points: Toward a History of Kāvya Literature*. New Delhi: Oxford University Press.

Brosius, Maria. 2006. *The Persians: An Introduction*. London and New York: Routledge.

Brown, Robert L. 2004. 'Vākāṭaka-Period Hindu Sculpture.' In Hans T. Bakker. (Ed.). *The Vākāṭaka Heritage: Indian Culture at the Crossroads*. Groningen: Egbert Forsten. pp. 59–69.

_______. 2011. 'The Importance of Gupta-period Sculpture in Southeast Asian Art History.' In Pierre-Yves Manguin, A. Mani, and Geoff Wade, *Early Interactions between South and Southeast Asia: Reflections on Cross-Cultural Exchange*. New Delhi, Manohar. pp. 317–31.

Bryant, Edwin. 2001. *The Quest for the Origins of Vedic Culture: The Indo-Aryan Migration Debate*. New Delhi: Oxford University Press.

Casson, Lionel. 1989. *The Periplus Maris Erythraei: Text with Introduction, Translation, and Commentary*. Princeton: Princeton University Press.

Cederlöf, Gunnal and Rangarajan, Mahesh. (Eds.). 2018. *At Nature's Edge: The Global Present and Long-term History*. New Delhi: Oxford University Press.

Chanchani, Nachiket. 2019. *Mountain Temples & Temple Mountains: Architecture, Religion, and Nature in the Central Himalayas*. Delhi: Niyogi Books.

Chakrabarti, Dilip K. 1984. 'Origin of the Indus Civilization: Theories and Problem.' In B. B. Lal and S. P. Gupta. (Eds.). *Frontiers of the Indus Civilization*. New Delhi: Books and Books.

_______. 1990. *The External Trade of the Indus Civilization*. New Delhi: Munshiram Manoharlal.

_______. 1992. *The Early Use of Iron in India*. Delhi: Oxford University Press.

_______. 1995. *The Archaeology of Ancient Indian Cities*. Delhi:Oxford University Press.

_______. 2001. 'The Archaeology of Hinduism.' In Timothy Insoll. (Ed.). *Archaeology and World Religion*. London and New York: Routledge. pp. 33–59.

_______. 2006. *The Oxford Companion to Indian Archaeology: The Archaeological Foundations of Ancient India, Stone Age to AD 13th Century*. New Delhi: Oxford University Press.

Chakrabarti, Dilip K. and Nayanjot Lahiri. 1986. 'A Preliminary Report on theStone Age of the Union Territory of Delhi and Haryana.' *Man and Environment* 11: 109–16.

Chakrabarti, Dilip K. and Makkhan Lal. (Eds.). 2014. *History of Ancient India*. 7 vols. New Delhi: Vivekanand International Foundation and Aryan Books International.

Chakrabarti, Kunal. 2001. *Religious Process: The Puranas and the Making of a Regional Tradition*. New Delhi: Oxford University Press.

Chakrabarti, Kunal. and Kanad Sinha. (Eds.). 2018. *State, Power and Legitimacy: The Gupta Kingdom*. Delhi: Primus Books.

Chakraborty, Kalyan Sekhar, Greg F. Slater, Heather M. L. Miller, Prabodh Shirvalkar, and Yadubirsingh Rawat. 2020. 'Compound specific isotope analysis of lipid residues provides the earliest direct evidence of dairy product processing in South Asia. *Nature* 10; https://doi.org/10.1038/s41598-020-72963-y

Chakravarti, Ranabir. (2002) 2020. *Trade and Traders in Early Indian Society*. New Delhi: Manohar.

_______. 2019. 'The Roman Empire, Berenike, Socotra and the Indian Seaboards: Maritime Interlocking (*c*. Late First Century BCE – 300 CE.' In Kumkum Roy and Naina Dayal. (Eds.). *Questioning Paradigms, Constructing Histories: A Festschrift for Romila Thapar*. New Delhi, Aleph in Association with The Book Review Literary Trust. pp. 346–62.

_______. 2020. *The Pull Towards the Coast and Other Essays: The Indian Ocean History and the Subcontinent Before 1500* CE. Delhi: Primus Books.

Chakravarti, Uma. 1987. *The Social Dimensions of Early Buddhism*. Delhi: Oxford University Press.

_______. (1989) 1999. 'The World of the Bhaktin in South Indian Traditions—The Body and Beyond.' In Kumkum Roy. (Ed.). *Women in Early Indian Societies*. New Delhi: Manohar. pp. 299–321.

_______. 2006. *Everyday Lives, Everyday Histories: Beyond the Kings and Brahmanas of 'Ancient' India*. New Delhi: Tulika.

Chakravarty, K. K. (Ed.). 1984. *Rock Art in India*. New Delhi: 1984.

Champakalakshmi, R. 1975–76. 'Archaeology and Tamil Literary Tradition.' *Puratattva* 8: 110–22.

_______. 1996. *Trade, Ideology and Urbanization: South India 300* BC *to AD 1300*. Delhi: Oxford University Press.

Chanana, Dev Raj. (1960) 1990. *Slavery in Ancient India*, New Delhi: People's Publishing House.

Chanda, Ramaprasad. 1926. 'The Indus Valley in the Vedic Period.' *Memoir of the Archaeological Survey of India 31*. Calcutta: Government of India Central Publications Branch.

Chandra, Moti. 1977. *Trade and Trade Routes in Ancient India*. New Delhi: Abhinav Publications.

Chandra, Pramod. (Ed.). 1975. 'The Study of Indian Temple Architecture.' *Studies in Indian Temple Architecture: Papers Presented at a Seminar Held in Varanasi, 1967*. New Delhi: American Institute of Indian Studies. pp. 1–46.

Chandramouli, N. 2002. *Rock Art of South India*. New Delhi: Bharatiya Kala Prakashan.

Chatterjee, Asim Kumar. 1984. *A Comprehensive History of Jainism*. 2 Vols. Calcutta: Firma KLM.

_______. 2000. *A Comprehensive History of Jainism. Vol 1: From the Earliest Beginnings to AD 1000*. New Delhi: Munshiram Manoharlal.

Chattopadhyay, R. N. 2014. 'Eastern Indian Neolithic-Chalcolithic. Dilip K. Chakrabarti and Makkhan Lal. (Eds.). *History of Ancient India*. Vol. 2: *Protohistoric Roots* (New Delhi: Vivekanand International Foundation and Aryan Books International). pp. 523–56.

_______. 2018. *The Archaeology of Coastal Bengal*. New Delhi: Oxford University Press.

Chattopadhyaya, B. D. (1973) 1997. 'Irrigation in Early Medieval Rajasthan.' In *The Making of Early Medieval India*. Delhi: Oxford University Press. pp. 38–56.

_______. (1976) 1997. 'The Origin of the Rajputs: The Political, Economic, and Social processes in Early Medieval Rajasthan.' *The Indian Historical Review*, 3: 57–88.

_______. 1977. *Coins and Currency Systems in South India c. 225–1300*. New Delhi: Munshiram Manoharlal.

_______. (1983) 1997. 'Political Process and Structure of Polity in Early Medieval India.' In *The Making of Early Medieval India*. Delhi: Oxford University Press.

_______. (1986) 1997. 'Urban Centres in Early Medieval India: An Overview.' In *The Making of Early Medieval India*. Delhi: Oxford University Press. pp. 155–82.

_______. (1987) 2003. 'Transition to the Early Historical Phase in the Deccan: A Note.' In *Studying Early India*. New Delhi: Permanent Black. pp. 39–47.

_______. 1990. *Aspects of Rural Settlements and Rural Society in Early Medieval India*. Calcutta and New Delhi: K. P. Bagchi and Co.

_______. (1994) 1997. *The Making of Early Medieval India*. Delhi: Oxford University Press.

_______. (1997) 2003. 'The City in Early India: Perspectives from Texts.' In *Studying Early India*, Delhi: Permanent Black. pp. 105–34.

_______. 1998. *Representing the Other? Sanskrit Sources and the Muslims (Eighth to Fourteenth Century)*. New Delhi: Manohar.

_______. (Ed.). 2002. *Combined Methods in Indology and Other Writings*. New Delhi: Oxford University Press.

Chattopadhyaya, Debiprasad. (1977) 1979. *Science and Society in Ancient India*. Calcutta: Research India Publication.

_______. 2019. *The Concept of Bharatavarsha and Other Essays*. Ranikhet: Permanent Black.

Chattopadhyaya, Umesh C. 1996. 'Settlement Pattern and the Spatial Organization of Subsistence and Mortuary Practices in the

Mesolithic Ganges Valley, North-Central India.' *World Archaeology* 27(3) Feb., *Hunter-Gatherer Land Use*: 461–76.

Chaudhuri, K. N. 1985. *Trade and Civilisation in the Indian Ocean: An Economic History from the Rise of Islam to 1750*. New Delhi: Munshiram Manoharlal.

Chauhan, Parth R. 2016. 'A Decade of Paleoanthropology in the Indian Subcontinent.' In Schug and Walimbe. (Eds.). *A Companion to South Asia in the Past*. Chap. 3. pp. 32–50.

Chowdhury, Abdul Momin and Ranabir Chakravarti. (Eds.). 2018. *History of Bangladesh: Early Bengal in Regional Perspectives (up to 1200 CE)*. 2 Vols. Dacca: Asiatic Society of Bangladesh.

Chelliah, J. V. 1962. *Pattupattu: Ten Tamil Idylls*. Tirunelveli: The South India Saiva Siddhanta Works Publishing Society.

Chhabra, B. 1965. *Expansion of Indo-Aryan Culture During Pallava Rule (as evidenced by inscriptions)*. Delhi: Munshiram Manoharlal.

Chhabra, B. and G. S. Gai. (Eds.). 1981. *Corpus Inscriptionum Indicarum. Vol. 3: Inscriptions of the Early Gupta Kings*. Revised by D. R. Bhandarkar. New Delhi: Archaeological Survey of India.

Childe, V. Gordon. 1950. 'The Urban Revolution.' In Gregory L. Possehl. (Ed.). 1979, *Ancient Cities of the Indus*. New Delhi: Vikas Publishing House. pp. 12–17.

_______. 1952. *New Light on the Most Ancient East*. New York: Praeger.

Choksi, Archana. 1995. 'Ceramic Vessels: Their Role in Illuminating Past and Present Social and Economic Relationships.' *Man and Environment* 20(1): 87–108.

Choudhary, Bijoy Kumar. 2016. 'Lesser-known Buddhist Monasteries: Tilaḍhaka and Yaśovermapura.' *Man and Environment* 41, 1: 17–28.

Claessen, Henri J. M. and Peter Skalnik. (Eds.). 1978. *The Early State*. The Hague: Mouton.

Clark, J. D. and Martin A. J. Williams. 1986. 'Palaeoenvironments and Prehistory in North Central India: A Preliminary Report.' In Jerome Jacobson. (Ed.). *Studies in the Archaeology of India and Pakistan*. Delhi: Oxford University Press and IBH. pp. 19–42.

Clark, Mathew. 2006. *The Daśanāmī Saṁnyāsīs: The Integration of Ascetic Lineages into an Order*, Leiden, Boston: Brill.

Cohen, Ronald. 1978. 'State Origins: A Reappraisal.' In Henri J. M. Claessen and Peter Skalnik. (Eds.). *The Early State*. The Hague: Mouton.

Collins, Steve. 1990. 'On the very idea of the Pali canon.' *Journal of the Pali Text Society* 15: 89–126.

Coningham, Robin A. E. 1995. 'Monks, Caves and Kings: A Reassessment of the Nature of Early Buddhism in Sri Lanka.' *World Archaeology* 27, 2: 222–42.

Coningham, Robin A. E. and F. R. Allchin. 1995. 'The rise of cities in Sri Lanka.' In F. R. Allchin, *The Archaeology of Early Historic South Asia*. Cambridge: Cambridge University Press. Chap. 9. pp. 152–83.

Coningham, Robin A. E, F. R. Allchin, C. M. Bhatt, and D. Lucy. 1996. 'Passage to India? Anuradhapura and the Early Use of the Brahmi script.' *Cambridge Archaeological Journal* 6, 1: 73–97.

Coningham, Robin A. E. and T. L. Sutherland. 1997. 'Dwellings or Granaries? The Pit Phenomenon of the Kashmir-Swat Neolithic.' *Man and Environment* 22(2): 29–34.

Coningham, Robin A. E., K. P. Acharya, K. M. Strickland, C. E. Davis, M. J. Manual, I. A. Simpson, K. Gilliland, J. Tremblay, T. C. Kinnaird, and D. C. W. Sanderson. 2013. 'The earliest Buddhist Shrine: Excavating the Birthplace of the Buddha, Lumbini (Nepal).' *Antiquity* 87:1104–23.

Coomaraswamy, Ananda K. (1928–31) 1980. *Yakshas*. 2nd Edn. New Delhi: MunshiramManoharlal.

Cort, John E. 1987. 'Medieval Jaina Goddess Traditions', *Numen*, 34. 2: 235–55.

_______. 2000. '"Intellectual Ahimsa" revisited: Jaina tolerance and the intolerance of others.' *Philosophy East and West* 50, 3: 324–47.

Cowell, E. B. and F. W. Thomas. (Trans.). 1993. *The Harsha-Charita of Bana*. Delhi: Motilal Banarsidass.

Cribb, Joe. 2005. *The Indian Coinage Tradition: Origins, Continuity and Change*. Nashik: Indian Institute of Research in Numismatic Studies.

Crone, Patricia. 1980. *Slaves on Horses: The Evolution of the Islamic Polity. Cambridge: Cambridge University Press.*

Cunningham, Alexander. 1871. *Four Reports Made During the Years 1862–65*. Archaeological Reports. Vol. 2. Simla.

Cunliffe, Barry. 2019. *The Scythians: Nomad Warriors of the Steppe*. Oxford: Oxford University Press.

Dales, George F. 1964. 'The Mythical Massacre at Mohenjo Daro.' *Expedition* 6(3): 36–43.

_______. 1966. 'The Decline of the Harappans.' *Scientific American*, 241(5): 92–100.

Dales, George F., J. M. Kenoyer, and the staff of the Harappa Project. 1991. 'Summaries of Five Seasons of Research at Harappa (District Sahiwal, Punjab, Pakistan), 1986–1990.' In R. H. Meadow. (Ed.). *Harappa Excavations, 1986–1990: A Multidisciplinary Approach*. Monographs in World Archaeology. Vol. 3. Madison: Prehistory Press.

Danino, Michel. 2016. 'Aryans and the Indus Civilization: Archeaological, Skeletal, and Molecular Evidence. In Gwen Robbins Schug and Subhash R. Walimbe. (Eds.). *A Companion to South Asia in the Past*. West Sussex: Wiley Blackwell. Chap. 13. pp. 205–224.

Darnal, Prakash. 2016. "Archaeology of Nepal." In Gwen Robbins Schug and Subhash R. Walimbe. (Eds.). *A Companion to South Asia in the Past*. West Sussex: Wiley Blackwell. Chap. 26.

Daryaee, Touraj. (Ed.). 2012. *The Oxford Handbook of Iranian History*. Oxford, New York: Oxford University Press.

Datta, Sanjukta. 2017. 'In the King's Shadow: Petitioner-donors of eighth-ninth century Pāla copper plate land grant charters. *Indian Economic and Social History Review* 54, 4: 457–76.

_______. 2019. 'Building for the Buddha: Patrons in the Pāla Kingdom.' *Studies in History* 35, 2: 1–17.

Datta, Swati. 1989. *Migrant Brahmanas in Northern India: Their Settlement and General Impact, c. A.D. 475–1030*. Delhi: Motilal Banarsidass.

Davidson, Ronald M. 2002. *Indian Esoteric Buddhism: A Social History of the Tantric Movement*. New York: Columbia University Press.

Davis, Richard H. (1997) 1999. *Lives of Indian Images*. Delhi: Motilal Banarsidass.

Dayal, Naina. 2019. 'Sūtas, Nāstikas and Retelling the Mahābhārata.' In Naina Dayal and Kumkum Roy (Eds.). *Questioning Paradigms, Constructing Histories: A Festschrift for Romila Thapar*, New Delhi: Aleph Book Company.

de Silva, K. M. 1981. A History of Sri Lanka. Delhi: Oxford University Press.

Deeg, Max. 2007. "Has Xuanzang really been in Mathurā? Interpretatio Dinica or Interpetatio Occidentalia – How to Critically Read the Records of the Chinese Pilgrim." In *Essays on East Asian Religion and Culture: Festscrift in honour of Nishiwaki Tsuneki on the occasion of his 65th birthday*, edited by Christian Withern and Shi Lishan. (Eds.). Kyoto: Editorial committee for the Festschrift in honour of Nishiwake Tsuneki.

Dehejia, Vidya. 1972. *Early Buddhist Rock Temples: A Chronological Study*. London: Thames and Hudson.

_______. 1988. *Slaves of the Lord: The Path of the Tamil Saints*. New Delhi: Munshiram Manoharlal.

_______. 1997a. *Discourse in Early Buddhist Art: Visual Narratives of India*. New Delhi: Munshiram Manoharlal.

_______. 2009. *The Body Adorned: Dissolving Boundaries Sacred and Profane in India's Art*. Ahmedabad: Mapin.

Dehejia, Vidya. and Peter Rockwell. 2016. *The Unfinished: Stone Carvers at Work on the Indian Subcontinent*. New Delhi: Roli Books.

Dehejia, Vidya. (Ed.). 1997. *Representing the Body: Gender Issues in Indian Art*. New Delhi: Kali for Women and The Book Review Literary Trust.

Deo, S. B. 1974. *Excavations at Bhokardan (Bhogavardhana). 1973*. Nagpur: Nagpur University; Aurangabad: Marathwada University.

Deraniyagala, S. U. (1988) 2004. *The Prehistory of Sri Lanka: An Ecological Perspective*. Colombo: Department of Archaeological Survey.

Desai, Devangana. 1975. *Erotic sculpture of India: A Socio-Cultural Study*. New Delhi: Tata McGraw Hill.

_______. 1978. 'Social Background of Ancient Indian Terracottas (*c*. 600 BC–AD 600).' In D. P. Chattopadhyaya. (Ed.). *History and Society: Essays in Honour of Professor Niharranjan Ray*. Calcutta: K. P. Bagchi. pp. 143–65.

Deshpande, Madhav. 1979. 'Genesis of Ṛgvedic Retroflexion, A Historical and Sociolinguistic Investigation.' In Madhav Deshpande and Peter Edwin Hook. (Eds.). *Aryan and Non-Aryan in India*. Michigan papers on South and Southeast Asia, No. 14. Ann Arbor: Centre for South and Southeast Asian Studies, University of Michigan. pp. 235–316.

Devadevan, Manu V. 2020. *The 'Early Medieval' Origins of India*. Cambridge: Cambridge University Press.

Devahuti, D. (1970) 1983. *Harsha: A Political Study*, 2nd Edn. Delhi: Oxford University Press.

_______. 2001. *The Unknown Hsuan-tsang*. Delhi: Oxford University Press.

Devaraja, D. V., J. G. Shaffer, C. S. Patil, and Balasubramanya. 1995. 'The Watgal Excavations: An Interim Report.' *Man and Environment* 20: 57–74.

Deyell, John S. 1990. *Living Without Silver: The Monetary History of Early Medieval North India*. Delhi: Oxford University Press.

_______. 2017. *Treasure, Trade and Tradition: Post-Kidarite Conis of the Gangetic Plains and the Punjab Foothills*, 590–820 CE. New Delhi: Manohar.

_______. 2019. '"Hard Money" and "Cashless" Economies in Medieval Bengal and the Greater Asian World. In John Deyell and Rila Mukherjee. (Eds.). 2019. *From Mountain Fastness to Coastal Kingdoms: Hard Money and 'Cashless' Economies in the Medieval Bay of Bengal World*. New Delhi: Manohar. pp. 175–222.

_______. and Rila Mukherjee. (Eds.). 2019. *From Mountain Fastness to Coastal Kingdoms: Hard Money and 'Cashless' Economies in the Medieval Bay of Bengal World*. New Delhi: Manohar.

Dhar, Parul Pandya. 2008. 'Historiography of Indian Temple Architecture: Some Methodological Concerns.' In Gautam Sengupta and Kaushik Gangopadhaya. (Eds.). *History of Archaeology in India: Ideas, Institutions and Individuals*. New Delhi: D. K. Printworld.

_______. 2011. 'A History of Art History: The Indian Context. In Parul Pandya. (Ed.). *Indian Art History: Changing Perspectives*. New Delhi: D. K. Printworld. pp. 1–32.

_______. (Ed.). 2011. *Indian Art History: Changing Perspectives*. New Delhi: D. K. Printworld.

_______. (Ed.). 2021. *The Multivalence of an Epic: Retelling the Ramayana in South India and Southeast Asia*. Manipal: Manipal University Press.

Dhavalikar, M. K. 1979a. 'Early Farming Communities of Central India.' In D. P. Agrawal and Dilip K. Chakrabarti. (Eds.). *Essays in Indian Protohistory*. Delhi: B. R. Publishing Corpn. pp. 229–45.

_______. 1979b. 'Early Farming Cultures of Deccan.' In D. P. Agrawaland Dilip K. Chakrabarti. (Eds.). *Essays in Indian Protohistory. pp.* 247–64.

_______, H. D. Sankalia, and Z. D. Ansari. 1988. *Excavations at Inamgaon*. Vol. 1, Parts I and II. Pune: Deccan College.

Dias, Malini. 2001. *The Growth of Buddhist Monastic Institutions in Sri Lanka from Brahmi Inscriptions. Epigraphia Zeylanica* 8. Colombo, Archaeological Survey of Sri Lanka.

Dikshit, K. N. (1938) 1999. 'Excavations at Paharpur, Bengal.' *Memoirs of the Archaeological Survey* 55. New Delhi: Archaeological Survey of India.

_______. (1971) 2018. 'Archaeological Remains of the Gupta Period.' In Kunal Chakrabarti and Kanad Sinha, *State, Power and Legitimacy: The Gupta Kingdom*. Delhi, Primus Books. pp. 89–104.

Divakaran, P. P. 2018. *The Mathematics of India: Concepts, Methods, Connections*. New Delhi: Hindustan Book Agency and Singapore: Springer. (Sources and Studies in the History of Mathematics and Physical Sciences series; managing editor Jed Z. Buchwald)

Divyabhanusinh. (2005) 2008. *The Story of Asia's Lions*. Mumbai: Marg.

Divyabhanusinh, Asok Kumar Das and Shibani Bose. 2018. *The Story of India's Unicorns*. Mumbai: Marg.

Dube, Leela. 1994. 'Kinship and Gender in South and Southeast Asia: Patterns and Contrasts', 9th J. P. Naik Memorial Lecture, 1994. Available at http://www.cwds.ac.in/wp-content/uploads/2016/09/Kinship-and-Gender.pdf.

Doniger, Wendy and Sudhir Kakar. (Trans). 2002. *Vatsyayana's Kamasutra*. Oxford World's Classics Series. Oxford: Oxford University Press.

Dundas, Paul. (1962) 1988. *Buddhist Monks and Monasteries of India: Their History and their Contribution to Indian Culture*. Rep. Edn. Delhi: Motilal Banarsidass.

_______. 1992. *The Jainas*. London and New York: Routledge. Dutt, Sukumar. (1924) 1984. *Early Buddhist Monachism*. New Delhi: Munshiram Manoharlal.

Eaton, Richard M. 2019. *India in the Persianate Age: 1000–1765*. **London:** Allen Lane.

_______. (Ed.). (2003) 2006. *India's Islamic Traditions, 711–1750*. Oxford in India Readings, Themes in India History series. New Delhi: Oxford University Press.

Ernst, Carl W. 2005. *Following Muhammad: Rethinking Islam in the Contemporary World*. New Delhi: Yoda Press.

Enzel, Y., L. L. Ely, S. Mishra, R. Ramesh, R. Amit, B. Lazar, S. N. Rajaguru, V. R. Baker, and A. Sandler. 1999. 'High-resolution Holocene Environmental Changes in the Thar Desert, Northwestern India.' In Nayanjot Lahiri. (Ed.). 2000, *The Decline and Fall of the Indus Civilization*. Delhi: Permanent Black. pp. 226–38.

Erdosy, George. 1988. *Urbanisation in Early Historical India*. BAR International Series 430. Oxford.

_______. 1995. 'City States of North India and Pakistan at the time of the Buddha.' In F. R. Allchin, *The Archaeology of Early Historic SouthAsia*. Cambridge: Cambridge University Press. pp. 99–122.

Eschmann, Anncharlott, Hermann Kulke, and Gaya Charan Tripathi. (Eds.). (1978) 2014. (Revised and enlarged Edn.) *The Cult of Jagannath and the Regional Tradition of Orissa*. New Delhi: Manohar.

Fairservis, Walter A. 1967. 'The Origin, Character and Decline of an Early Civilization.' In Gregory L. Possehl. (Ed.). 1979, *Ancient Cities of the Indus*. New Delhi: Vikas Publishing House. pp. 66–89.

Falk, Harry. 2001. 'The yuga of Sphujiddhvaja and the Era of the Kuṣāṇas. *Silk Road Art and Archaeology* 7: 121–36.

_______. 2006. Aśokan *Sites and Artefacts*. Mains am Rheim: Verlag Philipp Zabern.

_______. 2014. 'Owners' graffiti on pottery from Tissamaharama.' *Zeitschrift* Für *Archäologie Aussereuropäischer Kulturen*. Band 6. Wiesbaden: Reichert Verlag.

Falk, Harry and Chris Bennett. 2009. 'Macedonian Intercalary Months and the Era of Azes. *Acta Orientalia* 70: 197–216.

Falk, Harry. (Ed.). 2015. *Kushan Histories: Literary Sources and Selected Papers from a Symposium at Berlin, Decembers 5–7, 2013*. Bremen: Hempen Verlag.

Farmer, Steve, Richard Sproat, and Michael Witzel. 2004. 'The Collapse of the Indus Script Thesis: The Myth of a Literate Harappan Civilization.' *Electronic Journal of Vedic Studies* 11, 2: 19–57.

Feinman, Gary M. and Joyce Marcus. (Eds.). 1998. *Archaic States*. Santa Fe, New Mexico, School of American Research Press.

Fentress, Marcia A. 1984. 'The Indus Granaries: Illusion, Imagination and Archaeological Reconstruction.' In Kenneth A. R. Kennedy and Gregory L. Possehl. (Eds.). *Studies in the Archaeology and Palaeoanthropology of South Asia*. New Delhi: Oxford and IBH Publishing Co. and The American Institute of Indian Studies.

Fitzgerald, James L. 2004. 'Mahābhārata.' In Sushil Mittal and Gene Thursby. (Eds.). *The Hindu World*. Indian reprint Edn. New York and London: Routledge. pp. 52–74.

Flannery, Kent. 1969. 'Origins and Ecological Effects of Early Domestication in Iran and the Near East.' In Peter J. Ucko and G. W. Dimpleby. (Eds.). *The Domestication and Exploitation of Plants and Animals*. London: Gerald Duckworth.

Flecker, Michael. 2001. 'A Nineth-Century Arab or Indian Shipwreck in Indonesia: First Evidence for Direct trade with China.' *World Archaeology* 32, 3: 335–54.

Fogelin, Lars. 2006. *Archaeology of Early Buddhism*. Lanham: Alta Mira Press.

Folkert, Kendall W. 1993. *Scripture and Community: Collected Essays on the Jains*. John E. Cort. (Ed.). Atlanta: Scholars Press.

Forbes, Andrew. 1987. 'The Pre-Islamic Archaeology of the Maldive Islands.' *Bulletin de l'École française d'Extrême-Orient* 76: 281–88.

Francfort, H. P. 1992. 'Evidence for Harappan Irrigation System in Haryana and Rajasthan.' *Eastern Anthropologist* 45: 87–103.

Francis, Emmanuel. 2021. 'Imperial Languages and Public Writings in Tamil South India: A Bird's-Eye View in the Very Longue Durée. In Peter C. Bisschop and Elizabeth A. Cecil. (Eds.). 2021. *Primary Sources and Asian Pasts*. Berlin/Boston: de Gruyter. pp. 152–83.

Fried, Morton H. 1968. 'The State, the Chicken, and the Egg; or What came First.' In Ronald Cohen and Elman R. Service. (Eds.). *Origins of the State: the Anthropology of Political Evolution*. Philadelphia: Institute for the Study of Human Issues.

Fuller, Dorian Q., Nicole Boivin, and Ravi Korisettar. 2007. 'Dating the Neolithic of South India: New Radiometric Evidence for Key Economic, Social, and Ritual Transformations.' *Antiquity* 313: 755–78; DOI: https://doi.org/10.1017/S0003598X00095715. Furui, Ryosuke. 2019. 'Sujanagar Stone Inscription of the Time of Bhojavarman.' *Pratnasamiksha* 10: 115–22.

_______. 2020. *Land and Society in Early South Asia: Eastern India 400–1250 AD*. London and New York: Routledge.

Fussman, Gerard. 1987–88. 'Central and Provincial Administration in Ancient India: The Problem of the Mauryan Empire.' *Indian Historical Review* 14(1–2): 43–72.

Gaur, R. C. 1983. *Excavations at Atranjikhera: Early Civilization of the Upper Ganga Basin*. Delhi: Motilal Banarsidass.

Gaur, G. S. 1987. 'Semthan Excavation. A Step towards bridging the gap between the Neolithic and the Kushan Period in Kashmir.' In B. D. Chattopadhyaya and B. M. Pande. (Eds.). *Archaeology and History: Essays in Memory of Shri A. Ghosh*. Vol. 1. New Delhi: Agam Kala Prakashan. pp. 327–37.

Gaur, Rajan. 2016. 'Mammalian Palaeodiversity and the Ecology of Siwalik Primates in India and Nepal.' In Gwen Robbins Schug and Subhash R. Walimbe. (Eds.). *A Companion to South Asia in the Past*. West Sussex: Wiley Blackwell. Chap. 2.

Galway-Witham, James Cole and Chris Stringer. 2019. 'Aspects of Human Physical and Behavioral Evolution During the Last 1 million years.' *Journal of Quaternary Science*: Vol. 34, 6. pp. 1–24.

Gippert, Jost. 2004. 'A Glimpse into the Buddhist Past of the Maldives I. An Early Prakrit Inscription.' *Wiener Zeitschrift* Für Die Kunde *Südasiens (Vienna Journal of South Asian Studies)* 48: 81–109.

_______. 2013–14. 'A Glimpse into the Buddhist Past of the Maldives II. Two Sanskrit Inscriptions.' *Wiener Zeitschrift* Für Die Kunde *Südasiens* (*Vienna Journal of South Asian Studies*) 55: 111–44.

Gethin, Rupert. 1998. *The Foundations of Buddhism*. Oxford and New York: Oxford University Press.

Ghosh, A. (1939) 1986. *Nalanda*. New Delhi: Archaeological Survey of India.

Ghosh, A. 1965. 'The Indus Civilization: Its Origin, Authors, Extent and Chronology.' In V. N. Misra and M. S. Mate. (Ed.)., *Indian Prehistory: 1964*. Poona: Deccan College. pp. 113–56.

_______. 1967. 'The Pillars of Asoka: Their Purpose.' *East and West*, New Series 17(3–4): 273–75.

_______. 1989. *An Encyclopaedia of Indian Archaeology*. 2 Vols. New Delhi: Munshiram Manoharlal.

Goetz, H. 1963. 'The Gupta School.' In *The Encyclopaedia of World Art*. Vol. 6. London: McGraw-Hill.

Ghosh, Suchandra. 2017. *From the Oxus to the Indus: A Political and Cultural Study c. 300 BCE to c. 100 BCE*. Delhi: Primus.

_______. 2022. 'Cities as a point of convergence: case studies from early medieval India.' In Urvi Mukhopadhyay and Suchandra Ghosh. (Eds.). 2022. *Exploring South Asian Urbanity*. London and New York: Routledge. pp. 177–194.

Glover, Ian C. (1996) 2012. 'Recent Archaeological Evidence for Early Maritime Contacts Between Indian and Southeast Asia. In Himanshu Prabha Ray and Jean-François Salles. (Eds.). *Tradition and Archaeology: Early Maritime Contacts in the Indian Ocean*. New Delhi: Manohar. pp. 129–58.

Glover, Ian C. and Bérénice Bellina. 2011. 'Ban Don Ta Phet and Khao Sam Kaeo: The Earliest Indian Contacts Re-assessed.' In Pierre-Yves Manguin, A. Mani, and Geoff Wade. (Eds.). *Early Interactions between South and Southeast Asia*. Singapore, Institute of Southeast Asian Studies and New Delhi, Manohar. pp. 17–45.

Goldman, Robert P. and Sally J. Sutherland Goldman. 'Rāmāyaṇa.' 2004. In Sushil Mittal and Gene Thursby. (Eds.). *The Hindu World*. Indian reprint Edn. New York and London: Routledge. pp. 75–96.

Golzio, Karl-Heinz. (Ed.). 2004. *Inscriptions of Campa: based on the editions and translations of Abel Bergaigne, Etienne Aymonier, Louis Finot, Edouard Huber and other French scholars and of the work of R. C. Majumdar*. Aachen: Shaker Verlag.

Gomes, Mekhola, 2021. 'Decentring the King: Kinship and Ideations of Power in the Ikṣvāku Kingdom.' In Mekhola Gomes, Digvijay

Kumar Singh, and Meera Visvanathan. (Eds.). *Social Worlds of Premodern Transactions: Perspectives from Indian Epigraphy and History*. Delhi: Primus Books. pp. 25–44.

Gomes, Mekhola, Digvijay Kumar Singh and Meera Visvanathan. (Eds.). 2021. *Social Worlds of Premodern Transactions: Perspectives from Indian Epigraphy and History*. Delhi: Primus Books.

Gonda, Jan. (Gen. Ed.). (1973–87) 2022. *A History of Indian Literature*. 10 Vols. New Delhi: Manohar.

Good, I. L., J. M. Kenoyer, and R. H. Meadow. 2009. 'New Evidence for Early Silk in the Indus Civilization.' *Archaeometry* 50; DOI: 10.1111/j.1475-4754.2008.00454.

Goyal, S. R. 2005. *The Imperial Guptas: A Multidisciplinary Political Study*. Jodhpur, Kusumanjali Book World.

Green, Peter. 1991. *Alexander of Macedon 356–323 B. C.: A Historical Biography*. Berkeley: University of California Press.

Griffiths, Arlo. 2014. 'Early Indic Inscriptions of Southeast Asia.' In John Guy. (Ed.). *Lost Kingdoms: Hindu-Buddhist Sculpture of Early Southeast Asia*. New York, Metropolitan Museum of Art. pp. 53–57 (the book is available online at https://www.metmuseum.org/art/metpublications/Lost_Kingdoms_Hindu_Buddhist_Sculpture_of_Early_Southeast_Asia)

Grinin, Leonid E., Robert L. Carneiro, Dmitri M. Bondarnko, Nikolay N. Kradin, and Andray Y. Korotayev. 2004. *The Early State, its Alternatives and Analogues*. Volgograd: 'Uchitel' Publishing House.

Guha, Sumit. 2021. *Tribe and State in Asia through Twenty-Five Centuries*. Asia Shorts series, No. 10. Ann Arbor: Association for Asian Studies.

Guillaume, Olivier. (Ed. and comp.). 1991. *Graeco-Bactrian and Indian Coins from Afghanistan*. French Studies in South Asian Cultureand Society V. Osmund Boppearachchi. (Trans.). Delhi: Oxford University Press.

Gunawardana, R. A. L. H. 1995. *Historiography in a Time of Ethnic Conflict: Construction of the Past in Contemporary Sri Lanka*. Colombo, Social Scientists' Association.

_______. 2000. 'Prelude to the State: An Early Phase in the Evolution of Political Institutions in Ancient Sri Lanka.' In R. A. L. H. Gunawardana, S. Pathmanathan, and M. Rohanadeera. (Eds.). *Reflections on a Heritage: Historical Scholarship in Premodern Sri Lanka*. Colombo: Central Culture Fund. pp. 83–122.

Gunawardana, R. A. L. H., S. Pathmanathan, and M. Rohanadeera. (Eds.). *Reflections on a Heritage: Historical Scholarship in Premodern Sri Lanka*. Colombo: Central Culture Fund.

Gupta, P. L. (1969) 1996. *Coins*. 4th Edn. New Delhi: National Book Trust.

_______. (1974) 1979. *The Imperial Guptas*. 2 Vols. Varanasi: Vishwavidyalaya Prakashan.

Gupta, Vinay. 2009. *Buddhism in Mathura (A Detailed Study of Buddhist Tradition, Archaeology and Art*. Delhi: Bharatiya Kala Prakashan.

Gurukkal, Rajan. 1997. 'From Clan and Lineage to Hereditary Occupations and Caste in Early South India.' In Dev Nathan. (Ed.). *From Tribe to Caste*. Shimla: Indian Institute of Advanced Studies. pp. 205–22.

_______. (1981) 2006. 'Aspects of Early Iron Age Economy: Problems of Agrarian Expansion in Tamilakam.' In Bhairabi Prasad Sahu. (Ed.). 2006, *Iron and Social Change in Early India*. Oxford in India Readings: Debates in Indian History and Society. Delhi: Oxford University Press. pp. 220–31.

_______. 2010. *Social Formations of Early South India*. New Delhi, Oxford University Press.

Guy, John. 2014a. 'Introducing Early Southeast Asia. In Guy, John. (Ed.). 2014. *Lost Kingdoms: Hindu—Buddhist Sculpture of Early Southeast Asia*. New York: Metropolitan Museum of Art. pp. 3–13.

_______. 2014b. 'Principal Kingdoms of Early Southeast Asia. In Guy, John. (Ed.). 2014. *Lost Kingdoms: Hindu—Buddhist Sculpture of Early Southeast Asia*. New York: Metropolitan Museum of Art. pp. 14–21.

_______. 2019. 'Long Distance Arab Shipping in the 9th century Indian Ocean: recent shipwreck evidence from Southeast Asia.' *Current Science* 117, 10: 1647–53.

Guy, John. (Ed.). 2014. *Lost Kingdoms: Hindu—Buddhist Sculpture of Early Southeast Asia*. New York: Metropolitan Museum of Art. https://www.metmuseum.org/art/metpublications/Lost_Kingdoms_Hindu_Buddhist_Sculpture_of_Early_Southeast_Asia).

Haksar, A. N. D. (Trans.). 2011. *Kshemendra, Three Satires from Ancient Kashmir*, Gurgaon: Penguin Random House.

_______. (Trans.). 2014a. *Kshemendra, The Courtesan's Keeper: Samaya Mātrikā*. Gurgaon: Penguin Random House.

_______. (Trans.). 2014b. *Kshemendra, The Courtesan's Keeper: Samaya Mātrikā*. Gurgaon: Penguin Random House.

Halbfass, Wilhelm. 1991. *Tradition and Reflection: Explorations in Indian Thought*. New York: State University of New York Press.

Hanumanthan, K. R. 2004. 'Evolution of Untouchability in Tamil Nadu up to AD 1600'. In Aloka Parasher Sen ed., *Subordinate and Marginalized Groups in Early India*, New Delhi: Oxford University Press. pp. 125–56.

Haque, Enamul. 2001. *Chandraketugarh: Treasure-house of the Bengal Terracottas*. Studies in Bengal Art Series, No. 4. Dhaka: The International Centre for the Study of Bengal Art.

Hardy, Adam. 1995. *Indian Temple Architecture: Form and Transforma tion: The Karnata Dravida Tradition 7th to 13th Centuries*. New Delhi: Indira Gandhi Centre for the Arts and Abhinav Publications.

Hardy, Friedhelm. 1983. *Viraha-bhakti: The Early History of Krsn Devotion in South India*. Delhi: Oxford University Press.

Hargreaves, H. 1929. *Excavations in Baluchistan, 1925*. Calcutta: Government Printing Press.

Harle, J. C. (1974) 1996. *Gupta Sculpture of the Fourth to the Sixth Centuries AD*. New Delhi: Munshiram Manoharlal.

_______. (1986) 1990. *The Art and Architecture of the Indian Subcontinent*. The Pelican History of Art series. New York: Penguin Books.

Hart, George L. (Trans.). 2015. *The Four Hundred Songs of Love: An Anthology of Poems from Classical Tamil, the Akanāṉūṟu*. Puducherry: Institut Français de Pondichéry.

Hart, George L. and Hank Heifetz. (Trans.). 1988. *The Forest Book of the* Rāmāyaṇa *of Kampaṉ*. Berkeley and Los Angeles: University of California Press.

_______. (Trans.). 1999. *The Puṟanāṉūṟu: Four Hundred Songs of War and Wisdom*. Columbia University Press.

Hartel, H. 1993. *Excavations at Sonkh: 2500 Years of a Town in Mathura District*. Berlin: Dietrich Reimer Verlag.

Harvey, Peter. (1990) 2012. *An Introduction to Buddhism: Teachings, History and Practices*. Cambridge: Cambridge University Press.

Hawkes, Jason, and Akira Shimada. (Eds.). 2009. *Buddhist Stupas in South Asia: Recent Archaeological, Art-Historical, and Historical Perspectives*. New Delhi: Oxford University Press.

Hayashi, Takao. 1995. *The Bakhshālī Manuscript: An Ancient Indian Mathematical Treatise*. Groningen: Egbert Forsten.

_______. 2003. 'Indian Mathematics.' In Gavin Flood. (Ed.). *The Blackwell Companion to Hinduism*. Blackwell.

Hazarika, Manjil. 2017. *Prehistory and Archaeology of Northeast India: Multidisciplinary Investigations in an Archaeological Terra Incognita*. New Delhi: 2017.

Hazra, K. L. 2002. *Buddhism and Buddhist Literature in Early Indian Epigraphy*. New Delhi: Munshiram Manoharlal.

Heesterman, J. C. 1957. *The Ancient Indian Royal Consecration*. The Hague: Mouton.

Heitzman, James. 1997. *Gifts of Power: Lordship in an Early Indian State*. Delhi: Oxford University Press.

Hiltebeitel, A. 2001. *Rethinking the Mahabharata: A Reader's Guide to the Education of the Dharma King*. Chicago: Chicago University Press.

Hodgson, Marshall G. S. 1974. *The Venture of Islam: Consceince and History in a World Civilization*. Vol. 1: *The Classical Age of Islam*; Vol. 2: *The Expansion of Islam in the Middle Periods*. Chicago and London: University of Chicago Press.

Hooja, Rịma. 2004. 'Icons, Artefacts and Interpretations of the Past: Early Hinduism in Rajasthan.' In Elisabeth A. Bacus and Nayanjot Lahiri. (Eds.). *The Archaeology of Hinduism: World Archaeology* 36(3): 360–77.

Human Genome Project. National Human Genome Research Institute. Available at https://www.genome.gov.

Hoernle, A. F. Rudolf. 1893–1913. *The Bower Manuscript*. Edited with English Translation and Notes. Calcutta: Superintendent of Government Printing. Archaeological Survey of India, New Imperial Series. Vol. 22.

Hultzsch, E. (1925) 1969. *Corpus Inscriptionum Indicarum*. Vol. 1. *Inscriptions of Asoka*. Reprint Edn. Delhi: Indological Book House.

Huntingford, G. W. B. 1980. *The Periplus of the Erythraean Sea*. London: Hakluyt Society.

Huntington, Susan. 1985. *The Art of Ancient India: Buddhist, Hindu, Jain*. New York, Tokyo: Weather Hill.

Jackson, Peter. 1999. *The Delhi Sultanate*. Cambridge: Cambridge University Press.

Jacobi, Hermann. (1884) 1968. *Jaina Sutras*. Vol. 1. Delhi: Motilal Banarsidass.

Jacobson, Jerome 1986. 'The Harappan Civilization: An Early State.' In Jerome Jacobson. (Ed.). *Studies in the Archaeology of India and Pakistan*. Delhi: Oxford University Press, IBH, and The American Institute of Indian Studies. pp. 137–73.

Jagannathan, Bharati. 2015. *Approaching the Divine. The Integration of Āḻvār Bhakti in Śrīvaiṣṇavism*. Delhi: Primus Books.

Jahan, Shahnaj Husne. 2016. 'Prehistoric Archaeology in Bangladesh: An Overview.' In Gwen Robbins Schug and Subhash R. Walimbe. (Eds.). *A Companion to South Asia in the Past*. West Sussex: Wiley Blackwell., Chap. 25.

Jain, V. K. 1990. *Trade and Traders in Western India*. New Delhi: Munshiram Manoharlal.

Jaini, Padmanabh S. (1979) 2001. *The Jaina Path of Purification*. Berkeley: University of California Press.

_______. (1991) 1992. *Gender and Salvation: Jaina Debates on the Spiritual Liberation of Women*. New Delhi: Munshiram Manoharlal.

Jaiswal, Suvira. (1967) 1981. *The Origin and Development of Vaisnavism*. New Delhi: Munshiram Manoharlal. pp. 198–228.

_______. (1998) 2000. *Caste: Origin, Function and Dimensions of Change*. Delhi: Manohar.

Jamir, Tiatoshi and Hazarika, Manjil. (Eds.). 2014. *50 Years after Daojali-Hading: Emerging Perspectives in the Archaeology of Northeast India. Essays in Honour of Tarun Chandra Sharma*. New Delhi: Research India Press.

Jamison, Stephanie 2006. 'Women "Between the Empires" and "Between the Lines."' In Patrick Olivelle. (Ed.). *Between the Empires: Society in India 300 BCE to 400 CE*. Oxford, New York: Oxford University Press. pp. 191–214.

_______. 2019. 'The Term Gṛhastha and the (Pre)history of the Householder.' In Patrick Olivelle. (Ed.). *Gṛhastha: The Householder in Ancient Indian Religious Culture*. New Delhi: Oxford University Press. pp. 3–19.

Jamison, Stephanie W. and Joel P. Brereton. (Trans.). *The Rigveda: The Earliest Religious Poetry of India*. 2014. Oxford: Oxford University Press and Austin: South Asia Institute, University of Texas.

Jansen, M. 1989. 'Water Supply and Sewage Disposal at Mohenjo-Daro.' *World Archaeology* 21(2): 177–92.

Jarrige, Catherine, Jean-François Jarrige, Richard H. Meadow, and Gonzague Quivron. (Eds.). n.d. *Mehrgarh: Field Reports from Neolithic Times to the Indus Civilization*. Karachi: Department of Culture and Tourism, Government of Sindh, Pakistan, in collaboration with the French Ministry of Foreign Affairs.

Jayaswal, K. P. 1933–34. 'The Text of the Sohgaura Plate.' *Epigraphia Indica* 22: 1–3.

_______. 1943. *Hindu Polity: A Constitutional History of India in Hindu Times*. Parts I and II. Bangalore: Bangalore Printing and Publishing Co.

Jayaswal, K. P. and R. D. Banerji. 1929–20. 'The Hathigumpha inscription of Kharavela," *Epigraphia Indica*, 20: 71–89.

Jayaswal, Vidula. 1998. *From Stone Quarry to Sculpturing Workshop: A Report on the Archaeological investigations around Chunar, Varanasi and Sarnath*. Delhi: Agam Kala Prakashan.

Jha, D. N. 1967. *Revenue System in Post-Maurya and Gupta Times*. Calcutta: Punthi Pustak.

_______. 1974. 'Temples as Landed magnates in Early Medieval South India (*c*. AD 700–1300).' In R. S. Sharma (Ed.). *Indian Society: Historical Probing*. D. D. Kosambi Commemoration Volume. New Delhi: People's Publishing House.

_______. 1976. 'Temples and Merchants in South India: *c*. AD 900–1300.' In Barun De et al. (Eds.). *Essays in Honour of Professor S. C. Sarkar*. New Delhi: People's Publishing House. pp. 116–23.

_______. (Ed.). 2000. *The Feudal Order: State, Society and Ideology in Early Medieval India*. New Delhi: Manohar.

Jha, Vivekanand. 2004. 'Caṇḍāla and the Origin of Untouchability'. In Aloka Parasher-Sen. (Ed.). *Subordinate and Marginal Groups in Early India* (Themes in Indian History series), New Delhi: Oxford University Press. pp. 157–209.

Joglekar, P. P. and Pankaj Goyal, 'Animals.' 2014. In Dilip K. Chakrabarti and Makkhan Lal. (Eds.). *History of Ancient India*. Vol. 2: *Protohistoric Roots* (New Delhi: Vivekanand International Foundation and Aryan Books International). pp. 184–201.

Joshi, M. C. 1987. 'Aspects of Mauryan and Early post-Mauryan Art.' *Journal of the Indian Society of Oriental Art*, n.s., (16–17): 15–22.

_______. (Ed.). 1989. *King Chandra and the Mehrauli Pillar*. Meerut: Kusumanjali Prakashan.

Kailasapathy, K. (1968) 2002. *Tamil Heroic Poetry*. Reprint Edn. Colombo and Chennai: Kumaran Book House.

Kaimal, Padma. 1994. "Playful Ambiguity and Political Authority in the Large Relief at Māmallapuram." *Ars Orientalis*, 24: 1–27.

Kak, Subhash. 2001. 'On the Chronological Framework for Indian Culture.' *Journal of the Indian Council of Philosophical Research*. Special Issue: Chronology and Indian Philosophy: 1–24.

Kane, P. V. 1941a. *History of Dharmasastra (Ancient and Medieval Religious and Civil Law)*. Vol. 1, Part 2. Poona: Bhandarkar Oriental Research Institute.

_______. (1941b) 1974. *History of Dharmasastra*. Vol. 2, Part 1. 2nd Edn. Poona: Bhandarkar Oriental Research Institute.

_______. 1955. Extract from Presidential Address, Indian History Congress, *Proceedings of the Sixteenth Session, Waltair 1963.* Calcutta: Indian History Congress Association. pp. 12–17. Reprinted in Nayanjot Lahiri. (Ed.). 2000, *The Decline and Fall of the Indus Civilization.* Delhi: Permanent Black.

_______. (1946) 1973. *History of Dharmasastra.* Vol. 3. 2nd Edn. Poona. Bhandarkar Oriental Research Institute.

Kangle, R. P. 1960–65. *The Kautiliya Arthasastra* (Part I) 1960; *A Critical Edition with a Glossary* (Part II) 1963; *English Translation with Critical and Explanatory Notes* (reprinted in 1972); Part III (1965). Bombay: University of Bombay.

Karashima, Noboru. 1984. *South Indian History and Society: Studies from Inscriptions AD 850–1800.* Delhi: Oxford University Press.

_______. 2009. 'South Indian Merchant Guilds in the Indian Ocean and Southeast Asia.' In Hermann Kulke, K. Kesavapany, and Vijay Sakhuja. (Eds.). *Nagapattinam to Suvarnadwipa: Reflections on the Chola Naval Expeditions to Southeast Asia.* Singapore, Institute of Southeast Asian Studies. pp. 135–57.

Karashima, Noboru, Y. Subbarayalu, and Toru Matsui. 1978. 'A Concordance ofthe Names in the Chola Inscriptions.' 3 Vols. Madurai: SarvodayaIlakkiya Pannai.

_______. (Ed.). 2014. *A Concise History of South India: Issues and Interpretations.* New Delhi, Oxford University Press,

Karttunen, Klaus. 1989. *India in Early Greek Literature.* Studia Orientalia 65. Helsinki: Finnish Oriental Society.

Kashyap, Arunima. (1997) 2017. *India and the Hellenistic World.* Delhi: Motilal Banarsidass.

_______. 2006. *Use Wear and Starch Grain Analysis: An Integrated Approach to Understanding the Transition from Hunting Gathering to Food Production at Bagor, Rajasthan, India.* PhD dissertation. Michigan State University Department of Anthropology.

Kaul, Shonaleeka. 2010. *Imagining the Urban: Sanskrit and the City in Early India.* Delhi: Permanent Black.

_______. 2018. *The Making of Early Kashmir: Landscape and Identity in the Rajatarnagini.* New Delhi: Oxford University Press.

Kavork Dohanian, Diran. 1983. 'Sinhalese Sculptures in the Pallava Style.' *Archives of Asian Art* 36: 6–21

Kennedy, K. A. R. 1997. 'Have Aryans been Identified in the Pre-historic Skeletal Record from South Asia? Biological Anthropology and Concepts of Ancient Races.' In G. Erdosy. (Ed.). *The Indo-Aryans of Ancient South Asia.* Berlin and New York: Walter de Gruyter. pp. 46–66.

Kenoyer, Jonathan Mark. 1998. *Ancient Cities of the Indus Valley Civilization.* Karachi: Oxford University Press and American Institute of Pakistan Studies.

_______. 2011. 'Changing Perspectives of the Indus Civilization: New Discoveries and Challenges.' *Puratattva* 41:1–18.

Kenoyer, Jonathan Mark, Massimo Vidale, and Kuldeep K. Bhan. 1995. 'Carnelian Bead Production in Khambhat, India: An Ethnoarchaeological Study.' In Bridget Allchin. (Ed.). *Living Traditions: Studies in the Ethnoarchaeology of South Asia.* New Delhi: Oxford University Press and IBH. pp. 281–306.

Khanna, Gurcharan S. 1993. 'Patterns of Mobility in the Mesolithic of Rajasthan.' *Man and Environment* 18(1): 49–55.

Kharakwal, J. S., Y. S. Rawat, and Toshiki Osada. 2012. *Excavation at Kanmer 2005–06 — 2008–09.* Kanmer Archaeological Research Project. Kyoto: Indus Project, Research Institute for Humanity and Nature; Gandhinagar: Gujarat State Department of Archaeology; and Udaipur: Institute of Rajasthan Studies, JRN Rajasthan Vidyapeeth.

Khare M. D. 1967, 'Discovery of a Vishnu Temple Near the Heliodoros Pillar, Besnagar, Dist. Vidisha (M. P.)', *Lalit Kala* 13: 92–97.

Kishore Saxena, Kanika. 2021. *Before Kṛṣṇa: Religious Diversity in Ancient Mathura.* New Delhi: Oxford University Press.

Khongreiwo, Rammathot. 2014. 'Landscapes, Monuments, Collective Memories: Understanding Pre-Christian Belief Systems and Socio-Religious Practices of the Nagas.' In Tiatoshi Jamir and Manjil Hazarika. (Eds.). *50 Years after Daojali-Hading: Emerging Perspectives in the Archaeology of Northeast India. Essays in Honour of Tarun Chandra Sharma.* New Delhi: Research India Press, Chap. 26. pp. 292–317.

Kielhorn, F. 1900–01. 'Aihole Inscription of Pulakesin II, Saka-Samvat 556.' *Epigraphia Indica* 6: 1–12.

_______. 1905–06. 'Junagadh Rock Inscription of Rudradaman; the Year 72.' *Epigraphia Indica* 8: 36–49.

Korisettar, Ravi, P. P. Joglekar, Dorian Q. Fuller, and P. C. Venkatasubbaiah. 2001. 'Archaeological Re-investigation and Archaeozoology of Seven Southern Neolithic Sites in Karnatak and Andhra Pradesh.' *Manand Environment* 26(2): 46–66.

Korisettar, Ravi, P. C. Venkatasubbaiah, and Dorian Q. Fuller. 2003. 'Brahmagiri and Beyond: The Archaeology of the Southern Neo lithic.' In S. Settar and Ravi Korisettar. (Eds.). *Indian Archaeology in Retrospect.* Vol. 1: *Prehistory: Archaeology of South Asia.* New Delhi: Indian Council for Historical Research and Manohar. pp. 151–237.

Korisettar, Ravi and B. Janardhana. 2014. 'Jwalapuram.' In Dilip K. Chakrabarti and Makkhan Lal. (Eds.). *History of Ancient India.* Vol. 1: *Prehistoric Roots* (New Delhi: Vivekanand International Foundation and Aryan Books International). pp. 422–37.

Korisettar, Ravi and Nicole Boivin. 2014. 'Sanganakallu.' In Dilip K. Chakrabarti and Makkhan Lal. (Eds.). *History of Ancient India.* Vol. 1: *Prehistoric Roots* (New Delhi: Vivekanand International Foundation and Aryan Books International). pp. 823–42.

Kosambi, D. D. 1962. *Myth and Reality: Studies in the Formation of Indian Culture.* Bombay: Popular Prakashan.

_______. (1956) 1998. *An Introduction to the study of India History.* Reprint Edn. Bombay: Popular Prakashan.

Kramrisch, Stella. (1921) 1994. 'The Representation of Nature in Early Buddhist Sculpture (Bharhut-Sanchi).' In Barbara Stoler Miller. (Ed.). *Exploring India's Sacred Art: Selected Writings of Stella Kramrisch.* New Delhi: Indira Gandhi Centre for the Arts; Delhi: Motilal Banarsidass. pp. 123–29.

_______. (1928) 1994. 'Introduction to the Vishnudharmottara.' In Barbara Stoler Miller. (Ed.). *Exploring India's Sacred Art: Selected Writings of Stella Kramrisch.* New Delhi: Indira Gandhi Centre for the Arts and Delhi: Motilal Banarsidass.

_______. (1937) 1994. 'Ajanta.' In Barbara Stoler Miller. (Ed.). *Ex ploring India's Sacred Art: Selected Writings of Stella Kramrisch.* pp. 273–307.

_______. (1946) 1994. 'The Image of Mahadeva in the Cave-Temple on Elephanta Island.' In Barbara Stoler Miller. (Ed.). *Exploring India's Sacred Art: Selected Writings of Stella Kramrisch.* pp. 141–47.

Kropman, Martine. 2008. 'The seals and inscriptions from Mansar.' In Hans Bakker. (Ed.). *Mansar: The Discovery of Pravareśvara and Pravarapura Temple and Residence of the Vākāṭaka King Pravarasena.* Proceedings of a Symposium at the British Museum (London, 30 June – 1 July, 2008). http://mansar.eldoc.ub.rug.nl.

Kulatilake, 2016. 'The Peopling of Sri Lanka from Prehistoric to Historic Times: Biological and Archaeological Evidence.' In Gwen Robbins Schug and Subhash R. Walimbe. (Eds.). *A Companion to South Asia in the Past.* West Sussex: Wiley Blackwell. Chap. 27.

Kulke, Hermann. 1982. 'Fragmentation and Segmentation Versus Integration? Reflections on the Concepts of Indian Feudalism and the Segmentary State in Indian History.' *Studies in History* 4(2): 237–63.

_______. (1993) 2001. *Kings and Cults: State Formation and Legitimation in India and Southeast Asia*. New Delhi: Manohar.

_______. (Ed.). 1997. *The State in India 1000–1700*. Oxford in India Readings: Themes in Indian History. New Delhi: Oxford University Press.

Kulke, Hermann, K. Kesavapany, and Vijay Sakhuja. (Eds.). 2009. *Nagapattinam to Suvarnadwipa: Reflections on the Chola Naval Expeditions to Southeast Asia*. Singapore, Institute of Southeast Asian Studies.

Kulke, Hermann and Bhairabi Prasad Sahu. (Eds.). 2015. *Interrogating Political Systems: Integrative Prcoesses and States in Pre-Modern India*. New Delhi: Manohar.

_______. (Eds.). 2022. *The Routledge Handbook of the State in Premodern India*. London and New York: Routledge; Indian edition.

Kumar, Ajit. (Ed.). 2015. *Rock Art: Recent Researches and New Perspectives (Festschrift to Padma Shri Dr. Yashodhar Mathpal)*, 2 vols. Delhi: New Bharatiya Book Corporation.

Kumar, Giriraj. 'Rock Art.' 2014. In Dilip K. Chakrabarti and Makkhan Lal. (Eds.). *History of Ancient India*. Vol. 1: *Prehistoric Roots* (New Delhi: Vivekanand International Foundation and Aryan Books International). pp. 301–46.

Kumar, Sunil. 2007. *The Emergence of the Delhi Sultanate 1192–1286*. Ranikhet: Permanent Black in association with Ashoka University.

Kuppa, Meghana and Srikumar M. Menon. 2018. 'Stories from Silent Stones: On the Shape of Wedge Marks as a Diagnostic of Stone-Craft of Different Periods.' *Heritage: Journal of Multidisciplinary Studies in Archaeology* 6: 438–486

Lahiri, Nayanjot. 1991. *Pre-Ahom Assam: Studies in the Inscriptions of Assam between the Fifth and the Thirteenth Centuries AD*. New Delhi: Munshiram Manoharlal.

_______. 1992. *The Archaeology of Indian Trade Routes (up to c. 200 BC)*. Delhi: Oxford University Press.

_______. 1995. 'Indian Metal and Metal-related Artefacts as Cultural Signifiers: An Ethnographic perspective.' *World Archaeology* 27: 116–32.

_______. 2005. *Finding Forgotten Cities: How the Indus Civilization was Discover. (Ed.)*. Delhi: Permanent Black.

_______. 2015. *Ashoka in Ancient India*. Raniket: Permanent Black in association with Ashoka University.

_______. 2016. 'Buddhist Revival and Restoration of Sanchi.' In Nayanjot Lahiri and Upinder Singh. (Eds.). Buddhism in Asia: Revival and Reinvention. ICCR, Singapore: ISEAS, New Delhi: Manohar. pp. 53–80.

_______. 2022. *Searching for Ashoka: Questing for a Buddhist King from India to Thailand*. Permanent Black in association with Ashoka University.

Lahiri, Nayanjot, M. B. Rajani, Debdutta Sanyal and Samayita Banerjee. 2022. 'Exploring the Forest and Mapping its Archaeology: Bandhavargh National Pari and Tiger Reserve, India.' *Current Science* 123: 1–8.

Lahiri, Nayanjot. (Ed.). 2000. *The Decline and Fall of the Indus Civilization*. Delhi: Permanent Black.

Lal, B. B. 1954–55. 'Excavation at Hastinapura and other Explorations in the Upper Ganga and Sutlej Basins, 1950–52.' *Ancient India* (10–11): 5–151.

_______. 1993. *Excavations at Sringaverapura (1977–86)*. Vol 1. New Delhi: Archaeological Survey of India.

_______. 1997. *The Earliest Civilization of South Asia (Rise, Maturity and Decline)*. New Delhi: Aryan Books International.

Lal, B. B., Jagat Pati Joshi, Madhu Bala, A. K. Sharma, and K. S. Ramachandran. 2003. *Excavations at Kalibangan: The Early Harappans*. Part 1. New Delhi: Archaeological Survey of India.

_______. 2020. *Excavations at Kalibangan: The Harappans (1960–69)*. Part 2. New Delhi: Archaeological Survey of India.

Lal, Makkhan. 1984. *Settlement History and Rise of Civilization in Ganga-Yamuna Doab (from 1500 BC to 300 AD)*. Delhi: Orient Book Distributors. pp. 20–66.

Lal, Pranay. 2016. *India: A Deep Natural History of the Indian Subcontinent*. Gurgaon: Penguin Random House.

Lamberg-Karlovsky, C. C. 1972. 'Trade Mechanisms in Indus-Mesopotamian Interrelations.' In Gregory L. Possehl. (Ed.). 1979, *Ancient Cities of the Indus*. New Delhi: Vikas Publishing House. pp. 130–37.

Lambrick, H. T. 1967. The Indus Flood Plain and the "Indus" Civilization.' *Geographical Journal* 133(4): 483–95.

Law, Randall. 2011. *Inter-regional Interaction and Urbanism in the Ancient Indus Valley. A Geologic Provenance Study of Harappan Rock and Mineral Assemblage*. Kyoto: Research Institute for Humanity and Nature.

Leinhard, Siegfri. (Ed.). 1984. *A History of Classical Poetry: Sanskrit—Pali—Prakrit*. Wiesbaden: Otto Harrassowitz. (Jan Gonda (Gen. Ed.)., *A History of Indian Literature*. Vol. 3, Fasc. 1).

Legge, James. (1886) 1981. *The Travels of Fa-Hien: A Record of Bud dhistic Kingdoms, being an account by the Chinese monk Fa-hien of his travels in India and Ceylon (AD 399–414) in search of the Buddhist Books of Discipline*. Rep. Edn. New Delhi: Master Publishers.

Lerner, Gerda. 1986. *The Creation of Patriarchy*. New York: Oxford University Press.

Leshnik, L. 1968. 'The Harappan "Port" at Lothal: Another View.' *American Anthropologist* 70(5): 911–22.

Leslie, Julia. (Ed.). (1991) 2015. *Roles and Rituals for Hindu Women*. Delhi: Motilal Banarsidass.

Li, Rongxi. (2002) 2014. 'The Journey of the Eminent Monk Faxian.' In *Lives of Great Monks and Nuns*. Berkeley: Numata Center for Buddhist Translation and Research; dBET PDF version.

Liu, Xinriu. 1988. *Ancient India and Ancient China: Trade and Religious Exchanges*. Delhi: Oxford University Press.

_______. 1996. *Silk and Religion: An Exploration of Material Life and the Thought of People, AD 600–1200*. Delhi: Oxford University Press.

_______. 2022. Early Buddhist Society: The World of Gautama Buddha. Ranikhet: Permanent Black in Association with Ashoka University.

Liyanagamage, A. 2000. 'Conflicts in State—Sangha Relations in the Early History of Sri Lanka.' In R. A. L. H. Gunawardana, S. Pathmanathan, and M. Rohanadeera. (Eds.). *Reflections on a Heritage: Historical Scholarship in Premodern Sri Lanka*. Colombo: Central Culture Fund. pp. 165–206.

Lone, Abdul Rashid. 2019. 'A Site Catchment Analysis at Semthan, Anantnag District, Jammu and Kashmir.' *Man and Environment* 44: 90–104.

Lorenzen, David N. (1972) 1991. *The Kapalikas and Kalamukhas: Two Lost Saivite Sects*. 2nd rev. Edn. Delhi: Motilal Banarsidass.

_______. (1999) 2006. 'Who Invented Hinduism?' In David Lorenzen, *Who Invented Hinduism? Essays on Religion in History*. New Delhi: Yoda Press. pp. 1–36.

Lubin, Timothy. 2005. 'The Transmission, Patronage, and Prestige of Brahmanical Piety from the Mauryas to the Guptas.' In Federico Squarcini. (Ed.). *Boundaries, Dynamics and Construction of Traditions in South Asia*. Firenze: Firenze University Press.

Luders, H. (Ed.). 1963. *Bharhut Inscriptions*. Revised and supplemented by E. Waldschmidt and M. A. Mehendale. *Corpus Inscriptionum Indicarum*. Vol. II, Part 2. Ootacamund: Government Epigraphist for India.

Lukacs, J. R. 1985. 'Dental Pathology and Tooth Size in Early Neolithic Mehrgarh: An Anthropological Assessment.' In J. Schotsman and M. Taddei. (Eds.). *South Asian Archaeology, 1983*. pp. 121–50.

_______. 'Mesolithic Foragers of the Ganges Plain: Pathology, Stature, and Subsistence.' In Gwen Robbins Schug and Subhash R. Walimbe. (Eds.). 2016. *A Companion to South Asia in the Past*. West Sussex: Wiley Blackwell. Chap. 8.

Lukacs, J. R. and S. R. Walimbe. 1986. *Excavations at Inamgaon*. Vol. 2. *The Physical Anthropology of Human Skeletal Remains*. Pune: Deccan College.

Mahadevan, Iravatham. 1977. *The Indus Script: Texts, Concordance and Tables*. New Delhi: Archaeological Survey of India.

_______. 2003. *Early Tamil Epigraphy: From the Earliest Times to the Sixth Century AD* Chennai: Cre-A and the Department of Sanskrit and Indian Studies, Harvard University.

_______. 2007. 'A Megalithic Pottery Inscription and a Harappa Tablet: A Case of Extraordinary Resemblance.' *Journal of Tamil Studies*, June 2007: 80–87.

Mair, Victor H. 2004. 'Xie He's "Six Laws" of Painting and their Indian parallels.' In *Chinese Aesthetics: The Ordering of Literature, the Arts, and the Universe*, edited by Zongqi Cai, 81–122. Honolulu: University of Hawaii Press, 2004.

_______. and Mei, Tsu-Lin. 1991. 'The Sanskrit Origins of Recent Style Prosody.' *Harvard Journal of Asiatic Studies* 51, 2: 375–470.

Maity, S. K. (1957) 1970. *Economic Life in Northern India in the Gupta period (c. AD 300–550)*. 2nd rev. Edn. Delhi: Motilal Banarsidass.

_______. 1975. *The Imperial Guptas and their Times (c. AD 300–550)*. New Delhi. Munshiram Manoharlal.

Majumdar, G. P. and S. C. Banerji. (Eds. and Trans). 1960. *Krsiparasara*. Calcutta: The Asiatic Society.

Majumdar R. C. (Gen. Ed.) (1955) 1964. *The Age of Imperial Kanauj*. 2nd Edn. The History and Culture of the Indian People. Vol. 4. Bombay: Bharatiya Vidya Bhavan.

_______. (Gen. Ed.). (1957) 1966. *The Struggle for Empire*. 2nd Edn. The History and Culture of the Indian People. Vol. 5. Bombay Bharatiya Vidya Bhavan.

_______. (Ed.). (1960) 1981. *The Classical Accounts of India*. Calcutta: Firma KLM.

_______. (Ed.). 1981. *A Comprehensive History of India. Vol. 3, Part 1 (A. D. 300–985)*. New Delhi: People's Publishing House.

Majumdar R. C. et al. (Eds.). (1951) 1968. *The Age of Imperial Unity*. The History and Culture of the Indian People. Vol. 2. 4th Edn. Bombay: Bharatiya Vidya Bhavan.

Majumdar R. C. (Gen. Ed.). _______ et al. (Eds.). (1951) 1971. *The Vedic Age*. The History and Culture of the Indian People. Vol. 1. Bombay: Bharatiya Vidya Bhavan.

Malik, S. C. 1968. *Indian Civilization: The Formative Period—A Study of Archaeology as Anthropology*. Simla: Indian Institute of Advanced Study.

Manji, Hari, B. R. Mani, et al. 2003. *Ayodhya: 2002–03. Excavations at the Disputed Site. Report submitted to the Special Full Branch, Lucknow of the Hon'ble High Court, Allahabad*. New Delhi: Archaeological Survey of India.

Malhan, Tara Sheemar. 2017. *Plunging the Ocean: Courts, Castes, and Courtesans in the Kathāsaritsāgara*. Delhi: Primus Books.

Mallory, J. P. 1989. *In Search of the Indo-Europeans: Language, Archaeology and Myth*. London: Thames and Hudson.

Manguin, Pierre-Yves, A. Mani, and Geoff Wade. (Eds.). 2011. *Early Interactions between South and Southeast Asia*. Singapore, Institute of Southeast Asian Studies and New Delhi, Manohar.

Manjul, Sanjay Kumar and Arvin Manjul. 2018. 'Recent Discoveries at Sanauli, District Baghpat, UP: A Landmore of Indian Archaeology.' *Purātattva* 48: 220–25.

Marcus, Joyce, and Jeremy A. Sabloff. (Eds.). 2008. *The Ancient City: New Perspectives on Urbanism in the Old and New World*. New Mexico: School for Advanced Research Resident Scholar Series.

Marshall, John. 1915. 'Excavations at Bhita.' *Annual Report, 1911–12*. Delhi: Archaeological Survey of India. pp. 29–94.

_______. 1951. *Taxila, An Illustrated Account of Archaeological ExcavationsCarried out at Taxila under the Orders of the Government of India between1913 and 1934*. 3 Vols. Cambridge: Cambridge University Press.

———, Alfred Foucher, and N. G Majumdar. (1940) 1982. *Monuments of Sanchi*. Rep. Edn. Vol. I. Delhi: Swati Publications.

Mathpal, Yashodhar. 1974. *Prehistoric Rock Paintings of Bhimbetka in Central India*. New Delhi: Abhinav Publications.

Mathur, A. D. 2007. *Medieval Hindu Law: Historical Evolution and Enlightened Rebellion*. New Delhi: Oxford University Press.

Mauss, Marcel. (1954) 1980. *The Gift: Forms and Functions of Exchange in Archaic Societies*. Ian Cunnison. (Trans.). an Introduction by E. E. Evans-Pritchard. Rep. Edn. London and Henley: Routledge and Kegan Paul.

McC. Adams, Robert. 1966. *The Evolution of Urban Society*. London: Weidenfeld and Nicolson.

_______. 1968. 'The Natural History of Urbanism.' In Gregory L. Possehl. (Ed.). 1979, *Ancient Cities of the Indus*. New Delhi: Vikas Publishing House. pp. 18–26.

McClish, Mark. 2019. *The History of the Arthaśastra: Sovereignty and Sacred Law in Ancient India*. Cambridge: Cambridge University Press.

McGrindle, J. W. 1877. *Ancient India as described by Megasthenes and Arrian; being a translation of the fragments of the Indica of Megasthenes collected by Dr. Schwanbeck, and of the first part of the Indica of Arrian*. London: Trubner and Co.

Meadow, Richard H. and Ajita Patel. 1997. 'A Comment on "Horse Remains from Surkotada" by Sándor Bökönyi.' *South Asian Studies* 13: 308–18.

——— and Jonathan Mark Kenoyer. 2001. 'Recent Discoveries and Highlights from Excavations at Harappa: 1998–2000.' *Indo Koko Kenkyu* 22: 19–36. Tokyo: Indian Archaeological Society.

Mehrotra, Arvind Krishna. 1991. *The Absent Traveller: Prākrit Love Poetry from the Gāthāsaptaśatī of Sātavāhana Hāla*, Delhi: Ravi Dayal.

Mehta, R. N. and K. M. George. 1978. *Megaliths at Machad and Pazhayannur, Talppally Taluka, Trichur District, Kerala State (A Report of the Excavations conducted from 18th April to 12th May 1974)*. Baroda: University of Baroda.

Meister, Michael W. and M. A. Dhaky. (Eds.). 1989. *Encyclopaedia of Indian Temple Architecture. South India. Lower Dravidadesa*. Vol. 1. New Delhi: American Institute ofIndian Studies, Manohar.

Meister, Michael W., M. A. Dhaky, and Krishna Deva. (Eds.). 1989. *Encyclopaedia ofIndian Temple Architecture, North India: Foundations of North IndianStyle*. Vol. 2, Parts 1 & 2. Delhi: American Institute of Indian Studies, Oxford University Press.

Menon, Jaya and Supriya Varma. 2010a. "Reading Archaeological Evidence: Ceramic and Terracotta Production at Indor Khera, Uttar Pradesh (200 BCE–500 CE).' *Indian Historical Review* 37, 2: 187–216.

_______. 2010b. 'Children Playing and Learning: Crafting Ceramics in Ancient Indor Khera.' *Asian Perspectives* 49, 1: 85–109.

Michell, George. 2002. *Pattadakal*. (Monumental Legacy series). New Delhi: Oxford University Press.

Miksic, John N. and Geok Yian Goh. 2017. *Ancient Southeast Asia*. Routledge World Archaeology series. London and New York: Routledge.

Mirashi, V. V. 1981. *The History and Inscriptions of the Satavahanas and the Western Kshatrapas*. Bombay: Maharashtra Board for Literature and Culture.

_______. (Ed.). 1963. *Corpus Inscriptionum Indicarum. Vol. 5, Inscriptions of the Vakatakas*. Ootacamund: Archaeological Survey of India.

Mishra, Phani Kanta. 2001. 'Deorkothar Stupa: New Light on Early Buddhism.' *Marg* 52(1): 64–74.

Mishra, Sheila. 200–07. 'The Indian Palaeolithic.' *Bulletin of the Deccan College Research Institute*. 66/67: 47–94.

Mishra, Sheila, Naveen Chauhan, and Ashok K. Singhvi. 2013. 'Continuity of Microblade Technology in the Indian Subcontinent Since 45 ka.' *PLoS ONE* 8, 7: e69280.

Misra, Ram Nath. 1975. *Ancient Artists and Art-activity*. Simla: Indian Institute of Advanced Study.

_______. (1979) 1981. *Yaksha Cult and Iconography*. New Delhi: Munshiram Manoharlal.

Misra, V. D. and J. N. Pal. (Eds.). 2002. *Mesolithic India*. Allahabad: Department of Ancient History, Culture and Archaeology. University of Allahabad.

Misra, V. N. 1974. 'Archaeological and Ethnographic Evidence for the Hafting and Use of Microliths and Related Tools.' *Puratattva* 7: 3–12.

_______. 2019. *The Mesolithic Age in South Asia: Tradition and Transition*. New Delhi: Aryan Books International.

_______. and S. N. Rajaguru. 1985. 'Palaeoenvironments and Prehistory of the Thar Desert, Rajasthan, India.' *South Asian Archaeology*: 296–320.

Mital, S. K. 2000. *Kautiliya Arthasastra Revisit. (Ed.)*. Delhi: Centre for Studies in Civilization.

Mitchiner, Michael. 1973. *The Origins of Indian Coinage*. London: Hawkins Publications.

Mitra, Debala. 1971. *Buddhist Monuments*. Calcuta: Sahitya Samsad.

_______. 1992. *Udayagiri and Khandagiri*. New Delhi: Archaeological Survey of India.

Mittal, Sushil and Gene Thursby. (Eds.). 2004. *The Hindu World*. New York and London: Routledge. Indian Reprint Edn.

Mitter, Partha. 1977. *Much Maligned Monsters: History of European Reactions to Indian Art*. Oxford: Clarendon Press.

Mohan, Peggy. 2021. *Wanderers, Kings, Merchants: The Story of India Through its Languages*. Gurgaon: Penguin.

Mohanty, R. K. 1999. 'Significance of a Bead Manufacturing Centre at Mahurjhari, District Nagpur, Maharashtra, India.' *Man and Environment* 24(2): 79–89.

Mohanty, R. K. and Monica Smith. 2009. 'Excavations at Sisupalgarh, 2008.' *Man and Environment*, 34, 1: 47–56.

Monius, Anne E. 2001. *Imagining a Place for Buddhism: Literary Culture and Religious Community in Tamil-Speaking South India*. Oxford: Oxford University Press.

Morrison, K. D. 2005. 'Brahmagiri Revisited: A Reanalysis of the South Indian Sequence. *South Asian Archaeology 2001*: 257–261.

_______. 2007. 'Foragers and forager-traders in South Asian Worlds: Some thoughts from the last 10, 000 years.' In Michael D. Petraglia and Bridget Allchin. (Eds.). *The Evolution and History of Human Populations in South Asia: Interdisciplinary Studies in Archaeology, Biological Anthropology, Linguistics and Genetics*. Dordrecht: Springer. pp. 321–40.

Morrison, K. D., C. M. Sinopoli, K. Wilcox Black, M. Trivedi, A. Bauer, M. Lycett, S. Haricharan, J. Bates, and S. Reddy. 2017. 'From the Southern Neolithic to the Iron Age: A View from Kadebakale.' In Ravi Korisettar. (Ed.). *Beyond Stones and More Stones*. Vol. 3. Bangalore: Mythic Society.

Mughal, M. R. 1977. 'The Early Harappan Period in the Greater Indus Valley and North Baluchistan.' Unpublished Ph. D. dissertation, University of Pennsylvania.

_______. 1997. *Ancient Cholistan: Archaeology and Architecture*. Lahore: Ferozsons.

Mukherjee, B. N. 1970. *The Economic Factors in Kushana History*. Calcutta: Pilgrim Publisher.

_______. 1984. *Studies in Aramaic Edicts of Asoka*. Calcutta: Indian Museum.

_______. 1995. 'The Great Kushana Testament.' *Indian Museum Bulletin*. Kolkata: Indian Museum.

Mukherjee, Sabyasachi. 2022. *The Lost Stupa of Kahu-jo-daro: An Attempt at Reconstruction*. Mumbai: Chhatrapati Shivaji Vastu Sangrahalaya.

Mukherjee, Sraman. 2018. 'Relics in Transition: Material Mediations in Changing Worlds.' *Ars Orientalis* 48: 20–42.

Mukhia, Harbans. (Ed.). 1999. *The Feudalism Debate*. New Delhi: Manohar.

Mukhopadhyay, Urvi, and Suchandra Ghosh. (Eds.). 2022. *Exploring South Asian Urbanity*. London and New York: Routledge.

Murcott, Susan. 1991. *The First Buddhist Women: Translations and Commentaries on the Therigatha*. Berkeley, California: Parallax Press.

Murty, M. L. K. 1985. 'The Use of Wild Plant Foods by Aboriginal Communities in Central India.' In V. N. Misra and P. Bellwood. (Eds.). *Recent Advances in Indo-Pacific Prehistory*. Delhi: Indo-Pacific Prehistory Association. pp. 329–36.

Mushrif, V., N. Boivin, R. Korisettar, and S. R. Walimbe. 2002–03. 'Skeletal Remains from the Kudatini Sarcophagus Burial.' *Puratattva* 33: 74–85.

Muthucumarana, R. A. S. Gaur, W. M. Chandraratne, M. Manders, B. Ramlingeswara Rao, Ravi Bhushan, V. D. Khedekar and A. M. A. Dayananda. 2014. 'An Early Historic Assemblage Offshore of Godawaya, Sri Lanka: Evidence for Early Regional Seafaring in South Asia.' *Journal of Maritime Archaeology*, 9, 1: 41–58

Nagaraj, Nalini. 1980. *Sravanabelagola*. Bangalore: Art Publisher of India.

Nagaraju, S. 1981. *Buddhist Architecture of Western India (c. 250 B.C. – c. A.D. 300)*. Delhi, Agam Kala Prakashan.

Nakanishi, Maiko and Oskar von Hinüber. 2014. Kanaganahalli Inscriptions. *Annual Report if the International Research Institute of Advanced Buddhology at Soka University for the Academic Year 2013* 17, Supplement.

Nandi, R. N. 1989–90. 'Archaeology and the *RgVeda*.' *Indian Historical Review* 16(1–2): 35–79.

_______. 2000. *State Formation, Agrarian Growth and Social Change in Feudal South India c. AD 600–1200*. New Delhi: Manohar.

Narasimhan, Vagheesh M., et al. 2019. 'The Formation of Human Populations in South and Central Asia.' Science 356, 6457. 999.: DOI: 10.1126/science.aat7487.

Narain, A. K. 1993. 'A Clinching Evidence of the Date of Gotama the Buddha.' In *Dr. K. Isukamoto Felicitation Volume, Chi-no-Kaika: Buk-kyo-to-Kaguka*. Tokyo: Felicitation Committee. pp. 59–78.

Narayanan, M. G. S. (1996) 2013. *Perumāḷs of Kerala: Brahmin Oligarchy and Ritual Monarchy*. Thrissur: Cosmo Books.

Narayanan, M. G. S. and Keshavan Veluthat. 1978. 'The Bhakti Movement in South India.' In S. C. Malik. (Ed.). *Indian Movements: Some Aspects of Dissent, Protest and Reform*. Simla: Indian Institute of Advanced Studies.

Nath, Amarendra. 1999. 'Satavahana Antiquities from Adam.' In Ajay Mitra Shastri, *The Age of the Satavahanas*. Great Ages of Indian History. Vol. 2. New Delhi: Aryan Books International. pp. 260–66.

Nath, Vijay. 1993–94. 'Women and Property and Their Right to Inherit Property up to the Gupta Period.' *Indian Historical Review* 20(1–2): 1–15.

Neelis, Jason. 2011. *Early Buddhist Transmission and Trade Networks: Mobility and Exchange within and beyond the Northwestern Borderlands of South Asia*. Leiden, Boston: Brill.

Neumayer, Erwin. 1983. *Prehistoric Indian Rock Paintings*. Delhi: Oxford University Press.

________. 1993. *Lines on Stone: The Prehistoric Rock Art of India*. New Delhi: Manohar.

Nicolas, Arsenio. 2011. 'Early Musical Exchange between India and Southeast Asia.' In Pierre-Yves Manguin, A. Mani, and Geoff Wade, *Early Interactions between South and Southeast Asia: Reflections on Cross-Cultural Exchange*. New Delhi, Manohar. pp. 347–70.

Nicholson, Andrew J. (2010) 2011. *Unifying Hinduism: Philosophy and Identity in Indian Intellectual History*. Ranikhet, Permanent Black.

Nyberg, Harri. 1997. 'The Problem of the Aryans and the Soma:The Botanical Evidence.' In George Erdosy. (Ed.). *The Indo-Aryans of ancient South Asia: Language, Material Culture and Ethnicity*. pp.382–406.

O'Flaherty, Wendy Doniger. 1973. *Asceticism and Eroticism in the Mythology of Siva*. London, New York: Oxford University Press.

________. 1986. *The Rig Veda: An Anthology*. Middlesex: Penguin.

Obeyesekere, Gananath. (1984) 1987. *The Cult of the Goddess Pattini*. Delhi: Motilal Banarsidass.

Ollett, Andrew. 2017. *Language of the Snakes: Prakrit, Sanskrit, and the Language Order of Premodern India*. California, University of California Press.

Olivelle, Patrick. 1993. *The Ashrama System: The History and Hermeneutics of a Religious Institution*. Indian Edn. New York and Oxford: Oxford University Press.

________. 1998. *The Early Upanishads: Annotated Text and Translation*. New York, Oxford: Oxford University Press

________. (2000) 2003. *Dharmasutras: The Law Codes of Āpastamba, Gautama, Baudhāyana, and Vasiṣṭha*. Rep. Edn. Delhi. Motilal Banarsidass.

________. (2005) 2006. *Manu's Code of Law: A Critical Edition and Translation of the Manava-Dharmsastra*. New Delhi: Oxford University Press.

________. 2009. "The Semantic History of Dharma in the middle and late Vedic Periods." In Patrick Olivelle. (Ed.). *Dharma: Studies in Its Semantic, Cultural and Religious History*. Delhi: Motilal Banarsidass. pp. 69–89.

________. 2010. "Dharmaśastra: a textual history." In Timothy Lubin, Donald R. Davis Jr. and Jayanth K. Krishnan. (Eds.). *Hindusim and Law: An Introduction*. Cambridge: Cambridge University Press.

________. 2023. *Ashoka: Portrait of a Philosopher King*. Gurugram: Harper Collins.

Olivelle, Patrick. (Ed.). 2019. *Gṛhastha: The Householder in Ancient Indian Religious Culture*. New Delhi: Oxford University Press.

Olivelle, Patrick, Janice Leoshko, and Himanshu Prabha Ray. (Eds.). 2012. *Reimagining Aśoka: Memory and History*. New Delhi: Oxford University Press.

Orr, Leslie C. 2000a. *Donors, Devotees, and Daughters of God: Temple Women in Medieval Tamilnadu*. New York, Oxford: Oxford University Press.

________. 2000b. 'Women's Wealth and Worship: Female Patronage of Hinduism, Jainism, and Buddhism in Medieval Tamilnadu.' In Mandakranta Bose. (Ed.). *Faces of the Feminine in Ancient, Medieval, and Modern India*. Delhi: Oxford University Press. pp. 124–47.

Paddayya, K. 1982. *The Acheulian Culture of the Hunsgi Valley (Peninsular India): A Settlement System Perspective*. Pune: Deccan College.

________. 1985. 'The Acheulian Culture of the Hunsgi Valley, South India: Settlement and Subsistence Patterns.' In V. N. Misra and P. Bellwood. (Eds.). *Recent Advances in Indo-Pacific Prehistory*. Delhi: Indo-Pacific Prehistory Association. pp. 59–64.

________. 1993. 'Ash Mound Investigations at Budihal, Gulbarga District, Karnataka.' *Man and Environment* 18(1): 58–87.

________. 2014. 'Isampur.' in Dilip K. Chakrabarti and Makkhan Lal (Eds.). *History of Ancient India*. Vol. 1 (New Delhi, Vivekananda International Foundation and Aryan Books International. pp. 411–37.

Paddayya, K., Richa Jhaldiyal and Michael D. Petraglia. 1999–2000. 'The Significance of the Acheulian Site of Isampur, Karnataka, in the Lower Palaeolithic of India.' *Puratattva* 30: 1–24.

Paddayya, K. (Ed.). *Recent Studies in Indian Archaeology*. New Delhi. Munshiram Manoharlal. pp. 189–215.

Padoux, André. 2017. *The Hindu Tantric World: An Overview*, Chicago and London: University of Chicago Press.

Page, J. A. 1937. *A Memoir on Kotla Firoz Shah*. Memoirs of the Archaeological Survey of India No. 52. New Delhi: Archaeological Survey of India.

Pal, J. N. 2014. 'Microlithic Industries and the Issue of the Mesolithic.' In Dilip K. Chakrabarti and Makkhan Lal. (Eds.). *History of Ancient India*. Vol. 1: *Prehistoric Roots* (New Delhi: Vivekanand International Foundation and Aryan Books International). pp. 245–300.

Pande, G. C. (1994) 1998. *Life and Thought of Sankaracarya*. Rep. Edn. Delhi: Motilal Banarsidass.

Pandit, R. S. (Trans.). (1935) 1968. *Kalhana's Rajatarangini: The Saga of the Kings of Kasmir*. New Delhi: Sahitya Akademi.

Pant, P. C. and Vidula Jayaswal. 1991. *Paisra: The Stone Age Settlement of Bihar*. Delhi: Agam Kala Prakashan.

Pant, R. K. 1979. 'Microwear Studies on Burzahom Neolithic Tools.' *Man and Environment* 3: 11–18.

Pappu, Shanti, Yanni Gunnell, Kumar Akhilesh, Régis Braucher, Maurice Taieb, François Demory, and Nicolas Thouveny. 2011. 'Early Pleistcene Presence of Acheulian Hominins in South India.' *Science* 331: 1596–99.

Paranavitana, S. 1970. *Inscriptions of Ceylon*. Vol. 1: *Early Brāhmī Inscriptions: containing cave inscriptions from 3rd century B. C. to 1st century A. C. and other inscriptions in the early Brāhmī script*. Archaeological Survey of Ceylon. Colombo, Department of Archaeology.

Parasher, Aloka. 1991. *Mlecchas in Early India: A Study in Attitudes towards Outsiders upto AD 600*. Delhi: Munshiram Manoharlal.

________. 1992. 'Nature of Society and Civilization in Early Deccan.' *The Indian Economic and Social History Review* 29(4): 437–77.

Parpola, Asko. 1994. *Deciphering the Indus Script*. Cambridge, Cambridge University Press.

_______. 2008. 'Is the Indus Script Indeed not a Writing System?' In *Airāvati: Felicitation Volume in Honour of Iravatham Mahadevan*. Chennai: Varalaaru.com. pp. 111–31.

_______. 2020. 'Royal "Chariot" Burials of Sanauli Near Delhi and Archaeological Correlates of Prehistoric Indo-Iranian Languages.' *Studia Orientalia Electronica* 8(1) (2020): 175–198.

Patel, Alka. 2008. 'The Mosque in South Asia.' In Finbarr Barry Flood. (Ed.). *Piety and Politics in the Early Indian Mosque*. New Delhi: Oxford University Press. pp. 3–26.

_______. 2021. *Iran to India: The Sansabānīs of Afghanistan, c. 1145–1190 CE*. Edinburgh: Edinburgh University Press.

Pathak, V. S. 1966. *Ancient Historians of India: A Study in Historical Biographies*. Bombay: Asia Publishing House.

Patnaik, Sunil Kumar. (2020) 2021. *Buddhist Heritage of Odisha*. Bhubaneswar, Mayur Publications.

Pattanam Excavation 2011, Fifth Season Field Report. 2011. Trivandrum: Kerala Council for Historical Ressearch.

Paul, Diana Y. 1979. *Women in Buddhism: Images of the Feminine in Mahayana Tradition*. Berkeley: Asian Humanities Press.

Pearson, Michael. 2003. *The Indian Ocean*. London and New York: Routledge.

Perera, Nimal H. 2010. *Prehistoric Sri Lanka*. British Archaeological Reports, International Series 2042. Oxford: Archaeopress.

Petraglia, Michael D. and Bridget Allchin. (Eds.). 2007. *The Evolution and History of Human Populations in South Asia: Interdisciplinary Studies in Archaeology, Biological Anthropology, Linguistics and Genetics*. Dordrecht: Springer.

Plofker, Kim. 2009. *Mathematics in India*. Princeton and Oxford: Princeton University Press.

Pokharia, Anil. 2008. 'Record of Macrobotanical Remains from the Aravalli Hill, Ojiyana, Rajasthan: Evidence for Agricutlure-Based Subsistence Economy.' *Current Science* 94, 5: 612–22.

Pokharia, Anil K., J. N. Pal, and Alka Srivastava. 2009. 'Plant Macro-remains from Neolithic Jhusi in Ganga Plain: Evidence for Grain-based Agriculture.' *Current Science* 97, No. 4: 564–72.

Pokharia, Anil K., Tiatoshi Jamir, David Testo, and Zokho Venuh. 2013. 'Late first millennium BC to Second Millennium AD Agriculture in Nagaland: A Reconstruction Based on Archaeobotanical Evidence and Radiocarbon Dates.' *Current Science* 104, No. 10: 1341–53.

Pollock, Sheldon. (1984) 1991. *The Ramayana of Valmiki: Aranyakanda*. Vol. 3. Rep. Edn. Princeton: Princeton University Press.

_______. (2006) 2007. *The Language of the Gods in the World of Men: Sanskrit, Culture and Power in Premodern India*. Delhi: Permanent Black.

_______. (Ed.). 2003. *Literary Cultures in History: Reconstructions from South Asia*. New Delhi: Oxford University Press.

Poonacha, K. P. 2011. *Excavations at Kanaganahalli (Sannati, Dist. Gulbarga, Karnataka)*. New Delhi: Archaeological Survey of India.

Possehl, Gregory L. 2003. *The Indus Civilization: A Contemporary Perspective*. New Delhi: Vistaar Publications.

_______. (Ed.). 1979. *Ancient Cities of the Indus*. New Delhi: Vikas Publishing House.

Postel, Michel and Zarine Cooper. 1999. *Bastar Folk Art: Shrines, Figurines and Memorials*. Vol VIII. Mumbai: Project for Indian Cultural Studies Publications.

Pratap, Ajay. 2016. *Rock Art of the Vindhyas: An Archaeological Survey: The Documentation and Analysis of the Rock Art of Mirzapur District*, Uttar Pradesh. Oxford: Archaeopress.

Przyluski, J. 1967. *The Legend of Emperor Asoka in Indian and Chinese Texts*. Dilip Kumar Biswas. (Trans.). with additional notes and comments). Calcutta: Firma KLM.

Quigley, Declan. (1999) 2002. *The Interpretation of Caste*. Oxford Studies in Social and Cultural Anthropology. 4th Reprint Edn. Delhi: Oxford University Press.

Raikes, Robert L. 'The End of the Ancient Cities of the Indus.' *American Anthropologist* 66(2): 284–99.

Rajan, Chandra. 1989. *Kalidasa: The Loom of Time—A Selection of His Plays and Poems*. Translated from the Sanskrit and Prakrit with an Introduction. New Delhi: Penguin.

Rajan, K. 1990. 'New Light on the Megalithic Culture of the Kongu Region, Tamil Nadu.' *Man and Environment* 15(1): 93–102.

_______. 1991. 'Iron and Gemstone Industries as Revealed from Kodumanal Excavations.' *Puratattva* 20: 111–12.

_______.1998a. 'Archaeology of the South Arcot Region with Special Reference to Megalithic Burial Complexes.' *Man and Environment* 23(1): 93–105.

_______. 1998b. 'Further Excavations at Kodumanal, Tamil Nadu.' *Man and Environment* 23(2): 65–76.

_______. 2003. 'Archaeology of the Pudukottai Region, Tamil Nadu.' *Man and Environment* 28(1): 41–56.

_______. 2014. 'The Iron Age in Tamil Nadu.' In Chakrabarti and Lal. (Eds.). *History of Ancient India*. Vol. 2: *Protohistoric Roots*. New Delhi: Vivekanand International Foundation and Aryan Books International. pp. 592–614.

_______. 2015. *Early Writing System: A Journey from Graffiti to Brahmi*. Madurai: Pandya Nadu Centre for Historical Research.

Rajan, K., V. P. Yathees Kumar, M. Rajesh, R. Sivanantham, J. Ranjith, and J. Bhaskar. 2021 'Recent Radiometric Dates and Their Implications in Understanding the Early Writing Syestem and Early Archaeology of Tamil Nadu. *Man and Environment* 46, 1: 57–86.

Ramanujan, A. K. 1973. *Speaking of Siva*. Harmondsworth: Penguin.

_______. 1999a. 'Form in Classical Tamil Poetry.' In Vinay Dharwadker. (Ed.). *The Collected Essays of A. K. Ramanujan*. Delhi: Oxford University Press. pp. 197–218.

_______.1999b. 'Towards an Anthology of City Images. In Vinay Dharwadker. (Ed.). *The Collected Essays of A. K. Ramanujan*. Delhi: OxfordUniversity Press. pp. 52–72.

Ramaswamy, Vijaya. 1985. *Textiles and Weavers in Medieval South India*. Delhi: Oxford University Press.

_______. (1989) 1999. 'Aspects of Women and Work in Early South India.' In Kumkum Roy. (Ed.). *Women in Early Indian Societies*. New Delhi: Manohar. pp. 150–71.

_______. 1997. *Walking Naked: Women, Society, Spirituality in South India*. Simla: Indian Institute of Advanced Studies.

Rangachari, Devika. 2009. *Invisible Women, Visible Histories: Gender, Society and Polity in North India (Seventh to Twelfth Century AD)*. New Delhi, Manohar.

_______. 2020. *From Obscurity to Light: Women in Early Medieval Orissa (Seventh to Twelfth Centuries AD)*. New Delhi, Manohar.

Rangarajan, L. N. (Ed. and Trans.). 1992. *The Arthashastra*. New Delhi: Penguin. Rao, L. S., Nandini B. Sahu, Prabhash Sahu, Samir Diwan, and U. A. Shastry. 2004–05. 'New Light on the Excavation of Harappan Settlement at Bhirrana.' *Puratattva* 35: 60–75.

Ratnagar, Shereen. 1981. *Encounters: The Westerly Trade of the Harappa Civilization*. New Delhi: Oxford University Press.

_______. 1991. *Enquiries into the Political Organization of Harappan Society*. Pune: Ravish.

_______. 2016. *Harappan Archaeology: Early State Perspectives*. New Delhi: Primus.

Raven, Ellen M. 1994. "Invention and Innovation: Royal Gupta Gold Coins." In *Of Kings and Coins, Marg* 55, no. 4: 39–56.

_______. 2004. 'Kings in Copper.' In H. T. Bakker. (Ed.)., *The Vākāṭaka Heritage: Indian Culture at the Crossroads*. Groningen, Egbert Forsten. pp. 19–31.

Ray, Himanshu Prabha. 1986. *Monastery and Guild: Commerce Under the Satavahanas*. Delhi: Oxford University Press.

_______. 1994. *The Winds of Change: Buddhism and the Maritime Linksof Early South Asia*. Delhi: Oxford University Press.

_______. 2003. *The Archaeology of Seafaring in Ancient South Asia*. Cambridge: Cambridge University Press.

_______. 2014. 'The West Coast of India and the Maritime World of the Western Indian Ocean.' *The African Archaeological Review* 31, 4: 583–98.

_______. 2021. *Coastal Shrines and Transnational Maritime Networks Across India and Southeast Asia*. New York and London. Routledge.

Ray, Himanshu Prabha and Daniel T. Potts. (Eds.). 2007. *Memory as History: The Legacy of Alexander in Asia*. New Delhi: Aryan Books International.

Ray, Niharranjan. 1975. *Maurya and Post-Maurya Art: A Study in Social and Formal Contacts*. New Delhi: Indian Council of Historical Research.

Raychaudhuri, Hemachandra. (1923) 2000. *Political History of Ancient India: From the Accession of Parikshit to the Extinction of the Gupta Dynasty*. With a commentary by B. N. Mukherjee. Delhi: Oxford University Press.

Reade, Julian. 2008. 'The Indus-Mesopotamia Relationship Reconsidered.' In E. Olijdam and R. H. Spoor. (Eds.). *Intercultural Relations Between South and Southwest Asia. Studies in Commemoration of E. C. L. During Caspers (1934–1996)*. BAR International Series 1826: 12–18.

Reich, David. 2018. *Who We Are and How We Got Here: Ancient DNA and the new science of the human past*. Oxford: Oxford University Press.

Renou, Louis. 1971. *Vedic India. Classical India*. Vol. 3. Delhi, Varanasi: Indological Book House.

Renfrew, Colin and Paul Bahn. (1991) 2020. *Archaeology: Theories, Methods, and Practice*. 8th Edn. London: Thames and Hudson.

Rhys Davids, T. W. (1910) 1951. *Dialogues of the Buddha*. Part II. Sacred Books of the Buddhists Series, Pali Text Society. 3rd Edn. London: Luzac and Co.

_______. 1899. *Dialogues of the Buddha*. F. Max Muller. (Ed.)., *Sacred Books of the Buddhists*. Vol. 2. London: Henry Frowde.

Richman, Paula. (Ed.). 1992. *Many Ramayanas: The Diversity of a Narrative Tradition in South Asia*. Delhi: Oxford University Press.

Roberts, Alice. 2011. *Evolution: The Human Story*. London etc.: Dorling Kindersley.

Romani, Julie. 'Indian Architecture in the "Sanskrit Cosmopolis": The Temples of the Dieng Plateau.' In Pierre-Yves Manguin, A. Mani, and Geoff Wade, *Early Interactions between South and Southeast Asia: Reflections on Cross-Cultural Exchange*. New Delhi, Manohar. pp. 299–316.

Ross, E. J. 1946. 'A Chalcolithic Site in Northern Baluchistan.' *Journal of Near Eastern Studies* 5: 284–316.

Roy, Anamika. 2015. *Sixty-four Yoginis: Cult, Icons and Goddesses*. Delhi: Primus Books.

Roy, Kumkum. 1994a. 'Marriage as Communication: An Exploration of Norms and Narratives in Early India.' *Studies in History* 10(2), July–Dec: 183–98.

_______. 1994b. *The Emergence of Monarchy in North India: Eighth–fourth Centuries BC As Reflected in the Brahmanical Tradition*. Delhi: Oxford University Press.

_______. 1998. 'Unravelling the *Kamasutra*.' In Mary E. John and Janaki Nair. (Eds.). *A Question of Silence? The Sexual Economics of Modern India*. New Delhi: Kali for Women. pp. 52–74.

_______. 2018. *The Power of Gender and the Gender of Power: Explorations in Early Indian History*. New Delhi: Oxford University Press.

Roy, T. N. 1986. *A Study of Northern Black Polished Ware Culture: An Iron Age Culture of India*. New Delhi: Ramanand Vidya Bhawan.

Ruben, Walter. (1966) 1969. 'Some Problems of the Ancient Indian Republics.' In Horst Kruger. (Ed.). *Kunwar Mohammad Ashraf: An Indian Scholar and Revolutionary, 1903–1962*. Delhi: People's Publishing House. pp. 5–29.

Sachau, Edward C. 1964. *Alberuni's India*. Delhi: S. Chand & Co.

Sahni, M. R. 1956. 'Bio-geological Evidence Bearing on the Decline of the Indus Valley Civilization.' *Journal of the Palaeontological Society of India* 1(1): 101–07.

Sahni, Pragati. 2008. *Environmental Ethics in Buddhism*. London: Routledge.

Sahu, Bhairabi Prasad. 2013. *The Changing Gaze: Regions and the Constructions of Early India*. New Delhi: Oxford University Press.

_______. (Ed.). 2006. *Iron and Social Change in Early India*. Oxford in India Readings: Debates in Indian History and Society. Delhi: Oxford University Press. Saikia, Arupjyoti. 2019. *The Unquiet River: A Biography of the Brahmaputra*. New Delhi: Oxford University Press.

Sali, S. A. 1986. *Daimabad 1976–79*. Memoirs of the Archaeological Survey: 83. New Delhi: Archaeological Survey of India.

Salomon, Richard. 1998. *Indian Epigraphy: A Guide to the Study of Inscriptions in Sanskrit, Prakrit, and the other Indo-Aryan Languages*. New Delhi: Munshiram Manoharlal.

_______. 1999. *Ancient Buddhist Scrolls from Gandhara: The British Library Kharoshthi Fragments*. London: British Library.

Sanderson, Alexis. 2006. 'Śaivism and Brahmanism in the Early Medieval Period', Gonda lecture 2006, available on academia.edu.

_______. 2009. 'The Śaiva Age – The Rise and Dominance of Śaivism during the Early Medieval Period. In Shingo Einoo. (Ed.)., *Genesis and Development of Tantrism*. Tokyo: Institute of Oriental Culture. pp. 41–349.

_______. 2015a. 'Tolerance, Exclusivity, Inclusivity, and Persecution in Indian Religion During the Early Mediaeval Period.' In *Honoris Causa: Essays in Honour of Aveek Sarkar*. (Ed.). John Makinson, London: Allen Lane. pp. 155–224. Available on www.academia.edu.

_______. 2015b. 'How Public was Śaivism', Keynote Lecture at the Symposium (on) Tantric Communities in Context: Sacred Secrets and Public Rituals, Vienna, February 2015. pp. 3–5, also available at https://www.academia.eduSankalia, H. D. (1964) 1982. *Stone Age Tools: Their Techniques, Names and Probable Functions*. 2nd rep. Poona: Deccan College.

Sanderson, Alexis, Bendapudi Subbarao, and Shantaram Bhalchandra Deo. 1958. *The Excavations at Maheshwar and Navdatoli 1952–53*. Poona and Baroda: Deccan College Research Institute and M. S. University Publication No. 1.

Sankhyan, A. R. 'Hominin Fossil Remains from the Narmada Valley.' In Gwen Robbins Schug and Subhash R. Walimbe. (Eds.). *A Companion to South Asia in the Past*. West Sussex: Wiley Blackwell. Chap. 6.

Sanyal, Rajat. 2018 a. 'Antichak.' In Abdul Momin Chowdhury and Ranabir Chakravarti. (Eds.). *History of Bangladesh: Early Bengal in Regional Perspectives (up to 1200 CE)*. Vol. 1. Dacca: Asiatic Society of Bangladesh. pp. 131–43.

_______. 2018b. 'Bodhgaya.' In Abdul Momin Chowdhury and Ranabir Chakravarti. (Eds.). *History of Bangladesh: Early Bengal in Regional Perspectives (up to 1200 CE)*. Vol. 1. Dacca: Asiatic Society of Bangladesh. pp. 167–76.

_______. 2018c. 'Nalanda.' In Abdul Momin Chowdhury and Ranabir Chakravarti. (Eds.). *History of Bangladesh: Early Bengal in Regional Perspectives (up to 1200 CE)*. Vol. 1. Dacca: Asiatic Society of Bangladesh. pp. 291–316.

_______. 2018d. 'Moghalmari.' In Abdul Momin Chowdhury and Ranabir Chakravarti. (Eds.). *History of Bangladesh: Early Bengal in Regional Perspectives (up to 1200 CE)*. Vol. 1. Dacca: Asiatic Society of Bangladesh. Ranabir. pp. 281–90.

Sarao, K. T. S. (1990) 2007. *Urban Centres and Urbanization as Reflected in the Pali Vinaya and Sutta Pitaka.* 2nd Rev. Edn. Delhi: Department of Buddhist Studies, University of Delhi

Saraswat, K. S. 1996–97. 'Plant Economy of Barans at Ancient Sanghol (*c.* 1900–1400 BC) Punjab.' *Pragdhara* 7: 97–114.

Saraswat, K. S. and A. K. Pokharia. 1997–98. 'On the Remains of BotanicalMaterial Used in Fire-Sacrifice Ritualized During Kushana Periodat Sanghol (Punjab).' *Pragdhara* 8: 149–81.

_______. 2001–02. 'Harappan Plant Economy at Ancient Balu, Haryana.' *Pragdhara* 12: 153–71.

Sarkar, H. 1966. *Studies in Early Buddhist Architecture of India.* New Delhi: Munshiram Manoharlal.

Sarkar, H. and B. N. Misra. 1972. *Nagarjunakonda.* New Delhi: Archaeological Survey of India.

Sarma, I. K. 1994. *Parashuramesvara Temple at Gudimallam.* Nagpur: Dattsons.

Sarma, Pranab Jyoti and Hazarika, Manjil. 2014. 'Situation Northeast Indian Archaeology in Chronological Perspective: Fresh Observations.' In Tiatoshi Jamir and Manjil Hazarika. (Eds.). *50 Years After Daojali-Hading: Emerging Perspectives in the Archaeology of Northeast India. Essays in Honour of Tarun Chandra Sarma.* New Delhi, Research India Press. Chap. 4. pp. 37–59.

Sarma, Sreemula Rajeswara. 1986. 'Astronomical Instruments in Brahmagupta's *Brahmasputasiddhanta.*' *Indian Historical Review* 13(1–2): 63–74.

_______. 1988. 'Sunya: Mathematical Aspect.' In *Kalatattvakosa: A Lexicon of Fundamental Concepts of the Indian Arts.* New Delhi: Indira Gandhi National Centre for the Arts; Delhi: Motilal Banarsidass pp. 400–11.

_______. 2003. 'Sunya in Pingala's Chandahsutra.' In A. K. Baig and S. R. Sarma. (Eds.). *The Concept of Sunya.* New Delhi: Indira GandhiNational Centre for the Arts, Indian National Science Academy, Aryan Books International. pp. 126–36.

Sastri, K. A. Nilakanta. (1955) 1975. *A History of South India from Prehistoric Times to the Fall of Vijaynagar.* 4th Edn. Madras: Oxford University Press.

Sastry, V. V. Krishna, B. Subrahmanyam, and N. Rama Krishna Rao. 1992. *Thotlakonda: A Buddhist Site in Andhra Pradesh.* Hyderabad: Department of Archaeology and Museums, Government of Andhra Pradesh.

Saxena, Monika. 2019. *Women and the Purāṇic Tradition in India.* London and New York: Routledge.

Scarre, Chris, Brian Fagan and Charles Golden. (1997) 2021. *Ancient Civilizations.* 5th Revised Edn. New York and London: Routledge.

Schimmel, Annemarie. 1992. *Islam: An Introduction.* New York: State University of New York Press.

Schopen, Gregory. 1997. *Bones, Stones, and Buddhist Monks: Collected Papers on the Archaeology, Epigraphy, and Texts of Monastic Buddhism in India.* Honolulu: University of Hawaii Press.

Schug, Gwen Robbins and Walimbe, Subhash R. (Eds.). 2016. *A Companion to South Asia in the Past.* West Sussex: Wiley Blackwell.

Scott, James C. 2017. *Against the Grain: A Deep History of the Earliest States.* New Haven and London: Yale University Press.

Selby, Martha Ann. 2000. *Grow Long, Blessed Night: Love Poems from Classical India*, New York: Oxford University Press.

Selvakumar, V. 2011. 'Contacts between India and Southeast Asia in Ceramic and Boat Building Traditions.' In Pierre-Yves Manguin, A. Mani, and Geoff Wade, *Early Interactions between South and Southeast Asia: Reflections on Cross-Cultural Exchange.* New Delhi, Manohar. pp. 197–220.

Sen, D. C. 1954. *History of Bengali Language and Literature.* Calcutta: University of Calcutta.

Sen, Tansen. 2003. *Buddhism, Diplomacy, and Trade: The Realignment of Sino-Indian Relations, 600–1400.* Honolulu: Association for Asian Studies and University of Hawaii Press.

_______. 2006. 'The Travel Records of Chinese Pilgrims Faxian, Xuanzang, and Yijing: Sources for Cross-Cultural Encounters between Ancient China and Ancient India.' *Education About Asia* 11(3): 24–33.

_______. 2009. 'The Military Campaigns of Rajendra Chola and the Chola—Srivijaya—China Triangle.' In Hermann Kulke, K. Kesavapany, and Vijay Sakhuja. (Eds.). *Nagapattinam to Suvarnadwipa.* Singapore, Institute of Southeast Asian Studies. pp. 61–75.

_______. 2010. 'The Intricacies of Premodern Asian Connections. *Journal of Asian Studies* 69, 4: 991–99.

_______. 2018. *India, China and the World: A Connected History.* New Delhi, Oxford University Press.

Sen, Tansen. (Ed.). 2014. *Buddhism Across Asia: Networks of Material, Intellectual and Cultural Exchange.* Singapore: ISEAS and New Delhi: Manohar.

Sen, Swadhin. 2018. 'Paharpur.' In Abdul Momin Chowdhury and Ranabir Chakravarti. (Eds.). *History of Bangladesh: Early Bengal in Regional Perspectives (up to 1200 CE)*. Vol. 1. Dacca: Asiatic Society of Bangladesh. pp. 351–76.

Sen, Swadhin, A. K. M. Syufur Rahman, and S. M. K. Ahsan. 2014. 'Crossing the Boundaries of the Archaeology of Somapura Mahavihara: Alternative Approaches and Propositions.' *Pratnatattva* (Journal of the Dept. of Archaeology, Jahangirnagar University), 20: 49–79.

Swadhin Sen, Supriya Varman, and Bhairabi Prasad Sahu. (Eds). 2023. *The Archaeology of Early Medieval South Asia: Contesting Narratives from the Eastern Ganga—Brahmaputra Basin.* London and New York: Routledge.

Senart, E. 1905–06. "The Inscriptions in the Caves at Nasik." *Epigraphia Indica* 8: 59–96. Service, Elman R. 1975. *Origins of the State and Civilization: The Process of Cultural Evolution.* New York: W. W. Norton.

Settar, S. 2003. 'Footprints of Artisans in History: Some Reflections On Early Artisans of India.' Proceedings of the Indian History Congress, 64th Session. Mysore 2003. General President's Address. pp. 1–43.

_______. 2016. *Inviting Death: Historical Experiments on Sepulchral Hill.* (Revised Edn.). Delhi: Primus Books.

_______. 2017. *Pursuing Death: Philosophy and Practice of Voluntary Termination of Life.* (Revised Edn.)

_______. n.d. 'Memorial Stones in South India.' In S. Settar and Gunther D. Sontheimer. (Eds.). *Memorial Stones: A Study of Their Origin, Significance and Variety.* Institute of Indian Art History: Karnatak University, Dharwad and South Asia Institute, University of Heidelberg, Germany.

Setter, S. and Gunther D. Sontheimer. (Eds.). n.d. *Memorial Stones: A Study of their Origin, Significance and Variety*. Dharwad and Heidelberg: Institute of Indian Art History, Karnataka University and South Asia Institute, University of Heidelberg.

Shaffer, J. G. 1982a. 'Harappan Culture: A Reconsideration.' In Gregory Possehl. (Ed.). *Harappan Civilization: A Contemporary Perspective*. pp. 41–50.

_______. 1982b. 'Harappan Commerce: An Alternative Perspective.' In S. Pastner and L. Flam. (Eds.). *Anthropology in Pakistan: Recent Socio-cultural and Archaeological Perspectives*. Ithaca, New York: Cornell University. pp. 166–210.

_______. 1992. 'The Indus Valley, Baluchistan and Helmand Traditions: Neolithic through Bronze Age.' In R. W. Ehrich. (Ed.). *Chronologies in Old World Archaeology*. Vol. 2 (3rd Edn.). Chicago: University of Chicago Press. pp. 425–46.

Shah, A. M. (1964) 1998. 'Basic Terms and Concepts in Study of the Family in India.' In A. M. Shah. *The Family in India: Critical Essays*. Delhi: Orient Longman. pp. 14–51.

Shah, Kirit K. 2001. *The Problem of Identity: Women in Early Indian Inscriptions*. New Delhi: Oxford University Press.

Shali, S. L. 1993. *Kashmir: History and Archaeology through the Ages*. New Delhi: Indus Publishing Company.

Shanmugan, P. 1987. *The Revenue System of the Cholas, 850–1279*. Madras: New Era Publications.

Sharma, D. V., V. N. Prabhakar, R. Tewari, and R. K. Srivastava. 1999–2000. 'Harappan Jewellery Hoard from Mandi.' *Puratattva* 30: 36–41.

Sharma, D. V., A. Pradhan, V. N. Prabhakar, A. K. Bhargav, and K. A. Kabui. 2001–02. 'A Report on Excavation at Madarpur: A Copper Hoard Site.' *Puratattva* 32: 33–53.

Sharma, D. V., K. C. Nauriyal, and V. N. Prabhakar. 2005–06. 'Excavations at Sanauli 2005–06: A Harappan Necropolis in the Upper Ganga–Yamuna Doab.' *Puratattva* 36: 166–79.

Sharma, G. R. 1960. *The Excavations at Kausambi (1957–59)*. Allahabad: Department of Ancient History, Culture and Archaeology, University of Allahabad.

Sharma, G. R., V. D. Misra, D. Mandal, B. B. Misra, and J. N. Pal. 1980. *From Hunting and Food Gathering to Domestication of Plants and Animals: Beginnings of Agriculture (Epi-Palaeolithic to Neolithic: Excavations at Chopani-Mando, Mahadaha and Mahagara)*. Allahabad: Abinash Prakashan.

Sharma, J. P. 1968. *Republics in Ancient India c. 1500 BC–500 BC* Leiden: E. J. Brill.

Sharma, Prachi. 2021. 'Representations of Kingship: Epic Imagery in Kadamba Inscriptions. In pp. 45–71. In Mekhola Gomes, Digvijay Kumar Singh, and Meera Visvanathan. (Eds.). *Social Worlds of Premodern Transactions: Perspectives from Indian Epigraphy and History*. Delhi: Primus Books.

Sharma, R. S. (1958) 1980. *Sudras in Ancient India: A Social History of theLower Order Down to c. AD 600*. 2nd Rev. Edn. Delhi: Motilal Banarsidass.

_______. (1959) 1996. *Aspects of Political Ideas and Institutions in Ancient India*. Delhi: Motilal Banarsidass.

_______. (1965) 1980. *Indian Feudalism*. Madras: Macmillan.

_______. 1983. *Material Culture and Social Formations in Ancient India*.Delhi: Macmillan India.

_______. 1987. *Urban Decay in India (c. 300–c.1000)*. New Delhi: Munshiram Manoharlal.

_______. 'Material Milieu of Tantricism.' In R. S. Sharma. (Ed.). *Indian Society: Historical Probings (Essays in Memory of D. D. Kosambi)*. Delhi: People's Publishing House.

Sharma, R. S. and K. M. Shrimali. (Eds.). 1992. *A Comprehensive History of India. Vol. 4, Part 1 (AD 985–1206)*. New Delhi: People's Publishing House.

Shastri, Ajay Mitra. 1997. *Vakatakas: Sources and History*. Great Agesof Indian History. New Delhi: Aryan Books International.

Shaw, Julia. 2004. 'Nāga Sculptures in Sanchi's Archaeological Landscape: Buddhism, Vaiṣṇavism, and Local Agricultural Cults in Central India, First Century BCE to Fifth Century CE.' *Artibus Asiae*, 64, 1: 5–59.

Shaw, Julia, John Sutcliffe, Lindsay Lloyd-Smith, Jean-Luc Schewenninger and M. S. Chauhan. 2007. 'Ancient Irrigation and Buddhist History in Central India: Optically Stimulated Luminiscence Dates and Pollen Sequences from the Sanchi Dams.' *Asian Perspectives* 46, 1: 1666–201.

Shaw, Miranda. 1994. *Passionate Enlightenment: Women in Tantric Buddhism*. Princeton: Princeton University Press.

_______. 2006. *Buddhist Goddesses of India*. Princeton: Princeton University Press.

Shimada, Akira. 2013. *Early Buddhist Architecture in Context: The Great Stūpa at Amarāvatī (ca. 300 BCE – 300 CE)*. Leiden, Boston, Brill.

Shinde, Vasant. 1994. 'The Earliest Temple of Lajjagauri? The Recent Evidence from Padri in Gujarat.' *East and West* 44 (2–4): 481–85.

Shrimali, Krishna Mohan. 1987. *Agrarian Structure in Central India and the Northern Deccan (c. AD 300–500): A Study of Vakataka Inscriptions*. New Delhi: Munshiram Manoharlal.

Shinde, Vasant, Vagheesh M. Narasimhan, Nadin Rohland, Nick Patterson, Niraj Rai, David Reich et al. 2019. 'An Ancient Harappan Genome Lacks Ancestry from Steppe Pastoralists or Iranian Farmers,' *Cell* 176, 1–7.

Shinde, Vasant, Toshiki Osada and Manmohan Kumar. (Eds.). 2011. *Excavations at Farmana District Rohtak, Haryana, India 2006–2008*. Kyoto: Research Institute for Humanity and Nature.

Shulman, David. 2001. 'Poets and Patrons in Tamil Literature and Literary Legend'. In David Shulman, *The Wisdom of Poets: Studies in Tamil, Telugu, and Sanskrit*. New Delhi: Oxford University Press. pp. 63–102.

_______. 2016. *Tamil: A Biography*. Cambridge, MA: The Belknap Press of Harvard University Press.

Sidebotham, Steven E. 2011. *Berenike and the Ancient Maritime Spice Route* (The California World History Library). Berkeley, University of California Press.

Silva, Ronald. 2000. 'Developments of Ancient Cities in Sri Lanka: with special reference to Anurādhapura.' In R. A. L. H. Gunawardana, S. Pathmanathan, and M. Rohanadeera. (Eds.). *Reflections on a Heritage: Historical Scholarship in Premodern Sri Lanka*. Colombo: Central Culture Fund. pp. 49–81

Sims-Williams, N. and Joe Cribb. 1995–96. 'A New Bactrian Inscription of Kanishka the Great.' *Silk Road Art and Archaeology* 4: 75–142.

Singh, B. P. 2003. *Early Farming Communities of Kaimur: Excavations at Senuar.* 2 Vols. Jaipur: Publication Scheme.

Singh, Gurdip. 1971. 'The Indus Valley Culture.' *Archaeology and Physical Anthropology in Oceania* 6(2): 177–89.

Singh, H. N. 1979. 'Black and Red Ware: A Cultural Study.' In D. P. Agrawal and Dilip K. Chakrabarti. (Eds.). *Essays in Indian Protohistory*. pp. 267–83.

Singh, Purushottam. 1994. *Excavations at Narhan (1984–89)*. Varanasi: Banaras Hindu University and Delhi: B. R. Publishing Corpn.

Singh, S. B. 1979. *Archaeology of Panchala Region*. Delhi: Agam Kala Prakashan.

Singh, Ranjit Pratap. 2014. 'Agriculture.' In Dilip K. Chakrabarti and Makkhan Lal. (Eds.). *History of Ancient India*. Vol. 2: *Protohistoric Roots* (New Delhi: Vivekanand International Foundation and Aryan Books International). pp. 171–83.

Singh, Ravindra N. 2014. 'Metallurgy.' In Dilip K. Chakrabarti and Makkhan Lal. (Eds.). *History of Ancient India*. Vol. 2: *Protohistoric Roots* (New Delhi: Vivekanand International Foundation and Aryan Books International). pp. 212–34.

Singh, Snigdha. 2022. *Inscribing Identities, Proclaiming Piety: Exploring Recording Practices in Early Historic India*. Delhi: Primus Books.

Singh, Upinder. 1994. *Kings, Brahmanas and Temples in Orissa: An Epigraphic Study AD 300–1147*. New Delhi: Munshiram Manoharlal.

_______. (1996) 2023a. 'Sanchi: The History of the Patronage of an Ancient Buddhist Establishment.'In Upinder Singh, *The Idea of Ancient India*. Gurugram: Penguin. pp. 3–42.

_______. 1997–98. 'Texts on Stone: Understanding Asoka's Epigraph-Monuments and their Changing Contexts.' *Indian Historical Review* 24 (1–2): 1–19.

_______. (1999) 2006. *Ancient Delhi*. New Delhi: Oxford University Press.

_______. 2004. *The Discovery of Ancient India: Early Archaeologists and the Beginnings of Archaeology*. Delhi: Permanent Black.

_______. (2004) 2023b. 'Cults and Shrines in Early Historical Mathura (*c.*200 BC–AD 200).' *World Archaeology* 36(3): 378–98. In Upinder Singh, *The Idea of Ancient India*. Gurugram: Penguin. pp. 73–99.

_______. 2006. 'Early Medieval Orissa: The Data and the Debate.' In Martin Brandtner and Shishir Kumar Panda. (Eds.). *Interrogating History: Essays for Hermann Kulke*. New Delhi: Manohar.

_______2009. "Brahmana Settlements in Ancient and Early Medieval India." In B. D. Chattopadhyaya. (Ed.). *A Social History of Early India*. New Delhi: Pearson Longman (Project of History of Indian Science, Philosophy and Culture. Vol. 2, Part 5).

_______. 2010. Exile and Return: The Reinvention of Buddhism and Buddhist Sites in Modern India.' *South Asian Studies* 26, 2: 193–217.

_______. 2011. 'Introduction.' In Upinder Singh. (Ed.). *Rethinking Early Medieval India: A Reader*. New Delhi, Oxford University Press. pp. 1–44.

_______. 2014a. 'Varṇa and Jāti in ancient India: some questions.' In Kesavan Veluthat and Donald R. Davis Jr. (Eds.). *Irreverent History: Essays for M. G. S. Narayanan*. Delhi: Primus.

_______. 2014b. 'Gifts from Other Lands.' In Upinder Singh and Parul Pandya Dhar. (Eds.). *Asian Encounters: Exploring Connected Histories*. New Delhi, Oxford University Press.

_______. (2016) 2023c. 'Buddhism, Archaeology and the Nation: Nagarjunakonda, 1926–2006.' In Upinder Singh, *The Idea of Ancient India: Essays on Religion, Politics, and Archaeology*. Gurugram: Penguin. pp. 191–221.

_______. (2016) 2023d. 'Politics, Violence, and War in Kāmandaka's *Nītisāra*.' In Upinder Singh, *The Idea of Ancient India: Essays on Religion, Politics, and Archaeology*. Gurugram: Penguin. pp. 357–94

_______. (2016) 2023e. 'The Power of a Poet: Kingship, Empire, and War in Kālidāsa's Raghuvaṁśa.' In Upinder Singh, *The Idea of Ancient India: Essays on Religion, Politics, and Archaeology*. Gurugram: Penguin. pp. 395–421.

_______. 2017. *Political Violence in Ancient India*. Cambridge MA, Harvard University Press.

_______. 2021b. *Ancient India: Culture of Contradictions*. New Delhi: Aleph.

_______. 2022a. 'The State, violence and resistance.' In Hermann Kulke and Bhairabi Prasad Sahu. (Eds.). *The Routledge Handbook of the State in Premodern India*. Routledge. Chap. 4. pp. 101–15.

_______. 2022b. 'Inscribing power on the realm: royal ideology and religious policy in India, *c.* 200 BCE–300 CE.' Amsterdam, Royal Netherlands Academy of Arts and Science (KNAW) (available online).

Singh, Upinder. (Ed.). 2011. *Rethinking Early Medieval India: A Reader*. New Delhi, Oxford University Press.

_______. (Ed.). 2021. *The World of India's First Archaeologist: Letters from Alexander Cunningham to J. D. M. Beglar*. New Delhi: Oxford University Press.

Singh, Upinder and Parul Pandya Dhar. (Eds.). 2014. *Asian Encounters: Exploring Connected Histories*. New Delhi, Oxford University Press,

Sinha Kapur, Nandini. 2002. *State formation in Rajasthan: Mewar during the Seventh–Fifteenth Centuries*. New Delhi: Manohar.

Sinha, B. P. and Sita Ram Roy. 1969. *Vaisali Excavations 1958–1962*. Patna.

Sinha, Kanad. 2021. *From Dāśrājña to Kurukṣetra: Making of a Historical Tradition*. New Delhi: 2012.

_______. 2022. 'The city, the Kāma culture, and Daṇḍin: shades and varieties of urban life in the Daśakumāracarita. In Urvi Mukhopadhyay and Suchandra Ghosh. (Eds.). 2022. *Exploring South Asian Urbanity*. London and New York: Routledge. pp. 152–76.

Sinha, Prakash. 1989. 'Economic and Subsistence Activities at Baghor III, India: A Microwear Study.' In J. M. Kenoyer. (Ed.). *Old Problemsand New Perspectives in the Archaeology of South Asia*. Wisconsin.

Sircar, D. C. 1952. 'Some Kara-Sasanas of Ancient Orissa.' *Journal of the Royal Asiatic Society*. pp. 4–10.

_______. 1965. *Indian Epigraphy*. Delhi: Motilal Banarsidass.

_______. 1966a. *Indian Epigraphical Glossary*. Delhi: Motilal Banarsidass.

_______. 1966b. 'Ahraura Inscription of Asoka.' *Epigraphia Indica* 36: 239–48.

_______. 1969a. *Landlordism and Tenancy in Ancient and Early Medieval India as Revealed by Epigraphical Records*. Lucknow: University of Lucknow.

_______. 1969b. *Ancient Malwa and the Vikramāditya Tradition*. New Delhi, Munshiram Manoharlal.

_______. 1973. *The Shakta Pithas*. 2nd Rev. Edn. Delhi: Motilal Banarsidass.

Sivaramamurti, C. (1974) 1994. *Nataraja in Art, Thought and Literature*. Rep. Edn. New Delhi: Publications Division, Ministry of Information and Broadcasting.

Sjoberg, Gideon. 1964. 'The Rise and Fall of Cities: A Theoretical Perspective.' In Nels Anderson. (Ed.). *Urbanism and Urbanization*. Lieden: E. J. Brill.

Skilling, Peter. 2008. 'New Discoveries from South India: The life of the Buddha at Phanigiri, Andhra Pradesh.' *Arts Asiatique* 2008, 63: 96–118.

_______. 2011. 'Buddhism and the Circulation of Ritual. In Pierre-Yves Manguin, A. Mani, and Geoff Wade, *Early Interactions between South and Southeast Asia. Reflections on Cross-Cultural Exchange*. New Delhi, Manohar. pp. 371–84.

_______. 2012. 'Introduction.' In Peter Skilling, Jason A. Carbine and Claudio Cicuzza. (Eds.). *How Theravāda is Theravāda: Exploring Buddhist Identities*. Chiang Mai: Silkworm Books.

Smith, Brian K. 1994. *Classifying the Universe: The Ancient Indian Varna System and the Origins of Caste*. New York and Oxford: Oxford University Press.

Smith, Frederick M. 1991. 'Indra's Curse, Varuna's Noose, and the Suppression of the Woman in the Vedic Srauta Ritual.' In Julia Le slie. (Ed.). *Roles and Rituals for Hindu Women*. Rutherford: Fairleigh Dickinson University Press. pp. 17–45.

Smith, Monica L. (Ed.). (2003) 2010. *The Social Construction of Ancient Cities*. Washington D. C.: Smithsonian Books, Introduction.

Sontheimer, Günther-Dietz. 2022. 'The *Vana* and the *Kṣetra*: The Tribal Background of Some Famous Cults.' In Hermann Kulke and Bhairabi Prasad Sahu. (Eds.). *The Routledge Handbook of the State in Premodern India*. London and New York: Routledge. pp. 81–100.

Soundararajan, K. V. 1994. *Kaveripattinam Excavations 1963–73 (A PortCity on the Tamilnadu Coast)*. Memoirs of the Archaeological Surveyof India No. 90. New Delhi: Archaeological Survey of India.

________. (Ed.). with R. Subrahmanyam et al. 2006. *Nagarjunakonda (1954–60)*. Vol. II (The Historical Period). New Delhi: Archaeological Survey of India.

Southall, Aidan W. 1953. *Alur Society: A Study in Process and Types of Domination*. Cambridge: W. Heiffer & Sons.

Spencer, George. 1976. 'The Politics of Plunder: The Cholas in Eleventh-Century Ceylon.' *Journal of Asian Studies* 35, 3: 405–19.

________. 1983. 'The Politics of Expansion: The Chola conquest of Sri Lanka and Srivijaya.'Madras: New Era Publications.

Spink, Walter M. 2006. *Ajanta: History and Development*. 3 Vols. Lei den, Boston: E. J. Brill.

Spooner, D. B. 1912–13. *Mr. Ratan Tata's Excavations at Pataliputra: Annual Report of the Archaeological Survey of India*. pp. 53–86.

________. 1913–14. 'Excavations at Basarh, 1911–12.' *Annual Report of the Archaeological Survey of India*. Delhi: Archaeological Survey ofIndia. pp. 98–185.

Srinivasan, Doris M. 1989. 'Vaishnava Art and Iconography at Mathura.' In Srinivasan. (Ed.). *Mathura: The Cultural Heritage*. New Delhi: Manohar. pp. 383–92.

Srinivasan, Sharada. 2004. 'Shiva as Cosmic "Dancer": On Pallava Origins for the Nataraja Bronze.' In Elisabeth A. Bacus and Nayanjot Lahiri. (Eds.). *The Archaeology of Hinduism: World Archaeology* 36(3): 432–50.

Srivastava, K. M. 1996. *Excavations at Piprahwa and Ganwaria*. Memoirs of the Archaeological Survey of India No. 94. New Delhi: Archaeological Survey of India.

Staal, Fritz. 2003. 'The Science of Language.' In Gavin Flood. (Ed.). *The Blackwell Companion to Hinduism*. Blackwell.

Stargardt, Janice. 2021. 'Sri Ksetra, 3rd century BCE to 6th century CE: Indianization, Synergies. Creation.' In Peter C. Bisschop and Elizabeth A. Cecil. (Eds.). 2021. *Primary Sources and Asian Pasts*. Berlin/Boston: de Gruyter. pp. 220–65.

Stark, Miriam T. 2021. 'Landscapes, Linkages, and Luminiscence: First-Millennium CE Environmental and Social Change in Mainland Southeast Asia. In Peter C. Bisschop and Elizabeth A. Cecil. (Eds.). *Primary Sources and Asian Pasts*. Berlin/Boston: de Gruyter. pp. 184–219.

Stein, Burton. (1975) 1976. 'The State and the Agrarian Order in Medieval South Asia: A Historiographical Critique.' In Burton Stein. (Ed.). *Essays on South India*. Honolulu: University of Hawaii. pp. 64–91.

________. 1980. *Peasant State and Society in Medieval South India*. Delhi:Oxford University Press.

Stoneking, Mark. 'Archaic Genomes and the Peopling of South Asia.' In Gwen Robbins Schug and Subhash R. Walimbe. (Eds.). *A Companion to South Asia in the Past*. West Sussex: Wiley Blackwell. Chap. 4.

Stoneman, Richard. 2019. *The Greek Experience of India: From Alexander to the Indo-Greeks*. Princeton and Oxford: Princeton University Press.

Strauch, Ingo. 2016. 'Indian Inscriptions from Cave Hoq at Socotra.' In Boussac, Marie-Françoise, Jean-François Salles, and Jean-Baptiste Yon. (Eds.). 2016. *Ports of the Indian Ocean*. Delhi: Primus Books. pp. 79–98.

Strauch, Ingo. (Ed.). 2012. *Foreign Sailors on Socotra: The Inscriptions and Drawings from the Cave Hoq*. (Vergleichende Studien zu Antike und Orient 3), Bremen: Hempen Verlag.

Strong, John S. 1983. *The Legend of King Asoka: A Study and Translation of the Asokavadana*. Princeton: Princeton University Press.

________. 2004. *Relics of the Buddha*. Princeton and Oxford: Princeton University Press

Subbarayalu, Y. 1982. 'The Chola State.' *Studies in History* 4(2): 265–306.

________. 2002. 'State and Society During the Chola period.' In R. Champakalakshmi, Kesavan Veluthat and T. R. Venugopalan. (Eds.). *State and Society in Pre-Modern South India*. Thrissur: Cosmo Books. pp. 84–95.

________. 2009a. 'A Note on the Navy of the Chola State.' In Hermann Kulke, K. Kesavapany, and Vijay Sakhuja. (Eds.). *Nagapattinam to Suvarnadwipa: Reflections on the Chola Naval Expeditions to Southeast Asia*. Singapore, Institute of Southeast Asian Studies. pp. 91–95.

________. 2009b. 'Anjuvannam: A Maritime Trade Guild of Medieval Times. In Hermann Kulke, K. Kesavapany, and Vijay Sakhuja. (Eds.). *Nagapattinam to Suvarnadwipa: Reflections on the Chola Naval Expeditions to Southeast Asia*. Singapore, Institute of Southeast Asian Studies. pp. 158–167.

________. 2018. 'A Review of the Coins and Currency System of Early Historic Tamiḻakam.' In Manu Y. Devadevan. (Ed.). *Clio and her Descendants: Essays for Kesavan Veluthat*. Delhi: Primus Books. pp. 489–503.

Subbarayappa, B. V. 2013. *Science in India: A Historical Perspective*. New Delhi: Rupa.

Sundara, A. 1975. *The Early Chamber Tombs of South India*. Delhi: University Publishers.

Suresh, R. 2004. *Symbols of Trade: Roman and Pseudo-Roman Objects Found in India*. New Delhi: Manohar.

Suryanarayan, Akshyeta, Oliver Edward Craig, Miriam Cubas, and Ravindra Nath Singh. 2022. 'Lipid residues in pottery from the Indus Civilsation in northwest India.' *Journal of Archaeological Science* 125; https://doi.org/10.1016/j.jas.2020.105291

Sutherland, G. H. 1992. *Yaksha in Hinduism and Buddhism: The Disguises of the Demon*. New Delhi: Manohar.

Tandon, Pankaj. 2006. 'A Gold Coin of the Pāla Dharmapāla.' *The Numismatic Chronicle*, 166: 327–33.

________. *COININDIA: The Virtual Museum of Indian Coins*. Available at https://coinindia.com.

Tewari, Rakesh. 2014. 'The Beginning of Iron.' In Chakrabarti and Lal. (Eds.). *History of Ancient India*. Vol. 2: *Protohistoric Roots*. New Delhi: Vivekanand International Foundation and Aryan Books International. pp. 567–91.

Tewari, Rakesh and R. K. Srivastava (with contributions by A. Saxena, B, Seth, H. J. Tobschall, I. B. Singh, K. K. Singh, K. S. Saraswat, N. S. Tyagi, P. P. Joglekar, Randall Law, S. C. Yadava, S. Krumm, S. R. Dubey, and V. von Seekendorff). 2022. 'Excavations at Lahuradewa: 2001–92, 2002–03, 2004–05, 2005–06.' Part 1 and 2. *Pragdhara 27–28* (Joint Issue). *Journal of the U.P. State Archaeology Department*.

Talbot, Cynthia. 2016. *The Last Hindu Emperor: Prithviraj Chauhan and the Indian Past, 1200–2000*. Cambridge: Cambridge University Press.

Tarling, Nicholas. (Ed.). (1992) 1999. *The Cambridge History of Southeast Asia*. Vol. 1: *From early times to c. 1500*. Cambridge, Cambridge University Press.

Tartakov, Gary Michael. 1997. *The Durga Temple at Aihole: A Historiographical Study*. Delhi: Oxford University Press.

Thapar, Romila. (1963) 1987. *Asoka and the Decline of the Mauryas*. 7th rep.Delhi: Oxford University Press.

_______. 1984. *The Mauryas Revisit. (Ed.)*. Sakharam Ganesh Deuskar Lectures on Indian History. Centre for Studies in Social Science. Calcutta: K. P. Bagchi & Co.

_______. 2000. 'Society and Historical Consciousness: The *Itihasa-purana* Tradition.' In *Cultural Pasts: Essays in Early Indian History*. New Delhi: Oxford University Press. pp. 123–54.

_______. (2005) 2008. *Somanatha: The Many Voices of a History*. **Gurgaon:** Penguin.

Thaplyal, K. K. 1996. *Guilds in Ancient India: A Study of Guild Organi zation in Northern India and Western Deccan from circa 600 BC to circa 600 AD*. New Delhi: New Age International Ltd. Publishers.

_______. 2009. 'A New Aśokan Inscrption from Ratanpurwa.' *Jñāna-Pravāha*. Monograph 1.

Thomas, P. K. and P. P. Joglekar. 1995. 'Faunal Studies in Archaeology.' *Memoirs of the Geological Society of India* 32: 496–514.

Thomas, P. K., P. P. Joglekar, Arati Deshpande-Mukherjee, and S. J. Pawankar. 1995. 'Harappan Subsistence Patterns with Special Reference to Shikarpur, A Harappan Site in Gujarat.' *Man and Environment* 22(2): 33–41.

Tomber, Roberta. (2008) 2012. *Indo-Roman Trade: From Pots to Pepper*. London, Bristol Classical Press.

Tournier, Vincent. 2018. 'A Tide of Merit: Royal Donors, Tāmraparṇīya Monks, and the Buddha's Awakening in 5th–6th-century Āndhradeśa.' *Indo-Iranian Journal* 57, 20–96.

Trainor, Kevin. 1997. *Relics, Ritual, and Representation in Buddhism: Rematerializing the Sri Lankan Theravāda Tradition*. Cambridge: Cambridge University Press.

Trautmann, Thomas R. 1971. *Kautilya and the Arthasastra: A Statistical Investigation of the Authorship and Evolution of the Text*. Leiden: E. J. Brill.

_______. 2004. *Aryans and British India*. New Delhi: Yoda Press.

_______. 2015. *Elephants and Kings: An Environmental History*. Ranikhet: Permanent Black in association with Ashoka University.

_______. (Ed.). 2005. *The Aryan Debate*. Oxford in India Readings. Debates in Indian History and Society. New Delhi: Oxford University Press.

Tripathi, Vibha. 1984–85. 'From Copper to Iron—A Transition.' *Puratattva* 15: 75–79.

_______. 2002. 'The Protohistoric Cultures of the Ganga Valley.' In Truschke, Audrey. 2021. *The Language of History: Sanskrit Narratives of Muslim Pasts*. Gurgaon: Penguin Allan Lane.

Tsitsiridis, Stavros. 2011 'Greek Mime in the Roman Empire (P. Oxy. 413: *Charition* and *Moicheutria*).' *Logeion* 1: 184–232.

Tyagi, Jaya. 2008. *Engendering the Early Household: Brahmanical Precepts in the Early Gṛhyasūtras, Middle of the First Millennium B. C. E.* New Delhi: Orient Longman.

Ulrich, Katherine E. 2007. 'Food Fights: Buddhist, Hindu, and Jaina Dietary Polemics in South India.' *History of Religions* 46, 3: 228–61.

van Buitenan, J. A. B. 1981. *The Bhagavadgita in the Mahabharata*. Bilingual Edn. Chicago and London: University of Chicago Press.

van Kooij, Karel Rijk. 1972. *Worship of the Goddess According to the Kalikapurana*. Part 1. Leiden: E. J. Brill.

van Leur, J. C. (1934) 1955. *Indonesian Trade and Society: Essays in Asian Social and Economic History*. Translated from Dutch. The Hague: Bandung.

Varma, R. K., V. D. Mishra, and J. N. Pal. 2014. 'Madhya Pradesh and Adjoining Uttar Pradesh: Palaeolithic Cultures of the Belan and Son Valleys. In Dilip K. Chakrabarti and Makkhan Lal. (Eds.). *History of Ancient India*. Vol. 1: *Prehistoric Roots*. New Delhi: Vivekanand International Foundation and Aryan Books International. pp. 140–62.

Veluthat, Kesavan. 1993. *The Political Structure of Early Medieval South India*. New Delhi: Orient Longman.

Verardi, Giovanni. 2018. *The Gods and the Heretics: Crisis and Ruin of Indian Buddhism*; Appendices by Federica Barba. New Delhi: Aditya Prakashan and Buenos Aires: Fundación Bodhiyāna, 2018.

Wagle, Narendra. 1966. *Society at the Time of the Buddha*. Bombay: Popular Prakashan.

von Hinüber, Oskar. 2016. 'Buddhist Texts and Buddhist Images: New Evidence from Kanaganahalli (Karnataka/India).' *Annual Report of the International Research Institute of Advanced Buddhology at Soka University* 19, 7–20.

Wakankar, V. S. 2005. *Painted Rock-shelters of India*. Bhopal: Director, Archaeology, Archives and Museums, Government of Madhya Pradesh.

Wang, Bangwei. 2002. 'New Evidence on Wang Xuance's Missions to India.' In N. N. Vohra. (Ed.). *India and East Asia: Culture and Society*. Delhi: Shipra Publications.

Warder, A. K. 1972–2004. *Indian Kavya Literature*. 7 Vols. Delhi: Motilal Banarsidass.

Wedage, Oshan et al. 2019. 'Microliths in the South Asian rainforest -45-4 ka: New insights from Fa-Hien Lena Cave, Sri Lanka.' *PLoS ONE* 14 (10): e0222606.

_______. 2019a. 'Specialized rainforest hunting by *Homo Sapiens* 45,000 years ago.' *Nature Communications* 10.

Verma, B. S. 2011. *Antichak Excavations – 2 (1971–1981)*. New Delhi, Archaeological Survey of India.

Wheeler, R. E. M. 1947. 'Harappan Chronology and the Rig Veda.' *Ancient India* 3: 78–82.

Visvanathan, Meera. 2021. In Mekhola Gomes, Digvijay Kumar Singh, and Meera Visvanathan. (Eds.). *Social Worlds of Premodern Transactions: Perspectives from Indian Epigraphy and History*. Delhi: Primus Books. pp. 1–24.

Whitaker, Jarrod L. 2011. *Strong Arms and Drinking Strength: Masculinity, Violence, and the Body in Ancient India*. Oxford, New York: Oxford University Press.

Wijayaratne, Mohan. 1990. *Buddhist Monastic Life According to the Texts of the Theravada Tradition*. Claude Grangier and Steven Collins. (Trans. from French). Cambridge: Cambridge University Press.

_______. 2001. *Buddhist Nuns: The Birth and Development of a Woman'sMonastic Order*. Colombo: Wisdom.

Williams, Joanna. 1982. The *Art of Gupta India: Empire and Province*. Princeton, New Jersey: Princeton University Press.

Wink, Andre. 1999. *Al-Hind: The Making of the Indo-Islamic World*. Vol. 1: *Early Medieaval India and the Expansion of Islam 7th–11th Centuries*; Vol. 2: *Al-Hind: The Slave Kings and the Islamic Conquest 11th–13th Centuries*. New Delhi: Oxford University Press. New Delhi: Oxford University Press.

Williams, Michael. 2003. *Deforesting the Earth: From Prehistory to Global Crisis*. Chicago and London: University of Chicago Press.

_______. 1997a. 'The Development of the Vedic Canon and its Schools: The Social and Political Milieu.' In Michael Witzel. (Ed.). *Inside the Texts, Beyond the Texts: New Approaches to the Study of the Vedas*. Harvard Oriental Series Opera Minora. Vol. 2. Cambridge. Department of Sanskrit and Indian Studies, Harvard University. pp. 257–345.

_______. 1997b. 'Rgvedic History: Poets, Chieftains and Polities.' InGeorge Erdosy. (Ed.). *The Indo-Aryans of South Asia*. pp. 307–52.

_______. (Ed.). 1995. 'Early Sanskritization Origins and Development of the Kuru State.' *The Electronic Journal of Vedic Studies* (1–4): 1–26.

Wolters, O. W. 1982. *History, Culture, and Region in Southeast Asian Perspectives*. Singapore, Institute of Southeast Asian Studies.

Wujastyk, Dominik. (1998) 2001. *The Roots of Ayurveda: Selections from Sanskrit Medical Writings*. New Delhi: Penguin Books.

Yang, Bin. 2011. 'The Rise and Fall of Cowrie Shells.' *Journal of World History* 22, 1: 1–25.

Yoffee, Norman. 2005. *Myths of the Archaic State: Evolution of the Earliest Cities, States, and Civilizations*. Cambridge: Cambridge University Press.

Zeuner, Frederick E. 1963. *A History of Domesticated Animals*. New York: Harper Collins.

Zin, Monika. 2018. *The Kanaganahalli Stūpa: An Analysis of the 60 Massive Slabs Covering the Dome*. New Delhi: Aryan Books International.

_______. 2018a. 'Kanaganahalli in Sātavāhana art and Buddhism.' *Journal of the International Association of Buddhist Studies* 41: 537–55.

_______. 2018b. *The Kanaganahalli Stūpa: An Analysis of the 60 Massive Slabs Covering the Dome*. New Delhi: Aryan Books.

Zvelebil, K. 1973. *The Smile of Murugan: On Tamil Literature of South India*. Leiden: E. J. Brill.

_______. 1974. *Tamil Literature*. Jan Honda. (Ed.). *A History of Indian Literature*. Vol. X. Fasc. 1. Wiesbaden: Otto Harrassowitz.

_______. 1977. 'Beginnings of Bhakti in South India.' *Temenos* 13: 223–59.

Zysk, Kenneth G. 1991. *Asceticism and Healing in Ancient India: Medicine in the Buddhist Monastery*. New York and Bombay: Oxford University Press.

Index

M

N

Credits

Pearson India wishes to thank all authors and copyright holders. Every effort has been made to obtain permission from all copyright holders. However, in case of any oversight in this list the publisher would be grateful to be notified of corrections that should be incorporated in the next reprint.

Photograph Credits (Used with permission)

Abbreviations

American Institute of Indian Studies (AIIS)
Archaeological Survey of India, New Delhi (ASI)
Central Antiquity Collection, Purana Qila, ASI (CAC) Chhatrapati Shivaji Maharaj Vastu Sangrahalaya (CSMVS)
Indor Khera Archaeological Project (IKAP)
Kerala Council for Historical Research (KCHR)
NM, New Delhi (NM)

Cover images

Front: Sanchi Stupa no. 1, relief on Northern Gateway. Courtesy: Osmund Bopearachchi
Author image: ©Raghav Tankha

Introduction

2 (chapter opening) Auspicious Emblem with Five Revelers, Courtesy: Purchase, Bequest of Nina Bunshaft, by exchange, and funds from various donors, 2005 (Accessed from https://www.metmuseum.org on 8th May 2023) ; **3** (chapter opening) Plaque with a Dancer and a Vina Player India, 1st century BCE, Courtesy: Samuel Eilenberg Collection, Gift of Samuel Eilenberg, 1987 (Accessed from https://www.metmuseum.org on 8th May 2023); **5** Ramanagara rocks, ©Tanmay Haldar; **7** Brahmaputra river ©Ms. Rima Kalita; Harappan writing on seal—Egyptian hieroglyphics—Mesopotamian cuneiform, ©ASI; R. C. Majumdar ©Krishna Sen; **12** ©Meera Kosambi; **15** Plaque with a dancer and a vina player India, 1st century BCE, Courtesy: Samuel Eilenberg Collection, Gift of Samuel Eilenberg, 1987 (Accessed from https://www.metmuseum.org on 8th May 2023)

Chapter 1

17 (chapter opening) A 12th-century sandstone statue of an *apsara* from Madhya Pradesh, India, Courtesy: Gift of Florence and Herbert Irving, 2015, 1987 (Accessed from https://www.metmuseum.org on 10th April 2023); **19** Ancient palm leaf manuscripts, image 1, ©NM | A 12th century manuscript of the Prajnaparamita, ©Mudit Trivedi; **25** ©ASI; **41** ©ASI; **42** Alexander Cunningham ©ASI | JDM Beglar, Courtesy: Leiden University Libraries, Collection Kern Institute; **43** H. D. Sankalia ©B. R. Publishing Corporation, Daryaganj, Delhi, used with permission; **45** ©Alok Tripathi, reproduced with permission of Under Water Archaeology Wing, ASI; **48** ©ASI; **50** ©ASI; **51** J. F. Fleet, ©ASI; D. C. Sircar, ©Rajat Sanyal; **56** ©ASI; **57** ©AIIS; **59** ©ASI; **60–63, 65–66** ©NM; **67** Courtesy: Indian Museum, Kolkata; **69** A 12th-century sandstone statue of an *apsara* from Madhya Pradesh, India, Courtesy: Gift of Florence and Herbert Irving, 2015, 1987 (Accessed from https://www.metmuseum.org on 10th April 2023)

Chapter 2

70 (chapter opening) ©Aditya Arya; **71** Reproduced with permission of Erwin Neumayer; ©**78** ©Arun Sonakia; **85** ©Aditya Arya; **87–88** ©Aditya Arya; **89** ©Shanti Pappu, Sharma Centre for Heritage Education; **91–92, 100** ©Aditya Arya; **104** Reproduced with permission of Erwin Neumayer; **105** ©Oshan Wedage; **106–111** Reproduced with permission of Erwin Neumayer; **113** Reproduced with permission of Erwin Neumayer

Chapter 3

128 ©Aditya Arya; **132** ©U.P. State Archaeology Department; **133** ©U.P. State Archaeology Department; **134–135, 137** ©ASI; **146** ©Aditya Arya

Chapter 4

156 (chapter opening) ©D. P. Sharma; **157** (chapter opening) ©Aditya Arya; **158–161** ©ASI; **165**, **169** ©Aditya Arya; **172–175** ©Mohammad Rafique Mughal; **177–179** (B&W images) ©ASI; **179–180** ©Aditya Arya; **181–182** ©ASI; **184** Terracotta ©CM Dixon/Heritage Images | The Print Collector/Alamy | Rhino (Assam) ©Upinder Singh; **186–187** ©Aditya Arya; **188** Chert blades—stone gamesmen ©Aditya Arya | Copper arrowhead—celt—stone sealing—seal ©ASI; **189–191** ©ASI; **193** ©Aditya Arya; **199–200** ©ASI; **201** ©D. P. Sharma; **202** ©ASI; **203** Terracottas: Figurine—Games and Dice ©Aditya Arya | Perforated Bird-shaped rattle—bull with moveable head—cart ©ASI; **208** ©ASI; **209** ©Darshan Kumar/www.shutterstock.com; **213** ©Aditya Arya

Chapter 5

214 (chapter opening) ©D. P. Sharma; **215** (chapter opening) ©ASI; **235** ©Upinder Singh; **249** ©D. P. Sharma; **251**, **256–257**, **259**, **267**©ASI; **268** ©Aditya Arya; **269–270** ©ASI; **271** ©Aditya Arya; **272–273** ©ASI; **276** ©Aditya Arya; **278–279** ©Ravi Korisettar; **282** ©ASI; **285** ©Srikumar Menon; **286** ©Rammathot Khongreiwo; **287** ©ASI; **288** ©Aditya Arya; **292–293** ©K. Rajan; **294–295** ©ASI; **295** Megalithic Anthromorph ©K. Rajan; **296–297** ©Kathleen Morrison; **301** ©ASI

Chapter 6

302–303 (chapter opening) ©NM; **310** ©Aditya Arya; **312, 315** ©NM; **321** Courtesy: Indian Museum, Kolkata; **324** ©Osmund Bopearachchi; **329** ©Abdul Rashid Lone; **331** ©ASI; **332** ©Aditya Arya; **333** ©Mudit Trivedi; **334** Courtesy: Viren Desai/Alamy Stock Photo | Casper1774 Studio/www.shutterstock.com; **335** ©ASI; **336** ©Aditya Arya; **337** ©ASI; **338** ©Aditya Arya; **375** ©NM

Chapter 7

377 (chapter opening) ©Upinder Singh; **383** ©ASI; **389** ©Vijay Tankha; **392–393** ©Upinder Singh; **396** ©ASI; **397–399** ©Mudit Trivedi; **401** ©Upinder Singh; **404, 409** ©ASI; **411** ©Aditya Arya; **412** ©Vijay Tankha; **413** ©ASI; **414** ©ASI; **415–416** ©ASI; **417** ©Upinder Singh; **418** *stupa* no.1, Sanchi ©Upinder Singh | Didarganj *yakshi* SCHROEDER Alain/hemis.fr, Hemis/Alamy; **419** Lohanipur torso ©AIIS | Carved ring stones ©ASI; **420** (left image) ©ASI | (right image) ©Upinder Singh; **423** ©Upinder Singh

Chapter 8

424 ©NM; **425** ©Goutam Dey; **427** ©Central Cultural Fund, Sri Lanka, Courtesy: Osmund Bopearachchi; **431** ©NM; **432** ©Aditya Arya; **435** ©NM; **436–437** Courtesy: Late Paul Bernard; **438** ©NM; **440** ©NM; **442** Kanishka image from Mat ©Aditya Arya | Copper and gold coins ©NM; **443–444** ©NM; **447, 449** ©Upinder Singh; **450–452** ©NM; **460–462** ©ASI; **463** ©IKAP; **464** ©ASI; **465–466** ©Goutam Dey; **473** ©K. Rajan; **488** ©Ingo Strauch; **492–493** ©KCHR **508** ©Aditya Arya; **509** Mathura: sandstone Nagaraja from Chhargaon ©Aditya Arya | terracotta 'goddess' figurine ©ASI; **510** ©ASI; **514** ©Upinder Singh; **516** Courtesy: Osmund Bopearachchi; **518, 520** ©ASI; **523** Courtesy of late Paul Bernard; **528** ©ASI; **531–532** Courtesy: Indian Museum, Kolkata; **533** ©Aditya Arya; **534** Buddha image ©Upinder Singh | *stupa* with spoked-wheel plan ©ASI; **535** ©Upinder Singh; **536** ©Naman P. Ahuja; **537** ©Robert Arlt; **538–539** ©Upinder Singh; **540, 542** ©ASI; **543** ©Upinder Singh; **546** ©ASI; **547** ©AIIS; **548** Kayama elephant—Langudi ©Upinder Singh | Gandhara sculpture, Courtesy: ©AIIS; **549** ©AIIS; **550** ©ASI; **551** ©Aditya Arya; **552** Nagaraja ©Aditya Arya | seated *tirthankara*—Surya—Karttikeya ©AIIS; **553** Terracotta female figurine, Mathura ©ASI | Terracotta plaques—Chandraketugarh ©Goutam Dey; **558** Tiger striding out of Bandhavgarh cave ©Aditya Arya | Cave 4—Carvings of animals and hunters in Cave 4 ©Upinder Singh; **561** ©Goutam Dey

Chapter 9

563 (chapter opening) ©NM; **563** (chapter opening) Sigiriya paintings: Single female holding flower ©Upinder Singh; **565** ©ASI; **567** ©NM; **569** ©ASI; **570–571** ©NM; **573** ©Aditya Arya; **574** ©NM; **577** ©Hans Bakker; **581** ©Upinder Singh; **590, 592** Brahmi script, Allahabad *prashasti* ©ASI | Tiger slayer coin ©NM; **595** ©Aditya Arya; **606** ©ASI; **609** ©Aditya Arya; **610** Gaja–Lakshmi ©ASI | Ekamukhalinga from Khoh ©Aditya Arya; **611** ©AIIS; **614–615** ©ASI; **616** ©Upinder Singh; **620, 623** ©Aditya Arya; **624** Bhumara and Nachna-Kuthara temples—Lakshmana temple—detail of doorway—Nachna-Kuthara ©AIIS | Bhitargaon brick temple ©ASI; **625–627** ©Aditya Arya; **628** ©Benoy Behl; **629** Buddha figures on stone slab ©ASI | Buddha head (Mathura) ©Aditya Arya; **630–631** ©Upinder Singh; **632** Buddha seated in the preaching—standing Buddha ©Aditya Arya | Dancer and musicians, Aurangabad cave ©ASI; **633** ©Upinder Singh; **634** ©Hans Bakker; **635** Stucco head from Taxila ©AIIS | Mirpur Khas: seated Buddhas and devotee, Courtesy of the Trustees of the CSMVS; **636** Terracotta images of Ganga and Yamuna ©Aditya Arya | Aukana Buddha ©Upinder Singh; **647** ©Upinder Singh

Chapter 10

650 (chapter opening) ©NM; **651** (chapter opening) Child Saint Sambandar, Courtesy: Purchase, Lila Acheson Wallace and Doris Wiener Gifts, 2010 (Accessed from https://www.metmuseum.org on 8th May 2023); **661** ©ASI; **664** ©Bharat Kala Bhavan, Varanasi Courtesy: AIIS; **665–666** ©NM; **668** ©Aditya Arya; **672** ©Upinder Singh; **676–677** ©NM; **679** ©Aditya Arya; **680** ©NM; **682–683, 697** ©Pankaj Tandon; **706** ©Upinder Singh; **714** the *stupa* at Borobudur (Java) ©ASI | Vishnu temple, Angkor Vat—Cambodia: *apsara* reliefs, view of temple, Mahabharata relief, ©K. P. Shankaran; **719–721** ©Upinder Singh; **722** Spiti valley (HP): Key Monastery—Tabo Monastery ©Raghav Tankha | Clay statues in Assembly hall—Alchi, Ladakh: painting of shrine ©Benoy Behl; **723** ©Benoy Behl; **724** ©Jost Gippert; **725** ©ASI; **726** ©AIIS; **727** ©Srikumar Menon; **728–729** ©Kanika Kishore Saxena; **732–733** ©Upinder Singh; **734** ©Aditya Arya; **736** Kamakhya Temple, Assam ©Mazur Travel/www.shutterstock.com | Mahishasuramardini: Sivadol temple, Sibsagar—Virupaksha temple, Pattadakal—Nataraja temple, Chidambaram ©ASI; **737** Hirapur (Odisha): Chaunsat Yogini temple—yoginis ©Upinder Singh | Sapta-Matrika sculpture ©Aditya Arya; **739** ©Aditya Arya; **741** Karaikkal Ammaiyar, Shaiva Saint, Courtesy: Purchase, Edward J. Gallagher Jr. Bequest, in memory of his father, Edward Joseph Gallagher, his mother, Ann Hay Gallagher, and his son, Edward Joseph Gallagher III, 1982 (Accessed from https://www.metmuseum.org on 8th May 2023); **745–746, 750** ©ASI; **751** Khajuraho temple ©Aditya Arya | Khajuraho temple ©ASI; **752–753** ©AIIS; **754–756** ©Aditya Arya; **757–759** ©ASI; **760–761** ©Srikumar Menon; **762–763, 765–766** ©ASI; **767–768** ©Upinder Singh; **770–772** ©ASI; **773** ©Aditya Arya; **775** ©Alka Arvind Patel; **778** Child Saint Sambandar, Courtesy: Purchase, Lila Acheson Wallace and Doris Wiener Gifts, 2010 (Accessed from https://www.metmuseum.org on 8th May 2023)

Literary Credits

Chapter 1

30: Excerpt courtesy: ©Murcott, Susan. 1991: 81, 21, *The First Buddhist Women: Translations and Commentaries on the Therigatha*. Berkeley, California: Parallax Press, used with permission; **36** Excerpt courtesy: ©Cowell, E. B. and F. W. Thomas. (Trans.). 1993. *The Harsha-Charita of Bana*. Delhi: Motilal Banarsidass. Pathak, V. S. 1966. Ancient Historians of India: *A Study in Historical Biographies*. Bombay: Asia Publishing House; **39** Excerpt courtesy: *Alberuni's India*. London: Kegan Paul, Trench, Trübner & Co. 1910. Electronic reproduction. Vol. 1 and 2. New York, N.Y. Columbia University Libraries, 2006.

Chapter 5

52–54 Salomon, Richard. 1998. *Indian Epigraphy: A Guide to the Study of Inscriptions in Sanskrit, Prakrit, and the other Indo-Aryan Languages*. New Delhi: Munshiram Manoharlal; **222, 230, 239, 242** Excerpts courtesy: ©Oxford University Press, reproduced with permission of the Licensor through PLSclear; **244** Excerpt courtesy: *The Early Upanisads Annotated Text and Translation*, Patrick Olivelle ©Oxford University Press 2023, reproduced with permission of the Licensor through PLSclear; **246** Excerpt courtesy: ©Renou, Louis. *Vedic India*. Delhi: Indological Book House, 1971: 23–24.

Chapter 6

314 Excerpt courtesy: *The Ancient Geography of India* by Alexander Cunningham; **318** Excerpt courtesy: Rhys Davids. 1910. *Dialogues of the Buddha. Part II. Sacred Books of the Buddhists Series*, Pali Text Society. 3rd Edn. London: Luzac and Co. pp. 78–81; **325** Excerpt courtesy: *Arrian. The Anabasis of Alexander, or, The History of the Wars and Conquests of Alexander the Great: Literally Translated, with a Commentary, from the Greek of Arrian, the Nicomedian*. 1884. United Kingdom: Hodder and Stoughton; **344** Excerpt reprinted with permission by Ravindra Prakash Jain of Motilal Banarsidass (www.motilalbanarsidass.com); **357** Excerpt courtesy: ©Wisdom Books, United States. Reprinted by permission of Fred Courtright, The Permissions Company, Inc.; **362** Excerpt courtesy: Rhys Davids, T. W. 1899.

Dialogues of the Buddha. F. Max Muller. (Ed.). *Sacred Books of the Buddhists*. Vol. 2. London: Henry Frowde. pp. 112–33; **363** Excerpt courtesy: *The First Buddhist Women: Translations and Commentary on the Therigatha* (1991) 2006: 33–34 by Susan Murcott with permission of Parallax Press, Berkeley, California (www.parallax.org); **369, 370, 371** Excerpts reprinted with permission by Ravindra Prakash Jain of Motilal Banarsidass (www.motilalbanarsidass.com).

Chapter 7

386 Excerpt courtesy: H. L. Jones, cited in Majumdar (1960) 1981: 244 | McCrindle, 1877: 20–21, 194, 196–97, 21; **395** "Pataliputra and the palace, according to Arrian and Aelian". Courtesy: Arrian, Indica, 10. Translated by McCrindle, John Watson. 1876. | Claudius Aelianus, On the Peculiarities of Animals, 13.18; **401** Excerpt courtesy: Geography, Volume VII Books 15–16 by Strabo. Translated by Horace Leonard Jones; **402** Excerpt courtesy: Hultzsch, E. (1925) 1969. *Corpus Inscriptionum Indicarum*. Vol. 1. Inscriptions of Asoka. Rep. Edn. Delhi: Indological Book House. pp. 12–13; **405** Excerpt courtesy: Sircar (1966b). 'Ahraura Inscription of Asoka.' *Epigraphia Indica* 36, Archaeological Survey of India: 239–48 | Hultzsch, E. (1925) 1969. *Corpus Inscriptionum Indicarum*. Vol. 1, *Inscriptions of Asoka*. Rep. Edn. Delhi: Indological Book House. pp. 167–69; **407** Excerpt courtesy: Hultzsch, E. (1925) 1969. *Corpus Inscriptionum Indicarum*. Vol. 1, *Inscriptions of Asoka*. Rep. edn. Delhi: Indological Book House. pp. 127–28; **408** Excerpts courtesy: Hultzsch, E. (1925) 1969. *Corpus Inscriptionum Indicarum*. Vol. 1, *Inscriptions of Asoka*. Rep. Edn. Delhi: Indological Book House. pp. 68–70; **410** Excerpt courtesy: G. Pugliese Carratelli and G. Garbini. (Ed. and Trans.). *A bilingual Graeco-Aramaic edict by Asoka: the first Greek inscription discovered in Afghanistan*. (Serie Orientale Roma, XXIX.) XI, 62 pp., 4 plates. Eoma: Istituto Italiano per il Medio ed Estremo Oriente, 1964. L. 2, 500.

Chapter 8

432 Excerpt reprinted from *Indian Epigraphy*, Richard Salomon. 1998. Used with permission of Munshiram Manoharlal; **453** Excerpt reprinted from *The Four Hundred Songs of War and Wisdom An Anthology of Poems from Classical Tamil, the Purananuru*, by George L. Hart and Hank Heifetz. (Trans.). Copyright ©1999. Columbia University Press. Reprinted with permission of Columbia University Press; **472, 480** Excerpt courtesy: Chelliah, J. V. 1962. *Pattupattu: Ten Tamil Idylls*. Tirunelveli: The South India Saiva Siddhanta Works Publishing Society; **501** Excerpt courtesy: Poem 110. Neytal. ©George L. Hart, *Four Hundred Songs of Love: An Anthology of Poems* from Classical Tamil, the *Akanāṉūṟu* (Institut Français de Pondichéry. 2015. Used with permission. p. 121; **502** Excerpt reprinted from *The Four Hundred Songs of War and Wisdom An Anthology of Poems from Classical Tamil, the Purananuru*, by George L. Hart and Hank Heifetz. (Trans.). Copyright ©1999. Columbia University Press. Reprinted with permission of Columbia University Press; **506** Excerpt used with permission of University of Chicago Press - Books, from *The Bhagavadgita in the Mahābhārata: Text and Translation*, Buitenen, J. A. B. Van. 1997. (Permission conveyed through Copyright Clearance Center, Inc.); **555** Excerpt reprinted from *Indian Epigraphy*, Richard Salomon. 1998. Used with permission of Munshiram Manoharlal.

Chapter 9

566 Faxian's *Fuguo ji* ©Legge, James. (1886) 1981. *The Travels of Fa-Hien: A Record of Buddhistic Kingdoms, being an account by the Chinese monk Fa-hien of his travels in India and Ceylon (AD 399–414) in search of the Buddhist Books of Discipline*. Rep. Edn. New Delhi: Master Publishers; **576** Excerpt courtesy: Archaeological Survey of India, GODL-India https://data.gov.in/sites/default/files/Gazette_Notification_OGDL.pdf, via Wikimedia Commons; **594** Excerpt reprinted from *Vatsyayana's Kamasutra*. Translated by Wendy Doniger and Sudhir Kakar. 2002. Oxford World's Classics Series. Used with permission of Oxford University Press. pp. 18–20; **611** Excerpt reprinted with permission by Ravindra Prakash Jain of Motilal Banarsidass (www.motilalbanarsidass.com); **638** Excerpt reprinted from Kalidasa: *The Loom of Time: A Selection of His Plays and Poems* by Chandra Rajan. 1989. Used with permission of Penguin Books Ltd. pp. 156–57; 644 Excerpt reprinted from *The Roots of Ayurveda: Selections from Sanskrit Medical Writings* by Dominik Wujastyk. (1998) 2001. Used with permission of Penguin Books Ltd. pp. 77–78.

Chapter 10

660–661 Excert reprint courtesy: Kielhorn, F. 1900–01. 'Aihole Inscription of Pulakesin II, Saka-Samvat 556.' *Epigraphia Indica* 6: 1–12; **718** Excerpt reproduced from 'A letter from Xuanzang to Prajnadeva', ©Devahuti, Tan Chung. Used with permission; **739** Excerpts Courtesy: *Songs of the Nayanmar saint Appar: On Shiva Bhakti* ©Munshiram Manoharlal Publishers. Used with permission; **740** Excerpts courtesy: *Varanamayiram, Nachchiyar Tirumozhi, Srivatsan*, cited in Ramaswamy, 1997: 125 | K. C. Kamalaiah, cited in Ramaswamy, 1997: 126; **741** Excerpt courtesy: Vidya Dehejia. 1988. Used with permission of Munshiram Manoharlal Publishers; 743 Excerpts courtesy: A. K. Ramanujan. Used with permission of Penguin Books Ltd.

Figure Credits

Chapter 1

52–53 Courtesy Salomon, Richard. 1998. *Indian Epigraphy: A Guide to the Study of Inscriptions in Sanskrit, Prakrit, and the other Indo-Aryan Languages*. New Delhi: Munshiram Manoharlal.

Chapter 2

104, 106–111 Cave art reproduced with permission of Oxford University Press India, New Delhi, from *Prehistoric Indian Rock Art* (1983) by Erwin Neumayer. ©Erwin Neumayer.

Chapter 4

167 ©ASI, reproduced with permission

Access the resources in 4 simple steps!

1

Pearson eLibrary 2.0

Go to elibrary.in.pearson.com

2

Register and create your account as a New User (Enter **44A-n9U-F6h** as the Institute registration code) or Sign in as an Existing User.

3

Click the + icon, scan or enter the code mentioned in the box below.

4

Your content is available. To access the resources section, click on the three vertical dots located on the book card.

Access Code

Disclaimer: The QR /Access code can be redeemed only once. The validity of the course will be 2 years from the date of redemption.

Customer Support:

Toll-Free: 1800 123 463512

Website: in.pearson.com/Support/contact-support-center.html